# ILS Integrated Learning System

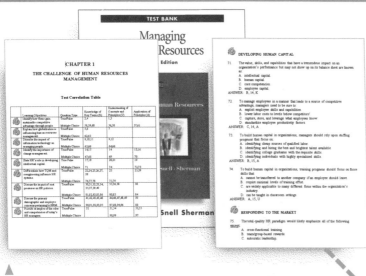

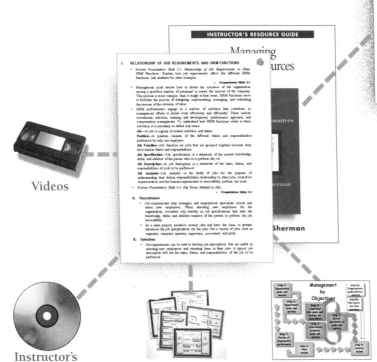

**Chapter Learning Objectives** from the text form the framework for organizing your lectures, selecting support materials, and customizing tests for your students.

**Test Bank Questions** are grouped by learning objective, so that you can thoroughly test all objectives – or emphasize the ones you feel are most important. Correlation tables at the beginning of each chapter make it easy to prepare tests that cover the objectives at the level of difficulty appropriate for your students.

**Exam View CD**

**Videos**

**Instructor's Resource CD**

**Transparencies**

**PowerPoint**

**All Lecture Support Materials** come together under their appropriate objectives in the *Instructor's Resource Guide* Lecture Outline. Annotations tell you where to integrate transparencies, PowerPoint slides, figures, cases, and activities from the text.

EDITION **12**

# Managing Human Resources

George Bohlander
Professor of Management
Arizona State University

Scott Snell
Professor of Management
The Pennsylvania State University

Arthur Sherman
Professor of Psychology
California State University, Sacramento

**South-Western College Publishing**
Thomson Learning™

Australia • Canada • Mexico • Singapore • Spain • United Kingdom • United States

*Managing Human Resources, 12e*
by George Bohlander, Scott Snell & Arthur Sherman

Publisher: Dave Shaut
Senior Acquisitions Editor: Charles McCormick, Jr.
Senior Marketing Manager: Joseph A. Sabatino
Senior Developmental Editor: Alice C. Denny
Production Editor: Elizabeth A. Shipp
Media Production Editor: Robin K. Browning
Manufacturing Coordinator: Sandee Milewski
Internal Design: Maureen McCutcheon Design
Cover Design: Joe Devine
Cover Illustration: © Diana Ong/Superstock
Photography Managers: Cary Benbow and Darren Wright
Photo Research: Feldman & Associates, Inc.
Production House: Lachina Publishing Services
Printer: RR Donnelley & Sons Company, Willard Manufacturing Division

1 2 3 4 5    03 02 01 00
Printed in the United States of America

For more information contact South-Western College Publishing, 5101 Madison Road,
Cincinnati, Ohio, 45227 or find us on the Internet at http://www.swcollege.com

For permission to use material from this text or product, contact us by
  • telephone: 1-800-730-2214
  • fax: 1-800-730-2215
  • web: http://www.thomsonrights.com

Library of Congress Cataloging-in-Publication Data:

Bohlander, George W.
    Managing human resources / George Bohlander, Scott Snell, Arthur Sherman.-- 12th ed.
        p. cm.
    Sherman's name appears first on the previous editions.
    Includes bibliographical references.
    ISBN 0-324-00724-8
        1. Personnel management. I. Snell, Scott, 1958- II. Sherman, Arthur W. III. Title.

HF5549 .C465 2000
658.3--dc21

                                                                            00-026939

This book is printed on acid-free paper.

*To my wife, Ronnie Bohlander, and to our children, Ryan and Kathryn*

*To my wife, Marybeth Snell, and to our children, Sara, Jack, and Emily*

*To my wife, Leneve Sherman, and to our children, Judy, Beverly, and Sandy*

# Special Features Tour

**B**efore You Open the Door to the 12th Edition of *Managing Human Resources*, take a walk through the special features of the text, detailed on the next few pages. The topic of human resources management holds special interest for us, and we are pleased to share what we know with you. As you'll see on the next few pages, we offer a variety of rich and interesting features to help you develop practical skills for managing a valuable and critical resource – people, as well as an awareness and appreciation for the challenges involved.

# Guided Tour for Readers

# Special Features

## INTEGRATED LEARNING SYSTEM

Beginning with the learning objectives that open each chapter, the text is organized as an integrated learning system. To keep the central ideas before you, the learning objectives are noted again in key places: at the beginning of the section where the objective is fulfilled and within the chapter summary and discussion questions where the key points of each objective are recapped.

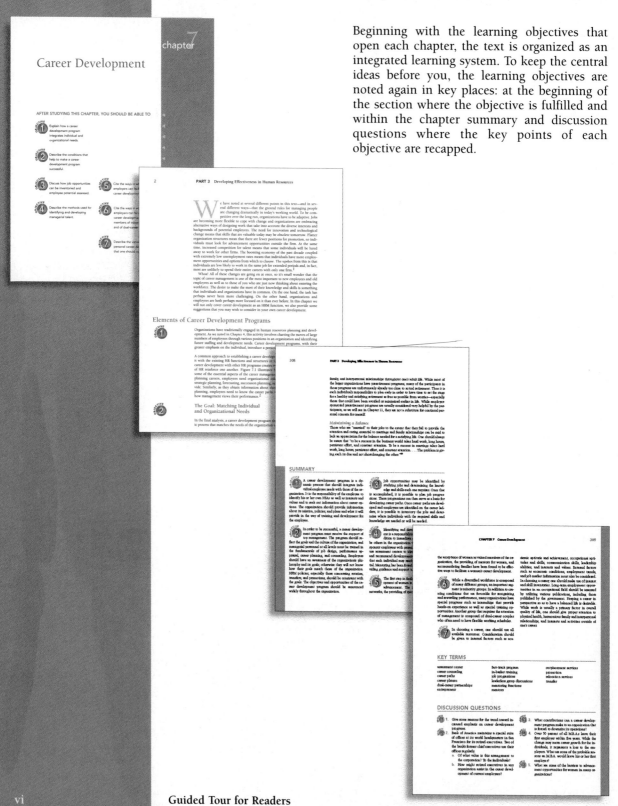

**Guided Tour for Readers**

To help you organize your study, we have structured the Study Guide around these same learning objectives. First we recap each key section in the chapter, grouped by learning objectives. Next come multiple choice, application, and true-false review questions—all organized according to the learning objectives they test. A matching section reviews important terms in the chapter. New for this edition is a "how-to" application activity.

---

6   Discuss significant court cases impacting equal employment opportunity.

7   Explain various enforcement procedures affecting equal employment opportunity.

8   Describe affirmative action and the basic steps in developing an affirmative action program.

**CHAPTER SUMMARY RELATING TO LEARNING OBJECTIVES**

1   U.S. employers have long practiced employment discrimination against African Americans, Hispanics, women, and other groups. Prejudice against minority groups is a major cause in their lack of employment gains. Government reports show that the wages and job opportunities of minorities typically lag behind those for whites.

2   Effective management requires knowing the legal aspects of the employment relationship. Pertinent legislation includes the Equal Pay Act, Title VII of the Civil Rights Act of 1964, Age Discrimination in Employment Act, Equal Employment Opportunity Act of 1972, Pregnancy Discrimination Act, Americans with Disabilities Act, Civil Rights Act of 1991, and various executive orders.

...ent is an area of particular importance to managers and ...ensive efforts should be made to ensure that both male and ...es are free from all forms of sexual harassment conduct. The ...orm and Control Act was passed to control unauthorized ...the United States. The law requires managers to maintain ...ment records, and they must not discriminate against job ...resent employees because of a person's national origin or ...us.

...idelines on Employment Selection Procedures is designed to ...in complying with federal prohibitions against employment ...scriminate on the basis of race, color, religion, gender, or ...The Uniform Guidelines provides employers with a framework for ...enforceable decisions. Employers must be able to show that ...dures are valid in predicting job performance.

...ative action and the basic steps in developing an affirmative

---

7   20. From the employer's standpoint, flextime can be most helpful in
a. predicting employee turnover.
b. recruiting and retaining personnel.
c. developing job sharing.
d. flexible and adaptable work schedules.

**True/False**

Identify the following statements as True or False.

1   1. Any discrepancies between the knowledge, skills, and abilities demonstrated by a jobholder and the requirements contained in the description and specification for that job provide clues to training needs.

1   2. The requirements contained in the description of a job provide the criteria for appraising the performance of the holder of that job is called job evaluation.

1   3. In determining the rate to be paid for performing a job, the relative worth of the job would be the least important factor to be considered.

  4. Job analysis is the process of obtaining information about jobs by determining what the duties, tasks, or activities of those jobs are.

  5. The job description and job specifications developed through job analysis should be as inaccurate as possible if they are to be of value to those who make Human Resources Management (HRM) decisions.

  ...onducting job analysis is usually the primary responsibility of ...e line manager.

2   ...ommon methods of analyzing jobs when undertaking job ...nalysis would include interviews, questionnaires, observation, ...nd diaries.

  ...eveloped by the U.S. Training and Employment Service, ...e functional job analysis (FJA) approach utilizes an inventory ...f the various types of functions or work activities that can ...onstitute any job.

---

5   3. To improve the workflow of its bank tellers, the Methods Improvement Group at First Interstate Bank used the concept of
a. leadership analysis.
b. industrial engineering.
c. decentralization of authority.
d. corporate downsizing.

5   4. By using safely designed equipment, Chrysler's Jefferson North facility employs the concept of
a. ergonomics.
b. re-engineering.
c. employee empowerment.
d. functional job analysis.

6   5. At such organizations as Federal Express, Steelcase Inc., Schreiber Foods, and Kent-Moore of Warren, Michigan, the benefits of employee teams have included the following, **EXCEPT FOR**
a. employee benchmarking.
b. improved integration of individual skills.
c. better performance in terms of quantity and quality of work.
d. a sense of confidence among team members.

**How To Inquire About a Realistic Job Preview**

A student may inquire how to pursue a realistic job preview when interviewing with an employer or the Human Resources Department.

A line manager or the Human Resources Department should state a realistic job preview in every interview. This process is an accurate portrayal of the job description that one is expected to perform. It would include the job title, duties and

---

The tightly integrated learning system is designed to help you study efficiently. After reading the chapter, review the summary. Next prepare verbal or written answers to the discussion questions to help you move from the concepts to applications. Then work through the review questions in the Study Guide. If you find from these review activities that you need further study on a particular objective, you can easily locate all of the applicable material by looking for the appropriate learning objective icon in the text and Study Guide.

# Special Features

Now in its 12th edition, this text has all the advantages of a time-tested product—and the added benefit of an author team committed to bringing you the most current and critical topics in HRM today. The excerpts shown here are only a small sample of the hot topics you'll encounter in this edition.

◀ **Age Discrimination**

◀ **Ergonomics**

**Virtual Teams** ▶

---

CHAPTER 2  Equal Employment Opportunity and Human Resources Management   49

The EEOC does not favor BFOQs, and both the EEOC and the courts have construed the concept narrowly. The exception does not apply to discrimination based on race or color. Where an organization claims a BFOQ, it must be able to prove that hiring on the basis of sex, religion, age, or national origin is a business necessity. **Business necessity** has been interpreted by the courts as a practice that is necessary to the safe and efficient operation of the organization. Students will often ask, "Why do Asian restaurants hire only Asian American food servers?" While restaurants generally cannot prefer one nationality over another (because the job of serving food can be performed equally well by all nationalities) to ensure the "authenticity" of the dining experience, an Asian restaurant may legitimately use the business-necessity defense to support the preference for hiring Asian American servers.

**Business necessity**
Work-related practice that is necessary to the safe and efficient operation of an organization

**Religious Preference.** Freedom to exercise religious choice is guaranteed under the U.S. Constitution. Title VII of the Civil Rights Act also prohibits discrimination based on religion in employment decisions, though it permits employer exemptions. The act defines religion to "include all aspects of religious observance and practice, as well as belief."

Title VII does not require employers to grant complete religious freedom in employment situations. Employers need only make a reasonable accommodation for a current employee's or job applicant's religious observance or practice without incurring undue hardship in the conduct of the business. Managers or supervisors may have to accommodate an employee's religion in the specific areas of (1) holidays and observances (scheduling), (2) personal appearance (wearing beards, veils, or turbans), and (3) religious conduct on the job (missionary work among other employees).

What constitutes "reasonable accommodation" has been difficult to define. In 1977, in the leading case of *TWA v Hardison*, the Supreme Court attempted to settle this dispute by ruling that employers...

**USING THE INTERNET**
To view the EEOC's Facts about Religious Discrimination, go to: www.eeoc.gov/facts/fs-relig.html

*Age Discrimination in Employment Act of 1967*

With the aging of the baby boomers—a group of 76 million... Age discrimination by employers increases dramatically...

---

CHAPTER 3  Job Requirements and the Design of Organizations   105

workforce whose average age is 51 years. Instead of dangling auto chassis from overhead assembly lines, which would require workers to crane upward, auto chassis are tilted at an angle for ease of access. Marilyn Joyce, head of Arthur D. Little's ergonomic unit, notes, "You simply have to adapt your workplace to the labor force; ignore it, and you could be sacrificing quality and productivity."

Ergonomics contributes to improvements in productivity. It has proven cost-effective at organizations such as the U.S. Postal Service, West Bend Mutual Insurance, Pitney Bowes, and the Bureau of National Affairs (BNA). With the increasing use of computers at these organizations and others, ergonomics has particular application at employee workstations. Although computers provide benefits to organizations, Figure 3.5 provides a checklist of potential problem areas for employees utilizing workstations.

**FIGURE 3.5** ➤ Computer Workstation Ergonomics Checklist

Use the following list to identify potential problem areas that should receive further investigation. Any "no" response may point to a problem.

1. Does the workstation ensure proper worker posture, such as:
   - Thighs in the horizontal position?
   - Lower legs in the vertical position?
   - Feet flat on the floor or on a footrest?
   - Wrists straight and relaxed?
2. Does the chair:
   - Adjust easily?
   - Have a padded seat with a rounded front?
   - Have an adjustable backrest?
   - Provide lumbar support?
   - Have casters?
3. Are the height and tilt of the work surface on which...
4. Is the keyboard detachable?
5. Do keying actions require minimal force?
6. Is there an adjustable document holder?
7. Are armrests provided where needed?
8. Are glare and reflections minimized?
9. Does the monitor have brightness and contrast con...
10. Is there sufficient space for knees and feet?
11. Can the workstation be used for either right- or left...

Source: The National Institute for Occupational Safety and Health (NIOSH), *Working Safely with Video Display Terminals*...

---

CHAPTER 3  Job Requirements and the Design of Organizations   109

**HRM 3**

**HIGHLIGHTS IN HRM**

### What Self-Managed Teams Manage

More self-managing teams are taking on tasks formerly the purview of supervisors or managers. Among organizations with self-directed teams, the percentages indicate that teams perform these functions on their own.

| Function | Percentage |
|---|---|
| Set work schedules | 79% |
| Deal directly with external customers | 59% |
| Training | 56% |
| Deal with vendors/suppliers | 52% |
| Set production quotas/performance targets | 50% |
| Budgeting | 49% |
| Purchase equipment or services | 43% |
| Performance appraisals | 36% |
| Hiring | 36% |
| Firing | 15% |

Source: Reprinted with permission from the October 1995 issue of *TRAINING* Magazine. Copyright 1995, Bill Communications, Inc., Minneapolis, MN. All rights reserved. Not for resale.

**Virtual team**
A team with widely dispersed members linked together through computer and telecommunications technology

To compete in today's national and international markets, managers have formed virtual teams. **Virtual teams** use advanced computer and telecommunications technology to link team members who are geographically dispersed—often worldwide. Management may form a cross-functional team (see Figure 3.7) to develop a new pharmaceutical drug and have the team operate in a virtual environment to achieve its goal. Virtual teams provide new opportunities for training,

---

The Internet now plays an important role in human resource management. Examples of recruitment and training are illustrated here, but other uses appear throughout the new edition of *Managing Human Resources*. New and updated Using the Internet Boxes will be the starting points for you to explore the wealth of HRM resources available on the Internet.

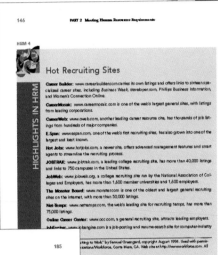

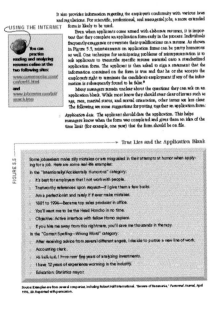

# Special Features
## HUMAN RESOURCES MANAGEMENT IN THE REAL WORLD

Throughout the text, we integrate real-world experiences using Highlights in HRM boxed features. Some Highlights in HRM boxes use real experiences to illustrate how businesses and other organizations cope with human resources issues. Other Highlights in HRM boxes allow the reader to test his or her knowledge or attitudes concerning HR issues. Still other Highlights in HRM boxes provide how-to suggestions taken from real-world experience.

**HRM 2**

**HIGHLIGHTS IN HRM**

### How Successful Is Succession Planning at . . .

*. . . Sun Microsystems?* There are 600 directors (the entry-level executive job) who report to 110 vice presidents. According to Ken Alvares, VP of HR, "We watch the directors closely, but give more attention to the VPs. . . . When you look at our bench strength, I don't get the feeling that we've got ourselves covered. I worry about developing people who can step up to the next level."

*. . . U.S. Postal Service?* The program focuses on 800 senior managers who may be selected to move up the ladder to the elite 45-person officer team. Steve Levy, the organization's corporate HR manager says it's "4,000 people backing up 800 jobs." Since the program was initiated, it has accounted for 90 percent of the senior management and executive hiring. According to Levy, "We're in the process of pushing the process below the executive level."

*. . . Sonoco?* The company's succession plan targets 300 executives in its top management group. About 20 percent of Sonoco's executive jobs turn over each year as a result of retirements, job changes, and departures. According to Cindy Hartley, VP of HR, the company's policy is to promote from within. "We meet with our division presidents and general managers to discuss our key people; we explore what we want to do to develop them and identify who we have tapped as potential successors."

*. . . UNUM?* The insurance company targets 200 managers out of its 7,000 employees. Tammie Snow, head of training, explains that the company puts the most promising candidates through management internship programs. "We provide management assistantships to a select number of people, about 12 each year, who have reached the director level. We identify the high potential people and for a year or a year and a half, they shadow a key executive."

*. . . Sears?* Recently, Sears created its Corporate Strategic Leadership Team (CSLT, pronounced "seasalt") to develop bench strength from among its top 220 executives to support the top twenty-four executive positions. Steve Kim, VP of organizational learning and development, explains, "We look at each position, identify the unique experiences and challenges that the job provides, then look at the people on the bench and match them with the appropriate position."

Adapted from Robert J. Grossman, "Heirs Unapparent," *HRMagazine* 44, no. 2 (February 1999): 36–44. Reprinted with the permission of *HRMagazine*, published by the Society for Human Resource Management, Alexandria, VA.

Figure 4.7 shows the distribution of college graduate employment. Other data predict that while the labor force is expected to grow at a rate of 14 percent between 1996 and 2006 (to reach 150.9 million workers), the growth rate for college-graduate-level jobs is expected to grow by more than 27 percent (to nearly 35 million workers). At the same time, estimates are that the number of individuals earning college degrees is actually declining but should resume growth in 2001 (see Figure 4.8). These kinds of data provide a much clearer picture to organizations attempting to project external labor supply.[19]

**HRM 1**

**HIGHLIGHTS IN HRM**

### Notes on Doing Needs Assessment Quick Time

**NOTE 1: Look at Problem Scope.** Common sense suggests that small, local matters may require less information gathering than big problems with a major impact on the organization. Ask managers a series of questions about the nature of the problem and its impact on the organization and gear your analysis accordingly.

**NOTE 2: Do Organizational Scanning.** Stay connected with what is going on in the organization in order to anticipate upcoming training needs. If a new technology is about to be launched, the need for training should take no one by surprise. In short, needs assessment isn't an event with a start-and-stop switch. It is the process of being engaged in your business.

**NOTE 3: Play "Give & Take."** Get the information you need, but don't drag your feet with excessive analysis before reporting back to managers. Show them that you are sensitive to their need for action by giving them updates on the information you have collected. If necessary, explain that better value may be gained by further analysis.

**NOTE 4: Check "Lost and Found."** Often, information gathered for a different purpose may bear on your training issue. Performance data (such as errors, sales customer complaints) and staffing data (such as proficiency testing, turnover, absenteeism) can be very helpful as a starting point.

**NOTE 5: Use Plain Talk.** Instead of using clinical terms such as "analysis or assessment," use straight talk with managers that tells them what you are doing: (1) identify the problem, (2) identify alternative ways to get there, (3) implement a solution based on cost/benefit concerns, (4) determine the effectiveness and efficiency of the solution.

**NOTE 6: Use the Web.** Information technology allows you to communicate with others, perhaps setting up a listserv to post questions, synthesize responses, share resources, get feedback, gather information on trends, and the like.

**NOTE 7: Use Rapid Prototyping.** Often the most effective and efficient training is that which is "just-in-time, just enough, and just for me." Create a rapid prototype of a training program, evaluating and revising as you implement and learn more about the problems.

**NOTE 8: Seek Out Exemplars.** Find those in the organization that currently demonstrate the performance the organization wants. Bring others together with them to talk about the performance issues, and let the exemplars share their experiences and insights. This avoids the risk of packaging the wrong information, and people learn just what they need to know from each other.

Condensed from: Ron Zemke, "How to Do a Needs Assessment When You Think You Don't Have Time," *Training* 35, no. 3 (March 1996): 36–44. Reprinted with permission from the March 1996 issue of *TRAINING Magazine*. Copyright 1996. Bill Communications, Inc., Minneapolis, MN. All rights reserved. Not for resale.

## Case Studies

To become a successful manager of people, you will need practice. In addition to offering practical information ready to put to use, each chapter of the textbook concludes with at least two Case Studies. These case studies present current HRM issues in real-life settings that allow for critical analysis.

CHAPTER 5 Selection 213

3. What characteristics do job knowledge and job sample tests have that often make them more acceptable to the examinees than other types of tests?

4. Personality tests, like other tests used in employee selection, have been under attack for several decades. What are some of the reasons applicants find personality tests objectionable? On what basis could their use for selection purposes be justified?

5. Compare briefly the major types of employment interviews described in this chapter. Which type would you prefer to conduct? Why?

6. In what ways does the clinical approach to selection differ from the statistical approach? How do you account for the fact that one approach is superior to the other?

Nike: Hiring Gets Off on the Right Foot

Technology is changing how companies recruit and select in ways that couldn't have been anticipated a few years ago. While automated hiring technologies are still in their infancy recruiters envision a world in which they can reduce the hiring cycle time by 90 percent, anticipate what skills will be in demand before they can be articulated, and call up information about a potential hire on their computer screens. Interactive voice response technology (IVR), which has been in use for a long time, is being used along with other database technologies to capture information about potential employees, giving the company more flexibility and speeding hiring decisions.

Nike is one example of a company using computer-assisted interviewing. The company has used an Aspen Tree product to hire employees for Niketowns, retail stores that showcase Nike products. At a recently opened store in Las Vegas, 6,000 people responded to ads for workers needed to fill 250 positions. Nike used IVR technology to make the first cut. Applicants responded to eight questions over the telephone; 3,500 applicants were screened out because they weren't available when needed or didn't have retail experience. The rest had a computer-assisted interview at the store, followed by a personal interview.

"We think it's important to give a personal interview to anyone who comes to the store," says Brian Rogers, Nike's manager of human resources for the retail division. "Applicants are customers as well as potential hires."

The computer interview identified those candidates who had been in customer service environments, had a passion for sports, and would make good Nike customer service representatives. Interviews were done in batches. The computer interview (which includes a video showing three scenarios for helping a customer and asks the applicant to choose the best one) was given every forty-five minutes to a group of applicants. As applicants completed the interview, a printer in the next room printed their responses. Areas that needed to be probed further were flagged, as were areas that indicated particular strengths.

While the applicant completed an application form on-line, the interviewer used the printout to prepare for the applicant's human interview. Some applicants would be given only a short interview; other, more likely candidates would be interviewed at greater length. The computer not only helped interviewers screen for

## Cases

Case 1      **ConnectPlus: Aligning Human Resources Functions with Strategic Objectives**

Jim Heinrich founded ConnectPlus and has managed the company's operations from its inception. ConnectPlus designs and produces communications software that is sold to customers ranging from the computer industry to independent businesses. Though ConnectPlus has been profitable over the decade of its existence, productivity at the company has recently decreased. Specifically, in the past several years the workers have displayed diminished innovation, higher turnover and absenteeism, and overall sluggish performance.

Because of these trends, Heinrich called a meeting of all the managers to discuss potential courses of action to correct the problems. After a series of discussions, Heinrich and the other managers agreed that they needed to hire a full-time manager to assume sole responsibility for human resources management. In the past, the department managers had assumed basic responsibilities for managing their employees. However, the growth of the company—there are now over 100 employees—coupled with recent increases in absenteeism and turnover, suggested that the human resources responsibilities were large enough to warrant hiring a full-time manager.

After careful consideration, Heinrich decided to hire Judith Thompson to assume the primary responsibilities of developing a systematic HRM function for ConnectPlus. Once Thompson arrived at ConnectPlus, she and Heinrich met to discuss the strategic objectives and long-term goals of the company. Heinrich stated that ConnectPlus must achieve two primary objectives to be successful in the future. First, the company must continue its growth strategy to respond to the expanding demands for its services. Second, it must enhance the innovative nature of its workforce to ensure that it remains up-to-date with competitors and market changes. At the end of their meeting, Heinrich gave Thompson the task of developing an HRM function that could address the absenteeism and turnover problems while helping ConnectPlus attain the two goals he has outlined.

7

## Comprehensive Cases

Ten comprehensive cases are located at the back of the text. These longer cases include topics found in more than just a single text chapter. The more complicated issues found in these cases enable you to put a variety of concepts into practice.

# Contents in Brief

# Contents

P A R T

## 3 Developing Effectiveness in Human Resources

## P A R T

## 6  Expanding Human Resources Management Horizons

# Preface

While maintaining many of the features that have made it the leader in introductory textbooks, the new twelfth edition of *Managing Human Resources* brings into clear focus the changes that are occurring in management at all levels. The role of HR managers is no longer limited to service functions such as recruiting and selecting employees. Today HR managers assume an active role in strategic planning and decision making at their organizations. Meeting challenges head-on and using human resources effectively are critical to the success of any work organization.

Also, many functions that may have been done by HR specialists in the past are now done in partnership with line managers and team directors. To ensure effectiveness, HR policies and procedures must be placed into a comprehensive program that managers can use effectively in their day-to-day interactions with employees.

The twelfth edition of *Managing Human Resources* will place your students at the forefront in understanding how organizations can gain sustainable competitive advantage through people. In the first chapter we begin by explaining the key challenges to HRM in developing the flexible and skilled workforce needed to compete effectively—going global, embracing new technology, managing change, developing intellectual capital, responding to the market, and containing costs. Side-by-side with these competitive challenges, HRM must also address important concerns such as managing a diverse workforce, recognizing employee rights, and adjusting to new work attitudes. The chapter also discusses HR's important partnership with line managers and the competencies required of HR management.

Then the textbook continues with the introduction, explanation, and discussion of the individual practices and policies that make up HRM. We recognize the manager's changing role and emphasize current issues and real-world problems and the policies and practices of HRM used to meet them. While the focus is on the HR role of managers, we do not exclude the impact and importance of the HR department's role in developing, coordinating, and enforcing policies and procedures relating to HR functions. Whether the reader becomes a manager or supervisor, an HR specialist, or an employee in other areas of the organization, *Managing Human Resources* provides a functional and practical understanding of HR programs to enable students to see how HR affects all employees, the organization, the community, and the larger society.

Organizations in today's competitive world are discovering that it is how the individual HR topics are combined that makes all the difference. Managers typically don't focus on HR issues like staffing, training, and compensation in isolation from one another. Each of these HR practices is combined into an overall system to enhance employee involvement and productivity. This edition of *Managing Human Resources* ends with a final chapter that focuses on development of high-performance work systems. We outline the various components of the system, including work-flow design, HR practices, management processes, and supporting technologies. We also discuss the strategic processes used to implement high-performance work systems and the outcomes that benefit both the employee and the organization as a whole.

## A Salute and Best Wishes to Arthur Sherman

The twelfth edition of *Managing Human Resources* will be the last to carry the name of Arthur Sherman as an author. The management and editors of South-Western College Publishing/Thomson Learning salute Professor Sherman for the many, many years of quality authorship that helped to make this textbook the standard in the field. George Bohlander acknowledges with appreciation Arthur Sherman's support as an active and caring mentor, and friend, for the years they worked together. Although his role in the writing and preparation of the manuscript has ended, Arthur Sherman's dedication to instructors and students alike remains the hallmark of this textbook.

## Organization of the Twelfth Edition

The new edition of *Managing Human Resources* is divided into six parts and seventeen chapters covering the following major topics:

- Part 1 Human Resources Management in Perspective

  The Challenge of Human Resources Management
  Equal Employment Opportunity and Human Resources Management

- Part 2 Meeting Human Resources Requirements

  Job Requirements and the Design of Organizations to Achieve Human Resources Productivity
  Human Resources Planning and Recruitment
  Selection

- Part 3 Developing Effectiveness in Human Resources

  Training and Development
  Career Development
  Appraising and Improving Performance

- Part 4 Implementing Compensation and Security

  Managing Compensation
  Incentive Rewards
  Employee Benefits
  Safety and Health

- Part 5 Enhancing Employee Relations

  Employee Rights and Discipline
  The Dynamics of Labor Relations
  Collective Bargaining and Contract Administration

- Part 6 Expanding Human Resources Management Horizons

  International Human Resources Management
  Creating High-Performance Work Systems

## What's New in the Twelfth Edition

There are many new features and information provided in this revision. We introduce overall text improvements that more accurately reflect HR in today's business world and help the reader understand HR issues more effectively.

- Internet references and addresses throughout the text point students to the latest on-line sources for HR information and examples.
- A complete update of all laws and court decisions governing HRM includes such recent developments as same-gender sexual harassment and recent changes regarding e-mail, constructive discharge, and other employee rights issues. In Chapter 2 we have added a new section on preventing employment discrimination charges.
- A new section in Chapter 3 describes work-design techniques to increase employee contributions: employee empowerment and employee involvement groups. A comprehensive discussion of teams is included.
- Expanded discussions cover major current issues, including

| | |
|---|---|
| Safety training | Conflict resolution |
| HR technologies | HR in small businesses |
| Ergonomics | Benefits changes |
| Employee competencies | Violence in the workplace |
| Diversity in the workplace | HRM in the global setting |
| High-performance work systems | Employee rights and management |
| Stress management | responsibilities |
| Employee empowerment | New union organizing tactics |

- Many new Highlights in HRM boxes present the student with up-to-date, real-world examples from a variety of large and small organizations.
- Improved Test Your Knowledge quizzes throughout the chapters will spark interest in a subject as well as provide for knowledge accumulation.
- References to and examples of the policies and practices of hundreds of organizations show HR concepts in action in the business world today.
- Two Case Studies per chapter and four new comprehensive cases at the end of the text reinforce critical thinking skills and problem-solving techniques.
- Use of the Integrated Learning System, which is carefully described on the front endsheet, continues for the twelfth edition. This integrated structure creates a comprehensive teaching and testing system.
- A completely revised test bank plays a strategic role in the Integrated Learning System.
- The inclusion of PowerPoint slides and acetates makes teaching and preparation easier and more convenient.

## Features of the Book

Designed to facilitate understanding and retention of the material presented, each chapter contains the following pedagogical features:

- **Learning objectives** listed at the beginning of each chapter provide the basis for the Integrated Learning System. Icons for identifying the learning objectives appear throughout the text and end-of-chapter material and on all print ancillaries.
- **Key terms** appear in boldface in the text and are defined in margin notes next to the text discussion. The key terms are also listed at the end of the chapter and appear in the glossary at the end of the book.

- **Figures** include an abundance of graphic materials, flowcharts, and summaries of research data and provide a visual, dynamic presentation of concepts and HR activities. All figures are systematically referenced in the text discussion.
- **Highlights in HRM**, the popular boxed feature, provide real-world examples of how organizations perform HR functions. The Highlights are introduced in the text discussion and include topics such as small-business practices and international issues.
- **Illustrations**, including captioned, full-color photographs and carefully selected cartoons, create student interest and reinforce points made in the text.
- A **summary**, containing a paragraph or two for each learning objective, provides a brief review of the chapter.
- **Discussion questions** following the chapter summary offer an opportunity to focus on each of the learning objectives in the chapter and to stimulate critical thinking. Many of these questions allow for group analysis and class discussion.
- At least **two case studies** per chapter present current HRM issues in real-life settings that allow for student consideration and critical analysis.
- **Notes and References**, found at the end of each chapter, include references from academic and practitioner journals and books. Author notes cite some historical information as well as personal observations and experiences.

In addition to the features found in each of the seventeen chapters, the text provides

- **Ten comprehensive cases** at the end of the book that portray current issues/problems in HRM. New cases cover redesign in employee jobs that results from technological advances, how corporate vision can emphasize competitiveness through diversity, the role of training and education in the consulting industry, and a company's efforts to revamp its performance appraisal system.
- A **glossary** of all the key terms introduced in the text that provides students with easy access to their definitions.
- **Name, organization, and subject indexes** that allow the book to become a valuable reference source.

## Ancillary Teaching and Learning Materials

Two ancillaries are available to students, either through bookstores or for direct purchase through the on-line catalog at www.swcollege.com:

- *Study Guide* to accompany *Managing Human Resources* (ISBN: 0-324-00989-5). Thomas Lloyd of Westmoreland County Community College prepared this new study guide. His many years of teaching experience allow him to bring new insight to this popular student supplement. It now includes review questions that can be used to check understanding and prepare for examinations on each chapter in the textbook. Using the Integrated Learning System, Study Guide questions are arranged by chapter learning objective so the student can quickly refer back to the textbook if further review is needed.

- *Applications in Human Resource Management: Cases, Exercises, and Skill Builders,* fourth edition, by Stella M. Nkomo, Myron D. Fottler, and R. Bruce McAfee (ISBN: 0-324-00711-6). This text supplement includes eighty-seven new and updated cases, exercises, incidents, and skill builders. These activities will supplement many of the topics covered in *Managing Human Resources,* twelfth edition.

The following instructor support materials are available to adopters from the Thomson Learning Academic Resource Center at 800-354-3906 or through www.swcollege.com. All printed ancillary materials were prepared by or under the direction of the text authors to guarantee full integration with the text. Multimedia supplements were prepared by experts in those fields.

- *Instructor's Resource Guide* (ISBN: 0-324-00987-9). For each chapter in the textbook, the resource guide for the twelfth edition contains the following:

  Chapter synopses and learning objectives

  A very detailed lecture outline, based on the textbook chapter outline, complete with notes for incorporating the transparencies

  Answers to the end-of-chapter discussion questions and case studies in the textbook

  Solutions to the comprehensive cases in the textbook

- *Test Bank* (ISBN: 0-324-00990-9). The test bank includes at least 100 questions for each text chapter. Each test bank chapter includes a matrix table that classifies each question according to type and learning objective. There are true/false, multiple-choice, and essay items for each chapter, arranged by learning objective. Page references to the text are included. Each objective question is coded to indicate whether it covers knowledge of key terms, understanding of concepts and principles, or application of principles.

- *Computerized Test Bank* (ISBN: 0-324-00992-5). *ExamView* testing software contains all the questions from the printed test bank and allows the instructor to edit, add, delete, or randomly mix questions for customized tests.

- *PowerPoint Presentation Slides* (ISBN: 0-324-00988-7). These screens will add color and interest to your lectures. The transparencies are also included within the presentation slide package.

- *Instructor's Resource CD* (ISBN: 0-324-05578-1). South-Western College Publishing is pleased to present the twelfth edition instructor ancillaries in a new, convenient format. The *Instructor's Resource Guide, Test Bank, ExamView,* and PowerPoint slides are provided on a single CD-ROM.

- *Video: South-Western College Publishing's HRM Video Library* (ISBN: 0-324-00991-7). Video segments taken from real companies as well as business features shown on CNN, the cable business news network, were chosen to accompany the text chapters. Descriptions of the videos are provided on the text's web site at bohlander.swcollege.com. Use them to introduce a topic, cover lecture material, or stimulate discussion.

- *Transparency Acetates* (ISBN: 0-324-05579-X). Also available with this edition is a set of transparencies. Only a few of these transparencies duplicate the figures in the textbook.

## Acknowledgments

We were fortunate in having the expertise of a number of reviewers. Some offered suggestions based on their actual use of the text in their courses, and others provided a careful review of the eleventh edition of the text. Our appreciation and thanks go to

Julia Morrison, Bloomfield College
Sharon Davis, Central Texas College
Scott L. Stevens, Detroit College of Business
Veronica Meyers, San Diego State University
Kenneth Kovach, University of Maryland
Barbara Luck, Jackson Community College
Marjorie L. McInerney, Marshall University
Tom Sedwick, Indiana University of Pennsylvania
Doug McCabe, Georgetown University

Because preparation of manuscript for a project as large as *Managing Human Resources* is a continuing process, we would also like to acknowledge the work of those colleagues who reviewed manuscript for the past two editions of the text:

Phyllis Alderdice, Jefferson Community College
Robert Allen, California State Polytechnic University
Timothy Barnett, Louisiana Tech University
Walter Bogumil, University of Central Florida
Bob S. Bulls, Reynolds Community College
Alan Cabelly, Portland State University
Barbara Chrispin, California State University–Dominguez Hills
Roy Cook, Fort Lewis College
Jack Dustman, Northern Arizona University
Wendy Eager, Eastern Washington University
Jan Feldhauer, Austin Community College
Mary Gowan, University of Texas at El Paso
Walter Greene, University of Texas–Pan American
Kathryn Hegar, Mountain View College
Lori Howard, University of Southern California
Vicki Kaman, Colorado State University
Harriet Kandelman, Barat College
Katherine Karl, Western Michigan University
Richard Kogelman, Delta College
Corrine Livesay, Liberty University
Thomas Lloyd, Westmoreland County Community College
Richard Magjuka, Indiana University
Wayne E. Nelson, Central Missouri State University
Larry A. Pace, Louisiana State University–Shreveport
Floyd Patrick, Eastern Michigan University
Alex S. Pomnichowski, Ferris State University
Joan Rivera, West Texas A&M University

Nestor St. Charles, Duchess Community College
Rodney Sherman, Central Missouri State University
Jeffrey Stauffer, Ventura College
Charles Toftoy, George Washington University
Robert Ulbrich, Parkland College
Nancy E. Waldeck, Ohio State University
Sandy J. Wayne, University of Illinois
Jon Werner, University of Wisconsin–Whitewater

In preparing the manuscript for this edition, we have drawn not only on the current literature but also on the current practices of organizations that furnished information and illustrations relating to their HR programs. We are indebted to the leaders in the field who have developed the available heritage of information and practices of HRM and who have influenced us through their writings and personal association. We have also been aided by students in our classes, by former students, by the participants in the management development programs with which we have been associated, by HR managers, and by our colleagues. In particular, we would like to express our appreciation to Mark Tier, Dorothy Galvez, and Chuck Huggins.

We appreciate the efforts of everyone at South-Western College Publishing who helped to develop and produce this text. They include Dave Shaut, publisher and team director; Charles McCormick, senior acquisitions editor; Alice Denny, senior developmental editor; Libby Shipp, production editor; and Joe Sabatino, senior marketing manager. Others who contributed include Joe Devine and Cary Benbow of the Art and Design group at South-Western; Cathy Kuryk of Feldman & Associates, Inc., photo researcher; and at Lachina Publishing, Elaine Clark, project manager.

Our greatest indebtedness is to our wives—Ronnie Bohlander, Marybeth Snell, and Leneve Sherman—who have contributed in so many ways to this book over the years. They are always sources of invaluable guidance and assistance. Furthermore, by their continued enthusiasm and support, they have made the process a more pleasant and rewarding experience. We are most grateful to them for their many contributions to this publication, to our lives, and to our families.

George W. Bohlander
Arizona State University

Scott A. Snell
The Pennsylvania State University

Arthur W. Sherman, Jr.
California State University, Sacramento

# Authors

## George W. Bohlander

George W. Bohlander is Professor of Management at Arizona State University. He teaches undergraduate, graduate, and executive development programs in the field of human resources and labor relations. His areas of expertise include employment law, training and development, work teams, public policy, and labor relations. He is the recipient of six outstanding teaching awards at ASU and has received the Outstanding Undergraduate Teaching Excellence Award given by the College of Business at ASU. In 1996, Dr. Bohlander received the prestigious ASU Parents Association Professorship for his contributions to students and teaching.

Dr. Bohlander is an active researcher and author. He has published over 50 articles and monographs covering various topics in the human resources area, ranging from labor-management cooperation to team training. His articles appear in such academic and practitioner journals as *Labor Studies Journal, HRMagazine, Labor Law Journal, Journal of Collective Negotiations in the Public Sector, Public Personnel Management, National Productivity Review, Personnel, Employee Relations Law Journal,* and *Journal of Individual Employment Rights.*

Before beginning his teaching career, Dr. Bohlander served as Human Resource administrator for General Telephone Company of California. His duties included recruitment and selection, training and development, equal employment opportunity, and labor relations. He was very active in resolving employee grievances and in arbitration preparation. Dr. Bohlander continues to be a consultant to both public- and private-sector organizations, and he has worked with such organizations as the U.S. Postal Service, Kaiser Cement, McDonnell Douglas, Arizona Public Service, American Productivity Center, Rural Metro Corporation, BFGoodrich, and Del Webb. Dr. Bohlander is also an active labor arbitrator. He received his Ph.D. from the University of California at Los Angeles and his M.B.A. from the University of Southern California.

## Scott A. Snell

Scott A. Snell is Professor of Management at The Pennsylvania State University. During his career, Dr. Snell has taught courses in human resource management, principles of management, and strategic management to undergraduates, graduates, and executives. In addition to his teaching duties, Dr. Snell also serves as director of research for Penn State's Institute for the Study of Organizational Effectiveness.

As an industry consultant, Professor Snell has worked with companies such as Arthur Andersen, AT&T, GE, IBM, and Shell Chemical to redesign human resource systems to cope with changes in the competitive environment. His specialization is the realignment of staffing, training, and reward systems to complement technology, quality, and other strategic initiatives. Recently his work has centered on the development of human capital as a source of competitive advantage.

Dr. Snell's research has been published in the *Academy of Management Journal, Academy of Management Review, Human Resource Management Review, Industrial Relations, Journal of Business Research, Journal of Management, Journal of Managerial Issues, Organizational Dynamics, Organization Studies, Personnel Administrator, Personnel Psychology, Strategic Management Journal,* and *Working Woman.* With Thomas S. Bateman he is also co-author of *Management: Building Competitive Human Resource Management Advantage.* In addition, Dr. Snell has served on the editorial boards of *Journal of Managerial Issues, Digest of Management Research, Human Resource Management Review, Human Resource Management,* and *Academy of Management Journal.*

He holds a B.A. in psychology from Miami University (Ohio) as well as M.B.A. and Ph.D. degrees in business administration from Michigan State University. His professional associations include the Strategic Management Society, Academy of Management, and the Society for Human Resource Management.

## Arthur W. Sherman, Jr.

Arthur W. Sherman, Jr., is Professor of Psychology, California State University, Sacramento. During most of his academic career he has taught undergraduate and graduate courses in organizational psychology, personnel psychology, human resources management, psychological testing, and professional development in psychology. Dr. Sherman has served as a consultant to several organizations, including the Department of Consumer Affairs of the State of California and the Social Security Administration. He has been a participant in seminars and workshops for twelve consecutive years as a lecturer in the management development program conducted by the CSUS School of Business Administration for the federal government. For over twenty years he had a private practice as a licensed psychologist specializing in career counseling.

He has been an author of this book since its first edition as well as of *Personnel Practices of American Companies in Europe,* published by the American Management Association.

As an undergraduate, Dr. Sherman attended Oberlin College and Ohio University, receiving a B.A. in psychology from Ohio University. He received an M.A. from Indiana University and a Ph.D. in industrial and counseling psychology from The Ohio State University. His professional affiliations include the American Psychological Association, the Society for Industrial and Organizational Psychology, and the Academy of Management.

EDITION 12

# Managing Human Resources

# chapter 1

# The Challenge of Human Resources Management

## AFTER STUDYING THIS CHAPTER, YOU SHOULD BE ABLE TO

 **OBJECTIVE 1** Identify how firms gain sustainable competitive advantage through people.

 **OBJECTIVE 2** Explain how globalization is influencing human resources management.

 **OBJECTIVE 3** Describe the impact of information technology on managing people.

 **OBJECTIVE 4** Identify the importance of change management.

 **OBJECTIVE 5** State HR's role in developing intellectual capital.

 **OBJECTIVE 6** Differentiate how TQM and reengineering influence HR systems.

 **OBJECTIVE 7** Discuss the impact of cost pressures on HR policies.

 **OBJECTIVE 8** Discuss the primary demographic and employee concerns pertaining to HRM.

 **OBJECTIVE 9** Provide examples of the roles and competencies of today's HR managers.

There's an old joke that goes . . .

*The organization of the future will be so technologically advanced that it will be run by just one person and a dog. The person will be there to feed the dog, and the dog will be there to make sure that the person doesn't touch anything.*

In the past, observers feared that machines might one day eliminate the need for people at work. In reality, just the opposite has been occurring. People are more important in today's organizations than ever before. According to former U.S. Secretary of Labor Robert Reich, "competitiveness is what a company can do uniquely," and the thing that is most unique within each company is the capability of its people.[1]

We use a lot of words to describe the importance of people to organizations. The term "human resources" implies that people have capabilities that drive organizational performance (along with other resources such as money, materials, information, and the like). Other terms such as "human capital" and "intellectual assets" all have in common the idea that people make the difference in how an organization performs. Successful organizations are particularly adept at bringing together different kinds of people to achieve a common purpose. This is the essence of human resources management (HRM).

# Why Study Human Resources Management?

As you embark on this course, you may be wondering how the topic of human resources management relates to your interests and career aspirations. The answer to the question "Why study HRM?" is pretty much the same regardless of whether you plan on working in an HR department or not. Staffing the organization, designing jobs and teams, developing skillful employees, identifying approaches for improving their performance, and rewarding employee successes—all typically labeled HRM issues—are as relevant to line managers as they are to managers in the HR department.

To work with people effectively, we have to understand human behavior, and we have to be knowledgeable about the various systems and practices available to help us build a skilled and motivated workforce. At the same time, we have to be aware of economic, technological, social, and legal issues that either facilitate or constrain our efforts to achieve organizational goals.

## Competitive Advantage through People

**Core competencies**
Integrated knowledge sets within an organization that distinguish it from its competitors and deliver value to customers

While people have always been central to organizations, today they have taken on an even more central role in building a firm's competitive advantage. Particularly in knowledge-based industries such as software and information services, success increasingly depends on "people-embodied know-how." This includes the knowledge, skills, and abilities imbedded in an organization's members.[2] In fact, a growing number of experts now argue that the key to a firm's success is based on establishing a set of **core competencies**—integrated knowledge sets within an organization that distinguish it from its competitors and deliver value to customers. McDonald's, for example, has developed core competencies in management efficiency and training. Federal Express has core competencies in package routing, delivery, and employee relations. Canon Corporation has core competencies in precision mechanics, fine optics, and microelectronics. British Petroleum has core competencies in oil exploration.[3] Core competencies tend to be limited in number, but they provide a long-term basis for technology innovation, product development, and service delivery.

Organizations can achieve sustained competitive advantage through people if they are able to meet the following criteria:[4]

1. *The resources must be of value.* People are a source of competitive advantage when they improve the efficiency or effectiveness of the company. Value is increased when employees find ways to decrease costs, provide something unique to customers, or some combination of the two. Empowerment programs, total-quality initiatives, and continuous improvement efforts at companies such as Corning and Schreiber Foods are intentionally designed to increase the value that employees represent on the bottom line.

2. *The resources must be rare.* People are a source of competitive advantage when their skills, knowledge, and abilities are not equally available to competitors. Companies such as Microsoft, Sun Microsystems, and McKinsey invest a great deal to hire and train the best and the brightest employees in order to gain advantage over their competitors.

3. *The resources must be difficult to imitate.* People are a source of competitive advantage when employee capabilities and contributions cannot be copied by others. Disney, Southwest Airlines, and Mirage Resorts are each known for creating unique cultures that get the most from employees (through teamwork) and are difficult to imitate.

4. *The resources must be organized.* People are a source of competitive advantage when their talents can be combined and deployed to work on new assignments at a moment's notice. Companies such as Spyglass Inc., a software company, and AT&T have invested in information technology to help allocate and track employee assignments to temporary projects. Teamwork and cooperation are two other pervasive methods for ensuring an organized workforce.

These four criteria highlight the importance of people and show the closeness of HRM to strategic management. In a recent survey by *USA Today* and Deloitte & Touche, nearly 80 percent of corporate executives said the importance of HRM in their firms has grown substantially over the past ten years, and two-thirds said that HR expenditures are now viewed as a strategic investment rather than simply a cost to be minimized.[5] Because employee skills, knowledge, and abilities are among the most distinctive and renewable resources upon which a company can draw, their strategic management is more important than ever. As Thomas J. Watson, founder of IBM, said, "You can get capital and erect buildings, but it takes people to build a business."[6]

While "competing through people" may be a theme for human resources management, the idea remains only a framework for action. On a day-to-day basis, managers focus on specific challenges and issues that pertain to human resources. Figure 1.1 provides an overall framework for human resources management. From

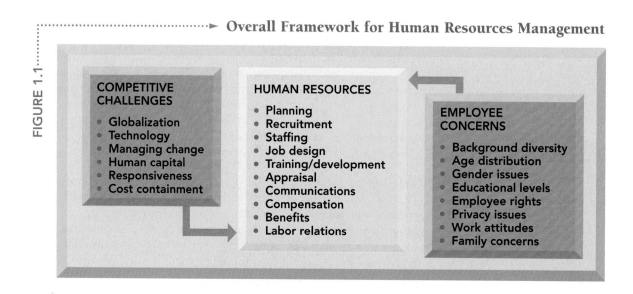

FIGURE 1.1 ▸ **Overall Framework for Human Resources Management**

**COMPETITIVE CHALLENGES**

- Globalization
- Technology
- Managing change
- Human capital
- Responsiveness
- Cost containment

**HUMAN RESOURCES**

- Planning
- Recruitment
- Staffing
- Job design
- Training/development
- Appraisal
- Communications
- Compensation
- Benefits
- Labor relations

**EMPLOYEE CONCERNS**

- Background diversity
- Age distribution
- Gender issues
- Educational levels
- Employee rights
- Privacy issues
- Work attitudes
- Family concerns

this figure, we can see that HRM has to help blend many aspects of management; at this point we will simply classify them as either "competitive challenges" or "employee concerns." By balancing sometimes competing demands, HRM plays an important role in getting the most from employees and providing a work environment that meets their short-term and long-term needs. We will use this framework as a basis for our discussion throughout the rest of this chapter.

# Competitive Challenges and Human Resources Management

For over a decade, the Society for Human Resource Management and the Commerce Clearing House have sponsored an ongoing study of the most important competitive trends and issues facing HR. These key trends extend beyond "people issues" per se, but they all focus on the need to develop a skilled and flexible workforce in order to compete in the twenty-first century:[7]

- Going global
- Embracing new technology
- Managing change
- Developing human capital
- Responding to the market
- Containing costs

## Challenge 1: Going Global

In order to grow and prosper, many companies are seeking business opportunities in global markets. Competition and cooperation with foreign companies have become increasingly important focal points for business since the early 1980s. Indeed, nearly 17 percent of U.S. corporate assets are invested overseas.

### Impact of Globalization

By partnering with firms in other regions of the world and using information technologies to coordinate distant parts of their businesses, companies such as Motorola, General Electric, and Nissan have shown that their vision for the future is to offer customers "anything, anytime, anywhere" around the world. But **globalization** is not just something of interest to large firms. While estimates vary widely, approximately 70 to 85 percent of the U.S. economy today is affected by international competition. Seven Seas Petroleum, for example, is a small company of only six full-time employees based in Houston, Texas, that works in the oil and gas exploration business around the globe. Since its beginning in 1995, the company has worked on more than sixty projects in more than twenty countries, including Colombia, Argentina, Australia, and Papua New Guinea. Other small companies, such as SpringHill Greenhouses in Lodi, Ohio, partner with florists through associations like FTD and Teleflora to work with growers in countries such as Holland (tulips and lilies) and Colombia (roses) to serve customers around the world.[8]

**Globalization**
Trend toward opening up foreign markets to international trade and investment

Efforts to lower trade barriers and open up global markets to free flow of goods, services, and capital among nations has created three zones of economic activity. Within North America, the North American Free Trade Agreement (NAFTA) was created to facilitate commerce between Mexico, Canada, and the United States. Although some U.S. opponents of NAFTA have feared the loss of jobs to Canada and Mexico, where wages are lower, proponents of NAFTA argue that the agreement is helping to remove impediments to trade and investment, thereby creating jobs.[9] While NAFTA focuses on markets in the Western Hemisphere, European Union (EU) focuses on the integration of Europe, and the Asia Pacific Economic Cooperation (APEC) has helped establish freer trade among Pacific Rim countries. The impact of these trade agreements has been impressive. For example, the General Agreement on Tariffs and Trade (GATT) alone is expected to add $330 billion to the world economy by allowing companies to compete in markets that were previously closed to them.[10]

> **USING THE INTERNET**
>
> Learn more about NAFTA by checking out NAFTAnet, sponsored by the North American Forum. The web page is devoted to providing information and resources about NAFTA.
>
> http://www.nafta.net/naftagre.htm

### Effect of Globalization on HRM

For all of the opportunities afforded by international business, when managers talk about "going global," they have to balance a complicated set of issues related to different geographies, cultures, laws, and business practices. Human resource issues underlie each of these concerns and include such things as identifying capable *expatriate managers* who live and work overseas; designing training programs and development opportunities to enhance the managers' understanding of foreign cultures and work practices; and adjusting compensation plans to ensure that pay schemes are fair and equitable across individuals in different regions with different costs of living.

So, while managing across borders provides new and broader opportunities for organizations, it also represents a quantum leap in the complexity of human resources management. In fact, the international arena for HRM is so involved that we have devoted an entire chapter (Chapter 16) to discussing its competitive, cultural, and practical implications.

## Challenge 2: Embracing New Technology

Advancements in computer technology have enabled organizations to take advantage of the information explosion. With computer networks, unlimited amounts of data can be stored, retrieved, and used in a wide variety of ways, from simple record keeping to controlling complex equipment. The effect is so dramatic that at a broader level, organizations are changing the way they do business. Use of the Internet to transact business has become so pervasive for both large and small companies that *e-commerce* is rapidly becoming the organizational challenge of the new millennium. "Virtual organizations" are connected via computer-mediated relationships, and they are giving rise to a new generation of "virtual" workers who work from home, hotels, their cars, or wherever their work takes them. The implications for HRM are at times mind-boggling.

### USING THE INTERNET

For more information about Manpower, see the company's web site at:

http://www.manpower.com/

**From there, you can also access Manpower's Global Learning Center:**

http://www.manpowernet.com/

**Knowledge workers**
Workers whose responsibilities extend beyond the physical execution of work to include planning, decision making, and problem solving

**Human resources information system (HRIS)**
Computerized system that provides current and accurate data for purposes of control and decision making

### *From Touch Labor to Knowledge Workers*

The introduction of advanced technology tends to reduce the number of jobs that require little skill and to increase the number of jobs that require considerable skill. In general, this transformation is referred to as a shift from "touch labor" to **"knowledge workers,"** where employee responsibilities expand to include a richer array of activities such as planning, decision making, and problem solving.[11] In many cases, current employees are being retrained to assume new roles and responsibilities. Even in those cases where employees are displaced, they also require retraining. We thus experience the paradox of having pages of newspaper advertisements for applicants with technical or scientific training while jobseekers without such training register for work with employment agencies.

Technology training makes up a growing portion of all formal training provided by U.S. employers. Today, fully one-third of all courses are devoted to computer skills training (compared with 25 percent in 1996). Manpower Inc., the largest employment agency in the United States, offers free information technology training through its Manpower Global Learning Center (www.manpowernet.com), a new on-line university for its 2 million employees. The learning center enables employees to access material at their leisure on a variety of technical subjects. In fact, Manpower is so focused on developing technical skills in potential employees that it has set up the system so that some training and career planning information is available to those who simply send the company a resume.[12]

### *Influence of Technology in HRM*

Information technology has, of course, changed the face of HRM in the United States and abroad. Perhaps the most central use of technology in HRM is an organization's **human resources information system (HRIS).** An HRIS provides current and accurate data for purposes of control and decision making; in this sense it moves beyond simply storing and retrieving information to include broader applications such as producing reports, forecasting HR needs, strategic planning, career and promotion planning, and evaluating HR policies and practices—a topic discussed further in Chapter 4.

One recent survey found that the most frequent uses of information technology in HRM include maintaining employee records, overseeing payroll operations,

"I'M GLAD TO SEE THE BANK HASN'T BECOME TOTALLY AUTOMATED."

©1998 by Nick Downes; from *Harvard Business Review*.

handling absence and vacation records, and administering recruitment and train-ing programs.[13] The U.S. Army's Career and Alumni Program (ACAP), for exam-ple, uses an HRIS to integrate all available federal and local transition activities for army alumni. The HRIS matches the skills of army veterans with the needs of pri-vate industry.[14] Federal Express recently merged its employee survey feedback process with its corporate human resources information system and created an automated program that taps 99 percent of employees throughout the United States and Canada. Alcoa's PeopleView project has integrated all human resources and payroll data worldwide into one central information system. The tech-nology streamlines HR transactions, processes them more quickly, provides better analytical capability, and along with other changes within HR has saved the company more than $40 million a year.[15]

The Internet has, of course, revolutionized our ability to access technol-ogy. A growing number of companies such as Sun Microsystems, Intel, and Silicon Graphics are using the Internet, and company-specific "intranets," to establish home pages that allow employees to read current job postings and even apply for the positions on-line (see Chapter 4). Equipped with only a PC and a modem, managers can take advantage of on-line services designed especially for HR departments (see Highlights in HRM 1). One such service is provided by ManCom Team, Inc. (www.mancom.com/index.html), an on-line human resources service provider that helps clients to manage, recruit,

**USING THE INTERNET**

For more information about The Mancom Team, Inc., an online HR service provider, check out the company's web site at:

http://mancom. com/

# A Guide to Internet Sites

Cyberspace offers the HR professional a large and growing set of resources for research, news, recruitment, and networking with people and organizations. Listed below are some Internet sites related to the HR field.

- *AFL-CIO's Labor Web (www.aflcio.org/home.htm)* Union news, issue papers, press releases, links to labor sites.
- *American Management Association (www.amanet.org/start.htm)* AMA membership, programs, training, etc.
- *BenefitsLink Homepage (www.magicnet.net/benefits)* Legal information, publications, and benefits yellow pages.
- *FedWorld (www.fedworld.gov/)* A gateway to many government websites.
- *HR Professional's Gateway to the Internet (www.hrisolution.com/index2.html)* Links to HR-related www pages.
- *HRM Resources (www.nbs.ntu.ac.uk/staff/lyerj/hrm_link.htm)* HR publications, consultants, services, etc.
- *Monster.com (www.monster.com)* Home of the Monster Board, news forums, recruitment, and job searches.
- *Occupational Safety and Health Resources (http://osh.net/)* OSHA-related sites, government pages, resources, etc.
- *Society for Human Resource Management (www.shrm.org)*, Current events, information, connections, articles.
- *Technology, HR & Communication (www.inforamp.net/~bcroft/)* HR videoconferencing, groupware, etc.
- *Telecommuting, Teleworking, and Alternative Officing (www.gilgordon.com/)* Telecommuting and flexible hours.
- *Training & Development Homepage (www.tcm.com/trdev/)* Job mart, training links, T&D listserv links.
- *U.S. Department of Labor (www.dol.gov/)* Job bank, labor statistics, press releases, grants, contract information.

train, and develop their workforce. ManCom provides up-to-date information and web pages in several categories, including staffing, careers, employee feedback, training, occupational safety and health, safety, and the like. In addition, the Society for Human Resource Management has a web page (www.shrm.org/) that connects users with over 73,000 HR professionals and allows them to quickly search reference materials, learn about seminars and conferences, read press releases, scan government affairs, and purchase HR-related software products. Highlights in HRM 2 lists just some software companies and the products they provide for managing people.

**HRM 2**

# Human Resource Software Companies

- *Abra Software (www.abra.com)*, St. Petersburg, Florida, (800) 847-2272. PC-based software for tracking and reporting for benefits, attendance, payroll and taxes, job costing, EEO, workers compensation, OSHA, etc.
- *Advanced Personnel Systems, Inc. (www.aps.com)*, Oceanside, California, (619) 941-2800. SmartSearch2 (SS2), a scanning-based employment management system.
- *Criterion Incorporated (www.criterioninc.com)*, Irving, Texas, (800) 782-1818. Strategic-Suite solutions to manage diversity/affirmative action; automate succession planning/career development; online training admin.
- *Cyborg Systems, Inc. (www.cyborg.com)*, Chicago, Illinois, (312) 454-1865. The Solution Series HR management system offers human resources management, payroll processing, and benefits administration.
- *HRDirect, Inc. (www.hrdirect)*, Dover, Delaware, (800) 346-1231. Human resources software, labor law posters, personnel forms, and motivational products. Call 1-800-346-1231 to request a catalog.
- *HRSoft, Inc. (www.hrsoft.com)*, Fairfield, Iowa, (800) 437-6781. HR planning, management, development, competency management, etc.
- *Human Resource Microsystems (www.hrms.com)*, San Francisco, California, (415) 362-8400. Employee tracking and flexible benefits administration system, and applicant tracking software.
- *Infinium Software, Inc. (www.s2k.com)*, Hyannis, Massachusetts, (800) 725-7668. Payroll, training, benefits administration, and industrial health modules. Career planning, succession planning, and work flow.
- *PRI Associates, Inc. (www.priassoc.com)*, Durham, North Carolina, (919) 493-7534. Affirmative action reports, utilization, goals, work force, job group, and adverse impact.
- *Resumix, Inc. (www.resumix.com)*, Sunnyvale, California, (408) 744-3800. Automated staffing and skills management solutions, expert system technology, image processing, client/server architecture, and database technology to produce electronic resume processing systems.
- *PeopleSoft Human Resources (www.peoplesoft.com)*, Pleasanton, California, (800) 947-7753. Recruitment, position management, salary administration, training and development, health and safety, skills inventory, career planning, EEO/affirmative action planning, benefits, etc.
- *Spectrum Human Resource Systems Corporation (www.spectrumhr.com)*, Denver, Colorado, (303) 534-8813. Payroll, training and development, and benefits administration needs.
- *Watson Wyatt Software (www.watsonwyatt.com/homepage/index.asp)*, Lake Oswego, Oregon, (503) 620-9800. Benefits administration, pensions, compensation management, employee surveys/performance management, time and attendance tracking.

Each of these examples shows that technology is changing the face of HRM—altering the methods of collecting employment information, speeding up the processing of that data, and improving the process of internal and external communication. Because of these implications, HR and line managers should jointly plan for its implementation. In small companies, in particular, managers should consider the following factors in their needs assessment for an HRIS:

- Initial costs and annual maintenance costs
- Fit of software packages to the employee base
- Ability to upgrade
- Increased efficiency and time savings
- Compatibility with current systems
- User-friendliness
- Availability of technical support
- Needs for customizing
- Time required to implement
- Training time required for HR and payroll[16]

On the front end, HR and line managers can identify methods for introducing new technology that minimize disruption and also minimize fears and concerns of employees. Communication with employees clearly plays a crucial role, as management must demonstrate a real commitment to supporting change through staffing, training, job redesign, and reward systems. Specifically, HR managers can provide guidance to line managers to ensure that the right technological skills are identified and sought in new employees, as well as in developing technology-literacy training programs. HR can also identify and evaluate the changes in organizational relationships brought about by new technology. In this regard, privacy issues are becoming more of a concern. Finally, HR should work with line managers to develop new structures that use technology to improve service, increase productivity, and reduce costs.[17]

## Challenge 3: Managing Change

Technology and globalization are only two of the forces driving change in organizations and HRM. As Jack Welch, CEO of General Electric, put it, "You've got to be on the cutting edge of change. You can't simply maintain the status quo, because somebody's always coming from another country with another product, or consumer tastes change, or the cost structure does, or there's a technology breakthrough. If you're not fast and adaptable, you're vulnerable. This is true for every segment of every business in every country in the world."[18]

### Types of Changes

Programs focused on total quality, continuous improvement, downsizing, reengineering, outsourcing, and the like are all examples of the means organizations are using to modify the way they operate in order to be more successful. Some of these changes are **reactive,** resulting when external forces have already affected an organization's performance. Other changes are more **proactive,** being initiated by managers to take advantage of targeted opportunities, particularly in fast-changing

**Reactive change**
Change that occurs after external forces have already affected performance

**Proactive change**
Change initiated to take advantage of targeted opportunities

industries where followers are not successful. Jack Welch, for example, recognized GE's need for change while the company was performing quite well and set in motion a series of actions to make GE a leader in all of its businesses. His goal was to bring about "boundarylessness" within the company by fostering better cooperation among parts of the business. To accomplish this goal, Welch and Steve Kerr, GE's vice president of learning, instituted a program called "Workout!" This program was designed to involve employees in instituting continuous innovation and improvement.[19] These types of change initiatives are not designed to fix problems that have arisen in the organization so much as they are designed to help renew everyone's focus on key success factors.

### Managing Change through HR

In a recent survey by the American Management Association (AMA), 84 percent of executives polled said that they have at least one change initiative going on in their organizations. Yet surprisingly, in contrast to the GE experience, only about two-thirds said that their companies have any sort of formal change-management program to support these initiatives![20] This is unfortunate since successful change rarely occurs naturally or easily. Most of the major reasons why change efforts can fail come down to HR issues. Some of the top reasons are as follows:[21]

1.   Not establishing a sense of urgency
2.   Not creating a powerful coalition to guide the effort
3.   Lacking leaders who have a vision
4.   Lacking leaders who communicate the vision
5.   Not removing obstacles to the new vision
6.   Not systematically planning for and creating short-term "wins"
7.   Declaring victory too soon
8.   Not anchoring changes in the corporate culture

Most employees—regardless of occupation—understand that the way things were done five or ten years ago is very different from how they are done today (or will be done five or ten years from now). Responsibilities change, job assignments change, work processes change. And this change is continuous—a part of the job—rather than temporary. Nevertheless, people often resist change because it requires them to modify or abandon ways of working that have been successful or at least familiar to them. As Dr. Marilyn Buckner, president of National Training Systems, put it: "Nontechnical, unattended human factors are, in fact, most often the problem in failed change projects." To manage change, executives and managers have to envision the future, communicate this vision to employees, set clear expectations for performance, and develop the capability to execute by reorganizing people and reallocating assets. Of course, this is easier said than done. Therefore all managers, including those in HR, have an important role in facilitating change processes, particularly in helping communicate business needs to employees and in listening to employee concerns.[22]

**Human capital**
The knowledge, skills, and capabilities of individuals that have economic value to an organization

## Challenge 4: Developing Human Capital

The idea that organizations "compete through people" highlights the fact that success increasingly depends on an organization's ability to manage **human capital**. The term "human capital" describes the economic value of knowledge, skills, and capabilities. Although the value of these assets may not show up directly on a company's balance sheet, it nevertheless has tremendous impact on an organization's performance. According to Lewis Platt, CEO of Hewlett-Packard, "Successful companies of the twenty-first century will be those who do the best jobs of capturing, storing and leveraging what their employees know."[23]

### Human Capital and HRM

Human capital is intangible and elusive and cannot be managed the way organizations manage jobs, products, and technologies. One of the reasons for this is that the employees, *not* the organization, own their own human capital. If valued employees leave a company, they take their human capital with them, and any investment the company has made in training and developing those people is lost.

**USING THE INTERNET**

For more information about how Skandia manages its human capital, check out the company's web site, which has a special section on intellectual capital:

http://www.skandia-afs.com/

To build human capital in organizations, managers must begin to develop strategies for ensuring superior knowledge, skills, and experience within their workforce. Staffing programs focus on identifying, recruiting, and hiring the best and the brightest talent available. Training programs complement these staffing practices to provide skill enhancement, particularly in areas that cannot be transferred to another company if an employee should leave.[24] In addition, employees need opportunities for development on the job. The most highly valued intelligence tends to be associated with competencies and capabilities that are learned from experience and are not easily taught.[25] Consequently, managers have to do a good job of providing developmental assignments to employees and making certain that job duties and requirements are flexible enough to allow for growth and learning.

Beyond the need to invest in employee development, organizations have to find ways of utilizing the knowledge that currently exists. Too often, employees have skills that go unused. According to Lief Edvinsson, director of intellectual capital for Skandia Insurance, "The value of knowledge management comes from application, not storage." Efforts to empower employees and encourage their participation and involvement more fully utilize the human capital available.[26] (Employee empowerment is discussed fully in Chapter 3.)

In companies such as Fidelity, Goldstar, and Texas Instruments, managers and employees are evaluated on their progress toward meeting developmental goals. These goals focus on skill development and gaining new competencies and capabilities. In a growing number of instances, pay is attached to this knowledge and skill acquisition. Skill-based pay, for example, rewards employees for each new class of jobs they are capable of performing. We will discuss skill-based pay (or pay-for-knowledge) more in Chapter 9.

Developmental assignments, particularly those involving teamwork, can also be a valuable way of facilitating knowledge exchange and mutual learning. Effective communications (whether face to face or through information technology) is instrumental in sharing knowledge and making it widely available throughout the organization. As Dave Ulrich, professor of business at the University of Michigan, noted: "Learning capability is *g* times *g*—a business's ability to *generate* new ideas multiplied by its adeptness at *generalizing* them throughout the company."[27]

HR programs and assignments are often the conduit through which knowledge is transferred among employees. A recent survey by the Human Resource Planning Society revealed that 65 percent of responding companies believed that their HR group plays a key role in developing human capital. Hughes Space & Communications Company, for example, the world's largest producer of commercial communications satellites, has created a "lessons learned architecture" on the Internet where all areas of the company can store the knowledge they have learned. Using the World Wide Web, initial pieces of information and intellectual capital are posted to the company's electronic news groups. This information is then analyzed and consolidated by editorial teams. Employees can access and use this new codified knowledge directly from the Internet. Executives at Hughes estimate that this form of structural capital has reduced the cost of developing a satellite by as much as $25 million.[28]

HR managers and line managers each play an important role in creating an organization that understands the value of knowledge, documents the skills and capabilities available to the organization, and identifies ways of utilizing that knowledge to benefit the firm. We will address these issues throughout the text, but particularly in Chapters 6 and 7 on training and career development.

## Challenge 5: Responding to the Market

Meeting customer expectations is essential for any organization. In addition to focusing on internal management issues, managers must also meet customer requirements of quality, innovation, variety, and responsiveness. These standards often separate the winners from the losers in today's competitive world. How well does a company understand its customers' needs? How fast can it develop and get a new product to market? How effectively has it responded to special concerns? *"Better, faster, cheaper . . . "* These standards require organizations to constantly align their processes with customer needs. Management innovations such as total-quality management (TQM) and process reengineering are but two of the comprehensive approaches to responding to customers. Each has direct implications for HR.

### Total Quality Management and HRM

**Total quality management (TQM)**

A set of principles and practices whose core ideas include understanding customer needs, doing things right the first time, and striving for continuous improvement

**Total quality management (TQM)** is a set of principles and practices whose core ideas include understanding customer needs, doing things right the first time, and striving for continuous improvement. The TQM revolution began in the mid-1980s, pioneered by companies such as Motorola, Xerox, and Ford. But since that time, criteria spelled out in the Malcolm Baldrige National Quality Award have provided the impetus for both large and small companies to rethink their approach to HRM. One of the most recent winners, Custom Research Inc., is a fairly small marketing research firm with only 105 employees.[29]

Unfortunately, TQM programs have not proved to be a panacea for responding to customer needs and improving productivity. In many cases, managers view quality as a quick fix and are disillusioned when results do not come easily. When TQM initiatives do work, it is usually because managers have made major changes in their philosophies and HR programs. A survey of 307 executives from *Fortune* 1000 companies and 308 executives from smaller firms (twenty-plus employees) found that the most important quality-improvement techniques stressed human resources issues: employee motivation, change in corporate culture, and employee education. Organizations known for product and service quality strongly believe that employees are the key to that quality.[30]

One of the reasons that HR programs are so essential to TQM is that they help balance two opposing forces. According to Laurie Broedling, senior vice president of HR and quality at McDonnell Douglas, "One set of forces (the need for order and control) pulls every business toward stagnation, while another set of forces (the need for growth and creativity) drives it toward disintegration."[31] TQM's focus on continuous improvement drives the system toward disequilibrium, while TQM's focus on customers, management systems, and the like provide the restraining forces that keep the system together. HR practices help managers balance these two forces.

### Reengineering and HRM

**Reengineering**

Fundamental rethinking and radical redesign of business processes to achieve dramatic improvements in cost, quality, service, and speed

In recent years, organizations have gone beyond TQM programs to a more comprehensive approach to process redesign called reengineering. **Reengineering** has been described as "the fundamental rethinking and radical redesign of business processes to achieve dramatic improvements in cost, quality, service and speed."[32] Reengineering often requires that managers start over from scratch in rethinking how work should be done, how technology and people should interact, and how entire organizations should be structured.[33] HR issues are central to these decisions. First, reengineering requires that managers create an environment for change and, as we mentioned previously, HR issues drive change. Second, reengineering efforts depend on effective leadership and communication processes, two other areas related to HRM. Third, reengineering requires that administrative systems be reviewed and modified. Selection, job descriptions, training, career planning, performance appraisal, compensation, and labor relations are all candidates for change to complement and support reengineering efforts. We will return to these issues, and speak more directly to the organizational development tools necessary for reengineering, in Chapter 7.

## Challenge 6: Containing Costs

Investments in reengineering, TQM, human capital, technology, globalization, and the like are all very important for organizational competitiveness. Yet, at the same time, there are increasing pressures on companies to lower costs and improve productivity to maximize efficiency. Labor costs are one of the largest expenditures of any organization, particularly in service and knowledge-intensive companies. Organizations have tried a number of approaches to lower costs, particularly labor costs. These include downsizing, outsourcing and employee leasing, and productivity enhancements, each of which has direct impact on HR policies and practices.

### Downsizing

**Downsizing**

The planned elimination of jobs

**Downsizing** is the planned elimination of jobs. For example, when L. L. Bean saw that sales had fallen in 1995, the company undertook a number of efforts to identify what they called "smart cost reductions." Bean's TQM activities helped the company target quality problems and saved an estimated $30 million. But the cuts were not enough, and ultimately Leon Gorman, president of the firm, and Bob Peixotto, vice president of HR and quality, realized the company needed to eliminate some jobs. Instead of simply laying off people, however, the company started early retirement and "sweetened" voluntary separation programs. Then in 1996, the company offered employee sabbaticals for continuing education.[34]

These efforts, combined with better employee communications, helped to soften the blow of layoffs at L. L. Bean. But the pain of downsizing has been widespread throughout the United States. Virtually every major corporation within the country has undergone some cycle of downsizing. In the 1990s, as many as 3,100 layoffs per day were announced, with over 650,000 jobs lost each year. That represents layoffs affecting nearly three-quarters of all the households in our country. Historically, layoffs tended to affect manufacturing firms, and line workers in particular. However, more recently, white-collar and managerial jobs have been the hardest hit. In the largest U.S. firms, 77 percent of the jobs lost in the last decade have been white-collar jobs.[35]

Figure 1.2 shows that the top ten job cutters of the 1990s found substantial productivity increases as a result. Unfortunately, the record on downsizing for most other firms was not quite so positive. Only about half of the companies that have eliminated jobs have seen an increase in profits. In fact, in about 20 percent of the cases, profits actually dropped after downsizing. A recent survey of 500 HR executives found that about one-third felt that their company had let go too many workers. The survey also found that one-third of companies that downsized since 1994 later restored jobs that had been cut.[36]

From a human resources standpoint, these results are not particularly surprising. As Dick Lidstad, vice president of HR for 3M, put it, "You don't get productivity and committed employees if at the first sign of bad times you show them they're expendable." In addition to poor morale among survivors, downsizing incurs additional HR

**FIGURE 1.2**

**▶ Top Ten Corporate Job Cutters**

|  | PERCENT CHANGE (1990 TO 1995) | |
| --- | --- | --- |
|  | IN EMPLOYEES | IN PRODUCTIVITY |
| Digital Equipment | −50.2% | +82.0% |
| McDonnell Douglas | −47.5 | +43.2 |
| General Electric | −25.5 | +38.0 |
| Kmart | −32.4 | +37.1 |
| GTE | −31.2 | +35.3 |
| IBM | −32.5 | +32.5 |
| General Motors | −6.9 | +23.4 |
| General Dynamics | −71.7 | +5.7 |
| Boeing | −35.1 | −6.6 |
| Sears | −40.2 | −9.8 |
| 10-COMPANY TOTAL | −29.1 | +27.9 |

Source: Gene Koretz, "Big Payoffs from Layoffs," *Business Week* (February 24, 1997): 30. Reproduced from the February 24, 1997, issue of *Business Week* by special permission, copyright © 1997 by The McGraw-Hill Companies, Inc.

costs to the company such as severance pay, accrued vacation and sick-day pay-outs, outplacement, pension and benefit payoffs, and administrative costs.

To approach downsizing more intelligently, companies such as Continental Airlines, Dial Corporation, and L. L. Bean (mentioned earlier) have made special efforts to reassign and retrain employees for new positions when their jobs are eliminated. This is consistent with a philosophy of employees as assets, as intel-lectual capital. According to Dick Lidstad, 3M's policy is that "HR has an obliga-tion to help maintain the relationship between a company and its employees. Downsizing ought to be painful—you need to sweat and bleed a little before you take that last step."[37]

### Outsourcing and Employee Leasing

**Outsourcing**
Contracting outside the organization to have work done that formerly was done by internal em-ployees

**Outsourcing** simply means hiring someone outside the company to perform tasks that could be done internally. Companies often hire the services of accounting firms, for example, to take care of financial services. They may hire advertising firms to handle promotions, software firms to develop data-processing systems, or law firms to handle legal issues. Interest in outsourcing has been spurred by exec-utives who want to focus their organization's activities on what they do best—their core competencies. Increasingly, activities such as maintenance, security, catering, and payroll are being outsourced in order to increase the organization's flexibility, lower its overhead costs, and gain access to expertise that others may have. Lewis Galoob Toys, based in San Francisco, is an example of a small company of only about 100 employees that uses outsourcing as a way to compete against industry giants. Independent inventors dream up most of Galoob's products, while outside designers and engineers make the ideas more concrete. Galoob subcontracts man-ufacturing and packaging to vendors in Hong Kong and distributes the toys through mass retailers such as Toys R Us, Wal-Mart, and Kmart.

There are several HR concerns with regard to outsourcing, not the least of which is that if employees are likely to lose their jobs when the work is out-sourced, morale and productivity can drop rapidly. To minimize problems, line and HR managers have to work together to define and communicate transitions plans, minimize the number of unknowns, and help employees identify their employ-ment options.[38]

**Employee leasing**
Process of dismissing employees who are then hired by a leasing company (which handles all HR-related activities) and contracting with that company to lease back the employees

In some cases, the outside vendors may actually hire the displaced employees. For example, M. W. Kellogg, Inc., a petroleum services company based in Hous-ton, recently outsourced its entire clerical staff to the McBer Company, a tempo-rary employment agency. McBer hired most of Kellogg's secretarial staff, so even though the people were employed by a different company, their jobs and locations stayed the same. This process is known as **employee leasing** and will be discussed in more detail in Chapter 4. Employee leasing has been growing rapidly, and according to an analysis by Bankers Trust, the industry could involve $185 billion in revenues and more than 9 million employees by 2005. The value of employee leasing lies in the fact that an organization can essentially maintain its working relationships but shift the administrative costs of health care, retirement, and other benefits to the vendor.[39]

### Productivity Enhancements

Pure cost-cutting efforts such as downsizing, outsourcing, and leasing may prove to be disappointing interventions if managers use them as simple solutions to complex performance problems. Overemphasis on labor costs perhaps misses the broader issue of productivity enhancement.

Since productivity can be defined as the "output gained from a fixed amount of inputs," organizations can increase productivity by either reducing the inputs (the cost approach) or by increasing the amount that employees produce. It is quite possible for managers to cut costs only to find that productivity falls at even a more rapid rate. Conversely, managers may find that increasing investment in employees (raising labor costs) may lead to even greater returns in enhanced productivity. Except in extremely cash-poor organizations, managers may find that looking for additional ways to boost productivity may be the best way to increase the value of their organizations.

In absolute terms, the United States remains the world's most productive nation. However, of major concern to most Americans is the fact that the United States now ranks twelfth among the top thirteen industrialized nations in "growth in output per worker." U.S. annual growth in output per worker averaged 1 percent for most of the 1980s. During the 1990s productivity in basic manufacturing operations improved slightly. Following a cycle of downsizing, the forging of new union agreements, and the closing or modernization of obsolete plants, the U.S. manufacturing sector has been back on a 3 percent growth track.[40]

Employee productivity is the result of a combination of employee abilities, motivation, and work environment. When productivity falls off—or more positively, when productivity improves—the change is usually traceable to enhanced skill, motivation, or a work environment conducive to high performance. In general, this can be summarized in the following equation:

$$\text{Performance} = f(\text{ability, motivation, environment})$$

If any of these three dimensions is low, productivity is likely to suffer. According to the *USA Today*/Deloitte & Touche survey mentioned earlier, three-fourths of executives said their firms will be able to increase productivity over the coming years by focusing more on HR issues. Figure 1.3 shows some of the topics that we cover in this textbook that help managers increase productivity in their organizations.

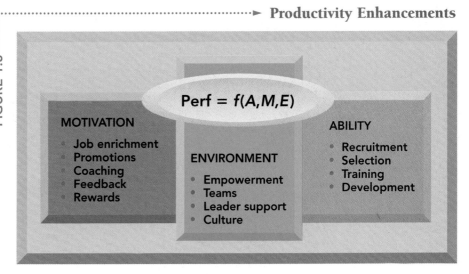

FIGURE 1.3  ▶ **Productivity Enhancements**

Perf = $f(A,M,E)$

**MOTIVATION**
- Job enrichment
- Promotions
- Coaching
- Feedback
- Rewards

**ENVIRONMENT**
- Empowerment
- Teams
- Leader support
- Culture

**ABILITY**
- Recruitment
- Selection
- Training
- Development

# Demographic and Employee Concerns

In addition to the competitive challenges facing organizations, managers in general—and HR managers in particular—need to be concerned about changes in the makeup and the expectations of their employees. As we noted at the beginning of this chapter, HRM involves being an advocate for employees, being aware of their concerns, and making sure that the exchange between the organization and its employees is *mutually* beneficial. Highlights in HRM 3 shows a summary of social concerns in HRM. We will discuss some of these issues here and address all of these issues in greater detail throughout the book.

## Demographic Changes

Among the most significant challenges to managers are the demographic changes occurring in the United States. Because they affect the workforce of an employer, these changes—in employee background, age, gender, and education—are important topics for discussion.

**HRM 3**

**HIGHLIGHTS IN HRM**

## Social Issues in HRM

**Changing Demographics:** The coming decades will bring a more diverse and aging workforce. This has major implications for all aspects of HRM as it alters traditional experience and expectations regarding the labor pool. Among the issues in this area are

- Shrinking pool of entry-level workers
- Individual differences
- Social Security contributions
- Use of temporary employees
- Productivity
- Retirement benefits
- Skills development

**Employer/Employee Rights:** This area reflects the shift toward organizations and individuals attempting to define rights, obligations, and responsibilities. Among the issues here are

- Job as an entitlement
- Whistle-blowing
- AIDS
- Concern for privacy
- Right to work
- Employment at will
- Comparable worth
- Mandated benefits

**Attitudes toward Work and Family:** Because of the increase of working women as well as employee mobility and a growing concern about family issues, there is demand for recognizing and supporting family-related concerns. Among the issues are

- Day care
- Job sharing
- Elder care
- Parental leave
- Flextime
- Alternative work schedules
- Job rotation
- Telecommuting

*As part of their training to become medical assistants, these two minority women are learning how to use a microscope.*

### Diversity of Backgrounds

Of course, American workers will continue to be a diverse group. In the year 2006 minorities will make up an even larger share of the U.S. labor force than they do today. Although whites will still constitute the largest percentage of the labor force, blacks will increase their share from 10 to 11.6 percent, Hispanics from 7 to 11.7 percent, and Asian Americans and others from 3 to 5.4 percent. These nonwhite groups are expected to account for about 70 percent of labor-force growth between now and 2006. Much of this growth is due to the arrival of immigrants who often are of working age but have different educational and occupational backgrounds from those of the U.S. population.[41] In cities such as New York, Houston, Chicago, Los Angeles, Atlanta, and Detroit, minorities currently represent more than half the population.

To accommodate the shift in demographics, many organizations have increased their efforts to recruit and train a more diverse workforce. In this regard, a group of 600 firms such as Chevron, AT&T, and Monsanto has developed an organization called Inroads, which for the past twenty-five years has identified promising minority students during their senior year in high school and offered them summer internships. Darden Restaurants, best known for its Olive Garden and Red Lobster chains, has a long history of recruiting minorities employees. Even further, 7-Eleven, the convenience store chain, has stepped up its efforts to attract minority candidates to be owners of its franchises.[42]

### Age Distribution of Employees

Past fluctuations in the birthrates of Americans are producing abrupt changes in the makeup of the labor force. The number of older workers (age 55 and above) is beginning to rise as baby boomers approach retirement age and is projected to

**USING THE INTERNET**

For more information about 7-Eleven's success attracting minority franchisees, see the company's web site, which has a section devoted to franchise information under "investor relations":

http://www.7-eleven.com/

reach 15.2 percent by 2006. In contrast, the youth share of the labor force (ages 16 to 24) is projected to drop to 16 percent by 2006, placing a strain on those businesses looking for employees just entering the job market.[43]

Imbalance in the age distribution of our labor force has significant implications for employers. Companies such as Pacific Gas and Electric and Bethlehem Steel are finding that large portions of their workforces are nearing retirement. Beyond the sheer number of employees they will have to replace, managers are concerned that the expertise of these employees is likely to be drained too rapidly from the company. As a stopgap measure, employers are making positive efforts to attract older workers, especially those who have taken early retirement. "We're looking to recruit additional senior workers," says Lynn Taylor, director of research at staffing firm Robert Half International based in Menlo Park, California. "They have a vast amount of experience that is invaluable and irreplaceable—and our clients are thrilled to tap that expertise." Older workers, for example, have significantly lower accident rates and absenteeism than younger workers. Further, they tend to report higher job satisfaction scores. And while some motor skills and cognitive abilities may start to decline (starting around age 25), most individuals find ways to compensate for this fact so that there is no discernible impact on their performance.[44]

There is an old cliche that "You can't teach an old dog new tricks." Probably we should revise this to say, "You can't teach an old dog the same way you teach a puppy." To address the fact that seniors learn in different ways, McDonald's, a heavy recruiter of older workers, has developed its McMasters program in which newly hired seniors work alongside experienced employees so that in a matter of four weeks they can be turned loose to work on their own. The training program is designed to help seniors "unlearn" old behaviors while acquiring new skills. More programs like these will be talked about throughout the book.

The other problem that accompanies age imbalances in the workforce might be referred to as the "echo boom" effect. Similar to the trends with baby boomers, those who constitute the new population bulge are experiencing greater competition for advancement from others of approximately the same age. This situation challenges the ingenuity of managers to develop career patterns for employees to smooth out gaps in the numbers and kinds of workers.[45]

## Gender Distribution of the Workforce

According to projections by the Bureau of Labor Statistics, women will continue to join the U.S. labor force and are expected to account for about 47.4 percent by the year 2006.[46] Employers are under constant pressure to ensure equality for women with respect to employment, advancement opportunities, and compensation. They also need to accommodate working mothers and fathers through parental leaves, part-time employment, flexible work schedules, job sharing, telecommuting, and child care assistance. In addition, because more women are working, employers are more sensitive to the growing need for policies and procedures to eliminate sexual harassment in the workplace. Some organizations have special orientation programs to acquaint all personnel with the problem and to warn potential offenders of the consequences. Many employers are demanding that managers and supervisors enforce their sexual harassment policy vigorously. (The basic components of such policies will be presented in Chapter 2.)

**USING THE INTERNET**

The U.S. Department of Labor and U.S. Department of Education web sites are helpful for providing more information about employment and education:

http://www.dol.gov/
http://www.ed.gov/

### Rising Levels of Education

In recent years the educational attainment of the U.S. labor force has risen dramatically. Not coincidentally, the most secure and fastest-growing sectors of employment over the past few decades have been in those areas requiring higher levels of education.[47] Figure 1.4 shows the average payoff in annual earnings from education.

It is important to observe that while the educational level of the workforce has continued to rise, there is a widening gap between the educated and noneducated. At the lower end of the educational spectrum, many employers are having to cope with individuals who are functionally illiterate—i.e., unable to read, write, calculate, or solve problems at a level that enables them to perform even the simplest technical tasks. Here are some frightening statistics: A recent study by the U.S. Department of Education suggests that less than half of all high school seniors are able to handle mathematics problems involving fractions, decimals, percents, elementary geometry, and

**FIGURE 1.4**

**► Education Pays**

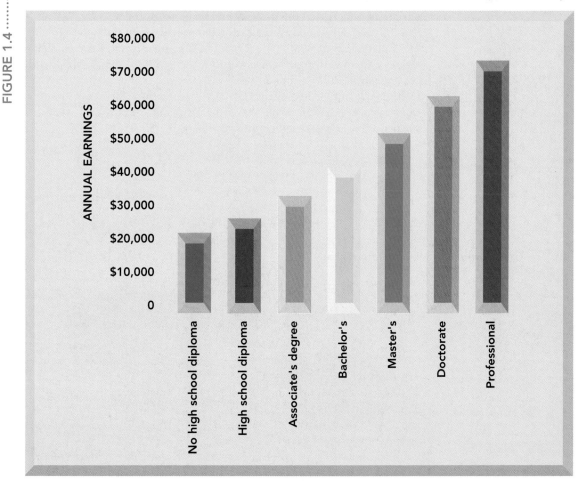

Source: U.S. Department of Labor

simple algebra. Further, a joint study by the Society for Human Resource Management and the Commerce Clearing House suggests that nearly 64 percent of organizations surveyed either knowingly or unknowingly hire workers lacking basic skills. In a speech to the Commonwealth Club of California, David Kearns, chairman and CEO of Xerox Corporation, said, "The American work force is in grave jeopardy. We are running out of qualified people. If current demographic and economic trends continue, American business will have to hire a million new workers a year who can't read, write, or count."[48]

HR managers are interested in these job trends because of their effects on all of the HRM functions. For example, given that minorities and women are increasing their share of the labor force, HR managers frequently analyze how each group is represented in both fast-growing and slow-growing occupations. Women, for example, are fairly well represented in fast-growing occupations such as health services but are also represented in some slow-growth occupations such as secretarial, computer processing, and financial records processing. For blacks and Hispanics, the data are less encouraging. Hispanics are poorly represented in all high-growth occupations, and blacks and Hispanics are heavily concentrated in several of the slow-growth and declining groups. Given these data, a number of efforts have been undertaken to encourage minority recruitment, selection, and training.

**Managing diversity**

Being aware of characteristics common to employees, while also managing employees as individuals

But these are only the initial efforts to provide an overall environment that values and utilizes a diverse workforce. **Managing diversity** means being acutely aware of characteristics *common* to employees, while also managing these employees as *individuals*. It means not just tolerating or accommodating all sorts of differences but supporting, nurturing, and utilizing these differences to the organization's advantage.[49] Figure 1.5 shows the results of a recent study that summarizes the major business-related reasons for managing diversity.

**FIGURE 1.5**

▶ **Diversity Rationale Poll**

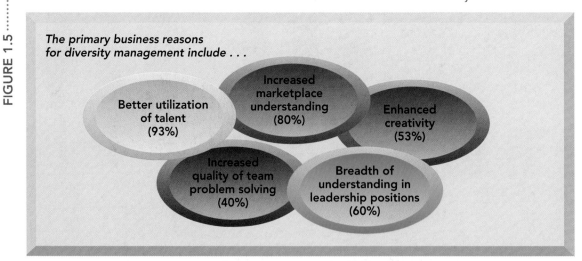

The primary business reasons for diversity management include . . .

Better utilization of talent (93%)

Increased marketplace understanding (80%)

Enhanced creativity (53%)

Increased quality of team problem solving (40%)

Breadth of understanding in leadership positions (60%)

Source: Survey data from Gail Robinson and Kathleen Dechant, "Building a Business Case for Diversity," *Academy of Management Executive* 11, no. 3 (August 1997): 21–31; permission conveyed through the Copyright Clearance Center, Inc.

## Cultural Changes

The attitudes, beliefs, values, and customs of people in a society are an integral part of their culture. Naturally, their culture affects their behavior on the job and the environment within the organization, influencing their reactions to work assignments, leadership styles, and reward systems. Like the external and internal environments of which it is a part, culture is undergoing continual change. HR policies and procedures therefore must be adjusted to cope with this change.

### Employee Rights

Over the past few decades, federal legislation has radically changed the rules for management of employees by granting them many specific rights. Among these are laws granting the right to equal employment opportunity (Chapter 2), union representation if desired (Chapters 14 and 15), a safe and healthful work environment (Chapter 12), a pension plan that is fiscally sound (Chapter 11), equal pay for men and women performing essentially the same job (Chapter 9), and privacy in the workplace. An expanded discussion of the specific areas in which rights and responsibilities are of concern to employers and employees, including the often-cited employment-at-will doctrine, will be presented in Chapter 13.

### Concern for Privacy

HR managers and their staffs, as well as line managers in positions of responsibility, generally recognize the importance of discretion in handling all types of information about employees. Since the passage of the federal Privacy Act of 1974, increased attention to privacy has been evident. While the act applies almost exclusively to records maintained by federal agencies, it has drawn attention to the importance of privacy and has led to the passage of privacy legislation in several states.

Employer responses to the issue of information privacy vary widely. IBM was one of the first companies to show concern for how personal information about employees was handled. It began restricting the release of information as early as 1965 and in 1971 developed a comprehensive privacy policy. Cummins Engine Company, Dow Corning Corporation, Avis, and Corning Glass Works are among other employers that have developed privacy programs.[50] We will discuss the content of such programs and present some recommended privacy guidelines in Chapter 13.

### Changing Attitudes toward Work

Another well-established trend is for employees to define success in terms of personal self-expression and fulfillment of potential on the job. They are frequently less obsessed with the acquisition of wealth and now view life satisfaction as more likely to result from balancing the challenges and rewards of work with those in their personal lives. Though most people still enjoy work, and want to excel at it, they tend to be focused on finding interesting work and may pursue multiple careers rather than being satisfied with just "having a job." People also appear to be seeking ways of living that are less complicated but more meaningful. These new lifestyles cannot help but have an impact on the way employees must be motivated and managed. Consequently, HRM has become more complex than it was when employees were concerned primarily with economic survival.[51]

*As more and more employees strive to balance the demands of their jobs with the needs of their families, employers are responding by offering greater flexibility in the workplace.*

### Balancing Work and Family

Work and the family are connected in many subtle and not-so-subtle social, economic, and psychological ways. Because of the new forms that the family has taken—e.g., the two-wage-earner and the single-parent family—work organizations find it necessary to provide employees with more family-friendly options. "Family friendly" is a broad term that may include unconventional hours, day care, part-time work, job sharing, pregnancy leave, parental leave, executive transfers, spousal involvement in career planning, assistance with family problems, and telecommuting. These issues have become important considerations for all managers and are more fully discussed in Chapter 11. Figure 1.6 shows some of the top concerns managers have about balancing work and home.

Some of the most progressive companies, such as American Express, Levi Strauss, Bank of America, PepsiCo, and Schering-Plough, promote flexibility throughout their organizations. In general, these companies calculate that accommodating individual needs and circumstances is a powerful way to attract and retain top-caliber people. Aetna Life and Casualty, for example, has cut turnover by 50 percent since it began to offer six-month parental leaves, coupled with an option for part-time work when employees return to the job. Bank of America provides up to six weeks of paid leave for fathers. Further, Bank of America encourages all its employees to

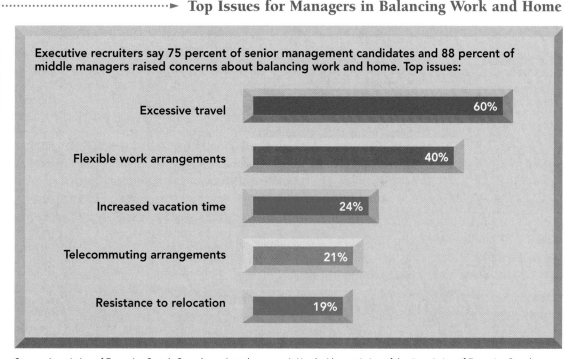

FIGURE 1.6

▶ **Top Issues for Managers in Balancing Work and Home**

**Executive recruiters say 75 percent of senior management candidates and 88 percent of middle managers raised concerns about balancing work and home. Top issues:**

| Issue | Percent |
|---|---|
| Excessive travel | 60% |
| Flexible work arrangements | 40% |
| Increased vacation time | 24% |
| Telecommuting arrangements | 21% |
| Resistance to relocation | 19% |

Source: Association of Executive Search Consultants (member survey). Used with permission of the Association of Executive Search Consultants, http://www.aesc.org.

spend two hours each week visiting their children's schools or volunteering at any school—on company time. Hugh McColl, the company's chairman, sees it this way: "It may seem inconsistent that we're asking employees to work harder now, but the need to pinch pennies and reduce head count plays to the short term, while flexibility is important to our long-term health."[52]

Arthur Andersen has developed a flexible work program that allows new parents to lighten their workloads for up to three years. There are acknowledged costs, however. In professional firms, such as accounting and law, career paths and promotion sequences are programmed in a lockstep manner. Time away from work can slow down—and in some cases derail—an individual's career advancement.

Further, family-friendly companies may risk alienating those who cannot capitalize on the benefits. Only a small minority of employees can actually take advantage of such policies. More than 60 percent of labor-force members have no children under 18. Women with children under age 6 (the core group targeted by such policies) represent only 8 percent of the labor force. A recent Conference Board survey of companies with family-friendly programs found that 56 percent of the companies acknowledge that childless employees harbor resentment against those with children.[53]

# The Partnership of Line Managers and HR Departments

We have taken a good deal of time up front in this book to outline today's competitive and social challenges to reinforce the idea that managing people is not something that occurs in a back room called the HR department. Managing people is every manager's business, and successful organizations are those that combine the experience of line managers with the expertise of HR specialists to develop and utilize the talents of employees to their greatest potential. Addressing HR issues is rarely the exclusive responsibility of HR departments acting alone. Instead, HR managers work side by side with line managers to address people-related issues of the organization. And while this relationship has not always achieved its ideal, the situation is rapidly improving. HR managers are assuming a greater role in top-management planning and decision making, a trend that reflects the growing awareness among executives that HRM can make important contributions to the success of an organization. A recent issue of the *Academy of Management Journal* was completely devoted to research demonstrating that effective management of human resources has a clear relationship to an organization's performance.[54]

## Responsibilities of the Human Resources Manager

Although line managers and HR managers need to work together, their responsibilities are different, as are their competencies and expertise. The major activities for which an HR manager is typically responsible are as follows:

1. *Advice and counsel.* The HR manager often serves as an in-house consultant to supervisors, managers, and executives. Given their knowledge of internal employment issues (policies, labor agreements, past practices, and the needs of employees) as well as their awareness of external trends (economic and employment data, legal issues, and the like), HR managers can be an invaluable resource for making decisions. As in-house consultants, HR managers should be concerned with the operating goals of the managers and supervisors. In turn, these managers must be convinced that the HR staff is there to assist them in increasing their productivity rather than to impose obstacles to their goals. This requires not only the ability on the part of the HR executive to consider problems from the viewpoint of line managers and supervisors but also skill in communicating with the managers and supervisors.[55]

2. *Service.* HR managers also engage in a host of service activities such as recruiting, selecting, testing, planning and conducting training programs, and hearing employee concerns and complaints. Technical expertise in these areas is essential for HR managers and forms the basis of HR program design and implementation.

3. *Policy formulation and implementation.* HR managers generally propose and draft new policies or policy revisions to cover recurring problems or to prevent anticipated problems. Ordinarily, these are proposed to the senior executives of the organization, who actually issue the policies. HR managers may monitor performance of line departments and other staff departments to ensure conformity with established HR policies, procedures, and practice. Perhaps more importantly, they are a resource to whom managers can turn for policy interpretation.

4. *Employee advocacy.* One of the enduring roles of HR managers is to serve as an employee advocate—listening to the employees' concerns and representing their needs to managers. Effective employee relations provides a support structure when disruptive changes interfere with normal daily activities.

In the process of managing human resources, increasing attention is being given to the personal needs of the participants. Thus throughout this book we will not only emphasize the importance of the contributions that HRM makes to the organization but also give serious consideration to its effects on the individual and on society.

Increasingly, employees and the public at large are demanding that employers demonstrate greater social responsibility in managing their human resources. Complaints that some jobs are devitalizing the lives and injuring the health of employees are not uncommon. Charges of discrimination against women, minorities, the physically and mentally disabled, and the elderly with respect to hiring, training, advancement, and compensation are being leveled against some employers. Issues such as comparable pay for comparable work, the high cost of health benefits, day care for children of employees, and alternative work schedules are concerns that many employers must address as our workforce grows more diverse.

All employers are finding that privacy and confidentiality of information about employees are serious matters and deserve the greatest protection that can be provided.

Where employees are organized into unions (covered in Chapters 14 and 15), employers can encounter costly collective bargaining proposals, threats of strike, and charges of unfair labor practices. Court litigation, demands for corrective action by governmental agencies, sizable damage awards in response to employee lawsuits, and attempts to erode the employment-at-will doctrine valued by employers are still other hazards that contemporary employers must try to avoid. (We will discuss these issues in detail in Chapter 13.)

Top management generally recognizes the contributions that the HR program can make to the organization and thus expects HR managers to assume a broader role in the overall organizational strategy. Thus HR managers must remember the bottom line if they are to fulfill their role.

## Competencies of the Human Resources Manager

As top executives expect HR managers to assume a broader role in overall organizational strategy, many of these managers will need to acquire a complementary set of competencies.[56] These competencies are summarized below and shown graphically in Figure 1.7.

1.  *Business mastery.* HR professionals need to know the business of their organization thoroughly. This requires an understanding of its economic and financial capabilities so that they can "join the team" of business managers. It also requires that HR professionals develop skills at external relations focused on their customers.

2.  *HR mastery.* HR professionals are the organization's behavioral science experts. In areas such as staffing, development, appraisal, rewards, team building, and communication, HR professionals should develop competencies that keep them abreast of changes.

3.  *Change mastery.* HR professionals have to be able to manage change processes so that HR activities are effectively merged with the business needs of the organization. This involves interpersonal and problem-solving skills, as well as innovativeness and creativity.

FIGURE 1.7

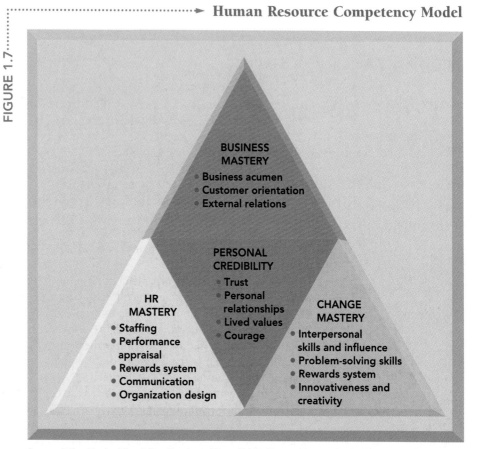

## Human Resource Competency Model

**BUSINESS MASTERY**
- Business acumen
- Customer orientation
- External relations

**PERSONAL CREDIBILITY**
- Trust
- Personal relationships
- Lived values
- Courage

**HR MASTERY**
- Staffing
- Performance appraisal
- Rewards system
- Communication
- Organization design

**CHANGE MASTERY**
- Interpersonal skills and influence
- Problem-solving skills
- Rewards system
- Innovativeness and creativity

Source: Arthur Yeung, Wayne Brockbank, and Dave Ulrich, "Lower Cost, Higher Value: Human Resource Function in Transformation." Reprinted with permission from *Human Resource Planning*, Vol. 17, No. 3 (1994). Copyright 1994 by The Human Resource Planning Society, 317 Madison Avenue, Suite 1509, New York, NY 10017, Phone: (212) 490-6387, Fax: (212) 682-6851.

4.  *Personal credibility.* HR professionals must establish personal credibility in the eyes of their internal and external customers. Credibility and trust are earned by developing personal relationships with customers, by demonstrating the values of the firm, by standing up for one's own beliefs, and by being fair-minded in dealing with others.

The ability to integrate business, HR, and change competencies is essential. By helping their organizations build a sustained competitive advantage and by learning to manage many activities well, HR professionals are becoming full business partners. Forward-looking CEOs such as Carly Fiorina at Hewlett-Packard, Herb Kelleher at Southwest Airlines, and George Fisher at Eastman Kodak make certain that their top HR executives report directly to them and help them address key issues.

At lower levels in the organization, a rapidly growing number of companies such as Ford, Intel, and Corning assign HR representatives to business teams to make certain that HR issues are addressed on the job and that HR representatives, in turn, are knowledgeable about business issues rather than simply focusing on the administrative function.

## Role of the Line Manager

As much as we might say about the role of the HR department, in the final analysis managing people depends upon effective supervisors and line managers. As one executive at Merck put it, "Human resources are far too important to be left to the personnel department." Although HR managers have the responsibility for coordinating programs and policies pertaining to people-related issues, managers and employees themselves are ultimately responsible for performing these functions.

We understand that most readers of this book will be line managers and supervisors, rather than HR specialists. The text is, therefore, oriented to *helping people manage people more effectively,* whether they become first-line supervisors or chief executive officers. Students now preparing for careers in organizations will find that the study of HRM provides a background that will be valuable in managerial and supervisory positions. Discussions concerning the role of the HR department can serve to provide a better understanding of the functions performed by this department. A familiarity with the role of HR should help to facilitate closer cooperation with the department's staff and to utilize more fully the assistance and services available from this resource.

# SUMMARY

**OBJECTIVE 1** People have always been central to organizations, but their strategic importance is growing in today's knowledge-based industries. An organization's success increasingly depends on the knowledge, skills, and abilities of employees, particularly as they help establish a set of core competencies that distinguish an organization from its competitors. When employees' talents are valuable, rare, difficult to imitate, and organized, an organization can achieve a sustained competitive advantage through people.

**OBJECTIVE 2** Globalization influences approximately 70 to 85 percent of the U.S. economy and affects the free flow of trade among countries. This influences the number and kinds of jobs that are available and requires that organizations balance a complicated set of issues related to managing people in different geographies, cultures, legal environments, and business conditions. HR functions such as staffing, training, compensation, and the like have to be adjusted to take into account the differences in global management.

**OBJECTIVE 3** Advanced technology has tended to reduce the number of jobs that require little skill and to increase the number of jobs that require considerable skill, a shift we refer to as moving from touch labor to knowledge work. This displaces some employees and requires that others be retrained. In addition, information technology has influenced HRM through human resources information systems (HRIS) that streamline the processing of data and make employee information more readily available to managers.

**OBJECTIVE 4** Both proactive and reactive change initiatives require HR managers to work with line managers and executives to create a vision for the future, establish an architecture that enables change, and communicate with employees about the processes of change.

**OBJECTIVE 5** In order to "compete through people" organizations have to do a good job of managing human capital: the knowledge, skills, and capabilities that have value to organizations. Managers must develop strategies for identifying, recruiting, and hiring the best talent available; for developing these employees in ways that are firm-specific; for helping them to generate new ideas and generalize them through the company; for encouraging information sharing; and for rewarding collaboration and teamwork.

In order to respond to customer needs better, faster, and more cheaply, organizations have instituted total-quality management (TQM) and reengineering programs. Each of these programs requires that HR be involved in changing work processes, training, job design, compensation, and the like. HR issues also arise when communicating with employees about the new work systems, just as with any change initiative.

 In order to contain costs, organizations have been downsizing, outsourcing and leasing employees, and enhancing productivity. HR's role is to maintain the relationship between a company and its employees, while implementing the changes.

 The workforce is becoming increasingly diverse and organizations are doing more to address employee concerns and to maximize the benefit of different kinds of employees. Demographic changes, social and cultural differences, and changing attitudes toward work can provide a rich source of variety for organizations. But to benefit from diversity, managers need to recognize the potential concerns of employees and make certain that the exchange between the organization and employees is mutually beneficial.

 In working with line managers to address the organization's challenges, HR managers play a number of important roles; they are called on for advice and counsel, for various service activities, for policy formulation and implementation, and for employee advocacy. To perform these roles effectively, HR managers must contribute business competencies, state-of-the-art HR competencies, and change-management competencies. Ultimately, managing people is rarely the exclusive responsibility of the HR function. Every manager's job is managing people, and successful companies are those that combine the expertise of HR specialists with the experience of line managers to develop and utilize the talents of employees to their greatest potential.

## KEY TERMS

core competencies
downsizing
employee leasing
globalization
human capital

human resources information
 system (HRIS)
knowledge workers
managing diversity
outsourcing

proactive change
reactive change
reengineering
total quality management (TQM)

## DISCUSSION QUESTIONS

 1. Are people always an organization's most valuable asset? Why or why not?

 2. Suppose you were asked by your boss to summarize the major people-related concerns in opening up an office in Tokyo. What issues would be on your list?

 3. Will technology eliminate the need for human resources managers?

 4. What are the pros and cons of change? Does it help or hurt organizational performance? Do you like change? Why or why not?

 5. Can you think of a situation where, if a particular person left an organization, the organization's expertise would drop rapidly?

 6. Someone once said that TQM is like paving cowpaths." What do you suppose this means in relation to reengineering?

 7. Do pressures on cost containment work against effective management of people? Why or why not?

 8. What are the pros and cons of having a more diverse workforce? Is the United States in a better position to compete globally because of our diverse population?

 9. In your opinion, what is the most important role of HR managers?

## The Role of HR in Reengineering and Change at Siemens Rolm

Siemens Rolm Communications, based in Santa Clara, California, is an operating company for Siemens, the electrical and electronics systems supplier. Rolm, which employs 5,800 people, was previously owned by IBM, but in 1988 when the company was losing $1 million a day, IBM sold Rolm. As the new owners, executives at Siemens were determined to turn the company around, but they realized that to do so would require a lot of changes. Because Siemens is a knowledge-based company, it had to restructure itself as a learning organization to stay competitive in the new business environment.

To start the change process, Bonnie Hathcock, vice president of HR, put together a team of managers to design a new appraisal process. The new system raised the bar on performance and encouraged employee self-development. The company president and CEO, Karl Geng, was committed to tracking appraisals of key players. The company also worked on a cultural transformation that emphasized "speed, guts, and dramatic moves." More than 600 managers—in small groups across the United States—attended a two-day "world-class management institute," a development conference that reinforced the message. Finally, the company reengineered its pay and rewards policies. HR carved out a portion of the merit budget pool to award employees who had advanced their skills in the previous period. In addition, the new flexible rewards program was instituted to allow managers to award up to $25,000 to employees who "go the extra five miles."

As the company is evolving into a learning organization, HR itself is becoming a new creature, one that brings Siemens Rolm's bid for excellence to fruition. Hathcock asks HR people to work on three skills: (1) business mastery, (2) change and process mastery, and (3) personal credibility. To accomplish this, HR has torn down the "silos" between staffing, training, compensation, and the like and reorganized into five business-driven teams. The Strategy and Design team studies Siemens Rolm's business plans and sets HR strategies that complement those plans. The Consulting Services group helps influence the company's culture and decides how to best deploy people to meet HR goals. The HR Program Integration area ensures that HR managers clone their expertise across the company, so it can maintain its own best practices system. The Education division assists with employee development, and the HR Service Center handles employees' day-to-day administrative HR questions.

According to Bonnie Hathcock, "We can't just think of ourselves as support. We have to be right out there." These efforts, taken together, have helped turn the company around, and in 1996, the firm won *Personnel Journal*'s Optimas Award for Managing Change.

Source: "HR's Advances Reengineer a Restructuring," *Personnel Journal*, January 1996: 60. Reprinted with permission.

### QUESTIONS

1. How can HR practices help Siemens Rolm become a learning organization?
2. What other methods might help the HR organization develop the competencies it needs?
3. What problems, if any, do you see in the Siemens change strategy?

# Managing "Daddy Stress" at Baxter Healthcare

For many years women have been torn between family and career. Now it's time for the men to be torn. In today's environment, some men are starting to rethink their priorities. Sometimes it's because they want to be closer to their kids than their dads were to them. Or sometimes they change unwillingly, pushed by their wives to spend more time on family matters. Whatever the reasons, combine them with a tight labor market, technology that allows employees to work from home, and a younger generation of chief executives, and you're seeing the beginnings of change in the corporate workplace.

"Some chief executives are beginning to acknowledge the problem, both for themselves and their employees. People like Harry M. Jansen Kraemer Jr., the 44-year-old chief of Baxter International, who makes it a point to leave his office at 6 p.m. to have dinner with his wife and four kids." "Harry Kraemer is part of a new generation. He woke up to the problem [of work/life balance] three years ago when Baxter, which manufactures medical products, surveyed employees and found that conflicts between work and home were roiling the company. Surprisingly, even more men than women reported feeling stress. Look at the gender split: Forty-nine percent of men versus 39 percent of women said they were looking for a new job because of work/life conflicts.

"Kraemer could understand. Unlike the bosses of a previous generation, whose wives supported them every inch of their climb, his wife was a banker until after their fourth child was born eighteen months ago. Both had heavy travel schedules. They took turns bringing the kids to day care. One day Kraemer was late to a meeting because when he arrived at his Deerfield, Illinois, office he found his 3-year-old daughter in the backseat of his car. "Dad, where are we?" she said. Rushed, he thought he had dropped her off at the baby-sitter's house.

"Kraemer is not merely a sympathizer; he's a practical employer in a tight labor market. So he supports employees working flexible schedules. In the past three years the number of Baxter employees (men and women) in the United States using alternative work arrangements doubled, to 2,310. They don't necessarily have to take pay cuts; they're simply not in the office during traditional hours, instead working part or all of the time from home or getting their work done in four days rather than five. Some employees post 'office hours' on their doors.

"To make sure his managers practice what he preaches, their raises hinge in part on an evaluation by their subordinates on how well they do in providing a supportive work/life environment. Kraemer also writes a monthly newsletter that typically leads with a funny account of life at the Kraemer household.

"Kraemer knows employees will gauge the sincerity of the change by how he leads his life. He hasn't given up his travel schedule, but when he's in town he's usually out of the office by 6 to have dinner with his family, helping his kids practice baseball, or do homework with them. From 10 p.m. to 1 a.m. he takes a run and does voice mail and e-mail. 'In any company, people are looking for signals,' he says. 'When they see me leave at a reasonable hour, they know this isn't being done for effect.'

"Is any of this good for business? Kraemer is convinced it is. He points to Baxter's logistics department: Thirty of its 100 employees—four of them men—work some kind of alternative work schedules. Yet volume has doubled in the last six years.

"As for his immediate subordinates, Kraemer says he no longer insists they hang around all the time. 'Whether your people are in Chicago, whether they're at home, whether they are in another country, as long as there is reasonable communication, why do you care how often you see any of those people?' It's results he wants."

Source: Mary Beth Grover, "Daddy Stress," *Forbes* 164 no. 5 (September 6, 1999): 202–8. Reprinted by Permission of Forbes Magazine ©1999 Forbes.

### QUESTIONS

1.  How do the pressures of the family/work balance differ for men and women?
2.  What can companies do to ensure a family-friendly work environment?
3.  What specific HRM practices would support a family friendly organization?

## Managing Diversity for Competitive Advantage at Deloitte & Touche

In 1992, Deloitte & Touche, LLP, was celebrating the tenth year in which approximately 50 percent of its new hires were women. Because it takes nearly a decade to become a partner, the Big Six accounting firm based in Wilton, Connecticut, was now sitting back waiting for all the women in the pipeline to start making bids for partnership.

But something unexpected happened. Instead of seeing an increase in the number of women applying for partnership, Deloitte & Touche saw a *decline*. Talented women were leaving the firm and this represented a huge drain of capable people. In a knowledge-intensive business such as theirs, this problem went beyond social consciousness. The success of the firm was at stake. They could not afford to lose valued partners.

To address the problem, the company formed the Task Force on the Retention and Advancement of Women to pinpoint the reason women were leaving. The task force conducted a massive information-gathering initiative, interviewing women at all levels of the company, even contacting women who had left the firm. The task force uncovered three main areas of complaint: (1) a work environment that limited opportunity for advancement, (2) exclusion from mentoring and networking, and (3) work and family issues.

The networking and mentoring concerns seemed to be the most troublesome. In a male-dominated business, men often network, sometimes to the exclusion of women. To tackle this problem, Deloitte & Touche retooled the work environment. It made changes such as a renewed commitment to flexible work arrangements, reduced workload, and flextime. The firm also developed plans for company-sponsored networking and formal career planning for women. In addition, the firm's 5,000 partners and managers attended two-day workshops called "Men and Women as Colleagues" at a price to the company of approximately $3 million.

The results have been terrific. Retention of women at all levels has risen, and for the first time in the history of the firm, turnover rates for senior managers (just before making partner) have been lower for women than for men. In addition, in 1995 the company promoted its highest percentage of new partners who were women (21 percent). Deloitte & Touche is basking in its new reputation as a woman-friendly firm: It now has the most female employees in the Big Six (52 percent of new hires). This gives them external recognition in the marketplace and not only helps them with recruiting but also gives them a laudable reputation with their customers. Apart from strictly diversity concerns, the business reasons for making these changes are coming home very quickly. For its efforts, Deloitte & Touche received *Personnel Journal*'s 1996 Optimas Award for Competitive Advantage.

Source: Excerpted from "Firm's Diversity Efforts Even the Playing Field," *Personnel Journal*, January 1996: 56.

### QUESTIONS

1. How did the problems at Deloitte & Touche occur in the first place?
2. Did their changes fix the underlying problems? Explain.
3. What other advice would you give their managers?

## NOTES AND REFERENCES

1. Michael A. Verespej, "Invest in People," *Industry Week* 248, no. 3 (February 1, 1999): 6–7.
2. C. K. Prahalad and G. Hamel, "The Core Competence of the Corporation," *Harvard Business Review* 68, no. 3 (1990): 79–91.
3. Dorothy Griffiths, Max Boisot, Veronica Mole, "Strategies for Managing Knowledge Assets: A Tale of Two Companies," *Technovation* 18, no. 8/9 (August/September 1998): 529–539; P. M. Wright, G. C. McMahan, B. McCormick, S. W. Sherman, "Strategy, Core Competence, and HR Involvement as Determinants of HR Effectiveness and Refinery Performance," *Human Resource Management* 37, no. 1 (Spring 1998): 17–29. See also G. Hamel and C. K. Prahalad, *Competing for the Future* (Boston: Harvard Business School Press, 1994); J. B. Quinn, "The Intelligent Enterprise: A New Paradigm," *Academy of Management Executive* no. 4 (1992): 48–63.
4. Russell W. Coff, "Human Assets and Management Dilemmas: Coping with Hazards on the Road to Resource-Based Theory," *Academy of Management Review* 22, no. 2 (April 1997): 374–402; S. A. Snell, M. A. Youndt, and P. M. Wright, "Establishing a Framework for Research in Strategic Human Resource Management: Merging Resource Theory and Organiza-

tional Learning," in G. Ferris (ed.), *Research in Personnel and Human Resource Management*, vol. 14 (Greenwich, Conn.: JAI Press, 1996), 61–90.
5. "The Importance of HR," *HRFocus* 73, no. 3, March 1996, 14.
6. T. J. Watson, Jr., *A Business and Its Beliefs: The Ideas That Helped Build IBM* (New York: McGraw-Hill, 1963).
7. William J. Rothwell, "Trends in HRM," Commerce Clearing House and Society for Human Resource Management. See also Dave Ulrich, "The Future Calls for Change," *Workforce* 77, no. 1 (January 1998): 87–91; William J. Rothwell, Robert K. Prescott, and Maria Taylor, "Tranforming HR into a Global Powerhouse," *HRFocus* 76, no. 3 (March 1999): 7–8; Gerald R. Ferris, Wayne A. Hochwarter, M. Ronald Buckley, Gloria Harrell-Cook, and Dwight D. Frink, "Human Resources Management: Some New Directions," *Journal of Management* 25, no. 3 (1999): 385–415; R. A. Shafer, A. B. Shostak, R. J. Flanagan, J. A. Alutto, and B. H. Harvey, "Professing HR Trends," *HRMagazine* 44, no. 11 (1999): 44–59.
8. Bruce E. Lazier, "Seven Seas Petroleum Inc.," *Oil & Gas Investor* 18, no. 4 (April 1998): 84; Leslie Haines, "Spreading Their Wings," *Oil & Gas Investor* 19, no. 1 (January 1999): 46–50.

9. "The Real NAFTA Winner," *Business Week* (September 27, 1999), 34; David Ensign, "NAFTA: Two Sides of the Coin," *Spectrum* 70, no. 4 (Fall 1997): 1–4.

10. I. M. Destler, "Trade Policy at a Cross Roads," *Brookings Review* 17, no. 1 (Winter 1999): 26–30.

11. Peter F. Drucker, "Knowledge-Worker Productivity: The Biggest Challenge," *California Management Review* 41 no. 2 (Winter 1999): 79–94; Michael Schrage, "It Seemed Brilliant at the Time," *Fortune* 140, no. 7 (October 11, 1999): 324. See also D. P. Lepak and S. A. Snell, "The Human Resource Architecture: Toward a Theory of Human Capital Development and Allocation," *Academy of Management Review* 24, no. 1 (1999): 31–48.

12. "Industry Report 1998: Information-Technology Training," *Training* 35, no. 10 (October 1998): 63–68; Barb Cole-Gomolski, "Recruiters Lure Temps with Free IT Training," *Computerworld* 33, no. 31 (August 2, 1999): 10.

13. Colin Richards-Carpenter, "Make a Difference by Doing IT Better," *People Management,* June 13, 1996, 39–40. See also Kenneth A. Kovach and Charles E. Cathcart, Jr., "Human Resource Information Systems (HRIS): Providing Business with Rapid Data Access, Information Exchange and Strategic Advantage," *Public Personnel Management* 28, no. 2 (Summer 1999): 275–82.

14. Scott A. Snell, Patricia Pedigo, and George M. Krawiec, "Managing the Impact of Information Technology on Human Resource Management," in Gerald R. Ferris, Sherman D. Rosen, and Darold T. Barnum (eds.), *Handbook of Human Resources Management* (Oxford, U.K.: Blackwell Publishers, 1995): 159–74. See also Bill Roberts, "Focus on Making Employee Data Pay," *HRMagazine* 44, no. 11 (1999): 86–96.

15. Rosa V. Lindahl, "Automation Breaks the Language Barrier," *HRMagazine* 41, no. 3, March 1996, 79–83; "Alcoa Heads toward Eliminating Administration," *Employee Benefit Plan Review,* 1996, 50.

16. Ruth E. Thaler-Carter, "The HRIS in Small Companies: Tips for Weighing the Options," *HRMagazine* 43, no. 8 (July 1998): 30–37.

17. Erik R. Eddy, Dianna L. Stone, and Eugene F. Stone-Romero, "The Effects of Information Management Policies on Reactions to Human Resource Information Systems: An Integration of Privacy and Procedural Justice Perspectives," *Personnel Psychology* 52, no. 2 (Summer 1999): 335–58; Joan C. Hubbard, Karen A. Forcht, and Daphyne S. Thomas, "Human Resource Information Systems: An Overview of Current Ethical and Legal Issues," *Journal of Business Ethics* 17, no. 12 (September 1998): 1319–23.

18. P. M. Senge, *The Fifth Discipline: The Art and Practice of the Learning Organization* (New York: Doubleday Currency, 1990); I. Nonaka and H. Takeuchi, *The Knowledge-Creating Company: How Japanese Companies Create the Dynamics of Innovation* (New York: Oxford Press, 1995).

19. Stratford Sherman, "A Master Class in Radical Change," *Fortune,* December 13, 1993, 95–96.

20. Jennifer J. Laabs, "Change," *Personnel Journal,* July 1996, 54–63.

21. John P. Kotter, "Leading Change: Why Transformation Efforts Fail," *Harvard Business Review,* March-April 1995, 59–67.

22. Lee G. Bolman and Terry E. Deal, "Four Steps to Keeping Change Efforts Heading in the Right Direction," *Journal of Quality and Participation* 22, no. 3 (May/June 1999): 6–11; Shannon Beske and Kevin Stallings, "Current Practices: Leading Strategic Change: Tools and Techniques," *Human Resource Planning* 21 no. 2 (1998): 9–10; Brenda Paik Sunoo, "Reinventing Government," *Workforce* 77, no. 2 (February 1998): 60–61; Gillian Flynn, "It Takes Values to Capitalize on Change," *Workforce* 76, no. 4 (April 1997): 27–34; Noel Tichy, "Revolutionize Your Company," *Fortune,* December 13, 1993, 115.

23. Marilyn Martiny, "Knowledge Management at HP Consulting," *Organizational Dynamics,* Autumn 1998, 71–77; Jerry Bowles and Josh Hammond, "Competing on Knowledge," *Fortune,* September 9, 1996, S1–S18.

24. Thomas A. Stewart, "Intellectual Capital," *Fortune,* October 3, 1994, 68–74.

25. Gary S. Becker, *Human Capital* (New York: Columbia University Press, 1964); S. A. Snell and J. W. Dean, Jr., "Integrated Manufacturing and Human Resource Management: A Human Capital Perspective," *Academy of Management Journal* 35, no. 3: 467–504.

26. K. T. Huang, "Capitalizing in Intellectual Assets," *IBM Systems Journal* 37, no. 4 (1998): 570–83; Roberta Fusaro, "IBM/Lotus to Tackle Information Overload," *Computerworld* 32, no. 26 (June 29, 1998): 24; Nick Bontis, "There's a Price on Your Head: Managing Intellectual Capital Strategically," *Business Quarterly,* Summer 1996, 41–47; Jerry Bowles and Josh Hammond, "Competing on Knowledge," *Fortune,* September 9, 1996, S1–S18.

27. Sherman, "Master Class," 95–96.

28. Joseph E. McCann, *Managing Intellectual Capital: Setting the Agenda for Human Resource Professionals* (New York: Human Resource Planning Society, 1999); Bowles and Hammond, "Competing on Knowledge," S1–S18.

29. Susan Greco, "Choose or Lose," *Inc.* 20, no. 18 (December 1998): 57–66; Ron Zemke, "The Little Company That Could," *Training* 34, no. 1 (January 1997): 59–64.

30. Y. K. Shetty, "The Human Side of Product Quality," *National Productivity Review* 8, no. 2 (Spring 1989), 175–82. See also Rosabeth Moss Kanter, Barry A. Stein, and Todd Jick, *The Challenge of Organizational Change—How People Experience It and Manage It* (New York: Free Press, 1991).

31. Laurie A. Broedling, "The Business of Business Is People," speech delivered to the Quality Conference, Washington Deming Study Group, George Washington University, Washington, D.C., April 8, 1996.

32. M. Hammer and J. Champy, *Reengineering the Corporation* (New York: HarperCollins, 1994). See also Michael Hammer, *Beyond Reengineering : How the Process-Centered Organization Is Changing Our Work and Our Lives* (New York: Harper Business, August 1996).

33. Ellen J. Quinn and Sharron L. Emmons, "Riding Roughshod over Reengineering," *Workforce* 77, no. 4 (April 1998): 101–4; Shari Caudron, "Integrate HR and Training: Working Together toward Shared Goals," *Workforce* 77, no. 5 (May 1998): 88–93; David H. Freed, "The Role of the Human Resource Department in Hospital Reengineering," *Health Care Supervisor* 14, no. 3 (1996); 37–45; S. Davis and W. Davidson, *2020 Vision: Transform Your Business Today to Succeed in Tomorrow's Economy* (New York: Simon & Schuster, 1991).

34. "Up to Speed: L. L. Bean Moves Employees as Workloads Shift," *Chief Executive*, July-August 1996, 15.

35. Charles R. Greer, Stuart A. Youngblood, and David A. Gray, "Human Resource Management Outsourcing: The Make or Buy Decision," *Academy of Management Executive* 13, no. 3 (August 1999): 85–96; Dawn Anfuso, "Save Jobs: Strategies to Stop the Layoffs," *Personnel Journal,* June 1996, 66–69; Jennifer J. Laabs, "Detailing HR's Top Two Concerns in 2005," *Personnel Journal,* January 1996, 36.

36. Gene Koretz, "Big Payoffs from Layoffs," *Business Week,* February 24, 1997, 30; Sherry Kuczynski, "Help! I Shrunk the Company!" *HRMagazine* 44, no. 6 (June 1999): 40–45.

37. Anfuso, "Save Jobs," 66–69.

38. James Brian Quinn, "Strategic Outsourcing: Leveraging Knowledge Capabilities," *Sloan Management Review,* Summer 1999, 9–21; William C. Byham and Sheryl Riddle, "Outsourcing: A Strategic Tool for a More Strategic HR," *Employment Relations Today* 26, no. 1 (Spring 1999): 37–55; Grover N. Wray, "The Role of Human Resources in Successful Outsourcing," *Employment Relations Today* 23, no. 1 (Spring 1996): 17–23.

39. Jay Finegan, "Look before You Lease," *Inc.* 19, no. 2 (February 1997): 106–7; Alex Morton, "How to Cut Costs with Employee Leasing," *Folio,* 1996, 54; Sarah Bergin, "Flexible Employees: Your Most Valuable Assets," *Training and Development,* March 1996, 112–16.

40. Shlomo Z. Reifman, "The Forbes/Bridge Economic Forecast Report," *Forbes* 163, no. 7 (April 5, 1999): 48; Robert E Hall and Charles I. Jones, "Levels of Economic Activity across Countries," *American Economic Review* 87, no. 2 (May 1997): 173–77.

41. The U.S. Department of Labor's Bureau of Labor Statistics keeps up-to-date projections and percentages in these categories. Interested readers can access this information through www.stats.bls.gov/. Also see A. M. Rappaport, C. A. Bogosian, and C. A. Klann, "Population Trends and the Labor Force in the Years Ahead," *Benefits Quarterly,* fourth quarter, 1998, 8–9.

42. Milford Prewitt, "Hispanics Find Job Niche in Restaurant Industry," *Nation's Restaurant News* 33, no. 5 (February 1, 1999): 41–46; "Doors Opening for Minority Students," *Advertising Age* 70, no. 7 (February 15, 1999): 7.

43. The U.S. Department of Labor's Bureau of Labor Statistics keeps up-to-date projections and percentages in these categories. Interested readers can access this information through www.stats.bls.gov/. Also see Rappaport, Bogosian, and Klann, "Population Trends," 8–9.

44. Shelley Donald Coolidge, "Retired. And Ready to Work. Selling Slow-Built Wisdom in a Churn-It-Out World, Senior Workers Get a Handle on the Hot Job Market," *Christian Science Monitor*, October 25, 1999, 11.

45. Lisa Goff, "Don't Miss the Bus!" *American Demographics* 21, no. 8 (August 1999): 48–54; Alison Stein Wellner, "Workplace Trends," *Incentive* 173, no. 9 (September 1999): 153-56.

46. The U.S. Department of Labor's Bureau of Labor Statistics keeps up-to-date projections and percentages in these categories. Interested readers can access this information through www.stats.bls.gov/.

47. The U.S. Department of Labor's Bureau of Labor Statistics keeps up-to-date projections and percentages on educational requirements for different kinds of jobs. Interested readers can access this information through www.stats.bls.gov/news.release/ecopro.table5.htm.

48. The U.S. Department of Education has either commissioned or conducted several studies on literacy rates in the United States. Interested readers can access this information on the web at www.ed.gov/offices/OVAE/AdultEd/InfoBoard/f-4.html.

49. Rose Mary Wentling and Nilda Palma-Rivas, "Current Status and Future Trends of Diversity Initiatives in the workplace: Diversity experts' perspective," *Human*

*Resource Development Quarterly* 9, no. 3 (Fall 1998): 235–53.

50. For practical recommendations on how to avoid lawsuits over invasion of privacy, see Linda E. Shostak, Gregory D. Wong, and Jocelyn S. Sperling, "Protecting Employers Against E-Mail Lawsuits," *HRFocus* (October 1999) *Supplement: Special Report on Employment Law,* S4; James A. Burns, Jr., "Personal Relationships of Employees: Are They Any Business of an Employer?" *Employee Relations Law Journal* 23, no. 4 (Spring 1998): 171–77. See also N. Ben Fairweather, "Surveillance in Employment: The Case of Teleworking," *Journal of Business Ethics* 22, no. 1 (October 1999): 39–49.

51. Julian Barling, Kathryne E. Dupre, and C. Gail Hepburn, "Effects of Parents' Job Insecurity on Children's Work Beliefs and Attitudes," *Journal of Applied Psychology* 83, no. 1 (February 1998): 112–18; Patricia L. Smith, Stanley J. Smits, and Frank Hoy, "Employee Work Attitudes: The Subtle Influence of Gender," *Human Relations* 51, no. 5 (May 1998): 649–66; Yue-Wah Chay and Samuel Aryee, "Potential Moderating Influence of Career Growth Opportunities on Careerist Orientation and Work Attitudes: Evidence of the Protean Career Era in Singapore," *Journal of Organizational Behavior* 20, no. 5 (September 1999): 613–23; Brian Dumaine, "Why Do We Work?" *Fortune,* December 26, 1994, 196–204.

52. Alan Deutschman, "Pioneers of the New Balance," *Fortune,* May 20, 1991, 60–68; William H. Miller, "A New Perspective for Tomorrow's Workforce," *Industry Week* 240, no. 6 (May 6, 1991): 6.

53. Dan Seligman, "Who Needs Family-Friendly Companies?" *Forbes* 163, no. 1 (January 11, 1999): 72–76.

54. For current research on the performance impact of HR, see the entire issue of *Academy of Management Journal* 39, no. 4.

55. Bill Leonard, "What Do HR Executives Want from CEOs?" *HRMagazine* 43, no. 13 (December 1998): 92–98; Jennifer Laabs, "Why HR Can't Win Today," *Workforce* 77, no. 5 (May 1998): 62–74; Robert Galford, Laurie Broedling, Edward E. Lawler III, and Tim Riley, "Why Doesn't This HR Department Get Any Respect?" *Harvard Business Review* 76, no. 2 (March/April 1998): 24–40.

56. Michael R. Losey, "Mastering the Competencies of HR Management," *Human Resource Management* 38, no. 2 (Summer 1999): 99–102; Wayne Brockbank, Dave Ulrich, and Richard W. Beatty, "HR Professional Development: Creating the Future Creators at the University of Michigan Business School," *Human Resource Management* 38, no. 2 (Summer 1999): 111–17; Dave Ulrich, "The Future Calls for Change," *Workforce* 77, no. 1 (January 1998): 87–91; David Ulrich, Wayne Brockbank, Arthur Yeung, and Dale G. Lake, "Human Resource Competencies: An Empirical Assessment," *Human Resource Management* 34, no. 4 (Winter 1995): 473–95.

# Equal Employment Opportunity and Human Resources Management

## AFTER STUDYING THIS CHAPTER, YOU SHOULD BE ABLE TO

**OBJECTIVE 1** Explain the reasons behind passage of EEO legislation.

**OBJECTIVE 2** Identify and describe the major laws affecting equal employment opportunity. Describe bona fide occupational qualification and religious preference as EEO issues.

**OBJECTIVE 3** Discuss sexual harassment and immigration reform and control as EEO concerns.

**OBJECTIVE 4** Explain the use of the *Uniform Guidelines on Employee Selection Procedures*.

**OBJECTIVE 5** Explain the concept of adverse impact and apply the four-fifths rule.

**OBJECTIVE 6** Discuss significant court cases impacting equal employment opportunity.

**OBJECTIVE 7** Explain various enforcement procedures affecting equal employment opportunity.

**OBJECTIVE 8** Describe affirmative action and the basic steps in developing an affirmative action program.

**Equal employment opportunity**
The treatment of individuals in all aspects of employment—hiring, promotion, training, etc.—in a fair and nonbiased manner

W ithin the field of HRM perhaps no topics have received more attention during the past thirty-five years than equal employment opportunity (EEO) and affirmative action (AA). **Equal employment opportunity,** or the employment of individuals in a fair and nonbiased manner, has consumed the attention of the media, the courts, practitioners, and legislators. Not surprisingly, a more diverse and multicultural workforce has mandated that managers know and comply with a myriad of legal requirements affecting all aspects of the employment relationship. These mandates create legal responsibilities for an organization and each of its managers to comply with various laws and administrative guidelines. Importantly, practitioners agree that when all functions of HRM comply with the law, the organization becomes a better place to work.

However, when managers ignore the legal aspects of HRM, they risk incurring costly and time-consuming litigation, negative public attitudes, and damages to their individual careers. Two highly publicized cases illustrate these points. In 1998, Astra USA agreed to pay $9.85 million to settle numerous sexual harassment claims. The monetary agreement is the largest sexual harassment settlement ever obtained by the Equal Employment Opportunity Commission. Astra USA admitted it had created a hostile work environment, including requests for sexual favors in exchange for favorable treatment for women. Lelia Bush, a former Astra sales representative, described the work climate as "unreal. It was fraternity-like. It was not a professional atmosphere."[1] In late 1997, Westinghouse Electric Corporation and Northrop Grumman agreed to pay $14 million to settle lawsuits filed by fired workers at two plants. Westinghouse was accused of discrimination against more than 800 older workers let go from 1991 to 1996 on the basis of their ages, higher salaries, and pension eligibility.[2]

Equal employment opportunity is not only a legal topic, it is also an emotional issue. It concerns all individuals, regardless of their sex, race, religion, age, national origin, color, physical condition, or position in an organization. Supervisors should be aware of their personal biases and how these attitudes can influence their dealings with subordinates. It should be emphasized that covert, as well as blatantly intentional, discrimination in employment is illegal.

In recent decades, employers have been compelled to develop employment policies that incorporate different laws, executive orders (EOs), administrative regulations, and court decisions (case law) designed to end job discrimination. The role of these legal requirements in shaping employment policies will be emphasized in this chapter. We will also discuss the process of affirmative action, which attempts to correct past practices of discrimination by actively recruiting minority group members.

# Historical Perspective of EEO Legislation

Equal employment opportunity as a national priority has emerged slowly in the United States. Not until the mid-1950s and early 1960s did nondiscriminatory employment become a strong social concern. Three factors seem to have influenced the growth of EEO legislation: (1) changing attitudes toward employment discrimination; (2) published reports highlighting the economic problems of women, minorities, and older workers; and (3) a growing body of disparate laws and government regulations covering discrimination.

## Changing National Values

The United States was founded on the principles of individual merit, hard work, and equality. The Constitution grants to all citizens the right to life, liberty, and the pursuit of happiness. The Fifth, Thirteenth, and Fourteenth Amendments expanded these guarantees by providing for due process of law (Fifth Amendment), outlawing slavery (Thirteenth Amendment), and guaranteeing equal protection under the law (Fourteenth Amendment). A central aim of political action has been to establish justice for all people of the nation.

In spite of these constitutional guarantees, employment discrimination has a long history in the United States. Organizations that claim to offer fair treatment to employees have openly or covertly engaged in discriminatory practices. Well-known organizations such as Continental Airlines, Gerber Products, Lennox Industries, First Union Corporation, Dillard Department Stores, and New York City have violated equal employment laws.[3]

Public attitudes changed dramatically with the beginning of the civil rights movement. During the late 1950s and early 1960s, minorities—especially blacks—publicized their low economic and occupational position through marches, sit-ins, rallies, and clashes with public authorities. The low employment status of women also gained recognition during this period. Supported by concerned individuals and church and civic leaders, the civil rights movement and the women's movement received wide attention through television and print media. These movements had a pronounced influence on changing the attitudes of society at large, of the business community, of civic leaders, and of government officials, resulting in improvements in the civil rights of all individuals. No longer was blatant discrimination to be accepted.

*Protests during the civil rights movement helped to change public attitudes toward discrimination, such as this sit-in staged by black students in 1960 at a Woolworth's lunch counter that refused to serve them.*

## Economic Disparity

The change in government and societal attitudes toward discrimination was further prompted by increasing public awareness of the economic imbalance between nonwhites and whites. Even today, civil rights activists cite government statistics to emphasize this disparity. For example, the January 1998 unemployment rate for black males over 20 years old was 7.9 percent, compared with 3.8 percent for white males the same age.[4] When employed, nonwhites tend to hold unskilled or semi-skilled jobs characterized by unstable employment, low status, and low pay. In the third quarter of 1998, the median weekly earnings of white males were $610; of black males, $462; and of Hispanic males, $398.[5] These inequities in employment rates and income figures were constant in the preceding years as well, lending support for legislative change.[6]

## Early Legal Developments

Since as early as the nineteenth century, the public has been aware of discriminatory employment practices in the United States. In 1866 Congress passed the Civil Rights Act, which extended to all persons the right to enjoy full and equal benefits of all laws, regardless of race. Beginning in the 1930s and 1940s, more-specific federal policies covering nondiscrimination began to emerge. In 1933 Congress enacted the Unemployment Relief Act, which prohibited employment discrimination on account of race, color, or creed. In 1941 President Franklin D. Roosevelt issued Executive Order 8802, which was to ensure that every American citizen, "regardless of race, creed, color, or national origin," would be guaranteed equal employment opportunities in World War II defense contracts. Over the next twenty years a variety of other legislative efforts were promoted to resolve inequities in employment practices.

Unfortunately, these early efforts did little to correct employment discrimination. First, at both the state and federal levels, nondiscrimination laws often failed to give any enforcement power to the agency charged with upholding the law. Second, the laws that were passed frequently neglected to list specific discriminatory practices or methods for their correction. Third, employers covered by the acts were only required to comply voluntarily with the equal employment opportunity legislation. Without a compulsory requirement, employers often violated legislation with impunity. Despite these faults, however, early executive orders and laws laid the groundwork for passage of the Civil Rights Act of 1964.

# Government Regulation of Equal Employment Opportunity

Significant laws have been passed barring employment discrimination. These laws influence all of the HRM functions, including recruitment, selection, performance appraisal, promotion, and compensation. Because all managers are involved in employment activities, knowledge of these statutes is critical. It should be understood that managers and supervisors perform their jobs as agents of the employer.

Under the business concept of agency, managers and supervisors authorized to deal with employees on the employers' behalf subject themselves, and their employers, to responsibility for illegal acts taken against employees. Both the manager and the organization can be sued by an employee alleging discrimination. Organizations cannot afford to have managers make HRM decisions without considering the possible legal implications of their actions for the organization and themselves. Highlights in HRM 1 will test your current understanding of EEO laws.[7]

## Major Federal Laws

**Protected classes**
Individuals of a minority race, women, older persons, and those with disabilities who are covered by federal laws on equal employment opportunity

Major federal equal employment opportunity laws have attempted to correct social problems of interest to particular groups of workers, called **protected classes.** Defined broadly, these include individuals of a minority race, women, older persons, and those with physical or mental disabilities. Separate federal laws cover each of these classes. Figure 2.1 lists the major federal laws and their provisions governing equal employment opportunity.

### Equal Pay Act of 1963

The Equal Pay Act outlaws discrimination in pay, employee benefits, and pensions based on the worker's gender. Employers are prohibited from paying employees of one gender at a rate lower than that paid to members of the other gender for doing equal work. Jobs are considered "equal" when they require substantially the same skill, effort, and responsibility under similar working conditions and in the same establishment. For example, male and female plastic molders working for Medical Plastics Laboratory, a company of 125 employees manufacturing medical education products, must not be paid differently because of their gender. However, other employers in this specialized industry may pay their plastic molders wage rates that differ on the basis of different job content or economic conditions from those of Medical Plastics.

**USING THE INTERNET**

Details explaining the responsibilities of the EEOC and complete texts of all the EEO laws may be found at:

www.eeoc.gov/laws.html

Employers do not violate the Equal Pay Act when differences in wages paid to men and women for equal work are based on seniority systems, merit considerations, or incentive pay plans. However, these exceptions must not be based on the employee's gender or serve to discriminate against one particular gender. Employers may not lower the wages of one gender to comply with the law; rather, they must raise the wages of the gender being underpaid.

The Equal Pay Act was passed as an amendment to the Fair Labor Standards Act (FLSA) and is administered by the Equal Employment Opportunity Commission (EEOC). It covers employers engaged in interstate commerce and most government employees.

### Civil Rights Act of 1964

Title VII of the Civil Rights Act of 1964 is the broadest and most significant of the antidiscrimination statutes. The act bars discrimination in all HR activities, including hiring, training, promotion, pay, employee benefits, and other conditions of employment. Discrimination is prohibited on the basis of race, color, religion, sex (also referred to as gender), or national origin. Also prohibited is discrimination

**HRM 1**

# Test Your Knowledge of Equal Employment Opportunity Law

The following questions have been used as "icebreakers" by employers and consultants when training supervisors and managers in EEO legislation. What is your knowledge of EEO laws? Answers are found at the end of this chapter.

1. Two male employees tell a sexually dirty joke. The joke is overheard by a female employee who complains to her supervisor that this is sexual harassment. Is her complaint legitimate?

    _____ Yes        _____ No

2. To be covered by Title VII of the Civil Rights Act, an employer must be engaged in interstate commerce and employ twenty-five or more employees.

    _____ True        _____ False

3. Persons addicted to illegal drugs are classified as disabled under the Americans with Disabilities Act of 1990.

    _____ Yes        _____ No

4. The Equal Pay Act of 1963 allows employers to pay different wages to men and women who are performing substantially similar work. What are the three defenses for paying a different wage?

    1. _____

    2. _____

    3. _____

5. A person applies with you for a job as a janitor. During the interview the person mentions that since birth he has sometimes suffered from short periods of memory loss. Must you consider this individual as a disabled person under the Americans with Disabilities Act of 1990?

    _____ Yes        _____ No

6. On Friday afternoon you tell Nancy Penley, a computer analyst, that she must work overtime the next day. She refuses, saying that Saturday is her regular religious holiday and she can't work. Do you have the legal right to order her to work on Saturday?

    _____ Yes        _____ No

7. You have just told an applicant that she will not receive the job she applied for. She claims that you denied her employment because of her age (she's 52). You claim she is not protected under the age discrimination law. Is your reasoning correct?

    _____ Yes        _____ No

8. As an employer, you can select those applicants who are the most qualified in terms of education and experience.

    _____ Yes        _____ No

9. As a manager, you have the legal right to mandate dates for pregnancy leaves.

    _____ True        _____ False

10. State fair employment practice laws cover smaller employers not covered by federal legislation.

    _____ True        _____ False

FIGURE 2.1

## Major Laws Affecting Equal Employment Opportunity

| LAW | PROVISIONS |
|---|---|
| Equal Pay Act of 1963 | Requires all employers covered by the Fair Labor Standards Act and others to provide equal pay for equal work, regardless of sex. |
| Title VII of Civil Rights Act of 1964 (amended in 1972, 1991, and 1994) | Prohibits discrimination in employment on the basis of race, color, religion, sex, or national origin; created the Equal Employment Opportunity Commission (EEOC) to enforce the provisions of Title VII. |
| Age Discrimination in Employment Act of 1967 (amended in 1986 and 1990) | Prohibits private and public employers from discriminating against persons 40 years of age or older in any area of employment because of age; exceptions are permitted where age is a bona fide occupational qualification. |
| Equal Employment Opportunity Act of 1972 | Amended Title VII of Civil Rights Act of 1964; strengthens EEOC's enforcement powers and extends coverage of Title VII to government employees, employees in higher education, and other employers and employees. |
| Pregnancy Discrimination Act of 1978 | Broadens the definition of sex discrimination to include pregnancy, childbirth, or related medical conditions; prohibits employers from discriminating against pregnant women in employment benefits if they are capable of performing their job duties. |
| Americans with Disabilities Act of 1990 | Prohibits discrimination in employment against persons with physical or mental disabilities or the chronically ill; enjoins employers to make reasonable accommodation to the employment needs of the disabled; covers employers with fifteen or more employees. |
| Civil Rights Act of 1991 | Provides for compensatory and punitive damages and jury trials in cases involving intentional discrimination; requires employers to demonstrate that job practices are job-related and consistent with business necessity; extends coverage to U.S. citizens working for American companies overseas. |
| Uniformed Services Employment and Reemployment Rights Act of 1994 | Protects the employment rights of individuals who enter the military for short periods of service. |

based on pregnancy.[8] The law protects hourly employees, supervisors, professional employees, managers, and executives from discriminatory practices. Section 703(a) of Title VII of the Civil Rights Act specifically provides that

> It shall be unlawful employment practice for an employer:
> 1. To fail or refuse to hire or to discharge any individual, or otherwise to discriminate against any individual with respect to his [or her] compensation, terms, conditions, or privileges of employment because of such individual's race, color, religion, sex, or national origin; or

2. To limit, segregate, or classify his [or her] employees or applicants for employment in any way which would deprive or tend to deprive any individual of employment opportunities or otherwise adversely affect his [or her] status as an employee because of such individual's race, color, religion, sex, or national origin.

While the purpose and the coverage of Title VII are extensive, the law does permit various exemptions. For example, as with the Equal Pay Act, managers are permitted to apply employment conditions differently if those differences are based on such objective factors as merit, seniority, or incentive payments. Nowhere does the law require employers to hire, promote, or retain workers who are not qualified to perform their job duties. And managers may still reward employees differently, provided these differences are not predicated on the employees' race, color, sex, religion, or national origin.

The Civil Rights Act of 1964, as amended by the Equal Employment Opportunity Act of 1972 and the Civil Rights Act of 1991, covers a broad range of organizations. The law includes under its jurisdiction the following:

1. All private employers in interstate commerce who employ fifteen or more employees for twenty or more weeks per year
2. State and local governments
3. Private and public employment agencies, including the U.S. Employment Service
4. Joint labor-management committees that govern apprenticeship or training programs
5. Labor unions having fifteen or more members or employees
6. Public and private educational institutions
7. Foreign subsidiaries of U.S. organizations employing U.S. citizens

Certain employers are excluded from coverage of the Civil Rights Act. Broadly defined, these are (1) U.S. government-owned corporations, (2) bona fide, tax-exempt private clubs, (3) religious organizations employing persons of a specific religion, and (4) organizations hiring Native Americans on or near a reservation.

The Civil Rights Act of 1964 established the Equal Employment Opportunity Commission to administer the law and promote equal employment opportunity. The commission's structure and operations will be reviewed later in this chapter.

*Bona Fide Occupational Qualification.*    Under Title VII of the Civil Rights Act, employers are permitted limited exemptions from antidiscrimination regulations if employment preferences are based on a bona fide occupational qualification. A **bona fide occupational qualification (BFOQ)** permits discrimination where employer hiring preferences are a reasonable necessity for the normal operation of the business. However, a BFOQ is a suitable defense against a discrimination charge only where age, religion, sex, or national origin is an actual qualification for performing the job. For example, an older person could legitimately be excluded from consideration for employment as a model for teenage designer jeans. It is reasonable to expect the San Francisco 49ers of the National Football League to hire male locker-room attendants or for Macy's department store to employ females as models for women's fashions. Likewise, religion is a BFOQ in organizations that require employees to share a particular religious doctrine.

**Bona fide occupational qualification (BFOQ)**
Suitable defense against a discrimination charge only where age, religion, sex, or national origin is an actual qualification for performing the job

The EEOC does not favor BFOQs, and both the EEOC and the courts have construed the concept narrowly. The exception does not apply to discrimination based on race or color. Where an organization claims a BFOQ, it must be able to prove that hiring on the basis of sex, religion, age, or national origin is a business necessity. **Business necessity** has been interpreted by the courts as a practice that is necessary to the safe and efficient operation of the organization. Students will often ask, "Why do Asian restaurants hire only Asian American food servers?" While restaurants generally cannot prefer one nationality over another (because the job of serving food can be performed equally well by all nationalities) to ensure the "authenticity" of the dining experience, an Asian restaurant may legitimately use the business-necessity defense to support the preference for hiring Asian American servers.

**Business necessity**
Work-related practice that is necessary to the safe and efficient operation of an organization

*Religious Preference.*   Freedom to exercise religious choice is guaranteed under the U.S. Constitution. Title VII of the Civil Rights Act also prohibits discrimination based on religion in employment decisions, though it permits employer exemptions. The act defines religion to "include all aspects of religious observance and practice, as well as belief."[9]

Title VII does not require employers to grant complete religious freedom in employment situations. Employers need only make a reasonable accommodation for a current employee's or job applicant's religious observance or practice without incurring undue hardship in the conduct of the business. Managers or supervisors may have to accommodate an employee's religion in the specific areas of (1) holidays and observances (scheduling), (2) personal appearance (wearing beards, veils, or turbans), and (3) religious conduct on the job (missionary work among other employees).[10]

What constitutes "reasonable accommodation" has been difficult to define.[11] In 1977, in the leading case of *TWA v Hardison*, the Supreme Court attempted to settle this dispute by ruling that employers had only to bear a minimum cost to show accommodation.[12] The Court said that to require otherwise would be discrimination against other employees for whom the expense of permitting time off for religious observance was not incurred. The *Hardison* case is important because it supported union management seniority systems where the employer had made a reasonable attempt to adjust employee work schedules without undue hardship. While *Hardison* permits reasonable accommodation and undue hardship as a defense against religious discrimination charges, the EEOC will investigate complaints on a case-by-case basis; and employers are still responsible for supporting their decisions to deny an employee's religious requests.[13]

**USING THE INTERNET**

To view the EEOC's Facts about Religious Discrimination, go to:

www.eeoc.gov/facts/fs-relig.html

### Age Discrimination in Employment Act of 1967

With the aging of the baby boomers—a group of 76 million people—the chances of age discrimination by employers increases dramatically. Recent figures from the EEOC show that age discrimination complaints compose about 20 percent of all discrimination charges. Furthermore, settlements and jury awards in age discrimination cases are substantially higher than those awarded in other types of discrimination cases. Managers or supervisors may discriminate against older employees by

- Excluding older workers from important work activities
- Making negative changes in the performance evaluations of older employees

- Denying older employees job-related education, career development, or promotional opportunities
- Selecting younger job applicants over older, better qualified candidates
- Pressuring older employees into taking early retirement
- Reducing the job duties and responsibilities of older employees[14]

Additionally, since older workers are less likely to agree to relocate or adapt to new job demands, they are prone to employer discrimination.

To make employment decisions based on age illegal, the Age Discrimination in Employment Act (ADEA), as amended, was passed in 1967. The act prohibits specific employers from discriminating against persons 40 years of age or older in any area of employment, including selection, because of age. Employers affected are those with twenty or more employees; unions with twenty-five or more members; employment agencies; and federal, state, and local governments.

Exceptions to the law are permitted where age is a bona fide occupational qualification. A BFOQ may exist where an employer can show that advanced age may affect public safety or organizational efficiency. For example, such conditions might exist for bus or truck drivers or for locomotive engineers. The greater the safety factor, measured by the likelihood of harm thorough accidents, the more stringent may be the job qualification designed to ensure safety. A BFOQ does not exist where an employer argues that younger employees foster a youthful or more energetic organizational image. Employers must also be careful to avoid making offhand remarks (e.g., "the old man") or expressing negative opinions (e.g., "People over 50 years old have more accidents") about older individuals. These remarks and attitudes can be used as proof of discrimination in age-bias suits.[15]

**USING THE INTERNET**

The American Association of Retired Persons (AARP) offers a number of resources to employers who want to maximize their use of older workers. Find this information at:

www.aarp.org

### Equal Employment Opportunity Act of 1972

In 1972 the Civil Rights Act of 1964 was amended by the Equal Employment Opportunity Act. Two important changes were made. First, the coverage of the act was broadened to include state and local governments and public and private educational institutions. Colleges and universities such as Central Texas College in Killeen, San Diego State University, and Bloomfield College in Bloomfield, New Jersey, are now covered by this statute. Second, the law strengthened the enforcement powers of the EEOC by allowing the agency itself to sue employers in court to enforce the provisions of the act. Regional litigation centers now exist to provide faster and more effective court action.

### Pregnancy Discrimination Act of 1978

Prior to the passage of the Pregnancy Discrimination Act, pregnant women could be forced to resign or take a leave of absence because of their condition. In addition, employers did not have to provide disability or medical coverage for pregnancy. The Pregnancy Discrimination Act amended the Civil Rights Act of 1964 by stating that pregnancy is a disability and that pregnant employees in covered organizations must be treated on an equal basis with employees having other medical conditions. Under the law, it is illegal for employers to deny sick leave for morning sickness or related pregnancy illness if sick leave is permitted for other medical conditions such as flu or surgical operations.[16]

Furthermore, the law prohibits discrimination in the hiring, promotion, or termination of women because of pregnancy. Women must be evaluated on their ability to perform the job, and employers may not set arbitrary dates for mandatory pregnancy leaves.[17] Leave dates are to be based on the individual pregnant employee's ability to work.

### Americans with Disabilities Act of 1990

Discrimination against the disabled was first prohibited in federally funded activities by the Vocational Rehabilitation Act of 1973 (to be discussed below). However, the disabled were not among the protected classes covered by the Civil Rights Act of 1964. To remedy this shortcoming, Congress in 1990 passed the Americans with Disabilities Act (ADA), prohibiting employers from discriminating against individuals with physical and mental handicaps and the chronically ill. The law defines a disability as "(a) a physical or mental impairment that substantially limits one or more of the major life activities; (b) a record of such impairment; or (c) being regarded as having such an impairment." Note that the law also protects persons "regarded" as having a disability—for example, individuals with disfiguring burns.

Managers and supervisors remark that the ADA is difficult to administer because of the ambiguous definition of a disability, particularly mental impairment.[18] The issue is, what is a disability? It sounds like a simple question, yet it is not. Not every mental or physical impairment is considered a disability under the law. For example, significant personality disorders are covered under the EEOC's "Enforcement Guidance on the Americans with Disabilities Act and Psychiatric Disabilities."[19] Covered personality disorders include schizophrenia, bipolar disorders, major affective disorders, personality disorders, and anxiety disorders. These impairments are characterized by aberrant behavior, self-defeating behavior, manipulation of others, and troublesome manners of behavior. However, mental impairments described as "adjustment disorders" or attributed to stress have generally not been subject to ADA coverage. Therefore, employees who claim to be "stressed" over marital problems, financial hardships, demands of the work environment, job duties, or harsh, unreasonable treatment from a supervisor would not be classified as disabled under the ADA.[20]

The act does not cover

1. Homosexuality or bisexuality
2. Gender-identity disorders not resulting from physical impairment or other sexual-behavior disorders
3. Compulsive gambling, kleptomania, or pyromania
4. Psychoactive substance-use disorders resulting from current illegal use of drugs
5. Current illegal use of drugs
6. Infectious or communicable diseases of public health significance (applied to food-handling jobs only and excluding AIDS)[21]

**Reasonable accommodation**
Attempt by employers to adjust, without undue hardship, the working conditions or schedules of employees with disabilities or religious preferences

In the cases it does cover, the act requires employers to make a reasonable accommodation for disabled persons who are otherwise qualified to work, unless doing so would cause undue hardship to the employer. "Undue hardship" refers to unusual work modifications or excessive expenses that might be incurred by an employer in providing an accommodation. **Reasonable accommodation** "includes

**USING THE INTERNET**

Retailer Sears has long had a commitment to hiring people with disabilities. Read about it at:

www.annenberg.nwu.edu/pubs/sears/

making facilities accessible and usable to disabled persons, restructuring jobs, permitting part-time or modified work schedules, reassigning to a vacant position, changing equipment, and/or expense." "Reasonable" is to be determined according to (1) the nature and cost of the accommodation and (2) the financial resources, size, and profitability of the facility and parent organization.[22] Furthermore, employers cannot use selection procedures that screen out or tend to screen out disabled persons, unless the selection procedure "is shown to be job-related for the position in question and is consistent with business necessity" and acceptable job performance cannot be achieved through reasonable accommodation. ("Essential functions," a pivotal issue for ensuring reasonable accommodation, will be discussed in Chapter 4.)

The act prohibits covered employers from discriminating against a qualified individual regarding application for employment, hiring, advancement, discharge, compensation, training, or other employment conditions. The law incorporates the procedures and remedies found in Title VII of the Civil Rights Act, allowing job applicants or employees initial employment, reinstatement, back pay, and other injunctive relief against employers who violate the statute.[23] The act covers employers with fifteen or more employees. The EEOC enforces the law in the same manner that Title VII of the Civil Rights Act is enforced.

Employers subject to the ADA, and those who value the varied abilities of the disabled, approach the law in a proactive manner. Because of the success experienced in the employment of disabled persons, the slogan "Hire the disabled—it's good business" is a standard policy for organizations like Little Tykes Co. of Hudson, Ohio, and Magnum Assembly Inc. of Austin, Texas. These employers place emphasis on what employees *can* do rather than what they *cannot* do. It is not suggested that disabled persons can be placed in any job without giving careful consideration to their disabilities, nor that employers can always make the workplace "user-friendly," but rather that it is good business to hire qualified disabled persons who can work safely and productively. Fortunately, there exist today manual and electronic devices to aid the hearing-impaired, visually-impaired, and mobility-impaired employee.[24] In many cases, the simple restructuring of jobs permits disabled persons to qualify for employment. Figure 2.2 identifies specific ways to make the workplace more accessible to the disabled.

### Civil Rights Act of 1991

After extensive U.S. House and Senate debate, the Civil Rights Act of 1991 was signed into law. The act amends Title VII of the Civil Rights Act of 1964. One of the major elements of the law is the awarding of damages in cases of intentional discrimination or unlawful harassment. For the first time under federal law, damages are provided to victims of intentional discrimination or unlawful harassment on the basis of sex, religion, national origin, and disability. An employee who claims intentional discrimination can seek compensatory or punitive damages. Compensatory damages include payment for future money losses, emotional pain, suffering, mental anguish, and other nonmonetary losses. Punitive damages are awarded if it can be shown that the employer engaged in discrimination with malice or reckless indifference to the law. Most significantly, the act allows juries rather than federal judges to decide discrimination claims.[25] Compensatory or punitive damages cannot be awarded in cases where an employment practice not intended to be dis-

FIGURE 2.2

**ADA Suggestions for an Accessible Workplace**

- Install easy-to-reach switches.
- Provide sloping sidewalks and entrances.
- Install wheelchair ramps.
- Reposition shelves for the easy reach of materials.
- Rearrange tables, chairs, vending machines, dispensers, and other furniture and fixtures.
- Widen doors and hallways.
- Add raised markings on control buttons.
- Provide designated accessible parking spaces.
- Install hand controls or manipulation devices.

- Provide flashing alarm lights.
- Remove turnstiles and revolving doors or provide alternative accessible paths.
- Install holding bars in toilet areas.
- Redesign toilet partitions to increase access space.
- Add paper cup dispensers at water fountains.
- Replace high-pile, low-density carpeting.
- Reposition telephones, water fountains, and other needed equipment.
- Add raised toilet seats.
- Provide a full-length bathroom mirror.

criminatory is shown to have an unlawful adverse impact on persons of a protected class. The total damages any one person can receive cannot be more than

$50,000 for employers having between 15 and 100 employees
$100,000 for employers having between 101 and 200 employees
$200,000 for employers having between 201 and 500 employees
$300,000 for employers having over 500 employees

In each case the aggrieved individual must have been employed with the organization for twenty or more calendar weeks.

The act requires that employers defending against a charge of discrimination demonstrate that employment practices are *job-related* and consistent with *business necessity*. Additionally, the act provides that an employer may not avoid liability in mixed-motive discrimination cases by proving it would have taken the same action without the discriminatory motive.

Under its other provisions, the law

- Prohibits employers from adjusting employment test scores or using different cutoff test scores on the basis of race, color, religion, sex, or national origin
- Prohibits litigation involving charges of reverse discrimination where employers are under a consent order (court order) to implement an affirmative action program

The Civil Rights Act of 1991 states that employees who are sent abroad to work for American-based companies are protected by U.S. antidiscrimination legislation governing age, disability, and Title VII of the Civil Rights Act of 1964. Thus employees can sue their American employers for claims of discriminatory treatment while employed in a foreign country. This could occur, for example, in Middle Eastern countries where women are prohibited from holding certain jobs or where a foreign country's mandatory retirement law conflicts with the Age Discrimination in Employment Act.[26]

### Uniformed Services Employment and Reemployment Rights Act of 1994

Under this act, individuals who enter the military for a short period of service can return to their private-sector jobs without risk of loss of seniority or benefits. The act protects against discrimination on the basis of military obligation in the areas of hiring, job retention, and advancement. Other provisions under the act require employers to make reasonable efforts to retrain or upgrade skills to qualify employees for reemployment, expand health care and employee pension plan coverage, and extend the length of time an individual may be absent for military duty from four to five years. For their part, service members must provide their employers advance notice of their military obligations in order to be protected by the reemployment rights statute. The Labor Department's Veterans Employment and Training Service is responsible for enforcing the law.

## Other Federal Laws and Executive Orders

Because the major laws affecting equal employment opportunity do not cover agencies of the federal government and because state laws do not apply to federal employees, it has at times been necessary for the president to issue executive orders to protect federal employees. Executive orders are also used to provide equal employment opportunity to individuals employed by government contractors. Since many large employers—like General Dynamics, AT&T, Allied-Signal, and Motorola—and numerous small companies have contracts with the federal government, managers are expected to know and comply with the provisions of executive orders and other laws. The federal laws and executive orders that apply to government agencies and government contractors are summarized in Figure 2.3.

### Vocational Rehabilitation Act of 1973

People with disabilities experience discrimination both because of negative attitudes regarding their ability to perform work and because of physical barriers imposed by organizational facilities.[27] The Vocational Rehabilitation Act was passed in 1973 to correct these problems by requiring private employers with federal contracts over $2,500 to take affirmative action to hire individuals with a mental or physical disability. Recipients of federal financial assistance, such as public and private colleges and universities, are also covered. Employers must make a reasonable accommodation to hire disabled individuals but are not required to employ unqualified persons. In applying the safeguards of this law, the term **disabled individual** means "any person who (1) has a physical or mental impairment which substantially limits one or more of such person's major life activities, (2) has a record of such an impairment, or (3) is regarded as having such an impairment." This definition closely parallels the definition of disabled individual provided in the Americans with Disabilities Act just discussed.

Individuals may be regarded as "substantially limited" when they experience difficulty in securing, retaining, or advancing in employment because of their

---

**Disabled individual**

Any person who (1) has a physical or mental impairment that substantially limits one or more of such person's major life activities, (2) has a record of such impairment, or (3) is regarded as having such an impairment

FIGURE 2.3

► **EEO Rules Applicable to Federal Contractors and Agencies**

| LAW | PROVISIONS |
|---|---|
| Vocational Rehabilitation Act of 1973 (amended in 1974) | Prohibits federal contractors from discriminating against disabled individuals in any program or activity receiving federal financial assistance; requires federal contractors to develop affirmative action plans to hire and promote disabled persons. |
| Executive Order 11246 (1965), as amended by Order 11375 (1966) | Prohibits employment discrimination based on race, color, religion, sex, or national origin by government contractors with contracts exceeding $10,000; requires contractors employing fifty or more workers to develop affirmative action plans when government contracts exceed $50,000 a year. |
| Executive Order 11478 (1969) | Obligates the federal government to ensure that all personnel actions affecting applicants for employment be free from discrimination based on race, color, religion, sex, or national origin. |

disability. Since the act was passed, a growing number of mental and physical impairments have been classified as disabilities within the meaning of the law. For example, disabilities such as blindness and paralysis are clearly covered. But other, less obvious impairments such as diabetes, high blood pressure, and heart disease also fall within the definition of disability established under the act.

In 1987, the Supreme Court ruled in *Nassau County, Florida v Arline* that employees afflicted with contagious diseases, such as tuberculosis, are disabled individuals and subject to the act's coverage.[28] In cases where persons with contagious diseases are "otherwise qualified" to do their jobs, the law requires employers to make a reasonable accommodation to allow the disabled to perform their jobs.[29] Individuals with AIDS are also disabled within the meaning of the Rehabilitation Act. Therefore, discrimination on the basis of AIDS violates the law, and employers must accommodate the employment needs of AIDS victims.[30] Public interest in AIDS has presented management with a challenge to address work-related concerns about AIDS. Many organizations, including BankAmerica Corporation, have developed specific policies to deal with the issue of AIDS in the workplace. (See Highlights in HRM 2.)

The Rehabilitation Act does not require employers to hire or retain a disabled person if he or she has a contagious disease that poses a direct threat to the health or safety of others and the individual cannot be accommodated. Also, employment is not required when some aspect of the employee's disability prevents that person from carrying out essential parts of the job; nor is it required if the disabled person is not otherwise qualified.

### Executive Order 11246

Federal agencies and government contractors with contracts of $10,000 or more must comply with the antidiscrimination provisions of Executive Order 11246.

**HRM 2**

# Bank of America NT & SA Corporation's Policy on Assisting Employees with Life-Threatening Illnesses

The company recognizes that employees with life-threatening illnesses—including but not limited to cancer, heart disease, and HIV disease—may wish to continue to engage in as many of their normal pursuits as their condition allows, including work. As long as these employees are able to meet acceptable performance standards, and medical evidence indicates that their conditions are not a threat to themselves or others, managers should be sensitive to their conditions and ensure that they are treated consistently with other employees. At the same time, the company seeks to provide a safe work environment for all employees and customers. Therefore, precautions should be taken to ensure that an employee's condition does not present a health and/or safety threat to other employees or customers.

Consistent with this concern for employees with life-threatening illnesses, the company offers the following range of resources available through your Human Resources representative:

- Management and employee education and information on terminal illness and specific life-threatening illnesses.
- Referral to agencies and organizations that offer supportive services to employees and dependents directly or indirectly affected by life-threatening illnesses.
- Benefits consultation to assist employees in effectively managing health, leave, and other benefits.

**Guidelines to help you deal with a situation**

When dealing with situations involving employees with life-threatening illnesses, managers should:

- Remember that an employee's health condition is personal, should be treated as confidential, and reasonable precautions should be taken to protect information regarding an employee's health condition.
- Contact your Human Resources representative if you believe that you or other employees need information about terminal illness, or a specific life-threatening illness, or if you need further guidance in managing a situation that involves an employee with a life-threatening illness.
- Contact your Human Resources representative if you have any concern about the possible contagious nature of an employee's illness.
- Contact your Human Resources representative to determine if a statement should be obtained from the employee's attending physician that continued presence at work will pose no threat to the employee, co-workers, or customers. The company reserves the right to require an examination by a medical doctor appointed by the company.
- If warranted, make reasonable accommodation, consistent with the business needs of the unit, for employees with life-threatening illnesses.

- Make a reasonable attempt upon request to transfer employees who have life-threatening illnesses and are experiencing undue emotional stress.
- Be sensitive and responsive to co-workers' concerns, and emphasize employee education available through your Human Resources representative.
- Give no special consideration beyond normal transfer requests to employees who feel threatened by a co-worker's life-threatening illness.
- Be sensitive to the fact that continued employment for an employee with a life-threatening illness may sometimes be therapeutically important in the remission or recovery process, or may help to prolong that employee's life.
- Encourage employees to seek assistance from established community support groups for medical treatment and counseling services. Information on these can be requested through a Human Resources representative or Corporate Health Programs #3666.

Source: Bank of America NT & SA. Used with permission.

The order prohibits discrimination based on race, color, religion, sex, or national origin in all employment activities. Furthermore, it requires that government contractors or subcontractors having fifty or more employees with contracts in excess of $50,000 develop affirmative action plans; such plans will be discussed later in the chapter.

Executive Order 11246 created the Office of Federal Contract Compliance Programs (OFCCP) to ensure equal employment opportunity in the federal procurement area. The agency issues nondiscriminatory guidelines and regulations similar to those issued by the EEOC. Noncompliance with OFCCP policies can result in the cancellation or suspension of contracts. The OFCCP is further charged with requiring that contractors provide job opportunities to the disabled, disabled veterans, and veterans of the Vietnam War.

## Fair Employment Practice Laws

**Fair employment practices (FEPs)**

State and local laws governing equal employment opportunity that are often more comprehensive than federal laws

Federal laws and executive orders provide the major regulations governing equal employment opportunity. But, in addition, almost all states and many local governments have passed laws barring employment discrimination. Referred to as **fair employment practices (FEPs)**, these statutes are often more comprehensive than the federal laws. While state and local laws are too numerous to review here, managers should be aware of them and how they affect HRM in their organizations.

State and local FEPs also promote the employment of individuals in a fair and unbiased way. They are patterned after federal legislation, although they frequently extend jurisdiction to employers exempt from federal coverage and therefore pertain mainly to smaller employers. While Title VII of the Civil Rights Act exempts employers with fewer than fifteen employees, many states extend antidiscrimination laws to employers with one or more workers. Thus managers and entrepreneurs operating a small business must pay close attention to these laws. Local or state legislation may bar discrimination based on physical appearance, marital status, sexual orientation, arrest records, color blindness, or political affiliation.

States with FEPs establish independent agencies to administer and enforce the statutes. The Ohio Civil Rights Commission, Massachusetts Commission against Discrimination, Colorado Civil Rights Division, and Pittsburgh Commission on Human Relations are examples. State agencies play an important role in the investigation and resolution of employment discrimination charges. FEP agencies and the Equal Employment Opportunity Commission often work together to resolve discrimination complaints.

# Other Equal Employment Opportunity Issues

Federal laws, executive orders, court cases, and state and local statutes provide the broad legal framework for equal employment opportunity. Within these major laws, specific issues are of particular interest to supervisors and managers. The situations discussed here occur in the day-to-day supervision of employees.

## Sexual Harassment

Sexual situations in the work environment are not new to organizational life. Sexual feelings are a part of group dynamics, and people who work together may come to develop these kinds of feelings for one another. Unfortunately, however, often these encounters are unpleasant and unwelcome, as witnessed by the many reported instances of sexual harassment.[31] Nationwide, 17,176 sexual harassment complaints were filed in 1998 with the EEOC and state fair employment practice agencies by employees of both small and large employers.[32] Ten percent of these charges were filed by males. Problems often arise from lack of knowledge of the specific on-the-job behaviors that constitute sexual harassment under the law. Through a questionnaire it is possible to test employee understanding of what is and what is not sexual harassment. Highlights in HRM 3 is a sampling of questions that could be used during a sexual harassment audit. Such an instrument, which is essentially a test, is a valuable tool for determining what employees know and do not know about sexual harassment.

The EEOC guidelines on sexual harassment are specific, stating that "unwelcome advances, requests for sexual favors, and other verbal or physical conduct of a sexual nature" constitute **sexual harassment** when submission to the conduct is tied to continuing employment or advancement. The EEOC recognizes two forms of sexual harassment as being illegal under Title VII. The first, *quid pro quo harassment*, occurs when "submission to or rejection of sexual conduct is used as a basis for employment decisions."[33] This type of harassment involves a tangible or economic consequence, such as a demotion or loss of pay. If a supervisor promotes a female employee only after she agrees to an after-work date, the conduct is clearly illegal.

The second type of harassment, *hostile environment,* can occur when unwelcome sexual conduct "has the purpose or effect of unreasonably interfering with job performance or creating an intimidating, hostile, or offensive working environment."[34] Thus dirty jokes, vulgar slang, nude pictures, swearing, and personal ridicule and insult constitute sexual harassment when an employee finds them offensive.

**Sexual harassment**
Unwelcome advances, requests for sexual favors, and other verbal or physical conduct of a sexual nature in the working environment

**HRM 3**

# Questions Used in Auditing Sexual Harassment

| ACTIVITY | IS THIS SEXUAL HARASSMENT? | | | ARE YOU AWARE OF THIS BEHAVIOR IN THE ORGANIZATION? | |
|---|---|---|---|---|---|
| Employees post cartoons on bulletin boards containing sexually related material. | Yes | No | Uncertain | Yes | No |
| A male employee says to a female employee that she has beautiful eyes and hair. | Yes | No | Uncertain | Yes | No |
| A male manager habitually calls all female employees "sweetie" or "darling." | Yes | No | Uncertain | Yes | No |
| A manager fails to promote a female (male) employee for not granting sexual favors. | Yes | No | Uncertain | Yes | No |
| Male employees use vulgar language and tell sexual jokes that are overheard by, but not directed at, female employees. | Yes | No | Uncertain | Yes | No |
| A male employee leans and peers over the back of a female employee when she wears a low-cut dress. | Yes | No | Uncertain | Yes | No |
| A supervisor gives a female (male) subordinate a nice gift on her (his) birthday. | Yes | No | Uncertain | Yes | No |
| Two male employees share a sexually explicit magazine while observed by a female employee. | Yes | No | Uncertain | Yes | No |
| Female office workers are "rated" by male employees as they pass the men's desks. | Yes | No | Uncertain | Yes | No |
| Revealing female clothing is given as a gift at an office birthday party. | Yes | No | Uncertain | Yes | No |

For example, the Paradise Valley Unified School District of Phoenix, Arizona, defines sexual harassment as including, but not limited to, suggestive or obscene letters, notes, or invitations; derogatory comments, slurs, jokes, and epithets; assault; blocking movements; leering gestures; and displays of sexually suggestive

To them, it's harmless conversation.

TO HER, IT'S A VIOLATION OF HER CIVIL RIGHTS.

*It's actually much more than that. It's a frightening and insulting experience, too.*

SEXUAL HARASSMENT COMES IN MANY FORMS. SOME ARE NOT AS OBVIOUS AS YOU THINK. WHAT MAY SEEM HARMLESS OR INNOCENT CAN, IN FACT, HAVE A DEVASTATING EFFECT, HARMING MUCH MORE THAN THE VICTIM.

SEXUAL HARASSMENT ISN'T SIMPLY ABOUT WHAT BEHAVIOR IS PERMITTED BY LAW.

*It's about treating people with respect.*

IT'S ABOUT TREATING PEOPLE THE WAY YOU WANT THEM TO TREAT YOU OR SOMEONE YOU CARE ABOUT.

AT THE UNITED STATES POSTAL SERVICE, WE BELIEVE PREVENTING SEXUAL HARASSMENT STARTS BY TREATING PEOPLE WITH THE RESPECT THEY DESERVE. IT MEANS SETTING A HIGHER STANDARD OF PROFESSIONAL BEHAVIOR TO MAKE OUR COMMUNITY A BETTER PLACE TO WORK AND LIVE.

**UNITED STATES POSTAL SERVICE**
Diversity Programs/Diversity Development
National Sexual Harassment Prevention Task Team

*We're part of your community. We care.*

*This United States Postal Service ad dramatically illustrates how sexual harassment can create a hostile environment in the workplace.*

objects, pictures, or cartoons where such conduct may create a hostile environment for the employee.[35]

In 1986, the Supreme Court issued its first sexual harassment decision, in *Meritor Savings Bank v Vinson.* This ruling provided employers with the Court's interpretation of how sexual harassment is viewed under EEOC guidelines.[36] The EEOC considers an employer guilty of sexual harassment when the employer knew or should have known about the unlawful conduct and failed to remedy it or to take corrective action. Employers are also guilty of sexual harassment when they allow nonemployees (customers or salespersons) to sexually harass employees.[37]

It is noteworthy that both the Supreme Court and the EEOC hold employers strictly accountable to prevent sexual harassment of both female and male employees. In 1998, the Supreme Court held in *Oncale v Sundowner Offshore Services* that same-sex sexual harassment (male-to-male, female-to-female) is covered under Title VII.[38] In the opinion of Justice Antonin Scalia, "What matters is the conduct at issue, not the sex of the people involved and not the presence or absence of sexual desire, whether heterosexual or homosexual."[39] Where charges of sexual harassment have been proved, the EEOC has imposed remedies including back pay; reinstatement; and payment of lost benefits, interest charges, and attorney's fees. Sexual harassment involving physical conduct can invite criminal charges, and damages may be assessed against both the employer and the individual offender.[40]

In 1993 the Supreme Court held in *Harris v Forklift Systems Inc.* that an individual alleging hostile work environment harassment need not show that the defendant's conduct caused psychological injury.[41] As long as a reasonable person would perceive the conduct to be hostile or abusive, and the individual perceives the conduct as such, there is no need for the conduct to cause psychological injury as well. Additionally, in *Burlington Industries, Inc. v Ellerth* (1998), the Supreme Court ruled that sexual harassment can take place even when there is no tangible job detriment such as a salary reduction, a less desirable job assignment, or denial of a promotion.[42] To determine whether the misconduct is hostile or abusive, courts must look at all the circumstances surrounding the charge of harassment. Important factors include the frequency of the misconduct; the severity of the misconduct; whether it is physically threatening or humiliating, as opposed to merely offensive; and whether it unreasonably interferes with the employee's work performance.[43]

Despite legislation against it, however, sexual harassment is still common in the workplace. Managers and supervisors must take special precautions to try to prevent it. Highlights in HRM 4 presents the Court's suggestions and the EEOC guidelines for an effective policy to minimize sexual harassment in the work environment.[44]

**HIGHLIGHTS IN HRM**

# Basic Components of an Effective Sexual Harassment Policy

1. Develop a comprehensive organization-wide policy on sexual harassment and present it to all current and new employees. Stress that sexual harassment will not be tolerated under any circumstances. Emphasis is best achieved when the policy is publicized and supported by top management.

2. Hold training sessions with supervisors to explain Title VII requirements, their role in providing an environment free of sexual harassment, and proper investigative procedures when charges occur.

3. Establish a formal complaint procedure in which employees can discuss problems without fear of retaliation. The complaint procedure should spell out how charges will be investigated and resolved.

4. Act immediately when employees complain of sexual harassment. Communicate widely that investigations will be conducted objectively and with appreciation for the sensitivity of the issue.

5. When an investigation supports employee charges, discipline the offender at once. For extremely serious offenses, discipline should include penalties up to and including discharge. Discipline should be applied consistently across similar cases and among managers and hourly employees alike.

6. Follow up on all cases to ensure a satisfactory resolution of the problem.

## Immigration Reform and Control

Good employment is the magnet that attracts many people to the United States. Unfortunately, illegal immigration has adversely affected welfare services and educational and Social Security benefits. To preserve our tradition of legal immigration while closing the door to illegal entry, in 1986 Congress passed the Immigration Reform and Control Act. The act was passed to control unauthorized immigration by making it unlawful for a person or organization to hire, recruit, or refer for a fee persons not legally eligible for employment in the United States.

Employers must comply with the law by verifying and maintaining records on the legal rights of applicants to work in the United States. The *Handbook for Employers*, published by the U.S. Department of Justice, lists five actions that employers must take to comply with the law:

1. Have employees fill out their part of Form I-9.
2. Check documents establishing an employee's identity and eligibility to work.
3. Complete the employer's section of Form I-9.
4. Retain Form I-9 for at least three years.
5. Present Form I-9 for inspection to an Immigration and Naturalization Service officer or to a Department of Labor officer upon request.[45]

Section 102 of the law also prohibits discrimination. Employers with four or more employees may not discriminate against any individual (other than an unauthorized alien) in hiring, discharge, recruiting, or referring for a fee because of that individual's national origin or, in the case of a citizen or intending citizen, because of citizenship status. Employers found to have violated the act will be ordered to cease the discriminatory practice. They may also be directed to hire, with or without back pay, individuals harmed by the discrimination and pay a fine of up to $1,000 for each person discriminated against. Charges of discrimination based on national origin or citizenship are filed with the Office of Special Counsel in the Department of Justice.

## Uniform Guidelines on Employee Selection Procedures

**Uniform Guidelines on Employee Selection Procedures**
Procedural document published in the *Federal Register* to assist employers in complying with federal regulations against discriminatory actions

Employers are often uncertain about the appropriateness of specific selection procedures, especially those related to testing and selection. To remedy this concern, in 1978 the Equal Employment Opportunity Commission, along with three other government agencies, adopted the current **Uniform Guidelines on Employee Selection Procedures**.[46] Since it was first published in 1970, the *Uniform Guidelines* has become a very important procedural document for managers because it applies to employee selection procedures in the areas of hiring, retention, promotion, transfer, demotion, dismissal, and referral. It is designed to assist employers, labor organizations, employment agencies, and licensing and certification boards in complying with the requirements of federal laws prohibiting discrimination in employment.

Essentially the *Uniform Guidelines* recommends that an employer be able to demonstrate that selection procedures are valid in predicting or measuring performance in a particular job. It defines "discrimination" as follows:

> The use of any selection procedure which has an adverse impact on the hiring, promotion, or other employment or membership opportunities of members of any race, sex, or ethnic group will be considered to be discriminatory and inconsistent with these guidelines, unless the procedure has been validated in accordance with these guidelines (or, certain other provisions are satisfied).[47]

### Validity

**Adverse impact**
A concept that refers to the rejection of a significantly higher percentage of a protected class for employment, placement, or promotion when compared with the successful, nonprotected class

When using a test or other selection instrument to choose individuals for employment, employers must be able to prove that the selection instrument bears a direct relationship to job success. This proof is established through validation studies that show the job relatedness or lack thereof for the selection instrument under study. The *Uniform Guidelines*, along with several of the court cases we discuss later, provides strict standards for employers to follow as they validate selection procedures. The different methods of testing validity are reviewed in detail in Chapter 5.

### Adverse Impact

For an applicant or employee to pursue a discrimination case successfully, the individual must establish that the employer's selection procedures resulted in an adverse impact on a protected class. **Adverse impact** refers to the rejection for employment, placement, or promotion of a significantly higher percentage of a protected class when compared with a nonprotected class.[48] Additionally, when pursuing an adverse impact claim, an individual is alleging that the employer's selection practice has *unintentionally* discriminated against a protected group.

In EEO cases it is important to distinguish between adverse impact and disparate treatment discrimination. Adverse impact cases deal with unintentional discrimination; **disparate treatment** cases involve instances of purposeful discrimination. For example, disparate treatment would arise where an employer hires men, but no women, with school-age children. Allowing men to apply for craft jobs, such as carpentry or electrical work, but denying this opportunity to women would also show disparate treatment. To win a disparate treatment case, the plaintiff must prove that the employer's actions intended to discriminate, a situation often difficult to substantiate.

There are three basic ways to show that adverse impact exists:

*Adverse Rejection Rate, or Four-Fifths Rule.*   According to the *Uniform Guidelines,* a selection program has an adverse impact when the selection rate for any racial, ethnic, or sex class is less than four-fifths (or 80 percent) of the rate of the class with the highest selection rate. The Equal Employment Opportunity Commission has adopted the **four-fifths rule** as a rule of thumb to determine adverse impact in enforcement proceedings. The four-fifths rule is not a legal definition of discrimination; rather, it is a method by which the EEOC or any other enforcement agency monitors serious discrepancies in hiring, promotion, or other employment decisions. Highlights in HRM 5 explains how adverse impact is determined and gives a realistic example of how the four-fifths rule is computed.

An alternative to the four-fifths rule, and one increasingly used in discrimination lawsuits, is to apply *standard deviation analysis* to the observed applicant flow data. In 1977, the Supreme Court, in *Hazelwood School District v United States,* set forth a standard deviation analysis that has been followed by numerous lower courts.[49] This statistical procedure determines whether the difference between the expected selection rates for protected groups and the actual selection rates could be attributed to chance. If chance is eliminated for the lower selection rates of the protected class, it is assumed that the employer's selection technique has an adverse impact on the employment opportunities of that group.

*Restricted Policy.*   Any evidence that an employer has a selection procedure that excludes members of a protected class, whether intentional or not, constitutes adverse impact. For example, hiring individuals who must meet a minimum height or appearance standard (at the expense of protected class members) is evidence of a restricted policy. In one case known to the authors, an organization when downsizing discharged employees primarily 40 years of age or older. These employees filed a class-action suit claiming adverse impact under the Age Discrimination in Employment Act.

*McDonnell Douglas Test.*   Individuals who believe they have been unjustly rejected for employment may demonstrate adverse impact through the McDonnell Douglas test.[50] This test, named for the Supreme Court case *McDonnell Douglas Corp. v Green* (1973), provides four guidelines for individuals to follow in establishing a case:[51]

1. The person is a member of a protected class.
2. The person applied for a job for which he or she was qualified.

---

**Disparate treatment**
Situation in which protected-class members receive unequal treatment or are evaluated by different standards

**Four-fifths rule**
Rule of thumb followed by the EEOC in determining adverse impact for use in enforcement proceedings

HRM 5

**HIGHLIGHTS IN HRM**

# Determining Adverse Impact: The Four-Fifths Rule

Employers can determine adverse impact by using the method outlined in the interpretive manual for the *Uniform Guidelines on Employee Selection Procedures.*

**A.**   Calculate the rate of selection for each group (divide the number of persons selected from a group by the number of total applicants from that group).

**B.**   Observe which group has the highest selection.

**C.**   Calculate the impact ratios by comparing the selection rate for each group with that of the highest group (divide the selection rate for a group by the selection rate for the highest group).

**D.**   Observe whether the selection rate for any group is substantially less (i.e., usually less than four-fifths, or 80 percent) than the selection rate for the highest group. If it is, adverse impact is indicated in most circumstances.

Example

| | JOB APPLICANTS | NUMBER HIRED | SELECTION RATE PERCENT HIRED |
|---|---|---|---|
| Step A | Whites 100 | 52 | 52/100 = 52% |
| | Blacks 50 | 14 | 14/50 = 28% |
| Step B | The group with the highest selection rate is whites, 52 percent. | | |
| Step C | Divide the black selection rate (28 percent) by the white selection rate (52 percent). The black rate is 53.8 percent of the white rate. | | |
| Step D | Since 53.8 percent is less than four-fifths, or 80 percent, adverse impact is indicated. | | |

Source: Adoption of Questions and Answers to Clarify and Provide a Common Interpretation of the *Uniform Guidelines on Employee Selection Procedures, Federal Register* 44, no. 43 (March 2, 1979): 11998.

**3.**   The person was rejected, despite being qualified.

**4.**   After rejection, the employer continued to seek other applicants with similar qualifications.

Provided these four guidelines are met, then a prima facie (i.e., before further examination) case of discrimination is shown. The burden now shifts to the employer to prove that the action taken against the individual was not discriminatory. For example, in a selection case where female applicants were denied employment, the supervisor may claim the male hired was the only applicant qualified to perform the job.

While the *Uniform Guidelines* does not require an employer to conduct validity studies of selection procedures where no adverse impact exists, it does encourage employers to use selection procedures that are valid. Organizations that validate their selection procedures on a regular basis and use interviews, tests, and other procedures in such a manner as to avoid adverse impact will generally be in compliance with the principles of equal employment legislation. Affirmative action programs also reflect employer intent. The motivation for using valid selection procedures, however, should be the desire to achieve effective management of human resources rather than the fear of legal pressure.

### Workforce Utilization Analysis

While employers must be aware of the impact of their selection procedures on protected-class members, they must also be concerned with the composition of their internal workforce when compared with their external labor market. The EEOC refers to this comparison as **workforce utilization analysis**. This concept simply compares an employer's workforce by race and sex for specific job categories against the surrounding labor market. The employer's relevant labor market is that area from which employees are drawn who have the skills needed to successfully perform the job. For example, if the Vision Track Golf Corporation is hiring computer technicians from a labor market composed of 10 percent black workers, 8 percent Hispanic workers, and 2 percent Native American workers, all of whom possess the qualifications for the job, the employer's internal workforce should reflect this racial composition. When this occurs, the employer's workforce is said to be *at parity* with the relevant labor market. If the employer's racial workforce composition is below external figures, then the protected class is said to be *underutilized* and the employer should take affirmative steps to correct the imbalance. Workforce utilization analysis is the cornerstone upon which affirmative action programs (discussed shortly) are developed and maintained.

**Workforce utilization analysis**

Process of classifying protected class members by number and by the type of job they hold within the organization

### Significant Court Cases

The *Uniform Guidelines* has been given added importance through three leading Supreme Court cases. Each case is noteworthy because it elaborates on the concepts of adverse impact, validity testing, and job relatedness. Managers of both large and small organizations must constantly be alert to new court decisions and be prepared to implement those rulings. The Bureau of National Affairs, Commerce Clearing House, and Prentice-Hall provide legal information on a subscription basis to interested managers. Local and regional seminars offered by professional organizations such as the American Management Association also provide information.

The benchmark case in employment selection procedures is *Griggs v Duke Power Company* (1971). Willie Griggs had applied for the position of coal handler with the Duke Power Company. His request for the position was denied because he was not a high school graduate, a requirement for the position. Griggs claimed the job standard was discriminatory because it did not relate to job success and because the standard had an adverse impact on a protected class.

In the *Griggs* decision, the Supreme Court established two important principles affecting equal employment opportunity.[52] First, the Court ruled that employer discrimination need not be overt or intentional to be present. Rather, employment practices can be illegal even when applied equally to all employees. For example, under this ruling, a new venture pharmaceutical company requiring all salespersons to be six feet tall would impose an adverse impact on Asians and women, limiting their employment opportunities.

Second, under *Griggs*, employment practices must be job-related. When discrimination charges arise, employers have the burden of proving that employment requirements are job-related or constitute a business necessity. Where employers use education, physical, or intelligence standards as a basis for hiring or promotion, these requirements must be absolutely necessary for job success. Under Title VII, good intent, or absence of intent to discriminate, is not a sufficient defense.

In 1975 the Supreme Court decided *Albemarle Paper Company v Moody.*[53] The Albemarle Paper Company required job applicants to pass a variety of employment tests, some of which were believed to be poor predictors of job success. The *Albemarle* case is important because in it the Supreme Court strengthened the principles established in *Griggs*. Specifically, more-stringent requirements were placed on employers to demonstrate the job relatedness of tests. Where tests are used for hiring or promotion decisions (tests are defined to include performance appraisals), they must be valid predictors of job success.

In *Wards Cove Packing Co. v Antonio,* decided in 1989, the Supreme Court handed down a major decision involving the burden of proof in a discrimination charge.[54] The Court ruled that in an adverse impact case, the burden of proving a charge of discrimination fell on the charging party. This decision made it more difficult for individuals to substantiate discrimination claims. The *Wards Cove* case, in effect, reversed the *Griggs* decision, which required employers to justify their employment practices. Additionally, the Court held that a statistical disparity among protected members of a workforce does not, in itself, show proof of discrimination. Rather, the relevant statistical comparison is to *qualified applicants* in the employer's relevant labor market.

The Civil Rights Act of 1991 overturned important parts of *Wards Cove*. The act once again places the burden of persuasion back upon the employer. If a discrimination case is made by showing a statistical disparity, the employer must again prove that the employment practice bears a relationship to the requirements of the job—a business necessity defense. Thus the Civil Rights Act of 1991 supports the *Griggs* decision.

# Enforcing Equal Employment Opportunity Legislation

Along with prohibiting employment discrimination, Title VII of the Civil Rights Act created the Equal Employment Opportunity Commission. As the federal government's leading civil rights agency, the EEOC is responsible for ensuring that covered employers comply with the intent of this act. The commission accomplishes this goal primarily by (1) issuing various employment guidelines and monitoring the employment practices of organizations and (2) protecting employee rights through the investigation and prosecution of discrimination charges. Figure 2.4 illustrates the case load of the EEOC for recent years.

It is important to remember that the EEOC's guidelines are not federal law but administrative rules and regulations published in the *Federal Register*. However, the different guidelines have been given weight by the courts as they interpret the law and therefore should not be taken lightly. In addition to enforcing Title VII, the EEOC has the authority to enforce the Age Discrimination in Employment Act and the Equal Pay Act. Executive Order 12067, which requires the coordination of all federal equal employment opportunity regulations, practices, and policies, is also administered by the EEOC.

**FIGURE 2.4**

### U.S. Equal Employment Opportunity Commission Case Figures, Fiscal Years 1992–1998

| BASIS | FY 1992 | FY 1993 | FY 1994 | FY 1995 | FY 1996 | FY 1997 | FY 1998 |
|---|---|---|---|---|---|---|---|
| Race | 29,042 | 31,688 | 31,656 | 29,986 | 26,287 | 29,199 | 28,820 |
| Sex | 21,482 | 23,905 | 25,860 | 26,181 | 23,813 | 24,728 | 24,454 |
| Disability | 999 | 15,242 | 18,808 | 19,778 | 18,046 | 18,108 | 17,806 |
| Age | 19,264 | 19,887 | 19,571 | 17,401 | 15,719 | 15,785 | 15,191 |
| Retaliation | 10,932 | 12,644 | 14,415 | 15,342 | 16,080 | 18,198 | 19,114 |
| National origin | 7,126 | 7,393 | 7,414 | 7,035 | 6,687 | 6,712 | 6,778 |
| Religion | 1,337 | 1,444 | 1,546 | 1,581 | 1,564 | 1,709 | 1,786 |
| Equal pay | 1,302 | 1,187 | 1,395 | 1,273 | 969 | 1,134 | 1,071 |
| Total* | 72,302 | 87,942 | 91,189 | 87,529 | 77,990 | 80,680 | 79,591 |

*The number for total charges reflects the number of individual charge filings. Because individuals often file charges under multiple bases, the number of total charges for any given fiscal year will be less than the total of the eight bases listed.

Source:  Data compiled by the Office of Research, Information and Planning from EEOC's Charge Data System's national database.

## The Equal Employment Opportunity Commission

The EEOC consists of five commissioners and a general counsel, all appointed by the president of the United States and confirmed by the Senate. The president appoints commissioners for staggered five-year terms, and no more than three members of the commission can be of the same political party. One commissioner is appointed to be the EEOC chairperson, who is responsible for the overall administration of the agency. The commission's work consists of formulating EEO policy and approving all litigation involved in maintaining equal employment opportunity.[55]

Appointed for a four-year term, the general counsel is responsible for investigating discrimination charges, conducting agency litigation, and providing legal opinions, in addition to reviewing EEOC regulations, guidelines, and contracts.

The day-to-day operation of the commission is performed through administrative headquarters, districts, and area offices. *District offices* handle discrimination charges and all compliance and litigation enforcement functions. *Area offices* are less than full-service organizations and generally serve as charge-processing and initial investigation units. Much of the EEOC's work is delegated to the district offices and other designated representatives. District directors have authority to receive or consent to the withdrawal of Title VII charges, issue subpoenas, send notices of the filing of charges, dismiss charges, enter into and sign conciliation agreements (voluntary employer settlements), and send out notices of the employee's right to sue. Employees who wish to file discrimination charges and employers responding to complaints work with district or area office personnel.

## Record-Keeping and Posting Requirements

Organizations subject to Title VII are required by law to maintain specific employment records and reports. In addition, employers are required to post selected equal employment opportunity notices and to summarize the composition of their workforce in order to determine the distribution of protected individuals. These records are for establishing minority-group statistical reports. Equal employment opportunity legislation covering federal contractors and subcontractors has special reporting requirements for these employers. Those failing to comply with record-keeping and posting requirements or willfully falsifying records can incur penalties, including fines and imprisonment.

It is important to note that record-keeping requirements are both detailed and comprehensive. For example, managers must generate and retain for specific time periods different employment data under each of the following laws: Title VII, the Age Discrimination in Employment Act, and the Equal Pay Act. Where federal contractors are required to have written affirmative action programs, these must be retained along with supporting documents (e.g., names of job applicants, rejection ratios, and seniority lists).

**EEO-1 report**

An employer information report that must be filed annually by employers of 100 or more employees (except state and local government employers) and government contractors and subcontractors to determine an employer's workforce composition

Employers of 100 or more employees (except state and local government employers) and government contractors and subcontractors subject to Executive Order 11286 must file annually an **EEO-1 report** (Employer Information Report). Figure 2.5 shows Section D of the EEO-1 report, which requires the reporting of minority employees. This comprehensive report is the EEOC's basic document for determining an employer's workforce composition. In preparing the EEO-1 report, the organization may collect records concerning racial or ethnic identity either by visual survey or through postemployment questionnaires, if not prohibited by state fair employment practice law.

To show evidence of its equal employment opportunity and affirmative action efforts, an organization should retain copies of recruitment letters sent to minority agencies, announcements of job openings, and other significant information concerning employee recruitment. Other employment records to keep include data on promotions, demotions, transfers, layoffs or terminations, rates of pay or other terms of compensation, and selections for training or apprenticeship programs. Title VII requires retention of all personnel or employment records, including application forms, for at least six months or until resolution of any HR action, whichever occurs later.

During the employment process, employers are permitted to collect racial data on job applicants for compiling statistical reports; however, these data must be collected on a separate information sheet, not on the formal job application form. Where a charge of discrimination has been filed, the respondent organization must retain all HR records relevant to the case until final disposition of the charge.

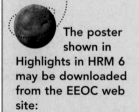

**USING THE INTERNET**

The poster shown in Highlights in HRM 6 may be downloaded from the EEOC web site:

www.eeoc.gov/poster.html

Posters explaining to individuals what their employment rights are and how to file complaints of discrimination have been developed by the EEOC and other administrative agencies. (See Highlights in HRM 6.) The law requires that employers display these posters and other federally required posters related to HRM in prominent places easily accessible to employees. HR employment offices, cafeterias, centrally located bulletin boards, and time clocks are popular locations. Posting requirements should not be taken lightly. For example, EEO posters

FIGURE 2.5

Section D, EEO-1 Report

**Section D—EMPLOYMENT DATA**

Employment at this establishment—Report all permanent full-time and part-time employees including apprentices and on-the-job trainees unless specifically excluded as set forth in the instructions. Enter the appropriate figures on all lines and in all columns. Blank spaces will be considered as zeros.

| JOB CATEGORIES | | OVERALL TOTALS (SUM OF COL. B THRU K) | MALE | | | | | FEMALE | | | | |
|---|---|---|---|---|---|---|---|---|---|---|---|---|
| | | | WHITE (NOT OF HISPANIC ORIGIN) | BLACK (NOT OF HISPANIC ORIGIN) | HISPANIC | ASIAN OR PACIFIC ISLANDER | AMERICAN INDIAN OR ALASKAN NATIVE | WHITE (NOT OF HISPANIC ORIGIN) | BLACK (NOT OF HISPANIC ORIGIN) | HISPANIC | ASIAN OR PACIFIC ISLANDER | AMERICAN INDIAN OR ALASKAN NATIVE |
| | | A | B | C | D | E | F | G | H | I | J | K |
| Officials and Managers | 1 | | | | | | | | | | | |
| Professionals | 2 | | | | | | | | | | | |
| Technicians | 3 | | | | | | | | | | | |
| Sales Workers | 4 | | | | | | | | | | | |
| Office and Clerical | 5 | | | | | | | | | | | |
| Craft Workers (Skilled) | 6 | | | | | | | | | | | |
| Operatives (Semi-Skilled) | 7 | | | | | | | | | | | |
| Laborers (Unskilled) | 8 | | | | | | | | | | | |
| Service Workers | 9 | | | | | | | | | | | |
| **TOTAL** | 10 | | | | | | | | | | | |
| Total employment reported in previous EEO–1 report | 11 | | | | | | | | | | | |

NOTE: Omit questions 1 and 2 on the Consolidated Report.
1. Date(s) of payroll period used:        2.   Does this establishment employ apprentices?
                                                    1 ☐ Yes      2 ☐ No

show the time limits for filing a charge of discrimination. Failure to post these notices may be used as a basis for excusing the late filing of a discrimination charge.

## Processing Discrimination Charges

**Charge form**

Discrimination complaint filed with the EEOC by employees or job applicants

Employees or job applicants who believe they have been discriminated against may file a discrimination complaint, or **charge form,** with the EEOC. Filing a charge form initiates an administrative procedure that can be lengthy, time-consuming, and costly for the employer. Both parties, the plaintiff (employee) and the defendant (organization), must be prepared to support their beliefs or actions. If litigation follows, employers will normally take an aggressive approach to defend their position.

Figure 2.6 summarizes the process of filing a discrimination charge with the EEOC. Under the law, charges must be filed within 180 days (300 days in deferral states)[56] of the alleged unlawful practice. The processing of a charge includes notifying the employer that a charge of employment discrimination has been filed. Employers will receive a copy of the charge within ten days of filing.

In states that have FEP laws with appropriate enforcement machinery, the discrimination charge is deferred to the state agency for resolution before action is taken by the EEOC. The EEOC will accept the recommendation of the state agency because deferral states must comply with federal standards. If the state agency fails to resolve the complaint or if the sixty-day deferral period lapses, the case is given back to the EEOC for final investigation.

**HRM 6**

## EEOC Poster

# Equal Employment Opportunity is
# THE LAW

### Employers Holding Federal Contracts or Subcontracts

Applicants to and employees of companies with a Federal government contract or subcontract are protected under the following Federal authorities:

**RACE, COLOR, RELIGION, SEX, NATIONAL ORIGIN**

Executive Order 11246, as amended, prohibits job discrimination on the basis of race, color, religion, sex or national origin, and requires affirmative action to ensure equality of opportunity in all aspects of employment.

**INDIVIDUALS WITH HANDICAPS**

Section 503 of the Rehabilitation Act of 1973, as amended, prohibits job discrimination because of handicap and requires affirmative action to employ and advance in employment qualified individuals with handicaps who, with reasonable accommodation, can perform the essential functions of a job.

**VIETNAM ERA AND SPECIAL DISABLED VETERANS**

38 U.S.C. 4212 of the Vietnam Era Veterans Readjustment Assistance Act of 1974 prohibits job discrimination and requires affirmative action to employ and advance in employment qualified Vietnam era veterans and qualified special disabled veterans.

Any person who believes a contractor has violated its nondiscrimination or affirmative action obligations under the authorities above should contact immediately:

The Office of Federal Contract Compliance Programs (OFCCP), Employment Standards Administration, U.S. Department of Labor, 200 Constitution Avenue, N.W., Washington, D.C. 20210 or call (202) 523-9368, or an OFCCP regional or district office, listed in most telephone directories under U.S. Government, Department of Labor.

### Private Employment, State and Local Governments, Educational Institutions

Applicants to and employees of most private employers, state and local governments, educational institutions, employment agencies and labor organizations are protected under the following Federal laws:

**RACE, COLOR, RELIGION, SEX, NATIONAL ORIGIN**

Title VII of the Civil Rights Act of 1964, as amended, prohibits discrimination in hiring, promotion, discharge, pay, fringe benefits, job training, classification, referral, and other aspects of employment, on the basis of race, color, religion, sex or national origin.

**DISABILITY**

The Americans with Disabilities Act of 1990, as amended, protects qualified applicants and employees with disabilities from discrimination in hiring, promotion, discharge, pay, job training, fringe benefits, classification, referral, and other aspects of employment on the basis of disability. The law also requires that covered entities provide qualified applicants and employees with disabilities with reasonable accommodations that do not impose undue hardship.

**AGE**

The Age Discrimination in Employment Act of 1967, as amended, protects applicants and employees 40 years of age or older from discrimination on the basis of age in hiring, promotion, discharge, compensation, terms, conditions or privileges of employment.

**SEX (WAGES)**

In addition to sex discrimination prohibited by Title VII of the Civil Rights Act (see above), the Equal Pay Act of 1963, as amended, prohibits sex discrimination in payment of wages to women and men performing substantially equal work in the same establishment.

Retaliation against a person who files a charge of discrimination, participates in an investigation, or opposes an unlawful employment practice is prohibited by all of these Federal laws.

If you believe that you have been discriminated against under any of the above laws, you immediately should contact:

The U.S. Equal Employment Opportunity Commission (EEOC), 1801 L Street, N.W., Washington, D.C. 20507 or an EEOC field office by calling toll free (800) 669-4000. For individuals with hearing impairments, EEOC's toll free TDD number is (800) 800-3302.

### Programs or Activities Receiving Federal Financial Assistance

**RACE, COLOR, NATIONAL ORIGIN, SEX**

In addition to the protection of Title VII of the Civil Rights Act of 1964, Title VI of the Civil Rights Act prohibits discrimination on the basis of race, color or national origin in programs or activities receiving Federal financial assistance. Employment discrimination is covered by Title VI if the primary objective of the financial assistance is provision of employment, or where employment discrimination causes or may cause discrimination in providing services under such programs. Title IX of the Education Amendments of 1972 prohibits employment discrimination on the basis of sex in educational programs or activities which receive Federal assistance.

**INDIVIDUALS WITH HANDICAPS**

Section 504 of the Rehabilitation Act of 1973, as amended, prohibits employment discrimination on the basis of handicap in any program or activity which receives Federal financial assistance. Discrimination is prohibited in all aspects of employment against handicapped persons who, with reasonable accommodation, can perform the essential functions of a job.

If you believe you have been discriminated against in a program of any institution which receives Federal assistance, you should contact immediately the Federal agency providing such assistance.

EEOC-P/E-1

FIGURE 2.6

## Filing a Charge of Employment Discrimination

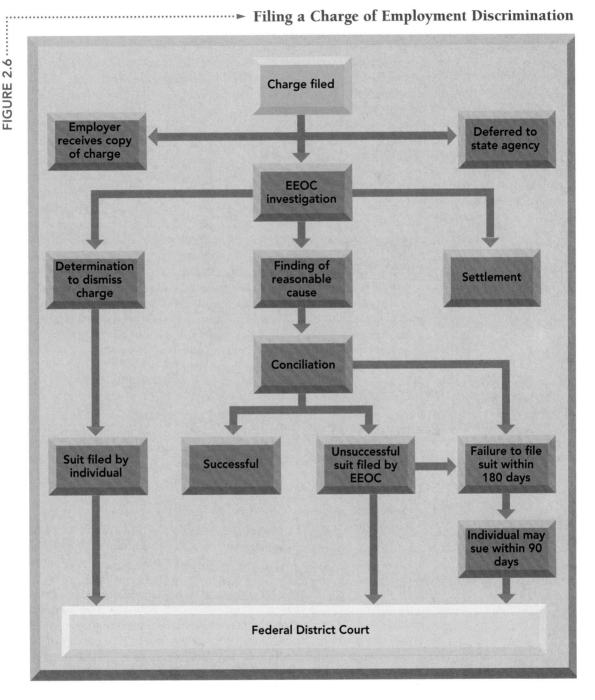

EEOC investigations are conducted by fully trained equal opportunity specialists (EOSs) who have extensive experience in investigative procedures, theories of discrimination, and relief and remedy techniques. The EOS will gather facts from both sides through telephone calls, letters and questionnaires, field visits, or jointly arranged meetings. While it is generally advisable for them to cooperate in EEOC investigations, employers may legally resist the commission's efforts by refusing to submit documents or give relevant testimony. However, the EEOC may obtain this information through a court subpoena. Employers who then refuse to supply the information will face contempt-of-court charges.

Once the investigation is under way or completed, several decision points occur. First, the employer may offer a settlement to resolve the case without further investigation. If the offer is accepted, the case is closed. Second, the EEOC may find no violation of law and dismiss the charge. In this case, the charging party is sent a *right-to-sue notice,* which permits the individual to start private litigation, if he or she so desires, in federal court within ninety days. Third, if the EEOC finds "reasonable cause" of discrimination, the commission will attempt to conciliate (settle) the matter between the charging party and the employer. The conciliation process is a voluntary procedure and will not always lead to a settlement.

Employers should keep in mind that when the EEOC negotiates a settlement, it will attempt to obtain full remedial, corrective, and preventive relief. Back pay, reinstatement, transfers, promotions, seniority rights, bonuses, and other "make whole" perquisites of employment are considered to be appropriate remedies. These settlements can frequently be costly.

If the employer and the EEOC cannot reach a negotiated settlement, the commission has the power to prosecute the organization in court. However, this decision is made on a case-by-case basis and may depend on the importance of the issue. Failure of the EEOC to take court action or to resolve the charge in 180 days from filing permits employees to pursue litigation within 90 days after receiving a right-to-sue letter issued by the commission.

### Retaliation

Importantly, managers and supervisors must not retaliate against individuals who invoke their legal right to file charges or to support other employees during EEOC proceedings. In one case, a black woman was awarded $64,000 in damages when she was fired in retaliation for filing a racial bias suit with the Indiana Civil Rights Commission, an FEP commission.[57] Retaliation can include any punitive action taken against employees who elect to exercise their legal rights before any EEO agency. These actions include discharge, demotion, salary reduction, reduced work responsibilities, transfer to a less desirable job, etc.[58]

## Preventing Discrimination Charges

Both large and small employers understand that the foundation to preventing any form of discrimination is a comprehensive EEO policy. The Supreme Court's emphasis on the prevention and correction of discrimination means that employers that do not have an EEO policy are legally vulnerable. Antidiscrimination policy statements must be inclusive; they must cover all applicable laws and EEOC guidelines and contain practical illustrations of specific inappropriate behavior.[59] For the policy to have value it must be widely disseminated to managers, supervisors, and all nonmanagerial employees. A complete policy will include specific sanctions for those found guilty of discriminatory behavior.

Since managers and supervisors are key to preventing and correcting discrimination, they, in particular, must be trained to understand employee rights and managerial obligations. A comprehensive training program will include (1) the prohibitions covered in the various EEO statutes, (2) guidance on how to respond to complaints of discrimination, (3) procedures for investigating complaints (see Chapter 13), and (4) suggestions for remedying inappropriate behavior. Perhaps the ultimate key to preventing employment discrimination is for managers and supervisors to create an organizational climate where the principles of dignity, respect, and the acceptance of a diverse workforce are expected.

# Affirmative Action

**Affirmative action**
Policy that goes beyond equal employment opportunity by requiring organizations to comply with the law and correct past discriminatory practices by increasing the numbers of minorities and women in specific positions

Equal employment opportunity legislation requires managers to provide the same opportunities to all job applicants and employees regardless of race, color, religion, sex, national origin, or age. While EEO law is largely a policy of nondiscrimination, **affirmative action** requires employers to analyze their workforce and develop a plan of action to correct areas of past discrimination. Affirmative action is achieved by having organizations follow specific guidelines and goals to ensure that they have a balanced and representative workforce. To achieve these goals, employers must make a concerted effort to recruit, select, train, and promote members of protected classes. Employers must locate not only minority candidates who are qualified, but also those who, with a reasonable amount of training or physical accommodation, can be made to qualify for job openings.

## Establishing Affirmative Action Programs

Employers establish affirmative action programs for several reasons. As noted in Figure 2.3, affirmative action programs are required by the OFCCP for employers with federal contracts greater than $50,000. Revised Order No. 4, issued by the OFCCP, provided regulations and suggestions for establishing affirmative action

From *The Wall Street Journal*—Permission, Cartoon Features Syndicate

plans. Specifically, employers must (1) perform a workforce utilization analysis, (2) establish goals and timetables for employment of underutilized protected classes, (3) develop actions and plans to reduce underutilization, including initiating proactive recruitment and selection methods, and (4) monitor progress of the entire affirmative action program.

Affirmative action programs may also be required by court order where an employer has been found guilty of past discrimination. Court-ordered programs will require the setting of hiring and promotion quotas along with stated timetables for compliance. Finally, many employers voluntarily develop their own affirmative action programs to ensure that protected-class members receive fair treatment in all aspects of employment. General Electric, the City of Portland, and Hilton Hotels use these programs as a useful way of monitoring the progress of employees while demonstrating good-faith employment effort. The EEOC recommends that organizations developing affirmative action programs follow specific steps, as shown in Highlights in HRM 7.

**Reverse discrimination**
Act of giving preference to members of protected classes to the extent that unprotected individuals believe they are suffering discrimination

In pursuing affirmative action, employers may be accused of **reverse discrimination,** or giving preference to members of protected classes to the extent that unprotected individuals believe they are suffering discrimination. When these charges occur, organizations are caught between attempting to correct past discriminatory practices and handling present complaints from unprotected members alleging that HR policies are unfair. It is exactly this "catch-22" that has made affirmative action one of the most controversial issues of the past fifty years. Two highly publicized cases illustrate the controversy.

**HRM 7**

**HIGHLIGHTS IN HRM**

# Basic Steps in Developing an Effective Affirmative Action Program

1. Issue a written equal employment opportunity policy and affirmative action commitment.
2. Appoint a top official with responsibility and authority to direct and implement the program.
3. Publicize the policy and affirmative action commitment.
4. Survey present minority and female employment by department and job classification.
5. Develop goals and timetables to improve utilization of minorities and women in each area where underutilization has been identified.
6. Develop and implement specific programs to achieve goals.
7. Establish an internal audit and reporting system to monitor and evaluate progress in each aspect of the program.
8. Develop supportive in-house and community programs.

Source: *Affirmative Action and Equal Employment: A Guidebook for Employers,* vol. 1 (Washington, D.C.: Equal Employment Opportunity Commission, 1974), 16–17.

In *University of California Regents v Bakke* (1978), the Supreme Court settled one of the most famous reverse discrimination cases.[60] Allen Bakke, a white male, charged that the University of California at Davis was guilty of reverse discrimination by admitting minority group members he believed were less qualified than he. The central issue before the Court was equal treatment under the law as guaranteed in the equal protection clause of the Fourteenth Amendment. The Court ruled that applicants must be evaluated on an individual basis, and race can be one factor used in the evaluation process as long as other competitive factors are considered. The Court stated that affirmative action programs were not illegal per se as long as rigid quota systems were not specified for different protected classes.

One year later the Supreme Court decided *United Steelworkers of America v Weber.*[61] In 1974 Kaiser Aluminum and its union, the United Steelworkers, had joined in a voluntary affirmative action program designed to increase the number of black workers in craft jobs at Kaiser's Louisiana plant. Brian Weber, a white production employee who was passed over for craft training in favor of a less-senior black worker, filed a suit charging violation of Title VII. The Supreme Court ruled against Weber, holding that under Title VII voluntary affirmative action programs are permissible where they attempt to eliminate racial imbalances in "traditionally segregated job categories." In *Weber*, the Supreme Court did not endorse all voluntary affirmative action programs, but it did give an important push to those programs voluntarily implemented and designed to correct past racial imbalances.

## Affirmative Action and Diversity

Affirmative action is a highly emotional and controversial subject since affirmative action programs affect all employees regardless of gender, race, or ethnicity. At the core of the debate is the concern that affirmative action leads to preferential treatment and quotas for selected individuals and thus results in reverse discrimination against others. Today there is a clear and growing objection by the courts, and the public, against affirmative action and preferential treatment. Additionally, affirmative action as a national priority has been challenged for the following reasons:

- Affirmative action has not consistently resulted in the improvement in the employment status of protected groups.
- Individuals hired under affirmative action programs sometimes feel prejudged, assumed capable only of inferior performance, and, in fact, these individuals *are* sometimes viewed by others as "tokens."
- Affirmative action programs of either voluntary or forced compliance have failed to effectively assimilate protected classes into an organization's workforce.

Since the beginning of the 1990s, federal courts have increasingly restricted the use of race and ethnicity in awarding scholarships, determining college admissions, making layoff decisions, selecting employees, promoting employees, and awarding government contracts.[62] For example, in 1989, the Court dealt affirmative action a blow when it ruled in *City of Richmond v Croson* that state and local governments cannot reserve a percentage of their business for minority contractors based only upon a "general assumption" of discrimination in the construction industry.[63] Writing for the majority, Justice Sandra O'Connor stated, "None of the evidence presented by the city points to any identified discrimination in the Richmond construction industry. Adoption of such quotas nationwide would obliterate the goal of a colorblind America." In *Adarand Constructors v Peña* (1995), the court ruled that federal programs that use race or ethnicity as a basis for decision making must be strictly scrutinized to ensure that they promote "compelling" governmental interests.[64] In the majority opinion the Court declared that "strict scrutiny of all governmental racial classifications is essential" to distinguish between legitimate programs that redress past discrimination and programs that "are in fact motivated by illegitimate notions of racial inferiority or simple racial politics."

Then, in a 1996 decision affecting admission standards at the University of Texas law school, the Court ruled in *Hopwood v State of Texas* that diversity could not constitute a competing state interest justifying racial preference in selection decisions.[65] The Court noted that the school could not discriminate "because there was no compelling justification under the Fourteenth Amendment or Supreme Court precedent for such conduct even if it was designed to correct perceived racial imbalance in the student body."[66]

And, finally, affirmative action proponents were dealt a most serious blow in 1998 when California voters ratified the California Civil Rights Initiative. This law proclaims that the State of California "shall not discriminate against or grant preferential treatment to any individual or group on the basis of race, sex, color, ethnicity or national origin in the operation of public employment, public education, or public contracting."[67]

The future of affirmative action may rest not in voluntary programs or mandated quota systems but in managerial attitudes that value diversity in the workforce. Managers who embrace a diverse workforce acknowledge individual employee differences and the contributions made by persons of varied abilities. Organizations that approach diversity from a practical, business-oriented perspective (rather than a court-ordered affirmative action mandate) will employ and promote protected-class members as a means for developing competitive advantage.[68] Viewed in this manner, greater workforce diversity will significantly enhance organizational performance through knowledge of diverse marketplaces and creative problem solving. For example, Michael Goldstein, chairman of Toys R Us, supports both affirmative action and diversity because "Our customers are not one group; they comprise all of America. It's important to be able to serve them." Eastman Kodak maintains it is committed to diversity because the composition of its customer base and of the workforce is changing.[69] For both of these organizations, commitment to the advantages of diversity automatically achieves the goals of affirmative action.

# SUMMARY

 Employment discrimination against blacks, Hispanics, women, and other groups has long been practiced by U.S. employers. Prejudice against minority groups is a major cause in their lack of employment gains. Government reports show that the wages and job opportunities of minorities typically lag behind those for whites.

 Effective management requires knowing the legal aspects of the employment relationship. Pertinent legislation includes the Equal Pay Act, Title VII of the Civil Rights Act of 1964, Age Discrimination in Employment Act, Equal Employment Opportunity Act of 1972, Pregnancy Discrimination Act, Americans with Disabilities Act,

Civil Rights Act of 1991, and various executive orders. Employers are permitted to discriminate against selected protected classes where hiring preferences are a reasonable necessity, constituting a bona fide occupational qualification for normal business operation. The religious preferences of employees must be accommodated as required by law.

**OBJECTIVE 3** Sexual harassment is an area of particular importance to managers and supervisors. Extensive efforts should be made to ensure that both male and female employees are free from all forms of sexually harassing conduct. The Immigration Reform and Control Act was passed to control unauthorized immigration into the United States. The law requires managers to maintain various employment records, and they must not discriminate against job applicants or present employees because of a person's national origin or citizenship status.

**OBJECTIVE 4** The *Uniform Guidelines on Employee Selection Procedures* is designed to assist employers in complying with federal prohibitions against employment practices that discriminate on the basis of race, color, religion, gender, or national origin. The *Uniform Guidelines* provides employers a framework for making legally enforceable employment decisions. Employers must be able to show that selection procedures are valid in predicting job performance.

**OBJECTIVE 5** Adverse impact plays an important role in proving employment discrimination. Adverse impact means that an employer's employment practices result in the rejection of a significantly higher percentage of members of minority and other protected groups for some employment activity. The four-fifths rule is a guideline to determine whether employment discrimination might exist.

Highlights in HRM 5 demonstrates calculation of the four-fifths rule.

**OBJECTIVE 6** The United States court system continually interprets employment law, and managers must formulate organizational policy in response to court decisions. Violations of the law will invite discrimination charges from protected groups or self-initiated investigation from government agencies. *Griggs v Duke Power, Albemarle Paper Company v Moody,* and *Wards Cove Packing Co. v Antonio* provided added importance to the *Uniform Guidelines. Meritor Savings Bank v Vinson, Harris v Forklift Systems Inc.,* and *TWA v Hardison* are instructive in the areas of sexual harassment and religious preference. Important cases in affirmative action include *University of California Regents v Bakke, United Steelworkers of America v Weber, City of Richmond v Croson, Adarand Constructors v Peña,* and *Hopwood v State of Texas.*

**OBJECTIVE 7** To ensure that organizations comply with antidiscrimination legislation, the EEOC was established to monitor employers' actions. Employers subject to federal laws must maintain required records and report requested employment statistics where mandated. The EEOC maintains a complaint procedure for individuals who believe they have been discriminated against. Figure 2.6 illustrates the steps in filing a charge of employment discrimination.

**OBJECTIVE 8** Affirmative action goes beyond providing equal employment opportunity to employees. Affirmative action requires employers to become proactive and correct areas of past discrimination. This is accomplished by employing protected classes for jobs where they are underrepresented. The employer's goal is to have a balanced internal workforce representative of the employer's relevant labor market.

# KEY TERMS

adverse impact
affirmative action
bona fide occupational
    qualification (BFOQ)
business necessity
charge form
disabled individual

disparate treatment
EEO-1 report
equal employment opportunity
fair employment practices (FEPs)
four-fifths rule
protected classes
reasonable accommodation

reverse discrimination
sexual harassment
*Uniform Guidelines on Employee
    Selection Procedures*
workforce utilization analysis

## DISCUSSION QUESTIONS

**1.** EEO legislation was prompted by significant social events. List those events and describe how they influenced the passage of various EEO laws.

**2.** Cite and describe the major federal laws and court decisions that affect the employment process of both large and small organizations.

**3.** After receiving several complaints of sexual harassment, the HR department of a city library decided to establish a sexual harassment policy. What should be included in the policy? How should it be implemented?

**4.** What is the *Uniform Guidelines on Employee Selection Procedures*? To whom do the guidelines apply? What do they cover?

**5.** What is meant by adverse impact? How is it determined? Give an example in calculating the four-fifths rule.

**6.** Throughout the chapter, specific court cases have been highlighted to signify their impact on shaping federal antidiscrimination policy. Identify these cases and explain their significance in defining employee or employer rights and duties.

**7.** As a marketing manager you have recently turned down Nancy Conrad for a position as sales supervisor. Nancy believes the denial was due to her gender and she has filed a sex discrimination charge with the EEOC. Explain the steps the EEOC will use to process the charge; include Nancy's options during the process.

**8.** Affirmative action is both a legal and emotional issue affecting employees and employers. Develop as many arguments as you can both supporting and opposing affirmative action as an employer policy. If you were asked to implement such a program, what steps would you follow?

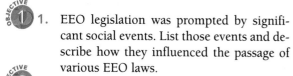

## Misplaced Affections: Discharge for Sexual Harassment*

Peter Lewiston was terminated on July 15, 1999, by the governing board of the Pine Circle Unified School District (PCUSD) for violation of the district's sexual harassment policy. Prior to Lewiston's termination he was a senior maintenance employee with an above-average work record who had worked for the PCUSD for eleven years. He had been a widower since 1992 and was described by his co-workers as a friendly, outgoing, but lonely individual. Beverly Gilbury was a fifth-grade teacher working in the district's Advanced Learning Program. She was 28 years old, married, and had worked for PCUSD for six years. At the time of the incidents, Lewiston and Gilbury both worked at the Simpson Elementary School, where their relationship was described as "cooperative." The following sequence of events was reported separately by Lewiston and Gilbury during the district's investigation of this sexual harassment case.

Gilbury reported that her relationship with Lewiston began to change during the last month of the 1998–1999 school year. She believed that Lewiston was paying her more attention and that his behavior was "out of the ordinary" and "sometimes weird." He began spending more time in her classroom talking with the children and with her. At the time she didn't say anything to Lewiston because "I didn't want to hurt his feelings since he is a nice, lonely, older man." However, on May 25, when Lewiston told Gilbury that he was "very fond" of her and that she had "very beautiful eyes," she replied, "Remember, Peter, we're just friends." For the remainder of the school year there was little contact between them; however, when they did see each other, Lewiston seemed "overly friendly" to her.

*June 7, 1999.* On the first day of summer school, Gilbury returned to school to find a dozen roses and a card from Lewiston. The card read, "Please forgive me for thinking you could like me. I played the big fool. Yours always, P.L." Later in the day Lewiston asked Gilbury to lunch. She replied, "It's been a long time since anyone sent me roses, but I can't go to lunch. We need to remain just friends." Gilbury told another teacher that she was uncomfortable about receiving the roses and card and that Lewiston wouldn't leave her alone. She expressed concern that Lewiston might get "more romantic" with her.

*June 8, 1999.* Gilbury arrived at school to find another card from Lewiston. Inside was a handwritten note that read, "I hope you can someday return my affections for you. I need you so much." Later in the day Lewiston again asked her to lunch and she declined saying, "I'm a happily married woman." At the close of the school day, when Gilbury went to her car, Lewiston suddenly appeared. He asked to explain himself but Gilbury became agitated and shouted, "I have to leave right now." Lewiston reached inside the car, supposedly to pat her shoulder, but touched her head instead. She believed he meant to stroke her hair. He stated that he was only trying to calm her down. She drove away, very upset.

*June 9, 1999.* Gilbury received another card and a lengthy letter from Lewiston, stating that he was wrong in trying to develop a relationship with her and he hoped they could still remain friends. He wished her all happiness with her family and job.

*June 11, 1999.* Gilbury obtained from the Western Justice Court an injunction prohibiting sexual harassment by Lewiston. Shortly thereafter Lewiston appealed the injunction. A notice was mailed to Gilbury giving the dates of the appeal hearing. The notice stated in part, "If you fail to appear, the injunction may be vacated and the petition dismissed." Gilbury failed to appear at the hearing and the injunction was set aside. Additionally, on June 11 she had filed with the district's EEOC officer a sexual harassment complaint against Lewiston. After the investigation the district concluded that Lewiston's actions created an intimidating, hostile, and offensive employment environment for Gilbury. The investigative report recommended dismissal based upon the grievous conduct of Lewiston and the initial injunction granted by the Justice Court.

*This case is adapted from an actual experience. The background information is factual. All names are fictitious.

## QUESTIONS

1. Evaluate the conduct of Peter Lewiston against the EEOC's definition of sexual harassment.
2. Should the intent or motive behind Lewiston's conduct be considered when deciding sexual harassment activities? Explain.
3. If you were the district's EEOC officer, what would you conclude? What disciplinary action, if any, would you take?

## Hair Today, Gone Tomorrow*

What seemed to Don Lim as a reasonable HR policy on personal grooming unfortunately backfired into a major EEO lawsuit.

As HR director of Movies for Less, a national retailer of videotapes, Don Lim is responsible for all corporate HR policy. Throughout its existence, Movies for Less has strived to be customer-friendly and has continually emphasized to employees the need to be "pleasing in attitude" and "conservative in all manners of appearance." To facilitate these standards, in April of 1999 Lim wrote a comprehensive dress code for employees of the organization. In part, the code stated that male employees had to maintain a hair style no longer than collar length. There was no standard on the length of hair for women.

After the dress code was disseminated and explained to employees, six male employees working in the Austin, Texas, store—all of whom had extremely long but well-groomed hair—chose to ignore the rule and were terminated. All six complained of discrimination and filed a formal charge with the EEOC. The terminated employees charged Movies for Less with sex discrimination and retaliation under Title VII of the Civil Rights Act.

*This case is adapted from Lynn Atkinson, "Hair Today, Gone Tomorrow," *HRFocus* 75, no. 10 (October 1998): 3. ©1998 American Management Association International. Reprinted by permission of American Management Association International, New York, NY. All rights reserved. http://www.amanet.org.

### QUESTIONS

1. Should employers be allowed to set different dress codes for each gender? Explain.
2. If an employer has a dress code requiring uniforms or other necessary apparel, should the employer or the employee be required to pay for the clothing? Explain.
3. If you had to decide this case for the EEOC, how would you settle the charge? What is the rationale for your decision?

## NOTES AND REFERENCES

1. Leslie Miller, "Pharmaceutical Firm to Pay $10 Million in Sexual Harassment Suit," *Mesa Tribune*, February 6, 1998, B10. See also JoAnn Muller, "Ford: The High Cost of Harassment," *Business Week*, November 15, 1999: 94–96.
2. Sheldon Steinhauser, "Costly Settlements Cross Industries," *HRMagazine* 43, no. 8 (July 1998): 98.
3. For an interesting case regarding the discharge of pregnant employees, see Lynn Atkinson, "Too Fat to Work, But Not to Collect $786,000," *HRFocus* 75, no. 8 (August 1998): 15.

4. "Current Labor Statistics," *Monthly Labor Review* 121, no. 7 (July 1998): Table 6.
5. "Median Usual Weekly Earnings of Full-Time Wage and Salary Workers by Selected Characteristics, Quarterly Average not Adjusted," *Labor Force Statistics from Current Population Survey* (Washington, D.C.: Bureau of Labor Statistics, October 1998): Table 1.
6. During 1996, the U.S. Department of Labor surveyed about 60,000 households to determine which race categories to use in employment, wage, and other statistics. Among the households, polled by race, about

44 percent prefer to be called *black,* 28 percent prefer *African-American,* and 12 percent prefer *Afro-American.* Based on the results of this survey, and on the government's current practice of classifying race, we have elected to use the term "black" throughout this text. Asra Q. Nomani, "Labor Letter," *The Wall Street Journal,* November 7, 1996, A-1.

7. Continuous training in EEO legislation is a requirement for successful employee supervision. A recent report on the in-house training activities of organizations listed EEO training as a training topic surpassed in popularity only by diversity training. This study found results to be consistent across both public and private organizations as well as large and small employers. See Kola Bliss, *Training Trends in the Workplace* (Glendale, Ariz.: Associated Consultants, 1996): 6.

8. For an overview of EEO law, see David P. Twomey, *Employment Discrimination Law: A Manager's Guide,* 4th ed. (Cincinnati, Ohio: South-Western Publishing, 1998); Fred S. Steingold, *The Employer's Legal Handbook,* 2nd ed. (Berkeley, Calif.: Nolo Press, 1997); *Employer EEO Responsibilities* (Washington, D.C.: Equal Employment Opportunity Commission, U.S. Government Printing Office, 1996).

9. Michael D. Malone, Sandra J. Hartman, and Dinah Payne, "Religion in the Workplace: How Much Is Too Much?" *Labor Law Journal* 49, no. 6 (June 1998): 1074–81.

10. Michael D. Malone, Sandra J. Hartman, and Dinah Payne, "Religion in the Workplace: Religious Activities on the Job," *Labor Law Journal* 49, no. 6 (June 1998): 1090–98.

11. Tim Howlett, "Accommodating Religion on the Job: Few Rules, Lots of Common Sense," *Workforce* 77, no. 9 (September 1998): 94–97. See also Patricia Digh, "Religion in the Workplace: Making a Good-Faith Effort to Accommodate," *HRMagazine* 43, no. 13 (December 1998): 85–91.

12. *TWA v Hardison,* 432 U.S. 63 (1977).

13. Michael D. Malone, Sandra J. Hartman, and Dinah Payne, "Religion in the Workplace: Accommodating for Scheduling and Personal Appearance," *Labor Law Journal* 49, no. 6 (June 1998): 1082–89.

14. Sheldon Steinhauser, "Is Your Corporate Culture in Need of an Overhaul?", *HRMagazine* 43, no. 8 (July 1998): 87–91.

15. Stephen Cabot, "When Words Mask Discrimination," *HRFocus* 74, no. 2 (February 1997): 11. See also Sheldon Steinhauser, "Minimizing Your Potential for Age Discrimination Lawsuits," *HRFocus* 75, no. 8 (August 1998): 3.

16. James A. Burns, Jr., "Accommodating Pregnant Employees," *Employee Relations Law Journal* 23, no. 1 (Summer 1997): 139–44.

17. Amy Oakes, Ronald E. Kidwell, Jr., and Linda Achey Kidwell, "Managing Pregnancy in the Workplace," *Business Horizons* 39, no. 6 (November 1996): 61–67.

18. James J. McDonald, Jr., and Jonathan P. Rosman, "EEOC Guidance on Psychiatric Disabilities: Many Problems, Few Workable Solutions," *Employee Relations Law Journal* 23, no. 2 (Autumn 1997): 5–29.

19. Larry Frierson, "ADA Accommodation in Psychiatric Cases," *HRFocus* 75, no. 12 (December 1998): 59. As noted in this article, "According to the ADA, an employer is not required to retain an employee who presents a 'direct threat,' [implying] a significant risk of substantial harm to the health and safety of the individual or others that cannot be eliminated or reduced by reasonable accommodation." Also, some court cases have held that an employee with a psychiatric disability is not a qualified individual because he or she cannot perform the essential functions of the job.

20. James J. McDonald, Jr., and Ronald M. Broudy, "Job Stress and the ADA," *Employee Relations Law Journal* 23, no. 3 (Winter 1997): 67–81. See also Simon R. Malko, "On the Defensive with the ADA," *HRFocus* 75, no. 2 (February 1998): 5.

21. Lawrence J. Rosenfeld, "AIDS and the ADA," *HRFocus* 75, no. 12 (December 1998): 56.

22. Barbara Gamble Magill, "ADA Accommodations Don't Have to Break the Bank," *HRMagazine* 42, no. 7 (July 1997): 85–88. See also Sandra M. Tomkowicz, "Beyond a Reasonable Accommodation: Hostile Work Environment Claims under the ADA," *Employee Relations Law Journal* 23, no. 3 (Winter 1997): 97–109.

23. Denise L. Hummel, "Anatomy of an ADA Case," *Employee Relations Law Journal* 19, no. 1 (Summer 1993): 103–16.

24. Brian Croft, "Assisting the Disabled," *Personnel Journal* 7, no. 7 (July 1996): 89–91. See also Jay W. Spechler, *Reasonable Accommodation: Profitable Compliance with the Americans with Disabilities Act* (Del Ray Beach, Fla.: St. Lucie Press, 1996).

25. Mary Chlopecki and Ellen Duffy McKay, "The Dollar Impact of the 1991 Civil Rights Act," *HRFocus* 74, no. 9 (September 1997): 15.

26. Joseph J. Ortego and Amy L. Ventry, "Sexual Harassment Abroad," *HRFocus* 75, no. 12 (December 1998): 53.

27. Terry Thomason, John F. Burton, Jr., and Douglas E. Hyatt, "New Approaches to Disability in the Workplace," *Labor Law Journal* 49, no. 7 (September 1998): 1175–87.

28. *Nassau County, Florida v Arline,* U.S, 43 FEP 81 (1987).

29. As currently defined, an "otherwise qualified" employee is one who can perform "the essential functions" of the job under consideration.

30. Michael D. Esposito and Jeffrey E. Myers, "Managing AIDS in the Workplace," *Employee Relations Law Journal* 19, no. 1 (Summer 1993): 53–74.

31. For an excellent reference guide on sexual harassment, see William Petrocelli and Barbara Kate Repa, *Sexual Harassment on the Job: What It Is and How to Stop It* (Berkeley, Calif.: Nolo Press, 1998).

32. EEOC charge statistics can be found at www.eeoc.gov. EEOC figures do not include the thousands of sexual harassment incidents not reported to governmental agencies or complaints reported to employers and settled internally through in-house complaint procedures.

33. *Guidelines on Discrimination Because of Sex,* 29 C.F.R. Sec. 1604.11(a) (1995).

34. *Guidelines on Discrimination,* Sec. 1605.11(a).

35. Paradise Valley Unified School District No. 69, Phoenix, Arizona.

36. *Meritor Savings Bank v Vinson,* 106 U.S. 2399 (1986).

37. "Third-Party Sexual Harassment," *HRFocus* 73, no. 7 (July 1996): 4.

38. *Oncale v Sundowner Offshore Services, Inc.,* 72 EPD ¶45, 175; WL 88039 (U.S. 1998); Dawn D. Bennett-Alexander, "Same-Gender Sexual Harassment: The Supreme Court Allows Coverage under Title VII," *Labor Law Journal* 49, no. 4 (April 1998): 927–40. See also Delaney J. Kirk and Maria M. Clapham, "Is It 'Men Behaving Badly' or Sexual Harassment? The Supreme Court Ruling on Same-Sex Harassment," *Labor Law Journal* 49, no. 4 (April 1998): 954–61.

39. Jennifer Laabs, "What You're Liable for Now," *Workplace* 77, no. 10 (October 1998): 35; see also "Sex on the Job," *Business Week,* February 16, 1998, 30.

40. Gerald Skoning, "Explanations of Sexual Harassment: Are They Viable Defenses?" *HRMagazine* 43, no. 8 (July 1998): 130–134.

41. *Harris v Forklift Systems Inc.,* 62 USLW 4004 (1993), 60 EPD at 42,072.

42. *Burlington Industries, Inc. v Ellerth,* No. 97–569 (1998).

43. Charlene Marmer Solomon, "Don't Forget the Emotional Stakes," *Workforce* 77, no. 10 (October 1998): 52–57.

44. Melissa Raphan and Max Heerman, "Eight Steps to Harassment-Proof Your Office, *HRFocus* 74, no. 8 (August 1997): 11–12. See also Nancy Bertrando, "Sexual Harassment and the CEO," *HRFocus* 72, no. 12 (December 1998): 55; and Jonathan A. Segal, "Sexual Harassment Prevention: Cement for the Glass Ceiling," *HRMagazine* 43, no. 12 (November 1998): 129–34.

45. U.S. Department of Justice, Immigration and Naturalization Service, *Handbook for Employers: Instructions for Completing Form I-9* (Washington, D.C.: U.S. Government Printing Office, 1987). See also Carl Shusterman and Scott Laurent, "Bills Toughen Standards for Hiring Alien Workers," *National Law Journal,* November 13, 1995, C2.

46. Equal Employment Opportunity Commission, Civil Service Commission, Department of Labor, and Department of Justice, Adoption by Four Agencies of *Uniform Guidelines on Employee Selection Procedures* (1978), as reproduced in the *Federal Register* 43, no. 166 (August 25, 1978): 38290–315. Discussion relating to the adoption of the *Uniform Guidelines* by four agencies comprises several pages. The guidelines themselves are published on pages 38295–309. Further clarification and expansion on the guidelines may be found in the *Federal Register* 44, no. 43 (March 2, 1979): 11996–12009.

47. *Uniform Guidelines,* Sec. 3A.

48. *Uniform Guidelines,* Sec. 40. Adverse impact need not be considered for groups that constitute less than 2 percent of the relevant labor force.

49. *Hazelwood School District v United States,* 433 U.S. 299, 15 FEP 1 (1977).

50. Adam C. Wit, "The 'Similarly Situated Individual': Evidence of Comparable Employees and Its Application in Employment Discrimination Litigation," *Employee Relations Law Journal* 23, no. 3 (Winter 1997): 34.

51. *McDonnell Douglas Corp. v Green,* 411 U.S. 792, 80 (1973).

52. *Griggs v Duke Power Company,* 401 U.S. 424 (1971).

53. *Albemarle Paper Company v Moody,* 422 U.S. 405 (1975).

54. *Wards Cove Packing Co. v Antonio,* FEPC 1519 (1989).

55. Bill Leonard, "Life at the EEOC," *HRMagazine* 43, no. 1 (January 1998): 83–90.

56. A *deferral state* is one in which the state EEOC office complies with minimum operating guidelines established by the federal agency. In a deferral state, discrimination charges filed with the federal EEOC office will be deferred to the state agency for investigation and determination. If the state agency is unwilling or unable to resolve the complaint in a specified time period, the complaint is referred back to the federal EEOC office for final disposition.

57. Lynn Atkinson, "Nondiscriminating Employer Must Pay for Retaliation," *HRFocus* 74, no. 4 (April 1997): 20.

58. William L. Kandel, "The Evolution in Claims from Discrimination to Retaliation," *Employee Relations Law Journal* 22, no. 4 (Spring 1997): 101–17. See also Keith R. Fentonmiller, "When Does Retaliation Count under Title VII?" *Employee Relations Law Journal* 23, no. 4 (Autumn 1997): 31–44.

59. Jonathan A. Segal, "Prevent Now or Pay Later," *HRMagazine* 43, no. 11 (October 1998): 145–49.

60. *University of California Regents v Bakke,* 438 U.S. 193 (1978).

61. *United Steelworkers of America v Weber,* 443 U.S. 193 (1979).

62. Robert K. Robinson, Ross L. Fink, and Billie Morgan Allen, "Affirmative Action in the Public Sector: The Increasing Burden of Strict Scrutiny," *Labor Law Journal* 49, no. 1 (January 1998): 801–9.

63. *City of Richmond v Croson,* 109 S. Ct. 706 (1989).

64. *Adarand Constructors v. Peña,* 67 FEP Cases 1828 (1995).

65. *Hopwood v State of Texas,* 78 F. 3d 932 (5th Cir. 1996).

66. Charles S. Mishkind, "Reverse Discrimination/Affirmative Action Litigation Update: Where Is It Going?" *Employee Relations Law Journal* 22, no. 3 (1996): 109.

67. Cal. Const. Art. 1 § 31(a).

68. Thomas S. Bateman and Scott A. Snell, *Management: Building Competitive Advantage,* 4th ed. (Chicago, Ill.: Richard D. Irwin, 1999).

69. "How Workplaces May Look without Affirmative Action," *The Wall Street Journal,* March 20, 1995, B1.

**Answers to Highlights in HRM 1**

1. Yes
2. False
3. No
4. Merit, seniority, incentive pay plans
5. Yes
6. Yes, if no reasonable accommodation can be made
7. No
8. Yes, except if under a court order
9. False
10. True

# Job Requirements and the Design of Organizations to Achieve Human Resources Productivity

# chapter 3

## AFTER STUDYING THIS CHAPTER, YOU SHOULD BE ABLE TO

 **OBJECTIVE 1**
Discuss the relationship between job requirements and the performance of HRM functions.

 **OBJECTIVE 2**
Describe the methods by which job analysis typically is completed.

 **OBJECTIVE 3**
Explain the various sections of job descriptions.

 **OBJECTIVE 4**
List the various factors that must be taken into account in designing a job.

 **OBJECTIVE 5**
Discuss the various job characteristics that motivate employees.

 **OBJECTIVE 6**
Describe the different group techniques used to maximize employee contributions.

 **OBJECTIVE 7**
Explain the different adjustments in work schedules.

Organizations are "reengineering" themselves in an attempt to become more effective. Companies like Darden Restaurants, United Technologies, and Sports Authority are breaking into smaller units and getting flatter. There is emphasis on smaller scale, less hierarchy, fewer layers, and more decentralized work units. As organizational reshaping takes place, managers want employees to operate more independently and flexibly to meet customer demands. To do this, they require that decisions be made by the people who are closest to the information and who are directly involved in the product or service delivered. At Ford, CEO Jacques Nasser "wants all 350,000 of Ford's employees—who together control 20 percent of the company's shares—to act more like owners and entrepreneurs and less like bean counters, engineers, or hourly workers."[1] The objective is to develop jobs and basic work units that are adaptable enough to thrive in a world of high-velocity change.

In this chapter, we will discuss how jobs can be designed so as to best contribute to the objectives of the organization and at the same time satisfy the needs of the employees who are to perform them. The value of job analysis, which defines clearly and precisely the requirements of each job, will be stressed. We will emphasize that these job requirements provide the foundation for making objective and legally defensible decisions in managing human resources. The chapter concludes by reviewing several innovative job design and employee contribution techniques that increase job satisfaction while improving organizational performance. Teamwork and the characteristics of successful teams are highlighted.

# Relationship of Job Requirements and HRM Functions

**Job**
A group of related activities and duties

**Position**
The different duties and responsibilities performed by only one employee

**Job family**
A group of individual jobs with similar characteristics

**Job specification**
Statement of the needed knowledge, skills, and abilities of the person who is to perform the job

A **job** consists of a group of related activities and duties. Ideally, the duties of a job should consist of natural units of work that are similar and related. They should be clear and distinct from those of other jobs to minimize misunderstanding and conflict among employees and to enable employees to recognize what is expected of them. For some jobs, several employees may be required, each of whom will occupy a separate position. A **position** consists of different duties and responsibilities performed by only one employee. In a city library, for example, four employees (four positions) may be involved in reference work, but all of them have only one job (reference librarian). Where different jobs have similar duties and responsibilities, they may be grouped into a **job family** for purposes of recruitment, training, compensation, or advancement opportunities.

## Recruitment

Before they can find capable employees for an organization, recruiters need to know the job specifications for the positions they are to fill. A **job specification** is a statement of the knowledge, skills, and abilities required of the person performing the job. In the HR department for the City of Mesa, Arizona, the job specification for senior personnel analyst includes the following:

1.  Graduation from a four-year college with major course work (minimum fifteen hours) in human resources management

2. Three to five years' experience in employee classification and compensation or selection or recruitment

3. Two years' experience in developing/improving job-related compensation and testing instruments and procedures[2]

Because job specifications establish the qualifications required of applicants for a job opening, they serve an essential role in the recruiting function. These qualifications typically are contained in the notices of job openings. Whether posted on organization bulletin boards or included in help-wanted advertisements or employment agency listings, job specifications provide a basis for attracting qualified applicants and discouraging unqualified ones.

## Selection

**Job description**
Statement of the tasks, duties, and responsibilities of a job to be performed

In addition to job specifications, managers and supervisors will use job descriptions to select and orient employees to jobs. A **job description** is a statement of the tasks, duties, and responsibilities of a job.

In the past, job specifications used as a basis for selection sometimes bore little relation to the duties to be performed under the job description. Examples of such nonjob-related specifications abounded. Applicants for the job of laborer were required to have a high school diploma. Firefighters were required to be at least six feet tall. And applicants for the job of truck driver were required to be male. These kinds of job specifications served to discriminate against members of certain protected classes, many of whom were excluded from these jobs.

Since the landmark *Griggs v Duke Power* case and the Civil Rights Act of 1991 (see Chapter 2), employers must be able to show that the job specifications used in selecting employees for a particular job relate specifically to the duties of that job. An organization must be careful to ensure that managers with job openings do not hire employees on the basis of "individualized" job requirements that satisfy personal whims but bear little relation to successful job performance.

## Training and Development

Any discrepancies between the knowledge, skills, and abilities (often referred to as KSA) demonstrated by a jobholder and the requirements contained in the description and specification for that job provide clues to training needs. Also, career development as a part of the training function is concerned with preparing employees for advancement to jobs where their capacities can be utilized to the fullest extent possible. The formal qualification requirements set forth in high-level jobs serve to indicate how much more training and development are needed for employees to advance to those jobs.

## Performance Appraisal

The requirements contained in the description of a job provide the criteria for evaluating the performance of the holder of that job. The results of performance appraisal may reveal, however, that certain requirements established for a job are not completely valid. As we have already stressed, these criteria must be specific and job-related. If the criteria used to evaluate employee performance are vague and not job-related, employers may find themselves being charged with unfair discrimination.

## Compensation Management

In determining the rate to be paid for performing a job, the relative worth of the job is one of the most important factors. This worth is based on what the job demands of an employee in terms of skill, effort, and responsibility, as well as the conditions and hazards under which the work is performed. The systems of job evaluation by which this worth may be measured are discussed in Chapter 9.

# Job Analysis

**Job analysis**
Process of obtaining information about jobs by determining what the duties, tasks, or activities of jobs are

Job analysis is sometimes called the cornerstone of HRM because the information it collects serves so many HRM functions. **Job analysis** is the process of obtaining information about jobs by determining what the duties, tasks, or activities of those jobs are. The procedure involves undertaking a systematic investigation of jobs by following a number of predetermined steps specified in advance of the study.[3] When completed, job analysis results in a written report summarizing the information obtained from the analysis of twenty or thirty individual job tasks or activities.[4] HR managers will use these data to develop job descriptions and job specifications. These documents, in turn, will be used to perform and enhance the different HR functions such as the development of performance appraisal criteria or the content of training classes.[5] The ultimate purpose of job analysis is to improve organizational performance and productivity. Figure 3.1 illustrates how job analysis is performed, including the functions for which it is used.

As contrasted with job design, which reflects subjective opinions about the ideal requirements of a job, job analysis is concerned with objective and verifiable information about the actual requirements of a job. The job descriptions and job specifications developed through job analysis should be as accurate as possible if they are to be of value to those who make HRM decisions. These decisions may involve any of the HR functions—from recruitment to termination of employees.

## Job Analysis and the Law

It should be emphasized that a major goal of modern job analysis is to help the organization establish the *job relatedness* of its selection and performance requirements. Job analysis helps both large and small employers to meet their legal duty under EEO law. Section 14.C.2. of the *Uniform Guidelines* states: "There shall be a job analysis which includes an analysis of the important work behaviors required for successful performance. . . . Any job analysis should focus on work behavior(s) and the tasks associated with them." (The *Uniform Guidelines* are discussed more fully in Chapter 2.)

The passage of the Americans with Disabilities Act also had a marked impact on the process of job analysis. Specifically, when preparing job descriptions and job specifications managers and supervisors must adhere to the legal mandates of the ADA.[6] The act requires that job duties and responsibilities be *essential functions* for job success. The purpose of essential functions is to help match and accommodate

FIGURE 3.1

The Process of Job Analysis

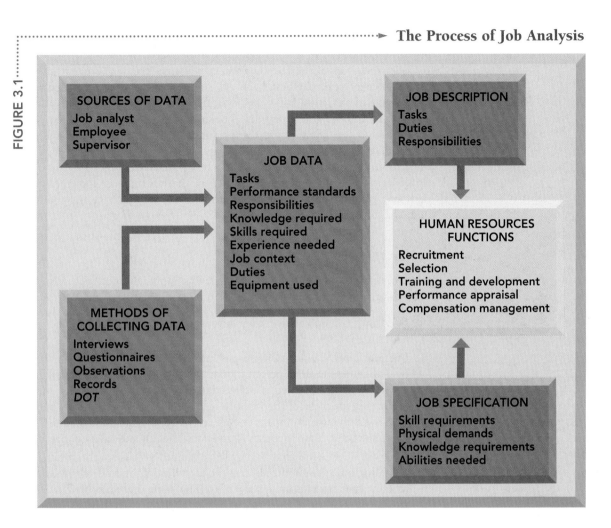

**SOURCES OF DATA**
Job analyst
Employee
Supervisor

**JOB DATA**
Tasks
Performance standards
Responsibilities
Knowledge required
Skills required
Experience needed
Job context
Duties
Equipment used

**JOB DESCRIPTION**
Tasks
Duties
Responsibilities

**HUMAN RESOURCES FUNCTIONS**
Recruitment
Selection
Training and development
Performance appraisal
Compensation management

**METHODS OF COLLECTING DATA**
Interviews
Questionnaires
Observations
Records
DOT

**JOB SPECIFICATION**
Skill requirements
Physical demands
Knowledge requirements
Abilities needed

human capabilities to job requirements. For example, if the job requires the job-holder to read extremely fine print, to climb ladders, or to memorize stock codes, these physical and mental requirements should be stated within the job description. Section 1630.2(n) of the act gives three guidelines for rendering a job function essential. These include (1) the reason the position exists is to perform the function, (2) a limited number of employees are available among whom the performance of the function may be distributed, and (3) the function may be highly specialized, requiring needed expertise or abilities to complete the job.[7] Managers who write job descriptions and job specifications in terms of essential functions reduce the risk of discriminating on the basis of a disability. Remember also that once essential functions for a job are defined the organization is legally required to make a reasonable accommodation to the disability of the individual.

## The Job Analyst's Responsibilities

Conducting job analysis is usually the primary responsibility of the HR department. If this department is large enough to have a division for compensation management, job analysis may be performed by members of that division. For example, in the HR department of General Telephone Company of California, job analysis is performed by the section titled Compensation and Organization.

Staff members of the HR department who specialize in job analysis have the title of job analyst or personnel analyst. Since the job carrying this title requires a high degree of analytical ability and writing skill, it sometimes serves as an entry-level job for college graduates who choose a career in HRM.

Although job analysts are the personnel primarily responsible for the job analysis program, they usually enlist the cooperation of the employees and managers in the departments where jobs are being analyzed. It is these managers and employees who are the sources of much of the information about the jobs, and they may be asked to prepare rough drafts of the job descriptions and specifications the job analysts need.

## Gathering Job Information

Job data may be obtained in several ways. The more common methods of analyzing jobs are through interviews, questionnaires, observation, and diaries.

- *Interviews.* The job analyst may question individual employees and managers about the job under review.
- *Questionnaires.* The job analyst may circulate carefully prepared questionnaires to be filled out individually by jobholders and managers. These forms will be used to obtain data in the areas of job duties and tasks performed, purpose of the job, physical setting, requirements for performing the job (skill, education, experience, physical and mental demands), equipment and materials used, and special health and safety concerns.
- *Observation.* The job analyst may learn about the jobs by observing and recording on a standardized form the activities of jobholders. Videotaping jobs for later study is an approach used by some organizations.
- *Diaries.* Jobholders themselves may be asked to keep a diary of their work activities during an entire work cycle. Diaries are normally filled out at specific times of the work shift (e.g., every half-hour or hour) and maintained for a two- to four-week period.

## Controlling the Accuracy of Job Information

If job analysis is to accomplish its intended purpose, the job data collected must be accurate. Care must be taken to ensure that all important facts are included. A job analyst should be alert for employees who tend to exaggerate the difficulty of their jobs in order to inflate their egos and their paychecks. When interviewing employees or reviewing their questionnaires, the job analyst must look for any responses that do not agree with other facts or impressions the analyst has received. Furthermore, when job information is collected from employees, a representative group of individuals should be surveyed. For example, the results of one study indicated that the information obtained from job analysis was related to race. In another study, the experience level of job incumbents influenced job analysis outcomes.

Whenever a job analyst doubts the accuracy of information provided by employees, he or she should obtain additional information from them, from their managers, or from other individuals who are familiar with or perform the same job. It is common practice to have the descriptions for each job reviewed by the jobholders and their managers. The job description summaries contained in the *Dictionary of Occupational Titles* can also serve as a basis for the job analyst's review.

## The *DOT* and Job Analysis

**⁙USING THE INTERNET**

You may view a portion of the *DOT* index at the web site below. The example shows the detailed job classification system and the codes:

www.immigrations-usa.com/dot_r3.html

Commonly referred to as the *DOT*, the *Dictionary of Occupational Titles* is compiled by the U.S. Department of Labor. It contains standardized and comprehensive descriptions of about 20,000 jobs. The purpose of the DOT is to "group occupations into a systematic occupational classification structure based on interrelationships of job tasks and requirements." This grouping of occupational classifications is done under a coding system.[8]

The *DOT* has helped to bring about a greater degree of uniformity in the job titles and descriptions used by employers in different sections of the country. This uniformity has facilitated the movement of workers from sections of the country that may be experiencing widespread unemployment to areas where employment opportunities are greater. The *DOT* code numbers also facilitate the exchange of statistical information about jobs. In addition, these code numbers are useful in reporting research in the HR area, in vocational counseling, and in charting career paths through job transfers and/or advancements.

## Approaches to Job Analysis

The systematic and quantitative definition of job content that job analysis provides is the foundation of many HRM practices. Specifically, the job analysis serves to justify job descriptions and other HRM selection procedures. Several different job analysis approaches are used to gather data, each with specific advantages and disadvantages. Four of the more popular methods are functional job analysis, the position analysis questionnaire system, the critical incident method, and computerized job analysis.

### Functional Job Analysis

**Functional job analysis (FJA)**

Quantitative approach to job analysis that utilizes a compiled inventory of the various functions or work activities that can make up any job and that assumes that each job involves three broad worker functions: (1) data, (2) people, and (3) things

Developed by the U.S. Training and Employment Service, the **functional job analysis (FJA)** approach utilizes an inventory of the various types of functions or work activities that can constitute any job. FJA thus assumes that each job involves performing certain functions. Specifically, there are three broad worker functions that form the bases of this system: (1) data, (2) people, and (3) things. These three categories are subdivided to form a hierarchy of worker-function scales, as shown in Figure 3.2. The job analyst, when studying the job under review, will indicate the functional level for each of the three categories (for example, "copying" under DATA) and then reflect the relative involvement of the worker in the function by assigning a percentage figure to each function (i.e., 50 percent to "copying"). This is done for each of the three areas, and the three functional levels must equal 100 percent. The end result is a quantitatively evaluated job. FJA can easily be used to describe the content of jobs and to assist in writing job descriptions and specifications; it is used as a basis for the *DOT* code.

FIGURE 3.2

**Difficulty Levels of Worker Functions**

| DATA (4TH DIGIT) | PEOPLE (5TH DIGIT) | THINGS (6TH DIGIT) |
|---|---|---|
| 0 Synthesizing | 0 Mentoring | 0 Setting up |
| 1 Coordinating | 1 Negotiating | 1 Precision working |
| 2 Analyzing | 2 Instructing | 2 Operating-controlling* |
| 3 Compiling | 3 Supervising | 3 Driving-operating* |
| 4 Computing | 4 Diverting | 4 Manipulating |
| 5 Copying | 5 Persuading | 5 Tending |
| 6 Comparing | 6 Speaking-signaling* | 6 Feeding-offbearing* |
| | 7 Serving | 7 Handling |
| | 8 Taking instructions–helping* | |

*Hyphenated factors are single factors.

Source: U.S. Department of Labor, Employment and Training Administration, *Revised Handbook for Analyzing Jobs* (Washington, D.C.: U.S. Government Printing Office, 1991), 5.

### The Position Analysis Questionnaire System

**Position analysis questionnaire (PAQ)**
Questionnaire covering 194 different tasks which, by means of a five-point scale, seeks to determine the degree to which different tasks are involved in performing a particular job

The **position analysis questionnaire (PAQ)** is a quantifiable data collection method covering 194 different worker-oriented tasks. Using a five-point scale, the PAQ seeks to determine the degree, if any, to which the different tasks, or job elements, are involved in performing a particular job.

A sample page from the PAQ covering eleven elements of the Information Input Division is shown in Figure 3.3. The person conducting an analysis with this questionnaire would rate each of the elements using the five-point scale shown in the upper-right-hand corner of the sample page. The results obtained with the PAQ are quantitative and can be subjected to statistical analysis. The PAQ also permits dimensions of behavior to be compared across a number of jobs and permits jobs to be grouped on the basis of common characteristics.[9]

### The Critical Incident Method

**Critical incident method**
Job analysis method by which important job tasks are identified for job success

The objective of the **critical incident method** is to identify critical job tasks. Critical job tasks are those important duties and job responsibilities performed by the jobholder that lead to job success. Information about critical job tasks can be collected through interviews with employees or managers or through self-report statements written by employees.

Suppose, for example, that the job analyst is studying the job of reference librarian. The interviewer will ask the employee to describe the job on the basis of what is done, how the job is performed, and what tools and equipment are used. The reference librarian may describe the job as follows:

> I assist patrons by answering their questions related to finding books, periodicals, or other library materials. I also give them directions to help them find

FIGURE 3.3

**A Sample Page from the PAQ**

---

**INFORMATION INPUT**

---

1          INFORMATION INPUT

1.1        Sources of Job Information

Rate each of the following items in terms of the extent to which it is used by the worker as a source of information in performing his job.

| | Extent of Use (U) |
|---|---|
| NA | Does not apply |
| 1 | Nominal/very infrequent |
| 2 | Occasional |
| 3 | Moderate |
| 4 | Considerable |
| 5 | Very substantial |

1.1.1 Visual Sources of Job Information

01 U   Written materials (books, reports, office notes, articles, job instructions, signs, etc.)

02 U   Quantitative materials (materials which deal with quantities or amounts, such as graphs, accounts, specifications, tables of numbers, etc.)

03 U   Pictorial materials (pictures or picturelike materials used as *sources* of information, for example, drawings, blueprints, diagrams, maps, tracings, photographic films, x-ray films, TV pictures, etc.)

04 U   Patterns/related devices (templates, stencils, patterns, etc., used as *sources* of information when *observed* during use; do *not* include here materials described in item 3 above)

05 U   Visual displays (dials, gauges, signal lights, radarscopes, speedometers, clocks, etc.)

06 U   Measuring devices (rulers, calipers, tire pressure gauges, scales, thickness gauges, pipettes, thermometers, protractors, etc., used to obtain visual information about physical measurements; do *not* include here devices described in item 5 above)

07 U   Mechanical devices (tools, equipment, machinery, and other mechanical devices which are *sources* of information when *observed* during use or operation)

08 U   Materials in process (parts, materials, objects, etc., which are *sources* of information when being modified, worked on, or otherwise processed, such as bread dough being mixed, workpiece being turned in a lathe, fabric being cut, shoe being resoled, etc.)

09 U   Materials *not* in process (parts, materials, objects, etc., not in the process of being changed or modified, which are *sources* of information when being inspected, handled, packaged, distributed, or selected, etc., such as items or materials in inventory, storage, or distribution channels, items being inspected, etc.)

10 U   Features of nature (landscapes, fields, geological samples, vegetation, cloud formations, and other features of nature which are observed or inspected to provide information)

11 U   Man-made features of environment (structures, buildings, dams, highways, bridges, docks, railroads, and other "man-made" or altered aspects of the indoor or outdoor environment which are *observed or inspected* to provide job information; do *not* consider equipment, machines, etc., that an individual uses in his work, as covered by item 7)

Source: *Position Analysis Questionnaire,* copyright 1969, 1989 by Purdue Research Foundation, West Lafayette, Ind. 47907. Reprinted with permission.

materials within the building. To perform my job I may have to look up materials myself or refer patrons to someone who can directly assist them. Some individuals may need training in how to use reference materials or special library facilities. I also give library tours to new patrons. I use computers and a variety of reference books to carry out my job.

After the job data are collected, the analyst will then write separate task statements that represent important job activities. For the reference librarian one task statement might be "Listens to patrons and answers their questions related to locating library materials." Typically the job analyst will write five to ten important task statements for each job under study. The final product will be written task statements that are clear, complete, and easily understood by those unfamiliar with the job. The critical incident method is an important job analysis method since it teaches the analyst to focus on employee behaviors critical to job success.

### Computerized Job Analysis

Human resource information systems have greatly facilitated the job analysis process. Available today are various software programs designed specifically to analyze jobs and to write job descriptions and job specifications based on those analyses. These programs normally contain generalized task statements that can apply to many different jobs. Managers and employees select those statements that best describe the job under review, indicating the importance of the task to the total job where appropriate. Advanced computer applications of job analysis combine job analysis with job evaluation (see Chapter 9) and the pricing of organizational jobs. Computerized job analysis systems can be expensive to initiate but where the organization has many jobs to analyze the cost per job may be low.

## Job Analysis in a Changing Environment

The traditional approach to job analysis assumes a static job environment where jobs remain relatively stable apart from incumbents who might hold these jobs. Here, jobs can be meaningfully defined in terms of tasks, duties, processes, and behaviors necessary for job success. This assumption, unfortunately, discounts technological advances that are often so accelerated that jobs, as they are defined today, may be obsolete tomorrow. The following quote given by the head of operations at a computer firm expresses this concern: "You know, I just can't move the boxes around fast enough any longer. I can't write out new job descriptions every week. So we still hire people by job descriptions but as soon as they are in the door, we forget about those job descriptions."[10]

Furthermore, downsizing, the demands of small organizations, or the need to respond to global change can alter the nature of jobs and the requirements of individuals needed to successfully perform them. For organizations using "virtual jobs" and "virtual teams" there is a shift away from narrow job specifications and descriptions to a world where work is "dejobbed" and emphasis is placed on the distribution of work.[11] In a dynamic environment where job demands rapidly change, job analysis data can quickly become outdated and inaccurate, and obsolete job analysis information can hinder an organization's ability to adapt to change.

Where organizations operate in a fast-moving environment, several novel approaches to job analysis may accommodate needed change. First, managers might adopt a future-oriented approach to job analysis. This "strategic" analysis of jobs requires that managers have a clear view of how jobs should be restructured in terms of duties and tasks in order to meet future organizational requirements. Second, organizations might adopt a competency-based approach to job analysis where emphasis is placed on characteristics of successful performers rather than on standard job duties, tasks, etc.[12] These competencies would match the organization's culture and strategy and might include such things as interpersonal communication skills, decision-making ability, conflict resolution skills, adaptability, and self-motivation.[13] This technique of job analysis serves to enhance a culture of TQM and continuous improvement since organizational improvement is the constant aim. Either of these two approaches is not without concerns, including the ability of managers to accurately predict future job needs, the necessity of job analysis to comply with EEOC guidelines, and the possibility of role ambiguity created by generically written job descriptions.

## Job Descriptions

As previously noted, a job description is a written description of a job and the types of duties it includes. Since there is no standard format for job descriptions, they tend to vary in appearance and content from one organization to another. However, most job descriptions will contain at least three parts: the job title, a job identification section, and a job duties section. If the job specifications are not prepared as a separate document, they are usually stated in the concluding section of the job description. Highlights in HRM 1 shows a job description for an HR employment assistant. This sample job description includes both job duties and job specifications and should satisfy most of the job information needs of managers who must recruit, interview, and orient a new employee.

Job descriptions are of value to both the employees and the employer. From the employees' standpoint, job descriptions can be used to help them learn their job duties and to remind them of the results they are expected to achieve. From the employer's standpoint, written job descriptions can serve as a basis for minimizing the misunderstandings that occur between managers and their subordinates concerning job requirements. They also establish management's right to take corrective action when the duties covered by the job description are not performed as required.

### Job Title

Selection of a job title is important for several reasons. First, the job title is of psychological importance, providing status to the employee. For instance, "sanitation engineer" is a more appealing title than "garbage collector." Second, if possible, the title should provide some indication of what the duties of the job entail. Titles like "meat inspector," "electronics assembler," "salesperson," and "engineer" obviously hint at the nature of the duties of these jobs. The job title also should indicate the relative level occupied by its holder in the organizational hierarchy. For example, the title "junior engineer" implies that this job occupies a lower level than that of "senior engineer." Other titles that indicate the relative level in the organizational hierarchy are "welder's helper" and "laboratory assistant."

**HRM 1**

# Job Description for an Employment Assistant

## Job Identification

**JOB TITLE:** Employment Assistant

Division: Southern Area

Department:     Human Resources Management

Job Analyst:     Virginia Sasaki

Date Analyzed:     12/3/99

Wage Category: Exempt

Report to:     HR Manager

Job Code:     11-17

Date Verified:     12/17/99

## Brief Listing of Major Job Duties

### JOB STATEMENT

Performs professional human resources work in the areas of employee *recruitment and selection, testing, orientation, transfers, and maintenance of employee human resources files.* May handle special assignments and projects in *EEO/ Affirmative Action, employee grievances, training,* or *classification and compensation.* Works under general supervision. Incumbent exercises initiative and independent judgment in the performance of assigned tasks.

## Essential Functions and Responsibilities

### ESSENTIAL FUNCTIONS

1. Prepares recruitment literature and job advertisements for applicant placement.
2. Schedules and conducts personal interviews to determine applicant suitability for employment. Includes reviewing mailed applications and resumes for qualified personnel.
3. Supervises administration of testing program. Responsible for developing or improving testing instruments and procedures.
4. Presents orientation program to all new employees. Reviews and develops all materials and procedures for orientation program.
5. Coordinates division job posting and transfer program. Establishes job posting procedures. Responsible for reviewing transfer applications, arranging transfer interviews, and determining effective transfer dates.
6. Maintains a daily working relationship with division managers on human resource matters, including recruitment concerns, retention or release of probationary employees, and discipline or discharge of permanent employees.
7. Distributes new or revised human resources policies and procedures to all employees and managers through bulletins, meetings, memorandums, and/or personal contact.
8. Performs related duties as assigned by the human resource manager.

**JOB SPECIFICATIONS**

1. Four-year college or university degree with major course work in human resources management, business administration, or industrial psychology; OR a combination of experience, education, and training equivalent to a four-year college degree in human resources management.
2. Considerable knowledge of principles of employee selection and assignment of personnel.
3. Ability to express ideas clearly in both written and oral communications.
4. Ability to independently plan and organize one's own activities.
5. Knowledge of human resource computer applications desirable.

Job Specifications and Requirements

### *Job Identification Section*

The job identification section of a job description usually follows the job title. It includes such items as the departmental location of the job, the person to whom the jobholder reports, and the date the job description was last revised. Sometimes it also contains a payroll or code number, the number of employees performing the job, the number of employees in the department where the job is located, and the *DOT* code number. "Statement of the Job" usually appears at the bottom of this section and serves to distinguish the job from other jobs—something the job title may fail to do.

### *Job Duties, or Essential Functions, Section*

Statements covering job duties are typically arranged in order of importance. These statements should indicate the weight, or value, of each duty. Usually, but not always, the weight of a duty can be gauged by the percentage of time devoted to it. The statements should stress the responsibilities all the duties entail and the results they are to accomplish. It is also general practice to indicate the tools and equipment used by the employee in performing the job. Remember, the job duties section must comply with law by listing only the essential functions of the job to be performed (see previous section on Job Analysis and the Law).

### *Job Specifications Section*

As stated earlier, the personal qualifications an individual must possess in order to perform the duties and responsibilities contained in a job description are compiled in the job specification. Typically the job specification covers two areas: (1) the skill required to perform the job and (2) the physical demands the job places upon the employee performing it.

Skills relevant to a job include education or experience, specialized training, personal traits or abilities, and manual dexterities. The physical demands of a job refer to how much walking, standing, reaching, lifting, or talking must be done on the job. The condition of the physical work environment and the hazards employees may encounter are also among the physical demands of a job.

## Problems with Job Descriptions

Managers consider job descriptions a valuable tool for performing HRM functions. Nevertheless, several problems are frequently associated with these documents, including the following:

1. If they are poorly written, using vague rather than specific terms, they provide little guidance to the jobholder.
2. They are sometimes not updated as job duties or specifications change.
3. They may violate the law by containing specifications not related to job success.
4. They can limit the scope of activities of the jobholder, reducing organizational flexibility.

## Writing Clear and Specific Job Descriptions

When writing a job description, it is essential to use statements that are terse, direct, and simply worded. Unnecessary words or phrases should be eliminated. Typically, the sentences that describe job duties begin with a present-tense verb, with the implied subject of the sentence being the employee performing the job. The term "occasionally" is used to describe those duties that are performed once in a while. The term "may" is used in connection with those duties performed only by some workers on the job.

Even when set forth in writing, job descriptions and specifications can still be vague. To the consternation of many employers, however, today's legal environment has created what might be called an "age of specifics." Federal guidelines and court decisions now require that the specific performance requirements of a job be based on *valid* job-related criteria.[14] Personnel decisions that involve either job applicants or employees and are based on criteria that are vague or not job-related are increasingly successfully challenged. Managers of small businesses, where employees may perform many different job tasks, must be particularly concerned about writing specific job descriptions.

Managers may find that writing job descriptions is a tedious process that distracts from other supervisory responsibilities. Fortunately, software packages are available to simplify this time-consuming yet necessary task. In one program, the user is provided an initial library of more than 2,500 prewritten job descriptions. Since the program works much like a word processor, text can be easily deleted, inserted, or modified to user demands. Various software packages can be found in HR journals such as *HRMagazine, Personnel,* and *Workforce* (formerly *Personnel Journal*).

# Job Design

It is not uncommon for managers and supervisors to confuse the processes of job analysis and job design. Job analysis is the study of jobs as currently performed by employees. It identifies job duties and the requirements needed to perform the

**Job design**
Outgrowth of job analysis that improves jobs through technological and human considerations in order to enhance organization efficiency and employee job satisfaction

work successfully. **Job design,** which is an outgrowth of job analysis, is concerned with structuring jobs in order to improve organization efficiency and employee job satisfaction. Job design is concerned with changing, modifying, and enriching jobs in order to capture the talents of employees while improving organization performance. For example, companies like Metawave Communications, Lucent Technologies, and PageNet, which are engaged in continuous improvement, or process reengineering, may revamp their jobs in order to eliminate unnecessary job tasks or find better ways of performing work. Job design should facilitate the achievement of organizational objectives. At the same time, the design should recognize the capabilities and needs of those who are to perform the job.

As Figure 3.4 illustrates, job design is a combination of four basic considerations: (1) the organizational objectives the job was created to fulfill; (2) industrial engineering considerations, including ways to make the job technologically efficient; (3) ergonomic concerns, including workers' physical and mental capabilities; and (4) behavioral concerns that influence an employee's job satisfaction.

## Behavioral Concerns

There are two job design methods that seek to incorporate the behavioral needs of employees as they perform their individual jobs. Both methods strive to satisfy the

FIGURE 3.4

**Basis for Job Design**

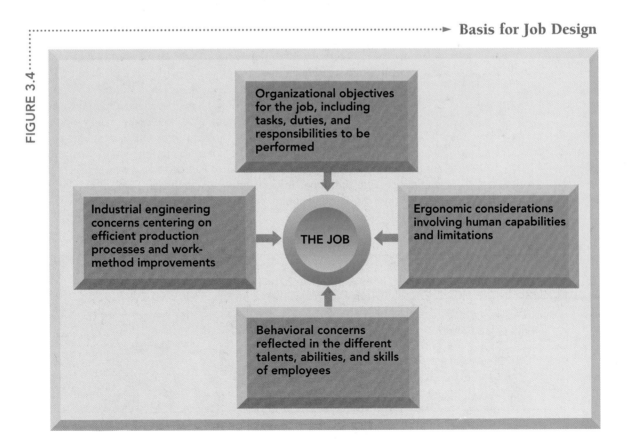

Organizational objectives for the job, including tasks, duties, and responsibilities to be performed

Industrial engineering concerns centering on efficient production processes and work-method improvements

THE JOB

Ergonomic considerations involving human capabilities and limitations

Behavioral concerns reflected in the different talents, abilities, and skills of employees

intrinsic needs of employees. The job enrichment model and the job characteristics model have long been popular with researchers and practitioners as ways to increase the job satisfaction of employees.

### Job Enrichment

**Job enrichment**

Enhancing a job by adding more meaningful tasks and duties to make the work more rewarding or satisfying

Any effort that makes work more rewarding or satisfying by adding more meaningful tasks to an employee's job is called **job enrichment.** Originally popularized by Frederick Herzberg, job enrichment is touted as fulfilling the high motivational needs of employees, such as self-fulfillment and self-esteem, while achieving long-term job satisfaction and performance goals.[15] Job enrichment, or the *vertical expansion* of jobs, may be accomplished by increasing the autonomy and responsibility of employees. Herzberg discusses five factors for enriching jobs and thereby motivating employees: achievement, recognition, growth, responsibility, and performance of the whole job versus only parts of the job. For example, managers can use these five factors to enrich the jobs of employees by

- Increasing the level of difficulty and responsibility of the job
- Allowing employees to retain more authority and control over work outcomes
- Providing unit or individual job performance reports directly to employees
- Adding new tasks to the job that require training and growth
- Assigning individuals specific tasks, thus enabling them to become experts

These factors allow employees to assume a greater role in the decision-making process and become more involved in planning, organizing, directing, and controlling their own work. Vertical job enrichment can also be accomplished by organizing workers into teams and giving these teams greater authority for self-management.

In spite of the benefits to be achieved through job enrichment, it must not be considered a panacea for overcoming production problems and employee discontent. Job enrichment programs are more likely to succeed in some jobs and work situations than in others. They are *not* the solution to such problems as dissatisfaction with pay, with employee benefits, or with employment security. Moreover, not all employees object to the mechanical pacing of an assembly line, nor do all employees seek additional responsibility or challenge. Some prefer routine jobs because they can let their minds wander while performing their work.[16]

PEANUTS © Distributed by United Feature Syndicate. Reprinted by Permission.

**Job characteristics model**
Job design that purports that three psychological states (experiencing meaningfulness of the work performed, responsibility for work outcomes, and knowledge of the results of the work performed) of a jobholder result in improved work performance, internal motivation, and lower absenteeism and turnover

## Job Characteristics

Job design studies explored a new field when behavioral scientists focused on identifying various job dimensions that would improve simultaneously the efficiency of organizations and the job satisfaction of employees. Perhaps the theory that best exemplifies this research is the one advanced by Richard Hackman and Greg Oldham.[17] Their **job characteristics model** proposes that three psychological states of a jobholder result in improved work performance, internal motivation, and lower absenteeism and turnover. The motivated, satisfied, and productive employee is one who (1) experiences *meaningfulness* of the work performed, (2) experiences *responsibility* for work outcomes, and (3) has *knowledge of the results* of the work performed. Achieving these three psychological states serves as reinforcement to the employee and as a source of internal motivation to continue doing the job well. As Hackman and Oldham state, "The net result is a self-perpetuating cycle of positive work motivation powered by self-generated rewards, that is predicted to continue until one or more of the three psychological states is no longer present, or until the individual no longer values the internal rewards that derive from good performance."[18]

Hackman and Oldham believe that five core job dimensions produce the three psychological states. The five job characteristics are as follows:

1. *Skill variety.* The degree to which a job entails a variety of different activities, which demand the use of a number of different skills and talents by the jobholder

2. *Task identity.* The degree to which the job requires completion of a whole and identifiable piece of work, that is, doing a job from beginning to end with a visible outcome

3. *Task significance.* The degree to which the job has a substantial impact on the lives or work of other people, whether in the immediate organization or in the external environment

4. *Autonomy.* The degree to which the job provides substantial freedom, independence, and discretion to the individual in scheduling the work and in determining the procedures to be used in carrying it out

5. *Feedback.* The degree to which carrying out the work activities required by the job results in the individual being given direct and clear information about the effectiveness of his or her performance[19]

It is important to realize that each of the five job characteristics affects employee performance differently. Therefore employees will experience the greatest motivation when all five characteristics are present, since the job characteristics combine to produce the three psychological states. Since the works of Hackman and Oldham and Herzberg are similar, suggestions for redesigning jobs through job enrichment also apply to the job characteristics model.[20]

The job characteristics model appears to work best when certain conditions are met. One of these conditions is that employees must have the psychological desire for the autonomy, variety, responsibility, and challenge of enriched jobs. When this personal characteristic is absent, employees may resist the job redesign effort. In addition, job redesign efforts almost always fail when employees lack the physical or mental skills, abilities, or education needed to perform the job. Forcing enriched jobs on individuals lacking these traits can result in frustrated employees.

## *Employee Empowerment*

**Employee empowerment**
Granting employees power to initiate change, thereby encouraging them to take charge of what they do

Job enrichment and job characteristics are specific programs by which managers or supervisors can formally change the jobs of employees. A less structured method is to allow employees to initiate their own job changes through the concept of empowerment. **Employee empowerment** is a technique of involving employees in their work through the process of inclusion.[21] Empowerment encourages employees to become innovators and managers of their own work, and it involves them in their jobs in ways that give them more control and autonomous decision-making capabilities (see Highlights in HRM 2).[22] Ann Howard from Development Dimensions International defines empowerment as "pushing down decision-making responsibility to those close to internal and external customers." To support high involvement, organizations must share information, knowledge, power to act, and rewards throughout the workforce.[23]

While defining empowerment can become the first step to achieving it, in order for empowerment to grow and thrive, organizations must encourage these conditions:

- *Participation.* Employees must be encouraged to take control of their work tasks. Employees, in turn, must care about improving their work process and interpersonal work relationships.
- *Innovation.* The environment must be receptive to people with innovative ideas and encourage people to explore new paths and to take reasonable risks at reasonable costs. An empowered environment is created when curiosity is as highly regarded as is technical expertise.
- *Access to information.* Employees must have access to a wide range of information. Involved individuals make decisions about what kind of information they need for performing their jobs.
- *Accountability.* Empowerment does not involve being able to do whatever you want. Empowered employees should be held accountable for their behavior toward others, producing agreed-upon results, achieving credibility, and operating with a positive approach.

Additionally, employee empowerment succeeds when the culture of the organization is open and receptive to change.[24] An organization's culture is largely created through the philosophies of senior managers and their leadership traits and behaviors. Effective leadership in an empowered organization is highlighted by managers who are honest, caring, and receptive to new ideas and who exhibit dignity and respect for employees as partners in organizational success.[25]

## Industrial Engineering Considerations

**Industrial engineering**
A field of study concerned with analyzing work methods and establishing time standards

The study of work is an important contribution of the scientific management movement. **Industrial engineering**, which evolved with this movement, is concerned with analyzing work methods and establishing time standards. Specifically, it involves the study of work cycles to determine which, if any, elements can be modified, combined, rearranged, or eliminated to reduce the time needed to complete the cycle. Next, time standards are established by recording the time required to complete each element in the work cycle, using a stopwatch or work-sampling technique. By combining the times for each element, the total time required is

**HIGHLIGHTS IN HRM**

# Examples of Employee Empowerment

All types of organizations have successfully empowered their employees. Examples come from organizations as diverse as Cigna Health Care, DuPont, PPG Industries, Wal-Mart, General Dynamics, the State of Illinois, Colgate-Palmolive, AT&T, Magma Copper Company, and Mesa (Arizona) Community College. Empowered employees have made improvements in product and service quality, have reduced costs, and have modified or, in some cases, designed products.

- At Chrysler Corporation, a six-member design team that developed the Dodge Copperhead decided that the vehicle would have snakeskin seats and tire treads. Nobody at the top interfered.
- Miners at Magma Copper Company are encouraged to design and implement innovative methods to extract ore from the company's extremely deep underground mining facilities at San Manuel, Arizona. Design and implementation were processes previously performed only by managers and engineers.
- Herman Miller, Inc., a manufacturer of office furniture, expects its employees to participate with managers in discussions involving product quality and service. Herman Miller prides itself on a corporate culture regarded as highly egalitarian.
- Avon Products empowered its minority managers to improve sales and service in inner-city markets. Grounded in the belief that minority managers better understand the culture of inner-city residents, Avon turned an unprofitable market into a highly productive sales area.
- Johnsonville Foods, a small, family-owned sausage manufacturer, allows employees to hire and fire one another, to select and purchase needed equipment, and generally to act as their own bosses.
- The State of Kentucky allowed public school teachers to have more control over public school administration. This change represented a dramatic shift in power from school boards to governing councils formed by teachers, who now have the authority to direct policy in education, including curriculum issues.
- At Ford's Escort factory in Wayne, Michigan, one group of employees made a suggestion saving $115,000 a year on the purchase of gloves used to protect workers who handle sheet metal and glass. The group figured out how to have the $4.72 per pair gloves washed so they could be used more than once.

determined. This time is subsequently adjusted to allow for the skill and effort demonstrated by the observed worker and for interruptions that may occur in performing the work. The adjusted time becomes the time standard for that particular work cycle. The Methods Improvement Group of First Interstate Bank employs the principles of industrial engineering to improve the work flow of its tellers. This may include eliminating any seemingly duplicate processes in the work cycle, or it may involve combining the tasks of two employees.

Industrial engineering constitutes a disciplined and objective approach to job design. Unfortunately, the concern of industrial engineering for improving efficiency and simplifying work methods may cause the behavioral considerations in job design to be neglected. What may be improvements in job design and efficiency from an engineering standpoint can sometimes prove to be psychologically unsound. For example, the assembly line with its simplified and repetitive tasks embodies sound principles of industrial engineering, but these tasks are often not psychologically rewarding for those who must perform them. Thus, to be effective, job design must also provide for the satisfaction of behavioral needs.

## Ergonomic Considerations

**Ergonomics**

An interdisciplinary approach to designing equipment and systems that can be easily and efficiently used by human beings

**Ergonomics** attempts to accommodate the human capabilities and deficiencies of those who are to perform a job. It is concerned with adapting the entire job system—the work, the work environment, the machines, the equipment, and the processes—to match human characteristics.[26] In short, *it seeks to fit the machine to the person rather than the person to the machine.* Also referred to as *human engineering* and *engineering psychology,* ergonomics attempts to minimize the harmful effects of carelessness, negligence, and other human fallibilities that otherwise may cause product defects, damage to equipment, or even the injury or death of employees.

Equipment design must take into consideration the physical ability of operators to use the equipment and to react through vision, hearing, and touch to the information the equipment conveys. Designing equipment controls to be compatible with both the physical characteristics and the reaction capabilities of the people who must operate them and the environment in which they work is increasingly important. Ergonomics also considers the requirements of a diverse workforce, accommodating, for example, women who may lack the strength to operate equipment requiring intense physical force or Asian Americans who may lack the stature to reach equipment controls. At Chrysler's Jefferson North assembly facility, the plant uses ergonomically designed equipment to accommodate an experienced

*The National Aeronautics and Space Administration (NASA) widely employed the principles of ergonomics on the space shuttle Discovery to improve the visual and auditory displays of information in the cockpit.*

workforce whose average age is 51 years. Instead of dangling auto chassis from overhead assembly lines, which would require workers to crane upward, auto chassis are tilted at an angle for ease of access. Marilyn Joyce, head of Arthur D. Little's ergonomic unit, notes, "You simply have to adapt your workplace to the labor force; ignore it, and you could be sacrificing quality and productivity."[27]

Ergonomics contributes to improvements in productivity. It has proven cost-effective at organizations such as the U.S. Postal Service, West Bend Mutual Insurance, Pitney Bowes, and the Bureau of National Affairs (BNA). With the increasing use of computers at these organizations and others, ergonomics has particular application at employee workstations.[28] Although computers provide benefits to organizations, Figure 3.5 provides a checklist of potential problem areas for employees utilizing workstations.

**FIGURE 3.5**

## ▶ Computer Workstation Ergonomics Checklist

Use the following list to identify potential problem areas that should receive further investigation. Any "no" response may point to a problem.

1. Does the workstation ensure proper worker posture, such as

   - Thighs in the horizontal position?
   - Lower legs in the vertical position?
   - Feet flat on the floor or on a footrest?
   - Wrists straight and relaxed?

2. Does the chair

   - Adjust easily?
   - Have a padded seat with a rounded front?
   - Have an adjustable backrest?
   - Provide lumbar support?
   - Have casters?

3. Are the height and tilt of the work surface on which the keyboard is located adjustable?

4. Is the keyboard detachable?

5. Do keying actions require minimal force?

6. Is there an adjustable document holder?

7. Are armrests provided where needed?

8. Are glare and reflections minimized?

9. Does the monitor have brightness and contrast controls?

10. Is there sufficient space for knees and feet?

11. Can the workstation be used for either right- or left-handed activity?

Source: The National Institute for Occupational Safety and Health (NIOSH), *Elements of Ergonomics Programs: A Primer Based on Workplace Evaluations of Musculoskeletal Disorders* (Washington, D.C.: U.S. Government Printing Office, March 1997).

# Designing Work for Group Contributions

Although a variety of group techniques have been developed to involve employees more fully in their organizations, all of these techniques have two characteristics in common—enhancing collaboration and increasing synergy. In increasing the degree of collaboration in the work environment, these techniques can improve work processes and organizational decision making. In increasing group synergy, the techniques underline the adage that the contributions of two or more employees are greater than the sum of their individual efforts. Furthermore, research has shown that working in a group setting strengthens employee commitment to the organization's goals, increases employee acceptance of decisions, and encourages a cooperative approach to workplace tasks. Two collaborative techniques are discussed here: employee involvement groups and employee teams.

### Employee Involvement Groups

Groups of five to ten employees doing similar or related work who meet together regularly to identify, analyze, and suggest solutions to shared problems are often referred to as **employee involvement groups (EIs)**. Also widely known as *quality circles* (QCs), EIs are used principally as a means of involving employees in the larger goals of the organization through their suggestions for improving product or service quality and cutting costs.[29] Generally, EIs recommend their solutions to management, which decides whether or not to implement them.

The employee involvement group process, illustrated in Figure 3.6, begins with EI members brainstorming job-related problems or concerns and gathering data about these issues. The process continues through the generation of solutions and recommendations that are then communicated to management. If the solutions are implemented, results are measured, and the EI and its members are usually recognized for the contributions they have made. EIs typically meet four or more hours per month, and the meetings are chaired by a group leader chosen from the group. The leader does not hold an authority position but instead serves as a discussion facilitator.

Although EIs have become an important employee contribution system, they are not without their problems and their critics. First, in order to achieve the results desired, those participating in EIs must receive comprehensive training in problem identification, problem analysis, and various decision-making tools such as statistical analysis and cause-and-effect diagrams. Comprehensive training for EIs is often cited as the most important factor leading to their success. Second, managers should recognize the group when a recommendation is made, regardless of whether the recommendation is adopted. This approach encourages the group to continue coming up with ideas even when they are not all implemented by management. Third, some organizations have found that EIs run out of ideas, and management must feed them ideas to keep the process going. Finally, other objections to EIs come from their basic design. Some critics argue that EIs do not fundamentally change the organization in which they are established. As a form of suggestion system, they may work well, but they do not alter organizational culture. Therefore, these critics argue, employees who participate may realize the benefits of participation, but most employees, who are not included in EIs, are unaffected by their efforts.

**Employee involvement groups (EIs)**

Groups of employees who meet to resolve problems or offer suggestions for organizational improvement

FIGURE 3.6

The Employee Involvement Group

Group members brainstorm, gather data, and establish cause and effect.

Group members prepare solutions and recommendations.

THE EMPLOYEE INVOLVEMENT GROUP PROCESS

EI group is recognized by management and, if recommendation is implemented, results are measured and feedback is provided to EI group.

Management considers EI group recommendations and makes decisions.

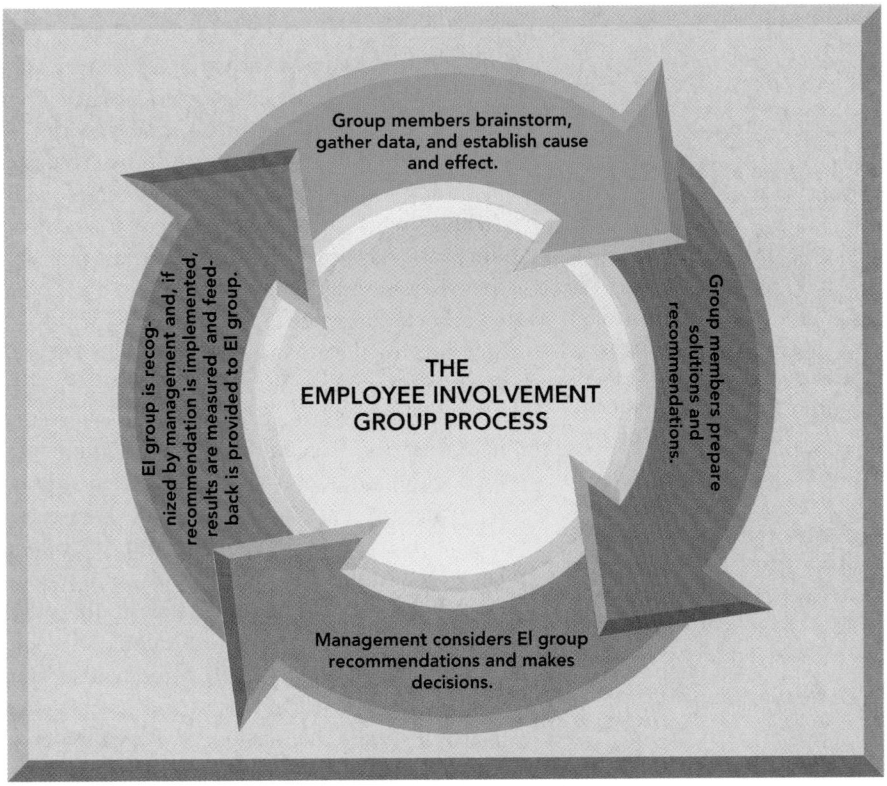

Source: The Family and Relationship Center, 7946 Ivanhoe Ave., Suite 201, La Jolla, Calif., 92037.

## Employee Teams

Jim Barksdale, president and CEO of Netscape Communications, states, "These days it seems as if every time a task needs to be accomplished within an organization, a team is formed to do it."[30] This statement simply emphasizes the increasing importance of teams to organization success in an ever-dynamic business climate. At such diverse organizations as Federal Express, Steelcase Inc., Schreiber Foods, the City of Phoenix, and Kent-Moore of Warren, Michigan, the benefits of employee teams have included more integration of individual skills, better performance in terms of quantity and quality, reduced turnover and absenteeism, and a sense of confidence and accomplishment among team members.

**Employee teams** are a logical outgrowth of employee involvement and the philosophy of empowerment. Teams are groups of employees who assume a greater role in the production or service process.[31] Teams provide a forum through which employees can contribute their ideas about daily operations or identify and solve organizational problems. Employee contributions can also include joint decision making in which employees are encouraged to share their knowledge to resolve operations concerns. Furthermore, teams seek to make members of the work group share responsibility for their group's performance. Inherent in the concept of employee teams is that employees, not managers, are in the best position to con-

**Employee teams**

An employee contributions technique whereby work functions are structured for groups rather than for individuals and team members are given discretion in matters traditionally considered management prerogatives, such as process improvements, product or service development, and individual work assignments

tribute to workplace improvements. With work teams, managers accept the notion that the group is the logical work unit to apply resources to resolve organizational problems and concerns.[32]

Teams can operate in a variety of structures, each with different strategic purposes or functional activities. Figure 3.7 describes common team forms. One form, self-directed teams, has sparked wide interest with U.S. organizations.[33] Self-directed teams, also called *autonomous work groups, self-managed teams,* or *high-performance teams,* are groups of employees who are accountable for a "whole" work process or segment that delivers a product or service to an internal or external customer. Team members acquire multiple skills enabling them to perform a variety of job tasks. To varying degrees, team members work together to improve their operations, handle day-to-day concerns, and plan and control their work. Highlights in HRM 3 shows the results from one study of the functions commonly performed by self-managed teams.

Self-directed teams are designed to give the team "ownership" of a product or service. In manufacturing environments, a team might be responsible for a whole product or a clearly defined segment of the production process.[34] At Tennessee Eastman, a division of Eastman Kodak Company, teams are responsible for manufacturing entire "product lines," including processing, lab work, and packaging. Similarly, in a service environment, a team usually has responsibility for entire groupings of products and services, often serving clients in a designated geographic area. For example, Aid Association for Lutherans (AAL), a fraternal benefits life insurer, has combined separate life insurance, health insurance, and support service functions and given these responsibilities to teams that serve clients in specific regional areas. Providing employees this type of ownership usually requires broader job categories and the sharing of work assignments.

**USING THE INTERNET**

To obtain a wide variety of information on teams, including free pamphlets and articles, view Center for the Study of Teams at:

www.workteams.unt.edu

**FIGURE 3.7**

## Forms of Employee Teams

**Cross-Functional Teams.** A group staffed with a mix of specialists (e.g., marketing, production, engineering) and formed to accomplish a specific objective. Cross-functional teams are based on assigned rather than voluntary membership.

**Project Teams.** A group formed specifically to design a new product or service. Members are assigned by management on the basis of their ability to contribute to success. The group normally disbands after task completion.

**Self-Directed Teams.** Groups of highly trained individuals performing a set of interdependent job tasks within a natural work unit. Team members use consensus decision making to perform work duties, solve problems, or deal with internal or external customers.

**Task Force Teams.** A task force is formed by management to immediately resolve a major problem. The group is responsible for developing a long-term plan for problem resolution that may include a charge for implementing the solution proposed.

**Process-Improvement Teams.** A group made up of experienced people from different departments or functions and charged with improving quality, decreasing waste, or enhancing productivity in processes that affect all departments or functions involved. Team members are normally appointed by management.

**HRM 3**

# What Self-Managed Teams Manage

More self-managing teams are taking on tasks formerly the purview of supervisors or managers. Among organizations with self-directed teams, the percentages indicate that teams perform these functions on their own.

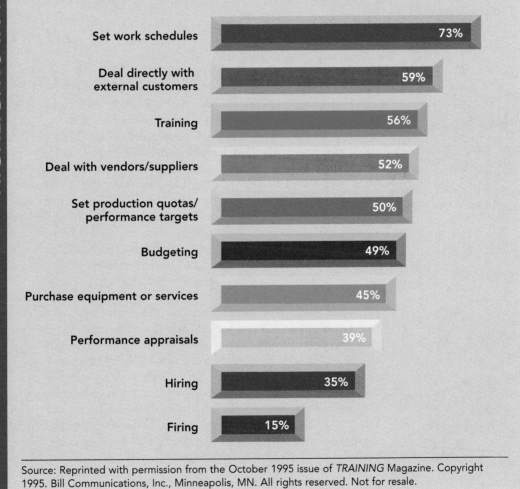

| | |
|---|---|
| Set work schedules | 73% |
| Deal directly with external customers | 59% |
| Training | 56% |
| Deal with vendors/suppliers | 52% |
| Set production quotas/performance targets | 50% |
| Budgeting | 49% |
| Purchase equipment or services | 45% |
| Performance appraisals | 39% |
| Hiring | 35% |
| Firing | 15% |

Source: Reprinted with permission from the October 1995 issue of *TRAINING* Magazine. Copyright 1995. Bill Communications, Inc., Minneapolis, MN. All rights reserved. Not for resale.

**Virtual team**
> A team with widely dispersed members linked together through computer and telecommunications technology

To compete in today's national and international markets, managers have formed virtual teams. **Virtual teams** use advanced computer and telecommunications technology to link team members who are geographically dispersed—often worldwide.[35] Management may form a cross-functional team (see Figure 3.7) to develop a new pharmaceutical drug and have the team operate in a virtual environment to achieve its goal. Virtual teams provide new opportunities for training, product development, and product market analysis. Importantly, virtual teams provide access to previously unavailable expertise and enhance cross-functional interactions.[36] However, while the benefits of virtual teams are many, they are not without their problems, including language and cultural barriers, time conflicts due to worldwide locations, and different goals and objectives across departments.

Regardless of the structure or purpose of the team, the following characteristics have been identified with successful teams:

- Commitment to shared goals and objectives
- Consensus decision making
- Open and honest communication
- Shared leadership
- Climate of cooperation, collaboration, trust, and support
- Valuing of individuals for their diversity
- Recognition of conflict and its positive resolution

Unfortunately, not all teams succeed or operate to their full potential. Therefore, in adopting the work-team concept, organizations must address several issues that could present obstacles to effective team function, including overly high expectations, group compensation, training, career movement, and power. For example, new team members must be retrained to work outside their primary functional areas, and compensation systems must be constructed to reward individuals for team accomplishments. Since team membership demands more general skills and since it moves an employee out of the historical career path, new career paths to general management must be created from the team experience. Finally, as the team members become capable of carrying out functions, such as strategic planning, that were previously restricted to higher levels of management, managers must be prepared to utilize their newfound expertise.

Another difficulty with work teams is that they alter the traditional manager-employee relationship. Managers often find it hard to adapt to the role of leader rather than supervisor and sometimes feel threatened by the growing power of the team and the reduced power of management.[37] Furthermore, some employees may also have difficulty adapting to a role that includes traditional supervisory responsibilities. Therefore, from our experience in working with teams, extensive attention must be given to training team members as they move through the four stages of team development—forming, storming, norming, and performing. *Complete* training would cover the importance of skills in (1) team leadership, (2) mission/goal setting, (3) conduct of meetings, (4) team decision making, (5) conflict resolution, (6) effective communication, and (7) diversity awareness.[38]

## Adjustments in Work Schedules

Adjustments in work schedules are not a true part of job design since job tasks and responsibilities are not changed. Nevertheless, we discuss adjustments in work schedules here because they alter the normal workweek of five eight-hour days in which all employees begin and end their workday at the same time. Employers may depart from the traditional workday or workweek in their attempt to improve organizational productivity and morale by giving employees increased control over the hours they work. The more common alternative work schedules include the compressed workweek, flextime, job sharing, and telecommuting.

### The Compressed Workweek

Under the compressed workweek, the number of days in the workweek is shortened by lengthening the number of hours worked per day.[39] This schedule is best illustrated by the four-day, forty-hour week, generally referred to as 4/10 or 4/40. Employees working a four-day workweek might work ten hours a day, Monday through Thursday. Although the 4/10 schedule is probably the best known, other compressed arrangements include reducing weekly hours to thirty-eight or thirty-six hours or scheduling eighty hours over nine days (9/80), taking one day off every other week.

Organizations that operate batch-processing systems (e.g., oil companies like Exxon or Shell Oil) use shorter workweeks to coordinate work schedules with production schedules. Compressed workweeks may assist with scheduling arrangements by improving plant and equipment utilization. The keying of work schedules to processing time for a specific operation rather than to a standard workweek reduces startup and closedown time and often results in higher weekly output.

Two of the strongest advantages for the compressed work schedule are that it accommodates the leisure-time activities of employees and facilitates the employee's scheduling of medical, dental, and other types of personal appointments. Other advantages include the improvement of employee job satisfaction and morale, reduced absenteeism, and the facilitation of recruitment.

The major disadvantage of the compressed workweek involves federal laws regarding overtime.[40] The Fair Labor Standards Act has stringent rules requiring the payment of overtime to nonsupervisory employees who work more than forty hours a week. (See Chapter 9.) Another disadvantage of the compressed workweek is that it increases the amount of stress on managers and employees, and long workdays can be exhausting.

### Flextime

**Flextime**
Flexible working hours that permit employees the option of choosing daily starting and quitting times, provided that they work a set number of hours per day or week

**Flextime,** or flexible working hours, permits employees the option of choosing daily starting and quitting times, provided that they work a certain number of hours per day or week.[41] With flextime, employees are given considerable latitude in scheduling their work. However, there is a "core period" during the morning and afternoon when *all* employees are required to be on the job. Flexible working hours are most common in service-type organizations—financial institutions, government agencies, or other organizations with large clerical operations. The regional office of Sentry Insurance Company in Scottsdale, Arizona, has found that flextime provides many advantages for employees working in claims, underwriting, and HR areas. Highlights in HRM 4 illustrates the flextime schedule used by Sentry Insurance.

Flextime provides both employees and employers with several advantages. By allowing employees greater flexibility in work scheduling, employers can reduce some of the traditional causes of tardiness and absenteeism. Employees can adjust their work to accommodate their particular lifestyles and, in doing so, gain greater job satisfaction. Employees can also schedule their working hours for the time of day when they are most productive. In addition, variations in arrival and departure times can help reduce traffic congestion at the peak commuting hours. In some cases, employees require less time to commute, and the pressures of meeting a rigid schedule are reduced.

From the employer's standpoint, flextime can be most helpful in recruiting and retaining personnel. It has proved invaluable to organizations wishing to improve service to customers or clients by extending operating hours. US West, a telecommunications company, uses flextime to keep its business offices open for customers who cannot get there during the day. Research demonstrates that flextime can have a positive impact on the performance measures of reliability, quality, and quantity of employee work.

There are, of course, several disadvantages to flextime. First, it is not suited to some jobs. It is not feasible, for example, where specific workstations must be staffed at all times. Second, it can create problems for managers in communicating with and instructing employees. Flextime schedules may also force these managers to extend their workweek if they are to exercise control over their subordinates.

### Job Sharing

The arrangement whereby two part-time employees perform a job that otherwise would be held by one full-time employee is called "job sharing." Job sharers usually work three days a week, "creating an overlap day for extended face-to-face conferencing." Their pay is three-fifths of a regular salary; however, job sharers usually take on additional responsibilities beyond what the original job would require. Companies that use job sharing are primarily in the legal, advertising, and financial-services businesses. Among more notable national programs, US Sprint began an extensive job sharing program for its attorneys, and Kaiser Permanente, one of the nation's largest health maintenance organizations, developed a job sharing program for physicians in its Northern California region. American Express, Lotus Development

**HRM 4**

HIGHLIGHTS IN HRM

# Sentry Insurance Company's Flextime Schedule

| Flextime (arrival) | Core Time (everyone present) | Lunch | Core Time (everyone present) | Flextime (departure) |
|---|---|---|---|---|

| 6 | 7 | 8 | 9 | 10 | 11 | 12 | 12:30 | 1:30 | 2:30 | 3:30 | 4:30 | 5:30 |
|---|---|---|---|---|---|---|---|---|---|---|---|---|

HOURS

- Employees arriving at 6:00 a.m. would leave at 2:30 p.m.
- Employees arriving at 9:00 a.m. would leave at 5:30 p.m.

Company, and Carter Hawley Hale Stores also use job sharing extensively. Employers note that without job sharing two good employees might otherwise be lost.

Job sharing is suited to the needs of families where one or both spouses desire to work only part-time. It is suited also to the needs of older workers who want to phase into retirement by shortening their workweek. For the employer, the work of part-time employees can be scheduled to conform to peaks in the daily workload. Job sharing can also limit layoffs in hard economic times. A final benefit is that employees engaged in job sharing have time off during the week to accommodate personal needs, so they are less likely to be absent.

Job sharing does have several problems, however.[42] Employers may not want to employ two people to do the work of one because the time required to orient and train a second employee constitutes an added burden. They may also want to avoid prorating the employee benefits between two part-time employees. This problem may be reduced, however, by permitting the employees to contribute the difference between the health insurance (or life insurance) premiums for a full-time employee and the pro rata amount the employer would otherwise contribute for a part-time employee. The key to making job sharing work is good communications between partners, who can use a number of ways to stay in contact—phone calls, written updates, electronic mail, and voice mail.

### Telecommuting

**Telecommuting**

Use of microcomputers, networks, and other communications technology such as fax machines to do work in the home that is traditionally done in the workplace

One of the more recent changes, and potentially the most far-reaching, is telecommuting.[43] It is estimated that in the year 2000, approximately 25 percent of the workforce were telecommuting either full-time or part-time. **Telecommuting** is the use of microcomputers, networks, and other communications technology such as fax machines to do work in the home that is traditionally done in the workplace. A variant of telecommunicating is the *virtual office* where employees are in the field selling to, or servicing, customers or stationed at other remote locations working as if they were in the home office.[44]

Respondents from one study noted that they implemented telecommuting for these reasons: improved customer service, 11 percent; environmental issues, 9

*Rapid advances in technology have given rise to the practice of telecommuting. Here a woman does bookkeeping on a computer in her home office.*

percent; reduced costs, 33 percent; improved productivity, 16 percent; increased employee retention, 16 percent; and improved employee morale, 15 percent.[45] Savings in expensive office space can be substantial. By supplementing its traditional offices, AT&T has freed up some $550 million in cash flow—a 30 percent improvement—by eliminating offices people don't need, consolidating others, and reducing related overload costs.[46]

While telecommuting offers significant benefits to employers, it also presents potential drawbacks. These include the loss of creativity as employees are not interacting with one another on a regular basis, the difficulty of developing appropriate performance standards and evaluation systems for telecommunicators, and the need to formulate an appropriate technology strategy for allocating the necessary equipment.[47] Employers wishing to have their employees telecommute must also comply with wage and hour laws, workers' compensation regulations, equipment purchase or rental agreement with employees, and federal EEO posting requirements (see Chapter 2). Where some employees are denied the opportunity to work from home, they may feel discriminated against and elect to pursue legal action or simply become disgruntled employees.[48]

# SUMMARY

**OBJECTIVE 1** Job requirements reflect the different duties, tasks, and responsibilities contained in jobs. Job requirements, in turn, influence the HR function performed by managers, including recruitment, selection, training and development, performance appraisal, compensation, and various labor relations activities.

**OBJECTIVE 2** Job analysis data may be gathered using one of several collection methods—interviews, questionnaires, observations, or diaries. Other more quantitative approaches include use of the functional job analysis, the position analysis questionnaire system, the critical incident method, and computerized job analysis. It is the prevailing opinion of the courts that HRM decisions on employment, performance appraisal, and promotions must be based on specific criteria that are job-related. These criteria can be determined objectively only by analyzing the requirements of each job.

**OBJECTIVE 3** The format of job descriptions varies widely, often reflecting the needs of the organization and the expertise of the writer. As a minimum, job descriptions should contain a job title,

a job identification section, and an essential functions section. A job specification section also may be included. Job descriptions should be written in clear and specific terms with consideration given to their legal implications.

**OBJECTIVE 4** Job design is a combination of four basic considerations: organizational objectives, industrial engineering concerns of analyzing work methods and establishing time standards; ergonomic considerations, which accommodate human capabilities and limitations to job tasks; and employee contributions.

**OBJECTIVE 5** In the job characteristics model, five job factors contribute to increased job performance and satisfaction—skill variety, task identity, task significance, autonomy, and feedback. All factors should be built into jobs since each factor influences different employee psychological states. When jobs are enriched through the job characteristics model, then employees experience more meaningfulness in their jobs, they acquire more job responsibility, and they receive direct feedback from the tasks they perform.

To improve the internal process of organizations and increase American productivity, greater efforts are being made by organizations to involve groups of employees in work operations. Employee involvement groups are composed of employees in work units charged with offering suggestions for improving product or service quality or fostering workplace effectiveness. Employee teams stress employee collaboration over individual accomplishment. Teams rely on the expertise and different abilities of members to achieve a specific goal or objective.

Self-directed teams are characterized by their willingness to perform traditional managerial tasks.

 Changes in work schedules—which include the compressed workweek, flextime, job sharing, and telecommuting—permit employees to adjust their work periods to accommodate their particular lifestyles. Employees can select from among these HR techniques to accommodate diverse employee needs while fostering organizational effectiveness.

## KEY TERMS

critical incident method
employee empowerment
employee involvement groups
  (EIs)
employee teams
ergonomics
flextime
functional job analysis (FJA)

industrial engineering
job
job analysis
job characteristics model
job description
job design
job enrichment
job family

job specification
position
position analysis questionnaire
  (PAQ)
telecommuting
virtual team

## DISCUSSION QUESTIONS

 1. Place yourself in the position of general manager of a service department. How might formally written job requirements help you manage your work unit?

 2. Discuss the various methods by which job analysis can be completed. Compare and contrast these methods, noting the pros or cons of each.

 3. Working with a group of three or four students, collect at least five different job descriptions from organizations in your area. Compare the descriptions, highlighting similarities and differences.

4. Explain how industrial engineering and ergonomics can both clash with and complement each other in the design of jobs.

 5. The job characteristics model has five components that serve to enhance employee jobs—skill variety, task identity, task significance, autonomy, and feedback. Give an example illustrating how each component can be used to improve the organization and the job of the employee. (Suggestion: Consider your present or a recent job to answer this question.)

6. Figure 3.7 shows the different forms of employee teams. Provide an example of where each type of team can be used. How do teams create synergy?

 7. As a small business employer, explain how nontraditional work schedules might make it easier for you to recruit employees.

## Job Design, Saturn Style

Automotive experts agree that Saturn Corporation, a General Motors subsidiary, has had a remarkable impact on the automobile industry. Saturn has achieved a significant sales niche in the U.S. market by offering a product with higher buyer satisfaction. Consumer surveys continue to rate Saturn cars as having high quality standards and resale value.

Saturn did not achieve these results by resorting to traditional production methods. Rather, it uses state-of-the-art manufacturing and job design techniques, including industrial engineering, ergonomics, and employee contributions. For example, workers stand on soft birch-wood floors instead of hard concrete. Cars pass through the assembly line on hydraulic lifts called "skillets," which allow employees to raise or lower the cars to the employee's height. Employees are allowed to ride the platform and take up to six minutes to correctly finish tasks. On traditional assembly lines, employees are given less than one minute to complete their individual duties. Industrial engineers videotape employees in action, looking for wasted motion. In one instance, employees were saved one-third of the steps walking to and from cars, thereby conserving employee energy.

Saturn managers agree, however, that the introduction of employee involvement teams is the key feature of the company's success. Teams are the basic organizational building block at Saturn. On the production floor, employees are formed into teams of five to fifteen people who manage themselves. Each team elects a leader called a "work-team counselor." Teams make decisions regarding scheduling, hiring, budgeting, and various production and quality concerns. Decisions are made by consensus, which requires a 70 percent "agreement rate" and a 100 percent "support rate" once a decision is reached.

Teams monitor themselves to ensure maximum efficiency. For example, one team member may check scrap and receive weekly reports on employee waste. Team members know the cost of parts and can calculate the added expense of wasted materials. Interestingly, each team forecasts yearly the amount of resources it plans to use in the coming year. Teams receive monthly breakdowns on budgeted items, even including telephone bills.

Above shop-floor teams are groups of employees called "work-unit module advisors." Advisors serve as troubleshooters and coordinators for all work teams within each of three business units—powertrain, body system, and vehicle systems. The entire Saturn complex is overseen by the manufacturing advisory committee composed of union and management representatives from each of the business units. At the pinnacle is the Strategic Action Committee (SAC), which is responsible for long-range planning and policy making for the company.

For an article on teams at Saturn, see Eleanor White, "Relying on the Power of People at Saturn," *National Productivity Review* 17, no. 1 (Winter 1997): 5–10.

### QUESTIONS

1.  What arguments could be advanced both for and against the use of employee involvement teams?

2. At Saturn, since team members are responsible for hiring decisions, what job specifications would be important for the hiring of employees?
3. How might a manager at a traditional auto-assembly plant react to Saturn's use of teams?

## Exactly Where Do You Work? AT&T's Shared Office

Richard S. Miller, vice president of Global Services (GS) at AT&T, leads a group that generates $4 billion in annual revenue. Global Services has an expense budget of about $200 million, of which real estate represents about 6 percent. To reduce this cost, GS implemented a "shared office" facility at its Morristown, New Jersey, location. Here, staff members who spend much of their time with customers outside the office can use the facilities as needed, without having assigned workstations.

Employees using the shared office include 58 salespeople, 101 technical specialists, and 66 management and support staff. Miller estimated that at least 60 percent of the sales and technical people would be out of the office with customers at any given time and, therefore, could share work space. The technical specialists become virtual resources who float from one account to another as needed, rather than individuals dedicated to specific customers.

The new shared office works as follows: Through their laptops, employees log onto a system to reserve a workstation either before they arrive at the building or when they enter the lobby. Once at the workstation, they retrieve their own mobile file cabinet and wheel it to their reserved space. The workstations are six feet square and are arranged in pairs with a C-shaped work surface so that two people can work apart privately or slide around to work side by side. The reservation system routes employees' personal phone numbers to their reserved space. Two large chalkboards allow people to leave messages for others; this feature also reduces the paper flow within the office. And three types of enclosed space—phone rooms, "personal harbors," and team rooms—accommodate private meetings and teleconferences.

Source: This case was written by George Bohlander, based on information found in Mahlon Apgar IV, "The Alternative Workplace: Changing Where and How People Work," *Harvard Business Review* 76, no. 3 (May–June 1998): 126.

### QUESTIONS

1. Is the alternative workplace like that used at GS for everyone? Explain.
2. Does an alternative workplace undermine teamwork and organizational cohesion? Explain.
3. If you were a manager hiring employees to work in an alternative workplace, what skills and abilities might those individuals need to possess?

# NOTES AND REFERENCES

1. Robert L. Simison, "Ford Rolls Out New Model of Corporate Culture," *The Wall Street Journal,* January 13, 1999, A-1.
2. Adapted from job description, "Senior Personnel Analyst, City of Mesa, Arizona." Provided by John Smoyer, personnel director, City of Mesa.
3. George T. Milkovich and Jerry M. Newman, *Compensation,* 6th rev. ed. (Homewood, Ill.: Irwin, 1999); see also Ronald A. Ash, "Job Analysis in the World of Work," in Sidney Gall (ed.), *The Job Analysis Handbook for Business, Industry and Government* (New York: Wiley, 1988): 3.
4. Richard Henderson, *Compensation Management,* 7th ed. (Englewood Cliffs, N.J.: Prentice-Hall, 1996).
5. James P. Clifford, "Job Analysis: Why Do It and How It Should Be Done," *Public Personnel Management* 23 (Summer 1994): 321–40.
6. Krystin E. Mitchell, George M. Alliger, and Richard Morfopoalos, "Toward an ADA-Appropriate Job Analysis," *Human Resource Management Review* 7, no. 1 (Spring 1997): 5–26. See also Richard Morfopoalos, "Job Analysis and the Americans with Disabilities Act," *Business Horizons* 39, no. 6 (November 1996): 68–72.
7. Equal Employment Opportunity Commission, *A Technical Assistance Manual on the Employment Provisions (Title I) of the Americans with Disabilities Act* (Washington, D.C.: EEOC, 1992); U.S. Department of Justice, Civil Rights Division, *Americans with Disabilities Act: Questions and Answers* (Washington, D.C.: U.S. Department of Justice, Civil Rights Division, 1991).
8. U.S. Department of Labor, *Dictionary of Occupational Titles,* 4th ed. (Washington, D.C.: U.S. Government Printing Office, 1991): xiv.
9. For one study on the PAQ, see James P. Clifford, "Manage Work Better to Better Manage Human Resources: A Comparative Study of Two Approaches to Job Analysis," *Public Personnel Management* 25, no. 1 (spring 1996): 89.
10. Caitlin Williams, "The End of the Job as We Know It," *Training and Development* 53, no. 1 (January 1999): 54.
11. Williams, "End of the Job," 3.
12. Steven T. Hunt, "Generic Work Behavior: An Investigation into the Dimensions of Entry-Level, Hourly Job Performance," *Personnel Psychology* 49, no. 1 (Spring 1996): 51–83.
13. Kenneth P. Carson and Greg L. Stewart, "Job Analysis and the Sociotechnical Approach to Quality: A Critical Examination," *Journal of Quality Management* 1, no. 1 (1996): 49–56.
14. Chapter 2 discusses the *Uniform Guidelines on Employee Selection Procedures* and the necessity for performance standards to be based on valid job-related criteria.
15. For Herzberg's important article on job enrichment, see Frederick Herzberg, "One More Time: How Do You Motivate Employees?" *Harvard Business Review* 46, no. 2 (January-February 1968): 53–62.
16. Timothy Aeppel, "Not All Workers Find Idea of Empowerment As Neat As It Sounds," *The Wall Street Journal,* September 8, 1997, A-1.
17. For the original article on the job characteristics model, see J. Richard Hackman and Greg R. Oldham, "Motivation through the Design of Work: Test of a Theory," *Organizational Behavior and Human Performance* 16, no. 2 (August 1976): 250–79.
18. Hackman and Oldham, "Motivation," 256.
19. Hackman and Oldham, "Motivation," 257–58.
20. Joan R. Rentsch and Robert P. Steel, "Testing the Durability of Job Characteristics as Predictors of Absenteeism over a Six-Year Period," *Personnel Psychology* 51, no. 1 (1998): 165–90.
21. James R. Lucas, *Balance of Power: Authority or Empowerment? How You Can Get the Best of Both in the "Interdependent" Organization* (New York, N.Y.: Amacom, 1998).
22. Barbara Ettorre, "The Empowerment Gap: Hype vs. Reality," *HRFocus* 74, no. 7 (July 1997): 1–6.
23. Simison, "Ford Rolls Out New Model," B-1.
24. John Garcia, "How's Your Organizational Commitment?" *HRFocus* 74, no. 1 (April 1997): 23–24.
25. Chris Argyris, "Empowerment: The Emperor's New Clothes," *Harvard Business Review* 76, no. 3 (May-June 1998): 98–105.
26. William A. Schaffer, *Ergowise: A Personal Guide to Making Your Workspace Comfortable and Safe* (New York, N.Y.: Amacom, 1996).
27. Kenneth Labich, "Making Diversity Pay," *Fortune,* September 9, 1996, 78.
28. Kathryn Tyler, "Sit Up Straight," *HRMagazine* 43, no. 10 (September 1998): 122–28. See also Michael S. Melnik, "Attitudinal Ergonomics," *HRFocus* 75, no. 4 (April 1998): 9–10.
29. Lizanne Lyons and Anthony D. Vivenzio, "Employee Involvement in Seattle: Reengineering Government in a City Lacking a Financial Crisis," *Public Personnel Management* 27, no. 1 (Spring 1998): 93–101.
30. "Teaching an Old Dog Some Virtual Tricks," *Association for Quality and Participation News,* May 1998, 6.

**31.** Paul Zuech and Nancy Finley, "Teamwork Enhances Customer Satisfaction and Manufacturing Capability at Kent-Moore," *National Productivity Review* 15, no. 2 (Spring 1996): 101–5.

**32.** With the popularity of teams, readers can find articles on many different team topics. See for example Allan B. Drexler and Russ Forrester, "Interdependence: The Crux of Teamwork," *HRMagazine* 43, no. 10 (September 1998): 52–62; Shari Caudron, "Keeping Team Conflict Alive," *Training and Development* 52, no. 9 (September 1998): 48–52; Jac Fitz-enz, "Measuring Team Effectiveness," *HRFocus* 74, no. 8 (August 1997): 3; Thomas J. Hackett, "Giving Teams a Tune-up," *HRFocus* 74, no. 11 (November 1997): 11–12.

**33.** Gill Robinson Hickman, "Diverse Self-Directed Work Teams: Developing Strategic Initiatives for 21st Century Organizations," *Public Personnel Management* 27, no. 2 (Summer 1998): 187–200. See also Bob Carroll, "The Self-Managed Payoff: Making Ten Years of Improvement in One," *National Productivity Review* 18, no. 1 (Winter 1998): 21–27; Irving H. Buchen, "Guiding Self-Directed Teams to Realize Their Potential," *National Productivity Review* 17, no. 1 (Winter 1997): 83–90.

**34.** Keith Denton, "How a Team Can Grow," *Quality Progress* 36, no. 6 (June 1999): 53–58. Eleanor White, "Relying on the Power of People at Saturn," *National Productivity Review* 17, no. 1 (Winter 1997): 5–10.

**35.** Anthony M. Townsend, Samuel M. DeMarie, and Anthony R. Hendrickson, "Virtual Teams: Technology and the Workplace of the Future," *Academy of Management Executive* 12, no. 3 (August 1998): 17–29.

**36.** Lynda McDermott, Bill Waite, and Nolan Brawley, "Putting Together a World-Class Team," *Training and Development* 53, no. 1 (January 1999): 47–51.

**37.** Richard L. Ratliff, Stephen M. Beckstead, and Steven H. Hanks, "The Use and Management of Teams: A How-to Guide," *Quality Progress* 36, no. 6 (June 1999): 31–38. See also, Mark Fenton-O'Creeny, "Employee Involvement and the Middle Manager," *Journal of Organizational Behavior* 19, no. 1 (January 1998): 67–84.

**38.** George W. Bohlander and Kathy McCarthy, "How To Get the Most from Team Training," *National Productivity Review* 20, no. 3 (Fall 1996): 25–35.

**39.** Dominic Bencivenga, "Compressed Weeks Fill an HR Niche," *HRMagazine* 40, no. 6 (June 1995): 71.

**40.** Susan N. Houseman, "Labor Standards in Alternative Work Arrangements," *Labor Law Journal* 49, no. 7 (September 1998): 1135–42.

**41.** "New Rules for the Workplace," *Arizona Republic,* October 13, 1998, WT-1.

**42.** Elizabeth Sheley, "Job Sharing Offers Unique Challenges," *HRMagazine* 41, no. 1 (January 1996): 46–49.

**43.** Michelle Conlin, "9 to 5 Isn't Working Anymore," *Business Week,* September 20, 1999, 94–98. See also Amy Dunkin, "Saying Adios to the Office," *Business Week,* October 12, 1998, 152–53.

**44.** Thomas L. Greenbaum, "Avoiding a Virtual Disaster," *HRFocus* 72, no. 2 (February 1998): 11–12.

**45.** Reported in Ellen M. Reilly, "Telecommuting: Putting Policy into Practice," *HRFocus* 74, no. 9 (September 1997): 5–6.

**46.** Mahlon Apgar IV, "The Alternative Workplace: Changing Where and How People Work," *Harvard Business Review* 76, no. 3 (May-June 1998): 121–36.

**47.** Lin Grensing-Pophal, "Training Employees to Telecommute: A Recipe for Success," *HRMagazine* 43, no. 13 (December 1998): 76–82. See also Genevieve Capowski, "Telecommuting: The New Frontier," *HRFocus* 75, no. 4 (April 1998): 2.

**48.** Jonathan A. Segal, "Home Sweet Office?" *HRMagazine* 43, no. 5 (April 1998): 119–29.

# Human Resources Planning and Recruitment

# chapter 4

AFTER STUDYING THIS CHAPTER, YOU SHOULD BE ABLE TO

 **OBJECTIVE 1**
Identify the advantages of integrating human resources planning and strategic planning.

 **OBJECTIVE 2**
Describe the basic approaches to human resources planning.

 **OBJECTIVE 3**
Explain the advantages and disadvantages of recruiting from within the organization.

 **OBJECTIVE 4**
Explain the advantages and disadvantages of external recruitment.

 **OBJECTIVE 5**
Describe how recruitment activities are integrated with diversity and equal employment opportunity initiatives.

I n earlier chapters we stressed that the challenges of human resources management all center on the idea that organizations increasingly compete on the basis of the talents and capabilities of their employees. It is therefore essential that managers do a careful job of recruiting, selecting, developing, and retaining valuable employees. In this chapter we focus on meeting these needs through effective human resources planning.

Essentially, we address two closely related processes: planning and recruitment. HR planning establishes a blueprint for staffing the organization, and recruitment sets this plan in motion. Employment recruiting has acquired new importance for managers since both manufacturing and service organizations are finding it increasingly difficult to secure qualified applicants to fill job openings. Virtually all of the available evidence suggests that employers have difficulty staffing jobs, ranging from the unskilled to the professional and highly technical; and this condition is not likely to abate in the near future.[1] No longer can managers rely solely upon unsolicited applications to fill openings. Changing employment conditions mandate that managers consider a variety of recruitment alternatives to attract the right employees to the organization. The process of planning for HR needs, finding sources of applicants, and attracting applicants will be discussed in this chapter.

# Human Resources Planning

OBJECTIVE 1

**Human resources planning (HRP)**

Process of anticipating and making provision for the movement of people into, within, and out of an organization

**Human resources planning (HRP)** is the process of anticipating and making provision for the movement of people into, within, and out of an organization. Its purpose is to deploy these resources as effectively as possible, where and when they are needed, in order to accomplish the organization's goals. Other, more specific purposes of HRP include anticipating labor shortages and surpluses; providing more employment opportunities for women, minorities, and the disabled; and mapping out employee training programs. In fact, HRP provides a launching point for most all of the activities that are subsumed under HRM.

## Importance of Human Resources Planning

Consider these facts about the U.S. labor force:

1.   Between 1996 and 2006, employment will rise from 132.4 million to 150.9 million workers.

2.   By 2006, the average age of the workforce will be 40.5, up from 34.7 in 1979. Yet while the group of workers age 45 to 54 will have increased by over 42 percent, the group between 25 and 39 will have shrunk by more than 11 percent.

3.   The fastest-growing segments of the workforce will be Asian Americans (40.1 percent increase) and Hispanics (36.4 percent increase), an increase primarily effected through immigration.

4.   Women will make up approximately 48 percent of the workforce (and 58 percent of college graduates) in 2006.

5.   Today nearly one-third of the workforce is composed of part-timers, temporary workers, and the self-employed.

6. The percentage of workers who have been with their employer for at least ten years has risen since the early 1990s, up from 54 to 57.6 percent.

7. The five occupations expected to experience faster-than-average growth are technicians, service workers, professionals, sales representatives, and executive and managerial employees. These occupations require the highest education and skill levels.

8. Over the next ten years another 1.3 million high-tech job openings will be created.

9. Two and a half million functionally illiterate Americans enter the workforce each year.[2]

How do managers cope with all these changes? How do they make certain they have the right people at the right time doing the right things for their organizations? Dramatic shifts in the composition of the labor force require that managers become more involved in HRP, since such changes affect not only employee recruitment but also methods of employee selection, training, compensation, and motivation. Although planning has always been an essential process of management, increased emphasis on HRP becomes especially critical when organizations consider mergers, relocation of plants, downsizing, or the closing of operating facilities.

An organization may incur several intangible costs as a result of inadequate HRP or, for that matter, the lack of HRP. For example, inadequate HRP can cause vacancies to remain unfilled. The resulting loss in efficiency can be costly, particularly when lead time is required to train replacements. Situations also may occur in which employees are laid off in one department while applicants are hired for similar jobs in another department. This may cause overhiring and result in the need to lay off those employees who were recently hired. Finally, lack of HRP makes it difficult for employees to make effective plans for career or personal development. As a result, some of the more competent and ambitious ones may seek other employment where they feel they will have better career opportunities.[3]

## HRP and Strategic Planning

As organizations plan for their future, HR managers must be concerned with meshing HRP and strategic planning for the organization as a whole.[4] HRP and strategic planning are linked in the three primary ways discussed below.

### Linking the Planning Processes

Through strategic planning, organizations set major objectives and develop comprehensive plans to achieve those objectives. Human resources planning relates to strategic planning on both the front end and the back end of this process. On the front end, human resource planning provides a set of inputs into the strategic *formulation* process in terms of what is possible, that is, whether the types and numbers of people are available to pursue a given strategy. For example, when Barnes & Noble executives contemplated the move into web-based commerce to compete with Amazon.com, one of the issues they had to address was whether they had the talent needed to succeed in that arena. On the back end, strategic planning and HRP are linked in terms of *implementation* concerns. Once the strategy is set, executives must make primary resource allocation decisions, including those pertaining to structure, processes, and human resources.[5]

Figure 4.1 illustrates the basic outline of how companies have begun aligning HRP and strategic planning. Companies such as Colgate-Palmolive, British Petroleum, and Delta Airlines have taken strides to combine these two aspects of management.[6] The integration of HRP and strategic planning tends to be most effective when there is a reciprocal relationship between the two processes. In this relationship, the top management team recognizes that strategic-planning decisions affect—and are affected by—HR concerns. As James Walker, noted HRP expert, put it, "Today, virtually *all* business issues have people implications; *all* human resource issues have business implications."[7]

In the best of companies, such as Merck, Honeywell, and Xerox, there is virtually no distinction between strategic planning and HRP; the planning cycles are the same and HR issues are seen as inherent in the management of the business. HR managers are important facilitators of the planning process and are viewed as credible and important contributors to creating the organization's future. This positive linkage occurs when the HR manager becomes a member of the organization's management steering committee or strategic-planning group. Once this interactive and dynamic structure exists, HR managers are recognized as contributing strategic planners alongside other top managers.[8]

## FIGURE 4.1

### Linking the Processes of HRP and Strategic Planning

**Strategic Analysis**

*Establish the context:*
- **Business goals**
- **Company strengths/ weaknesses**
- **External opportunities/ threats**
- **Source of competitive advantage**

**Strategy Formulation**

*Clarify performance expectations and future management methods:*
- **Values, guiding principles**
- **Business mission**
- **Objectives and priorities**
- **Resource allocations**

**Strategy Implementation**

*Implement processes to achieve desired results:*
- **Business goals**
- **Company strengths/ weaknesses**
- **External opportunities/ threats**
- **Source of competitive advantage**

**Identify people-related business issues**

**Define HR strategies, objectives, and action plans**

**Implement HR processes, policies, and practices**

**Human Resources Planning**

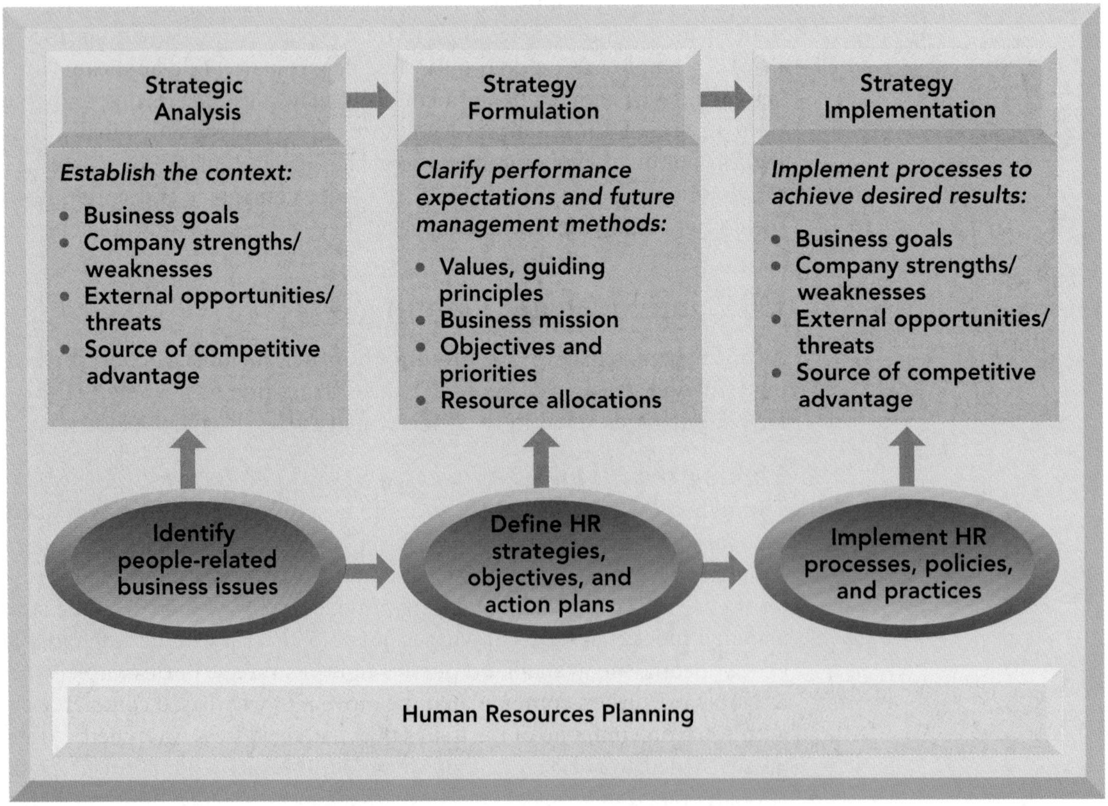

James W. Walker, "Integrating the Human Resource Function with the Business." Adapted with permission from *Human Resource Planning*, Vol. 14, No. 2 (1996). Copyright 1996 by the Human Resource Planning Society, 317 Madison Avenue, Suite 1509, New York, NY 10017, Phone: (212) 490-6387, Fax (212) 682-6851.

### *Mapping an Organization's Human Capital Architecture*

In addition to aligning the planning processes themselves, the linkage between strategy and HR today also focuses on the development of core competencies. Companies such as Domino's Pizza, Sony, Southwest Airlines, and Wal-Mart revolutionized their industries by developing skills—core competencies—that others didn't have. These competencies helped them gain advantage over their competitors and leverage this advantage by learning faster than others in their industries.

Underlying a firm's core competencies is a portfolio of employee skills and human capital. Figure 4.2 shows that different skill groups in any given organization can be classified according to the degree to which they create strategic value and are unique to the organization. Employment relationships and HR practices for different employees vary according to which cell they occupy in this matrix.

- *Core knowledge workers.* This group of employees has firm-specific skills that are directly linked to the company's strategy (e.g., R and D scientists in a pharmaceutical company, computer scientists in a software development company). These employees typically are engaged in knowledge work that involves considerable autonomy and discretion. Companies tend to make long-term commitments to these employees, investing in their continuous training and development and perhaps giving them an equity stake in the organization.

FIGURE 4.2

## Mapping an Organization's Human Capital Architecture

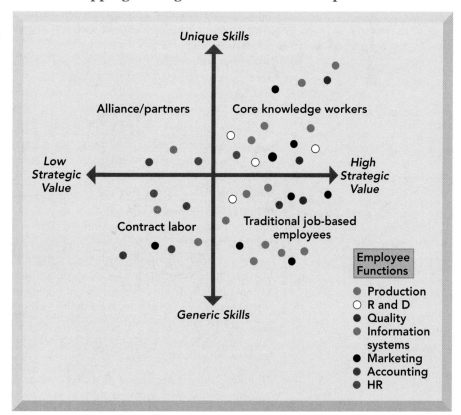

*A research scientist has knowledge and firm-specific skills that are directly linked to a company's strategy. Companies tend to make long-term investments in such core knowledge workers.*

- *Traditional job-based employees.* This group of employees has skills that are quite valuable to a company, but not unique (e.g., salespeople in a department store, truck drivers for a courier service). These employees are employed to perform a predefined job. As it is quite possible that they could leave to go to another firm, managers frequently make less investment in training and development and tend to focus more on paying for short-term performance achievements.
- *Contract labor.* This group of employees has skills that are of less strategic value and generally available to all firms (e.g., clerical workers, maintenance workers, staff workers in accounting and human resources). Individuals in these jobs are increasingly hired from external agencies on a contract basis, and the scope of their duties tends to be limited. Employment relationships tend to be transactional, focused on rules and procedures, with very little investment in development.
- *Alliance/partners.* This group of individuals has skills that are unique, but not directly related to a company's core strategy (e.g., attorneys, consultants, and research lab scientists). Although companies perhaps cannot justify their internal employment, given their tangential link to strategy, these individuals have skills that are specialized and not readily available to all firms. As a consequence, companies tend to establish longer-term alliances and partnerships with them and nurture an ongoing relationship focused on mutual learning. Considerable investment is made in the exchange of information and knowledge.[9]

An increasingly vital element of strategic planning for organizations that compete on competencies is determining if people are available, internally or externally, to execute an organization's strategy. Managers have to make tough decisions about whom to employ internally, whom to contract externally, and how to manage different types of employees with different skills who contribute in different ways to the organization. HRP plays an important role in helping managers weigh the costs and benefits of using one approach to employment versus another.

### Ensuring Fit and Flexibility

The third primary way that HRP and strategic planning are connected is in aligning the policies, programs, and practices in HR with the requirements of an organization's strategy. In this regard, HR policies and practices need to achieve two types of fit.[10]

*External fit* focuses on the connection between the business objectives and the major initiatives in HR. For example, if a company's strategy focuses on achieving low cost, HR policies and practices need to reinforce this idea by reinforcing efficient and reliable behavior. On the other hand, if the organization competes through innovation, new product development, and the like, HR policies and practices would be more aligned with the notion of creating flexibility and creativity. Highlights in HRM 1 shows the external fit between major business objectives and HR imperatives at AT&T's Global Business Communication Systems (now Lucent Technologies).

*Internal fit* means that HR practices are all aligned with one another to establish a configuration that is mutually reinforcing. For example, job design, staffing, training, performance appraisal, compensation, and the like would all focus on the same behavioral targets (such as efficiency and creativity). Unfortunately, it is all too often the case that training programs, for example, might be focused on teamwork and sharing all the while appraisal and compensation programs reinforce the ideas of individual achievement.

Apart from the need to establish a fit between HR and strategy, HRP is also focused on ensuring flexibility and agility when the environment changes. Ultimately, successful HRP helps to increase **organizational capability**—the capacity of the organization to act and change in pursuit of sustainable competitive advantage.[11]

**Organizational capability**
Capacity of the organization to act and change in pursuit of sustainable competitive advantage

Flexibility can be achieved in two primary ways: coordination flexibility and resource flexibility. *Coordination flexibility* occurs through rapid reallocation of resources to new or changing needs. Through HRP, managers can anticipate upcoming events, keep abreast of changes in legal regulations, forecast economic trends, recognize competitor moves, and the like. With advanced notice, managers can move people into and out of jobs, retrain them for new skill requirements, and modify the kinds of incentives they utilize. Use of a contingency workforce composed of part-timers, temporary employees, and external partners also helps to achieve coordination flexibility.[12]

*Resource flexibility,* on the other hand, results from having people who can do many different things in different ways. Cross-training, job rotations, team-based work modes, and the like are all focused on establishing a flexible workforce. We will discuss each of these issues at more length throughout the text. At this point, however, we want to emphasize that the process depends on a thorough understanding of the organization's environment. And this begins with environmental scanning.

**HIGHLIGHTS IN HRM**

# HR Strategy and Planning Model for AT&T's Global Business Communications Systems (GBCS)

| GBCS BUSINESS PRINCIPLES | GBCS HR STRATEGIC IMPERATIVES | HUMAN RESOURCES MISSION | FOCUS AREAS | HR PLAN INITIATIVES |
|---|---|---|---|---|
| Make *people* a key priority. → | I. Associates actively take ownership for the business success at all levels, individually and as teams, by improving associate value. | | | Learning forums, such as: <br> • Change Management and You <br> • GBCS Strategy Forum <br> • PEP Workshop <br> • Quality Curriculum |
| Use the *Total Quality Management* approach to run our business. → | II. GBCS HR contributes to increased shareholder value by achieving process improvements that increase productivity and customer satisfaction. | | Cultural Change → | Communication Platform <br> • Ask the President <br> • Answer Line <br> • All Associate Broadcasts <br> • Bureaucracy Busters <br> • Associate Dialogues |
| *Rapidly and profitably globalize* the business. → | III. Ensuring GBCS HR readiness to expand its business initiatives into global markets which requires a business partner that is sensitive to the unique needs of various cultures and people. → | To create an environment where the achievement of business goals is realized through an acceptance of individual accountability by each associate and by his/her commitment to performance excellence. | | Diversity Platform <br> • Pluralistic Leadership: Managing in a Global Society <br> • Celebration of Diversity <br> • National Diversity Council |
| *Profitably grow* by being the leader in customer-led applications of technology. → | IV. HR strategic plans and processes support and → are integrated with GBCS's strategic and business planning processes so that the HR management system attracts, develops, rewards, and retains associates who accept accountability for business success. | | Rewards and Recognition → | Progress Sharing Plan (PSP) <br><br> Special Long-Term Plan (SLTP) <br> Recognition Platform <br> • Partner of Choice <br> • Trailblazers <br> • President's Council <br> • Achiever's Club <br> • Local Recognition Programs <br> • Touch Award |

| GBCS BUSINESS PRINCIPLES | GBCS HR STRATEGIC IMPERATIVES | HUMAN RESOURCES MISSION | FOCUS AREAS | HR PLAN INITIATIVES |
|---|---|---|---|---|
| Be the *best value supplier*. | V. GBCS HR provides a level of service to internal and external customers that establishes the HR organization as their value added business partner. | | Ownership → | Performance Excellence Partnership (PEP) |
| | | | | Associate Surveys |
| | | | | ● ASI (Associate Satisfaction Index) |
| | VI. The HR leader and team are competent to provide leadership and support to GBCS by championing HR initiatives that contribute to GBCS's success | | | ● AOS (Associate Opinion Survey) |
| | | | | Organization Effectiveness |
| | | | | ● Work Teams |
| | | | | ● Process Teams |

M. J. Plevel, S. Nellis, F. Lane, and R. S. Schuler, "AT&T Global Business Communications Systems: Linking HR with Business Strategy." Reprinted from Organizational Dynamics, Winter/1994. © 1994 American Management Association International. Reprinted by permission of American Management Association International, New York, NY. All rights reserved. http://www.amanet.org.

## HRP and Environmental Scanning

Changes in the external environment have a direct impact on the way organizations are run and people are managed. *Environmental scanning* is the systematic monitoring of the major external forces influencing the organization.[13] Managers attend to a variety of external issues; however, the following six are monitored most frequently:

1. Economic factors, including general and regional conditions
2. Competitive trends, including new processes, services, and innovations
3. Technological changes, including robotics and office automation
4. Political and legislative issues, including laws and administrative rulings
5. Social concerns, including child care and educational priorities
6. Demographic trends, including age, composition, and literacy

By scanning the environment for changes that will likely affect an organization, managers can anticipate their impact and make adjustments early. In a rapidly changing environment, it is extremely dangerous to be caught off guard.

The labor-force trends listed earlier, for example, illustrate the importance of monitoring demographic changes as a part of HRP. Such changes can affect the composition and performance of an organization's workforce. These changes are important because EEO/AA plans must take into account the demographic composition of the population in the area where the organization is located. Furthermore, with a "maturing" American workforce, HRP must consider the many implications of this demographic fact on recruitment and replacement policies. You have seen the televised ads of McDonald's and other fast-food chains. Many other firms, including Days Inns of America, Travelers Insurance, and ABCO food stores have made a stronger effort in recent years to hire older workers.[14]

**Cultural audits**
Audits of the culture and quality of work life in an organization

In addition to scanning the external environment, organizations such as Syntex, Lotus Development, and Southwest Airlines are careful to also scan their internal environments. Because these companies view their employee-oriented cultures as critical to success, they conduct **cultural audits** to examine the attitudes and activities of the workforce. Sears has found that positive employee attitudes on ten essential factors—including workload and treatment by bosses—are directly linked to customer satisfaction and revenue increases.[15]

Cultural audits essentially involve discussions among top-level managers of how the organization's culture reveals itself to employees and how it can be influenced or improved. The cultural audit may include such questions as

- How do employees spend their time?
- How do they interact with each other?
- Are employees empowered?
- What is the predominant leadership style of managers?
- How do employees advance within the organization?

By conducting in-depth interviews and making observations over a period of time, managers are able to learn about the culture of their organization and the attitudes of its employees. With the increased diversity of the U.S. workplace, cultural audits can be used to determine whether there are different groups, or subcultures, within the organization that have distinctly different views about the nature of work, the quality of managers, and so on. Before any HR planning can take place, managers have to gain a clear idea of how employees view their organization.

# Elements of Effective HRP

Managers follow a systematic process, or model, when undertaking HRP, as shown in Figure 4.3. The three key elements of the process are forecasting the demand for labor, performing a supply analysis, and balancing supply and demand considerations. Careful attention to each factor will help top managers and supervisors to meet their staffing requirements.

## Forecasting Demand for Employees

A key component of HRP is forecasting the number and type of people needed to meet organizational objectives. A variety of organizational factors, including competitive strategy, technology, structure, and productivity, can influence the demand for labor. For example, as noted in Chapter 1, utilization of advanced technology is generally accompanied by less demand for low-skilled workers and more demand for knowledge workers. External factors such as business cycles—economic and seasonal trends—can also play a role. The Internal Revenue Service, for example, relies heavily on temporary employees between January and April when tax returns are received for processing.

Forecasting is frequently more an art than a science, providing inexact approximations rather than absolute results. The ever-changing environment in which an organization operates contributes to this problem. For example, estimating changes in product or service demand is a basic forecasting concern, as is anticipating

FIGURE 4.3

## Human Resource Planning Model

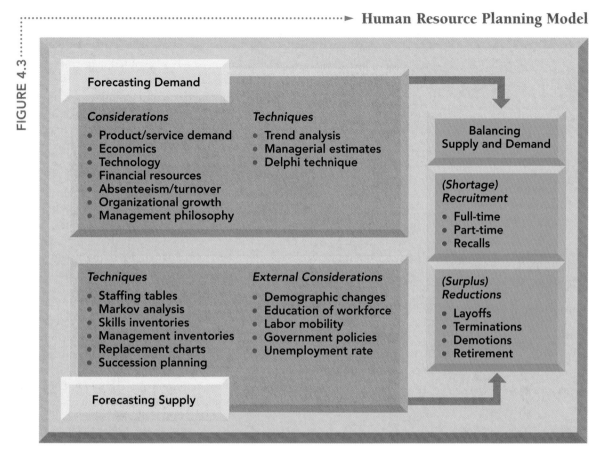

**Forecasting Demand**

*Considerations*
- Product/service demand
- Economics
- Technology
- Financial resources
- Absenteeism/turnover
- Organizational growth
- Management philosophy

*Techniques*
- Trend analysis
- Managerial estimates
- Delphi technique

**Balancing Supply and Demand**

*(Shortage) Recruitment*
- Full-time
- Part-time
- Recalls

*Techniques*
- Staffing tables
- Markov analysis
- Skills inventories
- Management inventories
- Replacement charts
- Succession planning

*External Considerations*
- Demographic changes
- Education of workforce
- Labor mobility
- Government policies
- Unemployment rate

*(Surplus) Reductions*
- Layoffs
- Terminations
- Demotions
- Retirement

**Forecasting Supply**

changes in national or regional economics. A community hospital anticipating internal changes in technology, organization, or administration must consider these environmental factors in its forecasts of staffing needs. Also, the forecasted staffing needs must be in line with the organization's financial resources.

There are two approaches to HR forecasting: quantitative and qualitative. When concentrating on human resources needs, forecasting is primarily quantitative in nature and, in large organizations, is accomplished by highly trained specialists. Quantitative approaches to forecasting can employ sophisticated analytical models, although forecasting may be as informal as having one person who knows the organization anticipate future HR requirements. Organizational demands will ultimately determine which technique is used. Regardless of the method, however, forecasting should not be neglected, even in relatively small organizations.

### Quantitative Approaches

**Trend analysis**
A quantitative approach to forecasting labor demand based on an organizational index such as sales

Quantitative approaches to forecasting involve the use of statistical or mathematical techniques; they are the approaches used by theoreticians and professional planners. One example is **trend analysis,** which forecasts employment requirements on the basis of some organizational index and is one of the most commonly used approaches for projecting HR demand. Trend analysis is typically done by following several steps:

First, select an appropriate business factor. This should be the best available predictor of human resources needs. Frequently, sales or value added (selling price minus costs of materials and supplies) is used as a predictor in trend analysis. Second, plot a historical trend of the business factor in relation to the number of employees. The ratio of employees to the business factor will provide a labor productivity ratio (for example, sales per employee). Third, compute the productivity ratio for at least the past five years. Fourth, calculate human resources demand by multiplying the business factor by the productivity ratio. Finally, project human resources demand out to the target year. This procedure is summarized in Figure 4.4 for a building contractor.

Other, more sophisticated statistical planning methods include modeling or multiple predictive techniques. Whereas trend analysis relies on a single factor (e.g., sales) to predict employment needs, the more advanced methods combine several factors, such as interest rates, gross national product, disposable income, and sales, to predict employment levels. While the costs of developing these forecasting methods used to be quite high, advances in technology and computer software have made rather sophisticated forecasting tools affordable to even small businesses.

## Qualitative Approaches

**Management forecasts**
The opinions (judgments) of supervisors, department managers, experts, or others knowledgeable about the organization's future employment needs

In contrast to quantitative approaches, qualitative approaches to forecasting are less statistical, attempting to reconcile the interests, abilities, and aspirations of individual employees with the current and future staffing needs of an organization. In both large and small organizations, HR planners may rely on experts who assist in preparing forecasts to anticipate staffing requirements. **Management forecasts** are the opinions (judgments) of supervisors, department managers, experts, or

**FIGURE 4.4**

## Example of Trend Analysis of HR Demand

| YEAR | BUSINESS FACTOR (Sales in thousands) | ÷ LABOR PRODUCTIVITY (Sales /employee) | = HUMAN RESOURCES DEMAND (Number of employees) |
|---|---|---|---|
| 1995 | $2,351 | 14.33 | 164 |
| 1996 | $2,613 | 11.12 | 235 |
| 1997 | $2,935 | 8.34 | 352 |
| 1998 | $3,306 | 10.02 | 330 |
| 1999 | $3,613 | 11.12 | 325 |
| 2000 | $3,748 | 11.12 | 337 |
| 2001 | $3,880 | 12.52 | 310 |
| 2002* | $4,095 | 12.52 | 327 |
| 2003* | $4,283 | 12.52 | 342 |
| 2004* | $4,446 | 12.52 | 355 |

*Projected figures

others knowledgeable about the organization's future employment needs. For example, at the Ripe Tomato, a growing family dining chain, each restaurant manager is responsible for employment forecasts.

Another qualitative forecasting method, the Delphi technique, attempts to decrease the subjectivity of forecasts by soliciting and summarizing the judgments of a preselected group of individuals. The final forecast thus represents a composite group judgment. The Delphi technique requires a great deal of coordination and cooperation in order to ensure satisfactory forecasts. This method works best in organizations where dynamic technological changes affect staffing levels.

Ideally, HRP should include the use of both quantitative and qualitative approaches. In combination, the two approaches serve to complement each other, providing a more complete forecast by bringing together the contributions of both theoreticians and practitioners.

## Forecasting Supply of Employees

Once an organization has forecast its future requirements for employees, it must then determine if there are sufficient numbers and types of employees available to staff anticipated openings. As with demand, the process involves both tracking current levels and making future projections.

### Internal Labor Supply

**Staffing tables**
Graphic representations of all organizational jobs, along with the numbers of employees currently occupying those jobs and future (monthly or yearly) employment requirements

**Markov analysis**
Method for tracking the pattern of employee movements through various jobs

**Skill inventories**
Files of personnel education, experience, interests, skills, etc., that allow managers to quickly match job openings with employee backgrounds

**Replacement charts**
Listings of current jobholders and persons who are potential replacements if an opening occurs

An internal supply analysis may begin with the preparation of staffing tables. **Staffing tables** are graphic representations of all organizational jobs, along with the numbers of employees currently occupying those jobs (and perhaps also future employment requirements derived from demand forecasts). Another technique, called **Markov analysis,** shows the percentage (and actual number) of employees who remain in each job from one year to the next, as well as the proportions of those who are promoted, demoted, transferred, or exit the organization. As shown in Figure 4.5, Markov analysis can be used to track the pattern of employee movements through various jobs and to develop a transition matrix for forecasting labor supply.[16]

Forecasting the supply of human resources requires that managers have a good understanding of employee turnover and absenteeism. We have included formulas for computing turnover and absenteeism rates in an appendix to this chapter. The calculations are easily made and used by managers of both large and small organizations.

While staffing tables, Markov analysis, turnover rates, and the like tend to focus on the number of employees in particular jobs, other techniques are more oriented toward the types of employees and their skills, knowledge, and experiences. **Skill inventories** can also be prepared that list each employee's education, past work experience, vocational interests, specific abilities and skills, compensation history, and job tenure. Of course, confidentiality is a vital concern in setting up any such inventory. Nevertheless, well-prepared and up-to-date skill inventories allow an organization to quickly match forthcoming job openings with employee backgrounds. Organizations like Zenith Data Systems, Westinghouse, and the State of Illinois use computers and special programs to perform this task. When data are gathered on managers, these inventories are called *management inventories.*

Both skill and management inventories—broadly referred to as talent inventories—can be used to develop employee **replacement charts,** which list current jobholders and identify possible replacements should openings occur. Figure 4.6

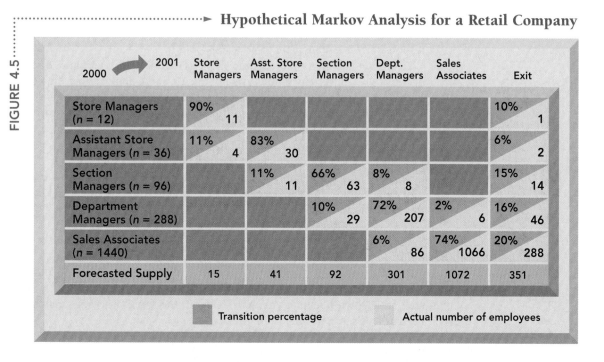

**FIGURE 4.5**

## Hypothetical Markov Analysis for a Retail Company

| 2000 → 2001 | Store Managers | Asst. Store Managers | Section Managers | Dept. Managers | Sales Associates | Exit |
|---|---|---|---|---|---|---|
| Store Managers (n = 12) | 90%   11 | | | | | 10%   1 |
| Assistant Store Managers (n = 36) | 11%   4 | 83%   30 | | | | 6%   2 |
| Section Managers (n = 96) | | 11%   11 | 66%   63 | 8%   8 | | 15%   14 |
| Department Managers (n = 288) | | | 10%   29 | 72%   207 | 2%   6 | 16%   46 |
| Sales Associates (n = 1440) | | | | 6%   86 | 74%   1066 | 20%   288 |
| Forecasted Supply | 15 | 41 | 92 | 301 | 1072 | 351 |

■ Transition percentage      ■ Actual number of employees

**Succession planning**
Process of identifying, developing, and tracking key individuals for executive positions

shows an example of how an organization might develop a replacement chart for the managers in one of its divisions. Note that this chart provides information on the current job performance and promotability of possible replacements. As such, it can be used side by side with other pieces of information for **succession planning**—the process of identifying, developing, and tracking key individuals so that they may eventually assume top-level positions.

In today's fast-moving environment, succession planning may be more important—and more difficult to conduct—than ever before. Seventy-five percent of corporate officers surveyed by McKinsey and Company said they were chronically short of talent at managerial levels. According to William Byam, CEO of Development Dimensions International (DDI), the typical company expects 33 percent turnover in the executive ranks in the next five years and, among these companies, roughly one-third are worried that they will not be able to find suitable replacements. And the cost of replacing these managers is extremely high, says Byam. "The average one-year estimated replacement cost is $750,000. That includes finding the new [person], training and development costs and opportunity costs of getting the new hire up to speed." Highlights in HRM 2 shows a sample of companies that are working to improve their succession planning systems.[17]

### External Labor Supply

When an organization lacks an internal supply of employees for promotions, or when it is staffing entry-level positions, managers must consider the external supply of labor. Many factors influence labor supply, including demographic changes in the population, national and regional economics, education level of the workforce, demand for specific employee skills, population mobility, and governmental policies. National and regional unemployment rates are often considered a general barometer of labor supply.

FIGURE 4.6

**An Executive Replacement Chart**

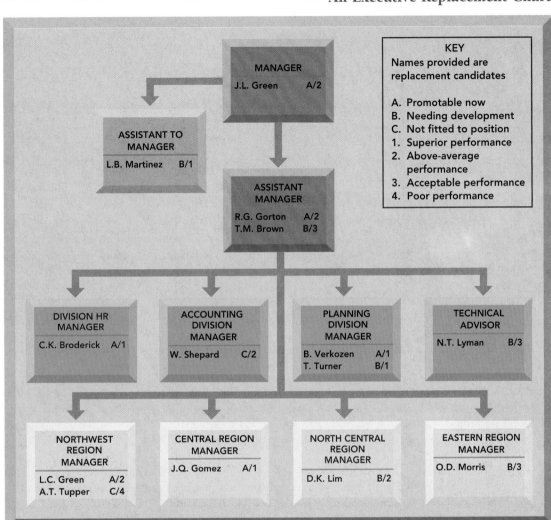

MANAGER
J.L. Green        A/2

ASSISTANT TO
MANAGER
L.B. Martinez    B/1

ASSISTANT
MANAGER
R.G. Gorton    A/2
T.M. Brown     B/3

KEY
Names provided are
replacement candidates

A.  Promotable now
B.  Needing development
C.  Not fitted to position
1.  Superior performance
2.  Above-average
    performance
3.  Acceptable performance
4.  Poor performance

DIVISION HR
MANAGER
C.K. Broderick    A/1

ACCOUNTING
DIVISION
MANAGER
W. Shepard      C/2

PLANNING
DIVISION
MANAGER
B. Verkozen    A/1
T. Turner      B/1

TECHNICAL
ADVISOR
N.T. Lyman      B/3

NORTHWEST
REGION
MANAGER
L.C. Green      A/2
A.T. Tupper     C/4

CENTRAL REGION
MANAGER
J.Q. Gomez      A/1

NORTH CENTRAL
REGION
MANAGER
D.K. Lim        B/2

EASTERN REGION
MANAGER
O.D. Morris     B/3

Fortunately, labor market analysis is aided by various published documents. Unemployment rates, labor-force projection figures, and population characteristics are reported by the U.S. Department of Labor.[18] The *Monthly Labor Review* and *Occupational Outlook Quarterly,* both published by the Bureau of Labor Statistics (BLS) of the U.S. Department of Labor, contain information on jobholder characteristics and predicted changes in the workforce. In addition, local chambers of commerce and individual state development and planning agencies also may assist both large organizations and new business ventures with labor market analysis.

For example, recent data from the BLS report that approximately 33 million college graduates are employed in the United States. These individuals work in a wide range of occupations, but the majority is found in two groups: (1) professional specialty occupations and (2) executive, administrative, and managerial occupations.

HRM 2

HIGHLIGHTS IN HRM

# How Successful Is Succession Planning at . . .

*. . . Sun Microsystems?* There are 600 directors (the entry-level executive job) who report to 110 vice presidents. According to Ken Alveres, VP of HR, "We watch the directors closely, but give more attention to the VPs. . . . When you look at our bench strength, I don't get the feeling that we've got ourselves covered. I worry about developing people who can step up to the next level."

*. . . U.S. Postal Service?* The program focuses on 800 senior managers who may be selected to move up the ladder to the elite 45-person officer team. Steve Levy, the organization's corporate HR manager, says it's "4,000 people backing up 800 jobs." Since the program was initiated, it has accounted for 90 percent of the senior management and executive hiring. According to Levy, "We're in the process of pushing the process below the executive level."

*. . . Sonoco?* The company's succession plan targets 300 executives in its top management group. About 20 percent of Sonoco's executive jobs turn over each year as a result of retirements, job changes, and departures. According to Cindy Hartley, VP of HR, the company's policy is to promote from within. "We meet with our division presidents and general managers to discuss our key people; we explore what we want to do to develop them and identify who we have tapped as potential successors."

*. . . UNUM?* The insurance company targets 200 managers out of its 7,000 employees. Tammie Snow, head of training, explains that the company puts the most promising candidates through management internship programs. "We provide management assistantships to a select number of people, about 12 each year, who have reached the director level. We identify the high potential people and for a year or a year and a half, they shadow a key executive."

*. . . Sears?* Recently, Sears created its Corporate Strategic Leadership Team (CSLT, pronounced "seasalt") to develop bench strength from among its top 220 executives to support the top twenty-four executive positions. Steve Kirn, VP of organizational learning and development, explains, "We look at each position, identify the unique experiences and challenges that the job provides, then look at the people on the bench and match them with the appropriate position."

Adapted from Robert J. Grossman, "Heirs Unapparent," *HRMagazine* 44, no. 2 (February 1999): 36–44. Reprinted with the permission of *HRMagazine*, published by the Society for Human Resource Management, Alexandria, VA.

Figure 4.7 shows the distribution of college graduate employment. Other data predict that while the labor force is expected to grow at a rate of 14 percent between 1996 and 2006 (to reach 150.9 million workers), the growth rate for college-graduate-level jobs is expected to grow by more than 27 percent (to nearly 35 million workers). At the same time, estimates are that the number of individuals earning college degrees is actually declining but should resume growth in 2001 (see Figure 4.8). These kinds of data provide a much clearer picture to organizations attempting to project external labor supply.[19]

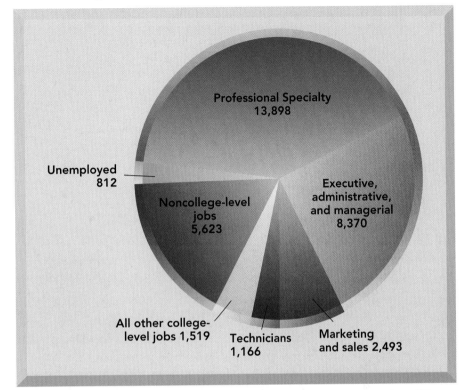

## College Graduates in the Labor Force, 1996 (Thousands)

FIGURE 4.7

Professional Specialty
13,898

Unemployed
812

Noncollege-level
jobs
5,623

Executive,
administrative,
and managerial
8,370

All other college-
level jobs 1,519

Technicians
1,166

Marketing
and sales 2,493

Source: Mark Mettelhauser, "The Outlook for College Graduates, 1996–2006: Prepare Yourself," *Occupational Outlook Quarterly*, Summer 1998, 3–9. Reproduced with permission of the copyright owner. Further reproduction prohibited without permission.

## Balancing Supply and Demand Considerations

Through HRP, organizations strive for a proper balance between demand considerations and supply considerations. Demand considerations are based on forecasted trends in business activity. Supply considerations involve the determination of where and how candidates with the required qualifications are to be found to fill vacancies. Because of the difficulty in locating applicants for the increasing number of jobs that require advanced training, this aspect of planning has been receiving a great deal more attention. Greater planning effort is also needed in recruiting members of protected classes for managerial jobs and technical jobs that require advanced levels of education.

In an effort to meet the demand for labor, organizations have several staffing possibilities, including hiring full-time employees, having employees work overtime, recalling laid-off workers, and using temporary employees. However, when HRP shows a surplus of jobholders, organizations may restrict hiring; reduce work hours; institute work sharing; or consider layoffs, demotions, and/or terminations. Additionally, over time organizations may try to reduce their workforce by relying on attrition (a gradual reduction of employees through resignations, retirements, or deaths). Over the past decade, early retirements have become a more and more common means for organizations to reduce excess labor supply. Organizations as diverse as state col-

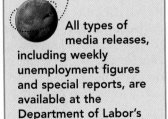

**USING THE INTERNET**

All types of media releases, including weekly unemployment figures and special reports, are available at the Department of Labor's web site:

www.dol.gov

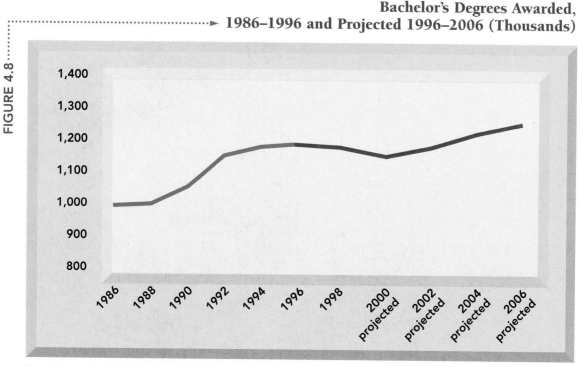

FIGURE 4.8

**Bachelor's Degrees Awarded, 1986–1996 and Projected 1996–2006 (Thousands)**

Note: Degrees awarded as of the end of the academic school year (May-June).

Source: Mark Mittelhauser, "The Outlook for College Graduates, 1996–2006: Prepare Yourself," *Occupational Outlook Quarterly*, Summer 1998, 3–9. Reproduced with permission of the copyright owner. Further reproduction prohibited without permission.

leges, health care facilities, and travel companies encourage employees to accept early retirement by offering "sweetened" retirement benefits. The various types of benefits are discussed in Chapter 11.

### Organizational Downsizing

As discussed in Chapter 1, organizations have undertaken the extremely painful task of downsizing and restructuring over the past decade to reduce "head count." Because of either economic or competitive pressures, organizations have found themselves with too many employees or with employees who have the wrong kinds of skills. In an effort to reconcile labor supply and demand considerations, companies such as Lockheed Martin and Cleveland-based KeyCorp have eliminated thousands of jobs.[20] These job cuts are not simply restricted to hourly workers. Technical, professional, and managerial positions have been (and are still being) eliminated at an unprecedented rate. In many cases, downsizing is part of a longer-term process of restructuring to take advantage of new technology, corporate partnerships, and cost minimization.

### Making Layoff Decisions

Decisions about employee layoffs are usually based on seniority and/or performance. In some organizations, especially those with labor agreements, seniority may be the primary consideration. In other organizations, such factors as ability and fitness may take precedence over seniority in determining layoffs.

In the case of unionized organizations, the criteria for determining an employee's eligibility for layoff are typically set forth in the union agreement. As a rule, seniority on the job receives significant weight in determining which employees are laid off first. Similar provisions in the union agreement provide for the right of employees to be recalled for jobs that they are still qualified to perform. Organizational policy, as well as provisions in the labor agreement, should therefore establish and define clearly the employment rights of each individual and the basis upon which layoff selections will be made and reemployment effected. The rights of employees during layoffs, the conditions concerning their eligibility for recall, and their obligations in accepting recall should also be clarified. It is common for labor agreements to preserve the reemployment rights of employees laid off for periods of up to two years, providing that they do not refuse to return to work if recalled sooner.

It has become customary, however, for employers to give some degree of recognition to seniority even among employees who are not unionized. Unions generally advocate recognition of seniority because they feel that their members should be entitled to certain rights proportionate to the years they have invested in their jobs. Nevertheless, whenever seniority provides a basis for determining or even influencing HR decisions, the discretion of management is reduced accordingly. One of the major disadvantages of overemphasizing seniority is that the less competent employees receive the same rewards and security as the more competent ones. Also, the practice of using seniority as the basis for deciding which workers to lay off may well have a disparate impact on women and minority workers, who often have less seniority than other groups.

In cases where economic conditions have brought about layoffs, employees who were let go while in good standing may be recalled to their jobs when the economic outlook brightens and job openings occur. However, in many cases these new jobs require a different set of skills than the jobs they replace. Identifying individuals for these jobs can be accomplished by searching among previous employees or among current employees who can be transferred, but frequently it requires searching externally in the broader labor market.[21]

# Recruiting within the Organization

Recruitment is the process of locating and encouraging potential applicants to apply for existing or anticipated job openings. During this process, efforts are made to inform the applicants fully about the qualifications required to perform the job and the career opportunities the organization can offer its employees. Whether or not a particular job vacancy will be filled by someone from within the organization or from outside will, of course, depend upon the availability of personnel, the organization's HR policies, and the requirements of the job to be staffed.

## Advantages of Recruiting from Within

Most organizations try to follow a policy of filling job vacancies above the entry-level position through promotions and transfers. By filling vacancies in this way, an organization can capitalize on the investment it has made in recruiting, selecting, training, and developing its current employees.

Promotion-from-within policies at Hard Rock America (operators of Hard Rock Cafes), Nordstrom's, Nucor Steel, and Wal-Mart have contributed to the companies' overall growth and success.[22] Promotion serves to reward employees for past performance and is intended to encourage them to continue their efforts. It also gives other employees reason to anticipate that similar efforts by them will lead to promotion, thus improving morale within the organization. This is particularly true for members of protected classes who have encountered difficulties in finding employment and have often faced even greater difficulty in advancing within an organization. Most organizations have integrated promotion policies as an essential part of their EEO/AA programs.

If an organization's promotion policy is to have maximum motivational value, employees must be made aware of that policy. The following is an example of a policy statement that an organization might prepare:

"Promotion from within" is generally recognized as a foundation of good employment practice, and it is the policy of our museum to promote from within whenever possible when filling a vacancy. The job vacancy will be posted for five calendar days to give all qualified full- and part-time personnel an equal opportunity to apply.

While a transfer lacks the motivational value of a promotion, it sometimes can serve to protect employees from layoff or to broaden their job experiences. Furthermore, the transferred employee's familiarity with the organization and its operations can eliminate the orientation and training costs that recruitment from the outside would entail. Most importantly, the transferee's performance record is likely to be a more accurate predictor of the candidate's success than the data gained about outside applicants.

## Methods of Locating Qualified Job Candidates

The effective use of internal sources requires a system for locating qualified job candidates and for enabling those who consider themselves qualified to apply for the opening. Qualified job candidates within the organization can be located by computerized record systems, by job posting and bidding, and by looking to those who have been laid off.

### Human Resources Information Systems

Information technology has made it possible for organizations to create databases that contain the complete records and qualifications of each employee within an organization. Combined with increasingly user-friendly search engines, managers can access this information and identify potential candidates for available jobs. Organizations as diverse as Sun Microsystems, Ford, and the U.S. military have developed resume-tracking systems that allow managers to query an on-line database of resumes. Companies such as PeopleSoft and Resumix are leaders in developing automated staffing and skills management software. Similar to the skills inventories mentioned earlier, these information systems allow an organization to rapidly screen its entire workforce to locate suitable candidates to fill an internal opening. These data can also be used to predict the career paths of employees and to anticipate when and where promotion opportunities may arise. Since the value of the data depends on its being kept up to date, the systems typically include provisions for recording changes in employee qualifications and job placements as they occur.[23]

### Job Posting and Bidding

**Job posting and bidding**
Posting vacancy notices and maintaining lists of employees looking for upgraded positions

Organizations may communicate information about job openings through a process referred to as **job posting and bidding.** In the past, this process has consisted largely of posting vacancy notices on bulletin boards. In addition, it may also include use of designated posting centers, employee publications, special handouts, direct mail, and public-address messages. Increasingly, companies such as Texas Instruments, Amoco, Household International, and Xerox are developing computerized job posting systems and maintaining voluntary lists of employees looking for upgraded positions. Case Study 2 at the end of this chapter highlights how Cisco Systems has developed a web site for internal (and external) job applicants. As a position becomes available, the list of employees seeking that position is retrieved from the computer, and the records of these employees are reviewed to select the best-qualified candidate.[24] Highlights in HRM 3 provides some guidelines for setting up an on-line job posting system.

**HRM 3**

**HIGHLIGHTS IN HRM**

# Guidelines for Setting Up an On-Line Job Posting System

To begin building an electronic job posting system, organizations need an electronic mail software program with the capability to display job postings and accept recruiting requests for available openings.

### Designing and Administering the System

To design and administer the system, organizations need:

- An automated process to enter job postings onto the system and to delete listings once they are filled
- The capability to automatically calculate each listing's expiration date
- A system that automatically assigns numbers to job postings
- The capability to preschedule job positions for future postings
- A way for coordinators to revise and delete postings after they are on the system
- Security measures that allow access to authorized users only
- A printing function

### Making It Easy for Applicants and Users

Applicants and other users need:

- Search capabilities for locating job openings by geographic area and job title
- Ways to display and print guidelines, policies, and procedures regarding the system
- Electronic application forms with job titles and departments already filled in
- Ways to address and send applications electronically to the appropriate HR managers

Source: Condensed from Sharon M. Tarrant, "Setting Up an Electronic Job-Posting System," *Training and Development*, January 1994, 39–42. Reprinted with permission.

The system of job posting and bidding can provide many benefits to an organization. However, these benefits may not be realized unless employees believe the system is being administered fairly. Furthermore, job bidding is more effective when it is part of a career development program in which employees are made aware of opportunities available to them within the organization. For example, HR departments may provide new employees with literature on job progression that describes the lines of job advancement, training requirements for each job, and skills and abilities needed as they move up the job-progression ladder.

## Limitations of Recruiting from Within

Sometimes certain jobs at the middle and upper levels that require specialized training and experience cannot be filled from within the organization and must be filled from the outside. This is especially common in small organizations. Also, for certain openings it may be necessary to hire individuals from the outside who have gained from another employer the knowledge and expertise required for these jobs.

Even though HR policy encourages job openings to be filled from within the organization, potential candidates from the outside should be considered in order to prevent the inbreeding of ideas and attitudes. Applicants hired from the outside, particularly for certain technical and managerial positions, can be a source of new ideas and may bring with them the latest knowledge acquired from their previous employers. Indeed, excessive reliance upon internal sources can create the risk of "employee cloning." Furthermore, it is not uncommon for firms in competitive fields such as high technology to attempt to gain secrets from competitors by hiring away their employees. Dow recently sued GE over just such an issue.[25]

# Recruiting outside the Organization

Unless there is to be a reduction in the workforce, a replacement from outside must be found to fill a vacancy when a jobholder moves to a new slot in the organization. Thus, when the president or CEO of the organization retires, a chain reaction of promotions may subsequently occur. This creates other managerial openings throughout the organization. The question therefore is not whether to bring people into the organization, but rather at which level they are to be brought in.

In the past few years, organizations such as Kellogg's, Pepsi, Cable and Wireless, and Goodyear have brought in outsiders to be their new CEOs. In fact, an astounding share of *Fortune* 500 companies who replace their CEOs do so by hiring executives from outside their companies. In many of these cases, hiring someone from the outside is seen as essential for revitalizing the organizations.[26]

## The Labor Market

**Labor market**
Area from which applicants are to be recruited

The **labor market,** or the area from which applicants are to be recruited, will vary with the type of position to be filled and the amount of compensation to be paid. Recruitment for executives and technical personnel who require a high degree of knowledge and skill may be national or even international in scope. Most colleges and universities, for example, conduct national employment searches to fill top administrative positions. Recruitment for jobs that require relatively little skill, however, may encompass only a small geographic area. The reluctance of people to relocate may cause them to turn down offers of employment, thereby eliminating them from employment consideration beyond the local labor market. However, by offering an attractive level of compensation and by helping to defray moving costs, employers may induce some applicants to move.[27]

The ease with which employees can commute to work will also influence the boundaries of the labor market. Insufficient public transportation or extreme traffic congestion on the streets and freeways can limit the distance employees are willing to travel to work, particularly to jobs of low pay. Also, population migration from the cities to the suburbs has had its effect on labor markets. If suitable employment can be obtained near where they live or if they can work at home, many suburbanites are less likely to accept or remain in jobs in the central city.

## Outside Sources of Recruitment

The outside sources from which employers recruit will vary with the type of position to be filled. A computer programmer, for example, is not likely to be recruited from the same source as a machine operator. Trade schools can provide applicants for entry-level positions, though these recruitment sources are not as useful when highly skilled employees are needed.

The condition of the labor market may also help to determine which recruiting sources an organization will use. During periods of high unemployment, organizations may be able to maintain an adequate supply of qualified applicants from unsolicited resumes alone. A tight labor market, one with low unemployment, may force the employer to advertise heavily and/or seek assistance from local employment agencies. How successful an organization has been in reaching its affirmative action goals may be still another factor in determining the sources from which to recruit. Typically, an employer at any given time will find it necessary to utilize several recruitment sources. Figure 4.9 shows how 201 HR executives in one study rated the effectiveness of nine different recruiting methods.

Several other studies have suggested that an employee's recruitment source can affect that employee's subsequent tenure and job performance in both large and small organizations.[28] In general, applicants who find employment through referral by a current employee tend to remain with the organization longer and give higher-quality performance than those employees recruited through the formal recruitment sources of advertisements and employment agencies. Informal recruiting sources may also yield higher selection rates than formal sources. Employers are cautioned, however, that relying on only one or two recruitment sources to secure job applicants could have an adverse effect on protected classes.

### *Advertisements*

One of the most common methods of attracting applicants is through advertisements. While newspapers and trade journals are the media used most often, radio, television, billboards, posters, and electronic mail are also utilized. Advertising has the advantage of reaching a large audience of possible applicants. Some degree of selectivity can be achieved by using newspapers and journals directed toward a particular group of readers. Professional journals, trade journals, and publications of unions and various fraternal or nonprofit organizations fall into this category.

FIGURE 4.9

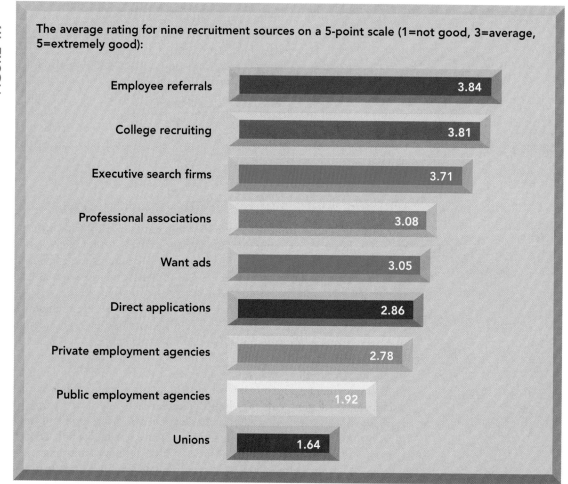

## Effectiveness of Recruitment Sources

The average rating for nine recruitment sources on a 5-point scale (1=not good, 3=average, 5=extremely good):

|  |  |
| --- | --- |
| Employee referrals | 3.84 |
| College recruiting | 3.81 |
| Executive search firms | 3.71 |
| Professional associations | 3.08 |
| Want ads | 3.05 |
| Direct applications | 2.86 |
| Private employment agencies | 2.78 |
| Public employment agencies | 1.92 |
| Unions | 1.64 |

Source: David E. Terpstra, "The Search for Effective Methods." Reprinted from *HR Focus*, May/1996. © 1996 American Management Association International. Reprinted by permission of American Management Association International, New York, NY. All rights reserved. http://www.amanet.org.

The preparation of recruiting advertisements is not only time-consuming, it also requires creativity in developing design and message content. Well-written advertisements highlight the major assets of the position while showing the responsiveness of the organization to the job and career needs of the applicants. Also, there appears to be a correlation between the accuracy and completeness of information provided in advertisements and the recruitment success of the organization. Among the information typically included in advertisements is that the recruiting organization is an equal opportunity employer.

Advertising can sometimes place a severe burden on an organization's employment office. Even though the specifications for the openings are described thoroughly in the advertisement, many applicants who know they do not meet the job requirements may still be attracted. They may apply with the hope that the employer will not be able to find applicants who do meet the specifications.

## Unsolicited Applications and Resumes

Many employers receive unsolicited applications and resumes from individuals who may or may not be good prospects for employment.[29] Even though the percentage of acceptable applicants from this source may not be high, it is a source that cannot be ignored. In fact, it is often believed that individuals who on their own initiative contact the employer will be better employees than those recruited through college placement services or newspaper advertisements.

Good public relations dictate that any person contacting an organization for a job be treated with courtesy and respect. If there is no possibility of employment in the organization at present or in the future, the applicant should be tactfully and frankly informed of this fact. Telling an applicant to "fill out an application, and we will keep it on file," when there is no hope for their employment, is not fair to the applicant.

## Using the Internet

According to IDC, a Massachusetts-based technology market research firm, 96 percent of all companies will use the Internet for recruitment needs within a few years. While still relatively new, web-based recruiting is not more expensive. Estimates from the Employee Management Association are that the cost per hire is about $377 versus $3,295 per hire using print media.[30] There are a variety of web sites available where applicants can submit their resumes and potential employers can check for qualified applicants. Estimates are that over 2,500 web sites exist that contain job postings, and over 1.5 million resumes are currently on line. Highlights in HRM 4 shows a list of some of the most useful sites.[31]

## Employee Referrals

The recruitment efforts of an organization can be aided by employee referrals, or recommendations made by current employees. Managers have found that the quality of employee-referred applicants is normally quite high, since employees are generally hesitant to recommend individuals who might not perform well. Keith Swenson, a human resources consultant with William M. Mercer, suggests several ways to increase the effectiveness of employee referral programs.

- *Up the ante.* Companies pay high commissions to employment agencies and search firms, so why not do the same thing with employees when they provide a good referral? Other recruitment incentives used by organizations include complimentary dinners, discounts on merchandise, all-expense-paid trips, and free insurance. By paying higher bonuses for "hot" skills, employees are more likely to focus on people they know in that area.

- *Pay for performance.* It is sometimes a good idea to save part of the referral bonus until the new hire has stayed for six months. This encourages referring employees to help the new hires succeed.

- *Tailor the program.* Companies typically need more of certain type of skills than others, but the referral programs do not always reflect this. Part of a good referral program is educating employees about the kinds of people the organization wants to hire. This includes some communication of the skills required, but also a reaffirmation of the values and ethics sought in applicants.

- *Increase visibility.* One of the best ways to publicize a referral program is to celebrate successes. Some companies use novel approaches such as "job of the month" or "celebrity endorsements" from managers. The idea is to keep everyone thinking about bringing in good people.

**HRM 4**

HIGHLIGHTS IN HRM

# Hot Recruiting Sites

**Career Builder:** www.careerbuilder.com carries its own listings and offers links to sixteen specialized career sites, including *Business Week*, developer.com, Phillips Business Information, and Women's Connection Online.

**CareerMosaic:** www.careermosaic.com is one of the web's largest general sites, with listings from leading corporations.

**CareerWeb:** www.cweb.com, another leading career resource cite, has thousands of job listings from hundreds of major companies.

**E.Span:** www.espan.com, one of the web's first recruiting sites, has also grown into one of the largest and best known.

**Hot Jobs:** www.hotjobs.com, a newer site, offers advanced management features and smart agents to streamline the recruiting process.

**JOBTRAK:** www.jobtrak.com, a leading college recruiting site, has more than 40,000 listings and links to 750 campuses in the United States.

**JobWeb:** www.jobweb.org, a college recruiting site run by the National Association of Colleges and Employers, has more than 1,600 member universities and 1,600 employers.

**The Monster Board:** www.monster.com is one of the oldest and largest general recruiting sites on the Internet, with more than 50,000 listings.

**Net-Temps:** www.nettemps.com, the web's leading site for recruiting temps, has more than 75,000 listings.

**Online Career Center:** www.occ.com, a general recruiting site, attracts leading employers.

**jobEngine:** www.jobengine.com is a job-posting and resume-search site for computer-industry professionals.

- *Keep the data.* Even if a referral does not get the job, it might be a good idea to keep the resume on file just in case another vacancy arises.
- *Rethink your taboos.* Some companies are reluctant to take on certain potential hires, such as former employees, relatives, and the like. In a tight labor market, it is a good idea to broaden the search.
- *Widen the program.* Just as it may make sense to consider hiring former employees, it may make sense to ask them for referrals even if they are not candidates for the jobs themselves. Most companies have mailing lists of "corporate friends" that can be used to seek out potential candidates.

● *Measure results.* No surprise here. After the program is implemented, managers need to take a hard look at the volume of referrals, the qualifications of candidates, and the success of new hires on the job. These results are then fed back to fine-tune the program.[32]

As noted above, there are some potential negative factors associated with employee referrals. They include the possibility of inbreeding and the violation of EEO regulations. Since employees and their referrals tend to have similar backgrounds, employers who rely heavily on employee referrals to fill job openings may intentionally or unintentionally screen out, and thereby discriminate against, protected classes. Furthermore, organizations may choose not to employ relatives of current employees. The practice of hiring relatives, referred to as **nepotism,** can invite charges of favoritism, especially in appointments to desirable positions.[33]

**Nepotism**
A preference for hiring relatives of current employees

### Executive Search Firms

In contrast to public and private employment agencies, which help jobseekers find the right job, executive search firms (often called "headhunters") help employers find the right person for a job. Firms such as Korn/Ferry, Heidrick and Struggles, Delta Consulting, and the Hunter Group seek out candidates with qualifications that match the requirements of the positions their client firm is seeking to fill. Executive search firms do not advertise in the media for job candidates, nor do they accept a fee from the individual being placed.

The fees charged by search firms may range from 30 to 40 percent of the annual salary for the position to be filled. For the recruitment of senior executives, this fee is paid by the client firm, whether or not the recruiting effort results in a hire. It is for this practice that search firms receive the greatest criticism.

Nevertheless, as noted earlier, it is an increasingly common occurrence that new chief executive officers (CEOs) are brought in from outside the organization. A large

"How do you do, sir? My name is
John L. Flagman, and I run a successful
executive search firm."

From *The Wall Street Journal*—Permission, Cartoon Features Syndicate number of these new CEOs are placed in those positions through the services of an executive search firm. Since high-caliber executives are in short supply, a significant number of the nation's largest corporations, including BMW, Texaco, Pillsbury, MONEY Financial Services, as well as the Rockefeller Foundation, use search firms to fill their top positions. Recently, when London-based Dunlop Slazenger Corporation wanted to replace the top executives in its Maxfli business unit, it used an executive search firm to lure Bill Olsen and Edward Hughes. The tactic was designed to revitalize sales from Maxfli's position as the third largest golf-ball manufacturer.[34]

Figure 4.10 shows the results of a study by McKinsey and Company that investigated the key factors that determine the likelihood executives would want to work for a particular company.

### Educational Institutions

Educational institutions typically are a source of young applicants with formal training but with relatively little full-time work experience. High schools are usually a source of employees for clerical and blue-collar jobs. Community colleges, with their various types of specialized training, can provide candidates for technical jobs. These institutions can also be a source of applicants for a variety of white-

FIGURE 4.10

**Factors That Motivate Top Talent**

Working for a great company and having a great job are more important to most executives than compensation.

**Great company (brand)**

| | |
|---|---|
| Values and culture | 58% |
| Well managed | 50% |
| Exciting challenges | 38% |
| Strong performance | 29% |
| Industry leader | 21% |
| Many talented people | 20% |
| Good at development | 17% |
| Inspiring mission | 16% |
| Fun with colleagues | 11% |
| Job security | 8% |

**Great jobs (products)**

| | |
|---|---|
| Freedom and autonomy | 56% |
| Exciting challenges | 51% |
| Career advancement and growth | 39% |
| Fit with boss I admire | 29% |

**Compensation and lifestyle (price)**

| | |
|---|---|
| Differentiated compensation | 29% |
| High total compensation | 23% |
| Geographic location | 19% |
| Respect for lifestyle | 14% |
| Acceptable pace and stress | 1% |

*Each number represents the percentage of the top 200 executives who agreed each factor was important.

Source: E.G. Chambers, H. Hanafield-Jones, S. M. Hankin, and E. G. Michaels, III, "Win the War for Top Talent," *Workforce* 77 no. 12 (December 1998): 50–56. Used with permission of McKinsey & Co.

collar jobs, including those in the sales and retail fields. Some management-trainee jobs are also staffed from this source.

For technical and managerial positions, colleges and universities are generally the primary source. However, the suitability of college graduates for open positions often depends on their major field of study. Organizations seeking applicants in the technical and professional areas, for example, are currently faced with a shortage of qualified candidates. To attract graduates in areas of high demand, managers employ innovative recruitment techniques such as work-study programs, internships, low-interest loans, and scholarships. Figure 4.11 shows which college graduates tend to be in highest and lowest demand as well as the top starting salaries for new graduates.

Some employers fail to take full advantage of college and university resources because of a poor recruitment program.[35] Consequently, their recruitment efforts fail to attract many potentially good applicants. Another common weakness is the failure to maintain a planned and continuing effort on a long-term basis. Furthermore, some recruiters sent to college campuses are not sufficiently trained or prepared to talk to interested candidates about career opportunities or the requirements of specific openings. Attempts to visit too many campuses instead of concentrating on selected institutions and the inability to use the campus placement office effectively are other recruiting weaknesses. Mismanagement of applicant visits to the organization's headquarters and the failure to follow up on individual prospects or to obtain hiring commitments from higher management are among other mistakes that have caused employers to lose well-qualified prospects.

### *Professional Organizations*

Many professional organizations and societies offer a placement service to members as one of their benefits. Listings of members seeking employment may be advertised in their journals or publicized at their national meetings. A placement center is usually established at national meetings for the mutual benefit of employers and jobseekers. The Society for Human Resource Management, for example, helps employers and prospective HR employees come together.

### *Labor Unions*

Labor unions can be a principal source of applicants for blue-collar and some professional jobs. Some unions, such as those in the maritime, printing, and construction industries, maintain hiring halls that can provide a supply of applicants, particularly for short-term needs. Employers wishing to use this recruitment source should contact the local union under consideration for employer-eligibility requirements and applicant availability.

### *Public Employment Agencies*

Each of the fifty states maintains an employment agency that is responsible for administering its unemployment insurance program. Many of the state agencies bear such titles as Department of Employment or Department of Human Resources. They are subject to certain regulations and controls administered by the U.S. Employment Service (USES).

State agencies maintain local public employment offices in most communities of any size. Individuals who become unemployed must register at one of these offices and be available for "suitable employment" in order to receive their weekly unemployment checks. Consequently, public employment

**USING THE INTERNET**

The computerized job bank is called America's Job Bank and can be used to access all of the individual state employment agencies:

www.ajb.dni.us/

**Best and Worst Majors for Job-Hunting Graduates**

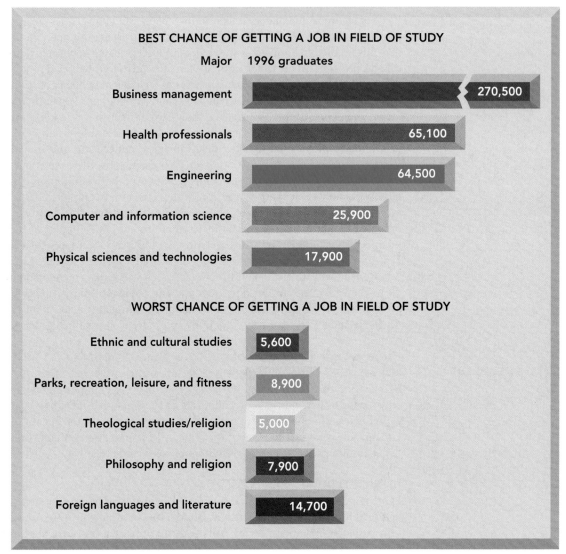

*(continued)*

agencies are able to refer to employers with job openings those applicants with the required skills who are available for employment.

USES has developed a nationwide computerized job bank that lists job openings, and state employment offices are connected to this job bank. The computerized job bank helps facilitate the movement of job applicants to different geographic areas. Most of these offices now have a local job-bank book that is published as a daily computer printout. Employer openings are listed along with other pertinent information, such as number of openings, pay rates, and job specifications. The local job bank makes it possible for employment interviewers in an agency to have a list of all job openings in the geographic area for which applicants assigned to

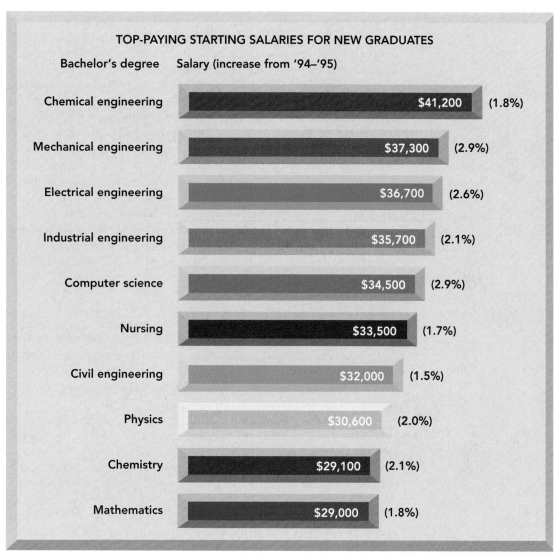

**TOP-PAYING STARTING SALARIES FOR NEW GRADUATES**

| Bachelor's degree | Salary (increase from '94–'95) | |
|---|---|---|
| Chemical engineering | $41,200 | (1.8%) |
| Mechanical engineering | $37,300 | (2.9%) |
| Electrical engineering | $36,700 | (2.6%) |
| Industrial engineering | $35,700 | (2.1%) |
| Computer science | $34,500 | (2.9%) |
| Nursing | $33,500 | (1.7%) |
| Civil engineering | $32,000 | (1.5%) |
| Physics | $30,600 | (2.0%) |
| Chemistry | $29,100 | (2.1%) |
| Mathematics | $29,000 | (1.8%) |

Source: Patrick Scheetz, Employment Research Institute, Michigan State University. From *USA Today*, Wednesday, May 29, 1996, 11B. Copyright 1996, *USA Today*. Reprinted with permission.

them might qualify. Furthermore, applicants looking for a specific job can review the computer printout and apply directly to the organization having the opening.

In addition to matching unemployed applicants with job openings, public employment agencies may assist employers with employment testing, job analysis, evaluation programs, and community wage surveys.

### Private Employment Agencies

Charging a fee enables private employment agencies to tailor their services to the specific needs of their clients. Snelling Personnel Services, Manpower, Kelly Services, and Olsten Staffing Services are among the largest private employment agencies. However, it is common for agencies to specialize in serving a specific occupational area or professional field. MacTemps, for example, specializes in providing businesses with the computer experts they need and in helping skilled employees find temporary and permanent positions. (For more on temporary help, see below.) Depending upon who is receiving the most service, the fee may be paid by either the employer or the jobseeker or both. It is not uncommon for private employment agencies to charge an employer a 25 to 30 percent fee, based on the position's annual salary, if they hire an applicant found by the agency.

Private employment agencies differ in the services they offer, their professionalism, and the caliber of their counselors. If counselors are paid on a commission basis, their desire to do a professional job may be offset by their desire to earn a commission. Thus they may encourage jobseekers to accept jobs for which they are not suited. Because of this, jobseekers would be wise to take the time to find a recruiter who is knowledgeable, experienced, and professional. When talking with potential recruiters, individuals should discuss openly their philosophies and practices with regard to recruiting strategies, including advertising, in-house recruiting, screening procedures, and costs for these efforts. They should try to find a recruiter who is flexible and who will consider their needs and wants.[36]

### Temporary Help Agencies

The temporary services industry is one of the fastest-growing recruitment sources. The number of people working as temporary employees has increased by almost 300 percent over the past decade (to nearly 2 million employees), and today there are over 7,000 temporary employment agencies. Because of these large increases, temporary services were among the strongest employers through the 1990s and are certain to continue as such in the new century.[37]

It is estimated that nine out of ten U.S. companies make some use of temporary employees. These include both large and small firms. "Temps" are typically used for short-term assignments or to help when managers cannot justify hiring a full-time employee, such as for vacation fill-ins, for peak work periods, or during an employee's pregnancy leave or sick leave. Increasingly, temps are being employed to fill positions once staffed by permanent employees. This practice is growing because temporaries can be laid off quickly, and with less cost, when work lessens. Some companies use a just-in-time staffing approach where a core staff of employees is augmented by a trained and highly skilled supplementary workforce. The use of temporaries thus becomes a viable way to maintain proper staffing levels. Also, the employment costs of temporaries are often lower than those of permanent employees because temps are not provided with benefits and can be dismissed without the need to file unemployment insurance claims. Used predominantly in office clerical positions, temporaries are becoming more and more common in legal work, engineering, computer programming, and other jobs requiring advanced professional training.[38]

### Employee Leasing

**Employee leasing**

Process of dismissing employees who are then hired by a leasing company (which handles all HR-related activities) and contracting with that company to lease back the employees

**Employee leasing** has become popular since 1982 with passage of the Tax Equity and Fiscal Responsibility Act. National Staff Network, Staff Services, Inc., and Action Staffing are three of a rapidly growing number of employee-leasing firms, also known as Professional Employment Organizations (PEOs). Unlike temporary help agencies, which supply workers only for limited periods, employee-leasing companies place their employees with subscribers on a permanent basis. Figure 4.12 shows the growth of PEOs from 1984 to 1996.

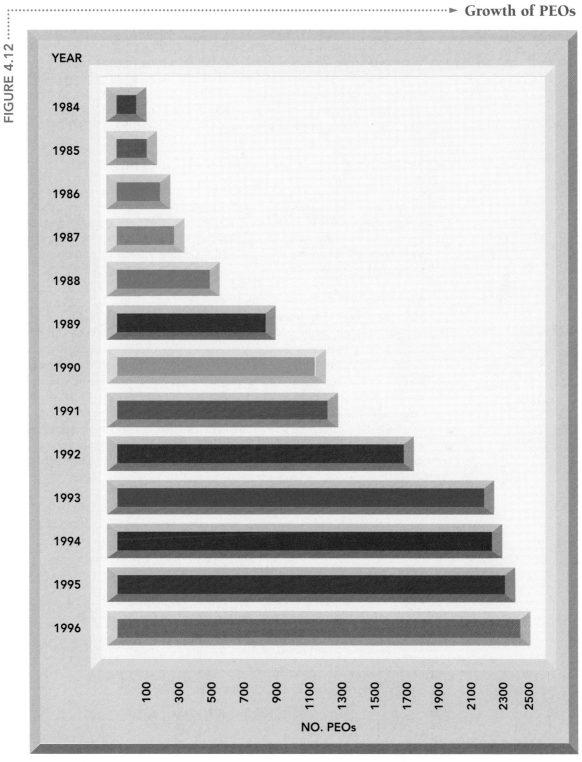

FIGURE 4.12 ···· Growth of PEOs

Source: Carolyn Hirschman, "All Aboard!" *HRMagazine* 42, no. 9 (September 1997): 80–85. Reprinted with the permission of *HRMagazine*, published by the Society for Human Resource Management, Alexandria, Va.

In its most common form, employee leasing is a process whereby an employer terminates a number of employees who are then hired by a third party—the PEO—which then leases the employees back to the original organization. However, PEOs also hire workers on a continual basis and then lease them to requesting organizations. The leasing company performs all the HR duties of an employer—hiring, payroll, performance appraisal, benefits administration, and other day-to-day HR activities—and in return is paid a placement fee of normally 2 to 5 percent of payroll cost plus 9 to 20 percent of gross wages to cover benefits and the PEO's profit.[39]

## Improving the Effectiveness of External Recruitment

With all of the uncertainties inherent in external recruiting, it is sometimes difficult to determine whether or not an organization's efforts to locate promising talent are effective and/or cost-efficient. However, there are several things that managers can do to maximize the probability of success. These include calculating yield ratios on recruiting sources, training organizational recruiters, and conducting realistic job previews.

### Yield Ratios

**Yield ratio**

Percentage of applicants from a recruitment source that make it to the next stage of the selection process

Yield ratios help indicate which recruitment sources are most effective at producing qualified job candidates. Quite simply, a **yield ratio** is the percentage of applicants from a particular source that make it to the next stage in the selection process. For example, if 100 resumes were obtained from an employment agency, and 17 of the applicants submitting those resumes were invited for an on-site interview, the yield ratio for that agency would be 17 percent (17/100). This yield ratio could then be recalculated for each subsequent stage in the selection process (e.g., after the interview and again after the final offer), which would result in a cumulative yield ratio. By calculating and comparing yield ratios for each recruitment source, it is possible to find out which sources produce qualified applicants.

### Costs of Recruitment

The cost of various recruiting procedures can be computed using a fairly simple set of calculations. For example, the average source cost per hire (SC/H) can be determined by the following formula:

$$\frac{SC}{H} = \frac{AC + AF + RB + NC}{H}$$

where  AC = advertising costs, total monthly expenditure (example: \$28,000)
 AF = agency fees, total for the month (example: \$19,000)
 RB = referral bonuses, total paid (example: \$2,300)
 NC = no-cost hires, walk-ins, nonprofit agencies, etc. (example: \$0)
 H = total hires (example: 119)

Substituting the example numbers into the formula gives

$$\frac{SC}{H} = \frac{\$28,000 + \$19,000 + \$2,300 + \$0}{119}$$

$$= \frac{\$49,300}{119}$$

$$= \$ 414 \text{ (source cost of recruits per hire)}$$

### *Organizational Recruiters*

Who performs the recruitment function depends mainly on the size of the organization. For large employers, professional HR recruiters are hired and trained to find new employees. In smaller organizations, recruitment may be done by an HR generalist; or if the organization has no HR position, recruitment may be carried out by managers and/or supervisors. At companies like Macy's and Microsoft, members of work teams take part in the selection of new team members.

Regardless of who does the recruiting, it is imperative that these individuals have a good understanding of the knowledge, skills, abilities, experiences, and other characteristics required for the job. All too often, a new person in the HR department or a line manager may be given a recruitment assignment, even before that person has been given interview training, before he or she fully understands the job, and before he or she fully comprehends the values and goals of the organization.

It is important to remember that recruiters have an influence on an applicant's job decision. Because recruiters can often enhance the perceived attractiveness of a job and an organization, they are often a main reason why applicants select one organization over another. On this basis we can conclude that personable, enthusiastic, and competent recruiters have an impact on the success of an organization's recruitment program.

### *Realistic Job Previews*

**Realistic job preview (RJP)**
Informing applicants about all aspects of the job, including both its desirable and undesirable facets

Another way organizations may be able to increase the effectiveness of their recruitment efforts is to provide job applicants with a **realistic job preview (RJP).** An RJP informs applicants about all aspects of the job, including both its desirable and undesirable facets. In contrast, a typical job preview presents the job in only positive terms. The RJP may also include a tour of the working area, combined with a discussion of any negative health or safety considerations. Proponents of the RJP believe that applicants who are given realistic information regarding a position are more likely to remain on the job and be successful, because there will be fewer unpleasant surprises. In fact, a number of research studies on RJP report these positive results:

- Improved employee job satisfaction
- Reduced voluntary turnover
- Enhanced communication through honesty and openness
- Realistic job expectations[40]

Like other HR techniques, however, RJPs must be tailored to the needs of the organization and should include a balanced presentation of positive and negative job information.

# Recruiting Protected Classes

In meeting their legal obligation to provide equal employment opportunity, employers often develop a formal EEO/AA program. An essential part of any EEO/AA policy must be an affirmative effort to recruit members of protected classes. The steps the EEOC recommends for organizations to follow in developing such a program were discussed in Chapter 2.

## Recruitment of Women

Women constitute the largest number among the protected classes. In 1995, they accounted for over 46 percent of all workers and 48 percent of all positions in management and professional occupations—a dramatic increase from 34 percent in the 1980s.[41] Women will be the major source of new entrants into the U.S. labor force over the next decade. They will make up 62 percent of the net labor-force growth, or 15 million workers, by the year 2005. Within this group, women of Hispanic and Asian origin will increase their labor-force participation by 80 percent between 1990 and 2005. However, even with the large numbers of women in the labor force, employers today often have difficulty in recruiting women for clerical, secretarial, and other jobs in which they have traditionally been employed. Furthermore, women still encounter barriers to landing the better-paying jobs that have been traditionally performed by men, particularly in rising to positions of top managerial responsibility.[42]

Contrary to a once-common belief, most women do not go to work merely to "get out of the house" or to fulfill psychological needs. Like men, they work for varying reasons, but primarily because of economic necessity. In recent years, over 60 percent of all women in the workforce have been responsible for supporting themselves, and three out of five of them are heads of households. While approximately 59 percent of all women work, the participation rate of working mothers is significantly higher. Almost 80 percent of mothers with school-age children (that is, ages 6 to 17) are employed in some capacity. In many cases, these women have the employment disadvantage of having completed, on average, fewer years of school than married women not in the workforce, and they are concentrated in lower-skilled, lower-paying jobs.[43]

A major employment obstacle for women is the stereotyped thinking that persists within our society. Still another barrier has been that women in the past were not as likely as men to have professional training and preparation for entrance or advancement into management positions. This situation is changing, however, with a significant increase in the enrollment of women in programs leading to degrees in management. In addition, more women are enrolling in management seminars and certification programs that will further prepare them for higher managerial positions.

As a consequence of these changes, an increasing number of women enter the labor force in managerial positions. Today women account for 43 percent of all managers and some of these are finally cracking the upper echelons of business. A recent Korn/Ferry survey found that 81 percent of all *Fortune* 500 companies have at least one female director. But overall there is a good deal more that can be done—only 9 percent of executive vice presidents in *Fortune* 1000 companies are women.[44] Highlights in HRM 5 shows a list of the top companies for women as compiled by *Working Woman* magazine.

## Recruitment of Minorities

Since the passage of the Civil Rights Act of 1964, many members of minority groups have been able to realize a substantial improvement in their social and economic well-being. Increasing numbers of blacks and Hispanics are now in the upper income-tax brackets by virtue of their entrance into professional, engineering, and managerial positions. However, the proportion of minorities in these areas is still substantially below their proportions in the total population. Unemployment among

**HRM 5**

HIGHLIGHTS IN HRM

# The Numbers Don't Lie

| | EMPLOYEES WORLDWIDE | | WOMEN ON BOARD OF DIRECTORS | PERCENTAGE OF WOMEN CORPORATE VP'S AND ABOVE | PERCENTAGE OF WOMAN MANAGERS | REVENUES 1997 |
|---|---|---|---|---|---|---|
| | Total | % of woman | | | | |
| 1. Avon Products | 8,100* | 70* | 6(46%) | 31.6* | 49.8* | $5.1 Bil |
| 2. Fannie Mae Corp. | 3,700 | 54 | 5(27.7%) | 56 | 50 | $27.8 Bil |
| 3. Pitney Bowes | 32,000 | 38 | 2(18.2%) | 58.3** | 24 | $4.1 Bil |
| 4. Procter & Gamble | 106,000 | 30.2 | 2(28.5%) | 8 | 31* | $35.8 Bil |
| 5. Gannett Co. | 39,000 | 46.1 | 3(33.3%) | 28.6 | 39.4 | $4.7 Bil |
| 6. Scholastic | 6,192 | 64.6 | 3(18.7%) | 45.4 | 61 | $966 Mil |
| 7. Gap | 80,000 | 71.6 | 2(16.6%) | 39.7 | 81.2 | $6.5 Bil |
| 8. Knight Ridder | 22,000 | 43 | 3(21.4%) | 27.7 | 28 | $2.9 Bil |
| 9. Nordstrom | 39,000 | 72 | 2(18%) | 38.8 | 71 | $4.9 Bil |
| 10. Sallie Mae | 4,205 | 68.6 | 3(20%) | 35.9 | 32.3 | $3.8 Mil |
| 11. Home Savings of America | 10,057 | 69.8 | 2(13.3%) | 32 | 58.8 | $3.73 Bil |
| 12. IBM Corp. | 269,000 | 29.3 | 2(18%) | 12.9 | 25.4* | $78.5 Bil |
| 13. Aetna | 28,000 | 73 | 4(33.3%) | 20.8 | 60 | $18.54 Bil |
| 14. Kelly Services | 6,000 | 80 | 1(20%)† | 38.7 | 78 | $3.85 Bil |
| 15. American Express Co. | 46,270* | 67* | 2(15.4%) | 32.7* | 54* | $17.7 Bil |
| 16. Dayton Hudson | 230,000 | 69 | 3(27%) | 25.9 | 51 | $27.76 Bil |
| 17. Merck & Co. | 32,527* | 52.8* | 2(15.3%) | 23.3 | 32 | $23.6 Bil |
| 18. Sara Lee Corp. | 141,000 | 57.5 | 2(11.1%) | 19 | 26 | $19.7 Bil |
| 19. Xerox Corp. | 50,000* | 33* | 3(21.4%) | 11.4 | 28* | $18.2 Bil |
| 20. Colgate-Palmolive Co. | 38,000 | 37 | 2(22%) | 9.3 | 30 | $9.05 Bil |
| 21. Johnson & Johnson | 90,500 | 49 | 3(23%) | 15.9 | 34 | $22.63 Bil |
| 22. Cigna | 48,000 | 74 | 2(18%) | 18.2 | 52 | $20 Bil |
| 23. Lincoln National Corp. | 8,300 | 70 | 2(16.6%) | 60 | 21 | $4.9 Bil |
| 24. Hannaford Bros. | 23,700 | 54 | 2(16.6%) | 25 | 28.9 | $3.2 Bil |
| 25. Bristol-Myers Squibb Co. | 53,000 | 49.7 | 2(18%) | 15.5 | 33.3 | $16.7 Bil |

*U.S. only
**VPs and above who report to chairman
†Company included because one woman represents 20 percent of the board, twice the national average

First appeared in *WORKING WOMAN*, September 1998. Written by Joanne Cleaver. Reprinted with the permission of MacDonald Communications Corporation. Copyright © 1999 by MacDonald Communications Corporation. www.workingwoman.com. For subscriptions call 1-800-234-9675.

**Read about the leadership development programs at Lockheed Martin's many businesses:**

www.careermosaic.com/cm/lockheed/lockheed53.html

minorities, particularly the youth, continues to be at a critically high level. Undoubtedly, these rates are considerably higher during periods of economic downturn when employment opportunities become harder to find.

For many minorities (who often live in the inner cities) employment opportunities still remain exceedingly limited because of educational and societal disadvantages. Also, because their social environment can sometimes lie apart from the mainstream, traditional recruitment methods may prove ineffective in reaching them. Community action agencies, civil rights organizations, and church groups within the communities can provide a means for recruiters to reach inner-city residents. Special media advertising targeted to this group also may prove effective. Highlights in HRM 6 shows how to design a tailored approach to diversity planning.

Unless minorities can be retained within an organization, diversity programs are likely to prove ineffective. If minority employees are to be retained, they, like any employee, must be made to feel welcome in their jobs and to feel that their efforts contribute to the success of the organization.[45] To build ongoing relationships with prospective employees, several companies have increased their sponsorship of internship programs. For example, Gannett Company and TeleCommunications Inc (TCI) have made substantial contributions to the Emma L. Bowen Foundation, which provides internships, college scholarships, and postgraduate employment for minorities. The program mentors students from their junior year in high school through college graduation. In another effort, Lockheed Martin has teamed up with Operation Enterprise, the American Management Association's summer program for high school and college students, to offer ten-week paid internships to students of America's historically black colleges and universities. Similarly, Dun & Bradstreet sponsors a summer internship program for minority M.B.A. students. These internships provide a trial period in which both the student and the company can learn more about one another. Ideally, these internships turn into opportunities for full-time employment.[46]

## Recruitment of the Disabled

While discrimination and obstacles still exist, we see many more disabled people on the job than ever before. Currently, half of the 29 million disabled Americans between the ages of 21 and 64 are working. The participation rate of those that are severely disabled is lower (about 25 percent). Altogether, persons with disabilities account for 14 percent of the workforce. The greatest numbers have impairments that are hearing-, vision-, or back-related.

Of those that do not work, the majority would like to. These individuals have often been rejected for employment because of the mistaken belief that there were no jobs within an organization that they might be able to perform effectively. Fears that the disabled might have more accidents or that they might aggravate existing disabilities have also deterred their employment. The lack of special facilities for physically impaired persons, particularly those in wheelchairs, has been a further employment restriction. However, physical obstructions are being eliminated as employers are making federally legislated improvements to accommodate disabled workers.

Efforts to eliminate discrimination in hiring, promotion, and compensation of people with disabilities are expected to increase dramatically as organizations come into compliance with the Americans with Disabilities Act of 1990 (see Chapter 2). Thanks to federal regulations, many organizations are beginning to recognize that

HRM 6

# Steps in Diversity Planning

Like affirmative action plans, voluntary workforce diversity plans are often based on numerical standards for the employment of minorities and women. Numerical standards are a critical element in planning, because they give managers something to strive for and benchmarks for measuring success. To be successful, the standards must be both realistic—tailored to the company's essential qualifications for filling jobs—and based on sound figures indicating the availability of qualified candidates in the labor markets.

**Calculating Realistic and Obtainable Standards**

*Step 1: Set general qualifications.* In order to understand the workforce and the general qualifications applicants must have to fill a position, HR managers must address four important questions:

- How much experience do people in this position generally have?
- What education is ordinarily needed for this job?
- What salary is ordinarily paid for this job?
- From what geographic regions are workers ordinarily recruited?

*Step 2: Match positions to U.S. census categories.* The U.S. Bureau of the Census reports the percentage of workers in each race and sex group for 501 occupational categories. Match each position in the company to one of the 501 categories. Job description information helps make this matching easier.

*Step 3: Identify qualified workers.* Qualified workers are those with the education, location, experience, and current salary level who fall within the range required for each position. Since the objective is to maximize diversity, the pool of workers should not be overly restrictive here.

*Step 4: Calculate percentages.* For each position, calculate the percentage of workers in the qualified pool who are minorities and women. Compare this number with the percentages in the census categories.

*Step 5: Set numerical standards.* Using these data, calculate hiring standards for jobs, groups of jobs, and the overall business unit. Long-term diversity goals can then be determined by evaluating where the company should be at some future date.

Source: Adapted from David S. Evans and Miriam Y. Oh, "Diversity Planning," *HRMagazine*, June 1996, 127–34. Reprinted with the permission of *HR Magazine*, published by the Society for Human Resource Management, Alexandria, VA.

physical disabilities may constitute limitations only with respect to certain job requirements. An employee in a wheelchair who might not be able to perform duties that involve certain physical activities may be quite capable of working at a bench or a desk.

The Workforce Recruitment Program for College Students with Disabilities (WRP) puts together profiles of more than 1,000 college students and recent grad-

*This elementary school teacher is conducting a reading group with her students. In America, people with disabilities make up about 14 percent of the workforce.*

uates seeking summer internships or permanent employment nationwide. These profiles are then made available free of charge to business owners. The candidates are skilled in a wide variety of fields, and each has a disability. This effort to help employers find workers and the disabled find jobs is co-sponsored by the U.S. Department of Defense and the President's Committee on Employment of People with Disabilities.[47]

### Advantages of Employing Disabled Persons

The most frequently cited advantages of employing disabled persons include their dependability, superior attendance, loyalty, and low turnover. Employers often find disabled workers to be more intelligent, better motivated, and better qualified than their nondisabled counterparts. However, the superior performance attributed to disabled workers could also be the result of hidden biases toward them. These biases may cause employers to require that the disabled be overqualified for an entry-level job and to avoid promoting them above it.

### Less Publicized Disabilities

In addition to the widely recognized forms of disability, there are others that can limit hiring and advancement opportunities. One such disability is unattractiveness, against which employers can be biased even if unconsciously. "Unattractive" individuals are those whose facial features are considered unpleasant but who do not possess physical disfiguration that would put them in the physically disabled category. Another less publicized disability in gaining and retaining employment is obesity. In some cases, courts have held obesity to be a legitimate physical disability. However, in December of 1998, the New York State Court of Appeals ruled that the use of weight standards as part of an employer's hiring criteria is not necessarily discriminatory. The case, *Delta Air Lines v New York State Division of Human Rights,* was brought by ten former Pam Am flight attendants who had hoped to work for Delta when it acquired Pan Am in 1991. Among their claims: Delta's weight standards were discriminatory and its preemployment questions about age, physical impairments, and other sensitive issues were illegal. New York's highest court unanimously ruled to the contrary.[48]

Finally, there is the disability of illiteracy. It is estimated that 90 million Americans demonstrate low literacy—that means about 47 percent of the adult population have only limited reading and writing abilities needed to handle the minimal demands of daily living or job performance.[49] Employers are encountering increasing numbers of employees, including college graduates, whose deficient reading and writing skills limit their performance on the job. A recent survey of *Fortune* 1000 CEOs found that 90 percent recognized the problems of illiteracy—yet just 38 percent acknowledged that it was a problem for their workers.[50]

The U.S. Department of Labor estimates that illiteracy costs U.S. businesses $225 billion a year in lost productivity. To address literacy problems, companies such as Magnavox, Motorola, and the City of Phoenix have instituted basic-skill-assessment programs and have begun teaching reading, math, and communication skills to employees who show some level of deficiency. The City of Phoenix has been recognized recently for instituting the Workplace Skills and Literacy Program for its basic-skills-seeking employees.[51]

## Recruitment of Older Persons

As previously noted, there is a definite trend by organizations to hire more older persons. The move has come as a result of changing workforce demographics and a change in the attitudes of employers and employees. Organizations realize that older workers have proven employment experience, have job "savvy," and are reliable employees. Older individuals are an excellent recruitment source to staff part-time and full-time positions otherwise hard to fill.

As the demand for skilled employees increases, organizations are offering flexible work schedules, better benefits, and additional training to attract older workers.[52] To recruit older workers, Home Shopping Network, the twenty-four-hour-a-day cable television company, located its headquarters in Florida where there are many retired people who need and want a little extra income. In 1990 the company established Prime Timer, a program that invites people over 55 to become part of their workforce. It systematically seeks out seniors and encourages them to join by offering flexible policies and part-time jobs. The company's HR director, Mount Burns, worked with the chamber of commerce and senior citizens' associations such as AARP (American Association of Retired Persons) to identify potential applicants. The Prime Timer program has been very successful, and more than 500 people have gone through the company's training program. According to Burns, the Prime Timers had a 30 percent lower turnover rate than other hires.[53] Figure 4.13 shows the results of a recent Conference Board survey that illustrates that the benefits of recruiting older workers often outweigh the costs.

FIGURE 4.13

## Perceived Benefits and Liabilities of Employing Older Workers

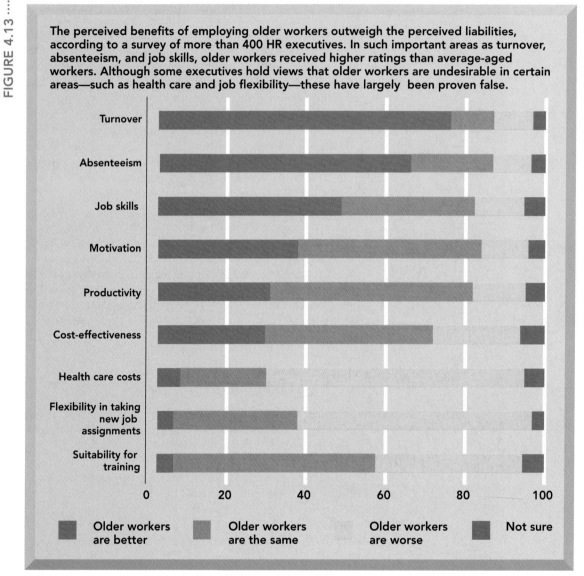

The perceived benefits of employing older workers outweigh the perceived liabilities, according to a survey of more than 400 HR executives. In such important areas as turnover, absenteeism, and job skills, older workers received higher ratings than average-aged workers. Although some executives hold views that older workers are undesirable in certain areas—such as health care and job flexibility—these have largely been proven false.

Source: The Conference Board, "Availability of a Quality Work Force," Personnel Journal, October 1995, 60. Used with permission of the Conference Board.

## SUMMARY

**OBJECTIVE 1**   As organizations plan for their future, top management and strategic planners must recognize that strategic-planning decisions affect—and are affected by—HR functions. On the one hand, HRP plays a reactive role in making certain the right number and type of employees are available to implement a chosen business plan. On the other hand, HRP can proactively identify and initiate programs needed to develop organizational capabilities upon which future strategies can be built.

**OBJECTIVE 2**   HRP is a systematic process that involves forecasting demand for labor, performing supply analysis, and balancing supply and demand considerations. Forecasting demand requires using either quantitative or qualitative methods to identify the number and type of people needed to meet organizational objectives. Supply analysis involves determining if there are sufficient employees available within the organization to meet demand and also determining whether potential employees are available on the job market. Reconciling supply and demand requires a host of activities, including internal and external recruitment.

 Employers usually find it advantageous to use internal promotion and transfer to fill as many openings as possible above the entry level. By recruiting from within, an organization can capitalize on previous investments made in recruiting, selecting, training, and developing its current employees. Further, internal promotions can reward employees for past performance and send a signal to other employees that their future efforts will pay off. However, potential candidates from the outside should occasionally be considered in order to prevent the inbreeding of ideas and attitudes.

Filling jobs above the entry level often requires managers to rely upon outside sources. These outside sources are also utilized to fill jobs with special qualifications, to avoid excessive inbreeding, and to acquire new ideas and technology. Which outside sources and methods are used in recruiting will depend on the recruitment goals of the organization, the conditions of the labor market, and the specifications of the jobs to be filled.

The legal requirements governing EEO make it mandatory that employers exert a positive effort to recruit and promote members of protected classes so that their representation at all levels within the organization will approximate their proportionate numbers in the labor market. These efforts include recruiting not only those members who are qualified but also those who can be made qualified with reasonable training and assistance.

## KEY TERMS

cultural audits
employee leasing
human resources planning (HRP)
job posting and bidding
labor market
management forecasts

Markov analysis
nepotism
organizational capability
realistic job preview (RJP)
replacement charts
skill inventories

staffing tables
succession planning
trend analysis
yield ratio

## DISCUSSION QUESTIONS

 1. Identify the three key elements of the human resources planning model and discuss the relationships among them.

 2. Distinguish between the quantitative and the qualitative approaches to forecasting the need for human resources.

 3. What are the advantages and disadvantages of filling openings from internal sources?

 4. In what ways do executive search firms differ from the traditional employment agencies?

 5. Explain how realistic job previews (RJPs) operate. Why do they appear to be an effective recruitment technique?

 6. Discuss some of the employment problems faced by members of protected classes.

## Human Resources Planning at Donna Karan International

Facing a challenge is one thing. Meeting it head-on is another. In 1997, New York City–based Donna Karan International experienced disappointing profits. As a young, fast-growing company, it had not always built its organization in the most profitable, efficient manner. Executives were forced to reevaluate the company's core operating groups' functions and relationships. Its new three-year strategic plan included a major downsizing driven by the reduction of the number of divisions from thirteen to six. Donna Karan also streamlined the company's senior management structure and made each of the six divisions fully integrated operating units. Below, HR vice president Christina Nichols discusses how her department is helping accomplish all of the changes.

*Q: What factors drove the recent downsizing?*

CN:  We're a very young company that has experienced tremendous rapid growth. When you grow very quickly, you don't always grow in the most profitable and efficient manner. So we made a difficult decision: to stop, evaluate what we've done, and readjust where necessary.

*Q: Which employees were the most impacted and why?*

CN:  It's interesting. I've been with the company for almost six years and have been through a few other "downsizing" efforts. Typically there had been a target percentage to be cut in each division. This time around, however, the downsizing was driven by actual restructuring within divisions in an effort to impact efficiency and cost savings.

Another significant impact on the restructuring was our entrance into strategic alliances with other companies. This included the licensing of the company's beauty business to The Estee Lauder Companies Inc., DKNY jeanswear and activewear products to Liz Claiborne, and DKNY Kids to Esprit de Corp. The employees impacted were from all levels of our population.

*Q: What were the HR implications?*

CN:  The restructuring process was draining to say the least! We were working with John Idol, our new CEO, trying to determine what the new structure would look like, trying to compile all the pertinent information for those employees who would be affected, coordinating outplacement services, and trying to coach management through the process. In the end, we managed to pull together as a team to make it happen successfully.

The aftermath of the restructuring process brings with it many new challenges. The employee population is dealing with the shock of losing co-workers, the stress of handling more responsibilities, and the uncertainty of their own job security. Responding to these concerns is difficult.

When we went through the restructuring process, we eliminated many jobs because of the decision to license various products. This was a fairly new direction for the company. You need to become the expert on the licensee's business so you can best educate the Donna Karan employees who will transition over [to working with them]. It's difficult to ensure that employees who transition to the licensee maintain the same level of compensation and benefits. It's a tough process because it doesn't end once the employees move over to the licensee's [work environment]. The role we play in this process already has evolved from working within the existing framework and facilitating the process to championing what's best for the employee.

*Q: What has been one of your most recent innovations with Human Resources?*

CN: I would say it has been the creation of the team I work with in human resources. This is the most talented group of people I have ever had the fortune to work with . . . and I'm a believer that you're only as good as your team.

With all the changes in the company, from the arrival of our new CEO to the restructure, the goals and focus of the human resources department have radically shifted to remain aligned with the company's direction. We've positioned ourselves as strategic business partners with the divisions in the company. We've evolved from putting out fires and creating policy to well-rounded business partners.

### QUESTIONS

1. How was the restructuring and downsizing process different for Donna Karan than for other firms?
2. How are survivors affected by the downsizing?
3. What have been the major challenges of the HR department at Donna Karan?

## Cisco Systems Goes to the Internet

The Internet is enjoying considerable buzz in corporate America these days. No longer relegated to the realm of techies, the Internet is being reframed as the new business tool. Of course, HR managers at Cisco Systems, based in San Jose, California, have known this for three years—the company is in the internetworking business. The midsized company, with 4,500 employees, began exploring how it could exploit the World Wide Web to better serve its internal and external customers way back in 1993. Two home pages were created: one to serve employees, the other to target people outside the company.

The internal home page is helping Cisco become a paperless company. It also allows employees to access a wide range of information, including a posting of available jobs. The external home page provides Internet explorers with information about the company and employment opportunities. When prospective employees click on the "Opportunities" button, they're treated to full job descriptions of open positions at Cisco. In addition, if Cisco is having difficulty filling a position, it may place the description under the rubric "Hot opportunities." In this section, which is limited to twenty descriptions, the openings are pitched with a more sales-minded, marketing approach.

Cisco hits all recruiting angles. A college page provides campus hopefuls with the dates and times that Cisco will hold job fairs at particular universities. Net surfers also can read about Cisco's mentoring and intern programs for college students. A culture page offers a little background on the firm: its compensation scales, benefits structure, and community-relations philosophy. Job listings are updated once a week and include information on how to fax or e-mail a resume. The company has corralled more than 20,000 active resumes in its database and receives another 50 to 75 from the Internet each day.

Like its internal counterpart, the external site saves HR a good deal of time: Resumes are automatically scanned in, and managers can conduct a key-word search rather than reading through piles of paper. For instance, if the company needs to hire an accountant, managers can type "ATM," and the computer will scan for all resumes containing the word "accountant." In addition to saving managers time, Internet recruiting yields higher-caliber candidates. According to Cisco's vice president of HR, Barbara Beck, "It provides a good method of self-selection. We're looking for people who are comfortable with technology, and those people are likely to be found on the Internet. This process is very inexpensive. It's better than a newspaper ad, where you get lots of resumes from people who may or may not have the kind of experience we're looking for."

Source: Condensed from "Cisco Systems' HR Is Wired for Success," *Personnel Journal*, January 1996, 59. Reprinted with permission.

## QUESTIONS

1. What advantages do you see in using the Internet to attract job candidates?
2. What potential problems need to be considered?
3. Would a system like this work for a wide range of companies of different sizes and in different industries?

# NOTES AND REFERENCES

1. Adam Lawrence, "Skill Shortage and Economic Pressures Combine to Hold Back Manufacturing," *Works Management* 51, no. 3 (August 1998): 14–17; D. A. Light, "Human Resources: Recruiting Generation 2001," *Harvard Business Review* 76, no. 4 (July/August 1998): 1316; Bill Leonard, "High Tech Boom Hits Labor Shortage Snag," *HRMagazine* 41, no. 1 (January 1996): 4; Patricia Martin, "Jobs Must Be Marketed," *Personnel Journal*, January 1996, 1–4.

2. Thomas J. Malott, "Creating Your Own Workforce: When You Need Skilled Workers, Will You Be Able to Find Them?" *Plan Engineering* 52, no. 7 (July 1998): 30–38; Eric Lofgren, "Workforce Management Is New Discipline for the Future," *Compensation and Benefits Management* 15, no. 1 (Winter 1999): 13–18; "Charting the Projections: 1994–2005," *Occupational Outlook Quarterly*, Fall 1995, 1–27.

3. Stephenie Overman, "Gearing Up for Tomorrow's Workforce," *HRFocus* 76, no. 2 (February 1999): 1, 15; Rick Mullin and Sylvia Pfeifer, "Hiring Becomes a Star Search," *Chemical Week* 159, no. 19 (May 14, 1997): 40–41; Douglas T. Hall, "Executive Careers and Learning: Aligning Selection, Strategy, and Development," *Human Resource Planning* 18, no. 2 (1995): 14–23.

4. Linda Gryton, "The New Rules of HR Strategy," *HRFocus* 75, no. 6 (June 1998): 13–14; Elaine McShulskis, "HR Failing to Tap the Future,"

*HRMagazine* 43, no. 1 (January 1998): 21; Bob Eichinger and Dave Ulrich, "Are You Future Agile?" *Human Resource Planning* 18, no. 4 (1996): 30–41.

5. Justin Hibard, "Web Service: Ready or Not," *Informationweek* 709 (November 16, 1998): 18–20; Dunstan Prial, "On-Line: Barnes & Noble Books: An IPO for Web Unit," *The Wall Street Journal*, August 21, 1998, B1; Chris Clark, "Trying to Sell Books over the Internet? Yeah, Right," *MC Technology Marketing Intelligence* 18, no. 8 (August 1998): 62.

6. Brian J. Smith, John W. Boroski, and George E. Davis, "Human Resource Planning," *Human Resource Management,* Spring/Summer 1992, 81–93. For other examples of how strategic planning and HRP are combined, see D. F. Beatty and F. M. K. Tampoe, "Human Resource Planning for ICL," *Long Range Planning* 23, no. 1 (1990): 17–28; Paul Michael Swiercz and Barbara A. Spencer, "HRM and Sustainable Competitive Advantage: Lessons from Delta Airlines," *Human Resource Planning* 15, no. 2 (1992): 35–46; Alan F. White, "Organizational Transformation at BP: An Interview with Chairman and CEO Robert Horton," *Human Resource Planning* 15, no. 1 (1992): 3–14.

7. James W. Walker, "Integrating the Human Resource Function with the Business," *Human Resource Planning* 14, no. 2 (1996): 59–77.

8. Patrick Wright, Gary McMahan, Scott Snell, and Barry Gerhart, *Strategic Human Resource Management: Building Human Capital and Organizational Capability,* technical report, Cornell University, Ithaca, N.Y., 1998; Arthur Yeung and Wayne Brockbank, "Lower Cost and Higher Value: Human Resource Function in Transformation," *Human Resource Planning* 17, no. 3 (1994): 1–16.

9. D. P. Lepak and S. A. Snell, "The Human Resource Architecture: Toward a Theory of Human Capital Development and Allocation," *Academy of Management Review* 24, no. 1 (1999): 31–48.

10. P. M. Wright and S. A. Snell, "Toward a Unifying Framework for Exploring Fit and Flexibility in Strategic Human Resource Management," *Academy of Management Review* 22, no. 4 (1998): 756–72.

11. Kotaro Kuwada, "Strategic Learning: The Continuous Side of Discontinuous Strategic Change," *Organization Science* 9, no. 6 (November/December 1998): 719–36; Dave Ulrich and Robert Eichinger, "Delivering HR with an Attitude," *HRMagazine* 43, no. 7 (June 1998): 154–60; Arthur Yeung and Bob Berman, "Adding Value through Human Resources: Reorienting Human Resources Measurement to Drive Business Performance," *Human Resource Management* 36, no. 3 (Fall 1997): 321–35.

12. R. Sanchez, "Strategic Flexibility in Product Competition," *Strategic Management Journal* 16 (1995): 135–59; Wright and Snell, "Toward a Unifying Framework."

13. Joseph Coates and Jennifer Jarratt, "The Future Is Now: A Review of a 1985 Forecast of HR Issues," *Employment Relations Today* 24, no. 4 (Winter 1998): 17–27; Abdalla Hagen and Sammy G. Amin, "Corporate Executives and Environmental Scanning Activities: An Empirical Examination," *Advanced Management Journal* 60, no. 2 (Spring 1995): 41–47.

14. Carolyn Walkup, "Companies Vie for Workers as Labor Pool Evaporates," *Nation's Restaurant News* 29, no. 8 (February 20, 1995): 1, 4.

15. Jennifer Laabs, "The HR Side of Sears' Comeback," *Workforce* 78, no. 3 (March 1999): 24–29; Odette Pollar, "A Diverse Workforce Requires Balanced Leadership," *Workforce* extra (December 1998): 4–5; Anthony Early, Jr., "A Passion for Personal Success," *Vital Speeches of the Day* 65, no. 6 (January 1, 1999): 184–87; Thomas Gilmore, Gregory Shea, and Michael Useem, "Side Effects of Corporate Cultural Transformations," *Journal of Applied Behavioral Science* 33, no. 2 (June 1997): 174–89.

16. James Ciecka, Thomas Donley, and Jerry Goldman, "A Markov Process Model of Work Life Expectancies Based on Labor Market Activity in 1994–95," *Journal of Legal Economics* 7, no. 1 (Spring 1997): 20–25; Oded Berman, Richard C. Larson and Edieal Pinker, "Scheduling Workforce and Workflow in a High Volume Factory," *Management Science* 43, no. 2 (February 1997): 158–72.

17. Robert Grossman, "Heirs Unapparent," *HRMagazine* 44, no. 2 (February 1999): 36–44.

18. For example, see U.S. Department of Labor, Bureau of Labor Statistics, *Geographic Profiles of Employment and Unemployment,* an annual bulletin. The data and information are accessible via the Office of Employment Projections home page at http://stats.bls.gov/emphome.htm.

19. "The Outlook for College Graduates, 1996–2006: Prepare Yourself," *Occupational Outlook Quarterly,* Summer 1998, 3–9.

20. Matt Murray, "KeyCorp Slashing Work Force, Branches," *The Wall Street Journal,* November 26, 1996, A2; Bruce Orwell, "Lockheed Martin to Close Eight Sites, Cut 1600 Jobs in Streamlining Effort," *The Wall Street Journal,* November 19, 1996, A2.

21. "The Rebirth of IBM: Blue Is the Colour," *The Economist* 347, no. 8071 (June 6, 1998): 65–68; Ronald Henkoff, "Getting beyond Downsizing," *Fortune,* January 10, 1994, 58–64; Susan Caminiti, "What Happens to Laid-Off Managers?" *Fortune,* June 13, 1994;

68–78; Del Jones, "Kodak to Eliminate 10,000 Jobs by '96," *USA Today,* August 19, 1993, B1; Tim Jones, "Retooling Unleashes Huge Wave of Layoffs," *Chicago Tribune,* June 22, 1994, 11.

22. "Nucor Adds Management Layer, Might Consider Acquisitions," *Iron Age New Steel* 15, no. 1 (January 1999): 8; Mike Troy, "Scott, Coughlin Set to Lead Wal-Mart," *Discount Store News* 38, no. 2 (January 25, 1999): 1, 48. See also Von Johnston and Herff Moore, "Pride Drives Wal-Mart to Service Excellence," *HRMagazine* 36, n. 10 (October 1991): 79–82; Gerald R. Ferris, Ronald M. Buckley, and Gillian M. Allen, "Promotion Systems in Organizations," *Human Resource Planning* 15, no. 3 (1992): 47–68.

23. Interested readers can check out the web sites of these companies at www.peoplesoft.com and www.resumix.com. Also see Natasha Wanchek, "People Who Need PeopleSoft," *MC Technology Marketing Intelligence* 18, no. 5 (May 1998): 22–29; "Resumix Once Again Pioneers Staffing Solutions Market with Introduction of Web-Based Product," *Business Wire,* September 22, 1998, Paul Gosling, "The Computer Is Going through Your CV Now," *The Independent,* August 23, 1998, 2.

24. Gillian Flynn, "Texas Instruments Engineers a Holistic HR," *Workforce* 77, no. 2 (February 1998): 30–35; Jeannette Brown, "Amoco Taps VAR to Post Jobs Online," *Computer Reseller News* 656 (November 6, 1995): 163; Shari Caudron, "Online Job-Posting Facilitates Lateral Transfers at Household International," *Personnel Journal* 73, no. 4 (April 1994): 64J; Carol Zarrow, "People Power," *CIO* 9, no. 14 (May 1, 1996): 86.

25. Micheline Maynard and Del Jones, "Keeping Secrets: High-Tech Tools Usher in Stolen-Information Age," *USA Today,* April 10, 1997, B1, 4.

26. Rekha Balu and L. Amante, "Kellogg Co. Shakes Up Management: Financial Officer among Those Quitting," *The Wall Street Journal,* March 4, 1999, B14; George Lazarus, "Pepsi Bottlers May Look Outside for New Chief," *Chicago Tribune,* February 12, 1999, 3; "Help Wanted: Creative Recruitment Tactics," *Personnel* 66, no. 10 (1989): 32–36.

27. Jennifer Laabs, "Cool Relo Benefits to Retain Top Talent," *Workforce* 78, no. 3 (March 1999): 89–94; Nancy Wong, "Do More than Make a Move," *Workforce* 78, no. 3 (March 1999): 95–97.

28. Herbert G. Heneman III and Robyn A. Berkley, "Applicant Attraction Practices and Outcomes among Small Businesses," *Journal of Small Business Management* 27, no. 1 (January 1999): 53–74; Jean Powell Kirnan, John A. Farley, and Kurt F. Geisinger, "The Relationship between Recruiting Source, Applicant Quality, and Hire Performance: An Analysis by Sex, Ethnicity, and Age," *Personnel Psychology* 42, no. 2 (Summer 1989): 293–308.

29. For additional articles on writing resumes, see Karen Sterkel Powell and Jackie L. Jankovich, "Student Portfolios: A Tool to Enhance the Traditional Job Search," *Business Communication Quarterly* 61, no. 4 (December 1998): 72–82; Christy Eidson, "Resume Embellishments," *Across the Board* 35, no. 10 (November/December 1998): 63; William H. Holly, Jr., Early Higgins, and Sally Speights, "Resumes and Cover Letters," *Personnel* 65, no. 12 (December 1988): 49–51.

30. "Resumix Once Again Pioneers Staffing Solutions."

31. Charlene Marmer Solomon, "Stellar Recruiting for a Tight Labor Market," *Workforce* 77, no. 8 (August 1998): 66–71; Samuel Greengard, "Putting Online Recruiting to Work," *Workforce* 77, no. 8 (August 1998): 73–76.

32. Keith Swenson, "Maximizing Employee Referrals," *HRFocus* 76, no. 1 (January 1999): 9–10; Thomas A. Stewart, "In Search of Elusive Tech Workers," *Fortune,* February 16, 1998, 171–72; Thomas Love, "Smart Tactics for Finding Workers," *Nation's Business,* January 1998, 20.

33. Steven Berglas, "Hiring In-laws: The Kiss of Death," *Inc.* 20, no. 16 (November 1998): 31–33; Paulette Thomas, "Workplace: An Ohio Design Shop Favors Family Ties," *The Wall Street Journal,* September 8, 1998, B1; Chad Kaydo, "Does Nepotism Work?" *Sales and Marketing Management* 150, no. 7 (July 1998): 161; Brenda Paik Sunoo, "Nepotism—Problem or Solution?" *Workforce* 77, no. 6 (June 1998): 17.

34. Carrick Mollenkamp, "Dunlop Maxfli Hopes New Golf Ball Will Drive Company's Sales Higher," *The Wall Street Journal,* July 15, 1998, S3. See also Thomas J. Hutton, "Increase the Odds for Successful Searches," *Personnel Journal,* November 1995, 1–5; Jacqueline M. Graves, "Bull Market for Senior Executives," *Fortune,* November 14, 1994, 14; Dave Kruger, "Executive Search Firms Riding High on Tidal Demand," *Japan Times Weekly International Edition* 36, no. 12 (March 25–31, 1996): 13.

35. "Pop Quiz: How Do You Recruit the Best College Grads?" *Personnel Journal,* August 1995, 12–18; Shannon Peters Talbott, "Boost Your Campus Image to Attract Top Grads," *Personnel Journal,* March 1996, 6–8; Holly Rawlinson, "Scholarships Recruit Future Employees Now," *Recruitment,* a supplement of *Personnel Journal,* August 1988, 14.

**36.** Donald A. Levenson, "Needed: Revamped Recruiting Services," *Personnel* 65, no. 7 (July 1988): 52. See also J. A. Breaugh, *Recruitment: Science and Practice* (Boston: PWS-Kent, 1992).

**37.** John W. Medcof and Brent Needham, "The Supra-Organizational HRM System," *Business Horizons* 41, no. 1 (January/February 1998): 43–50; Jaclyn Fierman, "The Contingency Work Force," *Fortune,* January 24, 1994, 30–36; Allison Thornson, "The Contingent Workforce," *Occupational Outlook Quarterly,* Spring 1995, 45–48; J. R. Brandstrater, "It's an Ill Wind," *Barron's,* March 25, 1996, 18–19; Michael R. Losey, "Temps: They're Not Just for Typing Anymore," *Modern Office Technology,* August 1991, 58–59. See also Louis S. Richman, "CEOs to Workers: Help Not Wanted," *Fortune,* July 12, 1993, 42–43.

**38.** David Lepak and Scott Snell, "The Human Resource Architecture: Toward a Theory of Human Capital Allocation and Development," *Academy of Management Review* 24, no. 1 (January 1999): 31–48; Jill E. Ellingson, Melissa I. Gruys, and Paul R. Sackett, "Factors Related to the Satisfaction and Performance of Temporary Employees," *Journal of Applied Psychology* 83, no. 6 (December 1998): 913–92; Kent Blake, "She's Just a Temporary," *HRMagazine* 43, no. 9 (August 1998): 45–52; Marianne A. Ferber and Jane Waldfogel, "The Long-Term Consequences of Nontraditional Employment," *Monthly Labor Review* 121, no. 5 (May 1998): 3–12.

**39.** Carolyn Hirschman, "All Aboard!" *HRMagazine* 42, no. 9 (September 1997): 80–85; "Who Is the Employer?" *HRMagazine* 42, no. 9 (September 1997): 84; Jay Finegan, "New Biz Puts 7,300 on Payroll," *Inc.* 19, no. 6 (May 1997): 17.

**40.** Robert D. Bretz Jr. And Timothy A. Judge, "Realistic Job Previews: A Test of the Adverse Self-Selection Hypothesis," *Journal of Applied Psychology* 83, no. 2 (April 1998): 330–37; Ben Pappas, "Accentuate the Negative," *Forbes,* December 28, 1998, 47; John P. Wanous, "Installing a Realistic Job Preview: Ten Tough Choices," *Personnel Psychology* 42, no. 1 (Spring 1989): 117–33.

**41.** Howard V. Hayghe, "Developments in Women's Labor Force Participation," *Monthly Labor Review* 120, no. 9 (September 1997): 41–46; Howard N. Fullerton Jr., "Evaluating the 1995 Labor Force Projections," *Monthly Labor Review* 120, no. 9 (September 1997): 5–9; Catherine Petrini and Rebecca Thomas, "Raising the Ceiling for Women," *Training and Development,* November 1995, 12. See also U.S. Department of Labor, Women's Bureau, *Facts on Working Women,* No. 93-2, June 1993.

**42.** Catherine M. Daily, S. Trevis Certo, and Dan R. Dalton, "A Decade of Corporate Women: Some Progress in the Boardroom, None in the Executive Suite," *Strategic Management Journal* 20, no. 1 (January 1999): 93–99; Christine Edwards, Oliver Robinson, Rosemary Welchman, and Jean Woodall, "Lost Opportunities? Organisational Restructuring and Women Managers," *Human Resource Management Journal* 9 no. 1 (1999): 55–64; U.S. Department of Labor, Women's Bureau, *Facts on Working Women,* No. 93-1, January 1992.

**43.** Hayghe, "Developments;" *Facts on Working Women,* No. 93-1.

**44.** Joanne Cleaver, "25 Top Leading Companies for Women," *Working Woman* 23, no. 8 September 1998, 50–64; Tom Dunkel, "The Front Runners," *Working Woman,* April 1996, 30–35, 72, 75; Rosemary Cafasso, "The Diversity Gap," *Computerworld,* June 1996, 35–37.

**45.** Shari Caudron and Cassandra Hayes, "Are Diversity Programs Benefiting African Americans?" *Black Enterprise* 27, no. 7 (February 1997): 121–32; Gillian Flynn, "Do You Have the Right Approach to Diversity?" *Personnel Journal,* October 1995, 68–75. See also Keith H. Hammonds, "Good Help Really Is Hard to Find," *Business Week,* April 4, 1994, 100–1; Leah Nathas Spiro, "Is Wall Street Finally Starting to Get It?" *Business Week,* September 26, 1994, 54.

**46.** Paige Albiniak and Bill McConnell, "Minority Internships," *Broadcasting & Cable* 128, no. 51 (December 14, 1998): 23; Barbara Ettorre, "Operation Enterprise: Training Tomorrow's Workers," *Management Review,* September 1993, 45–49; L. Winter, "Employers Go to School on Minority Recruiting," *The Wall Street Journal,* December 15, 1992, B1.

**47.** Paula Mergenhagen, "Enabling Disabled Workers," *American Demographic* 19, no. 7 (July 1997): 36–42; Albert G. Holzinger, "Service Matches Employers with Disabled Job Seekers," *Nation's Business,* June 1998, 10; Peter Sinton, "Wanted: New Hires/Firms Find Talent among Disabled, Welfare Recipients," *San Francisco Chronicle,* October 6, 1998, C1; "An ADA Checklist for Implementation and Review," *HRFocus* 71 no. 7 (July 1994): 19. See also *ADA Compliance: The Complete Planning and Practice Guide,* Business & Legal Reports (1993); Stephen Overall, "Firms Hire Fewer Disabled People in Unskilled Jobs," *People Management,* November 16, 1995, 10.

**48.** Helen Lippman, "Courts Weigh In on Obesity," *Business and Health,* February 1998, 53; "Increasing Sensitivity towards Obese Employees," *Business and Health,* August 1998, 27; Rudy M. Yandrick, "A Strategy for Managing Behavioral Problems at Work," *HRMagazine* 41, no. 6 (June 1996): 150–60. See also "320-Pound Woman Wins $100,000 Legal Appeal over Lost Job," *Arizona Republic,* November 24, 1993, A3.

**49.** Dawn Anfuso, "I Would Like to Go as Far as I Can Go," *Workforce* 77, no. 9 (September 1998): 112; "Low Literacy," *Training and Development* 48, no. 1 (January 1994): 12. See also Donald J. Ford, "Toward a More Literate Workforce," *Training and Development* 46, no. 11 (November 1992): 52–55.

**50.** Shelly Reese, "Illiteracy at Work," *American Demographics,* April 1996, 14–15.

**51.** Brenda Paik Sunoo, "Watching Phoenix Rise," *Workforce* 77, no. 2 (February 1998): 72–73; Anfuso, "I Would Like to Go as Far as I Can Go," 112; Donald J. Ford, "The Magnavox Experience," *Training and Development* 46, no. 11 (November 1992): 55–56.

**52.** Alison Kindelan, "Older Workers Can Alleviate Labor Shortages," *HRMagazine* 43, no. 10 (September 1998): 200; Heather Vogel Frederick, "Help Wanted," *Restaurant Business* 98, no. 1 (January 1, 1999): 24–25; "Encouraging Longer Careers and Attracting Young Workers," *HRMagazine* 40, no. 2 (February 1995): 44.

**53.** Charlene Marmer Solomon, "Unlock the Potential of Older Workers," *Personnel Journal,* October 1995, 56–66.

# Calculating Turnover and Absenteeism

Throughout this chapter we have emphasized that HRP depends on having an accurate picture of both the supply of and the demand for employees. Two factors, employee turnover and absenteeism, have a direct impact on HR planning and recruitment processes. In this appendix, we provide a detailed discussion of turnover and absenteeism, methods for measuring them, and suggestions for managing their impact.

## Employee Turnover Rates

"Employee turnover" refers simply to the movement of employees out of an organization. It is often cited as one of the factors behind the failure of U.S. employee productivity rates to keep pace with those of foreign competitors. It is also one of the chief determinants of labor supply. Even if everything else about an organization stays the same, as employees turn over, the supply of labor goes down. This involves both direct and indirect costs to the organization.

### Computing the Turnover Rate

The U.S. Department of Labor suggests the following formula for computing turnover rates:

$$\frac{\text{Number of separations during the month}}{\text{Total number of employees at midmonth}} \times 100$$

Thus, if there were 25 separations during a month and the total number of employees at midmonth was 500, the turnover rate would be

$$\frac{25}{500} \times 100 = 5 \text{ percent}$$

Turnover rates are computed on a regular basis to compare specific units such as departments, divisions, and work groups. In many cases, comparisons are made with data provided by other organizations. The *Bureau of National Affairs*

*Quarterly Report on Job Absence and Turnover* is a very good source of comparative turnover data.[1]

Another method of computing the turnover rate is one that reflects only the avoidable separations (S). This rate is computed by subtracting unavoidable separations (US)—for example, pregnancy, return to school, death, or marriage—from all separations. The formula for this method is as follows:

$$\frac{S - US}{M} \times 100 = T \text{ (turnover rate)}$$

where M represents the total number of employees at midmonth. For example, if there were 25 separations during a month, 5 of which were US, and the total number of employees at midmonth (M) was 500, the turnover rate would be

$$\frac{25 - 5}{500} \times 100 = 4 \text{ percent}$$

In looking at the impact of turnover on HR planning and recruitment, it is vitally important to recognize that quantitative rates of turnover are not the only factor to be considered. The *quality* of employees who leave an organization is equally important. If poor employees leave, what experts refer to as "functional turnover," this can prove to be beneficial to the organization. The costs of keeping unproductive workers may be far more than the costs to recruit and train a new, more effective performer.

## Determining the Costs of Turnover

Replacing an employee is time-consuming and expensive. Costs can generally be broken down into three categories: separation costs for the departing employee, replacement costs, and training costs for the new employee. These costs are conservatively estimated at two to three times the monthly salary of the departing employee, and they do not include indirect costs such as low productivity prior to quitting and lower morale and overtime for other employees because of the vacated job. Consequently, reducing turnover could result in significant savings to an organization. Highlights in HRM 7 details one organization's costs associated with the turnover of a single computer programmer. Note that the major expense is the cost involved in training a replacement.

# Employee Absenteeism Rates

How frequently employees are absent from their work—the absenteeism rate—is also directly related to HR planning and recruitment. When employees miss work, the organization incurs direct costs of lost wages and decreased productivity. It is not uncommon for organizations to hire extra workers just to make up for the number of absences totaled across all employees. In addition to these direct costs, there are indirect costs that may underlie excessive absenteeism. A certain amount of absenteeism is, of course, unavoidable. There will always be some who must be absent from work because of sickness, accidents, serious family problems, or other legitimate reasons. However, chronic absenteeism may signal some deeper problems in the work environment.

## Computing the Absenteeism Rates

Managers should determine the extent of the absenteeism problem, if any, by maintaining individual and departmental attendance records and by computing absenteeism rates. Although there is no universally accepted definition of "absence" nor a standard formula for computing absenteeism rates, the method most frequently used is that recommended by the U.S. Department of Labor:

$$\frac{\text{Number of worker-days lost through job absence during period}}{\text{Average number of employees} \times \text{number of workdays}} \times 100$$

**HRM 7**

**HIGHLIGHTS IN HRM**

# Costs Associated with the Turnover of One Computer Programmer

Turnover costs = Separation costs + Replacement costs + Training costs

**Separation costs**
1. Exit interview = cost for salary and benefits of both interviewer and departing employee during the exit interview = $30 + $30 = $60
2. Administrative and record-keeping action = $30
   Separation costs = $60 + $30 = $90

**Replacement costs**
1. Advertising for job opening = $2,500
2. Preemployment administrative functions and record-keeping action = $100
3. Selection interview = $250
4. Employment tests = $40
5. Meetings to discuss candidates (salary and benefits of managers while participating in meetings) = $250
   Replacement costs = $2,500 + $100 + $250 + $40 + $250 = $3,140

**Training costs**
1. Booklets, manuals, and reports = $50
2. Education = $240/day for new employee's salary and benefits × 10 days of workshops, seminars, or courses = $2,400
3. One-to-one coaching = ($240/day/new employee + $240/day/staff coach or job expert) × 20 days of one-to-one coaching = $9,600
4. Salary and benefits of new employee until he or she gets "up to par" = $240/day for salary and benefits × 20 days = $4,800
   Training costs = $50 + $2,400 + $9,600 + $4,800 = $16,850

**Total turnover costs = $90 + $3,140 + $16,850 = $20,080**

Source: Adapted from Michael W. Mercer, *Turning Your Human Resources Department into a Profit Center* (New York: AMACOM, 1993). Copyright 1993 Michael W. Mercer. Reproduced with permission from Michael W. Mercer, Ph.D., Industrial Psychologist, The Mercer Group, Inc., Chicago, Ill.

If 300 worker-days are lost through job absence during a month having 25 scheduled working days at an organization that employs 500 workers, the absenteeism rate for that month is

$$\frac{300}{500 \times 25} \times 100 = 2.4 \text{ percent}$$

The Department of Labor defines job absence as the failure of employees to report to work when their schedules require it, whether or not such failure to report is excused. Scheduled vacations, holidays, and prearranged leaves of absence are not counted as job absence.

## Comparing Absenteeism Data

The Bureau of Labor Statistics of the U.S. Department of Labor receives data on job absences from the Current Population Survey of Households conducted by the Bureau of the Census, and analyses of these data are published periodically. These analyses permit the identification of problem areas—those industries, occupations, or groups of workers with the highest incidence of absence or with rapidly increasing rates of absence. Comparison with other organizations may be made by referring to Bureau of Labor Statistics data reported in the *Monthly Labor Review* or by consulting such reporting services as the Bureau of National Affairs, Prentice-Hall, and Commerce Clearing House.[2]

## Costs of Absenteeism

Traditional accounting and information systems often do not generate data that reflect the costs of absenteeism. Consequently, their usefulness in HR planning is often limited. To accentuate the impact of absenteeism on organizational performance, managers should translate the data into dollar costs. A system for computing absenteeism costs for an individual organization is available. Organizations with computerized absence-reporting systems should find this additional information easy and inexpensive to generate. The cost of each person-hour lost to absenteeism is based on the hourly weighted-average salary, costs of employee benefits, supervisory costs, and incidental costs.

For example, XYZ Company, with 1,200 employees, has 78,000 person-hours lost to absenteeism; the total absence cost is $560,886. When this figure is divided by 1,200 employees, the cost per employee is $467.41. (In this example, we are assuming the absent workers are paid. If absent workers are not paid, their salary figures are omitted from the computation.)

## Absenteeism and HR Planning

While an employer may find that the overall absenteeism rate and costs are within an acceptable range, it is still advisable to study the statistics to determine if there are patterns in the data. Rarely does absenteeism spread itself evenly across an organization. It is very likely that employees in one area (or occupational group) may have nearly perfect attendance records, while others in a different area may be absent frequently. By monitoring these differential attendance records, managers can assess where problems might exist and, more importantly, begin planning ways to resolve or improve the underlying causes. For example, incentives could be provided for perfect attendance. Alternatively, progressive discipline procedures might be used with employees having a record of recurring absenteeism.

By establishing a comprehensive absenteeism policy, the Allen-Bradley Company was able to cut absenteeism 83.5 percent in a twenty-five-month period. This reduced the strain on labor costs and increased productivity. Part of the company's attendance policy reads:

> It is important to the successful operation of the Motion Control Division that employees be at work each scheduled workday. Each employee is performing an important set of tasks or activities. Excessive and/or avoidable absenteeism places unfair burdens on co-workers and increases the company's cost of doing business by disruption of work schedules, [creating] inefficiency and waste, delays, costly overtime, job pressures and customer complaints.[3]

**1.** This quarterly report is part of the *BNA Bulletin to Management.* For an excellent review of the relationship between performance and voluntary turnover, see Charles R. Williams and Linda Parrack Livingstone, "Another Look at the Relationship between Performance and Voluntary Turnover," *Academy of Management Journal* 37, no. 2 (April 1994): 269–98.

**2.** The loose-leaf publications of these organizations are sources of invaluable information for managers and HR professionals. These publications may be found in most libraries containing business reference books.

**3.** *Allen-Bradley Employee Handbook.*

# chapter 5

# Selection

**AFTER STUDYING THIS CHAPTER, YOU SHOULD BE ABLE TO**

**OBJECTIVE 1**
Explain the objectives of the personnel selection process.

**OBJECTIVE 2**
Identify the various sources of information used for personnel selection.

**OBJECTIVE 3**
Explain the value of different types of employment tests.

**OBJECTIVE 4**
Discuss the different approaches to conducting an employment interview.

**OBJECTIVE 5**
Describe the various decision strategies for selection.

There is perhaps no more important topic in HRM than employee selection. If it is true that organizations succeed or fail on the basis of talents of employees, then managers directly influence that success by the people they hire. Regardless of whether the company is large or small, hiring the best and the brightest employees lays a strong foundation for excellence. Alternatively, it is common to hear managers who don't recognize this point lament the inordinate amount of their time that is spent trying to fix bad selection decisions. In addition, equal employment opportunity legislation, court decisions, and the *Uniform Guidelines* (discussed in Chapter 2) have also provided an impetus for making sure that the selection process is done well. The bottom line is, good selection decisions make a difference. So do bad ones.

# Matching People and Jobs

**Selection**

Process of choosing individuals who have relevant qualifications to fill existing or projected job openings

In conjunction with the recruiting process, which is designed to increase the number of applicants whose qualifications meet job requirements and the needs of the organization, **selection** is the process of reducing that number and choosing from among those individuals who have the relevant qualifications.

Figure 5.1 shows in broad terms that the overall goal of selection is to maximize "hits" and avoid "misses." Hits are accurate predictions and misses are inaccurate ones. The cost of one type of miss would be the direct and indirect expense of hiring an employee who turns out to be unsuccessful. The cost of the other type of miss is an opportunity cost—someone who could have been successful didn't get a chance.

While the overall selection program is often the formal responsibility of the HR department, line managers typically make the final decision about hiring persons in their unit. It is important therefore that managers understand the objectives, policies, and practices used for selection. In that way, they can be highly involved in the process from the very beginning. Those responsible for making selection decisions should have adequate information upon which to base their decisions. Information about the jobs to be filled, knowledge of the ratio of job openings to the number of applicants, and as much relevant information as possible about the applicants themselves are essential for making sound decisions.

## Beginning with Job Analysis

In Chapter 3 we discussed the process of analyzing jobs to develop job descriptions and specifications. Job specifications, in particular, help identify the *individual competencies* employees need for success—the knowledge, skills, abilities, and other factors (KSAOs) that lead to superior performance. By identifying competencies through job analysis, managers can then use selection methods such as interviews, references, psychological tests, and the like to measure applicant KSAOs against the competencies required for the job and the needs of the organization.[1] Research has demonstrated that complete and unambiguous specification of required competencies (via job analysis) reduces the influence of racial and gender stereotypes and helps the interviewer to differentiate between qualified and unqualified applicants.[2]

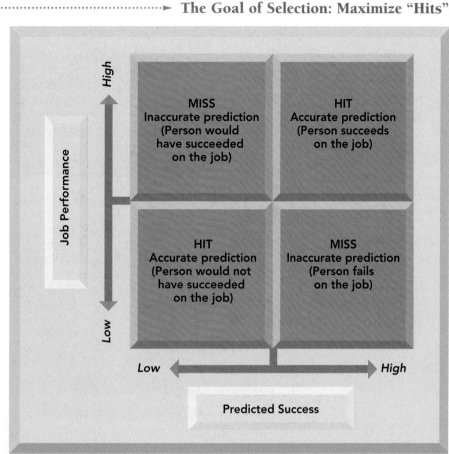

FIGURE 5.1

The Goal of Selection: Maximize "Hits"

Ordinarily, managers are well acquainted with the requirements pertaining to skill, physical demands, and other factors for jobs in their respective departments. Interviewers and other members of the HR department who participate in selection should maintain a close liaison with the various departments so that they can become thoroughly familiar with the jobs and competencies needed to perform them.

## The Selection Process

In most organizations, selection is a continuous process. Turnover inevitably occurs, leaving vacancies to be filled by applicants from inside or outside the organization or by individuals whose qualifications have been assessed previously. It is common to have a waiting list of applicants who can be called when permanent or temporary positions become open.

The number of steps in the selection process and their sequence will vary, not only with the organization but also with the type and level of jobs to be filled. Each step should be evaluated in terms of its contribution. The steps that typically make up the selection process are shown in Figure 5.2. Not all applicants will go through all of these steps. Some may be rejected after the preliminary interview, others after taking tests, and so on.

FIGURE 5.2

**Steps in the Selection Process**

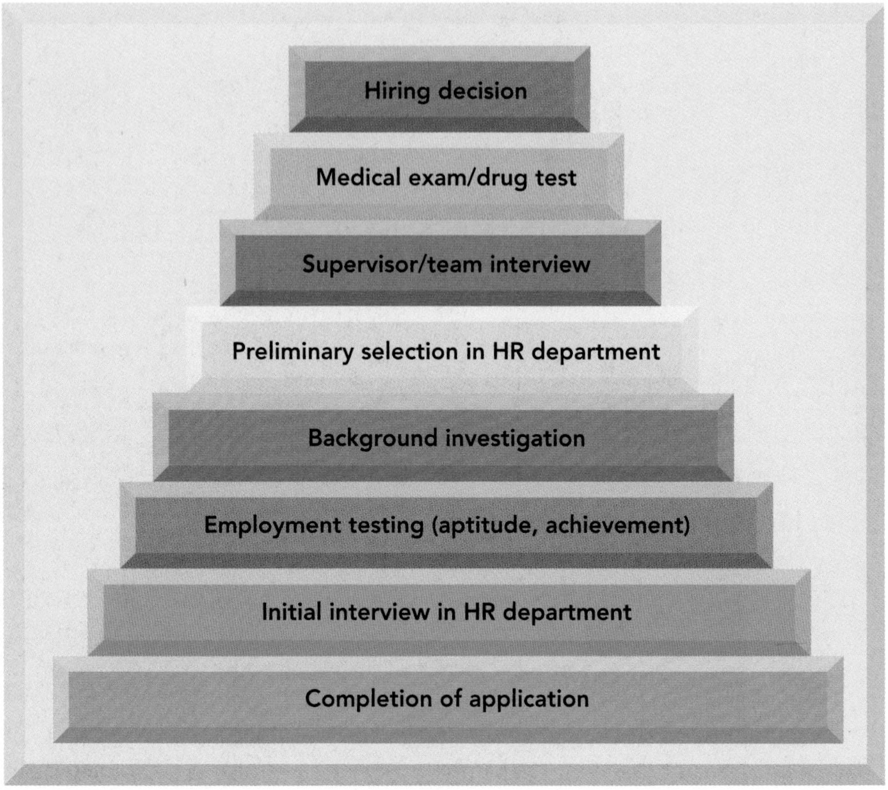

Hiring decision

Medical exam/drug test

Supervisor/team interview

Preliminary selection in HR department

Background investigation

Employment testing (aptitude, achievement)

Initial interview in HR department

Completion of application

Note: Steps may vary. An applicant may be rejected after any step in the process.

As shown in Figure 5.2, organizations use several different means to obtain information about applicants. These include application blanks, interviews, tests, medical examinations, and background investigations. Regardless of the method used, it is essential that it conform to accepted ethical standards, including privacy and confidentiality, as well as legal requirements. Above all, it is essential that the information obtained be sufficiently reliable and valid.

## Obtaining Reliable and Valid Information

**Reliability**
Degree to which interviews, tests, and other selection procedures yield comparable data over time and alternative measures

The degree to which interviews, tests, and other selection procedures yield comparable data over a period of time is known as **reliability.** For example, unless interviewers judge the capabilities of a group of applicants to be the same today as they did yesterday, their judgments are unreliable (i.e., unstable). Likewise, a test that gives widely different scores when it is administered to the same individual a few days apart is unreliable.

Reliability also refers to the extent to which two or more methods (interviews and tests, for example) yield similar results or are consistent. Interrater reliability—agreement between two or more raters—is one measure of a method's consistency. Unless the data upon which selection decisions are based are reliable, in terms of both stability and consistency, they cannot be used as predictors.

**Validity**
> Degree to which a test or selection procedure measures a person's attributes

In addition to having reliable information pertaining to a person's suitability for a job, the information must be as valid as possible. **Validity** refers to what a test or other selection procedure measures and how well it measures it. In the context of personnel selection, validity is essentially an indicator of the extent to which data from a procedure (interview or test, for example) are predictive of job performance. Like a new medicine, a selection procedure must be validated before it is used. There are two reasons for validating a procedure. First, validity is directly related to increases in employee productivity, as we will demonstrate later. Second, EEO regulations emphasize the importance of validity in selection procedures.[3] Although we commonly refer to "validating" a test or interview procedure, validity in the technical sense refers to the inferences made from the use of a procedure, not to the procedure itself.

The *Uniform Guidelines* (see Chapter 2) recognizes and accepts different approaches to validation. These are criterion-related validity, content validity, and construct validity.

### Criterion-Related Validity

**Criterion-related validity**
> Extent to which a selection tool predicts, or significantly correlates with, important elements of work behavior

The extent to which a selection tool predicts, or significantly correlates with, important elements of work behavior is known as **criterion-related validity.** Performance on a test, for example, is compared with actual production records, supervisory ratings, training outcomes, and other measures of success that are appropriate to each type of job. In a sales job, for example, it is common to use sales figures as a basis for comparison. In production jobs, quantity and quality of output may provide the best criteria of job success.

**Concurrent validity**
> The extent to which test scores (or other predictor information) match criterion data obtained at about the same time from current employees

There are two types of criterion-related validity, concurrent and predictive. **Concurrent validity** involves obtaining criterion data from *current employees* at about the same time that test scores (or other predictor information) are obtained. For example, a supervisor is asked to rate a group of clerical employees on the quantity and quality of their performance. These employees are then given a clerical aptitude test, and the test scores are compared with the supervisory ratings to determine the degree of relationship between them. **Predictive validity,** on the other hand, involves testing *applicants* and obtaining criterion data *after* those applicants have been hired and have been on the job for some indefinite period. For example, applicants are given a clerical aptitude test, which is then filed away for later study. After the individuals have been on the job for several months, supervisors, who should not know the employees' test scores, are asked to rate them on the quality and quantity of their performance. Test scores are then compared with the supervisors' ratings.

**Predictive validity**
> Extent to which applicants' test scores match criterion data obtained from those applicants/employees after they have been on the job for some indefinite period

Regardless of the method used, cross-validation is essential. **Cross-validation** is a process in which a test or battery of tests is administered to a different sample (drawn from the same population) for the purpose of verifying the results obtained from the original validation study.

**Cross-validation**
> Verifying the results obtained from a validation study by administering a test or test battery to a different sample (drawn from the same population)

Correlational methods are generally used to determine the relationship between predictor information such as test scores and criterion data. The correlation scatterplots in Figure 5.3 illustrate the difference between a selection test of zero validity (A) and one of high validity (B). Each dot represents a person. Note that in scatterplot A there is no relationship between test scores and success on the job; in other words, the validity is zero. In scatterplot B, those who score low on the test tend to have low success on the job, whereas those who score high on the test tend to have high success on the job, indicating high validity. In actual practice we would apply a statistical formula to the data to obtain a coefficient of correlation

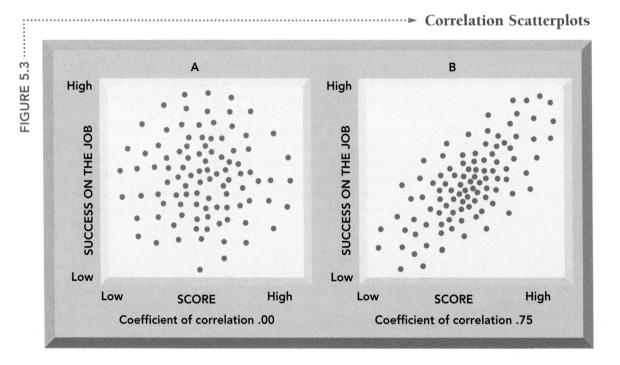

FIGURE 5.3

Correlation Scatterplots

referred to as a *validity coefficient*. Correlation coefficients range from 0.00, denoting a complete absence of relationship, to +1.00 and to −1.00, indicating a perfect positive and perfect negative relationship, respectively.

A thorough survey of the literature shows that the averages of the maximum validity coefficients are 0.45 where tests are validated against *training* criteria and 0.35 where tests are validated against job *proficiency* criteria. These figures represent the predictive power of single tests.[4] A higher validity may be obtained by combining two or more tests or other predictors (interview or biographical data, for instance), using the appropriate statistical formulas. The higher the overall validity, the greater the chances of hiring individuals who will be the better performers. The criterion-related method is generally preferred to other validation approaches because it is based on empirical data.

For several decades, personnel psychologists believed that validity coefficients had meaning only for the specific situation (job and organization). More recently, as a result of several research studies—many involving clerical jobs—it appears that validity coefficients can often be generalized across situations, hence the term **validity generalization.** Where there are adequate data to support the existence of validity generalization, the development of selection procedures can become less costly and time-consuming. The process involves analyzing jobs and situations and, on the basis of these analyses, consulting tables of generalized validities from previous studies using various predictors in similar circumstances. It is advisable for organizations to employ the services of an industrial-organizational psychologist experienced in test validation to develop the selection procedures.[5]

**Validity generalization**
Extent to which validity coefficients can be generalized across situations

**Content validity**
Extent to which a selection instrument, such as a test, adequately samples the knowledge and skills needed to perform a particular job

## Content Validity

Where it is not feasible to use the criterion-related approach, often because of limited samples of individuals, the content method is used. **Content validity** is assumed to exist when a selection instrument, such as a test, adequately samples the knowledge and skills needed to perform a particular job.

The closer the content of the selection instrument is to actual work samples or behaviors, the greater its content validity. For example, a civil service examination for accountants has high content validity when it requires the solution of accounting problems representative of those found on the job. Asking an accountant to lift a sixty-pound box, however, is a selection procedure that has content validity only if the job description indicates that accountants must be able to meet this requirement.

Content validity is the most direct and least complicated type of validity to assess. It is generally used to evaluate job knowledge and skill tests, to be described below. Unlike the criterion-related method, content validity is not expressed in correlational terms. Instead, an index is computed (from evaluations of an expert panel) that indicates the relationship between the content of the test items and performance on the job.[6] While content validity does have its limitations, it has made a positive contribution to job analysis procedures and to the role of expert judgment in sampling and scoring procedures.

### *Construct Validity*

**Construct validity**

Extent to which a selection tool measures a theoretical construct or trait

The extent to which a selection tool measures a theoretical construct, or trait, is known as **construct validity.** Typical constructs are intelligence, mechanical comprehension, and anxiety. They are in effect broad, general categories of human functions that are based on the measurement of many discrete behaviors. For example, the Bennett Mechanical Comprehension Test consists of a wide variety of tasks that measure the construct of mechanical comprehension.

Measuring construct validity requires showing that the psychological trait is related to satisfactory job performance and that the test accurately measures the psychological trait. There is a lack of literature covering this concept as it relates to employment practices, probably because it is difficult and expensive to validate a construct and to show how it is job-related.[7]

# Sources of Information about Job Candidates

Many sources of information are used to provide as reliable and valid a picture as possible of an applicant's potential for success on the job. Figure 5.4 shows the results of a recent survey that asked HR executives to evaluate the effectiveness of various selection techniques. In this section, we will study the potential contributions of application forms; biographical information blanks; background investigations; polygraph, or lie detector, tests; honesty and integrity tests; graphology; and medical examinations. Because interviewing plays such a major role in selection and because testing presents unique challenges, there will be expanded discussions of these sources of information later in the chapter. Assessment centers, which are often used in managerial selection, will be discussed in Chapter 7.

## Application Forms

Most organizations require application forms to be completed because they provide a fairly quick and systematic means of obtaining a variety of information about the applicant. As with interviews, the EEOC and the courts have found that

FIGURE 5.4

## The Effectiveness of Selection Methods

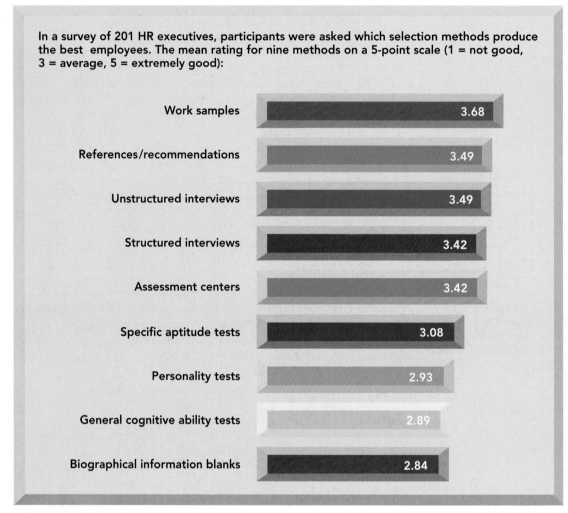

In a survey of 201 HR executives, participants were asked which selection methods produce the best employees. The mean rating for nine methods on a 5-point scale (1 = not good, 3 = average, 5 = extremely good):

|  |  |
|---|---|
| Work samples | 3.68 |
| References/recommendations | 3.49 |
| Unstructured interviews | 3.49 |
| Structured interviews | 3.42 |
| Assessment centers | 3.42 |
| Specific aptitude tests | 3.08 |
| Personality tests | 2.93 |
| General cognitive ability tests | 2.89 |
| Biographical information blanks | 2.84 |

Source: David E. Terpstra, "The Search for Effective Methods." Reprinted from *HRFocus*, May/1996. © 1996 American Management Association International. Reprinted by permission of American Management Association International, New York, NY. All rights reserved. http://www.amanet.org.

many questions asked on application forms disproportionately discriminate against females and minorities and often are not job-related. Application forms should therefore be developed with great care and revised as often as necessary. Because of differences in state laws on fair employment practices (FEPs) (see Chapter 2), organizations operating in more than one state will find it difficult to develop one form that can be used nationally.

Application forms serve several purposes. They provide information for deciding whether an applicant meets the minimum requirements for experience, education, etc. They provide a basis for questions the interviewer will ask about the applicant's background. They also offer sources for reference checks. For certain jobs, a short application form is appropriate. For example, McDonald's uses a form that is quite brief but asks for information that is highly relevant to job performance.

It also provides information regarding the employer's conformity with various laws and regulations. For scientific, professional, and managerial jobs, a more extended form is likely to be used.

**USING THE INTERNET**

 You can practice reading and analyzing resumes online at the two following sites:

www.careermosiac.com/cm/cm41.html

and

www.jobcenter.com/jol/search.htm

Even when applicants come armed with elaborate resumes, it is important that they complete an application form early in the process. Individuals frequently exaggerate or overstate their qualifications on a resume. As shown in Figure 5.5, misstatements on application forms can be pretty humorous as well. One technique for anticipating problems of misrepresentation is to ask applicants to transcribe specific resume material onto a standardized application form. The applicant is then asked to sign a statement that the information contained on the form is true and that he or she accepts the employer's right to terminate the candidate's employment if any of the information is subsequently found to be false.[8]

Many managers remain unclear about the questions they can ask on an application blank. While most know they should steer clear of issues such as age, race, marital status, and sexual orientation, other issues are less clear. The following are some suggestions for putting together an application form:

- *Application date.* The applicant should date the application. This helps managers know when the form was completed and gives them an idea of the time limit (for example, one year) that the form should be on file.

**FIGURE 5.5** ▶ **True Lies and the Application Blank**

Some jobseekers make silly mistakes or are misguided in their attempts at humor when applying for a job. Here are some real-life examples:

In the "Intentionally/Accidentally Humorous" category:

- It's best for employers that I not work with people.
- Trustworthy references upon request—if I give them a few bucks.
- Am a perfectionist and rarely if if ever make mistakes.
- 1881 to 1994—Became top sales producer in office.
- You'll want me to be the Head Honcho in no time.
- Objective: Active interface with fellow Homo sapiens.
- If you hire me away from this nightmare, you'll save me thousands in therapy.

In the "Correct Spelling—Wrong Word" category:

- After receiving advice from several different angels, I decide to pursue a new line of work.
- Accounting cleric.
- As indicted, I have over five years of analyzing investments.
- I have 12 years of experience worming in the industry.
- Education: Statistics mayor.

Source: Examples are from several companies, including Robert Half International. "Beware of Resumania," *Personnel Journal*, April 1996, 28. Reprinted with permission.

- *Educational background.* The applicant should also provide grade school, high school, college, and postcollege attendance—but not the dates attended, since that can be connected with age.
- *Experience.* Virtually any questions that focus on work experience related to the job are permissible.
- *Arrests and criminal convictions.* Questions about arrests alone are not permissible. But questions about convictions are fine. However, the Rehabilitation of Offenders Act of 1974 allows that, for some crimes, the applicant has no duty to disclose the conviction to a prospective employer after a certain time period has passed. The law allows the applicant to act as if the crime never occurred. There are certain professions such as teaching and nursing that are exceptions to this rule.
- *Country of citizenship.* Such questions are not permitted. It is allowable to ask if the person is legally prevented from working in the United States.
- *References.* It is both permissible and advisable that the names, addresses, and phone numbers of references be provided. (We will cover this in more detail below.)
- *Disabilities.* This is a potential problem area. With the most recent guidelines issued by the EEOC, employers may now ask if an applicant needs reasonable accommodation—*if* the disability is obvious or *if* the applicant has voluntarily disclosed the disability.[9]

Many of these issues will be addressed again, particularly in the section on employment interviews.

Some organizations use what is referred to as *a weighted application blank (WAB).* The WAB involves the use of a common standardized employment application that is designed to distinguish between successful and unsuccessful employees. If managers can identify application items (such as where someone went to school, etc.) that have predicted employee success in the past, they may use that information to screen other applicants. Some evidence suggests that use of the WAB has been especially helpful for reducing turnover costs in the hospitality industry.[10]

## Biographical Information Blanks

One of the oldest methods for predicting job success uses biographical information about job applicants. As early as 1917, the Life Insurance Agency Management Association constructed and validated a biographical information blank (BIB) for life insurance salespersons. BIBs cover such issues as family life, hobbies, club memberships, sales experience, and investments. Like application blanks, BIBs reveal information about a person's history that may have shaped his or her behavior. Sample questions from a BIB might include:

- At what age did you leave home?
- How large was the town/city in which you lived as a child?
- Did you ever build a model airplane that flew?
- Were sports a big part of your childhood?
- Do you play any musical instruments?

Both the BIB and the application form can be scored like tests. And because biographical questions rarely have obviously right or wrong answers, BIBs are difficult to fake. The development of a scoring system requires that the items that are valid predictors of job success (positively or negatively correlated) be identified and that weights be established for different responses to these items. By totaling the scores for each item, it is possible to obtain a composite score on the BIB as a whole for each applicant. Studies have shown that an objective scoring of BIB and application forms is one of the most potentially valid methods of predicting job success. This method has been useful in predicting all types of behavior, including employee theft, turnover, and performance in jobs such as sales, nursing, and management.[11]

**"You have to admit it's not a run of the mill resume."**

From *The Wall Street Journal*—Permission, Cartoon Features Syndicate

## Background Investigations

When the interviewer is satisfied that the applicant is potentially qualified, information about previous employment as well as other information provided by the applicant is investigated. For example, APCOA, Inc., a Cleveland-based company that operates airport parking facilities, conducts a number of background checks on potential employees. Former employers, school and college officials, credit bureaus, and individuals named as references may be contacted for verification of pertinent information such as length of time on the job, type of job, performance evaluation, highest wages, academic degrees earned, possible criminal record, and credit rating. Most of this information is now readily available on existing computer databases. One such database, called OPEN (Ohio Professional Electronic Network), provides on-line computer access to public record databases to allow individuals to conduct their own preemployment screening and background profiles on companies or individuals.[12] Figure 5.6 shows the results of a Society for Human Resource Management (SHRM) study on how managers check applicant backgrounds.

### Checking References

Organizations ranging from Canon to the Boston Philharmonic use both the mail and the telephone to check references. But while references are commonly used to screen and select employees, they have not proved successful for predicting employee performance. Written letters of reference are notoriously inflated, and this limits their validity. Generally, telephone checks are preferable because they save time and provide for greater candor. At Intuit, the Menlo Park, California, software company that produces *Quicken*, managerial applicants are asked to provide between five and nine references who are then called and asked specific job-related questions. The most reliable information usually comes from supervisors, who are in the best position to report on an applicant's work habits and perfor-

FIGURE 5.6

**How HR Uses Background Investigations**

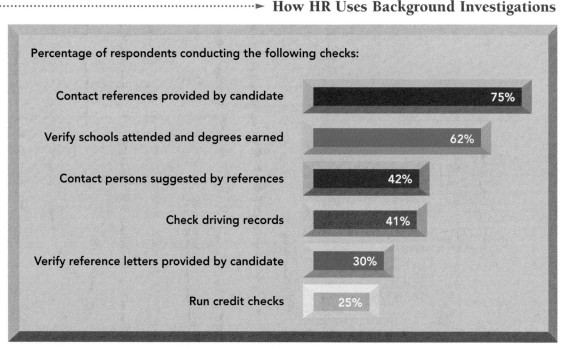

Source: Society for Human Resource Management (SHRM).

mance. Written verification of information relating to job titles, duties, and pay levels from the former employer's HR office is also very helpful.[13]

Since enactment of the Family Educational Rights Privacy Act of 1974 (FERPA), which gave students and their parents the right to inspect student personnel files, university administrators and faculty have been reluctant to provide anything other than general and often meaningless positive statements about student performance. The principles involved in FERPA came to apply to employees and their personnel records as well. As a result, most employers prefer using the telephone to check references.

Inadequate reference checking can contribute to high turnover, employee theft, and white-collar crime. By using sources in addition to former employers, organizations can obtain valuable information about an applicant's character and habits. For example, it is legal to use court records, litigation, bankruptcy, and workers' compensation records of applicants as long as the prospective employer is consistent in the use of information from these records.

### *Requiring Signed Requests for References*

Based on the Privacy Act of 1974, individuals have a legal right to examine letters of reference about them (unless they waive the right to do so). Although the Privacy Act applies only to the records maintained by federal government agencies, other forms of privacy legislation in most states has influenced employers to "clean up" personnel files and open them up to review and challenge by the employees concerned.[14]

As a legal protection for all concerned, it is important to ask the applicant to fill out forms permitting information to be solicited from former employers and other reference sources. Even with these safeguards, many organizations are reluctant to put into writing an evaluation of a former employee. One reason is that several firms have been sued by former employees who discovered that they had been given poor recommendations. As a result of such experiences, some employers even hesitate to answer questions and/or verify information about former employees over the phone. A recent survey by the Society for Human Resource Management (SHRM) found that although 75 percent of companies do provide references, many reported that the information consists only of employment dates and position.

Under these circumstances, it may be nearly impossible for potential employers to learn enough about the candidate to avoid hiring mistakes. There are really two problems here. First, new employers may be liable for negligent hiring if they fail to screen out applicants with histories of instability who become dangerous in the workplace. Second, recent court cases have held former employers liable when they knew an individual was dangerous but failed to disclose this fact to the new employer. Recognizing this predicament, thirty-two states so far have enacted statutes offering protection from liability for employers who give references in good faith.[15]

### Using Credit Reports

The use of consumer credit reports by employers as a basis for establishing an applicant's eligibility for employment has become more restricted. Under the 1997 Consumer Credit Reporting Reform Act (CCRRA) the term "credit report" extends beyond the financial arena to include almost any compilation of information on an individual that's prepared by a third-party agency. To rely on a report such as this in making employment decisions, organizations must follow four important steps.

First, organizations must advise and receive written consent from applicants if such a report will be requested. If an employer plans to use a more comprehensive type of third-party report, such as an investigative consumer report, the applicant must be advised in writing. An investigative consumer report includes information based upon personal interviews with the applicant's friends, neighbors, and associates rather than just from an existing database. The applicant must be told that additional disclosure concerning the complete nature and scope of the investigation will be provided to them upon written request.

Second, the organization must provide a written certification to the consumer reporting agency (the agency providing the information) about the purpose of the report and must assure them that it will not be used for any other purpose. In the case of investigative reports, the employer also has to certify that it will give an applicant the information if he or she asks for it.

Third, before taking any adverse action due to information in the report, organizations must provide applicants a copy of the consumer report as well as a summary of their rights under the CCRRA.

Fourth, if the organization decides not to hire the applicant based on the report, it must provide an adverse-action notice to that person. Although the notice can be provided verbally, in writing, or electronically, it must contain the name, address, and phone number of the agency that provided the report. The employer must also provide a statement that the reporting agency didn't make the hiring decision, that the applicant has a right to obtain an additional free copy of the report, and that the applicant has a right to dispute the accuracy of information with the reporting agency.[16]

## Polygraph Tests

The polygraph, or lie detector, is a device that measures the changes in breathing, blood pressure, and pulse of a person who is being questioned. It consists of a rubber tube around the chest, a cuff around the arm, and sensors attached to the fingers that record the physiological changes in the examinee as the examiner asks questions that call for an answer of yes or no. Questions typically cover such items as whether a person uses drugs, has stolen from an employer, or has committed a serious undetected crime.

The growing swell of objections to the use of polygraphs in employment situations culminated in the passage of the federal Employee Polygraph Protection Act of 1988. (See Highlights in HRM 1.) The act generally prohibits the use of a lie detector for prehire screening and random testing and applies to all private employers except pharmaceutical companies and companies that supply security guards for health and safety operations as well as government agencies.[17] It defines the term "lie detector" to include the polygraph, deceptograph, voice stress analyzer, psychological stress evaluator, and any similar mechanical or electrical device used to render a diagnostic opinion about the honesty or dishonesty of an individual.

Other provisions of the act set qualification standards for polygraph examiners, conditions for examinations, and disclosure of information where the use of the polygraph is authorized. Because of the law, employers have had to resort to such alternatives as written tests of honesty and background checks of applicants. Among the organizations most affected are Wall Street firms, banks, and retail companies, which used to rely heavily on polygraphs. Nevertheless, following a series of corruption scandals in the New York City Police Department, a special panel (Commission to Combat Police Corruption) established by Mayor Rudolph Giuliani recently recommended that the police department administer polygraph tests to new recruits.[18]

## Honesty and Integrity Tests

In response to the Employee Polygraph Protection Act, many employers have dramatically increased their use of pencil-and-paper honesty and integrity tests. These tests have commonly been used in settings such as retail stores where employees have access to cash or merchandise. Common areas of inquiry include beliefs about frequency and extent of theft in our society, punishment for theft, and perceived ease of theft. For example, Payless ShoeSource, based in Topeka, Kansas, has used a paper-and-pencil honesty test to reduce employee theft. When the company began its program, losses totaled nearly $21 million per year among its 4,700 stores. Within only one year of implementing its screening program, inventory shrinkage fell by 20 percent to less than 1 percent of sales. Nordstrom, the Seattle-based department store, also uses an integrity test, called the Reid Survey, which takes only about fifteen minutes to complete. Vice president of HR Joe Demarte argues that, using the Reid Survey, the company has about a 90 percent chance of screening out undesirable candidates. Popularity of the Reid test has grown substantially over the past decade. The Chicago-based company's client list—which ranges from retailers to airlines—has doubled since 1992.[19]

Potential items that might be used on an integrity test are shown in Figure 5.7. A comprehensive analysis of honesty tests reveals that they are valid for predicting job performance as well as a wide range of disruptive behaviors such as

**HRM 1**

# Employee Polygraph Protection Act

**U.S. DEPARTMENT OF LABOR**

EMPLOYMENT STANDARDS ADMINISTRATION

Wage and Hour Division
Washington, D.C. 20210

# NOTICE

## EMPLOYEE POLYGRAPH PROTECTION ACT

The Employee Polygraph Protection Act prohibits most private employers from using lie detector tests either for pre-employment screening or during the course of employment.

### PROHIBITIONS

Employers are generally prohibited from requiring or requesting any employee or job applicant to take a lie detector test, and from discharging, disciplining, or discriminating against an employee or prospective employee for refusing to take a test or for exercising other rights under the Act.

### EXEMPTIONS*

Federal, State and local governments are not affected by the law. Also, the law does not apply to tests given by the Federal Government to certain private individuals engaged in national security-related activities.

The Act permits *polygraph* (a kind of lie detector) tests to be administered in the private sector, subject to restrictions, to certain prospective employees of security service firms (armored car, alarm, and guard), and of pharmaceutical manufacturers, distributors and dispensers.

The Act also permits polygraph testing, subject to restrictions, of certain employees of private firms who are reasonably suspected of involvement in a workplace incident (theft, embezzlement, etc.) that resulted in economic loss to the employer.

### EXAMINEE RIGHTS

Where polygraph tests are permitted, they are subject to numerous strict standards concerning the conduct and length of the test. Examinees have a number of specific rights, including the right to a written notice before testing, the right to refuse or discontinue a test, and the right not to have test results disclosed to unauthorized persons.

### ENFORCEMENT

The Secretary of Labor may bring court actions to restrain violations and assess civil penalties up to $10,000 against violators. Employees or job applicants may also bring their own court actions.

### ADDITIONAL INFORMATION

Additional information may be obtained, and complaints of violations may be filed, at local offices of the Wage and Hour Division, which are listed in the telephone directory under U.S. Government, Department of Labor, Employment Standards Administration.

**THE LAW REQUIRES EMPLOYERS TO DISPLAY THIS POSTER WHERE EMPLOYEES AND JOB APPLICANTS CAN READILY SEE IT.**

*The law does not preempt any provision of any State or local law or any collective bargaining agreement which is more restrictive with respect to lie detector tests.*

**U.S. DEPARTMENT OF LABOR**
EMPLOYMENT STANDARDS ADMINISTRATION
Wage and Hour Division
Washington, D.C. 20210

WH Publication 1462
September 1988

**Integrity Test Question Examples**

FIGURE 5.7

| TO TEST TENDENCY TO | DESCRIPTION |
|---|---|
| Protect | Contains items that require individuals to indicate whether they would protect friends or co-workers who had engaged in counterproductive behaviors.<br><br>*Example:* I would turn in a fellow worker I saw stealing money. |
| Be lenient | Contains items in which test takers indicate whether they would be lenient with respect to the wrongdoings of others.<br><br>*Example:* An employee should be fired if the employer finds out the employee lied on the application blank. |
| Admit thought | Includes items that require test takers to indicate the degree to which they would engage in counterproductive thoughts or behaviors.<br><br>*Example:* I've thought about taking money from an employer without actually doing it. |
| Admit behavior | Contains items in which individuals admit to directly participating in actual counterproductive behaviors.<br><br>*Example:* Over the last three years, what's the total amount of money you've taken without permission from your employer? |
| Consider common | Includes items that require the individual to indicate the extent to which theft and other misbehaviors are common.<br><br>*Example:* Most people I've worked with have stolen something at one time or another. |
| Excuse | Contains items in which individuals indicate whether there are excuses or justifications for stealing or performing other questionable behaviors.<br><br>*Example:* Someone who steals because his family is in need should not be treated the same as a common thief. |
| Lie | Contains items that measure the extent to which the test taker is responding in a socially desirable manner.<br><br>*Example:* Never in my whole life have I wished for anything I was not entitled to. |

Note: The number of items in each category was 2, 8, 13, 9, 17, 8, and 7 respectively.
Stephen Dwight and George Alliger, "Reactions to overt integrity test items," *Educational and Psychological Measurement* 57, no. 6 (December 1997): 937–48, copyright © 1997 by Sage Publications, Inc. Reprinted with the permission of Sage Publications, Inc.

theft, disciplinary problems, and absenteeism.[20] Nevertheless, honesty tests have come under fire, too. According to Lewis Maltby, director of the Workplace Rights Office at the American Civil Liberties Union, "There are questions that will ask you for your reaction to hypothetical dishonest situations, and if you are a particularly kindhearted person who isn't sufficiently punitive, you fail. Mother Teresa would never pass some of these honesty tests." Given this possibility, HRM specialists should use the results from honesty tests very cautiously and most certainly in conjunction with other sources of information.[21]

## Graphology

Graphology, a term that refers to a variety of systems of handwriting analysis, is used by some employers to make employment decisions. Graphologists obtain a sample of handwriting and then examine such characteristics as the size and slant of letters, amount of pressure applied, and placement of the writing on the page. From their observations graphologists draw inferences about such things as the writer's personality traits, intelligence, energy level, organizational abilities, creativity, integrity, emotional maturity, self-image, people skills, and entrepreneurial tendencies. Graphology is used extensively in France, Germany, Switzerland, Israel, and the United Kingdom in making employment decisions.[22] Now handwriting analysis is quietly spreading through corporate America. Companies such as Ford and General Electric have used it for selection, as has the U.S. Central Intelligence Agency (CIA).

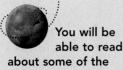

**USING THE INTERNET**

You will be able to read about some of the arguments against the use of graphology at the following text-heavy site:

condor.depaul.edu/ethics/hand.html

Organizations using handwriting analysis say they prefer it to typical personality tests because it only requires that job candidates take a few minutes to jot down a short essay. By contrast, a battery of personality tests and interviews with psychologists can take several hours and can cost thousands of dollars. In addition, the available evidence shows graphology to be a reliable predictor of personality when compared with other psychological tests. However, its predictive validity for job performance and occupational success remains questionable. In the academic community, where formal and rigorous validity studies are customary, use of graphology for employment decisions has been viewed with considerable skepticism.[23]

## Medical Examinations

The medical examination is one of the later steps in the selection process because it can be costly. A medical examination is generally given to ensure that the health of an applicant is adequate to meet the job requirements. It also provides a baseline against which subsequent medical examinations can be compared and interpreted. The latter objective is particularly important in determinations of work-caused disabilities under workers' compensation law.

In the past, requirements for such physical characteristics as strength, agility, height, and weight were often determined by an employer's unvalidated notion of what should be required. Many such requirements that tend to discriminate against women have been questioned and modified so as to represent typical job demands.

While there is much publicity about acquired immune deficiency syndrome (AIDS), corporate testing for the presence of HIV (human immunodeficiency virus) is conducted in only a small percentage of companies. And the vast majority of those that test for HIV are health care providers, government agencies, and military units.[24]

In some cases, medical testing can be considered an invasion of privacy and may be in violation of the law. For example, the Americans with Disabilities Act severely limits the types of medical inquiries and examinations that employers may use. The law explicitly states that all exams must be directly related to the requirements of the job and that a medical exam cannot be given until an offer of employment has been extended. Further, the ADA prohibits companies from screening out a prospective employee because he or she has an elevated risk of on-the-job injury or a medical condition that could be aggravated because of job demands. However, the ADA does not prevent testing of applicants or employees for illegal drug use, a topic discussed below.[25]

## Drug Testing

According to a recent American Management Association (AMA) study, the number of U.S. companies that test employment candidates for drug use has increased significantly. Since passage of the Drug-Free Workplace Act of 1988, applicants and employees of federal contractors, Department of Defense contractors, and those under Department of Transportation regulations are subject to testing for illegal drug use. (See Chapter 12 for an extended discussion of this topic, including a sample policy statement for a drug-free workplace.)

Urine sampling is the normal method used for drug testing; it is used by 96 percent of the AMA-surveyed employers who do drug testing. More-sophisticated tests are then used to validate positive findings. Some of the sharpest criticism of drug testing attacks the technology and standards by which tests are conducted—a topic we will discuss in detail in Chapter 13, in the context of employee rights.[26]

The wide range of firms that report using drug tests includes Federal Express, General Electric, Georgia Power, Westinghouse, Southern Pacific Railroad, and the New York Times Company. With most employers, applicants who test positive have virtually no chance of being hired. However, employees who test positive are typically referred for treatment or counseling and receive some sort of disciplinary action.

# Employment Tests

As the United States mobilized for World War I in the summer of 1917, some of the most talented psychologists in the country worked together to develop what later became known as the Army Alpha and Beta Tests of intelligence. (The Alpha exam was written for the general population and the Beta was designed for internationals and those with poor reading skills.) The tests were used to help identify potential officer candidates as well as select and place other potential recruits. Since that time, employment tests have played an important part in the HR programs of both public and private organizations.

Before the passage of the Civil Rights Act of 1964, over 90 percent of companies surveyed by the Bureau of National Affairs reported using tests. By the 1980s, however, far less than half were using tests. In the past decade, there has been a dramatic resurgence of employment testing.[27] In part, this indicates both that employers today are less fearful of lawsuits challenging the soundness of their tests and that there is a return to a focus on individual competence. Objective standards are coming back in both education and employment. Concurrently, methodological changes have made it easier to demonstrate test validity.[28] Too often employers have relied exclusively on the interview to measure or predict skills and abilities that can be measured or predicted more accurately by tests.

Tests have played a more important part in government HR programs where hiring on the basis of merit is required by law. Government agencies experienced the same types of problems with their testing programs as did organizations in the private sector. However, their staffs were forced to improve their testing programs rather than to abandon them.

Many organizations use professional test consultants such as Wonderlic Personnel Test Inc. in Libertyville, Illinois, to improve their testing programs and to meet EEO requirements. While it is often advisable to use consultants, especially

*This job candidate is taking a test that seeks to measure his aptitude for the skills he will need to perform the job.*

if an organization is considering the use of personality tests, managers should have a basic understanding of the technical aspects of testing and the contributions that tests can make to the HR program.

## Nature of Employment Tests

An employment test is an objective and standardized measure of a sample of behavior that is used to gauge a person's knowledge, skills, abilities, and other characteristics (KSAOs) in relation to other individuals.[29] The proper sampling of behavior—whether verbal, manipulative, or some other type—is the responsibility of the test author. It is also the responsibility of the test author to develop tests that meet accepted standards of reliability.[30] Data concerning reliability are ordinarily presented in the manual for the test. While high reliability is essential, it offers no assurance that the test provides the basis for making valid judgments. It is the responsibility of the HR staff to conduct validation studies before a test is adopted for regular use. Other considerations are cost, time, ease of administration and scoring, and the apparent relevance of the test to the individuals being tested—commonly referred to as "face validity." While face validity is desirable, it is no substitute for technical validity, described earlier in this chapter. Adopting a test just because it appears relevant is bad practice; many a "good-looking" test has poor validity.

**Aptitude tests**
   Measures of a person's capacity to learn or acquire skills

**Achievement tests**
   Measures of what a person knows or can do right now

## Classification of Employment Tests

Employment tests may be classified in different ways. Generally, they are viewed as measuring either aptitude or achievement. **Aptitude tests** measure a person's capacity to learn or acquire skills. **Achievement tests** measure what a person knows or can do right now.

### Cognitive Ability Tests

Cognitive ability tests measure mental capabilities such as general intelligence, verbal fluency, numerical ability, and reasoning ability. There are a host of paper-and-pencil tests that measure cognitive abilities, including the General Aptitude Test Battery (GATB), the Scholastic Aptitude Test (SAT), the Graduate Management Aptitude Test (GMAT), and the Bennett Mechanical Comprehension Test. Figure 5.8 shows some items that could be used to measure different cognitive abilities.

**FIGURE 5.8**

▶ **Sample Measures of Cognitive Ability**

**Verbal**

1. What is the meaning of the word "surreptitious"?

   a. covert
   b. winding
   c. lively
   d. sweet

2. How is the noun clause used in the following sentence? "I hope that I can learn this game."

   a. subject
   b. predicate nominative
   c. direct object
   d. object of the preposition

**Quantitative**

3. Divide 50 by 0.5 and add 5. What is the result?

   a. 25
   b. 30
   c. 95
   d. 105

4. What is the value of $144^2$?

   a. 12
   b. 72
   c. 288
   d. 20736

**Reasoning**

5. _____ is to *boat* as *snow* is to _____.

   a. Sail, ski
   b. Water, winter
   c. Water, ski
   d. Engine, water

6. Two women played 5 games of chess. Each woman won the same number of games, yet there were no ties. How can this be?

   a. There was a forfeit.
   b. One player cheated.
   c. They played different people.
   d. One game is still in progress.

**Mechanical**

7. If gear A and gear C are both turning counterclockwise, what is happening to gear B?

   a. It is turning counterclockwise.
   b. It is turning clockwise.
   c. It remains stationary.
   d. The whole system will jam.

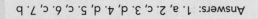

A       B       C

Answers: 1. a, 2. c, 3. d, 4. d, 5. c, 6. c, 7. b

Although cognitive ability tests can be developed to measure very specialized areas such as reading comprehension and spatial relations, many experts believe that the validity of cognitive ability tests simply reflects their connection to general intelligence. Measures of general intelligence (e.g., IQ) have been shown to be good predictors of performance across a wide variety of jobs.[31]

## Personality and Interest Inventories

Whereas cognitive ability tests measure a person's mental capacity, personality tests measure disposition and temperament. Years of research show that five dimensions can summarize personality traits. The "Big Five" factors include:

1. *Extroversion*—the degree to which someone is talkative, sociable, active, aggressive, and excitable
2. *Agreeableness*—the degree to which someone is trusting, amiable, generous, tolerant, honest, cooperative, and flexible
3. *Conscientiousness*—the degree to which someone is dependable and organized and perseveres in tasks
4. *Emotional stability*—the degree to which someone is secure, calm, independent, and autonomous
5. *Openness to experience*—the degree to which someone is intellectual, philosophical, insightful, creative, artistic, and curious[32]

The predictive validity of personality and interest inventories historically has been quite low. However, when used in combination with cognitive ability tests, measures of personality traits (such as conscientiousness) can lead to better prediction of job performance.[33]

**USING THE INTERNET**

Additional information about uses for Kuder and other interest inventories may be found at

job.careernet.org/mptc/interest.htm

As shown in Figure 5.9, personality tests can be problematic if they inadvertently discriminate against individuals who would otherwise perform effectively. Demonstrating job relatedness and validity of some personality characteristics is not always easy. The use of personality tests may also be seen as an invasion of privacy. For example, Target Stores, the national retailer, recently stopped using the Minnesota Multiphasic Personality Inventory (MMPI) and the California Psychological Inventory (CPI) as preemployment screening devices because they asked employees questions about their political views, belief in God, homosexuality, and bodily functions.[34] So many problems have stemmed from the use of personality tests for selection that several states, including Massachusetts, Minnesota, Rhode Island, and Wisconsin, severely restrict their usage.

Beyond the initial hiring decision, personality and interest inventories may be most useful for helping with occupational selection and career planning. Interest tests, such as the Kuder Inventory, measure an applicant's preferences for certain activities over others (such as sailing versus poker).

## Physical Ability Tests

In addition to learning about a job candidate's mental capabilities, employers frequently need to assess a person's physical abilities as well. These types of tests are reportedly being used more widely today for selection than ever before. Particularly for demanding and potentially dangerous jobs like those held by firefighters and police officers, physical abilities such as strength and endurance tend to be not only good predictors of performance, but of accidents and injuries.[35]

FIGURE 5.9

## Potentially Discriminatory Items on a Personality Test

The following are items taken from an actual personality test. Used for selecting employees, the items might unintentionally discriminate against certain individuals.

1. Do you prefer to associate with people younger than yourself?

2. When you are in low spirits, do you try to find someone to cheer you up?

3. Do you ever argue a point with an older person whom you respect?

4. Do ideas run through your head so that you cannot sleep?

5. Have you ever had dizzy spells?

6. Do you tend to be radical in your political, religious, or social beliefs?

7. Do your feelings alternate between happiness and sadness without apparent reason?

8. Do you feel that marriage is essential to your present or future happiness?

9. Are you usually considered to be indifferent to the opposite sex?

10. Would you like to be a church worker?

11. Would you like to be a minister, priest, or rabbi?

12. Would you like to read the Bible as a way of having fun?

13. Would you like to have day-to-day contact with religious people?

14. Would you like to have day-to-day contact with very old people?

15. Are you concerned about philosophical problems such as religion, the meaning of life, etc.?

Source: Daniel P. O'Meara, "Personality Tests Raise Questions of Legality and Effectiveness," *HRMagazine*, January 1994, 97–100. Reprinted with the permission of *HRMagazine*, published by the Society for Human Resource Management, Alexandria, Va.

Despite their potential value, physical ability tests tend to work to the disadvantage of women and disabled job applicants, a tendency that has led to several recent lawsuits. Evidence suggests that the average man is stronger, faster, and more powerful than the average woman, but women tend to have better balance, manual dexterity, flexibility, and coordination than men. On the basis of these differences, it is clear that (as with other methods for screening potential employees) the use of physical ability tests should be carefully validated on the basis of the essential functions of the job.[36]

### Job Knowledge Tests

Government agencies and licensing boards usually develop job knowledge tests, a type of achievement test designed to measure a person's level of understanding about a particular job. Most civil service examinations, for example, are used to determine whether an applicant possesses the information and understanding that will permit placement on the job without further training.[37] Job knowledge tests also play a major role in the enlisted personnel programs of the U.S. Army, Navy, Air Force, and Marines. They should be considered as useful tools for private and public organizations.

### Work Sample Tests

Work sample tests, or job sample tests, require the applicant to perform tasks that are actually a part of the work required on the job. Like job knowledge tests, work sample tests are constructed from a carefully developed outline that experts agree includes the major job functions; the tests are thus considered content-valid. Organizations that are interested in moving toward *competency-based selection*—that is, hiring based on observation of behaviors previously shown to distinguish successful employees—increasingly use work samples to see potential employees "in action."[38]

Work samples have been devised for many diverse jobs: a map-reading test for traffic control officers, a lathe test for machine operators, a complex coordination test for pilots, an in-basket test for managers, a group discussion test for supervisors, a judgment and decision-making test for administrators, to name a few. The City of Miami Beach has used work sample tests for jobs as diverse as plumbers, planners, and assistant chief accountants. The U.S. Air Force has used work samples for enlisted personnel in eight different specialty areas. In an increasing number of cases, work sample tests are aided by computer simulations, particularly when testing a candidate might prove dangerous. The reports are that this type of test is cost-effective, reliable, valid, fair, and acceptable to applicants.[39]

# The Employment Interview

Traditionally, the employment interview has a central role in the selection process—so much so that it is rare to find an instance where an employee is hired without some sort of interview. Depending upon the type of job, applicants may be interviewed by one person, by members of a work team, or other individuals in the organization. While researchers have raised some doubts about its validity, the interview remains a mainstay of selection because (1) it is especially practical when there are only a small number of applicants; (2) it serves other purposes, such as public relations; and (3) interviewers maintain great faith and confidence in their judgments. Nevertheless, the interview can be plagued by problems of subjectivity and personal bias. In those instances, the judgments of different interviewers may vary dramatically and the quality of the hire can be called into serious question.

In this section, we review the characteristics, advantages, and disadvantages of various types of employment interviews. We highlight the fact that the structure of the interview and the training of interviewers strongly influence the success of the hiring process.[40]

## Interviewing Methods

Interview methods differ in several ways, most significantly in terms of the amount of structure, or control, exercised by the interviewer. In highly structured interviews, the interviewer determines the course that the interview will follow as each question is asked. In the less structured interview, the applicant plays a larger role in determining the course the discussion will take. An examination of the different types of interviews from the least structured to the most structured reveals these differences.

## The Nondirective Interview

**Nondirective interview**
An interview in which the applicant is allowed the maximum amount of freedom in determining the course of the discussion, while the interviewer carefully refrains from influencing the applicant's remarks

In the **nondirective interview,** the interviewer carefully refrains from influencing the applicant's remarks. The applicant is allowed the maximum amount of freedom in determining the course of the discussion. The interviewer asks broad, open-ended questions—such as "Tell me more about your experiences on your last job"—and permits the applicant to talk freely with a minimum of interruption. Generally, the nondirective interviewer listens carefully and does not argue, interrupt, or change the subject abruptly. The interviewer also uses follow-up questions to allow the applicant to elaborate, makes only brief responses, and allows pauses in the conversation; the pausing technique is the most difficult for the beginning interviewer to master.

The greater freedom afforded to the applicant in the nondirective interview is particularly valuable in bringing to the interviewer's attention any information, attitudes, or feelings that may often be concealed by more structured questioning. However, because the applicant determines the course of the interview and no set procedure is followed, little information that comes from these interviews enables interviewers to cross-check agreement with other interviewers. Thus the reliability and validity of the nondirective interview may be expected to be minimal. This method is most likely to be used in interviewing candidates for high-level positions and in counseling, which we will discuss in Chapter 13.

## The Structured Interview

**Structured interview**
An interview in which a set of standardized questions having an established set of answers is used

More attention is being given to the structured interview as a result of EEO requirements and a concern for maximizing validity of selection decisions.[41] Because a **structured interview** has a set of standardized questions (based on job analysis) and an established set of answers against which applicant responses can be rated, it provides a more consistent basis for evaluating job candidates. For example, staff members of Weyerhauser Company's HR department have developed a structured interviewing process with the following characteristics:

1. The interview process is based exclusively on job duties and requirements critical to job performance.
2. It uses four types of questions: situational questions, job knowledge questions, job sample/simulation questions, and worker requirements questions.
3. There are sample (benchmark) answers, determined in advance, to each question. Interviewee responses are rated on a five-point scale relative to those answers.
4. The process involves an interview committee so that interviewee responses are evaluated by several raters.
5. It consistently follows the same procedures in all instances to ensure that each applicant has exactly the same chance as every other applicant.
6. The interviewer takes notes and documents the interview for future reference and in case of legal challenge.[42]

A structured interview is more likely to provide the type of information needed for making sound decisions. It also helps to reduce the possibility of legal charges of unfair discrimination. Employers must be aware that the interview is highly vulnerable to legal attack and that more litigation in this area can be expected in the future.

Most employment interviewers will tend toward either a nondirected or a structured format. However, within the general category of structured interviews, there are more specific differences that relate to the format of questions. These include the situational interview and behavioral description interview discussed below.

### The Situational Interview

**Situational interview**
An interview in which an applicant is given a hypothetical incident and asked how he or she would respond to it

One variation of the structured interview is called the **situational interview.**[43] With this approach, an applicant is given a *hypothetical* incident and asked how he or she would respond to it. The applicant's response is then evaluated relative to preestablished benchmark standards. Interestingly, many organizations are using the situational interview to select new college graduates. Highlights in HRM 2 shows a sample question from a situational interview used to select systems analysts at a chemical plant.

### The Behavioral Description Interview

**Behavioral description interview (BDI)**
An interview in which an applicant is asked questions about what he or she actually did in a given situation

In contrast to a situational interview, which focuses on hypothetical situations, a **behavioral description interview (BDI)** focuses on *actual* work incidents in the interviewee's past. The BDI format asks the job applicant what he or she actually did in a given situation. For example, to assess a potential manager's ability to handle a problem employee, an interviewer might ask, "Tell me about the last time you disciplined an employee." Such an approach to interviewing, based on a critical-incidents job analysis, assumes that past performance is the best predictor of future performance. It also may be somewhat less susceptible to applicant faking.

**HRM 2**

## HIGHLIGHTS IN HRM

# Sample Situational Interview Question

**QUESTION:**
It is the night before your scheduled vacation. You are all packed and ready to go. Just before you get into bed, you receive a phone call from the plant. A problem has arisen that only you can handle. You are asked to come in to take care of things. What would you do in this situation?

**RECORD ANSWER:**
_____
_____
_____

**SCORING GUIDE:**
Good: "I would go in to work and make certain that everything is O.K. Then I would go on vacation."
Good: "There are no problems that *only* I can handle. I would make certain that someone qualified was there to handle things."
Fair: "I would try to find someone else to deal with the problem."
Fair: "I would go on vacation."

*Panel interviews may result in higher validity because they allow input from several interviewers. Here, the man on the left is being interviewed by a panel of four.*

### The Panel Interview

**Panel interview**
An interview in which a board of interviewers questions and observes a single candidate

Another type of interview involves a panel of interviewers who question and observe a single candidate. In a typical **panel interview** the candidate meets with three to five interviewers who take turns asking questions. After the interview the interviewers pool their observations to reach a consensus about the suitability of the candidate. HRM specialists using this method at Philip Morris USA and Virginia Power report that panel interviews provide several significant advantages over traditional one-to-one interviews, including higher validity because of multiple inputs, greater acceptance of the decision, and shorter decision time.[44]

### The Computer Interview

With advances in information technology, more and more organizations are using computers and the Internet to help with the interviewing process. Nike (see end of chapter case), Cigna Insurance, Pinkerton Security, and Coopers & Lybrand have all developed expert systems to gather preliminary information as well as compare candidates.

Typically, a computer interview requires candidates to answer a series (75 to 125) of multiple-choice questions tailored to the job. These answers are compared with either an ideal profile or with profiles developed on the basis of other candidates' responses. Commercially available systems from companies such as TelServe or Aspen Tree allow organizations to generate printed reports that contain applicant response summaries, itemized lists of contradictory responses, latency response reports (time delays for each answer), summaries of potentially problematic responses, and lists of structured interview questions for the job interviewer to ask.[45]

A few years ago, Pic 'n Pay Shoe Stores partnered with MCI to create a computerized interview that could be conducted over the phone using an 800 number. The interview focused on honesty, work attitude, drug use, candor, dependability, and self-motivation. After implementing the system, the company cut turnover by 50 percent and reduced employee theft by almost 40 percent. Coopers & Lybrand took this idea one step further. Their system, called Springboard, is the first to put computer interview on the web (www.clspringboard.com). Coopers also has an on-line application system called Strategic Selection Advantage (SSA). Because the company recruits over 1,400 students a year, it developed an on-line application form that allows recruits to register their application and complete four initial screening modules at their convenience. Student answers are compared to a database of more than 300 first-year Coopers & Lybrand associates that has strong predictive validity with job performance.[46]

In addition to the benefits of objectivity, some research evidence suggests that applicants may be less likely to engage in "impression management" in computerized interviews than in face-to-face interviews.[47] So far, organizations have used the computer mainly as a complement to, rather than as a replacement for, conventional interviews.

## Guidelines for Employment Interviewers

Apart from the characteristics of the interviews themselves, there are several important tips for interviewers. Organizations should be cautious in selecting employment interviewers. Qualities that are desirable include humility, the ability to think objectively, maturity, and poise. Given the importance of diversity in the workforce, experience in associating with people from a variety of backgrounds is also desirable. Qualities to avoid in interviewers include overtalkativeness, extreme opinions, and biases.

### A Review of the Best

There have been several reviews of research studies on the employment interview.[48] Each of these reviews discusses and evaluates numerous studies concerned with such questions as "What traits can be assessed in the interview?" and "How do interviewers reach their decisions?" Highlights in HRM 3 presents some of the major findings of these studies. It shows that information is available that can be used to increase the validity of interviews.

Figure 5.10 summarizes the variables and processes involved in the employment interview. The figure shows that a number of applicant characteristics may influence the perception of the interviewer and thus the hiring decision. In addition, many interviewer and situational factors may also influence the perceptual and judgmental processes. For example, the race and sex of an applicant may shape the expectations, biases, and behaviors of an interviewer, which in turn may affect the interview outcome. Even a limited understanding of the variables shown in Figure 5.10 can help increase the interviewing effectiveness of managers and supervisors.

### Interviewer Training

Training has been shown to dramatically improve the competence of interviewers.[49] One "quick and dirty" source for interviewer training is Curry Business System's *Employment Interviewer Training Course*. More of a review than a training program per se, Curry Business System maintains a free web-based guide to effective interviewing (www.curryinc.com). The web site is divided into separate modules that review content, structure, legal issues, and planning.

HRM 3

# Some Major Findings from Research Studies on the Interview

1. Structured interviews are more reliable than unstructured interviews.
2. Interviewers are influenced more by unfavorable than by favorable information.
3. Interrater reliability is increased when there is a greater amount of information about the job to be filled.
4. A bias is established early in the interview, and this tends to be followed by either a favorable or an unfavorable decision.
5. Intelligence is the trait most validly estimated by an interview, but the interview information adds nothing to test data.
6. Interviewers can explain why they feel an applicant is likely to be an unsatisfactory employee but not why the applicant may be satisfactory.
7. Factual written data seem to be more important than physical appearance in determining judgments. This increases with interviewing experience.
8. An interviewee is given a more extreme evaluation (positive/negative) when preceded by an interviewee of opposing value (positive/negative).
9. Interpersonal skills and motivation are probably best evaluated by the interview.
10. Allowing the applicant time to talk makes rapid first impressions less likely and provides a larger behavior sample.
11. Nonverbal as well as verbal interactions influence decisions.
12. Experienced interviewers rank applicants in the same order, although they differ in the proportion that they will accept. There is a tendency for experienced interviewers to be more selective than less experienced ones.

If not done on a continuing basis, training should at least be done periodically for managers, supervisors, and HR representatives who conduct interviews. Interviewer training programs should include practice interviews conducted under guidance. Practice interviews may be recorded on videotape and evaluated later in a group training session. Some variation in technique is only natural. However, the following list presents ten ground rules for employment interviews that are commonly accepted and supported by research findings. Their apparent simplicity should not lead one to underestimate their importance.

1. *Establish an interview plan.* Examine the purposes of the interview and determine the areas and specific questions to be covered. Review job requirements, application-form data, test scores, and other available information before seeing the applicant.

2. *Establish and maintain rapport.* This is accomplished by greeting the applicant pleasantly, by explaining the purpose of the interview, by displaying sincere interest in the applicant, and by listening carefully.

FIGURE 5.10

Variables in the Employment Interview

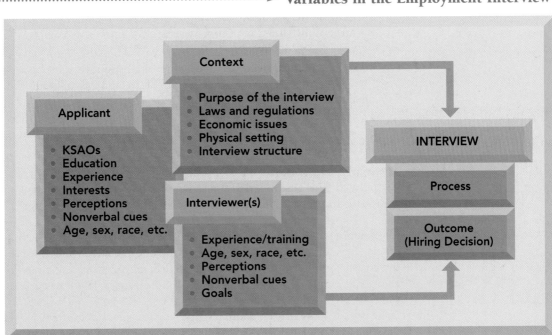

3. *Be an active listener.* Strive to understand, comprehend, and gain insight into what is only suggested or implied. A good listener's mind is alert, and face and posture usually reflect this fact.

4. *Pay attention to nonverbal cues.* An applicant's facial expressions, gestures, body position, and movements often provide clues to that person's attitudes and feelings. Interviewers should be aware of what they themselves are communicating nonverbally.

5. *Provide information as freely and honestly as possible.* Answer fully and frankly the applicant's questions. Present a realistic picture of the job.

6. *Use questions effectively.* To elicit a truthful answer, questions should be phrased as objectively as possible, giving no indication of what response is desired.

7. *Separate facts from inferences.* During the interview, record factual information. Later, record your inferences or interpretations of the facts. Compare your inferences with those of other interviewers.

8. *Recognize biases and stereotypes.* One typical bias is for interviewers to consider strangers who have interests, experiences, and backgrounds similar to their own to be more acceptable. Stereotyping involves forming generalized opinions of how people of a given gender, race, or ethnic background appear, think, feel, and act. The influence of sex-role stereotyping is central to sex discrimination in employment. Avoid the influence of "beautyism." Discrimination against unattractive persons is a persistent and pervasive form of employment discrimination. Also avoid "halo error," or judging an individual favorably or unfavorably overall on the basis of only one strong point (or weak point) on which you place high value.

9. *Control the course of the interview.* Establish an interview plan and stick to it. Provide the applicant with ample opportunity to talk but maintain control of the situation in order to reach the interview objectives.

10. *Standardize the questions asked.* To increase reliability and avoid discrimination, ask the same questions of all applicants for a particular job. Keep careful notes; record facts, impressions, and any relevant information, including what was told to the applicant.

## Are Your Questions Legal?

The entire subject of what is legal or illegal in an employment interview gets pretty complicated. There are differing and sometimes contradictory interpretations by the courts, the EEOC, and the OFCCP about what you can ask in an interview. Under federal laws there are no questions that are expressly prohibited. However, the EEOC looks with disfavor on direct or indirect questions related to race, color, age, religion, sex, or national origin. Some of the questions that interviewers once felt free to ask are now potentially hazardous. Federal courts have severely limited the area of questioning. An interviewer, for example, can ask about physical disabilities if the job involves manual labor, but not otherwise. Several states have fair employment practice laws that are more restrictive than federal legislation. In general, if a question is job-related, is asked of everyone, and does not discriminate against a certain class of applicants, it is likely to be acceptable to government authorities.

Particular care has to be given to questions asked of female applicants about their family responsibilities. It is inappropriate, for example, to ask, "Who will take care of your children while you are at work?" or "Do you plan to have children?" or "What is your husband's occupation?" or "Are you engaged?" It is, in fact, inappropriate to ask applicants of either gender questions about matters that have no relevance to job performance.

Employers have found it advisable to provide interviewers with instructions on how to avoid potentially discriminatory questions in their interviews. The examples of appropriate and inappropriate questions shown in Highlights in HRM 4 may serve as guidelines for application forms as well as preemployment interviews. Complete guidelines may be developed from current information available from district and regional EEOC offices and from state FEP offices. Once the individual is hired, the information needed but not asked in the interview may be obtained if there is a valid need for it and if it does not lead to discrimination.

# Reaching a Selection Decision

While all of the steps in the selection process are important, the most critical step is the decision to accept or reject applicants. Because of the cost of placing new employees on the payroll, the short probationary period in many organizations, and EEO/AA considerations, the final decision must be as sound as possible. Thus it requires systematic consideration of all the relevant information about applicants. It is common to use summary forms and checklists to ensure that all of the pertinent information has been included in the evaluation of applicants.

**HRM 4**

# Appropriate and Inappropriate Interview Questions

| | APPROPRIATE QUESTIONS | INAPPROPRIATE QUESTIONS |
|---|---|---|
| National origin | What is your name?<br>Have you ever worked under a different name?<br>Do you speak any foreign languages that may be pertinent to this job? | What's the origin of your name?<br>What is your ancestry? |
| Age | Are you over 18?<br>If hired, can you prove your age? | How old are you?<br>What is your date of birth? |
| Gender | (Say nothing unless it involves a bona fide occupational qualification.) | Are you a man or a woman? |
| Race | (Say nothing.) | What is your race? |
| Disabilities | Do you have any disabilities that may inhibit your job performance?<br>Are you willing to take a physical exam if the job requires it? | Do you have any physical defects?<br>When was your last physical?<br>What color are your eyes, hair, etc.? |
| Height and weight | (Not appropriate unless it is a bona fide occupational qualification.) | How tall are you?<br>How much do you weigh? |
| Residence | What is your address?<br>How long have you lived there? | What are the names/relationships of those with whom you live? |
| Religion | (You may inform a person of the required work schedule.) | Do you have any religious affiliation? |
| Military record | Did you have any military education/experience pertinent to this job? | What type of discharge did you receive? |
| Education and experience | Where did you go to school?<br>Did you finish school?<br>What is your prior work experience?<br>Why did you leave?<br>What is your salary history? | Is that a church-affiliated school?<br>When did you graduate?<br>What are your hobbies? |
| Criminal record | Have you ever been convicted of a crime? | Have you ever been arrested? |
| Citizenship | Do you have a legal right to work in the United States? | Are you a U.S. citizen? |
| Marital/family status | What is the name, address, and telephone number of a person we may contact in case of an emergency? | Are you married, divorced, single?<br>Do you prefer Miss, Mrs., or Ms.?<br>Do you have any children? How old are they? |

## Summarizing Information about Applicants

Fundamentally, an employer is interested in what an applicant can do and will do. An evaluation of candidates on the basis of assembled information should focus on these two factors, as shown in Figure 5.11. The "can-do" factors include knowledge and skills, as well as the aptitude (the potential) for acquiring new knowledge and skills. The "will-do" factors include motivation, interests, and other personality characteristics. Both factors are essential to successful performance on the job. The employee who has the ability (can do) but is not motivated to use it (will not do) is little better than the employee who lacks the necessary ability.

It is much easier to measure what individuals can do than what they will do. The can-do factors are readily evident from test scores and verified information. What the individual will do can only be inferred. Responses to interview and application-form questions may be used as a basis for obtaining information for making inferences about what an individual will do.

## Decision Strategy

The strategy used for making personnel decisions for one category of jobs may differ from that used for another category. The strategy for selecting managerial and executive personnel, for example, will differ from that used in selecting clerical and technical personnel. While many factors are to be considered in hiring decisions, the following are some of the questions that managers must consider:

1. Should the individuals be hired according to their highest potential or according to the needs of the organization?
2. At what grade or wage level should the individual be started?

**FIGURE 5.11** ▸ **"Can-Do" and "Will-Do" Factors in Selection Decisions**

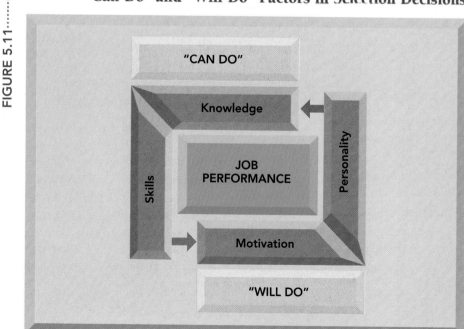

3. Should initial selection be concerned primarily with an ideal match of the employee to the job, or should potential for advancement in the organization be considered?

4. To what extent should those who are not qualified but are qualifiable be considered?

5. Should overqualified individuals be considered?

6. What effect will a decision have on meeting affirmative action plans and diversity considerations?

In addition to these types of factors, managers must also consider which approach they will use in making hiring decisions. There are two basic approaches to selection: clinical (personal judgment) and statistical.

### Clinical Approach

In the clinical approach to decision making, those making the selection decision review all the data on applicants. Then, on the basis of their understanding of the job and the individuals who have been successful in that job, they make a decision. Different individuals often arrive at different decisions about an applicant when they use this approach because each evaluator assigns different weights to the applicant's strengths and weaknesses. Furthermore, personal biases and stereotypes are frequently covered up by what appear to be rational bases for acceptance or rejection.

### Statistical Approach

In contrast to the clinical approach, the statistical approach to decision making is more objective. It involves identifying the most valid predictors and weighting them through statistical methods such as multiple regression.[50] Quantified data such as scores or ratings from interviews, tests, and other procedures are then combined according to their weighted value. Individuals with the highest combined scores are selected. A comparison of the clinical approach with the statistical approach in a wide variety of situations has shown that the statistical approach is superior. Although this superiority has been recognized for many decades, the clinical approach continues to be the one most commonly used.[51]

With a strictly statistical approach, a candidate's high score on one predictor (e.g., cognitive ability test) will make up for a low score on another predictor (e.g., the interview). For this reason, this model is a **compensatory model.** However, it is frequently important that applicants achieve some minimum level of proficiency on all selection dimensions. When this is the case, a **multiple cutoff model** can be used in which only those candidates who score above the cutoff on all dimensions are considered. The selection decision is made from that subset of candidates.

A variation of the multiple cutoff is referred to as the **multiple hurdle model.** This decision strategy is sequential in that after candidates go through an initial evaluation stage, the ones who score well are provisionally accepted and are assessed further at each successive stage. The process may continue through several stages (hurdles) before a final decision is made regarding the candidates. This approach is especially useful when either the testing or training procedures are lengthy and expensive.

Each of the statistical approaches requires that a decision be made about where the cutoff lies—that point in the distribution of scores above which a person should be considered and below which the person should be rejected. The

---

**Compensatory model**
Selection decision model in which a high score in one area can make up for a low score in another area

**Multiple cutoff model**
Selection decision model that requires an applicant to achieve some minimum level of proficiency on all selection dimensions

**Multiple hurdle model**
A sequential strategy in which only the applicants with the highest scores at an initial test stage go on to subsequent stages

score that the applicant must achieve is the cutoff score. Depending upon the labor supply, it may be necessary to lower or raise the cutoff score.

The effects of raising and lowering the cutoff score are illustrated in Figure 5.12. Each dot in the center of the figure represents the relationship between the test score (or a weighted combination of test scores) and the criterion of success for one individual. In this instance, the test has a fairly high validity, as represented by the elliptical pattern of dots. Note that the high-scoring individuals are concentrated in the satisfactory category on job success, whereas the low-scoring individuals are concentrated in the unsatisfactory category.

If the cutoff score is set at A, only the individuals represented by areas 1 and 2 will be accepted. Nearly all of them will be successful. If more employees are needed (i.e., there is an increase in the selection ratio), the cutoff score may be lowered to point B. In this case, a larger number of potential failures will be accepted, as shown in quadrants 2 and 4. Even if the cutoff is lowered to C, the total number of satisfactory individuals selected (represented by the dots in areas 1, 3, and 5) exceeds the total number selected who are unsatisfactory (areas 2, 4,

FIGURE 5.12

Test Score Scatterplot with Hypothetical Cutoffs

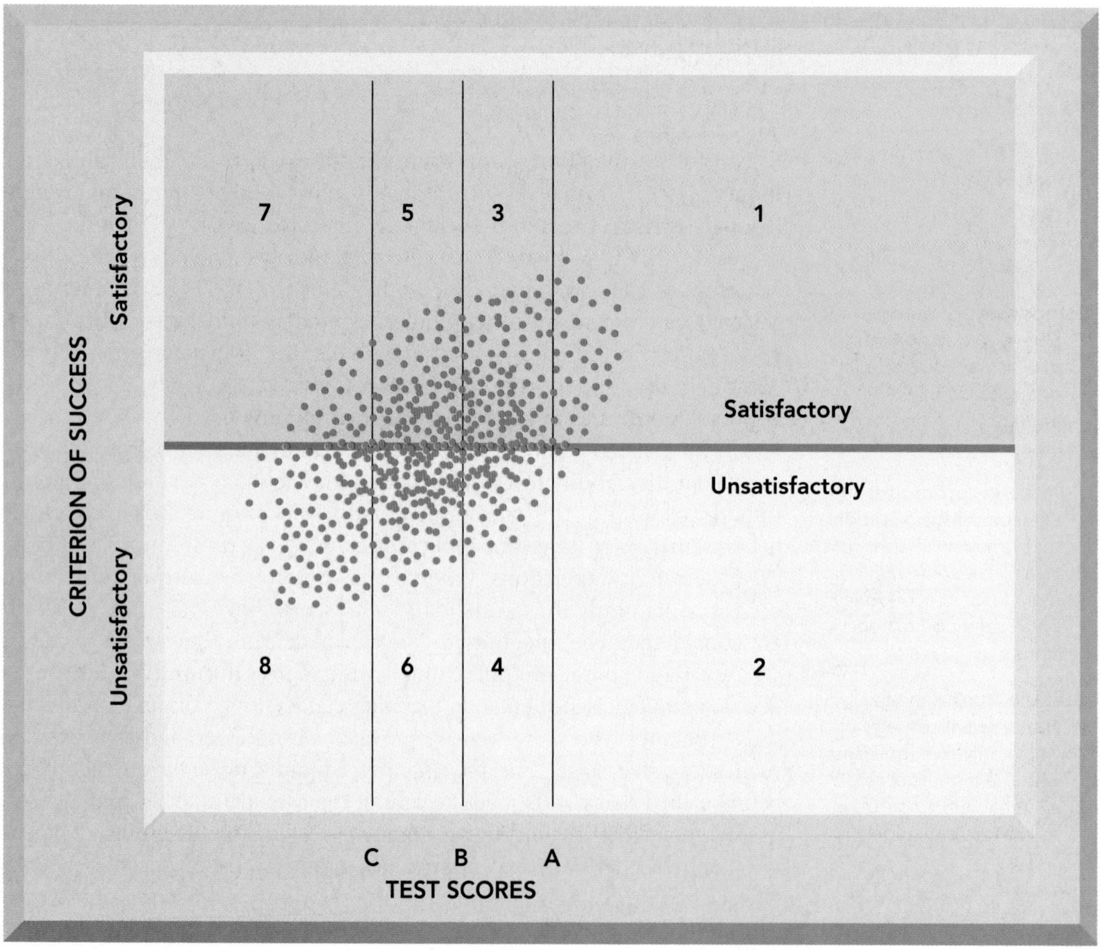

and 6). Thus the test serves to maximize the selection of probable successes and to minimize the selection of probable failures. This is all we can hope for in predicting job success: the probability of selecting a greater proportion of individuals who will be successful rather than unsuccessful.

While the most valid predictors should be used with any selection strategy, there is a related factor that contributes to selecting the best-qualified persons. It is selectivity, or having an adequate number of applicants or candidates from which to make a selection. Selectivity is typically expressed in terms of a **selection ratio,** which is the ratio of the number of applicants to be selected to the total number of applicants. A ratio of 0.10, for example, means that 10 percent of the applicants will be selected. A ratio of 0.90 means that 90 percent will be selected. If the selection ratio is low, only the most promising applicants will normally be hired. When the ratio is high, very little selectivity will be possible, since even applicants having mediocre ability will have to be hired if the vacancies are to be filled.

**Selection ratio**

The number of applicants compared with the number of persons to be hired

It should be noted that how much of a contribution any predictor will make to the improvement of a given selection process is a function not only of the validity of the predictor and the selection ratio, but also of the proportion of persons who are judged successful using current selection procedures.[52]

## Final Decision

After a preliminary selection has been made in the employment department, those applicants who appear to be most promising are then referred to departments having vacancies. There they are interviewed by the managers or supervisors, who usually make the final decision and communicate it to the employment department. Because of the weight that is usually given to their choices, managers and supervisors should be trained so that their role in the selection process does not negate the more rigorous efforts of the HR department staff.

In large organizations, notifying applicants of the decision and making job offers is often the responsibility of the HR department. This department should confirm the details of the job, working arrangements, wages, etc., and specify a deadline by which the applicant must reach a decision. If, at this point, findings from the medical examination are not yet available, an offer is often made contingent upon the applicant's passing the examination.

In government agencies, the selection of individuals to fill vacancies is made from lists or registers of eligible candidates. Ordinarily, three or more names of individuals at the top of the register are submitted to the requisitioning official. This arrangement provides some latitude for those making a selection and, at the same time, preserves the merit system.

# SUMMARY

**OBJECTIVE 1** The selection process should provide as much reliable and valid information as possible about applicants so that their qualifications can be carefully matched with job specifications. The information that is obtained should be clearly job-related or predictive of success on the job and free from potential discrimination. Reliability refers to the consistency of test scores over time and across measures. Validity refers to the accuracy of measurement. Validity can be assessed in terms of whether the measurement is based on a job specification (content validity), whether test scores correlate with performance criteria (predictive validity), and whether the test accurately measures what it purports to measure (construct validity).

**OBJECTIVE 2** Interviews are customarily used in conjunction with application forms, biographical information blanks, references, background investigations, medical examinations, cognitive ability tests, job knowledge tests, and work sample tests.

**OBJECTIVE 3** While the popularity of tests had declined somewhat with the passage of EEO laws, in recent years there has been a dramatic resurgence of testing. The value of tests should not be overlooked since they are more objective than the interview and can provide a broader sampling of behavior. Cognitive ability tests are especially valuable for assessing verbal, quantitative, and reasoning abilities. Personality and interest tests are perhaps best for placement. Physical ability tests are most useful for predicting job performance, accidents, and injuries, particularly for demanding work. Job knowledge and work sample tests are achievement tests that are useful for determining if a candidate can perform the duties of the job without further training.

**OBJECTIVE 4** The interview is an important source of information about job applicants. It can be unstructured, wherein the interviewer is free to pursue whatever approach and sequence of topics might seem appropriate. Alternatively, an interview can be structured, wherein each applicant receives the same set of questions, which have preestablished answers. Some interviews are situational and can focus on hypothetical situations or actual behavioral descriptions of previous work experiences. Interviews can be conducted by a single individual, by a panel, or via a computer interface. Regardless of the technique chosen, those who conduct interviews should receive special training to acquaint them with interviewing methods and EEO considerations. The training should also make them more aware of the major findings from research studies on the interview and how they can apply these findings.

**OBJECTIVE 5** In the process of making decisions, all "can-do" and "will-do" factors should be assembled and weighted systematically so that the final decision can be based on a composite of the most reliable and valid information. While the clinical approach to decision making is used more than the statistical approach, the former lacks the accuracy of the latter. Compensatory models allow a candidate's high score on one predictor to make up for a low score on another. However, multiple cutoff and multiple hurdle approaches require minimal competency on each selection criterion. Whichever of these approaches is used, the goal is to select a greater proportion of individuals who will be successful on the job.

# KEY TERMS

achievement tests
aptitude tests
behavioral description
   interview (BDI)
compensatory model
concurrent validity
construct validity
content validity

criterion-related validity
cross-validation
multiple cutoff model
multiple hurdle model
nondirective interview
panel interview
predictive validity
reliability

selection
selection ratio
situational interview
structured interview
validity
validity generalization

# DISCUSSION QUESTIONS

 **1.** What is meant by the term "criterion" as it is used in personnel selection? Give some examples of criteria used for jobs with which you are familiar.

 **2.** What are some of the problems that arise in checking references furnished by job applicants? Are there any solutions to these problems?

3. What characteristics do job knowledge and job sample tests have that often make them more acceptable to the examinees than other types of tests?

 4. Personality tests, like other tests used in employee selection, have been under attack for several decades. What are some of the reasons applicants find personality tests objectionable? On what basis could their use for selection purposes be justified?

 5. Compare briefly the major types of employment interviews described in this chapter. Which type would you prefer to conduct? Why?

 6. In what ways does the clinical approach to selection differ from the statistical approach? How do you account for the fact that one approach is superior to the other?

## Nike: Hiring Gets Off on the Right Foot

Technology is changing how companies recruit and select in ways that couldn't have been anticipated a few years ago. While automated hiring technologies are still in their infancy, recruiters envision a world in which they can reduce the hiring cycle time by 90 percent, anticipate what skills will be in demand before they can be articulated, and call up information about a potential hire on their computer screens. Interactive voice response technology (IVR), which has been in use for a long time, is being used along with other database technologies to capture information about potential employees, giving the company more flexibility and speeding hiring decisions.

Nike is one example of a company using computer-assisted interviewing. The company has used an Aspen Tree product to hire employees for Niketowns, retail stores that showcase Nike products. At a recently opened store in Las Vegas, 6,000 people responded to ads for workers needed to fill 250 positions. Nike used IVR technology to make the first cut. Applicants responded to eight questions over the telephone; 3,500 applicants were screened out because they weren't available when needed or didn't have retail experience. The rest had a computer-assisted interview at the store, followed by a personal interview.

"We think it's important to give a personal interview to anyone who comes to the store," says Brian Rogers, Nike's manager of human resources for the retail division. "Applicants are customers as well as potential hires."

The computer interview identified those candidates who had been in customer service environments, had a passion for sports, and would make good Nike customer service representatives. Interviews were done in batches. The computer interview (which includes a video showing three scenarios for helping a customer and asks the applicant to choose the best one) was given every forty-five minutes to a group of applicants. As applicants completed the interview, a printer in the next room printed their responses. Areas that needed to be probed further were flagged, as were areas that indicated particular strengths.

While the applicant completed an application form on-line, the interviewer used the printout to prepare for the applicant's human interview. Some applicants would be given only a short interview; other, more likely candidates would be interviewed at greater length. The computer not only helped interviewers screen for people who lost their temper in work situations or who demonstrated other undesirable behaviors, but it also helped the interviewers to determine what to ask to reconcile inconsistencies in the computer interview or to probe applicant strengths in desired areas. Because Nike uses behavioral-based interviewing, applicants must document their areas of strength with examples from their work. Some applicants were offered jobs on the spot. Others were called back for second interviews.

Rogers says using computer-assisted interviewing has helped Nike staff up fast as well as reduce turnover in the retail division. The company saved $2.4 million during a three-year period by reducing turnover from 87 to 51 percent, although other processes for coaching and leading within the stores have also played a part. Other areas of the company see the technology as promising, and Nike is exploring developing electronic profiles for manufacturing positions.

Source: Linda Thornburg, "Computer-Assisted Interviewing Shortens Hiring Cycle," *HRMagazine* 43, no. 2 (February 1998): 73–79. Reprinted with the permission of *HRMagazine*, published by the Society for Human Resource Management, Alexandria, Va.

### QUESTIONS

1. What do you think are the prime advantages and disadvantages of Nike's computer-based interviewing system?
2. Are there any EEO concerns regarding this system?
3. If interviews serve a public relations role, what should Nike be concerned about?
4. How would you suggest that Nike might modify and improve its system?

## Small Companies Need Diversity Too

When John Chuang started MacTemps, a temporary staffing firm, in 1987, he thought that if he hired strictly according to merit and turned a blind eye to race, age, and gender, he would get a diverse and balanced workforce without imposing rules or guidelines. As a small company, MacTemps wasn't closely scrutinized by the EEOC or the OFCCP. And as an Asian, himself, Chuang didn't like the idea of affirmative action because it allowed people to typecast him. As he said, "Did I get into Harvard University solely because I was a minority?" He felt as though his success was due to his hard work, not his ethnic background. He was certain that hiring talented people—regardless of race, gender, and the like—was the best approach.

After eight years of frenzied growth, MacTemps had $50 million in revenue and had made the *Inc.* 500 list twice. Chuang thought his "meritocracy" was working very well. Then, a *New York Times* reporter brought to his attention that MacTemps had a preponderance of white males at the top level of the company and a preponderance of white females in other positions. Despite Chuang's hope for a diverse workforce, a couple of staffing practices had moved the company off track.

First, the hiring decisions were based, quite fairly, on experience. But in the temporary help industry, which has historically been skewed toward secretarial and clerical jobs, the people with the most experience tended to be white females.

By hiring new managers based solely on their prior experience, Chuang had inadvertently hired a disproportionate number of women. Second, most start-ups depend on personal relationships. So entrepreneurs often hire friends, and Chuang was no different. As he put it, "When you're in the initial start-up phase, you're not thinking about diversity for the future, you're thinking about getting sales, and you count on the people you know. The pitfall of hiring friends, of course, is that they tend to be like you."

To rectify the problem, and maximize the potential benefits of hiring a diverse workforce, Chuang has undertaken a number of steps to improve the hiring process at MacTemps. For starters, the company brings in entry-level employees who reflect the ethnic composition of the countries in which it would like to do business. Accompanying this, the company has established a set of diversity goals—not quotas—and according to Chuang, "will never promote a less qualified person over a more qualified one." Nevertheless, the company is confident its efforts will create an internal staff with a wider perspective as well as cultivate a more diverse workforce for hire by its customers.

Source: John Chuang, "On Balance," *Inc.*, July 1995, 25–26. Adapted with permission, *Inc. Magazine*, July 1995. Copyright 1995 by Goldhirsh Group, Inc., 38 Commercial Wharf, Boston, Mass. 02110; permission conveyed through Copyright Clearance Center, Inc.

### QUESTIONS

1. Do you think MacTemps should have changed its hiring strategy? Explain.
2. Do you foresee any problems with the changes that Chuang instituted? Explain.
3. What *should* the diversity goals of MacTemps be?
4. If MacTemps also provides temporary employees for firms in other countries, how might managers in other countries view Chuang's staffing policies?

# NOTES AND REFERENCES

1. Edward L. Levine, Doris M. Maye, Ronald A. Ulm, and Thomas R. Gordon, "A Methodology for Developing and Validating Minimum Qualifications (MQs)," *Personnel Psychology* 50, no. 4 (Winter 1997): 1009–23; Jodi Barnes Nelson, "The Boundaryless Organization: Implications for Job Analysis, Recruitment, and Selection," *Human Resource Planning* 20, no. 4 (1997): 39–49; Greg L. Stewart and Kenneth P. Carson, "Moving beyond the Mechanistic Model: An Alternative Approach to Staffing for Contemporary Organizations," *Human Resource Management Review* 7, no. 2 (Summer 1997: 157–84; "Competencies Drive HR Practices," *HRFocus* 73, no. 8 (August 1996):15; Pat McLagan, "Great Ideas Revisited," *Training and Development* 50, no. 1 (January 1996): 60–65.

2. Kim Jones, "Be Specific to Give a Fair Deal to Disabled People, " *People Management* 3, no. 3 (February 6, 1997): 43; Bruce Meger, "A Critical Review of Competency-Based Systems," *Human Resource Professional* 9, no. 1 (January/February 1996): 22–25; Frank J. Landy and Laura J. Shankster, "Personnel Selection and Placement," in *Annual Review of Psychology* 45 (Palo Alto, Calif.: Annual Reviews 1994), 261–96.

3. Neal Schmitt, William Rogers, David Chan, Lori Sheppard, and Danielle Jennings, "Adverse Impact and Predictive Efficiency of Various Predictor Combinations," *Journal of Applied Psychology* 82, no. 5 (October 1997): 719–30; Charlene Marmer Solomon, "Testing at Odds with Diversity Efforts?" *Personnel Journal* 75, no. 4 (April 1996): 131–40; Scott E. Maxwell and Richard D. Arvey, "The Search for Predictors with High Validity and Low Adverse Impact: Compatible or Incompatible Goals?" *Journal of Applied Psychology* 78, no. 3 (June 1993): 433–37.

4. Frank J. Landy, "Test Validity Yearbook," *Journal of Business Psychology* 7, no. 2 (1992): 111–257. See also Edwin E. Ghiselli, "The Validity of Aptitude Tests in Personnel Selection," *Personnel Psychology* 26, no. 4 (Winter 1973): 461–77; J. E. Hunter and R. H. Hunter, "Validity and Utility of Alternative Predictors of Job Performance," *Psychological Bulletin* 96 (1984): 72–98; N. Schmitt, R. Z. Gooding, R. A. Noe, and M. Kirsch, "Meta-Analysis of Validity Studies Published between 1964 and 1982 and the Investigation of Study Characteristics," *Personnel Psychology* 37 (1984): 407–22.

5. Calvin C. Hoffman and S. Morton McPhail, "Exploring Options for Supporting Test Use in Situations Precluding Local Validation," *Personnel Psychology* 51, no. 4 (Winter 1998): 987–1003.

6. Levine, Maye, Ulm, and Gordon, "A Methodology"; S. Messick, "Foundations of Validity: Meaning and Consequences in Psychological Assessment," *European Journal of Psychological Assessment* 10 (1994): 1–9.

7. For examples of recent research on construct validity, see the following: Allison W. Harrison, Wayne A. Hochwarter, Pamela L. Perrewe, and David A. Ralston, "The Ingratiation Construct: An Assessment of the Validity of the Measure of Ingratiatory Behaviors in Organizational Settings (MIBOS)," *Journal of Applied Psychology* 83, no. 6 (December 1998): 932–43; David B. Schmidt, David Lubinski, and Camilla Persson Benbow, "Validity of Assessing Educational-Vocational Preference Dimensions among Intellectually Talented 13-Year-Olds," *Journal of Counseling Psychology* 45, no. 4 (October 1998): 436–53.

8. "Beware of Resumania," *Personnel Journal,* April 1996, 28; Marlene Brown, "Checking the Facts on a Resume," *Personnel Journal,* January 1993, SS6–SS7. See also T. Lammers, "How to Read between the Lines: Tactics for Evaluating a Resume," *Inc.,* March 1993, 105–7.

9. Teresa Brady, "Coming and Going," *American Management Association,* August 1996, 10–12.

10. Scott R. Kaak, Hubert S. Field, William F. Giles, and Dwight R. Norris, "The Weighted Application Blank," *Cornell Hotel and Restaurant Administration Quarterly* 39, no. 2 (April 1998): 18–24. See also J. S. Boles, L. E. Ross, and J. T. Johnson, "Reducing Employee Turnover through the Use of Preemployment Application Demographics: An Exploratory Study," *Council on Hotel, Restaurant, and Institutional Education* 19 (1995): 19–30. Mitchell, "BioData: Using Employment Applications to Screen New Hires," *Cornell Hotel and Restaurant Administration Quarterly* 29, no. 4 (February 1989): 56–61.

11. Margaret A. McManus and Mary L. Kelly, "Personality Measures and Biodata: Evidence Regarding Their Incremental Predictive Value in the Life Insurance Industry," *Personnel Psychology* 52, no. 1 (Spring 1999): 137–48; Andrew J. Vinchur, Jeffrey S. Schippmann, Fred S. Switzer III, and Philip L. Roth, "A Meta-Analytic Review of Predictors of Job Performance for Salespeople," *Journal of Applied Psychology* 83, no. 4 (August 1998): 586–97; Gary R. Kettlitz, Imad Zbib, and Jaideep Motwani, "Validity of Background Data as a Predictor of Employee Tenure among Nursing Aides in Long-Term Care Facilities," *Health Care Supervisor* 16, no. 3 (March 1998): 26–31; Anthony F. Buono, "Biodata Handbook: Theory, Research, and Use of Biographical Information for Selection and Performance Prediction," *Personnel Psychology* 47, no. 4 (Winter 1994): 890–94.

12. Deborah L. O'Mara, "Help Yourself to Background Checks," *Security* 34, no. 3 (March 1997): 91–92. In addition, organizations make use of other resources such as the following: *The Guide to Background Investigations: A Comprehensive Source Directory for Employee Screening and Background Investigations,* 8th ed. (TISI, 1998); *The Computerized Guide to Background Investigations,* Hi Tek Information Services, 4500 S. 129th East Avenue, Suite 200, Tulsa, Okla. 74134. For an article summarizing this system, see "Using Computers for Hiring," *The Futurist* 31, no. 1 (January/February 1997): 41.

13. Samuel Greengard, "Are You Well Armed to Screen Applicants?" *Personnel Journal,* December 1995, 84–95; "The Final Rung: References," *Across the Board,* March 1996, 40; Judith Howlings, "Staff Recruitment: Your Rights and Obligations," *People Management,* May 30, 1996, 47; "Read between the Lines," *Management Today,* February 1996, 14; M. G. Aamondt, D. A. Bryan, and A. J. Whitcomb, "Predicting Performance with Letters of Recommendation," *Public Personnel Management* 22 (Spring 1993): 81–90.

14. Robert L. Brady, "Employee Loses Defamation Suit over Bad Reference," *HRFocus* 73, no. 7 (July 1996): 20; Glenn Withiam, "Complexities of Employee References," *Cornell Hotel and Restaurant Administration Quarterly* 37, no. 3 (June 1996): 10. For a continuously updated listing of employment policy changes, see *Fair Employment Practices Bulletin* (Washington, D.C.: Bureau of National Affairs).

15. Jane Easter Bahls, "Available upon Request?" *HRMagazine* 44, no. 1 (January 1999): H2–H6; Ellen Duffy McKay, "Reference Checks: A Legal Minefield," *HRFocus* 74, no. 12 (December 1997): S11–S12.

16. Gillian Flynn, "Are You Legal under the Fair Credit Reporting Act?" *Workforce* 77, no. 3 (March 1998): 79, 81; Scott F. Cooper, "The Fair Credit Reporting

Act—Time for Employers to Change Their Use of Credit Information," *Employee Relations Law Journal* 24, no. 1 (1998): 57–71.

17. Bob Rosner, "How Do You Feel about the Use of Lie Detectors at Work?" *Workforce* 78, no. 6 (June 1999): 24–25. With some exceptions for jobs in law enforcement, government agencies, and drug-dispensing firms, the following states have banned compulsory or involuntary polygraphing in employment situations: Alaska, California, Connecticut, Delaware, Georgia, Hawaii, Idaho, Iowa, Kansas, Maine, Maryland, Massachusetts, Michigan, Minnesota, Montana, Nebraska, Nevada, New Jersey, New York, Oregon, Pennsylvania, Rhode Island, Tennessee, Texas, Utah, Vermont, Virginia, Washington, West Virginia, and Wisconsin. The District of Columbia also prohibits such testing. Several states have some restrictions. See *BNA Policy and Practice Series—Personnel Management*, 1988, 201–51.

18. Paul Zielbauer, "Small Changes Could Improve Police Hiring, Panel Says," *The New York Times*, January 7, 1999, 8; Del Jones, "Employers Going for Quality Hires, not Quantity," *USA Today*, December 11, 1997, 1B; John B. Miner and Michael H. Capps, *How Honesty Testing Works* (Westport, Conn.: Quorum Books, 1996).

19. Constance L. Hays, "Tests Are Becoming Common in Hiring," *The New York Times*, November 28, 1997, D1. See also Gregory M. Lousig-Nont, "Avoid Common Hiring Mistakes with Honesty Tests," *Nation's Restaurant News* 31, no. 11 (March 17, 1997): 30; "If the Shoe Fits," *Security Management* 40, no. 2 (February 1996): 11.

20. D. S. Ones, C. Viswesvaran, and F. L. Schmidt, "Comprehensive Meta-Analysis of Integrity Test Validities: Findings and Implications for Personnel Selection and Theories of Job Performance," *Journal of Applied Psychology* 78 (August 1993): 679–703. See also Deniz S. Ones and Chockalingam Viswesvaran, "Gender, Age and Race Differences on Overt Integrity Tests: Results across Four Large-Scale Job Applicant Data Sets," *Journal of Applied Psychology* 83, no. 1 (February 1998): 35–42.

21. "Honesty Tests Flawed," *People Management* 3, no. 2 (January 23, 1997): 15; Constance L. Hays, "Tests Are Becoming Common in Hiring," *The New York Times*, November 28, 1997, D1; Stephen A. Dwight and George M. Alliger, "Reactions to Overt Integrity Test Items," *Educational and Psychological Measurement* 57, no. 6 (December 1997): 937–48.

22. Bill Leonard, "Reading Employees," *HRMagazine* 44, no. 4 (April 1999): 67–73; Stephanie Armour, "Fine Print: Hiring through Handwriting Analysis," *USA Today*, July 21, 1998, 1B; Mike Thatcher, "A Test of Character," *People Management* 3, no. 10 (May 15, 1997): 34–38.

23. Dirk D. Steiner and Stephen W. Gilliland, "Fairness Reactions to Personnel Selection Techniques in France and the United States," *Journal of Applied Psychology* 81, no. 2 (April 1996): 134–41.

24. Michael Adams, Ben Van Houten, Robert Klara, and Elizabeth Bernstein, "Access Denied?" *Restaurant Business* 98, no. 2 (January 15, 1999): 36–48; Robert Ellis Smith, "Corporations That Fail the Fair Hiring Test," *Business and Society Review* 88 (Winter 1994): 29–33.

25. Kristina Rundquist, "Pre-employment testing: Making It Work For You," *Occupational Hazards* 59, no. 12 (December 1997): 38–40.

26. David May, "Testing by Necessity," *Occupational Health & Safety* 68, no. 4 (April 1999): 48–51; Ken Kunsman, "Cafeteria Plan Testing," *Occupational Health & Safety* 68, no. 4 (April 1999): 44–47; "Drug Testing Grows, AMA Study Finds," *Managing Office Technology* 41, no. 7 (July 1996): 23; Paul Farrell, "Pass or Fail: Managing a Drug and Alcohol Testing Program," *Risk Management* 43, no. 5 (May 1996): 34–37.

27. Jane Pickard, "The Wrong Turns to Avoid with Tests," *People Management* 2, no. 16 (August 8, 1996): 20–25. Eric Rolfe Greenberg, "Workplace Testing: The 1990 AMA Survey, Part 1," *Personnel*, June 1990, 43–51.

28. Jones, "Employers Going for Quality Hires"; Messick, "Foundations of Validity"; Messick, "Validity of Psychological Assessment." For a counter argument, see Kevin R. Murphy, Ann Harris Shiarella, "Implications of the Multidimensional Nature of Job Performance for the Validity of Selection Tests: Multivariate Frameworks for Studying Test Validity," *Personnel Psychology* 50, no. 4 (Winter 1997): 823–54.

29. For books with comprehensive coverage of testing, including employment testing, see Anne Anastasi and Susana Urbina, *Psychological Testing*, 7th ed. (New York: Macmillan, 1997); Gary Groth-Marnat, *Handbook of Psychological Assessment* (New York: Wiley, 1996); Lee J. Cronbach, *Essentials of Psychological Testing*, 5th ed. (New York: HarperCollins, 1990).

30. Standards that testing programs should meet are described in *Standards for Educational and Psychological Tests* (Washington, D.C.: American Psychological Association, 1986). HR managers who want to examine paper-and-pencil tests should obtain specimen sets that include a test manual, a copy of the test, an answer sheet, and a scoring key. The test manual provides the essential information about the construction of the test; its recommended use; and instructions for administering, scoring, and interpreting the

test. Test users should not rely entirely on the material furnished by the test author and publisher. A major source of consumer information about commercially available tests—the *Mental Measurements Yearbook (MMY)*—is available in most libraries. Published periodically, the *MMY* contains descriptive information plus critical reviews by experts in the various types of tests. The reviews are useful in evaluating a particular test for tryout in employment situations. Other sources of information about tests include *Test Critiques,* a set of volumes containing professional reviews of tests, and *Tests: A Comprehensive Reference for Assessments in Psychology, Education, and Business.* The latter describes more than 3,100 tests published in the English language. Another source, *Principles for the Validation and Use of Personnel Selection Procedures,* published by the Society for Industrial and Organizational Psychology, is a valuable guide for employers who use tests. Other publications are available that present detailed information on how to avoid discrimination and achieve fairness in testing.

31. Vinchur, Schippmann, Switzer, and Roth, "A Meta-Analytic Review"; Harold W. Goldstein, Kenneth P. Yusko, Eric P. Braverman, D. Brent Smith, and Beth Chung, "The Role of Cognitive Ability in the Subgroup Differences and Incremental Validity of Assessment Center Exercises," *Personnel Psychology* 51, no. 2 (Summer 1998): 357–74; Richard K. Wagner, "Intelligence, Training, and Employment," *American Psychologist* 52, no. 10 (October 1997): 1059–69.

32. McManus and Kelly, "Personality Measures"; M. R. Barrick and M. K. Mount, "The Big Five Personality Dimensions and Job Performance: A Meta-Analysis," *Personnel Psychology* 44, no. ___ (1991): 1–26.

33. Murphy and Shiarella, "Implications of the Multidimensional Nature"; Seymore Adler, "Personality Tests for Salesforce Selection: Worth a Fresh Look," *Review of Business* 16, no. 1 (Summer/Fall 1994): 27–31.

34. In the case of *Soroka v Dayton Hudson Corporation* (1993), plaintiffs sued on the grounds that the selection test violated California's Fair Employment laws and that certain items, especially MMPI items, constituted an unlawful invasion of privacy. Although the case was settled out of court, the California state appellate court, in a preliminary injunction, found that certain questions violated the plaintiffs' rights to privacy and that Target Stores had not shown these questions to be job-related. See Stephen A. Dwight and George M. Alliger, "Reactions to Overt Integrity Test Items," *Educational and Psychological Measurement* 57, no. 6 (December 1997): 937–48; Daniel P. O'Meara, "Personality Tests Raise Questions of Legality and Effectiveness," *HRMagazine* 39, no. 1 (January

1994): 97–100; Jeffrey A. Mello, "Personality Tests and Privacy Rights," *HRFocus* 73, no. 3 (March 1996): 22–23.

35. Walter C. Borman, Mary Ann Hanson, and Jerry W. Hedge, "Personnel Selection," *Annual Review of Psychology* 48 (1997): 299–337; Joyce Hogan and Ann Quigley, "Effects of Preparing for Physical Ability Tests," *Public Personnel Management* 23, no. 1 (Spring 1994): 85–104; J. Hogan, "The Structure of Physical Performance," *Journal of Applied Psychology* 76 (1991): 495–507.

36. Alisha Berger, "Physical Fitness as a Job Yardstick," *The New York Times,* June 29, 1999, 8; Charles Anderson, "Can Employees Physically Do the Job?" *Human Resources* 7, no. 5 (September/October 1994): 3–5.

37. It may be interesting to note that the origins of the civil service system go back to 2200 B.C., when the Chinese emperor examined officials every three years to determine their fitness for continuing in office. In 1115 B.C. candidates for government posts were examined for their proficiency in music, archery, horsemanship, writing, arithmetic, and the rites and ceremonies of public and private life. See Philip H. DuBois, *A History of Psychological Testing* (Boston: Allyn & Bacon, 1970), Chapter 1.

38. Leonard D. Goodstein and Alan D. Davidson, "Hiring the Right Stuff: Using Competency-Based Selection," *Compensation & Benefits Management* 14, no. 3 (Summer 1998): 1–10.

39. Linda Marsh, "By Their Actions Shall Ye Know Them," *Works Management* 50, no. 11 (November 1997): 52–53; Florence Berger and Ajay Ghei, "Employment Tests: A Facet of Hospitality Hiring," *Cornell Hotel and Restaurant Administration Quarterly* 36, no. 6 (December 1995): 28–31; Malcolm James Ree, Thomas R. Carretta, and Mark S. Teachout, "Role of Ability and Prior Job Knowledge in Complex Training Performance," *Journal of Applied Psychology* 80, no. 6 (December 1995): 721–30.

40. Cynthia Kay Stevens, "Antecedents of Interview Interactions, Interviewers' Ratings, and Applicants' Reactions," *Personnel Psychology* 51, no. 1 (Spring 1998): 55–85; Laura Gollub Williamson, James E. Campion, Stanley B. Malos, and Mark V. Roehling, "Employment Interview on Trial: Linking Interview Structure with Litigation Outcomes," *Journal of Applied Psychology* 82, no. 6 (December 1997): 900–12. See also James M. Conway, Robert A. Jako, and Deborah F. Goodman, "A Meta-Analysis of Interrater and Internal Consistency Reliability of Selection Interviews," *Journal of Applied Psychology* 80, no. 5 (October 1995): 565–79; Michael McDaniel, Deborah L. Whetzel, Frank L. Schmidt, and Steven D. Maurer,

"The Validity of Employment Interviews: A Comprehensive Review and Meta-Analysis," *Journal of Applied Psychology* 79, no. 4 (August 1994): 599–616.

**41.** Frank L. Schmidt and Mark Rader, "Exploring the Boundary Conditions for Interview Validity: Meta-Analytic Validity Findings for a New Interview Type," *Personnel Psychology* 52, no. 2 (Summer 1999): 445–50; Williamson, Campion, Malos, and Roehling, "Employment Interview on Trial"; Jennifer R. Burnett and Stephan J. Motowidlo, "Relations between Different Sources of Information in the Structured Selection Interview," *Personnel Psychology* 51, no. 4 (Winter 1998): 963–83. See also Geoffrey Colvin, "Looking to Hire the Very Best? Ask the Right Questions. Lots of Them," *Fortune,* June 21, 1999, 192–94; "Recruiting Practices That Get the EEOC's Attention," *HRMagazine* 42, no. 11 (November 1997): 60.

**42.** For an excellent review of research on the structured interview, see Michael A. Campion, David K. Palmer, and James E. Campion, "A Review of Structure in the Selection Interview," *Personnel Psychology* 50, no. 3 (Autumn 1997): 655–702. Also see Jennifer R. Burnett, Chenche Fan, Stephan J. Motowidlo, and Tim Degroot, "Interview Notes and Validity," *Personnel Psychology* 51, no. 2 (Summer 1998): 375–96; Burnett and Motowidlo, "Relations between Different Sources."

**43.** Todd Maurer, Jerry Solamon, and Deborah Troxtel, "Relationship of Coaching with Performance in Situational Employment Interviews," *Journal of Applied Psychology* 83, no. 1 (February 1998): 128–36; Steven D. Maurer, "The Potential of the Situational Interview: Existing Research and Unresolved Issues," *Human Resource Management Review* 7, no. 2 (Summer 1997): 185–201.

**44.** Amelia J. Prewett-Livingston, John G. Veres III, Hubert S. Feild, and Philip M. Lewis, "Effects of Race on Interview Ratings in a Situational Panel Interview," *Journal of Applied Psychology* 81, no. 2 (April 1996): 178–86. See also Damodar Y. Golhar and Satish P. Deshpande, "HRM Practices of Large and Small Canadian Manufacturing Firms," *Journal of Small Business Management* 35, no. 3 (July 1997): 30–38; Philip L. Roth and James E. Campion, "An Analysis of the Predictive Power of the Panel Interview and Pre-Employment Tests," *Journal of Occupational and Organizational Psychology* 65 (March 1992): 51–60.

**45.** Peter C. Sawyers, "Structured Interviewing: Your Key to the Best Hires," *Personnel Journal,* Special Supplement, December 1992. See also Bob Smith, "Pinkerton Keeps Its Eye on Recruitment," *HRFocus* 70, no. 9 (September 1993): 1, 8; Elizabeth Daniele, "PC-Based Screening Passes the Test at Cigna," *Insurance & Technology* 17 (January 1992): 15, 18.

**46.** Linda Thornburg, "Computer-Assisted Interviewing Shortens Hiring Cycle," *HRMagazine* 43, no. 2 (February 1998): 73–79; Lisa Arbetter, "Interview Coup," *Security Management* 38, no. 5 (May 1994): 12–13; Gary Robins, "Dial-an-Interview," *Stores* 76, no. 6 (June 1994): 34–35; "Recruitment Goes High Tech," *Personnel Journal,* August 1994, 6–10.

**47.** C. L. Martin and D. H. Nagao, "Some Effects of Computerized Interviewing on Job Applicant Responses," *Journal of Applied Psychology* 74 (1989): 72–80.

**48.** Campion, Palmer, and Campion, "A Review of Structure"; Burnett and Motowidlo, "Relations between Different Sources"; Steven J. Cesare, "Subjective Judgment and the Selection Interview: A Methodological Review," *Public Personnel Management* 25, no. 3 (Fall 1996): 291–310.

**49.** Burnett and Motowidlo, "Relations between Different Sources." See also Mike Frost, "Interviewing ABCs," *HRMagazine* 42, no. 3 (March 1997): 32–34.

**50.** Multiple regression is a statistical method for evaluating the magnitude of effects of more than one independent variable (e.g., selection predictors) on a dependent variable (e.g., job performance) using principles of correlation and regression. See W. P. Vogt, *Dictionary of Statistics and Methodology* (Newbury Park, Calif.: Sage Publications, 1993), 146; F. N. Kerlinger, *Foundations of Behavioral Research,* 3d ed. (Fort Worth, Tex.: Holt, Rinehart and Winston, 1986), 527.

**51.** P. E. Meehl, *Clinical v. Statistical Prediction* (Minneapolis: University of Minnesota Press, 1954); J. Sawyer, "Measurement and Prediction, Clinical and Statistical," *Psychological Bulletin* 66, no. 3 (September 1966): 178–200.

**52.** Wayne F. Cascio, *Applied Psychology in Personnel Management,* 5th ed. (Englewood Cliffs, N.J.: Prentice-Hall, 1998). In addition to Cascio's book, the reader may wish to consult George F. Dreher and Daniel W. Kendall, "Organizational Staffing," in Gerald R. Ferris, Sherman D. Rosen, and Darold T. Barnum (eds.), *Handbook of Human Resource Management* (Cambridge, Mass. Blackwell Publishers, 1995).

# chapter 6

# Training and Development

## AFTER STUDYING THIS CHAPTER, YOU SHOULD BE ABLE TO

Discuss the systems approach
to training and development.

Describe the components of
training-needs assessment.

Identify the principles of
learning and describe how they
facilitate training.

Identify the types of training
methods used for managers
and nonmanagers.

Discuss the advantages and
disadvantages of various
evaluation criteria.

Describe the special training
programs that are currently
popular.

Training has become increasingly vital to the success of modern organizations. Recall that in Chapter 1 we noted that organizations often compete on competencies—the core sets of knowledge and expertise that give them an edge over their competitors. Training plays a central role in nurturing and strengthening these competencies, and in this way has become part of the backbone of strategy implementation. In addition, rapidly changing technologies require that employees continuously hone their knowledge, skills, and abilities (KSAs) to cope with new processes and systems. Jobs that require little skill are rapidly being replaced by jobs that require technical, interpersonal, and problem-solving skills. Other trends toward empowerment, total-quality management, teamwork, and international business make it necessary for managers, as well as employees, to develop the skills that will enable them to handle new and more demanding assignments.

# The Scope of Training

Many new employees come equipped with most of the KSAs needed to start work. Others may require extensive training before they are ready to make much of a contribution to their organizations. Almost any employee, however, needs some type of training on an ongoing basis to maintain effective performance or to adjust to new ways of work.

The term "training" is often used casually to describe almost any effort initiated by an organization to foster learning among its members. However, many experts make a distinction between *training*, which tends to be more narrowly focused and oriented toward short-term performance concerns, and *development*, which tends to be oriented more toward broadening an individual's skills for the future responsibilities. The two terms tend to be combined into a single phrase—"training and development"—to recognize the combination of activities used by organizations to increase the skill base of employees.

The primary reason that organizations train new employees is to bring their KSAs up to the level required for satisfactory performance. As these employees continue on the job, additional training provides opportunities for them to acquire new knowledge and skills. As a result of this training, employees may be even more effective on the job and may be able to perform other jobs in other areas or at higher levels.

## Investments in Training

According to *Training Magazine's* ongoing industry report, U.S. businesses spend more than $60 billion each year to provide more than 1.7 billion hours of formal training. Industries such as transportation, communications, and utilities tend to spend the most on training. But overall, nearly 50 million individuals receive some formal training from their employers, typically amounting to over thirty hours of instruction per employee each year. Figure 6.1 shows that salespeople (thirty-eight hours) and professionals (thirty-seven hours) tend to receive the most training. However, a higher percentage of organizations (76 percent) provide training to administrative employees than any other group.[1]

**FIGURE 6.1**

**Who Gets the Training?**

| JOB CATEGORY | ORGANIZATIONS PROVIDING TRAINING (%)* | AVERAGE NUMBER OF INDIVIDUALS TRAINED† | PROJECTED TOTAL OF INDIVIDUALS TRAINED (IN MILLIONS) | AVERAGE HOURS OF TRAINING PER INDIVIDUAL‡ |
|---|---|---|---|---|
| Salespeople | 41 | 50 | 4.2 | 38 |
| Professionals | 72 | 67 | 10.0 | 37 |
| First-line supervisors | 64 | 32 | 4.2 | 34 |
| Middle managers | 72 | 24 | 3.6 | 32 |
| Customer-service people | 49 | 72 | 7.2 | 30 |
| Production workers | 37 | 222 | 16.9 | 30 |
| Senior managers | 64 | 13 | 1.7 | 30 |
| Executives | 70 | 9 | 1.3 | 29 |
| Administrative employees | 76 | 33 | 5.2 | 21 |
| Total | — | — | 54.5 | — |

*Percent of all U.S. organizations with 100 or more employees that provide formal training to people in these types of jobs.
†Per organization, based only on those organizations that do provide training to these types of workers.
‡One person receiving training for one hour equals one "hour of training."
Source: "Industry Report 1998," *Training* 35, no. 10 (October 1998): 43–75. Reprinted with permission from the October 1998 issue of TRAINING Magazine. Copyright 1998. Bill Communications, Inc. Minneapolis, MN. All rights reserved. Not for resale.

In addition to formal training, more than $180 billion is spent on informal instruction that goes on every day in organizations everywhere. These investments are directed at a variety of programs, ranging from basic computer skills to customer service. In today's organizations, fully one-third of all training is information-technology-based. We discuss this trend later in the chapter.

## A Systems Approach to Training

From the broadest perspective, the goal of training is to contribute to the organization's overall goals. Training programs should be developed with this in mind. Managers should keep a close eye on the organizational goals and strategies and orient training accordingly. Unfortunately, many organizations never make the connection between their strategic objectives and their training programs. Instead, fads, fashions, or "whatever the competition is doing" can sometimes be the main drivers of an organization's training agenda. As a result, much of an organization's investment can be wasted—training programs are often misdirected, poorly designed, inadequately evaluated—and these problems directly affect organizational performance.

To make certain that investments in training and development have maximum impact on individual and organizational performance, a systems approach to training should be used. The systems approach involves four phases: (1) needs assessment, (2) program design, (3) implementation, and (4) evaluation. A model that is useful to designers of training programs is presented in Figure 6.2. We will use this model as a framework for organizing the material throughout this chapter.

# Phase 1: Conducting the Needs Assessment

Managers and HR staffs should stay alert to the kinds of training that are needed, where they are needed, who needs them, and which methods will best deliver needed KSAs to employees. If workers consistently fail to achieve productivity objectives, this might be a signal that training is needed. Likewise, if organizations receive an excessive number of customer complaints, this too might suggest inadequate training. To make certain that training is timely and focused on priority issues, managers should approach needs assessment systematically by utilizing the three different types of analysis shown in Figure 6.3: organization analysis, task analysis, and person analysis. Each of these is discussed below.

A study by the American Society for Training and Development (ASTD) found that, unfortunately, because of the costs, expertise, and time required, organiza-

**FIGURE 6.2**

► **Systems Model of Training**

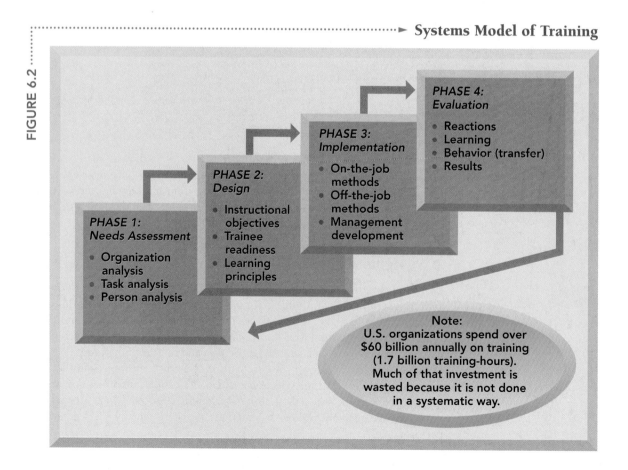

PHASE 4:
Evaluation
- Reactions
- Learning
- Behavior (transfer)
- Results

PHASE 3:
Implementation
- On-the-job methods
- Off-the-job methods
- Management development

PHASE 2:
Design
- Instructional objectives
- Trainee readiness
- Learning principles

PHASE 1:
Needs Assessment
- Organization analysis
- Task analysis
- Person analysis

Note:
U.S. organizations spend over $60 billion annually on training (1.7 billion training-hours). Much of that investment is wasted because it is not done in a systematic way.

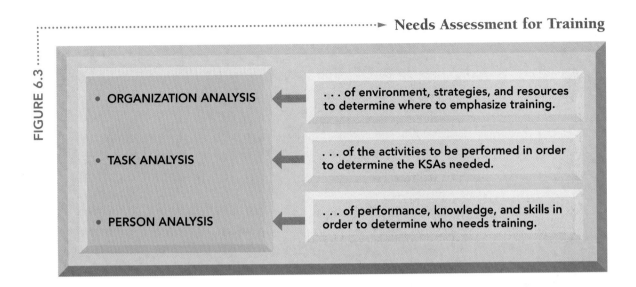

FIGURE 6.3

**Needs Assessment for Training**

- **ORGANIZATION ANALYSIS** ⬅ . . . of environment, strategies, and resources to determine where to emphasize training.

- **TASK ANALYSIS** ⬅ . . . of the activities to be performed in order to determine the KSAs needed.

- **PERSON ANALYSIS** ⬅ . . . of performance, knowledge, and skills in order to determine who needs training.

tions conduct needs assessment less than 50 percent of the time before initiating a training program. To overcome these obstacles, ASTD has teamed up with Insync Corporation, a training and development firm in McLean, Virginia, to develop a software program called ASTD ASSESS. This program enables managers to use a personal computer to develop surveys, analyze data, and prepare reports used in training-needs assessment. Companies such as Noxell, Marriott, and Minnesota Power have participated in the development of this software.[2]

Too frequently, managers lament that they simply don't have time to conduct needs assessment. Ironically, as the speed of change increases, and time and resources are at a premium, the need for good needs assessment actually increases. In these cases, the process need not be so daunting and laborious. Highlights in HRM 1 provides some tips for doing rapid assessment for training needs.

## Organization Analysis

**Organization analysis**
Examination of the environment, strategies, and resources of the organization to determine where training emphasis should be placed

The first step in needs assessment is identifying the broad forces that can influence training needs. **Organization analysis** is an examination of the environment, strategies, and resources of the organization to determine where training emphasis should be placed.

Economic and public policy issues tend to have widespread effect on the training needs of many organizations. For example, training programs focused on handling sexual harassment adopted by such organizations as Zenith, Smith Barney, and the City of Minneapolis reflect the influence of environmental concerns on training.

Other issues tend to revolve around the strategic initiatives of an organization. Mergers and acquisitions, for example, frequently require that employees take on new roles and responsibilities and adjust to new cultures and ways of conducting business. Nowhere is this more prevalent than in grooming new leaders within organizations. Other issues such as technological change, globalization, reengineering, and total-quality management all influence the way work is done and the types of skills needed to do it. Still other concerns may be more tactical, but no less important in their impact on training. Organizational restructuring, downsizing,

**HRM 1**

# Notes on Doing Needs Assessment Quick Time

**NOTE 1: Look at Problem Scope.** Common sense suggests that small, local matters may require less information gathering than big problems with a major impact on the organization. Ask managers a series of questions about the nature of the problem and its impact on the organization and gear your analysis accordingly.

**NOTE 2: Do Organizational Scanning.** Stay connected with what is going on in the organization in order to anticipate upcoming training needs. If a new technology is about to be launched, the need for training should take no one by surprise. In short, needs assessment isn't an event with a start-and-stop switch. It is the process of being engaged in your business.

**NOTE 3: Play "Give & Take."** Get the information you need, but don't drag your feet with excessive analysis before reporting back to managers. Show them that you are sensitive to their need for action by giving them updates on the information you have collected. If necessary, explain that better value may be gained by further analysis.

**NOTE 4: Check "Lost and Found."** Often, information gathered for a different purpose may bear on your training issue. Performance data (such as errors, sales customer complaints) and staffing data (such as proficiency testing, turnover, absenteeism) can be very helpful as a starting point.

**NOTE 5: Use Plain Talk.** Instead of using clinical terms such as "analysis or assessment," use straight talk with managers that tells them what you are doing: (1) Identify the problem, (2) identify alternative ways to get there, (3) implement a solution based on cost/benefit concerns, (4) determine the effectiveness and efficiency of the solution.

**NOTE 6: Use the Web.** Information technology allows you to communicate with others, perhaps setting up a listserv to post questions, synthesize responses, share resources, get feedback, gather information on trends, and the like.

**NOTE 7: Use Rapid Prototyping.** Often the most effective and efficient training is that which is "just-in-time, just enough, and just for me." Create a rapid prototype of a training program, evaluating and revising as you implement and learn more about the problems.

**NOTE 8: Seek Out Exemplars.** Find those in the organization that currently demonstrate the performance the organization wants. Bring others together with them to talk about the performance issues, and let the exemplars share their experiences and insights. This avoids the risk of packaging the wrong information, and people learn just what they need to know from each other.

---

Condensed from: Ron Zemke, "How to Do a Needs Assessment When You Think You Don't Have Time," *Training* 35, no. 3 (March 1998): 38–44. Reprinted with permission from the March 1998 issue of TRAINING Magazine. Copyright 1998. Bill Communications, Inc., Minneapolis, MN. All rights reserved. Not for resale.

empowerment, and teamwork, for example, have immediate training requirements. Finally, trends in the workforce itself have an impact on training needs. As we mentioned in Chapter 1, employees increasingly value self-development and personal growth, and with this has come an enormous desire for learning. At the same time, as older workers near retirement, younger workers need to focus on gaining the skills and knowledge needed to take their place. Organizations as diverse as Bethlehem Steel and Lockheed Martin are facing situations where they need to prepare the next generations of employees as the current groups approach retirement.[3]

Side by side with forces that influence training needs, organization analysis involves close examination of the resources—technological, financial, and human— that are available to meet training objectives. Organizations typically collect data to use in the analysis, data such as information on direct and indirect labor costs, quality of goods or services, absenteeism, turnover, and number of accidents. The availability of potential replacements and the time required to train them are other important factors in organization analysis.

In recent years, as organizations continue to keep a tight rein on costs, training budgets are often constrained—even while organizations recognize the need for more and better training. To cope with resource constraints while contributing to strategic imperatives, managers have to be more focused and efficient with their training budgets. Companies such as Motorola, Ford, and MCI-WorldCom have found that by using information technology wisely, they cut their training budget by as much as 30 to 50 percent while keeping services levels high.[4] In order to "do more with less," managers have to plan carefully where they will spend their training dollars, and this means doing rigorous organization analysis.

*A supervisor trains a factory worker on how a circuit board operates.*

## Task Analysis

**Task analysis**
Process of determining what the content of a training program should be on the basis of a study of the tasks and duties involved in the job

The second step in training-needs assessment is task analysis. **Task analysis** involves reviewing the job description and specification to identify the activities performed in a particular job and the KSAs needed to perform them. Task analysis oftentimes becomes more detailed than job analysis, but the overall purpose is to determine the exact content of the training program.

The first step in task analysis is to list all the tasks or duties included in the job. The second step is to list the steps performed by the employee to complete each task. Once the job is understood thoroughly, the type of performance required (e.g., speech, recall, discrimination, manipulation), along with the skills and knowledge necessary for performance, can be defined. For example, in the task of taking a chest x-ray, a radiologist correctly positions the patient (manipulation), gives special instructions (speech), and checks the proper distance of the x-ray tube from the patient (discrimination). The types of performance skills and knowledge that trainees need can be determined by observing and questioning skilled jobholders and/or by reviewing job descriptions. This information helps trainers to select program content and choose the most effective training method.

**Competency assessment**
Analysis of the sets of skills and knowledge needed for decision-oriented and knowledge-intensive jobs

However, like job analysis, task analysis appears to be shifting from an emphasis on a fixed sequence of tasks to the more flexible sets of competencies required for superior performance. Companies such as Case and the Principal Financial Group have found that as jobs change toward teamwork, flexibility requires that employees adjust their behavior as needed. **Competency assessment** focuses on the sets of skills and knowledge employees need to be successful, particularly for decision-oriented and knowledge-intensive jobs. While training programs based on work-oriented task analysis can become dated as work undergoes dynamic change, training programs based on competency assessment are more flexible and perhaps have more durability.[5] Highlights in HRM 2 shows a checklist for conducting a competency assessment.

## Person Analysis

**Person analysis**
Determination of the specific individuals who need training

Along with organization and task analyses, it is necessary to perform a person analysis. **Person analysis** involves determining which employees require training and, equally important, which do not. In this regard, person analysis is important for several reasons. First, thorough analysis helps organizations avoid the mistake of sending all employees into training when some do not need it. In addition, person analysis helps managers determine what prospective trainees are able to do when they enter training so that the programs can be designed to emphasize the areas in which they are deficient.

Companies such as Teradyne and Hewlett-Packard use performance appraisal information as an input for person analysis. However, while performance appraisals may reveal who is not meeting expectations, it typically does not reveal why. If performance deficiencies are due to ability problems, training may likely be a good intervention. However, if performance deficiencies are due to poor motivation or factors outside an employee's control, training may not be the answer. Ultimately managers have to sit down with employees to talk about areas for improvement so that they can jointly determine the developmental approaches that will have maximum benefit.[6]

**HIGHLIGHTS IN HRM**

# Tips for Conducting a Competency Assessment

Learning how to perform a competency assessment can be a lengthy process, but here's a simplified approach:

- *Clarify the purpose of the effort.* Will you be using the competency model for training purposes only or for other purposes as well?
- *Clarify the target for the effort.* Will you be constructing a competency model for the entire organization? For only part of it? For only one or for several job categories, such as senior executives or middle managers?
- *Network with others in your industry and in the training field.* Try to find a competency model that already has been developed. (Industry associations or professional societies may have developed models.)
- *Form a panel of exemplary performers within your organization from the group targeted for assessment and from the group to which they report (such as managers and executives).*
- *Ask a panel of eight to twelve people in your organization to review the competency study (or studies) obtained from other sources and to prioritize the competencies as they apply to success in your corporate culture.*
- *Verify the competency model and secure ownership of it by encouraging input from others, such as senior executives.*

# Phase 2: Designing the Training Program

Once the training needs have been determined, the next step is to design the type of learning environment necessary to enhance learning. The success of training programs depends on more than the organization's ability to identify training needs. Success hinges on taking the information gained from needs analysis and utilizing it to design first-rate training programs. Experts believe that training design should focus on at least four related issues: (1) instructional objectives, (2) trainee readiness and motivation, (3) principles of learning, and (4) characteristics of instructors.

## Instructional Objectives

As a result of conducting organization, task, and person analyses, managers will have a more complete picture of the training needs. On the basis of this information, they can more formally state the desired outcomes of training through written instructional objectives. Generally, **instructional objectives** describe the skills

**Instructional objectives**
Desired outcomes of a training program

or knowledge to be acquired and/or the attitudes to be changed. One type of instructional objective, the performance-centered objective, is widely used because it lends itself to an unbiased evaluation of results. For example, the stated objective for one training program might be that "Employees trained in team methods will be able to perform these different jobs within six months." Performance-centered objectives typically include precise terms, such as "to calculate," "to repair," "to adjust," "to construct," "to assemble," and "to classify."

Robert Mager, an internationally known training expert, emphasizes the importance of instructional objectives by noting that "before you prepare for instruction, before you select instructional procedures or subject matter or material, it is important to be able to state clearly just what you intend the results of that instruction to be. A clear statement of instructional objectives will provide a sound basis for choosing methods and materials and for selecting the means for assessing whether the instruction will be successful."[7]

## Trainee Readiness and Motivation

Two preconditions for learning affect the success of those who are to receive training: readiness and motivation. *Trainee readiness* refers to both maturity and experience factors in the trainee's background. Prospective trainees should be screened to determine that they have the background knowledge and the skills necessary to absorb what will be presented to them. Recognizing individual differences in readiness is as important in organizational training as it is in any other teaching situation. It is often desirable to group individuals according to their capacity to learn, as determined by test scores, and to provide an alternative type of instruction for those who need it.

The receptiveness and readiness of participants in training programs can be increased by having them complete questionnaires about why they are attending training and what they hope to accomplish. Participants may also be asked to give copies of their completed questionnaires to their managers.

The other precondition for learning is *trainee motivation*. Individuals who are conscientious, goal-oriented, self-disciplined, and persevering are more likely to perceive a link between effort they put into training and higher performance on the job. For optimum learning to take place, trainees must recognize the need for new knowledge or skills, and they must maintain a desire to learn as training progresses. By focusing on the trainees themselves rather than on the trainer or training topic, managers can create a training environment that is conducive to learning. Six strategies can be essential:

1. Use positive reinforcement.
2. Eliminate threats and punishment.
3. Be flexible.
4. Have participants set personal goals.
5. Design interesting instruction.
6. Break down physical and psychological obstacles to learning.[8]

While most employees are motivated by certain common needs, they differ from one another in the relative importance of these needs at any given time. For example, new college graduates often have a high desire for advancement, and they have established specific goals for career progression. Training objectives that are clearly related to trainees' individual needs will increase the motivation of employees to succeed in training programs.

## Principles of Learning

OBJECTIVE 3

As we move from needs assessment and instructional objectives to employee readiness and motivation, we are shifting from a focus on the organization to a focus on employees. Ultimately, training has to build a bridge between employees and the organization. One important step in this transition is giving full consideration to the psychological principles of learning, that is, the characteristics of training programs that help employees grasp new material, make sense of it in their own lives, and transfer it back to the job.

Because the success or failure of a training program is frequently related to certain principles of learning, managers as well as employees should understand that different training methods or techniques vary in the extent to which they utilize these principles. All things considered, training programs are likely to be more effective if they incorporate the principles of learning shown in Figure 6.4.

### Goal Setting
The value of goal setting for focusing and motivating behavior extends into training. When trainers take the time to explain the goals and objectives to trainees—

**FIGURE 6.4**

**Principles of Learning**

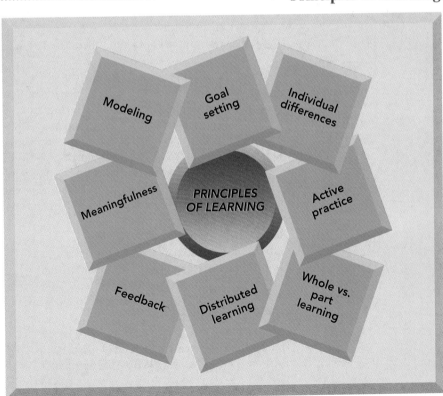

Modeling · Goal setting · Individual differences · Meaningfulness · PRINCIPLES OF LEARNING · Active practice · Feedback · Distributed learning · Whole vs. part learning

or when trainees are encouraged to set goals on their own—the level of interest, understanding, and effort directed toward training is likely to increase. In some cases, goal setting can simply take the form of a "road map" of the course/program, its objectives, and learning points.[9]

### Meaningfulness of Presentation

One principle of learning is that the material to be learned should be presented in as meaningful a manner as possible. Quite simply, trainees are better able to learn new information (from training) if they can connect it with things that are already familiar to them. Trainers frequently use colorful examples to which trainees can relate. The examples make the material meaningful. In addition, material should be arranged so that each experience builds upon preceding ones. In this way, trainees are able to integrate the experiences into a usable pattern of knowledge and skills.

### Modeling

The old saying "A picture is worth a thousand words" applies to training. Just as examples increase the meaningfulness of factual material or new knowledge in a training environment, modeling increases the salience of behavioral training. Work by Albert Bandura and others on social learning theory underscores the point that we learn vicariously. Quite simply, we learn by watching. For example, if you were learning to ride a horse, it would be much easier to watch someone do it—and then try it yourself—than to read a book or listen to a lecture and hope you can do it right.[10]

Modeling can take many forms. For example, real-life demonstrations or videotapes are often helpful; even pictures and drawings can get the visual message across. The point is that modeling demonstrates the desired behavior or method to be learned. In some cases, modeling the wrong behavior can even be helpful if it shows trainees what not to do and then clarifies the appropriate behavior.

### Individual Differences

People learn at different rates and in different ways. For example, some individuals can remember new information after hearing it only once (echoic memory) or seeing it only once (iconic memory). Others may have to work longer or find other techniques for retrieving the information, but this may have nothing to do with their intelligence. Some students do horribly in large lecture settings but then excel in small discussion classes. Others may have the opposite ability. To the extent possible, training programs should try to account for and accommodate these individual differences in order to facilitate each person's style and rate of learning.[11]

### Active Practice and Repetition

Those things we do daily become a part of our repertoire of skills. Trainees should be given frequent opportunity to practice their job tasks in the way that they will ultimately be expected to perform them. The individual who is being taught how to operate a machine should have an opportunity to practice on it. The manager who is being taught how to train should be given supervised practice in training.

In some cases, the value of practice is that it causes behaviors to become second nature. For example, when you first learned to drive a car, you focused a great deal on the mechanics: "Where are my hands, where are my feet, how fast am I going?" As you practiced driving, you began to think less about the mechanics and more about the road, the weather, and the traffic. Other forms of learning are no different—by practicing, a trainee can forget about distinct behaviors and concentrate on the subtleties of how they are used.

### Whole-versus-Part Learning

Most jobs and tasks can be broken down into parts that lend themselves to further analysis. Determining the most effective manner for completing each part then provides a basis for giving specific instruction. Typing, for example, is made up of several skills that are part of the total process. The typist starts by learning the proper use of each finger; eventually, with practice, the individual finger movements become integrated into a total pattern. Practice by moving individual fingers is an example of part learning. In evaluating whole-versus-part learning, it is necessary to consider the nature of the task to be learned. If the task can be broken down successfully, it probably should be broken down to facilitate learning; otherwise, it should probably be taught as a unit.

### Massed-versus-Distributed Learning

Another factor that determines the effectiveness of training is the amount of time devoted to practice in one session. Should trainees be given training in five two-hour periods or in ten one-hour periods? It has been found in most cases that spacing out the training will result in faster learning and longer retention. This is the principle of *distributed learning*. Since the efficiency of the distribution will vary with the type and complexity of the task, managers should refer to the rapidly growing body of research in this area when they require guidance in designing a specific training situation.

### Feedback and Reinforcement

Can any learning occur without feedback? Some feedback comes from self-monitoring while other feedback comes from trainers, fellow trainees, and the like. As an employee's training progresses, feedback serves two related purposes: (1) knowledge of results and (2) motivation.

The informational aspects of feedback help individuals focus in on what they are doing right and what they are doing wrong. In this way, feedback serves a "shaping" role in helping individuals approach the objectives of training. Think about when you first learned how to throw a baseball, ride a bicycle, or swim. Someone, perhaps a parent, told you what you were doing right and what things to correct. As you did, you perhaps got better.

In addition to its informational aspects, feedback also serves an important motivational role. At times, progress in training, measured either in terms of mistakes or successes, may be plotted on a chart commonly referred to as a "learning curve." Figure 6.5 presents an example of a learning curve common in the acquisition of many job skills. In many learning situations there are times when progress does not occur. Such periods show up on the curve as a fairly straight horizontal line called a *plateau*. A plateau may be the result of reduced motivation or of ineffective methods of task performance. It is a natural phenomenon of learning, and there is usually a spontaneous recovery, as Figure 6.5 shows.

Verbal encouragement or more extrinsic rewards may help to reinforce desired behavior over time. At times, reinforcement is simply the feeling of accomplishment that follows successful performance. (In some cases it may be impossible to distinguish between feedback and rewards.) Reinforcement is generally most effective when it occurs immediately after a task has been performed.

FIGURE 6.5

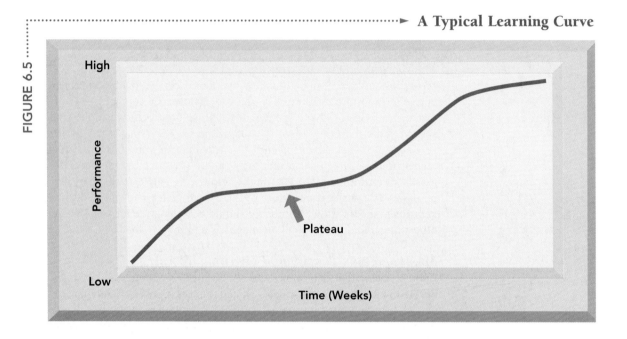

**A Typical Learning Curve**

**Behavior modification**
Technique that operates on the principle that behavior that is rewarded, or positively reinforced, will be exhibited more frequently in the future, whereas behavior that is penalized or unrewarded will decrease in frequency

In recent years some work organizations have used **behavior modification,** a technique that operates on the principle that behavior that is rewarded—positively reinforced—will be exhibited more frequently in the future, whereas behavior that is penalized or unrewarded will decrease in frequency.[12]

## Characteristics of Instructors

The success of any training effort will depend in large part on the teaching skills and personal characteristics of those responsible for conducting the training. What separates the good trainers from the mediocre ones? Often a good trainer is one who shows a little more effort or demonstrates more instructional preparation. However, training is also influenced by the trainer's personal manner and characteristics. Here is a short list of desirable traits:

1.  *Knowledge of subject.* Employees expect trainers to know their job or subject thoroughly. Furthermore, they are expected to demonstrate that knowledge (what some experts call "active intelligence").

2.  *Adaptability.* Some individuals learn faster or slower than others, and instruction should be matched to the trainee's learning ability.

3.  *Sincerity.* Trainees appreciate sincerity in trainers. Along with this, trainers need to be patient with trainees and demonstrate tact in addressing their concerns.

4.  *Sense of humor.* Learning can be fun; very often a point can be made with a story or anecdote.

5.  *Interest.* Good trainers have a keen interest in the subject they are teaching; this interest is readily conveyed to trainees.

6.  *Clear instructions.* Naturally, training is accomplished more quickly and retained longer when trainers give clear instructions.

7.  *Individual assistance.* When training more than one employee, successful trainers always provide individual assistance.

8.  *Enthusiasm.* A dynamic presentation and a vibrant personality show trainees that the trainer enjoys training; employees tend to respond positively to an enthusiastic climate.[13]

For training programs to be most successful, organizations should reward managers who prove to be excellent trainers. Too often managers are not recognized for their contributions to this important aspect of HRM. Likewise, training specialists in the HR function should be recognized for their role in the training program.

# Phase 3: Implementing the Training Program

Despite the importance of needs assessment, instructional objectives, principles of learning, and the like, choices regarding instructional methods are where "the rubber meets the road" in implementing a training program. A major consideration in choosing among various training methods is determining which ones are appropriate for the KSAs to be learned. For example, if the material is mostly factual, methods such as lecture, classroom, or programmed instruction may be fine. However, if the training involves a large behavioral component, other methods such as on-the-job training, simulation, or computer-based training might work better.[14]

In order to organize our discussion of various training methods, we will break them down into two primary groups: those used for nonmanagerial employees and those used for managers.

## Training Methods for Nonmanagerial Employees

A wide variety of methods is available for training employees at all levels. Some of the methods have a long history of usage. Newer methods have emerged over the years out of a greater understanding of human behavior, particularly in the areas of learning, motivation, and interpersonal relationships. More recently, technological advances, especially in computer hardware and software, have resulted in training devices that in many instances are more effective and economical than the traditional training methods.

### On-the-Job Training

By far, the most common method used for training nonmanagerial employees is **on-the-job training (OJT).** In fact, one estimate suggests that organizations spend three to six times more on OJT than on classroom training. OJT has the advantage of providing hands-on experience under normal working conditions and an opportunity for the trainer—a manager or senior employee—to build good relationships with new employees. As time becomes a critical resource—and "just-in-time training" is needed most—OJT is viewed by some to be potentially the most effective means of facilitating learning in the workplace.[15]

Although it is used by all types of organizations, OJT is often one of the most poorly implemented training methods. Three common drawbacks include (1) the lack of a well-structured training environment, (2) poor training skills of managers,

**On-the-job training (OJT)**
Method by which employees are given hands-on experience with instructions from their supervisor or other trainer

and (3) the absence of well-defined job performance criteria. To overcome these problems, training experts suggest the following:

1. Develop realistic goals and/or measures for each OJT area.
2. Plan a specific training schedule for each trainee, including set periods for evaluation and feedback.
3. Help managers to establish a nonthreatening atmosphere conducive to learning.
4. Conduct periodic evaluations, after training is completed, to prevent regression.[16]

Many successful trainers use a system known as *job instruction training* to acquaint managers with techniques in instructing their employees. (See Highlights in HRM 3.) While the principles of job instruction training were developed during

**HIGHLIGHTS IN HRM**

# Job Instruction Training

**GET READY, GET SET . . .**
- Decide what the employee must be taught.
- Have the right equipment and materials ready.
- Have the workplace properly arranged.

**Step 1: Preparation**
Put the employee at ease.
Find out what the employee already knows.
Get the employee interested and desirous of learning the job.

**Step 2: Presentation**
Tell, show, illustrate, and question in order to put out the new knowledge.
Instruct slowly, clearly, completely, and patiently, one point at a time.
Check, question, and repeat.
Make sure the employee really knows.

**Step 3: Performance**
Test employee by having him/her perform the job.
Ask questions beginning with why, how, when, where.
Observe, correct errors, and repeat instructions.
Continue until you know the employee knows.

**Step 4: Follow-up**
Put employee on his/her own.
Check up frequently that instructions are followed.
Taper off extra supervision.

Source: *The Training within Industry Report* (Washington, D.C.: Bureau of Training, Training with Industry Service, War Manpower Commission).

*With assistance from a teacher, these apprentice butchers are learning how to prepare meat.*

World War II, the recommended training tips are clearly appropriate for today's organizations. The basic format, or an adaptation of it, is used by many small business managers for instructing a new person on the job or a present worker on a new job.

For example, KLM Royal Dutch Airlines uses OJT to train cabin attendants in customer service. The airline started an experimental program that places cabin attendant trainees in the classroom for a certain period and then gives them additional training during an evaluation flight. On these flights, experienced cabin attendants provide the trainees with OJT, based on a list of identified job tasks. Some tasks, such as serving meals and snacks, are demonstrated during the actual delivery of services to passengers. Other tasks are presented to trainees away from passengers between meal service.[17]

**Apprenticeship training**
System of training in which a worker entering the skilled trades is given thorough instruction and experience, both on and off the job, in the practical and theoretical aspects of the work

### Apprenticeship Training

An extension of OJT is **apprenticeship training.** With this method, individuals entering industry, particularly in the skilled trades such as machinist, laboratory technician, or electrician, are given thorough instruction and experience, both on and off the job, in the practical and theoretical aspects of the work. For example, Bonneville Power Administration and General Physics Corporation developed an apprenticeship program for substation operators to give employees both a strong technical foundation in the fundamentals of electricity and a hands-on ability to operate equipment within the power substation. Ultimately the program was also designed to help future electrical operators respond to emergencies. In Europe, organizations such as British Aerospace, Ford Motor Company, and Rover use apprenticeship programs extensively for their engineers. Highlights in HRM 4 shows how one organization, Siemens, has transferred its apprenticeship program to the United States.[18]

Interestingly, a Detroit-based organization called Focus: HOPE provides young, low-income, unemployed adults apprenticeship opportunities to

**USING THE INTERNET**

Siemens now has apprenticeship programs at several U.S. locations, and several more are planned. Some of the programs include college coursework. You can learn the latest details at:

www.sea.siemens.com/training/apprenticeship.html

## HIGHLIGHTS IN HRM

# European-Style Apprenticeships at Siemens

At Siemens Stromberg-Carlson, European apprenticeship practices are being adopted in a version well suited to American enterprise of the 1990s.

Siemens Stromberg-Carlson is the Lake Mary, Florida, location of the Siemens Corporation. A grant from the U.S. Department of Labor helped establish an apprenticeship program at that location. The initiative, begun in 1992, is a modified version of the Siemens apprenticeship model used in Germany. It includes areas of specialization in equipment engineering and telecommunications technology.

The Electronics Technician Apprenticeship Training Program has levels for high school and community-college students. Community-college students who participate in the program initially receive about twenty hours per week of hands-on instruction at the company's apprenticeship training center. In the second and third years of the program, the students receive part-time, on-the-job training that gives them the chance to apply their acquired skills and knowledge in a real production environment.

The company selects top high school students from area schools to participate in its pre-apprenticeship program—the secondary-education version of the company's full apprenticeship program. High school students learn the fundamentals in their classrooms at school; they receive hands-on training at the apprenticeship training center. After the young people finish high school, Siemens considers them for admission into the full apprenticeship program.

Early results show that the performance levels of students enrolled in the program are at least equal to those of their counterparts in Germany. In fact, results are so good that other businesses in the Lake Mary area are working with the local school district to develop similar apprenticeship programs within their industries. Siemens has expanded its own initiative beyond Lake Mary, with similar pilot programs in Franklin, Kentucky, and Raleigh, North Carolina. And designers are working on eleven more programs for other Siemens facilities.

Source: "Siemens European-Style Apprenticeships," *Training and Development*, November 1994, 35.

learn advanced manufacturing skills for today's high-tech jobs. Among other opportunities, Focus: HOPE has established the Center for Advanced Technology, which offers a six-year curriculum that integrates structured work experience and study in applied engineering with computer-integrated manufacturing.[19]

While apprenticeship programs originated in Europe as part of its guild system, they have been adapted for use in the United States. Typically, the programs involve cooperation between organizations and their labor unions, between industry and government, or between organizations and local school systems. In the United States today, nearly 35,000 organizations have registered their programs with the U.S. Department of Labor's Bureau of Apprenticeship and Training (MAP). And the number of apprentices, including minorities, women, youth, and dislocated workers, totals more than 350,000. (Approximately 66 percent of these are in construction and manufacturing industries.)

Although employee wages are typically less while the trainees are completing their apprenticeships, the method does provide compensation while individuals learn their trade. Registered apprenticeship programs range from one to six or more years in length. For the apprentice, this translates into an "industry scholarship" worth $40,000 to $150,000. In addition, the U.S. Department of Labor requires that apprenticeship-program operators take affirmative action in recruiting and hiring women and also requires that they establish goals and timetables for doing so.[20]

## Cooperative Training, Internships, and Governmental Training

Similar to apprenticeships, **cooperative training** programs combine practical on-the-job experience with formal classes. However, the term "cooperative training" is typically used in connection with high school and college programs that incorporate part- or full-time experiences. In recent years there has been an increased effort to expand opportunities that combine on-the-job skill training with regular classroom training so that students can pursue either technical work or a college degree program. Many organizations, including Fannie Mae, Burger King, Champion International, Pacific Telesis Foundation, Cray Research, and UNUM Life Insurance, have strong ties to public schools and invest millions of dollars in educational programs.

**Internship programs,** jointly sponsored by colleges, universities, and a variety of organizations, offer students the chance to get real-world experience while finding out how they will perform in work organizations. Organizations benefit by getting student-employees with new ideas, energy, and eagerness to accomplish their assignments. Arizona State University, Penn State, and many other universities allow students to earn college credits on the basis of successful job performance and fulfillment of established program requirements. Highlights in HRM 5 shows some of the more popular internship opportunities.

The federal government and various state governments sponsor a multitude of training programs for new and current employees. The federal government's largest job-skills program, funded by the Job Training Partnership Act (JTPA), has aided thousands of organizations to help local disadvantaged and disabled individuals get job training assistance. The Long Beach Summer Youth Program, for example, is funded by JTPA to provide work experience and academic enrichment for economically disadvantaged youths between 14 and 21 years old. The eight-week program sponsors 1,200 youths each year to help them improve their work and communications skills, build self-esteem, clarify life goals, and have opportunities to practice employment skills that will help them move toward permanent, sustaining jobs.[21]

Employers who are interested in participating in the JTPA program are advised to contact the local Private Industry Council (PIC). There are more than 600 PICs in the country that are responsible for administering the program. PICs are staffed by appointees of local elected officials and are the legal arm of the U.S. Department of Labor. Employers sign a contract with the PIC that stipulates how long the training will last, what the training will consist of, and how much the company will receive in reimbursement. Many of these PICs are collaborating with one another to better manage individuals within their particular regions. For example, nine PICs in the Washington, D.C.-Maryland-Virginia region are now linked by a database designed to facilitate the flow of potential technology workers to suitable jobs. The goal of "jump-starting" new workers into promising jobs seems to be working.[22]

**Cooperative training**
Training program that combines practical on-the-job experience with formal educational classes

**Internship programs**
Programs jointly sponsored by colleges, universities, and other organizations that offer students the opportunity to gain real-life experience while allowing them to find out how they will perform in work organizations

## Student Internships

### TEN BEST INTERNSHIPS

| | |
|---|---|
| *Academy of Television Arts and Sciences* | http://www.emmys.org/activities/ |
| *Boeing* | http://www.boeing.com/ |
| *Citibank* | http://www.citibank.com/ |
| *Frito-Lay* | http://www.fritolay.com/ |
| *Inroads* | http://www.inroadsinc.org/ |
| *J. P. Morgan* | http://www.jpmorgan.com/ |
| *Northwestern Mutual Life* | http://www.northwesternmutual.com/ |
| *QVC* | http://www.qvc.com/ |
| *United States Supreme Court* | http://www.uscourts.gov/ |
| *3M* | http://www.3m.com/ |

Source: Paul O'Donnell, Seth Stevenson, Beth Kwon, and Jesse Oxfeld, "Sun and Fun? Ha! Try Work and Network," *Newsweek*, April 26, 1999, 8.

### Classroom Instruction

When most people think about training, they think about classrooms. There is good reason for this. Beyond its pervasiveness in education, classroom training enables the maximum number of trainees to be handled by the minimum number of instructors. This method lends itself particularly to training in areas where information can be presented in lectures, demonstrations, films, and videotapes or through computer instruction. Where it is not possible to obtain videotapes, audiotapes can be very valuable. For example, to instruct flight-crew trainees, airlines might play a cockpit tape taken from a doomed aircraft. After listening to the tape, the trainees discuss the behavior of the crew during the crisis. By listening to the recorded statements of others and observing their failure to operate as a team, pilot trainees will develop an understanding of the need for balancing their sense of self-reliance with an ability to listen to subordinates.

A special type of classroom facility is used in *vestibule training*. Trainees are given instruction in the operation of equipment like that found in operating departments. Perhaps you have been given instructions on using a new computer system in a classroom/lab setting. In this way, vestibule training emphasizes instruction rather than production.

### Programmed Instruction

One method of instruction that is particularly good for allowing individuals to work at their own pace is programmed instruction. Programmed instruction—increasingly referred to as *self-directed learning*—involves the use of books, manuals, or computers to break down subject matter content into highly organized, logical sequences that demand continuous response on the part of the trainee. After being presented with a small segment of information, the trainee is required to answer a question, either by writing it in a response frame or by pushing a button. If the response is correct, the trainee is told so and is presented with the next step (frame) in the material. If the response is incorrect, further explanatory information is given and the trainee is told to try again.

A major advantage of programmed instruction is that it incorporates a number of the established learning principles discussed earlier in the chapter. With programmed instruction, training is individualized, trainees are actively involved in the instructional process, and feedback and reinforcement are immediate. While programmed instruction may not increase the amount an individual learns, it typically increases the speed at which he or she learns.[23]

## Audiovisual Methods

To teach skills and procedures for many production jobs, certain audiovisual devices can be used. At the simplest level, videotapes are often used to illustrate the steps in a procedure such as assembling electronic equipment or working with a problem employee. Using camcorders permits trainers and trainees to view an on-the-spot recording and to get immediate feedback about progress toward learning objectives. Golf and tennis coaches frequently tape their students to let them see their mistakes.

Other technologies, such as CDs, videodiscs, and more recently, DVD, take audiovisual technology further by providing trainees interactive capability. Students can access any segment of the instructional program, which is especially useful for individualized instruction when employees have different levels of knowledge and ability. Such technology is currently used to teach doctors to diagnose illness, to help dairy farmers to increase productivity, and to teach CPR trainees to revive victims of heart attacks. More-recent applications tackle the difficult managerial skills of leadership, supervision, and interpersonal relations.

Extending video technology, teleconferencing or videoconferencing allows an instructional program to be transmitted to many locations simultaneously and permits immediate interaction among trainees. These methods are becoming quite powerful as tools for bringing continuing and distance education to life. MIT, for example, has developed a two-year program—called the MIT System Design and Management (SDM) Program—that students attend via videoconference. The program comprises thirteen required courses, and graduates receive a master of science in both engineering and management. MIT's program has approximately 100 students, 75 percent of whom are off-site. Off-site students use their company's videoconferencing equipment to interact with other students to coordinate the video, audio, and data exchange. Boeing and PeopleSoft are two other organizations that use satellite-based systems to broadcast training to its employees. In contrast, Oracle recently dropped its satellite network and is now developing Internet-based training for its employees and customers. Highlights in HRM 6 shows how, on a smaller scale, one individual, Leslie Speidel, has created two organizations that provide consultation and instruction to managers of small businesses.[24]

## Computer-Based Training (CBT)

As development of technology proceeds at a rapid pace and the cost of computers continues to decline, high-technology training methods are finding increased use in industry, academia, and the military. Computer-based training (CBT) encompasses

**HIGHLIGHTS IN HRM**

# Teletraining for a Small Business

*Companies:*  Marketing Coach, Small Business University (SBU)
*Founder:*  Leslie Speidel
*Services:*  Offers small business courses through teleconferences and on-line
*Initial Capital:*  $10,000 for both ventures
*Combined Annual Revenues:*  $75,000 (projected)

### Size Doesn't Matter

Having dealt with scores of entrepreneurs as a seventeen-year advertising veteran, Leslie Speidel spotted a small business need that wasn't being met: Firms wanted counseling but couldn't afford the hefty fees consultants typically charged. So with $6,000, Speidel launched Marketing Coach (www.themarketingcoach.com), offering teletraining classes to small business owners on how to market via the web. Installed in Speidel's Raleigh, North Carolina, home office is a 150-line teleconference system, which students dial into for class. Each teleconference holds between 40 and 100 attendees, and tuition depends on the length of study. To date, Marketing Coach has counseled more than 1,400 entrepreneurs.

### There's No Place Like Cyberspace

After running Marketing Coach for three months, Speidel spied another opportunity: teaching entrepreneurship through an on-line university. Launched in November 1997, Small Business University's faculty includes Speidel as well as eleven other business professionals scattered across the nation. By logging on to SBU's web site (www.sbu.com), students can take courses—ranging from one to four weeks in length—on public relations, multilevel marketing, and management. Aspiring entrepreneurs pay tuitions of from $40 to $75 per course.

Source: Jenny C. McCune, "Cash In on Cyber-Coaching," *Home Office Computing* 16, no. 7 (July 1998): 132. Used with permission.

---

**Computer-assisted instruction (CAI)**
System that delivers instructional material directly through a computer terminal in an interactive format

**Computer-managed instruction (CMI)**
System normally employed in conjunction with CAI that uses a computer to generate and score tests and to determine the level of training proficiency

two distinct techniques: computer-assisted instruction and computer-managed instruction. A **computer-assisted instruction (CAI)** system delivers training material directly through a computer terminal in an interactive format. Computers make it possible to provide drill and practice, problem solving, simulation, gaming forms of instruction, and certain very sophisticated forms of individualized tutorial instruction.

A **computer-managed instruction (CMI)** system is normally used in conjunction with CAI, thereby providing an efficient means of managing the training function. CMI uses a computer to generate and score tests and to determine the level of trainee proficiency. CMI systems can also track the performance of trainees and direct them to appropriate study material to meet their specific needs. With CMI, the computer takes on some of the routine aspects of training, freeing the instructor to spend time on course development or individualized instruction. Additionally, when the CBT is structured in a way that makes it available to employees on the job whenever they need it, it is referred to as "just-in-time" training.

Hilton Reservations Worldwide (the reservations group for Hilton Hotels and Hilton International) recently implemented a CBT system called HILSTAR to train approximately 10,000 employees worldwide on all aspects of reservations. According to John Luke, vice president of Front-Office Operations and Systems, HILSTAR has reduced training times from three days to one. Additionally, the average success rate of trainees has risen to 88 percent. Currently, the company is investigating putting the system on the Internet. [25]

Other organizations are perhaps farther along the learning curve using web-based training. In addition to Oracle, mentioned earlier, Andersen Consulting also uses its intranet-based knowledge management system, called Knowledge Xchange, as a foundation for the entire educational process of its consultants. One program, Change Fundamentals, gives these Andersen employees on-demand access to the firm's latest thinking and establishes virtual classes and workshops that allow participants to communicate with their instructor and each other.[26]

Although systems can be very sophisticated, they need not be overly expensive. Highlights in HRM 7 provides some tips for getting into web-based training. Web-based training can be revised rapidly, thereby providing continuously updated training material. This not only makes it easier and cheaper to revise training curricula, it saves travel and classroom costs. When combined with other communications technology such as e-mail, teleconferencing, videoconferencing, groupware, and the like, web-based training becomes almost indistinguishable from real-time management. A summary of these advantages includes the following:

- Learning is self-paced.
- Training comes to the employee.
- Training is interactive.
- New employees do not have to wait for a scheduled training session.
- Training can focus on specific needs as revealed by built-in tests.
- Trainees can be referred to on-line help or written material.
- It is easier to revise a computer program than to change classroom-training materials.
- Record keeping is facilitated.
- The computer program can be linked to video presentations.
- The training can be cost-effective if used for a large number of employees.

One caveat of web-based training applications bears mentioning: Some have suggested there is a potential downside in that Internet users, in general, tend to "surf." Given the sometimes nondirect format of the Internet, it may be a challenge to focus trainee interaction. Of course, this could be an advantage as well. The Internet requires that users become adept at searching, comparing, and making sense of a large amount of information. These skills are particularly important for building other skills: troubleshooting, problem solving, and analytical thinking.[27]

### Simulation Method

Sometimes it is either impractical or unwise to train employees on the actual equipment used on the job. An obvious example is training employees to operate aircraft, spacecraft, and other highly technical and expensive equipment. The simulation

**USING THE INTERNET**

Motorola is a high-tech firm, and much of its training uses multimedia technologies. Read how Motorola University extends training worldwide by using the Internet and CD-ROM technologies; visit:

www.mot.com

**HRM 7**

HIGHLIGHTS IN HRM

# Web-Based Training for under $100!

Very tight budget? Look to the web. You'll find an array of software tools that can help you build every aspect of a web-based training course. Some of these tools are free; some require a small payment. For less than $100, you can put together a toolbox of software for building and managing WBT that includes graphics, interactive tests, conferencing, and animation. The following sites will get you started.

**Multimedia Editors, HTML Tools, and Discussion Forums**
Delphi Forums (www.delphi.com). Delphi is a free-use site that lets you create and maintain chat rooms, discussion lists, and meeting places that can be linked directly to your web site. The payoff for Delphi is the banner advertising posted throughout the site. It's a very cost-effective alternative to buying your own discussion software. Click the "Free Forum" icon at the Delphi home page for details on how to build your own forum.

Tucows (www.tucows.rom). The Tucows site, a huge collection of Internet software, is the best place to start looking for freeware and shareware. At the site, choose your operating system, Windows 95 or 98, Windows NT, Windows 3.x, and Macintosh, and take your pick from a vast library of resources. There are chat tools, HTML editors, animation and image editors, and Internet and browser accessories. Click on a software category, and you'll find a list of downloadable tools with ratings (up to five cows), system requirements, a description, download information, and cost (if any).

A random sampling of programs turned up an average price of $20 for most selections—with the exception of the multimedia tools, which ranged from free up to $200 per program.

**Tests, Surveys, and Forms**
CGI Resource Index (www.cgi-resources.com/Programs_and Scripts/). This is the site to visit when you want interactive elements but have zero programming skills and no interest in learning them. CGI (common gateway interface) scripts are preprogrammed elements that let you add forms, tests, animations, and more. You copy and paste the template onto your web site, then add your own text or details. The templates are almost always free, although some ask for a small fee if you decide to use them.

At the site, choose a programming language, such as Perl, and scroll through the categories to get an idea of what is available. There are several test forms that let you build trivia-like formats, offer feedback, and give hints. You can also use CGI scripts to create tables, monitor the number of users to your site, create surveys, and more.

Source: Sara Fister, "Web-Based Training for under $100," *Training* 35, no. 12 (December 1998): 44–45. Reprinted with permission from the December 1998 issue of TRAINING Magazine. Copyright 1998. Bill Communications, Inc., Minneapolis, MN. All rights reserved. Not for resale.

method emphasizes realism in equipment and its operation at minimum cost and maximum safety. For example, CAE Electronics worked closely with Boeing to develop flight simulators in parallel with the development of the 777 aircraft.

Southwest Airlines boasts perhaps the most technologically advanced simulator in the airline industry, a $10.8 million full-motion Boeing 737-700 unit that is housed in a 110,000-square-foot flight operations training center adjacent to its headquarters at Dallas's Love Field. The facility can house up to six 737 simulators and can train up to 300 (of Southwest's 2,676) pilots at one time. The center has a staff of fifty-one, including twenty-three instructors, fifteen technicians, and thirteen support personnel. In addition to the simulators and their associated briefing and computer programming rooms, the training center houses eight classrooms, each fully equipped with closed-circuit TV, computers, conventional audio/visual equipment, and telephone hookups; four computer-based training rooms; 737 cockpit procedure trainers; an emergency-equipment training area that includes an evacuation trainer that contains one of the new spring-loaded overwing exits.[28]

The sophistication of simulation training centers such as Southwest's are certainly impressive, but as information technology becomes more powerful the distinction between simulation and the simpler CBT is beginning to blur. For example, a simulation developed by Wicat in partnership with Airbus and Singapore Airlines runs on a PC and replicates a cockpit with control displays and throttle/flap controls. Even though the PC-based simulation is relatively inexpensive, it is powerful. Pilots are taken through a self-paced program that simulates "taxi, takeoff, climb, cruise, descent, approach, landing, and go-around." These types of technologies are making it easier to offer training in new and different ways. Denny Schmidt, director of training and development for Delta Airlines, has stated that his company's goal is to deliver simulation training to employees at their homes. Given advances in telecommunications, the possibilities seem limitless.[29]

## Training Methods for Management Development

While many of the methods used to train first-level employees are also used to train managers and supervisors, there are other methods that tend to be reserved for management development. Recall that development differs somewhat from training in that its purpose is to broaden an individual's experience and provide a longer-term view of that individual's role in the organization. Over the past decade, the importance of management development has grown as organizations attempt to compete through people. Organizational change and strategic revitalization depend on talented leaders, managers, and supervisors. Management development is instrumental for giving managers the skills and perspectives they need to be successful.[30]

As with training for nonmanagerial employees, the methods used for management development differ in terms of the principles of learning they incorporate and their appropriateness for delivering various SKAs.

### On-the-Job Experiences

Some skills and knowledge can be acquired just by listening and observing or by reading. But others must be acquired through actual practice and experience. By presenting managers with the opportunities to perform under pressure and to learn from their mistakes, on-the-job development experiences are some of the most powerful and commonly used techniques.

However, just as on-the-job training for first-level employees can be problematic if not well planned, on-the-job management development should be well organized, supervised, and challenging to the participants.[31] Methods of providing on-the-job experiences include the following:

1.  *Coaching* involves a continuing flow of instructions, comments, and suggestions from the manager to the subordinate. (*Mentoring*, discussed in Chapter 7, is a similar approach to personal and informal management development.)

2.  *Understudy assignments* groom an individual to take over a manager's job by gaining experience in handling important functions of the job.

3.  *Job rotation* provides, through a variety of work experiences, the broadened knowledge and understanding required to manage more effectively.

4.  *Lateral transfer* involves horizontal movement through different departments, along with upward movement in the organization.

5.  *Special projects* and *junior boards* provide an opportunity for individuals to become involved in the study of current organizational problems and in planning and decision-making activities.

6.  *Action learning* gives managers release time to work full-time on projects with others in the organization. In some cases, action learning is combined with classroom instruction, discussions, and conferences.

7.  *Staff meetings* enable participants to become more familiar with problems and events occurring outside their immediate area by exposing them to the ideas and thinking of other managers.

8.  *Planned career progressions* (discussed in Chapter 7) utilize all these different methods to provide employees with the training and development necessary to progress through a series of jobs requiring higher and higher levels of knowledge and/or skills.

Although these methods are used most often to develop managers for higher-level positions, they also provide valuable experiences for those who are being groomed for other types of positions in the organization. And while on-the-job experiences constitute the core of management training and development, other off-the-job methods of development can be used to supplement these experiences.

DILBERT reprinted by permission of United Feature Syndicate, Inc.

## Seminars and Conferences

Seminars and conferences, like classroom instruction, are useful for bringing groups of people together for training and development. In management development, seminars and conferences can be used to communicate ideas, policies, or procedures, but they are also good for raising points of debate or discussing issues (usually with the help of a qualified leader) that have no set answers or resolutions. In this regard, seminars and conferences are often used when attitude change is a goal.

Outside seminars and conferences are often conducted jointly with universities and consulting firms. One such program that is focused on management development is the Leadership Grid. The seminars are focused on two dimensions of effective leadership: *concern for people* and *concern for production*. These two dimensions are represented in the grid shown in Figure 6.6. Developers of the grid, Robert Blake and Jane Srygley Mouton, use a combination of seminars, discussions, and personal reflection to help managers achieve what they refer to as the "9,9" leadership style ("Team Management" in Figure 6.6). By participating in seminars, managers and supervisors learn to identify necessary personal and organizational changes and to become more effective in their interpersonal relationships and their work groups.

Other seminars, on topics ranging from communications to strategic planning, are offered by organizations such as the American Management Association, the Conference Board, and the Center for Creative Leadership.

## Case Studies

A particularly useful method used in classroom learning situations is the case study. The FBI, for example, uses its Integrated Case Scenario method to bring together new agents in a logical way. Using documented examples, participants learn how to analyze (take apart) and synthesize (put together) facts, to become conscious of the many variables on which management decisions are based, and, in general, to improve their decision-making skills. Experienced educators and trainers generally point out that the case study is most appropriate where

1. Analytic, problem-solving, and critical thinking skills are most important.
2. The KSAs are complex and participants need time to master them.
3. Active participation is desired.
4. The process of learning (questioning, interpreting, etc.) is as important as the content.
5. Team problem solving and interaction are possible.[32]

Even in those situations where case studies may be appropriate, they are often mismanaged. As with any other development technique, implementation is crucial for effectiveness. Figure 6.7 provides a set of guidelines for conducting case studies.

## Management Games

Training experiences have been brought to life and made more interesting through the development of management games, where players are faced with the task of making a series of decisions affecting a hypothetical organization. The effects that every decision has on each area within the organization can be simulated with a computer programmed for the game. A major advantage of this technique is the high degree of participation it requires.

Games are now widely used as a management development method. Many of them have been designed for general use but more recently have been adapted for

FIGURE 6.6

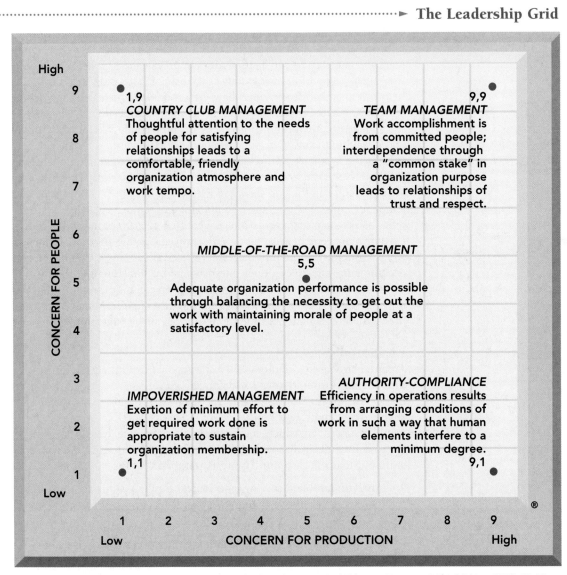

specific industries. It might be amusing to learn that the Marine Corps' basic warfare group has used a computer game called Doom to help trainees learn how to develop strategies. Similarly, Bell Canada has its managers play the game of TeleSim, a computer simulation for the telecommunications industry developed by Thinking Tools Inc. and Coopers & Lybrand Consulting to teach executives how to act in an increasingly open, competitive market.[33]

As the development of industry-specific games has increased, there are now simulations for a wide variety of organizations. Some are using simulations of organization dynamics as tools for change. General Electric, for example, uses a three-day simulation to wrap up its management development program. It is a cus-

**FIGURE 6.7**

**When Using Case Studies . . .**

- Be clear about learning objectives, and list possible ways to achieve the objectives.
- Decide which objectives would be best served by the case method.
- Identify available cases that might work, or consider writing your own.
- Set up the activity—including the case material, the room, and the schedule.
- Follow the principles of effective group dynamics.
- Provide a chance for all learners to take part and try to keep the groups small.
- Stop for process checks and be ready to intervene if group dynamics get out of hand.
- Allow for different learning styles.
- Clarify the trainer's role.
- Bridge the gap between theory and practice.

Source: Adapted from Albert A. Einsiedel, Jr., "Case Studies: Indispensable Tools for Trainers," *Training and Development*, August 1995, 50–53.

tomized computerized simulation that teaches managers to balance such variables as profit, cost, turnover, product schedules, and personnel changes.[34] Practitioners in the area of management training have come to realize that extensive preparation, planning, and debriefing are needed to realize the potential benefits of this method.

The game method does not always require a computer, however. Motorola has developed a game called "EEO: It's Your Job" to teach the basic principles of equal employment opportunity. Originally devised to fill Motorola's own affirmative action needs, it is now commercially available for use in training programs.[35] The game kit accommodates up to twenty-four players, divided into teams of four, at a single session. The players get caught up in the competitive spirit of a game and at the same time absorb and remember government regulations. They also become aware of how their own daily decisions affect their employer's compliance with these regulations. The game is reinforced with a slide presentation.

### Role Playing

Role playing consists of assuming the attitudes and behavior—that is, playing the role—of others, often a supervisor and a subordinate who are involved in a particular problem. By acting out another's position, participants in the role playing can improve their ability to understand and cope with others. Role playing should also help them to learn how to counsel others by helping them see situations from a different point of view. Role playing is used widely in training health care professionals to be empathic and sensitive to the concerns of patients. It is also used widely in training managers to handle employee issues relating to absenteeism, performance appraisal, and conflict situations.

At times, participants may be hesitant to try role playing. Successful role play takes planning. Instructors should

1. Ensure that members of the group are comfortable with each other.
2. Select and prepare the role players by introducing a specific situation.

3. To help participants prepare, ask them to describe potential characters.
4. Realize that volunteers make better role players.
5. Prepare the observers by giving them specific tasks (e.g., evaluation, feedback).
6. Guide the role-play enactment through its bumps (since it is not scripted).
7. Keep it short.
8. Discuss the enactment and prepare bulleted points of what was learned.[36]

Role play is a versatile teaching model, applicable to a variety of training experiences. Planned and implemented correctly, role play can bring realism and insight into dilemmas and experiences that otherwise might not be shared.

### Behavior Modeling

One technique that combines several different training methods, and therefore multiple principles of learning, is the behavior modeling technique. **Behavior modeling** involves four basic components:

1. *Learning points.* At the beginning of instruction, the essential goals and objectives of the program are enumerated. In some cases, the learning points are a sequence of behaviors that are to be taught. For example, the learning points might describe the recommended steps for giving employees feedback.
2. *Model.* Participants view films or videotapes in which a model manager is portrayed dealing with an employee in an effort to improve his or her performance. The model shows specifically how to deal with the situation and demonstrates the learning points.
3. *Practice and role play.* Trainees participate in extensive rehearsal of the behaviors demonstrated by the models. The greatest percentage of training time is spent in these skill-practice sessions.
4. *Feedback and reinforcement.* As the trainee's behavior increasingly resembles that of the model, the trainer and other trainees provide social reinforcers such as praise, approval, encouragement, and attention. Videotaping behavior rehearsals provides feedback and reinforcement. Emphasis throughout the training period is placed on transferring the training to the job.

Does behavior modeling work? Several controlled studies have demonstrated success in helping managers interact with employees, handle discipline, introduce change, and increase productivity.[37]

> **Behavior modeling**
> Approach that demonstrates desired behavior and gives trainees the chance to practice and role-play those behaviors and receive feedback

# Phase 4: Evaluating the Training Program

Training, like any other HRM function, should be evaluated to determine its effectiveness. A variety of methods are available to assess the extent to which training programs improve learning, affect behavior on the job, and impact the bottom-line performance of an organization. Unfortunately, few organizations adequately evaluate their training programs. In many ways, this goes beyond poor management; it is poor business practice. Given the substantial monetary stake that organizations have in training, it would seem prudent that managers would want to maximize the return on that investment.

Figure 6.8 shows that there are four basic criteria available to evaluate training: (1) reactions, (2) learning, (3) behavior, and (4) results. Some of these criteria are easier to measure than others, but each is important in that it provides different information about the success of the programs. The combination of these criteria can give a total picture of the training program in order to help managers decide where problem areas lie, what to change about the program, and whether or not to continue with a program.[38]

## Criterion 1: Reactions

One of the simplest and most common approaches to training evaluation is assessing participant reactions. Happy trainees will be more likely to want to focus on training principles and to utilize the information on the job. However, participants can do more than tell you whether they liked a program or not. They can give insights into the content and techniques they found most useful. They can critique the instructors or make suggestions about participant interactions, feedback, and the like. Potential questions might include the following:

- What were your learning goals for this program?
- Did you achieve them?
- Did you like this program?
- Would you recommend it to others who have similar learning goals?
- What suggestions do you have for improving the program?
- Should the organization continue to offer it?

While evaluation methods based on reactions are improving, too many conclusions about training effectiveness are still based on broad satisfaction measures that lack specific feedback. Furthermore, it should be noted that positive reactions are no guarantee that the training has been successful. It may be easy to collect glowing comments from trainees, but gratifying as this information is to management, it may

**FIGURE 6.8** ▶ **Criteria for Evaluating Training**

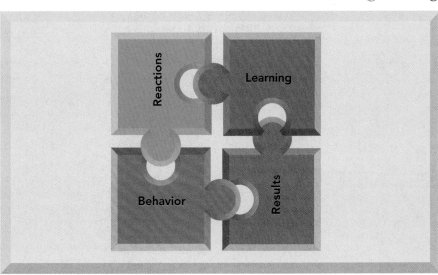

not be useful to the organization unless it somehow translates into improved behavior and job performance. In the final analysis, reaction measures should not stop with assessing the training's entertainment value.

## Criterion 2: Learning

Beyond what participants *think* about the training, it might be a good idea to see whether or not they actually learned anything. Testing knowledge and skills before beginning a training program gives a baseline standard on trainees that can be measured again after training to determine improvement. However, in addition to testing trainees before and after training, parallel standards can be measured for individuals in a control group to compare with those in training to make certain that improvements are due to training and not some other factor (such as change in jobs, compensation, and the like). The control group should be made up of employees who have not received the training but who match the trainees in such areas as experience, past training, and job level.[39]

Earlier in this chapter we discussed the principles of learning that are key ingredients of a well-designed training program. Revisiting those principles (such as goal setting, modeling, individual differences, practice, and feedback) should be done routinely as an element of evaluation. It is not enough to just know that learning did (or did not) occur; evaluation of training will, it is hoped, uncover "why."

## Criterion 3: Behavior

You might be surprised to learn that much of what is learned in a training program never gets used back on the job. It's not that the training was necessarily ineffective. In fact, on measures of employee reactions and learning, the program might score quite high. But for several reasons, trainees may not demonstrate behavior change back on the job. **Transfer of training** refers to the effective application of principles learned to what is required on the job. To maximize transfer, managers and trainers can take several approaches:

**Transfer of training**
Effective application of principles learned to what is required on the job

1. *Feature identical elements.* Transfer of training to the job can be facilitated by having conditions in the training program come as close as possible to those on the job.

2. *Focus on general principles.* In those cases where jobs change or where the work environment cannot be matched exactly, trainers often stress the general principles behind the training rather than focusing on rote behavior. This approach helps trainees learn how to apply the main learning points to varying conditions on the job.

3. *Establish a climate for transfer.* In some cases, trained behavior is not implemented because old approaches and routines are still reinforced by other managers, peers, and employees. To prevent this kind of problem, the manager should ensure that the work environment supports, reinforces, and rewards the trainee for applying the new skills or knowledge.

4. *Give employees transfer strategies.* Particularly in settings that are not conducive to transfer, managers should also provide trainees with strategies and tactics for dealing with their transfer environment. One approach, called *relapse prevention (RP)*, teaches individuals how to anticipate and cope with

the inevitable setbacks they will encounter back on the job—that is, a relapse into former behaviors. By identifying high-risk situations that jeopardize transfer and developing coping strategies, relapse prevention can help employees gain better control over maintaining learned behaviors.[40]

There are several methods for assessing transfer of learned skills back to the job. At Xerox, for example, managers use multiple methods, including observations of trainees once they return to their regular positions, interviews with the trainees' managers, and examination of trainees' post-training performance appraisals. They combine these indices to ascertain whether T and D has impacted job behaviors.[41]

## Criterion 4: Results

According to an American Society of Training and Development (ASTD) study, approximately two-thirds of training managers surveyed reported that they were coming under additional pressure to show that their programs produce "bottom-line" results.[42] Some of the results-based criteria used in evaluating training include increased productivity, fewer employee complaints, decreased costs and waste, and profitability.

### *Utility and Return on Investment*

Related to results criteria, many organizations are beginning to think in terms of the utility of the training programs. *Utility* refers to the benefits derived from training relative to the costs incurred. Motorola has conducted several studies to assess the value training brings to the company. In one such study, Motorola found that for every $1 spent on training, $33 was returned to the company. Based on a calculation of the dollar payoff, if the cost of training is high and the benefits are low, or if employees leave their jobs for other ones, the utility of training may be low.[43]

Increasingly, organizations with sophisticated training systems look to training to support long-term strategy and change more than they look for short-term financial returns from their investments. Instead of looking for a "payback," organizations such as Florida Power and Light, Motorola, and Arthur Andersen view training in terms of its "pay-forward," the extent to which the training provides knowledge and skills that create a competitive advantage and a culture that is ready for continuous change.[44]

### *Benchmarking*

**Benchmarking**

Process of measuring one's own services and practices against the recognized leaders in order to identify areas for improvement

As training and development are increasingly viewed from a strategic standpoint, there is increased interest in **benchmarking** developmental services and practices against those of recognized leaders in industry. While no single model for exact benchmarking exists, the simplest models are based on the late W. Edwards Deming's classic four-step process. The four-step process advocates that managers

1. *Plan*. Conduct a self-audit to define internal processes and measurements; decide on areas to be benchmarked and choose the comparison organization.
2. *Do*. Collect data through surveys, interviews, site visits, and/or historical records.
3. *Check*. Analyze data to discover performance gaps and communicate findings and suggested improvements to management.
4. *Act*. Establish goals, implement specific changes, monitor progress, and redefine benchmarks as a continuous improvement process.

To use benchmarking successfully, managers must clearly define the measures of competency and performance and must objectively assess the current situation and identify areas for improvement. To this end, experts in this area are attempting to work out ways of measuring what training departments do. Three broad areas that most HR training and developmental practitioners consider essential to measure are

1. *Training activity:* How much training is occurring?
2. *Training results:* Do training and development achieve their goals?
3. *Training efficiency:* Are resources utilized in the pursuit of this mission?

The American Society for Training and Development (ASTD) and its Institute for Workplace Learning have established a project that allows organizations to measure and benchmark training and development activities against each other. This benchmarking forum, which shares the findings from over 800 companies, compares data on training costs, staffing, administration, design, development, and delivery of training programs. Initiatives such as these not only help organizations evaluate their training programs but the process serves as a feedback loop to reinitiate needs assessment and design of future training.[45] Highlights in HRM 8 shows several aspects of training that can be benchmarked against organizations considered superior in the training function.

# Special Topics in Training and Development

While we have focused almost exclusively on the processes underlying a systems model of training—needs assessment, principles of learning, implementation methods, evaluation—it may be useful to discuss some of the more popular topics that are covered in these training programs. As we noted in the beginning of this chapter, there is a wide variety of training programs. In addition to the training that addresses SKAs reflecting the demands of a particular job, many employers develop training programs to meet the needs of a broader base of employees. In this final section, we summarize some of these programs, including orientation training, basic skills training, team training, and diversity training. Global training will be covered in Chapter 16.

## Orientation Training

**Orientation**
Formal process of familiarizing new employees with the organization, their jobs, and their work units

To get new employees off to a good start, organizations generally offer a formal orientation program. **Orientation** is the formal process of familiarizing new employees with the organization, their jobs, and their work units. Most executives, 82 percent in one survey conducted by Robert Half International, believe that formal orientation programs are effective in helping to retain and motivate employees. These and other reported benefits include the following:

1. Lower turnover
2. Increased productivity
3. Improved employee morale
4. Lower recruiting and training costs
5. Facilitation of learning
6. Reduction of the new employee's anxiety[46]

HRM 8

# Benchmarking HR Training

| MEASUREMENT NAME | MEASUREMENT TYPE | HOW TO CALCULATE | EXAMPLE |
|---|---|---|---|
| Percent of payroll spent on training | Training activity | Total training expenditures ÷ total payroll | U.S. average = 1.4 percent of payroll spent on training per year. |
| Training dollars spent per employee | Training activity | Total training expenditures ÷ total employees served | Three Baldrige winners spent $1,100 per employee on training in 1990. |
| Average training hours per employee | Training activity | Total number of training hours (hours × participants) ÷ total employees served | U.S. average for large firms (100+ employees) = 33 hours per employee in 1990. |
| Percent of employees trained per year | Training activity | Total number of employees receiving training ÷ total employee population | Three Baldrige winners trained an average of 92.5 percent of their workforces in 1990. |
| HRD staff per 1,000 employees | Training activity | Number of HRD staff ÷ total employee population × 1,000 | Three Baldrige winners had an average of 4.1 HRD staff members per 1,000 employees. |
| Cost savings as a ratio of training expenses | Training results: Bottom line | Total savings in scrap or waste ÷ dollars invested in training | A Baldrige winner reported saving $30 for every $1 spent on TQM training (for an ROI of 30:1). |
| Profits per employee per year | Training results: Bottom line | Total yearly gross profits ÷ total number of employees | An electronics firm earned average profits per employee of $21,000 in 1990. |
| Training costs per student hour | Training efficiency | Total costs of training ÷ total number of hours of training | Three Baldrige winners reported $27 in average training costs per hour of training in 1990. |

Source: Adapted from Donald J. Ford, "Benchmarking HRD," *Training and Development*, 36–41. Copyright 1993 by the American Society for Training and Development. Reprinted with permission. All rights reserved. See also Leslie F. Overmyer Day, "Benchmarking Training," *Training and Development*, November 1995, 26–30.

Southwest Airlines buys into the idea that employee orientation is important. The company approaches the new hire orientation program as a welcoming party (called "New Hire Celebration: You, Southwest, and Success"). According to Dena Wilson, a learning facilitator with the company, "We celebrate the individual becoming a part of our family at Southwest and what that signifies. . . . It's not easy to become a Southwest employee. We get over 100,000 applications a year and hire about 4,300."[47]

The more time and effort spent in helping new employees feel welcome, the more likely they are to identify with the organization and become valuable members of it. Unlike training, which emphasizes the *what* and the *how,* orientation often stresses the *why.* It is designed to influence employee attitudes about the work they will be doing and their role in the organization. It defines the philosophy behind the organization's rules and provides a framework for job-related tasks. And as plans, policies, and procedures change in organizations, even current employees need to be kept up to date and continually reoriented to changing conditions.

For a well-integrated orientation program, cooperation between line and staff is essential. The HR department ordinarily is responsible for coordinating orientation activities and for providing new employees with information about conditions of employment, pay, benefits, and other areas not directly under a supervisor's direction. However, the supervisor has the most important role in the orientation program. New employees are interested primarily in what the supervisor says and does and what their new co-workers are like. Before the arrival of a new employee, the supervisor should inform the work group that a new worker is joining the unit. It is also common practice for supervisors or other managerial personnel to recruit co-workers to serve as volunteer "sponsors" for incoming employees. In addition to providing practical help to newcomers, this approach conveys an emphasis on teamwork.

Given the immediate and lasting impact of orientation programs, careful planning—with emphasis on program goals, topics to be covered, and methods of organizing and presenting them—is essential. In many cases, organizations devise checklists for use by those responsible for conducting the orientation so that no item of importance to employees is overlooked. The checklist would include such things as (1) an introduction to other employees, (2) an outline of training, (3) expectations for attendance, conduct, and appearance, (4) the conditions of employment, such as hours, pay periods, etc., (5) an explanation of job duties, standards, and appraisal criteria, (6) safety regulations, (7) a list of the chain of command, and (8) an explanation of the organization's purpose and strategic goals. As shown in Figure 6.9, employees are often given a packet of orientation materials to read at their leisure. Because some of the materials might include policy statements that are legally binding—the bases for dismissal, benefits, and the like—someone should review the packet in the legal department.[48]

Some organizations are combining orientation programs with computer-based training to create multimedia capabilities. Using CBT, Lazarus Department Stores was able to cut orientation-training time in half, orienting 2,500 new employees in six weeks. Duracell International has developed an orientation program that lets employees around the world view video clips from company executives. IBM Global Services's orientation programs have eliminated paper in the classroom by giving students instruction on the web and facilitating their discussion of the materials (via Lotus Notes). This is in keeping with IBM's commitment to use the days and weeks of orientation to teach new hires the technology it sells to its customers. Of course, these types of programs *supplement*—but do not replace—the value of face-to-face orientation.[49]

► **Items for an Orientation Packet**

**FIGURE 6.9**

**For your orientation packet . . .**

- Company history
- Copy of specific job goals and descriptions
- List of unique terms in the industry, company, and job
- Copy of each important organizational publication
- Telephone numbers and locations of key personnel
- Copies of performance appraisal forms and procedures
- List of on-the-job training opportunities
- Safety and emergency procedures
- Copy of policy handbook
- Current organization chart
- Map of facility
- Copy of union contract
- List of holidays
- List of employee benefits
- Sources of information
- Copies of insurance plans

## Basic Skills Training

According to the National Adult Literacy Survey, some 90 million adults in the United States (about 40 percent of the adult population) are functionally illiterate. Experts define an illiterate individual as one having a sixth-grade education or less. Currently, over 65 percent of the workforce cannot read at the ninth-grade level. Further, the U.S. Department of Education reports that illiteracy will grow in the workforce because each year 1 million teenagers leave school without elementary skills and another 1.3 million non-English-speaking persons arrive in the United States. Estimates are that employees' lack of basic skills results in a $60 billion loss in productivity for American companies each year.[50]

These figures have important implications for society at large and for organizations that must work around these skill deficiencies. Never has this been more true, given tight labor markets on the one hand and increasing skill requirements (related to advances in technology) on the other. Basic skills have become essential occupational qualifications, having profound implications for product quality, customer service, internal efficiency, and workplace and environmental safety. A list of typical basic skills includes the following:

- Reading
- Writing
- Computing

- Speaking
- Listening
- Problem solving
- Managing oneself
- Knowing how to learn
- Working as part of a team
- Leading others

While there are different possible approaches to ensuring that employees have basic skills, the establishment of in-house basic skills programs has come increasingly into favor.[51] More than half of the *Fortune* 500 companies report that they conduct remedial employee training at costs upward of $300 million each year. Here is just a short list of examples: Ford offers reading courses at twenty-five of its plants; Domino's Pizza uses a videodisc program to teach reading and math (and making pizza dough); Polaroid United Technologies and AT&T have developed remedial training programs in math, English, and spelling; Standard Oil of Indiana reports hiring a schoolteacher to teach grammar and spelling to secretaries; RJR Nabisco offers employees at its Planters Peanuts factory in Suffolk, Virginia, four hours a week of elementary school courses on company time.[52] Figure 6.10 shows a list of training methods for basic skills, the most popular of which appears to be on-the-job training.

But grown-ups don't learn the way kids do, so many of the traditional basic skills training techniques are not successful with adults. To implement a successful program in basic and remedial skills, managers should

1. Explain to employees why and how the training will help them in their jobs.
2. Relate the training to the employees' goals.
3. Respect and consider participant experiences, and use these as a resource.
4. Use a task-centered or problem-centered approach so that participants "learn by doing."
5. Give feedback on progress toward meeting learning objectives.

The key to developing a successful basic-skills program is *flexibility*, reinforcing the principle of individual differences while acknowledging the reality of work and family constraints.[53]

## Team Training

As we discussed in Chapter 3, organizations rely on teams to attain strategic and operational goals. Whether it be an aircrew, a research team, or a manufacturing or service unit, the contributions of the individual members of the team are not only a function of the KSAs of each individual but of the interaction of the team members. Teamwork behaviors that differentiate effective teams are shown in Figure 6.11. They include both process dynamics and behavioral dynamics. The fact that these behaviors are observable and measurable provides a basis for training team members to function more effectively in the pursuit of their goals.[54]

Coca-Cola's Fountain Manufacturing Operation (the 104-person plant based in Baltimore, Maryland, that makes syrup for Coke and Diet Coke) recently worked with consultants from Moving On! to develop team training for its manufacturing employees. The program focuses on three skill categories: (1) technical,

FIGURE 6.10

**Remedial Programs in the Workplace**

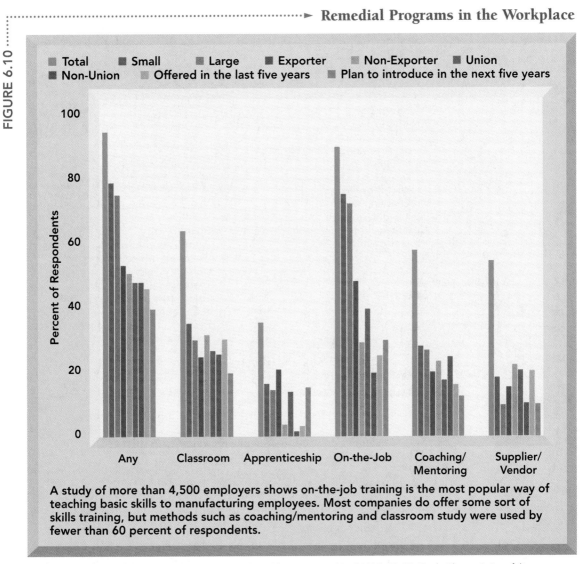

■ Total  ■ Small  ■ Large  ■ Exporter  ■ Non-Exporter  ■ Union
■ Non-Union  ■ Offered in the last five years  ■ Plan to introduce in the next five years

A study of more than 4,500 employers shows on-the-job training is the most popular way of teaching basic skills to manufacturing employees. Most companies do offer some sort of skills training, but methods such as coaching/mentoring and classroom study were used by fewer than 60 percent of respondents.

Source: Scott Hays, "The ABCs of Workplace Literacy," *Workforce* 78, no. 4 (April 1999): 70–74. Used with permission of the Manufacturing Institute's Center for Workforce Success.

(2) interpersonal, and (3) team action. The technical component is called Four-Deep Training, which implies that each individual should learn four different jobs to allow for team flexibility. The interpersonal skills component is called Adventures in Attitudes, and it focuses on listening, conflict resolution, influence, and negotiation. Team-action training focuses on team leadership, management of meetings, team roles, group dynamics, and problem solving: all skills needed to function effectively as a team. The training has not only increased quality and customer satisfaction, it has helped decrease costs and has set up a model for preparing employees for the future.[55]

In the last few years other organizations have developed exercises to generate enthusiasm and enhance team participation. Employees at Evart Glass in Michigan, for example, engage in the team-based activities listed in Highlights in HRM 9.

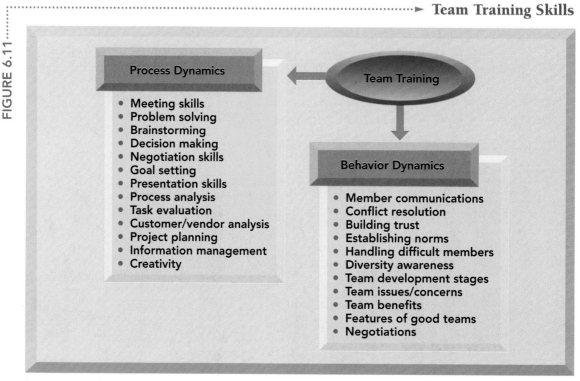

FIGURE 6.11

**Team Training Skills**

Source: George Bohlander and Kathy McCarthy, "How to Get the Most from Team Training," *National Productivity Review*, Autumn 1996, 25–35.

Managers who want to design team training for their organization should keep the following points in mind:

1. Team building is a difficult and comprehensive process. Since many new teams are under pressure to produce, there is little time for training. You cannot cover everything in a twenty-four-hour blitz. Team training works best when it is provided over time and parallels team development.

2. Team development is not always a linear sequence of "forming, storming, norming, and performing." Training initiatives can help a team work through each of these stages, but managers must be aware that lapses can occur.

3. Additional training is required to assimilate new members. Large membership changes may result in teams reverting to a previous developmental stage.

4. Behavioral and process skills need to be acquired through participative exercises. Team members cannot internalize subjects like conflict resolution through passive listening. Hands-on experiences are much better.[56]

## Diversity Training

More than 50 percent of all U.S. organizations sponsor some sort of diversity training. This emphasis is sparked by an awareness of the varied demographics of the workforce, the challenges of affirmative action, the dynamics of stereotyping, the changing values of the workforce, and the potential competitive payoffs from bringing different people together for a common purpose. There are basically two types

HRM 9

HIGHLIGHTS IN HRM

# Team Training at Evart Glass

Employees at Evart Glass in Evart, Michigan, engaged in a full-day experiential team-training program. A sampling of the activities they participated in is given below:

**Carpet-Square Maze of Life Activity**

*Challenge:* The group must find the hidden path through the carpet-square maze and then safely move each member of the group through the maze in a limited amount of time.

*Lesson:* By allowing each individual's strength to come out (some have better memories, others can move faster), the group discovers hidden leaders. Either the whole group finds success by making the deadline, or the group pays the consequence of starting a new maze from the beginning.

**Electric-Fence Activity**

*Challenge:* Each member of the group must move from one side of the "electric" fence to the other—without touching the fence.

*Lesson:* Support and trust are vital parts of teamwork. Sometimes you have to be willing to be vulnerable and ask for help in order to do your job successfully.

**Designing Vehicles Activity**

*Challenge:* Members must draw a vehicle that represents the training team and signify which part of the vehicle each member represents. Someone might be the air filter, cleaning out the negativity in the atmosphere; another might represent the headlights as someone who looks ahead to what lies in front of the team.

*Lesson:* The different strengths each member brings to the team are highlighted and it is seen how these strengths can be brought together to drive the plan ahead.

Source: "Team Activities Drive the Message Home," *Personnel Journal, May 1996, 58.*

of diversity training: (1) awareness building, which helps employees appreciate the benefits of diversity, and (2) skill building, which provides the KSAs necessary for working with people who are different. For example, a skill-building diversity program might teach managers how to conduct performance appraisals with people from different cultures or teach male supervisors how to coach female employees toward better career opportunities. All of the diverse dimensions—race, gender, age, disabilities, lifestyles, culture, education, ideas, and backgrounds—should be considered in the design of a diversity training program.[57]

Wisconsin Power and Light has established a diversity steering committee and workshop to help employees recognize the potential value of diversity. The fifteen-member steering committee represents all levels of the organization and has a mix of races, ages, and genders. The one-day workshop has several noteworthy features. A company executive kicks things off and sends a signal to employees about the importance of diversity. Each participant is given a workbook with support material and an

**USING THE INTERNET**

The focus of GE's commitment to leadership development is GE Crotonville, the world's first major corporate business school. Information about the development programs offered at Crotonville can be found at:

www.ge.com/ibcroa18. htm

outline of the important topics in the course, including company policies. The participants are asked to describe specific actions they would take to support diversity and to create a list of diversity ground rules, or "norms," that suggest how work groups can operate and what type of behavior might be accepted. The goal is to have employees and managers discuss and revise the diversity ground rules that are most important for their work areas.[58]

But not all diversity training is independently designed. Increasingly, diversity training is being combined with other training programs, an occurrence that some believe represents the "mainstreaming" of diversity with other strategic issues facing organizations. Honeywell, for example, subsumes diversity training within a week-long advanced management program and as part of its sales training programs. General Electric trains mentors and proteges in a program that isn't explicitly a diversity initiative but nevertheless clearly helps women and ethnic minorities.[59]

Organizations that have been successful with diversity training realize that it is a long-term process that requires the highest level of skill. Ineffective training in this area can be damaging and can create more problems than it solves. Unfortunately, many consulting firms have added diversity training to their list of programs without adequate personnel to handle the assignment. To avoid the pitfalls of substandard diversity training, managers will want to do the following:

1. *Forge a strategic link.* Begin by establishing the reasons for diversity training. Clarify the links between diversity and business goals in order to provide a context for training. Affirmative action and valuing diversity are not the same thing. Ultimately diversity enhances differences and unites those differences toward a common goal.

2. *Check out consultant qualifications.* Recognize that there are no certification criteria for consultants, so make certain they are qualified. Background and experience checks are essential.

3. *Don't settle for "off the shelf" programs.* Each company has somewhat different goals, and the training should reflect this.

4. *Choose training methods carefully.* Most diversity training is really education (awareness building). Managers may hope they are developing skills, but this requires more in-depth training. Employees may benefit from either awareness or skill building, but they are not the same.

5. *Document individual and organizational benefits.* Diversity training, when done well, can enhance communications, improve responsiveness to social issues, reduce lawsuits, create a climate of fairness, improve productivity on complex tasks, and increase revenues and profits. These criteria extend beyond affirmative action goals and support the competitive capability of the organization.[60]

# SUMMARY

Today we find that organizational operations cover a broad range of subjects and involve personnel at all levels, from orientation through management development. In addition to providing the training needed for effective job performance, employers offer training in such areas as personal growth and wellness. In order to have effective training programs the systems approach is recommended. This approach consists of four phases: (1) needs assessment, (2) program design, (3) implementation, and (4) evaluation.

**OBJECTIVE 2** Needs assessment begins with organization analysis. Managers must establish a context for training by deciding where training is needed, how it connects with strategic goals, and how organizational resources can best be used. Task analysis is used to identify the knowledge, skills, and abilities that are needed. Person analysis is used to identify which persons need training.

**OBJECTIVE 3** In designing a training program, managers must consider the two fundamental preconditions for learning: readiness and motivation. In addition, principles of learning should be considered in order to create an environment that is conducive to learning. These principles include goal setting, meaningfulness, modeling, individual differences, active practice, whole-versus-part learning, distributed learning, feedback, and rewards and reinforcement.

**OBJECTIVE 4** In the training of nonmanagerial personnel a wide variety of methods is available. On-the-job training is one of the most commonly used methods because it provides the advantage of hands-on experience and an opportunity to build a relationship between supervisor and employee. Apprenticeship training and internships are especially effective because they provide both on- and off-the-job experiences. Other off-the-job methods include the conference or discussion method, classroom training, programmed instruction, computer-based training, simulation, closed-circuit TV, teletraining, and interactive videodisc. All of these methods can make a contribution to the training effort with relatively little cost vis-à-vis the number of trainees who can be accommodated.

The training and development of managers is a multibillion-dollar business. As with nonmanagerial personnel, a wide variety of training methods are used for developing managers. On-the-job experiences include coaching, understudy assignment, job rotation, lateral transfer, project and committee assignments, and staff meetings. Off-the-job experiences include analysis of case studies, management games, role playing, and behavior modeling.

**OBJECTIVE 5** Evaluation of a training program should focus on several criteria: participant reactions, learning, behavior change on the job, and bottom-line results. Transfer of training is measured via examination of the degree to which trained skills are demonstrated back on the job. Benchmarking and utility analysis help evaluate the impact of training and provide the information for further needs assessment.

**OBJECTIVE 6** Special issues in training involve those programs that are important to a broad range of employees. Orientation training, for example, begins and continues throughout an employee's service with an organization. By participating in a formal orientation program, employees acquire the knowledge, skills, and attitudes that increase the probabilities of their success with the organization. To make an orientation effective there should be close cooperation between the HR department and other departments in all phases of the program, from initial planning through follow-up and evaluation. Basic skills training, team training, and diversity training are also critically important in today's organizations.

# KEY TERMS

apprenticeship training
behavior modeling
behavior modification
benchmarking
competency assessment
computer-assisted instruction (CAI)

computer-managed instruction (CMI)
cooperative training
instructional objectives
internship programs
on-the-job training (OJT)

organization analysis
orientation
person analysis
task analysis
transfer of training

# DISCUSSION QUESTIONS

 1. What economic, social, and political forces have made employee training even more important today than it was in the past?

 2. What analyses should be made to determine the training needs of an organization? After the needs are determined, what is the next step?

 3. Which principles of learning do you see demonstrated in your own class? In what ways might you bring other principles into the class?

 4. Indicate what training methods you would use for each of the following jobs. Give reasons for your choices.
   a.  File clerk
   b.  Computer operator
   c.  Automobile service station attendant
   d.  Pizza maker
   e.  Nurse's aide

 5. Compare computer-assisted instruction with the lecture method in regard to the way the two methods involve the different psychological principles of learning.

 6. Suppose that you are the manager of an accounts receivable unit in a large company. You are switching to a new system of billing and record keeping and need to train your three supervisors and twenty-eight employees in the new procedures. What training method(s) would you use? Why?

 7. Participants in a training course are often asked to evaluate the course by means of a questionnaire. What are the pros and cons of this approach? Are there better ways of evaluating a course?

 8. A new employee is likely to be anxious the first few days on the job.
   a.  What are some possible causes of this anxiety?
   b.  How may the anxiety be reduced?

 9. Why is employee orientation an important process? What are some benefits of a properly conducted orientation program?

## Creativity Training at Ingersoll-Rand

Today it is widely recognized in business that the only sustainable competitive advantage comes from being more innovative than the competition. This requires imagination, creativity, and "thinking outside the box." Executives at Ingersoll-Rand, a world leader in manufacturing tools, machinery, locks, and bearings, are keenly aware of this and have developed a series of creativity training programs with the help of their partner, creativity guru Michael T. Bagley.

In the late 1980s, Bagley helped company executives introduce a program called Innovative Thinking, a two-day skills workshop aimed primarily at engineers. The objectives of the training are to introduce a model for better understanding of the creative process and to demonstrate several creative thinking tools and methodologies to be used in designing new products. Workshops are held, training manuals are given out, specific exercises are demonstrated, and follow-ups are done to reinforce the learnings.

Creativity training methods are admittedly unconventional—but extremely powerful. For example, in his training workshop, Bagley commonly asks engineering design groups to pretend they are "molecules of air" that go on imaginary journeys through existing products and then through idealized innovative products. Other techniques such as "creative imagery" and "image repetition" require that participants visualize perfect or near-perfect solutions and products. By having participants get outside their common ways of approaching problems, Bagley helps Ingersoll-Rand employees generate new and different perspectives that lead to very creative ideas.

Managers at Ingersoll-Rand believe there are four major ingredients to a successful creativity program. First, participants must have the right focus—all the players must know both the problem and the goal of training beforehand. Second, the right group of people, oftentimes an intact team, must be put together. Third, it is very important to conduct the session in the right setting. It doesn't always have to be off-site, but it must be in a relaxed setting where concentration and motivation are increased. Finally, successful creativity training depends on having the right facilitator, someone who can help make participants comfortable and allow them to pursue nontraditional thinking.

From the initial success of the Innovative Thinking workshops, Ingersoll-Rand has incorporated creativity into many of its training courses such as Process Breakthrough, a two-day program focused on process design, and Design Concept Development, a three-day program focused on new product designs. Most recently, Ingersoll-Rand executives made creativity training methods the foundation of its Quality of Leadership program. Ultimately, the company's goal is to have all its managers and supervisors go through training that will allow them to tap their creative potential and that of their employees. The company has launched a major effort to use imagination as a competitive weapon and has established creativity as an integral part of its corporate culture.

Source: This case is based on conversations with Michael T. Bagley, Ph.D.

### QUESTIONS

1. What jobs besides engineering do you believe would benefit from creativity training?
2. Is creativity an individual or group phenomenon? Explain.
3. Where and at what times of the day are you most creative? As a manager, how would you try to accommodate individual differences such as this into a training program on creativity?
4. How would you evaluate the benefits of creativity training? How would you assess transfer? What results criteria would you try to measure?

## Kodak Gets the Picture in Executive Education

Eastman Kodak is changing dramatically to compete in a world of new technologies, emerging markets, and global customers. As a result, Kodak's efforts in executive education have pushed the limits to create innovative "learning events" for senior management. According to June Delano, Kodak's director of Executive Education and Development, these learning events are designed to be as dynamic and future-oriented as the company's business environment.

In the past, the highly successful Kodak was a citadel of stability. It enjoyed market dominance, worldwide brand recognition, extraordinary customer loyalty, and enviable profits. Understandably, few employees (or managers) wanted to do anything to upset the status quo as most of them looked forward to a lifetime of employment and security.

Then things changed. The company restructured in order to go head-to-head with competitors in a much tougher digital marketplace and, in the process, there has been a one-third reduction in executive positions. These events have driven complacency far from the environs of Rochester, New York, Kodak's headquarters city. "Agility" has replaced "stability" as the watchword of the future.

## Executive Education

As a consequence of Kodak's transformation—not to mention the personnel changes—the majority of senior managers have been in their positions for less than three years. Executive education is viewed as a critical tool for improving the managerial ranks. But Delano believed that the development programs needed to be as active, innovative, and future-oriented as the company. Off-the-shelf materials were out, as were case studies, lectures, and other passive learning approaches. A new approach meant inventing from scratch, letting go of control, and taking monumental risks. Skills in anticipating the business, pushing the culture, and networking were demanded. Delano wanted executive education to optimize opportunities to think collectively and to experiment and explore implications as a team. These objectives led to the creation of three new programs for the senior management team:

- *The Kodak Prosperity Game.* This program was developed in partnership with the Prosperity Institute and was conducted in June 1996 using staff drawn from industry and academia. Focusing on the imaging industry, the program innovatively teamed fifty Kodak executives with twenty-five peer executives from other companies. These "reality-based" teams worked on meaningful, implementable strategies, alliances, and deals.
- *The Digital Executive.* This program was held in October 1996. Its framework was a "scavenger hunt" exploring Kodak's digital present and future. Using digital products and the Internet, small teams researched digital competitors and interacted with a consumer focus group via videoconferencing. One innovative feature of this program was the upward mentoring of the participants by technology "whiz kids."
- *The Future of the Company.* This was a two-part program, developed in partnership with the Global Business Network and focused on learning about possible futures for the industry and the company. Part I was a two-day "conversation" about Kodak and its environment in the year 2007. Industry scenarios for growth were developed in small team discussions involving Kodak executives and customers, alliance partners, and futurists. The resulting scenarios launched Part II, in which additional outsiders and provocative thinkers mixed ideas with the participants. The outcomes were a set of new ideas and potential strategies for the Kodak businesses.

It is difficult at this point to quantify the results of these new programs in concrete terms, but there have been observable behavior changes and changes in the focus of executive conversations. In addition, the executives were energized by working together on real issues and rated the programs as valuable tools for achieving future growth and increasing market share.

William G. Stopper, "Agility in action: Picturing the lessons learned from Kodak and 23 other companies." Adapted with permission from *Human Resource Planning*, Vol. 21, No. 1 (1998). Copyright 1998 by The Human Resource Planning Society, 317 Madison Avenue, Suite 1509, New York, NY 10017, Phone: (212) 490-6387, Fax: (212) 682-6851.

### QUESTIONS

1. What can you tell about how Kodak did needs assessment for executive education? What recommendations would you give June Delano for improving this analysis?
2. From what you read, what principles of learning do you believe are imbedded in the three new programs?
3. How would you go about evaluating the effectiveness of these educational experiences? Do you believe that company profitability should be used as a criterion?

## NOTES AND REFERENCES

1. "Industry Report 1998," *Training* 35, no. 10 (October 1998): 43–75. See also Laurie J. Bassi and Mark E. Van Buren, "The 1999 ASTD State of the Industry Report," *Training and Development,* supplement (1999): 1–27.

2. Bob Rosner, "Training Is the Answer . . . But What Was the Question?" *Workforce* 78, no. 5 (May 1999): 42–52; Beverly Davis, "A Flexible, Convenient Way to Assess Your Training Needs," *HRMagazine* 40, no. 10 (August 1995): 114–17; Ryan R. Nelson, Ellen M. Whitener, and Henry H. Philcox, "The Assessment of End-User Training Needs," *Communications of the ACM* 38, no. 7 (July 1995): 27–39.

3. William C. Byham, "Grooming Leaders," *Executive Excellence* 16, no. 6 (June 1999): 18; Agnes Shanley and Charlene Crabb, "Who Will Operate Your Plant?" *Chemical Engineering* 106, no. 2 (February 1999): 30; Sam McClelland, "Gaining Competitive Advantage through Strategic Management Development," *Journal of Management Development* 13, no. 5 (1994): 4–13.

4. Samuel Greengard, "Web-Based Training Yields Maximum Returns," *Workforce* 78, no. 2 (February 1999): 95–96; Marc Hequet, "Doing More with Less—1995 Industry Report," *Training* 32, no. 10 (October 1995): 77–82.

5. Ron Zemke and Susan Zemke, "Putting Competencies to Work," *Training* 36, no. 1 (January 1999): 70–76; Jim Kochanski, "Competency-Based Management," *Training and Development* 51, no. 10 (October 1997): 40–44; Donald J. McNerney and Angela Briggins, "Competency Assessment Gains Favor among Trainers," *HRFocus* 72, no. 6 (June 1995): 19. See also Edward E. Lawler III, "From Job-Based to Competency-Based Organizations," *Human Resource Management* 15, no. 1 (1994): 3–15.

6. John Titus, "Annual Reviews Shape Career Paths," *Test & Measurement World* 18, no. 4 (March 1998): 37–40; Steven I. Thomas, "Performance Appraisals: Any Use for Training?" *Business Forum* 22, no. 1 (Winter 1997): 29. See also "Guidelines for Coaching and Mentoring," *Training and Development* 51, no. 8 (August 1997): 8; Geary Rummler, "In Search of the Holy Performance Grail," *Training and Development* 50, no. 4 (April 1996): 26–32.

7. Robert F. Mager, *Making Instruction Work, or, Skillbloomers* (London: Kogan Page, 1990). See also Robert F. Mager, *What Every Manager Should Know about Training* (Belmont, Calif.: Lake Publishing, 1999); Elwood F. Holton III and Curt Bailey, "Top-to-Bottom Curriculum Redesign," *Training and Development* 49, no. 3 (March 1995): 40–44.

8. Jason A. Colquitt and Marcia J. Simmering, "Conscientiousness, Goal Orientation, and Motivation to Learn During the Learning Process: A Longitudinal Study," *Journal of Applied Psychology* 83, no. 4 (August 1998): 654–65; Jeffrey D. Facteau, Gregory H. Dobbins, and Joyce E. Russell, "The Influence of General Perceptions of the Training Environment on Pretraining Motivation and Perceived Training Trans-

fer," *Journal of Management* 12, no. 1 (Spring 1995): 1–25; Kimberly A. Smith-Jentsch, Florian G. Jentsch, Stephanie C. Payne, and Eduardo Salas, "Can Pre-training Experiences Explain Individual Differences in Learning?" *Journal of Applied Psychology* 81, no. 1 (February 1996): 110–16.

9. J. Kevin Ford, Eleanor M. Smith, Daniel A. Weissbein, Stanley M. Gully, and Eduardo Salas, "Relationships of Goal Orientation, Metacognitive Activity, and Practice Strategies with Learning Outcomes and Transfer," *Journal of Applied Psychology* 83, no. 2 (April 1998): 218–33.

10. The classics by Albert Bandura here include *Social Foundations of Thought and Action: A Social Cognitive Theory* (Englewood Cliffs, N.J.: Prentice-Hall, 1986) and *A Social Learning Theory* (Englewood Cliffs, N.J.: Prentice-Hall, 1977).

11. J. Kevin Ford, Eleanor M. Smith, Daniel A. Weissbein, Stanley M. Gully, and Eduardo Salas, "Relationships of Goal Orientation, Metacognitive Activity, and Practice Strategies with Learning Outcomes and Transfer," *Journal of Applied Psychology* 83, no. 2 (April 1998): 218–33; M. K. Kacmar, P. W. Wright, and G. C. McMahan, "The Effect of Individual Differences on Technological Training," *Journal of Managerial Issues* 9, no. 1 (Spring 1997): 104–20; Candice G. Harp, Sandra C. Taylor, and John W. Satzinger, "Computer Training and Individual Differences: When Method Matters," *Human Resource Development Quarterly* 9, no. 3 (Fall 1998): 271–83.

12. Fred Luthans and Alexander D. Stajkovic, "Reinforce for Performance: The Need to Go beyond Pay and Even Rewards," *Academy of Management Executive* 13, no. 2 (May 1999): 49–57; M. R. Dixon, L. J. Hayes, L. M. Binder, and S. Manthey, "Using a Self-Control Training Procedure to Increase Appropriate Behavior," *Journal of Applied Behavior Analysis* 31, no. 2 (Summer 1998): 203–10; W. W. Fisher, D. E. Kuhn, and R. H. Thompson, "Establishing Discriminative Control of Responding Using Functional and Alternative Reinforcers during Functional Communication Training," *Journal of Applied Behavior Analysis* 31, no. 4 (Winter 1998): 543–60.

13. For recent discussions on the desired characteristics of trainers as well as their effects on training, see Greg Hopkins, "How to Design an Instructor Evaluation," *Training and Development* 53, no. 3 (March 1999): 51–52; Beth Thomas, "How to Hire Instructors Who Love Training," *Training and Development* 53, no. 3 (March 1999): 14–15; Chris Lee, "Certified to Train," *Training* 35, no. 9 (September 1998): 32–40. See also Kathryn Tyler, "Simon Says, 'Make Learning Fun,'" *HRMagazine* 41, no. 6 (June 1996):

162–68; Dale Ballou and Michael Podgursky, "Education Policy and Teacher Effort," *Industrial Relations* 34, no. 1 (January 1995): 21–39; Andy Hubbard, "People and Money," *Mortgage Banking* 55, no. 4 (January 1995): 91–92.

14. Alan Fowler, "How to Decide on Training Methods," *People Management* 1, no. 25 (December 21, 1995): 36–37.

15. William J. Rothwell and H. C. Kazanas, *Improving On-The-Job Training: How to Establish and Operate a Comprehensive OJT Program* (San Francisco: Jossey-Bass, 1994).

16. Nancy Chase, "OJT Doesn't Mean 'Sit by Joe,'" *Quality* 36, no. 11 (November 1997): 84; Polly A. Phipps, "On-the-Job Training and Employee Productivity," *Monthly Labor Review*, March 1996, 33; Reed Neil Olsen and Edwin A. Sexton, "Gender Differences in the Returns to and the Acquisition of On-the-Job Training," *Industrial Relations* 35, no. 1 (January 1996): 59–77; W. H. Weiss, "Techniques for Training and Instructing Manufacturing Plant Employees," *Supervision* 55, no. 10 (October 1994): 18–20.

17. Ronald L. Jacobs and Michael J. Jones, "Teaching Tools: When to Use On-the-Job Training," *Security Management* 41, no. 9 (September 1997): 35–39.

18. Howard Gospel and Alison Fuller, "The Modern Apprenticeship: New Wine in Old Bottles?" *Human Resource Management Journal* 8, no. 1 (1998): 5–22; Dan Darr, Kurt Hawkins, and David J. Scott, "Apprenticeship Program Trains Future Operators," *Transmission and Distribution World* 48, no. 4 (April 1996): 44–52.

19. "Focus: HOPE Prepares Apprentices for a Future in Manufacturing," *Material Handling Engineering* 50, no. 11 (October 1995): 126.

20. The interested reader can check out the Department of Labor's (Bureau of Apprenticeship and Training) web site: www.doleta.gov/bat/operator.htm. "The Survival of Apprenticeship Training," *Journal of Management Development* 14, no. 9 (1995): 21–24; Bernard Elbaum and Nirvikar Singh, "The Economic Rationale of Apprenticeship Training: Some Lessons from British and U.S. Experience," *Industrial Relations* 34, no. 4 (October 1995): 593–622.

21. Jennifer J. Laabs, "Disadvantaged Teens Work toward a Better Future," *Personnel Journal* 73, no. 12 (December 1994): 34–43. For research evidence on the effectiveness of JTPA-sponsored programs, interested persons might read the following: H. S. Bloom, L. L. Orr, S. H. Bell, G. Cave, F. L. Doolittle, and B. H. Winston, "The Benefits and Costs of JTPA Title II-A Programs: Key Findings from the National JTPA Study," *Journal of Human Resources* 32 (Summer

1997): 549–76; Robert Kornfeld and Howard S. Bloom, "Measuring Program Impacts on Earnings and Employment: Do Unemployment Insurance Wage Reports from Employers Agree with Surveys of Individuals?" *Journal of Labor Economics* 187, no. 1 (January 1999): 168–97.

22. Edward Cone, "Priming the Pump," *Informationweek* 655 (November 3, 1997): 48; Kathleen Barnes, "Government Program Supports On-the-Job Training," *HRFocus* 71, no. 6 (June 1994): 12–13.

23. K. M. Kritch and D. E. Bostow, "Degree of Constructed-Response Interaction in Computer-Based Programmed Instruction," *Journal of Applied Behavior Analysis* 31, no. 3 (Fall 1998): 387–98; Glenn Kelly and John Crosbie, "Immediate and Delayed Effects of Imposed Postfeedback Delays in Computerized Programmed Instruction," *Psychological Record* 47, no. 4 (Fall 1997): 687–98.

24. Nancy Dillon, "MIT Mixes, MBA, Technology Training," *Computerworld* 32, no. 21 (May 25, 1998): 39–42; Jenny C. McCune, "Cash In on Cyber-Coaching," *Home Office Computing* 16, no. 7 (July 1998): 132; Craig Stedman, "Oracle, PeopleSoft Offer New Approaches to Live Training," *Computerworld* 26, no. 8 (June 28, 1999): 8.

25. Ed Rubinstein, "The Learning Imperative: Operators Tap CBT, the 'Net,' to Train and Retain Employees," *Nation's Restaurant News* 33, no. 23 (June 7, 1999): 51, 56. For information on how a similar system is being used at Days Inns, see Bill Roberts, "://Training via the Desktop://," *HRMagazine* 43, no. 9 (August 1998): 98–104.

26. Robert H. Hunter, "The 'New HR' and the New HR Consultant: Developing Human Resource Consultants at Andersen Consulting," *Human Resource Management* 38, no. 2 (Summer 1999): 147–55; Samuel Greengard, "Web-Based Training Yields Maximum Returns," *Workforce* 78, no. 2 (February 1999): 95–96.

27. Tim Ouellette, "Training: Pros and Cons," *Computerworld,* 33, no. 17 (April 26, 1999): 61–62; "Web-Based Training in the Future?" *Computerworld* 29, no. 51 (December 18, 1995): 81; Donald Forlenza, "Computer-Based Training," *Professional Safety* 40, no. 5 (May 1995): 28–29.

28. Danna K. Henderson, "Next-Generation Training," *Air Transport World* 35, no. 6 (June 1998): 77–79; Bruce D. Nordwall, "CAE about to Ship First 777 Full Flight Simulator," *Aviation Week and Space Technology* 140, no. 25 (June 20, 1994): 22; Michael Mecham, "Boeing Extends Training Help to China's Airlines," *Aviation Week and Space Technology* 143, no. 1 (July 3, 1995): 51.

29. For other applications of simulation in training, see Chang Dahai and Andrew Wike, "PLC, Simulation Training Helping Personnel Cope with Growing Complexity of China's Pipelines," *Oil & Gas Journal* 96, no. 32 (August 10, 1998): 57–63; A. J. Vogl, "The Army after Next," *Across the Board* 36, no. 6 (June 1999): 43–47; Mike Fillon, "Strategic Fun and Games," *Informationweek* 654 (October 27, 1997): 122; Danna K. Henderson, "Virtual Work," *Air Transport World* 33, no. 4 (April 1996): 69–71; "Where Will You Be in 10 Years?" *Training and Development* 50, no. 4 (April 1996): 14.

30. William G. Stopper, "Agility in Action: Picturing the Lessons Learned from Kodak and 23 Other Companies," *Human Resource Planning* 21, no. 1 (1998): 11–13; J. Bernard Keys and Robert M. Fulmer, *Executive Development and Organizational Learning for Global Business* (New York: International Business Press, 1998). See also Robert M. Fulmer and Albert Vicere, *Executive Education and Leadership Development: The State of the Practice* (State College, Pa.: Penn State Institute for the Study of Organizational Effectiveness, 1995).

31. Darcy Hitchcock, "Learning from Chaos," *Journal for Quality and Participation* 19, no. 1 (January/February 1996): 42–45.

32. Chris Whitcomb, "Scenario-Based Training to the F.B.I.," *Training and Development* 53, no. 6 (June 1999): 42–46; Albert A. Einsiedel, Jr., "Case Studies: Indispensable Tools for Trainers," *Training and Development* 49, no. 8 (August 1995): 50–53. See also Alan Fowler, "How to Decide on Training Methods," *People Management* 1, no. 25 (December 21, 1995): 36–37.

33. Jenny C. McCune, "The Game of Business," *Management Review* 87, no. 2 (February 1998): 56–58; Phaedra Brotherton, "Let the Games Begin," *American Gas* 81, no. 3 (April 1999): 19–20; "The IMS Management Game 1997/98," *Management Services* 42, no. 4 (April 1998): 39; David C. Lane, "On a Resurgence of Management Simulations and Games," *Journal of the Operational Research Society* 46, no. 5 (May 1995): 604–25. For more information on a variety of commercially available management games, see "Handbook of Management Games," *HRFocus* 71, no. 5 (May 1994): 20.

34. Kim Slack, "Training for the Real Thing," *Training and Development* 47, no. 5 (May 1993): 79–89.

35. For more information, contact Corporate Affirmative Action and Compliance Department, Motorola, Inc., 1303 East Algonquin Road, Schaumburg, Ill. 60196.

36. Sandra J. Balli, "Oh No . . . Not Role Play Again," *Training and Development* 49, no. 2 (February 1995): 14–15.

**37.** Jon M. Werner, Anne O'Leary-Kelly, Timothy T. Baldwin, and Kenneth N. Wexley, "Augmenting Behavior-Modeling Training: Testing the Effects of Pre- and Post-Training Interventions," *Human Resource Development Quarterly* 5, no. 2 (Summer 1994): 169–83.

**38.** Donald Kirkpatrick, "Great Ideas Revisited: Revisiting Kirkpatrick's Four-Level Model," *Training and Development* 50, no. 1 (January 1996): 54–57. Also see Dean R. Spitzer, "Embracing Evaluation," *Training* 36, no. 6 (June 1999): 42–47; Mike Miller, "Learn to Measure Your Return on Training," *Credit Union Magazine* 65, no. 6 (June 1999): 31–32. For a counter view on this model, see Elwood F. Holton III, "The Flawed Four-Level Evaluation Model," *Human Resource Development Quarterly* 7, no. 1 (Spring 1996): 5–21.

**39.** Robert R. Haccoun and Thierry Hamtiaux, "Optimizing Knowledge Tests for Inferring Learning Acquisition Levels in Single Group Training Evaluation Designs: The Internal Referencing Strategy," *Personnel Psychology* 47, no. 3 (Autumn 1994): 593–604.

**40.** Robert E. Haskell, *Reengineering Corporate Training* (New York: Greenwood Publishing, 1998); Joel B. Bennett, Wayne E. K. Lehman, and Jamie K. Forst, "Change, Transfer Climate, and Customer Orientation: A Contextual Model and Analysis of Change-Driving Training," *Group & Organization Management* 24, no. 2 (June 1999): 188–216; Ford, Smith, Weissbein, Gully, and Salas, "Relationships of Goal Orientation," M. E. Gist and C. K. Stevens, "Effects of Practice Conditions and Supplemental Training Method on Cognitive Learning and Interpersonal Skill Generalization," *Organizational Behavior and Human Decision Processes* 75, no. 2 (August 1998): 142–69; Lisa Burke, "Improving Positive Transfer: A Test of Relapse Prevention Training on Transfer Outcomes," *Human Resource Development Quarterly* 8, no. 2 (Summer 1997): 115–28.

**41.** Judy D. Olian, Cathy C. Durham, Amy L. Kristof, Kenneth G. Brown, et al., "Designing Management Training and Development for Competitive Advantage: Lessons from the Best," *Human Resource Planning* 21, no. 1 (1998): 20–31.

**42.** A. P. Carnevale and E. R. Schulz, "Evaluation Practices," *Training and Development* 44 (1990): S23–S29. See also Jean M. Cook, "On Showing ROI," *Training*, Supplement (July 1998): OS62; Anthony R. Montebello and Maureen Haga, "To Justify Training, Test, Test Again," *Personnel Journal* 73, no. 1 (January 1994): 83–87.

**43.** Mike Miller, "Evaluate Training on These Four Levels," *Credit Union Magazine* 65, no. 5 (May 1999): 25–26; Dean R. Spitzer, "Embracing Evaluation,"

*Training* 36, no. 6 (June 1999): 42–47; Jeff Moad, "Calculating the Real Benefit of Training," *Datamation* 41, no. 7 (April 15, 1995): 45–47; Jac Fitz-enz, "Yes . . . You Can Weigh Training's Value," *Training* 31, no. 7 (July 1994): 54–58.

**44.** Richard Lee, "The 'Pay-Forward' View of Training," *People Management* 2, no. 3 (February 8, 1996): 30–32; Nancy Dixon, "New Routes to Evaluation," *Training and Development* 50, no. 5 (May 1996): 82–85.

**45.** Laurie J. Bassi and Mark E. Van Buren, "The 1999 ASTD State of the Industry Report," *Training and Development*, supplement (1999): 1–26; Laurie J. Bassi, Scott Cheney, and Daniel McMurrer, "A Common Standard for Measuring Training Results," *Training and Development* 52, no. 3 (March 1998): 10–11; Leslie F. Overmyer Day, "Benchmarking Training," *Training and Development* 49, no. 11 (November 1995): 26–30; DeAnn Christinat, "Benchmarking Executive Training," *CFO* 14, no. 9 (September 1998): 27.

**46.** "Employee Orientation Must Be Good," *America's Community Banker* 8, no. 1 (January 1999): 40.

**47.** Kathryn Tyler, "Take New Employee Orientation off the Back Burner," *HRMagazine* 43, no. 6 (May 1998): 49–57.

**48.** David K. Lindo, "Employee Orientation: Not a Self-Study Course," *Training* 32, no. 11 (November 1995): 16; Kaye Loraine, "How to Cut the Cost of Job Orientation," *Supervision*, November 1994, 3–7.

**49.** Rebecca Ganzel, "More Than a Handshake," *Training* 35, no. 3 (March 1998): 60; Marc Hequet, Michele Picard, and Ron Zemke, "Training on the Quick," *Training* 32, no. 9 (September 1995): 14; Tim Ouellett, "Multimedia Jolts Duracell Training Program," *Computerworld* 29, no. 40 (October 2, 1995): 64.

**50.** "Literacy Rates Linked to Employment, Earnings," *Occupational Outlook Quarterly* 42, no. 2 (Summer 1998): 41; Teresa L. Smith, "The Resource Center: Finding Solutions for Illiteracy," *HRFocus* 72, no. 2 (February 1995): 7; Erica Gordon Sorohan, "Low Literacy," *Training and Development* 48, no. 1 (January 1994): 12.

**51.** Scott Hays, "Basic Skills Training 101," *Workforce* 78, no. 4 (April 1999): 76–78; Scott Hays, "The ABCs of Workplace Literacy," *Workforce* 78, no. 4 (April 1999): 70–74; Erica Gordon Sorohan, "Basic Skills Training on the Rise," *Training and Development* 49, no. 5 (May 1995): 12–13. See also David Stamps, "Solutions 101," *Training* 32, no. 12 (December 1995): 38; Patrick J. O'Connor, "Getting Down to Basics," *Training and Development* 47, no. 7 (July 1993): 62–64; Edward E. Gordon, Judith A. Ponticell, and Ronald R. Morgan, *Closing the Literacy Gap in*

*American Business: A Guide for Trainers and Human Resource Specialists* (New York: Quorom Books, 1991).

52. Michael A. Verespej, "The Education Difference," *Industry Week* 245, no. 9 (May 6, 1996): 11–14; Richard D. Zalman, "The Basics of In-House Skills Training," *HRMagazine* 34, no. 2 (February 1990): 74–78; Ron Zemke, "Workplace Illiteracy—Shall We Overcome?" *Training* 26, no. 6 (June 1989): 33–39.

53. Teresa L. Smith, "The Basics of Basic-Skills Training," *Training and Development* 49, no. 4 (April 1995): 44–46; Teresa L. Smith, "Job Related Materials Reinforce Basic Skills," *HRMagazine* 40, no. 7 (July 1995): 84–90.

54. Irving H. Buchen, "Guiding Self-Directed Teams to Realize Their Potential," *National Productivity Review* 17, no. 1 (Winter 1997): 83–90; "How to Get the Most from Team Training," *HRFocus* 72, no. 3 (March 1995): 20; Steven Crom and Herbert France, "Teamwork Brings Breakthrough Improvements in Quality and Climate," *Quality Progress* 29, no. 3 (March 1996): 39–42.

55. Sandra N. Phillips, "Team Training Puts Fizz in Coke Plant's Future," *Personnel Journal* 75, no. 1 (January 1996): 87–92.

56. George W. Bohlander and Kathy McCarthy, "How to Get the Most from Team Training," *National Productivity Review,* Autumn 1996, 25–35.

57. Parshotam Dass and Barbara Parker, "Strategies for Managing Human Resource Diversity: From Resistance to Learning," *Academy of Management Executive* 13, no. 2 (May 1999): 68–80; Odette Pollar, "A Diverse Workforce Requires Balanced Leadership," *Workforce* supplement (December 1998): 4–5; Patricia L. Nemetz and Sandra L. Christensen, "The Challenge of Cultural Diversity: Harnessing a Diversity of Views to Understand Multiculturalism," *Academy of Management Review* 21, no. 2 (April 1996): 434–62; William Beaver, "Let's Stop Diversity Training and Start Managing for Diversity," *Industrial Management* 37, no. 4 (July/August 1995): 7–9.

58. Nancy L. Mueller, "Wisconsin Power and Light's Model Diversity Program," *Training and Development* 50, no. 3 (March 1996): 57–60; Shari Caudron, "Training Can Damage Diversity Efforts," *Personnel Journal* 72, no. 4 (April 1993): 51–62.

59. Jack Gordon, Marc Hequet, Chris Lee, Michele Picard, et al., "Is Diversity Training Heading South?" *Training* 33, no. 2 (February 1996): 12–14.

60. Rose Mary Wentling and Nilda Palma-Rivas, "Current Status and Future Trends of Diversity Initiatives in the Workplace: Diversity Experts' Perspective," *Human Resource Development Quarterly* 9, no. 3 (Fall 1998): 235–53; Katrina Jordan, "Diversity Training in the Workplace Today: A Status Report," *Journal of Career Planning & Employment* 59, no. 1 (Fall 1998): 46–51; Leslie E. Overmyer Day, "The Pitfalls of Diversity Training," *Training and Development* 49, no. 12 (December 1995): 24–29; Sara Rynes and Benson Rosen, "A Field Survey of Factors Affecting the Adoption and Perceived Success of Diversity Training," *Personnel Psychology* 48, no. 2 (Summer 1995): 247–70.

# chapter 7

# Career Development

## AFTER STUDYING THIS CHAPTER, YOU SHOULD BE ABLE TO

 **OBJECTIVE 1**
Explain how a career development program integrates individual and organizational needs.

 **OBJECTIVE 2**
Describe the conditions that help to make a career development program successful.

 **OBJECTIVE 3**
Discuss how job opportunities can be inventoried and employee potential assessed.

 **OBJECTIVE 4**
Describe the methods used for identifying and developing managerial talent.

 **OBJECTIVE 5**
Cite the ways in which employers can facilitate the career development of women.

 **OBJECTIVE 6**
Cite the ways in which employers can facilitate the career development of members of minority groups and of dual-career couples.

 **OBJECTIVE 7**
Describe the various aspects of personal career development that one should consider.

W e have noted at several different points in this text—and in several different ways—that the ground rules for managing people are changing dramatically in today's working world. To be competitive over the long run, organizations have to be adaptive. Jobs are becoming more flexible to cope with change and organizations are embracing alternative ways of designing work that take into account the diverse interests and backgrounds of potential employees. The need for innovation and technological change means that skills that are valuable today may be obsolete tomorrow. Flatter organization structures mean that there are fewer positions for promotion, so individuals must look for advancement opportunities outside the firm. At the same time, increased competition for talent means that some individuals will be lured away to work for other firms. The booming economy of the past decade coupled with extremely low unemployment rates means that individuals have more employment opportunities and options from which to choose. The upshot from this is that individuals are less likely to work in the same job for extended periods and, in fact, most are unlikely to spend their entire careers with only one firm.[1]

Whoa! All of these changes are going on at once, so it's small wonder that the topic of career management is one of the most important to new employees and old employees as well as to those of you who are just now thinking about entering the workforce. The desire to make the most of their knowledge and skills is something that individuals and organizations have in common. On the one hand, the task has perhaps never been more challenging. On the other hand, organizations and employees are both perhaps more focused on it than ever before. In this chapter we will not only cover career development as an HRM function, we also provide some suggestions that you may wish to consider in your own career development.

# Elements of Career Development Programs

Organizations have traditionally engaged in human resources planning and development. As we noted in Chapter 4, this activity involves charting the moves of large numbers of employees through various positions in an organization and identifying future staffing and development needs. Career development programs, with their greater emphasis on the individual, introduce a personalized aspect to the process.

A common approach to establishing a career development program is to integrate it with the existing HR functions and structures in the organization. Integrating career development with other HR programs creates synergies in which all aspects of HR reinforce one another. Figure 7.1 illustrates how HR structures relate to some of the essential aspects of the career management process. For example, in planning careers, employees need organizational information—information that strategic planning, forecasting, succession planning, and skills inventories can provide. Similarly, as they obtain information about themselves and use it in career planning, employees need to know the career paths within the organization and how management views their performance.[2]

## The Goal: Matching Individual and Organizational Needs

In the final analysis, a career development program should be viewed as a dynamic process that matches the needs of the organization with the needs of employees.

FIGURE 7.1

► **HR's Role in Career Development**

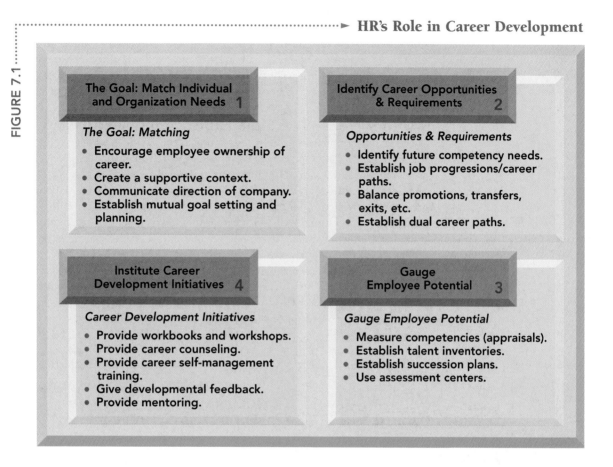

**The Goal: Match Individual and Organization Needs   1**

*The Goal: Matching*
- Encourage employee ownership of career.
- Create a supportive context.
- Communicate direction of company.
- Establish mutual goal setting and planning.

**Identify Career Opportunities & Requirements   2**

*Opportunities & Requirements*
- Identify future competency needs.
- Establish job progressions/career paths.
- Balance promotions, transfers, exits, etc.
- Establish dual career paths.

**Institute Career Development Initiatives   4**

*Career Development Initiatives*
- Provide workbooks and workshops.
- Provide career counseling.
- Provide career self-management training.
- Give developmental feedback.
- Provide mentoring.

**Gauge Employee Potential   3**

*Gauge Employee Potential*
- Measure competencies (appraisals).
- Establish talent inventories.
- Establish succession plans.
- Use assessment centers.

## The Employee's Role

In today's organizations, individuals are responsible for initiating and managing their own career planning. It is up to each individual to identify his or her own knowledge, skills, abilities, interests, and values and seek out information about career options in order to set goals and develop career plans. Managers should encourage employees to take responsibility for their own careers, offering continuing assistance in the form of feedback on individual performance and making available information about the organization, about the job, and about career opportunities that might be of interest.

The organization is responsible for supplying information about its mission, policies, and plans and for providing support for employee self-assessment, training, and development. Significant career growth can occur when individual initiative combines with organizational opportunity. Career development programs benefit managers by giving them increased skill in managing their own careers, greater retention of valued employees, increased understanding of the organization, and enhanced reputations as people-developers. As with other HR programs, the inauguration of a career development program should be based on the organization's needs as well.

Assessment of needs should take a variety of approaches (surveys, informal group discussions, interviews, etc.) and should involve personnel from different groups, such as new employees, managers, plateaued employees, minority employees, and technical and professional employees. Identifying the needs and problems of these groups provides the starting point for the organization's career development efforts. As shown in Figure 7.2, organizational needs should be linked with individual career needs in a way that joins personal effectiveness and satisfaction of employees with the achievement of the organization's strategic objectives.

### The Organization's Role: Establishing a Favorable Context

If career development is to succeed, it must receive the complete support of top management. Ideally, senior line managers and HR department managers should work together to design and implement a career development system. The system should reflect the goals and culture of the organization, and the HR philosophy should be woven throughout. An HR philosophy can provide employees with a clear set of expectations and directions for their own career development. For a program to be effective, managerial personnel at all levels must be trained in the fundamentals of job design, performance appraisal, career planning, and counseling.

One of the most important indicators of management support comes in the form of mentoring. This is true regardless of whether it is done formally as part of an ongoing program or informally as merely a kind gesture to a less experienced employee. Dealing with uncertainty is one of the biggest challenges any individual

FIGURE 7.2

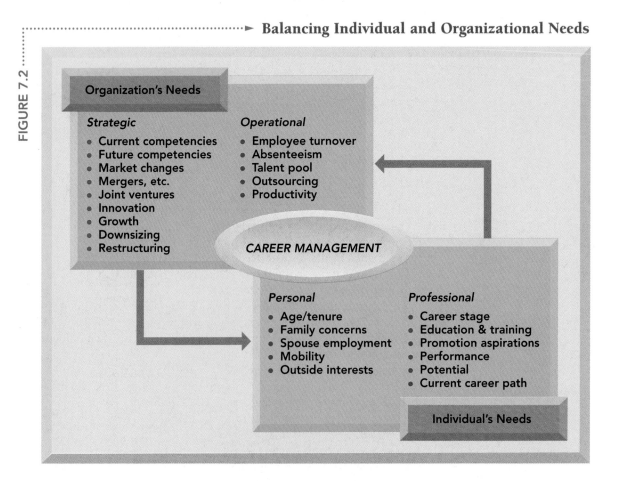

**Balancing Individual and Organizational Needs**

**Organization's Needs**

*Strategic*
- Current competencies
- Future competencies
- Market changes
- Mergers, etc.
- Joint ventures
- Innovation
- Growth
- Downsizing
- Restructuring

*Operational*
- Employee turnover
- Absenteeism
- Talent pool
- Outsourcing
- Productivity

**CAREER MANAGEMENT**

*Personal*
- Age/tenure
- Family concerns
- Spouse employment
- Mobility
- Outside interests

*Professional*
- Career stage
- Education & training
- Promotion aspirations
- Performance
- Potential
- Current career path

**Individual's Needs**

faces in his or her career. Receiving advice and council from someone who has gone through similar experiences can prove to be invaluable to employees. We discussed mentoring briefly in Chapter 6 (Training and Development) and devote an entire section to the topic later in this chapter.

### Blending Individual and Organizational Goals

Before individuals can engage in meaningful career planning, they must not only have an awareness of the organization's philosophy, but they must also have a good understanding of the organization's more immediate goals. Otherwise, they may plan for personal change and growth without knowing if or how their own goals match those of the organization. For example, if the technology of a business is changing and new skills are needed, will the organization retrain to meet this need or hire new talent? Is there growth, stability, or decline in the number of employees needed? How will turnover affect this need? Clearly, an organizational plan that answers these kinds of questions is essential to support individual career planning.

At the same time, it would be unrealistic to expect that individuals can establish their career goals with *perfect* understanding of where they are going or—for that matter—where the organization is going. Individuals change over time, and because of that, their needs and interests change. Similarly, organizations also change their directions and adjust their strategies to cope with change. So while goal setting is critical, building in some flexibility is probably a good idea.

## Identifying Career Opportunities and Requirements

While career development integrates a number of related HR activities, those who direct the process have to keep a steady watch on the needs and requirements of the organization. This involves an analysis of the competencies required for jobs, the progression among related jobs, and the supply of ready (and potential) talent available to fill those jobs.

### Competency Analysis

It is important for an organization to study its jobs carefully in order to identify and assign weights to the knowledge and skills that each one requires. This can be achieved with job analysis and evaluation systems such as those used in compensation programs. The system used at Sears measures three basic competencies for each job: know-how, problem solving, and accountability. Know-how is broken down into three types of job knowledge: technical, managerial, and human relations. Problem solving and accountability also have several dimensions. Scores for each of these three major competencies are assigned to each job, and a total value is computed for each job. For any planned job transfer, the amount of increase (or decrease) the next job represents in each of the skill areas, as well as in the total point values, can be computed. This information is then used to make certain that a transfer to a different job is a move that requires growth on the part of the employee.

Sears designs career development paths to provide the following experiences: (1) an increase in at least one skill area on each new assignment, (2) an increase of at least 10 percent in total points on each new assignment, and (3) assignments in several different functional areas.[3]

**Job progressions**
> Hierarchy of jobs a new employee might experience, ranging from a starting job to jobs that successively require more knowledge and/or skill

**Career paths**
> Lines of advancement in an occupational field within an organization

## *Job Progressions*

Once the skill demands of jobs are identified and weighted according to their importance, it is then possible to plan **job progressions.** A new employee with no experience is typically assigned to a "starting job." After a period of time in that job, the employee can be promoted to one that requires more knowledge and/or skill. While most organizations concentrate on developing job progressions for managerial, professional, and technical jobs, progressions can be developed for all categories of jobs. These job progressions then can serve as a basis for developing **career paths**—the lines of advancement within an organization—for individuals.

Figure 7.3 illustrates a typical line of advancement in the human resources area of a large multinational corporation. It is apparent that one must be prepared to move geographically in order to advance very far in HRM with this firm. This would also be true of other career fields within the organization.

Many organizations prepare interesting and attractive brochures to describe the career paths that are available to employees. General Motors has prepared a career development guide that groups jobs by fields of work such as engineering, manufacturing, communications, data processing, financial, HR, and scientific. These categories give employees an understanding of the career possibilities in the various fields.

Although these analyses can be quite helpful to employees—and are perhaps essential for organizations—a word of caution is appropriate here for readers. Many successful careers are not this methodical, nor do they proceed in a lockstep manner. In today's working world, career progressions often occur as much through creating and capitalizing on arising opportunities as they do through rational plan-

**FIGURE 7.3**

## ► Typical Line of Advancement in HR Management

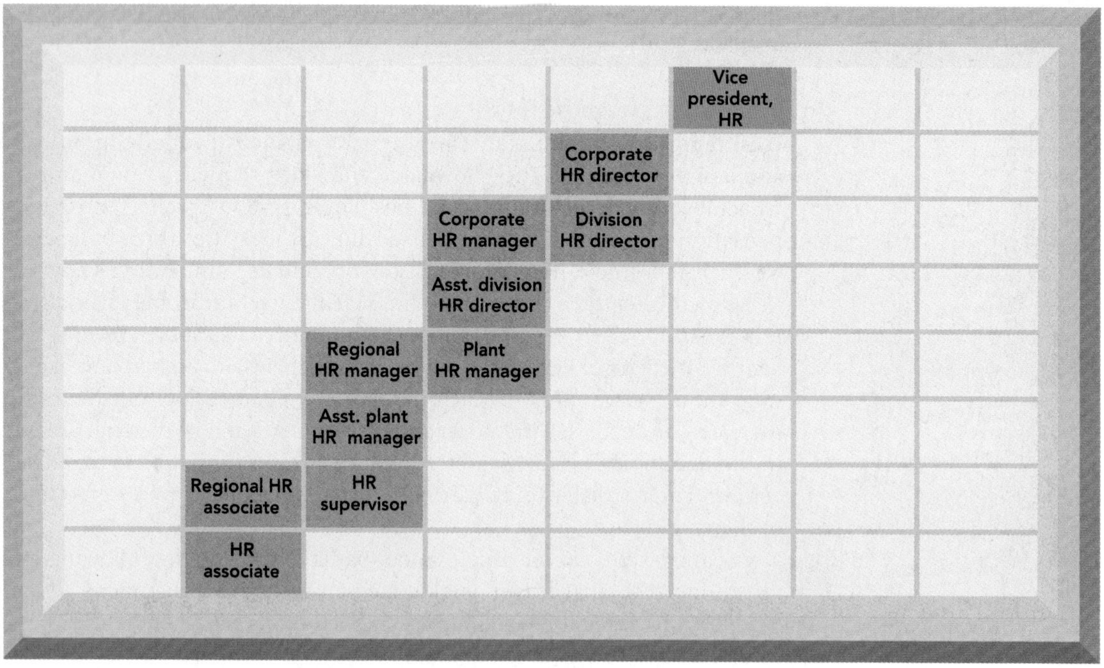

| | | | | | | Vice president, HR | | |
|---|---|---|---|---|---|---|---|---|
| | | | | | Corporate HR director | | | |
| | | | | Corporate HR manager | Division HR director | | | |
| | | | | Asst. division HR director | | | | |
| | | | Regional HR manager | Plant HR manager | | | | |
| | | | Asst. plant HR manager | | | | | |
| | | Regional HR associate | HR supervisor | | | | | |
| | | HR associate | | | | | | |

ning. So while it is a good idea for organizations to map out a career path, and individuals would do well to establish a strategy for advancement, many successful individuals readily admit that their career paths are quite idiosyncratic to their circumstances. These people often note that they have been fortunate to be "in the right place at the right time." Of course, others describe them as being extremely career savvy. Highlights in HRM 1 shows one such example, the career path of U.S. Trade Representative Charlene Barshefsky.

### Lots of Possibilities

It used to be that career development and planning systems were primarily focused on promotions and hierarchical advancement. However, in today's flatter organizations and more dynamic work environment, an individual's career advancement can occur along several different paths: transfers, demotions—even exits—as well as promotions. HR policies have to be flexible enough to adapt as well as helpful enough to support the career change.

**Promotion**
Change of assignment to a job at a higher level in the organization

As illustrated in Figure 7.4, a **promotion** is a change of assignment to a job at a higher level in the organization. The new job normally provides an increase in pay and status and demands more skill or carries more responsibility. Promotions

---

**HRM 1**

**HIGHLIGHTS IN HRM**

## Career Path of Charlene Barshefsky, U.S. Trade Representative

**1999**   Chairs the World Trade Organization's global trade ministers' conference.

**1998**   President Clinton approves her appointment as U.S. trade representative; becomes one of the leading architects of Africa Trade Initiative, which was a focal point of Clinton's 1998 visit.

**1996**   China is slow to enforce previous year's agreement and a second deal is negotiated. Chinese president Jiang Zemin asks her to help bring China into the World Trade Organization.

**1995**   Negotiates Intellectual Property Rights Agreement with China, which protects the competitive advantage of U.S. film, music, and video companies on the international market.

**1993**   While mulling over the offer from Mickey Kantor to serve as deputy U.S. trade representative, she sees a license plate that reads "GO 4 IT" and accepts the post.

**1982**   At Steptoe & Johnson, represents Harley-Davidson; gets the nickname "the Harley woman in briefs."

**1979**   Meets Armand Hammer while working on a case for Occidental Petroleum; is fascinated by Hammer's role as "private ambassador of the U.S."

**1975**   After graduating from Catholic University of America–Columbus School of Law, she joins Steptoe & Johnson in Washington, D.C.

Source: Kerry McIlroy, "Career Path," *George* 4 no. 2 (February 1999): 24.

FIGURE 7.4

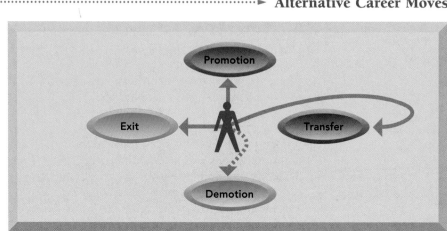

**► Alternative Career Moves**

enable an organization to utilize the skills and abilities of its personnel more effectively, and the opportunity to gain a promotion serves as an incentive for good performance. The three principal criteria for determining promotions are merit, seniority, and potential. Often the problem is to determine how much consideration to give to each factor. A common problem in organizations that promote primarily on past performance and seniority is called the Peter Principle. This refers to the situation where individuals are promoted as long as they have done a good job in their previous job. Trouble is, this continues until someone does poorly in his or her new job. Then they are no longer promoted. This results in people being promoted to their level of incompetence.[4]

In flatter organizations, there are fewer promotional opportunities and many individuals have found career advancement through lateral moves. A **transfer** is the placement of an employee in another job for which the duties, responsibilities, status, and remuneration are approximately equal to those of the previous job (although as an incentive, organizations may offer a salary adjustment). Individuals who look forward to change or want a chance to learn more may seek out transfers. In addition, transfers frequently provide a broader foundation for individuals to prepare them for an eventual promotion. A transfer may require the employee to change work group, workplace, work shift, or organizational unit; it may even necessitate moving to another geographic area. Transfers make it possible for an organization to place its employees in jobs where there is a greater need for their services and where they can acquire new knowledge and skills.

A downward transfer, or *demotion*, moves an individual into a lower-level job that can provide developmental opportunities. Although such a move is ordinarily considered unfavorable, some individuals actually may request it in order to return to their "technical roots." It is not uncommon, for example, that organizations appoint temporary leaders (especially in team environments) with the proviso that they will eventually step down from this position to reassume their former position.

Transfers, promotions, and demotions require individuals to adjust to new job demands and usually to a different work environment. A transfer that involves moving to a new location within the United States or abroad places greater demands on an employee, because it requires that employee to adapt not only to a new work

**Transfer**
Placement of an individual in another job for which the duties, responsibilities, status, and remuneration are approximately equal to those of the previous job

**Relocation services**
Services provided to an employee who is transferred to a new location, which might include help in moving, in selling a home, in orienting to a new culture, and/or in learning a new language

environment but also to new living conditions. The employee with a family has the added responsibility of helping family members adjust to the new living arrangements. Even though some employers provide all types of **relocation services**—including covering moving expenses, helping to sell a home, and providing cultural orientation and language training—there is always some loss of productive time. Pretransfer training, whether related to job skills or to lifestyle, has been suggested as one of the most effective ways to reduce lost productivity.

When one considers the numerous changes that may be accompany a career move within an organization, it should come as no surprise that many individuals are opting to accept career changes that involve *organizational exit*. Given limited career opportunities within firms, coupled with the need for talent in other companies, many individuals are discovering that their best career options may involve switching companies.

While some employees leave voluntarily, some employees are forced to leave. Even so, many organizations now provide **outplacement services** to help terminated employees find a job elsewhere. These services can be used to enhance a productive employee's career as well as to terminate an employee who is unproductive. If an organization cannot meet its career development responsibilities to its productive workers, HR policy should provide for assistance to be given them in finding more suitable career opportunities elsewhere. Jack Welch, CEO of General Electric, was one of the first executives to make a commitment to employees that while the company could no longer guarantee lifetime employment, it would try to ensure *employability*. That is, GE has committed to providing employees with the skills and support they would need to find a job in another organization.[5]

**Outplacement services**
Services provided by organizations to help terminated employees find a new job

### Dual Career Paths

One of the most obvious places where career paths have been changing is in technical and professional areas. One of the ironies of organizations in the past has been that the most successful engineers, scientists, and professionals were often promoted right out of their area of specialization into management. Instead of doing what they were good at, they were promoted into a job they often didn't understand and often didn't enjoy. It has become apparent that there must be another way to compensate such individuals without elevating them to a management position. The solution has been to develop dual career paths, or tracks, that provide for progression in special areas such as finance, marketing, and engineering with compensation that is comparable to that received by managers at different levels.[6]

Many organizations have found that this is the solution to keeping employees with valuable knowledge and skills performing tasks that are as important to the organization as those performed by managers. Highlights in HRM 2 shows the dual career path devised by Xenova Corporation, a bio-pharmaceutical company, to recognize both the scientific and the managerial paths of employees.

**USING THE INTERNET**

**Ford Motor Company** provides an excellent illustration of the dual career path. See the description of the Ford Technical Specialist Program at:

www.ford.com/careercenter/tech-sp.html

## Gauging Employee Potential

Side by side with mapping the career opportunities and requirements with their organizations, managers must also establish a clear understanding of the talent base they have at their disposal. This typically begins with the use of performance appraisal and moves into other potentially sophisticated methods.

# Dual Career Tracks: Xenova System

**Scientist**

Plans and undertakes laboratory work to achieve agreed-upon project goals, using inputs from colleagues, the external scientific community, literature, and suppliers.

**Senior Scientist**

Plans and undertakes experimental programs and laboratory work to achieve agreed-upon project or scientific goals, uses inputs from and provides outputs to colleagues, community, and suppliers.

**Section Leader**

Leads and manages a team of scientists from both science and operational management standpoint; makes significant contribution to management of groups of scientists and the general management of the department.

**Research Associate**

Provides expertise and direction to programs and projects through in-depth understanding of a scientific specialism; leads or forms part of a scientific team with the main purpose of providing expertise in a scientific discipline.

**Department Head**

Leads and manages a department of scientists to provide Xenova with a well-managed and motivated scientific resource; makes a significant contribution to the general management of the company or division of the company.

**Principal Scientist**

Provides scientific expertise and understanding of the highest level to ensure scientific leadership and direction; maintains a personal standing as a world-recognized and highly respected scientist and uses this to further the aims of the company through science.

Source: Adapted from Alan Garmonsway of Xenova and Michael Wellin of Behavioral Transformation, "Creating the Right Natural Chemistry," *People Management* 1, no. 19 (September 21, 1995): 36–39.

## Using Performance Appraisals

Performance appraisals are discussed more fully in the next chapter (Chapter 8). For our purposes here, we want to note that managers measure and evaluate an employee's performance for several reasons, none more important than for making developmental and career decisions. Successful performers are often good candidates for a promotion. In contrast, poor performing employees may need—and benefit from—a transfer to another area or even a demotion.

Identifying and developing talent in individuals is a role that all managers should take seriously. As they conduct formal appraisals, they should be concerned with their subordinates' potential for managerial or advanced technical jobs and encourage their growth in that direction. In addition to immediate managers, there should be others in the organization who have the power to evaluate, nominate, and sponsor employees with promise.

### Inventorying Management Talent

As we discussed in Chapter 4, skill inventories are an important tool for succession planning. These inventories provide an indication of the skills employees have as well as their interests and experiences. In this way, they help managers pay better attention to the developmental needs of employees, both in their present jobs and in managerial jobs to which they may be promoted. An equally important part of this process is identifying high-potential employees who may be groomed as replacements for managers who are reassigned, retire, or otherwise vacate a position.

Unfortunately, many companies do a poor job of managing their talent. In a study conducted by McKinsey and Company, three-quarters of corporate officers said their companies were chronically short of talent. At the same time, half of the respondents to a similar survey acknowledged that they were not doing effective succession planning and were unprepared to replace key executives. [7]

Organizations that emphasize developing human assets as well as turning a profit typically have the talent they need and some to spare. Some companies— Xerox, Intel, and Wal-Mart, to name a few—have become "academy" companies that unintentionally provide a source of talented managers to organizations that lack good management career development programs of their own.

### Using Assessment Centers

There are other very effective ways to assess a person's career potential. Pioneered in the mid-1950s by Douglas Bray and his associates at AT&T, assessment centers are considered one of the most valuable methods for evaluating personnel. An **assessment center** is a process (not a place) by which individuals are evaluated as they participate in a series of situations that resemble what they might be called upon to handle on the job. The popularity of the assessment center can be attributed to its capacity for increasing an organization's ability to select employees who will perform successfully in management positions or to assist and promote the development of skills for their current position. These centers may use in-basket exercises, leaderless group discussions, and approaches discussed in Chapter 6:

- *In-basket training.* This method is used to simulate a problem situation. The participants are given several documents, each describing some problem or situation requiring an immediate response. They are thus forced to make decisions under the pressure of time and also to determine what priority to give each problem.

- *Leaderless group discussions.* With this activity, trainees are gathered in a conference setting to discuss an assigned topic, either with or without designated group roles. The participants are given little or no instruction in how to approach the topic, nor are they told what decision to reach. Leaderless group trainees are evaluated on their initiative, leadership skills, and ability to work effectively in a group setting.

The assessment-center schedule of the various activities at the California Highway Patrol Academy assessment center is shown in Highlights in HRM 3. Participation in these activities provides samples of behavior that are representative of

---

**Assessment center**
Process by which individuals are evaluated as they participate in a series of situations that resemble what they might be called upon to handle on the job

**In-basket training**
Assessment-center process for evaluating trainees by simulating a real-life work situation

**Leaderless group discussions**
Assessment-center process that places trainees in a conference setting to discuss an assigned topic, either with or without designated group roles

what is required for advancement. At the end of the assessment-center period, the assessors' observations are combined and integrated to develop an overall picture of the strengths and needs of the participants. A report is normally submitted to senior management, and feedback is given to the participants.

Increasing attention is being given to the validity of assessment-center procedures. As with employment tests, the assessments provided must be valid. Before the

**HRM 3**

**HIGHLIGHTS IN HRM**

# Assessment-Center Program of the California Highway Patrol

| One week prior to to conduct of the centers | Five-day training for all assessors* |
|---|---|
| Monday—A.M. | Assessors review exercises. |
|  | Participants go through orientation. |
| Monday—P.M. | Leaderless group discussion: Participants divided into two groups of six each, observed by three assessors; each assessor observes two participants. |
|  | Assessors prepare final report on this exercise. |
|  | In-basket exercise: Each participant works individually for three hours on a 31-item in-basket. |
|  | Assessors review and score in-basket and prepare for in-basket interview the following day. |
| Tuesday—P.M. | Participants take a forty-minute reading test (*Davis Reading Test*). |
|  | Assessors review in-basket observations with participants and prepare final report on this exercise. |
| Wednesday—A.M. | Participants complete an individual analysis exercise and prepare a seven-minute presentation to the panel of assessors on solution to the problem. |
|  | Participants begin presentations to panel of assessors. |
| Wednesday—P.M. | Presentations continue through afternoon. |
|  | Participants are released to return to work site. |
|  | Assessors prepare final reports on this exercise. |
|  | Administrator prepares for discussion of each candidate the following day. |
| Thursday—All day | Assessors meet in teams of three to integrate observations of each participant's overall exercises, to reach a consensual rating on each skill evaluated, and to make specific developmental recommendations. |
| Within 45 days | Assessors meet with participants and their supervisors at the participant's work site to discuss observations of assessor panel. |
| Within 60 days | Participants and supervisors develop a career plan to assist participant in skill development. |

*All exercises and training take place on-site at the CHP Academy.

Source: California Highway Patrol Academy. Reproduced with permission.

assessment center is run, the characteristics or dimensions to be studied should be determined through job analyses. The exercises used in the center should reflect the job for which the person is being evaluated; i.e., the exercises should have content validity. While the assessment-center methodology lends itself readily to content validation, predictive validity has also been observed in many instances. A strong positive relationship is found between assessments and future performance on the job.[8]

While assessment centers have proved quite valuable in identifying managerial talent and in helping with the development of individuals, it should be noted that the method tends to favor those who are strong in interpersonal skills and have the ability to influence others. Some individuals find it difficult to perform at their best in a situation that for them is as threatening as taking a test. The manner in which assessment-center personnel conduct the exercises and provide feedback to the participants will play a major role in determining how individuals react to the experience.

## Career Development Initiatives

Although career management involves a good deal of analysis and planning, the reality is that it needs to provide a set of tools and techniques that help employees gauge their potential for success in the organization. Informal counseling by HR staff and supervisors is used widely. Many organizations give their employees information on educational assistance, EEO/AA programs and policies, salary administration, and job requirements. Career planning workbooks and workshops are also popular means of helping employees identify their potential and the strength of their interests.[9]

### Career Planning Workbooks

Several organizations have prepared workbooks to guide their employees individually through systematic self-assessment of values, interests, abilities, goals, and personal development plans. General Motors' *Career Development Guide* contains a section called "What Do You Want Your Future to Be?" in which the employee makes a personal evaluation. General Electric has developed an extensive set of manuals for its career development program, including two workbooks to help employees explore life issues that affect career decisions. Syntex's workbook, *How to Work for a Living and Like It,* may be used by individuals on their own or in a group workshop.

Some organizations prefer to use workbooks written for the general public. Popular ones include Richard N. Bolles's *What Color Is Your Parachute?,* Andrew H. Souerwine's *Career Strategies: Planning for Personal Growth,* John Holland's *Self-Directed Search,* and John W. Slocum and G. Scott King's *How to Pack Your Career Parachute.*[10] These same books are recommended to students for help in planning their careers.

### Career Planning Workshops

Workshops offer experiences similar to those provided by workbooks. However, they have the advantage of providing a chance to compare and discuss attitudes, concerns, and plans with others in similar situations. Some workshops focus on current job performance and development plans. Others deal with broader life and career plans and values. Case Study 1 (at the end of this chapter), on Amoco's career management system, highlights two different workshops used by that company.

As mentioned earlier, employees should be encouraged to assume responsibility for their own careers. A career workshop can help them do that. It can also help

**Career counseling**
Process of discussing with employees their current job activities and performance, their personal and career interests and goals, their personal skills, and suitable career development objectives

them learn how to make career decisions, set career goals, create career options, seek career planning information, and at the same time build confidence and self-esteem.[11] Highlights in HRM 4 describes a workshop used by Marriott Corporation.

### Career Counseling

**Career counseling** involves talking with employees about their current job activities and performance, their personal and career interests and goals, their personal skills, and suitable career development objectives. While some organizations make counseling a part of the annual performance appraisal, career counseling is usually voluntary. Career counseling may be provided by the HR staff, managers and super-

**HRM 4**

**HIGHLIGHTS IN HRM**

# Career Development Workshops at Marriott

Given the business realities of a highly competitive hotel industry, Marriott Corporation executives know that they can no longer take a paternalistic approach to career management. To provide managers and supervisors with assistance in managing their own careers—and the careers of their employees—Marriott has developed a workshop called "Partners in Career Management." The workshop is based on a four-step model that helps managers focus on the following questions:

- *Who am I?* The program helps employees identify their skills, values, and interests.
- *How am I seen?* The program offers ongoing feedback to help employees understand how others view their contribution.
- *What are my career objectives?* The workshop helps employees create a set of realistic career goals.
- *How can I achieve my goals?* The workshop helps individuals develop action plans that focus on leveraging their abilities and experiences to achieve their goals.

By training its managers to help company employees learn about career opportunities and resources, Marriott is moving toward shifting responsibility for career management away from the company and to the employee. At Marriott, employees are responsible for

- Assessing their own skills, values, interests, and developmental needs
- Determining long- and short-term career goals
- Creating with their managers career development plans to reach their goals
- Following through with their plans
- Learning about career management resources such as the on-line job posting system
- Meeting with their managers on a regular basis for career development discussions
- Recognizing that career discussions imply no promises or guarantees
- Recognizing that their development will depend directly on Marriott's organizational needs and opportunities as well as their own performance

Source: Shari Caudron, "Marriott Trains Managers to Become Partners in Career Management," *Personnel Journal* 73, no. 4 (April 1994): 641.

visors, specialized staff counselors, or outside consultants. Several techniques for career counseling are outlined at the end of this chapter. (See section, Personal Career Development.)

As employees approach retirement, they may be encouraged to participate in preretirement programs, which often include counseling along with other helping activities. Preretirement programs will be discussed in Chapter 11.

One interesting development in recent years has been the establishment of the Workforce Investment Act of 1998. With the signing of this act, Congress established a new law that consolidates a wide variety of federally sponsored career development and job training programs. Under the new arrangement, one-stop service centers will be set up in cooperation among businesses and local governments to provide job-seekers with a variety of services, including career counseling, skill assessments, training, job search assistance, and referrals to related programs and services.[12]

### *Determining Individual Development Needs*

Because the requirements of each position and the qualifications of each person are different, no two individuals will have identical developmental needs. For one individual, self-development may consist of developing the ability to write reports, give talks, and lead conferences. For another, it may require developing interpersonal skills in order to communicate and relate more effectively with a diverse workforce. Periodic performance appraisals can provide a basis for determining each manager's progress. Conferences in which these appraisals are discussed are an essential part of self-improvement efforts.

In helping individuals plan their careers, it is important for organizations to recognize that younger employees today seek meaningful training assignments that are interesting and involve challenge, responsibility, and a sense of empowerment. They also have a greater concern for the contribution that their work in the organization will make to society. Unfortunately, they are frequently given responsibilities they view as rudimentary, boring, and composed of too many "make-work" activities. Some organizations are attempting to retain young managers with high potential by offering a **fast-track program** that enables them to advance more rapidly than those with less potential. A fast-track program may provide for a relatively rapid progression—lateral transfers or promotions—through a number of managerial positions requiring exposure to different organizational functions; it may also provide opportunities to make meaningful decisions.

**Fast-track program**
Program that encourages young managers with high potential to remain with an organization by enabling them to advance more rapidly than those with less potential

### *Career Self-Management Training*

In response to the growing view that employees should assume greater responsibility for their own career management, many organizations such as AT&T and Chevron are establishing training programs for employees on how they can engage in *career self-management*. The training focuses on two major objectives: (1) helping employees learn to continuously gather feedback and information about their careers and (2) encouraging them to prepare for mobility.

The training is not geared to skills and behaviors associated with a specific job, but rather toward their long-term personal effectiveness. Employees typically undertake self-assessments to increase awareness of their own career attitudes and values. In addition, they are encouraged to widen their viewpoint beyond the next company promotion to broader opportunities in the marketplace. For many, these external opportunities have not been seen as viable options, much less something the company would acknowledge. Participants might be encouraged to engage in career networking or to identify other means to prepare for job mobility such as hearing reports from employees who made transitions to new job opportunities both within and outside of the organization.[13]

### Mentoring

When one talks with men and women about their employment experiences, it is common to hear them mention individuals at work who influenced them. They frequently refer to immediate managers who were especially helpful as career developers. But they also mention others at higher levels in the organization who provided guidance and support to them in the development of their careers. These executives and managers who coach, advise, and encourage employees of lesser rank are called **mentors.**

At times, individuals can be overly restrictive in their definitions of who constitutes a mentor, or what that mentor can do. The top ten myths about mentors are shown in Figure 7.5. In reality, informal mentoring goes on daily within every type

**Mentors**
Executives who coach, advise, and encourage individuals of lesser rank

**FIGURE 7.5**

### Top Ten Myths about Mentors

**Myth 1:** *Mentors exist only for career development.* Sometimes the mentor focuses on formal career development. Sometimes the mentor is teacher, counselor, and friend. Some mentors assume all these roles. This enhances both personal and professional development.

**Myth 2:** *You only need one mentor.* We can have multiple mentors in our lives. Different mentors provide different things and tap different facets of our lives.

**Myth 3:** *Mentoring is a one-way process.* Learning flows both ways. The mentor often learns from the protégé, so the growth is reciprocal.

**Myth 4:** *A mentor has to be older than the protégé.* Age does not matter. Experience and wisdom matter. Don't deprive yourself of learning opportunities from others who have rich experiences.

**Myth 5:** *A mentor has to be same gender and race as the protégé.* The purpose of mentoring is to learn. Don't deprive yourself. Seek mentors who are different from you.

**Myth 6:** *Mentor relationships just happen.* Being in the right place at the right time can help, but the key to selecting a good mentor is what (not whom) you need. Don't be afraid to actively seek a mentor.

**Myth 7:** *Highly profiled people make the best mentors.* Prestige and success can be good, but good advice, leadership styles, work ethics, and the like vary by individuals. Good mentors are people who challenge you according to your needs, readiness, and aspirations.

**Myth 8:** *Once a mentor, always a mentor.* Over time, the mentor should pull back and let the protégé go his or her own way. Although the two may maintain contact, the relationship changes over time.

**Myth 9:** *Mentoring is a complicated process.* The most complicated part is getting out of a bad mentor relationship. If the relationship is not productive, find a tactful way to disengage.

**Myth 10:** *Mentor-protégé expectations are the same for everyone.* Individuals seek mentors for the same reasons: resources, visibility, enhanced skills, and counsel. But each individual brings different expectations. The key is understanding where the protege is *now*, not where he or she *should be*.

of organization. Generally, the mentor initiates the relationship, but sometimes an employee will approach a potential mentor for advice. Most mentoring relationships develop over time on an informal basis. However, in proactive organizations there is an emphasis on formal mentoring plans that call for the assignment of a mentor to those employees considered for upward movement in the organization. Under a good mentor, learning focuses on goals, opportunities, expectations, standards, and assistance in fulfilling one's potential.[14]

Figure 7.6 shows a list of the most effective features of mentors as well as mentees. In general, **mentoring functions** can be divided into two broad categories: career functions and psychosocial functions:

**Mentoring functions**
Functions concerned with the career advancement and psychological aspects of the person being mentored

- *Career functions.* Career functions are those aspects of the relationship that enhance career advancement. They include sponsorship, exposure and visibility, coaching, protection, challenging assignments.

- *Psychosocial functions.* Psychosocial functions are those aspects that enhance the protégé's sense of competence, identity, and effectiveness in a professional role. They include role modeling, acceptance and confirmation, counseling, and friendship. Both functions are viewed as critical to management development.[15]

Organizations with formal mentoring programs include Shell International, Sun Express (part of Sun Microsystems), Johnson & Johnson, the federal Government Accounting Office, and the Bank of Montreal.[16] Alternatively, given the importance of the issue, a number of mentoring organizations have begun to spring up. One such organization, Menttium Corporation, helps create and monitor mentoring partnerships so that the right people are matched with one another. When done well, the mentoring process is beneficial for both the pupil and the mentor. Not surprisingly, mentoring is also being done over the Internet. Known as *e-mentoring,* the process is mediated via web sites that bring experienced business professionals

**FIGURE 7.6**

**Mentoring Functions**

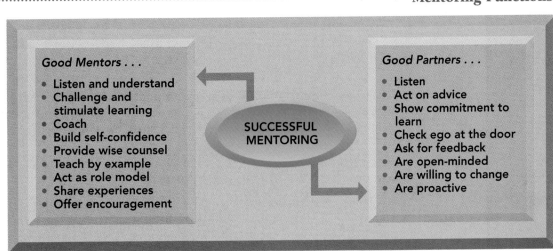

*Good Mentors . . .*
- Listen and understand
- Challenge and stimulate learning
- Coach
- Build self-confidence
- Provide wise counsel
- Teach by example
- Act as role model
- Share experiences
- Offer encouragement

**SUCCESSFUL MENTORING**

*Good Partners . . .*
- Listen
- Act on advice
- Show commitment to learn
- Check ego at the door
- Ask for feedback
- Are open-minded
- Are willing to change
- Are proactive

Source: Matt Starcevich, Ph.D. and Fred Friend, "Effective mentoring relationships from the Mentee's perspective," *Workforce,* supplement (July 1999): 2–3. Used with permission of the Center for Coaching and Mentoring, Inc., http://coachingandmentoring.com.

together with individuals needing counseling. A few examples include:

- *Women in Technology International (WITI)* is a Sherman Oaks, California–based association that has assembled thousands of women in technology fields who will act as on-line mentors to visitors of its web site.
- *Mighty Mentors* is a program by Mighty Media (Minneapolis, Minnesota) that provides interactive educational technology. The mentor service lets teachers mentor one another via e-mail after they connect on line.
- *NursingNet* is an on-line nursing forum that has mentoring programs for those in health care. The site hooks up experienced nurses with those who need guidance.[17]

*Mighty Mentors, launched by Mighty Media, facilitates on-line mentoring for teachers.*

Even though participants in e-mentoring typically never meet in person, many form long-lasting e-mail connections that tend to be very beneficial. Still, most participants see these connections as supplements to—rather than substitutes for—in-company mentors.

Another new form of mentoring, sponsored by the MS Foundation for Women, provides an opportunity for girls 9 to 15 years old to spend a day with mothers or friends on the job. The program is designed to give young women more attention and to provide them with career role models. Many of the larger organizations, including Nike, DuPont, Ford, and Valvoline, have participated in this program, and it has grown to include boys of the same age. Other groups, like the Girl Scouts in the Washington, D.C., area, have longer-term mentoring plans where young women ages 12 to 18 spend up to a month a year in the offices of women scientists, accountants, and other professionals. It is hoped that through such programs young women will think more broadly in their career planning.[18]

# Career Development for a Diverse Workforce

Today some organizations offer extensive career development programs that include programs geared to special groups, such as women, minorities, and/or dual-career couples. Let's examine some of these special programs more closely.

## Career Development for Women

In Chapter 4 we discussed some of the current trends in the employment of women in jobs that until recently were held predominantly by men. Included among these jobs are management-level positions. Organizations are continually concerned, as a result of EEO/AA requirements and because of the need for strong leadership, to increase the proportion of women they employ as managers.

## *Eliminating Barriers to Advancement*

Women in management have been at a disadvantage because they were not part of the so-called good old boys' network, an informal network of interpersonal relationships that has traditionally provided a means for senior (male) members of the organization to pass along news of advancement opportunities and other career tips to junior (male) members. Women have typically been outside the network, lacking role models to serve as mentors.

To combat their difficulty in advancing to management positions, women in several organizations have developed their own women's networks. At Ralston Purina in St. Louis, a women's network that any female employee may join serves as a system for encouraging and fostering women's career development and for sharing information, experiences, and insights. Corporate officers are invited to regularly scheduled network meetings to discuss such matters as planning, development, and company performance. Network members view these sessions as an opportunity to let corporate officers know of women who are interested in and capable of furthering their careers. Other corporations where women's networks have been established include Hoffman-LaRoche, Metropolitan Life Insurance, Atlantic Richfield, Scholastic Magazines, and CBS.[19]

As we mentioned previously, there are several on-line e-mentoring networks available. Two that are expressly devoted to working women are WomenConnect (www.womenconnect.com) and Advancing Women (www.advancingwomen.com). In addition, an organization that is devoted to helping employers break down barriers to upward mobility for women is Catalyst, a New York City–based not-for-profit organization. Catalyst not only courts corporate officers but also offers career advice, job placement, continuing education, and related professional development for women of all ages. At its New York headquarters, Catalyst houses an extensive library and audiovisual center that is regarded as the country's leading resource for information on women and work.[20]

The advancement of women in management has been hindered by a series of sex-role stereotypes that have shaped the destiny of women, working women in particular. Some of the more prominent myths were discussed in Chapter 4. Fortunately, there is substantial evidence that stereotyped attitudes toward women are changing. As women pursue career goals assertively and attitudes continue to change, the climate for women in management will be even more favorable. Research has shown that newer male managers tend to be more receptive to the advancement of women managers. Also, the U.S. Supreme Court ruling in *Price Waterhouse v Hopkins* (1989), which states unequivocally that sex stereotyping is discriminatory, has helped to push organizations in a progressive direction.

The good news is that women have made substantial progress in securing mid- and lower-level management positions over the past decade; women hold more than 40 percent of all managerial positions and over 23 percent of executive positions. However, despite these numbers, the proportion of women in top echelons of management—board chair, CEO, president, executive VP—remains extremely low, around 3 percent. One notable exception to this trend among companies was the appointment of Carley Fiorino to the CEO position of Hewlett-Packard. While these data suggest there that has been some progress, there is much left to do to break the glass ceiling, that invisible barrier of attitudes, prejudices, and "old boy" networks that blocks the progress of women who seek important positions in an organization. Figure 7.7 lists the top female executives as compiled by *Working Woman* magazine.[21]

FIGURE 7.7

## Women in Ownership or Top Management Positions

| NAME | COMPANY | LOCATION | ANNUAL SALES | NO. OF EMPLOYEES |
|------|---------|----------|--------------|------------------|
| Loida N. Lewis | TLC Beatrice | New York | $1.82 billion | 4,200 |
| Joyce Raley Teel | Raley's | Sacramento | 1.8 billion | 10,500 |
| Lynda Resnick | Roll International | Los Angeles | 1.4 billion | 7,500 |
| Marian Ilitch | Little Caesar Enterprises | Detroit | 1.0 billion | 8,100 |
| Antonia Axson Johnson | Axel Johnson | Stockholm | 815 million (U.S.) | 2,000 |
| Liz Minyard and Gretchen Minyard Williams | Minyard Food Stores | Coppell, Tex. | 800 million | 6,500 |
| Linda Wachner | Warnaco | New York | 789 million | 14,800 |
| Donna Karan | Donna Karan | New York | 465 million | 1,288 |
| Donna Wolf Steigerwaldt | Jockey International | Kenosha, Wisc. | 450 million | 4,000 |
| Helen Copley | Copley Press | La Jolla, Calif. | 380 million | 3,250 |
| Jenny Craig | Jenny Craig | Del Mar, Calif. | 376 million | 4,300 |
| Carole Little | Carole Little | Los Angeles | 375 million | 950 |
| Irma Elder | Troy Motors | Troy, Mich. | 364 million | 200 |
| Dian Graves Owen | Owen Healthcare | Houston | 320 million* | 2,983 |
| Susie Tompkins | Esprit de Corp. | San Francisco | 300 million† | 1,250 |
| Annabelle Lundy Fetterman | Lundy Packing | Clinton, N.C. | 299 million | 900 |
| Ellen Gordon | Tootsie Roll Industries | Chicago | 298 million | 1,700 |
| Barbara Levy Kipper | Chas. Levy | Chicago | 285 million | 1,885 |
| Gertrude Boyle | Columbia Sportswear | Portland, Ore. | 265 million | 800 |
| Christel DeHaan | Resort Condominiums | Indianapolis | 259 million | 1,971 |
| Donna L. Reeves | Norm Reeves Honda | Cerritos, Calif. | 252 million | 418 |
| Patricia Gallup | PC Connection | Marlow, N.H. | 250 million | 900 |
| Kavelle Bajaj | INET | Bethesda, Md. | 230 million | 2,570 |
| Rachelle Friedman | J&R Music World | New York | 223 million | 600 |
| Lillian Vernon | Lillian Vernon | New Rochelle, N.Y. | 221 million | 3,000 |

*As of November 30, 1994.
†Estimated.

Source: Adapted from Susan McHenry, "The Working Woman 50: America's Top Women Business Owners," *Working Woman*, May 1996, 38–48.

### Glass-Ceiling Audits

The U.S. Department of Labor defines the glass ceiling as "those artificial barriers based on attitudinal or organizational bias that prevent qualified individuals from advancing upward in their organizations into management level positions."[22] "Glass-ceiling reviews," also known as "corporate reviews," are conducted by the Department of Labor to identify practices that appear to hinder the upward mobility of qualified women (and minorities). The Department of Labor looks for such things as equal access to

- Upper-level management and executive training
- Rotational assignments
- International assignments
- Opportunities for promotion
- Opportunities for executive development programs at universities
- Desirable compensation packages
- Opportunities to participate on high-profile project teams
- Upper-level special assignments

Organizations are increasingly conducting their own glass-ceiling audits prior to government review to avoid fines and externally imposed corrective action. These audits can document any ceilings and the reasons they exist. Self-audits are one step to tapping the potentials of a diversified workforce.

### Preparing Women for Management

As noted above, opportunities for women to move into management positions are definitely improving. In addition to breaking down the barriers to advancement, the development of women managers demands a better understanding of women's needs and the requirements of the management world.

According to Rose Mary Wentling, business today needs all the leadership, talent, quality, competence, productivity, innovation, and creativity possible, as U.S. firms face more-demanding worldwide competition. Companies committed to equal opportunities for women and men will undoubtedly keep the best talent available. Wentling has devised a list of actions organizations can take to maximize the human resource represented by women. These actions are presented in Highlights in HRM 5.[23]

Many employers now offer special training to women who are on a management career path. They may use their own staff or outside firms to conduct this training. Opportunities are also available for women to participate in seminars and workshops that provide instruction and experiences in a wide variety of management topics.

In the past several years, the number of women enrolled in college and university degree programs in management has increased significantly. At the same time, more women trained in management have joined management department faculties at business schools, thus creating an environment that fosters the mentoring and development of women as professionals capable of assuming higher-level positions in work organizations.

In addition to formal training opportunities, women today are provided with a wealth of information and guidance in books and magazines. Business sections in bookstores are stocked with numerous books written especially for women who

**HIGHLIGHTS IN HRM**

# Maximizing the Human Resources of Female Managers

1. Ensure that women receive frequent and specific feedback on their job performance. Women need and want candid reviews of their work. Clearly articulated suggestions for improvement, standards for work performance, and plans for career advancement will make women feel more involved in their jobs and help make them better employees.

2. Accept women as valued members of the management team. Include them in every kind of communication. Listen to their needs and concerns, and encourage their contributions.

3. Give talented women the same opportunities given to talented men to grow, develop, and contribute to company profitability. Give them the responsibility to direct major projects and to plan and implement systems and programs. Expect them to travel and relocate and to make the same commitment to the company as men aspiring to leadership positions.

4. Give women the same level of counseling on professional career advancement opportunities as that given to men.

5. Identify women as potential managers early in their employment and facilitate their advancement through training and other developmental activities.

6. Assist women in strengthening their assertion skills. Reinforce strategic career planning to encourage women's commitment to their careers and long-term career plans.

7. Accelerate the development of qualified women through fast-track programs. Either formally or informally, this method will provide women with the exposure, knowledge, and positioning for career advancement.

8. Provide opportunities for women to develop mentoring or sponsoring relationships with employees. Women do not often have equal or easy access (compared with their male colleagues) to senior employees. The overall goal should be to provide advice, counsel, and support to promising female employees by knowledgeable, senior-level men and women.

9. Encourage company co-ed management support systems and networks. Sharing experiences and information with other men and women who are managers provides invaluable support to peers. These activities provide the opportunity for women to meet and learn from men and women in more advanced stages of their careers—a helpful way of identifying potential mentors or role models.

10. Examine the feasibility of increasing participation of women in company-sponsored planning retreats, use of company facilities, social functions, and so forth. With notable exceptions, men are still generally more comfortable with other men, and as a result, women miss many of the career and business opportunities that arise during social functions. In addition, women may not have access to information about the company's informal political and social systems. Encourage male managers to include women when socializing with other business associates.

Source: R. M. Wentling, "Women in Middle Management: Their Career Development and Aspirations." Reprinted from *Business Horizons*, January/February 1992, copyright 1992 by the Foundation for the School of Business at Indiana University. Used with permission.

want a better idea of the career opportunities available to them. Many books are devoted to the pursuit of careers in specific fields.[24]

Popular magazines that contain many articles about women and jobs include *Working Woman, New Woman, Savvy, The Executive Female,* and *Enterprising Women.* These magazines are also recommended reading for men who want a better understanding of the problems that women face in the world of work.

### Accommodating Families

One of the major problems women have faced is that of having both a managerial career and a family. Women managers whose children are at an age requiring close parental attention often experience conflict between their responsibility to the children and their duty to the employer. If the conflict becomes too painful, they may decide to forgo their careers, at least temporarily, and leave their jobs. Companies with 300 or more employees lose an average of $88,000 a year because of absenteeism, shortened workdays, and lost workhours due to child care problems.[25]

In recent years many employers, including Paine Webber, SunTrust Bank, Quaker Oats Company, Corning Inc., and Pacific Telesis, have inaugurated programs that are mutually advantageous to the career-oriented woman and the employer. These programs, which include alternative career paths, extended leave, flextime, job sharing, and telecommuting, provide new ways to balance career and family. The number of employers moving to protect their investment in top-flight women is still small, but more of them are defining a separate track for women managers.[26]

These efforts are paying off. Recent evidence suggests that women no longer have to choose between careers and families. In 1982, only 49 percent of women executives were married and only 39 percent had children. Today, nearly 70 percent of women executives are married and 63 percent have children.

Nevertheless, there is still a fairly controversial debate about the so-called mommy track, a separate track designed to help women be productive but not necessarily upwardly mobile.[27] Many women, as well as men, criticize the use of a separate track as perpetuating the inequities of a double standard and as pitting women against women—those with children against those without. On the other hand, there are those who believe that this approach at least gives women choices.

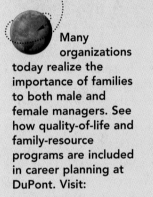

**USING THE INTERNET**

Many organizations today realize the importance of families to both male and female managers. See how quality-of-life and family-resource programs are included in career planning at DuPont. Visit:

www.dupont.com/ career.html#family

## Career Development for Minorities

Many organizations have specific career planning programs for minority employees. These programs are intended to equip employees with career planning skills and development opportunities that will help them compete effectively for advancement.

We observed in Chapter 4 that many employers make a special effort to recruit minorities. Once individuals from minority groups are on the job, it is important for employers to provide opportunities for them to move ahead in the organization as they improve their job skills and abilities.

### Advancement of Minorities to Management

The area of employment that has been the slowest to respond to affirmative action appeals is the advancement of minorities to middle- and top-management positions.

*Opportunities to make presentations provide development experiences for young minority managers.*

For example, while blacks constitute approximately 10 percent of the employed U.S. civilian population, they hold only about 7 percent of executive, administrative, and managerial positions. With about 8 percent of the employed civilian population, Hispanics hold only about 4 percent of executive, administrative, and managerial positions.[28]

The male black or Hispanic manager who aspires to higher levels in an organization is likely to find that his career will start off like a rocket but that as he reaches the middle ranks a barrier makes it very difficult to move to the top. Support groups like the Black Professionals Organization at United Airlines alert management to the concerns of black employees. Sara Lee and BankBoston are two among a growing number of companies that are committed to increasing their ranks of minority managers. Given the talent shortages existing in most industries, few organizations can afford to neglect the development of potential managers.

In recent years black women have been rising more rapidly than black men in corporate America. Over the past decade, this group has grown by over 125 percent. The reasons black women are overtaking black men are many and complex. However, in spite of their progress, both black women and black men need continued support in their development and advancement.[29]

While minority managers do play a part in creating a better climate for groups that are discriminated against in advancement opportunities, top management and the HR department have the primary responsibility to create conditions in the organization that are favorable for recognizing and rewarding performance on the basis of objective, nondiscriminatory criteria.

### Providing Internships

One approach to helping minority students prepare for management careers is to give them employment experiences while they are still in college. An internship program offers students an opportunity to learn on the job and gain hands-on experience. One organization, Inroads, Inc., offers qualified minority college students a package of tutoring, counseling, and summer internships with large corporations. It has about 800 corporate sponsors that pay an annual fee for each intern they sponsor. Among the sponsors are Pitney Bowes, Kaiser Permanente, Arthur Andersen & Company, TRW, Macy's California, and Shell Oil Company. The program considers only students who graduate in the top 10 percent of their high school class. In college, the students must maintain a 2.7 grade-point average out of a possible 4.0. Participants report that Inroads has raised their aspirations and has taught them how to adjust to the corporate world. Benefits for the corporation include early access to talented minorities, opportunities to hire college graduates who understand the company's business and its culture, and a greater number of minorities pursuing careers in the traditionally underrepresented fields of engineering and business.[30]

For example, blacks make up a very small percentage of the enrollment in U.S. business schools. Presently, the four schools with the highest percentages of black enrollment are University of Michigan (15 percent), Penn State (14 percent), University of Pittsburgh (9 percent), and Duke (8 percent). The three schools that have graduated the highest-ranking black executives are Harvard, the University of Chicago, and Stanford.[31]

### Organizing Training Courses

Training opportunities for minority managers are offered by such organizations as the American Management Association. Specifically addressing the advancement difficulties of blacks, the AMA conducts a course titled "Self-Development Strategies for Black Managers" in several cities throughout the country. Major topics include the realities of corporate life, race-related stresses, effective interpersonal relationships, situational leadership, handling of racial discrimination, and personal self-assessment.

## Dual-Career Couples

As discussed throughout this book, the employment of both members of a couple has become a way of life in North America. Economic necessity and social forces have encouraged this trend to the point that over 80 percent of all marriages are now **dual-career partnerships** in which both members follow their own careers and actively support each other's career development.

As with most lifestyles, the dual-career arrangement has its positive and negative sides. A significant number of organizations are concerned with the problems facing dual-career couples and offer assistance to them. Flexible working schedules are the most frequent organizational accommodation to these couples. Other arrangements include leave policies where either parent may stay home with a newborn, policies that allow work to be performed at home, day care on organization premises, and job sharing.

The difficulties that dual-career couples face include the need for quality child care, the time demands, and the emotional stress. However, the main problem these couples face is the threat of relocation. Many large organizations now offer some kind of job-finding assistance for spouses of employees who are relocated, including payment of fees charged by employment agencies, job counseling firms, and executive search firms. Organizations are also developing networking relationships with other employers to find jobs for the spouses of their relocating

**Dual-career partnerships**
Couples in which both members follow their own careers and actively support each other's career development

employees. These networks can provide a way to "share the wealth and talent" in a community while simultaneously assisting in the recruitment efforts of the participating organizations.[32]

The relocating of dual-career couples to foreign facilities is a major issue that international employers face. Fewer employees are willing to relocate without assistance for their spouses. Many employers have developed effective approaches for integrating the various allowances typically paid for overseas assignments when husband and wife work for the same employer. Far more complex are the problems that arise when couples work for two different employers. The problems associated with overseas assignments of dual-career couples will be examined in greater detail in Chapter 16.

# Personal Career Development

We have observed that there are numerous ways for an employer to contribute to an individual employee's career development and at the same time meet the organization's HR needs. The organization can certainly be a positive force in the development process, but the primary responsibility for personal career growth still rests with the individual. One's career may begin before and often continue after a period of employment with an organization. To help employees achieve their career objectives, managers and HRM professionals should have an understanding of the stages one goes through in developing a career and the actions one should take to be successful.

## Stages of Career Development

Knowledge, skills, abilities, and attitudes as well as career aspirations change as one matures. While the work that individuals in different occupations perform can vary significantly, the challenges and frustrations that they face at the same stage in their careers are remarkably similar. A model describing these stages is shown in Figure 7.8. The stages are (1) preparation for work, (2) organizational entry, (3) early career, (4) midcareer, and (5) late career. The typical age range and the major tasks of each stage are also presented in the figure.

Copyright 1983 Pat Brady. Reprinted with permission.

FIGURE 7.8

**Stages of Career Development**

*Stage 5: Late Career (ages 55–retirement):*

Remain productive in work, maintain self-esteem, prepare for effective retirement.

*Stage 4: Midcareer (ages 40–55):*

Reappraise early career and early adulthood goals, reaffirm or modify goals, make choices appropriate to middle adult years, remain productive.

*Stage 3: Early Career (ages 25–40):*

Learn job, learn organizational rules and norms, fit into chosen occupation and organization, increase competence, pursue goals.

*Stage 2: Organizational Entry (ages 18–25):*

Obtain job offer(s) from desired organization(s), select appropriate job based on complete and accurate information.

*Stage 1: Preparation for Work (ages 0–25):*

Develop occupational self-image, assess alternative occupations, develop initial occupational choice, pursue necessary education.

The first stage—preparation for work—encompasses the period prior to entering an organization, often extending until age 25. It is a period in which individuals must acquire the knowledge, abilities, and skills they will need to compete in the marketplace. It is a time when careful planning, based on sound information, should be the focus. The second stage, typically from ages 18 to 25, is devoted to soliciting job offers and selecting an appropriate job. During this period one may also be involved in preparing for work. The next three stages entail fitting into a chosen occupation and organization, modifying goals, making choices, remaining productive, and finally, preparing for retirement. In the remainder of the chapter we will examine some of the activities of primary concern to the student, who is likely to be in the early stages. Retirement planning will be discussed in Chapter 11.

## Developing Personal Skills and Competencies

In planning a career, one should attend to more than simply acquiring specific job knowledge and skills. Job know-how is clearly essential, but there are other skills one must develop to be successful as an employee. To succeed as a manager, one must achieve a still-higher level of proficiency in such major areas as communication, time management, self-motivation, interpersonal relationships, and the broad area of leadership.

Hundreds of self-help books have been written on these topics, and myriad opportunities to participate in workshops are available, often under the sponsorship of one's employer.[33] One should not overlook sources of valuable information such as articles in general-interest magazines and professional journals. For example, the pointers on the basic skills of successful career management listed in Highlights in HRM 6 are taken from a competency assessment conducted at Caterpillar.

**HRM 6**

**HIGHLIGHTS IN HRM**

# Career Competencies at Caterpillar

During the Caterpillar business unit's career development training process in Joliet, Illinois, the company compiled the following competencies as necessary for success within the reorganized, changing organization:

- *Interpersonal skills:* Possesses team-building and leadership skills; can effectively lead groups and facilitate group interaction
- *Problem-solving skills:* Can analyze and use problem-solving approaches
- *Communication skills:* Able to verbalize articulately, make presentations, and write cogently
- *Leadership skills:* Is recognized by peers as a natural leader; accomplishes results without formal authority
- *Organization and planning skills:* Able to manage time; sets and achieves goals
- *Technical skills:* Possesses education specific to assignments and job content; understands and uses appropriate level of technical skills
- *Responsibility:* Takes initiative; accepts accountability for own work and additional tasks for the good of the group
- *Assertiveness:* Able and comfortable with communicating openly and directly; demonstrates self-confidence and awareness of others' perceptions
- *Flexibility:* Able to adapt to organizational changes and changing market needs; willingly considers new ideas and implements new ways of doing things
- *Judgment:* Able to determine level of risk and appropriate action; accepts accountability for significant decisions

Source: Peggy Simonsen and Cathy Wells, "African Americans Take Control of Their Careers," *Personnel Journal* 73, no. 4 (April 1994): 99–108.

## Choosing a Career

Many years ago, when Peter Drucker was asked about career choice, he said, "The probability that the first job choice you make is the right one for you is roughly one in a million. If you decide your first choice is the right one, chances are that you are just plain lazy."[34] The implications of this statement are just as true today. One must often do a lot of searching and changing to find a career path that is psychologically and financially satisfying. Highlights in HRM 7 shows a list of some of the hottest career tracks.

### Use of Available Resources

A variety of resources is available to aid in the process of choosing a satisfying career. Counselors at colleges and universities, as well as those in private practice, are equipped to assist individuals in evaluating their aptitudes, abilities, interests, and values as they relate to career selection. There is broad interest among business

**HRM 7**

**HIGHLIGHTS IN HRM**

# Twenty Hot Career Tracks

| CAREER TRACK | SALARY |
| --- | --- |
| Accounting: *Environmental Accountant* | $ 32,750–67,000 |
| Advertising: *Web Specialist* | $ 48,000–90,200 |
| Arts/entertainment: *Musician* | $ 20,000–700,000+ |
| Child care: *Nanny* | $ 10,300–48,000 |
| Communications: *Technical Writer* | $ 35,500–54,510 |
| Construction: *Project Manager* | $ 50,000–86,000 |
| Consulting: *IT Consultant* | $ 51,200–250,000 |
| Education: *Speech Pathologist* | $ 38,000–52,000 |
| Engineering: *Communications Engineer* | $ 60,800–99,000 |
| Banking: *Relationship Manager* | $ 40,000–59,000 |
| Health care: *Physical Therapist* | $ 39,780–65,000 |
| Hospitality: *Catering Director* | $ 22,800–42,600 |
| Human resources: *Executive Recruiter* | $ 50,000–250,000+ |
| IT: *Networking Architect* | $ 53,900–87,000 |
| Law: *Real Estate Attorney* | $ 95,924–208,181 |
| Medicine: *Primary Care Physician* | $ 120,000–140,000+ |
| New media: *Web Site Developer* | $ 30,300–74,000 |
| Sales: *On-Line Sales Manager* | $ 80,000–150,000 |
| Scientific research: *Molecular Biologist* | $ 41,200–106,000 |
| Social work: *Counselor* | $ 32,500–52,500 |

Source: "20 Hot Job Tracks," *U.S. News & World Report*, October 26, 1998, 84–90.

schools in a formal instructional program in career planning and development, and other units in the institutions, such as placement offices and continuing education centers, offer some type of career planning assistance.

### Accuracy of Self-Evaluation

Successful career development depends in part on an individual's ability to conduct an accurate self-evaluation. In making a self-evaluation, one needs to consider those factors that are personally significant. The most important internal factors are one's academic aptitude and achievement, occupational aptitudes and skills, social skills, communication skills, leadership abilities, and interests and values. The latter should include consideration of salary level, status, opportunities for advancement, and growth on the job. External factors that should be assessed include family values and expectations, economic conditions, employment trends, job market information, and perceived effect of physical or psychological disabilities on success.[35]

### Significance of Interest Inventories

Psychologists who specialize in career counseling typically administer a battery of tests such as those mentioned in Chapter 5. The *Strong Vocational Interest Blank* (SVIB), developed by E. K. Strong, Jr., was among the first of the interest tests.[36] Somewhat later, G. Frederic Kuder developed inventories to measure degree of interest in mechanical, clerical, scientific, and persuasive activities, among others. Both the Strong and the Kuder interest inventories have been used widely in vocational counseling.

Strong found that there are substantial differences in interests that vary from occupation to occupation and that a person's interest pattern, especially after age 21, tends to become quite stable. By taking his test, now known as the *Strong Interest Inventory,* one can learn the degree to which his or her interests correspond with those of successful people in a wide range of occupations. Personality type can also be obtained by using a special scoring key on an individual's *Strong Interest Inventory* answer sheet. This key, developed by John Holland, provides scores on six personality types: (1) realistic, (2) investigative, (3) artistic, (4) social, (5) enterprising, and (6) conventional. These categories characterize not only a type of personality, but also the type of working environment that a person would find most satisfying. In the actual application of Holland's theory, combinations of the six types are examined. For example, a person may be classified as realistic-investigative-enterprising (RIE). Jobs in the RIE category include mechanical engineer, lineperson, and air-traffic controller. To facilitate searching for occupations that match one's category, such as RIE, Holland has devised a series of tables that correlate the Holland categories with jobs in the *Dictionary of Occupational Titles (DOT),* described in Chapter 3.[37]

Another inventory that measures both interests and skills is the *Campbell™ Interest and Skill Survey (CISS®).*[38] The CISS can be used not only to assist employees in exploring career paths and options but to help organizations develop their employees or to reassign them because of major organizational changes. In completing the inventory, individuals report their levels of interest and skill using a six-point response scale on 200 interest items and 120 skill items. CISS item responses are translated into seven orientations—influencing, organizing, helping, creating, analyzing, producing, and adventuring—and further categorized into twenty-nine basic scales such as leadership and supervision, to identify occupations that reflect today's workplace.

Highlights in HRM 8 shows a sample profile for one individual. Note that at the top of the profile the range of scores is from 30 to 70, with 50 in the midrange. Corresponding verbal descriptions of scores range from very low to very high. Also note that on the profile two types of scores are profiled: interest (a solid diamond ◆) and skill (an open diamond ◇). The interest score ◆ shows how much the individual likes the specified activities; the skill score shows how confident the individual feels about performing these activities.

There are four noteworthy patterns of combinations of the interest and skill scores as shown in Figure 7.9: Pursue, Develop, Explore, and Avoid. For the individual whose scores are profiled in Highlights in HRM 8, one would interpret the scores on the seven orientation scales (as shown in the right-hand column of the profile) as follows:

| | |
|---|---|
| Influencing | Pursue |
| Organizing | Indeterminate |
| Helping | Pursue |
| Creating | Avoid |
| Analyzing | Avoid |
| Producing | Indeterminate |
| Adventuring | Develop |

On the basis of such profiles, individuals can see how their interests and skills compare with those of a sample of people happily employed in a wide range of occupations. Completed answer sheets can be mailed to a scoring center, or software is available and may be obtained for in-house scoring.

### Evaluation of Long-Term Employment Opportunities

In making a career choice, one should attempt to determine the probable long-term opportunities in the occupational fields one is considering. While even the experts can err in their predictions, one should give at least some attention to the opinions that are available. A source of information that has proved valuable over the years is the *Occupational Outlook Handbook,* published by the U.S. Department of Labor and available at most libraries. Many libraries also have publications that provide details about jobs and career fields. In recent years, a considerable amount of computer software has been developed to facilitate access to information about career fields and to enable individuals to match their abilities, aptitudes, interests, and experiences with the requirements of occupational areas.

## Choosing an Employer

Once an individual has made a career choice, even if only tentatively, the next major step is deciding where to work. The choice of employer may be based primarily on location, on immediate availability of a position, on starting salary, or on other basic considerations. However, the college graduate who has prepared for a professional or managerial career is likely to have more sophisticated concerns. Douglas Hall proposes that people frequently choose an organization on the basis of its climate and how it appears to fit their needs. According to Hall, people with

**HRM 8**

# Campbell Interest and Skill Survey: Individual Profile

SAMPLE                    ORIENTATIONS AND BASIC SCALES                    DATE SCORED 10/20/96

| ORIENTATIONS AND BASIC SCALES | INTEREST | SKILL | VERY LOW | LOW | MID-RANGE | HIGH | VERY HIGH | INTEREST/SKILL PATTERN |
|---|---|---|---|---|---|---|---|---|
| | ◆ | ◇ | 30    35 | 40    45 | 50    55 | 60 | 65    70 | |
| **Influencing** | **61** | **60** | | | | | | Pursue |
| Leadership | 65 | 64 | | | | | | Pursue |
| Law/Politics | 48 | 57 | | | | | | Explore |
| Public Speaking | 63 | 59 | | | | | | Pursue |
| Sales | 46 | 58 | | | | | | Explore |
| Advertising/Marketing | 47 | 42 | | | | | | |
| **Organizing** | **46** | **37** | | | | | | |
| Supervision | 68 | 58 | | | | | | Pursue |
| Financial Services | 35 | 31 | | | | | | Avoid |
| Office Practices | 44 | 42 | | | | | | Avoid |
| **Helping** | **60** | **68** | | | | | | Pursue |
| Adult Development | 62 | 58 | | | | | | Pursue |
| Counseling | 58 | 68 | | | | | | Pursue |
| Child Development | 56 | 43 | | | | | | Develop |
| Religious Activities | 70 | 60 | | | | | | Pursue |
| Medical Practice | 52 | 56 | | | | | | Explore |
| **Creating** | **23** | **37** | | | | | | Avoid |
| Art/Design | 19 | 32 | | | | | | Avoid |
| Performing Arts | 41 | 39 | | | | | | Avoid |
| Writing | 32 | 36 | | | | | | Avoid |
| International Activities | 50 | 64 | | | | | | Explore |
| Fashion | 35 | 48 | | | | | | |
| Culinary Arts | 48 | 43 | | | | | | |
| **Analyzing** | **33** | **33** | | | | | | Avoid |
| Mathematics | 34 | 33 | | | | | | Avoid |
| Science | 31 | 36 | | | | | | Avoid |
| **Producing** | **37** | **46** | | | | | | |
| Mechanical Crafts | 33 | 35 | | | | | | Avoid |
| Woodworking | 32 | 39 | | | | | | Avoid |
| Farming/Forestry | 46 | 44 | | | | | | |
| Plants/Gardens | 51 | 51 | | | | | | |
| Animal Care | 50 | 49 | | | | | | |
| **Adventuring** | **59** | **54** | | | | | | Develop |
| Athletics/Physical Fitness | 58 | 47 | | | | | | Develop |
| Military/Law Enforcement | 63 | 66 | | | | | | Pursue |
| Risks/Adventure | 46 | 52 | | | | | | |

FIGURE 7.9

**Combinations of Career Interests and Skills**

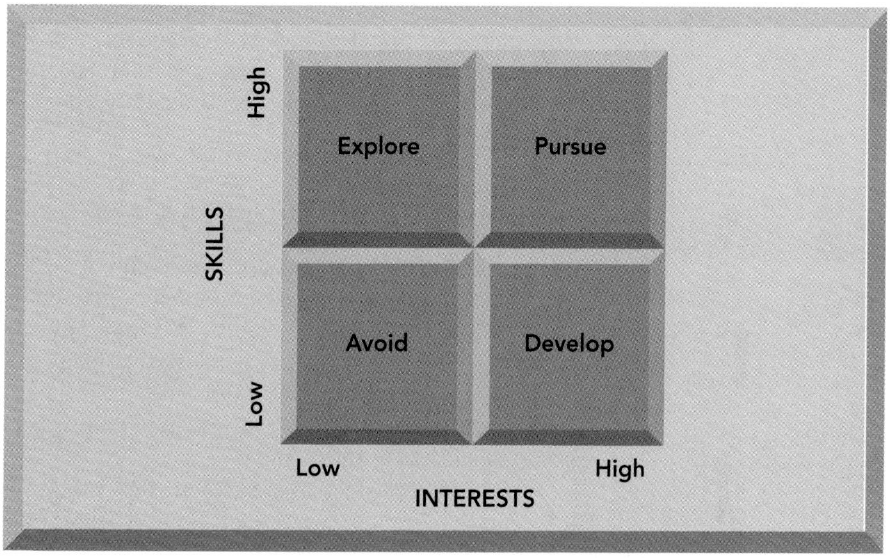

high needs for achievement may choose aggressive, achievement-oriented organizations. Power-oriented people may choose influential, prestigious, power-oriented organizations. Affiliative people may choose warm, friendly, supportive organizations. We know that people whose needs fit with the climate of an organization are rewarded more and are more satisfied than those who fit in less well, so it is natural to reason that fit would also be a factor in one's choice of an organization. Given change, it is increasingly unlikely that individuals will remain with only one organization for their entire career. The old model of "the organization man" who starts and stays with the same company is being replaced by a more flexible career model that Hall calls a "protean" career (based on the Greek god Proteus, who could change shape at will).[39]

## The Plateauing Trap

**Career plateau**
Situation in which for either organizational or personal reasons the probability of moving up the career ladder is low

Judith Bardwick was the first to label the plateauing phenomenon.[40] A **career plateau** is a situation in which for either organizational or personal reasons the probability of moving up the career ladder is low. According to Bardwick, only 1 percent of the labor force will not plateau in their working lives. There are three types of plateaus: structural, content, and life. A *structural plateau* marks the end of promotions; one will now have to leave the organization to find new opportunities and challenges. A *content plateau* occurs when a person has learned a job too well and is bored with day-to-day activities. According to Susan Brooks, a *life plateau* is more profound and may feel like a midlife crisis.[41] People who experience life plateaus often have allowed work or some other major factor to become the most significant aspect of their lives, and they experience a loss of identity and self-esteem when there is no longer success in that area.

Organizations can help individuals cope with plateaus by providing opportunities for lateral growth where opportunities for advancement do not exist. Brooks makes reference to Beverly Kaye, a partner in Career Systems, Inc., and Jane Michel, training services consultant at Chevron, who work with Chevron employees in a career enrichment program. According to Michel, "It is a process for helping people learn more about what gives them satisfaction within the company, as well as what kinds of opportunities will make them happiest if they go elsewhere."[42] Other employers using an approach that encourages career self-management include John Hancock, Apple Computer, the Times Mirror Company, and Marriott International.[43]

## Becoming an Entrepreneur

**Entrepreneur**
One who starts, organizes, manages, and assumes responsibility for a business or other enterprise

At the opening of the century, no discussion of careers would be complete if entrepreneurship opportunities were not mentioned. Being an **entrepreneur**—one who starts, organizes, manages, and assumes responsibility for a business or other enterprise—offers a personal challenge that many individuals prefer over being an employee. Small businesses are typically run by entrepreneurs who accept the personal financial risks that go with owning a business but who also benefit directly from the success of the business.[44]

Small businesses are actually big employers. Over 87 percent of all businesses employ fewer than twenty people. But in total those small firms employ 27 percent of the U.S. workforce. Businesses with ninety-nine or fewer employees account for 56 percent of the workforce.[45] Hence small business is the source of over half of wage and salary jobs in this country.

The individual who considers starting a small business can obtain assistance from the Small Business Administration (SBA), which advises and assists the millions of small businesses in the United States. It is essential for one considering a small business to obtain as much information as possible from the SBA, from libraries, and from organizations and individuals who are knowledgeable about the type of business one is considering. For instance, valuable assistance may be obtained from members of the Service Corps of Retired Executives (SCORE), who offer advisory services under the auspices of the SBA.

Since the details of organizing a business are beyond the scope of this book, Figure 7.10 is presented to provide an overview of the basic steps in starting a new business.[46] *Nation's Business,* published monthly by the U.S. Chamber of Commerce, has a column entitled "Entrepreneur's Notebook" in each issue.

**USING THE INTERNET**

Information about starting a business can also be found at the Small Business Administration's web site. Material concerning SCORE (as a small-business resource or a retirement activity) is also available on the Internet. Visit:

www.sba.gov

and

sba.gov/SCORE

## Keeping a Career in Perspective

For most people, work is a primary factor in the overall quality of their lives. It provides a setting for satisfying practically the whole range of human needs and is thus of considerable value to the individual. Nevertheless, it is advisable to keep one's career in perspective so that other important areas of life are not neglected.

### Off-the-Job Interests

Satisfaction with one's life is a product of many forces. Some of the more important ingredients are physical health, emotional well-being, financial security, harmonious interpersonal relationships, freedom from too much stress, and achievement of one's goals. While a career can provide some of the satisfaction that one needs, most people find it necessary to turn to interests and activities outside their

FIGURE 7.10

**Twelve Steps for Starting a New Business**

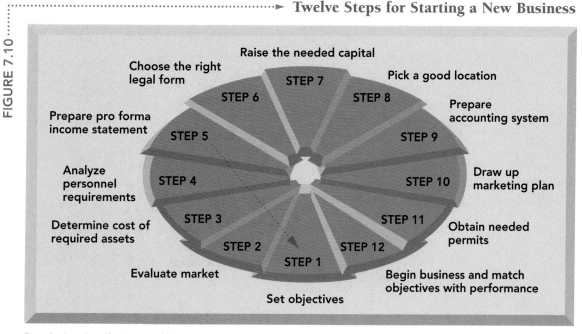

From *Business in a Changing World*, 3rd edition, by W. Cunningham, R. Aldag, and S. Block: 139 © 1993. Reprinted with permission of South-Western College Publishing, a division of Thomson Learning. Fax 800-730-2215.

career. Off-the-job activities not only provide a respite from daily work responsibilities but also offer satisfaction in areas unrelated to work.

### Marital and/or Family Life

The career development plans of an individual as well as of an organization must take into account the needs of spouses and children. As we have said, the one event that often poses the greatest threat to family needs is relocation. Conflict between a desire to advance in one's career and a desire to stay in one place and put down family roots often borders on the disastrous. Many employers now provide assistance in this area, including relocation counseling, in an effort to reduce the severity of the pain that can accompany relocations.

While relocation may be the most serious threat to employees with families, there are also other sources of conflict between career and family. Some of the work-related sources of conflict are number of hours worked per week, frequency of overtime, and the presence and irregularity of shift work. In addition, ambiguity and/or conflict within the employee's work role, low level of leader support, and disappointments due to unfulfilled expectations affect one's life away from the job. Some of the family-related sources of conflict include the need to spend an unusually large amount of time with the family and its concerns, spouse employment patterns, and dissimilarity in a couple's career orientations.[47]

### Planning for Retirement

While retirement appears to be a long way off for the individual who is still in the early stages of a career, it is never too early to make plans for it. In order to enjoy retirement one should prepare for it by giving careful attention to health, finances, family, and interpersonal relationships throughout one's adult life. While most of the larger organizations have preretirement programs, many of the participants in those programs are unfortunately already too close to actual retirement. Thus it is each individual's responsibility to plan early in order to have time to set the stage for a healthy and satisfying retirement as free as possible from worries—especially those that could have been avoided or minimized earlier in life. While employer-sponsored preretirement programs are usually considered very helpful by the participants, as we will see in Chapter 11, they are not a substitute for continual personal concern for oneself.

### Maintaining a Balance

Those who are "married" to their jobs to the extent that they fail to provide the attention and caring essential to marriage and family relationships can be said to lack an appreciation for the balance needed for a satisfying life. One should always be aware that "to be a success in the business world takes hard work, long hours, persistent effort, and constant attention. To be a success in marriage takes hard work, long hours, persistent effort, and constant attention. . . . The problem is giving each its due and not shortchanging the other."[48]

## SUMMARY

**OBJECTIVE 1** A career development program is a dynamic process that should integrate individual employee needs with those of the organization. It is the responsibility of the employee to identify his or her own KSAs as well as interests and values and to seek out information about career options. The organization should provide information about its mission, policies, and plans and what it will provide in the way of training and development for the employee.

**OBJECTIVE 2** In order to be successful, a career development program must receive the support of top management. The program should reflect the goals and the culture of the organization, and managerial personnel at all levels must be trained in the fundamentals of job design, performance appraisal, career planning, and counseling. Employees should have an awareness of the organization's philosophy and its goals; otherwise they will not know how their goals match those of the organization. HRM policies, especially those concerning rotation, transfers, and promotions, should be consistent with the goals. The objectives and opportunities of the career development program should be announced widely throughout the organization.

**OBJECTIVE 3** Job opportunities may be identified by studying jobs and determining the knowledge and skills each one requires. Once that is accomplished, it is possible to plan job progressions. These progressions can then serve as a basis for developing career paths. Once career paths are developed and employees are identified on the career ladders, it is possible to inventory the jobs and determine where individuals with the required skills and knowledge are needed or will be needed.

**OBJECTIVE 4** Identifying and developing managerial talent is a responsibility of all managers. In addition to immediate superiors, there should be others in the organization who can nominate and sponsor employees with promise. Many organizations use assessment centers to identify managerial talent and recommend developmental experiences in order that each individual may reach her or his full potential. Mentoring has been found to be valuable for providing guidance and support to potential managers.

**OBJECTIVE 5** The first step in facilitating the career development of women is to eliminate barriers to advancement. The formation of women's networks, the providing of special training for women, the acceptance of women as valued members of the organization, the providing of mentors for women, and accommodating families have been found to be effective ways to facilitate a woman's career development.

 While a diversified workforce is composed of many different groups, an important segment is minority groups. In addition to creating conditions that are favorable for recognizing and rewarding performance, many organizations have special programs such as internships that provide hands-on experience as well as special training opportunities. Another group that requires the attention of management is composed of dual-career couples who often need to have flexible working schedules.

 In choosing a career, one should use all available resources. Consideration should be given to internal factors such as academic aptitude and achievement, occupational aptitudes and skills, communication skills, leadership abilities, and interests and values. External factors such as economic conditions, employment trends, and job market information must also be considered. In choosing a career, one should make use of interest and skill inventories. Long-term employment opportunities in an occupational field should be assessed by utilizing various publications, including those published by the government. Keeping a career in perspective so as to have a balanced life is desirable. While work is usually a primary factor in overall quality of life, one should give proper attention to physical health, harmonious family and interpersonal relationships, and interests and activities outside of one's career.

## KEY TERMS

assessment center
career counseling
career paths
career plateau
dual-career partnerships
entrepreneur

fast-track program
in-basket training
job progressions
leaderless group discussions
mentoring functions
mentors

outplacement services
promotion
relocation services
transfer

## DISCUSSION QUESTIONS

 1. Give some reasons for the trend toward increased emphasis on career development programs.

 2. Bank of America maintains a special suite of offices at its world headquarters in San Francisco for its retired executives. Two of the bank's former chief executives use their offices regularly.
   a. Of what value is this arrangement to the corporation? To the individuals?
   b. How might retired executives in any organization assist in the career development of current employees?

 3. What contributions can a career development program make to an organization that is forced to downsize its operations?

 4. Over 50 percent of all M.B.A.s leave their first employer within five years. While the change may mean career growth for the individuals, it represents a loss to the employers. What are some of the probable reasons an M.B.A. would leave his or her first employer?

 5. What are some of the barriers to advancement opportunities for women in many organizations?

6. How are the career challenges of minorities both similar to and different from those of women?

7. List the advantages and disadvantages of being an entrepreneur.

8. In your opinion, what personal characteristics are employers looking for in individuals whom they are considering for long-term employment and probable advancement in the organization? To what extent can one develop these characteristics?

9. One recruiter has said, "Next to talent, the second most important factor in career success is taking the time and effort to develop visibility." What are some ways of developing visibility?

## Managing Amoco's Career Pipeline

Executives at Amoco, the Chicago-based oil company, know the importance of keeping pipelines full. And these days, company executives are as concerned about the talent pipeline as they are about the oil pipelines. As the company has gone through changes in strategy, structure, and technology, Amoco employees have had to adapt rapidly to new skill requirements. To ensure success, there has to be a careful balancing of individual competencies and business needs.

As part of Chairman H. Laurance "Larry" Fuller's plan to revitalize the company, a task force was put together to design the career management system. The task force included high-level executives (with support from the HR function); in addition, each member of the task force had a personal "advisory board" of employees with whom he or she could meet. This resulted in a partnership of more than 500 employees from all levels within Amoco, who provided input into the design of the career management system.

Amoco's Career Management System (ACM) took two and a half years to develop and, when completed, had four key components: (1) education, (2) assessment, (3) development, and (4) outcomes. Education was initiated via launch meetings led by the top-management teams of each business unit and attended by all employees. This was followed by a voluntary half-day educational program called Exploring ACM. Assessment, the second component of ACM, is accomplished through subsequent training sessions in which employees analyze their skills relative to company goals. Employees can choose between two assessment workshops: one that focuses on current skills and another, called Maximizing Career Choices, that focuses on future career planning and job enrichment. In both workshops managers and employees work together to identify strengths and weaknesses relative to their career goals.

Development is the third component of ACM. Ongoing career discussions are held between employees and their managers. Employees bring completed individual development plans to the meeting, while managers bring a clearly articulated team development plan to the meeting. In this way, the employee and the manager contribute equally to the career discussion.

Finally, ACM is tied to measurable business outcomes. Since the goal of ACM is to align employee abilities and organizational goals, outcomes are measured in terms of contributions to teams and units, rather than by rapid rates of promotion.

Amoco continues to learn from the ACM system. Executives believe its key lessons so far include:

- Development must be tied to business strategy in order to gain support from top management.
- Individuals must be allowed to customize the program rather than trying to force a "one-size-fits-all" approach.
- Communication must be considered at least as important as design and implementation.
- Career management must be linked to other HR practices such as recruitment and training to create synergies that reinforce organizational and individual goals.
- The ultimate objective of the system—getting people thinking about how to make themselves more marketable in the long run, not just more promotable in the short run—must be the focus of the program.

The company culture around career management has been enhanced through ACM. Amoco employees are taking charge of their careers, and the company has a pipeline of people with the right skills in the right jobs at the right times.

Source: Adapted from Barbara Baumann, John Duncan, Stephen E. Forrer, and Zandy Leibowitz, "Amoco Primes the Talent Pump," *Personnel Journal*, February 1996, 79–84.

### QUESTIONS

1. How do you think career development is affected by changes in technology and by changes in structure?
2. Does Amoco's career management system sound complete? What else would you do?
3. Are there other HR practices that you would connect with career development? Which ones?
4. How would executives at Amoco know if their new career management system is working?

## Preparing a Career Development Plan

Sue Ann Scott was a receptionist at the headquarters of a large corporation. A high school graduate, she had no particular skills other than an ability to organize her job duties and a pleasant personality. Unfortunately, she did not have any particular plan for career development; nevertheless, she wanted very much to improve her economic position. Recognizing her educational limitations, she began taking accounting courses on a random basis in an evening adult education program.

Scott also took advantage of the corporation's job bidding system by applying for openings that were posted, even though in many instances she did not meet the specifications listed for them. After being rejected several times, she became discouraged. Her depressed spirits were observed by Elizabeth Burroughs, one of the department managers in the corporation. Burroughs invited Scott to come to her office for a talk about the problems she was having. Scott took full advantage of this opportunity to express her frustrations and disappointments. As she unburdened herself, it became apparent both to her and to Burroughs that during interviews she repeatedly apologized for having "only a high school education," an attitude that had probably made it difficult for the interviewers to select her over other candidates who were more positive about their backgrounds and skills. Burroughs suggested that Scott might try taking a more positive approach during her interviews. For example, she could stress her self-improvement efforts at night school and the fact that she was a dependable and cooperative person who was willing to work hard to succeed in the job for which she was applying.

Following Burroughs's advice, Scott applied for a position as invoice clerk, a job for which she felt she was qualified. She made a very forceful and positive presentation during her interview, stressing the favorable qualities she possessed. As a result of this approach, she got the job. While the pay for an invoice clerk was not much more than that for a receptionist, the position did offer an avenue for possible advancement into the accounting field, where the accounting courses she was taking would be of value.

### QUESTIONS

1.  What are some of the possible reasons Scott did not seek or receive advice from her immediate supervisor?
2.  After reviewing the chapter, suggest all possible ways that Scott can prepare herself for career advancement.

## NOTES AND REFERENCES

1.  Valentin Fernandez, "Career Strategies for the 21st Century," *Executive Speeches* 13, no. 6 (June/July 1999): 20–23; Brent B. Allred, Charles C. Snow, and Raymond E. Miles, "Characteristics of Managerial Careers in the 21st Century," *Academy of Management Executive* 10, no. 4 (1996): 17–27; Stephen A. Laser, "Employees, Careers, and Job Creation: Developing Growth-Oriented Human Resource Strategies and Programs," *Personnel Psychology* 49, no. 2 (summer 1996): 504–8.

2.  Ellen Ernst Kossek, Karen Roberts, Sandra Fisher, and Beverly Demarr, "Career Self-Management: A Quasi-Experimental Assessment of the Effects of a Training Intervention," *Personnel Psychology* 51, no. 4 (Winter 1998): 935–62; Ann G. Colby, "Making the New Career Development Model Work," *HRMagazine* 40, no. 6 (June 1995): 150–52; Shari Caudron, "HR Revamps Career Itineraries," *Business Credit* 97, no. 9 (September 1995): 20–27.

3.  Peg O'Herron and Peggy Simonsen, "Career Development Gets a Charge at Sears Credit," *Personnel Journal* 74, no. 5 (May 1995): 103–6. See also Jules Abend, "Behind the Scenes at: Sears," *Bobbin* 39, no. 11 (June 1998): 22–26; Shari Caudron, "The De-Jobbing of America," *Industry Week* 243, no. 16 (September 5, 1994): 30–36; Edward E. Lawler III, "From Job-Based to Competency-Based Organizations," *Journal of Organizational Behavior* 15, no. 1 (January 1994): 3–15.

4.  Laurence J. Peter and Raymond Hull, *The Peter Principle* (Cutchogue, NY: Buccaneer Books, 1996).

5.  Sumantra Ghoshal, Christopher A. Bartlett, and Peter Moran, "A New Manifesto for Management," *Sloan Management Review* 40, no. 3 (Spring 1999): 9–20.

6.  Ann M. Thayer, "Dual Career Ladders," *Chemical & Engineering News* 76, no. 44 (November 2, 1998): 51–55; Alan Garmonsway and Michael Wellin, "Creating the Right Natural Chemistry," *People Management* 1, no. 19 (September 21, 1995): 36–39; Shari Caudron, "Downshift Yourself," *Industry Week* 245, no. 10 (May 20, 1996): 126–30; Jerome A. Katz, "Which Track Are You On?" *Inc.* 17, no. 14 (October 1995): 27–28.

7. Robert J. Grossman, "Heirs Unapparent," *HRMagazine* 44, no. 2 (February 1999): 36–44; Amy Barrett, "How to Keep Rising Stars from Straying," *Business Week,* June 7, 1999, 80.

8. Peter Carrick and Richard Williams, "Development Centres—A Review of Assumptions," *Human Resource Management Journal* 9, no. 2 (1999): 77–92; Maria M. Chapham, "A Comparison of Assessor and Self-Dimension Ratings in an Advanced Management Assessment Centre," *Journal of Occupational and Organizational Psychology* 71, no. 3 (September 1998): 193–203; Harold W. Goldstein, Kenneth P. Yusko, Eric P. Braverman, D. Brent Smith, and Beth Chung, "The Role of Cognitive Ability in the Subgroup Differences and Incremental Validity of Assessment Center Exercises," *Personnel Psychology* 51, no. 2 (Summer 1998): 357–74; Amos S. Engelbrecht and Hermann Fischer, "The Managerial Performance Implications of a Developmental Assessment Center," *Human Relations* 48, no. 4 (April 1995): 387–404; Robert G. Jones and Mark D. Whitmore, "Evaluating Developmental Assessment Centers as Interventions," *Personnel Psychology* 48, no. 2 (Summer 1995): 377–88.

9. Lisa A. Burke, "Developing High-Potential Employees in the New Business Reality," *Business Horizons* 40, no. 2 (March/April 1997): 18–24.

10. For up-to-date career information and guidance as well as an opportunity for self-analysis, see Richard Boles, *What Color is Your Parachute 1999: A Practical Manual for Job-Hunters & Career-Changers* (Berkeley, CA: Ten Sped Press, 1999); James D. Porterfield, *Business Career Planning Guide* (Cincinnati, Ohio: South-Western Publishing, 1993); and Julie Griffin Levitt, *Your Career—How to Make It Happen,* 3d ed. (Cincinnati, Ohio: South-Western Publishing, 1995). Interested persons might also wish to obtain a copy of the video "Planning Your Career," TMW/Media Group (1998) (run time: 22 minutes).

11. Shari Caudron, "Marriott Trains Managers to Become Partners in Career Development," *Personnel Journal* 73, no. 4 (April 1994): 641. [Also published as "Marriott Trains Managers to Become Partners in Career Development," *Business Credit* 97, no. 9 (September 1995): 22.] See also Shari Caudron, "HR Revamps Career Itineraries," *Business Credit* 83, no. 4 (April 1994): 35; Jean R. Haskell, "Getting Employees to Take Charge of Their Careers," *Training and Development* 47, no. 2 (February 1993): 51–54.

12. Cynthia Pantazis, "The New Workforce Investment Act," *Training and Development* 53, no. 8 (August 1999): 48–50; The Workforce Investment Partnership Act," *HRMagazine* 43, no. 11 (October 1998): 89.

13. Ellen Ernst Kossek, Karen Roberts, Sandra Fisher, and Beverly Demarr, "Career Self-Management: A Quasi-Experimental Assessment of the Effects of a Training Intervention," *Personnel Psychology* 51, no. 4 (Winter 1998): 935–62.

14. Matt Starcevich and Fred Friend, "Effective mentoring relationships from the Mentee's perspective," *Workforce,* supplement, July 1999, 2–3; Samuel Aryee, Thomas Wyatt, and Raymond Stone, "Early Career Outcomes of Graduate Employees: The Effect of Mentoring and Integration," *Journal of Management* 33, no. 1 (January 1996): 95–118.

15. Kathryn H. Dansky, "The Effects of Group Mentoring on Career Outcomes," *Group and Organization Management* 21, no. 1 (March 1996): 5–21; Stephen G. Green and Talya N. Bauer, "Supervisory Mentoring by Advisors: Relationships with Doctoral Student Potential, Productivity and Commitment," *Personnel Psychology* 48, no. 3 (Autumn 1995): 537–61. Kathy Kram, *Mentoring at Work* (Lanham, Md.: University Press of America, 1988).

16. Tony Stott and Jenny Sweeney, "More Than a Match," *People Management* 5, no. 13 (June 30, 1999): 44–48; Neave Connolly and Gerrold Walker, "Resource for Junior Executives," *Transportation and Distribution* 36, no. 4 (April 1995): 92–93; Janet Dreyfus Gray, Michael J. Lee, and Johanne M. Totta, "Mentoring at the Bank of Montreal," *Human Resource Planning* 18, no. 4 (1995): 45–49; Marshall Loeb, "The New Mentoring," *Fortune,* November 27, 1965, 213.

17. Stephanie Armour, "Mentoring with a Twist: Workers Connect on Line," *USA Today,* August 18, 1999, 1B.

18. Audrey L. Mathews, "The Diversity Connections: Mentoring and Networking," *Public Manager* 23, no. 4 (Winter 1994/1995): 23–26; Barbara Addison Reid, "Mentorships Ensure Equal Opportunity," *Personnel Journal* 73, no. 11 (November 1994): 122–23.

19. Anne M. Walsh and Susan C. Borkowski, "Cross-Gender Mentoring and Career Development in the Health Care Industry," *Health Care Management Review* 24, no. 3 (Summer 1999): 7–17; Victoria Parker and Kathy Kram, "Women Mentoring Women: Creating Conditions for Connection," *Business Horizons* 36, no. 2 (March–April 1993): 42–51.

20. Headquarters for Catalyst is at 250 Park Avenue South, 5th floor, New York, N.Y. 10003-8900. Articles that summarize research sponsored by Catalyst include Sheila Wellington, "Advancing Women in Business: You've Come a Long Way—Maybe!" *Vital Speeches of the Day* 65, no. 20 (August 1, 1999): 637–39; Robert W. Thompson, "More Women Are Expected to Ascend Corporate Ladder," *HRMagazine* 44, no. 1 (January 1999): 10; Elaine McShulskis,

"Women's Progress in Corporate Leadership," *HRMagazine* 41, no. 6 (June 1996): 21–22.

21. Peter Burrows and Peter Elstrom, "The Boss," *Business Week*, August 2, 1999, 76; Dan R. Dalton and Catherine M. Daily, "Not There Yet," *Across the Board* 35, no. 10 (November/December 1998): 16–20; Joanne Cleaver, "25 Top Leading Companies for Women," *Working Woman* 23, no. 8 (September 1998): 50–64; Thomas R. Miller and Mary A. Lemons, "Breaking the Glass Ceiling: Lessons from a Management Pioneer," *S.A.M. Advanced Management Journal* 63, no. 1 (Winter 1998): 4–9.

22. A host of reports on glass ceiling issues can be found on the U.S. Department of Labor's website: www.dol.gov.

23. Rose Mary Wentling, "Women in Middle Management: Their Career Development and Aspirations," *Business Horizons* 35, no. 1 (January-February 1992): 47–54. See also Harris Collingwood, "Women as Managers: Not Just Different—Better," *Working Woman* 20, no. 11 (November 1995): 14; Elyse Mall, "Why Getting Ahead Is (Still) Tougher for Women," *Working Woman* 19, no. 7 (July 1994): 11.

24. The interested reader should find the following books very informative: Johanna Hunsaker and Phillip Hunsaker, *Strategies and Skills for Managerial Women* (Cincinnati, Ohio: South-Western Publishing, 1991); and Helen Gurley Brown, *Having It All* (New York: Simon & Schuster, 1982).

25. Nancy Hatch Woodward, "Child Care to the Rescue," *HRMagazine* 44, no. 8 (August 1999): 82–88.

26. Stephenie Overman, "Make Family-Friendly Initiatives Fly," *HRFocus* 76, no. 7 (July 1999): 1–14; "Work-Family Concern Tops List," *HRFocus* 76, no. 7 (July 1999): 4; Kathleen Cannings and William Lazonick, "Equal Employment Opportunity and the 'Managerial Woman,'" *Industrial Relations* 33, no. 1 (January 1994): 44–69.

27. Theodore Gideonse, "Mommy Track at the *Times*," *Newsweek*, June 1, 1998, 61; Yvonne Benschop and Hans Doorewaard, "Covered by Equality: The Gender Subtext of Organizations," *Organization Studies* 19, no. 5 (1998): 787–805; "Why Law Firms Cannot Afford to Maintain the Mommy Track," *Harvard Law Review* 109, no. 6 (April 1996): 1375–92.

28. U.S. Department of Commerce, Bureau of the Census, *Statistical Abstract of the United States* (Washington, D.C.: U.S. Government Printing Office, 1994), 407.

29. John H. Bryan, "The Diversity Imperative," *Executive Excellence* 16, no. 5 (May 1999): 6; Debra Lau, "BankBoston Development Co. Strikes a Chord in Urban America," *Venture Capital Journal*, May 1, 1999, 35–36; Herminia Ibarra, "Personal Networks of Women and Minorities in Management: A Conceptual Framework," *Academy of Management Review* 18, no. 1 (January 1993): 56–87. See also Dorothy J. Gaiter, "Black Women's Gains in Corporate America Outstrip Black Men's," *The Wall Street Journal*, March 8, 1994, A-1.

30. "Bolstering Diversity Programs," *HRFocus* 75, no. 7 (July 1998): S4. See also Inroads brochure, *Partnership for a Diverse Workforce*. The national headquarters of Inroads, Inc., is located at Suite 800, 1221 Locust, St. Louis, Mo. 63103.

31. Theodore Cross and Robert Bruce Slater, "The Impact of a Rollback of Affirmative Action on the Nation's Major MBA Programs," *Business and Society Review* 100/101 (1998): 81–84; Milton R. Moskowitz, "The Best Business Schools for Blacks," *Business and Society Review* 19, no. 1 (January 1994): 38–41.

32. Valerie Frazee, "Expert Help for Dual-Career Spouses," *Workforce* 4, no. 2 (March 1999): 18–20; Charlene Marmer Solomon, "One Assignment, Two Lives," *Personnel Journal* 75, no. 5 (May 1996): 36–74; Gillian Flynn, "Heck No—We Won't Go!" *Personnel Journal* 75, no. 3 (March 1996): 37–43.

33. A selection of self-help publications on a variety of topics may be found in any bookstore. College and university bookstores typically have a wide selection in their trade or general books department. Two recent popular books by Stephen R. Covey that present a principle-centered approach to time management are *First Things First Everyday* (New York: Fireside, 1997) and *The Seven Habits of Highly Effective People: Powerful Lessons in Personal Change* (New York: Fireside, 1990).

34. Mary Harrington Hall, "A Conversation with Peter Drucker," *Psychology Today*, March 1968, 22.

35. Candace Jones and Robert J. DeFillippi, "Back to the Future in Film: Combining Industry and Self-Knowledge to Meet the Career Challenges of the 21st Century," *Academy of Management Executive* 10, no. 4 (November 1996): 89–104; Walter Kiechel III, "A Manager's Career in the New Economy," *Fortune*, April 4, 1994, 68–72.

36. E. K. Strong, Jr., of Stanford University, was active in the measurement of interests from the early 1920s to the time of his death in 1963. Since then his work has been carried on by the staff of the Measurement Research Center, University of Minnesota. *The Strong Interest Inventory* is distributed by Consulting Psychologists Press, Inc., P. O. Box 60070, Palo Alto, Calif. 94306, to qualified persons under an exclusive license from the publisher, Stanford University Press.

37. Gary D. Gottfredson and John L. Holland, *Dictionary of Holland Occupational Codes* (Lutz, FL: Psychological Assessment Resources, December 1996).

38. The *Campbell Interest and Skill Survey* (copyright 1992) is published and distributed by NCS Assessments, P. O. Box 1416, Minneapolis, Minn. 55440. For recent research in this area, see David Lubinski, Camilla P. Benbow, and Jennifer Ryan, "Stability of Vocational Interests among the Intellectually Gifted from Adolescence to Adulthood: A 15-Year Longitudinal Study," *Journal of Applied Psychology* 80, no. 1 (February 1995): 196–200.

39. Douglas T. Hall and Jonathan E. Moss, "The New Protean Career Contract: Helping Organizations and Employees Adapt," *Organizational Dynamics* 26, no. 3 (Winter 1998): 22–37. Also see Douglas T. Hall, *The Career Is Dead, Long Live the Career: A Relational Approach to Careers* (San Francisco: Jossey-Bass, 1996); Douglas T. Hall, "Protean Careers of the 21st Century," *Academy of Management Executive* 10, no. 4 (1996): 8–16; Douglas T. Hall and Associates, *Career Development in Organizations* (San Francisco: Jossey-Bass, 1986).

40. Judith Bardwick, *The Plateauing Trap* (New York: AMACOM, 1986). See also Judith Bardwick, *Danger in the Comfort Zone: From Boardroom to Mailroom— How to Break the Entitlement Habit That's Killing American Business* (New York: AMACOM Book Division, 1995).

41. Susan Sonnsesyn Brooks, "Moving Up Is Not the Only Option," *HRMagazine* 39, no. 3 (March 1994): 79–82.

42. Susan Sonnsesyn Brooks, "Moving Up." See also Michel Tremblay, Alain Roger, and Jean-Marie Toulouse, "Career Plateau and Work Attitudes: An Empirical Study of Managers," *Human Relations* 48, no. 3 (March 1995): 221–37.

43. Betsy Morris, "Executive Women Confront Midlife Crisis," *Fortune,* September 18, 1995, 60–86; Brian O'Reilly, "Men at Midlife: Crisis? What Crisis?" *Fortune,* September 18, 1995, 72.

44. Abraham Sagie and Dov Abraham, "Achievement Motive and Entrepreneurial Orientation: A Structural Analysis," *Journal of Organizational Behavior* 20, no. 3 (May 1999): 375–87; Eleni T. Stavrous, "Succession in Family Businesses: Exploring the Effects of Demographic Factors on Offspring Intentions to Join and Take Over the Business," *Journal of Small Business Management* 37, no. 3 (July 1999): 43–61.

45. U.S. Department of Commerce, Bureau of the Census, *County Business Patterns* (Washington, D.C.: U.S. Government Printing Office, 1994): ix. See also "Manager's Handbook," *Manager's Magazine* 69, no. 6 (June 1994): 25–31; Matthew Mariani, "The Young and the Entrepreneurial," *Occupational Outlook Quarterly* 38, no. 3 (Fall 1994): 2–4.

46. For information on starting a business, the interested reader might look into Bob Adams, *Adams Streetwise Small Business Startup* (Holbrook, MA: Adams Media Corporation, 1996); Linda Pinson and Jerry Jinnett, *Anatomy of a Business Plan: Starting Smart, Building a Business and Securing Your Company's Future* (Upstart Publishing, 1996); Kenneth Cook, AMA *Complete Guide to Strategic Planning for Small Business* (NTC Business Books, 1995); Priscilla Y. Huff, *101 Best Small Businesses for Women* (Prima Pub., 1996); Constance Jones, *The 220 Best Franchises to Buy: The Sourcebook for Evaluating the Best Franchise Opportunities* (New York: Bantam Doubleday Dell, 1993).

47. Charlene Marmer Solomon, "Workers Want a Life! Do Managers Care?" *Workforce* 78, no. 8 (August 1999): 54–58; Katherine J. Sweetman, "Family and Careers," *Harvard Business Review* 73, no. 4 (July/August 1995): 14–15.

48. Christopher Caggiano, "Married . . . with Companies," *Inc.* 17, no. 6 (May 1995): 68–76; Andrew E. Scharlach and Janice K. Stanger, "Mandated Family and Medical Leave: Boon or Bane?" *Compensation and Benefits Management* 11, no. 3 (Summer 1995): 1–9; Timothy A. Judge, John W. Boudreau, and Robert D. Bretz, Jr., "Job and Life Attitudes of Male Executives," *Journal of Applied Psychology* 79, no. 5 (October 1994): 767–82; Samuel Aryee and Vivienne Luk, "Balancing Two Major Parts of Adult Life Experience: Work and Family Identity among Dual-Earner Couples," *Human Relations* 49, no. 4 (April 1996): 465–87; Stewart L. Stokes, Jr., "A Line in the Sand: Maintaining Work-Life Balance," *Information Systems Management* 13, no. 2 (Spring 1996): 83–85; Gillian Flynn, "Hallmark Cares," *Personnel Journal* 75, no. 3 (March 1996): 50–53.

# Appraising and Improving Performance

## AFTER STUDYING THIS CHAPTER, YOU SHOULD BE ABLE TO

**OBJECTIVE 1**
Explain the purposes of performance appraisals and the reasons they can sometimes fail.

**OBJECTIVE 2**
Identify the characteristics of an effective appraisal program.

**OBJECTIVE 3**
Describe the different sources of appraisal information.

**OBJECTIVE 4**
Explain the various methods used for performance evaluation.

**OBJECTIVE 5**
Outline the characteristics of an effective performance appraisal interview.

In the preceding chapters, we have discussed some of the most effective methods available to managers for acquiring and developing top-notch employees. But talented employees are not enough—successful organizations are particularly adept at engaging their workforce to achieve goals that benefit the organization as well as the individuals.

In this chapter we turn to performance appraisal programs, which are among the most helpful tools an organization can use to maintain and enhance productivity and facilitate progress toward strategic goals. While we will focus mainly on formal performance appraisal procedures, the processes of managing and evaluating performance can be informal as well. All managers monitor the way employees work and assess how this matches organizational needs. They form impressions about the relative value of employees to the organization and seek to maximize the contribution of every individual. Yet while these ongoing informal processes are vitally important, most organizations also have a formal performance appraisal once or twice a year.

The success or failure of a performance appraisal program depends on the philosophy underlying it, its connection with business goals, and the attitudes and skills of those responsible for its administration. Many different methods can be used to gather information about employee performance. However, gathering information is only one step in the appraisal process. The information must be evaluated in the context of organizational needs and communicated to employees so that it will result in high levels of performance.[1]

# Performance Appraisal Programs

Formal programs for performance appraisal and merit ratings are by no means new to organizations. The federal government began evaluating employees in 1842, when Congress passed a law mandating yearly performance reviews for department clerks. From this early beginning, performance appraisal programs have spread to large and small organizations in both the public and private sectors. Advocates see these HR programs as among the most logical means to appraise, develop, and effectively utilize the knowledge and abilities of employees. However, a growing number of observers point out that performance appraisals frequently fall short of their potential.[2]

Interest in total-quality management (TQM), for example, has caused numerous organizations to rethink their approach to performance appraisal. The late W. Edwards Deming, a pioneer in TQM, identified performance appraisal as one of seven deadly diseases of U.S. management. While most managers still recognize the benefits of performance appraisal, TQM challenges some long-standing assumptions about how it should be conducted.[3] Motorola, Eastman Chemical, Merrill Lynch, and Procter & Gamble, for example, have modified their appraisal systems to better acknowledge quality of performance (in addition to quantity), teamwork (in addition to individual accomplishments), and process improvements (in addition to performance outcomes).[4] Each of these issues is discussed at greater length throughout the chapter.

## Purposes of Performance Appraisal

It might seem at first glance that performance appraisals are used for a rather narrow purpose—to evaluate who is doing a good job (or not). But in reality performance appraisals are one of the most versatile tools available to managers. They can serve many purposes that benefit both the organization and the employee whose performance is being appraised. The following are just a sample of objectives:

1. To give employees the opportunity to discuss performance and performance standards regularly with their supervisor

2. To provide the supervisor with a means of identifying the strengths and weaknesses of an employee's performance

3. To provide a format enabling the supervisor to recommend a specific program designed to help an employee improve performance

4. To provide a basis for salary recommendations.

Figure 8.1 shows the most common uses of performance appraisals. In general, these can be classified as either *administrative* or *developmental.*

## Uses of Performance Appraisal

**FIGURE 8.1**

| RANKING | RATING* |
|---------|---------|
| 1.  Salary administration | 5.85 |
| 2.  Performance feedback | 5.67 |
| 3.  Identification of individual strengths and weaknesses | 5.41 |
| 4.  Documentation of personnel decisions | 5.15 |
| 5.  Recognition of individual performance | 5.02 |
| 6.  Determination of promotion | 4.80 |
| 7.  Identification of poor performance | 4.96 |
| 8.  Assistance in goal identification | 4.90 |
| 9.  Decision in retention or termination | 4.75 |
| 10. Evaluation of goal achievement | 4.72 |
| 11. Meeting legal requirements | 4.58 |
| 12. Determination of transfers and assignments | 3.66 |
| 13. Decision on layoffs | 3.51 |
| 14. Identification of individual training needs | 3.42 |
| 15. Determination of organizational training needs | 2.74 |
| 16. Personnel planning | 2.72 |
| 17. Reinforcement of authority structure | 2.65 |
| 18. Identification of organizational development needs | 2.63 |
| 19. Establishment of criteria for validation research | 2.30 |
| 20. Evaluation of personnel systems | 2.04 |

*Ratings are on a seven-point scale.

Jeanette N. Cleveland, Kevin R. Murphy, and Richard E. Williams, "Multiple Uses of Performance Appraisal: Prevalence and Correlates," *Journal of Applied Psychology* 74 (1989): 130–35. Copyright © 1989 by the American Psychological Association. Adapted with permission.

## Administrative Purposes

From the standpoint of administration, appraisal programs provide input that can be used for the entire range of HRM activities. For example, research has shown that performance appraisals are used most widely as a basis for compensation decisions.[5] The practice of "pay-for-performance" is found in all types of organizations. Performance appraisal is also directly related to a number of other major HR functions, such as promotion, transfer, and layoff decisions. Performance appraisal data may also be used in HR planning, in determining the relative worth of jobs under a job evaluation program, and as criteria for validating selection tests. Performance appraisals also provide a "paper trail" for documenting HRM actions that may result in legal action. Because of government EEO/AA directives, employers must maintain accurate, objective records of employee performance in order to defend themselves against possible charges of discrimination in connection with such HRM actions as promotion, salary determination, and termination. Finally, it is important to recognize that the success of the entire HR program depends on knowing how the performance of employees compares with the goals established for them. This knowledge is best derived from a carefully planned and administered HR appraisal program. Appraisal systems have the capability to influence employee behavior, thereby leading directly to improved organizational performance.

## Developmental Purposes

From the standpoint of individual development, appraisal provides the feedback essential for discussing strengths and weaknesses as well as improving performance. Regardless of the employee's level of performance, the appraisal process provides an opportunity to identify issues for discussion, eliminate any potential problems, and set new goals for achieving high performance. Newer approaches to performance appraisal emphasize training as well as development and growth plans for employees. A developmental approach to appraisal recognizes that the purpose of a manager is to improve job behavior, not simply to evaluate past performance. Having a sound basis for improving performance is one of the major benefits of an appraisal program.

Monsanto, for example, recently changed its performance appraisal system (referred to as the Performance Enhancement Process) to manage the *context* in which performance occurs, rather than just "calling the fouls." By focusing on employee development, Monsanto hopes to transfer the manager's role in performance appraisal from that of judge to one of a coach.[6]

## Reasons Appraisal Programs Sometimes Fail

In actual practice, and for a number of reasons, formal performance appraisal programs sometimes yield disappointing results. Figure 8.2 shows that the primary culprits include lack of top-management information and support, unclear performance standards, rater bias, too many forms to complete, and use of the program for conflicting purposes. For example, if an appraisal program is used to provide a written appraisal for salary action and at the same time to motivate employees to improve their work, the administrative and developmental purposes may be in conflict. As a result, the appraisal interview may become a discussion about salary in which the manager seeks to justify the action taken. In such cases, the discussion might have little influence on the employee's future job performance.

FIGURE 8.2

**▶ Top 10 Reasons Performance Appraisals Can Fail**

1. Manager lacks information concerning an employee's actual performance.
2. Standards by which to evaluate an employee's performance are unclear.
3. Manager does not take the appraisal seriously.
4. Manager is not prepared for the appraisal review with the employee.
5. Manager is not honest/sincere during the evaluation.
6. Manage lacks appraisal skills.
7. Employee does not receive ongoing performance feedback.
8. Insufficient resources are provided to reward performance.
9. There is ineffective discussion of employee development.
10. Manager uses unclear/ambiguous language in the evaluation process.

Source: Adapted with permission from Clinton O. Longnecker and Denise R. McGinnis, "Appraising Technical People: Pitfalls and Solutions," *Journal of Systems Management,* December 1992, 12–16; and Clinton O. Longnecker and Stephen J. Goff, "Why Performance Appraisals Still Fail," *Journal of Compensation and Benefits* 6, no. 3 (November/December 1990): 36–41. Copyright 1992 and 1990 by Warren, Gorham & Lamont, Park Square Building, 31 St. James Avenue, Boston, MA 02116-4112. 1-800-950-1216. All rights reserved. *See also* Clinton O. Longnecker and Dennis A. Gioia, "The Politics of Executive Appraisals," *Journal of Compensation and Benefits* 10, no. 2 (September/October 1994): 5–11; Ken Blanchard, "Performance Appraisals," *Executive Excellence* 11, no. 10 (October 1994): 15–16; Allan J. Weber, "Making Performance Appraisals Consistent with a Quality Environment," *Quality Progress* 28, no. 6 (June 1995): 65–69; Paul Falcone, "The Integrated Performance Appraisal," *Management Review* 84, no. 12 (December 1995): 46; "Seven Deadly Sins of Performance Appraisals," *Supervisory Management* 39, no. 1 (January 1994): 7–8.

As with all HR functions, if the support of top management is lacking, the appraisal program will not be successful. Even the best-conceived program will not work in an environment where appraisers are not encouraged by their superiors to take the program seriously. To underscore the importance of this responsibility, top management should announce that effectiveness in appraising subordinates is a standard by which the appraisers themselves will be evaluated.

Other reasons performance appraisal programs can fail to yield the desired results include the following:

1. Managers feel that little or no benefit will be derived from the time and energy spent in the process.
2. Managers dislike the face-to-face confrontation of appraisal interviews.
3. Managers are not sufficiently adept in providing appraisal feedback.
4. The judgmental role of appraisal conflicts with the helping role of developing employees.

Performance appraisal in many organizations is a once-a-year activity in which the appraisal interview becomes a source of friction for both managers and employees. An important principle of performance appraisal is that continual feedback and employee coaching must be a positive daily activity. The annual or semiannual performance review should simply be a logical extension of the day-to-day supervision process.

One of the main concerns of employees is the fairness of the performance appraisal system, since the process is central to so many HRM decisions. Employees who believe the system is unfair may consider the appraisal interview a waste of time and leave the interview with feelings of anxiety or frustration. Also, they may view compliance with the appraisal system as perfunctory and thus play only a passive role during the interview process. By addressing these employee concerns during the planning stage of the appraisal process, the organization will help the appraisal program to succeed in reaching its goals.[7]

Finally, organizational politics can introduce a bias even in fairly administered employee appraisals.[8] For example, managers may inflate evaluations because they desire higher salaries for their employees or because higher subordinate ratings make them look good as managers. Alternatively, managers may want to get rid of troublesome employees, passing them off to another department by inflating their ratings.

# Developing an Effective Appraisal Program

The HR department ordinarily has the primary responsibility for overseeing and coordinating the appraisal program. Managers from the operating departments must also be actively involved, particularly in helping to establish the objectives for the program. Furthermore, employees are more likely to accept and be satisfied with the performance appraisal program when they have the chance to participate in its development. Their concerns about fairness and accuracy in determining raises, promotions, and the like tend to be alleviated somewhat when they have been involved at the planning stage and have helped develop the performance standards themselves.

## What Are the Performance Standards?

Before any appraisal is conducted, the standards by which performance is to be evaluated should be clearly defined and communicated to the employee. As discussed in Chapter 3, these standards should be based on job-related requirements derived from job analysis and reflected in the job descriptions and job specifications. When performance standards are properly established, they help translate organizational goals and objectives into job requirements that convey acceptable and unacceptable levels of performance to employees.[9]

As shown in Figure 8.3, there are four basic considerations in establishing performance standards: strategic relevance, criterion deficiency, criterion contamination, and reliability.

### Strategic Relevance

Strategic relevance refers to the extent to which standards relate to the strategic objectives of the organization. For example, if a TQM program has established a standard that "95 percent of all customer complaints are to be resolved in one day," then it is relevant for the customer service representatives to use such a standard for their evaluations. Companies such as 3M and Rubbermaid have strategic objectives that 25 to 30 percent of their sales are to be generated from products developed within the past five years. These objectives are translated into performance standards for their employees.[10]

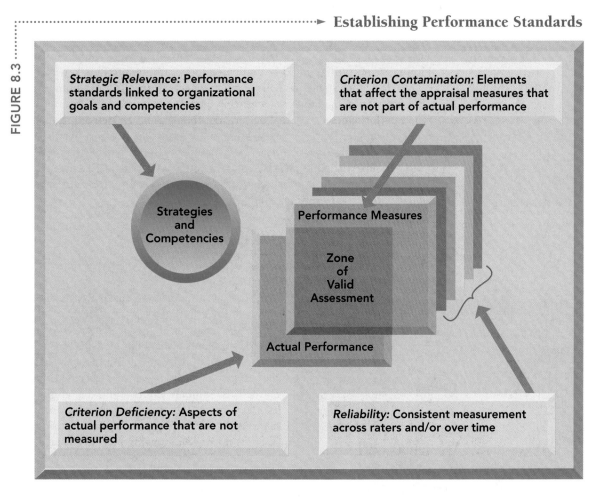

**FIGURE 8.3**

**Establishing Performance Standards**

*Strategic Relevance:* Performance standards linked to organizational goals and competencies

*Criterion Contamination:* Elements that affect the appraisal measures that are not part of actual performance

Strategies and Competencies

Performance Measures

Zone of Valid Assessment

Actual Performance

*Criterion Deficiency:* Aspects of actual performance that are not measured

*Reliability:* Consistent measurement across raters and/or over time

### Criterion Deficiency

A second consideration in establishing performance standards is the extent to which the standards capture the entire range of an employee's responsibilities. When performance standards focus on a single criterion (e.g., sales revenues) to the exclusion of other important but less quantifiable performance dimensions (e.g., customer service), then the appraisal system is said to suffer from criterion deficiency.[11]

### Criterion Contamination

Just as performance criteria can be deficient, they can also be contaminated. There are factors outside an employee's control that can influence his or her performance. A comparison of performance of production workers, for example, should not be contaminated by the fact that some have newer machines than others do. A comparison of the performance of traveling salespeople should not be contaminated by the fact that territories differ in sales potential.

### Reliability

As discussed in Chapter 5, reliability refers to the stability or consistency of a standard, or the extent to which individuals tend to maintain a certain level of performance over time. In ratings, reliability may be measured by correlating two sets of ratings made by a single rater or by two different raters. For example, two managers may rate the same individual and estimate his or her suitability for a promotion. Their ratings could be compared to determine interrater reliability.

Performance standards will permit managers to specify and communicate precise information to employees regarding quality and quantity of output. Therefore, when performance standards are written, they should be defined in quantifiable and measurable terms. For example, "ability and willingness to handle customer orders" is not as good a performance standard as "all customer orders will be filled in four hours with a 98 percent accuracy rate." When standards are expressed in specific, measurable terms, comparing the employee's performance against the standard results in a more justifiable appraisal.

## Are You Complying with the Law?

Since performance appraisals are used as one basis for HRM actions, they must meet certain legal requirements. In *Brito v Zia,* for example, the Supreme Court ruled that performance appraisals were subject to the same validity criteria as selection procedures.[12] As the courts have made clear, a central issue is to have carefully defined and measurable performance standards. In one landmark case involving test validation, *Albemarle Paper Company v Moody* (discussed in Chapter 2), the U.S. Supreme Court found that employees had been ranked against a vague standard, open to each supervisor's own interpretation. The court stated that "there is no way of knowing precisely what criteria of job performance the supervisors were considering, whether each supervisor was considering the same criteria, or whether indeed, any of the supervisors actually applied a focused and stable body of criteria of any kind."[13] This decision has prompted organizations to try to eliminate vagueness in descriptions of traits such as attitude, cooperation, dependability, initiative, and leadership. For example, the trait "dependability" can be made much less vague if it is spelled out in terms of employee tardiness and/or unexcused absences. In general, reducing room for subjective judgments will improve the entire appraisal process.

Furthermore, other court decisions show that employers might face legal challenges to their appraisal systems when appraisals indicate acceptable or above-average performance but employees are later passed over for promotion, disciplined for poor performance, discharged, or laid off from the organization. In these cases, the performance appraisals can

*Specific, measurable job standards help remove vagueness and subjectivity from performance appraisals.*

undermine the legitimacy of the subsequent personnel decision. Intel, for example, was recently taken to court by a group of former employees on grounds that the performance appraisal system (used for layoff decisions) was unreliable and invalid. In light of court cases such as this, performance appraisals should meet the following legal guidelines:

- Performance ratings must be job-related, with performance standards developed through job analysis.
- Employees must be given a written copy of their job standards in advance of appraisals.
- Managers who conduct the appraisal must be able to observe the behavior they are rating. This implies having a measurable standard with which to compare employee behavior.
- Supervisors should be trained to use the appraisal form correctly. They should be instructed in how to apply appraisal standards when making judgments.
- Appraisals should be discussed openly with employees and counseling or corrective guidance offered to help poor performers improve their performance.
- An appeals procedure should be established to enable employees to express disagreement with the appraisal.[14]

To comply with the legal requirements of performance appraisals, employers must ensure that managers and supervisors document appraisals and reasons for subsequent HRM actions. (See Chapter 16 on documentation.) This information may prove decisive should an employee take legal action. An employer's credibility is strengthened when it can support performance appraisal ratings by documenting instances of poor performance.[15]

## Who Should Appraise Performance?

Just as there are multiple standards by which to evaluate performance, there are also multiple candidates for appraising performance. Given the complexity of today's jobs, it is often unrealistic to presume that one person can fully observe and evaluate an employee's performance. As shown in Figure 8.4, raters may include supervisors, peers, team members, self, subordinates, and customers. And each may be more or less useful for the administrative and developmental purposes we

**FIGURE 8.4**

**Alternative Sources of Appraisal**

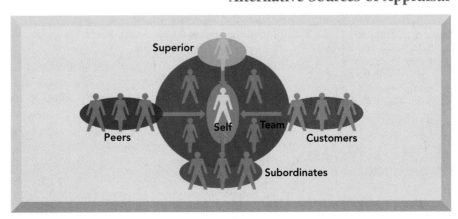

discussed earlier. Companies such as US West, Westinghouse, and the Walt Disney Company have begun to use a multiple-rater approach—or 360-degree appraisal—to evaluate employee performance.[16] We will talk more about 360-degree appraisal at the end of this section.

### Manager/Supervisor Appraisal

**Manager and/or supervisor appraisal**
Performance appraisal done by an employee's manager and often reviewed by a manager one level higher

**Manager and/or supervisor appraisal** has been the traditional approach to evaluating an employee's performance. In most instances supervisors are in the best position to perform this function, although it may not always be possible for them to do so. Managers often complain that they do not have the time to fully observe the performance of employees. These managers must then rely on performance records to evaluate an employee's performance. If reliable and valid measures are not available, the appraisal may be less than accurate. (Recall our earlier discussion of criterion deficiency and contamination.)

Where a supervisor appraises employees independently, provision is often made for a review of the appraisals by the supervisor's superior. Having appraisals reviewed by a supervisor's superior reduces the chance of superficial or biased evaluations. Reviews by superiors generally are more objective and provide a broader perspective of employee performance than do appraisals by immediate supervisors.

### Self-Appraisal

**Self-appraisal**
Performance appraisal done by the employee being evaluated, generally on an appraisal form completed by the employee prior to the performance interview

Sometimes employees are asked to evaluate themselves on a self-appraisal form. The **self-appraisal** is beneficial when managers seek to increase an employee's involvement in the review process. A self-appraisal system requires an employee to complete the appraisal form prior to the performance interview. At a minimum, this gets the employee thinking about his or her strengths and weaknesses and may lead to discussions about barriers to effective performance. During the performance interview, the manager and the employee discuss job performance and agree on a final appraisal. This approach also works well when the manager and the employee jointly establish future performance goals or employee development plans. Critics of self-appraisal argue that self-raters are more lenient than managers in their assessments and tend to present themselves in a highly favorable light. For this reason, self-appraisals may be best for developmental purposes rather than for administrative decisions. Used in conjunction with other methods, self-appraisals can be a valuable source of appraisal information.[17]

### Subordinate Appraisal

**Subordinate appraisal**
Performance appraisal of a superior by an employee, which is more appropriate for developmental than for administrative purposes

**Subordinate appraisal** has been used by both large organizations (such as Xerox and Pratt & Whitney) and small organizations (such as Hyde Manufacturing and Halifax Building Society) to give managers feedback on how their subordinates view them.[18] Subordinates are in a good position to evaluate their managers since they are in frequent contact with their superiors and occupy a unique position from which to observe many performance-related behaviors. Those performance dimensions judged most appropriate for subordinate appraisals include leadership, oral communication, delegation of authority, coordination of team efforts, and interest in subordinates. However, dimensions related to managers' specific job tasks, such as planning and organizing, budgeting, creativity, and analytical ability, are not usually seen as appropriate for subordinate appraisal.

Since subordinate appraisals give employees power over their bosses, the managers themselves may be hesitant to endorse such a system, particularly when it might be used as a basis for compensation decisions. However, when the information is used for developmental purposes, managers tend to be more open to the idea. And available evidence suggests that when managers heed the advice of their subordinates, their own performance can improve substantially. Nevertheless, to avoid potential problems, subordinate appraisals should be submitted anonymously and combined across several individual raters.[19]

### Peer Appraisal

Peer appraisal
Performance appraisal done by one's fellow employees, generally on forms that are compiled into a single profile for use in the performance interview conducted by the employee's manager

Individuals of equal rank who work together are increasingly asked to evaluate each other. A **peer appraisal** provides information that differs to some degree from ratings by a superior, since peers often see different dimensions of performance. Peers can readily identify leadership and interpersonal skills along with other strengths and weaknesses of their co-workers. A superior asked to rate a patrol officer on a dimension such as "dealing with the public" may not have had much opportunity to observe it. Fellow officers, on the other hand, have the opportunity to observe this behavior regularly.

One advantage of peer appraisals is the belief that they furnish more accurate and valid information than appraisals by superiors. The supervisor often sees employees putting their best foot forward, while those who work with their fellow employees on a regular basis may see a more realistic picture. With peer appraisals, co-workers complete an evaluation on the employee. The forms are then usually compiled into a single profile, which is given to the supervisor for use in the final appraisal.[20]

Despite the evidence that peer appraisals are possibly the most accurate method of judging employee behavior, there are reasons why they have not been used more frequently.[21] The reasons commonly cited include the following:

1. Peer ratings are simply a popularity contest.
2. Managers are reluctant to give up control over the appraisal process.
3. Those receiving low ratings might retaliate against their peers.
4. Peers rely on stereotypes in ratings.

When peers are in competition with one another, such as with sales associates, peer appraisals may not be advisable for administrative decisions such as salary or bonuses. Employers using peer appraisals must also be sure to safeguard confidentiality in handling the review forms. Any breach of confidentiality can create interpersonal rivalries or hurt feelings and bring about hostility among fellow employees.

**USING THE INTERNET**

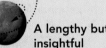

A lengthy but insightful description of the implementation of a peer appraisal system in conjunction with self-directed work teams at the Racine liquid manufacturing facility of S. C. Johnson & Son, Inc., appears at:

www.workteams.unt.edu80/proceed/jwax.htm

### Team Appraisal

Team appraisal
Performance appraisal, based on TQM concepts, that recognizes team accomplishment rather than individual performance

An extension of the peer appraisal is the **team appraisal.** While peers are on equal standing with one another, they may not work closely together. In a team setting, it may be nearly impossible to separate out an individual's contribution. Advocates of team appraisal argue that, in such cases, individual appraisal can be dysfunctional since it detracts from the critical issues of the team. To address this issue, organizations ranging from Boeing and Texas Instruments to Jostens and

## kinko's
### Express Yourself.™

**You are a valued Kinko's customer. What you have to say is important to us.**

Please take a moment to let us know how we are doing by filling out this card,
calling Kinko's Customer Service at 1-800-2-KINKOS
or visiting our web site at www.kinkos.com.

Overall, how satisfied were you with your experience at Kinko's today? (Circle one)

1        2        3        4        5        6        7        8        9
Extremely Dissatisfied                                              Extremely Satisfied

What do we do well?_____

_____

What should we change?_____

_____

What can we do to serve you better?_____

_____

Additional comments?_____

_____

_____

_____

_____

Date of visit: _____ Time of day: _____

Name: _____

Address: _____

City/State/Zip: _____

Area Code: _____ Telephone: _____

Occupation: _____

*Thanks* for visiting
Kinko's Glenview IL Glenview North Plaza
#02-08-047-3614

©1999 Kinko's, Inc. Kinko's and Kinko's Express Yourself are proprietary marks of Kinko's Ventures, Inc. and are used by permission. All rights reserved.    Printed on recycled paper.

*Kinko's invites customers to rate the company on its service.*

**Customer appraisal**
Performance appraisal, which, like team appraisal, is based on TQM concepts and seeks evaluation from both external and internal customers

Otis Engineering have begun developing team appraisals to evaluate the performance of the team as a whole.[22]

A company's interest in team appraisals is frequently driven by its commitment to TQM principles and practices. At its root, TQM is a control system that involves setting standards (based on customer requirements), measuring performance against those standards, and identifying opportunities for continuous improvement. In this regard TQM and performance appraisal are perfectly complementary. However, a basic tenet of TQM is that performance is best understood at the level of the system as a whole, whereas performance appraisal traditionally has focused on individual performance. Team appraisals represent one way to break down barriers between individuals and encourage their collective effort.[23] Frequently, the system is complemented by use of team incentives or group variable pay. (See Chapters 10 and 17.)

### Customer Appraisal

Also driven by TQM concerns, an increasing number of organizations use internal and external **customer appraisal** as a source of performance appraisal information. External customers' evaluations, of course, have been used for some time to appraise restaurant personnel. However, companies such as Federal Express, AT&T, and Granite Rock have begun utilizing external customers as well. Managers establish customer service measures (CSMs) and set goals for employees (linked to company goals). Often the CSM goals are linked to employee pay through incentive programs. Customer survey data are then incorporated into the performance evaluation. By including CSMs in their performance reviews, AT&T, Granite Rock, and Federal Express hope to produce more objective evaluations, more effective employees, more satisfied customers, and better business performance.[24]

In contrast to external customers, internal customers include anyone inside the organization who depends upon an employee's work output. For example, managers who rely on the HR department for selection and training services would be candidates for conducting internal customer evaluations of that department. For both developmental and administrative purposes, internal customers can provide extremely useful feedback about the value added by an employee or team of employees.[25]

## Putting It All Together: 360-Degree Appraisal

As mentioned previously, many companies are combining various sources of performance appraisal information to create multirater—or 360-degree—appraisal and feedback systems. Jobs are multifaceted, and different people see different

**USING THE INTERNET**

Software used to help prepare 360-degree appraisal systems is available from a number of companies. The web site of Organizational Universe Systems not only sells its software but also provides an interesting discussion of 360-degree feedback to managers. The site is located at:

ous.usa.net/msasbro.htm

things. As the name implies, 360-degree feedback is intended to provide employees with as accurate a view of their performance as possible by getting input from all angles: supervisors, peers, subordinates, customers, and the like. Although in the beginning, 360-degree systems were purely developmental and were restricted mainly to management and career development, they have migrated to performance appraisal and other administrative applications. A recent survey found that over 90 percent of *Fortune* 1000 companies have implemented some form of 360-degree feedback system for career development, performance appraisal, or both. Because the system combines more information than a typical performance appraisal, it can become administratively complex. For that reason, organizations have recently begun using web technology (Internet, intranet) to compile and aggregate the information.[26]

Figure 8.5 shows a list of pros and cons of 360-degree appraisal. Although 360-degree feedback can be useful for both developmental and administrative purposes, most companies start with an exclusive focus on development. Employees may be understandably nervous about the possibility of everyone "ganging up" on them in their evaluations. If an organization

**FIGURE 8.5**

▶ **Pros and Cons of 360-Degree Appraisal**

**PROS**

- The system is more comprehensive in that responses are gathered from multiple perspectives.
- Quality of information is better. (Quality of respondents is more important than quantity.)
- It complements TQM initiatives by emphasizing internal/external customers and teams.
- It may lessen bias/prejudice since feedback comes from more people, not one individual.
- Feedback from peers and others may increase employee self-development.

**CONS**

- The system is complex in combining all the responses.
- Feedback can abe intimidating and cause resentment if employee feels the respondents have "ganged up."
- There may be conflicting opinions, though they may all be accurate from the respective standpoints.
- The system requires training to work effectively.
- Employees may collude or "game" the system by giving invalid evaluations to one another.
- Appraisers may not be accountable if their evaluations are anonymous.

Sources: Compiled from David A. Waldman, Leanne E. Atwater, and David Antonioni, "Has 360 Feedback Gone Amok?" *Academy of Management Executive* 12, no. 2 (May 1998): 86–94; David Antonioni, "Designing an Effective 360-Degree Appraisal Feedback Process," *Organizational Dynamics* 25, no. 2 (Autumn 1996): 24–38; Mark Edwards and Ann J. Ewen, "How to Manage Performance and Pay with 360 Degree Feedback," *Compensation and Benefits Review* 28, no. 3 (May/June 1996): 41–46; Mary N. Vinson, "The Pros and Cons of 360 Degree Feedback: Making It Work," *Training and Development* 50, no. 4 (April 1996): 11–12.

starts with only developmental feedback—not tied to compensation, promotions, and the like—employees will become accustomed to the process and will likely value the input they get from various parties.

When Intel established a 360-degree system, they observed the following safeguards to ensure its maximum quality and acceptance:

- *Assure anonymity.* Make certain that no employee ever knows how any evaluation-team member responded. (The supervisor's rating is an exception to this rule.)
- *Make respondents accountable.* Supervisors should discuss each evaluation-team member's input, letting each member know whether she or he used the rating scales appropriately, whether their responses were reliable, and how other participants rated the employee.
- *Prevent "gaming" of the system.* Some individuals may try to help or hurt an employee by giving either too high or too low an evaluation. Team members may try to collude with one another by agreeing to give each other uniformly high ratings. Supervisors should check for obviously invalid responses.
- *Use statistical procedures.* Use weighted averages or other quantitative approaches to combining evaluations. Supervisors should be careful about using subjective combinations of data, which could undermine the system.
- *Identify and quantify biases.* Check for prejudices or preferences related to age, gender, ethnicity, or other group factors.[27]

Based on the experiences of companies like Intel, Disney, and Monsanto, it appears as though 360-degree feedback can provide a valuable approach to performance appraisal. Its success, as with any appraisal technique, depends on how managers use the information and how fairly employees are treated.

## Training Appraisers

A weakness of many performance appraisal programs is that managers and supervisors are not adequately trained for the appraisal task and provide little meaningful feedback to subordinates. Because they lack precise standards for appraising subordinates' performance and have not developed the necessary observational and feedback skills, their appraisals often become nondirective and meaningless. Therefore, training appraisers can vastly improve the performance appraisal process.

### Establishing an Appraisal Plan

Training programs are most effective when they follow a systematic process that begins with an explanation of the objectives of the performance appraisal system.[28] It is important for the rater to know the purpose for which the appraisal is to be used. For example, using the appraisal for compensation decisions rather than development purposes may affect how the rater evaluates the employee, and it may change the rater's opinion of how the appraisal form should be completed. The mechanics of the rating system should also be explained, including how frequently the appraisals are to be conducted, who will conduct them, and what the standards of performance are. In addition, appraisal training should alert raters to the weaknesses and problems of appraisal systems so they can be avoided.

### Eliminating Rater Error

Appraisal training should focus on eliminating the subjective errors made by managers in the rating process. Gary Latham and Kenneth Wexley stress the importance of performance appraisal training by noting that

> [R]egardless of whether evaluations are obtained from multiple appraisers or from only the employee's immediate superior, all appraisers should be trained to reduce errors of judgment that occur when one person evaluates another. This training is necessary because to the degree to which a performance appraisal is biased, distorted, or inaccurate, the probability of increasing the productivity of the employee is greatly decreased. Moreover, wrong decisions could be made regarding whom to promote, retain, or replace, which in turn will penalize the organization's bottom line. In addition, when a performance appraisal is affected by rating errors, the employee may be justified in filing a discrimination charge.[29]

With any rating method, certain types of errors can arise that should be considered. The "halo error" discussed in Chapter 5 is also common with respect to rating scales, especially those that do not include carefully developed descriptions of the employee behaviors being rated.[30] Provision for comments on the rating form tends to reduce halo error.

Some types of rating errors are *distributional errors* in that they involve a group of ratings given across various employees. For example, raters who are reluctant to assign either extremely high or extremely low ratings commit the **error of central tendency.** In this case, all employees are rated about average. To such raters it is a good idea to explain that, among large numbers of employees, one should expect to find significant differences in behavior, productivity, and other characteristics.

In contrast to central tendency errors, it is also common for some raters to give unusually high or low ratings. For example, a manager may erroneously assert, "All my employees are excellent" or "None of my people are good enough." These beliefs give rise to what is called **leniency or strictness error**.[31] One way to reduce this error is to clearly define the characteristics or dimensions of performance and to provide meaningful descriptions of behavior, known as "anchors," on the scale. Another approach is to require ratings to conform to a *forced distribution*. Managers appraising employees under a forced-distribution system are required to place a certain percentage of employees into various performance categories. For example, it may be required that 10 percent of ratings be poor (or excellent). This is similar to the requirement in some schools that instructors grade on a curve. However, while a forced distribution may solve leniency and strictness error, it may create other errors in the accuracy of ratings—particularly if most employees are performing above standard. In addition, since employees are usually compared only in terms of overall suitability, this method may result in a legal challenge. (See *Albemarle Paper Company v Moody*.) Companies such as Xerox and Cadillac have recently abandoned their forced-distribution systems completely, but a modified version is still being used at Merck for determining merit pay.[32]

Some rating errors are *temporal* in that the performance review is biased either favorably or unfavorably, depending on the way performance information is selected, evaluated, and organized by the rater over time. For example, when the appraisal is based largely on the employee's recent behavior, good or bad, the rater has committed the **recency error.** Managers who give higher ratings because they believe an employee is "showing improvement" may unwittingly be committing

**Error of central tendency**
Performance-rating error in which all employees are rated about average

**Leniency or strictness error**
Performance-rating error in which the appraiser tends to give employees either unusually high or unusually low ratings

**Recency error**
Performance-rating error in which the appraisal is based largely on the employee's most recent behavior rather than on behavior throughout the appraisal period

recency error. Without work-record documentation for the entire appraisal period, the rater is forced to recall recent employee behavior to establish the rating. Having the rater routinely document employee accomplishments and failures throughout the whole appraisal period can minimize the recency error. Rater training also will help reduce this error.

**Contrast error**

Performance-rating error in which an employee's evaluation is biased either upward or downward because of comparison with another employee just previously evaluated

**Contrast error** occurs when an employee's evaluation is biased either upward or downward because of another employee's performance, evaluated just previously. For example, an average employee may appear especially productive when compared with a poor performer. However, that same employee may appear unproductive when compared with a star performer. Contrast errors are most likely when raters are required to rank employees in order from the best to the poorest. Employees are evaluated against one another, usually on the basis of some organizational standard or guideline. For example, they may be compared on the basis of their ability to meet production standards or their "overall" ability to perform their job. As with other types of rating error, contrast error can be reduced through training that focuses on using objective standards and behavioral anchors to appraise performance.

**Similar-to-me error**

Performance-rating error in which an appraiser inflates the evaluation of an employee because of a mutual personal connection

**Similar-to-me error** occurs when appraisers inflate the evaluations of people with whom they have something in common. For example, if both the manager and the employee are from small towns, the manager may unwittingly have a more favorable impression of the employee. The effects of a similar-to-me error can be powerful, and when the similarity is based on race, religion, gender, or some other protected category, it may result in discrimination.

Furthermore, raters should be aware of any stereotypes they may hold toward particular groups—e.g., male/female, white/black—because the observation and interpretation of performance can be clouded by these stereotypes. Results from a study examining how stereotypes of women affect performance ratings suggested that women evaluated by raters who hold traditional stereotypes of women will be at a disadvantage in obtaining merit pay increases and promotions.[33] This problem will be aggravated when employees are appraised on the basis of poorly defined performance standards and subjective performance traits.

A host of organizations such as Sears, Weyerhauser, and Allied Chemical have developed formal training programs to reduce the subjective errors commonly made during the rating process. This training can pay off, particularly when participants have the opportunity to (1) observe other managers making errors, (2) actively participate in discovering their own errors, and (3) practice job-related tasks to reduce the errors they tend to make.[34]

## Feedback Training

Finally, a training program for raters should provide some general points to consider for planning and conducting the feedback interview. The interview not only provides employees with knowledge of results of their evaluation, but it allows the manager and employee to discuss current problems and set future goals.

Training in specific skills should cover at least three basic areas: (1) communicating effectively, (2) diagnosing the root causes of performance problems, and (3) setting goals and objectives.[35] A checklist can be used to assist supervisors in preparing for the appraisal interview. A checklist suggested by AT&T is shown in Highlights in HRM 1. The AT&T checklist reflects the growing tendency of organizations to have employees assess their own performance prior to the appraisal interview. The performance appraisal interview will be discussed in detail later in the chapter.

**HRM 1**

HIGHLIGHTS IN HRM

# Supervisor's Checklist for the Performance Appraisal

**Scheduling**

1. Schedule the review and notify the employee ten days or two weeks in advance.
2. Ask the employee to prepare for the session by reviewing his or her performance, job objectives, and development goals.
3. Clearly state that this will be the formal annual performance appraisal.

**Preparing for the Review**

1. Review the performance documentation collected throughout the year. Concentrate on work patterns that have developed.
2. Be prepared to give specific examples of above- or below-average performance.
3. When performance falls short of expectations, determine what changes need to be made. If performance meets or exceeds expectations, discuss this and plan how to reinforce it.
4. After the appraisal is written, set it aside for a few days and then review it again.
5. Follow whatever steps are required by your organization's performance appraisal system.

**Conducting the Review**

1. Select a location that is comfortable and free of distractions. The location should encourage a frank and candid conversation.
2. Discuss each time in the appraisal one at a time, considering both strengths and shortcomings.
3. Be specific and descriptive, not general and judgmental. Report occurrences rather than evaluating them.
4. Discuss your differences and resolve them. Solicit agreement with the evaluation.
5. Jointly discuss and design plans for taking corrective action for growth and development.
6. Maintain a professional and supportive approach to the appraisal discussion.

Source: Adapted from "The Performance-Management Process, Part 1 and 2," *Straight Talk* (AT&T) 1, nos. 8 and 9 (December 1987).

# Performance Appraisal Methods

Since the early years of their use by the federal government, methods of evaluating personnel have evolved considerably. Old systems have been replaced by new methods that reflect technical improvements and legal requirements and are more consistent with the purposes of appraisal. In the discussion that follows, we will examine in some detail those methods that have found widespread use, and we will briefly touch on other methods that are used less frequently. Performance appraisal methods can be broadly classified as measuring traits, behaviors, or results. Trait approaches continue to be the more popular systems despite their inherent subjectivity. Behavioral approaches provide more action-oriented information to employees and therefore may be best for development. The results-oriented approach is gaining popularity because it focuses on the measurable contributions that employees make to the organization.

## Trait Methods

Trait approaches to performance appraisal are designed to measure the extent to which an employee possesses certain characteristics—such as dependability, creativity, initiative, and leadership—that are viewed as important for the job and the organization in general. The fact that trait methods are the most popular is due in large part to the ease with which they are developed. However, if not designed carefully on the basis of job analysis, trait appraisals can be notoriously biased and subjective.

### Graphic Rating Scales

**Graphic rating-scale method**

A trait approach to performance appraisal whereby each employee is rated according to a scale of characteristics

In the **graphic rating-scale method** each trait or characteristic to be rated is represented by a scale on which a rater indicates the degree to which an employee possesses that trait or characteristic. An example of this type of scale is shown in Highlights in HRM 2. There are many variations of the graphic rating scale. The differences are to be found in (1) the characteristics or dimensions on which individuals are rated, (2) the degree to which the performance dimension is defined for the rater, and (3) how clearly the points on the scale are defined. In Highlights in HRM 2 the dimensions are defined briefly, and some attempt is made to define the points on the scale. Subjectivity bias is reduced somewhat when the dimensions on the scale and the scale points are defined as precisely as possible. This can be achieved by training raters and by including descriptive appraisal guidelines in a performance appraisal reference packet.[36]

Also, the rating form should provide sufficient space for comments on the behavior associated with each scale. These comments improve the accuracy of the appraisal since they require the rater to think in terms of observable employee behaviors while providing specific examples to discuss with the employee during the appraisal interview.

### Mixed-Standard Scales

**Mixed-standard scale method**

A trait approach to performance appraisal similar to other scale methods but based on comparison with (better than, equal to, or worse than) a standard

The **mixed-standard scale method** is a modification of the basic rating-scale method. Rather than evaluating traits according to a single scale, the rater is given three specific descriptions of each trait. These descriptions reflect three levels of performance: superior, average, and inferior. After the three descriptions for each trait are written, they are randomly sequenced to form the mixed-standard scale. As shown in Highlights in HRM 3, supervisors evaluate employees by indicating whether their performance is better than, equal to, or worse than the standard for each behavior.

### Forced-Choice Method

**Forced-choice method**

A trait approach to performance appraisal that requires the rater to choose from statements designed to distinguish between successful and unsuccessful performance

The **forced-choice method** requires the rater to choose from statements, often in pairs, that appear equally favorable or equally unfavorable. The statements, however, are designed to distinguish between successful and unsuccessful performance. The rater selects one statement from the pair without knowing which

## HRM 2

# Graphic Rating Scale with Provision for Comments

Appraise employee's performance in PRESENT ASSIGNMENT. Check (✔) most appropriate square. Appraisers are *urged to freely use* the "Remarks" sections for significant comments descriptive of the individual.

| 1. KNOWLEDGE OF WORK: Understanding of all phases of his/her work and related matters | Needs instruction or guidance ☐ ☐ | Has required knowledge of own and related work ☐ | Has exceptional knowledge of own and related work ✔ ☐ |
|---|---|---|---|
| | Remarks: *Is particularly good on gas engines.* | | |

| 2. INITIATIVE: Ability to originate or develop ideas and to get things started | Lacks imagination ☐ | Meets necessary requirements ✔ ☐ | Unusually resourceful ☐ ☐ |
|---|---|---|---|
| | Remarks: *Has good ideas when asked for an opinion, but otherwise will not offer them. Somewhat lacking in self-confidence.* | | |

| 3. APPLICATION: Attention and application to his/her work | Wastes time Needs close supervision ☐ ☐ | Steady and willing worker ✔ | Exceptionally industrious ☐ ☐ |
|---|---|---|---|
| | Remarks: *Accepts new jobs when assigned.* | | |

| 4. QUALITY OF WORK: Thoroughness, neatness, and accuracy of work | Needs improvement ☐ ☐ | Regularly meets recognized standards ☐ | Consistently maintains highest quality ✔ ☐ |
|---|---|---|---|
| | Remarks: *The work he turns out is always of the highest possible quality.* | | |

| 5. VOLUME OF WORK: Quantity of acceptable work | Should be increased ☐ ☐ | Regularly meets recognized standards ✔ | Unusually high output ☐ ☐ |
|---|---|---|---|
| | Remarks: *Would be higher if he did not spend so much time checking and rechecking his work.* | | |

statement correctly describes successful job behavior. For example, forced-choice pairs might include the following:

1. _____ a) Works hard          _____ b) Works quickly
2. _____ a) Shows initiative     _____ b) Is responsive to customers
3. _____ a) Produces poor quality  _____ b) Lacks good work habits

**HRM 3**

# Example of a Mixed-Standard Scale

DIRECTIONS: Please indicate whether the individual's performance is above (+), equal to (0), or lower (−) than each of the following standards.

1. _____ Employee uses good judgment when addressing problems and provides workable alternatives; however, at times does not take actions to prevent problems. (*medium PROBLEM SOLVING*)

2. _____ Employee lacks supervisory skills; frequently handles employees poorly and is at times argumentative. (*low LEADERSHIP*)

3. _____ Employee is extremely cooperative; can be expected to take the lead in developing cooperation among employees; completes job tasks with a positive attitude. (*High COOPERATION*)

4. _____ Employee has effective supervision skills; encourages productivity, quality, and employee development. (*medium LEADERSHIP*)

5. _____ Employee normally displays an argumentative or defensive attitude toward fellow employees and job assignments. (*low COOPERATION*)

6. _____ Employee is generally agreeable but becomes argumentative at times when given job assignments; cooperates with other employees as expected. (*medium COOPERATION*)

7. _____ Employee is not good at solving problems; uses poor judgment and does not anticipate potential difficulties. (*low PROBLEM SOLVING*)

8. _____ Employee anticipates potential problems and provides creative, proactive alternative solutions; has good attention to follow-up. (*high PROBLEM SOLVING*)

9. _____ Employee displays skilled direction; effectively coordinates unit activities; is generally a dynamic leader and motivates employees to high performance. (*high LEADERSHIP*)

---

The forced-choice method is not without limitations, the primary one being the cost of establishing and maintaining its validity. The fact that it has been a source of frustration to many raters has sometimes caused the method to be eliminated from appraisal programs. In addition, it cannot be used as effectively as some of the other methods to help achieve the commonly held objective of using appraisals as a tool for developing employees by such means as the appraisal interview.

## *Essay Method*

**Essay method**
A trait approach to performance appraisal that requires the rater to compose a statement describing employee behavior

Unlike rating scales, which provide a structured form of appraisal, the **essay method** requires the appraiser to compose a statement that best describes the employee being appraised. The appraiser is usually instructed to describe the employee's strengths and weaknesses and to make recommendations for his or her development. Often the essay method is combined with other rating methods. Essays may provide additional descriptive information on performance that is not obtained with a structured rating scale, for example.

The essay method provides an excellent opportunity to point out the unique characteristics of the employee being appraised. This aspect of the method is heightened when a supervisor is instructed to describe specific points about the employee's promotability, special talents, skills, strengths, and weaknesses. A major limitation of the essay method is that composing an essay that attempts to cover all of an employee's essential characteristics is a very time-consuming task (though when combined with other methods, this method does not require a lengthy statement). Another disadvantage of the essay method is that the quality of the performance appraisal may be influenced by the supervisor's writing skills and composition style. Good writers may simply be able to produce more-favorable appraisals. A final drawback of this appraisal method is that it tends to be subjective and may not focus on relevant aspects of job performance.

## Behavioral Methods

As mentioned above, one of the potential drawbacks of a trait-oriented performance appraisal is that traits tend to be vague and subjective. We discussed earlier that one way to improve a rating scale is to have descriptions of behavior along a scale, or continuum. These descriptions permit the rater to readily identify the point where a particular employee falls on the scale. Behavioral methods have been developed to specifically describe which actions should (or should not) be exhibited on the job. They are frequently more useful for providing employees with developmental feedback.

### Critical Incident Method

**Critical incident**
Unusual event that denotes superior or inferior employee performance in some part of the job

The critical incident method, described in Chapter 3 in connection with job analysis, is also used as a method of appraisal. Recall that a **critical incident** occurs when employee behavior results in unusual success or unusual failure in some part of the job. A favorable critical incident is illustrated by the janitor who observed that a file cabinet containing classified documents had been left unlocked at the close of business. The janitor called the security officer, who took the necessary action to correct the problem. An unfavorable incident is illustrated by the mail clerk who failed to deliver an Express Mail package immediately, instead putting it in with regular mail to be routed two hours later. One advantage of the critical incident method is that it covers the entire appraisal period (and therefore may guard against recency error). And because the behavioral incidents are specific, they can facilitate employee feedback and development. However, unless both favorable and unfavorable incidents are discussed, employees who are appraised may have negative feelings about this method. Some employees have been known to refer to it as the "little black book" approach. Perhaps its greatest contribution is in developing job specifications and in constructing other types of appraisal procedures. (See below.)

### Behavioral Checklist Method

One of the oldest appraisal techniques is the behavioral checklist method. It consists of having the rater check those statements on a list that the rater believes are characteristic of the employee's performance or behavior. A checklist developed for computer salespersons might include a number of statements like the following:

_____ Is able to explain equipment clearly
_____ Keeps abreast of new developments in technology
_____ Tends to be a steady worker
_____ Reacts quickly to customer needs
_____ Processes orders correctly

### Behaviorally Anchored Rating Scale (BARS)

**Behaviorally anchored rating scale (BARS)**
A behavioral approach to performance appraisal that consists of a series of vertical scales, one for each important dimension of job performance

A **behaviorally anchored rating scale (BARS)** consists of a series of five to ten vertical scales—one for each important dimension of performance identified through job analysis. These dimensions are anchored by behaviors identified through a critical incidents job analysis. The critical incidents are placed along the scale and are assigned point values according to the opinions of experts. A BARS for the job of firefighter is shown in Highlights in HRM 4. Note that this particular scale is for the dimension described as "Firefighting Strategy: Knowledge of Fire Characteristics."

A BARS is typically developed by a committee that includes both subordinates and managers.[37] The committee's task is to identify all the relevant characteristics or dimensions of the job. Behavioral anchors in the form of statements are then established for each of the job dimensions. Several participants are asked to review the anchor statements and indicate which job dimension each anchor illustrates. The only anchors retained are those which at least 70 percent of the group agree belong with a particular dimension. Finally, anchors are attached to their job dimensions and placed on the appropriate scales according to values that the group assigns to them.

**⌁USING THE INTERNET**

Historical background concerning the development of BARS can be found at:

wissago.uwex.edu/test/joe/1987winter/a5.html

At present there is no strong evidence that a BARS reduces all of the rating errors mentioned previously. However, some studies have shown that scales of this type can yield more-accurate ratings.[38] One major advantage of a BARS is that personnel outside of the HR department participate with HR staff in its development. Employee participation can lead to greater acceptance of the performance appraisal process and of the performance measures that it uses.

The procedures followed in developing a BARS also result in scales that have a high degree of content validity. The main disadvantage of a BARS is that it requires considerable time and effort to develop. In addition, because the scales are specific to particular jobs, a scale designed for one job may not apply to another.

### Behavior Observation Scales (BOS)

**Behavior observation scale (BOS)**
A behavioral approach to performance appraisal that measures the frequency of observed behavior

A **behavior observation scale (BOS)** is similar to a BARS in that they are both based on critical incidents. However, Highlights in HRM 5 shows that rather than asking the evaluator to choose the most representative behavioral anchor, a BOS is designed to measure how frequently each of the behaviors has been observed.

The value of a BOS is that this approach allows the appraiser to play the role of observer rather than of judge. In this way, he or she may more easily provide constructive feedback to the employee. Companies such as AT&T, Weyerhauser, and Dayton-Hudson have used the BOS, and research shows that users of the system frequently prefer it over the BARS or trait scales for (1) maintaining objectivity,

HRM 4

**HIGHLIGHTS IN HRM**

# Example of a BARS for Municipal Fire Companies

*FIREFIGHTING STRATEGY: Knowledge of Fire Characteristics.* This area of performance concerns the ability of a firefighter to use his or her knowledge of fire characteristics to develop the best strategy for fighting a fire. It involves the following activities: Observe fire and smoke conditions and locate source of fire. Size up fire and identify appropriate extinguishing techniques and ventilation procedures. Consult preplan reports. Apply knowledge of heat and fluid mechanics to anticipate fire behavior. Identify and screen or saturate potential exposures using direct or fog streams or water curtains. Identify and remove or protect flammable or hazardous materials.

| | | |
|---|---|---|
| HIGH | 7 | |
| | 6 | —Finds the fire when no one else can |
| | | —Correctly assesses best point of entry for fighting fire |
| | | —Uses type of smoke as indicator of type of fire |
| | 5 | |
| | | —Understands basic hydraulics |
| AVERAGE | 4 | |
| | 3 | —Cannot tell the type of fire by observing the color of flame |
| | | —Cannot identify location of the fire |
| | 2 | |
| | | —Will not change firefighting strategy in spite of flashbacks and other signs that accelerants are present |
| LOW | 1 | |

Source: Adapted from Landy, Jacobs, and Associates. Reprinted with permission.

(2) distinguishing good from poor performers, (3) providing feedback, and (4) identifying training needs.[39]

## Results Methods

Rather than looking at the traits of employees or the behaviors they exhibit on the job, many organizations evaluate employee accomplishments—the results they achieve through their work. Advocates of results appraisals argue that they are more objective and empowering for employees. Looking at results such as sales figures, production output, and the like involves less subjectivity and therefore may be less open to bias. Furthermore, results appraisals often give employees responsibility for their outcomes, while giving them discretion over the methods they use to accomplish them (within limits). This is empowerment in action.

# Sample Items from Behavior Observation Scales

**INSTRUCTIONS:** Please consider the Sales Representative's behavior on the job in the past rating period. Read each statement carefully, then circle the number that indicates the extent to which the employee has demonstrated this *effective* or *ineffective* behavior. For each behavior observed, use the following scale:

5 represents *almost always*      95–100% of the time
4 represents *frequently*         85–94% of the time
3 represents *sometimes*          75–84% of the time
2 represents *seldom*             65–74% of the time
1 represents *almost never*       0–64% of the time

| SALES PRODUCTIVITY | ALMOST NEVER | | | | ALMOST ALWAYS |
|---|---|---|---|---|---|
| 1. Reviews individual productivity results with manager | 1 | 2 | 3 | 4 | 5 |
| 2. Suggests to peers ways of building sales | 1 | 2 | 3 | 4 | 5 |
| 3. Formulates specific objectives for each contact | 1 | 2 | 3 | 4 | 5 |
| 4. Focuses on product rather than customer problem | 1 | 2 | 3 | 4 | 5 |
| 5. Keeps account plans updated | 1 | 2 | 3 | 4 | 5 |
| 6. Keeps customer waiting for service | 1 | 2 | 3 | 4 | 5 |
| 7. Anticipates and prepares for customer concerns | 1 | 2 | 3 | 4 | 5 |
| 8. Follows up on customer leads | 1 | 2 | 3 | 4 | 5 |

## *Productivity Measures*

There are a number of results measures available to evaluate performance. Salespeople are evaluated on the basis of their sales volume (both the number of units sold and the dollar amount in revenues). Production workers are evaluated on the basis of the number of units they produce and perhaps the scrap rate or number of defects that are detected. Executives are frequently evaluated on the basis of company profits or growth rate. Each of these measures directly links what employees accomplish and results that benefit the organization. In this way, results appraisals can directly align employee and organizational goals.

But there are some problems with results appraisals. First, recall our earlier discussion of criteria contamination. Results appraisals may be contaminated by external factors that employees cannot influence. Sales representatives who have extremely bad markets or production employees who can't get the materials will not be able to perform up to their abilities. It may be unfair to hold these employees accountable for results that are contaminated by circumstances beyond their control.

Furthermore, results appraisals may inadvertently encourage employees to "look good" on a short-term basis, while ignoring the long-term ramifications. Line supervisors, for example, may let their equipment suffer to reduce maintenance costs. If the appraisal focuses on a narrow set of results criteria to the exclusion of other important process issues, the system may suffer from criterion deficiency and may unintentionally foster the attitude that "what gets measured gets done." In fact, in any job involving interaction with others, it is not enough to simply look at production or sales figures. Factors such as cooperation, adaptability, initiative, and concern for human relations may be important to job success. If these factors are important job standards, they should be added to the appraisal review. Thus, to be realistic, both the results and the methods or processes used to achieve them should be considered.[40]

## Management by Objectives

**Management by objectives (MBO)**

Philosophy of management that rates performance on the basis of employee achievement of goals set by mutual agreement of employee and manager

One method that attempts to overcome some of the limitations of results appraisals is **management by objectives (MBO).** MBO is a philosophy of management first proposed by Peter Drucker in 1954 that has employees establish objectives (e.g., production costs, sales per product, quality standards, profits) through consultation with their superiors and then uses these objectives as a basis for evaluation.[41] MBO is a system involving a cycle (Figure 8.6) that begins with setting the organization's common goals and objectives and ultimately returns to that step. The system acts as a goal-setting process whereby objectives are established for the organization (step 1), departments (step 2), and individual managers and employees (step 3).

As Figure 8.6 illustrates, a significant feature of the cycle is the establishment of specific goals by the employee, but those goals are based on a broad statement of

**FIGURE 8.6** ▸ **Performance Appraisal under an MBO Program**

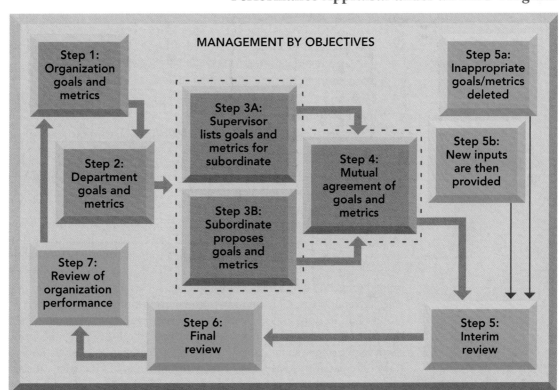

**MANAGEMENT BY OBJECTIVES**

Step 1: Organization goals and metrics

Step 2: Department goals and metrics

Step 3A: Supervisor lists goals and metrics for subordinate

Step 3B: Subordinate proposes goals and metrics

Step 4: Mutual agreement of goals and metrics

Step 5a: Inappropriate goals/metrics deleted

Step 5b: New inputs are then provided

Step 5: Interim review

Step 6: Final review

Step 7: Review of organization performance

employee responsibilities prepared by the supervisor. Employee-established goals are discussed with the supervisor and jointly reviewed and modified until both parties are satisfied with them (step 4). The goal statements are accompanied by a detailed account of the actions the employee proposes to take in order to reach the goals. During periodic reviews, as objective data are made available, the progress that the employee is making toward the goals is then assessed (step 5). Goals may be changed at this time as new or additional data are received. At the conclusion of a period of time (usually six months or one year), the employee makes a self-appraisal of what she or he has accomplished, substantiating the self-appraisal with factual data wherever possible. The "interview" is an examination of the employee's self-appraisal by the supervisor and the employee together (step 6). The final step (step 7) is reviewing the connection between individual and organizational performance.

To ensure success, MBO programs should be viewed as part of a total system for managing, not as merely an addition to the manager's job. Managers must be willing to empower employees to accomplish their objectives on their own, giving them discretion over the methods they use (but holding them accountable for outcomes). The following guidelines may be especially helpful:

1. Managers and employees must be willing to establish goals and objectives together. Goal setting has been shown to improve employee performance, typically ranging from 10 to 25 percent. Goal setting works because it helps employees to focus on important tasks and makes them accountable for completing these tasks. It also establishes an automatic feedback system that aids learning, since employees can regularly evaluate their performance against their goals. [42]

2. Objectives should be quantifiable and measurable for the long and short term. However, goal statements should be accompanied by a description of how that goal will be accomplished.

3. Expected results must be under the employee's control. Recall our early discussion of criterion contamination.

4. Goals and objectives must be consistent for each level (top executive, manager, and employee).

5. Managers and employees must establish specific times when goals are to be reviewed and evaluated.

Highlights in HRM 6 presents the goal-setting worksheet used by Universal Service Corporation. Note that this worksheet contains sections for the setting of goals and the evaluation of goal achievement.

MBO is used extensively in the "Big Five" public accounting firms (Arthur Andersen, Ernst & Young, Pricewaterhouse Coopers, Deloitte & Touche, and KPMG). The systems are typically designed to help situate partners' actions in the larger context of the organization as a whole. By arranging firm, office, and individual goals into a hierarchical structure, each partner's objectives are nested in the firm's overall plans. Consistent with the prescriptions of MBO advocates, periodic counseling sessions are held between supervisors and subordinates to discuss areas for performance improvement. In most cases, the MBO programs are integrated with mentoring systems as well. In addition, companies such as Roberts Express have integrated their MBO systems with measures of customer satisfaction, providing yet another means by which to merge TQM initiatives with MBO. [43]

**HRM 6**

# Example of a Goal-Setting Worksheet

**UNIVERSAL SERVICE CORPORATION**

Employee's Rating Record

Name                                                    Date

Job Title                                               Department

Appraised by                                            Date Started

*Summary of Appraisal*

*Development Needs*

| Major Responsibilities and Period Goals | Evaluation of Attainment Goals |
|---|---|
| Responsibility | |
| Goal | |
| Responsibility | |
| Goal | |
| Responsibility | |
| Goal | |

## Which Performance Appraisal Method to Use?

The choice of method should be based largely on the purpose of the appraisal. Figure 8.7 lists some of the strengths and weaknesses of trait, behavior, and results approaches to appraisal. Note that the simplest and least expensive techniques often yield the least-accurate information. However, research has not always supported a clear choice among appraisal methods.[44] While researchers and HR managers generally believe that the more sophisticated and more time-consuming methods offer more useful information, this may not always be the case. Managers must make cost-benefit decisions about which methods to use.

The bigger picture here focuses on *how* the performance appraisal systems are used. Having a first-rate method does no good if the manager simply "shoves it in

**FIGURE 8.7**

Summary of Various Appraisal Methods

|  | ADVANTAGES | DISADVANTAGES |
|---|---|---|
| **Trait Methods** | 1. Are inexpensive to develop | 1. Have high potential for rating errors |
|  | 2. Use meaningful dimensions | 2. Are not useful for employee counseling |
|  | 3. Are easy to use | 3. Are not useful for allocating rewards |
|  |  | 4. Are not useful for promotion decisions |
| **Behavioral Methods** | 1. Use specific performance dimensions | 1. Can be time-consuming to develop/use |
|  | 2. Are acceptable to employees and superiors | 2. Can be costly to develop |
|  | 3. Are useful for providing feedback | 3. Have some potential for rating error |
|  | 4. Are fair for reward and promotion decisions |  |
| **Results Methods** | 1. Have less subjectivity bias | 1. Are time-consuming to develop/use |
|  | 2. Are acceptable to employees and superiors | 2. May encourage short-term perspective |
|  | 3. Link individual performance to organizational performance | 3. May use contaminated criteria |
|  | 4. Encourage mutual goal setting | 4. May use deficient criteria |
|  | 5. Are good for reward and promotion decisions |  |

a drawer." Alternatively, even a rudimentary system, when used properly, can initiate a discussion between managers and employees that genuinely drives superior performance. These issues are discussed next under the topic of performance appraisal interviews.

# Appraisal Interviews

OBJECTIVE 5

The appraisal interview is perhaps the most important part of the entire performance appraisal process. The appraisal interview gives a manager the opportunity to discuss a subordinate's performance record and to explore areas of possible improvement and growth. It also provides an opportunity to identify the subordinate's attitudes and feelings more thoroughly and thus to improve communication.

Unfortunately, the interviewer can become overburdened by attempting to discuss too much, such as the employee's past performance and future development goals. Dividing the appraisal interview into two sessions, one for the performance review and the other for the employee's growth plans, can alleviate time pressures. Moreover, by separating the interview into two sessions, the interviewer can give each session the proper attention it deserves. It can be difficult for a supervisor to perform the role of both evaluator and counselor in the same review period. Dividing the sessions may also improve communication between the parties, thereby reducing stress and defensiveness.

The format for the appraisal interview will be determined in large part by the purpose of the interview, the type of appraisal system used, and the organization of the interview form. Most appraisal interviews attempt to give feedback to employees on how well they are performing their jobs and on planning for their future development. Interviews should be scheduled far enough in advance to allow the interviewee, as well as the interviewer, to prepare for the discussion. Usually ten days to two weeks is a sufficient amount of lead time.

## Three Types of Appraisal Interviews

The individual who has probably studied different approaches to performance appraisal interviews most thoroughly is Norman R. F. Maier. In his classic book, *The Appraisal Interview,* he analyzes the cause-and-effect relationships in three types of appraisal interviews: tell-and-sell, tell-and-listen, and problem solving.[45]

### Tell-and-Sell Interview

The skills required in the tell-and-sell interview include the ability to persuade an employee to change in a prescribed manner. This may require the development of new behaviors on the part of the employee and skillful use of motivational incentives on the part of the appraiser/supervisor.

### Tell-and-Listen Interview

In the tell-and-listen interview the skills required include the ability to communicate the strong and weak points of an employee's job performance during the first part of the interview. During the second part of the interview, the employee's feelings about the appraisal are thoroughly explored. The supervisor is still in the role of appraiser, but the method requires listening to disagreement and coping with defensive behavior without attempting to refute any statements. The tell-and-listen method assumes that the opportunity to release frustrated feelings will help to reduce or remove those feelings.

### Problem-Solving Interview

The skills associated with the problem-solving interview are consistent with the nondirective procedures of the tell-and-listen method. Listening, accepting, and responding to feelings are essential elements of the problem-solving interview. However, this method goes beyond an interest in the employee's feelings. It seeks to stimulate growth and development in the employee by discussing the problems, needs, innovations, satisfactions, and dissatisfactions the employee has encountered on the job since the last appraisal interview. Maier recommends this method, since the objective of appraisal is normally to stimulate growth and development in the employee.

Managers should not assume that only one type of appraisal interview is appropriate for every review session. Rather, they should be able to use one or more of the interview types, depending on the topic being discussed or on the behavior of the employee being appraised. The interview should be seen as requiring a flexible approach.[46]

DILBERT reprinted by permission of United Feature Syndicate, Inc.

## Conducting the Appraisal Interview

While there are probably no hard-and-fast rules for how to conduct an appraisal interview, there are some guidelines that may increase the employee's acceptance of the feedback, satisfaction with the interview, and intention to improve in the future. Many of the principles of effective interviewing discussed in Chapter 5 apply to performance appraisal interviews as well. Here are some other guidelines that should also be considered.

### Ask for a Self-Assessment

As noted earlier in the chapter, it is useful to have employees evaluate their own performance prior to the appraisal interview. Even if this information is not used formally, the self-appraisal starts the employee thinking about his or her accomplishments. Self-appraisal also ensures that the employee knows against what criteria he or she is being evaluated, thus eliminating any potential surprises.

Recent research evidence suggests that employees are more satisfied and view the appraisal system as providing more *procedural justice* when they have input into the process. When the employee has evaluated his or her own performance, the interview can be used to discuss those areas where the manager and the employee have reached different conclusions—not so much to resolve the "truth," but to work toward a resolution of problems.[47]

### Invite Participation

The core purpose of a performance appraisal interview is to initiate a dialogue that will help an employee improve her or his performance. To the extent that an employee is an active participant in that discussion, the more likely it is that the root causes and obstacles to performance will be uncovered, and the more likely it is that constructive ideas for improvement will be raised. In addition, research evidence suggests that participation is strongly related to an employee's satisfaction with the appraisal feedback, the extent to which the employee believes it is fair and useful, as well as her or his intention to improve performance.[48] As a rule of thumb, supervisors should spend only about 30 to 35 percent of the time talking during the interview. The rest of the time they should be listening to employees respond to questions.

### Express Appreciation

Praise is a powerful motivator, and in an appraisal interview, particularly, employees are seeking positive feedback. It is frequently beneficial to start the appraisal interview by expressing appreciation for what the employee has done well. In this way, he or she may be less defensive and more likely to talk about aspects of the job that are not going so well. However, try to avoid obvious use of the "sandwich technique" in which positive statements are followed by negative ones, which are then followed by positive statements. This approach may not work for several reasons. Praise often alerts the employee that criticism will be coming. Positive comments following the criticism then suggest to the employee that no more negative comments will come for a while. If managers follow an appraisal form, the problem of the sandwich technique will oftentimes be avoided. Furthermore, if employees are kept informed of their behavior on a regular basis, there will be no need for this appraisal technique to be used.

### Minimize Criticism

Employees who have a good relationship with their managers may be able to handle criticism better than those who do not. However, even the most stoic employees can absorb only so much criticism before they start to get defensive. If an employee has many areas in need of improvement, managers should focus on those few objective issues that are most problematic or most important to the job. Some tips for using criticism constructively include the following:

- *Consider whether it is really necessary.* Frustration with performance problems sometimes leads to criticism that is little more than a manager "letting off steam." Make certain that the criticism focuses on a recurrent problem or a consistent pattern of behavior.
- *Don't exaggerate.* Even managers who dislike criticizing may find that, once they get started, they tend to overdo it. Sometimes we overstate problems in order to be convincing or to demonstrate our concern. Try to keep criticism simple, factual, and to the point. Avoid using terms like "always," "completely," or "never."
- *Make improvement your goal.* "Laying it on the line" is not likely to be useful unless it clarifies a path to improved performance. Criticism needs to be complemented with managerial support. This point is elaborated upon below.[49]

### Change the Behavior, not the Person

Managers frequently try to play psychologist, to "figure out" why an employee has acted a certain way. However, when dealing with a problem area, in particular, remember that it is not the person who is bad, but the actions exhibited on the job.

Avoid suggestions about personal traits to change; instead suggest more acceptable ways of performing. For example, instead of focusing on a person's "unreliability," a manager might focus on the fact that the employee "has been late to work seven times this month." It is difficult for employees to change who they are; it is usually much easier for them to change how they act.

### Focus on Solving Problems

In addressing performance issues, it is frequently tempting to get into the "blame game" in which both manager and employee enter into a potentially endless discussion of why a situation has arisen. Frequently, solving problems requires an analysis of the causes, but ultimately the appraisal interview should be directed at devising a solution to the problem.

### Be Supportive

One of the better techniques for engaging an employee in the problem-solving process is for the manager to ask, "What can I do to help?" Employees frequently attribute performance problems to either real or perceived obstacles (such as bureaucratic procedures or inadequate resources). By being open and supportive, the manager conveys to the employee that he or she will try to eliminate external roadblocks and will work with the employee to achieve higher standards.

### Establish Goals

Since a major purpose of the appraisal interview is to make plans for improvement, it is important to focus the interviewee's attention on the future rather than the past. In setting goals with an employee, the manager should observe the following points:

- Emphasize strengths on which the employee can build rather than weaknesses to overcome.
- Concentrate on opportunities for growth that exist within the framework of the employee's present position.
- Limit plans for growth to a few important items that can be accomplished within a reasonable period of time.
- Establish specific action plans that spell out how each goal will be achieved. These action plans may also include a list of contacts, resources, and timetables for follow-up.

### Follow Up Day to Day

Ideally, performance feedback should be an ongoing part of a manager's job. Feedback is most useful when it is immediate and specific to a particular situation. Unfortunately, both managers and employees are frequently happy to finish the interview and file away the appraisal form. A better approach is to have informal talks periodically to follow up on the issues raised in the appraisal interview. Levi Strauss, for example, recently redesigned its performance appraisal system to explicitly include informal feedback and coaching sessions on an ongoing basis. The changes, referred to as the Partners in Performance Program, help Levi Strauss managers adopt more of a coaching role (versus that of a judge) and are designed to enhance continuous improvement and business objectives.[50]

## Improving Performance

In many instances the appraisal interview will provide the basis for noting deficiencies in employee performance and for making plans for improvement. Unless these deficiencies are brought to the employee's attention, they are likely to continue until they become quite serious. Sometimes underperformers may not understand exactly what is expected of them. However, once their responsibilities are clarified, they are in a position to take the corrective action needed to improve their performance.

### Identifying Sources of Ineffective Performance

Performance is a function of several factors, but perhaps it can be boiled down to three primary concerns: ability, motivation, and environment. Each individual has a unique pattern of strengths and weaknesses that play a part. But talented employees with low motivation are not likely to succeed. In addition, other factors in the work environment—or even in the external environment which includes personal, family, and community concerns—can impact performance either positively or negatively. Figure 8.8 may provide a better picture of how these three factors (ability, motivation, and environment) can influence performance.

It is recommended that a diagnosis of poor employee performance focus on these three interactive elements. For example, if an employee's performance is not up to standards, the cause could be a skill problem (knowledge, abilities, technical competencies), an effort problem (motivation to get the job done), and/or some problem in the external conditions of work (poor economic conditions, supply shortages, difficult sales territories).[51] Any one of these problem areas could cause performance to suffer.

**FIGURE 8.8**

**Factors That Influence Performance**

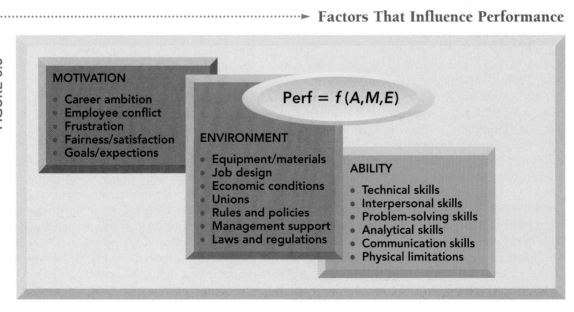

**MOTIVATION**
- Career ambition
- Employee conflict
- Frustration
- Fairness/satisfaction
- Goals/expectations

$$Perf = f(A,M,E)$$

**ENVIRONMENT**
- Equipment/materials
- Job design
- Economic conditions
- Unions
- Rules and policies
- Management support
- Laws and regulations

**ABILITY**
- Technical skills
- Interpersonal skills
- Problem-solving skills
- Analytical skills
- Communication skills
- Physical limitations

### *Managing Ineffective Performance*

Once the sources of performance problems are known, a course of action can be planned. This action may lie in providing training in areas that would increase the knowledge and/or skills needed for effective performance. A transfer to another job or department might give an employee a chance to become a more effective member of the organization. In other instances, greater attention may have to be focused on ways to motivate the individual.[52]

If ineffective performance persists, it may be necessary to transfer the employee, take disciplinary action, or discharge the person from the organization. Whatever action is taken to cope with ineffective performance, it should be done with objectivity, fairness, and a recognition of the feelings of the individual involved.

A final word of caution when it comes to managing performance problems: Research consistently shows that managers often attribute poor performance to characteristics of the individuals (ability or motivation), while employees themselves typically blame external factors for their miscues. This can establish a negative cycle if not handled properly. Managers who assume employees are not motivated or not capable may begin to treat them differently (perhaps supervising them too closely or watching for their next mistake). This can actually decrease an employee's motivation and cause him or her to withdraw. Seeing this, the manager may confirm his or her initial beliefs that the employee does not "measure up." As you can see, this "set-up-to-fail" syndrome can be self-fulfilling and self-reinforcing. It is hoped that the ideas and suggestions given in this chapter will help managers accurately identify who is performing well (and why) and give them some focus for improving employee productivity.[53]

## SUMMARY

**OBJECTIVE 1** Performance appraisal programs serve many purposes, but in general those purposes can be clustered into two categories: administrative and developmental. The administrative purposes include decisions about who will be promoted, transferred, or laid off. They can also include compensation decisions and the like. Developmental decisions include those related to improving and enhancing an individual's capabilities. These include identifying a person's strengths and weaknesses, eliminating external performance obstacles, establishing training needs, and so on. The combination of administrative and developmental purposes of performance appraisal reflect, in a specific way, human resources management's larger role of integrating the individual with the organization.

In many organizations, performance appraisals are seen as a necessary evil. Managers frequently avoid conducting appraisals because they dislike playing the role of judge. Further, if managers are not adequately trained, subjectivity and organizational politics can distort the reviews. This situation tends to be self-defeating in that such managers frequently do not develop good feedback skills and are often not prepared to conduct an appraisal. As a consequence, the appraisal is done begrudgingly once a year and then forgotten about.

**OBJECTIVE 2** The success of an organization depends largely on the performance of its human resources. To determine the contributions of each individual, it is necessary to have a formal appraisal program with clearly stated objectives. Carefully defined performance standards that are reliable, strategically relevant, and free from either criterion deficiency or contamination are essential foundations for evaluation. Appraisal systems must also comply with the law. Appraisals should be treated with the same concerns for validity as are selection tests. For example, ratings must be job-related, employees must understand their performance standards in advance, appraisers must be able to observe job performance, appraisers must be trained, feedback must be given, and an appeals procedure must be established.

 Using multiple raters is frequently a good idea because different individuals see different facets of an employee's performance. The supervisor, for example, has legitimate authority over an employee and is in a good position to discern whether he or she is contributing to the goals of the organization. Peers and team members, on the other hand, often have an unfiltered view of an employee's work activity, particularly related to issues such as co-operation and dependability. Subordinates often provide good information about whether an employee is facilitating their work, and customers (both internal and external) can convey the extent to which an employee adds value and meets their requirements. Self-appraisal is useful, if for no other reason than it encourages employees to think about their strengths, weaknesses, and future goals. An increasing number of organizations are using multiple raters—or 360-degree appraisal—to get a more comprehensive picture of employee performance. Regardless of the source of appraisal information, appraisers should be thoroughly trained in the particular methods they will use in evaluating their subordinates. Participation in developing rating scales, such as a BARS, automatically provides such training.

There are several methods that can be used for performance appraisal. These include trait approaches (such as graphic rating scales, mixed-standard scales, forced-choice forms, and essays), behavioral methods (such as critical incidents ratings, checklists, BARS, and BOS), and results methods (MBO). The choice of method depends on the purpose of the appraisal. Trait appraisals are simple to develop and complete, but they have problems in subjectivity and are not useful for feedback. Behavioral methods provide more specific information for giving feedback but can be time-consuming and costly to develop. Results appraisals are more objective and can link individual performance to the organization as a whole, but they may encourage a short-term perspective (e.g., annual goals) and may not include subtle yet important aspects of performance.

The degree to which the performance appraisal program benefits the organization and its members is directly related to the quality of the appraisal interviews that are conducted. Interviewing skills are best developed through instruction and supervised practice. Although there are various approaches to the interview, research suggests that employee participation and goal setting lead to higher satisfaction and improved performance. Discussing problems, showing support, minimizing criticism, and rewarding effective performance are also beneficial practices. In the interview, deficiencies in employee performance can be discussed and plans for improvement can be made.

## KEY TERMS

behavior observation scale (BOS)
behaviorally anchored rating scale (BARS)
contrast error
critical incident
customer appraisal
error of central tendency

essay method
forced-choice method
graphic rating-scale method
leniency or strictness error
management by objectives (MBO)
manager and/or supervisor appraisal

mixed-standard scale method
peer appraisal
recency error
self-appraisal
similar-to-me error
subordinate appraisal
team appraisal

## DISCUSSION QUESTIONS

1. What are the major purposes of performance appraisal? In what ways might these purposes be contradictory?

2. Describe the relationships among performance appraisal and selection, training, and development.

3. How can performance appraisals be adjusted to include the principles underlying total-quality management (TQM)?

 4. Describe the characteristics of the ideal appraisal system.

 5. Discuss the guidelines that performance appraisals should meet in order to be legally defensible.

 6. What sources could be used to evaluate the performance of people working in the following jobs?

   a. Sales representative
   b. TV repairer
   c. Director of nursing in a hospital
   d. HR manager
   e. Air-traffic controller

7. In many organizations, evaluators submit ratings to their immediate superiors for review before discussing them with the individual employees they have rated. What advantages are there to this procedure?

 8. What are the pros and cons of trait, behavior, and results appraisals?

 9. Three types of appraisal interviews are described in this chapter.

   a. What different skills are required for each type of appraisal interview? What reactions can one expect from using these different skills?

   b. How can one develop the skills needed for the problem-solving type of interview?

   c. Which method do you feel is the least desirable? Why?

 10. Discuss how you would diagnose poor performance. List several factors to consider.

# 360-Degree Appraisal at Johnson & Johnson

In order to provide a broader perspective for performance appraisal and encourage employee development, Johnson & Johnson Advanced Behavioral Technology (JJABT), based in Denver, Colorado, has instituted a new 360-degree feedback system. The new system allows employees to compare their own perceptions with the views of others such as superiors, peers, subordinates, and external customers.

According to company executives, the most important consideration in implementing the system is choosing the right individuals to be raters. To assemble the rating group, JJABT employees develop a list of key internal and external customers with whom they interact and then recommend five to ten individuals to serve as raters. Each employee's supervisor still has the ultimate responsibility for the appraisal and ensures that the appropriate raters are selected. This helps prevent ratees from stacking the deck with supportive customers or colleagues who will give high ratings.

Once managers decide who will do the rating, the criteria by which the ratee will be evaluated are made clear. Since the supervisor is most aware of the ratee's individual work tasks and goals, the various raters ideally evaluate the ratee only on the behaviors or work incidents that they have directly observed. The JJABT 360-degree appraisal form includes items such as

Does the employee

- Follow up on problems, decisions, and requests in a timely fashion?
- Clearly communicate his or her needs/expectations?
- Share information or help others?
- Listen to others?
- Establish plans to meet future needs?
- Adhere to schedules?

Raters score these items on a scale ranging from 1 (needs improvement) to 5 (outstanding). Space is also provided for the raters to make written comments.

The employee's supervisor is responsible for summarizing the data and determining the final performance rating. This represents a combination of the comments and ratings from the various raters and the supervisor's own feedback on the ratee's performance. Typically, managers include a mean score and distribution range for each item.

On the basis of the company's experience so far, it seems clear that feedback can't always be taken at face value. For instance, care must be exercised when one rater has given highly negative or positive feedback. JJABT managers stress that the key is to look for trends or patterns in the data. If there are questions or ambiguities in the raters' feedback, supervisors will often solicit additional feedback from the same or new raters. After summarizing the data, the supervisor conducts the formal appraisal interview with the ratee.

To ensure fairness, raters are provided the option of being anonymous or open in their feedback. If the rater requests anonymity, then the supervisor must not reveal his or her identity to the ratee when discussing the performance review. However, if the rater is willing to be open, then the supervisor may refer the ratee with questions about his or her feedback to the rater. In this way, it is hoped that the 360-degree appraisal can become less an evaluative tool and more a comprehensive system for enhancing communication, facilitating self-development, and improving performance.

Source: John F. Milliman, Robert A. Zawacki, Carol Norman, Lynda Powell, and Jay Kirksey, "Companies Evaluate Employees from All Perspectives," *Personnel Journal*, November 1994, 99–103. Printed with permission of *Personnel Journal*.

### QUESTIONS

1. What are the advantages and disadvantages of Johnson & Johnson's 360-degree appraisal?
2. Do you think the rating system is useful? How might you suggest improving it?
3. What are your views on the anonymity issue? Should raters be encouraged to be open? Explain.

## How Does the Bank of Montreal Keep Score on Success?

In 1990, when Matthew W. Barrett became Bank of Montreal's chairman and Tony Comper became president, they had one major goal: To focus the entire workforce on success. It's a simple idea, but not so easy in execution. How would they get entry-level tellers to think of their work not just as a means to a paycheck, but as a direct contribution to BMO shareholders? How would they remind corporate executives that their jobs were not just to boost the bottom line, but to charm entire communities?

The answer was what BMO executives call a balanced scorecard approach. To be competitive, executives decided, the bank had to meet the needs of four stakeholders: BMO shareholders, customers, employees, and communities. Executives translated that idea into four goals: Shareholders needed a return on equity, customers needed good service, employees needed to feel loyal and satisfied, and communities needed to feel the bank made a difference in their neighborhoods. Return on investment would determine satisfaction for shareholders; surveys and feedback would determine satisfaction for customers, employees, and communities.

So far, so good, but every single department and every employee in every department had to understand how their work contributed to the success of those four goals. So each employee's and each department's performance ratings now are dependent on their contribution toward each goal. Employees in the customer-service department, for instance, are rated by their return on equity (judged by their cost-effectiveness), their customer satisfaction (judged by customer feed-back), and their community involvement (judged by any outreach programs or increase in customers).

Departments may be assigned a specific stakeholder. HR is in charge of the employee piece, ensuring competent, committed workers in a cost-effective way. Harriet Stairs, senior vice president of HR, uses training and education to ensure competency and work/life and career-development programs to help commitment. Knowing she's rated on the cost-effectiveness of all this, she also keeps her eye on the price tag. "It encourages everyone to do his or her job with the exact same issues in mind," Stairs says.

At the end of the year, the scores from everyone's performance ratings are trans-lated into indexes, ratings from 1 to 10. The index for the employee stakeholder piece would be determined by ratings for competency, commitment, and cost-effectiveness. The four indexes for BMO shareholders, customers, employees, and communities are then rolled up into one figure of merit. At the end of each year, Barrett presents this to the board of directors, who use it to determine his bonus.

### QUESTIONS

1. What are the strengths and weaknesses of a balanced scorecard approach to performance appraisal?
2. Do you think that such an approach would be integrated well with an MBO system? Why or why not?
3. Do you believe that a balanced scorecard approach would be more effective for the administrative or for the developmental purposes of appraisal discussed in this chapter?

CASE STUDY 3

## Setting Performance Standards at General Telephone Company of California

Raymond Sanchez, a new college graduate with a degree in human resources, was recently hired by General Telephone Company of California. His job assignment is as college recruiter, with the responsibility to fill entry-level supervisory positions and staff assignments in accounting, finance, data processing, and marketing. He is in charge of a recruiting schedule that includes twelve colleges and universities. Six of the schools are located in California, three in Arizona, two in Oregon, and one in Nevada.

Over the past two years, the company has made a concerted effort to develop a comprehensive and effective college recruiting program. It was decided that part of this effort should be devoted to creating a positive and continuing relationship with college placement offices, as well as with certain professors who are in a position to refer students for job openings. Establishing this relationship with the schools, which is viewed as critical for identifying and selecting high-potential employees, is Sanchez's responsibility, equally important as filling positions for General Telephone.

Daniel Turner, manager of the company's HR department, has established yearly performance standards for each of his subordinates. Company guidelines indicate that, where possible, observable and measurable performance standards should be set. Upon completing his first three months with the company, Sanchez agrees to set his performance standards with Turner for the upcoming recruitment period, although both acknowledge that setting measurable standards might be somewhat difficult because of the subjective nature of college recruiting. The job description stated only that the person who held the position should develop and maintain rapport with the colleges and universities, that openings should be filled in a timely manner, and that college graduates selected for company interviews should be of high quality. (The company's annual HR planning schedule, listing the types and numbers of college graduates needed by each department and operating area, is completed by December of each year, and managers requesting new graduates state on the employment requisition form the date by which the positions are to be filled.)

Now Turner asks Sanchez to come up with four to six observable and measurable performance standards that will capture the duties and responsibilities of the college recruiter's job.

Source: Based on an actual case known to the authors; employee names are fictitious.

### QUESTIONS

1. Develop four to six observable and measurable performance standards suitable to Sanchez's position as college recruiter.
2. Discuss any obstacles that might make this task difficult.

## NOTES AND REFERENCES

1. Brian D. Cawley, Lisa M. Keeping, and Paul E. Levy, "Participation in the Performance Appraisal Process and Employee Reactions: A Meta-Analytic Review of Field Investigations," *Journal of Applied Psychology* 83, no. 4 (August 1998): 615–33; Mike Deblieux, "Encouraging Great Performance," *HRFocus* 75, no. 1 (January 1998): 13; Birgit Benkhoff, "Ignoring Commitment Is Costly: New Approaches Establish the Missing Link between Commitment and Performance," *Human Relations* 50, no. 6 (June 1997): 701–26.

2. Philip Schofield, "Do Appraisals Need Review?" *Works Management* 52, no. 2 (February 1999): 24–26; Marilyn Moats Kennedy. "The Case against Performance Appraisals," *Across the Board* 36, no. 1 (January 1999): 51–52; Gillian Flynn, "Employee Evaluations Get So-So Grades," *Personnel Journal* 74, no. 6 (June 1995): 21–23.

3. For recent work on performance appraisal and TQM, see Simon S. K. Lam and John Schaubroeck, "Total Quality Management and Performance Appraisal: An Experimental Study of Process versus Results and Group versus Individual Approaches," *Journal of Organizational Behavior* 20, no. 4 (July 1999): 445–57; Allan J. Weber, "Making Performance Appraisals Consistent with a Quality Environment," *Quality Progress* 28, no. 6 (June 1995): 65–69; Jai Ghorpade, Milton M. Chen, and Joseph Caggiano, "Creating Quality-Driven Performance Appraisal Systems: Executive Commentary," *Academy of Management Executive* 9, no. 1 (February 1995): 32–41.

4. Ann Monroe, "Compensation: How Merrill Rewards Its Team Players," *Investment Dealers Digest* 62, no. 22 (May 27, 1996): 15; Nancy K. Austin, "It's Time for Your Review," *Incentive* 168, no. 3 (March 1994): 19.

5. Matt Bloom, "The Performance Effects of Pay Dispersion on Individuals and Organizations," *Academy of Management Journal* 42, no. 1 (February 1999): 25–40; Donald J. Campbell, Kathleen M. Campbell, and Ho-Beng Chia, "Merit Pay, Performance Appraisal, and Individual Motivation: An Analysis and Alternative," *Human Resource Management* 37, no. 2 (Summer 1998): 131–46; Robert H. Woods, Michael Sciarini, and Deborah Breiter, "Performance Appraisals in Hotels," *Cornell Hotel and Restaurant Administration Quarterly* 39, no. 2 (April 1998): 25–29.

6. Jon Younger and Kurt Sandholtz, "Helping R & D Professionals Build Successful Careers," *Research Technology Management* 40, no. 6 (November/December 1997): 23–28; Thomas W. Jones, "Performance Management in a Changing Context: Monsanto Pioneers a Competency-Based Developmental Approach," *Human Resource Management* 34, no. 3 (Fall 1995): 425–42; "Performance Management: What's Hot—What's Not," *Compensation and Benefits Review* 26, no. 3 (May/June 1994): 71–75.

7. Ronald J. Deluga, "The Quest for Justice on the Job: Essays and Experiments," *Journal of Occupational and Organizational Psychology* 72, no. 1 (March 1999): 122–24; Cawley, Keeping, and Levy, "Participation in the Performance Appraisal Process."

8. Robert Bookman, "Tools for Cultivating Constructive Feedback," *Association Management* 51, no. 2 (February 1999): 73–79; Clinton O. Longnecker and Dennis A. Gioia, "The Politics of Executive Appraisals," *Journal of Compensation and Benefits* 10, no. 2 (September/October 1994): 5–11; Aharon Tziner, Gary P. Latham, Bruce S. Price, and Robert Haccoun, "Development and Validation of a Questionnaire for Measuring Perceived Political Considerations in Performance Appraisal," *Journal of Organizational Behavior* 17, no. 2 (March 1996): 179–90.

9. David C. Martin and Kathryn M. Bartol, "Performance Appraisal: Maintaining System Effectiveness," *Public Personnel Management* 27, no. 2 (Summer 1998): 223–30; William H. Bommer, Jonathan L. Johnson, Gregory A. Rich, Philip M. Podsakoff, and Scott B. Mackenzie, "On the Interchangeability of Objective and Subjective Measures of Employee Performance: A Meta-Analysis," *Personnel Psychology* 48, no. 3 (Autumn 1995): 587–605.

10. "Strategic Planning Viewed from the Bottom Up," *The Futurist* 32, no. 4 (May 1998): 46; Anthony Johnson, "Performance Monitoring and Policy-Making: Making Effective Use of Evaluation Strategies," *Total Quality Management* 9, nos. 2/3 (May 1998): 259–67; Tracy B. Weiss and Franklin Hartle, *Reengineering Performance Management: Breakthroughs in Achieving Strategy Through People* (Winter Park, FL: St. Lucie Press, 1997); Milan Moravec, Ron Juliff, and Kathleen Hesler, "Partnerships Help a Company Manage Performance," *Personnel Journal,* January 1995, 104–8.

11. Gregory D. Streib and Theodore H. Poister, "Assessing the Validity, Legitimacy, and Functionality of Performance Measurement Systems in Municipal Governments," *American Review of Public Administration* 29, no. 2 (June 1999): 107–23; Margaret A. McManus and Steven H. Brown, "Adjusting Sales Results Measures for Use as Criteria," *Personnel Psychology* 48, no. 2 (Summer 1995): 391–400.

12. *Brito v Zia Company,* 478 F.2d 1200 (10th. Cir. 1973).

13. *Albemarle Paper Company v Moody,* 422 U.S. 405 (1975).

14. Jon M. Werner and Mark C. Bolino, "Explaining U.S. Courts of Appeals Decisions Involving Performance Appraisal: Accuracy, Fairness, and Validation," *Personnel Psychology* 50, no. 1 (Sprint 1997): 1–24; Jilly Welch, "Intel Faces Fight over Termination Quotas," *People Management* 3, no. 13 (June 26, 1997): 9. For a review of other performance appraisal court cases, see Clinton O. Longnecker and Frederick R. Post, "Effective and Legally Defensible Performance Appraisals," *Journal of Compensation and Benefits* 11, no. 6 (May/June 1996): 41–46.

15. Werner and Bolino, "Explaining U.S. courts of appeals decisions"; "Legalities of Documenting Performance," *Credit Union Executive* 35, no. 6 (November/December 1995): 11–12; John Edward Davidson, "The Temptation of Performance Appraisal Abuse in Employment Litigation," *Virginia Law Review* 81, no. 6 (September 1995): 1605–29. For an informative video on performance appraisal issues in the courtroom, see *The Legal Side of Performance Appraisal: You Be the Judge,* produced by the Bureau of Business Practice (24 Hope Road, Waterford, Conn. 06386).

16. Clive Fletcher, "The Implication of Research on Gender Differences in Self-Assessment and 360 Degree Appraisal," *Human Resource Management Journal* 9, no. 1 (1999): 39–46; David A. Waldman and David E. Bowen, "The Acceptability of 360 Degree Appraisals: A Customer-Supplier Relationship Perspective," *Human Resource Management* 37, no. 2 (Summer 1998):117–29; James M. Conway, "Analysis and Design of Multitrait-Multirater Performance Appraisal Studies," *Journal of Management* 22, no. 1 (1996): 139–62.

17. Adrian Furnham and Paul Stringfield, "Congruence in Job-Performance Ratings: A Study of 360 Degree Feedback Examining Self, Manager, Peers, and Consultant Ratings," *Human Relations* 51, no. 4 (April

1998): 517–30; Shaul Fox, Tamir Caspy, and Avner Reisler, "Variables Affecting Leniency, Halo, and Validity of Self Appraisal," *Journal of Occupational and Organizational Psychology* 67, no. 1 (March 1994): 45–56; Paul E. Levy, "Self-Appraisal and Attributions: A Test of a Model," *Journal of Management* 19 (Spring 1993): 51–62.

18.  Jerrell D. Coggburn, "Subordinate Appraisals of Managers: Lessons from a State Agency," *Review of Public Personnel Administration* 18, no. 1 (Winter 1998): 68–79; Stephanie Gruner, "Turning the Tables," *Inc.* 18, no. 6 (May 1996): 87–89; David Littlefield, "Halifax Employees to Assess Management," *People Management* 2, no. 3 (February 8, 1996): 5.

19.  Alan G. Walker and James W. Smither, "A Five-Year Study of Upward Feedback: What Managers Do with Their Results Matters," *Personnel Psychology* 52, no. 2 (Summer 1999): 393–423; Michael K. Mount, Timothy A. Judge, Steven E. Scullen, Marcia R. Sytsma, and Sarah A. Hezlett, "Trait, Rater and Level Effects in 360-Degree Performance Ratings," *Personnel Psychology* 51, no. 3 (Autumn 1998): 557–76.

20.  Donald B. Fedor, Kenneth L. Bettenhausen, and Walter Davis, "Peer Reviews: Employees' Dual Roles as Raters and Recipients," *Group & Organization Management* 24, no. 1 (March 1999): 92–120.

21.  Vanessa Urch Druskat and Steven B. Wolff, "Effects and Timing of Developmental Peer Appraisals in Self-Managing Work Groups," *Journal of Applied Psychology* 84, no. 1 (February 1999): 58–74; Kenneth L. Bettenhausen and Donald B. Fedor, "Peer and Upward Appraisals: A Comparison of Their Benefits and Problems," *Group & Organization Management* 22, no. 2 (June 1997): 236–63.

22.  Michael M. Beyerlein, Douglas A. Johnson, and Susan T. Beyerlein, *Advances in Interdisciplinary Studies of Work Teams*, Vol. 4 (Greenwich, Conn: JAI Press, 1997); Dale E. Yeatts, Martha Hipskind, and Debra Barnes, "Lessons Learned from Self-Managed Work Teams," *Business Horizons* 37, no. 4 (July/August 1994): 11–18.

23.  Leslie B. Hammer and Karen M. Barbera, "Toward an Integration of Alternative Work," *Human Resource Planning* 20, no. 2 (1997): 28–36; Patricia K. Zingheim and Jay R. Schuster, "Supporting Teams with Multi-Rater Performance Reviews," *Compensation and Benefits Management* 11, no. 3 (Summer 1995): 41–45.

24.  Michelle A. Yakovac, "Paying for Satisfaction," *HRFocus* 73, no. 6 (June 1996): 10–11; John Milliman, Robert A. Zawacki, and Brian Schultz, "Customer Service Drives 360-Degree Goal Setting," *Personnel Journal* 74, no. 6 (June 1995): 136–42; Margaret

Kaeter, "Driving toward Sales and Satisfaction," *Training,* August 1990, 19–22.

25.  George Eckes, "Practical Alternatives to Performance Appraisals," *Quality Progress* 27, no. 11 (November 1994): 57–60; James P. Muuss, "Security and the Surrogate Shopper," *Security Management* 39, no. 12 (December 1995): 55–57. Benjamin Schneider, Paul J. Hanges, and Harold W. Goldstein, "Do Customer Service Perceptions Generalize? The Case of Student and Chair Ratings of Faculty Effectiveness," *Journal of Applied Psychology* 27, no. 4 (April 1994): 65–69.

26.  David W. Bracken, Lynn Summers, and John Fleenor, "High-Tech 360," *Training and Development* 52, no. 8 (Aug 1998): 42–45.

27.  David A. Waldman, Leanne E. Atwater, and David Antonioni, "Has 360 Feedback Gone Amok?" *Academy of Management Executive* 12, no. 2 (May 1998): 86–94; David Antonioni, "Designing an Effective 360-Degree Appraisal Feedback Process," *Organizational Dynamics* 25, no. 2 (Autumn 1996): 24–38.

28.  Gary E. Roberts, "Perspectives on Enduring and Emerging Issues in Performance Appraisal," *Public Personnel Management* 27, no. 3 (Fall 1998): 301–20; William Hubbartt, "Bring Performance Appraisal Training to Life," *HRMagazine* 40, no. 5 (May 1995): 166, 168.

29.  Gary P. Latham and Kenneth N. Wexley, *Increasing Productivity through Performance Appraisal,* 2d ed. (Reading, Mass.: Addison-Wesley, 1994), 137.

30.  Andrew L. Solomonson and Charles E. Lance, "Examination of the Relationship between True Halo and Halo Error in Performance Ratings," *Journal of Applied Psychology* 82, no. 5 (October 1997): 665–74; Charles E. Lance, Julie A. LaPointe, and Amy M. Stewart, "A Test of the Context Dependency of Three Causal Models of Halo Rater Error," *Journal of Applied Psychology* 79, no. 3 (June 1994): 332–40; Kevin Murphy, Robert A. Jako, and Rebecca L. Anhalt, "Nature and Consequences of Halo Error: A Critical Analysis," *Journal of Applied Psychology* 78, no. 2 (April 1993): 218–25.

31.  Deidra J. Schleicher and David V. Day, "A Cognitive Evaluation of Frame-of-Reference Rater Training: Content and Process Issues," *Organizational Behavior and Human Decision Processes* 73, no. 1 (January 1998): 76–101; Jeffrey S. Kane, John H. Bernardin, Peter Villanova, and Joseph Peyrefitte, "Stability of Rater Leniency: Three Studies," *Academy of Management Journal* 38, no. 4 (August 1995): 1036–51.

32.  Kevin J. Murphy, "Performance Measurement and Appraisal: Merck Tries to Motivate Managers to Do It Right," *Employment Relations Today* 20, no. 1 (Spring 1993): 47–62. Also see Diana L. Deadrick and Donald

G. Gardner, "Distributional Ratings of Performance Levels and Variability," *Group & Organization Management* 22, no. 3 (September 1997): 317–42.

33. Sandy Wayne and Robert Liden, "Effects of Impression Management on Performance Ratings: A Longitudinal Study," *Academy of Management Journal* 38, no. 1 (February 1995): 232–60.

34. Roberts, "Perspectives on Enduring and Emerging issues"; David J. Woehr, "Understanding Frame-of-Reference Training: The Impact of Training on the Recall of Performance Information," *Journal of Applied Psychology* 79, no. 4 (August 1994): 525–34.

35. Terry Gillen, "Why Appraisal Should Climb the Skills Agenda," *People Management* 2, no. 9 (May 2, 1996): 43.

36. Stephen C. Behrenbrinker, "Conducting Productive Performance Evaluations in the Assessor's Office," *Assessment Journal* 2, no. 5 (September/October 1995): 48–54.

37. Joseph Maiorca, "How to Construct Behaviorally Anchored Rating Scales (BARS) for Employee Evaluations," *Supervision* 58, no. 8 (August 1997): 15–18; Jeffrey M. Conte, Frank J. Landy, and John E. Mathieu, "Time Urgency: Conceptual and Construct Development," *Journal of Applied Psychology* 80, no. 1 (February 1995): 178–85.

38. For a comprehensive review of the research on BARS, see Chapter 6 in H. John Bernardin and Richard W. Beatty, *Performance Appraisal: Assessing Human Behavior at Work* (Boston: Kent, 1984). Also see Latham and Wexley, *Increasing Productivity*; Kevin R. Murphy and Jeanette N. Cleveland, *Understanding Performance Appraisal* (Thousand Oaks, Calif.: Sage, 1995).

39. Latham and Wexley, *Increasing Productivity*; Aharon Tziner, Richard Kopelman, and Christine Joanis, "Investigation of Raters' and Ratees' Reactions to Three Methods of Performance Appraisal: BOS, BARS, and GRS," *Revue Canadienne des Sciences de l'Administration* 14, no. 4 (December 1997): 396–404.

40. Lam and Schaubroeck, "Total Quality Management"; James D. Van Tassel, "Death to MBO," *Training and Development* 49, no. 3 (March 1995): 2–5.

41. Peter F. Drucker, *The Practice of Management* (New York: Harper & Brothers, 1954). Reissued by HarperCollins in 1993.

42. E. Locke and G. Latham, *A Theory of Goal Setting and Task Performance* (Englewood Cliffs, N.J.: Prentice-Hall, 1990). See also John J. Donovan and David J. Radosevich, "The Moderating Role of Goal Commitment on the Goal Difficulty-Performance Relationship: A Meta-Analytic Review and Critical Reanalysis," *Journal of Applied Psychology* 83, no. 2 (April 1998): 308–15; Don Vande Walle, Steven P. Brown,

William L. Cron, and John W. Slocum Jr., "The Influence of Goal Orientation and Self-Regulation Tactics on Sales Performance: A Longitudinal Field Test," *Journal of Applied Psychology* 84, no. 2 (April 1999): 249–59.

43. Mark A. Covaleski, Mark W. Dirsmith, James B. Heian, and Sajay Samuel, "The Calculated and the Avowed: Techniques of Discipline and Struggles over Identity in Big Six Public Accounting Firms," *Administrative Science Quarterly* 43, no. 2 (June 1998): 293–327. For an example of how Roberts Express has integrated its MBO system with TQM and customer requirements, see Jack Pickard, "Motivate Employees to Delight Customers," *Transportation and Distribution* 34, no. 7 (July 1993): 48. See also Jim M. Graber, Roger E. Breisch, and Walter E. Breisch, "Performance Appraisal and Deming: A Misunderstanding?" *Quality Progress* 25, no. 6 (June 1992): 59–62; Dennis M. Daley, "Pay for Performance, Performance Appraisal, and Total Quality," *Public Productivity and Management Review* 16, no. 1 (Fall 1992): 39–51.

44. Deloris McGee Wanguri, "A Review, an Integration, and a Critique of Cross-Disciplinary Research on Performance Appraisals, Evaluations, and Feedback," *Journal of Business Communications* 32, no. 3 (July 1995): 267–93; Peter Allan, "Designing and Implementing an Effective Performance Appraisal System," *Review of Business* 16, no. 2 (Winter 1994): 3–8.

45. Norman R. F. Maier, *The Appraisal Interview* (New York: Wiley, 1958); Norman R. F. Maier, *The Appraisal Interview—Three Basic Approaches* (San Diego: University Associates, 1976).

46. John F. Kikoski, "Effective Communication in the Performance Appraisal Interview: Face-to-Face Communication for Public Managers in the Culturally Diverse Workplace," *Public Personnel Management* 28, no. 2 (Summer 1999): 301–22; Howard J. Klein and Scott A. Snell, "The Impact of Interview Process and Context on Performance Appraisal Interview Effectiveness," *Journal of Managerial Issues* 6, no. 2 (Summer 1994): 160–75.

47. David E. Bowen, Stephen W. Gilliland, and Robert Folger; "HRM and Service Fairness: How Being Fair with Employees Spills Over to Customers," *Organizational Dynamics* 27, no. 3 (Winter 1999): 7–23; Audrey M. Korsgaard and Loriann Roberson, "Procedural Justice in Performance Evaluation: The Role of Instrumental and Non-Instrumental Voice in Performance Appraisal Discussions," *Journal of Management* 21, no. 4 (1995): 657–69; Susan M. Taylor, Kay B. Tracy, Monika K. Renard, J. Kline Harrison, and Stephen J. Carroll, "Due Process in Performance Appraisal: A Quasi-Experiment in Procedural Jus-

tice," *Administrative Science Quarterly* 40, no. 3 (September 1995): 495–523.

48. Martin Geller, "Participation in the Performance Appraisal Review: Inflexible Manager Behavior and Variable Worker Needs," *Human Relations* 51, no. 8 (August 1998): 1061–83; Cawley, Keeping, and Levy, "Participation in the Performance Appraisal Process."

49. Ted Pollock, "Make Your Criticism Pay Off," *Automotive Manufacturing & Production* 110, no. 6 (June 1998): 10; Helaine Olen, "The Pitfalls of Perfectionism," *Working Woman* 21, no. 3 (March 1996): 55–57; Ted Pollock, "The Positive Power of Criticism," *Automotive Production* 108, no. 5 (May 1996): 13.

50. "Levi Strauss and Company Implements New Pay and Performance System," *Employee Benefit Plan Review* 48, no. 7 (January 1994): 46–48.

51. Scott A. Snell and Kenneth N. Wexley, "Performance Diagnosis: Identifying the Causes of Poor Performance," *Personnel Administrator* 30, no. 4 (April 1985): 117–27.

52. Robert Crow, "You Cannot Improve My Performance by Measuring It!" *Journal of Quality and Participation* 19, no. 1 (January/February 1996): 62–64; Allan M. Mohrman and Susan Albers Mohrman, "Performance Management Is 'Running the Business,'" *Compensation and Benefits Review* 27, no. 4 (July/August 1995): 69–75.

53. Jean François Manzoni and Jean-Louis Barsoux, "The set-up-to-fail syndrome," *Harvard Business Review* 76, no. 2 (March/April 1998): 101–13.

# chapter 9

# Managing Compensation

## AFTER STUDYING THIS CHAPTER, YOU SHOULD BE ABLE TO

OBJECTIVE **1** Explain employer concerns in developing a strategic compensation program.

OBJECTIVE **2** Identify the various factors that influence the setting of wages.

OBJECTIVE **3** Discuss the mechanics of each of the major job evaluation systems.

OBJECTIVE **4** Explain the purpose of a wage survey.

OBJECTIVE **5** Define the wage curve, pay grades, and rate ranges as parts of the compensation structure.

OBJECTIVE **6** Identify the major provisions of the federal laws affecting compensation.

OBJECTIVE **7** Discuss the current issues of equal pay for comparable worth, pay compression, and low wage budgets.

An extensive review of the literature indicates that important work-related variables leading to job satisfaction include challenging work, interesting job assignments, equitable rewards, competent supervision, and rewarding careers.[1] It is doubtful, however, whether many employees would continue working were it not for the money they earn. Employees desire compensation systems that they perceive as being fair and commensurate with their skills and expectations.[2] Pay, therefore, is a major consideration in HRM because it provides employees with a tangible reward for their services, as well as a source of recognition and livelihood. Employee compensation includes all forms of pay and rewards received by employees for the performance of their jobs. *Direct compensation* encompasses employee wages and salaries, incentives, bonuses, and commissions. *Indirect compensation* comprises the many benefits supplied by employers, and *nonfinancial compensation* includes employee recognition programs, rewarding jobs, and flexible work hours to accommodate personal needs.

Both managers and scholars agree that the way compensation is allocated among employees sends a message about what management believes is important and the types of activities it encourages. Furthermore, for an employer, the payroll constitutes a sizable operating cost. In manufacturing firms compensation is seldom as low as 20 percent of total expenditures, and in service enterprises it often exceeds 80 percent. A strategic compensation program, therefore, is essential so that pay can serve to motivate employee production sufficiently to keep labor costs at an acceptable level. This chapter will be concerned with the management of a compensation program, job evaluation systems, and pay structures for determining compensation payments. Included will be a discussion of federal regulations that affect wage and salary rates. Chapter 10 will review financial incentive plans for employees. Employee benefits that are part of the total compensation package are then discussed in Chapter 11.

# Strategic Compensation Planning

What is strategic compensation planning? Simply stated, it is the compensation of employees in ways that enhance motivation and growth while, at the same time, aligning their efforts with the objectives, philosophies, and culture of the organization. Strategic compensation planning goes beyond determining what market rates to pay employees—although market rates are one element of compensation planning—to purposefully linking compensation to the organization's mission and general business objectives.[3]

Additionally, strategic compensation planning serves to mesh the monetary payments made to employees with specific functions of the HR program. For example, in the recruitment of new employees, the rate of pay for jobs can increase or limit the supply of applicants. Howard W. Risher, a compensation specialist, notes, "The linkage of pay levels to labor markets is a strategic policy issue because it affects the caliber of the workforce and the organization's relative payroll costs."[4] Many fast-food restaurants, traditionally low-wage employers, have needed to raise their starting wages to attract a sufficient number of job applicants to meet staffing requirements. If rates of pay are high, creating a large applicant pool, then organizations may choose to raise their selection standards and hire better-qualified employees. This in turn can reduce employer training costs. When employees perform at exceptional levels, their performance appraisals may justify an increased pay rate. For these reasons and others, an organization should develop a formal HR program to manage employee compensation.

We will discuss three important aspects of strategic compensation planning: linking compensation to organizational objectives, the pay-for-performance standard, and the motivating value of compensation.

## Linking Compensation to Organizational Objectives

When organizations undertake to downsize, restructure, outsource, or reengineer, they intend to become leaner and flatter in order to gain flexibility and respond more quickly to ever-changing customer demands. With fewer employees, these organizations must manage compensation programs in ways that remaining employees are motivated to make meaningful contributions while assuming ownership of their jobs. An outcome of today's dynamic business environment is that managers have needed to change their pay philosophies from paying for a specific position or job title to rewarding employees on the basis of their individual contributions to organizational success. A compensation program, therefore, must be tailored to the needs of the organization and its employees.

**Value-added compensation**

Evaluating the individual components of the compensation program to see if they advance the needs of employees and the goals of the organization

Increasingly, compensation specialists speak of value-added compensation.[5] A **value-added compensation** program, also called value-chain compensation, is one in which the components of the compensation package (benefits, base pay, incentives, etc.), both separately and in combination, create value for the organization and its employees.[6] Using a value-added viewpoint, managers will ask questions such as "How does this compensation practice benefit the organization?" and "Does the benefit offset the administrative cost?" Payments that fail to advance either the employee or the organization are removed from the compensation program.

It is not uncommon for organizations to establish very specific goals for joining their organizational objectives to their compensation program.[7] Formalized compensation goals serve as guidelines for managers to ensure that wage and benefit policies achieve their intended purpose.[8] The more common goals of a strategic compensation policy include the following:

1.  To reward employees' past performance
2.  To remain competitive in the labor market
3.  To maintain salary equity among employees
4.  To mesh employees' future performance with organizational goals
5.  To control the compensation budget
6.  To attract new employees
7.  To reduce unnecessary turnover

To achieve these goals, policies must be established to guide management in making decisions. Formal statements of compensation policies typically include the following:

1.  The rate of pay within the organization and whether it is to be above, below, or at the prevailing community rate
2.  The ability of the pay program to gain employee acceptance while motivating employees to perform to the best of their abilities

3. The pay level at which employees may be recruited and the pay differential between new and more senior employees
4. The intervals at which pay raises are to be granted and the extent to which merit and/or seniority will influence the raises
5. The pay levels needed to facilitate the achievement of a sound financial position in relation to the products or services offered

## The Pay-for-Performance Standard

**Pay-for-performance standard**
Standard by which managers tie compensation to employee effort and performance

To raise productivity and lower labor costs in today's competitive economic environment, organizations are increasingly setting compensation objectives based on a **pay-for-performance standard.** It is agreed that managers must tie at least some reward to employee effort and performance. Without this standard, motivation to perform with greater effort will be low, resulting in higher wage costs to the organization.[9]

The term "pay for performance" refers to a wide range of compensation options, including merit-based pay, bonuses, salary commissions, job and pay banding, team/group incentives, and various gainsharing programs. (Gainsharing plans are discussed in Chapter 10.) Each of these compensation systems seeks to differentiate between the pay of average performers and outstanding performers. When Peoples Natural Gas Company of Pittsburgh revamped its compensation program, it had as its goals "to clarify job expectations, to provide communication and feedback, and to provide recognition and rewards for meeting or exceeding performance expectations."[10] Interestingly, productivity studies show that employees will increase their output by 15 to 35 percent when an organization installs a pay-for-performance program.

Unfortunately, designing a sound pay-for-performance system is not easy. Considerations must be given to how employee performance will be measured, the monies to be allocated for compensation increases, which employees to cover, the payout method, and the periods when payments will be made.[11] A critical issue concerns the size of the monetary increase and its perceived value to employees. Rose Stanley, compensation specialist with the American Compensation Association, reports that annual salary budgets for 1998 averaged 4.2 percent, a decline of a tenth of a percentage point from 1997.[12] These percentages only slightly exceed yearly increases in the cost of living. While differences exist as to how large a wage or salary increase must be before it is perceived as meaningful, a pay-for-performance program will lack its full potential when pay increases only approximate rises in the cost of living.

**USING THE INTERNET**

A variety of wage and benefit information can be obtained from the American Compensation Association at:

www.acaonline.org

## The Motivating Value of Compensation

Pay constitutes a quantitative measure of an employee's relative worth. For most employees, pay has a direct bearing not only on their standard of living, but also on the status and recognition they may be able to achieve both on and off the job. Since pay represents a reward received in exchange for an employee's contributions, it is essential, according to the equity theory, that the pay be equitable in terms of those contributions. It is essential also that an employee's pay be equitable in terms of what other employees are receiving for their contributions.

### Pay Equity

Equity can be defined as anything of value earned through the investment of something of value. Equity theory, from which pay equity is derived, is a motivation theory that explains how employees respond to situations in which they feel they have received less (or more) than they deserve.[13] Central to the theory is the role of perception in motivation and the fact that individuals make comparisons. It states that individuals form a ratio of their inputs (abilities, skills, experiences) in a situation to their outcomes (salary, benefits) in that situation. They then compare the value of that ratio with the value of the input/output ratio for other individuals in a similar class of jobs either internal or external to the organization. If the value of their ratio equals the value of another's, they perceive the situation as equitable and no tension exists. However, if they perceive their input/output ratio as inequitable relative to others', this creates tension and motivates them to eliminate or reduce the inequity. The strength of their motivation is proportional to the magnitude of the perceived inequity. Figure 9.1 illustrates pay equity and feelings of being fairly paid.

For employees, **pay equity** is achieved when the compensation received is equal to the value of the work performed. Research clearly demonstrates that employees' perceptions of pay equity, or inequity, can have dramatic effects on their motivation for both work behavior and productivity. Managers must therefore develop strategic pay practices that are both internally and externally equitable. Compensation policies are *internally* equitable when employees believe that the wage rates for their jobs approximate the job's worth to the organization. Perceptions of *external* pay equity exist when the organization is paying wages that are relatively equal to what other employers are paying for similar types of work.

**Pay equity**
An employee's perception that compensation received is equal to the value of the work performed

### Expectancy Theory and Pay

The expectancy theory of motivation predicts that one's level of motivation depends on the attractiveness of the rewards sought and the probability of obtaining those

FIGURE 9.1

**Relationship between Pay Equity and Motivation**

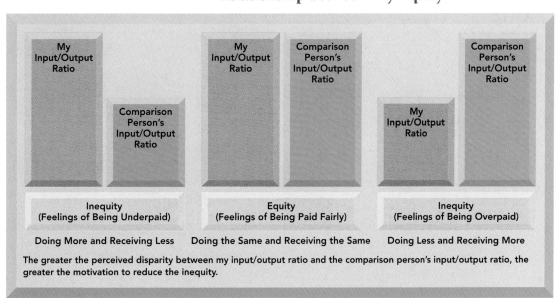

| My Input/Output Ratio | Comparison Person's Input/Output Ratio | My Input/Output Ratio | Comparison Person's Input/Output Ratio | My Input/Output Ratio | Comparison Person's Input/Output Ratio |

| Inequity (Feelings of Being Underpaid) | Equity (Feelings of Being Paid Fairly) | Inequity (Feelings of Being Overpaid) |

Doing More and Receiving Less     Doing the Same and Receiving the Same     Doing Less and Receiving More

The greater the perceived disparity between my input/output ratio and the comparison person's input/output ratio, the greater the motivation to reduce the inequity.

rewards.[14] The theory has developed from the work of psychologists who consider humans as thinking, reasoning persons who have beliefs and anticipations concerning future life events. Expectancy theory therefore holds that employees should exert greater work effort if they have reason to expect that it will result in a reward that is valued.[15] To motivate this effort, the value of any monetary reward should be attractive. Employees also must believe that good performance is valued by their employer and will result in their receiving the expected reward.

Figure 9.2 shows the relationship between pay-for-performance and the expectancy theory of motivation. The model predicts, first, that high effort will lead to high performance (expectancy). For example, if an employee believes she has the skills and abilities to perform her job, and if she works hard (effort), then her performance will improve or be high. Second, high performance should result in rewards that are appreciated (valued). Elements of the compensation package are said to have *instrumentality* when an employee's high performance leads to monetary rewards that are valued. Since we previously stated that pay-for-performance leads to a feeling of pay satisfaction, this feeling should reinforce one's high level of effort.

Thus, how employees view compensation can be an important factor in determining the motivational value of compensation. Furthermore, the effective communication of pay information together with an organizational environment that elicits employee trust in management can contribute to employees having more accurate perceptions of their pay. The perceptions employees develop concerning their pay are influenced by the accuracy of their knowledge and understanding of the compensation program's strategic objectives.

## Pay Secrecy

Misperceptions by employees concerning the equity of their pay and its relationship to performance can be created by secrecy about the pay that others receive. There is reason to believe that secrecy can generate distrust in the compensation

**FIGURE 9.2**

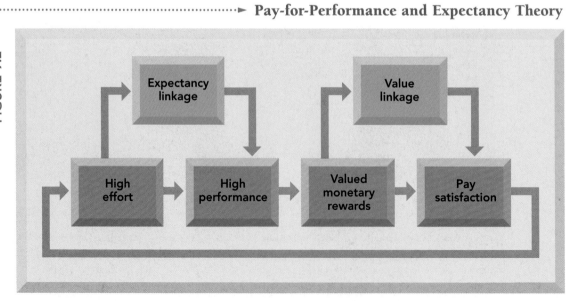

**Pay-for-Performance and Expectancy Theory**

system, reduce employee motivation, and inhibit organizational effectiveness. Yet pay secrecy seems to be an accepted practice in many organizations in both the private and the public sector.

Managers may justify secrecy on the grounds that most employees prefer to have their own pay kept secret. Probably one of the reasons for pay secrecy that managers may be unwilling to admit is that it gives them greater freedom in compensation management, since pay decisions are not disclosed and there is no need to justify or defend them. Employees who are not supposed to know what others are being paid have no objective base for pursuing complaints about their own pay. Secrecy also serves to cover up inequities existing within the internal pay structure. Furthermore, secrecy surrounding compensation decisions may lead employees to believe that there is no direct relationship between pay and performance.

## The Bases for Compensation

**Hourly work**
Work paid on an hourly basis

**Piecework**
Work paid according to the number of units produced

Work performed in most private, public, and not-for-profit organizations has traditionally been compensated on an hourly basis. It is referred to as **hourly work,** in contrast to **piecework,** in which employees are paid according to the number of units they produce. Hourly work, however, is far more prevalent than piecework as a basis for compensating employees.

Employees compensated on an hourly basis are classified as *hourly employees,* or wage earners. Those whose compensation is computed on the basis of weekly, biweekly, or monthly pay periods are classified as *salaried employees.*[16] Hourly employees are normally paid only for the time they work. Salaried employees, by contrast, are generally paid the same for each pay period, even though they occasionally may work more hours or fewer than the regular number of hours in a period. They also usually receive certain benefits not provided to hourly employees.

**Nonexempt employees**
Employees covered by the overtime provisions of the Fair Labor Standards Act

**Exempt employees**
Employees not covered in the overtime provisions of the Fair Labor Standards Act

Another basis for compensation centers on whether employees are classified as *nonexempt* or *exempt* under the Fair Labor Standards Act (FLSA). **Nonexempt employees** are covered by the act and must be paid at a rate of $1\frac{1}{2}$ times their *regular* pay rate for time worked in excess of forty hours in their workweek. Most hourly workers employed in interstate commerce are considered nonexempt workers under the FLSA. Employees not covered by the overtime provision of the FLSA are classified as **exempt employees.** Managers and supervisors as well as a large number of white-collar employees are in the exempt category. The U.S. Department of Labor (DOL) imposes a narrow definition of exempt status, and employers wishing to classify employees as exempt must convince the DOL that the job is exempt on the basis of the independent judgment of the jobholder and other criteria. Therefore employers should check the exact terms and conditions of exemption before classifying employees as either exempt or nonexempt. (See Exemptions under the Act later in this chapter.)

# Components of the Wage Mix

A combination of *internal* and *external* factors can influence, directly or indirectly, the rates at which employees are paid. Through their interaction these factors constitute the wage mix, as shown in Figure 9.3. For example, the area wage rate for administrative assistants might be $9.75 per hour. However, one employer may

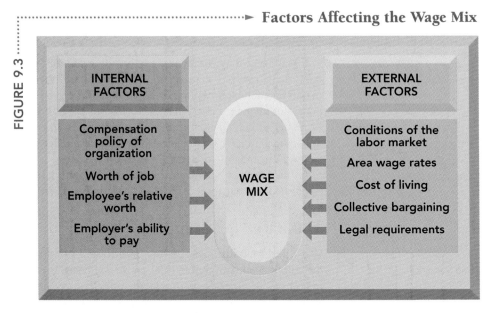

FIGURE 9.3    Factors Affecting the Wage Mix

elect to pay its administrative assistants $11.50 per hour because of their excellent performance. The influence of government legislation on the wage mix will be discussed later in the chapter.

## Internal Factors

The internal factors that influence wage rates are the employer's compensation policy, the worth of a job, an employee's relative worth in meeting job requirements, and an employer's ability to pay.

### Employer's Compensation Policy

Highlights in HRM 1 illustrates the compensation objectives of two organizations, Longmore Manufacturing and Eye-Tech Vision Care. The pay objective of Eye-Tech Vision Care is to be an industry pay leader, while Longmore Manufacturing seeks to be wage-competitive. Both employers strive to promote a compensation policy that is internally fair.

Longmore Manufacturing and Eye-Tech Vision Care, like other employers, will establish numerous compensation objectives that affect the pay employees receive. As a minimum, both large and small employers should set pay policies reflecting (1) the internal wage relationship among jobs and skill levels, (2) the external competition or an employer's pay position relative to what competitors are paying, (3) a policy of rewarding employee performance, and (4) administrative decisions concerning elements of the pay system such as overtime premiums, payment periods, and short-term or long-term incentives.[17]

### Worth of a Job

Organizations without a formal compensation program generally base the worth of jobs on the subjective opinions of people familiar with the jobs. In such instances, pay rates may be influenced heavily by the labor market or, in the case of union-

## HRM 1

# Compensation Objectives of Two Organizations

Compensation policies and objectives can differ widely across large and small employers as well as across employers in the private and public sectors. Here are the compensation objectives at Longmore Manufacturing and Eye-Tech Vision Care.

| Longmore Manufacturing | Eye-Tech Vision Care |
|---|---|
| • Pay market-competitive compensation | • Be a pay leader in the vision care industry |
| • Achieve internal and external pay equity | • Promote open and understandable pay practices |
| • Achieve simplicity in compensation programs | • Ensure fair employee treatment |
| • Strive for employee commitment and a collaborative work environment | • Offer benefits promoting individual employee needs |
| • Promote gender fairness in pay and benefits | • Offer compensation rewarding employee creativity and achievements |
| • Comply with all governmental compensation regulations | • Offer compensation to foster the strategic mission of the organization |
| • Promote pay-for-performance practices | • Obtain employee input when developing compensation practices |

ized employers, by collective bargaining. Organizations with formal compensation programs, however, are more likely to rely on a system of *job evaluation* to aid in rate determination. Even when rates are subject to collective bargaining, job evaluation can assist the organization in maintaining some degree of control over its wage structure.

The use of job evaluation is widespread in both the public and the private sector. The cities of Chicago and Miami use job evaluation in establishing wage structures, as do Levi Strauss and J.C. Penney. The jobs covered most frequently by job evaluation comprise clerical, technical, and various blue-collar groups, whereas those jobs covered least frequently are managerial and top-executive positions.

### Employee's Relative Worth

In both hourly and salary jobs, employee performance can be recognized and rewarded through promotion and with various incentive systems. (The incentive systems used most often will be discussed in the next chapter.) Superior performance can also be rewarded by granting merit raises on the basis of steps within a rate range established for a job class. If merit raises are to have their intended value, however, they must be determined by an effective performance appraisal system that differentiates between those employees who deserve the raises and those who do not. This system, moreover, must provide a visible and credible relationship between

"A raise just isn't feasible at this time, Osgood.
But we're going to give you the 'wave.'"

©1999; Reprinted courtesy of Bunny Hoest and Parade Magazine.

performance and any raises received. Unfortunately, too many so-called merit systems provide for raises to be granted automatically. As a result, employees tend to be rewarded more for merely being present than for being productive on the job.

### Employer's Ability to Pay

In the public sector, the amount of pay and benefits employees can receive is limited by the funds budgeted for this purpose and by the willingness of taxpayers to provide them. In the private sector, pay levels are limited by profits and other financial resources available to employers. Thus an organization's ability to pay is determined in part by the productivity of its employees. This productivity is a result not only of their performance, but also of the amount of capital the organization has invested in labor-saving equipment. Generally, increases in capital investment reduce the number of employees required to perform the work and increase an employer's ability to provide higher pay for those it employs.

Economic conditions and competition faced by employers can also significantly affect the rates they are able to pay. Competition and recessions can force prices down and reduce the income from which compensation payments are derived. In such situations, employers have little choice but to reduce wages and/or lay off employees, or, even worse, to go out of business.

## External Factors

The major external factors that influence wage rates include labor market conditions, area wage rates, cost of living, collective bargaining if the employer is unionized, and legal requirements.

### Labor Market Conditions

The labor market reflects the forces of supply and demand for qualified labor within an area. These forces help to influence the wage rates required to recruit or retain competent employees. It must be recognized, however, that counterforces can reduce the full impact of supply and demand on the labor market. The economic power of unions, for example, may prevent employers from lowering wage rates even when unemployment is high among union members. Government regulations also may prevent an employer from paying at a market rate less than an established minimum.

### Area Wage Rates

A formal wage structure should provide rates that are in line with those being paid by other employers for comparable jobs within the area. Data pertaining to area wage rates may be obtained from local wage surveys. For example, the Arizona Department of Economic Security conducts an annual wage survey for both large and small employers in various cities throughout the state. Wage-survey data also may be obtained from a variety of sources, including the American Management Association, Administrative Management Society, U.S. Department of Labor, and Federal Reserve Banks. Smaller employers such as the Woodsmith Corporation and Golden State Container, Inc., use government surveys to establish rates of pay for new and senior employees. Many organizations, like the City of Atlanta, Northwest Airlines, and Wang Laboratories, conduct their own surveys. Others engage in a cooperative exchange of wage information or rely on various professional associations for these data. A high percentage of wage data is inexpensive—under $100—and is therefore available to all employers, regardless of size.

Wage surveys (discussed fully later in the chapter) serve the important function of providing external wage equity between the surveying organization and other organizations competing for labor in the surrounding labor market. Importantly, data from area wage surveys can be used to prevent the rates for jobs from drifting too far above or below those of other employers in the region. When rates rise above existing area levels, an employer's labor costs may become excessive. Conversely, if they drop too far below area levels, it may be difficult to recruit and retain competent personnel. Wage-survey data must also take into account indirect wages paid in the form of benefits.

**Consumer price index (CPI)**

Measure of the average change in prices over time in a fixed "market basket" of goods and services

## Cost of Living

Because of inflation, compensation rates have had to be adjusted upward periodically to help employees maintain their purchasing power. Employers make these changes with the help of the **consumer price index (CPI).** The CPI is a measure of the average change in prices over time in a fixed "market basket" of goods and services.[18] The consumer price index is based on prices of food, clothing, shelter, and fuels; transportation fares; charges for medical services; and prices of other goods and services that people buy for day-to-day living. The Bureau of Labor Statistics collects price information on a monthly basis and calculates the CPI for the nation as a whole and various U.S. city averages. Separate indexes are also published by size of city and by region of the country. Employers in a number of communities monitor changes in the CPI as a basis for compensation decisions.

Changes in the CPI can have important effects on pay rates. Granting wage increases solely on the basis of the CPI helps to compress pay rates within a pay structure, thereby creating inequities among those who receive

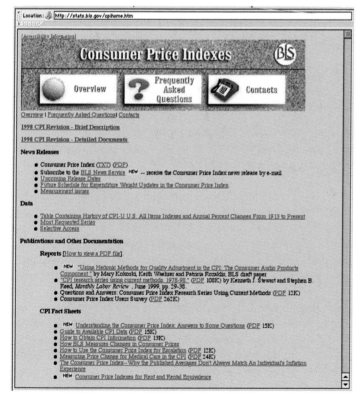

*The CPI is calculated each month using price information collected by the Bureau of Labor Statistics. See stats.bls.gov/cpihome.htm.*

the wage increase. Inequities also result from the fact that adjustments are made on a cent-per-hour rather than a percentage basis. For example, a cost-of-living adjustment of 50 cents represents a 7.1 percent increase for an employee earning $7 per hour, but only a 4.2 percent increase for one earning $12 per hour. Unless adjustments are made periodically in employee base rates, the desired differential between higher- and lower-paying jobs will gradually be reduced. The incentive to accept more-demanding jobs will also be reduced.

Employees who work under a union contract may receive wage increases through **escalator clauses** found in their labor agreement. These clauses provide for quarterly cost-of-living adjustments (COLA) in wages based on changes in the CPI. The most common adjustments are 1 cent per hour for each 0.3- or 0.4-point change in the CPI. COLAs are favored by unions during particularly high periods of inflation.

### Collective Bargaining

One of the primary functions of a labor union, as emphasized in Chapter 14, is to bargain collectively over conditions of employment, the most important of which is compensation.[19] The union's goal in each new agreement is to achieve increases in **real wages**—wage increases larger than the increase in the CPI—thereby improving the purchasing power and standard of living of its members. This goal includes gaining wage settlements that equal if not exceed the pattern established by other unions within the area.

The agreements negotiated by unions tend to establish rate patterns within the labor market. As a result, wages are generally higher in areas where organized labor is strong. To recruit and retain competent personnel and avoid unionization, nonunion employers must either meet or exceed these rates. The "union scale" also becomes the prevailing rate that all employers must pay for work performed under government contract. The impact of collective bargaining therefore extends beyond that segment of the labor force that is unionized.

**Escalator clauses**
Clauses in labor agreements that provide for quarterly cost-of-living adjustments in wages, basing the adjustments upon changes in the consumer price index

**Real wages**
Wage increases larger than rises in the consumer price index; that is, the real earning power of wages

# Job Evaluation Systems

**Job evaluation**
Systematic process of determining the relative worth of jobs in order to establish which jobs should be paid more than others within an organization

As we discussed earlier, one important component of the wage mix is the worth of the job. Organizations formally determine the value of jobs through the process of job evaluation. **Job evaluation** is the systematic process of determining the *relative* worth of jobs in order to establish which jobs should be paid more than others within the organization. Job evaluation helps to establish internal equity between various jobs. The relative worth of a job may be determined by comparing it with others within the organization or by comparing it with a scale that has been constructed for this purpose. Each method of comparison, furthermore, may be made on the basis of the jobs as a whole or on the basis of the parts that constitute the jobs.

Four methods of comparison are shown in Figure 9.4. They provide the basis for the principal systems of job evaluation. We will begin by discussing the simpler, nonquantitative approaches and conclude by reviewing the more popular, quantitative systems. Regardless of the methodology used, it is important to remember that all job evaluation methods require varying degrees of managerial judgment. Also, those involved in evaluating jobs must consider the impact of the Americans with Disabilities Act on the process. (See Chapter 3.)

## Job Ranking System

**Job ranking system**
Simplest and oldest system of job evaluation by which jobs are arrayed on the basis of their relative worth

The simplest and oldest system of job evaluation is the **job ranking system,** which arrays jobs on the basis of their relative worth. One technique used to rank jobs

Different Job Evaluation Systems

FIGURE 9.4

| BASIS FOR COMPARISON | SCOPE OF COMPARISON | |
| | JOB AS A WHOLE (NONQUANTITATIVE) | JOB PARTS OR FACTORS (QUANTITATIVE) |
|---|---|---|
| Job vs. job | Job ranking system | Factor comparison system |
| Job vs. scale | Job classification system | Point system |

consists of having the raters arrange cards listing the duties and responsibilities of each job in order of the importance of the jobs. Job ranking can be done by a single individual knowledgeable about all jobs or by a committee composed of management and employee representatives.

Another common approach to job ranking is the paired-comparison method. Raters compare each job with all other jobs by means of a paired-comparison ranking table that lists the jobs in both rows and columns, as shown in Figure 9.5. To use the table, raters compare a job from a row with the jobs from each of the columns. If the row job is ranked higher than a column job, an X is placed in the appropriate cell. After all the jobs have been compared, raters total the Xs for row jobs. The total number of Xs for a row job will establish its worth relative to other

Paired-Comparison Job Ranking Table

FIGURE 9.5

| Row Jobs \ Column Jobs | Senior Administrative Secretary | Data-Entry Operator | Data-Processing Director | File Clerk | Systems Analyst | Programmer | Total |
|---|---|---|---|---|---|---|---|
| Senior Administrative Secretary | — | X | | X | | X | 3 |
| Data-Entry Operator | | — | | X | | | 1 |
| Data-Processing Director | X | X | — | X | X | X | 5 |
| File Clerk | | | | — | | | 0 |
| Systems Analyst | X | X | | X | — | X | 4 |
| Programmer | | X | | X | | — | 2 |

*Directions:* Place an X in the cell where the value of a row job is higher than that of a column job.

jobs. Differences in rankings should then be reconciled into a single rating for all jobs. After jobs are evaluated, wage rates can be assigned to them through use of the salary survey discussed later in the chapter.

The basic weakness of the job ranking system is that it does not provide a very refined measure of each job's worth. Since the comparisons are normally made on the basis of the job as a whole, it is quite easy for one or more of the factors of a job to bias the ranking given to a job, particularly if the job is complex. This drawback can be partially eliminated by having the raters—prior to the evaluation process—agree on one or two important factors with which to evaluate jobs and the weights to be assigned these factors. Another disadvantage of the job ranking system is that the final ranking of jobs merely indicates the relative importance of the jobs, not the differences in the degree of importance that may exist between jobs. A final limitation of the job ranking method is that it can only be used with a small number of jobs, probably no more than fifteen. Its simplicity, however, makes it ideal for use by smaller employers.

## Job Classification System

**Job classification system**
System of job evaluation in which jobs are classified and grouped according to a series of predetermined wage grades

In the **job classification system,** jobs are classified and grouped according to a series of predetermined grades. Successive grades require increasing amounts of job responsibility, skill, knowledge, ability, or other factors selected to compare jobs. For example, Grade GS-1 from the federal government grade descriptions reads as follows:

> GS-1 includes those classes of positions the duties of which are to perform, under immediate supervision, with little or no latitude for the exercise of independent judgment (A) the simplest routine work in office, business, or fiscal operations; or (B) elementary work of a subordinate technical character in a professional, scientific, or technical field.

The descriptions of each of the job classes constitute the scale against which the specifications for the various jobs are compared. Managers then evaluate jobs by comparing job descriptions with the different wage grades in order to "slot" the job into the appropriate grade. While this system has the advantage of simplicity, it is less precise than the point and factor comparison systems (discussed in the next sections) because the job is evaluated as a whole. The federal civil service job classification system is probably the best-known system of this type. The job classification system is widely used by municipal and state governments.

## Point System

**Point system**
Quantitative job evaluation procedure that determines the relative value of a job by the total points assigned to it

The **point system** is a quantitative job evaluation procedure that determines a job's relative value by calculating the total points assigned to it. It has been successfully used by high-visibility organizations such as Digital Equipment Company, TRW, Johnson Wax Company, Boeing, TransAmerica, and many other public and private organizations, both large and small. Although point systems are rather complicated to establish, once in place they are relatively simple to understand and use. The principal advantage of the point system is that it provides a more refined basis for making judgments than either the ranking or classification systems and thereby can produce results that are more valid and less easy to manipulate.

The point system permits jobs to be evaluated quantitatively on the basis of factors or elements—commonly called *compensable factors*—that constitute the job. The skills, efforts, responsibilities, and working conditions that a job usually entails are the more common major compensable factors that serve to rank one job as more or less important than another. The number of compensable factors an organization uses depends on the nature of the organization and the jobs to be evaluated. Once selected, compensable factors will be assigned weights according to their relative importance to the organization. For example, if responsibility is considered extremely important to the organization, it could be assigned a weight of 40 percent. Next, each factor will be divided into a number of degrees. Degrees represent different levels of difficulty associated with each factor.

The point system requires the use of a *point manual*. The point manual is, in effect, a handbook that contains a description of the compensable factors and the degrees to which these factors may exist within the jobs. A manual also will indicate—usually by means of a table (see Highlights in HRM 2)—the number of points allocated to each factor and to each of the degrees into which these factors are divided. The point value assigned to a job represents the sum of the numerical degree values of each compensable factor that the job possesses.

**HRM 2**

HIGHLIGHTS IN HRM

# Point Values for Job Factors of the American Association of Industrial Management

| FACTORS | 1ST DEGREE | 2ND DEGREE | 3RD DEGREE | 4TH DEGREE | 5TH DEGREE |
|---|---|---|---|---|---|
| **Skill** | | | | | |
| 1. Job knowledge | 14 | 28 | 42 | 56 | 70 |
| 2. Experience | 22 | 44 | 66 | 88 | 110 |
| 3. Initiative and ingenuity | 14 | 28 | 42 | 56 | 70 |
| **Effort** | | | | | |
| 4. Physical demand | 10 | 20 | 30 | 40 | 50 |
| 5. Mental or visual demand | 5 | 10 | 15 | 20 | 25 |
| **Responsibility** | | | | | |
| 6. Equipment or press | 5 | 10 | 15 | 20 | 25 |
| 7. Material or product | 5 | 10 | 15 | 20 | 25 |
| 8. Safety of others | 5 | 10 | 15 | 20 | 25 |
| 9. Work of others | 5 | 10 | 15 | 20 | 25 |
| **Job Conditions** | | | | | |
| 10. Working conditions | 10 | 20 | 30 | 40 | 50 |
| 11. Hazards | 5 | 10 | 15 | 20 | 25 |

Source: Developed by the National Metal Trades Association. Reproduced with permission of the American Association of Industrial Management, Springfield, Mass.

## Developing a Point Manual

A variety of point manuals have been developed by organizations, trade associations, and management consultants. An organization that seeks to use one of these existing manuals should make certain that the manual is suited to its particular jobs and conditions of operation. If necessary, the organization should modify the manual or develop its own to suit its needs.

The job factors that are illustrated in Highlights in HRM 2 represent those covered by the American Association of Industrial Management point manual. Each of the factors listed in this manual has been divided into five degrees. The number of degrees into which the factors in a manual are to be divided, however, can be greater or smaller than this number, depending on the relative weight assigned to each factor and the ease with which the individual degrees can be defined or distinguished.

After the job factors in the point manual have been divided into degrees, a statement must be prepared defining each of these degrees, as well as each factor as a whole. The definitions should be concise and yet distinguish the factors and each of their degrees. Highlights in HRM 3 represents another portion of the point manual used by the American Association of Industrial Management to describe each of the degrees for the job knowledge factor. These descriptions enable those conducting a job evaluation to determine the degree to which the factors exist in each job being evaluated.

The final step in developing a point manual is to determine the number of points to be assigned to each factor and to each degree within these factors. Although the total number of points is arbitrary, 500 points is often the maximum.

## Using the Point Manual

Job evaluation under the point system is accomplished by comparing the job descriptions and job specifications, factor by factor, against the various factor-degree descriptions contained in the manual. Each factor within the job being evaluated is then assigned the number of points specified in the manual. When the points for each factor have been determined from the manual, the total point value for the job as a whole can be calculated. The relative worth of the job is then determined from the total points that have been assigned to that job.

# Factor Comparison System

**Factor comparison system**
Job evaluation system that permits the evaluation process to be accomplished on a factor-by-factor basis by developing a factor comparison scale

The **factor comparison system,** like the point system, permits the job evaluation process to be accomplished on a factor-by-factor basis. It differs from the point system, however, in that the compensable factors of the jobs to be evaluated are compared against the compensable factors of *key jobs* within the organization that serve as the job evaluation scale. Key jobs can be defined as those jobs that are important for wage-setting purposes and are widely known in the labor market. Key jobs have the following characteristics:

1.  They are important to employees and the organization.
2.  They vary in terms of job requirements.
3.  They have relatively stable job content.
4.  They are used in salary surveys for wage determination.

Key jobs are evaluated against five compensable factors—skill, mental effort, physical effort, responsibility, and working conditions—resulting in a ranking of the different factors for each key job. Normally a committee is selected to rank the

HRM 3

HIGHLIGHTS IN HRM

# Description of Job Knowledge Factor and Degrees of the American Association of Industrial Management

### 1.  Job Knowledge

*This factor measures the knowledge or equivalent training required to perform the position duties.*

**1st Degree**   Use of reading and writing, adding and subtracting of whole numbers; following of instructions; use of fixed gauges, direct reading instruments, and similar devices where interpretation is not required.

**2nd Degree**   Use of addition, subtraction, multiplication, and division of numbers including decimals and fractions; simple use of formulas, charts, tablets, drawings, specifications, schedules, wiring diagrams; use of adjustable measuring instruments; checking of reports, forms, records, and comparable data where interpretation is required.

**3rd Degree**   Use of mathematics together with the use of complicated drawings, specifications, charts, tables; various types of precision measuring instruments. Equivalent to one to three years applied trades training in a particular or specialized occupation.

**4th Degree**   Use of advanced trades mathematics, together with the use of complicated drawings, specifications, charts, tables, handbook formulas; all varieties of precision measuring instruments. Equivalent to complete accredited apprenticeship in a recognized trade, craft, or occupation; or equivalent to a two-year technical college education.

**5th Degree**   Use of higher mathematics involved in the application of engineering principles and their performance of related practical operations, together with a comprehensive knowledge of the theories and practices of mechanical, electrical, chemical, civil, or like engineering field. Equivalent to complete four years of technical college or university education.

Source: Developed by the National Metal Trades Association. Reproduced with permission of the American Association of Industrial Management, Springfield, Mass.

criteria across key jobs. Committee members must also assign monetary rates of pay to each compensable factor for each key job. When this task is completed, a factor comparison scale is developed for use in evaluating all other jobs.

## Job Evaluation for Management Positions

Because management positions are more difficult to evaluate and involve certain demands not found in jobs at the lower levels, some organizations do not attempt to include them in their job evaluation programs. Those employers that do evaluate these positions, however, may extend their regular system of evaluation to include such positions, or they may develop a separate evaluation system for management positions.

**Hay profile method**
Job evaluation technique using three factors—knowledge, mental activity, and accountability—to evaluate executive and managerial positions

Several systems have been developed especially for the evaluation of executive, managerial, and professional positions. One of the better-known is the **Hay profile method,** developed by Edward N. Hay. The three broad factors that constitute the evaluation in the "profile" include knowledge (or know-how), mental activity (or problem solving), and accountability.[20] The Hay method uses only three factors because it is assumed that these factors represent the most important aspects of all executive and managerial positions. The profile for each position is developed by determining the percentage value to be assigned to each of the three factors. Jobs are then ranked on the basis of each factor, and point values that make up the profile are assigned to each job on the basis of the percentage-value level at which the job is ranked.

# The Compensation Structure

Job evaluation systems provide for internal equity and serve as the basis for wage-rate determination. They do not in themselves determine the wage rate. The evaluated worth of each job in terms of its rank, class, points, or monetary worth must be converted into an hourly, daily, weekly, or monthly wage rate. The compensation tool used to help set wages is the wage and salary survey.

**Wage and salary survey**
Survey of the wages paid to employees of other employers in the surveying organization's relevant labor market

## Wage and Salary Surveys

The **wage and salary survey** is a survey of the wages paid by employers in an organization's relevant labor market—local, regional, or national, depending on the job. The labor market is frequently defined as that area from which employers obtain certain types of workers. The labor market for office personnel would be local, whereas the labor market for engineers would be national. It is the wage and salary survey that permits an organization to maintain external equity, that is, to pay its employees wages equivalent to the wages similar employees earn in other establishments.

When job evaluation and wage-survey data are used jointly, they serve to link the likelihood of both internal and external equity. Although surveys are primarily conducted to gather competitive wage data, they can also collect information on employee benefits or organizational pay practices (e.g., overtime rates or shift differentials).

### Collecting Survey Data
While many organizations conduct their own wage and salary surveys, a variety of "preconducted" pay surveys are available to satisfy the requirements of most public and not-for-profit or private employers. The Bureau of Labor Statistics (BLS) is the major publisher of wage and salary data. In 1997, the BLS began publishing the National Compensation Survey (NCS), a statistically valid and comprehensive compensation program of wage, salary, and benefit information. (See Highlights in HRM 4.) As described by William J. Wiatrowski, economist with the BLS, "The National Compensation Survey is the umbrella program that combines several BLS compensation programs into a single vehicle that can produce local, regional, and national statistics on levels, trends, and characteristics of pay and benefits."[21]

Many states conduct surveys on either a municipal or county basis and make them available to employers. Besides these government surveys, trade groups such as the Dallas Personnel Association, the Administrative Management Society, the

**HRM 4**

# Bureau of Labor Statistics National Compensation Survey

NCS data are used by managers and compensation specialists in large and small organizations to answer such questions as

- How much must I pay accountants in Atlanta, Georgia?
- Is a 3 percent benefits increase comparable to that of other employers in the manufacturing industry?
- Is vision coverage a prevalent benefit among large employers in the Northeast?
- How have wage costs changed over the past year?

**How the NCS Survey Works**

The National Compensation Survey is an area-based survey. Wage and benefit data are collected from a predetermined set of 154 metropolitan and nonmetropolitan areas through the fifty states and the District of Columbia to represent the United States. Compensation information is collected from such diverse locations as Knoxville, Tennessee; Pittsburgh, Pennsylvania; Reno, Nevada; and Richland-Kennewick-Pasco, Washington. All areas are selected to produce regional estimates for nine broad geographic divisions and four broad regions.

Within each area, a scientific sample of establishments represents all area establishments. An "establishment" is a single physical location, such as a plant, a warehouse, a corporate office, or a retail outlet. State and local government offices are also included in the survey.

Once an establishment has been chosen for inclusion in the survey, a BLS economist selects occupations within that establishment to represent all occupations in the establishment. The BLS limits the selection to a small number of occupations to reduce the survey burden for employers. Data are collected for all incumbents in a selected occupation.

The selected occupations are then classified based on the Census Bureau's occupation classification system. The census classification categorizes approximately 450 individual occupations into ten major groupings such as sales, professional specialty and technical, and machine operators, assemblers, and inspectors. For the occupations selected, wage and benefit data are collected. Items included in the collection of wages are time-based payments, piece rates, commissions, hazard pay, and other items directly related to the work being performed. A variety of benefit data are collected, including paid vacations, paid holidays, paid sick leave, shift differentials, and nonproduction bonuses.

Source: William J. Wiatrowski, "Bureau of Labor Statistics' New National Compensation Survey." Adapted from *Compensation and Benefits Review*, September-October/1998. © 1998 American Management Association International. Reprinted by permission of American Management Association International, New York, NY. All rights reserved. http://www.amanet.org.

Society for Human Resource Management, the American Management Association, the National Society of Professional Engineers, and the Financial Executive Institute conduct special surveys tailored to their members' needs. Employers with global operations can purchase international surveys through large consulting firms. The overseas compensation survey offered by *TPF&C* reports on the payment practices in twenty countries. While all of these third-party surveys provide certain benefits to their users, they also have various limitations. Two problems with all published surveys are that (1) they are not always compatible with the user's jobs and (2) the user cannot specify what specific data to collect. To overcome these problems, organizations may collect their own compensation data.

### Employer-Initiated Surveys

Employers wishing to conduct their own wage and salary survey must first select the jobs to be used in the survey and identify the organizations with whom they actually compete for employees.[22] Since it is not feasible to survey all the jobs in an organization, normally only key jobs, also called benchmark jobs, are used. The survey of key jobs will usually be sent to ten or fifteen organizations that represent a valid sample of other employers likely to compete for the employees of the surveying organization. A diversity of organizations should be selected—large and small, public and private, new and established, and union and nonunion—since each classification of employer is likely to pay different wage rates for surveyed jobs.

After the key jobs and the employers to be surveyed have been identified, the surveying organization must decide what information to gather on wages, benefit types, and pay policies. For example, when requesting pay data, it is important to specify whether hourly, daily, or weekly pay figures are needed. In addition, those conducting surveys must state if the wage data are needed for new hires or for senior employees. Precisely defining the compensation data needed will greatly increase the accuracy of the information received and the number of purposes for which it can be used. Once the survey data are tabulated, the compensation structure can be completed.

## Wage Surveys and Virtual Jobs

As jobs constantly change to match the dynamic needs of the organization and its customers, compensation specialists are asking questions such as, "How do you conduct salary surveys when there are no stable jobs?" "How do you match jobs when there are no jobs to match?" or, with the growth of virtual jobs, "How should internal and external pay equity be addressed?"[23] The answers to these concerns lie in developing creative pay surveys to match the organization's compensation strategy. For example, where organizations pay employees on the basis of their competencies and skills, then pay surveys will need to address the compensation of core competencies that span all work and all jobs. The use of maturity-curve surveys is another method to compensate ever-changing job content.[24] Traditionally used to compensate scientific and technical personnel, maturity-curve surveys can also be used to compensate employees on the basis of a relationship between market value and experience. (See Chapter 10.)

## The Wage Curve

**OBJECTIVE 5**

**Wage curve**
Curve in a scattergram representing the relationship between relative worth of jobs and wage rates

The relationship between the relative worth of jobs and their wage rates can be represented by means of a **wage curve.** This curve may indicate the rates currently paid for jobs within an organization, the new rates resulting from job evaluation, or the rates for similar jobs currently being paid by other organizations within the labor market. A curve may be constructed graphically by preparing a scattergram consisting of a series of dots that represent the current wage rates. As shown in Figure 9.6, a freehand curve is then drawn through the cluster of dots in such a

FIGURE 9.6

**Freehand Wage Curve**

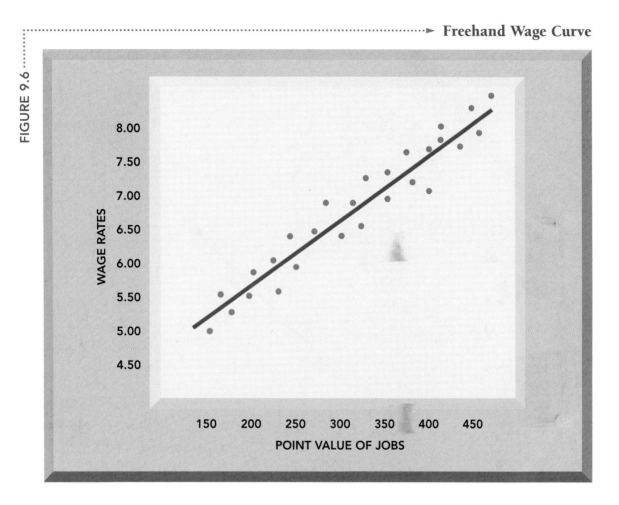

manner as to leave approximately an equal number of dots above and below the curve. The wage curve can be relatively straight or curved. This curve can then be used to determine the relationship between the value of a job and its wage rate at any given point on the line.

## Pay Grades

**Pay grades**
Groups of jobs within a particular class that are paid the same rate

From an administrative standpoint, it is generally preferable to group jobs into **pay grades** and to pay all jobs within a particular grade the same rate or rate range. When the classification system of job evaluation is used, jobs are grouped into grades as part of the evaluation process. When the point and factor comparison systems are used, however, pay grades must be established at selected intervals that represent either the point or the evaluated monetary value of these jobs. The graph in Figure 9.7 illustrates a series of pay grades designated along the horizontal axis at fifty-point intervals.

The grades within a wage structure may vary in number. The number is determined by such factors as the slope of the wage curve, the number and distribution of the jobs within the structure, and the organization's wage administration and

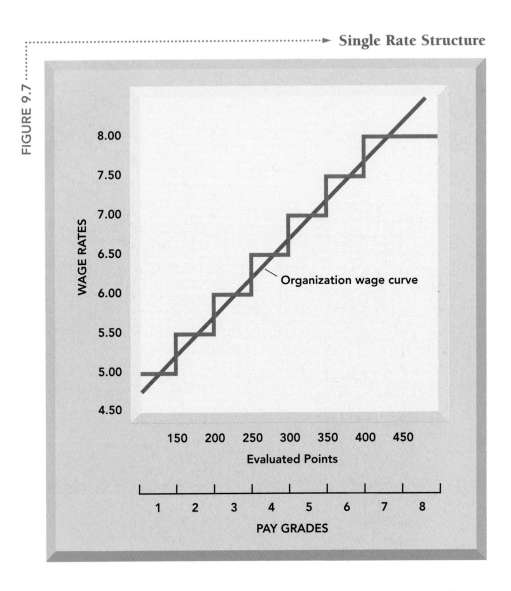

FIGURE 9.7

**Single Rate Structure**

promotion policies. The number utilized should be sufficient to permit difficulty levels to be distinguished, but not so great as to make the distinction between two adjoining grades insignificant.

## Rate Ranges

Although a single rate may be created for each pay grade, as shown in Figure 9.7, it is more common to provide a range of rates for each pay grade. The rate ranges may be the same for each grade or proportionately greater for each successive grade, as shown in Figure 9.8. Rate ranges constructed on the latter basis provide a greater incentive for employees to accept a promotion to a job in a higher grade.

Rate ranges generally are divided into a series of steps that permit employees to receive increases up to the maximum rate for the range on the basis of merit or seniority or a combination of the two. Most salary structures provide for the ranges

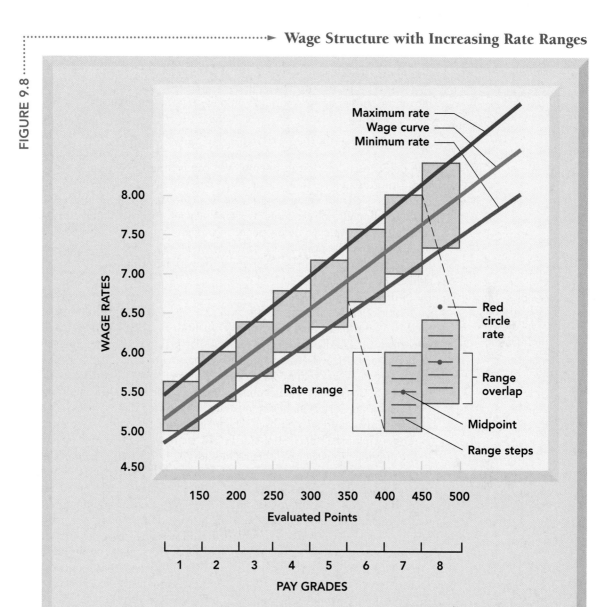

FIGURE 9.8

**Wage Structure with Increasing Rate Ranges**

of adjoining pay grades to overlap. The purpose of the overlap is to permit an employee with experience to earn as much as or more than a person with less experience in the next-higher job classification.

The final step in setting up a wage structure is to determine the appropriate pay grade into which each job should be placed on the basis of its evaluated worth. Traditionally, this worth is determined on the basis of job requirements without regard to the performance of the person in that job. Under this system, the performance of those who exceed the requirements of a job may be acknowledged by merit increases within the grade range or by promotion to a job in the next-higher pay grade.

**Red circle rates**
Payment rates above the maximum of the pay range

Organizations may pay individuals above the maximum of the pay range when employees have high seniority or promotional opportunities are scarce. Wages paid above the range maximum are called **red circle rates.** Because these rates are exceptions to the pay structure, employers will often "freeze" these rates until all ranges are shifted upward through market wage adjustments.

## Alternatives to Traditional Job-Based Pay

The predominant approach to employee compensation is still the job-based system. Unfortunately, such a system often fails to reward employees for their skills or the knowledge they possess or to encourage them to learn a new job-related skill. Additionally, job-based pay systems may not reinforce an organizational culture stressing employee involvement or provide increased employee flexibility to meet overall production or service requirements. Therefore, organizations such as Frito-Lay, Nortel Networks, Sherwin-Williams, and Honeywell have introduced skill-based pay plans.[25]

**Skill-based pay**
Pay based on how many skills employees have or how many jobs they can perform

**Skill-based pay,** also referred to as knowledge-based pay, pay-for-knowledge, or multiskilled-based pay, compensates employees for the different skills or increased knowledge they possess rather than for the job they hold in a designated job category. Regardless of the name, these pay plans encourage employees to earn higher base wages by learning and performing a wider variety of skills (or jobs) or displaying an array of competencies that can be applied to a variety of organizational requirements.[26] Organizations will grant an increase in pay after each skill has been mastered and can be demonstrated according to a predetermined standard. Skill-based pay is frequently used where employees are part of autonomous work groups or employee teams. Skill-based pay systems represent a fundamental change in the attitude of management regarding how work should be organized and how employees should be paid for their work efforts. The most frequently cited benefits of skill-based pay include greater productivity, increased employee learning and commitment to work, improved staffing flexibility to meet production or service demands, and the reduced effects of absenteeism and turnover since managers can assign employees where and when needed. Skill-based pay also encourages employees to acquire training when new or updated skills are needed by an organization.

Unfortunately, skill-based pay plans may bring some long-term difficulties. Some plans limit the amount of compensation employees can earn, regardless of the new skills or competencies they acquire. Thus, after achieving the top wage, employees may be reluctant to continue their educational training. Furthermore, employees can become discouraged when they acquire new abilities but find there are no higher-rated jobs to which they can transfer. Unless all employees have the opportunity to increase their pay through the attainment of new skills, employees who are not given this opportunity may feel disgruntled.

### Broadbanding

Organizations that adopt a skill-based or competency-based pay system frequently use *broadbanding* to structure their compensation payments to employees. Broadbanding simply collapses many traditional salary grades into a few wide salary bands.[27] For example, Marriott International now places its 14,500 managers into four broad salary levels.[28] Instead of being assigned to specific grade levels, Marriott managers now have wide latitude to receive more pay and added experience.

Banding encourages lateral skill building while addressing the need to pay employees performing multiple jobs with different skill-level requirements. According to one authority, "Broadbands help eliminate the obsession with grades and, instead, encourage employees to move to jobs where they can develop in their careers and add value to the organization."[29] Paying employees through broadbands enables organizations to consider job responsibilities, individual skills and competencies, and career mobility patterns in assigning employees to bands.

# Governmental Regulation of Compensation

Compensation management, like the other areas of HRM, is subject to state and federal regulations. A majority of states have minimum wage laws or wage boards that fix minimum wage rates on an industry-by-industry basis. Most states also regulate hours of work and overtime payments.

The three principal federal laws affecting wages are the Davis-Bacon Act, the Walsh-Healy Act, and the Fair Labor Standards Act. These laws were enacted during the 1930s to prevent the payment of abnormally low wage rates and to encourage the spreading of work among a greater number of workers. The latter objective was accomplished by forcing organizations to pay a premium rate for overtime work (all hours worked in excess of a prescribed number).

## Davis-Bacon Act of 1931

The Davis-Bacon Act, also referred to as the Prevailing Wage Law, was passed in 1931 and is the oldest of the three federal wage laws. It requires that the minimum wage rates paid to persons employed on federal public works projects worth more than $2,000 be at least equal to the prevailing rates and that overtime be paid at $1\frac{1}{2}$ times this rate. The act is criticized because the prevailing rates are often the union rates for jobs in the area and are often higher than the average (nonunion) rates.[30]

## Walsh-Healy Act of 1936

The Walsh-Healy Act, which is officially called the Public Contracts Act, was passed in 1936 and covers workers employed on government contract work for supplies, equipment, and materials worth in excess of $10,000. The act requires contractors to pay employees at least the prevailing wage rates established for the area by the Secretary of Labor, and overtime of $1\frac{1}{2}$ times the regular rate for all work performed in excess of eight hours in one day or forty hours in one week, depending on which basis provides the larger premium.

## Fair Labor Standards Act of 1938 (as Amended)

The Fair Labor Standards Act (FLSA), commonly referred to as the Wage and Hour Act, was passed in 1938 and since then has been amended many times. It covers those employees who are engaged in the production of goods for interstate and foreign commerce, including those whose work is closely related to or essential to such production. The act also covers agricultural workers, as well as employees of certain retail and service establishments whose sales volume exceeds a prescribed

## USING THE INTERNET

At its web site, the Department of Labor provides extensive information about the minimum wage, including a photo of the signing ceremony for the 1996 amendment. You can also download a copy of the FLSA minimum wage poster:

www.dol.gov/dol/esa/
public/minwage/main.
htm

amount. The major provisions of the FLSA are concerned with minimum wage rates and overtime payments, child labor, and equal rights.[31]

### Wage and Hour Provisions

The minimum wage prescribed by federal law has been raised many times, from an original figure of 25 cents per hour to $5.15 per hour on September 1, 1997. (See Highlights in HRM 5 for the federal minimum wage poster that employers are required to display.) This minimum rate applies to the actual earning rate before any overtime premiums have been added. An overtime rate of $1\frac{1}{2}$ times the base rate must be paid for all hours worked in excess of forty during a given week. The base wage rate from which the overtime rate is computed must include incentive payments or bonuses that are received during the period. For example, if a person employed at a base rate of $6 an hour works a total of forty-five hours in a given week and receives a bonus of $90, that person is actually working at the rate of $8 an hour. (The $90 bonus divided by the forty-five hours required to earn it equals $2 per hour, which, when added to the base rate of $6 per hour, increases the employee's earning rate to $8 per hour for the week.) Earnings for the week would total $380, computed as follows:

| | | |
|---|---|---|
| Regular time | 40 × $8 = | $320 |
| Overtime | 5 × $12 = | 60 |
| Total earnings | | $380 |

If the bonus is paid on a monthly or quarterly basis, earnings for the period must be recalculated to include this bonus in the hourly rate for overtime payments. When employees are given time off in return for overtime work, it must be granted at $1\frac{1}{2}$ times the number of hours that were worked as overtime. Employees who are paid on a piece-rate basis also must receive a premium for overtime

*Young workers in a Carolina cotton mill before child labor was illegal (circa 1908).*

HRM 5

# The Federal Minimum Wage Poster

*Your Rights Under the Fair Labor Standards Act*

## Federal Minimum Wage

### $4.75 per hour
beginning October 1, 1996

### $5.15 per hour
beginning September 1, 1997

Employees under 20 years of age may be paid $4.25 per hour during their first 90 consecutive calendar days of employment with an employer.

Certain full-time students, student learners, apprentices, and workers with disabilities may be paid less than the minimum wage under special certificates issued by the Department of Labor.

Tip Credit – Employers of "tipped employees" must pay a cash wage of at least $2.13 per hour if they claim a tip credit against their minimum wage obligation. If an employee's tips combined with the employer's cash wage of at least $2.13 per hour do not equal the minimum hourly wage, the employer must make up the difference. Certain other conditions must also be met.

### Overtime Pay

At least 1$^{1}/_{2}$ times your regular rate of pay for all hours worked over 40 in a workweek.

### Child Labor

An employee must be at least 16 years old to work in most non-farm jobs and at least 18 to work in non-farm jobs declared hazardous by the Secretary of Labor. Youths 14 and 15 years old may work outside school hours in various non-manufacturing, non-mining, non-hazardous jobs under the following conditions:

No more than –
 • 3 hours on a school day or 18 hours in a school week;
 • 8 hours on a non-school day or 40 hours in a non-school week.

Also, work may not begin before 7 a.m. or end after 7 p.m., except from June 1 through **Labor Day**, when evening hours are extended to 9 p.m. Different rules apply in agricultural employment.

### Enforcement

The Department of Labor may recover back wages either administratively or through court action, for the employees that have been underpaid in violation of the law. Violations may result in civil or criminal action.

Fines of up to $10,000 per violation may be assessed against employers who violate the child labor provisions of the law and up to $1,000 per violation against employers who willfully or repeatedly violate the minimum wage or overtime pay provisions. This law prohibits discriminating against or discharging workers who file a complaint or participate in any proceedings under the Act.

*Note:*  • Certain occupations and establishments are exempt from the minimum wage and/or overtime pay provisions.
 • Special provisions apply to workers in American Samoa.
 • Where state law requires a higher minimum wage, the higher standard applies.

*For Additional Information, Contact* the Wage and Hour Division office nearest you — listed in your telephone directory under United States Government, Labor Department.

This poster may be viewed on the world wide web at this address: http://www.dol.gov./dol/esa/public/minwage/main.htm

*The law requires employers to display this poster where employees can readily see it.*

U.S. Department of Labor
Employment Standards Administration
Wage and Hour Division
Washington, D.C.  20210

WH Publication 1088
Revised October 1996

*U.S. Government Printing Office: 1996 — 414-534

work. The hourly rate on which overtime is to be based is computed by dividing earnings from piecework by the total number of hours of work required to earn this amount. For example, if an employee produced 1,250 units of work at 25 cents per unit during a fifty-hour week, the earning rate would be $6.25 per hour, computed as follows:

$$\frac{1{,}250 \text{ units} \times 20 \text{ cents}}{50 \text{ hours}} = \$6.25 \text{ per hour}$$

Since the ten hours in excess of a forty-hour week constitute overtime at $1\frac{1}{2}$ times the regular rate, total earnings for the week would be $343.80, computed as follows:

| | | |
|---|---|---|
| Regular time | 40 × $6.25 = | $250.00 |
| Overtime | 10 × $9.38 = | 93.80 |
| Total earnings | | $343.80 |

A few minutes of extra work a day may seem trivial to a manager or supervisor but not to the U.S. Department of Labor. In one case investigated by the DOL's Wage and Hour Division, an Iowa beef processor failed to pay 23,500 employees for setup and cleanup work done before and after their shifts. Although the time amounted to only 14 minutes per employee each day, that violation of law cost the meatpacker $7.1 million in back wages and interest.[32] Failure to include all periods of work can often lead to overtime miscalculations. Some important compensable situations include

- Downtime or call-in time, where the employee must be readily available for work
- Payment for required classes, meetings, or other periods of instruction
- Travel between job sites
- Preparation and cleanup before and after shifts
- Break periods shorter than twenty minutes

Clearly, a complete understanding of when and how to pay employees is the best protection against a DOL investigation into overtime violation. Furthermore, under the FLSA, an employer must pay an employee for whatever work the employer "suffers or permits" the employee to perform, even if the work is done away from the workplace and even if it is not specifically expected or requested. This condition could likely occur where employees work away from headquarters and are unsupervised or they telecommunicate on a frequent basis.[33]

Under the FLSA it doesn't matter that the supervisor never asked the employee to work extra time; all that matters is that the supervisor knew the employee was putting in the time and did nothing to prevent it. This rule, as well as the overtime and bonus rules discussed earlier, applies only to nonexempt employees.

Some argue that the "floor" imposed by the minimum wage makes it more difficult for high school students and young adults to find jobs. Many employers who might otherwise be willing to hire these individuals are unwilling to pay them the same rate as adults because of their lack of experience. For unskilled workers, the FLSA permits employers to pay a "training wage" of $4.25 per hour for employees younger than 20 during their first ninety days of employment.

**USING THE INTERNET**

Various states have web pages explaining their wage and hour and labor standard legislation. In New York, the site is:

www.labor.state.ny.us/wages

### Child Labor Provisions

The FLSA forbids the employment of minors between 16 and 18 years of age in hazardous occupations such as mining, logging, woodworking, meatpacking, and certain types of manufacturing. Minors under 16 cannot be employed in any work destined for interstate commerce except that which is performed in a nonhazardous occupation for a parent or guardian or for an employer under a temporary work permit issued by the Department of Labor.

### Exemptions under the Act

The feature of the FLSA that perhaps creates the most confusion is the exemption of certain groups of employees from coverage by the act or from coverage by certain of its provisions. The act now provides more than forty separate exemptions, some of which apply only to a certain group of personnel or to certain provisions of the act, such as those relating to child labor and to overtime. One of the most common exemptions concerns the overtime provisions of the act. Four employee groups—executives, administrators, professionals, and outside salespersons—are specifically excluded from the overtime provisions. However, persons performing jobs in these groups must meet specific job requirements as stated under the law. For example, a manager is defined as someone whose *primary* duty is the direction of two or more other employees. "Primary duty" means that the manager generally devotes more than 50 percent of his or her time to supervising others. Because exemptions are generally narrowly defined under FLSA, an employer should carefully check the exact terms and conditions for each. Detailed information is available from local wage-hour offices.[34]

### Equal Rights Provisions

One of the most significant amendments to the FLSA was the Equal Pay Act passed in 1963. (See Chapter 2.) The federal Age Discrimination Act of 1967, as amended, extends the equal rights provisions by forbidding wage discrimination based on age for employees 40 years of age and older. Neither of these acts, however, prohibits wage differentials based on factors other than age or sex. Seniority, merit, and individual incentive plans, for instance, are not affected.

In spite of the Equal Pay Act, the achievement of parity by women in the labor market has been slow in coming. In the third quarter, 1998, the median earnings level of all women workers in the United States was 76.7 percent of the median for all working men. This figure is about 14 percentage points higher than in 1980, with little change since 1990.[35] Fortunately, the median earnings of young women (ages 16 to 24) are 93 percent of those of similar-age men—up from 78 percent in 1980. If this trend toward greater comparability in earnings continues as these women become older, this age group may set the stage for more equitable treatment in the future. However, it is still important to remember that young women, and young men as well, typically work in low-paying, entry-level jobs. For women, these are often clerical or sales positions.

Because of the continued differences in pay for women and men, some HR professionals are suggesting that the wage differences could be reduced if women were paid on the basis of equal pay for comparable work, which will be discussed in the next section.

# Significant Compensation Issues

As with other HR activities, compensation management operates in a dynamic environment. For example, as managers strive to reward employees in a fair manner, they must consider controls over labor costs, legal issues regarding male and female wage payments, and internal pay equity concerns. Each of these concerns is highlighted in three important compensation issues: equal pay for comparable worth, wage-rate compression, and low salary budgets.

## The Issue of Equal Pay for Comparable Worth

One of the most important gender issues in compensation is equal pay for comparable worth. The issue stems from the fact that jobs performed predominantly by women are paid less than those performed by men. This practice results in what critics term *institutionalized sex discrimination,* causing women to receive less pay for jobs that may be different from but comparable in worth to those performed by men. The issue of **comparable worth** goes beyond providing equal pay for jobs that involve the same duties for women as for men. It is not concerned with whether a female secretary should receive the same pay as a male secretary. Rather, the argument for comparable worth is that jobs held by women are not compensated the same as those held by men, even though both job types may contribute equally to organizational success.[36]

**Comparable worth**
The concept that male and female jobs that are dissimilar, but equal in terms of value or worth to the employer, should be paid the same

### Problem of Measuring Comparability

Advocates of comparable worth argue that the difference in wage rates for predominantly male and female occupations rests in the undervaluing of traditional female occupations. To remedy this situation, they propose that wages should be equal for jobs that are "somehow" equivalent in total worth or compensation to the organization. Unfortunately, there is no consensus on a comparable worth standard by which to evaluate jobs, nor is there agreement on the ability of present job evaluation techniques to remedy the problem.[37] Indeed, organizations may dodge the comparable worth issue by using one job evaluation system for clerical and secretarial jobs and another system for other jobs. Furthermore, the advocates of comparable worth argue that current job evaluation techniques simply serve to continue the differences in pay between the sexes.

The argument over comparable worth is likely to remain an HR issue for many years to come. Unanswered questions such as the following will serve to keep the issue alive:

1. If comparable worth is adopted, who will determine the worth of jobs, and by what means?
2. How much would comparable worth cost employers?
3. Would comparable worth reduce the wage gap between men and women caused by labor market supply-and-demand forces?
4. Would comparable worth reduce the number of employment opportunities for women?

### Current State of Comparable Worth

The issue of comparable worth has been addressed in two important court cases, *Washington County v Gunther* (1981) and *AFSCME v State of Washington* (1983).[38] While each case brought comparable worth to the attention of the public, neither case has caused a large number of employers to accept comparable worth as a strategic pay policy. In addition, some believe that comparable worth is a societal problem, not just a legal one. Nonjudicial determination of comparable worth through collective bargaining and pressure-group action may be a better way to achieve gender-based pay equity. The compensation gap between men and women will not disappear overnight, but the persistence of comparable worth advocates will help shrink it.

## The Issue of Wage-Rate Compression

**Wage-rate compression**
Compression of differentials between job classes, particularly the differential between hourly workers and their managers

Earlier, when we discussed the compensation structure, it was noted that the primary purpose of the pay differentials between the wage classes is to provide an incentive for employees to prepare for and accept more-demanding jobs. Unfortunately, this incentive is being significantly reduced by **wage-rate compression**—the reduction of differences between job classes. Wage-rate compression is largely an internal pay-equity concern. The problem occurs when employees perceive that there is too narrow a difference between their compensation and that of colleagues in lower-rated jobs.

HR professionals acknowledge that wage-rate compression is a widespread organizational problem affecting diverse occupational groups: white-collar and blue-collar workers, technical and professional employees, and managerial personnel.[39] It can cause low employee morale, leading to issues of reduced employee performance, higher absenteeism and turnover, and even delinquent behavior such as employee theft.

There is no single cause of wage-rate compression. For example, it can occur when unions negotiate across-the-board increases for hourly employees but managerial personnel are not granted corresponding wage differentials. Such increases can result in part from COLAs provided for in labor agreements. Other inequities have resulted from the scarcity of applicants in computers, engineering, and other professional and technical fields. Job applicants in these fields frequently have been offered starting salaries not far below those paid to employees with considerable experience and seniority. Wage-rate compression often occurs when organizations grant pay adjustments for lower-rated jobs without providing commensurate adjustments for occupations at the top of the job hierarchy.

Identifying wage-rate compression and its causes is far simpler than implementing organizational policies to alleviate its effect. Organizations wishing to minimize the problem may incorporate the following ideas into their pay policies:

1. Give larger compensation increases to more-senior employees.
2. Emphasize pay-for-performance and reward merit-worthy employees.
3. Limit the hiring of new applicants seeking exorbitant salaries.
4. Design the pay structure to allow a wide spread between hourly and supervisory jobs or between new hires and senior employees.
5. Provide equity adjustments for selected employees hardest hit by pay compression.

Other options include permitting more flexibility in employees' work schedules, including four-day workweeks and work at home. Hallmark Cards is offering selected employees different types of benefits to retain valued individuals.

## The Issue of Low Salary Budgets

At a recent compensation seminar attended by one of the authors, a speaker noted, "The blank-check days for large salary increases are over." While workers may not have as tough a time as Dagwood in convincing employers that a raise is in order, as reported by the American Compensation Association, the sizes of salary increases have been modest compared with periods before 1990. Figure 9.9 shows salary budgets by type of employee from 1989 to 1999. These figures are not projected to increase greatly in future years. While current inflation rates have been stable, and are even declining—allowing most employees to realize a real earnings gain—these gains are small compared with prior years.

Interestingly, low wage increases exist at a period when many industries have reported strong financial performance. Although smaller raises may seem an odd response to strong results, they reflect a general trend toward tight compensation-cost controls caused by the global competition for jobs, the reductions in workforce because of technology, and the growing use of temporary and part-time employees who receive low wages and few benefits.[40] Unfortunately, low wages could portend unfavorable effects for employers and society, including (1) increased turnover as employees change jobs for higher wages, (2) diminished employee output as employees perceive a low pay-for-performance relationship, and (3) the creation of a two-tier wage system.

**FIGURE 9.9**

## ▶ Salary Budgets by Type of Employee, 1989–1999

| TYPE OF EMPLOYEE | ACTUAL | | | | | | | | | | | PROJECTED |
| | 1989 | 1990 | 1991 | 1992 | 1993 | 1994 | 1995 | 1996 | 1997 | 1998 | 1999 | 2000 |
| --- | --- | --- | --- | --- | --- | --- | --- | --- | --- | --- | --- | --- |
| Nonexempt hourly nonunion | | | | | | | | 3.8% | 4.1% | 4.0% | 4.1% | 4.1% |
| Nonexempt salaried | 5.2% | 5.4% | 5.0% | 4.6% | 4.2% | 4.0% | 3.9% | 4.0% | 4.1% | 4.2% | 4.2% | 4.2% |
| Exempt salaried | 5.4% | 5.5% | 5.0% | 4.7% | 4.3% | 4.0% | 4.0% | 4.1% | 4.3% | 4.3% | 4.4% | 4.4% |
| Officers/ executives | 5.7% | 5.8% | 5.1% | 4.8% | 4.4% | 4.1% | 4.1% | 4.3% | 4.5% | 4.4% | 4.5% | 4.5% |

Reprinted from *Report on the 1999–2000 Total Salary Increase Budget Survey* with permission from the American Compensation Association (ACA), 14040 North Northsight Blvd., Scottsdale, Ariz. 85260 USA; (480) 951-9191; fax (480) 483-8352. ©ACA, www.acaonline.org.

# SUMMARY

**OBJECTIVE 1** Establishing compensation programs requires both large and small organizations to consider specific goals—employee retention, compensation distribution, and adherence to a budget, for instance. Compensation must reward employees for past efforts (pay-for-performance) while serving to motivate employees' future performance. Internal and external equity of the pay program affects employees' concepts of fairness. Organizations must balance each of these concerns while still remaining competitive. The ability to attract qualified employees while controlling labor costs is a major factor in allowing organizations to remain viable in the domestic or international markets.

**OBJECTIVE 2** The basis on which compensation payments are determined, and the way they are administered, can significantly affect employee productivity and the achievement of organizational goals. Internal influences include the employer's compensation policy, the worth of the job, the performance of the employee, and the employer's ability to pay. External factors influencing wage rates include labor market conditions, area wage rates, cost of living, the outcomes of collective bargaining, and legal requirements.

**OBJECTIVE 3** Organizations use one of four basic job evaluation techniques to determine the relative worth of jobs. The job ranking system arranges jobs in numerical order on the basis of the importance of the job's duties and responsibilities to the organization. The job classification system slots jobs into preestablished grades. Higher-rated grades will require more responsibilities, working conditions, and job duties. The point system of job evaluation uses a point scheme based upon the compensable job factors of skill, effort, responsibility, and working conditions. The more compensable factors a job possesses, the more points are assigned to it. Jobs with higher accumulated points are considered more valuable to the organization. The factor comparison system evaluates jobs on a factor-by-factor basis against key jobs in the organization.

**OBJECTIVE 4** Wage surveys determine the external equity of jobs. Data obtained from surveys will facilitate establishing the organization's wage policy while ensuring that the employer does not pay more, or less, than needed for jobs in the relevant labor market.

**OBJECTIVE 5** The wage structure is composed of the wage curve, pay grades, and rate ranges. The wage curve depicts graphically the pay rates assigned to jobs within each pay grade. Pay grades represent the grouping of similar jobs on the basis of their relative worth. Each pay grade will include a rate range. Rate ranges will have a midpoint and minimum and maximum pay rates for all jobs in the pay grade.

**OBJECTIVE 6** Both the Davis-Bacon Act and the Walsh-Healy Act are prevailing wage statutes. These laws require government contractors to pay wages normally based on the union scale in the employer's operating area. The Walsh-Healy Act also requires payment of $1\frac{1}{2}$ the regular pay for hours over eight per day or forty per week. The Fair Labor Standards Act contains provisions covering the federal minimum wage, hours worked, and child labor.

**OBJECTIVE 7** The concept of comparable worth seeks to overcome the fact that jobs held by women are compensated at a lower rate than those performed by men. This happens even though both types of jobs may contribute equally to organizational productivity. Wage-rate compression largely affects managerial and senior employees as the pay given to new employees or the wage increases gained through union agreements erode the pay differences between these groups. Low wage increases are a prominent compensation strategy as employers seek to adjust to competitive challenges.

## KEY TERMS

comparable worth
consumer price index (CPI)
escalator clauses
exempt employees
factor comparison system
Hay profile method
hourly work
job classification system

job evaluation
job ranking system
nonexempt employees
pay equity
pay-for-performance standard
pay grades
piecework
point system

real wages
red circle rates
skill-based pay
value-added compensation
wage and salary survey
wage curve
wage-rate compression

## DISCUSSION QUESTIONS

 1. Tomax Corporation has 400 employees and wishes to develop a compensation policy to correspond to its dynamic business strategy. The company wishes to employ a high-quality workforce capable of responding to a competitive business environment. Suggest different compensation objectives to match Tomax's business goals.

2. Since employees may differ in terms of their job performance, would it not be more feasible to determine the wage rate for each employee on the basis of his or her relative worth to the organization? Explain.

3. What is job evaluation? Describe the two nonquantitative and two quantitative approaches to job evaluation.

 4. Describe the basic steps in conducting a wage and salary survey. What are some factors to consider?

 5. One of the objections to granting wage increases on a percentage basis is that the lowest-paid employees, who are having the most trouble making ends meet, get the smallest increase, while the highest-paid employees get the largest increase. Is this objection a valid one? Explain.

 6. Federal laws governing compensation raise important issues for both employers and employees. Discuss the following:
   a. The effect of paying a prevailing wage as required by the Davis-Bacon Act
   b. The effects of raising the minimum wage

 7. What are some of the problems of developing a pay system based on equal pay for comparable worth?

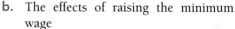

## Pay Decisions at Performance Sports

Katie Perkins' career objective while attending Rockford State College was to obtain a degree in small business management and upon graduation to start her own business. Her ultimate desire was to combine her love of sports and a strong interest in marketing to start a mail-order golf equipment business aimed specifically at beginning golfers.

In February 1996, after extensive development of a strategic business plan and a loan in the amount of $75,000 from the Small Business Administration, Performance Sports was begun. Based on a marketing plan that stressed fast delivery, error-free customer service, and large discount pricing, Performance Sports grew rapidly. At present the company employs sixteen people: eight customer service representatives earning between $9.75 and $11.25 per hour; four shipping and receiving associates paid between $7.50 and $8.50 per hour; two clerical employees, each earning $7.75 per hour; an assistant manager earning $13.10 per hour, and a general manager with a wage of $14.25 per hour. Both the manager and assistant manager are former customer service representatives.

Perkins intends to create a new managerial position, purchasing agent, to handle the complex duties of purchasing golf equipment from the company's numerous equipment manufacturers. Also, the mail-order catalog from Performance Sports will be expanded to handle a complete line of tennis equipment. Since the position of purchasing agent is new, Perkins isn't sure how much to pay this person. She wants to employ an individual with between five and eight years of experience in sports equipment purchasing.

While attending an equipment manufacturers' convention in Las Vegas, Nevada, Perkins learns that a competitor, East Valley Sports, pays its customer service representatives on a pay-for-performance basis. Intrigued by this compensation philosophy, Perkins asks her assistant manager, George Balkin, to research the pros and cons of this payment strategy. This request has become a priority since only last week two customer service representatives expressed dissatisfaction with their hourly wage. Both complained that they felt underpaid relative to the large amount of sales revenue each generates for the company.

### QUESTIONS

1. What factors should Perkins and Balkin consider when setting the wage for the purchasing agent position? What resources are available for them to consult when establishing this wage?
2. Suggest advantages and disadvantages of a pay-for-performance policy for Performance Sports.
3. Suggest a new payment plan for the customer service representatives.

CASE STUDY 2

## Strategic Compensation Planning at Southern California Edison

Southern California Edison (SCE) faced one of its biggest changes in history when the Public Utilities Commission of California (PUC) announced that it would deregulate electric utilities in California. The major challenge faced by SCE was increased competition. Unfortunately, the company's compensation program was appropriate for a monopoly but not for an organization operating in a competitive environment. Explained Dennis Spry, manager of total compensation for SCE, "Well, all our programs were designed for the [old kind of company]—our compensation, benefits, all our HR programs." The organization has been hard at work trying to align its business structure and systems to support the new changes. "We had to look at our compensation program to see what we could do to help it better support the goals that the corporation is striving to achieve," noted Spry.

One change made in 1996 by SCE was to introduce the Compensation Integration Program, or CIP. Part of CIP involved eliminating the company's traditional salary-grade system, with its 3,200 job titles, replacing them with only 170 job titles, which were organized in fewer but much wider salary bands. These salary bands allow great flexibility in paying employees. In some cases, there is a 250 percent spread in each band.

Another compensation strategy was to begin a gainsharing program called Results Sharing. For their agreement to return 5 percent of their base pay, employees now have the opportunity to earn as much as 10 percent of their annual pay if cost savings or profits are made. In the first year under the Results Sharing program, SCE generated $96 million in savings. With a payout of less than $40 million, Spry noted, "The way I see it, the company's about $60 million ahead of the game."

Source: Adapted from "A Utility Aligns Pay with Corporate Change," *Personnel Journal* 75, no. 7 (July 1996): 61. Printed with permission of the *Personnel Journal*.

### QUESTIONS

1. How might SCE have obtained the support of employees to accept the new pay program?
2. With new wide broadbands, won't salaries rise greatly as employees move to the top of their respective bands? Explain.
3. What kind of employee do you think would best operate under this type of system?
4. Do you think Results Sharing will continue to reap the large cost savings realized in the first year of operations? Explain.

## NOTES AND REFERENCES

1. Robert Kreitner and Angelo Kinicki, *Organizational Behavior,* 4th ed. (Burr Ridge, Ill.: Irwin, 1998), Chapter 6.
2. Peter V. LeBlanc and Paul W. Hulvey, "How American Workers See the Rewards of Work," *Compensation and Benefits Review* 30, no. 1 (January-February 1998): 24–28.
3. Kathryn Tyler, "Compensation Strategies Can Foster Lateral Moves and Growing in Place," *HRMagazine* 43, no. 5 (April 1998): 64–71.
4. Howard Risher, "Strategic Salary Planning," *Compensation and Benefits Review* 25, no. 1 (January-February 1993): 47.
5. Howard Risher, "Planning and Managing Rewards in the New Work Paradigm," *Compensation and Benefits Review* 29, no. 1 (January-February 1997): 16.
6. Jerry M. Newman and Frank J. Krzystofiak, "Value-Chain Compensation," *Compensation and Benefits Review* 30, no. 3 (May-June 1998): 60–66.

7. For a frequently referenced book on strategic compensation planning, see Edward E. Lawler III, *Strategic Pay: Aligning Organizational Strategies and Pay Systems* (San Francisco: Jossey-Bass, 1990).
8. "Stay for Pay: A Retention Solution," *HRFocus* 75, no. 9 (September 1998): 57.
9. Craig J. Cantoni, "Learn to Manage Pay and Performance Like an Entrepreneur," *Compensation and Benefits Review* 29, no. 1 (January-February 1997): 52–58.
10. Kathleen A. Guinn and Robert J. Corona, "Putting a Price on Performance," *Personnel Journal* 10, no. 5 (May 1991): 72.
11. Sam T. Johnson, "Plan Your Organization's Reward Strategy through Pay-for-Performance Dynamics," *Compensation and Benefits Review* 30, no. 3 (May-June 1998): 67–72.
12. Telephone conversation with Rose Stanley, American Compensation Association, Scottsdale, Arizona, February 2, 1999.

13. For one of the classic articles on equity theory, see J. Stacey Adams, "Integrity in Social Exchange," in L. Berkowitz (ed.), *Advances in Experimental Social Psychology* (New York: Academic Press, 1965): 276–99.

14. Victor H. Vroom, *Work and Motivation* (San Francisco: Jossey-Bass, 1994). This landmark book, originally published in 1964, integrates the work of hundreds of researchers seeking to explain choice of work, job satisfaction, and job performance.

15. Andrew DuBrin, *Fundamentals of Organizational Behavior: An Applied Approach* (Cincinnati, Ohio: South-Western Publishing, 1997).

16. Carla Joinson, "Pay Attention to Pay Cycles," *HRMagazine* 43, no. 12 (November 1998): 71–78.

17. George T. Milkovich and Jerry M. Newman, *Compensation*, 6th ed. (Chicago: Irwin, 1999): 13–15.

18. *CPI Detailed Report*, May 1996 (Washington, D.C.: U.S. Department of Labor, Bureau of Labor Statistics), 94.

19. Fay Hansen, "Union Membership and the Union Wage Differential," *Compensation and Benefits Review* 30, no. 3 (May-June 1998): 16–21.

20. Richard I. Henderson, *Compensation Management*, 7th ed. (Reston, Va.: Reston Publishing, 1996).

21. William J. Wiatrowski, "Bureau of Labor Statistics' New National Compensation Survey," *Compensation and Benefits Review* 30, no. 5 (September-October 1998): 29–41.

22. Robert L. Heneman, "Finding the Right Salary Survey," *HRFocus* 75, no. 7 (July 1998): 10.

23. John Yurkutat, "Is 'The End of Jobs' the End of Pay Surveys Too?" *Compensation and Benefits Review* 29, no. 4 (July-August 1997): 24. For a response to the Yurkutat article, see Joe Mays, "Why We Haven't Seen 'The End of Jobs' or the End of Salary Surveys," *Compensation and Benefits Review* 29, no. 4 (July-August, 1997): 25.

24. John H. Davis, "The Future of Salary Surveys When Jobs Disappear," *Compensation and Benefits Review* 29, no. 1 (January-February 1997): 18–26.

25. Reginald Shareef, "A Midterm Case Study Assessment of Skill-Based Pay in the Virginia Department of Transportation," *Public Personnel Administration* 18, no. 1 (Winter 1998): 5–17.

26. Darrell J. Cira and Ellen R. Benjamin, "Competency-Based Pay: A Concept in Evolution," *Compensation and Benefits Review* 30, no. 5 (September-October 1998): 21–28. See also Gail Grib and Susan O'Donnell, "Pay Plans That Reward Employee Achievement," *HRMagazine* 40, no. 7 (July 1995): 49–50; Bill Leonard, "New Ways to Pay Employees," *HRMagazine* 39, no. 2 (February 1994): 62.

27. Tyler, "Compensation Strategies." See also Susan Hallett, "Broadbanding: A Strategic Tool for Organizational Change," *Compensation and Benefits Review* 27, no. 6 (May 1995): 40–46; Gary I. Bergel, "Choosing the Right Pay Delivery System to Fit Broadbanding," *Compensation and Benefits Review* 25, no. 4 (July-August 1994): 34–38.

28. Aaron Bernstein, "We Want You to Stay: Really," *Newsweek*, June 22, 1998, 70.

29. Larry Reissman, "Nine Common Myths about Broadbanding," *HRMagazine* 40, no. 8 (August 1995): 79–86.

30. A. J. Thieblot, "A New Evaluation of Impacts of Prevailing Wage Law Repeal," *Journal of Labor Research* 17, no. 2 (Spring 1996): 297–322.

31. Because the FLSA is always subject to amendment, an employer should consult the appropriate publications of one of the labor services previously mentioned or the Wage and Hour Division of the U.S. Department of Labor in order to obtain the latest information regarding its current provisions, particularly the minimum wage rate.

32. Carla Joinson, "Killing Time," *HRMagazine* 43, no. 11 (October 1998): 120–28. For an interesting article on the effects of "on-call" policies and paying overtime, see Christopher S. Miller, Steven J. Whitehead, and Elizabeth Clark-Morrison, "On-Call Policies Help Avoid Overtime Pay, " *HRMagazine* 41, no. 7 (July 1996): 57–64.

33. Jonathan A. Segal, "Home Sweet Office," *HRMagazine* 43, no. 5 (April 1998): 119–29.

34. The U.S. Department of Labor has several pamphlets that highlight the provisions of the FLSA. These include *Employers Guide to the Fair Labor Standards Act, Handy Reference Guide to the Fair Labor Standards Act,* and *A Look at Hours Worked under the Fair Labor Standards Act.* Pamphlets are available upon request from the Wage and Hour Division Office, U.S. Labor Department in your vicinity.

35. *Employment and Earnings,* Bureau of Labor Statistics, U.S. Department of Labor, October 1998, 157.

36. The issue of comparable worth largely exists in public-sector employment. Ten states have comparable worth legislation focusing on public-sector jobs: Connecticut, Hawaii, Iowa, Minnesota, Montana, New York, Ohio, Oregon, Washington, and Wisconsin.

37. Susan E. Gardner, "Implementing Comparable Worth/Pay Equity: Experiences of Cutting-Edge States," *Public Personnel Management* 27, no. 4 (Winter 1998): 475–89.

38. *Washington County v Gunther,* 101 Sup. Ct. 2242 (1981), 452 U.W. 161; AFSCME v State of Washington, 578 F. Supp. 846 (W.D. Wash. 1983).

39. Timothy D. Schellhardt, "Rookie Gains in Pay Wars Rile Veterans," *The Wall Street Journal*, June 4, 1998, B-1.

40. "The Best of Times, the Worst of Times," *HRFocus* 73, no. 2 (February 1996): 15.

# chapter 11

# Employee Benefits

## AFTER STUDYING THIS CHAPTER, YOU SHOULD BE ABLE TO

**OBJECTIVE 1** Describe the characteristics of a sound benefits program.

**OBJECTIVE 2** Recognize management concerns about the costs of employee benefits and discuss ways to control those costs.

**OBJECTIVE 3** Explain the employee benefits required by law.

**OBJECTIVE 4** Discuss suggested ways to control the costs of health care programs.

**OBJECTIVE 5** Describe those benefits that involve payment for time not worked.

**OBJECTIVE 6** Discuss the recent trends in retirement policies and programs.

**OBJECTIVE 7** Describe the major factors involved in the management of pension plans.

**OBJECTIVE 8** List the types of service benefits that employers may provide.

W hat is the best kept secret in America today? The answer, according to a recent report of the U.S. Chamber of Commerce labeled "The Hidden Payroll," is employee benefits. Compensation surveys indicate that a majority of employees are unable to accurately name the benefits they receive and "more than 75 percent of employees perceive the value of their benefits at less than half the actual cost to their employers."[1] Unfortunately, while benefits are largely undervalued and misidentified, they continue to be an important issue for both employers and employees. It is clear that benefits are no longer a "fringe" but rather an integral part of the compensation package. Additionally, since most benefits (almost 80 percent) are provided voluntarily by employers, they become both a significant cost and an employment advantage to employers, while providing needed psychological and physical assistance to employees. The importance of benefits to both sides simply cannot be overstated.

Virtually all employers provide a variety of benefits to supplement the wages or salaries paid to their employees. These benefits, some of which are required by law, must be considered a part of their total compensation. Therefore, in this chapter we examine the characteristics of employee benefits programs. We will study the types of benefits required by law, the major discretionary benefits that employers offer, the employee services they provide, and the retirement programs in use. The chapter concludes with a discussion of popular work/life benefit programs.

# Employee Benefits Programs

Employee benefits constitute an indirect form of compensation intended to improve the quality of the work lives and the personal lives of employees. As discussed later, benefits represent 40 percent of total payroll costs to employers. In return, employers generally expect employees to be supportive of the organization and to be productive. Since employees have come to expect an increasing number of benefits, the motivational value of these benefits depends on how the benefits program is designed and communicated. Once viewed as a gift from the employer, benefits are now considered rights to which all employees are entitled, and they have become one of the fastest-growing areas of employment law and litigation.

*ee-"entitlement"*

## Information Technology and Employee Benefits

With the large number of benefits offered to employees today, administering an organization's benefits program can be both costly and time-consuming. Even for small employers with thirty to forty employees, keeping track of each employee's use of a benefit, or request for a change of benefits, can be cumbersome. For example, even the rather straightforward task of monitoring employee sick-leave usage becomes complex as the size of the organization grows.

Fortunately, interactive employee benefit systems are becoming mainstream at a large majority of both large and small employers, such as Public Service Enterprise Group, Wells Fargo Bank, and LG&E Energy.[2] Through the technology of the Internet, a double-click on the computer permits employees access to their benefits package, allowing both greater control and ownership of the benefits offered them. Part of the advantage of an Internet benefits system is that employees are able to obtain information on their own timetable. Priscilla Craven, U.S. benefits communications and vendor manager at Digital, explains, "You no longer need to call a person when an office is open to get a form or make an enrollment choice."[3]

On-line benefits programs create a form of self-service benefits administration. One intent of on-line programs is to completely eliminate the annual open enrollment period for various benefits, thereby providing greater flexibility in benefits selection. An important advantage to an interactive benefits program is the significant cost savings in benefits administration. Once an on-line system is operational, it is easy and inexpensive to adapt to employer and employee demands. However, while the Internet can be used effectively in benefits administration, security must always be a concern when transmitting benefits information.[4]

Perhaps no part of the HR function is more technologically advanced than the administration of employee benefits programs. There exists a wide variety of commercially developed software packages that serve to facilitate benefits administration in such areas as pension, variable pay, workers' compensation, health benefits, and time-off programs. Descriptions of and advertisements for a variety of benefits software programs are readily found in HR journals like *Workforce* and *HRMagazine*. Software programs represent a cost-effective way to manage employee benefits programs where employers lack the resources or expertise to manage such programs.

## Requirements for a Sound Benefits Program

Too often a particular benefit is provided because other employers are doing it, because someone in authority believes it is a good idea, or because there is union pressure. However, the contributions that benefits will make to the HR program depend on how much attention is paid to certain basic considerations.

### Establishing Specific Objectives

Like any other component of the HR program, an employee benefits program should be based on specific objectives. The objectives an organization establishes will depend on many factors, including the size of the firm; its location, degree of unionization, and profitability; and industry patterns.[5] Most important, these aims must be compatible with the organization's strategic compensation plan (see Chapter 9), including its philosophy and policies.[6]

The chief objectives of most benefits programs are to

- Improve employee work satisfaction ✓
- Meet employee health and security requirements ✓
- Attract and motivate employees ✓
- Reduce turnover ✓
- Maintain a favorable competitive position ✓

Further, these objectives must be considered within the framework of cost containment—a major issue to today's programs.

Unless an organization has a flexible benefits plan (to be discussed later), a uniform package of benefits should be developed. This involves careful consideration of the various benefits that can be offered, the relative preference shown for each benefit by management and the employees, the estimated cost of each benefit, and the total amount of money available for the entire benefits package.

### Allowing for Employee Input

Before a new benefit is introduced, the need for it should first be determined through consultation with employees. Many organizations establish committees composed of managers and employees to administer, interpret, and oversee their benefits policies. Opinion surveys are also used to obtain employee input. Having employees participate in designing benefits programs helps to ensure that management is moving in the direction of satisfying employee wants. Pitney Bowes, Quaker Oats, Nike, and Salomon Brothers ask employees to help them improve benefit plans. The companies then ask teams to design a new benefit package that offers more choices without raising costs.

*[handwritten margin note: ee opinion survey / ensure satisfaction to ees]*

### Modifying Employee Benefits

To serve their intended purpose, employee benefits programs must reflect the changes that are continually occurring within our society. Particularly significant are changes in the composition and lifestyles of the workforce. These changes make it necessary to develop new types of benefits to meet shifting needs. Therefore more employers are tailoring their benefit programs to be family-friendly.[7] (Specific work/life benefits are discussed later in the chapter.) For example, as we have indicated throughout this book, the number of women in the workforce is continuing to grow. Which benefits are most valuable to them (and to men) will be determined largely by whether they have dependent children and whether they have a spouse who has benefits coverage.

Unfortunately, benefit plans sometimes provide little advantage to employees, limiting the organization's ability to attract or retain quality employees. For example, many employers provide unneeded medical benefits to the young and single in the form of dependents' coverage. Likewise, a well-designed—and costly—defined-benefits pension program may not serve the needs of employees or the employer of a predominately younger workforce. Similarly, the employer's contribution to the pension plan for a 30-year-old employee is approximately one-fourth the contribution for a 50-year-old employee for the same amount of pension commencing at age 65. This difference in funds spent on older workers in effect discriminates against the younger worker, although legally it is not regarded as discriminatory. These examples illustrate the need for benefits programs that take into account the differing needs of a variety of workers in order to attract a highly capable workforce.

### Providing for Flexibility

**Flexible benefits plans (cafeteria plans)**
Benefit plans that enable individual employees to choose the benefits that are best suited to their particular needs

To accommodate the individual needs of employees, there is a trend toward **flexible benefits plans,** also known as **cafeteria plans.** These plans enable individual employees to choose the benefits that are best suited to their particular needs. They also prevent certain benefits from being wasted on employees who have no need for them. Typically, employees are offered a basic or core benefits package of life and health insurance, sick leave, and vacation. Requiring a core set of benefits ensures that employees have a minimum level of coverage to protect against unforeseen financial hardships. Employees are then given a specified number of credits they may use to "buy" whatever other benefits they need. Other benefit options might include prepaid legal services, financial planning, or long-term care insurance.[8] Compensation specialists often see flexible benefits plans as ideal. Employees select the benefits of greatest value to them, while employers manage benefits costs by limiting the dollars employees have to spend. Figure 11.1 lists the most frequently cited advantages and disadvantages of flexible benefits programs.

Because cafeteria plans increase the complexity of administering the entire benefits program, organizations may elect to "contract out" the handling of this function to a professional benefits vendor. Paying a service or contract fee to these firms may be particularly cost-effective for the smaller employer. Furthermore, benefits programs must be flexible enough to accommodate the constant flow of new legislation and IRS regulations that affect them. A number of benefits-consulting firms are available to help managers keep up with changes in all phases of the programs they oversee.

## Communicating Employee Benefits Information

The true measure of a successful benefits program is the degree of trust, understanding, and appreciation it earns from the employees.[9] Employers should carefully communicate information about complicated insurance and pension plans so that there will be no misunderstanding about what the plans will and will not provide.

The communication of employee benefits information improved significantly with passage of the Employee Retirement Income Security Act (ERISA) in 1974. The act requires that employees be informed about their pension and certain other benefits in a manner calculated to be understood by the average employee. Additionally, employees can sue their employers for misleading them about health and welfare benefits under ERISA.[10] In an important case, the U.S. Supreme Court ruled in *Varity Corp. v Howe* (1996) that employees are entitled to relief (in this case, restoration of health and welfare benefits) when employers deliberately mislead them about these plans.[11] Problems can arise when managers discuss benefits with

**FIGURE 11.1**

▶ **Flexible Benefits Plans: Advantages and Disadvantages**

**ADVANTAGES**

- Employees select benefits to match their individual needs.
- Benefit selections adapt to a constantly changing (diversified) workforce.
- Employees gain greater understanding of the benefits offered to them and the costs incurred.
- Employers maximize the psychological value of their benefits program by paying only for highly desired benefits.
- Employers limit benefit costs by allowing employees to "buy" benefits only up to a maximum (defined) amount.
- Employers gain competitive advantage in the recruiting and retention of employees.

**DISADVANTAGES**

- Poor employee benefits selection results in unwanted financial costs.
- There are certain added costs to establishing and maintaining the flexible plan.
- Employees may choose benefits of high use to them that increase employer premium costs.

groups of employees or in one-on-one talks and employees receive inaccurate information. Or a manager could mislead an employee by stating that the organization's insurance policy does not cover a particular condition when, in fact, it does or that a maternity leave provision is 120 days when the plan is actually 60 days. As noted by one benefits professional, "This case [*Varity*] brings new questions as to what information management needs to provide employees and underscores the importance of communicating such information accurately and unambiguously."[12]

Employers use an array of methods to communicate benefits to employees. A widely used method of communication is in-house publications, including employee handbooks and organization newsletters.[13] To ensure that employees are familiar with the benefits program, managers should be allowed sufficient time in new-hire orientation and other training classes to present information regarding benefits and to answer questions. Some employers summarize benefits information on a paycheck stub as a reminder to employees of their total compensation.

New employee self-service (ESS) systems have made it possible for employees to gain information about their benefits plans, enroll in their plans of choice, change benefits coverage, alter W-4 designations, or simply inquire about the status of their various benefit accounts without ever contacting an HR representative.[14] Coopers & Lybrand offers a Benefits Information Line that allows employers to provide employees with instant access to a wide variety of benefits and HR information by telephone. Individual account information is available upon entering a personal identification number (PIN). Other organizations use networked PCs or multimedia kiosks as the basis of their self-service system.[15] These approaches permit employees to click on icons to access different benefits and type in new information to update their records. Once an update or change is made, the new information is permanently entered into the organization's HR information system without the need for paperwork. Highlights in HRM 1 presents suggestions for designing a professional benefits communication program.

In addition to having general information, it is important for each employee to have a current statement of the status of her or his benefits.[16] The usual means is the personalized computer-generated statement of benefits. As Highlights in HRM 2 shows, this benefits cost statement can be one of the best ways of slicing through a maze of technicalities to provide concise data to employees about the status of their personal benefits.[17]

## Concerns of Management

Managing an employee benefits program requires close attention to the many forces that must be kept in balance if the program is to succeed. Management must consider union demands, the benefits other employers are offering, tax consequences, rising costs, and legal ramifications. We will briefly examine the last two concerns.

### Significant Costs

According to a 1996 U.S. Chamber of Commerce study, the cost of employee benefits in that year averaged 41.3 percent of payroll, as shown in Figure 11.2.[18] The average distribution of these benefits was $14,086 per employee per year. Costs of benefits were higher in manufacturing than in nonmanufacturing industries. Study Figure 11.2 to obtain an overview of the type of benefits to be discussed in this chapter.

**HIGHLIGHTS IN HRM**

# Crafting an Effective Benefits Communication Program

A well-designed benefits communication program will greatly enhance employees' appreciation of their benefits while ensuring that employers receive the intended value of these offerings. An effective program will provide frequent information to employees in a cost-effective and timely manner. Compensation specialists recommend the following points when administering a benefits communication program.

**In building an identity:**
- Design materials that are eye-catching and of high interest to employees.
- Develop a graphic logo for all material.
- Identify a theme for the benefits program.

**In writing benefits materials:**
- Avoid complex language when describing benefits. Clear, concise, and understandable language is a must.
- Provide numerous examples to illustrate benefit specifics.
- Explain all benefits in an open and honest manner. Do not attempt to conceal unpleasant news.
- Explain the purpose behind the benefit and the value of the benefit to employees.

**In publicizing benefits information:**
- Use all popular employee communication techniques.
- Maintain employee self-service (ESS) technology to disseminate benefits information and to update employee benefits selections.
- Use voice mail to send benefits information.
- Employ presentation software such as PowerPoint or Lotus Freelance to present information to groups of employees.
- Maintain a benefits hot line to answer employee questions.

Since many benefits represent a fixed rather than a variable cost, management must decide whether or not it can afford this cost under less favorable economic conditions. As managers can readily attest, if an organization is forced to discontinue a benefit, the negative effects of cutting it may outweigh any positive effects that accrued from providing it.

To minimize negative effects and avoid unnecessary expense, many employers enlist the cooperation of employees in evaluating the importance of particular benefits. Increasingly, employers are requiring employees to pay part of the costs of certain benefits (e.g., through copayments or higher deductibles), especially medical coverage. At all times, benefit plan administrators are expected to select vendors of benefit services who have the most to offer for the cost.

**HIGHLIGHTS IN HRM**

# A Personalized Statement of Benefits Costs

### Highlights of Your Telstar Global, Inc., Benefits Program

ID: 000-00-0000                    Nancy Doe                    Statement Date:   3-15-2000

| Benefits | Annual Cost | | Total |
| --- | --- | --- | --- |
| | You | Company | |
| *Insurance Programs* | | | |
| 1. Health insurance | 942.48 | 2,318.32 | 3,260.80 |
| 2. Dental Insurance | 254.28 | 301.00 | 555.28 |
| 3. Life Insurance | | | |
|     Employee—$80,000 | 303.80 | | 303.80 |
|     Spouse—$10,000 | 457.60 | 37.68 | 495.28 |
|     Dependent—$5,000 | 11.04 | | 11.04 |
| 4. Short-term disability | 201.04 | | 201.04 |
| 5. Long-term disability | | 207.16 | 207.16 |
| 6. Workers' compensation | | 252.84 | 252.84 |
| 7. Unemployment compensation | | 31.60 | 31.60 |
| *Retirement program* | 3,547.44 | 3,547.44 | 7,094.88 |
| *Social Security* | | | |
|   FICA/OASDI | 2,501.20 | 2,501.20 | 5,002.40 |
|   Medicare | 786.27 | 786.27 | 1,572.54 |
| Totals | $9,005.15 | $9,983.51 | $18,988.66 |

Hourly Rate:  $21.92                                        Annual Salary:  $44,719.00

Holidays (8 Days)          80.00 Hrs.          Value:  $1,753.60

Besides the actual costs of employee benefits, there are costs of administering them. The federal reporting requirements under ERISA require a considerable amount of paperwork for employers. In addition, new requirements, such as those mandated by the Consolidated Omnibus Budget Reconciliation Act of 1986 (COBRA), now require employers to make health coverage—at the same rate the employer would pay—available to employees, their spouses, and their dependents upon termination of employment, death, or divorce.[19] Thus former employees and their families benefit by paying a lower premium for health coverage than

FIGURE 11.2

## Employee Benefits by Type

| TYPE OF BENEFIT | TOTAL, ALL COMPANIES | TOTAL, ALL MANUFACTURING | TOTAL, ALL NON-MANUFACTURING |
|---|---|---|---|
| Total employee benefits as percent of payroll | 41.3 | 44.1 | 40.7 |
| **1.** Legally required payments (employers' share only) | 8.8 | 9.7 | 8.7 |
|   **a.** Old-Age, Survivors, Disability and Health Insurance (employer FICA taxes) and Railroad Retirement Tax | 7.0 | 7.3 | 7.0 |
|   **b.** Unemployment compensation | 0.7 | 1.0 | 0.6 |
|   **c.** Workers' compensation (including estimated cost of self-insured) | 1.1 | 1.4 | 1.1 |
|   **d.** State sickness benefit insurance and other | 0.1 | 0.0 | 0.1 |
| **2.** Retirement and savings plan payments (employer's share only) | 6.3 | 6.2 | 6.3 |
|   **a.** Defined benefit pension plan contributions | 3.4 | 4.0 | 3.2 |
|   **b.** Defined contribution plan payments (401(k) type) | 1.5 | 1.3 | 1.6 |
|   **c.** Profit sharing | 0.5 | 0.6 | 0.4 |
|   **d.** Stock bonus and employee stock ownership plans (ESOP) | 0.1 | 0.1 | 0.1 |
|   **e.** Pension plan premiums (net) under insurance and annuity contracts (insured and trusted) | 0.5 | 0.0 | 0.6 |
|   **f.** Administrative and other costs | 0.3 | 0.2 | 0.4 |
| **3.** Life insurance and death benefit payments (employers' share only) | 0.4 | 0.4 | 0.3 |
| **4.** Medical & medically related benefit payments (employers' share only) | 9.6 | 10.4 | 9.5 |
|   **a.** Hospital, surgical, medical, and major medical insurance premiums (net) | 7.0 | 7.7 | 6.9 |
|   **b.** Retiree (payments for retired employees) hospital, surgical, medical, and major medical insurance premiums (net) | 1.0 | 1.1 | 0.9 |
|   **c.** Short-term disability, sickness or accident insurance (company plan or insured plan) | 0.4 | 0.6 | 0.4 |

*(continued)*

| TYPE OF BENEFIT | TOTAL, ALL COMPANIES | TOTAL, ALL MANUFACTURING | TOTAL, ALL NON-MANUFACTURING |
|---|---|---|---|
| d. Long-term disability or wage continuation (insured, self-administered, or trusts) | 0.3 | 0.3 | 0.3 |
| e. Dental insurance premiums | 0.5 | 0.3 | 0.6 |
| f. Other (vision care, physical and mental fitness benefits for former employees) | 0.4 | 0.5 | 0.4 |
| 5. Paid rest periods, coffee breaks, lunch periods, wash-up time, travel time, clothes-change time, get ready time, etc. | 3.7 | 4.6 | 3.5 |
| 6. Payments for time not worked | 10.2 | 10.2 | 10.2 |
| a. Payment for or in lieu of vacations | 5.3 | 5.1 | 5.3 |
| b. Payment for or in lieu of holidays | 3.1 | 3.7 | 3.0 |
| c. Sick leave pay | 1.2 | 0.3 | 1.4 |
| d. Parental leave (maternity and paternity leave payments) | 0.0 | 0.0 | 0.0 |
| e. Other | 0.6 | 1.1 | 0.5 |
| 7. Miscellaneous benefit payments | 2.3 | 2.6 | 2.2 |
| a. Discounts on goods and services purchased from company by employees | 0.4 | 0.0 | 0.4 |
| b. Severance pay | 0.3 | 0.1 | 0.4 |
| c. Employee education expenditures | 0.4 | 0.9 | 0.3 |
| d. Child care | 0.0 | 0.0 | 0.0 |
| e. Other | 1.2 | 1.5 | 1.1 |
| Total employee benefits as cents per hour | 679.9¢ | 887.8¢ | 646.4¢ |
| Total employee benefits as dollars per year per employee | $14,086 | $19,217 | $13,299 |

Source: Reprinted with permission of the U.S. Chamber of Commerce from the 1997 edition of *Employee Benefits*. To order call 1-800-638-6582.

is available to individual policyholders. While the former employee pays the premiums, employers have to establish procedures to collect premiums and to keep track of former employees and their dependents.

### *Domestic Partnership Benefits*

With a diverse workforce, more employers are willing to provide benefits to employees who establish a *domestic partnership*. In some industries, domestic partner coverage is so prevalent that companies lose competitive advantage in attracting and retaining quality employees if this coverage is denied specific individuals. While the definition of a domestic partnership varies, the description used by Apple Computer is compatible with most definitions. A domestic partner, the company says, is "a person over age 18 who shares living quarters with another adult in an exclusive, committed relationship in which the partners are responsible for each other's common welfare."[20] A standard definition of domestic partnership contains

- A minimum age requirement
- A requirement that the couple live together
- A specification of financial interdependence
- A requirement that the relationship be a permanent one
- A requirement that each not be a blood relative.[21]

Employers who offer domestic partnership coverage typically require employees to sign a form attesting to their relationship.

Organizations that offer benefits to domestic partners are simply extending current benefits, normally full medical and dental plans, to employees.[22] Cost increases to employers are those associated with adding new members to a current benefits plan and those that come with unfavorable tax advantages for both the employer and employee. The Internal Revenue Service has ruled that health benefits offered to employees as domestic partners are taxable as wages to the employee if the partner is not considered a spouse under state law or as a dependent for other federal tax purposes. Despite these conditions, organizations like Viacom International, Stanford University, and the City of Berkeley, California, offer benefits to their domestic partner employees.

# Employee Benefits Required by Law

Legally required employee benefits constitute nearly a quarter of the benefits package that employers provide. These benefits include employer contributions to Social Security, unemployment insurance, workers' compensation insurance, and state disability insurance. We will discuss all but the last of these benefits.

## Social Security Insurance

Passed in 1935, the Social Security Act provides an insurance plan designed to protect covered individuals against loss of earnings resulting from various causes. These causes may include retirement, unemployment, disability, or, in the case of dependents, the death of the worker supporting them. Thus, as with any type of casualty insurance, Social Security does not pay off except in the case where a loss of income is actually incurred through loss of employment.

To be eligible for old-age and survivors' insurance (OASI) as well as disability and unemployment insurance under the Social Security Act, an individual must have been engaged in employment covered by the act. Most employment in private enterprise, most types of self-employment, active military service after 1956, and employment in certain nonprofit organizations and governmental agencies are subject to coverage under the act.[23] Railroad workers and civil service employees who are covered by their own systems and some occupational groups, under certain conditions, are exempted from the act.[24]

The Social Security program is supported by means of a tax levied against an employee's earnings that must be matched by the employer in each pay period.[25] The tax revenues are used to pay three major types of benefits: (1) old-age insurance benefits, (2) disability benefits, and (3) survivors' insurance benefits. Because of the continual changes that result from legislation and administrative rulings, as well as the complexities of making determinations of an individual's rights under Social Security, we will describe these benefits only in general terms.

To qualify for old-age insurance benefits, a person must have reached retirement age and be fully insured. A *fully insured person* has earned forty credits—a maximum of four credits a year for ten years, based on annual earnings of $2,360 (a figure adjusted annually) or more. Having enough credits to be fully insured makes one eligible for retirement benefits, but it does not determine the amount. The amount of monthly Social Security retirement benefits is based on earnings, adjusted for inflation, over the years an individual is covered by Social Security.[26]

To receive old-age insurance benefits, covered individuals must also meet the *retirement earnings test*. Persons under 70 years of age cannot be earning more than the established annual exempt amount through gainful employment without a reduction in benefits. This limitation on earnings does not include income from sources other than gainful employment, such as investments or pensions.

The Social Security program provides disability benefits to workers too severely disabled to engage in "substantial gainful work." To be eligible for such benefits, however, an individual's disability must have existed for at least six months and must be expected to continue for at least twelve months or be expected to result in death. After receiving disability payments for twenty-four months, a disabled person receives Medicare protection. Those eligible for disability benefits, furthermore, must have worked under Social Security long enough and recently enough before becoming disabled. Disability benefits, which include auxiliary benefits for dependents, are computed on the same basis as retirement benefits and are converted to retirement benefits when the individual reaches the age of 65.

Survivors' insurance benefits represent a form of life insurance paid to members of a deceased person's family who meet the eligibility requirements. As with life insurance, the benefits that the survivors of a covered individual receive may greatly exceed their cost to this individual. Survivors' benefits can be paid only if the deceased worker had credit for a certain amount of time spent in work covered by Social Security. The exact amount of work credit needed depends on the worker's age at death. Generally, older workers need more years of Social Security work credit than younger workers, but never more than forty credits. As with other benefits discussed earlier, the *amount* of benefit survivors receive is based on the worker's lifetime earnings in work covered by Social Security.

## Unemployment Insurance

Employees who have been working in employment covered by the Social Security Act and who are laid off may be eligible for up to twenty-six weeks of unemployment insurance benefits during their unemployment. Eligible persons must submit an application for unemployment compensation with their state employment agency, register for available work, and be willing to accept any suitable employment that may be offered to them. However, the term "suitable" gives individuals considerable discretion in accepting or rejecting job offers.

The amount of compensation that workers are eligible to receive, which varies among states, is determined by their previous wage rate and previous period of employment. Funds for unemployment compensation are derived from a federal payroll tax based on the wages paid to each employee, up to an established maximum. The major portion of this tax is refunded to the individual states, which in turn operate their unemployment compensation programs in accordance with minimum standards prescribed by the federal government.

## Workers' Compensation Insurance

**Workers' compensation insurance**
Federal- or state-mandated insurance provided to workers to defray the loss of income and cost of treatment due to work-related injuries or illness

Both state and federal **workers' compensation insurance** is based on the theory that the cost of work-related accidents and illnesses should be considered one of the costs of doing business and should ultimately be passed on to the consumer.[27] Individual employees should not be required to bear the cost of their treatment or loss of income, nor should they be subjected to complicated, delaying, and expensive legal procedures.

In all states, except New Jersey, South Carolina, and Texas, workers' compensation insurance is compulsory. When compulsory, every employer subject to it is required to comply with the law's provisions for the compensation of work-related injuries. The law is compulsory for the employee also. In the three states where it is elective, employers have the option of either accepting or rejecting the law. If they reject it, and suits are filed against them, they lose the customary common-law defenses: (1) assumed risk of employment, (2) negligence of a fellow employee, and (3) contributory negligence.[28]

Three methods of providing for workers' compensation coverage are commonly used. One method is for the state to operate an insurance system that employers may join—in some states, are *required* to join. A second method is for the states to permit employers to insure with private companies. Third, in some states, employers may be certified by the commission handling workers' compensation to handle their own coverage without any type of insurance.

Workers' compensation laws typically provide that employees will be paid a disability benefit based on a percentage of their wages. Each state also specifies the length of the period of payment and usually indicates a maximum amount that may be paid. Benefits, which vary from state to state, are generally provided for four types of disability: (1) permanent partial disability, (2) permanent total disability, (3) temporary partial disability, and (4) temporary total disability. Disabilities may result from injuries or accidents, as well as from occupational diseases such as black lung, radiation illness, and asbestosis. Before any workers' compensation claim will be allowed, though, the work relatedness of the disability must be established. Also, the evaluation of the claimant by a physician trained in occupational medicine is an essential part of the claim process.

In addition to the disability benefits, provision is made for payment of medical and hospitalization expenses up to certain limits, and in all states, death benefits are paid to survivors of the employee. Commissions are established to resolve claims at little or no legal expense to the claimant.

A major concern to employers nationwide is the high cost of workers' compensation claims. The direct cost of claims to U.S. businesses has been around $70 billion annually. Swelling medical costs and benefits paid to workers are the major factors. In addition, there are more disorders today that are harder to assess objectively, such as back pain. Then too, claims are sometimes made for ailments that may have little to do with the workplace, such as hearing loss, stress, and cancer.[29] Steps that managers and supervisors can take to control workers' compensation costs are given in Figure 11.3.

Managers should recognize that a workplace injury presents several problems to the injured worker—medical, financial, insurance, and employment security, and possibly legal problems. Injured employees are likely to feel isolated, and complain when they receive insufficient information about their rights and obligations. Therefore an important step in developing a smoothly functioning system for "comp" cases is for managers and professionals to consider the perspective of the injured worker and to provide the information and assistance needed in a positive, supportive manner.

## Leaves without Pay

Most employers grant leaves of absence to their employees for personal reasons. These leaves are usually taken without pay, but also without loss of seniority or benefits. An unpaid leave may be granted for a variety of reasons, including extended illness, illness in the family, pregnancy, the birth or adoption of a child, educational or political activities, and social service activities.

## The Family and Medical Leave Act

The Family and Medical Leave Act (FMLA) was passed and became effective on August 5, 1993.[30] The FMLA applies to employers having fifty or more employees

**FIGURE 11.3**

**▶ Reducing Workers' Comp Costs: Key Areas**

1. Perform an audit to assess high-risk areas within a workplace.

2. Prevent injuries by proper ergonomic design of the job and effective assessment of job candidates.

3. Provide quality medical care to injured employees by physicians with experience and preferably with training in occupational health.

4. Reduce litigation by effective communication between the employer and the injured worker.

5. Manage the care of an injured worker from the injury until return to work. Keep a partially recovered employee at the work site.

6. Provide extensive worker training in all related health and safety areas.

during twenty or more calendar workweeks in the current or preceding year. It requires the employer to provide up to twelve weeks of unpaid, job-protected leave to eligible employees for certain family and medical reasons. The specific reasons for taking leave are listed on the federally required poster reproduced in Highlights in HRM 3. In studying the poster, note the other important stipulations, such as enforcement and unlawful acts, which are of direct concern to managers.

Like many laws pertaining to HRM, the FMLA is simple in principle but requires revising policies and procedures for compliance.[31] This law affects an organization's benefits program in several of its provisions: It mandates continuation of medical coverage, it prohibits loss of accrued benefits, it provides for restoration of benefits after leave, it permits substitution of paid leave and vacation during leave, it makes communication and notice compulsory, and it prohibits waiver of benefits.[32]

It is apparent that employees as a group will benefit from FMLA at critical times in their lives. Supporters say that it will especially help today's "sandwich generation"—baby boomers born from 1946 to 1964—as they enter middle age and rear children while simultaneously caring for aging parents. Temporary-help firms expect to profit from FLMA by providing workers to fill in for permanent employees who take time off to care for relatives. The temp agencies are prepared to provide temporary managers and executives as well as clerical help. However, in a move designed to protect contingent workers (see Chapter 4), the Department of Labor has ruled that organizations that employ contingent workers must extend coverage of the law to these individuals.[33]

## The Older Workers Benefit Protection Act

Passed by Congress in 1990, the Older Workers Benefit Protection Act (OWBPA) is a companion piece of legislation to the Age Discrimination in Employment Act (ADEA).[34] (See Chapter 2.) Specifically, the OWBPA prohibits age-based discrimination in early retirement and other benefit plans. The act imposes strict guidelines on employers who seek to have employees sign release forms waiving their right to pursue age discrimination claims under the ADEA.[35]

Where employers desire to obtain release waivers from employees, the OWBPA requires that a valid waiver must be voluntary and written in a manner that is understandable to the parties involved. Additionally, the OWBPA requires that

- The waiver specify employee rights under the ADEA
- Employees signing the waiver be given benefits greater than those to which they would already be entitled
- Employees be given twenty-one days to sign the release and seven days to revoke the agreement after signing

Furthermore, employers must inform employees that they have the right to consult with an attorney before signing the waiver.[36]

# Discretionary Major Employee Benefits

Employee benefits may be categorized in different ways. In Figure 11.2 we saw the categories of benefits that have been used by the U.S. Chamber of Commerce in studies of benefits since 1951. In the discussion that follows, we will use a somewhat

**HRM 3**

HIGHLIGHTS IN HRM

# "Your Rights": Another Federally Required Poster

## Your Rights
### Under The
## Family and Medical Leave Act of 1993

FMLA requires covered employers to provide up to 12 weeks of unpaid, job-protected leave to "eligible" employees for certain family and medical reasons. Employees are eligible if they have worked for a covered employer for at least one year, and for 1,250 hours over the previous 12 months, and if there are at least 50 employees within 75 miles.

### Reasons For Taking Leave:

Unpaid leave must be granted for *any* of the following reasons:

- to care for the employee's child after birth, or placement for adoption or foster care;
- to care for the employee's spouse, son or daughter, or parent, who has a serious health condition; or
- for a serious health condition that makes the employee unable to perform the employee's job.

At the employee's or employer's option, certain kinds of *paid* leave may be substituted for unpaid leave.

### Advance Notice and Medical Certification:

The employee may be required to provide advance leave notice and medical certification. Taking of leave may be denied if requirements are not met.

- The employee ordinarily must provide 30 days advance notice when the leave is "foreseeable."
- An employer may require medical certification to support a request for leave because of a serious health condition, and may require second or third opinions (at the employer's expense) and a fitness for duty report to return to work.

### Job Benefits and Protection:

- For the duration of FMLA leave, the employer must maintain the employee's health coverage under any "group health plan."

- Upon return from FMLA leave, most employees must be restored to their original or equivalent positions with equivalent pay, benefits, and other employment terms.
- The use of FMLA leave cannot result in the loss of any employment benefit that accrued prior to the start of an employee's leave.

### Unlawful Acts By Employers:

FMLA makes it unlawful for any employer to:

- interfere with, restrain, or deny the exercise of any right provided under FMLA:
- discharge or discriminate against any person for opposing any practice made unlawful by FMLA or for involvement in any proceeding under or relating to FMLA.

### Enforcement:

- The U.S. Department of Labor is authorized to investigate and resolve complaints of violations.
- An eligible employee may bring a civil action against an employer for violations.

FMLA does not affect any Federal or State law prohibiting discrimination, or supersede any State or local law or collective bargaining agreement which provides greater family or medical leave rights.

### For Additional Information:

**Contact the nearest office of the Wage and Hour Division, listed in most telephone directories under U.S. Government, Department of Labor.**

 U.S. Department of Labor
Employment Standards Administration
Wage and Hour Division
Washington, D.C. 20210

WH Publication 1420
June 1993

GPO : 1993 0 – 355–556

Note: Other federally required posters are reproduced in Chapters 2, 5, 9, and 12.

# Incentive Rewards

**AFTER STUDYING THIS CHAPTER, YOU SHOULD BE ABLE TO** ◄

 **OBJECTIVE 1** Discuss the basic requirements for successful implementation of incentive programs.

 **OBJECTIVE 2** List the types of, and reasons for implementing, individual incentive plans.

 **OBJECTIVE 3** Explain why merit raises may fail to motivate employees adequately and discuss ways to increase their motivational value.

 **OBJECTIVE 4** State and identify the advantage of each of the principal methods used to compensate salespersons.

 **OBJECTIVE 5** Differentiate how gains may be shared with employees under the Scanlon, Rucker, Improshare, and earnings-at-risk gainsharing systems.

 **OBJECTIVE 6** Explain what profit-sharing plans are and the advantages and disadvantages of these programs.

 **OBJECTIVE 7** Describe the main types of ESOP plans and discuss the advantages of ESOP to employers and employees.

In the previous chapter we emphasized that the worth of a job is a significant factor in determining the pay rate for that job. However, pay based solely on this measure may fail to motivate employees to perform to their full capacity. Unmotivated employees are likely to meet only minimum performance standards. Recognizing this fact, diverse organizations such as Continental Bank, AmeriSteel, Rhino Foods, Alliant Health Systems, Compaq Computers, and BFGoodrich offer some form of incentive to workers.[1] These organizations are attempting to get more motivational mileage out of employee compensation by tying it more clearly to organizational objectives and employee performance. Managers at Magma Copper Company note that incentive linked with output "causes workers to more fully apply their skills and knowledge to their jobs while encouraging them to work together as a team." Marshall Campbell, vice president of human resources at Magma, remarked, "If we increase production of ore extraction, and tie output to employee compensation, we operate with lower costs and that makes us more competitive in the national and international marketplace."[2] In their attempt to raise productivity, managers are focusing on the many variables that help to determine the effectiveness of pay as a motivator.

In this chapter we will discuss incentive plans in terms of the objectives they hope to achieve and the various factors that may affect their success. Since many organizations have implemented broad-based incentive programs, for discussion purposes we have grouped incentive plans into three broad categories: individual incentive plans, group incentive plans, and enterprise incentive plans, as shown in Figure 10.1.

# Reasons and Requirements for Incentive Plans

**Variable Pay**
Tying pay to some measure of individual, group, or organizational performance

A clear trend in strategic compensation management is the growth of incentive plans, also called **variable pay** programs, for employees throughout the organization. Variable pay programs establish a performance "threshold" (a baseline performance level) an employee or group of employees must reach in order to qualify for variable payments. According to one compensation specialist, "The performance threshold is the minimum level an employee must reach in order to qualify for variable pay."[3]

A 1998 salary survey conducted by the American Compensation Association showed that 63 percent of respondents used at least one form of variable pay.[4] Of the 37 percent that did not, 28.5 percent were planning to introduce variable pay during 1999. Incentive plans emphasize a shared focus on organizational objectives by broadening the opportunities for incentives to employees throughout the organization. Incentive plans create an operating environment that champions a philosophy of shared commitment through the belief that every individual contributes to organizational performance and success.

## Incentive Plans as Links to Organizational Objectives

Over the years, organizations have implemented incentive plans for a variety of reasons: high labor costs, competitive product markets, slow technological advances, and high potential for production bottlenecks. While these reasons are still cited,

FIGURE 10.1

**Types of Incentive Plans**

| INDIVIDUAL | GROUP | ENTERPRISE |
|---|---|---|
| Piecework | Team compensation | Profit sharing |
| Standard hour plan | Scanlon Plan | Stock options |
| Bonuses | Rucker Plan | Employee stock ownership plans (ESOPs) |
| Merit pay | Improshare | |
| Lump-sum merit pay | Earnings-at-risk plans | |
| Sales incentives | | |
| Maturity curves | | |
| Executive compensation | | |

contemporary arguments for incentive plans focus on pay-for-performance and link compensation rewards to organizational goals.[5] By meshing compensation and organizational objectives, managers believe that employees will assume "ownership" of their jobs, thereby improving their effort and overall job performance. Incentives are designed to encourage employees to put out more effort to complete their job tasks—effort they might not be motivated to expend under hourly and/or seniority-based compensation systems. Financial incentives are therefore offered to improve or maintain high levels of productivity and quality, which in turn improves the market for U.S. goods and services in a global economy. Figure 10.2 summarizes the major advantages of incentive pay programs as noted by researchers and HR professionals.

Do incentive plans work? Various studies have demonstrated a measurable relationship between incentive plans and improved organizational performance.

FIGURE 10.2

**Advantages of Incentive Pay Programs**

- Incentives focus employee efforts on specific performance targets. They provide real motivation that produces important employee and organizational gains.

- Incentive payouts are variable costs linked to the achievement of results. Base salaries are fixed costs largely unrelated to output.

- Incentive compensation is directly related to operating performance. If performance objectives (quantity and/or quality) are met, incentives are paid. If objectives are not achieved, incentives are withheld.

- Incentives foster teamwork and unit cohesiveness when payments to individuals are based on team results.

- Incentives are a way to distribute success among those responsible for producing that success.

According to the nonprofit Employment Policy Foundation in Washington, D.C., the typical incentive program yields organizational productivity increases between 5 and 49 percent.[6] In the area of manufacturing, productivity will often improve by as much as 20 percent after the adoption of incentive plans. Improvements, however, are not limited to goods-producing industries. Service organizations, not-for-profits, and government agencies also show productivity gains when incentives are linked to organizational goals. For example, after beginning a skill-based pay-for-performance plan, the City of Englewood, Colorado, reduced operating costs and improved employee-management communications. Taco Bell Corporation reduced food costs and improved customer service after it began an employee bonus program.

Unfortunately, studies also show that variable pay plans may not achieve their proposed objectives or lead to organizational improvements.[7] First, incentive plans sometimes fail to satisfy employee needs. Second, management may have failed to give adequate attention to the design and implementation of the plan. And third, employees may have little ability to affect performance standards. Furthermore, the success of an incentive plan will depend on the environment that exists within an organization. A plan is more likely to work in an organization where morale is high, employees believe they are being treated fairly, and there is harmony between employees and management.

## Requirements for a Successful Incentive Plan

For an incentive plan to succeed, employees must have some desire for the plan.[8] This desire can be influenced in part by how successful management is in introducing the plan and convincing employees of its benefits.[9] Encouraging employees to participate in developing and administering the plan is likely to increase their willingness to accept it.[10]

Employees must be able to see a clear connection between the incentive payments they receive and their job performance. This connection is more visible if there are objective quality or quantity standards by which they can judge their performance. Commitment by employees to meet these standards is also essential for incentive plans to succeed. This requires mutual trust and understanding between employees and their supervisors, which can only be achieved through open, two-way channels of communication. Management should never allow incentive payments to be seen as an *entitlement*. Instead, these payments should be viewed as a reward that must be earned through effort. This perception can be strengthened if the incentive money is distributed to employees in a separate check. Compensation specialists also note the following as characteristics of a successful incentive plan:

- Financial incentives are linked to valued behavior.
- The incentive program seems fair to employees.
- Productivity/quality standards are challenging but achievable.
- Payout formulas are simple and understandable.

# Setting Performance Measures

Measurement is key to the success of incentive plans because it communicates the importance of established organizational goals. What gets measured and rewarded

gets attention. For example, if the organization desires to be a leader in quality, then performance indexes may focus on customer satisfaction, timeliness, or being error-free. If being a low-priced producer is the goal, then emphasis should be on cost reduction or increased productivity with lower acceptable levels of quality. While a variety of performance options are available, most focus on quality, cost control, or productivity. Highlights in HRM 1 describes how one new performance measure, customer satisfaction measures (CSMs), can be linked with customer service goals.

**HRM 1**

**HIGHLIGHTS IN HRM**

# Setting Performance Goals through Customer Satisfaction Measures (CSMs)

As organizations continue to focus on customer opinions as a way to gauge organizational success, there is a growing interest in using customer satisfaction measures (CSMs) as the basis for performance reviews and compensation rewards. In a study by Walker Information, at least six winners of the Malcolm Baldrige National Quality Award—Federal Express, Xerox, AT&T Network Systems, Granite Rock, IBM Rochester, and AT&T Universal Card—said they used the CSM process as a basis for employee compensation because it (1) demonstrates a commitment to the customer, (2) holds employees accountable, and (3) fosters change. Perhaps the most compelling reason for establishing CSMs is to focus employees on the all-important goal of giving careful attention to each and every customer interaction. While organizations can tie CSMs to reward systems in a variety of ways, the process generally follows the following format:

- The organization collects survey data that identify the key factors related to the customer's purchase satisfaction. It then conducts a survey across customers to quantify the organization's current performance levels in those areas.
- The organization sets CSM goals. These goals identify the areas for improvement, the levels of improvement expected, and the time frame for goal attainment. The targets may be fixed—for example, improve customers' rating of product quality by two percentage points in 2000—or they may call for continuous improvements for each quarter or year.
- CSM goals are linked to incentive pay, basing anywhere from 10 to 100 percent of an employee's total potential bonus on the achievement of CSM goals.
- The organization communicates the goals to employees and develops supporting action plans. These plans determine how participants will go about achieving the objectives.
- At the end of the period, the organization surveys customers to remeasure its performance in the targeted areas. It then incorporates the results into performance reviews, giving employees an objective look at how their work affects customers. One benefit of a CSM program is that it replaces the traditionally "soft" process used to measure customer satisfaction with quantified results. The cycle continues with the setting of new CSM goals.

One authority on incentive plans notes that the failure of most incentive plans can be traced to the choice of performance measures.[11] Therefore measures that are quantitative, simple, and structured to show a clear relationship to improved performance are best. Overly quantitative, complex measures are to be avoided. Also, when selecting a performance measure, it is necessary to evaluate the extent to which the employees involved can actually influence the measurement. Finally, employers must guard against "ratcheting up" performance goals by continually trying to exceed previous results. This eventually leads to employee frustration and employee perception that the standards are unattainable. The result will be a mistrust of management and a backlash against the entire incentive program.

# Administering Incentive Plans

While incentive plans based on productivity can reduce direct labor costs, to achieve their full benefit they must be carefully thought out, implemented, and maintained. A cardinal rule is that thorough planning must be combined with a "proceed with caution" approach. Compensation managers repeatedly stress a number of points related to the effective administration of incentive plans. Three of the more important points are, by consensus:

1.  Incentive systems are effective only when managers are willing to grant incentives based on differences in individual, team, or organizational performance. Allowing incentive payments to become pay guarantees defeats the motivational intent of the incentive. The primary purpose of an incentive compensation plan is not to pay off under almost all circumstances, but rather to motivate performance. Thus, if the plan is to succeed, poor performance must go unrewarded.

2.  Annual salary budgets must be large enough to reward and reinforce exceptional performance. When compensation budgets are set to ensure that pay increases do not exceed certain limits (often established as a percentage of payroll or sales), these constraints may prohibit rewarding outstanding individual or group performance.

3.  The overhead costs associated with plan implementation and administration must be determined. These may include the cost of establishing performance standards and the added cost of record keeping. The time consumed in communicating the plan to employees, answering questions, and resolving any complaints about it must also be included in these costs.[12]

# Individual Incentive Plans

In today's competitive world, one word, "flexibility," describes the design of individual incentive plans. For example, technology, job tasks and duties, and/or organizational goals (e.g., being a low-cost producer) impact the organization's choice of incentive pay programs. Incentive payments may be determined by the number of units produced, by the achievement of specific performance goals, or by productivity improvements in the organization as a whole. In addition, in highly competitive industries such as foods and retailing, low profit margins will affect the

availability of monies for incentive payouts. All of these considerations suggest that tradition and philosophy, as well as economics and technology, help to govern the design of individual incentive systems.

## Piecework

**Straight piecework**
Incentive plan under which employees receive a certain rate for each unit produced

**Differential piece rate**
Compensation rate under which employees whose production exceeds the standard amount of output receive a higher rate for all of their work than the rate paid to those who do not exceed the standard amount

One of the oldest incentive plans is based on piecework. Under **straight piecework,** employees receive a certain rate for each unit produced. Their compensation is determined by the number of units they produce during a pay period. At Steelcase, an office furniture maker, employees can earn more than their base pay, often as much as 35 percent more, through piecework for each slab of metal they cut or chair they upholster. Under a **differential piece rate,** employees whose production exceeds the standard output receive a higher rate for *all* of their work than the rate paid to those who do not exceed the standard.

Employers will include piecework in their compensation strategy for several reasons. The wage payment for each employee is simple to compute, and the plan permits an organization to predict its labor costs with considerable accuracy, since these costs are the same for each unit of output. The piecework system is more likely to succeed when units of output can be measured readily, when the quality of the product is less critical, when the job is fairly standardized, and when a constant flow of work can be maintained.

### Computing the Piece Rate

Although time standards establish the time required to perform a given amount of work, they do not by themselves determine what the incentive rate should be. The incentive rates must be based on hourly wage rates that would otherwise be paid for the type of work being performed. Say, for example, the standard time for producing one unit of work in a job paying $7.50 per hour was set at twelve minutes. The piece rate would be $1.50 per unit, computed as follows:

$$\frac{60 \text{ (minutes per hour)}}{12 \text{ (standard time per unit)}} = 5 \text{ units per hour}$$

$$\frac{\$7.50 \text{ (hourly rate)}}{5 \text{ (units per hour)}} = \$1.50 \text{ per unit}$$

### Piecework: The Drawbacks

Despite their obvious advantages—including their direct tie to a pay-for-performance philosophy—piecework systems have a number of disadvantages that offset their usefulness. Production standards on which piecework must be based can be difficult to develop for many types of jobs. Jobs in which individual contributions are difficult to distinguish or measure, or in which the work is mechanized to the point that the employee exercises very little control over output, also may be unsuited to piecework. Importantly, piecework incentive systems can work against an organizational culture promoting workforce cooperation, creativity, or problem solving since each of these goals can infringe on an employee's time and productivity and, therefore, total incentive earned.

One of the most significant weaknesses of piecework, as well as of other incentive plans based on individual effort, is that it may not always be an effective motivator. If employees believe that an increase in their output will provoke disapproval

*Piecework incentive programs have been used for many years in the garment industry.*

from fellow workers (often referred to as "rate busting"), they may avoid exerting maximum effort because their desire for peer approval outweighs their desire for more money.[13] Over a period of time, the standards on which piece rates are based tend to loosen, either because of peer pressure to relax the standards or because employees discover ways to do the work in less than standard time. In either case, employees are not required to exert as much effort to receive the same amount of incentive pay, so the incentive value is reduced.

Some union leaders have feared that management will use piecework or similar systems to try to speed up production, getting more work from employees for the same amount of money. Piecework may also be inappropriate where

- Quality is more important than quantity.
- Technology changes are frequent.
- Cross-training is desired to promote scheduling flexibility.

## Standard Hour Plan

**Standard hour plan**
Incentive plan that sets rates based upon the completion of a job in a predetermined standard time

Another common incentive technique is the **standard hour plan,** which sets incentive rates on the basis of a predetermined "standard time" for completing a job. If employees finish the work in less than the expected time, their pay is still based on the standard time for the job multiplied by their hourly rate. For example, if the standard time to install an engine in a half-ton truck is five hours and the mechanic completes the job in four and a half hours, the payment would be the mechanic's hourly rate times five hours. Standard hour plans are particularly suited to long-cycle operations or those jobs or tasks that are nonrepetitive and require a variety of skills.[14]

The Wood Products Southern Division of Potlatch Corporation has successfully used a standard hour plan for the production of numerous wood products. The incentive payment is based on the standard hours calculated to produce and

*Much better than a raise, Fredericks, I've promoted you to V.P. You'll oversee our coffee distribution and trash removal teams.*

Reprinted with permission of Jerry King.

**Bonus**
Incentive payment that is supplemental to the base wage

**Spot bonus**
Unplanned bonus given for employee effort unrelated to an established performance measure

package 1,000 feet of wood paneling. If employees can produce the paneling in less time than the standard, incentives are paid on the basis of the percentage improvement. Thus, with a 1,000-hour standard and completion of the wood paneling in 900 hours, a 10 percent incentive is paid. Each employee's base hourly wage is increased by 10 percent and then multiplied by the hours worked.

While standard hour plans can motivate employees to produce more, employers must ensure that equipment maintenance and product quality do not suffer as employees strive to do their work faster to earn additional income.

## Bonuses

A **bonus** is an incentive payment that is given to an employee beyond one's normal base wage. It is frequently given at the end of the year and does not become part of base pay. Bonuses have the advantage of providing employees with more pay for exerting greater effort, while at the same time the employees still have the security of a basic wage. Bonus payments are common among managerial and executive employees but recent trends show they are increasingly given to employees throughout the organization.

Depending on who is to receive the bonus, the incentive payment may be determined on the basis of cost reduction, quality improvement, or performance criteria established by the organization. At the executive level, for example, performance criteria might include earnings growth or enterprise-specific agreed-upon objectives. For hourly employees, a bonus payment may be based on the number of units that an individual produces, as in the case of piecework. For example, at the basic wage rate of $7 an hour plus a bonus of 15 cents per unit, an employee who produces 100 units during an eight-hour period is paid $71, computed as follows:

$$(\text{Hours} \times \text{wage rate}) + (\text{number of units} \times \text{unit rate}) = \text{Wages}$$
$$(8 = \$7) + (100 \times 15\text{¢}) = \$71$$

When some special employee contribution is to be rewarded, a spot bonus is used. A **spot bonus,** as the name implies, is given "on the spot," normally for some employee effort not directly tied to an established performance standard. For example, a customer service representative might receive a spot bonus for working long hours to fill a new customer's large order.

## Merit Pay

A merit pay program (merit raise) links an increase in base pay to how successfully an employee performs his or her job.[15] The merit increase is normally given on the basis of an employee's having achieved some objective performance standard—although a superior's subjective evaluation of subordinate performance may

play a large role in the increase given. Merit raises can serve to motivate if employees perceive the raise to be related to the performance required to earn them.

Theories of motivation, in addition to behavioral science research, provide justification for merit pay plans as well as other pay-for-performance programs. For employees to see the link between pay and performance, however, their performance must be evaluated in light of objective criteria. If this evaluation also includes the use of subjective judgment by their superiors, employees must have confidence in the validity of this judgment. Most important, any increases granted on the basis of merit should be distinguishable from employees' regular pay and from any cost-of-living or other general increases. Where merit increases are based on pay-for-performance, merit pay should be withheld when performance is seen to decline.[16]

### Problems with Merit Raises

Merit raises may not always achieve their intended purpose.[17] Unlike a bonus, a merit raise may be perpetuated year after year even when performance declines. When this happens, employees come to expect the increase and see it as being unrelated to their performance. Furthermore, employees in some organizations are opposed to merit raises because, among other reasons, they do not really trust management. What are referred to as merit raises often turn out to be increases based on seniority or favoritism, or raises to accommodate increases in cost of living or in area wage rates.[18]

As noted by two compensation specialists, "Some subordinates have better political connections within the company than others. Subordinates who are politically, socially, and familially connected inside and outside the organization, who carry clout, and who can hurt the supervisor in some way are likely to receive a larger share of the merit pie than their performance might warrant."[19] Even when merit raises are determined by performance, the employee's gains may be offset by inflation and higher income taxes. Compensation specialists also recognize the following problems with merit pay plans:

1. Money available for merit increases may be inadequate to satisfactorily raise employees' base pay.
2. Managers may have no guidance in how to define and measure performance; there may be vagueness regarding merit award criteria.
3. Employees may not believe that their compensation is tied to effort and performance; they may be unable to differentiate between merit pay and other types of pay increases.
4. Employees may believe that organizational politics plays a significant factor in merit pay decisions, despite the presence of a formal merit pay system.
5. There may be a lack of honesty and cooperation between management and employees.
6. It has been shown that "overall" merit pay plans do not motivate higher levels of employee performance.

Probably one of the major weaknesses of merit raises lies in the performance appraisal system on which the increases are based. Even with an effective system, performance may be difficult to measure. Furthermore, any deficiencies in the performance appraisal program (these were discussed in Chapter 8) can impair the operation of a merit pay plan. Moreover, the performance appraisal objectives of

employees and their superiors are often at odds. Employees typically want to maximize their pay increases, whereas superiors may seek to reward employees in an equitable manner on the basis of their performance. In some instances, employee pressures for pay increases actually may have a harmful effect on their performance appraisal.

**Merit guidelines**
Guidelines for awarding merit raises that are tied to performance objectives

While there are no easy solutions to these problems, organizations using a true merit pay plan often base the percentage pay raise on **merit guidelines** tied to performance appraisals. For example, Highlights in HRM 2 illustrates a guideline chart for awarding merit raises. The percentages may change each year, depending on various internal or external concerns such as profit levels or national economic conditions as indicated by changes in the consumer price index. Under the illustrated merit plan, to prevent all employees from being rated outstanding or above average, managers may be required to distribute the performance rating according to some preestablished formula (e.g., only 10 percent can be rated outstanding). Additionally, when setting merit percentage guidelines, organizations should consider individual performance along with such factors as training, experience, and current earnings.

## Lump-Sum Merit Pay

**Lump-sum merit program**
Program under which employees receive a year-end merit payment, which is not added to their base pay

To make merit increases more flexible and visible, organizations such as Boeing, Timex, and Westinghouse have implemented a **lump-sum merit program.** Under this type of plan, employees receive a single lump-sum increase at the time of their review, an increase that is not added to their base salary. Unless management takes further steps to compensate employees, their base salary is essentially frozen until they receive a promotion.

Lump-sum merit programs offer several advantages. For employers, this innovative approach provides financial control by maintaining annual salary expenses. Merit increases granted on a lump-sum basis do not contribute to escalating base salary levels. In addition, organizations can contain employee benefit costs, since the levels of benefits are normally calculated from current salary levels. For employees, an advantage is that receiving a single lump-sum merit payment can provide a clear link between pay and performance. For example, a 6 percent merit increase granted to an industrial engineer earning $42,000 a year translates into a weekly increase of $48.46—a figure that looks small compared with a lump-sum payment of $2,520. Organizations using a lump-sum merit program will want to adjust base salaries upward after a certain period of time. This can be done yearly or after several years. These adjustments should keep pace with the rising cost of living and increases in the general market wage.

## Sales Incentives

The enthusiasm and drive required in most types of sales work demand that sales employees be highly motivated. This fact, as well as the competitive nature of selling, explains why financial incentives for salespeople are widely used. These incentive plans must provide a source of motivation that will elicit cooperation and trust. Motivation is particularly important for employees away from the office who cannot be supervised closely and who, as a result, must exercise a high degree of self-discipline.

# Merit Pay Guidelines Chart

A merit pay guidelines chart is a "look-up" table for awarding merit increases on the basis of (1) employee performance, (2) position in the pay range, and, in a few cases, (3) time since the last pay increase. One feature of most merit pay guidelines charts is that they are designed to move new jobholders relatively quickly up to the midpoint of their pay range (see Chapter 9) once they can competently perform the job. The purpose of getting employees' pay to the midpoint is to ensure that they are competitively compensated and not tempted to move to other employers who pay higher wages or salaries. A second feature of the chart is to slow the employees' progress in the pay range above the midpoint to ensure that only top performers move toward the upper limit of the range. If too many employees are paid above the mid-point, the organization is paying a premium for labor, and top performers who are at the top of the pay range cannot receive pay increases unless the pay range is adjusted.

The merit pay guidelines chart below shows the pay range for each pay grade as divided into five levels (quintiles), with 1 at the bottom of the pay range and 5 at the top. On the left, employee performance (as determined by the annual appraisal) is arranged in five levels from high (outstanding) to low (unsatisfactory). An employee's position in his or her salary range and performance level indicates the percentage pay increase to be awarded. For example, a person at the top of the pay range (5) who gets a performance rating of "outstanding" will be awarded a 6 percent pay increase. However, an outstanding performer at the bottom of the pay range (1) will receive a 9 percent increase.

Because the purpose of the guidelines chart is to balance conflicting pay goals, it compromises, by design, the relationship between merit increases and performance appraisal ratings. The highest-rated performers will not always be the employees with the highest percentage increase. Notice that a superior performer in quintiles 1, 2, and 3 can receive a percentage increase as much as or more than that of an outstanding performer in quintile 5. As a result, employees are likely to learn that pay increases are not determined just by performance. However, as we learned in Chapter 9, if money is to serve as a motivator, expectancy theory specifies that employees must believe there is a link between performance and pay increases if performance is to remain at a high level.

### MERIT PAY GUIDE CHART

| PERFORMANCE LEVEL | QUINTILE (POSITION IN RANGE), % | | | | |
|---|---|---|---|---|---|
| | 1 | 2 | 3 | 4 | 5 |
| Outstanding (5) | 9 | 9 | 8 | 7 | 6 |
| Superior (4) | 7 | 7 | 6 | 5 | 4 |
| Competent (3) | 5 | 5 | 4 | 3 | 3 |
| Needs improvement (2) | 0 | 0 | 0 | 0 | 0 |
| Unsatisfactory (1) | 0 | 0 | 0 | 0 | 0 |

Source: Adapted from K. Dow Scott, Steven E. Markham, and Michael J. Vest, "The Influence of a Merit Pay Guide Chart on Employee Attitudes toward Pay at a Transit Authority," *Public Personnel Management* 25, no. 1 (Spring 1996): 103–15. Published with permission.

## Unique Needs of Sales Incentive Plans

Incentive systems for salespeople are complicated by the wide differences in the types of sales jobs.[20] These range from department store clerks who ring up customer purchases to industrial salespersons from McGraw-Edison who provide consultation and other highly technical services. Salespersons' performance may be measured by the dollar volume of their sales and by their ability to establish new accounts. Other measures are the ability to promote new products or services and to provide various forms of customer service and assistance that do not produce immediate sales revenues.

Performance standards for sales employees are difficult to develop, however, because their performance is often affected by external factors beyond their control.[21] Economic and seasonal fluctuations, sales competition, changes in demand, and the nature of the sales territory can all affect an individual's sales record. Sales volume alone therefore may not be an accurate indicator of the effort salespeople have expended.

In developing incentive plans for salespeople, managers are also confronted with the problem of how to reward extra sales effort and at the same time compensate for activities that do not contribute directly or immediately to sales. Furthermore, sales employees must be able to enjoy some degree of income stability.

## Types of Sales Incentive Plans

Compensation plans for sales employees may consist of a straight salary plan, a straight commission plan, or a combination salary and commission plan.[22] A **straight salary plan** permits salespeople to be paid for performing various duties not reflected immediately in their sales volume. It enables them to devote more time to providing services and building up the goodwill of customers without jeopardizing their income. The principal limitation of the straight salary plan is that it may not motivate salespeople to exert sufficient effort in maximizing their sales volume.

On the other hand, the **straight commission plan,** based on a percentage of sales, provides maximum incentive and is easy to compute and understand. For example, organizations that pay a straight commission based on total volume may use the following simple formulas:

$$\text{Total cash compensation} = 2\% \times \text{total volume}$$

or

$$\text{Total cash compensation} = 2\% \times \text{total volume up to quota}$$
$$+ 4\% \times \text{volume over quota}$$

However, the straight commission plan is limited by the following disadvantages:

1. Emphasis is on sales volume rather than on profits.
2. Customer service after the sale is likely to be neglected.
3. Earnings tend to fluctuate widely between good and poor periods of business, and turnover of trained sales employees tends to increase in poor periods.
4. Salespeople are tempted to grant price concessions.

When a **combined salary and commission plan** is used, the percentage of cash compensation paid out in commissions (i.e., incentives) is called "leverage." Leverage is usually expressed as a ratio of base salary to commission. For example, a salesperson working under a 70/30 combination plan would receive total cash compensation paid out as 70 percent base salary and 30 percent commission. The amount of leverage will be determined after considering the constraining factors

**Straight salary plan**
Compensation plan that permits salespeople to be paid for performing various duties that are not reflected immediately in their sales volume

**Straight commission plan**
Compensation plan based upon a percentage of sales

**Combined salary and commission plan**
Compensation plan that includes a straight salary and a commission

affecting performance discussed earlier and the sales objectives of the organization. The following advantages indicate why the combination salary and commission plan is so widely used.[23]

1. The right kind of incentive compensation, if linked to salary in the right proportion, has most of the advantages of both the straight salary and the straight commission forms of compensation.
2. A salary-plus-incentive compensation plan offers greater design flexibility and can therefore be more readily set up to help maximize company profits.
3. The plan can develop the most favorable ratio of selling expense to sales.
4. The field sales force can be motivated to achieve specific company marketing objectives in addition to sales volume.

## Maturity Curves

Like other salaried workers, professional employees—engineers, scientists, and attorneys, for example—may be motivated through bonuses and merit increases. In some organizations, unfortunately, professional employees cannot advance beyond a certain point in the salary structure unless they are willing to take an administrative assignment. When they are promoted, their professional talents are no longer utilized fully. In the process, the organization may lose a good professional employee and gain a poor administrator. To avoid this situation, some organizations have extended the salary range for professional positions to equal or nearly equal that for administrative positions. The extension of this range provides a double-track wage system, as illustrated in Chapter 7, whereby professionals who do not aspire to become administrators still have an opportunity to earn comparable salaries.

Organizations also use career curves or **maturity curves** as a basis for providing salary increases to professional employees. These curves, such as the ones

**Maturity curves**
Experience or performance bases for providing salary increases for professional employees

*An engineer working on high-tech projects like this gamma ray detector could expect to be part of a performance-based incentive program.*

shown in Figure 10.3, provide for the annual salary rate to be based on experience and performance. Separate curves are established to reflect different levels of performance and to provide for annual increases. The curves representing higher levels of performance tend to rise to a higher level and at a faster rate than the curves representing lower performance levels.

Professional employees can receive compensation beyond base pay. For example, scientists and engineers employed by high-tech firms are included in performance-based incentive programs such as profit sharing or stock ownership. These plans encourage greater levels of individual performance. Cash bonuses can be awarded to those who complete projects on or before deadline dates. Payments may also be given to individuals elected to professional societies, granted patents, or meeting professional licensing standards.

## Executive Compensation

A major function of incentive plans for executives is to motivate them to develop and use their abilities and contribute their energies to the fullest possible extent.

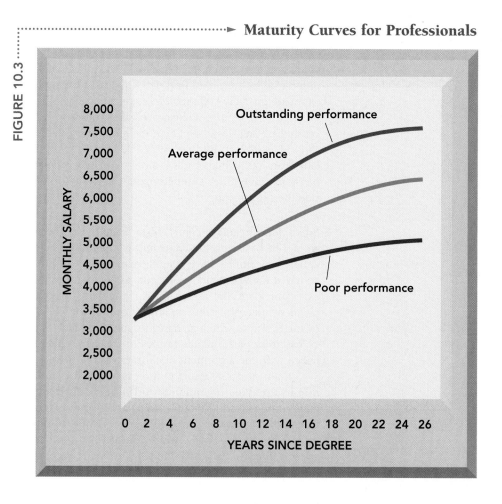

**FIGURE 10.3**    ► **Maturity Curves for Professionals**

Incentive plans should also facilitate the recruitment and retention of competent executive employees. This can be accomplished with plans that will enable them to accumulate a financial estate and to shelter a portion of their compensation from current income taxes.

### Components of Executive Compensation

Organizations commonly have more than one compensation strategy for executives in order to meet various organizational goals and executive needs. For example, chief executive officers (CEOs) may have their compensation packages heavily weighted toward long-term incentives, because CEOs should be more concerned about the long-term impact of their decisions than the short-term implications. Group vice presidents, on the other hand, may receive more short-term incentives since their decisions affect operations on a six- to twelve-month basis. Regardless of the mix, executive compensation plans consist of four basic components: (1) base salary, (2) short-term incentives or bonuses, (3) long-term incentives or stock plans, and (4) perquisites. Another important element in compensation strategy is the compensation mix to be paid to managers and executives accepting overseas assignments. (We will elaborate on this topic in Chapter 16.)

***Bases for Executive Salaries.*** The levels of competitive salaries in the job market exert perhaps the greatest influence on executive base salaries. An organization's compensation committee—normally members of the board of directors—will order a salary survey to find out what executives earn in comparable enterprises. Comparisons may be based on organization size, sales volume, or industry grouping. In a 1998 survey of executive base salaries by industry, results showed that the yearly base salaries of CEOs in the automotive industry were $814,000; in health care, $764,000; in mining, $992,000; and in retail, $733,000.[24] By analyzing the data from published studies, along with self-generated salary surveys, the compensation committee can determine the equity of the compensation package outside the organization.[25]

***Bases for Executive Short-Term Incentives.*** Incentive bonuses for executives should be based on the contribution the individual makes to the organization. A variety of formulas have been developed for this purpose. Incentive bonuses may be based on a percentage of a company's total profits or a percentage of profits in excess of a specific return on stockholders' investments. In other instances the payments may be tied to an annual profit plan whereby the amount is determined by the extent to which an agreed-upon profit level is exceeded. Payments may also be based on performance ratings or the achievement of specific objectives established with the agreement of executives and the board of directors.

In a continuing effort to monitor the pulse of the marketplace, more organizations are tying operational yardsticks to the traditional financial gauges when computing executive pay. Called *balanced scorecards,* these yardsticks may measure things like customer satisfaction, the ability to innovate, or product or service leadership. Notes David Cates, a compensation principal with Towers Perrin, a balanced scorecard "allows companies to focus on building future economic value, rather than be driven solely by short-term financial results."[26] Mobil Oil uses a bal-

anced scorecard that better indicates exactly where the company is successful and where improvement is needed.

A bonus payment may take the form of cash or stock. Also, the timing of the payment may vary. Payment can be immediate (which is frequently the case), deferred for a short term, or deferred until retirement. Most organizations pay their short-term incentive bonuses in cash (in the form of a supplemental check), in keeping with their pay-for-performance strategy. By providing a reward soon after the performance, and thus linking it to the effort on which it is based, they can use cash bonuses as a significant motivator.

A deferred bonus can be used to provide the sole source of retirement benefits or to supplement a regular pension plan. If they are in a lower tax bracket when the deferred benefits are ultimately received—which is not always the case—executives can realize income tax savings. In addition, interest on the deferred amount can allow it to appreciate without being taxed until it is received. To the organization's advantage, deferred bonuses are not subject to the reporting requirement of the Employee Retirement Income Security Act (ERISA). However, deferred income funds do become a part of the company's indebtedness, and may be lost in part or in toto should the company become insolvent. Also, if these funds do not appreciate with inflation, participants also stand to suffer a loss from inflation.

*Bases for Executive Long-Term Incentives.*    Short-term incentive bonuses are criticized for causing top executives to focus on quarterly profit goals to the detriment of long-term survival and growth objectives. Therefore corporations such as Sears, Combustion Engineering, Borden, and Enhart have adopted compensation strategies that tie executive pay to long-term performance measures. Each of these organizations recognizes that, while incentive payments for executives may be based on the achievement of specific goals relating to their positions, the plans must also take into account the performance of the organization as a whole. Important to stockholders are such performance results as growth in earnings per share, return on stockholders' equity, and, ultimately, stock price appreciation. A variety of incentive plans, therefore, has been developed to tie rewards to these performance results, particularly over the long term.

Stock options are the primary long-term incentive offered to executives. Stock options can be extremely lavish for executives. For example, senior executives at Consero stand to receive more than $590 million if the company is sold during their tenure.[27] According to Ira Kay, compensation specialist, "The principal reason driving executive stock ownership is the desire on the part of both the company and outside investors for senior managers to have a significant stake in the success of the business—to have their fortunes rise and fall with the value they create for shareholders."[28] The major long-term incentives fall into three broad categories:

1.  Stock price appreciation grants
2.  Restricted stock and restricted cash grants
3.  Performance-based grants

Each of these broad categories includes various stock grants or cash incentives for the payment of executive performance. See Figure 10.4 for definitions of the different grant types. The granting of stock options contributes substantially to executives' million-dollar compensation packages, which we will shortly highlight.

FIGURE 10.4

► Types of Long-Term Incentive Plans

### STOCK PRICE APPRECIATION PLANS

| | |
|---|---|
| Stock options | Rights granted to executives to purchase shares of their organization's stock at an established price for a fixed period of time. Stock price is usually set at market value at the time the option is granted. |
| Stock appreciation rights (SARs) | Cash or stock award determined by increase in stock price during any time chosen by the executive in the option period; does not require executive financing. |
| Stock purchase | Opportunities for executives to purchase shares of their organization's stock valued at full market or a discount price, often with the organization providing financial assistance. |
| Phantom stock | Grant of units equal in value to the fair market value or book value of a share of stock; on a specified date the executive will be paid the appreciation in the value of the units up to that time. |

### RESTRICTED STOCK/CASH PLANS

| | |
|---|---|
| Restricted stock | Grant of stock or stock units at a reduced price with the condition that the stock not be transferred or sold (by risk of forfeiture) before a specified employment date. |
| Restricted cash | Grant of fixed-dollar amounts subject to transfer or forfeiture restrictions before a specified employment date. |

### PERFORMANCE-BASED PLANS

| | |
|---|---|
| Performance units | Grants analogous to annual bonuses except that the measurement period exceeds one year. The value of the grant can be expressed as a flat dollar amount or converted to a number of "units" of equivalent aggregate value. |
| Performance shares | Grants of actual stock or phantom stock units. Value is contingent on both predetermined performance objectives over a specified period of time and the stock market. |
| Formula-value grants | Rights to receive units or the gain in value of units determined by a formula (such as book value or an earnings multiplier) rather than changes in market price. |
| Dividend units | Rights to receive an amount equal to the dividends paid on a specified number of shares; typically granted in conjunction with other grant types, such as performance shares. |

**Perquisites**
Special benefits given to executives; often referred to as perks

**Executive Perquisites.**  In addition to incentive programs, executive employees are often given special benefits and perquisites. **Perquisites,** or "perks," are a means of demonstrating the executives' importance to the organization while giving them an incentive to improve their performance. Furthermore, perks serve as a status symbol both inside and outside the organization. Perquisites can also provide a tax saving to executives, since some are not taxed as income. Highlights in HRM 3 shows the more common perks offered to executives.

HRM 3

# The "Sweetness" of Executive Perks

Compensation consulting firms such as Coopers and Lybrand LLP, the American Compensation Association, and Hewitt Associates regularly survey companies nationwide to identify the perks they provide for executives and other top managers. Below are listed popular executive perks along with some less popular perquisites.

## PREVALENT PERQUISITES

- Company car
- Company plane
- Financial consulting
- Company-paid parking
- Estate planning
- First-class air travel

- Physical exams
- Mobile phones
- Large insurance policies
- Income tax preparation
- Country club membership
- Luncheon club membership

## LESS PREVALENT PERQUISITES

- Chauffeur service
- Children's education
- Spouse travel

- Personal home repairs
- Legal counseling
- Vacation cabins

## Executive Compensation: The Issue of Amount

Consider the total direct compensation drawn in 1998 by the following top executives:[29]

| | |
|---|---|
| Kenneth L. Lay, Enron | $21,394,900 |
| Robert B. Shapiro, Monsanto | 19,641,600 |
| Frederick W. Smith, Fox | 17,654,200 |
| Robert S. Evans, Crane | 17,110,700 |
| Charles F. Knight, Emerson Electric | 15,300,700 |

While the majority of total executive compensation is received in bonuses and long-term incentives, the question asked by many is "Are top executives worth the salaries and bonuses they receive?" The answer may depend on whom you ask. Corporate compensation committees justify big bonuses in the following ways:

1. Large financial incentives are a way to reward superior performance.
2. Business competition is pressure-filled and demanding.
3. Good executive talent is in great demand.
4. Effective executives create shareholder value.

Others justify high compensation as a fact of business life, reflecting market compensation trends.[30]

Nevertheless, in an era of massive downsizing, low wage increases, and increased workloads for layoff survivors, strong criticism is voiced regarding the high monetary awards given to the senior executives.[31] Furthermore, with the large compensation packages awarded to senior managers and top-level executives, cries for performance accountability and openness abound. During the years ahead, compensation professionals note several challenges facing executive compensation including (1) performance measurement techniques that reflect individual contributions and (2) executive compensation practices that will support global value-creating strategies with well-considered incentive pay programs. Hard questions to be answered include: "What exactly are the implications of global competitiveness and the corresponding strategies required to improve U.S. corporations' effectiveness?" and "How do these new strategies affect organizations and their compensation systems?"

# Group Incentive Plans

The emphasis on cost reduction and total quality management has led many organizations to implement a variety of group incentive plans. Group plans enable employees to share in the benefits of improved efficiency realized by major organizational units or various individual work teams. These plans encourage a cooperative—rather than individualistic—spirit among all employees and reward them for their total contribution to the organization. Such features are particularly desirable when working conditions make individual performance difficult, if not impossible, to measure.

## Team Compensation

As production has become more automated, as teamwork and coordination among workers have become more important, and as the contributions of those engaged indirectly in production or service tasks have increased, team incentive plans have grown more popular. **Team incentive plans** reward team members with an incentive bonus when agreed-upon performance standards are met or exceeded. Furthermore, the incentive will seek to establish a psychological climate that fosters team cooperation.

**Team incentive plan**
Compensation plan where all team members receive an incentive bonus payment when production or service standards are met or exceeded

One catch with setting team compensation is that not all teams are alike (see Chapter 3). For example, cross-functional teams, self-directed teams, and task force teams make it impossible to develop one consistent type of team incentive plan. And, with a variety of teams, managers find it difficult to adopt uniform measurement standards or payout formulas for team pay.[32] According to Steven Gross, Hay manager, "Each type of team requires a specific pay structure to function at its peak."[33]

In spite of this caveat, organizations will typically use the three-step approach to establishing team incentive payments.[34] First, they will set performance measures upon which incentive payments are based. Improvements in efficiency, product quality, or reduction in materials or labor costs are common benchmark criteria. For example, if labor costs for a team represent 30 percent of the organization's sales dollars, and the organization pays a bonus for labor cost savings, then whenever team labor costs are less than 30 percent of sales dollars, those savings are paid as an incentive bonus to team members. Information on the size of the incentive bonus is reported to employees on a weekly or monthly basis, explaining why

incentive pay was or was not earned. Second, the size of the incentive bonus must be determined. At Aid Association for Lutherans (AAL), health insurance underwriters can receive team incentive bonuses of up to 10 percent of base salary; however, the exact level of incentive pay depends on overall team performance and the company's performance over one year. Team incentives at AAL are paid annually. Third, a payout formula is established and fully explained to employees. The team bonus may be distributed to employees equally, in proportion to their base pay, or on the basis of their relative contribution to the team. With discretionary formulas, managers, or in some cases, team members themselves, agree on the payouts to individual team members. Figure 10.5 presents the commonly stated advantages and disadvantages of team incentive pay.

## Gainsharing Incentive Plans

**Gainsharing plans**
Programs under which both employees and the organization share the financial gains according to a predetermined formula that reflects improved productivity and profitability

**Gainsharing plans** are organizational programs designed to increase productivity or decrease labor costs and share monetary gains with employees.[35] These plans are based on a mathematical formula that compares a baseline of performance with actual productivity during a given period. When productivity exceeds the baseline, an agreed-upon savings is shared with employees. Inherent in gainsharing is the idea that involved employees will improve productivity through more effective use of organizational resources.

Although productivity can be measured in various ways, it is usually calculated as a ratio of outputs to inputs. Sales, pieces produced, pounds, total standard costs, direct labor dollars earned, and customer orders are common output measures.

**FIGURE 10.5**

### The Pros and Cons of Team Incentive Plans

**PROS**

- Team incentives support group planning and problem solving, thereby building a team culture.
- The contributions of individual employees are dependent on group cooperation.
- Unlike incentive plans based solely on output, team incentives can broaden the scope of the contribution that employees are motivated to make.
- Team bonuses tend to reduce employee jealousies and complaints over "tight" or "loose" individual standards.
- Team incentives encourage cross-training and the acquiring of new interpersonal competencies.

**CONS**

- Individual team members may perceive that "their" efforts contribute little to team success or to the attainment of the incentive bonus.
- Intergroup social problems—pressure to limit performance (e.g., team members are afraid one individual may make the others look bad) and the "free-ride" effect (one individual puts in less effort than others but shares equally in team rewards)—may arise.
- Complex payout formulas can be difficult for team members to understand.

Inputs frequently measured include materials, labor, energy, inventory, purchased goods or services, and total costs. An increase in productivity is normally gained when

- Greater output is obtained with less or equal input.
- Equal production output is obtained with less input.[36]

Although gainsharing is a popular reward system for employees, experience with these techniques has pointed up a number of factors that contribute to either their success or their failure. Highlights in HRM 4 discusses common considerations when establishing a gainsharing program.[37]

There are four unique gainsharing plans. Two plans, which bear the names of their originators, Joe Scanlon and Alan Rucker, are similar in their philosophy. Both plans emphasize participative management. Both encourage cost reduction

**OBJECTIVE 5**

**HRM 4**

**HIGHLIGHTS IN HRM**

# Lessons Learned: Designing Effective Gainsharing Programs

Will your gainsharing program be successful? While there are no exact keys to success, gainsharing proponents cite the following as important components of a meaningful gainsharing plan.

- Enlist *total* managerial support for the gainsharing effort. While top-management support is critical, without the encouragement of middle- and lower-level managers (those directly involved in program implementation), gainsharing efforts invariably fail.
- When developing new programs, include representatives from all groups affected by the gainsharing effort—labor, management, employees. Inclusion, not exclusion, serves to build trust and understanding of the program's intent and operation.
- Prevent political gamesmanship whereby involved parties are more interested in preserving their self-interests than in supporting the group effort. The political manipulation of the bonus calculation to hold down payouts is a certain obstacle to all gainsharing programs.
- Bonus payout formulas must be seen as fair, must be easy for employees to calculate, must offer payouts on a frequent basis, and must be large enough to encourage future employee effort. The goal is to create a pay-for-performance environment.
- Establish effective, fair, and precise measurement standards. Standards must encourage increased effort without being unreasonable.
- Be certain that employees are predisposed to a gainsharing reward system. Is there a "cultural readiness" for gainsharing? If changes are indicated, what needs to be done? Will employees need additional skills training or training in other competencies in order to make anticipated organizational improvements?
- Launch the plan during a favorable business period. Business downturns jeopardize payments. A plan is likely to fail if it does not pay out under normal conditions in its first two or three years of operation.

by sharing with employees any savings resulting from these reductions. The formulas on which the bonuses are based, however, are somewhat different. The third plan, Improshare, is a gainsharing program based on the number of finished goods that employee work teams complete in an established period. The fourth plan, earnings-at-risk, encourages employees to achieve higher output and quality standards by placing a portion of their base salary at risk of loss.

### The Scanlon Plan

**Scanlon Plan**
Bonus incentive plan using employee and management committees to gain cost-reduction improvements

The philosophy behind the **Scanlon Plan** is that employees should offer ideas and suggestions to improve productivity and, in turn, be rewarded for their constructive efforts. The plan requires good management, leadership, trust and respect between employees and managers, and a workforce dedicated to responsible decision making. When correctly implemented, the Scanlon Plan can result in improved efficiency and profitability for the organization and steady employment and high compensation for employees.

According to Scanlon's proponents, effective employee participation, which includes the use of committees on which employees are represented, is the most significant feature of the Scanlon Plan.[38] This gives employees the opportunity to communicate their ideas and opinions and to exercise some degree of influence over decisions affecting their work and their welfare within the organization. Employees have an opportunity to become managers of their time and energy, equipment usage, the quality and quantity of their production, and other factors relating to their work. They accept changes in production methods more readily and volunteer new ideas. The Scanlon Plan encourages greater teamwork and sharing of knowledge at the lower levels. It demands more efficient management and better planning as workers try to reduce overtime and to work smarter rather than harder or faster.

The primary mechanisms for employee participation in the Scanlon Plan are the shop committees established in each department. (See Figure 10.6 for an illustration of the Scanlon Plan suggestion process.) These committees consider production problems and make suggestions for improvement within their respective departments to an organization-wide screening committee. The function of the screening committee is to oversee the operation of the plan, to act on suggestions received from the shop committees, and to review the data on which monthly bonuses are to be based. The screening committee is also responsible for consulting with and advising top management, which retains decision-making authority. Both the shop committees and the screening committee are composed of equal numbers of employees and managers.

Financial incentives under the Scanlon Plan are ordinarily offered to all employees (a significant feature of the plan) on the basis of an established formula. This formula is based on increases in employee productivity as determined by a norm that has been established for labor costs. The norm, which is subject to review, reflects the relationship between labor costs and the sales value of production (SVOP). The SVOP includes sales revenue and the value of goods in inventory. Figure 10.7 illustrates how the two figures are used to determine the Scanlon Plan incentive bonus.

The plan also provides for the establishment of a reserve fund into which 25 percent of any earned bonus is paid to cover deficits during the months when labor costs exceed the norm. After the reserve portion has been deducted, the remainder of the bonus is distributed, with 25 percent going to the organization and 50 percent to the employees. At the end of the year, any surplus that has been accumulated in

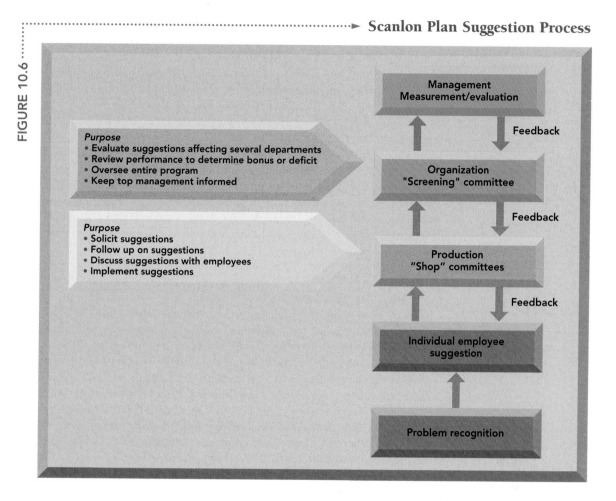

FIGURE 10.6

**Scanlon Plan Suggestion Process**

Management
Measurement/evaluation

Feedback

*Purpose*
• Evaluate suggestions affecting several departments
• Review performance to determine bonus or deficit
• Oversee entire program
• Keep top management informed

Organization
"Screening" committee

Feedback

*Purpose*
• Solicit suggestions
• Follow up on suggestions
• Discuss suggestions with employees
• Implement suggestions

Production
"Shop" committees

Feedback

Individual employee
suggestion

Problem recognition

the reserve fund is distributed to employees according to the same formula. The Scanlon Plan (and variations of it) has become a fundamental way of managing, if not a way of life, in organizations such as American Valve Company, TRW, Weyerhauser, and the Xaloy Corporation.

### The Rucker Plan

**Rucker Plan**

Bonus incentive plan based on the historic relationship between the total earnings of hourly employees and the production value created by the employees

The share-of-production plan (SOP), or **Rucker Plan,** normally covers just production workers but may be expanded to cover all employees. As with the Scanlon Plan, committees are formed to elicit and evaluate employee suggestions. The Rucker Plan, however, uses a far less elaborate participatory structure. As one authority noted, "It commonly represents a type of program that is used as an alternative to the Scanlon Plan in firms attempting to move from a traditional style of management toward a higher level of employee involvement."[39]

The financial incentive of the Rucker Plan is based on the historic relationship between the total earnings of hourly employees and the production value that employees create. The bonus is based on any improvement in this relationship that employees are able to realize. Thus, for every 1 percent increase in production value that is achieved, workers receive a bonus of 1 percent of their total payroll costs.[40]

**FIGURE 10.7** ▸ **Determining the Monthly Scanlon Plan Incentive Bonus**

| | | | |
|---|---|---|---|
| 1. | Sales revenue | | $100,000 |
| 2. | Plus value of goods in inventory | | 10,000 |
| 3. | Sales value of production (SVOP) | | $110,000 |
| 4. | Target payroll costs (40% of no. 3) | $44,000 | |
| 5. | Minus actual labor costs | 35,000 | |
| 6. | Available incentive bonus | | $9,000 |
| 7. | Deficit reserve | 2,250 | |
| 8. | Company share | 2,250 | |
| 9. | Employee share | 4,500 | |

Employee bonus (percent of actual payroll) = 12.8% ($4,500/$35,000)

## Lessons from the Scanlon and Rucker Plans

Perhaps the most important lesson to be learned from the Scanlon and Rucker Plans is that any management expecting to gain the cooperation of its employees in improving efficiency must permit them to become involved psychologically as well as financially in the organization. If employees are to contribute maximum effort, they must have a feeling of involvement and identification with their organization, which does not come out of the traditional manager-subordinate relationship. Consequently, it is important for organizations to realize that while employee cooperation is essential to the successful administration of the Scanlon and Rucker Plans, the plans themselves do not necessarily stimulate this cooperation. Furthermore, the attitude of management is of paramount importance to the success of either plan. For example, where managers show little confidence and trust in their employees, the plans tend to fail.

## Improshare

**Improshare**
Gainsharing program under which bonuses are based upon the overall productivity of the work team

**Improshare**—improved productivity through sharing—is a gainsharing program developed by Mitchell Fain, an industrial engineer with experience in traditional individual incentive systems. Whereas individual production bonuses are typically based on how much an employee produces above some standard amount, Improshare bonuses are based on the overall productivity of the *work team*. Improshare output is measured by the number of finished products that a work team produces in a given period. Both production (direct) employees and nonproduction (indirect) employees are included in the determination of the bonus.[41] Since a cooperative environment benefits all, Improshare promotes increased interaction and support between employees and management.

The bonus is based not on dollar savings, as in the Scanlon and Rucker Plans, but on productivity gains that result from reducing the time it takes to produce a finished product. Bonuses are determined monthly by calculating the difference between standard hours (Improshare hours) and actual hours, and dividing the result by actual hours. The employees and the company each receive payment for

## USING THE INTERNET

*Quality Digest Magazine* provides extensive coverage of quality-and-productivity-related issues. For information on the Scanlon, Rucker, and Improshare incentive plans, go to:

www.qualitydigest.com/jul/gainshre.html

**Earnings-at-risk incentive plans**

> Incentive pay plans placing a portion of the employee's base pay at risk, but giving the opportunity to earn income above base pay when goals are met or exceeded

50 percent of the improvement. Companies such as Hinderliter Energy Equipment Corporation and Dowe Cheatum and Howe, the world's premiere kite manufacturer, pay the bonus as a separate check to emphasize that it is extra income.

### Earnings-at-Risk Plans

As the name implies, **earnings-at-risk incentive plans** place a portion of an employee's base pay at risk. The philosophy behind these programs is that employees should not expect substantial rewards without assuming some risk for their performance. These plans, however, allow employees to recapture lower wages, or reap additional income above full base pay when quality, service, or productivity goals are met or exceeded. An employee's base pay might be set at 90 percent (i.e., 10 percent below market value—the risk part), the loss to be regained through performance. For example, at Saturn Corporation, employee total compensation is made up of base pay, risk pay, and reward pay. The risk/reward incentive encourages team members to continuously improve job performance. The risk portion of pay requires that 12 percent of base pay be withheld until specific organizational performance goals are met. When these goals are achieved, the money withheld is paid back in a quarterly lump sum. The reward portion of compensation is paid only if the risk goals are met. The maximum achievable reward is $12,500. Production rewards are paid quarterly and profitability rewards are paid annually.[42]

# Enterprise Incentive Plans

Enterprise incentive plans differ from individual and group incentive plans in that all organizational members participate in the plan's compensation payout. Enterprise incentive plans reward employees on the basis of the success of the organization over an extended time period—normally one year, but the period can be longer. Enterprise incentive plans seek to create a "culture of ownership" by fostering a philosophy of cooperation and teamwork among all organizational members. Common enterprise incentive plans include profit-sharing, stock options, and employee stock ownership plans (ESOPs).

**OBJECTIVE 6**

**Profit sharing**

> Any procedure by which an employer pays, or makes available to all regular employees, in addition to base pay, special current or deferred sums based upon the profits of the enterprise

## Profit-Sharing Plans

Probably no incentive plan has been the subject of more widespread interest, attention, and misunderstanding than profit sharing. **Profit sharing** is any procedure by which an employer pays, or makes available to all regular employees, special current or deferred sums based on the organization's profits. As defined here, profit sharing represents cash payments made to eligible employees at designated time periods, as distinct from profit sharing in the form of contributions to employee pension funds.

Profit-sharing plans are intended to give employees the opportunity to increase their earnings by contributing to the growth of their organization's profits. These contributions may be directed toward improving product quality, reducing operating costs, improving work methods, and building goodwill rather than just increasing

rates of production. Profit sharing can help to stimulate employees to think and feel more like partners in the enterprise and thus to concern themselves with the welfare of the organization as a whole. Its purpose therefore is to motivate a total commitment from employees rather than simply to have them contribute in specific areas.

A popular example of a highly successful profit-sharing plan is the one in use at Lincoln Electric Company, a manufacturer of arc welding equipment and supplies.[43] This plan was started in 1934 by J. F. Lincoln, president of the company. Each year the company distributes a large percentage of its profits to employees in accordance with their salary level and merit ratings. In recent years the annual bonus has ranged from a low of 55 percent to a high of 115 percent of annual wages. In addition, Lincoln's program includes a piecework plan with a guarantee, cash awards for employee suggestions, a guarantee of employment for thirty hours of the forty-hour workweek, and an employee stock purchase plan.

The success of Lincoln Electric's incentive system depends on a high level of contribution by each employee. The performance evaluations employees receive twice a year are based on four factors—dependability, quality, output, and ideas and cooperation. There is a high degree of respect among employees and management for Lincoln's organizational goals and for the profit-sharing program.[44]

**USING THE INTERNET**

Lincoln Electric's web site provides a description of its incentive management system. It also presents information concerning career opportunities with the company. The address is:

www.lincolnelectric.com

### Variations in Profit-Sharing Plans

Profit-sharing plans differ in the proportion of profits shared with employees and in the distribution and form of payment. The amount shared with employees may range from 5 to 50 percent of the net profit. In most plans, however, about 20 to 25 percent of the net profit is shared. Profit distributions may be made to all employees on an equal basis, or they may be based on regular salaries or some formula that takes into account seniority and/or merit. The payments may be disbursed in cash, deferred, or made on the basis of combining the two forms of payments.

### Weaknesses of Profit-Sharing Plans

In spite of their potential advantages, profit-sharing plans are also prone to certain weaknesses. The profits shared with employees may be the result of inventory speculation, climatic factors, economic conditions, national emergencies, or other factors over which employees have no control. Conversely, losses may occur during years when employee contributions have been at a maximum. The fact that profit-sharing payments are made only once a year or deferred until retirement may reduce their motivational value. If a plan fails to pay off for several years in a row, this can have an adverse effect on productivity and employee morale.

## Stock Options

What do the following companies—Apple Computer, Wang Laboratories, Air-Touch, Bristol-Myers Squibb, Nike, Quaker Oats, and Sara Lee—have in common? The answer: Each of these diverse organizations offers a stock option program to its employees. According to the American Compensation Association, the use of stock options has become a very prevalent method of motivating and compensating hourly employees, as well as salaried and executive personnel. This appears true regardless of the industry surveyed or the organization's size.[45]

Stock option programs are sometimes implemented as part of an employee benefit plan or as part of a corporate culture linking employee effort to stock performance. However, organizations that offer stock option programs to employees do so with the belief that there is some incentive value to the systems. By allowing employees to purchase stock, the organization hopes they will increase their productivity, assume a partnership role in the organization, and thus cause the stock price to rise. Furthermore, stock option programs have become a popular way to boost morale of disenfranchised employees caught in mergers, acquisitions, and downsizing.

Stock option plans grant to employees the right to purchase a specific number of shares of the company's stock at a guaranteed price (the option price) during a designated time period. Although there are many types of options, most options are granted at the stock's fair market value.[46] Not uncommon are plans for purchasing stock through payroll deductions. At Chemical Bank, full-time employees receive options, called "success share," to purchase a set amount of company stock at a fixed price. When the company's stock price reaches a certain level, employees can exercise a portion of the option and collect the cash. Stock ownership plans serve as productivity incentives for booksellers at Borders, tellers at NationsBank, box packers at Pfizer, baggage handlers at Delta Airlines, and expresso coffee servers at Starbucks.[47]

## Employee Stock Ownership Plans (ESOPs)

**Employee stock ownership plans (ESOPs)**
Stock plans in which an organization contributes shares of its stock to an established trust for the purpose of stock purchases by its employees

**Employee stock ownership plans (ESOPs)** have grown significantly during the past years. The Chicago Tribune Company, Southwest Airlines, Roadway Services, and Cincinnati Bell are organizations with established ESOPs. Continental Bank also decided that employee stock ownership was an effective and innovative way to give employees a share of Continental's success.

Employee stock ownership plans take two primary forms: a stock bonus plan and a leveraged plan. With either plan, the public or private employer establishes an ESOP trust that qualifies as a tax-exempt employee trust under Section 401(a) of the Internal Revenue Code. With a stock bonus plan, each year the organization gives stock to the ESOP or gives cash to the ESOP to buy outstanding stock. The ESOP holds the stock for employees, and they are routinely informed of the value of their accounts. Stock allocations can be based on employee wages or seniority. When employees leave the organization or retire, they can sell their stock back to the organization, or they can sell it on the open market if it is traded publicly. Leveraged ESOPs work in much the same way as do stock bonus plans, except that the ESOP borrows money from a bank or other financial institution to purchase stock. The organization then makes annual tax-deductible payments to the ESOP, which in turn repays the lending institution. Organizations may also use the stock placed in an ESOP trust as collateral for a bank loan. As the loan is repaid, the stock used as collateral is allocated to employee accounts. Payments of both the principal and interest can be deducted from the organization's income tax liability.

### *Advantages of ESOPs*

Encouraged by favorable federal income tax provisions, employers utilize ESOPs as a means of providing retirement benefits for their employees. Favorable tax incentives permit a portion of earnings to be excluded from taxation if that portion is assigned to employees in the form of shares of stock. Employers can therefore provide retirement benefits for their employees at relatively low cost, because stock contributions are in effect subsidized by the federal government. ESOPs can also increase employ-

ees' pride of ownership in the organization, providing an incentive for them to increase productivity and help the organization prosper and grow. Enthusiastic promoters of ESOPs go so far as to claim that these plans will make U.S. organizations more competitive in world markets. The plans, they maintain, will increase productivity, improve employee-management relations, and promote economic justice.

### Problems with ESOPs

Generally, ESOPs are more likely to serve their intended purposes in publicly held companies than in privately held ones. A major problem with the privately held company is its potential inability to pay back the stock of employees when they retire. These employees do not have the alternative of disposing of their stock on the open market. Even large organizations, such as Carter Hawley Hale, Thomson McKinnon, and Burlington Holdings, have suffered financial difficulties that have lowered the value of the companies' stocks and, thus, the value of the employees' retirement plans. Requiring organizations to establish a sinking fund to be used exclusively for repurchasing stock could eliminate this problem.

Other problems with ESOPs include the following:

- As more retirement income comes from these plans, the more dependent a pensioner becomes on the price of company stock. Future retirees are vulnerable to stock market fluctuations as well as to management mistakes.

- Unlike traditional pension plans, ESOP contributions are not guaranteed by the federally established Pension Benefit Guaranty Corporation (see Chapter 11), a major drawback to employees should their employer face serious financial setbacks or closure.

- Finally, although studies show that productivity improves when ESOPs are implemented, these gains are not guaranteed. ESOPs help little unless managers are willing to involve employees in organizational decision making. Unfortunately, ESOPs are sometimes set up in ways that restrict employee decision making and expose the ESOP to risk, though providing investors with large potential gains.

## SUMMARY

**OBJECTIVE 1** The success of an incentive pay plan depends on the organizational climate in which it must operate, employee confidence in it, and its suitability to employee and organizational needs. Importantly, employees must view their incentive pay as being equitable and related to their performance. Performance measures should be quantifiable, easily understood, and bear a demonstrated relationship to organizational performance.

**OBJECTIVE 2** Piecework plans pay employees a given rate for each unit satisfactorily completed. Employers implement these plans when output is easily measured and when the production process is

fairly standardized. Bonuses are incentive payments above base wages paid on either an individual or team basis. A bonus is offered to encourage employees to exert greater effort. Standard hour plans establish a standard time for job completion. An incentive is paid for finishing the job in less than the preestablished time. These plans are popular for jobs with a fixed time for completion.

**OBJECTIVE 3** Merit raises will not serve to motivate employees when they are seen as entitlements, which occurs when these raises are given yearly without regard to changes in employee performance. Merit raises are not motivational when

they are given because of seniority or favoritism or when merit budgets are inadequate to sufficiently reward employee performance. To be motivational, merit raises must be such that employees see a clear relationship between pay and performance and the salary increase must be large enough to exceed inflation and higher income taxes.

 Salespersons may be compensated by a straight salary, a combination of salary and commission, or a commission only. Paying employees a straight salary allows them to focus on tasks other than sales, such as service and customer goodwill. A straight commission plan causes employees to emphasize sales goals. A combination of salary and commission provides the advantages of both the straight salary and the straight commission form of payments.

The Scanlon, Rucker, Improshare, and earnings-at-risk gainshare plans pay bonuses to employees unrelated to profit levels. Each of these plans encourages employees to maximize their performance and cooperation through suggestions offered to improve organizational performance. The Scanlon Plan pays an employee a bonus based on saved labor cost measured against the organization's sales value of production. The bonus under the Rucker Plan is based on any improvement in the relationship between the total earnings of hourly employees and the value of production that employees create. The Improshare bonus is paid when employees increase production output above a given target level. With earnings-at-risk programs, employees earn bonuses when production quotas are met or exceeded, as well as wages that had been put at risk.

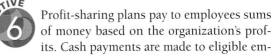 Profit-sharing plans pay to employees sums of money based on the organization's profits. Cash payments are made to eligible employees at specified times, normally yearly. The primary purpose of profit sharing is to provide employees with additional income through their participation in organizational achievement. Employee commitment to improved productivity, quality, and customer service will contribute to organizational success and, in turn, to their compensation. Profit-sharing plans may not achieve their stated gains when employee performance is unrelated to organizational success or failure. This may occur because of economic conditions, other competition, or environmental conditions. Profit-sharing plans can have a negative effect on employee morale when plans fail to consistently reward employees.

With a stock bonus ESOP, each year the organization contributes stock or cash to buy stock that is then placed in an ESOP trust. With a leveraged ESOP, the organization borrows money from a lending institution to purchase stock for the trust. With either plan, the ESOP holds the stock for employees until they either retire or leave the company, at which time the stock is sold back to the company or through a brokerage firm. Employers receive tax benefits for qualified ESOPs; they also hope to receive their employees' commitment to organizational improvement. Employees, however, may lose their retirement income should the company fail or stock prices fall. Another drawback to ESOPs is that they are not guaranteed by any federal agency.

# KEY TERMS

bonus
combined salary and commission
  plan
differential piece rate
earnings-at-risk incentive plans
employee stock ownership plans
  (ESOPs)
gainsharing plans

Improshare
lump-sum merit program
maturity curves
merit guidelines
perquisites
profit sharing
Rucker Plan
Scanlon Plan

spot bonus
standard hour plan
straight commission plan
straight piecework
straight salary plan
team incentive plan
variable pay

# DISCUSSION QUESTIONS

**1.** Working individually or in groups, identify the factors for a successful incentive plan.

**2.** Contrast the differences between straight piecework, differential piece rate, and standard hour plans. Explain where each plan might best be used.

**3.** A frequently heard complaint about merit raises is that they do little to increase employee effort. What are the causes of this belief? Suggest ways in which the motivating value of merit raises may be increased.

**4.** What are the reasons behind the different payment methods for sales employees?

**5.** What are the reasons for the success of the Scanlon and Rucker Plans?

**6.** Because of competitive forces within your industry, you have decided to implement a profit-sharing plan for your employees. Discuss the advantages of profit sharing and identify specific characteristics that will assure success for your plan.

**7.** What are some of the reasons for the rapid growth of ESOPs? Cite some of the potential problems concerning their use.

## Get Productive or Go Broke

Viking Steel Fabrication has reversed a disastrous trend of financial losses, declining market share, and low employee morale. What caused the turnaround? While several changes are noteworthy, management credits the implementation of a team-based gainsharing program as a major cause of the improvement. Over a three-year period—since the start of the incentive program—the company has renewed sales growth, increased productivity (an 11 percent annual productivity gain), and reduced fixed costs while stimulating a growth in employee compensation. In 1999, employees earned an average 32 percent of their base compensation in additional variable pay.

Viking Steel operates three mini-steel mills in Arizona, Texas, and New Mexico. Each mill employs approximately 325 employees. The company produces a specialty low-margin steel reinforcing bar (rebar) used in various construction applications. Prior to introducing the team compensation plan, employees worked in a highly autocratic environment where orders were given and compliance was expected. Employees were afforded little or no opportunity to influence their individual job tasks or the overall operation of the mill. As one manager stated, "There was little desire for change, and wages and benefits were viewed as entitlements by employees for minimal job performance."

Fortunately, the production of steel rebar allows for vast improvements in the manufacturing process. This can largely be accomplished by reducing the fixed costs of producing a ton of steel. Employees can impact the amount of steel produced daily through various "setup" techniques and through "change-over" time— that time between different production runs. Change-over periods can vary between four and nine hours, depending on the requirements of the customer's order. Since the market for rebar is highly price-sensitive, lower production costs result in low prices and increased demand, thereby improving market share.

At the heart of Viking's gainsharing plan is an earnings-at-risk incentive program. Employee base pay is reduced by 15 percent. All employees, from the CEO to support personnel, are included in the incentive scheme. The pay reduction is replaced with an incentive that pays employees 0.5 percent of their base pay for every 1 percent improvement in productivity over 70 percent of a 1995 historical base standard. At 100 percent of the 1995 standard, employees recover their at-risk base pay. Employees can earn an additional 1.5 percent of their base pay for each 1 percent improvement over 100 percent of standard. The plan's goal is for average incentive awards to reap between 30 and 35 percent of base pay over the life of the program. Interestingly, incentive payments were realized after the first week of program implementation, showing that gainsharing plans can and do work when implemented with careful planning and consideration.

Source: Steven E. Gross and Dan Duncan, "Gainsharing Plan Spurs Record Productivity and Payout at AmeriSteel." Adapted from *Compensation and Benefits Review*, November-December/1998. © 1998 American Management Association International. Reprinted by permission of American Management Association International, New York, NY. All rights reserved. http://www.amanet.org.

### QUESTIONS

1. What barriers might a proposed earnings-at-risk gainsharing program face from employees?
2. How might Viking Steel have implemented their gainsharing plan in order to obtain employee acceptance?
3. Suggest methods by which Viking Steel could elicit performance improvements from employees.

## To Merit or Not to Merit

In January 1993, the Samaritan Memorial Hospital implemented a formal performance appraisal program for its 127 staff nurses. The program originally met with some resistance from a few nurses and supervisors, but generally the system was welcomed as an objective way to appraise nursing performance. Complaints centered around the increase in time it took to complete the appraisal review process and the fact that supervisors disliked having to confront nurses who disagreed with their performance review. Nursing supervisors are required to appraise employee performance annually and to forward to the HR department a copy of each appraisal form.

In July 1997, Thomas Tittle, HR manager for the hospital, reviewed all nurses' appraisals on file since the beginning of the program. From this study he concluded that the large majority (82 percent) of nurses were evaluated as performing at an "average" level, as indicated by a global rating at the bottom of the form. Approximately 10 percent were rated "above average" or "superior," and the remainder received "below standard" performance reviews. As a response to these findings, Tittle decided to base the annual raise for all nurses on the consumer price index for the hospital's metropolitan area. This, he concluded, would allow

the nurses to maintain their standard of living while guaranteeing all nurses a yearly raise. For the past three years, nurses have received their annual wage increase according to this policy.

As part of the hospital's employee involvement program, Tittle holds quarterly meetings with groups of employees to solicit their feelings regarding hospital policy and their jobs. Both positive and negative opinions are expressed at these gatherings. These opinions are used to modify hospital policy. At meetings in the past year, a number of both junior and senior nurses have expressed dissatisfaction with the across-the-board pay policy for annual raises. The biggest complaint concerns the lack of motivation to increase output, since all nurses are paid the same regardless of individual performance. These comments have been numerous enough that Tittle has considered changing the nurses' compensation policy. During the past seven months, nine of the better nurses have quit to take jobs with area hospitals that award annual increases on a merit or pay-for-performance basis.

### QUESTIONS

1. What are the advantages of adopting a merit pay plan for hospital nurses? Are there any disadvantages to starting a merit pay program?
2. What problems might arise with a supervisor's appraisals of nurses?
3. Develop a merit pay guideline chart based on the following levels of performance evaluation: superior, above average, average, below average, and poor. Use current cost-of-living figures for your area or salary survey data available to you to guide your merit percentage increases.
4. It is not uncommon for hospital nurses to work in teams. Explain how a team-based incentive program for nurses might be developed. What criteria might be used to evaluate team performance?

# NOTES AND REFERENCES

1. Steven E. Gross and Dan Duncan, "Gainsharing Plan Spurs Record Productivity and Payouts at AmeriSteel," *Compensation and Benefits Review* 30, no. 6 (November-December 1998): 46–50. See also Gillian Flynn, "Why Rhino Won't Wait 'til Tomorrow," *Personnel Journal* 75, no. 7 (July 1996): 36–43. See also Michelle Conlin, Peter Coy, Theresa Palmer, and Gabrielle Saveri, "The Wild New Workforce," *Business Week* (December 6, 1999): 39.

2. Ongoing productivity and compensation research conducted by one of the authors with Magma Copper Company, Tucson, Arizona.

3. Sam T. Johnson, "Plan Your Organization's Reward Strategy through Pay-for-Performance Dynamics," *Compensation and Benefits Review* 30, no. 3 (May-June 1998): 67–72.

4. Telephone conversation with Rose Stanley, compensation specialist, American Compensation Association, Scottsdale, Ariz., February 10, 1999.

5. Richard P. Semler, "Developing Management Incentives That Drive Results," *Compensation and Benefits Review* 30, no. 4 (July-August 1998): 41–48. See also Richard B. McKenzie and Dwight R. Lee, *Managing through Incentives: How to Develop a More Collaborative, Productive, and Profitable Organization* (New York: Oxford University Press, 1998).

6. Larry Reynolds, "Variable Pay Laws May Benefit Employers," *HRFocus* 75, no. 12 (December 1998): 3. See also Nina Gupta and Jason D. Shaw, "Financial Incentives Are Effective," *Compensation and Benefits Review* 30, no. 2 (March-April 1998): 26–32.

7. "Perception vs. Reality with Variable Pay Success," *HRFocus* 75, no. 6 (June 1998): 7.

8. Regina F. Bento and Lourdes F. White, "Participants' Values and Incentive Plans," *Human Resource Management* 37, no. 1 (Spring 1998): 47–59. See also Jamie Hale and George Bailey, "Seven Dimensions of Suc-

cessful Reward Plans," *Compensation and Benefits Review* 30, no. 4 (July-August 1998): 71–77.

9. Francine C. McKenzie and Matthew D. Shilling, "Ensuring Effective Incentive Design and Implementation," *Compensation and Benefits Review* 30, no. 4 (July-August 1998): 57–65.

10. Robert L. Heneman, Julie A. Fox, and Don E. Eskew, "Using Employee Attitude Surveys to Evaluate a New Incentive Pay Program," *Compensation and Benefits Review* 30, no. 1 (January-February 1998): 40–44.

11. David Beck, "Implementing a Gainsharing Plan: What Companies Need to Know," *Compensation and Benefits Review* 24, no. 1 (January-February 1992): 23.

12. Don Barksdale, "Leading Employees Through the Variable Pay Jungle," *HRMagazine* 43, no. 8 (July 1998): 111–18. See also Kenan S. Abosch, "Variable Pay: Do We Have the Basics in Place?" *Compensation and Benefits Review* 30, no. 4 (July-August 1998): 12–22.

13. George T. Milkovich and Jerry M. Newman, *Compensation,* 6th ed. (Chicago: Irwin, 1996): 305.

14. Milkovich and Newman, *Compensation,* 303.

15. Peter V. LeBlanc and Paul W. Mulvey, "How American Workers See the Rewards of Work," *Compensation and Benefits Review* 30, no. 1 (January-February 1998): 24–28.

16. Barry L. Wisdom, "Before Implementing a Merit System . . . Know the Environment and Situations That Demand Caution," *Personnel Administrator* 34, no. 10 (October 1989): 46–49.

17. Donald J. Campbell, Kathleen M. Campbell, and Ho-Beng Chia, "Merit Pay, Performance Appraisal, and Individual Motivation: An Analysis and Alternative," *Human Resource Management* 37, no. 2 (Summer 1998): 131–46.

18. Glenn Bassett, "Merit Pay Increases Are a Mistake," *Compensation and Benefits Review* 26, no. 2 (March-April 1994): 20–25.

19. Nina Gupta and G. Douglas Jenkins, Jr., "The Politics of Pay," *Compensation and Benefits Review* 28, no. 2 (March-April 1996): 23–30.

20. Bill O'Connell, "Dead Solid Perfect: Achieving Sales Compensation Alignment," *Compensation and Benefits Review* 28, no. 2 (March-April 1996): 41.

21. John K. Moynahan, *The Sales Compensation Handbook,* 2d ed. (New York: Amacom, 1998).

22. To promote higher sales efforts, organizations may also offer special cash incentives and noncash incentives such as merchandise, travel awards, and status and recognition awards. One study showed that the majority of responding organizations use noncash incentives in addition to their standard compensation plan. See Alfred J. Candrilli, "Success through a Quality-Based

Sales Incentive Program," *Compensation and Benefits Review* 22, no. 5 (September-October 1990): 54–59.

23. John Tallitsch and John Moynahan, "Fine-Tuning Sales Compensation Programs," *Compensation and Benefits Review* 26, no. 7 (March-April 1994): 34–37.

24. Jack L. Lederer and Carl R. Weinberg, "Setting Executive Compensation: Does the Industry You're In Really Matter?" *Compensation and Benefits Review* 31, no. 1 (January-February 1999): 13–24.

25. Matt Bloom, "The Art and Context of the Deal: A Balanced View of Executive Incentives," *Compensation and Benefits Review* 31, no. 1 (January-February 1999): 25–31. See also Roger Brassy and John E. Balkcom, "Executive Compensation: Finding a Balance in the Quest for Value," *Compensation and Benefits Review* 30, no. 1 (January-February 1998): 29–34.

26. "Balancing the 'Score' in Executive Pay," *HRFocus* 73, no. 3 (June 1996): 17.

27. Debra Sparks, "The Mother of All Stock Option Plans," *Business Week,* November 23, 1998, p. 158. See also Joann S. Lublin and Leslie Scism, "Stock Options at Firms Irk Some Investors," *The Wall Street Journal,* January 12, 1999, C-1.

28. Ira T. Kay, "Growing Shareholder Value: Why Executive Stock Ownership Works," *Compensation and Benefits Review* 31, no. 1 (January-February 1999): 32–37. See also Alan Johnson, "Should Options Reward Absolute or Relative Shareholder Returns?" *Compensation and Benefits Review* 31, no. 1 (January-February 1999): 38–43.

29. "Executive Pay Survey," *The Wall Street Journal,* April 8, 1999, R-12.

30. Bloom, "The Art and Context of the Deal." See also "CEO Hires Getting Costly," *HRFocus* 75, no. 1 (July 1998): 6.

31. David N. Swinford, "Don't Pay for Executive Failure," *Compensation and Benefits Review* 31, no. 1 (January-February 1999): 54–60.

32. Richard Seaman, "Rejuvenating an Organization with Team Pay," *Compensation and Benefits Review* 29, no. 5 (September-October 1997): 25–30.

33. Steven E. Gross, "When Jobs Become Team Roles, What Do You Pay For?" *Compensation and Benefits Review* 29, no. 1 (January-February 1997): 48–51.

34. Steven E. Gross, *Compensation for Teams* (New York: American Management Association, 1996).

35. Linda Bennett, "Research from the Trenches . . . Making Group Incentives Work," *Compensation and Benefits Review* 29, no. 4 (July-August 1997): 37–39.

36. Ronald J. Recardo and Diane Pricone, "Is Gainsharing for You?" at www.qualitydigest.com/jul/gainshre.html, 1–7.

37. Robert Masternak, "How to Make Gainsharing Successful: The Collective Experience of 17 Facilities," *Compensation and Benefits Review* 29, no. 5 (September-October 1997): 43–52.

38. For an excellent discussion on the development of a Scanlon Plan, see Steven E. Markham, K. Dow Scott, and Walter G. Cox, Jr., "The Evolutionary Development of a Scanlon Plan," *Compensation and Benefits Review* 24, no. 2 (March-April 1992): 50–56.

39. Edward Ost, "Gain Sharing's Potential," *Personnel Administrator* 34, no. 7 (July 1989): 94.

40. The Rucker Plan uses a somewhat more complex formula for determining employee bonuses. For a detailed example of the Rucker bonus, see Milkovich and Newman, *Compensation,* 315.

41. The standard of Improshare's measurement system is the base productivity factor (BPF), which is the ratio of standard direct labor hours produced to total actual hours worked in a base period. The productivity of subsequent periods is then measured by enlarging standard direct labor hours earned by the BPF ratio to establish Improshare hours (IH). The IH is then compared with actual hours worked in the same period. If earned hours exceed actual hours, 50 percent of the gain is divided by actual hours worked in order to establish a bonus percentage for all employees in the plan.

42. Eleanor White, "Relying on the Power of People at Saturn," *National Productivity Review* 17, no. 1 (Winter 1997): 5–10. See also Don L. Bohl, "Saturn Corporation—A Different Kind of Pay," *Compensation and Benefits Review* 26, no. 6 (November-December 1997): 51–56.

43. Richard M. Hodgetts, "Discussing Incentive Compensation with Donald Hastings of Lincoln Electric," *Compensation and Benefits Review* 29, no. 5 (September-October 1997): 60–66. See also Kenneth W. Chilton, "Lincoln Electric's Incentive System: A Reservoir of Trust," *Compensation and Benefits Review* 25, no. 6 (November 1994): 29–34.

44. For an article explaining the philosophy behind the Lincoln Electric incentive program, see Harry C. Hanolin, "The Company Built Upon the Golden Rule: Lincoln Electric," *Journal of Organizational Behavior* 12, no. 1 (January 1992): 151–63.

45. Arthur H. Kroll, "Exploring Options," *HRMagazine* 42, no. 10 (October 1997): 96–100.

46. Jeff Stainman and Kerry Tompson, "Designing and Implementing a Broad-Based Stock Option Plan," *Compensation and Benefits Review* 30, no. 4 (July-August 1998): 23–40.

47. Brenda Deming, "Stock Options: DeVry Shares Its Success," *HRFocus* 75, no. 11 (November 1998): S-7.

different but compatible grouping of benefits to highlight the important issues and trends in managing an employee benefits program.

## Health Care Benefits

The benefits that receive the most attention from employers today because of high costs and employee concern are health care benefits. In the past, health insurance plans covered only medical, surgical, and hospital expenses. Today employers include prescription drugs as well as dental, optical, and mental health care benefits in the package they offer their workers.

### High Health Care Costs

According to a U.S. Chamber of Commerce study, medical and medical-related benefits costs (employers' share) average 9.6 percent of payroll costs. This represents an annual expense of $2,568 for medical insurance premiums for each active employee.[37] Importantly, since 1980, the employer cost of providing medical and dental insurance has increased by more than 250 percent. The main reason for the increase is that the cost of medical care has risen more than twice the increase in CPI for all items. Health insurance premiums paid by employers increased more than 50 percent faster than medical care costs, compounding the problems facing employers.

The growth in health care costs is attributed to a number of factors, including federal legislation, changes in Medicare pricing, the greater need for health care by an aging population, the costs of technological advances in medicine, skyrocketing malpractice insurance rates, rising costs of health care labor, and overuse of costly health care services.[38]

### Cost Containment

With the significant rise in health care costs, it is understandable that employers seek relief from these expenses. The approaches used to contain the costs of health care benefits include reductions in coverage, increased deductibles or copayments, and increased coordination of benefits to make sure the same expense is not paid by more than one insurance reimbursement. Other cost-containment efforts involve alternatives to traditional medical care: the use of health maintenance organizations and preferred providers, incentives for outpatient surgery and testing, and mandatory second opinions for surgical procedures.[39] Employee assistance programs and wellness programs may also allow an organization to cut the costs of its health care benefits.[40]

**Health maintenance organizations (HMOs)** are organizations of physicians and other health care professionals that provide a wide range of services to subscribers and their dependents on a prepaid basis. HMOs offer routine medical services at a specific site for a fixed fee for each employee visit. Employers pay a fixed annual fee to the HMO to cover the majority of their employees' medical costs. Because they must provide all covered services for a fixed dollar amount, HMOs generally emphasize preventive care and early intervention. As a result of the federal HMO Act of 1973, employers having twenty-five or more employees and a health insurance plan must offer a federally qualified HMO as a voluntary option.

Although HMOs have clearly lowered health care costs, there is growing concern that quality care is being sacrificed in the name of cost savings. Increasing health care competition, price battles, high usage rates, and, in some cases, medical

**Health maintenance organizations (HMOs)**
Organizations of physicians and health care professionals that provide a wide range of services to subscribers and dependents on a prepaid basis

"You'll hate it here. The pay is low, conditions are fairly chaotic, and I myself am quite impossible. Nevertheless, we have a pretty good dental plan."

Reprinted with permission of J.B. Handelsman.

**Preferred provider organization (PPO)**

A group of physicians who establish an organization that guarantees lower health care costs to the employer

apathy are all cited as causes of lower-quality HMO health care. Fortunately, employers can monitor the quality of care provided by the HMO by conducting a process evaluation of the providers' effectiveness. A survey of employees focusing on (1) employee satisfaction with various HMO services, (2) access to care, (3) monitoring performance and efficiency of services offered, and (4) measuring medical outcomes will tell whether the HMO is meeting employee (and employer) expectations and needs.[41]

Preferred provider organizations have also helped to contain costs. The **preferred provider organization (PPO)** is a group of physicians who establish an organization or a network of doctors that guarantees lower costs to the employer through lower service charges or agreed-upon utilization controls (e.g., a reduced number of diagnostic tests per employee). Unlike HMOs, where employees may have little choice in the doctor they see, PPOs allow employees to select from a list of physicians (participating doctors) their doctor of choice. Normally, a number of physicians are available to choose from for different medical needs.

According to one study, employees enrolled in preferred provider organizations are more likely to receive options that include popular alternative medical treatments and/or alternative therapy than members of other health plans. For example, chiropractic care, acupressure and/or acupuncture, massage therapy, homeopathy, and biofeedback are offered on a larger basis with PPOs than with traditional indemnity plans and HMOs.[42] Since employees and the federal government will continue to push for improved health care, employers will find it necessary to have an active managed care program for their employees emphasizing both quality service and cost containment.

Another important medical cost containment program is *medical savings accounts (MSAs)*. Employer-offered MSA plans provide employees with comprehensive medical insurance carrying high deductibles. Employers establish a fund from which to pay employee medical costs "before" the deductible is satisfied. For example, ABC Company might offer its employees a comprehensive medical program with a $2,500 deductible while depositing up to $2,500 in an employee account from which employee-incurred health expenses are paid up to the established deductible. If an employee does not spend all the money in his or her personalized account, the remainder is refunded as a cash reward. The benefits of an MSA include

- The employer pays lower medical care premiums.
- Employees retain discretion over medical spending.
- Employees can "shop" for the best cost/quality medical care available commensurate with their individual needs.

Employees of small businesses find MSAs particularly beneficial to their health care needs. Under the Health Insurance Portability and Accountability Act of 1996, employees of small employers may establish a tax-free, interest-bearing MSA. Under the MSA, individuals enrolled in a high-deductible plan may make tax-free contributions to an account created primarily for the purpose of paying for qualified medical expenses.[43]

### Other Health Benefits

Dental plans are designed to help pay for dental care costs and to encourage employees to receive regular dental attention. Like medical plans, dental care plans may be operated by insurance companies, dental service corporations, those administering Blue Cross/Blue Shield plans, HMOs, and groups of dental care providers. Typically, the insurance pays a portion of the charges, and the subscriber pays the remainder.

Optical care insurance is another, relatively new benefit that many employers are offering. Coverage can include visual examinations and a percentage of the costs of lenses and frames.

## Payment for Time Not Worked

The "payment for time not worked" category of benefits includes paid vacations, bonuses given in lieu of paid vacations, payments for holidays not worked, paid sick leave, military and jury duty, and payments for absence due to a death in the family or other personal reasons. As Figure 11.2 showed, these benefits constitute another large expenditure—10.2 percent—of the employer's total payroll costs.

### Vacations with Pay

It is generally agreed that vacations are essential to the well-being of an employee. Eligibility for vacations varies by industry, locale, and organization size. To qualify for longer vacations of three, four, or five weeks, one may expect to work for seven, fifteen, and twenty years, respectively.

A new benefit offered by 11 percent of 1,000 employers surveyed nationwide allows employees to "buy" an extra week of vacation. The cost to employees is a lost week of pay, making the extra vacation period simply time off without pay.[44] Vacation-buying programs appeal to relatively new employees who haven't acquired the time for longer vacation periods. This benefit also favors employees who need extra time to care for aging parents or those simply wishing to extend a vacation period.

While vacations are a relatively easy benefit to manage, employers should, nevertheless, remember that vacation scheduling must meet the employer's state wage laws and state contract law principles.[45]

### Paid Holidays

Both hourly and salaried workers can usually expect to be paid for ten holidays a year. The type of business tends to influence both the number and observance of holidays. Virtually all employers in the United States, however, observe and pay their employees for New Year's Day, Memorial Day, Independence Day, Labor Day, Thanksgiving Day, and Christmas Day. Many employers give workers an additional two or three personal days off to use at their discretion.

### Sick Leave

There are several ways in which employees may be compensated during periods when they are unable to work because of illness or injury. Most

**USING THE INTERNET**

The benefits information source for employees of the University of California is an example of the kinds of services an HR department can provide for its employees. It provides detailed information about available benefits and allows changes by using online forms:

www.ucop.edu/bencom

public employees, as well as many in private firms, receive a set number of sick-leave days each year to cover such absences. Where permitted, sick leave that employees do not use can be accumulated to cover prolonged absences. Accumulated vacation leave may sometimes be used as a source of income when sick-leave benefits have been exhausted. Group insurance that provides income protection during a long-term disability is also made available by some employers. As discussed earlier in the chapter, income lost during absences resulting from job-related injuries may be reimbursed, at least partially, through workers' compensation insurance.

### Severance Pay

A one-time payment is sometimes given to employees who are being terminated. Known as *severance pay,* it may cover only a few days' wages or wages for several months. The pay received is usually dependent on the employee's years of service. However, severance pay can also be based on the reason for termination, the salary or grade level of the employee, the title or level in the organization, or a combination of factors. Employers that are downsizing often use severance pay as a means of lessening the negative effects of unexpected termination of employees. Other triggers for severance pay include job elimination, voluntary separation programs, or refusal of reassignment or relocation.

## Supplemental Unemployment Benefits

**Supplemental unemployment benefits (SUBs)**

A plan that enables an employee who is laid off to draw, in addition to state unemployment compensation, weekly benefits from the employer that are paid from a fund created for this purpose

While *not* required by law, in some industries unemployment compensation is augmented by **supplemental unemployment benefits (SUBs),** which are financed by the employer. These plans enable an employee who is laid off to draw, in addition to state unemployment compensation, weekly benefits from the employer that are paid from a fund created for this purpose. Many SUB plans in recent years have been liberalized to permit employees to receive weekly benefits when the length of their workweek is reduced and to receive a lump-sum payment if their employment is terminated permanently. The amount of benefits is determined by length of service and wage rate. Employer liability under the plan is limited to the amount of money accumulated within the fund from employer contributions based on the total hours of work performed by employees.

## Life Insurance

One of the oldest and most popular employee benefits is group term life insurance, which provides death benefits to beneficiaries and may also provide accidental death and dismemberment benefits. The premium costs are normally paid by the employer, with the face value of the life insurance equal to two times the employee's yearly wages. These programs frequently allow employees to purchase additional amounts of insurance for nominal charges. Where employers operate a cafeteria benefits program, selection of extra life insurance may be part of the choices offered employees. Also as one benefits expert notes, "Employers can provide—in advance and at minimal or no cost—a substantial portion of life insurance benefits to employees diagnosed with terminal illnesses such as cancer or AIDS."[46]

## Long-Term Care Insurance

A small but growing number of employers are offering long-term care insurance as part of their benefits package. Long-term care insurance is designed to pay for nursing home and other medical-related costs during old age. An advantage of employer-sponsored long-term care insurance is that enrolled employees receive coverage automatically and do not need to pass a physical examination.

## Retirement Programs

As discussed in Chapters 1 and 4, a significant trend in workforce demographics is the increased age of U.S. workers. A prominent cause of this change is the "aging" of the baby boom generation—a demographic group born between 1946 and 1964. Given their sheer numbers, Michael Dickerman, director of Towers Perrin's Professional Development Institute, has labeled this group the "El Niño" of retirement."[47] Therefore, retirement becomes an important part of life, requiring sufficient and careful preparation. In convincing job applicants that theirs is a good organization to work for, employers usually emphasize the retirement benefits that can be expected after a certain number of years of employment.

### Retirement Policies

With an increasing older workforce (see Figure 11.4), a trend of recent years has been the early retirement of employees before the traditional retirement age of 65.[48] While the United States has no law mandating a specific retirement age, there have

**FIGURE 11.4**

**Trends Affecting Retirement**

- Number of people age 65 and older tripled to about 34 million between 1940 and 1995.

- According to U.S. census projections, people 65 and older are expected to number 80 million by 2050.

- In 1960, 45.4 percent of male workers over age 65 were still in the labor force; in 1990, only 27.4 percent were still working. While the labor force participation rates of women between the ages of 55 and 64 have been rising, further increases are not expected.

- Eight baby boomers turn 50 every ten minutes.

- The U.S. net national savings rate was relatively stable at about 7 percent of GDP from 1951 to 1980. It has collapsed since 1980, most recently dropping to less than 1 percent of GDP.

- In 1940, a 65-year-old had a normal life expectancy of 12.7 more years. Currently, it is about 17 more years.

Source: Adapted from Jenny C. McCune, "The Future of Retirement," *HRFocus* 75, no. 6 (June 1998): 1–4; and Sylvester J. Schieber, "The Sleeping Giant Awakens," *HRFocus* 73, no. 4 (April 1996): 23.

not been an overwhelming number of older persons who remain on the job. The early retirement trend partly reflects voluntary departures. Others choose partial retirement or work part-time for a period preceding complete retirement. Recently, however, large numbers of workers have been pushed into premature retirement—the victims of organizational downsizing. Whether the trend in early retirement will continue as more baby boomers enter retirement age is open to speculation.

To avoid layoffs, particularly of more recently hired members of protected classes, and to reduce salary and benefit costs, employers often encourage early retirement. Encouragement comes in the form of increased pension benefits for several years or cash bonuses, sometimes referred to as the **silver handshake.** The cost of these retirement incentives can frequently be offset by the lower compensation paid to replacements and/or by a reduction in the workforce.

The major factors affecting the decision to retire early are the individual's personal financial condition and health and the extent to which he or she receives satisfaction from the work. Attractive pension benefits, possibilities of future layoffs, and inability to meet the demands of their jobs are also among the reasons workers choose to retire early.

**Silver handshake**

An early-retirement incentive in the form of increased pension benefits for several years or a cash bonus

### *Preretirement Programs*

While most people eagerly anticipate retirement, many are bitterly disappointed once they reach this stage of life. Employers may offer preretirement planning programs to help make employees aware of the kinds of adjustments they may need to make when they retire. These adjustments may include learning to live on a reduced, fixed income and having to cope with the problems of lost prestige, family problems, and idleness that retirement may create.

Preretirement programs typically include seminars and workshops that include lectures, videos, and printed materials. Topics covered include pension plans, health insurance coverage, Social Security and Medicare, personal financial planning, wellness and lifestyles, and adjustment to retirement. The numerous publications of the American Association of Retired Persons (AARP), including its popular magazine, *Modern Maturity,* are valuable sources of information.

The National Council on Aging has developed a retirement planning program for employers. Atlantic Richfield, Travelers Insurance, and Alcoa are among the more than seventy-five organizations using this program. In many communities, hospitals are developing resource centers for health and retirement planning. To help older workers get used to the idea of retirement, some organizations experiment with retirement rehearsal. Polaroid, for example, offers employees an opportunity to try out retirement through an unpaid three-month leave program. They also offer a program that permits employees to gradually cut their hours before retirement. Employees are paid only for hours worked, but they receive full medical insurance and prorated pension credits. Most experts agree that preretirement planning is a much-needed, cost-effective employee benefit.

**USING THE INTERNET**

AARP is the nation's leading organization for people age 50 and older. It serves their needs through information, education, advocacy, and community service. AARP retirement information can be found at:

www.aarp.org

## Pension Plans

Originally, pensions were based on a *reward philosophy,* which viewed pensions primarily as a way to retain personnel by rewarding them for staying with the organization until they retired. Because of the vesting requirements negotiated into most union contracts and more recently required by law, pensions are now based on an *earnings philosophy*. This philosophy regards a pension as deferred income that employees accumulate during their working lives and that belongs to them after a specified number of years of service, whether or not they remain with the employer until retirement. Since the passage of the Social Security Act of 1935, pension plans have been used to supplement the floor of protection provided by Social Security. However, the decision whether or not to offer a pension plan is up to the employer.

### Types of Pension Plans

There are two major ways to categorize pension plans: (1) according to contributions made by the employer and (2) according to the amount of pension benefits to be paid. In a **contributory plan**, contributions to a pension plan are made jointly by employees and employers. In a **noncontributory plan,** the contributions are made solely by the employer. Most of the plans existing in privately held organizations are noncontributory, whereas those in government are contributory plans.

When pension plans are classified by the amount of pension benefits to be paid, there are two basic types: the defined-benefit plan and the defined-contribution plan. Under a **defined-benefit plan,** the amount an employee is to receive upon retirement is specifically set forth. This amount is usually based on the employee's years of service, average earnings during a specific period of time, and age at time of retirement. While a variety of formulas exist for determining pension benefits, the one used most often is based on the employee's average earnings (usually over a three- to five-year period immediately preceding retirement), multiplied by the number of years of service with the organization. A deduction is then made for each year the retiree is under age 65. As noted earlier, pension benefits are usually integrated with Social Security benefits.

A **defined-contribution plan** establishes the basis on which an employer will contribute to the pension fund.[49] The contributions may be made through profit sharing, thrift plans, matches of employee contributions, employer-sponsored Individual Retirement Accounts (IRAs), and various other means. The amount of benefits employees receive on retirement is determined by the funds accumulated in their account at the time of retirement and what retirement benefits (usually an annuity) these funds will purchase. These plans do not offer the benefit-security predictability of a defined-benefit plan. However, even under defined-benefit plans, retirees may not receive the benefits promised them if the plan is not adequately funded.

The use of traditional defined-benefit plans, with their fixed payouts, is in decline. Defined-benefit plans are less popular with employers because they cost more and because they require compliance with complicated government rules. Some experts, however, believe that employers may want to consider returning to defined-benefit plans, which allow for flexibility in plan design such as opening paths for the advancement of younger employees while enabling older workers to retire.

### 401(k) Savings Plans

A significant change in pension coverage is the tremendous growth of tax-deferred 401(k) savings plans, which are named after section 401(k) of the Internal Revenue Code. Currently, 25 million people have about $1 trillion invested in 401(k) plans.[50] The 401(k) savings plans are particularly popular with smaller employers

**OBJECTIVE 7**

**Contributory plan**
A pension plan where contributions are made jointly by employees and employers

**Noncontributory plan**
A pension plan where contributions are made solely by the employer

**Defined-benefit plan**
A pension plan in which the amount an employee is to receive upon retirement is specifically set forth

**Defined-contribution plan**
A pension plan that establishes the basis on which an employer will contribute to the pension fund

who find these pension plans less costly than defined-benefit programs. Changes in the Fair Labor Standards Act encourage smaller employers to set up 401(k) plans by removing complicated filing rules in exchange for employer contributions of 3 percent of pay for workers who participate in the plan or 2 percent of pay for all workers whether or not they participate.

The 401(k) savings plans allow employees to save through payroll deductions and to have their contributions matched by the employer. Usually the employer matches the employee contributions at the rate of fifty cents for every worker dollar contributed up to 6 percent of salary. An organization's contribution can, however, run the gamut from doubling the worker's contribution to zero contribution.[51] In fact, a current concern in retirement planning is the disparity between company 401(k) plans. For example, Allied-Signal matches dollar for dollar on the first 8 percent of pay contributed by employees. Columbia/HCA Healthcare, the nation's largest service firm, matches 25 cents per employee dollar on the first 3 percent of pay. Some organizations, such as Sara Lee, Caterpillar, Procter & Gamble, and PepsiCo, have no match.[52] The percentage of the employer's contribution will likely depend on the allowable saving rate of the employee (i.e., higher allowable employee saving rates will decrease the percentage of the employer's contribution).

Interestingly, to encourage employees to save for retirement, some employers are making enrollment in their 401(k) plan mandatory.[53] Motorola, for example, makes 401(k) saving mandatory, while McDonald's enrolls all employees in its plan unless an employee specifically declines. At these employers, the intent is to have employees see the importance of putting money aside for retirement.

Unlike traditional defined-benefit pension plans, which guarantee payments based on years of service, the 401(k) plans guarantee nothing. Return depends entirely on how much money goes into the plan and the rate of return on investments. A current trend is for organizations to allow their employees considerable control over the investment of their 401(k) savings.[54] Since employees often need assistance in making informed investment decisions, Department of Labor standards provide employers with "sufficient information" standards to follow in putting participants legally in control of their investment. Highlights in HRM 4 illustrates the important features of the 401(k) program.

### Cash-Balance Pension Plans

Along with 401(k) saving plans, the largest development in pension planning has been cash-balance saving plans. Pension experts predict that within a decade most large corporations will convert their traditional pension plan to a cash-balance program. Cash-balance plans offer large monetary savings to employers while providing financial security to employees.[55]

Cash-balance plans work by having the employer make a yearly contribution into an employee's retirement savings account. Contributions are based on a percentage of the employee's pay—typically 4 percent. Additionally, the employee's account earns annual interest, often tied to the thirty-year Treasury rate.[56] For example, an employee earning $35,000 a year would receive a yearly contribution of $1,400 to his or her account. After a year, the account would receive an interest credit, typically 5 percent. Employees can normally roll the balance of their account into an IRA should they change jobs.

HRM 4

# Important Features of a 401(k) Savings Plan

All retirement saving programs have requirements for "putting money in" and "taking money out." Here are the ground rules for 401(k) plans.

---
## Putting Money In
---

### WHO QUALIFIES?

Employees eligible to take part in their company's plan
Typical eligibility rules:

- At least 21 years old
- One year of service

### WHO BENEFITS MOST?

People in plans with generous terms, such as matching contributions from employer

### DEADLINES FOR SETUP AND ANNUAL CONTRIBUTION

Not your problem. Your company sets up the plan and automatically deducts your contributions from your paycheck.

### HOW MUCH CAN YOU SAVE EACH YEAR?

- Tax-deferred up to $10,000, or the maximum permitted by your plan
- After-tax, if allowed: up to the maximum permitted by your plan, but combined savings can't top $30,000 or 25% of pay

### ARE CONTRIBUTIONS TAX-DEFERRED?

Yes. (Some plans also allow after-tax savings.)

---
## Taking Money Out
---

### TRANSFERS BETWEEN ACCOUNTS

Rollovers permitted into IRAs and other qualified plans.

### HOW ARE WITHDRAWALS TAXED?

- Ordinary income-tax rates apply to withdrawals of tax-deferred contributions and any investment earnings
- No tax on withdrawals of after-tax contributions, loans from your account, or rollovers to an IRA or new employer's 401(k)

### PENALTIES FOR EARLY WITHDRAWALS

Additional 10% tax on withdrawals made before age $59\frac{1}{2}$.

*(continued)*

**EXCEPTIONS TO PENALTIES**

Early withdrawals made

- By your beneficiaries at your death
- On diagnosis of severe disability
- To pay medical expenses in excess of 7.5% of gross income
- In equal installments intended to last the rest of your life
- Upon leaving your job after age 55

**MINIMUM-DISTRIBUTION RULES**

Employees can continue to contribute as long as they're working. But if you're a 5% or more owner or retired, you generally must begin withdrawing money from the plan by April 1 of the year after you turn $70^1/_2$. The minimum payout depends on your life expectancy or the joint life expectancy of you and a beneficiary.

**IN SHORT**

*Special Advantages*

- An employer match sharply boosts the return on each dollar you save.
- If your plan offers loans, you can get quick access to your savings by borrowing against your account.

*Drawbacks*

- Not all companies match your savings.
- You may have to remain in the job several years to become vested in your employer's matching contributions.

---

Source: Eileen P. Gunn, "Sorting Out the Savings Plans," *Fortune* 38, no. 4 (August 17, 1998): 121. © 1998 Time Inc. Reprinted by permission.

Whether an individual employee benefits from a cash-balance retirement plan depends on the employee's age and years of service with the company. Employees in their 20s or 30s with low years of service can build substantial retirement savings starting at an early age. However, employees in their 40s, 50s, or 60s, with lengthy years of service, can lose from 20 to 50 percent of their pension by switching from a traditional pension plan to a cash-balance program.[57] Why? With a traditional pension plan, employee benefits rise sharply during later years of employment. Remember, typical pension formulas multiply years of service by the highest final years of pay. Therefore, employees normally earn half of their pension during the last five years on the job. With a cash-balance plan, all employees receive the same steady annual credit; thus older employees lose those last big years of accruals. Companies reap financial savings because pension contributions for older employees are significantly reduced.

To lessen the financial impact on older employees, some companies may increase the annual pay credit for older employees as compared with younger workers. Others have allowed older employees to remain in the traditional pension plan until retirement, or they grant older employees a "boost" in their opening cash-balance account.

## Federal Regulation of Pension Plans

Private pension plans are subject to federal regulation under the Employee Retirement Income Security Act (ERISA).[58] Although the act does not require employers to establish a pension plan, it provides certain standards and controls for pension plans. It requires minimum funding standards to ensure that benefits will be available when an employee retires. It also requires that the soundness of the actuarial assumptions on which the funding is based be certified by an actuary at least every three years. Of special concern to the individual employee is the matter of vesting.

**Vesting**
A guarantee of accrued benefits to participants at retirement age, regardless of their employment status at that time

**Vesting** is a guarantee of accrued benefits to participants at retirement age, regardless of their employment status at that time. Vested benefits that have been earned by an employee cannot be revoked by an employer. Under ERISA, all pension plans must provide that employees will have vested rights in their accrued benefits after certain minimum-years-of-service requirements have been met. However, employers can pay out a departing employee's vested benefits if the present value of the benefit is small. Also, while vesting is required by ERISA, portability—the ability to move pension funds between employers—is optional. Employees are well advised to seek out pension options that are portable if at all possible.

Three government agencies administer ERISA: the Internal Revenue Service (IRS), the Department of Labor, and the Pension Benefit Guaranty Corporation (PBGC). The IRS is concerned primarily with qualified retirement plans—those that offer employers and employees favorable income tax treatment under a special section of the tax law. The Department of Labor's main responsibility is to protect participants' rights.

About 40 million of the 76 million covered workers have their pensions insured by the federal government's Pension Benefit Guaranty Corporation. Pensions in workplaces with fewer than twenty-five employees are not covered. The PBGC ensures that if a plan is terminated, guaranteed minimum benefits are paid to participants. The PBGC is supported by premiums paid by employers.

In 1984 the Retirement Equity Act (REA) amended ERISA.[59] REA is intended to provide greater equity under private pension plans for workers and their spouses by taking into account changes in work patterns, the status of marriage as an economic partnership, and the substantial contributions made by both spouses. All qualified pension plans are affected by the act, which brought major changes in eligibility and vesting provisions, parental leave, spouse survivor benefits, assignments of benefits in divorce cases, and other areas. If an employee declines to elect survivors' benefits, the employer is required to inform prospective beneficiaries of this fact. The Deficit Reduction Act of 1984 has had a significant impact on employee benefits, such as pension and group insurance plans, in determining what is taxable and nontaxable to employees.[60]

## Pension Portability

A weakness in most traditional pension plans is that they lack the portability to enable employees who change employment to maintain equity in a single pension. Before ERISA, unions sought to address this problem by encouraging multiple-employer plans that covered the employees of two or more unrelated organizations in accordance with a collective bargaining agreement. Such plans are governed by employer and union representatives who constitute the plan's board of trustees. Multiple-employer plans tend to be found in industries where the typical company has too few employees to justify an individual plan. They are also found more frequently in industries where there is seasonal or irregular employment. Manufacturing industries where these plans exist include apparel, printing, furniture, leather, and metalworking. They are also used in such nonmanufacturing industries as mining, construction, transport, entertainment, and private higher education.

### Pension Funds

Pension funds may be administered through either a trusteed or an insured plan. In a trusteed pension plan, pension contributions are placed in a trust fund. The investment and administration of the fund are handled by trustees appointed by the employer or, if the employees are unionized, by either the employer or the union. Contributions to an insured pension plan are used to purchase insurance annuities. The responsibility for administering these funds rests with the insurance company providing the annuities.

Private and public pension funds constitute the largest pool of investment capital in the world, with over $4 trillion in assets. Still, one cannot be complacent about the future. Social Security will be stretched thin as baby boomers age, and some private pensions may be vulnerable to poorly performing investments. It should also be noted that the pension funds of some organizations are not adequate to cover their obligations. Such deficiencies present legal and ethical problems that must be addressed.

Current pension fund difficulties have been caused in part by the fact that the wages on which pension benefits are based today drastically exceed the wages on which pension fund contributions were based in earlier years. Furthermore, those drawing pensions are living beyond the life expectancies on which their pension benefits were calculated.

# Employee Services: Creating a Work/Life Setting

OBJECTIVE 8

ConAgra, Inc., of Omaha, Nebraska, provides a home nurse for up to twelve hours to care for a sick child or elder parent. Lincoln National Corp., a financial services company, offers a "homework-assistance help line" staffed with teachers for children of employees, and Eddie Bauer, an outdoor clothing and equipment supplier, offers its employees take-out dinners and one paid "Balance Day" off a year.[61] These organizations, like many others, are seeking to create a work/life (also called family-friendly) organizational climate that allows employees to balance work and personal needs. For example, a national survey conducted by Hewitt Associates, a consulting firm, found that 85 percent of surveyed employers offered some type of child care assistance to employees, 97 percent offered dependent-care spending accounts, 42 percent offered resource and referral services, 15 percent offered sick/emergency child care programs, and 33 percent provided elder care programs.[62] While each of these programs helps employees manage time, employers benefit through competitive recruitment and reductions in the various employee hassles and interruptions that affect workplace productivity. Figure 11.5 lists some of the more popular employer-sponsored work/life benefits.

**USING THE INTERNET**

The U.S. Department of Labor maintains a web site for work/life policies and other business practices that treat employees as important assets:

www.ttrc.doleta.gov/citizen/

FIGURE 11.5

### Work/Life Benefits: Balancing Work and Home Needs

- Child care/elder care referral services
- Time off for children's school activities
- Employer-paid on-site or near-site child care facilities
- Flexible work hours scheduling
- Employee-accumulated leave days for dependent care
- Subsidized temporary or emergency dependent care costs
- Extended leave policies for child/elder care
- Sick-child programs (caregiver on call)
- Work-at-home arrangements/telecommuting
- Partial funding of child care costs
- Customized career paths

## Employee Assistance Programs

**Employee assistance programs (EAPs)**
Services provided by employers to help workers cope with a wide variety of problems that interfere with the way they perform their jobs

To help workers cope with a wide variety of problems that interfere with the way they perform their jobs, organizations such as the New York Mets, the Los Angeles Police Department, and Levi-Strauss have developed **employee assistance programs (EAPs).**[63] An employee assistance program typically provides diagnosis, counseling, and referral for advice or treatment when necessary for problems related to alcohol or drug abuse, emotional difficulties, and financial or family difficulties. (EAPs will be discussed in detail in Chapter 12.) The main intent is to

*A wide variety of personal problems may force employees to seek counseling through employee assistance programs.*

*ConAgra, Inc., creates a family-friendly atmosphere for its employees by providing up to 12 hours of home-nurse care for a sick child.*

help employees solve their personal problems or at least to prevent problems from turning into crises that affect their ability to work productively. To handle crises, many EAPs offer twenty-four-hour hot lines.

## Counseling Services

An important part of an EAP is the counseling services it provides to employees. While most organizations expect managers to counsel subordinates, some employees may have problems that require the services of professional counselors. Most organizations refer such individuals to outside counseling services such as family counseling services, marriage counselors, and mental health clinics. Some organizations have a clinical psychologist, counselor, or comparable specialist on staff, to whom employees may be referred.

## Child and Elder Care

The increased employment of women with dependent children has created an unprecedented demand for child care arrangements. In the past, working parents had to make their own arrangements with sitters or with nursery schools for preschool children. Today benefits may include financial assistance, alternative work schedules, and family leave. The most common child care benefit offered by employers, however, is the dependent-care spending account. With this account, a portion of a worker's pay before taxes is set aside for caring for a dependent child.

For many employees, on-site or near-site child care centers are the most visible, prestigious, and desired solutions. Employee-parents often express the importance of having their children near them with available quality child care. Hoffman-LaRoche has a center only one block from its Nutley, New Jersey, plant. The facility has several classrooms and uses innovative teaching methods. Among other companies that offer child care at the work site are Fel-Pro, Merck, Syntex, Baptist Hospital of Miami, and Ben & Jerry's Homemade Ice Cream.

If an employer decides to operate its own center, it must decide how to fund this cost. While some companies want parents to pay full operating costs, a more acceptable approach is for the employer to pay for capital costs, while parents' tuition payments subsidize operating expenses.[64] While on-site child care centers are normally offered by larger employers, smaller employers have the opportunity of collaborating with other employers to run a joint facility.

Responsibility for the care of aging parents and other relatives is another fact of life for increasing numbers of employees. A report issued by the National Council on the Aging estimates that nearly 12 percent of today's workforce assists elderly parents.[65] The term **elder care,** as used in the context of employment, refers to the circumstance where an employee provides care to an elderly relative while remaining actively at work. The majority of caregivers are women. The following quote from two researchers highlights the workplace consequences of caring for relatives.

**Elder care**
Care provided to an elderly relative by an employee who remains actively at work

There is no doubt that elder care responsibilities detract from work efficiency: from time lost to take a parent to the doctor, to loss of concentration due to worry, work time being spent making care arrangements, never knowing when an emergency will occur, and calls from neighbors and relatives disrupting the workday. When combined, these responsibilities lead to a situation where neither the care giver nor employee role is filled adequately. Lost productivity due to absenteeism of those caring for elders can cost a 1,000 employee company without an elder care program as much as $400,000 per year. TransAmerica Corporation reported that 1,600 missed workdays per year were attributed to 22% of the employees who were caring for an elderly relative, for an annual loss to the corporation of $250,000. For larger companies, these costs can run into the millions.[66]

To reduce the negative effects of caregiving on productivity, organizations may offer elder care counseling, educational fairs and seminars, printed resource material, support groups, and special flexible schedules and leaves of absence. Schering-Plough, a pharmaceutical manufacturer, uses an 800 telephone line for elder care referrals, while IBM has a national telephone network of more than 200 community-based referral agencies. Employers may also band together for better elder care. The Partnership for Elder Care—a consortium of American Express Company, J. P. Morgan, and Philip Morris Company—and other companies use the resources of the New York City Department of Aging, a public information and aging support agency.

Interest in and demand for elder care programs will increase dramatically as baby boomers move into their fifties and find themselves managing organizations and experiencing elder care problems with their own parents.

## Other Services

The variety of benefits and services that employers offer today could not have been imagined a few years ago. Some are fairly standard, and we will cover them briefly. Some are unique and obviously grew out of specific concerns, needs, and interests. Some of the more unique benefits are group insurance for employee pets,[67] tickets for employees of the Los Angeles Dodgers, tanning beds for workers of Volvo,[68] and unlimited paid sick leave at Leo Burnett and Syntex. These examples represent only a few of the possibilities for benefits that go beyond those typically offered.

**USING THE INTERNET**

The BenefitLink home page provides a link to benefits-related information and services on the Internet. Coverage includes legal information, regulations, articles, advertisements, and benefits job openings.

www.benefitslink.com

### Food Services

Many organizations offer food services to their employees through vending machines, cafeterias, coffee trucks, and lunch wagons. These services are frequently offered at low cost or, in some cases, at below cost to the employer. The intent is to provide a convenience to employees while keeping them close to the work location. Offering quality nutrition may be a component of an organization's wellness program, a topic discussed in the next chapter.

### On-Site Health Services

Most of the larger organizations provide some form of on-site health services. The extent of these services varies considerably, but they are generally designed to handle minor illnesses and injuries. They may also include alcohol- and drug-abuse referral services, in-house counseling programs, and wellness clinics. We will discuss these and related programs in detail in the next chapter.

### Legal Services

One of the fastest-growing employee benefits is the prepaid legal service plan. There are two general types: access plans and comprehensive plans.[69] Access plans provide free telephone or office consultation, document review, and discounts on legal fees for more complex matters. Comprehensive plans cover other services such as representation in divorce cases, real estate transactions, and civil and criminal trials.

Covered employees normally pay a monthly or an annual fee to be enrolled in the plan. When the need for legal assistance arises, the employee may choose an attorney from a directory of providers and incur no expenses for attorney fees.[70] One benefits consultant remarked, "The whole idea behind prepaid legal plans is that the employer can use its purchase power and shift it to employees without incurring a lot of expense."[71] Prepaid legal programs are typically offered as part of an employer's cafeteria benefits plan.

### Financial Planning

One of the newer benefits is financial planning. As yet offered primarily to executives and middle-level managers, it is likely to become available to more employees through flexible benefits programs. Financial planning programs cover investments, tax planning and management, estate planning, and related topics.

### Housing and Moving Expenses

The days of "company houses" are now past, except in mining or logging operations, construction projects in remote areas, and the armed forces. However, a variety of housing services is usually provided in nearly all organizations that move employees from one office or plant to another in connection with a transfer or plant relocation. These services may include helping employees find living quarters, paying for travel and moving expenses, and protecting transferred employees from loss when selling their homes.[72]

### Transportation Pooling

Daily transportation to and from work is often a major concern of employees. The result may be considerable time and energy devoted to organizing car pools and scrambling for parking spaces. Many employers, like the Arizona Public Service Company and RCA in Bloomington, Indiana, attempt to ease conditions by offering transportation in vans. Employer-organized van pooling is common among private and public organizations with operations in metropolitan areas. Many employers report that tardiness and absenteeism are reduced by van pooling.

### Purchasing Assistance

Organizations may use various methods to assist their employees in purchasing merchandise more conveniently and at a discount. Retailers often offer their employees a discount on purchases made at the store. Most firms sell their own products at a discount to their employees, and in some instances they procure certain items from other manufacturers that they then offer to employees at a discount. For example, Costco, a high volume/low cost retailer in the Southwest, negotiates with local automobile dealerships special purchase prices for selected cars or trucks.

### Credit Unions

Credit unions exist in many organizations to serve the financial needs of employees. They offer a variety of deposits as well as other banking services and make loans to their members. Although the employer may provide office space and a payroll deduction service, credit unions are operated by the employees under federal and state legislation and supervision. At the end of December 1998, there were more than 11,212 credit unions in the United States with 73.4 million members and combined assets of $376 billion. In almost all credit unions, deposits are insured up to $100,000 per account by the National Credit Union Share Insurance Fund, a U.S. government agency.[73]

### Recreational and Social Services

Many organizations offer some type of sports program in which personnel may participate on a voluntary basis. Bowling, softball, golf, baseball, and tennis are quite often included in an intramural program. In addition to intramurals, many organizations have teams that represent them in competitions with other local organizations. Memberships or discounts on membership fees at health clubs and fitness centers are also popular offerings. (See Chapter 12.)

Many social functions are organized for employees and their families. Employees should have a major part in planning if these functions are to be successful. However, the employer should retain control of all events associated with the organization because of possible legal liability. For example, in Florida and California employers may be held liable for injuries to third persons caused by an employee's actions arising *within the course and scope of employment.* Thus accidents occurring while an employee is driving to or from an employer-sponsored event that the employee was encouraged to attend could trigger liability for an employer.

### Awards

Awards are often used to recognize productivity, special contributions, and service to an organization. Typically they are presented by top management at special meetings, banquets, and other functions where the honored employees will receive wide recognition. While cash awards are usually given for cost-saving suggestions from employees, a noncash gift is often a more appropriate way to recognize special achievement. For example, travel has emerged as an important part of many sales incentive programs. An all-expense-paid trip for two to Paris is likely to be a unique experience, more memorable than a cash gift.

## SUMMARY

 Benefits are an established and integral part of the total compensation package. In order to have a sound benefits program there are certain basic considerations. It is essential that a program be based on specific objectives that are compatible with organizational philosophy and policies as well as affordable. Through committees and surveys a benefit package can be developed to meet employees' needs. Through the use of flexible benefit plans, employees are able to choose those benefits that are best suited for their individual needs. An important factor in how employees view the program is the full communication of benefits information through meetings, printed material, and annual personalized statements of benefits.

According to a 1996 study, the costs of employee benefits in that year averaged 41.3 percent of payroll, or $14,086 per employee. Since many of the benefits represent a fixed cost, management must pay close attention in assuming more benefit expense. Increasingly, employers are requiring employees to pay part of the costs of certain benefits. Employers also shop for benefit services that are competitively priced.

**OBJECTIVE 3** Nearly a quarter of the benefits package that employers provide is legally required. These benefits include employer contributions to Social Security, unemployment insurance, workers' compensation insurance, and state disability insurance. Social Security taxes collected from employers and employees are used to pay three major types of benefits: (1) old-age insurance benefits, (2) disability benefits, and (3) survivors' insurance benefits.

**OBJECTIVE 4** The cost of health care programs has become the major concern in the area of employee benefits. Several approaches are used to contain health care costs, including reduction in coverage, increased coordination of benefits, increased deductible or copayments, use of health maintenance and preferred provider organizations, medical savings accounts, incentives for outpatient surgery and testing, and mandatory second opinions where surgery is indicated. Employee assistance programs and wellness programs may also contribute to cutting the costs of health care benefits.

**OBJECTIVE 5** Included in the category of benefits that involve payments for time not worked are vacations with pay, paid holidays, sick leave, and severance pay. The typical practice in the United States is to give twenty days' vacation leave and ten holidays. In addition to vacation time, most employees, particularly in white-collar jobs, receive a set number of sick-leave days. A one-time payment of severance pay may be given to employees who are being terminated.

**OBJECTIVE 6** Prior to 1979 employers were permitted to determine the age (usually 65) at which their employees would be required to retire. While there is now no ceiling, a growing number of workers choose to retire before age 65. Many employers provide incentives for early retirement in the form of increased pension benefits or cash bonuses. Some organizations provide preretirement programs that may include seminars, workshops, and informational materials. The National Council on Aging, the American Association of Retired Persons, and many other organizations are available to assist both employers and employees in preretirement activities.

**OBJECTIVE 7** Whether or not to offer a pension plan is the employer's prerogative. However, once a plan is established it is then subject to federal regulation under ERISA to ensure that benefits will be available when an employee retires. There are two traditional pension plans available—defined benefit and defined contribution. The amount an employee receives upon retirement is based on years of service, average earnings, and age at time of retirement. Pension benefits are typically integrated with Social Security benefits. Two of the most significant trends are the growth of 401(k) salary reduction plans and cash-balance pension plans. Pension funds may be administered through either a trusteed or an insurance plan. While ERISA requires that funds be invested where the return will be the greatest, employees often demand a voice in determining where funds will be invested.

**OBJECTIVE 8** The types of service benefits that employers typically provide include employee assistance programs, counseling services, educational assistance plans, child care, and elder care. Other benefits are food services, on-site health services, prepaid legal services, financial planning, housing and moving, transportation pooling, purchase assistance, credit unions, social and recreational services, and awards.

# KEY TERMS

contributory plan
defined-benefit plan
defined-contribution
  plan
elder care
employee assistance
  programs (EAPs)

flexible benefits plans (cafeteria
  plans)
health maintenance
  organizations (HMOs)
noncontributory plan
preferred provider
  organization (PPO)

silver handshake
supplemental unemployment
  benefits (SUBs)
vesting
workers' compensation
  insurance

## DISCUSSION QUESTIONS

 1. You are a small employer wishing to establish a benefits program for your employees. What things should you consider to ensure that the program is a success for your employees?

 2. Many organizations are concerned about the rising cost of employee benefits and question their value to the organization and to the employees.

    a. In your opinion, what benefits are of greatest value to employees? To the organization? Why?

    b. What can management do to increase the value to the organization of the benefits provided to employees?

 3. Employers are required by law to provide specific benefits to employees. What laws mandate benefits to employees and what are the provisions of those laws?

 4. Identify and contrast the various ways employers can control the costs of health care.

 5. Do you agree with the argument that benefits for time-not-worked are those most readily available to reduce employer costs? Explain.

 6. Prior to 1979, all employers could prescribe a mandatory retirement age—usually 65 years. What would you think are the advantages and disadvantages of a mandatory retirement age? What factors may affect an individual's decision to retire at a particular time, and what factors may affect his or her ability to adjust to retirement?

 7. Describe 401(k) pension plans, listing their advantages and disadvantages. As an employee, would you want control over the investment decisions of your 401(k) plan? Explain.

8. a. Working in teams of three or four, list and discuss the various benefits offered by your employer (or former employer). How are (were) the costs of these benefits paid for?

    b. Assume your team was hired as a benefits consultant to a small business having fifty to sixty employees. What benefits do you believe this employer should offer, given limited resources? Justify your reasons for offering these benefits.

## 401(k) Plans: Selecting the Best Options

In 1989, Sandra Perkins and Bethany McLean started Interior Designs, a manufacturer of high-end specialty furniture. A successful venture, the company has grown to over 1,500 employees and is recognized in the Seattle area as an "employee-friendly" employer. The workforce at Interior Designs is diverse in gender, age, and education.

Interior Designs has offered its employees a traditional defined-benefit pension plan but wishes to change to a 401(k) program. Unfortunately, after studying 401(k) plans, Joel Weisblatt, HR director, is unsure of the best program to select for Interior Designs employees. Here are some of the questions he faces:

- What percentage of wages should employees be allowed to invest: 3, 4, 5, 6, or 7 percent? Should there even be a cap on investment dollars?

- Should Interior Designs contribute to employee investments, and, if so, what should the matching rate be: 50 percent, 100 percent, 200 percent?

- Should the number of investment options be limited or should employee choices be unrestricted?
- What should the mix of investments be? Only stocks and bonds or some combination of investment alternatives?
- How often and how many times will employees be allowed to switch their investments? If changes are allowed, will the employee or Interior Designs assume these transfer costs?
- Is it reasonable to expect that Interior Designs will offer investment advice to employees?
- Should employees be allowed to borrow on their 401(k) savings? Will borrowing affect the security of an individual's pension plan?

While Weisblatt would like to offer the maximum options and financial advantages to employees, Interior Designs cannot do "everything" for its employees. And since each of the considerations noted above has pluses and minuses for both employees and the company, the details of the final plan are undecided.

### QUESTIONS

Work individually or in teams to cover the following points:

1. Discuss the advantages and disadvantages of the above choices.
2. Should an employee's age or time with Interior Designs influence option choices? Explain.
3. How concerned or knowledgeable do you believe employees are about investing their retirement funds through a 401(k) program? Explain.
4. Make a recommendation as to what you feel would be the best 401(k) plan for employees and Interior Designs. Defend your recommendation.

## Pitney Bowes: Benefit Choices with Value-Added Services

Mirroring other large and small organizations, Pitney Bowes faced double-digit annual cost inflation for employee benefits. Additionally, the workforce had adopted an entitlement mentality, assuming that their many benefits would always be available. Forgotten by employees was that the high cost of benefits inhibited the company's ability to invest in the firm's infrastructure such as new product development and training. Facing these challenges, Pitney Bowes felt a need to effectively communicate to employees the value of their benefits while satisfying the benefit demands of its many diversified employees.

Pitney Bowes decided to offer a cafeteria-style benefits plan to employees. A price was attached to a wide array of benefits and employees were told they had a certain number of flex dollars available to spend on the benefits of their choice. Employees "buy" benefits specific to their needs until their flex dollars are used up. Flex dollars are calculated separately for each individual on the basis of the employee's salary, years of service, age, and number of household dependents covered by benefits. The following example illustrates how flex dollars are awarded and what they can buy.

- Mrs. Elstrom is 45 years old, earns $35,000 a year, and has been with Pitney Bowes for ten years. Her flex dollars total $6,525.

- Mr. Goode is also 45 and earns $35,000. But he has been with Pitney Bowes for just five years and he wishes to cover only himself. His flex dollars total $2,265.

The Pitney Bowes benefits program allows employees to buy more benefits than granted under flex dollars by contributing cash from their paychecks. Or, should they purchase fewer benefits than allotted, they can receive their extra flex dollars as a cash reward.

Source: David Hom and Jeannie Mandelker, "How Pitney Bowes Broadens Benefit Choices with Value-Added Services." Adapted from *Compensation and Benefits Review,* March-April/1996. © 1996 American Management Association International. Reprinted by permission of American Management Association International, New York, NY. All rights reserved. http://www.amanet.org.

### QUESTIONS

1. Working individually or in teams, suggest a wide array of benefits that should be available to employees. Explain why each benefit is being offered and to which employee group it would appeal.

2. Explain several ways by which employees could select their benefits. How often should employees be allowed to change the mix of their benefits? Why?

3. If employees are performing similar jobs, shouldn't they be given the same flex dollars to spend? Explain.

4. With a cafeteria benefits program, won't employees make decisions about immediate needs (medical care) at the expense of their future needs (retirement)? Explain.

## NOTES AND REFERENCES

1. *Employee Benefits,* 1997 (Washington, D.C.: U.S. Chamber of Commerce, 1997): 5.

2. Frank E. Kuzmits, "Communicating Benefits: A Double-Click Away," *Compensation and Benefits Review* 30, no. 5 (September-October 1998): 60–64.

3. Lynn Asinof, "Click and Shift: Workers Control Their Benefits On-Line," *The Wall Street Journal,* November 27, 1997, C-1.

4. Jim Everett, "Internet Security," *Employee Benefits Journal* 23, no. 3 (September 1998): 14–18. Also see Alan R. Parham, "Developing a Technology Policy," *Employee Benefits Journal* 23, no. 3 (September 1998): 3–5.

5. Effective Benefits for Retaining Employees," *Bulletin to Management* 50, no. 6 (February 11, 1999): 44.

6. Scott J. Macey, "Corporate Restructuring—Strategic Planning and Redesign of Employee Benefits," *Employee Benefits Journal* 21, no. 4 (December 1996): 13-19.

7. Helen Box Reynolds, "Mid-management's Influence on Work/Life Programs," *Employee Benefits Journal* 23, no. 4 (December 1998): 44–46. See also Ann Vin-

cola, "Work and Life: In Search of the Missing Link," *HRFocus* 75, no. 8 (August 1998): 53–54.

8. Ronald W. Perry and N. Joseph Cayer, "Cafeteria Style Health Plans in Municipal Government," *Public Personnel Management* 28, no. 1 (Spring 1999): 107–17.

9. Kathryn M. Wall, "Enhancing Your Credibility: Does Your Audience Believe You?" *Employee Benefits Journal* 23, no. 2 (June 1998): 34–40.

10. Paul T. Shultz and Jane F. Greenman, "Supreme Court Muddies Employer versus Fiduciary Distinction in *Varity," Employee Relations Law Journal* 22, no. 1 (Summer 1996): 155–70.

11. *Varity Corp. v Howe,* 1996 WL 116994 (U.S. March 19, 1996).

12. "Employees Sue over Medical Benefits," *HRFocus* 73, no. 3 (June 1996): 7.

13. Madelon Lubin Finkel, "Evaluate and Communicate Health Care Benefits," *Employee Benefits Journal* 22, no. 4 (December 1997): 29–32.

14. Robert D. Perussina, "Fire That Elusive 'Somebody' in HR by Redefining ESS," *Employee Benefits Journal* 23, no. 4 (December 1998): 28–31.

**15.** Maureen E. Simons, "Multimedia Technology in Benefits Communication," *Employee Benefits Journal* 22, no. 1 (March 1997): 27–30.

**16.** Jeffrey M. Everson, "Effective Benefits Communication on a Shoestring Budget," *Employee Benefits Journal* 21, no. 4 (December 1996): 2–5.

**17.** Computerized data also enable management to keep accurate records of the cost of each benefit. To assist employers with the administrative and communication functions, the International Foundation of Employee Benefit Plans in Brookfield, Wisconsin, maintains an extensive library of employee benefits publications. It also prepares publications on this subject. The foundation has an on-line database that members can use to get immediate, comprehensive responses to questions about employee benefits. In cooperation with the Wharton School at the University of Pennsylvania and with Dalhousie University in Canada, the foundation offers a college-level program leading to the Certified Employee Benefit Specialist (CEBS) designation. For over forty years benefits professionals have relied on the International Foundation of Employee Benefit Plans for education and information about employee benefits. Total membership consists of 35,000 individuals who represent more than 7,400 trust funds, corporations, professional firms, and public employee funds throughout the United States, Canada, and overseas. The headquarters address is P.O. Box 69, Brookfield, WI 53008-0069. One of their many publications is a valuable reference book, *Employee Benefit Plans: A Glossary of Terms,* 8th ed. (Brookfield, WI: International Foundation of Employee Benefit Plans, 1993).

**18.** *Employee Benefits, 1997,* 7.

**19.** COBRA: April 7, 1986, P.L. 99-272, 100 Stat. 82.

**20.** Mark E. Brossman and Rebecca K. Kramnick, "Domestic Partnership Benefits," *Employee Benefits Journal* 19, no. 1 (March 1994): 2.

**21.** Elizabeth A. Rutherford, "Domestic Partner Benefits: Are You Doing It Right?" *Employee Relations Law Journal* 23, no. 1 (Summer 1997): 125–32.

**22.** Julie Cohen Mason, "Extending Benefits to Domestic Partners," *HRFocus* 73, no. 2 (February 1996): 17–18.

**23.** Active military service completed between 1940 and 1956 inclusive was granted Social Security credit based on monthly earnings of $160 per month. Since the Social Security Act is continually subject to amendment, readers should refer to the literature provided by the nearest Social Security office for the most current details pertaining to the tax rates and benefit provisions of the act.

**24.** For a more detailed account of exempted groups, see the current edition of *Labor Course* or *Tax Course* (Englewood Cliffs, N.J.: Prentice-Hall).

**25.** Peter Coy, "Social Security: Let It Be," *Business Week,* November 30, 1998, 34–35.

**26.** U.S. Department of Health and Human Services, *Social Security Handbook,* 13th ed. (Washington, D.C.: U.S. Government Printing Office, 1997): ¶212. The amount changes annually and is published in the *Federal Register.*

**27.** "Workers' Comp Often Overlooked—Until Needed," *Arizona Department of Economic Security* 22, no. 1 (Spring 1998): 1–8.

**28.** (1) The doctrine of the assumption of risk holds that when employees accept a job, they assume the ordinary risks of the job. (2) The fellow-servant rule provides that if the employee is injured as a result of the negligence of a fellow employee, the employer is not liable for the injury. (3) The doctrine of contributory negligence states that the employer is not liable if the injury of the employee is due wholly or in part to negligence.

**29.** Steve Lattanzio, "What Can an Employer Do to Influence the Cost of Its Workers' Compensation Program?" *Compensation and Benefits Review* 29, no. 3 (May-June 1997): 20–28.

**30.** FMLA: February 5, 1993, P.L. 103-3, 107 Stat. 6.

**31.** Alice E. Conway, "A Guide to Practical Knowledge of the FMLA and Its Complex New Final Regulations," *Labor Law Journal* 46, no. 9 (September 1995): 515–42.

**32.** Janell M. Kurtz and Theressa Arrick-Kruger, "Coordination-of-Leave Benefits: An Important Component in Preventing Employee Abuse of the Family and Medical Leave Act," *Employee Benefits Journal* 21, no. 1 (March 1996): 25–29. See also Brenda Park Sunoo, "Managing the FMLA—A Big or Little Challenge?" *Personnel Journal* 75, no. 9 (September 1996): 149–50.

**33.** Aaron Bernstein, "When Is a Temp Not a Temp?" *Business Week,* December 7, 1998, 90–92.

**34.** *Older Workers Benefit Protection Act* (29 U.S.C. 1990) §§623, 626, and 630.

**35.** By signing a waiver (also called a release not to sue), an employee agrees not to take any legal action against the employer. Legal action could be an age discrimination lawsuit. In return for the signed waiver, the employer gives the employee an incentive to leave voluntarily, such as a severance pay package that is larger than the company's normal offer.

**36.** Paul J. Kennedy, "Take the Money and Sue," *HRMagazine* 43, no. 5 (April 1998): 105–8.

**37.** *Employee Benefits, 1996,* 12.

**38.** Michael Meyer, "Oh No, Here We Go Again," *Newsweek,* December 14, 1998, 46–47.

**39.** Forrest Briscoe and James Maxwell, "Hands-On Health Care Benefits," *HRMagazine* 44, no. 2 (February 1999): 73–78.

**40.** Greg Jaffe, "Corporate Carrots, Sticks Cut Health Bills," *The Wall Street Journal,* February 3, 1998, B-1.

**41.** Madelon Lubin Finkel and Susan Oliveria, "Focus on Quality Assessment: The Need for Evaluation," *Employee Benefits Journal* 23, no. 1 (March 1998): 21–22.

42. "PPOs Lead the Way in Alternative Therapies," *Bulletin to Management* 50, no. 10 (March 11, 1999): 76.

43. Scott M. Stevens, "Medical Savings Accounts (MSAs)—Big Benefits for Small Business," *Employee Benefits Journal* 22, no. 2 (June 1997): 10–11.

44. Brenda Park Sunoo, "Vacations: Going Once, Going Twice, Sold," *Personnel Journal* 75, no. 8 (August 1996): 72–80.

45. Judy C. Bauserman, "Designing Vacation Programs That Comply with State Law Restrictions," *Employee Relations Law Journal* 23, no. 4 (Spring 1998): 153–62.

46. David S. Landay, "Living: An Affordable Compassionate Option," *HRMagazine* 41, no. 6 (June 1996): 118–25.

47. Jenny C. McCune, "The Future of Retirement," *HRFocus* 75, no. 6 (June 1998): 1–4.

48. Prior to 1979, employers were permitted to determine the age (usually 65) at which their employees would be required to retire. A 1978 amendment to the Age Discrimination in Employment Act of 1967 prohibited mandatory retirement under the age of 70 in private employment and at any age in federal employment. A 1986 amendment removed the ceiling age of 70 and prohibits age-based employment discrimination for *ages 40 and older*. However, for some specific occupations, there are legally mandated retirement ages. For airline pilots, for instance, the age is 60.

49. John D. Abraham and Krista Schneider, "A Comparison of Income Replacement Rates in Defined Benefit and Defined Contribution Pension Plans," *Employee Benefits Journal* 23, no. 3 (September 1998): 31–40.

50. Anne Willette, "Gap Widens among 401(k)s," *Mesa Tribune*, January 18, 1998, B-6.

51. Eileen P. Gunn, "Sorting Out the Savings Plans," *Fortune*, August 17, 1998, 121–25.

52. Willette, "Gap Widens" B-1. See also Ellen E. Schultz, "Rich-Poor Gap in 401(k) Plans Widens, " *The Wall Street Journal*, August 21, 1997, C-23.

53. Diane Youden, "Automatic 401(k) Enrollment: Retirement Cure-All or Bitter Pill?" *Compensation and Benefits Review* 31, no. 2 (March/April 1999): 54–60.

54. "Educating Employees on 401(k) Investments," *HRFocus* 75, no. 11 (November 1998): 2. See also "401(k) Participants More Comfortable with Equities," *HRFocus* 75, no. 11 (November 1998); S-3.

55. Ellen E. Schultz, "Ins and Outs of Cash-Balance Plans," *The Wall Street Journal*, December 4, 1998, C-1.

56. Jon G. Auerbach, "IBM Considers Adopting New Pension Plan," *The Wall Street Journal*, March 18, 1999, A-3. See also Ellen E. Schultz, "Employers Win Big with a Pension Shift: Employees Often Lose," *The Wall Street Journal*, December 4, 1998, A-1.

57. Schultz, "Employers Win Big."

58. ERISA: September 2, 1974, P.L. 93-406, 88 Stat. 829.

59. REA: August 23, 1984, P.L. 98-397, 98 Stat. 1426.

60. Deficit Reduction Act of 1984: July 18, 1984, P.L. 98-369, 98 Stat. 494.

61. Leslie Faught, "At Eddie Bauer You Can Work and Have a Life," *Workforce* 76, no. 4 (April 1997): 83–98. See also Kate Fralin, "Case Study: Fannie Mae Creates a Balance, " *HRFocus* 75, no. 8 (August 1998): 5–11; Anne Szostak, "Fleet Financial Tests Work/Life," *HRFocus* 75, no. 11 (November 1998): 5–13; Keith H. Hammonds and Ann Therese Palmer, "The Daddy Trap," *Business Week*, September 21, 1998, 56–64; Teresa J. Rothausen, Jorge A. Gonzales, Nicole E. Clarke, and Lisa L. O'Dell, "Family-Friendly Backlash—Fact or Fiction? The Case of Organization's On-Site Child Care Centers," *Personnel Psychology* 51, no. 3 (Autumn 1998): 685–706.

62. "Employers Help Workers Achieve Balance in Life," *HRFocus* 75, no. 11 (November 1998): S-3.

63. Gary L. Wirt, "The ABCs of EAPs," *HRFocus* 75, no. 11 (November 1998): S-2.

64. Eric Lekus, "Will On-Site Centers Become Regular Workplace Features?"*Bulletin to Management* 50, no. 9 (March 9, 1999): 71.

65. Maureen Mineham, "The Aging of America Will Increase Elder Care Responsibilities," *HRMagazine* 42, no. 7 (July 1997): 184.

66. Elaine Davis and Mary Kay Krouze, "A Maturing Benefit: Elder Care after a Decade," *Employee Benefits Journal* 19, no. 3 (September 1994): 16–19. See also Meridy M. Rachor, "When Worlds Collide: Elder Caregiving Poses New Challenges for Balancing Work and Life," *Employee Benefits Journal* 23, no. 3 (September 1998): 20–23.

67. "Pet Insurance?" *HRFocus* 75, no. 11 (November 1998): S-10.

68. Almar Latour, "Detroit Meets a 'Workers Paradise'—Will Volvo's Perks Give Ford Sticker Shock?" *The Wall Street Journal*, March 3, 1999, B-1.

69. Sandra H. DeMent, "Advice for Employers: How to Select a Prepaid Legal Benefit," *Employee Benefits Journal* 23, no. 2 (June 1998): 22–24.

70. Jennifer Click, "The Ins and Outs of Prepaid Legal Plans, " *HRMagazine* 43, no. 1 (January 1998): 66–69.

71. "Sears Tries on a Pre-paid Legal Plan," *HRFocus* 73, no. 5 (May 1996): 7.

72. Judy C. Bauserman, "Allowing Employees to Choose Transportation Fringe Benefits," *Employee Relations Law Journal* 24, no. 4 (Spring 1999): 123–34. See also Alan S. Mileski, "It's Time to Relocate Employees: Will They Accept the Transfer?" *Compensation and Benefits Review* 30, no. 2 (March/April 1998): 57–58.

73. Data obtained April 22, 1999, from the Credit Union National Association, P.O. Box 431, Madison, WI 53701, (608) 231-4000.

# chapter 12

# Safety and Health

## AFTER STUDYING THIS CHAPTER, YOU SHOULD BE ABLE TO

 **OBJECTIVE 1**
Summarize the general provisions of the Occupational Safety and Health Act (OSHA).

 **OBJECTIVE 2**
Describe what management can do to create a safe work environment.

 **OBJECTIVE 3**
Cite the measures that should be taken to control and eliminate health hazards.

 **OBJECTIVE 4**
Describe the organizational services and programs for building better health.

 **OBJECTIVE 5**
Explain the role of employee assistance programs in HRM.

 **OBJECTIVE 6**
Describe methods for coping with stress.

Occupational safety and health accidents are both numerous and costly to employers. As one example, corporate security and safety directors consider the spillover of domestic problems into the workplace a high-risk safety concern. Some 13,000 acts of domestic-related violence against women occur in the workplace annually. It is projected that employees miss 175,000 days of work per year due to domestic violence, costing employers between $3 billion and $5 billion yearly in lost productivity, greater absenteeism, and increased health care costs.[1] To prevent losses such as these, employers are concerned about limiting violence in the workplace along with providing working conditions—in all areas of employment—that provide for the safety and health of their employees.

While the laws safeguarding employees' physical and emotional well-being are certainly an incentive, many employers are motivated to provide desirable working conditions by virtue of their sensitivity to human needs and rights. The more cost-oriented employer recognizes the importance of avoiding accidents and illnesses wherever possible. Costs associated with sick leave, disability payments, replacement of employees who are injured or killed, and workers' compensation far exceed the costs of maintaining a safety and health program. Accidents and illnesses attributable to the workplace may also have pronounced effects on employee morale and on the goodwill that the organization enjoys in the community and in the business world.

Managers at all levels are expected to know and enforce safety and health standards throughout the organization. They must ensure a work environment that protects employees from physical hazards, unhealthy conditions, and unsafe acts of other personnel. Through effective safety and health programs, the physical and emotional well-being of employees may be preserved and even enhanced.

We begin this chapter by inviting readers to examine their safety and health knowledge by taking the test in Highlights in HRM 1. After discussing the legal requirements for safety and health, we shall focus in the rest of the chapter on the creation of a safe and healthy work environment and on the management of stress.

# Safety and Health: It's the Law

Consider these facts:

- A fifteen-year study conducted by the National Institute for Occupational Safety and Health reported 88,622 work-related deaths; 23.1 percent of the deaths were due to traffic accidents.[2]
- Repetitive motion injuries soared from 50,000 cases in 1986 to 280,000 cases in 1998.
- In any year, approximately 75 million working days are lost because of on-the-job injuries.
- In 1996, 6,112 employees died from work accidents.
- The cost to employers for job-related injuries and illnesses for truck drivers, laborers, machine operators, carpenters, janitors, and assemblers exceeds $1.75 billion annually.[3]

**HIGHLIGHTS IN HRM**

# Test Your Safety Smarts

Take the following quiz to evaluate your knowledge and awareness of safety and health issues. Answers are found at the end of this chapter.

1. What is the maximum fine for a nondeath OSHA citation?
   **a.** $500        **b.** $750        **c.** $20,000        **d.** $70,000

2. Name one of the OSHA four-point safety and health guidelines.

3. What is the OSHA "general duty clause"?

4. What percent of the U.S. population will be affected by back injuries?
   **a.** 23        **b.** 47        **c.** 60        **d.** 80

5. During 1998, the Occupational Safety and Health Administration issued the most citations for safety and health violations in which area?
   **a.** Hazard communications        **c.** Electrical wiring
   **b.** Ladders and scaffolds        **d.** Engines and machinery

6. In the first quarter of 1999, OSHA conducted approximately _____ general industry workplace inspections.
   **a.** 1,800        **b.** 3,500        **c.** 4,700        **d.** 6,200

7. Which causes more accidents: unsafe acts or unsafe conditions?

8. List five areas regarding safety that should be covered during a new employee orientation.

9. OSHA standards reflect
   **a.** Minimum standards        **c.** State guidelines
   **b.** Suggested requirements        **d.** Both a and c

10. True or false? Carpal tunnel syndrome is the fear of enclosed areas such as silos, tanks, and hallways.

11. True or false? Employers are required to allow OSHA inspectors on premises for unannounced inspections.

The burden on the nation's commerce as a result of lost productivity and wages, medical expenses, and disability compensation is staggering. And there is no way to calculate the human suffering involved.

It was to forestall even worse losses that Congress passed the Occupational Safety and Health Act (OSHA) in 1970.[4] In spite of the figures cited above, the act, which was designed "to assure so far as possible every working man and woman in the Nation safe and healthful working conditions and to preserve our human resources," has been very effective in reducing the number of injuries resulting in lost work time, as well as the number of job-related deaths.[5] For example, in 1996, with almost twice as many workers as in the 1960s, the 6,112 fatalities reported were almost one-third the number of worker deaths reported in the late 1960s.

*OSHA standards require the use of protective gear and equipment in certain work environments.*

## OSHA's Coverage

In general, the act extends to all employers and their employees, with only a few exceptions, which include the federal government and any state or political subdivision of a state. Each federal agency, however, is required to establish and maintain a safety and health program that is monitored by the Occupational Safety and Health Administration. Likewise, a state seeking OSHA approval of its safety and health program for the private sector must provide a similar program that covers its state and local government employees and is at least as effective as its program for private employers. Where state programs for the private sector have been approved by the federal government as meeting federal standards, the state carries out the enforcement functions that would otherwise be performed by the federal government. Approximately one-half of the states currently have their own OSHA-approved programs.

## OSHA Standards

One of the responsibilities of the Occupational Safety and Health Administration is to develop and enforce mandatory job safety and health standards. OSHA standards fall into four major categories: general industry, maritime, construction, and agriculture. These standards cover the workplace, machinery and equipment, material, power sources, processing, protective clothing, first aid, and administrative requirements. It is the responsibility of employers to become familiar with those standards that are applicable to their establishments and to ensure that their employees use personal protective gear and equipment when required for safety. The *Federal Register* is the principal source of information on proposed, adopted, amended, and deleted OSHA standards. Large employers usually subscribe to it and/or the OSHA Subscription Service.[6]

The Occupational Safety and Health Administration can begin standards-setting procedures on its own initiative or on petition from other parties, including the Secretary of Health and Human Services (HHS) and the National Institute for Occupational Safety and Health (NIOSH). Other bodies that may also initiate standards-setting procedures are state and local governments and any nationally recognized standards-producing organization, employer, or labor representative. NIOSH, however, is the major source of standards.[7] As an agency of the Department of Health and Human Services, it is responsible for conducting research on various safety and health problems, including the psychological factors involved.[8]

## Enforcing OSHA Standards

The Secretary of Labor is authorized by the Occupational Safety and Health Act to conduct workplace inspections, to issue citations, and to impose penal-

### USING THE INTERNET

For a variety of information on OSHA, including recent regulations, standards, and statistics, go to:

www.osha.gov./

ties on employers. Inspections have been delegated to the Occupational Safety and Health Administration of the U.S. Department of Labor.

## Workplace Inspections

Under the act, "upon presenting appropriate credentials to the owner, operator, or agent in charge," an OSHA compliance officer is authorized to do the following:

- Enter without delay and at reasonable times any factory, plant, establishment, construction site or other areas, workplace, or environment where work is performed by an employee of an employer; and to
- Inspect and investigate during regular working hours, and at other reasonable times, and within reasonable limits and in a reasonable manner, any such place of employment and all pertinent conditions, structures, machines, apparatus, devices, equipment and materials therein, and to question privately any such employer, owner, operator, agent, or employee.[9]

OSHA has further established a system of inspection priorities:[10]

First level: Inspection of imminent danger situations

Second level: Investigation of catastrophes, fatalities, and accidents that result in hospitalization of five or more employees

Third level: Investigation of valid employee complaints of alleged violations of standards or of unsafe or unhealthful working conditions

Fourth level: Special-emphasis inspections aimed at specific high-hazard industries, occupations, or substances that are injurious to health

Typically, OSHA inspectors will arrive at a work site unannounced and ask for a meeting with a representative of the employer. At the meeting the inspectors will explain the purpose of the visit, describe the procedure for the inspection, and ask to review the employer's safety and health records. An employer may either agree voluntarily to the inspection or require the inspectors to obtain a search warrant.

The act gives both the employer and the employees the right to accompany inspectors on their tour of the work site. After the tour the OSHA officials will conduct a closing conference to inform the employer and employee representatives, if any, of the results of their inspection. They will point out conditions or practices that appear to be hazardous and issue a written citation if warranted.[11]

## Citations and Penalties

OSHA citations may be issued immediately following the inspection or later by mail. Citations tell the employer and employees which regulations and standards are alleged to have been violated and the amount of time allowed for their correction. The employer must post a copy of each citation at or near the place the violation occurred for three days or until the violation is abated, whichever is longer.

OSHA has a wide range of penalties for violations. Fines of as much as $7,000 are imposed for serious violations, including violations of posting requirements. For willful or repeated violations, OSHA can assess penalties of up to $70,000 for each violation, or if a willful violation results in the death of an employee, a fine of up to $250,000 for an individual or $500,000 for a corporation plus imprisonment of up to six months or both. The law provides for appeal by employers and by employees under specified circumstances.[12]

The following examples illustrate the seriousness of OSHA citations and penalties.

- The Erik K. Ho Company was cited for an asbestos fire. Proposed penalty: $1.5 million.
- Archer Daniels Midland was issued citations for confined space. Proposed penalty: $1.6 million.
- The Claremont Steel Company was cited for faulty hydraulic jacks. Proposed penalty: $463,000.[13]

### On-site Consultation

OSHA provides a free on-site consultation service. Consultants from the state government or private contractors help employers identify hazardous conditions and determine corrective measures. No citations are issued in connection with a consultation, and the consultant's files cannot be used to trigger an OSHA inspection.

### Voluntary Protection Programs

**Voluntary protection programs (VPPs)**

Programs that encourage employers to go beyond the minimum requirements of OSHA

The **voluntary protection programs (VPPs)** represent one component of OSHA's effort to extend worker protection beyond the minimum required by OSHA standards.[14] There are three specific VPPs—Star, Merit, and Demonstration—which are designed to do the following:

1. Recognize outstanding achievement of those who have successfully incorporated comprehensive safety and health programs into their total management system.

2. Motivate others to achieve excellent safety and health results in the same outstanding way.

3. Establish a relationship among employers, employees, and OSHA that is based on cooperation rather than coercion.

Once it has been approved for a VPP, an organization is then taken off OSHA's list for routine inspections.[15]

OSHA's area offices provide a variety of informational services to employers. The OSHA Training Institute in Des Plaines, Illinois, provides basic and advanced training in safety and health. Over sixty courses are available. OSHA also provides funds to nonprofit organizations to conduct workplace training.

Highlights in HRM 2 describes OSHA's four-point recommended safety and health program for small businesses.

## Responsibilities and Rights under OSHA

Both employers and employees have certain responsibilities and rights under OSHA. We will discuss only those that relate directly to the management of human resources.

### Employers' Responsibilities and Rights

In addition to providing a hazard-free workplace and complying with the applicable standards, employers must inform all of their employees about the safety and health requirements of OSHA. Employers are also required to display the OSHA poster that lists employees' rights and responsibilities (see Highlights in HRM 3), to keep certain records, and to compile and post an annual summary of work-

**HRM 2**

# OSHA's Four-Point Safety and Health Program for Small Businesses

The Four-Point Workplace Program is based upon the safety and health management guidelines issued by OSHA. Although voluntary, these guidelines represent OSHA's policy on what every work site should have in place to protect workers from occupational hazards. The guidelines are based heavily on OSHA's experience with the voluntary protection programs. Additional information can be obtained from OSHA's Office of Cooperative Programs, U.S. Department of Labor, 200 Constitution Avenue, N.W., Washington, D.C. 20210, (202) 219-7266.

*Point 1: Management Commitment and Employee Involvement* As the owner or manager of a small business, your attitude toward job safety and health will be reflected by your employees. Demonstrate to employees the depth of management's commitment by involving them in planning and carrying out all safety efforts.

*Point 2: Work Site Analysis* Work site analysis combines a group of processes that helps managers know what is needed to ensure workplace safety and health. OSHA area offices can provide assistance with in-depth investigations of the work environment.

*Point 3: Hazard Prevention and Control* You must establish safe work procedures and policies based on the analysis of the hazards previously identified. Be ready, if necessary, to enforce the rules for safe work through a fair and clearly understood disciplinary system.

*Point 4: Train Employees, Supervisors, Managers* As an owner or manager, ensure that all employees know about any hazardous materials and equipment they work with and know how to control the hazards. An effective accident prevention program requires proper job performance from everyone in the workplace.

related injuries and illnesses. From these records, organizations can compute their *incidence rate,* the number of injuries and illnesses per 100 full-time employees during a given year. The standard formula for computing the incidence rate is shown by the following equation, where 200,000 equals the base for 100 full-time workers who work forty hours a week, fifty weeks a year:

$$\text{Incidence rate} = \frac{\text{Number of injuries and illnesses} \times 200{,}000}{\text{Total hours worked by all employees during period covered}}$$

It should be noted that the same formula can be used to compute incidence rates for (1) the number of workdays lost because of injuries and illnesses, (2) the number of nonfatal injuries and illnesses without lost workdays, and (3) cases involving only injuries or only illnesses.

Incidence rates are useful for making comparisons between work groups, between departments, and between similar units within an organization. They also provide a basis for making comparisons with other organizations doing similar work. The Bureau of Labor Statistics and other organizations, such as the National

**HRM 3**

# Job Safety and Health Protection Poster

## JOB SAFETY & HEALTH PROTECTION

The Occupational Safety and Health Act of 1970 provides job safety and health protection for workers by promoting safe and healthful working conditions throughout the Nation. Provisions of the Act include the following:

### Employers

All employers must furnish to employees employment and a place of employment free from recognized hazards that are causing or are likely to cause death or serious harm to employees. Employers must comply with occupational safety and health standards issued under the Act.

### Employees

Employees must comply with all occupational safety and health standards, rules, regulations and orders issued under the Act that apply to their own actions and conduct on the job.

The Occupational Safety and Health Administration (OSHA) of the U.S. Department of Labor has the primary responsibility for administering the Act. OSHA issues occupational safety and health standards, and its Compliance Safety and Health Officers conduct jobsite inspections to help ensure compliance with the Act.

### Inspection

The Act requires that a representative of the employer and a representative authorized by the employees be given an opportunity to accompany the OSHA inspector for the purpose of aiding the inspection.

Where there is no authorized employee representative, the OSHA Compliance Officer must consult with a reasonable number of employees concerning safety and health conditions in the workplace.

### Complaint

Employees or their representatives have the right to file a complaint with the nearest OSHA office requesting an inspection if they believe unsafe or unhealthful conditions exist in their workplace. OSHA will withhold, on request, names of employees complaining.

The Act provides that employees may not be discharged or discriminated against in any way for filing safety and health complaints or for otherwise exercising their rights under the Act.

Employees who believe they have been discriminated against may file a complaint with their nearest OSHA office within 30 days of the alleged discriminatory action.

### Citation

If upon inspection OSHA believes an employer has violated the Act, a citation alleging such violations will be issued to the employer. Each citation will specify a time period within which the alleged violation must be corrected.

The OSHA citation must be prominently displayed at or near the place of alleged violation for three days, or until it is corrected, whichever is later, to warn employees of dangers that may exist there.

### Proposed Penalty

The Act provides for mandatory civil penalties against employers of up to $7,000 for each serious violation and for optional penalties of up to $7,000 for each nonserious violation. Penalties of up to $7,000 per day may be proposed for failure to correct violations within the proposed time period and for each day the violation continues beyond the prescribed abatement date. Also, any employer who willfully or repeatedly violates the Act may be assessed penalties of up to $70,000 for each such violation. A minimum penalty of $5,000 may be imposed for each willful violation. A violation of posting requirements can bring a penalty of up to $7,000.

There are also provisions for criminal penalties. Any willful violation resulting in the death of any employee, upon conviction, is punishable by a fine of up to $250,000 (or $500,000 if the employer is a corporation), or by imprisonment for up to six months, or both. A second conviction of an employer doubles the possible term of imprisonment. Falsifying records, reports, or applications is punishable by a fine of $10,000 or up to six months in jail or both.

### Voluntary Activity

While providing penalties for violations, the Act also encourages efforts by labor and management, before an OSHA inspection, to reduce workplace hazards voluntarily and to develop and improve safety and health programs in all workplaces and industries. OSHA's Voluntary Protection Programs recognize outstanding efforts of this nature.

OSHA has published Safety and Health Program Management Guidelines to assist employers in establishing or perfecting programs to prevent or control employee exposure to workplace hazards. There are many public and private organizations that can provide information and assistance in this effort, if requested. Also, your local OSHA office can provide considerable help and advice on solving safety and health problems or can refer you to other sources for help such as training.

### Consultation

Free assistance in identifying and correcting hazards and in improving safety and health management is available to employers, without citation or penalty, through OSHA-supported programs in each State. These programs are usually administered by the State Labor or Health department or a State university.

### Posting Instructions

Employers in States operating OSHA approved State Plans should obtain and post the State's equivalent poster.

*Under provisions of Title 29, Code of Federal Regulations, Part 1903.2(a)(1) employers must post this notice (or facsimile) in a conspicuous place where notices to employees are customarily posted.*

### More Information

Additional information and copies of the Act, specific OSHA safety and health standards, and other applicable regulations may be obtained from your employer or from the nearest OSHA Regional Office in the following locations:

| | |
|---|---|
| Atlanta, GA | (404) 347-3573 |
| Boston, MA | (617) 565-7164 |
| Chicago, IL | (312) 353-2220 |
| Dallas, TX | (214) 767-4731 |
| Denver, CO | (303) 844-3061 |
| Kansas City, MO | (816) 426-5861 |
| New York, NY | (212) 337-2378 |
| Philadelphia, PA | (215) 596-1201 |
| San Francisco, CA | (415) 744-6670 |
| Seattle, WA | (206) 553-5930 |

**To report suspected fire hazards, imminent danger safety and health hazards in the workplace, or other job safety and health emergencies, such as toxic waste in the workplace, call OSHA's 24-hour hotline: 1-800-321-OSHA.**

Washington, DC
1992 (Reprinted)
OSHA 2203

Robert B. Reich, Secretary of Labor

**U.S. Department of Labor**
Occupational Safety and Health Administration

This information will be made available to sensory impaired individuals upon request.
Voice phone: (202) 219-8615; TDD message referral phone: 1-800-326-2577

GPO : 1993 O – 355-763 QL

Safety Council, compile data that an employer can use as a basis for comparing its safety record with other organizations. These comparisons provide a starting point for analyzing problem areas, making changes in the working environment, and motivating personnel to promote safety and health.

It is the employer's responsibility to make sure employees use protective equipment when necessary. Employers must therefore engage in safety training and be prepared to discipline employees for failing to comply with safety rules. And employers must not discriminate against employees who exercise their rights under the act by filing complaints. On the other hand, employers are afforded many rights under the law, most of which pertain to receiving information, applying for variances in standards, and contesting citations.[16]

### Employees' Responsibilities and Rights

Employees are required to comply with all applicable OSHA standards, to report hazardous conditions, and to follow all employer safety and health rules and regulations, including those prescribing the use of protective equipment. Workers have a right to demand safe and healthy conditions on the job without fear of punishment. They also have many rights that pertain to requesting and receiving information about safety and health conditions.[17]

## Right-to-Know Laws

**Right-to-know laws**
Laws that require employers to advise employees about the hazardous chemicals they handle

Exposure to hazardous chemicals is currently one of the most serious health concerns for both employers and employees. Therefore, most states—and federal law—require that employers provide information to employees about the hazardous chemicals they handle. Commonly known as **right-to-know laws,** these statutes address such issues as the definition of toxic and hazardous substances, the duties of employers and manufacturers to provide health-risk information to employees, trade-secret protection, and enforcement provisions. Since state right-to-know laws can be more stringent then federal law, employers are encouraged to contact their state's health and safety agency for a copy of their appropriate hazard communication standards.[18]

**Material Safety Data Sheets (MSDSs)**
Documents that contain vital information about hazardous substances

To understand the right-to-know laws, employers must first become familiar with OSHA-published hazardous chemical regulations known as the Hazard Communication Standard (HCS). The HCS prescribes a system for communicating data on health hazards to employees. It includes a format for **Material Safety Data Sheets (MSDSs).** MSDSs should include the chemical name of a hazardous substance; all of the risks involved in using it, including potential health risks; safe handling practices; personal protective equipment needed; first aid in the event of an accident; and information identifying the manufacturer.

## OSHA's Enforcement Record

Perhaps no federal government agency has been more severely criticized than the Occupational Safety and Health Administration. Complaints often concern what employers consider to be picky or unrealistic standards and the proliferation of rules under agency personnel. According to one safety manager known to the authors, "It seems OSHA administration conducts research and sets safety and health standards in an ivory tower, not knowing or caring if standards are valid for the real world."

However, the complaint most registered against OSHA is the uneven enforcement efforts by the agency from one political administration to the next.

Under some administrations, enforcement efforts have been seen as virtually nonexistent (or at least very lax), while under others, regulatory enforcement has seemed more proactive. Employers often view OSHA as overly zealous, while unions and safety groups continue to worry that OSHA is lax in monitoring its agreements with organizations. These groups would prefer mandatory standards instead of voluntary guidelines for problems such as injuries related to jobs involving repetitive motion—a topic to be considered later in the chapter.

# Creating a Safe Work Environment

We have seen that employers are required by law to provide safe working conditions for their employees. To achieve this objective, the majority of employers have a formal safety program.[19] Typically, the HR department or the industrial relations department is responsible for the safety program. While the success of a safety program depends largely on managers and supervisors of operating departments, the HR department typically coordinates the safety communication and training programs, maintains safety records required by OSHA, and works closely with managers and supervisors in a cooperative effort to make the program a success.

Organizations with formal safety programs generally have an employee-management safety committee that includes representatives from management, each department or manufacturing/service unit, and employee representatives. Committees are typically involved in investigating accidents and helping to publicize the importance of safety rules and their enforcement.

*Safety begins with preparedness, as these employees demonstrate in this dress rehearsal.*

## Safety Motivation and Knowledge

Probably the most important role of a safety program is motivating managers, supervisors, and subordinates to be aware of safety considerations. In one study conducted by the American Institute of Plant Engineers, "survey results showed a direct correlation between an increase in management's commitment to safety in the workplace and a decrease in accidents."[20] If managers and supervisors fail to demonstrate awareness, their subordinates can hardly be expected to do so. Unfortunately, most managers and supervisors wear their "safety hats" far less often than their "production, quality control, and methods improvement hats." Just as important as safety motivation are a knowledge of safety and an understanding of where to place safety efforts. Training can help personnel on all levels understand the organization's policy on safety, its safety procedures, and its system of establishing accountability.

## Promoting Safety Awareness

Most organizations have a safety awareness program that entails the use of several different media. Safety lectures, commercially produced films, specially developed videocassettes, and other media such as pamphlets are useful for teaching and motivating employees to follow safe work procedures.[21] A page from one of these pamphlets is shown in Highlights in HRM 4. Posters have been found to be very effective because they can be displayed in strategic locations where workers will be sure to see them. For example, a shipyard found that placing posters at the work site helped reduce accidents by making employees more conscious of the hazards of using scaffolds. At another employer, Stanley Works, Inc., the company's Internet is the number 1 tool for reducing health and safety problems. According to Kevin Nelson, employee health and safety director, "The Internet functions as the organization's SWAT team to develop and implement timely and efficient health and safety programs."[22] Interactive CD-ROM training is another method ideal for standardized safety, environmental, and health instruction.[23]

### Safety and TQM

Interestingly, the concepts that promote product and service quality through TQM are equally applicable to safety awareness programs. These concepts include (1) safety as a product that demands continuous improvement, (2) a strong organizational culture stressing no tolerance for unsafe practices, (3) employee empowerment, which allows employees to participate in forming safety policy and in-field safety decisions, and (4) safety management based on information, measurement, data, and analysis. In TQM safety terms, what gets measured gets managed and improved.

### The Key Role of the Supervisor

One of a supervisor's major responsibilities is to communicate to an employee the need to work safely.[24] Beginning with new employee orientation, safety should be emphasized continually. Proper work procedures, the use of protective clothing and devices, and potential hazards should be explained thoroughly. Furthermore, employees' understanding of all these considerations should be verified during training sessions, and employees should be encouraged to take some initiative in maintaining a concern for safety. Since training by itself does not ensure continual adherence to safe work practices, supervisors must observe employees at work and

**HRM 4**

# Page from a Safety Awareness Pamphlet

## Hard hat care

**Clean the shell of your hard hat at least once a month.**

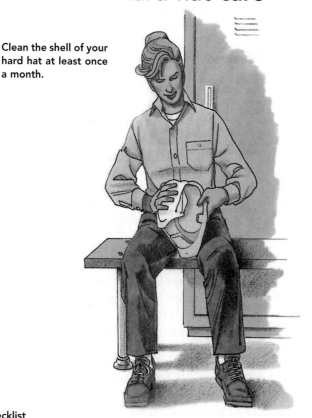

**Your Checklist**

❏ Make sure your hat fits right. There should be approximately 1″ between the harness and the shell so air can circulate and keep your scalp cool. If your hat is too loose, it will fall off when you bend over. Too tight and it may cause headaches.

❏ Wear a color-coded hat if you need identification. Don't paint or scratch your hard hat to identify it.

❏ Add light-attracting tape to your hat if you work at night or in darkness. This will make it easier for others to see you.

❏ Clean the shell of your hard hat at least once a month to remove oil, grease, chemicals and sweat. Soak it for five minutes in mild detergent and water that's at least 140 degrees Fahrenheit (60 degrees Centigrade). Then wipe the hat and let the air dry it. Clean the hat according to the instructions provided.

❏ Take good care of your hat; don't drop it, throw it or drill holes in it.

❏ Sunlight and heat can rot the harness and straps. Don't leave your hard hat on the front or back window ledge of your car.

Source: Used by permission of the National Safety Council, Itasca, Illinois

reinforce safe practices. Where unsafe acts are detected, supervisors should take immediate action to find the cause. Supervisors should also foster a team spirit of safety among the work group.

### Proactive Safety Training Program

What are the most popular subjects in safety training programs? One study found the most frequent topics to be (1) first aid, (2) defensive driving, (3) accident prevention techniques, (4) hazardous materials, and (5) emergency procedures.

Most programs emphasize the use of emergency first-aid equipment and personal safety equipment. Furthermore, many organizations provide training in off-the-job safety—at home, on the highway, etc.—as well as in first aid. Injuries and fatalities away from the job occur much more frequently than do those on the job and are reflected in employer costs for insurance premiums, wage continuation, and interrupted production.

A current trend in safety instruction is behavior-based safety (BBS) training and implementation.[25] This instructional technique has become a priority for organizations wanting to offer proactive safety training programs to improve their safety record. Behavior-based training is built upon the principles of behavior modification.[26] The goal of training is behavioral change by helping trainees reduce the frequency of their identified at-risk (i.e., unsafe) work behaviors. Training begins by having employees identify barriers that make particular safety-related behaviors difficult. Management's role is then to remove these barriers while additionally rewarding employees for their new safety behaviors.[27]

### Incentives in Safety Programs

Boise Cascade offers espresso coffee machines and shortwave radios as part of its incentive program. At Turner Bros. Trucking, an oil field transportation company, employees receive specialty work gloves and coveralls for improved safety records below an established benchmark.[28] Other organizations offer gift certificates, cash awards, trips, dinners, and gifts such as jewelry or clothing as safety incentives.[29]

For safety programs to reach their objectives, special attention must be given to the incentives used to motivate safe behavior in employees. One authority suggests "surveying employees to find out their interests and what type of rewards would have the most value to them."[30] Furthermore, safety awards should be obtainable by a large number of employees. In support of safety incentives, two researchers looked at twenty-four studies where positive reinforcement and feedback were used to enhance safe behavior. In all of the studies, incentives were found to be successful in improving safety conditions or reducing accidents.[31] Figure 12.1 provides recommended steps for a successful safety incentive program.

## Enforcing Safety Rules

Specific rules and regulations concerning safety are communicated through supervisors, bulletin-board notices, employee handbooks, and signs attached to equipment. Safety rules are also emphasized in regular safety meetings, at new employee orientations, and in manuals of standard operating procedures. Such rules typically refer to the following types of employee behaviors:

- Using proper safety devices
- Using proper work procedures
- Following good housekeeping practices

FIGURE 12.1

**Steps to a Successful Safety Incentive Program**

- Obtain the full support and involvement of management by providing cost benefits.
- Review current injury and health statistics to determine where change is needed.
- Decide upon a program of action and set an appropriate budget.
- Select a realistic safety goal such as reducing accidents by a set percentage, improving safety suggestions, or achieving a length of time without a lost-time injury. Communicate your objectives to everyone involved.
- Select incentive rewards on the basis of their attractiveness to employees and their fit with your budget.
- Develop a program that is both interesting and fun. Use kickoff meetings, posters, banners, quizzes, and/or games to spark employee interest. Give all employees a chance to win.
- Communicate continually the success of your program. Provide specific examples of positive changes in behavior.
- Reward safety gains immediately. Providing rewards shortly after improvements reinforces changed behavior and encourages additional support for the safety program.

- Complying with accident-and-injury reporting procedures
- Wearing required safety clothing and equipment
- Avoiding carelessness and horseplay

Penalties for violation of safety rules are usually stated in the employee handbook. In a large percentage of organizations, the penalties imposed on violators are the same as those for violations of other rules. They include an oral or written warning for the first violation, suspension for repeated violations, and, as a last resort, dismissal. However, for serious violations—such as smoking around volatile substances—even the first offense may be cause for termination.

While discipline may force employees to work safely, safety managers understand that the most effective enforcement of safety rules occurs when employees willingly obey and "champion" safety rules and procedures.[32] This can be achieved when employees are actively encouraged by management to participate in all aspects of the organization's safety program. For example, opportunities for employee involvement include (1) jointly setting safety standards with management, (2) participation in safety training, (3) involvement in designing and implementing special safety training programs, (4) involvement in establishing safety incentives and rewards, and (5) inclusion in accident investigations. At Federal Mogel, employees are invited to become Danger Rangers. These employees spot near-miss accidents and take corrective action. Danger Rangers who report near-miss accidents are enrolled in monthly drawings for prizes, such as gift certificates and clothing.[33]

## Investigating and Recording Accidents

Every accident, even those considered minor, should be investigated by the supervisor and a member of the safety committee. Such an investigation may determine the factors contributing to the accident and may reveal what corrections are needed to prevent it from happening again. Correction may require rearranging workstations, installing safety guards or controls, or, more often, giving employees additional safety training and reassessing their motivation for safety.

OSHA requirements mandate that employers with eleven or more employees maintain records of occupational injuries and illnesses. As stated in an earlier section, OSHA also requires that a Log and Summary of Occupational Injuries and Illnesses (OSHA Form 200) be maintained by the organization.[34] All recordable cases are to be entered in the log. A **recordable case** is any occupational death, occupational illness, or occupational injury (except those involving only first aid).[35] Each year the Summary portion of the log is to be posted for one month where employee notices are customarily posted. For every recordable case written in the log, a Supplementary Record of Occupational Injuries and Illnesses (OSHA Form 101) is to be completed. OSHA Form 101 requires answers to questions about the case. Since managers can become confused about what is a recordable case, Figure 12.2 illustrates OSHA's diagram for classifying accidents under the law.

**Recordable case**

Any occupational death, illness, or injury to be recorded in the log (OSHA Form 200)

**FIGURE 12.2**

## ▶ Guide to Recording Cases under the Occupational Safety and Health Act

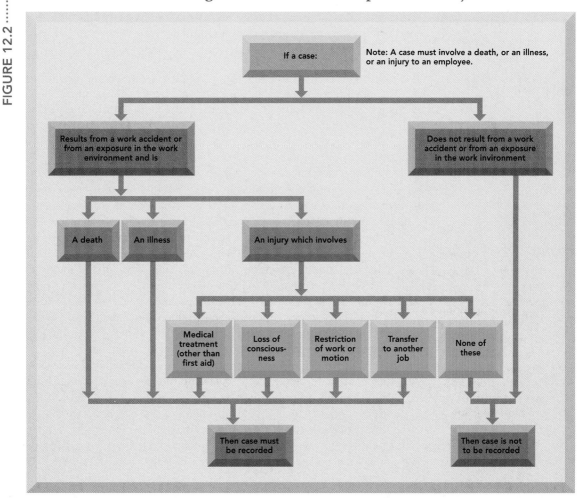

# Creating a Healthy Work Environment

From its title alone, the Occupational Safety and Health Act was clearly designed to protect the health, as well as the safety, of employees. Because of the dramatic impact of workplace accidents, however, managers and employees alike may pay more attention to these kinds of immediate safety concerns than to job conditions that are dangerous to their health. It is essential, therefore, that health hazards be identified and controlled. Furthermore, pressure from the federal government and unions, as well as increased public concern, has given employers a definite incentive to provide the safest and healthiest work environment possible.

## Health Hazards and Issues

At one time health hazards were associated primarily with jobs found in industrial processing operations. In recent years, however, hazards in jobs outside the plant, such as in offices, health care facilities, and airports, have been recognized and preventive methods adopted. Substituting materials, altering processes, enclosing or isolating a process, issuing protective equipment, and improving ventilation are some of the common preventions. General conditions of health with respect to sanitation, housekeeping, cleanliness, ventilation, water supply, pest control, and food handling are also important to monitor.

### Chemical Hazards

It is estimated that there are more than 65,000 different chemicals currently in use in the United States with which humans may come into contact. Many of these chemicals are harmful, lurking for years in the body with no outward symptoms until the disease they cause is well established. It is not surprising, therefore, that the OSHA Hazard Communication standard is the most frequently cited OSHA standard for general industry as well as for the construction industry.[36] The purpose of the law is to ensure the testing and evaluation of chemicals by producers and the distribution of the chemical hazard information to users of the chemical.

All hazardous chemical containers must be labeled with the identity of the contents and must state any appropriate hazard warnings. The labels must be in English and employees must be able to cross-reference the label to the material safety data sheet (MSDS) for the hazardous chemical. OSHA-required chemical training includes informing employees of the methods used to detect the presence or release of hazardous chemicals, the physical and health problems posed by hazardous chemicals, and the ways in which employees can protect themselves from chemical dangers.

In 1982 Johnson Controls, Inc., the largest maker of automobile batteries, instituted a policy that excluded all women capable of bearing children from its battery factories because they could be exposed to lead—a known danger to a developing fetus. A lawsuit filed by women working in the Johnson Controls plant in Fullerton, California, finally resulted in a U.S. Supreme Court decision (6 to 3 vote). In *International Union v Johnson Controls,* the Court ruled in 1991 that employers may not bar women of childbearing age from certain jobs because of potential risk to their fetuses. The Court said that such policies are a form of sex bias that is prohibited by federal civil rights law. The decision has made it important for employers to inform and to warn women workers about fetal health risks on the job.[37]

**USING THE INTERNET**

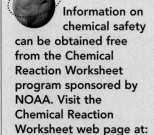

Information on chemical safety can be obtained free from the Chemical Reaction Worksheet program sponsored by NOAA. Visit the Chemical Reaction Worksheet web page at:

www.orca.nos.noaa.gov/ projects/hazmat/chemai ds/react.html

*Indoor Air Quality*

As a consequence of energy concerns, commercial and residential construction techniques have been changed to increase energy efficiency of heating, ventilating, and air-conditioning systems. This has included sealing windows, reducing outside air, and in general "buttoning up" buildings—thus resulting in the "sick building" phenomenon that gives rise to such employee complaints as headaches, dizziness, disorientation, fatigue, and eye, ear, and throat irritation. In addition to these complaints are others documented by research reprinted by the National Safety Council.

According to the American Lung Association, four basic ways to overcome polluted buildings are to (1) eliminate tobacco smoke, (2) provide adequate ventilation, (3) maintain the ventilating system, and (4) remove sources of pollution. Figure 12.3 shows the common sources of emissions released by office equipment. Study the figure carefully in order to have a better understanding of the sources of irritants that can affect the well-being and job performance of office employees.

**FIGURE 12.3**

**Office Equipment Emissions—Health complaints include increased perception of headache; mucous irritation; eye, nose, and throat irritation; dry and tight facial skin.**

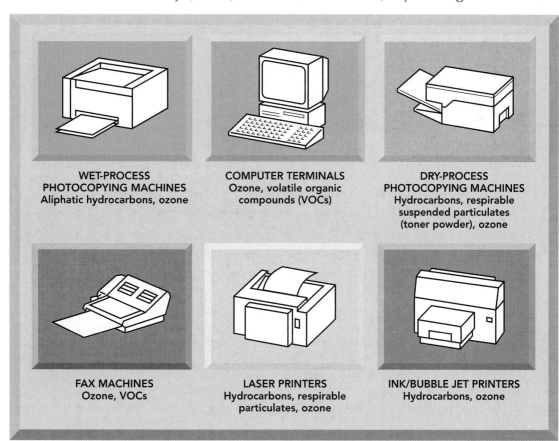

| WET-PROCESS PHOTOCOPYING MACHINES<br>Aliphatic hydrocarbons, ozone | COMPUTER TERMINALS<br>Ozone, volatile organic compounds (VOCs) | DRY-PROCESS PHOTOCOPYING MACHINES<br>Hydrocarbons, respirable suspended particulates (toner powder), ozone |
| FAX MACHINES<br>Ozone, VOCs | LASER PRINTERS<br>Hydrocarbons, respirable particulates, ozone | INK/BUBBLE JET PRINTERS<br>Hydrocarbons, ozone |

Source: Air and Energy Engineering Research, EPA.

*Tobacco smoke.* Probably the most heated workplace health issue of the 1990s was smoking. Nonsmokers, fueled by studies linking "passive smoking" (inhaling other people's smoke) with disease and death and irritated by smoke getting in their eyes, noses, throats, and clothes, were extremely vocal in demanding a smoke-free environment. The American Medical Association reported that about 8,000 nonsmokers died annually from lung cancer due to breathing secondhand smoke.[38] At least forty-two states and the District of Columbia, as well as numerous cities, towns, and counties, have passed laws restricting smoking in offices and other public places. Often, as in California, the local ordinances are broader and more stringent than the state law and frequently mandate stiffer fines for violators. Virtually all large organizations and even smaller ones have initiated smoking policies. (See Highlights in HRM 5).

**HRM 5**

**HIGHLIGHTS IN HRM**

# Hallmarkers Prepare for a Smoke-Free Workplace

Kicking the smoking habit has become a priority for many Hallmarkers. Smoking cessation classes, offered by Hallmark through St. Luke's Hospital, Kansas City, Missouri, are designed to help smokers adopt healthy lifestyle habits and become nonsmokers. Classes focus on breaking the smoking habit, mastering smoking urges, and developing strategies and support systems for maintaining a smoke-free commitment. They also cover counseling in nutrition, stress management, and weight control.

The cost of the class is $100. Hallmark pays $50 of the fee when you enroll. You may use payroll deductions. If you complete the program and do not smoke for a year, the company will reimburse the $50 you paid.

The classes are being offered as part of the company commitment to health and wellness. They are a resource that Hallmark smokers can use to prepare for the implementation of a smoke-free workplace in Hallmark facilities at headquarters and in the Crown Center complex. The decision for a smoke-free program was made because of Hallmark's concern about the health and well-being of its employees and was based on research from both within and without the organization:

- The U.S. Surgeon General, in his 1986 report, "The Health Effects of Involuntary Smoking," concluded that "involuntary smoking is a cause of disease, including lung cancer, in healthy non-smokers. The simple separation of smokers and non-smokers within the same air space can reduce, but does not eliminate, the exposure of non-smokers to environmental tobacco smoke."
- About 350,000 Americans die prematurely each year from diseases related to cigarette smoking.
- A survey of 1,800 headquarters Hallmarkers showed that nearly 60 percent favored a smoke-free environment.

Source: Adapted with permission from Hallmark Cards.

In a study published in the *Journal of the American Medical Association,* findings showed that, "in businesses that permitted smoking, more than 60 percent of the office air samples contained nicotine levels above the 'significant risk' level of 6.8 micrograms per cubic meter. That's comparable to the level considered significant by OSHA's proposed standard on indoor air quality, which would limit the level of tobacco smoke and other pollutions in the workplace."[39] By contrast, nearly all nonsmoking workplaces, or those that restricted smoking to designated areas, had nicotine levels considered to be insignificant. In developing smoking policies, it is advisable to have the involvement of both smokers and nonsmokers. Organizations emphasizing employee involvement include GTE Northwest, Michigan Bell, Merck, and Comerica, Inc.

Because of documented higher health care costs for smokers, some employers are charging smokers more for health insurance or are reducing their benefits. Many employers, however, prefer positive reinforcement through wellness programs to encourage their employees to stop smoking.

## Video Display Terminals

The expanding use of computers and video display terminals (VDTs) in the workplace has generated intense debate over the possible hazards to which VDT users may be exposed. Many fears about VDT use have been shown to be unfounded, but serious health complaints remain an issue. Problems that managers have to confront in this area fall into four major groups:

1. *Visual difficulties.* VDT operators frequently complain of blurred vision, sore eyes, burning and itching eyes, and glare.
2. *Radiation hazards.* Cataract formation and reproductive problems, including miscarriages and birth defects, have been attributed to VDT use, but the risks of exposure to VDT radiation have yet to be determined.
3. *Muscular aches and pains.* Pains in the back, neck, and shoulders are common complaints of VDT operators.
4. *Job stress.* Eye strain, postural problems, noise, insufficient training, excessive workloads, and monotonous work are complaints reported by three-quarters of VDT users.[40]

To capitalize on the benefits of VDTs while safeguarding employee health, Dr. James Sheedy, a VDT and vision expert, offers these tips on how to minimize the negative effects of computer use on the eyes and body:

- Place the computer screen four to nine inches below eye level.
- Keep the monitor directly in front of you.[41]
- Sit in an adjustable-height chair and use a copyholder that attaches to both the desk and the monitor.
- Use a screen with adjustable brightness and contrast controls.
- Use shades or blinds to reduce the computer-screen glare created by window lighting.[42]

## Repetitive Motion Injuries

Meat cutters, fish filleters, cooks, dental hygienists, textile workers, violinists, flight attendants, office workers at computer terminals, and others whose jobs require

**Repetitive motion injuries**
Injuries involving tendons of the fingers, hands, and arms that become inflamed from repeated stresses and strains

repetitive motion of the fingers, hands, or arms are reporting injuries in growing percentages. Known as **repetitive motion injuries,** these injuries involve tendons that become inflamed from repeated stresses and strains. One of the more common conditions is *carpal tunnel syndrome,* which is characterized by tingling or numbness in the fingers occurring when a tunnel of bones and ligaments in the wrist narrows and pinches nerves that reach the fingers and base of the thumb.[43] To prevent repetitive motion injuries, minibreaks involving exercises, properly designed workstations, the changing of positions, and improvement in tool design have been found helpful. These kinds of injuries often go away if they are caught early. If they are not, they may require months or years of treatment or even surgical correction.[44]

The levying of OSHA fines has prompted employers to take action to prevent these injuries. Also when repetitive motion injuries result from work activities, these injuries have been held by courts to be compensable injuries entailing workers' compensation payment.[45]

### AIDS

In recent years, few workplace issues have received as much attention as AIDS (acquired immune deficiency syndrome). Many legal and medical questions have arisen that have made it imperative for employers to provide answers to everyone concerned.

As we observed in Chapter 2, AIDS is a disability covered by federal, state, and local protective statutes. Employers subject to statutes under which AIDS victims are likely to be considered disabled are required to hire or retain an AIDS victim qualified to perform the essential functions of his or her job. The federal Rehabilitation Act, the Americans with Disabilities Act, and statutes of several states also require employers to give reasonable accommodation to the person through such adjustments as job restructuring, modified work schedules, and less rigid physical requirements.

While there is still no evidence that AIDS can be spread through casual contact in the typical workplace, one of the major problems employers face is the concern that many people have about contracting it. Employers have found it important to have programs to educate managers about the transmission of AIDS and to educate the entire workforce through newsletters, posters, and seminars.[46] The manager's job of obtaining AIDS information has been assisted by various organizations, including the Centers for Disease Control, which has a special office to assist employers and labor organizations.[47] A comprehensive and widely distributed AIDS policy (see Highlights in HRM 2 in Chapter 2) contributes to reducing fears about this illness.

## Workplace Violence

Workplace violence has been called the "deadly virus" of crime in America.[48] Statistics on workplace violence are sobering. Workplace slayings account for one of every six deaths at work in the United States. It is estimated that more than 1,000 persons are murdered each year in acts of workplace violence. Most job-related homicides occur to taxi drivers while those working in the health care, community services, and retail establishments are at the greatest risk of nonfatal assaults. Women are the victims in nearly three-fifths of reported cases of workplace aggression. More than 500,000 rapes, robberies, and aggravated assaults take place each year at U.S. workplaces.[49]

### Reducing Workplace Violence

A NIOSH study has identified risk factors associated with higher incidents of work-related violence. Employees who have contact with the public; exchange money; deliver passengers, goods, or services; work in health care, social services, or criminal settings; or work alone or in small numbers are at a greater risk of encountering workplace assaults. Employers are cautioned to afford increased protection to these individuals.

In 1998, OSHA issued five recommendations for preventing workplace violence. These guidelines include

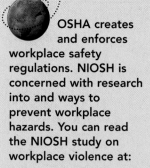

**USING THE INTERNET**

OSHA creates and enforces workplace safety regulations. NIOSH is concerned with research into and ways to prevent workplace hazards. You can read the NIOSH study on workplace violence at:

www.cdc.gov/niosh/violcont.html

- Management commitment to and employee involvement in preventing acts of violence
- Analyzing the workplace to uncover areas of potential violence
- Preventing and controlling violence by designing safe workplaces and work practices
- Providing violence prevention training throughout the organization
- Evaluating violence program effectiveness[50]

The appendix to this chapter provides an OSHA-developed risk assessment survey form. Managers can use this form to identify likely points of workplace aggression.

In addition to OSHA guidelines, specialists recommend that employers take specific actions to reduce workplace violence. For example, it is recommended that organizations screen job applicants for histories showing a propensity to violence.[51] For small employers, there are outside investigators who will perform background checks for very small fees. (Remember, employers may be found legally negligent in their hiring practices if they fail to properly investigate applicants.) Additionally, managers and supervisors can be trained to recognize violence indicators such as those given in Figure 12.4. Awareness of these threatening behaviors can provide an opportunity to intervene and prevent disruptive, abusive, or violent acts.[52] Managers must effectively communicate a zero-tolerance policy for violence and encourage employees to report any possible or observed incidents of workplace violence.[53] A meaningful reporting procedure with clear lines of responsibility can ensure that management is promptly notified of potential security risks in order to take immediate steps to resolve the issues. Finally, organizations like Garden Fresh, a growing restaurant chain, have formalized workplace violence-prevention policies, informing employees that aggressive employee behavior will not be tolerated (see Highlights in HRM 6).

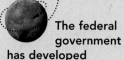

**USING THE INTERNET**

The federal government has developed guidelines to help federal agencies detect, reduce, and prevent workplace violence. A copy of "Dealing with Workplace Violence: A Guide for Agency Planners" is available under the topic "Violence" at:

www.opm.gov

### Violence Response Teams

Organizations like Allied-Signal, Motorola, and Circle K Corporation have formal violence response teams. These teams, composed of both hourly and managerial employees, conduct initial risk assessment surveys, develop action plans to respond to violent situations, and, importantly, perform crisis intervention during violent, or potentially violent, encounters. For example, a violence response team would investigate a threat reported by an employee. The team's mandate would be to gather facts about the threat, decide if the organization should intervene, and, if so, determine the most appropriate

**FIGURE 12.4**

....................................................................► **Violence Indicators: Know the Warning Signs**

Most people leave a trail of indicators before they become violent. Similarly, disgruntled former employees who commit acts of violence leave warning signs of their intent before and after termination. The following behaviors should be taken seriously when assessing situations of potential violence:

- Direct or veiled threatening statements
- Recent performance declines, including concentration problems and excessive excuses
- Prominent mood or behavior changes; despondence
- Preoccupation with guns, knives, or other weapons
- Deliberate destruction of workplace equipment; sabotage
- Fascination with stories of violence
- Reckless or antisocial behavior; evidence of prior assaultive behavior
- Aggressive behavior or intimidating statements
- Written messages of violent intent; exaggerated perceptions of injustice
- Serious stress in personal life
- Obsessive desire to harm a specific group or person
- Violence against a family member
- Substance abuse

Source: Adapted from Christine McGovern, "Take Action, Heed Warnings to End Workplace Violence," *Occupational Hazards* 61, no. 3 (March 1999): 61–63; and Rebecca A. Speer, "Can Workplace Violence Be Prevented?" *Occupational Hazards* 60, no. 8 (August 1998): 27.

method of doing so. Occasionally, a member of the team, or an individual manager, will be called upon to intervene and calm an angry employee. When this occurs, the steps given in Figure 12.5 will help to defuse a volatile situation.

When violent incidents, such as the death of a co-worker, happen at work, employees can experience shock, guilt, grief, apathy, resentment, cynicism, and a host of other emotions. Jim Martin, an employee assistant program professional with the Detroit fire department, notes that after an incident of violence, employees become frightened and they may not want to return to work.[54] Such incidents may require the violence response team to perform crisis intervention through positive counseling techniques.

## Building Better Health

Along with improving working conditions that are hazardous to employee health, many employers provide health services and have programs that encourage employees to improve their health habits. It is recognized that better health not only benefits the individual, but also pays off for the organization in reduced absenteeism, increased efficiency, better morale, and other savings. An increased understanding of the close relationship between physical and emotional health and job performance has made broad health-building programs attractive to employers as well as to employees.

**HRM 6**

# Garden Fresh's Workplace Violence Prevention Policy

Garden Fresh is committed to conducting its operations in a safe manner. Consistent with this policy, acts or threats (either verbal or implied) of physical violence, including intimidation, harassment, and/or coercion, which involve or affect Garden Fresh or which occur on Garden Fresh property will not be tolerated.

Acts or threats of violence include, but are not limited to, the following:

- All threats or acts of violence occurring on Garden Fresh premises, regardless of the relationship between Garden Fresh and the parties involved in the incident.
- All threats or acts of violence occurring off of Garden Fresh premises involving someone who is acting in the capacity of a representative of the company.
- All threats or acts of violence occurring off of Garden Fresh premises involving an employee of GFRC if the threats or acts affect the legitimate interests of Garden Fresh.
- Any acts or threats resulting in the conviction of an employee or agent of Garden Fresh, or of an individual performing services for Garden Fresh on a contract or temporary basis, under any criminal code provision relating to violence or threats of violence which adversely affect the legitimate interests and goals of Garden Fresh.

Specific examples of conduct which may be considered threats or acts of violence include, but are not limited to, the following:

- Hitting or shoving an individual.
- Threatening an individual or his/her family, friends, associates, or property with harm.
- The intentional destruction or threat of destruction of company property.
- Harassing or threatening phone calls.
- Harassing surveillance or stalking.
- The suggestion or intimation that violence is appropriate.
- Possession or use of firearms or weapons.

Garden Fresh's prohibition against threats and acts of violence applies to all persons involved in the company's operation, including Garden Fresh personnel, contract and temporary workers, and anyone else on Garden Fresh property.

Violations of this policy by any individual on Garden Fresh's property, by any individual acting as a representative of Garden Fresh while off of Garden Fresh property, or by an individual acting off of Garden Fresh's property when his/her actions affect the company's business interests will lead to disciplinary action (up to and including termination) and/or legal action as appropriate.

Employees should learn to recognize and respond to behaviors by potential perpetrators that may indicate a risk of violence.

Employees shall place safety as the highest concern, and shall report all acts or threats of violence immediately. Every employee and every person on Garden Fresh's property is encouraged to report incidents of threats or acts of physical violence of which he/she is aware. The report should be made to the Director of Human Resources, the reporting individual's immediate supervisor, or another supervisory employee if the immediate supervisor is not available.

It is the responsibility of managers and supervisors to make safety their highest concern. When made aware of a real or perceived threat of violence, management shall conduct a thorough investigation and take specific actions to help prevent acts of violence.

Nothing in this policy alters any other reporting obligation established by Garden Fresh policies or in state, federal, or other applicable law.

Source: Used with permission from Garden Fresh, 17180 Bernardo Center Drive, San Diego, Calif. 92128.

**FIGURE 12.5**

▶ **Calming an Angry Employee**

If you try to defuse a tense situation, remember that anger frequently results from a person's feeling of being wronged, misunderstood, or unheard. Keep the following tips in mind to guide you.

- Confront the employee privately to prevent embarrassment.

- Don't lose your temper, overreact, or gesture aggressively; these will trigger a similar response in the employee.

- Listen without judgment. Many people simply want someone to hear what they have to say.

- Validate the employee's feelings or position. Say, "You have a good point," or agree that there is a problem.

- Help the employee save face during an anger situation. Don't pounce on a rash statement or pursue a muddled line of reasoning.

- If necessary, suggest a delay so people can cool off. Say, "Let's meet at 2 p.m. to discuss this."

- Withdraw if necessary.

If you sense that the situation is escalating or if you are part of the employee's problem, offer to find someone else to help. Leave if the employee becomes so agitated that you become uneasy.

Source: Carla Joinson, "Controlling Hostility," *HRMagazine* 43, no. 9 (August 1998): 65–70. Reprinted with the permission of *HRMagazine*, published by the Society for Human Resource Management, Alexandria, Va.

### Ensuring Healthful Employees

Importantly, about one-half of all employers give preemployment medical examinations to prospective employees. Generally, these examinations are required to assure employers that the health of applicants is adequate for the job. The preemployment examination should include a medical history with special reference to previous hazardous exposures. Exposure to hazards whose effects may be cumulative, such as noise, lead, and radiation, are especially relevant. For jobs involving unusual physical demands, the applicant's muscular development, flexibility, agility, range of motion, and cardiac and respiratory functions should be evaluated. The preemployment medical examination that includes laboratory analyses can help screen those applicants who abuse drugs. Many organizations also give periodic examinations on either a required or a voluntary basis. Such examinations are useful in determining the effects of potential hazards in the workplace as well as in detecting any health problems to which an employee's particular lifestyle or health habits may contribute.

### Alternative Approaches to Health

In a discussion of health services as well as health benefits it should be emphasized that there are many nontraditional approaches to better health. These are typically referred to as *alternative approaches*. Many of the approaches differ from traditional medicine in that they are less invasive and they empower the patient by enlisting patient participation in health care decisions.

Relaxation techniques, chiropractic, therapeutic massage, acupuncture, homeopathy, megavitamin and herbal therapy, special diets, and many other alternative approaches are used to treat a wide variety of health problems. These and other approaches are examined in various publications such as *Alternatives—For the Health Conscious Individual,* a monthly newsletter, and books like Jane Heimlich's *What the Doctor Won't Tell You* and Linda Rector-Page's *Healthy Healing.*[55] Interest in these alternative approaches influences employee concerns about health plan coverage.

## Promoting Employee Health

Many organizations such as Tenneco, with headquarters in Houston, have developed programs that emphasize regular exercise, proper nutrition, weight control, and avoidance of substances harmful to health.[56] For example, the employee health management program at Xerox includes cardiovascular fitness through aerobic exercises such as jogging, skipping rope, and racquet sports. The company gives its employees a publication called *Fitbook,* which provides instructions and illustrations for a variety of exercises. The book also includes chapters on the hazards of smoking and the effects of alcohol and drug abuse, facts on nutrition and weight control, and guidelines for managing stress and learning to relax. Smaller organizations may distribute wellness literature obtained from the Association for Worksite Health Promotion; the National Wellness Institute; the Department of Health and Human Services, Office of Disease Prevention and Health Promotion; and the American Institute for Preventive Medicine.[57]

Importantly, wellness programs produce measurable cost savings to employers.[58] Wellness efforts are particularly effective when organizations target their wellness initiatives at specific health risks such as high cholesterol or blood pressure counts, high body-fat levels, or smoking. Thanks to FitWorks, Pacific Bell's wellness program, employees achieved a 20 percent reduction in cardiovascular risks in two years. San Francisco–based Charles Schwab and Co. attributes its reduction in heart disease to its Pro-Fit wellness program.[59] Figure 12.6 gives nine tips for launching a successful wellness program, even on a limited budget.

**FIGURE 12.6**

⋯⋯⋯⋯⋯⋯⋯⋯⋯⋯⋯⋯⋯⋯⋯⋯⋯⋯⋯⋯▶ **Tips for Starting a Successful Wellness Program**

1. Conduct a health risk assessment of employees.
2. Determine where medically related money is spent.
3. Include family members and retirees in wellness instruction.
4. Provide nutritional advice from a registered dietitian.
5. Include healthy, low-fat choices among snacks and meals provided in cafeterias and through vending machines.
6. Eliminate smoking from the work setting.
7. Negotiate discounts from area health clubs.
8. Start a health and fitness newsletter.
9. Focus on reducing one or two high-risk factors among employees.

Source: Adapted from Pamela Witting, "Starting a Health Promotion Program," *Occupational Hazards* 58, no. 4 (April 1996): 53.

As part of their wellness program, employers should encourage employees to adopt healthful eating habits. There is mounting evidence to support the link between certain nutritional deficiencies and various physiological and psychological disorders, including alcoholism, depression, nervousness, low energy level, perceptual inaccuracy, and lack of reasonability. In fact, a person's mental and emotional states are affected by the foods he or she consumes, hence the wisdom of such sayings as "You are what you eat" and "What you eat today you walk and talk tomorrow." Proponents suggest that the potential return on a minimal investment in a sound nutritional plan is great, in terms of both dollars and morale, because human behavior might be more easily and quickly modified by dietary changes than by more sophisticated modification techniques.

## Employee Assistance Programs

A broad view of health includes the emotional, as well as the physical, aspects of one's life. While emotional problems, personal crises, alcoholism, and drug abuse are considered to be personal matters, they become organizational problems when they affect behavior at work and interfere with job performance. To be able to handle such problems, organizations such as DuPont,[60] Arizona State University, and Stewart Warner, manufacturer of automotive parts, offer an employee assistance program (EAP). Typically, such a program refers employees in need of assistance to in-house counselors or outside professionals. Supervisors are often given training and policy guidance in the type of help they can offer their subordinates.[61] In contracting with professional counselors outside the organization, the HR department needs to give special attention to their credentials, cost, accountability, and service capabilities.[62]

### Personal Crises

The most prevalent problems among employees are personal crises involving marital, family, financial, or legal matters. Furthermore, according to one study, EAPs have been directing increased attention to the problem of domestic violence.[63] Such problems often come to a supervisor's attention. In most instances, the supervisor can usually provide the best help simply by being understanding and supportive and by helping the individual find the type of assistance he or she needs. In many cases, in-house counseling or referral to an outside professional is recommended. In recent years, crisis hot lines have been set up in many communities to provide counseling by telephone for those too distraught to wait for an appointment with a counselor.

### Emotional Problems

While personal crises are typically fraught with emotion, most of them are resolved in a reasonable period of time and the troubled individual's equilibrium is restored. Unfortunately, when personal crises linger, stress and tension may cause or intensify a mood disorder like depression. **Depression** is the decrease in functional activity accompanied by symptoms of low spirits, gloominess, and sadness. The National Institute of Mental Health estimates that nearly 17 million Americans suffer from depression each year. With available treatment, however, 70 percent of afflicted individuals will significantly improve, usually within a matter of weeks.[64]

Since depression lowers individual productivity, causes morale problems, increases absenteeism, and contributes to substance abuse, it is important for man-

**Depression**

Negative emotional state marked by feelings of low spirits, gloominess, sadness, and loss of pleasure in ordinary activities

agers to identify signs of depression on the job and to learn to deal with depressed employees.[65] The more likely workplace signs of depression are decreased energy, concentration and memory problems, guilt feelings, irritability, and chronic aches and pains that don't respond to treatment. When confronted with depressed employees, managers and supervisors are encouraged to be concerned with the employee's problem, be an active listener, and—should the depression persist—suggest professional help. Under no circumstances should managers attempt to play amateur psychologist and try to diagnose an employee's condition. Mood disorders, like depression, are complex in nature and do not lend themselves to quick diagnoses.[66] Furthermore, in reviewing such cases, the organization should pay particular attention to workplace safety factors, since there is general agreement that emotional disturbances are primary or secondary factors in a large portion of industrial accidents and violence.

### Alcoholism

Business and industry lose an estimated $20.6 billion each year because of alcoholism, according to the Conference Board. The National Council for Alcoholism reports that in this country alone there are more than 10.5 million alcoholics. Alcoholism affects workers in every occupational category—blue-collar and white-collar.

In confronting the problem, employers must recognize that alcoholism is a disease that follows a rather predictable course. Thus they can take specific actions to deal with employees showing symptoms of the disease at particular stages of its progression. Alcoholism typically begins with social drinking getting out of control. As the disease progresses, the alcoholic loses control over how much to drink and eventually cannot keep from drinking, even at inappropriate times. The person uses denial to avoid facing the problems created by the abuse of alcohol and often blames others for these problems. The first step in helping the alcoholic is to awaken the person to the reality of his or her situation.[67]

To identify alcoholism as early as possible, it is essential that supervisors monitor the performance of all personnel regularly and systematically. A supervisor should carefully document evidence of declining performance on the job and then confront the employee with unequivocal proof that the job is suffering. The employee should be assured that help will be made available without penalty. Since the evaluations are made solely in terms of lagging job performance, a supervisor can avoid any mention of alcoholism and allow such employees to seek aid as they would for any other problem.

Employers must remember that alcoholism is classified as a disability under the Americans with Disabilities Act (see Chapter 2). Alcoholism is regarded as a disease, similar to a mental impairment. Therefore, a person disabled by alcoholism is entitled to the same protection from job discrimination as any other person with a disability. However, under the ADA, employers can discipline or discharge employees when job performance is so badly affected by alcohol usage that the employee is unable to perform the job.[68]

### Abuse of Illegal Drugs

The abuse of drugs by employees is one of the major employment issues today. Once confined to a small segment of the population, drug abuse is now a national problem that has spread to every industry and occupation as well

*A poster such as this is usually found in the employment office.*

as employee level. In one study it was estimated that drug abuse costs businesses $75 billion annually in terms of safety risks, theft, reduced productivity, and accidents. According to Irwin Lerner, former chairman and CEO of Nutlex, "Businesses need to stay focused on this issue, not only because drugs can impact bottom-line performance, but because we have a responsibility to our communities."[69]

In the past, most efforts to curb workplace drug abuse have been voluntary actions on the part of management. Now, however, a wide range of employers, including federal contractors and private and public transportation firms, are subject to regulations aimed at eliminating the use of illegal drugs on the job. The federal antidrug initiatives include the following:

1. Drug-Free Workplace Act of 1988, which requires federal contractors and recipients of federal grants to take specific steps to ensure a drug-free work environment. One of the main provisions of the act is the preparation and distribution of an antidrug policy statement, a sample of which is shown in Highlights in HRM 7.

2. Department of Defense (DOD) contract rules, which specify that employers entering into contracts with the DOD must agree to a clause certifying their intention to maintain a drug-free workplace.

3. Department of Transportation (DOT) regulations, which require that employees whose jobs include safety- or security-related duties be tested for illegal drug use under DOT rules.

The ADA considers an individual using drugs as disabled, provided the person is enrolled in a recognized drug treatment program. The prudent employer will, therefore, make a reasonable accommodation to the specific needs of this employee. Reasonable accommodation may include time off from work or a modified work schedule to obtain treatment. Illegal drug users are, however, not covered under the ADA.

We observed in Chapter 5 that a number of employers test for substance abuse in the final stages of the employee selection process. At this point it is often easy to screen out applicants who may become problem employees. Once an applicant is accepted, however, the employer is faced with the problem of controlling drug abuse. For this reason, an increasing number of employers are instituting drug-testing programs.

As noted earlier, employers operating under the federal requirements are required to test for drug use under certain specified conditions. However, employers that are exempt from the federal requirement may operate under state or local laws restricting or prohibiting drug tests. Issues related to drug testing under state or local laws are discussed in Chapter 13 in the context of employee rights.

While attention is usually focused on the abuse of illegal drugs, it should be noted that the abuse of legal drugs can also pose a problem for employees. Employees who abuse legal drugs—i.e., those prescribed by physicians—often do not realize they have become addicted or how their behavior has changed as a result of their addiction. Also, managers should be aware that some employees may be taking legal sedatives or stimulants as part of their medical treatment and that their behavior at work may be affected by their use of these drugs. A standard reference book of legal drugs is the *Physicians' Desk Reference (PDR)*.[70]

HRM 7

HIGHLIGHTS IN HRM

# Kinko's Policies and Procedures for a Drug-Free Workplace

## Purpose

Co-workers are Kinko's most valuable resource and for that reason, their health and safety is of paramount concern. Kinko's does not tolerate any drug or alcohol use which imperils the health and well-being of its co-workers or threatens its business. The use of illegal drugs and abuse of other controlled substances, on or off duty, is normally inconsistent with law-abiding behavior expected of all citizens. Co-workers who use illegal drugs or abuse other controlled substances or alcohol, on or off duty, tend to be less productive, less reliable, and prone to greater absenteeism resulting in the potential for increased cost, delay, and risk in business. In addition, drug and alcohol abuse inflicts a terrible toll on the nation's productive resources and the health and well-being of American workers and their families.

Kinko's is therefore committed to maintaining a safe work place free from the influence of alcohol and drugs. It is the policy of Kinko's to prohibit the use, sale, distribution, dispensing, possession, and manufacture of all controlled substances in Kinko's work place.

## Procedures

### Definitions

*Under the Influence:*

Co-workers who are considered unable to perform their work in a safe and productive manner, or whose physical or mental condition creates a risk to the safety or well-being of the co-worker, other co-workers, the public, or company property, will be deemed to be under the influence.

### Procedures

Co-worker infractions of this policy are defined as misconduct. When infractions occur, the supervisor will refer to the Human Resources policy titled *Termination of Employment*.

Any co-worker who is taking a drug or other medication, whether or not prescribed by a physician for a medical condition, which is known or advertised as possibly affecting or impairing judgment, coordination or senses, or which may adversely affect the co-worker's ability to perform work in a safe manner or may prevent the co-worker from performing the essential functions of his or her position, is required to notify his or her supervisor prior to starting work. The supervisor is required to seek guidance from a trained medical provider, if necessary. The supervisor is required to decide if the co-worker can remain at work or on the company premises or what work restrictions or reasonable accommodations, if any, are deemed necessary.

### Assistance in Overcoming Alcohol or Drug Abuse

Early recognition and treatment of alcohol or drug abuse is important for successful rehabilitation, return to Kinko's, and reduced personal, family, and social disruption. Kinko's encourages the earliest possible diagnosis and treatment of alcohol or drug abuse. Kinko's supports sound treatment efforts. Whenever feasible, Kinko's will assist co-workers in overcoming drug or alcohol abuse. However, the decision to seek diagnosis and accept treatment for alcohol or drug abuse is primarily the individual co-worker's responsibility.

Co-workers with personal alcohol or drug abuse problems should request assistance from management. Management is to refer the co-worker, on a confidential basis, to any agency able to provide appropriate treatment and counseling, or to LifeBalance, Kinko's employee advisory resource.

*(continued)*

### Prohibitions

Kinko's prohibits the following:

1. Use, possession, manufacture, distribution, dispensation, or sale of illegal drugs, controlled substances whose use is unauthorized, or alcohol on Kinko's premises, in Kinko's supplied vehicles, or during working hours

2. Storing in desks, automobiles, or other property on Kinko's premises any illegal drug, any controlled substance whose use is unauthorized, or any alcohol

3. Being under the influence of a controlled substance whose use is unauthorized or illegal drug or alcohol on Kinko's premises or during Kinko's business, in Kinko's vehicles, or during working hours

4. Use of alcohol off Kinko's premises that adversely affects the co-worker's work performance, his or her own or others' safety at work, or Kinko's regard or reputation in the community

5. Possession, use, manufacture, distribution, dispensation, or sale of illegal drugs off Kinko's premises that adversely affects the individual's work performance, his or her or others' safety at work, or Kinko's regard or reputation in the community

6. Refusing to submit to a search when requested by a manager or supervisor during working hours in accordance with the Human Resources policy titled *Surveillance/Searches*

7. Failing to adhere to the requirements of any drug or alcohol treatment or counseling program in which the co-worker is enrolled

8. Conviction under any criminal drug statute for violation occurring in the workplace

9. Failure to notify Kinko's of any arrest or conviction under any criminal drug statute for a violation occurring in the work place within five days of the arrest or conviction

10. Failure to report to management the use of any prescribed drug which may alter the co-worker's ability to safely perform his or her duties

### Searches

If Kinko's suspects that any co-worker's performance or on-the-job behavior may have been affected in any way by alcohol or drugs, two Kinko's representatives may search the co-worker's work area including desk, or any Kinko's property under the control of the co-worker as well as the co-worker's personal effects or automobile on Kinko's property.

If Kinko's suspects that the co-worker possesses alcohol or drugs on Kinko's premises, two Kinko's representatives may search the co-worker's work area including desk or locker, or any Kinko's property under the control of the co-worker, as well as the co-worker's personal effects or automobile on Kinko's property.

### Consequences for Violation

Violation of this policy may result in severe disciplinary action up to and including termination at Kinko's sole discretion. In addition to any disciplinary action, Kinko's may, in its sole discretion through management, refer the co-worker to a treatment and counseling program for alcohol or drug abuse. Co-workers referred to such a program by Kinko's must immediately cease any alcohol or drug abuse, and are required to comply with all conditions of the treatment and counseling program. Any co-worker referred to such a program will not be permitted to return to work until certification is presented to management and the co-worker is capable of performing his or her job. Failure to cooperate with the agreed-upon treatment plan may result in disciplinary action, up to and including termination. KCO Human Resources will determine whether any co-worker it has referred for drug or alcohol treatment and counseling shall be temporarily or permanently reassigned to another position. Management is required to consult with KCO Human Resources.

Source: All depictions of Kinko's are the exclusive property of Kinko's, Inc. KINKO'S® is a registered trademark of Kinko's Ventures, Inc. All depictions of Kinko's and its trademark are used by permission.

Reprinted with permission of Wayne Stayskal.

# The Management of Stress

Many jobs require employees to adjust to conditions that place unusual demands on them. In time these demands create stresses that can affect the health of employees as well as their productivity and satisfaction. Fortunately, increasing attention is being given to ways of identifying and preventing undue stress on the job. Even greater attention must be given to identifying and removing sources of stress to protect the well-being of employees and to reduce the costs to organizations. The costs of stress in health insurance claims, disability claims, and lost productivity alone are between $50 billion and $150 billion per year, and NIOSH has predicted a need for greater emphasis on ways to reduce stress in the workplace.

## What Is Stress?

**Stress** is any demand on the individual that requires coping behavior. Stress comes from two basic sources: physical activity and mental or emotional activity. The physical reaction of the body to both types of stress is the same. Psychologists use two separate terms to distinguish between positive and negative forms of stress, even though reactions to the two forms are the same biochemically. **Eustress** is positive stress that accompanies achievement and exhilaration. Eustress is the stress of meeting challenges such as those found in a managerial, technical, or public contact job. Eustress is regarded as a beneficial force that helps us to forge ahead against obstacles. What is harmful is **distress.** Stress becomes distress when we begin to sense a loss of our feelings of security and adequacy. Helplessness, desperation, and disappointment turn stress into distress.

**Stress**
> Any adjustive demand caused by physical, mental, or emotional factors that requires coping behavior

**Eustress**
> Positive stress that accompanies achievement and exhilaration

**Distress**
> Harmful stress characterized by a loss of feelings of security and adequacy

The stress reaction is a coordinated chemical mobilization of the entire body to meet the requirements of fight-or-flight in a situation perceived to be stressful. The sympathetic nervous system activates the secretion of hormones from the endocrine glands that places the body on a "war footing." This response, commonly referred to as the **alarm reaction,** basically involves an elevated heart rate, increased respiration, elevated levels of adrenaline in the blood, and increased blood pressure. It persists until one's estimate of the relative threat to well-being has been reevaluated. If distress persists long enough, it can result in fatigue, exhaustion, and even physical and/or emotional breakdown. Some research has linked stress to heart disease. Other studies have shown a connection between chronic stress and hypertension (high blood pressure). High blood pressure, the most common cause of strokes, contributes to heart disease.

**Alarm reaction**
Response to stress that basically involves an elevated heart rate, increased respiration, elevated levels of adrenaline in the blood, and increased blood pressure

## Job-Related Stress

Although the body experiences a certain degree of stress (either eustress or distress) in all situations, here we are primarily concerned with the stress related to the work setting. It is in this setting that management can use some preventive approaches.

### Sources of Job-Related Stress

Causes of workplace stress are many; however, high workloads, excessive job pressures, layoffs and organizational restructuring, and global economic conditions are identified as the primary factors of employee stress.[71] Additionally, disagreements with managers or fellow employees are a common cause of distress, along with little or no say about how a job is performed, lack of communication on the job, and lack of recognition for a job well done. Even minor irritations such as lack of privacy, unappealing music, excessive noise, and other conditions can be distressful to one person or another.

### Burnout

**Burnout** is the most severe stage of distress. Career burnout generally occurs when a person begins questioning his or her own personal values. Quite simply, one no longer feels that what he or she is doing is important. Depression, frustration, and a loss of productivity are all symptoms of burnout. Burnout is due primarily to a lack of personal fulfillment in the job or a lack of positive feedback about performance.[72] In organizations that have downsized, remaining employees can experience burnout since they must perform more work with fewer co-workers. Overachievers can experience burnout when unrealistic work goals are unattainable.

**Burnout**
Most severe stage of distress, manifesting itself in depression, frustration, and loss of productivity

## Coping with Stress

The issue of stress on the job has received considerable publicity in the various media. Furthermore, in the past decade the number of mental-stress workers' compensation claims have mushroomed because of (1) the growing number of employees in service jobs where the work is more mental than manual, (2) the repetitive nature of tasks, (3) the trend toward seeking compensation for mental as well as physical injuries, and (4) the receptivity of the courts to such cases.[73]

Coping with organizational stress begins by having managers recognize the universal symptoms of work stress as well as the stressful situations particular to their work unit. Major stressors include

- Responsibility without authority
- Inability to voice complaints
- Prejudice because of age, gender, race, or religion
- Poor working conditions
- Inadequate recognition
- Lack of a clear job description or chain of command
- Unfriendly interpersonal relationships[74]

Many employers have developed stress-management programs to teach employees how to minimize the negative effects of job-related stress. A typical program might include instruction in relaxation techniques, coping skills, listening skills, methods of dealing with difficult people, time management, and assertiveness. All of these techniques are designed to break the pattern of tension that accompanies stress situations and to help participants achieve greater control of their lives. Organizational techniques, such as clarifying the employee's work role, redesigning and enriching jobs, correcting physical factors in the environment, and effectively handling interpersonal factors, should not be overlooked in the process of teaching employees how to handle stress.[75]

Even though the number and severity of organizational stressors can be reduced, everyone encounters situations that may be described as distressful. Those in good physical health are generally better able to cope with the stressors they encounter. Figure 12.7 describes several ways to resolve job-related stress.

**FIGURE 12.7**

**► Tips for Reducing Job-Related Stress**

- Build rewarding relationships with co-workers.
- Talk openly with managers or employees about job or personal concerns.
- Prepare for the future by keeping abreast of likely changes in job demands.
- Don't greatly exceed your skills and abilities.
- Set realistic deadlines; negotiate reasonable deadlines with managers.
- Act now on problems or concerns of importance.
- Designate dedicated work periods during which time interruptions are avoided.
- When feeling stressed, find time for detachment or relaxation.
- Don't let trivial items take on importance; handle them quickly or assign them to others.
- Take short breaks from your work area as a change of pace.

Before concluding this discussion, we should observe that stress that is harmful to some employees may be healthy for others. Most executives learn to handle distress effectively and find that it actually stimulates better performance. However, there will always be those who are unable to handle stress and need assistance in learning to cope with it. The increased interest of young and old alike in developing habits that will enable them to lead happier and more productive lives will undoubtedly be beneficial to them as individuals, to the organizations where they work, and to a society where people are becoming more and more interdependent.

# SUMMARY

**OBJECTIVE 1**

The Occupational Safety and Health Act was designed to assure, so far as possible, safe and healthful working conditions to every working person. In general, the act extends to all employers and employees. OSHA administration involves setting standards, ensuring employer and employee compliance, and providing safety and health consultation and training where needed. Both employers and employees have certain responsibilities and rights under OSHA. Employers are not only required to provide a hazard-free work environment, but also must keep employees informed about OSHA requirements and must require their employees to use protective equipment when necessary. Under the "right to know" regulations, employers are required to keep employees informed of hazardous substances and instruct them in avoiding the dangers presented. Employees, in turn, are required to comply with OSHA standards, to report hazardous conditions, and to follow all employer safety and health regulations.

**OBJECTIVE 2**

In order to provide safe working conditions for their employees, employers typically establish a formal program that, in a large percentage of organizations, is under the direction of the HR manager. The program may have many facets, including providing safety knowledge and motivating employees to use it, making employees aware of the need for safety, and rewarding them for safe behavior. Such incentives as praise, public recognition, and awards are used to involve employees in the safety program. Maintenance of required records from accident investigations provides a basis for information that can be used to create a safer work environment.

**OBJECTIVE 3**

Job conditions that are dangerous to the health of employees are now receiving much greater attention than in the past. There is special concern for toxic chemicals that proliferate at a rapid rate and may lurk in the body for years without outward symptoms. Concern for health hazards other than those found in industrial processing operations—indoor air pollution, video display terminals, and repetitive motion injuries—present special problems that must be addressed. Today tobacco smoke is rarely tolerated in the work environment. While there is no evidence that AIDS can be spread through casual contact in the workplace, employers have found that it is important to educate managers and employees about AIDS and to assist those who are afflicted.

**OBJECTIVE 4**

Along with providing safer and healthier work environments, many employers establish programs that encourage employees to improve their health habits. Some of the larger employers have opened primary care clinics for employees and their dependents to provide better health care service and to reduce costs. Wellness programs that emphasize exercise, nutrition, weight control, and avoidance of harmful substances serve employees at all organizational levels.

**OBJECTIVE 5**

Virtually all of the larger organizations and many of the smaller ones have found that an employee assistance program is beneficial to all concerned. While emotional problems, personal crises, alcoholism, and drug abuse are often viewed as personal matters, it is apparent that they affect behavior at work and interfere with job performance. An employee assistance program typically provides professional assistance by in-house counselors or outside professionals where needed. In contracting with professional persons outside the organization, the HR department should give special attention to their credentials.

 An important dimension to health and safety is stress that comes from physical activity and mental or emotional activity. While stress is an integral part of being alive, when it turns into distress it becomes harmful. We have seen that there are many sources of stress that are job-related. In recognizing the need for reducing stress, employers can develop stress-management programs to assist employees in acquiring techniques for coping with stress. In addition, organizations need to take action to redesign and enrich jobs, to clarify the employee's work role, to correct physical factors in the environment, and to take any other actions that will help reduce stress on the job.

## KEY TERMS

alarm reaction
burnout
depression
distress
eustress

Material Safety Data Sheets
  (MSDSs)
recordable case
repetitive motion injuries
right-to-know laws

stress
voluntary protection programs
  (VPPs)

## DISCUSSION QUESTIONS

 1. When OSHA was enacted in 1970, it was heralded as the most important new source of protection for the American worker in this half of the twentieth century. What opinions about the effectiveness or the ineffectiveness of the act or its implementation have you heard from acquaintances who have been affected by it?

2. What steps should be taken by management to increase motivation for safety?

3. An unhealthy work environment can lower productivity, contribute to low morale, and increase medical and workers' compensation costs. Working individually or in teams, list specific ways managers can
   a. Improve indoor air quality
   b. Accommodate the desires of smokers and nonsmokers
   c. Reduce the harmful affects of VDTs
   d. Address the fears of employees caused by AIDS.

4. To live a healthier life, medical professionals say we need to identify those things we currently do that either impair or contribute to our health. Prepare a list of those activities you do that are beneficial or harmful to your overall health. Discuss with others a way to develop a lifetime program for a healthy lifestyle.

5. In several states employers can require an employee to take a drug test only if there is a "reasonable cause" for testing. What are some behaviors that would indicate that a worker may be under the influence of drugs?

6. Identify the sources of stress in an organization.
   a. In what ways do they affect the individual employee? The organization?
   b. What can managers and supervisors do to make the workplace less stressful?

## Violence Prevention in the Postal Service

Not rain, nor sleet nor snow can stop postal workers from doing their jobs. But bullets can, and indeed have. During the 1990s, nearly three dozen postal workers were killed on the job, gunned down by fellow employees.

These facts prompted the Postal Service to reexamine its work practices in regard to employee safety. Its examination led to the development of a six-strategy violence prevention program, coordinated through the agency's national employee relations function. The strategies involve:

1. *Selection.* The goal of the Postal Service is to hire selectively, ensuring it gets the right people in the jobs in the first place. Its prescreening process includes performing competency tests and contracting with an outside firm to do thorough background checks.

2. *Security.* The Postal Service is providing increased security to its 47,000 facilities nationwide. The amount and type of security vary from facility to facility.

3. *Policy.* A clear, direct, absolute, and well-communicated policy related to violence has been made known to employees. The policy prohibits any kind of weapon on postal property, including parking lots; promotes a zero-tolerance attitude toward threats of any type; and establishes a protocol to intervene early. The policy outlines a method for reporting all incidents of violence.

4. *Climate.* A healthy workplace is a safe workplace, so the Postal Service has an intense initiative to improve the agency's environment. It's putting managers and supervisors through a series of training sessions that deal with such issues as employee empowerment, conflict resolution, and positive reinforcement. It's also working with its unions to improve the grievance process.

5. *Employee support.* The Postal Service beefed up its employee assistance program (EAP) and began conducting training with supervisors and managers on how best to use the EAP and how to educate employees on how to use it. The agency also implemented an orientation program for all the employees. And in addition to the EAP, the Postal Service installed a 24-hour, toll-free hot line that employees can call to report threats or concerns.

6. *Separation.* Because termination does become necessary at times, the agency has created policies and procedures for terminating employees in the most effective way. It has also evaluated methods for making assessments on whether the people being dismissed may be dangerous.

### QUESTIONS

1. Identify and discuss various techniques the Postal Service could use to increase security at its various locations.

2. While all six strategies used by the Postal Service are important, which ones do you believe deserve the highest priority? Why?

3.  a.  Use the Workplace Violence Checklist found in the appendix to this chapter to assess the potential for violence at your place of work.
    b.  Working individually, or in a group, identify points that should be included in a violence prevention policy.

## Coping with Stress at U.S. Customs

Growing numbers of air and sea passengers and expanding amounts of cargo, along with illegal smuggling and drug trafficking, have brought added pressure to the job of U.S. Custom employees. Coupled with these stressors is the added pressure of an expanding workforce characterized as more diverse and less well trained. Work-weeks sometimes average eleven hours a day for six days, increasing the number and intensity of personal stressors such as child care issues and financial problems.

Heightening these problems is the fact that roughly one-half of U.S. Custom employees also serve as law enforcement officials. These persons face the pressures of shift work, exposure to society's worst social illnesses, frustration in dealing with a bureaucratic criminal justice system, and long periods of boredom followed by adrenaline-pumping excitement. Another common complaint of employees is that their managers lack good supervisory skills. Employees describe the work environment as one of criticism, negative feedback, and emphasis on mistakes while good performers are taken for granted and go unrewarded.

During stress-management training classes at the U.S. Customs Service, employees identified five factors as the major causes of their workplace stress:

- Supervisory pressures
- Deadlines/time pressures
- Boredom/meaninglessness of work
- Frustration with co-workers
- Working conditions

### QUESTIONS

1.  Working individually or in a group, discuss ways that each of the stressors mentioned by U.S. Customs employees might be reduced or eliminated.
2.  How might employers reduce or eliminate personal off-the-job stressors?

## NOTES AND REFERENCES

1.  Larry Reynolds, "Fighting Domestic Violence in the Workplace," *HRFocus* 74, no. 11 (November 1997): 8.
2.  "Top On-Job Killers: Traffic Accidents, Homicide," *Cincinnati Enquirer,* April 24, 1998, C-1.
3.  "The Cost of Doing Business," *Occupational Hazards* 60, no. 2 (February 1998): 26.
4.  Stephen G. Minter, "The Birth of OSHA," *Occupational Hazards* 60, no. 7 (July 1998): 59–60. See also Lisa Finnegan, "Is 1999 OSHA's Year?" *Occupational Hazards* 16, no. 12 (December 1998): 27–29.
5.  U.S. Department of Labor, Occupational Safety and Health Administration. *All about OSHA,* rev. ed.

(Washington, D.C.: U.S. Government Printing Office, 1995), 1.

6. *All about OSHA,* 5, 6.

7. S. L. Smith, "The Rebirth of NIOSH," *Occupational Hazards* 60, no. 12 (December 1998): 30–32.

8. *All about OSHA,* 6, 7.

9. *All about OSHA,* 17.

10. Charles M. Chadd and Jerome K. Bowman, "Targeted for Inspection," *Occupational Health and Safety* 67, no. 3 (March 1998): 22–26. See also "OSHA's Most Wanted," *HRFocus* 75, no. 2 (February 1998): 6.

11. *All about OSHA,* 19–23.

12. *All about OSHA,* 28–30. See also "Trial Program Sets Up Settlement Procedures," *Bulletin to Management* 50, no. 9 (March 1999): 68.

13. "OSHA Releases Citation, Inspection Figures," *Bulletin to Management* 50, no. 7 (February 1999): 52.

14. Lisa Finnegan, "Industry Partners with OSHA," *Occupational Hazards* 61, no. 2 (February 1999): 43–45.

15. *All about OSHA,* 34–36.

16. *All about OSHA,* 37–40.

17. *All about OSHA,* 41.

18. Fred S. Steingold, *The Employer's Legal Handbook,* 2nd ed. (Berkeley, Calif.: Nolo Press, 1998): 7/27.

19. Stephen G. Minter, "Safety Wisdom," *Occupational Hazards* 60, no. 10 (October 1998): 89–94. See also Bob Latham, "The Paper Pyramid," *Occupational Health and Safety* 67, no. 10 (October 1998): 6.

20. "Workplace Accidents Decrease as Safety Commitment Increases," *HRFocus* 71, no. 9 (September 1994): 16.

21. Stephen G. Minter, "Safety Training That Sticks," *Occupational Hazards* 58, no. 7 (June 1996): 36–38.

22. Peter Salwen, "The Internet Edge," *Occupational Health and Safety* 67, no. 5 (May 1998): 114–16.

23. Joe E. Beck, "High-End Training," *Occupational Health and Safety* 68, no. 1 (January 1999): 50–54.

24. F. David Pierce, "10 Rules for Better Communication," *Occupational Hazards* 58, no. 5 (May 1996): 78–80.

25. E. Scott Geller, "Behavior-Based Safety: Confusion, Controversy, and Confusion," *Occupational Health and Safety* 68, no. 1 (January 1999): 40–49.

26. Debra L. Nelson and James C. Quick, *Organizational Behavior,* 3rd ed. (Cincinnati, Ohio: South-Western College Publishing, 2000): 178–84.

27. Don Groover, "Behavior-Based Training for Safety and Health," *Occupational Hazards* 60, no. 9 (September 1998): 46–51.

28. Garry M. Ritzky, "Turner Bros. Wins Safety Game with Behavioral Incentives," *HRMagazine* 43, no. 7 (June 1998): 79–83.

29. Thomas R. Krause, "A Close Look at Safety Incentives, Part II," *Occupational Health and Safety* 67, no. 6 (June 1998): 32.

30. S. L. Smith, "Reaping the Rewards of Safety Incentives," *Occupational Hazards* 58, no. 1 (January 1996): 100. See also "Choosing the Right Incentive Reward," *Occupational Hazard* 58, no. 3 (March 1996): 63–65.

31. James W. Coonts, "Sizing Up Safety Awards," *Occupational Health and Safety* 67, no. 10 (October 1998): 166–67.

32. "From 703 to Zero, Zero, Zero…," *Occupational Health and Safety* 67, no. 5 (May 1998): 24–26.

33. Virginia Sutcliffe, "COS Finalists Team Up for Safety," *Occupational Hazards* 60, no. 11 (November 1998): 49–50.

34. Kathy McNeese and Roxanna Balden-Anslyn, "Beyond OSHA 200," *Occupational Health and Safety* 67, no. 2 (February 1998): 50–51.

35. OSHA defines an occupational injury as any injury, such as a cut, fracture, sprain, or amputation, that results from a work accident or from an exposure involving a single accident in the work environment. An *occupational illness* is any abnormal condition or disorder, other than one resulting from an occupational injury, caused by exposure to environmental factors associated with employment. This category includes acute and chronic illnesses or diseases that may be caused by inhalation, absorption, ingestion, or direct contact. Not recordable are first-aid cases that involve one-time treatment and subsequent observation of minor scratches, cuts, burns, splinters, etc., that do not ordinarily require medical care, even though such treatment is provided by a physician or registered professional personnel.

36. "OSHA Releases Citation, Inspection Figures," *Bulletin to Management* 50, no. 7 (February 1998): 52. See also John F. Rekus, "Hazard Communication: OSHA's Most Frequently Cited Standard," *Occupational Hazards* 60, no. 2 (February 1998): 39–42.

37. The Supreme Court decision in *International Union v Johnson Controls* may be found in 59 U.S. Law Week 4029. For additional information on chemicals and the reproductive system, see Catherine Arnst, "Is Your Reproductive System in Danger?" *Business Week,* September 14, 1998, 105–8.

38. "Smoke Gets in Your Lungs," *HRFocus* 73, no. 2 (February 1996): 17.

39. "Smoke Gets in Your Lungs," 19. See also Lin Grensing-Pophal, "Smoking in the Workplace," *HRMagazine* 44, no. 5 (May 1999): 59–66.

**40.** *BNA Policy and Practice Series—Personnel Management* (Washington, D.C.: Bureau of National Affairs, 1988), 247:164.

**41.** Ganga Subramanian, "Computer Screens an Eyesore for Unblinked Lids, Doctors Say," *Arizona State Press,* October 21, 1998, 7.

**42.** For other suggestions on maintaining VDT safety and health see "Laptop Fitness," *HRFocus* 73, no. 9 (September 1996): 18.

**43.** Patricia M. Fernberg, "Is It Carpal Tunnel Syndrome?" *Occupational Hazards* 60, no. 6 (June 1998): 34–38.

**44.** Elizabeth Sheley, "Preventing Repetitive Motion Injuries," *HRMagazine* 40, no. 10 (October 1995): 57–60.

**45.** "Is Carpal Tunnel Syndrome a Compensable Disease?" *Occupational Hazards* 58, no. 2 (February 1996): 70. See also Robert S. Sand, "Repetitive Stress Injuries: Will the Focus Shift from the Agencies to the Courts?" *Employee Relations Law Journal* 23, no. 1 (Summer 1997): 133–38.

**46.** Eileen Oswald, "Workplace AIDS/HIV: Are You Immune?" *Occupational Health and Safety* 65, no. 4 (April 1996): 39–40.

**47.** CDC Business and Labor Responds to AIDS, P.O. Box 6003, Rockville, Md. 20849, (800) 458-5281.

**48.** Errol Chenier, "The Workplace: A Battleground for Violence," *Public Personnel Management* 27, no. 4 (Winter 1998): 557–68.

**49.** Rick Kaletsky, "A Violence Reality Check," *Occupational Health and Safety* 67, no. 10 (October 1998): 188.

**50.** For a copy of *Recommendations for Workplace Violence Prevention Programs in Late-Night Retail Establishments* (OSHA Publication No. 3153), call (202) 219-4667.

**51.** Christine McGovern, "Take Action, Heed Warnings to End Workplace Violence," *Occupational Hazards* 61, no. 3 (March 1999): 61–63. See also Kaletsky, "Violence Reality Check," 188–90; and Gregory K. Moffatt, "Subjective Fear: Preventing Workplace Homicide," *HRFocus* 75, no. 8 (August 1998): 11–12.

**52.** Dominic Bencivenga, "Dealing with the Dark Side," *HRMagazine* 44, no. 1 (January 1999): 50–58. See also Nancy Hatch Woodward, "Domestic Abuse Policies in the Workplace," *HRMagazine* 43, no. 6 (May 1998): 117–23.

**53.** Rebecca A. Speer, "Can Workplace Violence Be Prevented?" *Occupational Hazards* 60, no. 8 (August 1998): 26–30.

**54.** Linda Thornburg, "When Violence Hits Business," *HRMagazine* 38, no. 7 (July 1993): 40–45.

**55.** *Alternatives—for the Health Conscious Individual,* published by Mountain Home Publishing Company, P.O. Box 829, Ingram, Tex. 78025; Jane Heimlich, *What Your Doctor Won't Tell You* (New York: Harper Collins, 1990); Linda G. Rector-Page, *Healthy Healing: An Alternative Healing Reference,* 10th ed. (Sonora, Calif.: Healthy Healing Publications, 1996).

**56.** Stephen G. Minter, "Tenneco: Pursuing Health for the Long Term," *Occupational Hazards* 58, no. 4 (April 1996): 53–54.

**57.** Wellness Resources: Association for Worksite Health Promotion, 60 Revere Dr., Suite 500, Northbrook, Ill. 60062, (847) 480-9574; Department of Health and Human Services, Office of Disease Prevention and Health Promotion, Washington, D.C. 20201, (202) 401-7780; National Wellness Institute, 1045 Clark St., Suite 210, P.O. Box 827, Stevens Point, Wisc. 54481-0828, (715) 342-2969; American Institute for Preventive Medicine, 30445 Northwestern Highway, Suite 350, Farmington Hills, Mich. 48334, (810) 539-1800.

**58.** "Here's to Your Health," *HRFocus* 73, no. 1 (January 1996): 18.

**59.** Nancy Ann Jeffrey, "Wellness Plans Try to Target the Not-So-Well," *The Wall Street Journal,* June 20, 1996, B-1.

**60.** Brent Chartier, "Reaffirming EAP at DuPont," *EAP Digest* 17, no. 1 (November/December 1996): 26–28.

**61.** Ted Larrison, "Clearing the Supervision Logjam," *EAP Digest* 19, no. 2 (January/February 1999): 27–29. See also Karen M. Hopkins, "Influences on Formal and Informal Supervisor Intervention with Troubled Employees," *Employee Assistance Quarterly* 13, no. 1 (1997): 33–54.

**62.** Jane Easter Bahls, "Handle with Care," *HRMagazine* 44, no. 3 (March 1999): 60–66. See also Gary L. Wirt, "The ABCs of EAPs," *HRFocus* 75, no. 11 (November 1998): S-2; George T. Watkins, "Finding the Right Provider," *EAP Digest* 18, no. 5 (July/August 1998): 7.

**63.** Nancy E. Isaac, "Corporate Response to Domestic Violence," *EAP Digest* 19, no. 3 (March/April 1999): 16–21.

**64.** "More Businesses Helping Workers Deal with the Blues," *Sacramento Bee,* April 21, 1996, sec. D.

**65.** David Chaudron, "Mood Disorders: Warning Signs and Action Steps," *HRFocus* 71, no. 10 (October 1994): 9.

**66.** Sandra Turner, "Identifying Depression in the Workplace," *HRMagazine* 40, no. 10 (October 1995): 82–84.

**67.** Rudy M. Yandrick, "A Better Way to Identify Substance Abusers," *EAP Digest* 18, no. 4 (May/June 1998): 28–29.

**68.** *The Employer's Legal Handbook,* 7/43.

**69.** "Substance Abuse Soaring," *HRFocus* 75, no. 9 (September 1998): 5.

**70.** The *Physician's Desk Reference* is published annually. The 2000 edition is the fifty-fifth edition.

**71.** Chris L. Peterson, *Stress at Work: A Sociological Perspective* (Amityville, N.Y.: Baywood Publishing Company, 1998). See also Terry A. Beehr, "Research on Occupational Stress: An Unfinished Enterprise," *Personnel Psychology* 51, no. 4 (Fall 1998): 835–44.

**72.** Lin Grensing-Pophal, "Recognizing and Conquering Burnout," *HRMagazine* 44, no. 3 (March 1999): 82–88. See also Guy H. Ross, "Preventing Burnout with Solution-Focused Assessments," *EAP Digest* 17, no. 2 (January/February 1997): 26–27.

**73.** Karen E. Semenuk, "Stress Test," *EAP Digest* 16, no. 6 (September/October 1996): 20–21.

**74.** Gail Dutton, "Cutting Edge Stressbusters," *HRFocus* 75, no. 9 (September 1998): 11–12.

**75.** Lawrence T. Woodburn and Suzanne Simpson, "Coping with the Stages of Job Stress," *EAP Digest* 18, no. 4 (May/June 1998): 22–25.

# Identifying the Risk of Workplace Violence:
## A Survey for Large and Small Employers

The OSHA-developed survey form shown below can be used to address workplace violence head on. Any statement marked T indicates a potential for serious security hazard. One should remember that employers can be cited for violating the Occupational Safety and Health Act's "general duty clause" if there is a recognized hazard of workplace violence in their establishments and "they do nothing to prevent or abate it." Copies of OSHA's guidelines on workplace violence can be obtained free by writing OSHA Publications Office, P.O. Box 37535, Washington, D.C. 20013-7535, or by faxing a request to 202-219-9266.

---

### WORKPLACE VIOLENCE CHECKLIST

**T   F**   This industry frequently confronts violent behavior and assaults of staff.

**T   F**   Violence occurs regularly where this facility is located.

**T   F**   Violence has occurred on the premises or in conducting business.

**T   F**   Customers, clients or co-workers assault, threaten, yell, push, or verbally abuse employees or use racial or sexual remarks.

**T   F**   Employees are NOT required to report incidents or threats of violence, regardless of injury or severity.

**T   F**   Employees have NOT been trained to recognize and handle threatening, aggressive, or violent behavior.

**T   F**   Alarm systems such as panic alarm buttons, silent alarms, or personal electronic alarm systems are NOT being used for prompt security assistance.

**T   F**   There is no regular training provided on the correct response to an alarm sounding.

**T   F**   Alarm systems are NOT tested on a monthly basis to assure correct function.

**T   F**   Security guards are NOT employed at the workplace.

**T   F**   Closed circuit cameras and mirrors are NOT used to monitor dangerous areas.

**T   F**   Metal detectors are NOT available or NOT used in the facility.

**T   F**   Violence is accepted as "part of the job" by some managers, supervisors, or employees.

**T   F**   Access and freedom of movement within the workplace are NOT re-

*(continued)*

stricted to those persons who have a legitimate reason for being there.

T F The workplace security system is inadequate—i.e., door locks malfunction, windows are not secure, and there are no physical barriers or containment systems.

T F Employees or staff members have been assaulted, threatened, or verbally abused by clients and patients.

T F Medical and counseling services have NOT been offered to employees who have been assaulted.

T F Employees have NOT been trained to recognize and control hostile and es-

calating aggressive behaviors and to manage assaultive behavior.

T F Employees CANNOT adjust work schedules to use the "buddy system" for visits to clients in areas where they feel threatened.

T F Cellular phones or other communication devices are NOT made available to field staff to enable them to request aid.

T F Vehicles are NOT maintained on a regular basis to ensure reliability and safety.

T F Employees work where assistance is NOT quickly available.

**Answers to Highlights in HRM 1**

1. d.  $70,000
2. Management commitment and employee involvement
   Work site analysis
   Hazard prevention and control
   Training
3. The clause requires the employer to provide a safe and healthy work environment for all employees.
4. d.  80
5. a.  Hazard communications
6. d.  6,200. OSHA is a busy federal agency.
7. Unsafe acts (85 percent of all accidents)
8. The company position on safety and health
   The identity of the safety coordinator
   Rules and regulations
   Hazard Communication program elements
   Safety programs in place
   Employee and employer responsibilities
   Safety communication in the workplace
9. a.  Minimum standards
10. False
11. True

# chapter 13

# Employee Rights and Discipline

AFTER STUDYING THIS CHAPTER, YOU SHOULD BE ABLE TO

**OBJECTIVE 1**

Explain the concepts of employment-at-will, wrongful discharge, implied contract, and constructive discharge.

**OBJECTIVE 2**

Identify the job expectancy rights of employees.

**OBJECTIVE 3**

Explain the process of establishing disciplinary policies, including the proper implementation of organizational rules.

**OBJECTIVE 4**

Discuss the meaning of discipline and how to investigate a disciplinary problem.

**OBJECTIVE 5**

Explain two approaches to disciplinary action.

**OBJECTIVE 6**

Identify the different types of alternative dispute-resolution procedures.

**OBJECTIVE 7**

Discuss the role of ethics in the management of human resources.

I n this chapter we discuss employee rights, workplace privacy, and employee discipline. Managers note that these topics have a major influence on the activities of both employees and supervisors. Robert J. Deeny, an employment attorney, has stated that employee rights and workplace privacy will "continue to be the hottest employment law topics into the twenty-first century."[1] Managers are discovering that the right to discipline and discharge employees—a traditional responsibility of management—is more difficult to exercise in light of the growing attention to employee rights. Furthermore, disciplining employees is a difficult and unpleasant task for most managers and supervisors; many of them report that taking disciplinary action against an employee is the most stressful duty they perform. Balancing employee rights and employee discipline may not be easy, but it is a universal requirement and a critical aspect of good management.

Because the growth of employee rights issues has led to an increase in the number of lawsuits filed by employees, we include in this chapter a discussion of alternative dispute resolution as a way to foster organizational justice. Since disciplinary actions are subject to challenge and possible reversal through governmental agencies or the courts, management should make a positive effort to prevent the need for such action. When disciplinary action becomes impossible to avoid, however, that action should be taken in accordance with carefully developed HR policies and practices. Since ethics is an important element of organizational justice, the chapter concludes with a discussion of organizational ethics in employee relations.

In a discussion of organizational discipline, the role of counseling in the achievement of individual and organizational objectives deserves special attention. We have included a review of counseling purposes and techniques in the appendix to this chapter.

# Employee Rights

Various antidiscrimination laws, wage and hour statutes, and safety and health legislation have secured basic employee rights and brought numerous job improvements to the workplace. Now employee rights litigation has shifted to such workplace issues as employees' rights to protest unfair disciplinary action, to refuse to take drug tests, to have access to their personnel files, to challenge employer searches and surveillance, and to receive advance notice of a plant closing.[2]

**Employee rights**
Guarantees of fair treatment from employers, particularly regarding an employee's right to privacy

The current emphasis on employee rights is a natural result of the evolution of societal, business, and employee interests. **Employee rights** can be defined as the guarantees of fair treatment that employees expect in protection of their employment status.[3] These expectations become rights when they are granted to employees by the courts, legislatures, or employers. Employee rights frequently involve an employer's alleged invasion of an employee's right to privacy. Unfortunately, the difference between an employee's legal right to privacy and the moral or personal right to privacy is not always clear. The confusion is due to the lack of a comprehensive and consistent body of privacy protection, whether from laws or from court decisions.

Balanced against employee rights is the employer's responsibility to provide a safe workplace for employees while guaranteeing safe, quality goods and services to consumers. An employee who uses drugs may exercise his or her privacy right and refuse to submit to a drug test. But should that employee produce a faulty product as a result of drug impairment, the employer can be held liable for any harm caused by that product. Employers must therefore exercise *reasonable care* in the hiring, training, and assignment of employees to jobs. Without the exercise of reasonable care, employers can be held negligent by outside parties or other employees injured by a dishonest, unfit, or incompetent employee. In law, **negligence** is the failure to use a reasonable amount of care where such failure results in injury to another person.

It is here that employee rights and employer responsibilities can come most pointedly into conflict. The failure of employers to honor employee rights can result in costly lawsuits, damage the organization's reputation, and hurt employee morale. But failure to protect the safety and welfare of employees or consumer interests can invite litigation from both groups. In the remainder of this section we will discuss various rights employees have come to expect from their employers.

**Negligence**
Failure to provide reasonable care where such failure results in injury to consumers or other employees

## Employment Protection Rights

It is not surprising that employees should regard their jobs as an established right—a right that should not be taken away without just cause.[4] Without the opportunity to hold a job our personal well-being would be greatly curtailed. This line of reasoning has led to the emergence of four legal considerations regarding the security of one's job: the employment-at-will principle, the concept of the implied contract, constructive discharge, and plant closing notification.

It should be understood, however, that although employees might have cause to regard jobs as an established right, there is no legal protection affording employees a permanent or continuous job. The U.S. Constitution carries no mandate guaranteeing that jobs are among the specific property rights of employees. Regardless, the concept of job as property right does obligate management to act in a consistent manner that is fair and equitable to all employees. Employees do have the right to expect sound employment practices and to be treated as individuals of dignity and substantial worth.

### Employment-at-Will

**Employment-at-will principle**
The right of an employer to fire an employee without giving a reason and the right of an employee to quit when he or she chooses

The employment relationship has traditionally followed the common-law doctrine of employment-at-will. The **employment-at-will principle** assumes that an employee has a right to sever the employment relationship for a better job opportunity or for other personal reasons. Employers, likewise, are free to terminate the employment relationship at any time—and without notice—for any reason, no reason, or even a bad reason.[5] In essence, employees are said to work "at the will" of the employer.[6]

The employment-at-will relationship is created when an employee agrees to work for an employer for an unspecified period of time. Since the employment is of an indefinite duration, it can, in general, be terminated at the whim of either party. This freedom includes the right of management to unilaterally determine the conditions of employment and to make personnel decisions. In 1908, the Supreme Court upheld the employment-at-will doctrine in *Adair v United States,* and this principle continues to be the basic rule governing the private-sector employment relationship.[7]

Public-sector employees have additional constitutional protection of their employment rights under the Fifth and Fourteenth Amendments to the Constitution. The Fifth Amendment applies to federal employees, while the Fourteenth applies to employees working for state, county, and local governments. Both amendments act to limit the methods and reasons that may be utilized to discipline or dismiss an incumbent employee in the public sector. The clauses of the Fifth Amendment that prohibit denial of life, liberty, and property without due process of law, as well as the Fourteenth Amendment, provide the principal constitutional protection afforded public-sector employees.

### Wrongful Discharge

Estimates of the American workforce subject to arbitrary discharge under the employment-at-will doctrine range from 55 million to 65 million employees. Approximately 2 million workers are discharged each year. Estimates of unfair employee dismissals range from 50,000 to 200,000 a year. In recent years, a substantial number of these employees have sued their former employers for "wrongful or unjust discharge."

The significance of wrongful discharge suits is that they challenge the employer's right under the employment-at-will concept to unilaterally discharge employees. Various state courts now recognize the following three important exceptions to the employment-at-will doctrine:

1. *Violation of public policy.* This exception occurs in instances where an employee is terminated for refusing to commit a crime; for reporting criminal activity to government authorities; for disclosing illegal, unethical, or unsafe practices of the employer; or for exercising employment rights.[8] (See Figure 13.1 for examples of public policy violations.)

2. *Implied contract.* This exception occurs when employees are discharged despite the employer's promise (expressed or implied) of job security or contrary to established termination procedures. An employer's oral or written statements may constitute a contractual obligation if they are communicated to employees and employees rely on them as conditions of employment.

3. *Implied covenant.* This exception occurs where a lack of good faith and fair dealing by the employer has been suggested. By inflicting harm without justification, the employer violates the implied covenant. Discharged employees may seek tort damages for mental distress or defamation.

**FIGURE 13.1**

▶ **Discharges That Violate Public Policy**

An employer may *not* terminate an employee for

- Refusing to commit perjury in court on the employer's behalf
- Cooperating with a government agency in the investigation of a charge or giving testimony
- Refusing to violate a professional code of conduct
- Reporting Occupational Safety and Health Administration (OSHA) infractions
- Refusing to support a law or a political candidate favored by the employer
- "Whistle-blowing," or reporting illegal conduct by the employer
- Informing a customer that the employer has stolen property from the customer
- Complying with summons to jury duty

"I'm sensing confidence, boldness and moral sensibility. You're not going to turn out to be a whistle-blower are you?"

From *The Wall Street Journal*—Permission, Cartoon Features Syndicate

At the present time the confusion and conflict between the traditional right of employers to terminate at will and the right of employees to be protected from unjust discharge are far from resolved. Therefore, to protect themselves from large jury awards—sometimes exceeding $1 million—more organizations are insuring themselves against workers' claims. Known as employment-practice liability insurance, these policies protect employers facing huge legal bills or damage awards from wrongful discharge lawsuits.[9] To help prevent wrongful discharge termination, HR specialists recommend the suggestions given in Figure 13.2.

To further limit large jury awards, various states have imposed damage caps and limitations on monetary settlements. Punitive damage awards have also been under attack. At issue is the "reasonableness" of the high settlements in light of the principle that any award of punitive damages must bear a reasonable relationship to the actual injury suffered by the employees.

### Implied Contract

Although it is estimated that 70 percent of employees in the United States work without benefit of an employment contract, under certain conditions these employees may be granted contractual employment rights. This can occur when an implied promise by the employer suggests some form of job security to the employee. These implied contractual rights can be based on either oral or written statements made

**FIGURE 13.2**

▶ **Tips to Avoid Wrongful Employment Termination Lawsuits**

- *Terminate an employee only if there is an articulated reason.* An employer should have clearly articulated, easily understandable reasons for discharging an employee. The reasons should be stated as objectively as possible and should reflect company rules, policies, and practices.

- *Set and follow termination rules and schedules.* Make sure every termination follows a documented set of procedures. Procedures can be from an employee handbook, a supervisory manual, or even an intraoffice memorandum. Before terminating, give employees notices of unsatisfactory performance and improvement opportunities through a system of warnings and suspensions.

- *Document all performance problems.* A lack of documented problems in an employee's personnel record may be used as circumstantial evidence of pretextual discharge if the employee is "suddenly" discharged.

- *Be consistent with employees in similar situations.* Document reasons given for all disciplinary actions, even if they do not lead to termination. Terminated employees may claim exception-to-the-rule cases are discriminatory. Detailed documentation will help employers explain why these "exceptions" did not warrant termination.

during the preemployment process or subsequent to hiring. Often these promises are contained in employee handbooks, HR manuals, or employment applications or are made during the selection interview.[10] Once these explicit or implicit promises of job security have been made, courts have generally prohibited the employer from terminating the employee without first exhausting the conditions of the contract. For example, a leading case, *Toussaint v Blue Cross and Blue Shield of Michigan*, found an employee handbook enforceable as a unilateral contract.[11] The following are some examples of how an implied contract may become binding:

- Telling employees their jobs are secure as long as they perform satisfactorily and are loyal to the organization.
- Stating in the employee handbook that employees will not be terminated without the right of defense or access to an appeal procedure—that is, due process.
- Urging an employee to leave another organization by promising higher wages and benefits, then denying those promises after the person has been hired.

Fortunately, employers may lessen their vulnerability to implied-contract lawsuits by prudent managerial practices, training, and HR policies. HR experts recommend the following approaches:

1. Training supervisors and managers not to imply contract benefits in conversations with new or present employees.
2. Including in employment offers a statement that an employee may voluntarily terminate employment with proper notice and the employee may be dismissed by the employer at any time and for a justified reason. The language in this statement must be appropriate, clear, and easily understood.
3. Including employment-at-will statements in all employment documents—for example, employee handbooks, employment applications, and letters of employment.[12] (See Highlights in HRM 1.)
4. Having written proof that employees have read and understood the employment-at-will disclaimers.

### Constructive Discharge

**Constructive discharge**

An employee voluntarily terminates his or her employment because of harsh, unreasonable employment conditions placed upon the individual by the employer

It is increasingly common for employees to quit or resign their employment because of acts of alleged discrimination and subsequently claim their employment rights were violated through a **constructive discharge**. That is, they were "forced" to resign because of intolerable working conditions purposefully placed upon them by the employer. Put simply, the employer has forced on an employee working conditions so unreasonable and unfair that the employee has no choice but to quit.[13] In a leading constructive discharge case, *Young v Southwestern Savings and Loan Association*, the court noted:

> The general rule is that if the employer deliberately makes an employee's working conditions so intolerable that the employee is forced into involuntary resignation, then the employer has encompassed a constructive discharge and is as liable for any illegal conduct involved therein as if he had formally discharged the aggrieved employee.[14]

The courts, by formulating the constructive-discharge doctrine, attempt to prevent employers from accomplishing covertly that which they are prohibited by

# Examples of Employment-at-Will Statements

Employment handbooks frequently include an opening statement that employees are employed at will; that is, there are no duration guarantees. Also no supervisors or managers, except specified individuals (that is, the HR director or company president), have the authority to promise any employment benefit—including salary, job position, and the like. All handbooks should include a disclaimer that expressly provides that all employment policies and benefits contained in the handbook are subject to change or removal at the sole and exclusive discretion of the employer.

Two examples of at-will statements are

I acknowledge that if hired, I will be an at-will employee. I will be subject to dismissal or discipline without notice or cause, at the discretion of the employer. I understand that no representative of the company, other than the president, has authority to change the terms of an at-will employment and that any such change can occur only in a written employment contract.

I understand that my employment is not governed by any written or oral contract and is considered an at-will arrangement. This means that I am free, as is the company, to terminate the employment relationship at any time for any reason, so long as there is no violation of applicable federal or state law. In the event of employment, I understand that my employment is not for any definite period or succession of periods and is considered an at-will arrangement. That means I am free to terminate my employment at any time for any reason, as is the company, so long as there is no violation of applicable federal or state law.

law from achieving overtly. For example, unscrupulous employers may desire to rid themselves of seemingly undesirable employees by deliberately forcing on them unfavorable working conditions so grievous that employees would rather quit than tolerate the disagreeable conditions. Under this action, the employer may be attempting to limit liability should an employee seek redress through various protective employment statutes.

Currently U.S. circuit courts disagree on how employees must prove a constructive-discharge claim. A majority of circuit courts favor a *reasonable-person* standard. Under this standard, the plaintiff must merely show that working conditions were intolerable to a "reasonable person," leaving the employee with no recourse but to resign.[15] A minority of circuit courts adopt the reasonable-person standard, but plaintiffs must additionally prove that the employer intended to force the quit. This approach is called the *employer-intent* standard.[16] The employer-intent test is highly subjective and, therefore, more difficult for an employee to substantiate. It should be noted that the constructive-discharge doctrine does not provide employees with any new employment rights. Rather, through a constructive-discharge suit, the employee is only protecting employment safeguards previously granted through laws or court rulings.

### Plant Closing Notification

Millions of jobs have been lost in the United States as a result of the closing of large firms. Plant closings have a tragic impact on the lives of employees and their communities. It is estimated that for every 100 jobs lost from a plant closing, the local community loses 200 to 300 jobs through a ripple effect.

The federal government, several states, and local jurisdictions have passed legislation restricting the unilateral right of employers to close or relocate their facilities. In 1989 Congress passed the Workers' Adjustment Retraining and Notification Act (WARN), which requires organizations with more than 100 employees to give employees and their communities sixty days' notice of any closure or layoff affecting fifty or more full-time employees.[17] Notice must be given to collective bargaining representatives, unrepresented employees, the appropriate state dislocated-worker agency, and the highest-elected local official. Terminated employees must be notified individually in writing. The act allows several exemptions, including "unforeseeable circumstances" and "faltering businesses." Failure to comply with the law can subject employers to liability for back pay, fringe benefits, prejudgment interest, and attorney's fees. WARN does not prohibit employer closings, layoffs, or loss of jobs; the law simply seeks to lessen the hardships caused by job loss.

**USING THE INTERNET**

You can read about the details of the WARN Act by going through the Department of Labor's web site:

www.dol.gov/dol/asp/public/programs/handbook/warn.htm

**OBJECTIVE 2**

# Privacy Rights

The right of privacy can be regarded as a matter of personal freedom from unwarranted government or business intrusion into personal affairs. The right of privacy—a right well recognized in both law and legal commentary—includes the general principle of "personal autonomy."[18] It largely involves the individual's right to be left alone.[19]

Interestingly, a recent survey found more than 89 percent of Americans concerned about their invasion of privacy.[20] Employer challenges to privacy rights in the workplace have sparked a heated debate over the extent to which fundamental rights previously thought untouchable may be lessened through the employment relationship.[21] Through extensive media coverage, employees now realize that privacy rights on the job are more limited than those at home.[22] According to one writer, "employee privacy is recognized as one of the most significant workplace issues facing companies today."[23]

Employers defend their intrusion into employee privacy by noting their legitimate interest in some of the personal affairs of employees, particularly where those affairs (e.g., drug use, criminal activity, co-worker dating) may directly affect employee productivity and workplace safety and/or morale. Court cases regarding workplace privacy generally attempt to establish a balance between an employee's legitimate expectation of privacy against the employer's need to supervise and control the efficient operation of the organization. In this section we address the important workplace privacy issues of substance abuse and drug testing, searches and surveillance, access to personnel files, e-mail privacy, employee conduct outside the workplace, and genetic testing.

### Substance Abuse and Drug Testing

Consider these facts. Compared with nonabusing employees, substance abusers have been found to

- Be involved in 65 percent of all on-the-job accidents
- File six times more workers' compensation claims
- Use sixteen times as many health care benefits
- Be absent three times more often
- Make twice as many mistakes[24]

It is estimated that drug abuse by employees costs U.S. employers $75 billion every year in terms of safety risks, theft, reduced productivity, accidents, and benefits costs.[25] Furthermore, in these litigious times, the failure of an employer to ensure a safe and drug-free workplace can result in astronomical liability claims when consumers are injured because of a negligent employee or a faulty product. In response to the workplace drug issues, an increasing number of companies are battling the problem through drug-free workplace policies, employee education, drug testing, employee assistance programs, and undercover drug busts.[26]

Drug testing is most prevalent among employees in sensitive positions within the public sector, in organizations doing business with the federal government, and in public and private transportation outfits.[27] The definition of *sensitive position* has been formulated by the courts to include employees holding positions requiring top-secret national security clearance (*Harmon v Thornburgh*), those working in the interdiction of dangerous drugs (*Treasury Employees Union v Von Raab*), uniformed police officers and firefighters (*City of Annapolis v United Food and Commercial Workers Local 400*), and employees in transportation safety positions (*Skinner v Railway Labor Executives Association*). These employees can be required to submit to a drug test even without an "individualized suspicion" of drug usage.[28] The Federal Aviation Administration (FAA) mandatory drug testing program for flight crew members, flight attendants, air traffic controllers, maintenance personnel, aircraft dispatchers, and aviation security was upheld in *Bluestein v Skinner*.[29]

The courts in these cases have held that an employer's interest in maintaining a drug-free workplace outweighs any privacy interest the employee may have. At the federal level, the Drug-Free Workplace Act of 1988 requires, among other things, that organizations with government contracts of $25,000 or more publish and furnish to employees a policy statement prohibiting drug usage at work, establish awareness programs, and notify the federal contracting agency of any employees who have been convicted of a drug-related criminal offense. (See Chapter 12 for a sample policy statement.)

Employers subject to the Americans with Disabilities Act (see Chapter 2) must comply with the law's provisions regarding drug addiction.[30] The ADA clearly exempts from coverage any employee or job applicant who "is currently engaging in the illegal use of drugs." Illegal drug users are not considered to be "individuals with a disability." However, recovering or recovered drug addicts are included under the law's provisions. As the law states,

> Nothing in the ADA shall be construed to exclude as an individual with a disability an individual who—

**USING THE INTERNET**

For help in developing a drug policy, contact the Substance Abuse and Mental Health Services Administration at:

www.health.org

(1) has successfully completed a supervised drug rehabilitation program and is no longer engaging in the illegal use of drugs, or has otherwise been rehabilitated successfully and is no longer engaging in such use;

(2) is participating in a supervised rehabilitation program and is no longer engaging in such use.[31]

The ADA also protects employees addicted to legal drugs obtained legally. For example, an employee who lawfully takes pain medication and subsequently becomes addicted to the medication satisfies the ADA definition of an individual with a disability.

Legislation on drug testing in the private sector is varied and largely regulated by individual states. As one authority noted, "State statutes may be broadly categorized as either 'anti–drug testing' or 'pro–drug testing.'"[32] Anti–drug testing laws generally prohibit the testing for drugs except in very specific circumstances. Pro-drug testing states generally permit testing, provided that strict testing procedures are followed. Unless state or local laws either restrict or prohibit drug testing, private employers have a right to require employees to submit to a urinalysis or blood test where *reasonable suspicion* or *probable cause* exists.[33] Probable cause could include observable safety, conduct, or performance problems; excessive absenteeism or tardiness; or increased difficulty in working cooperatively with supervisors or co-workers. Employers who want to implement mandatory or random drug testing programs may face more stringent state court restrictions. Organizations cannot usually conduct blanket drug tests of all employees; the testing must usually be focused on an individual. (The best way to get up-to-date details on drug laws in your state is to research them in a local library or request information from an appropriate state agency.[34]) Figure 13.3 lists the prominent reasons for employer drug testing.

**FIGURE 13.3**

▶ **Reasons for Employer Drug Testing**

- *Preemployment:* To screen all job applicants or newly hired employees
- *Safety-sensitive positions:* To avoid endangerment of the jobholder or others where errant acts could compromise safety
- *Security-sensitive positions:* To screen employees who handle highly confidential materials or safekeep large amounts of valuables, deal in the interdiction of drugs, or carry firearms
- *Reasonable suspicion:* To confirm reasonable suspicion or find probable cause that employees are doing illegal drugs or are dealing in drugs
- *Postaccident:* To test immediately after an accident has caused serious injury or property damage
- *Return-to-duty:* To ensure the absence of drugs following an employee's return to work from rehabilitation
- *Follow-up:* To check after an employee has failed an initial drug test
- *Random:* To deter drug use through unannounced drug testing

Urinalysis is the most common form of drug testing, although employers also use blood sampling, hair sampling, and performance testing. Illegal substances remain in urine for various periods of time: cocaine for approximately seventy-two hours, marijuana for three weeks or longer. Hair samples provide a record of past drug use. Because hair grows about half an inch per month, a relatively small sample can provide a long record of drug use. Typically, state laws set out the testing method that must be used.

Some of the sharpest criticism of drug testing concerns the technology and standards with which the tests are conducted. Drug testing involves a number of different steps in which human error can occur. Testing equipment can be miscalibrated or insufficiently cleaned, samples can become contaminated, and chain-of-custody problems can occur. (*Chain-of-custody* documentation accounts for the integrity of each urine specimen by tracking its handling and storage from point of collection to final disposition.) Any of these difficulties can cause a *false positive* test result in which a particular drug is mistakenly identified in a specimen. To overcome these problems, the National Institute on Drug Abuse (NIDA) has established standards for drug testing labs. Employers should use only NIDA-certified labs. Also, large and small employers can use medical review officers as a safeguard in the testing procedure. TWA and 3M believe that medical review officers help both managers and employees to understand the complexities of drug testing.

Finally, when drug testing, employers must be careful not to defame the individual involved—employee or job applicant. The issue here concerns revealing the results of drug tests to others or "broadcasting" someone's drug problem. Defamation suits normally involve costly monetary damages for pain and suffering. Provide the results of drug tests only to those who need to know, for example, supervisors or HR staff members, and not to other co-workers or disinterested managers.

### Employee Searches and Surveillance

The U.S. Chamber of Commerce estimates that employee theft costs U.S. businesses $40 billion annually. Estimates are that 33 percent of workers steal from their employers and approximately 20 percent of all businesses fail (more than 16,000 U.S. firms annually) because of internal theft. To help fight these employee crimes, the courts have allowed random searches of lockers, desks, suitcases, toolboxes, and general work areas where adequate justification exists and employees have received proper notification beforehand.[35] Employees have no reasonable expectation of privacy in places where work rules that provide for inspections have been put into effect. They must comply with probable-cause searches by employers. And they can be appropriately disciplined, normally for insubordination, for refusing to comply with search requests.

Managers must be diligent when conducting employee searches. Improper searches can lead to employee lawsuits charging the employer with invasion of privacy, defamation of character, and negligent infliction of emotional distress. Employers are advised to develop an HR search policy based on the following guidelines:[36]

1. The search policy should be widely publicized and should advocate a probable or compelling reason for the search.
2. The search policy should be applied in a reasonable, evenhanded manner.
3. Where possible, searches should be conducted in private.
4. The employer should attempt to obtain the employee's consent prior to the search.

5.  The search should be conducted in a humane and discreet manner to avoid infliction of emotional distress.

6.  The penalty for refusing to consent to a search should be specified.

It is not uncommon for employers to monitor the conduct of employees through surveillance techniques. In some cases managers act as stationary surveillance covers or as moving surveillance covers, following the subject from point to point. Employers can use electronic surveillance equipment providing photographic or video images. General Electric employs tiny fish-eye lenses installed behind pinholes in walls and ceilings to observe employees suspected of crimes. DuPont uses long-distance cameras to monitor its loading docks. While most workplace surveillance must have some legitimate business purpose, there are very few federal legal controls protecting workers from being watched. State laws, however, set their own regulations on how much prying employees must tolerate.

One of the most common means of electronic surveillance by employers is telephone surveillance to ensure that customer requests are handled properly or to prevent theft. Employers have the right to monitor employees, provided they do it for compelling business reasons and employees have been informed that their calls will be monitored. However, a federal law, the Electronic Communications Privacy Act (ECPA), places some major limitations on that right.[37] The ECPA restricts employers from intercepting wire, oral, or electronic communications. Under the law, if an employee receives a personal call, the employer must hang up as soon as he or she realizes the call is personal. As noted by one legal authority, "An employer may monitor a personal call only if an employee knows the particular call is being monitored—and he or she consents to it."[38] Employees can sue for invasion of privacy, but courts have held that to win damages, an employee must show that the reasonable expectations of privacy outweigh the organization's reason for surveillance.

As a means of electronic security, this hand scanner device reads a person's palm once a code is entered on the keypad.

### Access to Personnel Files

The information kept in an employee's personnel file can have a significant impact—positive or negative—on career development. The personnel file, typically kept by the HR department, can contain performance appraisals, salary notices, investigatory reports, credit checks, criminal records, test scores, and family data. The Americans with Disabilities Act (discussed in Chapter 2) requires that an employee's medical history be kept in a file separate from other personnel information. Errors and/or omissions in personnel files, or access to the files by unauthorized persons, can create employment or personal hardships.[39]

Legislation at the federal level (see Figure 13.4) and laws in approximately half the states permit employees to inspect their own personnel files. How much

FIGURE 13.4

▸ **Right-to-Privacy Laws**

| LAW | EFFECT |
|---|---|
| Privacy Act (1974) | Applies to federal agencies and to organizations supplying goods or services to the federal government; gives individuals the right to examine references regarding employment decisions; allows employees to review their personnel records for accuracy. Employers who willfully violate the act are subject to civil suits. |
| Family Education Rights and Privacy Act—The Buckley Amendment (1974) | Prohibits educational institutions from supplying information about students without prior consent. Students have the right to inspect their educational records. |
| Fair Credit Reporting Act (1970) | Permits job applicants and employees to know of the existence and context of any credit files maintained on them. Employees have the right to know of the existence and nature of an investigative consumer report compiled by the employer. |
| Crime Control and Safe Streets Act (1968) | Prohibits employers from intercepting or listening to an employee's confidential communication without the employee's prior consent. |

access varies from state to state. For example, employers can prohibit employees from viewing information that might violate the privacy of others. Reference letters and criminal investigation reports are of this nature. A state law can limit the employee to copies of documents that he or she has signed, such as performance evaluations or job applications. The states that grant employees the privilege to see their personnel files generally provide

- The right to know of the existence of one's personnel file
- The right to inspect one's own personnel file
- The right to correct inaccurate data in the file

Typically, if a state law allows employees to examine their files, employers can insist that someone from HR, or a supervisor, be present to ensure that nothing is taken, added, or changed. Even in the absence of specific legislation, most employers give their employees access to their personnel files. Employment professionals recommend that organizations develop a policy on employee files that includes, as a minimum, the points noted in Figure 13.5.[40]

### E-Mail and Voice Mail Privacy

The benefits of e-mail and voice mail are many; they provide instant delivery of messages, they facilitate teamwork, they increase time efficiency, they offer access to global information, and they promote flexible work arrangements.[41] Unfortunately, the growth of HR information systems can create privacy problems by making per-

FIGURE 13.5

► **Personnel Files: Policy Guidelines**

- Ensure compliance with applicable state laws.
- Define exactly what information is to be kept in employee files.
- Develop different categories of personnel information, depending on legal requirements and organizational needs.
- Specify where, when, how, and under what circumstances employees may review or copy their files.
- Identify company individuals allowed to view personnel files.
- Prohibit the collection of information that could be viewed as discriminatory or could form the basis for an invasion-of-privacy suit.
- Audit employment records on a regular basis to remove irrelevant, outdated, or inaccurate information.

sonnel information more accessible to those with prying eyes or "hackers" who might use the information inappropriately. It is estimated that at least 20 million Americans may be subject to electronic monitoring through their computers.[42] Messages can be read or heard and deleted messages can be retrieved. Even log-on IDs and passwords will not prevent unauthorized access to computers by nonprivileged users.[43] Moreover, messages can be forwarded, replicated, and printed with ease.[44]

High technology creates a critical balance between employee privacy and the employer's need to know. Although employees may assume that their right to privacy extends to e-mail and voice messages, it does not. Employers routinely monitor e-mail messages that employees send and receive. Some e-mail systems copy all transmitted messages while others create backup copies of new messages. Employees who erase their messages may wrongly assume their messages are gone when deleted. Court cases governing e-mail generally grant to employers the right to monitor materials created, received, or sent for business-related reasons.[45] Furthermore, employees can be disciplined or terminated for inappropriate e-mail messages. Employers are strongly encouraged to develop clear policies and guidelines that explain to employees how e-mail and voice mail are to be used, including when and under what conditions employees can be monitored.[46] (See Figure 13.6.) As with other employment policies, employees should sign a form indicating they have read and understand the policy.

### Employee Conduct outside the Workplace

Consider the following case. On Monday morning the owner of ABC Corporation reads in the newspaper that a company employee has been charged with robbery and assault on a local convenience store owner. The employee has been released pending trial. A phone call to the employee's supervisor reveals that the employee has reported to work. What should the owner do?

Legal authorities generally conclude that the off-duty behavior of employees is not subject to employer disciplinary action. Case law suggests that misconduct

FIGURE 13.6

► **E-Mail and Voice Mail: Policy Guidelines**

- Ensure compliance with federal and state legislation.
- Specify the circumstances, if any, under which the system can be used for personal business.
- Specify that confidential information not be sent on the network.
- Set forth the condition under which monitoring will be done—by whom, how frequently, and with what notification to employees.
- Specify that e-mail and voice mail information be sent only to users who need it for business purposes.
- Expressly prohibit use of e-mail or voice mail to harass others or to send anonymous messages.
- Make clear that employees have no privacy rights in any material delivered or received through e-mail or voice mail.
- Specify that employees who violate the policy are subject to discipline, including discharge.

outside the workplace may not, in some circumstances, be a lawful justification for employee discipline. Organizations that want to discipline employees for off-duty misconduct must establish a clear relationship between the misconduct and its negative effect on other employees or the organization. This might be established, for example, in cases where off-duty criminal misconduct (e.g., child molestation) creates a disruptive impact on the workplace. Another example might be where the public nature of the employee's job (e.g., police or fire department personnel) creates an image problem for the organization. Generally, however, little of what an employee does outside the workplace bears discipline by the employer.

Workplace romances, however, create a particular dilemma for organizations. The concern is employer liability if a co-worker, supervisor-subordinate, or other power-differentiated romance goes sour, leading to charges of sexual harassment.[47] Acceptable behavior in a consensual relationship between employees can become harassing behavior if one party to the relationship no longer welcomes the conduct.[48] Organizations may also increase the potential for workplace violence should a scorned lover seek violent revenge at the work site.

Furthermore, workplace romances can lead to employee charges of favoritism against a co-worker involved in a supervisor-subordinate romance. These "reverse harassment" claims are based on preferential treatment given an employee engaged in a romantic affair. Workplace romances can also create morale problems when other employees feel unfairly treated; such situations can lead to jealousy, resentment, and hard feelings. Supervisor romances can have profound effects on organizational operations and productivity.

Interestingly, some employers are asking their employees to sign "love contracts" as a defense against retaliation claims in co-worker sexual harassment suits.[49] Love contracts emphasize the voluntary nature of the relationship. Currently love contracts are used exclusively for top-level executives and are not recommended for hourly or supervisory personnel.

### Genetic Testing

Advances in genetic research now make it possible to identify the genetic basis for human diseases and illnesses.[50] Genetic findings present opportunities for individualized prevention strategies and early detection and treatment. Unfortunately, knowledge gained through genetic testing can also be used discreetly by employers to discriminate against or stigmatize individuals applying for employment or individuals currently employed. For example, genetic testing can identify an individual's risk of developing common disorders such as cancer, heart disease, or diabetes.

Since employee diseases and illnesses raise employment costs, employers may avoid hiring or retaining individuals who they believe are likely to become unduly sick, resign, or retire early, thus creating additional recruitment, training, or medical costs. However, employers must remember that there is no scientific evidence to substantiate a relationship between unexpressed genetic factors and an individual's ability to perform his or her job. There are few federal or state laws, or court decisions, governing an employer's use of genetic information. Employers, therefore, are cautioned when gathering genetic data, regardless of its intended purpose.

## Disciplinary Policies and Procedures

The rights of managers to discipline and discharge employees is increasingly limited. There is thus a great need for managers at all levels to understand discipline procedures. Disciplinary action taken against an employee must be for justifiable reasons, and there must be effective policies and procedures to govern its use. Such policies and procedures serve to assist those responsible for taking disciplinary action and help to ensure that employees will receive fair and constructive treatment. Equally important, these guidelines help to prevent disciplinary action from being voided or from being reversed through the appeal system.

Disciplinary policies and procedures should extend to a number of important areas to ensure thorough coverage. Figure 13.7 presents a disciplinary model that illustrates the areas where provisions should be established. The model also

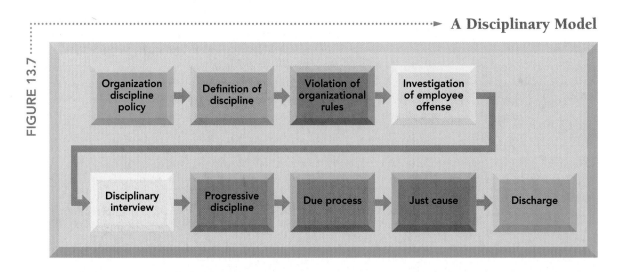

**FIGURE 13.7**

**A Disciplinary Model**

Organization discipline policy → Definition of discipline → Violation of organizational rules → Investigation of employee offense → Disciplinary interview → Progressive discipline → Due process → Just cause → Discharge shows the logical sequence in which disciplinary steps must be carried out to ensure enforceable decisions.

A major responsibility of the HR department is to develop, and to have top management approve, its disciplinary policies and procedures. The development, however, must involve the supervisors and managers who are to carry out these policies. Their experience can contribute to more effective coordination and consistency in the use of disciplinary action throughout the organization. The HR department is also responsible for ensuring that disciplinary policies, as well as any disciplinary actions taken against employees, are consistent with the labor agreement (if one exists) and conform with current law.

The primary responsibility for preventing or correcting disciplinary problems rests with an employee's immediate supervisor. This person is best able to observe evidence of unsatisfactory behavior or performance and to discuss the matter with the employee. Discussion is frequently all that is needed to correct the problem, and disciplinary action becomes unnecessary. However, when disciplinary action is needed, the supervisor should strive to use a problem-solving attitude. Causes underlying the problem are as important as the problem itself, and any attempt to prevent recurrence will require an understanding of them. Admittedly, it is often difficult for supervisors to maintain an objective attitude toward employee infractions. But if supervisors can maintain a problem-solving stance, they are likely to come up with a diagnosis that is nearer the truth than would be possible were they to use the approach of a trial lawyer.

## The Results of Inaction

Figure 13.8 lists the more common disciplinary problems identified by managers. Failure to take disciplinary action in any of these areas only serves to aggravate a problem that eventually must be resolved. Failure to act implies that the performance of the employee concerned has been satisfactory. If disciplinary action is eventually taken, the delay will make it more difficult to justify the action if appealed. In defending against such an appeal, the employer is likely to be asked why an employee who had not been performing or behaving satisfactorily was kept on the payroll. Or an even more damaging question might be "Why did that employee receive satisfactory performance ratings (or perhaps even merit raises)?"[51]

Such contradictions in practice can only aid employees in successfully challenging management's corrective actions. Unfortunately, there are supervisors who try to build a case to justify their corrective actions only after they have decided that a particular employee should be discharged. The following are common reasons given by supervisors for their failure to impose a disciplinary penalty:

1. The supervisor had failed to document earlier actions, so no record existed on which to base subsequent disciplinary action.
2. Supervisors believed they would receive little or no support from higher management for the disciplinary action.
3. The supervisor was uncertain of the facts underlying the situation requiring disciplinary action.
4. Failure by the supervisor to discipline employees in the past for a certain infraction caused the supervisor to forgo current disciplinary action in order to appear consistent.
5. The supervisor wanted to be seen as a likable person.

FIGURE 13.8

**Common Disciplinary Problems**

**ATTENDANCE PROBLEMS**

- Unexcused absence
- Chronic absenteeism
- Unexcused/excessive tardiness
- Leaving without permission

**DISHONESTY AND RELATED PROBLEMS**

- Theft
- Falsifying employment application
- Willfully damaging organizational property
- Punching another employee's time card
- Falsifying work records

**WORK PERFORMANCE PROBLEMS**

- Failure to complete work assignments
- Producing substandard products or services
- Failure to meet established production requirements

**ON-THE-JOB BEHAVIOR PROBLEMS**

- Intoxication at work
- Insubordination
- Horseplay
- Smoking in unauthorized places
- Fighting
- Gambling
- Failure to use safety devices
- Failure to report injuries
- Carelessness
- Sleeping on the job
- Using abusive or threatening language with supervisors
- Possession of narcotics or alcohol
- Possession of firearms or other weapons
- Sexual harassment

## Setting Organizational Rules

The setting of organizational rules is the foundation for an effective disciplinary system. These rules govern the type of behavior expected of employees. Organizations as diverse as Gerber Products, Wal-Mart, Steelcase, and Pitney Bowes have written policies explaining the type of conduct required of employees. Since employee behavior standards are established through the setting of organizational rules and regulations, the following suggestions may help reduce problems in this area:

1. Rules should be widely disseminated and known to all employees. It should not be assumed that employees know all the rules.

2. Rules should be reviewed periodically—perhaps annually—especially those rules critical to work success.

3. The reasons for a rule should always be explained. Acceptance of an organizational rule is greater when employees understand the reasons behind it.

4. Rules should always be written. Ambiguity should be avoided, since this can result in different interpretations of the rules by different supervisors.

5. Rules must be reasonable and relate to the safe and efficient operation of the organization. Rules should not be made simply because of personal likes or dislikes.

6.  If management has been lax in the enforcement of a rule, the rule must be restated, along with the consequences for its violation, before disciplinary action can begin.

7.  Have employees sign that they have read and understand the organizational rules.

When taken against employees, disciplinary action should never be thought of as punishment. Discipline can embody a penalty as a means of obtaining a desired result; however, punishment should not be the intent of disciplinary action. Rather, discipline must have as its goal the improvement of the employee's future behavior. To apply discipline in any other way—as punishment or as a way of getting even with employees—can only invite problems for management, including possible wrongful discharge suits.

When seeking reasons for unsatisfactory behavior, supervisors must keep in mind that employees may not be aware of certain work rules. Before initiating any disciplinary action, therefore, it is essential that supervisors determine whether they have given their employees careful and thorough orientation in the rules and regulations relating to their jobs. In fact, the proper communication of organizational rules and regulations is so important that labor arbitrators cite *neglect in communicating rules* as a major reason for reversing the disciplinary action taken against an employee.[52]

## The Hot-Stove Approach to Rule Enforcement

**Hot-stove rule**

Rule of discipline that can be compared with a hot stove in that it gives warning, is effective immediately, is enforced consistently, and applies to all employees in an impersonal and unbiased way

Regardless of the reason for the disciplinary action, it should be taken as soon as possible after the infraction has occurred and a complete investigation has been conducted. HR professionals often use the **hot-stove rule** to explain the correct application of discipline. A hot stove gives warning that it should not be touched. Those who ignore the warning and touch it are assured of being burned. The punishment is an immediate and direct consequence of breaking the rule never to touch a hot stove. Likewise, a work rule should apply to all employees and should be enforced consistently and in an impersonal and unbiased way. Employees should know the consequences of violating the rule, so that it has preventive value.

## Defining Discipline

**Discipline**

(1) Treatment that punishes; (2) orderly behavior in an organizational setting; or (3) training that molds and strengthens desirable conduct—or corrects undesirable conduct—and develops self-control

In management seminars conducted by the authors of this text, when managers are asked to define the word "discipline," their most frequent response is that discipline means punishment. Although this answer is not incorrect, it is only one of three possible meanings. As normally defined, **discipline** has these meanings:

1.  Treatment that punishes
2.  Orderly behavior in an organizational setting
3.  Training that molds and strengthens desirable conduct—or corrects undesirable conduct—and develops self-control

To some managers, discipline is synonymous with force. They equate the term with the punishment of employees who violate rules or regulations. Other managers think of discipline as a general state of affairs—a condition of orderliness where employees conduct themselves according to standards of acceptable behavior.

Discipline viewed in this manner can be considered positive when employees willingly practice self-control and respect organizational rules.

The third definition considers discipline a management tool used to correct undesirable employee behavior. Discipline is applied as a constructive means of getting employees to conform to acceptable standards of performance. Many organizations, such as Goodyear Aerospace and Arizona State University, define the term "discipline" in their policy manuals as training that "corrects, molds, or perfects knowledge, attitudes, behavior, or conduct." Discipline is thus viewed as a way to correct poor employee performance rather than simply as punishment for an offense. As these organizations emphasize, discipline should be seen as a method of training employees to perform better or to improve their job attitudes or work behavior. It is also interesting to note that the word "discipline" is derived from the word "disciple," which means follower or pupil. At least one group of researchers believes that the implication here is that good discipline is based on good supervisory leadership.[53]

## Investigating the Disciplinary Problem

It's a rare manager who has a good, intuitive sense of how to investigate employee misconduct. Too frequently investigations are conducted in a haphazard manner; worse, they overlook one or more investigative concerns. In conducting an employee investigation, it is important to be objective and to avoid the assumptions, suppositions, and biases that often surround discipline cases. Figure 13.9 lists seven questions to consider in investigating an employee offense. Attending to each question will help ensure a full and fair investigation while providing reliable information free from personal prejudice.

### Documentation of Employee Misconduct

"It's too complicated." "I just didn't take time to do it." "I have more important things to do." These are some of the frequent excuses used by managers who have failed to document cases of employee misconduct. The most significant cause of inadequate documentation, however, is that managers have no idea of what constitutes good documentation. Unfortunately, the failure of managers to record employee misconduct accurately can result in the reversal of any subsequent disciplinary action. The maintenance of *accurate* and *complete* work records, therefore, is an essential part of an effective disciplinary system.[54] For documentation to be complete, the following eight items should be included:

1. Date, time, and location of the incident(s)
2. Negative performance or behavior exhibited by the employee—the problem
3. Consequences of that action or behavior on the employee's overall work performance and/or the operation of the employee's work unit
4. Prior discussion(s) with the employee about the problem
5. Disciplinary action to be taken and specific improvement expected
6. Consequences if improvement is not made, and a follow-up date
7. The employee's reaction to the supervisor's attempt to change behavior
8. The names of witnesses to the incident (if appropriate)

FIGURE 13.9

▶ **Considerations in Disciplinary Investigations**

1. In very specific terms, what is the offense charged?
   - Is management sure it fully understands the charge against the employee?
   - Was the employee really terminated for insubordination, or did the employee merely refuse a request by management?

2. Did the employee know he or she was doing something wrong?
   - What rule or provision was violated?
   - How would the employee know of the existence of the rule?
   - Was the employee warned of the consequence?

3. Is the employee guilty?
   - What are the sources of facts?
   - Is there direct or only indirect evidence of guilt?
   - Has anyone talked to the employee to hear his or her side of the situation?

4. Are there extenuating circumstances?
   - Were conflicting orders given by different supervisors?
   - Does anybody have reason to want to "get" this employee?
   - Was the employee provoked by a manager or another employee?

5. Has the rule been uniformly enforced?
   - Have all managers applied this rule consistently?
   - What punishment have previous offenders received?
   - Were any other employees involved in this offense?

6. Is the offense related to the workplace?
   - Is there evidence that the offense hurt the organization?
   - Is management making a moral judgement or a business judgment?

7. What is the employee's past work record?
   - How many years of service has the employee given the organization?
   - How many years or months has the employee held the present job?
   - What is the employer's personnel record as a whole, especially his or her disciplinary record?

When preparing documentation, it is important for a manager to record the incident immediately after the infraction takes place, when the memory of it is still fresh, and to ensure that the record is complete and accurate. Documentation need not be lengthy, but it must include the eight points in the preceding list. Remember, a manager's records of employee misconduct are considered business documents, and as such they are admissible as evidence in arbitration hearings, administrative proceedings, and courts of law.[55]

## *The Investigative Interview*

Before any disciplinary action is initiated, an investigative interview should be conducted to make sure employees are fully aware of the offense. This interview is necessary because the supervisor's perceptions of the employee's behavior may not be entirely accurate. The interview should concentrate on how the offense violated the performance and behavior standards of the job. It should avoid getting into personalities or areas unrelated to job performance. Most important, the employee must be given a full opportunity to explain his or her side of the issue so that any deficiencies for which the organization may be responsible are revealed.

In the leading case *NLRB v Weingarten, Inc.,* the Supreme Court upheld a National Labor Relations Board ruling in favor of the employee's right to representation during an investigative interview in a unionized organization.[56] The Court reasoned that the presence of a union representative would serve the beneficial purpose of balancing the power between labor and management, since the union representative could aid an employee who was "too fearful or inarticulate to relate accurately the incident being investigated, or too ignorant to raise extenuating factors."[57] In the *Weingarten* case, the Court decided that since the employee had reason to believe that the investigative interview might result in action jeopardizing her job security, she had the right to representation. The *Weingarten* decision does not apply to nonunion employers, however.

It is important to note also that an employee's right to representation in a unionized organization does not extend to all interviews with management. The *Weingarten* case places some carefully defined limits on an employee's representation rights. The rules limiting these rights are as follows:

1. Representation rights apply only to *investigative interviews,* not to run-of-the-mill shop-floor discussions.
2. The rights arise only in incidents where the employee requests representation and where the employee *reasonably believes that discipline may result* from the interview.
3. Management has *no obligation to bargain* with the employee's representative.[58]

Even if employees and management comply with these rules, managers are still not required to hold an investigative interview. The *Weingarten* decision does not guarantee an employee an investigative interview; it only grants the right to representation *if requested.* The law does permit employers to cancel the interview if a representative is requested, and management may then continue the investigation by other appropriate means. Where employers violate the law, however, the NLRB can impose remedies, including cease-and-desist orders, reinstatement and back pay for discharged employees, and the removal of the record of disciplinary action.

**USING THE INTERNET**

A rather technical but very current discussion of *Weingarten* rights and nonunion workers, taken from *The New York Law Journal,* is found at:

www.ljx.com/corpcouns elor/0103labor.html

## Approaches to Disciplinary Action

**OBJECTIVE 5**

If a thorough investigation shows that an employee has violated some organization rule, disciplinary action must be imposed. Two approaches to disciplinary action are progressive discipline and positive discipline.

*Positive discipline is achieved by joint discussion and problem-solving between manager and employee.*

**Progressive discipline**
Application of corrective measures by increasing degrees

**Positive, or nonpunitive, discipline**
System of discipline that focuses on the early correction of employee misconduct, with the employee taking total responsibility for correcting the problem

## Progressive Discipline

Generally, discipline is imposed in a progressive manner. By definition, **progressive discipline** is the application of corrective measures by increasing degrees. Progressive discipline is designed to motivate an employee to correct his or her misconduct voluntarily. The technique is aimed at nipping the problem in the bud, using only enough corrective action to remedy the shortcoming. However, the sequence and severity of the disciplinary action vary with the type of offense and the circumstances surrounding it. Since each situation is unique, a number of factors must be considered in determining how severe a disciplinary action should be. Some of the factors to consider were listed in Figure 13.9.

The typical progressive discipline procedure includes four steps.[59] From an oral warning (or counseling) that subsequent unsatisfactory behavior or performance will not be tolerated, the action may progress to a written warning, to a suspension without pay, and ultimately to discharge. The progressive discipline used by Samaritan Health System is shown in Highlights in HRM 2. The "capital punishment" of discharge is utilized only as a last resort. Organizations normally use lower forms of disciplinary action for less severe performance problems. It is important for managers to remember that three important things occur when progressive discipline is applied properly:

1. Employees always know where they stand regarding offenses.
2. Employees know what improvement is expected of them.
3. Employees understand what will happen next if improvement is not made.

## Positive Discipline

Although progressive discipline is the most popular approach to correcting employee misconduct, recently some managers have questioned its logic. They have noted that it has certain flaws, including its intimidating and adversarial nature, which prevent it from achieving the intended purpose. For these reasons, organizations such as Tampa Electric Company, Ocean Spray, the Texas Department of Mental Health and Mental Retardation, Pennzoil, and Bay Area Rapid Transit are using an approach called **positive,** or **nonpunitive, discipline.** Positive discipline is based on the concept that employees must assume responsibility for their personal conduct and job performance.[60]

Positive discipline requires a cooperative environment where the employee and the supervisor engage in joint discussion and problem solving to resolve incidents of employee irresponsibility. The approach focuses on the early correction of misconduct, with the employee taking total responsibility for resolving the problem. Nothing is imposed by management; all solutions and affirmations are jointly reached. HR managers will often describe positive discipline as "nonpunitive discipline that replaces threats and punishment with encouragement."[61]

**HRM 2**

# The Samaritan Health System Corrective Action Process

When corrective action is necessary, managers should take the lowest-level action possible to correct the problem, even if that means repeating a step previously used. Samaritan believes that a progressive corrective action process is in the best interest of the employee and Samaritan. Progressive corrective action is not intended to be punishment, but rather to impress upon the employee the need for improvement. All facts, including length of service, previous performance, and attendance, will be considered.

An informal counseling with the employee may be all that is necessary to correct performance or attendance problems and should be used before beginning corrective action. This is an opportunity to discuss with the employee the problem, the resources available to him or her, and the ways to resolve the problem.

- *Step 1: Verbal warning.* Discuss the problem with the employee, pointing out what is needed to correct the problem. Be clear with the employee by saying, "This is a verbal warning," and by indicating that a written warning will result if performance or attendance is not improved as expected. This action should be documented and kept in the supervisor's file for future reference. No record of this warning is to be placed in the employee's official personnel record.

- *Step 2: Written warning.* If sufficient improvement is not observed in performance or attendance after issuing the verbal warning, a written warning is to follow. The problem and relevant facts should be described on the corrective action form. The employee must be told that if performance or attendance does not improve, further corrective action will occur in the form of a final written warning or suspension. A record of this warning should be placed in the employee's personnel record.

- *Step 3: Final written warning or suspension.* If sufficient improvement is not observed after the written warning, the supervisor should proceed to a final written warning or suspension. A suspension may be for one to three days and in the progressive action process is always without pay. Employees should be advised that the suspension is the last step before discharge and the time away from work is to be used to decide whether they can correct their performance or attendance problem. As with suspension, employees should be told that a final written warning is the final step before discharge. Suspensions and final written warnings are to be documented with relevant information and the dates of previous corrective action steps on the corrective action form.

- *Step 4: Discharge.* Before making the final decision to terminate, the supervisor should discuss with the employee the issue/incident that has caused the decision to discharge him or her. If the employee gives information that needs to be investigated, the supervisor should take time to do so. If there is no new information, then the human resources department should be consulted prior to discharging the employee. A Notice of Discharge form should be completed at the time the employee is discharged. The statement on the form should document the dates of the verbal, written, and final written warnings and the decree of suspension. It should also address the particular events that have brought about this decision and any other actions that have been taken or suggested to the employee to assist in the correction of the problem.

**Immediate Action**

Occasionally an infraction is so severe that immediate corrective action, up to and including termination, may appear to be warranted. If it is necessary to remove an employee from the work area, suspend him or her immediately, pending an investigation that should not last for more than a few days. There is no reason to terminate an employee "on the spot." The investigation may reveal that disciplinary action was not appropriate. In such cases the employee will be paid for the days of suspension.

**Source:** Adapted from *Samaritan Employee Handbook and Management Guideline.* Used with permission of Samaritan Health System, Phoenix, Ariz.

Figure 13.10 illustrates the procedure for implementing positive discipline. While positive discipline appears similar to progressive discipline, its emphasis is on giving employees reminders rather than reprimands as a way to improve performance. The technique is implemented in three steps. The first is a conference between the employee and the supervisor. The purpose of this meeting is to find a solution to the problem through discussion, with oral agreement by the employee to improve his or her performance. The supervisor refrains from reprimanding or threatening the employee with further disciplinary action. Supervisors may document

**FIGURE 13.10**

**Positive Discipline Procedure**

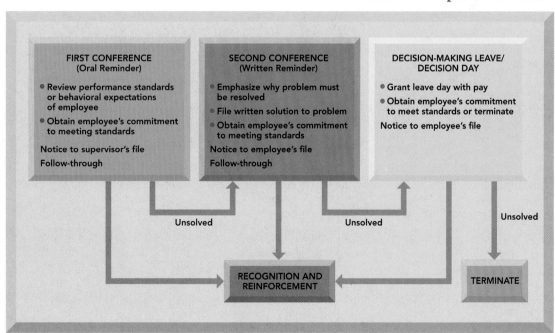

this conference, but a written record of this meeting is not placed in the employee's file unless the misconduct occurs again.

If improvement is not made after this first step, the supervisor holds a second conference with the employee to determine why the solution agreed to in the first conference did not work. At this stage, however, a written reminder is given to the employee. This document states the new or repeated solution to the problem, with an affirmation that improvement is the responsibility of the employee and a condition of continued employment.

When both conferences fail to produce the desired results, the third step is to give the employee a one-day *decision-making leave* (a paid leave). The purpose of this paid leave is for the employee to decide whether he or she wishes to continue working for the organization. The organization pays for this leave to demonstrate its desire to retain the person. Also, paying for the leave eliminates the negative effects for the employee of losing a day's pay. Employees given a decision-making leave are instructed to return the following day with a decision either to make a total commitment to improve performance or to quit the organization. If a commitment is not made, the employee is dismissed with the assumption that he or she lacked responsibility toward the organization.[62]

## Compiling a Disciplinary Record

In applying either progressive or positive discipline, it is important for managers to maintain complete records of each step of the procedure. When employees fail to meet the obligation of a disciplinary step, they should be given a warning, and the warning should be documented by their manager. A copy of this warning is usually placed in the employee's personnel file. After an established period—frequently six months—the warning is usually removed, provided that it has served its purpose. Otherwise it remains in the file to serve as evidence should a more severe penalty become necessary later.

An employee's personnel file contains the employee's complete work history. It serves as a basis for determining and supporting disciplinary action and for evaluating the organization's disciplinary policies and procedures. Maintenance of proper records also provides management with valuable information about the soundness of its rules and regulations. Those rules that are violated most frequently should receive particular attention, because the need for them may no longer exist or some change might be required to facilitate their enforcement. If the rule is shown to have little or no value, it should be revised or rescinded. Otherwise, employees are likely to feel they are being restricted unnecessarily.

## Discharging Employees

When employees fail to conform to organizational rules and regulations, the final disciplinary action in many cases is discharge. Since discharge has such serious consequences for the employee—and possibly for the organization—it should be undertaken only after a deliberate and thoughtful review of the case. If an employee is fired, he or she may file a wrongful discharge suit claiming the termination was "without just or sufficient cause," implying a lack of fair treatment by management.

If an employee termination is to be upheld for good cause, what constitutes fair employee treatment? This question is not easily answered, but standards governing just cause discharge do exist, in the form of rules developed in the field of labor arbitration.[63] These rules consist of a set of guidelines that are applied by arbitrators to dismissal cases to determine if management had just cause for the termination.[64] These guidelines are normally set forth in the form of questions, provided in Figure 13.11. For example, before discharging an employee, did the manager forewarn the person of possible disciplinary action? A no answer to any of the seven questions in the figure generally means that just cause was not established and that management's decision to terminate was arbitrary, capricious, or discriminatory. The significance of these guidelines is that they are being applied not only by arbitrators in discharge cases, but also by judges in wrongful discharge suits. It is critical that managers at all levels understand the just cause guidelines, including their proper application.[65]

### Informing the Employee

Regardless of the reasons for a discharge, it should be done with personal consideration for the employee affected. Every effort should be made to ease the trauma a discharge creates.[66] The employee must be informed honestly, yet tactfully, of the exact reasons for the action. Such candor can help the employee face the problem and adjust to it in a constructive manner.

Managers may wish to discuss, and even rehearse, with their peers the upcoming termination meeting. This practice can ensure that all important points are covered while giving confidence to the manager. While managers agree that there is no single right way to conduct the discharge meeting, the following guidelines will help to make the discussion more effective:

1. Come to the point within the first two or three minutes, and list in a logical order all reasons for the termination.
2. Be straightforward and firm, yet tactful, and remain resolute in your decision.
3. Make the discussion private, businesslike, and fairly brief.

**FIGURE 13.11**

**"Just Cause" Discharge Guidelines**

1. Did the organization forewarn the employee of the possible disciplinary consequences of his or her action?
2. Were management's requirements of the employee reasonable in relation to the orderly, efficient, and safe operation of the organization's business?
3. Did management, before discharging the employee, make a reasonable effort to establish that the employee's performance was unsatisfactory?
4. Was the organization's investigation conducted in a fair and objective manner?
5. Did the investigation produce sufficient evidence of proof of guilt as charged?
6. Has management treated this employee under its rules, orders, and penalties as it has other employees in similar circumstances?
7. Did the discharge fit the misconduct, considering the seriousness of the proven offense, the employee's service record, and any mitigating circumstances?

4. Avoid making accusations against the employee and injecting personal feelings into the discussion.

5. Avoid bringing up any personality differences between you and the employee.

6. Provide any information concerning severance pay and the status of benefits and coverage.

7. Explain how you will handle employment inquiries from future employers.

Termination meetings should be held in a neutral location, such as a conference room, so that the manager can leave if the meeting gets out of control. The prudent manager will also have determined, prior to the termination decision, that the dismissal does not violate any legal rights the employee may have. (We have discussed elsewhere certain federal and state laws and court decisions that limit an employer's freedom to discharge employees.)

Finally, when terminated employees are escorted off the premises the removal must not serve to defame the employee. Managers should not give peers the impression that the terminated employee was dishonest or untrustworthy. Increasingly, terminated employees are pursuing lawsuits that go beyond the issue of whether their discharge was for business-related reasons.[67]

### Due Process

**Due process**

Employee's right to present his or her position during a disciplinary action

Management has traditionally possessed the right to direct employees and to take corrective action when needed. Nevertheless, when employees are alleged to have violated organizational rules, many individuals also believe that employees should not be disciplined without the protection of due process. HR managers normally define **due process** as the employee's right to be heard—the right of the employee to tell his or her side of the story regarding the alleged infraction of organizational rules. Due process serves to ensure that a full and fair investigation of employee misconduct occurs. Normally, due process is provided employees through the employer's appeals procedure. However, proactive employers will additionally incorporate the following principles—or rights—in their interpretation of due process:

1. The right to know job expectations and the consequences of not fulfilling those expectations.

2. The right to consistent and predictable management action for the violation of rules.

3. The right to fair discipline based on facts, the right to question those facts, and the right to present a defense.

4. The right to appeal disciplinary action.

5. The right to progressive discipline.

# Appealing Disciplinary Actions

With growing frequency, organizations are taking steps to protect employees from arbitrary and inequitable treatment by their supervisors. A particular emphasis is placed on creating a climate in which employees are assured that they can voice their dissatisfaction with their superiors without fear of reprisal. This safeguard can be provided through the implementation of a formal procedure for appealing disciplinary actions.

# Alternative Dispute-Resolution Procedures

**OBJECTIVE 6**

In unionized workplaces, grievance procedures are stated in virtually all labor agreements. In nonunion organizations, however, **alternative dispute-resolution** (ADR) procedures are a relatively recent development.[68] The employer's interest stems from the desire to meet employees' expectations for fair treatment in the workplace while guaranteeing them due process—in the hope of minimizing discrimination claims or wrongful discharge suits.[69] ADR procedures received a boost from the U.S. Supreme Court when, in *Gilmer v Interstate/Johnson Lane Corp.*, the Court enforced a private agreement that required the arbitration of an age-discrimination claim.[70] Additionally, Section 118 of the Civil Rights Act of 1991 encourages the use of ADR procedures, including arbitration. In 1998, the Alternative Dispute Resolution Act was issued for use by employees in the federal sector.[71] The act causes litigants in civil cases filed in federal district court to consider using an ADR process to resolve their dispute.[72]

Some organizations champion these procedures as an avenue for upward communication for employees and as a way to gauge the temperament of the workforce. Others view these systems as a way to resolve minor problems before they mushroom into major issues, thus leading to improved employee morale and productivity.

The appeal procedures that will be described in this chapter are the step-review system, the peer-review system, the use of a hearing officer, the open-door policy, the use of an ombudsman, and arbitration.

## Step-Review Systems

As Figure 13.12 illustrates, a **step-review system** is based on a preestablished set of steps—normally four—for the review of an employee complaint by successively higher levels of management. These procedures are patterned after the union grievance systems we will discuss in Chapter 15. For example, they normally require that the employee's complaint be formalized as a written statement. Managers at each step are required to provide a full response to the complaint within a specified time period, perhaps three to five working days.

An employee is sometimes allowed to bypass the meeting with his or her immediate supervisor if the employee fears reprisal from this person. Unlike appeal systems in unionized organizations, however, nonunion appeal procedures ordinarily do not provide for a neutral third party—such as an arbitrator—to serve as the judge of last resort.[73] In most step-review systems, the president, chief executive officer, vice president, or HR director acts as the final authority, and this person's decision is

**USING THE INTERNET**

Current federal and state laws and leading court decisions regarding alternative dispute-resolution procedures can be found on the American Arbitration Association web site at:

http://www.adr.org/

**Alternative dispute resolution (ADR)**
Term applied to different types of employee complaint or dispute-resolution procedures

**Step-review system**
System for reviewing employee complaints and disputes by successively higher levels of management

**FIGURE 13.12**

**Conventional Step-Review Appeal Procedure**

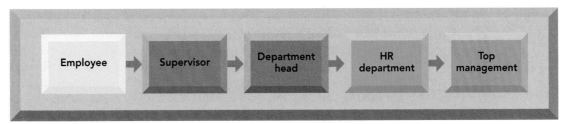

Employee → Supervisor → Department head → HR department → Top management

not appealable. Some organizations give employees assistance in preparing their complaint cases. For example, an employee who desires it may be able to get advice and counsel from a designated person in the HR department before discussing the issue with management.

Unfortunately, step-review systems may not yield their intended benefits. Employees may believe that management is slow in responding to complaints and that management's response often does not solve the problem. Furthermore, employees may believe that, regardless of policies forbidding reprisal, supervisors would still hold it against them if they exercised their rights as spelled out in the step-review system. These concerns should not lead to the conclusion that all step-review systems are ineffective, but rather that management must take special precautions to ensure the systems work and provide the benefits intended. We offer the following suggestions to make step-review systems successful:

1. Consult employees when designing the complaint system. Commitment to the process is enhanced when employees participate in its design.
2. Train supervisors in handling complaints.
3. Handle complaints in a timely manner.
4. Make sure that all employees know how to use the complaint procedure and *encourage* them to use the system when they feel aggrieved.
5. Handle cases in a fair manner and assure employees that they need not fear reprisal for filing complaints.

## Peer-Review Systems

**Peer-review system**

System for reviewing employee complaints that utilizes a group composed of equal numbers of employee representatives and management appointees, which functions as a jury since its members weigh evidence, consider arguments, and after deliberation vote independently to render a final decision

A **peer-review system**, also called a complaint committee, is composed of equal numbers of employee representatives and management appointees. Employee representatives are normally elected by secret ballot by their co-workers for a rotating term, whereas management representatives are assigned, also on a rotating basis. A peer-review system functions as a jury since its members weigh evidence, consider arguments, and, after deliberation, vote independently to render a final decision.

Organizations such as Turner Brothers Trucking, Northrop Corporation, Polaroid, and Citicorp consider one of the benefits of the peer-review system to be the sense of justice that it creates among employees. The peer-review system can be used as the sole method for resolving employee complaints, or it can be used in conjunction with a step-review system. For example, if an employee is not satisfied with management's action at step 1 or 2 in the step-review system, the employee can submit the complaint to the peer-review committee for final resolution.

## Use of a Hearing Officer

**Hearing officer**

Person who holds a full-time position with an organization but assumes a neutral role when deciding cases between the aggrieved employees and management

This procedure is ordinarily confined to large organizations, such as a state government, where employees may be represented by unions. The **hearing officer** holds a full-time position with the organization but assumes a neutral role when deciding cases between an aggrieved employee and management. Hearing officers are employed by the organization; however, they function independently from other managers and occupy a special place in the organizational hierarchy. Their success rests on being perceived as neutral, highly competent, and completely unbiased in handling employee complaints. They hear cases upon request, almost always made by the employee. After considering the evidence and facts presented, they render decisions or awards that are normally final and binding on both sides. Like the peer-review system, the hearing-officer system can be used by itself or as part of a step-review procedure.

### Open-Door Policy

The open-door policy is an old standby for settling employee complaints. In fact, most managers, regardless of whether their organization has adopted a formal open-door policy, profess to maintain one for their employees. The traditional **open-door policy** identifies various levels of management above the immediate supervisor that an aggrieved employee may contact; the levels may extend as high as a vice president, president, or chief executive officer. Typically the person who acts as "the court of last resort" is the HR director or a senior staff official.

The problems with an open-door policy are well documented. Two of its major weaknesses are the unwillingness of managers to listen honestly to employee complaints and worker reluctance to approach managers with their complaints. As an employee once told the authors of this text, "My manager has an open-door policy but the door is only open one inch." Obviously this employee felt he had little opportunity to get through to his manager. Other problems are attributed to this system as well. The open-door policy generally fails to guarantee consistent decision making since what is fair to one manager may seem unfair to another. Higher-level managers tend to support supervisors for fear of undermining authority. And, as a system of justice, open-door policies lack credibility with employees. Still, the open-door policy is often successful where it is supported by all levels of management and where management works to maintain a reputation for being fair and open-minded.[74]

**Open-door policy**
Policy of settling grievances that identifies various levels of management above the immediate supervisor for employee contact

### Ombudsman System

Rockwell, Johnson and Johnson, Herman Miller, Inc., Morley Builders, and Volvo are just a few of the companies who employ the expertise of an ombudsman.[75] An **ombudsman** is a designated individual from whom employees may seek counsel for the resolution of their complaints. The ombudsman listens to an employee's complaint and attempts to resolve it by mediating a solution between the employee and the supervisor. This individual works cooperatively with both sides to reach a settlement, often employing a clinical approach to problem solving. Since the ombudsman has no authority to finalize a solution to the problem, compromises are highly possible and all concerned tend to feel satisfied with the outcome.

**Ombudsman**
Designated individual from whom employees may seek counsel for the resolution of their complaints

To function successfully, ombudsmen must be able to operate in an atmosphere of confidentiality that does not threaten the security of the managers or subordinates who are involved in a complaint. While ombudsmen do not have power to overrule the decision made by an employee's supervisor, they should be able to appeal the decision up the line if they believe an employee is not being treated fairly. Apart from helping to achieve equity for employees, ombudsmen can help to provide management with a check on itself.

### Arbitration

Prompted by the *Gilmer* decision, private employers may require that employees submit their employment disputes for a binding resolution through arbitration. (Arbitration is fully explained in Chapter 15.) Arbitration is used primarily to resolve discrimination suits in areas of age, gender, sexual harassment, and race.[76] Employers cite savings in litigation costs and avoidance of time delays and unfavorable publicity as advantages for using arbitration. However, to ensure the legality of their arbitration policies, employers must

- Have a clear, well-defined, and widely communicated arbitration policy
- Specify those topics subject to arbitration
- Inform employees of the rights they are relinquishing by signing an arbitration agreement
- Provide a procedurally fair arbitration system
- Allow for the nonbiased selection of an arbitrator or arbitration panel[77]

As an alternative to arbitration, ADR proponents champion the use of mediation as an effective procedure to resolve employee disputes (see Chapter 15). According to one authority, "Mediation might be described as a private discussion assisted by an impartial third party."[78] A cornerstone of mediation is that the parties maintain control over the settlement outcome.[79] The EEOC supports mediation as an effective way of reducing employment discrimination.[80]

# Organizational Ethics in Employee Relations

**Ethics**
Set of standards of conduct and moral judgments that help to determine right and wrong behavior

Throughout this textbook we have emphasized the legal requirements of HRM. Laws, agency rulings, and court decisions impact all aspects of the employment process—recruitment, selection, performance appraisal, safety and health, labor relations, and testing. Managers must comply with governmental regulations to promote an environment free from litigation.

However, beyond what is required by the law is the question of organizational ethics and the ethical—or unethical—behavior engaged in by managers.[81] **Ethics** can be defined as a set of standards of acceptable conduct and moral judgment. Ethics provides cultural guidelines—organizational or societal—that help decide between proper or improper conduct. Therefore, ethics, like the legal aspects of HR, permeates all aspects of the employment relationship. For example, managers may adhere to the organization's objective of hiring more protected-class members, but how those employees are supervised and treated once employed gets to the issue of managerial ethics.

Compliance with laws and the behavioral treatment of employees are two completely different aspects of the manager's job. While ethical dilemmas will always occur in the supervision of employees, it is how employees are treated that largely distinguishes the ethical organization from the unethical one. We believe that an ethical organization recognizes and values the contributions of employees and respects their personal rights.

Many organizations have their own code of ethics that governs relations with employees and the public at large.[82] This written code focuses attention on ethical values and provides a basis for the organization, and individual managers, to evaluate their plans and actions. HR departments have been given a greater role in communicating the organization's values and standards, monitoring compliance with its code of ethics, and enforcing the standards throughout the organization. Organizations now have ethics committees and ethics ombudsmen to provide training in ethics to employees. The ultimate goal of ethics training is to avoid unethical behavior and adverse publicity; to gain a strategic advantage; but most of all, to treat employees in a fair and equitable manner, recognizing them as productive members of the organization.

# SUMMARY

**OBJECTIVE 1**
Both employees and employers have rights and expectations in the employment relationship. The employment-at-will doctrine regards the rights of employees and employers to terminate the employment relationship while the implied-contract concept is an exception to the employment-at-will doctrine. Under this concept, an employer's oral or written statements may form a contractual obligation that can preclude the automatic termination of employees. Constructive discharge occurs when an employee voluntarily terminates employment but subsequently alleges he or she was forced to quit because of intolerable working conditions imposed by the employer.

**OBJECTIVE 2**
Once employed, employees expect certain privacy rights regarding personal freedom from unwarranted intrusion into their personal affairs. These rights extend over such issues as substance abuse and drug testing, searches and surveillance, off-duty privacy rights, e-mail and voice mail privacy, and genetic testing.

**OBJECTIVE 3**
The HR department, in combination with other managers, should establish disciplinary policies. This will help achieve both acceptance of the policy and its consistent application. To reduce the need for discipline, organizational rules and procedures should be widely known, reviewed on a regular basis, and written and explained to employees. The rules must relate to the safe and efficient operation of the organization. When managers overlook the enforcement of rules, they must reemphasize the rule and its enforcement before disciplining an employee.

**OBJECTIVE 4**
The term "discipline" has three meanings—punishment, orderly behavior, and the training of employee conduct. When used with employees, discipline should serve to correct undesirable employee behavior, creating within the em-

ployee a desire for self-control. This third definition of discipline can be achieved only when managers conduct a complete and unbiased investigation of employee misconduct. The investigation of employee misconduct begins with the proper documentation of wrongdoing. When managers are investigating employee problems they need to know specifically the infraction of the employee, whether the employee knew of the rule violated, and any extenuating circumstances that might justify the employee's conduct. When employees are to receive discipline, the rule must be uniformly enforced and the past work record of the employee must be considered.

**OBJECTIVE 5**
The two approaches to discipline are progressive discipline and positive discipline. Progressive discipline follows a series of steps based upon increasing the degrees of corrective action. The corrective action applied should match the severity of the employee misconduct. Positive discipline, based upon reminders, is a cooperative discipline approach where employees accept responsibility for the desired employee improvement. The focus is on coping with the unsatisfactory performance and dissatisfactions of employees before the problems become major.

**OBJECTIVE 6**
Alternative dispute-resolution procedures present ways by which employees exercise their due process rights. The most common forms of ADRs are step-review systems, peer-review systems, the use of hearing officers, the open-door system, the ombudsman system, and arbitration.

**OBJECTIVE 7**
Ethics in HRM extends beyond the legal requirements of managing employees. Managers engage in ethical behavior when employees are treated in an objective and fair way and when an employee's personal and work-related rights are respected and valued.

## KEY TERMS

alternative dispute resolution
  (ADR)
constructive discharge
discipline
due process
employee rights

employment-at-will principle
ethics
hearing officer
hot-stove rule
negligence
ombudsman

open-door policy
peer-review system
positive, or nonpunitive,
  discipline
progressive discipline
step-review system

## DISCUSSION QUESTIONS

 1. Define the employment-at-will doctrine. What are the three major court exceptions to the doctrine?

 2. What are the legislative and court restrictions on employer drug testing in both the private and the public sector?

 3. If you were asked to develop a policy on discipline, what topics would you cover in the policy?

 4. What should be the purpose of an investigative interview, and what approach should be taken in conducting it?

 5. Discuss why documentation is so important to the disciplinary process. What constitutes correct documentation?

 6. Describe progressive and positive discipline, noting the differences between these two approaches.

 7. What do you think would constitute an effective alternative dispute-resolution system? What benefits would you expect from such a system? If you were asked to rule on a discharge case, what facts would you analyze in deciding whether to uphold or reverse the employer's action?

 8. Working by yourself, or in a team, identify ethical dilemmas that could arise in the HR areas of selection, performance appraisal, safety and health, privacy rights, and compensation.

## The Whistle-Blower's Dilemma

Tom Corbin has worked as a manager at Harbor Electric for eleven years. Shortly after being promoted to director of the electric generator division, he made a discovery that dramatically changed his managerial career. While cleaning out some old files, he stumbled across a seven-year-old report that clearly documented some design flaws in the company's large industrial R-1 electric generator. While these flaws presented no safety hazards, they held the potential to increase construction costs, creating cost overruns for the purchaser. Also, though breakdowns would probably not be immediate, the flaws made the units more susceptible to mechanical failure. If breakdowns occurred after the warranty period had expired, the costly repairs would have to be paid for by the purchasing organization. The R-1 generators were sold mainly to utility companies, so cost overruns or the cost of mechanical failures would ultimately be passed on to consumers.

Corbin was genuinely upset by the report and quickly decided to show it to Robert Medlock, the vice president of manufacturing. Their meeting was brief and to the point. Medlock expressed surprise and dismay at the report but seemed to have no great desire to correct the problems. While not denying the design flaws, Medlock explained that the R-1 generator was basically a well-designed unit that offered an excellent value to purchasers. He further noted that the success of the company rested largely on sales of the generator and to admit any design flaws at this time would be catastrophic to future sales. Public exposure could lead to complaints from consumer groups and government regulators while providing competitors with damaging product information. When Corbin argued that Harbor was essentially "ripping off" utility companies and consumers, he was told to cool down and to forget he ever saw the report. Corbin replied that he couldn't believe Harbor would risk its reputation by selling generators with potentially costly design flaws. He concluded the meeting by saying that he had joined the company because of its honesty and dedication to responsible customer relations, but now he had serious doubts.

Corbin stormed out of Medlock's office. On his way back to the generator division, he considered calling the state utility commission to report the design flaws. He recognized clearly what public knowledge of the problems would do to sales of the R-1 generator. He also considered the consequences of reporting the design flaws on his career with Harbor Electric.

### QUESTIONS

1. Discuss all the possible consequences of reporting the design flaws to the state utility commission, including the possible consequences for Corbin's career.
2. Suggest a proper course of action for Corbin in correcting the problems surrounding the design flaws in the R-1 generator.

## "You Can't Fire Me! I Passed the Test"

"We had no choice but to fire him, " explained supervisor Tim Walton. "Jerry knew our drug policy and he simply chose to violate it." The drug policy was clear and known to all employees, Walton said. "Employees suspected of drug use are required to submit to a drug test on demand by the employer. If employees could take drug tests when they wanted, we would never catch drug abusers." At the company's ADR hearing, employee Jerry Butler responded, "They can't fire me! I refused to take the test because I was sick in the hospital. Besides, I got sick due to heat exhaustion caused by excessive temperatures on the shop floor. I took the test the next day and passed it." Replied Walton, "All we know is that Jerry refused the test and that's good enough for us. No additional investigation was needed. Besides, some drugs leave the human system fairly quickly. We need an immediate drug test."

The case arose when two employees of the steel contractor observed Jerry Butler in the employees' locker room with white powder under his nose. Suspecting drug use, they reported the incident to Walton. Two days later, Butler was asked to submit to a drug test while recovering from heat exhaustion in the local hospital.

He refused the test, claiming he was too ill to comply with the demand. In support of his claim, Butler had the attending doctor explain that he was unable to take the test because of his illness. The following day Butler took and passed the required drug test. The company, however, refused to reconsider its termination decision. At the hearing, Jerry Butler also claimed that the company fired him to avoid paying his workers' compensation claims.

Source: Adapted from a case reported in *Bulletin to Management*, February 25, 1999, 64. All names are fictitious.

## QUESTIONS

1. If you were selected to hear this case, what would your decision be? Explain fully.
2. What other information might be useful to resolve this case?
3. Would the company create any ethical dilemmas by calling employees as witnesses against Jerry Butler? Explain fully.

## NOTES AND REFERENCES

1. Interview with Robert J. Deeny, Phoenix, Arizona, February 10, 1999.
2. Barbara Kate Repa, *Your Rights in the Workplace* (Berkeley, Calif.: Nolo Press, 1997).
3. Alfred G. Felio, *Primer on Individual Employee Rights* (Washington, D.C.: Bureau of National Affairs, 1996).
4. Samuel Greengard, "Privacy: Entitlement or Illusion?" *Personnel Journal* 75, no. 5 (May 1996): 74–88.
5. Benjamin B. Dunford and Dennis J. Devine, "Employment-At-Will and Employee Discharge: A Justice Perspective on Legal Action Following Termination," *Personnel Psychology* 51, no. 4 (Winter 1998): 903–34.
6. Christopher Bouvier, "Why At-Will Employment Is Dying," *Personnel Journal* 75, no. 5 (May 1996): 123–28.
7. *Adair v United States*, 2078 U.S. 161 (1908).
8. Susan E. Long, "Whistleblower Who Participates in Wrongdoing Still Protected," *HRFocus* 76, no. 2 (February 1999): 3.
9. David C. Skinner, William T. Edwards, and Gregory L. Gravlee, "Selecting Employment Practices Liability Insurance," *HRMagazine* 43, no. 10 (September 1998): 146–152. See also Leslie Scism, "More Firms Insure against Worker Suits," *The Wall Street Journal*, November 15, 1996, A-2.
10. John J. Myers, David V. Radack, and Paul M. Yenerall, "Making the Most of Employment Contracts," *HRMagazine* 43, no. 9 (August 1998): 106–9.

11. *Toussaint v Blue Cross and Blue Shield of Michigan*, 408 Mich. 579: 292 N.W.2d 880 (1980).
12. Jeffrey London, "Bring Your Employee Handbook into the Millennium," *HRFocus* 76, no.1 (January 1999): 6.
13. George W. Bohlander, "Constructive Discharge— A.K.A. Was It a Quit or a Discharge? Understanding the Doctrine and Prevention of Constructive Discharge Cases," *Journal of Individual Employment Rights* 8, no. 1 (1999–2000): 47–59.
14. *Young v Southwestern Savings and Loan Association*, 509 F.2d 140, 141 5th Cir. (1975).
15. For two instructive cases on constructive discharge, see *Faragher v City of Boca Raton*, 1998 WL 336322 (U.S.), and *Burlington Industries v Ellerth*, 1998 WL 336326 (U.S.).
16. George D. Mesritz, "Constructive Discharge and Employer Intent: Are the Courts Split over a Distinction without a Difference?" *Employee Relations Law Journal* 21, no. 4 (Spring 1996): 89–98.
17. Barclay J. Beery, "Small Break in the Clouds: Status of the WARN Act's Sales Exclusion," *Labor Law Journal* 49, no. 5 (May 1998): 1008–12.
18. Steven C. Bennett and Scott D. Locke, "Privacy in the Workplace," *Labor Law Journal* 49, no. 1 (January 1998): 781–87.
19. The common definition of privacy as a "general right of the individual to be let alone" is captured in the words of Samuel Warren and Louis Brandeis in their seminal article on privacy. See Samuel Warren and

Louis Brandeis, "The Right to Privacy," *Harvard Law Review* 193, 205 (1890).

20. Maureen Mineham, "Debate on Workplace Privacy Likely to Intensify," *HRMagazine* 44, no. 1 (January 1999): 142.

21. Gary Anton and Joseph J. Ward, "Every Breath You Take: Employee Privacy Rights in the Workpalce—An Orwellian Prophecy Come True?" *Labor Law Journal* 49, no. 3 (March 1998): 897–911.

22. Kathleen Menda, "The New Battle over Workplace Privacy," *HRMagazine* 43, no. 5 (April 1998): 130–32.

23. Anton and Ward, "Every Breath You Take," 897.

24. Jane Easter Bahls, "Drugs in the Workplace," *HRMagazine* 43, no. 2 (February 1998): 81–87.

25. "Substance Abuse Soaring," *HRFocus* 75, no. 9 (September 1998): 5.

26. Jane Easter Bahls, "Dealing with Drugs: Keep It Legal," *HRMagazine* 43, no. 4 (March 1998): 104–116.

27. David Schitt, "Ready for the Road," *Occupational Health and Safety* 65, no. 3 (March 1996): 51–54. See also Scott F. Cooper, "At Issue for Private Sector Employers: New DOT Regulations Mandate Alcohol Testing for Employees in Safety-Sensitive Positions," *Employee Relations Law Journal* 21, no. 1 (Summer 1995): 53–71.

28. *Harmon v Thornburgh,* CA, DC No. 88-5265 (July 30, 1989), *Treasury Employees Union v Von Raab,* US SupCt No. 86-18796 (March 21, 1989); *City of Annapolis v United Food & Commercial Workers Local 400,* Md. CtApp No. 38 (November 6, 1989), *Skinner v Railway Labor Executives Association,* US SupCt No. 87-1555 (March 21, 1989).

29. *Bluestein v Skinner,* 908 F.2d 451 9th Cir. (1990).

30. Jonathan R. Mook and Erin E. Powell, "Substance Abuse and the ADA: What Every Employer Should Know," *Employee Relations Law Journal* 22, no. 2 (Autumn 1996): 57–77.

31. 42 U.S.C. § 12210 (b).

32. John M. Moorwood, "Drug Testing in the Private Sector and Its Impact on Employees' Right to Privacy," *Labor Law Journal* 45, no. 12 (December 1994): 131–48.

33. Repa, *Your Rights,* 6/18–6/21.

34. Information on individual state laws can be obtained from *A Guide to State Drug Testing Laws and Legislation,* published annually by the Institute for a Drug-Free Workplace. A free copy of the institute's *Mandatory Guidelines for Federal Workplace Drug Testing Programs* and its official list of certified laboratories can be obtained by calling the National Clearing House for Alcohol and Drug Information at (800) 729-6686. The American Bar Association's *Model Drug Testing in Employment Statutes* is also useful.

35. David John Hoekstra, "Workplace Searches: A Legal Overview," *Labor Law Journal* 47, no. 2 (February 1996): 127–38.

36. Kevin J. Conlon, "Privacy in the Workplace," *Labor Law Journal* 48, no. 8 (August 1997): 444–52. See also Robert L. Brady, "Workplace Searches: Avoid Legal Problems," *HRFocus* 72, no. 4 (April 1995): 18.

37. Electronic Communications Privacy Act, 18 U.S.C. §§ 2510 to 2720.

38. Repa, *Your Rights,* 6/41.

39. Dan Wise, "Private Matters," *Business and Health* 13, no. 2 (February 1995): 22–28.

40. Robert L. Brady, "Personnel Files: Keep Your Policies Updated," *HRFocus* 72, no. 2 (February 1995): 18. See also Brenda Paik Sunoo, "When to View Personnel Files," *Personnel Journal* 7, no. 7 (July 1996): 92.

41. Richard Behar, "Who's Reading Your E-Mail?" *Fortune,* February 3, 1997, 57–70; Richard F. Federico and James M. Bowley, "The Great E-Mail Debate," *HRMagazine* 41, no. 1 (January 1996): 67–72.

42. Samuel A. Thumma, "E-Mail Laps the Workplace," *HRFocus* 73, no. 7 (July 1998): 9.

43. Kathy J. Lang and Elaine Davis, "Personnel E-Mail: An Employee Benefit Causing Increasing Privacy Concerns," *Employee Benfits Journal* 22, no. 2 (June 1996): 30–33.

44. Jim Everett, "Internet Security," *Employee Benefits Journal* 23, no. 3 (September 1998): 14–18.

45. Jonathan A. Segal, "The Perils of High Tech Talk," *HRMagazine* 42, no. 6 (July 1997): 159–68.

46. Alan R. Parham, "Developing a Technology Policy," *Employee Benefits Policy* 23, no. 3 (September 1998): 3–5. See also Joseph Maddaloni Jr., "Monitoring Employee Communications," *HRFocus* 75, no. 12 (December 1998): 57; and Robert L. Brady, "Electronic Mail: Drafting a Policy," *HRFocus* 72, no. 10 (October 1995): 19.

47. Melinda Socol Herbst, "Employers May Police Some Workplace Romances," *The National Law Journal,* February 26, 1996, C19; Douglas Massengill and Donald J. Petersen, "Legal Challenges to No Fraternization Rules," *Labor Law Journal* 46, no. 7 (July 1995): 429–35.

48. James A. Burns, Jr., "Personal Relationships of Employees: Are They Any Business of an Employer?" *Employee Relations Law Journal* 23, no. 4 (Spring 1998): 171–77.

49. Gillian Flynn, "Love Contracts Help Fend Off Harassment Suits," *Workforce* 78, no. 3 (March 1999): 106–8.

50. Material for this section was largely obtained from "Genetic Information in the Workforce," *Labor Law Journal* 49, no. 2 (February 1998): 867–76. The article is based on a report by the Department of Labor, the Department of Health and Human Services, the Equal Employment Opportunity Commission, and the Department of Justice.

51. Gary Bielous, "The Five Worst Discipline Mistakes," *Supervisory Management* 40, no. 1 (January 1995): 14–15.

52. George W. Bohlander, "Why Arbitrators Overturn Managers in Employee Supervision and Discharge Cases," *Journal of Collective Negotiations in the Public Sector* 23, no. 1 (Spring 1994): 73–89.

53. Donald C. Mosley, Leon C. Megginson, and Paul H. Pietri, *Supervisory Management: The Art of Developing and Empowering People,* 4th ed. (Cincinnati: South-Western, 1997).

54. Cecily A. Waterman and Teresa A. Maginn, "Investigating Suspect Employees," *HRMagazine* 38, no. 1 (January 1993): 85–87.

55. Rebecca K. Spar, "Keeping Internal Investigations Confidential," *HRMagazine* 41, no. 1 (January 1996): 33–36.

56. Neal Orkin and Miriam Heise, "*Weingarten* through the Looking Glass," *Labor Law Journal* 48, no. 3 (March 1997): 157–63.

57. *NLRB v Weingarten, Inc.,* 95 S.Ct. 959 (1975), 402 U.S. 251, 43 L. Ed. 2d. 171.

58. Christopher J. Martin, "Some Reflections on *Weingarten* and the Free Speech Rights of Union Stewards," *Employee Relations Law Journal* 18, no. 4 (Spring 1993): 647–53.

59. Paul Falcone, "The Fundamentals of Progressive Discipline," *HRMagazine* 42, no. 2 (February 1997): 90–94.

60. Readers interested in the pioneering work on positive discipline should see James R. Redeker, "Discipline, Part 1: Progressive Systems Work Only by Accident," *Personnel* 62, no. 10 (October 1985): 8–12; James R. Redeker, "Discipline, Part 2: The Nonpunitive Approach Works by Design," *Personnel* 62, no. 11 (November 1985): 7–14. See also Alan W. Bryant, "Replacing Punitive Discipline with a Positive Approach," *Personnel Administrator* 29, no. 2 (February 1984): 79–87.

61. Dick Grove, *Discipline without Punishment* (New York: American Management Association, 1996).

62. Brenda Paik Sunoo, "Positive Discipline: Sending the Right or Wrong Message," *Personnel Journal* 75, no. 8 (August 1996): 109–10.

63. For an excellent explanation of just cause discharge guidelines, see Adolph M. Koven and Susan N. Smith, *Just Cause: The Seven Tests,* 2nd ed. (Washington, D.C.: Bureau of National Affairs, 1992).

64. George W. Bohlander and Donna Blancero, "A Study of Reversal Determinants in Discipline and Discharge Arbitration Awards: The Impact of Just Cause Standards," *Labor Studies Journal* 21, no. 3 (Fall 1996): 3–18.

65. For an expanded discussion of just cause, see Frank Elkouri and Edna Asher Elkouri, *How Arbitration Works,* 4th ed. (Washington, D.C.: Bureau of National Affairs, 1985): 650–54.

66. Katherine A. Karl and Barry W. Hancock, "Expert Advice on Employment Termination Practices: How Expert Is It?" *Public Personnel Management* 28, no. 1 (Spring 1999): 51–61.

67. John E. Lyncheski, "Mishandling Termination Causes Legal Nightmare," *HRMagazine* 40, no. 5 (May 1995): 25–30.

68. Jean Baker, "ADR in the Federal Sector," *Newsletter of Dispute Resolution Law and Practice* 3, no. 3 (September 1998): 2–4. See also Susan A. Klein, "AAA President Slate Focuses on ADR Challenges," *Dispute Resolution Journal* 51, no. 2–3 (April 1996): 29–33, 130–35.

69. "Alternative Dispute Resolution Works Best before Battle Lines Are Drawn Too Deeply," *Bulletin to Management* 50, no. 8 (February 25, 1999): 1.

70. *Gilmer v Interstate/Johnson Lane Corp.,* 111 S. Ct. 1647 (1991).

71. Alternative Dispute Resolution Act (1998): P.L. 105–314.

72. "ADR Authorized in the Federal Courts," *Newsletter of Dispute Resolution Law and Practice* 3, no. 4 (December 1998): 4–5. See also Baker, "ADR in the Federal Sector," 5–7.

73. For an excellent review of ADR procedures, see Douglas M. McCabe, "Corporate Nonunion Grievance Arbitration Systems: A Procedural Analysis," *Labor Law Journal* 40, no. 7 (July 1989): 432–37.

74. Antonio Ruiz-Quintanilla and Donna Blancero, "Open Door Policies: Measuring Impact Using Attitude Surveys," *Human Resource Management* 35, no. 3 (Fall 1996): 269–89.

75. Olaf Isachson, "Do You Need an Ombudsman?" *HRFocus* 75, no. 9 (September 1998): 6.

76. Evan J. Spelfogel, "Mandatory Arbitration vs. Employment Litigation," *Dispute Resolution Journal* 54, no. 2 (May 1999): 78–81. See also Mei L. Bickner, Christine Ver Ploeg, and Charles Feigenbaum, *Devel-*

*opments in Employment Arbitration Dispute Resolution Journal* 52, no. 1 (January 1997): 8–15; Joseph D. Garrison, "Mandatory Binding Arbitration Constitutes Little More Than a Waiver of a Worker's Rights," *Dispute Resolution Journal* 52, no. 4 (Fall 1997): 15–18.

77. George W. Bohlander and Robert J. Denny, "Designing a Legally Defensible Alternative Dispute Resolution (ADR) Agreement," *Journal of Individual Employment Rights* 7, no. 3 (1998–99): 189–98. See also Larry C. Drapkin and Stefano G. Moscato, "Arbitration Agreements: Getting around the Roadblocks," *HRFocus* 75, no. 12 (December 1998): 54.

78. Nancy Kauffman and Barbara Davis, "What Type of Mediation Do You Need?" *Dispute Resolution Journal* 53, no. 2 (May 1998): 10.

79. Joel E. Davidson, "Successful Mediation: The Do's and Don'ts," *Dispute Resolution Journal* 53, no. 3 (August 1998): 26–29.

80. "EEOC Expands Mediation Program," *Dispute Resolution Journal* 54, no. 2 (May 1999): 7.

81. "Ethics Are Questionable in the Workplace," *HRFocus* 75, no. 6 (June 1998): 7. See also "Ethics vs. Ethical," *HRFocus* 75, no. 4 (April 1998): 7.

82. Louis V. Larimer, "Reflections on Ethics and Integrity," *HRFocus* 74, no. 4 (April 1997): 5.

# The Manager as Counselor

Without question, employee counseling is an important part of a manager's job. Unlike a disciplinary interview, which is often restricted to obtaining and giving specific information, counseling is a process involving a dynamic relationship between two parties in which a person is free to discuss needs, feelings, and problems of concern for the purpose of obtaining help. As shown in Figure 13.A, counseling involves many variables on the side of the helper as well as the helpee. The relationship is the chief means of meshing the helpee's problems with the counsel

FIGURE 13.A

## Developing the Counseling Relationship

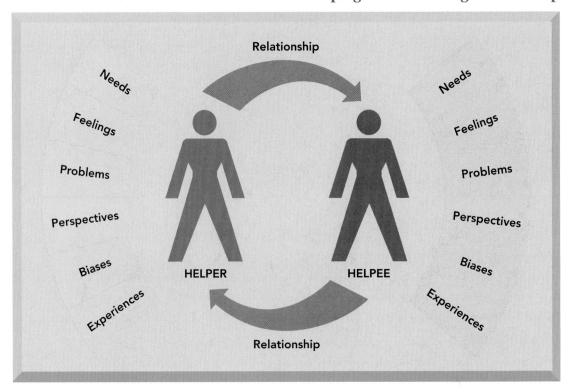

of the helper. While counseling can help employees with their personal problems—poor health, drug or alcohol abuse, family concerns, or financial difficulties—it can also help them deal with their job-related complaints or performance problems. The most effective way to reduce complaints is to encourage them to be brought out into the open.

# Nature of the Relationship

Counseling does not take place in a vacuum. The basic relationship between the two parties is the context in which counseling occurs. In organizations, authority affects the nature of the relationship between the two parties. An employee, for example, is not free to ignore a supervisor's help in matters related to the job, while in the counseling relationship, the helper is *advising* the helpee, not *instructing*. Another factor in the counseling relationship is confidentiality. Generally, what takes place in a counseling relationship is expected *not* to go beyond the two parties involved. There are times, however, when it is necessary to report certain types of information that may result in serious harm to others if not reported. Another factor that can affect the relationship is the manager's degree of commitment to be of assistance.

# Counseling Techniques

All of us have a natural tendency to judge, to evaluate, to approve or disapprove. Sometimes we engage in these judgments prematurely on the basis of our preconceived assumptions, thereby reducing our ability to communicate effectively. One way to limit these premature judgments is through a counseling technique called *active listening*. Active listening involves trying to understand what the other person is thinking by allowing this person to explain his or her perspective more fully without interruptions, questions, or introduction of new topics. The supervisor should maintain eye contact and should be relaxed and attentive to what the employee says or is trying to say.

While active listening is important in all circumstances, it is absolutely essential when

1. We do not understand how the other person feels and we need to understand the person's perspective.
2. We believe that what is being said is not as important as what is *not* being said.
3. The other person is so confused that a clear message cannot be communicated.

In addition to active listening, a manager will use a technique known as *reflecting feelings*. This technique involves expressing, in somewhat different words, the employee's feelings, either stated or implied. The goal is to focus on feelings rather than content, to bring vaguely expressed feelings into clearer focus, and to assist the person in talking about his or her feelings.

Examples of this technique include the use of expressions such as "You resent the way the boss treats you," and "You feel that you deserve more recognition from the company." The technique of reflecting feelings is especially useful in the early stages of counseling to bring out the employee's feelings. It is the standard procedure in nondirective counseling, a type of counseling to be discussed later.

Another way to assist the employee is to ask questions that will help that person understand his or her problem. Generally, they should be *open-ended questions,* i.e., those that cannot be answered with a yes or no—"Tell me more about your experiences with Mr. Jones." They should be questions that lead to clarification for the employee rather than information for the supervisor. Open-ended questions leave the employee free to take the interview in the direction that will do the most for him or her.

# Counseling Approaches

In attempting to help an employee who has a problem, a variety of counseling approaches are used. All of these approaches, however, depend on active listening. Sometimes the mere furnishing of information or advice may be the solution to what at first appeared to be a knotty problem. More frequently, however, the problem cannot be solved easily because of frustrations or conflicts that are accompanied by strong feelings such as fear, confusion, or hostility. A manager, therefore, needs to learn to use whatever approach appears to be suitable at the time. Flexibility is a key component of the counseling process.

## Directive Counseling

In *directive counseling,* the manager attempts to control, directly or indirectly, the topics the employee is talking about, describes the choices the employee faces, and/or advises the employee what to do. There are many instances in job counseling and contacts when it is appropriate to furnish information and advice in areas where the supervisor is knowledgeable and experienced, especially where information and/or advice is sought. However, where there are choices to be made and frustration and/or conflict are apparent, the use of the directive approach is to be avoided.

## Nondirective Counseling

In *nondirective counseling,* the employee is permitted to have maximum freedom in determining the course of the interview. The importance of nonevaluative listening as a communication skill is important here; it is the primary technique used in nondirective counseling. Fundamentally, the approach is to listen, with understanding and without criticism or appraisal, to the problem as it is described by the employee. The employee is encouraged, through the manager's attitude and reaction to what is said or not said, to express feelings without fear of shame, embarrassment, or reprisal.

The free expression that is encouraged in the nondirective approach tends to reduce tensions and frustrations. The employee who has had an opportunity to release pent-up feelings is usually in a better position to view the problem more objectively and with a problem-solving attitude. The permissive atmosphere allows the employee to try to work through the entanglements of the problem and to see it in a clearer perspective, often to reach a more desirable solution.

## Participative Counseling

The directive and nondirective approaches that have just been described are obviously at the extremes of a continuum. While a particular professional counselor may tend to be at one end of the continuum or the other, most managers vary their approach during the course of a session and/or in subsequent sessions. Many choose to emphasize a middle-of-the-road approach in which both parties work together in planning how a particular problem will be analyzed and solved. This approach, which may be thought of as *participative counseling*, is particularly suitable for use in work organizations.

Many of the problems that managers and supervisors are concerned with require not only that the subordinates' feelings be recognized, but also that subordinates be made aware of and adhere to management's expectations for them to be productive, responsible, and cooperative. On the other side of the coin, most people with problems would prefer to be actively involved in the solution once they see that there is a positive course of action available. In many of the work situations where counseling will be used, the participative approach is recommended in working with an individual over a period of time. To repeat: At different times, however, in the course of a single session, it may be advisable to be both directive and nondirective.

# When Counseling Doesn't Work

Counseling as a helping relationship has been discussed in order to present techniques that facilitate communication and help solve problems that affect the well-being of employees and the organization. It should be recognized, however, that counseling by managers will not always be successful in achieving this goal. Nevertheless, some progress can often be made by using counseling techniques where this type of action is appropriate. In cases where counseling apparently fails to yield results, it will often be necessary to take other measures, such as discipline or a transfer.

Since a manager or supervisor may not have the skill or time to handle the more complex personal problems of employees, there should be an established system for making referrals to trained counselors. Sometimes the problem area is one over which the supervisor has little or no influence, such as an employee's family relationships. Then it may be advisable for the supervisor to recommend the employee see a professional counselor. Usually the HR department has the responsibility for handling referrals to professionals who are competent and licensed to perform such services.

# chapter 14

# The Dynamics of Labor Relations

## AFTER STUDYING THIS CHAPTER, YOU SHOULD BE ABLE TO

**OBJECTIVE 1**

Identify and explain the principal federal laws that provide the framework for labor relations.

**OBJECTIVE 2**

Cite the reasons employees join unions.

**OBJECTIVE 3**

Describe the process by which unions organize employees and gain recognition as their bargaining agent.

**OBJECTIVE 4**

Describe the overall structure of the labor movement and the functions labor unions perform at the national and local levels.

**OBJECTIVE 5**

Describe the differences between private-sector and public-sector labor relations.

**OBJECTIVE 6**

Discuss some of the contemporary challenges to labor organizations.

Mention the word "union" and most people will have some opinion, positive or negative, regarding U.S. labor organizations. To some, the word evokes images of labor-management unrest—grievances, strikes, picketing, boycotts. To others, the word represents industrial democracy, fairness, opportunity, equal representation. Many think of unions as simply creating an adversarial relationship between employees and managers.

Regardless of attitudes toward them, since the mid-1800s unions have been an important force shaping organizational practices, legislation, and political thought in the United States. Today unions remain of interest because of their influence on organizational productivity, U.S. competitiveness, the development of labor law, and HR policies and practices. Like business organizations themselves, unions are undergoing changes in both operation and philosophy. Furthermore, after years of declining membership, unions are again actively organizing unrepresented employees. For example, the United Auto Workers is aggressively organizing workers at the Mercedes auto plant in Vance, Alabama, and at the Freightliner Corporation in Gastonia, North Carolina.[1] The AFL-CIO and national unions have targeted organizing as a top priority for the twenty-first century.

In spite of the long history of unions, the intricacies of labor relations are unfamiliar to many individuals. Therefore, this chapter describes government regulation of labor relations, the labor relations process, the reasons workers join labor organizations, the structure and leadership of labor unions, and contemporary challenges to labor organizations.

Unions and other labor organizations can affect significantly the ability of managers to direct and control the various functions of HRM. For example, union seniority provisions in the labor contract may influence who is selected for job promotions or training programs. Pay rates may be determined through union negotiations, or unions may impose restrictions on management's employee appraisal methods. Therefore, it is essential that managers in both the union and nonunion environment understand how unions operate and be thoroughly familiar with the important body of law governing labor relations. Remember, ignorance of labor legislation is no defense when managers and supervisors violate labor law. Before reading further, test your knowledge of labor relations law by answering the questions in Highlights in HRM 1.

# Government Regulation of Labor Relations

Unions have a long history in America, and the regulations governing labor relations have evolved from labor's historical developments. Prior to 1930, employers strongly opposed union growth, using court injunctions (e.g., court orders forbidding various union activities, such as picketing and strikes) and the "yellow-dog contract."[2] A yellow-dog contract was an employer's antiunion tactic by which employees bound themselves not to join a union while working for the employer's organization. Using strikebreakers, blacklisting employees (e.g., circulating the names of union supporters to other employers), and discriminating against those who favored unionization were other defensive maneuvers of employers.

As unions became stronger under federal laws passed during the 1930s, legislation was passed to curb union abuses of power and to protect the rights of union

**HRM 1**

# Test Your Labor Relations Know-How

**1.** An auto mechanic applied for a job with an automotive dealership. He was denied employment because of his union membership. Was the employer's action lawful?

      Yes_____          No_____

**2.** During a labor organizing drive, supervisors questioned individual employees about their union beliefs. Was this questioning permissible?

      Yes_____          No_____

**3.** When members of a union began wearing union buttons at work, management ordered the buttons to be removed. Was management within its rights?

      Yes_____          No_____

**4.** While an organizing drive was underway, an employer agreed—as a social gesture—to furnish refreshments at a holiday party. Was the employer acting within the law?

      Yes_____          No_____

**5.** A company distributed to other antiunion employers in the area a list of job applicants known to be union supporters. Was the distribution unlawful?

      Yes_____          No_____

**6.** During a union organizing drive, the owner of Servo Pipe promised her employees a wage increase if they would vote against the union. Can the owner legally make this promise to her employees?

      Yes_____          No_____

**7.** Employees have the right to file unfair labor practice charges against their union.

      Yes_____          No_____

**8.** An employee, who is a union member, has been scheduled for a disciplinary hearing. The employee requests that the union steward attend the meeting, but the request is denied. Can management legally deny this request?

      Yes_____          No_____

**9.** John Green, a maintenance engineer, has a poor work record. Management wishes to terminate his employment; however, Green is a union steward and he is highly critical of the company. Can management legally discharge this employee?

      Yes_____          No_____

**10.** During an organizing drive, an office manager expressed strong antiunion beliefs and called union officials "racketeers," "big stinkers," and a "bunch of radicals." He told employees who joined the union that they "ought to have their heads examined." Were the manager's comments legal?

      Yes_____          No_____

Answers are found at the end of this chapter.

members from unethical union activities. Today the laws governing labor relations seek to create an environment where both unions and employers can discharge their respective rights and responsibilities. Knowledge of labor relations laws will assist the understanding of how union-management relations operate in the United States. The first federal law pertaining to labor relations was the Railway Labor Act of 1926. Other major laws that affect labor relations in the private sector are the Norris-LaGuardia Act, the Wagner Act, the Taft-Hartley Act, and the Landrum-Griffin Act.

## The Railway Labor Act

The primary purpose of the Railway Labor Act (RLA) is to avoid service interruptions resulting from disputes between railroads and their operating unions. To achieve this end, the RLA contains two extensive procedures to handle these labor-management disputes. First, the National Mediation Board resolves negotiating impasses by using mediation and/or arbitration. The board is additionally charged with holding secret-ballot elections to determine if employees desire unionization. Second, the National Railway Adjustment Board functions to handle grievance and arbitration disputes arising during the life of an agreement.

## The Norris-LaGuardia Act

**USING THE INTERNET**

The U.S. National Labor Relations Board has its own web site. There you can find details of its organization, current cases, and decisions.
www.nlrb.gov/index.html

The Norris-LaGuardia Act, or Anti-Injunction Act, of 1932 severely restricts the ability of employers to obtain an injunction forbidding a union from engaging in peaceful picketing, boycotts, or various striking activities. Previously, federal court injunctions had been an effective antiunion weapon because they forced unions to either cease such activities or suffer the penalty of being held in contempt of court. Like the RLA, this act promotes collective bargaining and encourages the existence, formation, and effective operation of labor organizations.

Injunctions may still be granted in labor disputes. Before an injunction may be issued, however, employers must show that there were prior efforts to resolve the dispute peaceably, that law enforcement agencies are unable or unwilling to protect the employer's property, and that lack of an injunction will cause greater harm to the employer than to the union. This act also contains provisions that made the yellow-dog contract unenforceable in court.

## The Wagner Act

The Wagner Act of 1935 (or National Labor Relations Act) has had by far the most significant impact on union-management relations. It placed the protective power of the federal government firmly behind employee efforts to organize and bargain collectively through representatives of their choice.[3]

The Wagner Act created the National Labor Relations Board (NLRB) to govern labor relations in the United States. Although this act was amended by the Taft-Hartley Act, most of its major provisions that protected employee bargaining rights were retained. Section 7 of the law guarantees these rights as follows:

Employees shall have the right to self-organization, to form, join, or assist labor organizations, to bargain collectively through representatives of their own choosing, and to engage in concerted activities, for the purpose of collective bargaining or other mutual aid or protection, and shall also have the right to refrain from any or all of such activities except to the extent that such right may be affected by an agreement requiring membership in a labor organization as a condition of employment.[4]

To guarantee employees their Section 7 rights, Congress outlawed specific employer practices that deny employees the benefits of the law. Section 8 of the act lists five **unfair labor practices (ULPs)** of employers. These practices are defined as follows:

**Unfair labor practices (ULPs)**
Specific employer and union illegal practices that operate to deny employees their rights and benefits under federal labor law

1. Interfering with, restraining, or coercing employees in the exercise of their rights guaranteed in Section 7
2. Dominating or interfering with the formation or administration of any labor organization, or contributing financial or other support to it
3. Discriminating in regard to hiring or tenure of employment or any term or condition of employment so as to encourage or discourage membership in any labor organization
4. Discharging or otherwise discriminating against employees because they file charges or give testimony under this act
5. Refusing to bargain collectively with the duly chosen representatives of employees

Many ULPs are either knowingly or unknowingly committed each year by employers. In fiscal year 1998, for example, 30,439 unfair labor practices were filed with the NLRB. Alleged violations of the act by employers were filed in 23,630 cases.[5] The majority of all charges against employers concerned illegal discharge or other discrimination against employees. It is therefore imperative that managers at all levels receive training in employee rights and unfair labor practices. Where employers violate employee rights, the NLRB can "take such affirmative action including reinstatement of employment with or without back pay, as well as effectuate the policies of the Act, and make discriminated employees whole."[6] In 1998, the NLRB won for employees $92,133,616 in back pay because of employer violations of the act.

### The National Labor Relations Board

The agency responsible for administering and enforcing the Wagner Act is the National Labor Relations Board.[7] It serves the public interest by reducing interruptions in production or service caused by labor-management strife. To accomplish this goal the NLRB is given two primary charges: (1) to hold secret-ballot elections to determine whether employees wish to be represented by a union and (2) to prevent and remedy unfair labor practices. The NLRB does not act on its own initiative in either function. It processes only those charges of unfair labor practices and petitions for employee elections that may be filed at one of its regional offices or other smaller field offices.

## The Taft-Hartley Act

Because the bargaining power of unions increased significantly after the passage of the Wagner Act, certain restraints on unions were considered necessary. The Taft-Hartley Act of 1947 (also known as the Labor-Management Relations Act) defined the following activities as unfair union practices:

1. Restraint or coercion of employees in the exercise of their rights
2. Restraint or coercion of employers in the selection of the parties to bargain in their behalf
3. Persuasion of employers to discriminate against any of their employees
4. Refusal to bargain collectively with an employer
5. Participation in secondary boycotts and jurisdictional disputes
6. Attempt to force recognition from an employer when another union is already the certified representative
7. Charge of excessive initiation fees and dues
8. "Featherbedding" practices that require payment of wages for services not performed

In short, by passing the Taft-Hartley Act, Congress balanced the rights and duties of labor and management in the collective bargaining arena. No longer could the law be criticized as favoring unions.

Health care employees represent a large and important part of the workforce. In 1974 the Taft-Hartley Act was amended to include coverage of employees working in privately owned hospitals and nursing homes. Because of the critical nature of health care services, the 1974 amendments place special requirements on collective bargaining in this industry. For example, before a union of health care employees can strike, it must give a ten-day notice to the employer. Unions must also notify health care facilities of their intent to renegotiate a labor contract at least ninety days prior to the expiration of the agreement; there is a sixty-day requirement for other industries covered by the act.

### The Federal Mediation and Conciliation Service

Because of the high incidence of strikes after World War II, the Taft-Hartley Act created the Federal Mediation and Conciliation Service (FMCS) to help resolve negotiating disputes. The function of this independent agency is to help labor and management reach collective bargaining agreements through the processes of mediation and conciliation. These functions use a neutral party who maintains communications between bargainers in an attempt to gain agreement. Unlike the NLRB, the FMCS has no enforcement powers, nor can it prosecute anyone. Rather, the parties in a negotiating impasse must voluntarily elect to use the service. Once the FMCS is asked to mediate a dispute, however, its involvement in the process can greatly improve labor-management relations while providing a vehicle for the exchange of collective bargaining proposals.[8] According to Ron Collotta, commissioner, FMCS, Phoenix, Arizona, the agency mediates annually between 6,000 and 7,000 bargaining disputes.[9] In recent years, the FMCS has been highly visible in resolving deadlocks involving the communications, sports, education, and transportation industries.

### The Landrum-Griffin Act

In 1959 Congress passed the Landrum-Griffin Act (also known as the Labor-Management Reporting and Disclosure Act) to safeguard union member rights and prevent racketeering and other unscrupulous practices by employers and union officers.[10] The act also establishes certain ground rules governing the control that national unions may exert over local unions where locals are alleged to have violated member rights.

One of the most important provisions of the Landrum-Griffin Act is the Bill of Rights of Union Members, which requires that every union member must be given the right to (1) nominate candidates for union office, (2) vote in union elections or referendums, (3) attend union meetings, and (4) participate in union meetings and vote on union business.[11] Members who are deprived of these rights are permitted to seek appropriate relief in a federal court. The court's action may include obtaining an appropriate injunction. Union members are also granted the right to examine union accounts and records in order to verify information contained in union reports and to bring suit against union officers as necessary to protect union funds. Moreover, under the act, unions are required to submit a financial report annually to the Secretary of Labor, and employers must report any expenditures that are made in attempting to exercise their bargaining rights.

# The Labor Relations Process

**Labor relations process**
Logical sequence of four events: (1) workers desire collective representation, (2) union begins its organizing campaign, (3) collective negotiations lead to a contract, and (4) the contract is administered

Individually, employees may be able to exercise relatively little power in their relations with employers. The treatment and benefits they receive depend in large part on how their employers view their worth to the organization. Of course, if they believe they are not being treated fairly, they have the option of quitting. However, another way to correct the situation is to organize and bargain with the employer collectively. When employees pursue this direction, the labor relations process begins. As Figure 14.1 illustrates, the **labor relations process** consists of a logical sequence of four events: (1) workers desire collective representation, (2) union begins its organizing campaign, (3) collective negotiations lead to a contract, and (4) the contract is administered. Laws and administrative rulings influence each of the separate events by granting special privileges to, or imposing defined constraints on, workers, managers, and union officials.[12]

### Why Employees Unionize

**Union shop**
Provision of the labor agreement that requires employees to join the union as a requirement for their employment

The majority of research on why employees unionize comes from the study of blue-collar employees in the private sector. These studies generally conclude that employees unionize as a result of economic need, because of a general dissatisfaction with managerial practices, and/or as a way to fulfill social and status needs. In short, employees see unionism as a way to achieve results they cannot achieve acting individually.[13]

It should be pointed out that some employees join unions because of the union-shop provisions of the labor agreement. In states where it is permitted, a **union shop** is a provision of the labor agreement that requires employees to join as a condition

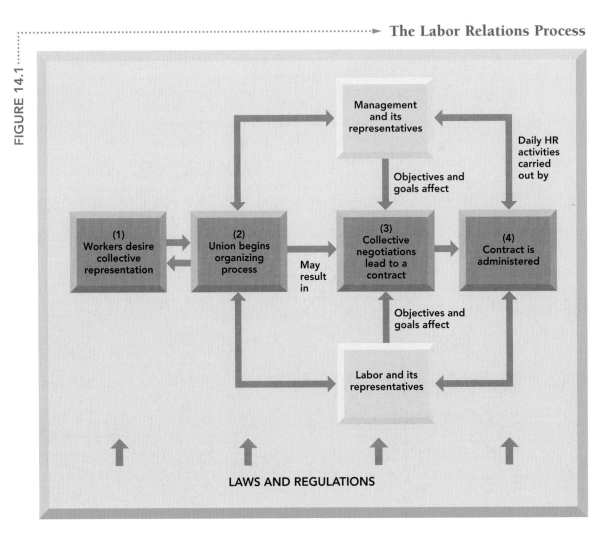

FIGURE 14.1

**The Labor Relations Process**

of employment. Even when compelled to join, however, many employees accept the concept of unionism once they become involved in the union as a member.

### Economic Needs

Whether or not a union can become the bargaining agent for a group of employees will be influenced by the employees' degree of dissatisfaction, if any, with their employment conditions. It will depend also on whether the employees perceive the union as likely to be effective in improving these conditions. Dissatisfaction with wages, benefits, and working conditions appears to provide the strongest reason to join a union. This point is continually supported by research studies that find that both union members and nonmembers have their highest expectations of union performance regarding the "bread and butter" issues of collective bargaining.[14] It is these traditional issues of wages and benefits on which unions are built.

### Dissatisfaction with Management

Employees may seek unionization when they perceive that managerial practices regarding promotion, transfer, shift assignment, or other job-related policies are

*These farmworkers use an organized demonstration to show their dissatisfaction with management.*

administered in an unfair or biased manner. Employees cite favoritism shown by managers as a major reason for joining unions. This is particularly true when the favoritism concerns the HR areas of discipline, promotion, and wage increases.

We have noted throughout this book that today's employees are better educated than those of the past, and they often express a desire to be more involved in decisions affecting their jobs. Chapter 3 discussed the concept of employee empowerment and highlighted various employee involvement techniques. The failure of employers to give employees an opportunity to participate in decisions affecting their welfare may encourage union membership. It is widely believed that one reason managers begin employee involvement programs and seek to empower their employees is to avoid collective action by employees. For example, employers in the auto, semiconductor, and financial industries involve employees in collaborative programs as a means to stifle unionization. In one organizing effort by the United Auto Workers at a Nissan plant, the union lost the election because workers were satisfied with the voice in decision making that Nissan's participatory style of management gave them.

### Social and Status Concerns

Employees whose needs for status and recognition are being frustrated may join unions as a means of satisfying these needs. Through their union, they have an opportunity to fraternize with other employees who have similar desires, interests, problems, and gripes. Joining the union also enables them to put leadership talents to use.

The limited studies conducted on employee unionization in the public sector generally find public employees unionizing for reasons similar to those of their private-sector counterparts. For example, higher wages and benefits, job security, and protection against arbitrary and unfair management treatment are primary motives for unionization among public-sector employees.[15] In the final analysis, the extent to which employees perceive that the benefits of joining a union outweigh the costs associated with membership is likely to be the deciding factor.

## Organizing Campaigns

Once employees desire to unionize, a formal organizing campaign may be started either by a union organizer or by employees acting on their own behalf. Contrary to popular belief, most organizing campaigns are begun by employees rather than by union organizers. Large national unions like the United Auto Workers, the United Brotherhood of Carpenters, the United Steelworkers, and the Teamsters, however, have formal organizing departments whose purpose is to identify organizing opportunities and launch organizing campaigns.

Since such campaigns can be expensive, union leaders carefully evaluate their chances of success and the possible benefits to be gained from their efforts.

Important in this evaluation is the employer's vulnerability to unionization. Union leaders also consider the effect that allowing an employer to remain nonunion may have on the strength of their union within the area. A nonunion employer can impair a union's efforts to standardize employment conditions within an industry or geographic area, as well as weaken the union's bargaining power with employers it has unionized.

## Organizing Steps

Terry Moser, former president, Teamster Local 104, once told the authors that the typical organizing campaign follows a series of progressive steps that can lead to employee representation. The organizing process as described by Moser normally includes the following steps:

1.  Employee/union contact
2.  Initial organizational meeting
3.  Formation of in-house organizing committee
4.  Election petition and voting preparation
5.  Contract negotiations

*Step 1.* The first step begins when employees and union officials make contact to explore the possibility of unionization. During these discussions, employees will investigate the advantages of labor representation, and union officials will begin to gather information on employee needs, problems, and grievances. Labor organizers will also seek specific information about the employer's financial health, supervisory styles, and organizational policies and practices. To win employee support, labor organizers must build a case *against* the employer and *for* the union.

*Step 2.* As an organizing campaign gathers momentum, the organizer will schedule an initial union meeting to attract more supporters. The organizer will use the information gathered in step 1 to address employee needs and explain how the union can secure these goals. Two additional purposes of organizational meetings are (1) to identify employees who can help the organizer direct the campaign and (2) to establish communication chains that reach all employees.

*Step 3.* The third important step in the organizing drive is to form an in-house organizing committee composed of employees willing to provide leadership to the campaign. The committee's role is to interest other employees in joining the union and in supporting its campaign. An important task of the committee is to have employees sign an **authorization card** (see Highlights in HRM 2) indicating their willingness to be represented by a labor union in collective bargaining with their employer. The number of signed authorization cards demonstrates the potential strength of the labor union.[16] At least 30 percent of the employees must sign authorization cards before the National Labor Relations Board will hold a representation election.

*Step 4.* If a sufficient number of employees support the union drive, the organizer will seek a government-sponsored election. A representation petition will be filed with the NLRB, asking that a secret-ballot election be held to determine if employees actually desire unionization. Before the election, a large publicity campaign will be directed toward employees, seeking their support and election votes. This is a period of intense emotions for the employees, the labor organization, and the employer.

**Authorization card**
A statement signed by an employee authorizing a union to act as a representative of the employee for purposes of collective bargaining

HRM 2

**HIGHLIGHTS IN HRM**

# United Food and Commercial Workers International Union Authorization Card

## United Food & Commercial Workers International Union

Affiliated with AFL-CIO-CLC

### AUTHORIZATION FOR REPRESENTATION

I hereby authorize the United Food & Commercial Workers International Union, AFL-CIO-CLC, or its chartered Local Union(s) to represent me for the purpose of collective bargaining.

_____     _____
(Print Name)                                                    (Date)

_____     _____
(Signature)                                                  (Home Phone)

_____     _____     _____     _____
(Home Address)                              (City)                     (State)             (Zip)

_____     _____
(Employer's Name)                                          (Address)

_____     _____     _____
(Hire Date)                        (Type Work Performed)                   (Department)

Day                   Night               Full              Part-
Shift _____       Shift _____       Time _____     Time _____
_____     _____
(Hourly Rate)         (Day Off)

Would you participate in an organizing committee?     Yes _____     No _____

*Step 5.* Union organizing is concluded when the union wins the election. The NLRB will "certify" the union as the legal bargaining representative of the employees. Contract negotiations will now begin; these negotiations represent another struggle between the union and employer. During negotiations each side will seek employment conditions favorable to its position. Members of the in-plant organizing committee and the union organizer will attempt to negotiate the employees' first contract. In about one out of four union campaigns, unions are unable to secure a first contract after winning a representation election.[17] Should the union fail to obtain an agreement within one year from winning the election, the Taft-Hartley Act allows the employees to vote the union out through an NLRB "decertification" election.

## Nontraditional Organizing Tactics

While the five organizing steps represent the traditional method of union recruitment, the labor movement has become much more *aggressive* and *creative* in its organizing tactics. Unions have been shocked into developing these "revolutionary" organizing strategies to compensate for a decline in membership and to counteract employer antiunion campaigns.[18] (Both topics will be discussed later.) To accomplish their agenda of "vitalizing" the labor movement, unions employ the following organizing weapons—in varying degrees—to achieve their goals:[19]

1.  *Political involvement.* Unions have become more selective in their support of public officials, giving union funds to candidates who specifically pledge support for prolabor legislation. Conversely, unions intend to "get tough" against politicians who champion antiunion sentiments. According to one union official, organized labor needs to generate "Street Heat" during political struggles.[20]

2.  *Union "salting."* Paid union organizers apply for employment at a company targeted for organizing, normally a nonunion construction firm. Once hired, these trained organizers actively work to unionize other employees.[21] In NLRB v Town and Country Electric, Inc., the U.S. Supreme Court (1995) held that employers cannot discriminate in regard to hire or other terms of employment against union salts.[22] A real thorn to managers, salting campaigns have been successful in the growth regions of our nation.

3.  *Organizer training.* Traditionally, organizing has been part-time work. Today, the AFL-CIO's Organizing Institute is actively training a new generation of professional, highly skilled, full-time organizers. The current goal is to train 1,000 new organizers.[23] Additionally, the AFL-CIO has challenged local unions to mobilize the local's entire membership around organizing— including spending 30 percent of local monies on recruitment efforts. An organizing tactic is to oversupply (flood) a community with well-trained organizers. The purpose is to focus on a particular company or industry ripe for organizing.

4.  *Corporate campaigns.* Unions may enlist political or community groups to boycott the product(s) of a targeted company. Other tactics include writing newspaper editorials chastising specific company decisions; filing charges with administrative agencies such as OSHA, the Department of Labor, and the NLRB; and pressuring an organization's financial institution to withhold loans or demand payments.[24] In a recent strategy, labor unions have petitioned the Securities and Exchange Commission to probe companies' alleged failure to disclose important financial information to stockholders. For example, the Paper, Allied-Industrial, Chemical, and Energy Workers union charged Crown Central Petroleum with a misleading 1998 financial statement regarding $70 million in costs, largely from environmental fines.[25]

5.  *Contract clauses.* Unions seek contract clauses that obligate managers to urge unionization on company suppliers. These clauses may also mandate that managers not assume an antiunion position at new facilities opened by the employer. In 1999, bargaining with the Big Three auto makers, the United Auto Workers leaned on the auto companies to persuade their parts suppliers and their nonunion subsidiaries to not oppose union organizing efforts.[26]

### Employer Tactics

In counteracting a union campaign, employers must not threaten employees with the loss of their jobs or loss or reduction of other employment benefits if they vote to unionize. However, within the limits permitted by the Taft-Hartley Act, employers can express their views about the disadvantages of being represented by a union. When possible, employers will stress the favorable employer-employee relationship they have experienced in the past without a union.[27] Employers may emphasize any advantages in wages, benefits, or working conditions the employees may enjoy in comparison with those provided by organizations that are already unionized. "While you have a right to join a union," the employers may remind their employees, "you also have a right not to join one and to deal directly with the organization free from outside interference." Highlights in HRM 3 lists some activities managers and supervisors should not engage in.

Employers *may* emphasize any unfavorable publicity the organizing union has received with respect to corruption or abuse of members' legal rights. Employers may also use government statistics to show that unions commit large numbers of unfair labor practices. For example, 6,751 unfair labor practices were charged against unions in 1998; the majority (5,720) alleged illegal restraint and coercion of employees.[28]

If the union has engaged in a number of strikes, employers may stress this fact to warn employees about possible work disruption and loss of income. Also, employers will point out to employees the cost of union dues and special assessments, along with any false promises made by the union in the course of its campaign.[29] Furthermore, employers may initiate legal action should union members and/or their leaders engage in any unfair labor practices during the organizing effort.

**HRM 3**

**HIGHLIGHTS IN HRM**

# Employer "Don'ts" during Union Organizing Campaigns

Union organizing drives are emotionally charged events. Furthermore, labor law, NLRB rulings, and court decisions greatly affect the behavior and actions of management and union representatives. During the drive, managers and supervisors should avoid

- Attending union meetings, spying on employee-union gatherings, or questioning employees about the content of union meetings
- Questioning present or current employees about their union sentiments, particularly about how they might vote in a union election
- Threatening or terminating employees for their union support or beliefs
- Changing the working conditions of employees because they actively work for the union or simply support its ideals
- Supplying the names, addresses, and phone numbers of employees to union representatives or other employees sympathetic to the union
- Promising employees improvements in working conditions (e.g., wage increases, benefit improvements, etc.) if they vote against the union
- Accepting or reviewing union authorization cards or prounion petitions, since employees' names are listed on these documents

## How Employees Become Unionized

**Bargaining unit**
Group of two or more employees who share common employment interests and conditions and may reasonably be grouped together for purposes of collective bargaining

The employees to be organized constitute the bargaining unit to be covered by the labor agreement. The NLRB defines a **bargaining unit** as a group of two or more employees who have common employment interests and conditions and may reasonably be grouped together for purposes of collective bargaining. If an employer and a union cannot agree on who should be in the bargaining unit, an appropriate bargaining unit will be determined by the NLRB on the basis of a similarity of interests (e.g. wages, job duties, training) among employees within the unit. For example, in hospitals, the NLRB has designated separate units for nurses, technicians, doctors, maintenance employees, office clerical personnel, all other non-professionals, and guards.

### Employer Recognition

If it succeeds in signing up at least 50 percent of employees within the bargaining unit, the union may request recognition by the employer. Typically, evidence is produced in the form of authorization cards signed by employees. If no other union is competing to represent the employees, the employer at this point can simply agree to recognize the union and negotiate an agreement with it.[30] This procedure is referred to as "certification on a card count." Smitty's food stores in Phoenix, Arizona, agreed to recognize the United Food & Commercial Workers (UFCW) as bargaining representatives of store employees when over 70 percent of the employees signed authorization cards. However, if the employer believes that a majority of its employees do not want to belong to the union or if more than one union is attempting to gain recognition, the employer can insist that a representation election be held. This election will determine which union, if any, will represent the employees. The petition to hold representation elections usually is initiated by the union, although employers, under certain conditions, have the right to petition for one. (See Highlights in HRM 4.)

### Types of NLRB Representation Elections

**Consent election**
NLRB election option wherein the petition to hold a representation election is not contested by either the employer or the union

**Stipulation election**
NLRB election option wherein the parties seek settlement of representation questions such as the NLRB's jurisdiction or the appropriate employees to be included in the bargaining unit

The NLRB offers two election options. The first option, called a **consent election,** is used when the petition to hold a representation election is not contested. Here there are no disagreements between the union and the employer. The NLRB sets a date to hold the election, and voting is conducted by secret ballot. Should the request for representation be contested by the employer or should more than one union be seeking recognition, then *preelection hearings* must be held.[31] This second option is called a **stipulation election.** At the preelection hearings several important issues will be discussed, including the NLRB's jurisdiction to hold the election, determination of the bargaining unit (if contested by the parties), and the voting choice(s) to appear on the ballot. The ballot lists the names of the unions that are seeking recognition and also provides for the choice of "no union."[32]

After the election is held, the winning party will be determined on the basis of the number of actual votes, not on the number of members of the bargaining unit. For example, suppose the bargaining unit at XYZ Corporation comprised 100 employees, but only 27 employees voted in the election. The union receiving 14 yes votes among the 27 voting (a majority) would be declared the winner, and the union would bargain for all 100 employees. By law the union would be granted

**HRM 4**

## NLRB Election Poster

# NOTICE TO EMPLOYEES

### FROM THE
## National Labor Relations Board

A PETITION has been filed with this Federal agency seeking an election to determine whether certain employees want to be represented by a union.

The case is being investigated and NO DETERMINATION HAS BEEN MADE AT THIS TIME by the National Labor Relations Board. IF an election is held Notices of Election will be posted giving complete details for voting.

It was suggested that your employer post this notice so the National Labor Relations Board could inform you of your basic rights under the National Labor Relations Act.

**YOU HAVE THE RIGHT under Federal Law**

- To self-organization
- To form, join, or assist labor organizations
- To bargain collectively through representatives of your own choosing
- To act together for the purposes of collective bargaining or other mutual aid or protection
- To refuse to do any or all of these things unless the union and employer, in a state where such agreements are permitted, enter into a lawful union-security agreement requiring employees to pay periodic dues and initiation fees. Nonmembers who inform the union that they object to the use of their payments for nonrepresentational purposes may be required to pay only their share of the union's costs of representational activities *(such as collective bargaining, contract administration, and grievance adjustments)*.

It is possible that some of you will be voting in an employee representation election as a result of the request for an election having been filed. While NO DETERMINATION HAS BEEN MADE AT THIS TIME, in the event an election is held, the NATIONAL LABOR RELATIONS BOARD wants all eligible voters to be familiar with their rights under the law IF it holds an election.

The Board applies rules that are intended to keep its elections fair and honest and that result in a free choice. If agents of either unions or employers act in such a way as to interfere with your right to a free election, the election can be set aside by the Board. Where appropriate the Board provides other remedies, such as reinstatement for employees fired for exercising their rights, including backpay from the party responsible for their discharge.

**NOTE:**

The following are examples of conduct that interfere with the rights of employees and may result in the setting aside of the election.

- Threatening loss of jobs or benefits by an employer or a union
- Promising or granting promotions, pay raises, or other benefits to influence an employee's vote by a party capable of carrying out such promises
- An employer firing employees to discourage or encourage union activity or a union causing them to be fired to encourage union activity
- Making campaign speeches to assembled groups of employees on company time within the 24-hour period before the election
- Incitement by either an employer or a union of racial or religious prejudice by inflammatory appeals
- Threatening physical force or violence to employees by a union or an employer to influence their votes

Please be assured that IF AN ELECTION IS HELD every effort will be made to protect your right to a free choice under the law. Improper conduct will not be permitted. All parties are expected to cooperate fully with this Agency in maintaining basic principles of a fair election as required by law. The National Labor Relations Board, as an agency of the United States Government, does not endorse any choice in the election.

**NATIONAL LABOR RELATIONS BOARD**
*an agency of the*
**UNITED STATES GOVERNMENT**

**THIS IS AN OFFICIAL GOVERNMENT NOTICE AND MUST NOT BE DEFACED BY ANYONE**

FORM NLRB-666 (5-90)                                        ☆ U.S. Government Printing Office: 1990-270-693/19127 *exclusive representation* over all bargaining unit employees. The union will be *certified* by the NLRB as the bargaining agent for a period of at least a year, or for the duration of the labor agreement. Once the union is certified, the employer is obligated to begin negotiations leading toward a labor agreement.

An important statistic in labor relations is the win/loss record of unions in certification elections. This statistic is often regarded as an indication of the general vitality of the union movement. As Figure 14.2 shows, from 1975 through 1998 unions consistently lost more than 50 percent of elections held by the NLRB. This contrasts sharply with the union win rate of 74.5 percent in 1950 and 60.2 percent in 1965. The conclusion can be drawn from Figure 14.2 that unions have lost much of their ability to unionize employees, although the percentage rate for union wins has stabilized at around 48 percent since 1996.

**FIGURE 14.2** ➤ **NLRB Elections, Selected Years**

| YEAR | ELECTIONS HELD | UNIONS WON | UNION PERCENTAGE WINS |
|------|------|------|------|
| 1950 | 5,619 | 4,186 | 74.5 |
| 1955 | 4,215 | 2,849 | 67.6 |
| 1965 | 7,775 | 4,880 | 60.2 |
| 1975 | 8,577 | 4,134 | 48.2 |
| 1985 | 4,614 | 1,956 | 42.4 |
| 1986 | 4,520 | 1,951 | 43.2 |
| 1987 | 4,069 | 1,788 | 43.9 |
| 1988 | 4,153 | 1,921 | 46.3 |
| 1989 | 4,413 | 2,059 | 46.7 |
| 1990 | 4,210 | 1,965 | 46.7 |
| 1991 | 3,752 | 1,663 | 44.3 |
| 1992 | 3,599 | 1,673 | 46.5 |
| 1993 | 3,586 | 1,706 | 47.6 |
| 1994 | 3,572 | 1,665 | 46.6 |
| 1995 | 3,399 | 1,611 | 47.4 |
| 1996 | 3,277 | 1,584 | 48.3 |
| 1997 | 3,480 | 1,677 | 48.2 |
| 1998 | 3,795 | 1,856 | 48.9 |

Source: *Annual Reports of the National Labor Relations Board*, U.S. Government Printing Office, Washington, D.C.

## Impact of Unionization on Managers

The unionization of employees can affect managers in several ways. Perhaps most significant is the effect it can have on the prerogatives exercised by management in making decisions about employees. Furthermore, unionization restricts the freedom of management to formulate HR policy unilaterally and can challenge the authority of supervisors.

### *Challenges to Management Prerogatives*

**Management prerogatives**
Decisions regarding organizational operations over which management claims exclusive rights

Unions typically attempt to achieve greater participation in management decisions that affect their members. Specifically, these decisions may involve such issues as the subcontracting of work, productivity standards, and job content. Employers quite naturally seek to claim many of these decisions as their exclusive **management prerogatives**—decisions over which management claims exclusive rights. However, these prerogatives are subject to challenge and erosion by the union. They may be challenged at the bargaining table, through the grievance procedure, and through strikes.

### *Loss of Supervisory Authority*

At a recent labor-management conference a union official commented, "Contract terms covering wages, benefits, job security, and working hours are of major importance to our membership." However, for managers and supervisors, the focal point of the union's impact is at the operating level (the shop floor or office facility), where the terms of the labor agreement are implemented on a daily basis. For example, these terms can determine what corrective action is to be taken in directing and in disciplining employees. When disciplining employees, supervisors must be certain they can demonstrate *just cause* (see Chapter 13) for their actions, because these actions can be challenged by the union and the supervisor called as defendant during a grievance hearing. If the challenge is upheld, the supervisor's effectiveness in coping with subsequent disciplinary problems may be impaired. Specific contract language can also reduce the supervisor's ability to manage in such areas as scheduling, training, transfers, performance evaluation, and promotions, to name a few.

# Structures, Functions, and Leadership of Labor Unions

**Craft unions**
Unions that represent skilled craft workers

**Industrial unions**
Unions that represent all workers—skilled, semi-skilled, unskilled—employed along industry lines

Unions that represent skilled craft workers, such as carpenters or masons, are called **craft unions.** Craft unions include the International Association of Iron Workers, the United Brotherhood of Carpenters, and the United Association of Plumbers and Pipefitters. Unions that represent unskilled and semiskilled workers employed along industry lines are known as **industrial unions.** The American Union of Postal Workers is an industrial union, as are the United Auto Workers; the United Steelworkers; the American Federation of State, County, and Municipal Employees; and the Office and Professional Employees International Union. While this distinction still exists, technological changes and competition among unions for members have helped to reduce it. Today skilled and unskilled workers, white-collar and blue-collar workers, and professional groups are being represented by both types of union.

**Employee associations**
Labor organizations that represent various groups of professional and white-collar employees in labor-management relations

Besides unions, there are also **employee associations** representing various groups of professional and white-collar employees. Examples of employee associations include the National Education Association, the Michigan State Employees Association, the American Nurses' Association, and the Air Line Pilots Association. In competing with unions, these associations, for all purposes, may function as unions and become just as aggressive as unions in representing members.

Regardless of their type, labor organizations are diverse organizations, each with its own method of governance and objectives. Furthermore, they have their own structures that serve to bind them together. For example, when describing labor organizations, most researchers divide them into three levels: (1) the American Federation of Labor and Congress of Industrial Organizations (AFL-CIO), (2) national unions, and (3) local unions belonging to a parent national union. Each level has its own purpose for existence as well as its own operating policies and procedures.

## Structure and Functions of the AFL-CIO

In 1955 the American Federation of Labor—composed largely of craft unions—and the Congress of Industrial Organizations—made up mainly of industrial unions—merged to form the AFL-CIO. The AFL-CIO is a federation of sixty-eight autonomous national and international unions.[33] Because the interests and organizing activities of these autonomous unions in the AFL-CIO do not always coincide, a chief advantage of belonging to the AFL-CIO is a provision that affords protection to member unions against "raiding" by other unions within the federation. A violation of this no-raiding provision can lead to expulsion from the federation.

In effect, the AFL-CIO is the "House of Labor" that serves to present a united front on behalf of organized labor. It disseminates labor policy developed by leaders of its affiliated unions, assists in coordinating organizing activities among its affiliated unions, and provides research and other assistance through its various departments. Most major unions belong to this federation. The AFL-CIO claims a membership of about 13 million, or about 80 percent of all union members.[34] Specifically, the AFL-CIO serves its members by

1. Lobbying before legislative bodies on subjects of interest to labor
2. Coordinating organizing efforts among its affiliated unions
3. Publicizing the concerns and benefits of unionization to the public
4. Resolving disputes between different unions as they occur

Besides offering these services, the AFL-CIO maintains an interest in international trade and domestic economic issues, foreign policy matters, and national and regional politics. For example, the AFL-CIO recently earmarked $35 million for political activities that included the training of political organizers and politicians in labor issues.

The federation is governed by its constitution and various policies set at its biennial conventions. National unions send a number of delegates to the convention according to the size of the unions. Thus larger unions have greater voting power on the resolutions adopted at the convention. Between conventions, the AFL-CIO is run by its executive council. The affiliated unions pay per capita dues (currently 50 cents per member per month) to support federation activities.

**USING THE INTERNET**

Many national unions have web sites for their members.

**Auto Workers at:**

www.uaw.org

**Transport Workers at:**

www.twu.com

**and Office and Professional Employees at:**

www.opieu.org

**The AFL-CIO, the federation of national unions, has a web site at:**

www.aflcio.org

## Structure and Functions of National Unions

The center of power in the labor movement resides with national and international unions. It is these organizations that set the broad guidelines for governing union members and for formulating collective bargaining goals in dealing with management. The only major difference between a national and an international union is that the international union organizes workers and charters local unions in foreign countries. For example, the International Brotherhood of Electrical Workers is an international union with locals in Canada.

A national union, through its constitution, establishes the rules and conditions under which the local unions may be chartered. Most national unions have regulations governing dues, initiation fees, and the internal administration of the locals. National unions also may require that certain standard provisions be included in labor agreements with employers. Standard contract terms covering safety or grievance procedures and seniority rights are examples. In return for these controls, they provide professional and financial assistance during organizing drives and strikes and help in the negotiation and administration of labor agreements. Other services provided by national unions include (1) training of union leaders, (2) legal assistance, (3) leadership in political activity, (4) educational and public relations programs, and (5) discipline of union members.

Like the AFL-CIO, national unions hold conventions to pass resolutions, amend their constitutions, and elect officers. This last function is very important to a national union because its president often exerts a large influence—if not control—over the union's policies and direction. Furthermore, many presidents, like Steve Yokich (United Auto Workers), Sandra Feldman (American Federation of Teachers), Arturo S. Rodriques (United Farm Workers), and Andrew Stern (Service Employees International Union), are highly visible individuals who represent the labor movement to the public. In addition, the president of a national union is responsible for the overall administration of the union and of the different union departments, as shown in Figure 14.3.

## Structure and Functions of Local Unions

The officers of a local union are usually responsible for negotiating the local labor agreement and for investigating and processing member grievances. Most important, they assist in preventing the members of the local union from being treated by their employers in ways that run counter to management-established HR policies.[35]

The officers of a local union typically include a president, vice president, secretary-treasurer, business representative, and various committee chairpersons. Depending on the size of the union, one or more of these officers, in addition to the business representative, may be paid by the union to serve on a full-time basis. The remaining officers are members who have regular jobs and who serve the union without pay except perhaps for token gratuities and expense allowances. In many locals, the business representative is the dominant power. In some locals, however, the dominant power is the secretary-treasurer or the president.

### Role of the Union Steward

The **union steward** represents the interests of union members in their relations with their immediate supervisors and other members of management. Stewards are

**Union steward**
Employee who as a non-paid union official represents the interests of members in their relations with management

FIGURE 14.3

## Typical Organization of a National Union

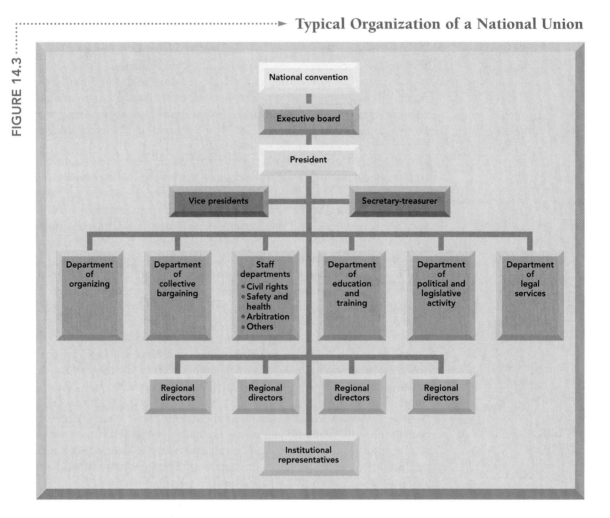

normally elected by union members within their department and serve without union pay. Since stewards are full-time employees of the organization, they often spend considerable time after working hours investigating and handling member problems. When stewards represent members during grievance meetings on organizational time, their lost earnings are paid by the local union.

A union steward can be viewed as a "person in the middle," caught between conflicting interests and groups. It cannot be assumed that stewards will always champion union members and routinely oppose managerial objectives. Union stewards are often insightful individuals working for the betterment of employees and the organization. Therefore it is *highly* encouraged that supervisors and managers at all levels develop a professional working relationship with stewards and all union officials. This relationship can have an important bearing on union-management cooperation and on the efficiency and morale of the workforce.[36]

**Business representative**
Normally a paid labor official responsible for negotiating and administering the labor agreement and working to resolve union members' problems

### Role of the Business Representative

Negotiating and administering the labor agreement and working to resolve problems arising in connection with it are major responsibilities of the **business representative.** In performing these duties, business representatives must be all things to all persons within their unions. They frequently are required to assume the role of counselor in helping union members with both personal and job-related problems. They are also expected to dispose satisfactorily of the members' grievances that cannot be settled by the union stewards. Administering the daily affairs of the local union is another significant part of the business representative's job.

## Union Leadership Approaches and Philosophies

To evaluate the role of union leaders accurately, one must understand the nature of their backgrounds and ambitions and recognize the political nature of the offices they occupy. The leaders of many national unions have been able to develop political machines that enable them to defeat opposition and to perpetuate themselves in office. Tenure for the leaders of a local union, however, is less secure. In the local union, officers, by federal law, must run for reelection at least every third year. If they are to remain in office, they must be able to convince a majority of the members that they are serving them effectively.

Although it is true that union leaders occupy positions of power within their organizations, rank-and-file members can and often do exercise a very strong influence over these leaders, particularly with respect to the negotiation and administration of the labor agreement. It is important for managers to understand that union officials are elected to office and, like any political officials, must be responsive to the views of their constituency. The union leader who ignores the demands of union members may risk (1) being voted out of office, (2) having members vote the union out as their bargaining agent, (3) having members refuse to ratify the union agreement, or (4) having members engage in wildcat strikes or work stoppages.

**Business unionism**
Term applied to the goals of U.S. labor organizations, which collectively bargain for improvements in wages, hours, job security, and working conditions

To be effective leaders, labor officials must also pay constant attention to the general goals and philosophies of the labor movement. **Business unionism** is the general label given to the goals of American labor organizations: increased pay and benefits, job security, and improved working conditions. Furthermore, union leaders also know that unions must address the broader social, economic, and legislative issues of concern to members.[37] For example, the United Auto Workers continually lobbies Congress for protective legislation affecting the auto industry. The American Federation of State, County, and Municipal Employees, the Union of Needletrades, Industrial and Textile Employees, and the Association of Flight Attendants representing flight attendants at America West Airlines have been active supporters of women's issues at both the state and national levels.

Finally, as part of America's adjustment to global competition, union leaders have been active in working with managers in order to make their employing industries more competitive.[38] For example, officials of the United Brotherhood of Carpenters, Communication Workers of America, the United Food & Commercial Workers Union, and the Office and Professional Employees International Union have implemented cooperative programs with managers in organizations where they represent employees.

# Labor Relations in the Public Sector

Collective bargaining among federal, state, and local government employees has been an area of growth for the union movement since the early 1960s. Today 7 million public workers belong to unions or employee associations. They constitute about 40 percent of government employees. The latest union membership figures show that some of the nation's largest labor organizations represent employees in the public sector—the National Education Association (2.4 million members), American Federation of Teachers (900,000 members), and State, County, and Municipal Employees (1.3 million members), for instance.[39] As unions and employee associations of teachers, police, firefighters, and state employees have grown in size and political power, they have demanded the same rights to bargain and strike that private-sector employees have.

While public- and private-sector collective bargaining have many features in common, a number of factors differentiate the two sectors. In this section, we will highlight several of the major differences between public-sector and private-sector industrial relations and discuss how these differences affect HRM. Three areas will be explored: (1) legislation governing collective bargaining in the public sector, (2) the political nature of the labor-management relationship, and (3) public-sector strikes.

## Public-Sector Legislation

Public-sector legislation affecting HRM includes executive orders, the Civil Service Reform Act of 1978, and state laws.

### Executive Orders

Issued in 1962 by President Kennedy, Executive Order 10988 contained provisions similar to those in Section 7 of the Taft-Hartley Act.[40] These provisions state that federal employees have the right freely and without fear of penalty or reprisal to form, join, or assist any labor organization or to refrain from such activity.[41] Included in this executive order are provisions for establishing bargaining units within government agencies. Labor organizations also are permitted to bargain collectively with the government in reaching a labor agreement for members.

Issued in 1971 by President Nixon, Executive Order 11491 defined the bargaining rights of federal employees more precisely and provided procedures for safeguarding these rights. This executive order created the Federal Labor Relations Council to hear appeals relating to unfair practices and bargaining issues. A body called the Federal Service Impasses Panel also was established to deal with collective bargaining deadlocks.[42]

### The Civil Service Reform Act of 1978

The Civil Service Reform Act of 1978 made the regulation of labor relations in the federal government even more consistent with that contained in the Taft-Hartley Act for the private sector. The Federal Labor Relations Authority (FLRA), an agency similar to the NLRB, was created to decide on unfair practices and representation cases and to enforce the provisions of the act. An office of general counsel, similar to that provided by the Taft-Hartley Act, also was created to investigate and decide which unfair labor practices and complaints are to be prosecuted.

Even with the Civil Service Reform Act, labor organizations representing federal employees do not have rights equal to those provided by the Taft-Hartley Act. Most important, they lack the legal right to strike to enforce their bargaining demands. Furthermore, management rights in the federal government are accorded greater protection than those of employers in the private sector. Rules, procedures, and area restrictions that govern bargaining further reduce the influence that labor organizations can exercise over employment conditions in federal agencies.

### State Legislation

One distinctive characteristic of public-sector collective bargaining at the state level is the great diversity among the various state laws.[43] This occurs because the regulation of public-sector labor-management relations falls within the separate jurisdiction of each state. For example, some states, like Arizona, Utah, and Mississippi, have no collective bargaining laws; other states, like Florida, Hawaii, and New York, have comprehensive laws granting collective bargaining rights to all public employees. Between these extremes are state laws granting collective bargaining rights only to specific employee groups such as teachers and the uniformed services (police and fire). Comprehensive state laws provide for an administrative agency analogous to the NLRB and the Federal Labor Relations Authority. A frequent state restriction concerns the right to negotiate labor agreements. Public employees may have only the right to "meet and confer" with representatives of management for the purpose of developing an agreement, often called "a memorandum of understanding."

## Political Nature of the Labor-Management Relationship

One significant difference between public- and private-sector labor relations is that labor relations in the private sector has an economic foundation, whereas in government its foundation is political. Since private employers must stay in business in order to sell their goods or services, their employees are not likely to make demands that could bankrupt them. A strike in the private sector is a test of the employer's economic staying power, and usually the employer's customers have alternative sources of supply. Governments, on the other hand, must stay in business because alternative services are usually not available. Nevertheless, unions representing government employees are not reluctant to press for financial gains that will be paid for by the public.

Another difference between the labor-management relationship in the public and private sectors is the source of management authority. In a private organization the authority flows downward from the board of directors and ultimately from the shareholders. In the public sector, however, authority flows upward from the public at large to their elected representatives and to the appointed or elected managers. Therefore public employees can exert influence not only as union members but also as pressure groups and voting citizens.

## Strikes in the Public Sector

Strikes by government employees create a problem for lawmakers and for the general public. Because the services that government employees provide are often considered essential to the well-being of the public, public policy is opposed to such strikes. Thus most state legislatures have not granted public employees the right to strike. In those states where striking is permitted, the right is limited to specific

**Compulsory binding arbitration**
  Binding method of resolving collective bargaining deadlocks by a neutral third party

**Final-offer arbitration**
  Method of resolving collective bargaining deadlocks whereby the arbitrator has no power to compromise but must select one or another of the final offers submitted by the two parties

groups of employees—normally nonuniformed employees—and the strike cannot endanger the public's health, safety, or welfare. Public-employee unions contend, however, that by denying them the same right to strike as employees in the private sector, their power during collective bargaining is greatly reduced.

In order to provide some equity in bargaining power, various arbitration methods are used for resolving collective bargaining deadlocks in the public sector. One is **compulsory binding arbitration** for employees such as police officers, firefighters, and others in jobs where strikes cannot be tolerated. Another method is **final-offer arbitration,** under which the arbitrator must select one or the other of the final offers submitted by the disputing parties. With this method, the arbitrator's award is more likely to go to the party whose final bargaining offer has moved the closest toward a reasonable settlement.

# Contemporary Challenges to Labor Organizations

Among the changes that pose challenges to labor organizations today are foreign competition and technological advances, a decline in labor's public image, the decrease of union membership, and employers' focus on maintaining nonunion status.

## Foreign Competition and Technological Change

The importation of steel, consumer electronics, automobiles, clothing, textiles, and shoes from foreign countries creates a loss of jobs in the United States for workers who produce these products. Furthermore, foreign subsidiaries of American corporations such as Rockwell, Westinghouse, and Xerox have been accused by labor unions of exporting the jobs of American workers. As a result, unions are demanding more government protection against imports. Such protection has spurred lively congressional debate between those who argue that protective trade barriers create higher prices for American consumers and those who seek to protect American jobs from low-cost overseas producers. U.S. unions were highly opposed to passage of the North American Free Trade Agreement (NAFTA), claiming American jobs would be lost to low-wage employers in Mexico.

Coupled with the threat of foreign competition is the challenge to labor brought about by rapid technological advances. Improvements in computer technology and highly automated operating systems have lowered the demand for certain types of employees. Decline in membership in the auto, steel, rubber, and transportation unions illustrates this fact. Technological advances have also diminished the effectiveness of strikes because highly automated organizations are capable of maintaining satisfactory levels of operation with minimum staffing levels during work stoppages.

## Labor's Unfavorable Public Image

Organized labor has suffered a decline in its public image. For example, critics of labor cite wage increases gained by labor unions as a factor that not only contributes to inflation but also helps to drive American products out of the foreign and domestic markets. Union leaders are viewed as overly powerful individuals who frequently act in their own self-interest, appear to be contemptuous of the public, are often dishonest and unethical, and are out of touch with the rank-and-file membership.

Well aware of its "dinosaur" image, the labor movement has programs under way that are designed to communicate to the American public, and especially to a new generation of workers, the benefits and relevance of organized labor.[44] The AFL-CIO created the Labor Institute for Public Affairs charged with telling "labor's story" to Congress and the public. The labor movement's "Union Yes" advertisements on billboards and bumper stickers seek to present a positive, upbeat view of unions. The ultimate goal of the campaign is to create a favorable image of unions that will help organizing efforts. At the local level, service projects such as the Labor's Community Services Agency in Phoenix, Arizona, attempt to improve labor's image at the community level.

## Decrease in Union Membership

A major challenge confronting organized labor is to halt the decline in union membership. The magnitude of the problem is shown in Figure 14.4, which illustrates

**FIGURE 14.4**

**Union Membership, Selected Years**

| YEAR | UNION MEMBERSHIP (IN THOUSANDS) | MEMBERSHIP AS A PERCENTAGE OF CIVILIAN LABOR FORCE |
|------|------|------|
| 1970 | 21,248 | 25.7 |
| 1980 | 22,366 | 20.9 |
| 1982 | 19,763 | 19.3 |
| 1984 | 17,340 | 18.8 |
| 1985 | 16,996 | 18.0 |
| 1986 | 16,975 | 17.5 |
| 1987 | 16,913 | 17.0 |
| 1988 | 17,002 | 16.8 |
| 1989 | 16,900 | 16.4 |
| 1990 | 16,740 | 16.1 |
| 1991 | 16,568 | 16.1 |
| 1992 | 16,390 | 15.8 |
| 1993 | 16,598 | 15.8 |
| 1994 | 16,748 | 15.5 |
| 1995 | 16,360 | 14.9 |
| 1996 | 16,269 | 14.5 |
| 1997 | 16,110 | 14.1 |
| 1998 | 16,211 | 13.9 |

Source: Bureau of Labor Statistics, Washington, D.C. Data obtained July 14, 1999.

*The growing number of workers entering the health care field has energized organizations that support professions such as nursing.*

how union membership has declined in total numbers and as a percentage of the total civilian labor force. The combination of a growing labor force and decreasing union membership dropped organized labor's share of the civilian workforce to a new modern-era low of 13.9 percent in 1998. In the private sector, union membership accounted for approximately 10 percent of all those employed, or about 9 million workers. The loss of union jobs reflects, in part, the decline in U.S. manufacturing jobs, coupled with the failure of unions to draw membership from among the white-collar ranks, where the labor force is growing more rapidly.

### Energized Organizing

According to the Employment Policy Institute, unions must increase membership by more than 300,000 a year just to maintain 14 percent of a growing workforce.[45] Therefore, in order to stem the decline in membership, organized labor has become highly aggressive in its unionizing efforts. College professors, doctors, high-tech white-collar workers, and recent-immigrant workers have attracted the attention of union organizers. This new energized attention to organizing U.S. workers has many important implications for nonunion organizations. While many examples illustrate labor's renewed organizing vigor, the following cases highlight the efforts:

- Unions are targeting workers they have long ignored: low-wage service workers on the bottom tier of the U.S. economy—for example, janitors, maids, and service workers; food service employees; and retail clerks.

- Unions see recent immigrants, the fastest-growing segment of working people, as potent prospects for union growth. Haitian cab drivers, Latino airport workers, Vietnamese warehouse distribution workers, Russian truck drivers, and Asian-American service workers are targeted for union representation.[46]

- The Service Employees International Union, the country's fastest-growing union, has unleashed aggressive campaigns against Kaiser Permanente, the nation's largest HMO, and Beverly Enterprises and Vencor, the two largest nursing home chains. These campaigns are part of a grand plan to organize all nonunion employees in health care.[47]

- The ranks of unionized doctors have grown 80 percent in the past several years, to about 40,000, or 6 percent of doctors in the United States[48] Doctors at various HMOs have unionized into the fast-growing Federation of Physicians and Dentists.[49] Even the American Medical Association (AMA), long opposed to the unionization of doctors, has plans to organize residents and physicians into unions.[50]

- John Sweeney, president of the AFL-CIO, has adopted "America Needs a Raise" as the AFL-CIO's motto for a $20-million-a-year organizing drive.[51]

Additionally, unions are stepping up their efforts to organize white-collar workers. In recent years, employers have tended to depersonalize the work of white-collar groups and to isolate them from management. The lack of job security during layoffs, together with growing difficulties in attempting to resolve grievances, has helped to push white-collar workers toward unionization. Unions are also capitalizing on new health and safety issues in white-collar jobs, such as the effects of working at video display terminals or working with potentially hazardous substances. Unions active in recruiting white-collar employees include the Service Employees International Union; the International Brotherhood of Teamsters; 9 to 5, the National Association of Working Women; the Office and Professional Employees International Union; the Insurance Workers International Union; the United Auto Workers; and the United Steelworkers of America.

## Employers' Focus on Maintaining Nonunion Status

Kirk Adams, AFL-CIO director of organizing, recently remarked that "employer resistance to organizing is growing."[52] Indeed, a significant fact in U.S. labor relations during the 1990s and into the twenty-first century is the prevalence of union avoidance programs. Managers in all types of organizations are vocal in their desire to maintain a union-free environment. To support this goal, employers are providing wages, benefits, and services designed to make unionism unattractive to employees.[53] In addition, a participative management style, profit-sharing plans, and alternative dispute-resolution procedures (see Chapter 13) are offered to counteract the long-established union goals of improved wages and working conditions. Highlights in HRM 5 lists the key strategies identified by HR specialists as means of avoiding unionization. It is important to recognize that these strategies react to the conditions cited at the beginning of the chapter as the main reasons why workers unionize. Since these conditions are under the direct control of management, they can be changed to help discourage or prevent unionism.

Organizations may even go so far as to provoke strikes in order to hire replacement workers and permanently lay off striking union members. The president of the North Carolina AFL-CIO noted, "Strikes are now a weapon of management. In a lot of cases, management wants you to go out on strike so they can bust the strike and bust the union."[54] In recent years unionized employees at Holsum Bakery and Phelps Dodge Corporation have lost their jobs after lengthy bitter strikes. It seems clear that a hard-line management approach to employee unionization contributes to the defeat of union organizing efforts.

**HRM 5**

# Strategies to Remain Union-Free

- Offer competitive wages and benefits based on labor market comparisons and salary and benefit surveys.
- Train supervisors in progressive human relations skills, including employee motivation, job design, and employment law.
- Institute formal procedures to resolve employee complaints and grievances; these may include peer-review committees, step-review complaint systems, or open-door policies.
- Involve employees in work decisions affecting job performance or the quality or quantity of the product or service provided.
- Give attention to employee growth and development needs; recognize that the workforce is growing older, more female, more vocal, better educated, less patient, and more demanding.
- Draft HR policies that reflect legal safeguards and that are fair and equitable in employment conditions such as discipline, promotions, training, and layoffs.

## SUMMARY

**OBJECTIVE 1**

The Railway Labor Act (1926) affords collective bargaining rights to workers employed in the railway and airline industries. The Norris-LaGuardia Act (1932) imposes limitations on the granting of injunctions in labor-management disputes. Most private employees are granted representation rights through the Wagner Act (1935), which has helped to protect and encourage union organizing and bargaining activities. The passage of the Taft-Hartley Act (1947) and the Landrum-Griffin Act (1959) has served to establish certain controls over the internal affairs of unions and their relations with employers.

**OBJECTIVE 2**

Studies show that workers unionize for different economic, psychological, and social reasons. While some employees may join unions because they are required to do so, most belong to unions because they are convinced that unions help them to improve their wages, benefits, and various working conditions. Employee unionization is largely caused by dissatisfaction with managerial practices and procedures.

**OBJECTIVE 3**

A formal union organizing campaign is used to solicit employee support for the union. Once employees demonstrate their desire to unionize through signing authorization cards, the union petitions the NLRB for a secret-ballot election. If 51 percent of those voting in the election vote for the union, the NLRB certifies the union as the bargaining representative for all employees in the bargaining unit. If employee support for the union is very high, management may avoid the election and recognize the union on the basis of authorization cards.

The U.S. labor movement is composed of three basic units: the AFL-CIO, a federation to which national and international unions can elect to belong; national unions; and local unions chartered by the different national labor organizations. National unions and their locals perform various functions for members which include negotiating the contract, handling grievances, training union officials, offering social functions, and providing legal and political activity.

 Legislation governing labor relations in the public and private sectors is vastly different. Public employees are largely denied the right to strike and public unions may be denied, by law, the right to bargain over specific topics such as grievance procedures or certain economic terms of employment. Another difference is that collective bargaining in the private sector has an economic base, whereas in government the base is political. Additionally, in the private sector, authority flows downward; in the public sector, authority flows upward.

 Challenges facing union leaders today include a declining membership caused by technological advancements and increased domestic and global competition. The general public has come to view unions in a less favorable light, which affects their efforts to recruit new members. Labor organizations experience less success in organizing when employers establish progressive HR policies or when they take a hard-line approach toward the unionization of their employees.

## KEY TERMS

authorization card
bargaining unit
business representative
business unionism
compulsory binding arbitration
consent election

craft unions
employee associations
final-offer arbitration
industrial unions
labor relations process
management prerogatives

stipulation election
unfair labor practices (ULPs)
union shop
union steward

## DISCUSSION QUESTIONS

 1. Under the provisions of the Taft-Hartley Act, which unfair labor practices apply to both unions and employers?

 2. Contrast the arguments concerning union membership that are likely to be presented by a union with those likely to be presented by an employer.

 3. Describe the steps in the traditional organizing drive. What "nontraditional" organizing tactics are unions using to increase their membership ranks?

 4. What are the functions of national unions and local unions?

5. What arguments would public-sector managers put forth in opposition to unionization?

6. a. What are some of the actions being taken by unions to cope with the contemporary challenges they face?

   b. Why have attitudes toward organized labor, on the part of certain segments of our society, become less favorable than they were in the past?

## The Unfair Labor Practice Charge against Apollo Corporation

Bob Thomas was discharged after nineteen years as a plant maintenance engineer with Apollo Corporation. During that time he had received average, and sometimes below-average, annual performance appraisals. Thomas was known as something of a complainer and troublemaker, and he was highly critical of management. Prior to his termination, his attendance record for the previous five years had been very poor. However, Apollo Corporation had never enforced its attendance policy, and Thomas had never been disciplined for his attendance problems. In fact, until recently, Apollo management had been rather laid-back in its dealings with employees.

Apollo Corporation produces general component parts for the communications industry—an industry beset since 1991 by intense competitive pressures. To meet this competitive challenge, Jean Lipski, HR director, held a series of meetings with managers in which she instructed them to tighten up their supervisory relationship with employees. They were told to enforce HR policies strictly and to begin disciplinary action against employees not conforming to company policy. These changes did not sit well with employees, particularly Bob Thomas. Upon hearing of the new management approach, Thomas became irate and announced, "They can't get away with this. I wrote the book around here." But secretly, Thomas believed his past conduct was catching up with him, and he became concerned about protecting his job.

One night after work, Thomas called a union organizer of the Brotherhood of Machine Engineers and asked that a union drive begin at Apollo. Within a week employees began handing out flyers announcing a union meeting. When Lipski heard of the organizing campaign and Thomas's leadership in it, she decided to terminate his employment. Thomas's termination paper read: "Discharged for poor work performance and unsatisfactory attendance." Thomas was called into Lipski's office and told of the discharge. After leaving her office, Thomas called the union organizer, and they both went to the regional office of the NLRB to file an unfair labor practice charge on Thomas's behalf. The ULP alleged that he was fired for his support of the union and the organizing drive.

### QUESTIONS

1. What, if any, violation of the law did the Apollo Corporation commit?
2. What arguments will Jean Lipski and Bob Thomas use to support their cases?
3. Will the discharge of Thomas help or hinder the union's organizing attempt? Explain fully.

## Apollo Corporation: The Organizing Drive

Jean Lipski, HR director for Apollo Corporation, had little experience with unions in general and no specific experience with union organizing campaigns. Unfortunately for Lipski, the Brotherhood of Machine Engineers, Local 1463, began an organizing drive against Apollo on June 1. While the union's initial efforts were confined to passing out flyers about an organizational meeting, by June 10 it was obvious that employee support for the union had grown and union campaigning had greatly intensified. The question faced by Lipski was no longer "Should Apollo do something?" but rather "What should Apollo do?" It was obvious to Lipski that the union was committed to a full-fledged effort to unionize the company's employees. Supervisors reported to her that union supporters were passing out authorization cards in order to petition the NLRB for a certification election.

### QUESTIONS

1.  Since the job of a labor organizer is to build a case for the union and against the company, what information about the organization do you think the union organizer would like to have?
2.  What should Apollo do—both strategically and tactically—to defeat the organizing drive? Be specific.
3.  List things that managers should *not* do lest they commit unfair labor practices.

## NOTES AND REFERENCES

1.  Aaron Bernstein, "The UAW's Next Battleground," *Business Week,* July 26, 1999, 28–29. See also Joann Muller, "Hey, Thanks for the Bargaining Chip," *Business Week,* May 17, 1999, 43.
2.  Bruce E. Kaufman, "Nonunion Employee Representation in the Pre-Wagner Act Years: A Reassessment," *Journal of Labor Research* 20, no. 1 (Winter 1999): 9–29.
3.  Bruce E. Kaufman and David Lewin, "Is the NLRA Still Relevant to Today's Economy and Workforce?" *Labor Law Journal* 49, no. 7 (September 1998): 1114–17.
4.  *Labor-Management Relations Act,* Public Law 101, 80th Congress, 1947.
5.  *Sixty-third Annual Report of the National Labor Relations Board—1998* (Washington, D.C.: U.S. Government Printing Office, 1999), Section 1.
6.  *Labor-Management Relations Act,* sec. 10(c), 1947, as amended.
7.  Michael O. Miller, "Thirty-Seven Years with the NLRB," *Perspectives on Work* 2, no. 1 (1998): 44–46.
8.  Joel E. Davidson, "Successful Mediation: The Do's and Don'ts," *Dispute Resolution Journal* 53, no. 3 (August 1998): 26–29. See also Nancy Kauffman and Barbara Davis, "The Mediation Solution," *Dispute Resolution Journal* 53, no. 2 (May 1998): 8–49.
9.  Telephone interview with Ron Collotta, commissioner, FMCS, Phoenix, Arizona, July 12, 1999.
10. Arthur L. Bowker, "Trust Violators in the Labor Movement: A Study of Union Embezzlements," *Journal of Labor Research* 19, no. 3 (Summer 1998): 571–79.
11. Helene Boetticher, "The Effects of a Violation of the LMRDA on the Outcome of an Election," *Labor Law Journal* 49, no. 8 (December 1998): 1191–94.
12. For an expanded model of the labor relations process, see John Dunlop, *Industrial Relations Systems* (New York: Henry Holt, 1958), Chapter 1. This book is a classic in the labor relations field. Also, those interested in labor relations may wish to explore in greater detail the historical developments of the U.S. labor movement. Much can be learned about the current operations of labor organizations and the philosophies of labor officials from labor's historical context. A brief but comprehensive history of labor unions can be found in *A Brief History of the American Labor Movement,* U.S. Department of Labor, Bureau of Labor Statistics, Bulletin 1000.
13. John A. McClendon, Hoyt N. Wheeler, and Roger D. Weikle, "The Individual Decision to Unionize," *Labor Studies Journal* 23, no. 3 (Fall 1998): 34–54.
14. John A. Fossum, *Labor Relations: Development, Structure, Process,* 7th ed. (Homewood, Ill.: Irwin, 1999).
15. Marc G. Singer and Thomas Li-Ping Tang, "Factors Related to Perceived Organizational Instrumentality," *Journal of Collective Negotiations in the Public Sector* 25, no. 3 (1996): 271–85.
16. William H. Holley and Kenneth M. Jennings, *The Labor Relations Process,* 6th ed. (Fort Worth, Tex.: Dryden Press, 1996).
17. Richard W. Hurd, "Union-Free Bargaining Strategies and First Contact Failures," *Proceedings of the Forty-eighth Annual Meeting* (San Francisco: Industrial Relations Research Association, 1996),145–52. See also

Kate Bronfen Brenner, "Lasting Victories, Successful Union Strategies for Winning First Contracts," *Proceedings of the Forty-eighth Annual Meeting,* 161–67; G. Pascal Zachary, "Long Litigation Often Holds Up Union Victories," *The Wall Street Journal,* November 17, 1995, B-1; Thomas F. Reed, "Securing a Union Contract: Impact of the Union Organizer,"*Industrial Relations* 32, no. 2 (Spring 1993): 188–203.

18. Glenn Burkins, "Union Membership Fell Further in 1997," *The Wall Street Journal,* March 18, 1998, A-2.

19. Teresa Conrow and Linda Delp, "Teaching Organizing Through Workers' Experiences," *Labor Studies Journal* 24, no. 1 (Spring 1999): 42–57. See also Larry Reynolds, "Jump-Starting Organized Labor," *HRFocus* 75, no. 10 (October 1998): 15.

20. Aaron Bernstein, "Labor Helps Turn the Tide—The Old Fashioned Way," *Business Week,* November 16, 1998, 45.

21. Jeffrey A. Mello, "The Enemy Within: When Paid Union Organizers Become Employees," *Labor Law Journal* 47, no. 10 (October 1996): 677–83; James A. Burns, Jr., "Refusing to Hire Union Organizers," *Employee Relations Law Journal* 21, no. 3 (Winter 1995–96): 161–66.

22. *NLRB v Town and Country Electric, Inc.,* 116 S. Ct. 450 (1995).

23. Scott D. Rechtschaffen, "The New Strategy of Union Organizing," *HRFocus* 75, no. 6 (June 1998): 3.

24. Daniel V. Yager and Joseph J. LoBue, "Corporate Campaigns and Card Checks: Creating the Company Union of the Twenty-First Century," *Employee Relations Law Journal* 24, no. 4 (Spring 1999): 21–56. See also Herbert R. Northrup, "Corporate Campaigns: The Perversion of the Regulatory Process," *Journal of Labor Research* 17, no. 3 (Summer 1996): 345–55; Charles R. Perry, "Corporate Campaigns in Context," *Journal of Labor Research* 17, no. 3 (Summer 1996): 329–41; Kenneth A. Jenero and Mark A. Spognardi, "Defending Against the Corporate Campaign: Selected Legal Responses to Common Union Tactics," *Journal of Labor Research* 17, no. 3 (Summer 1996): 119–37; Columbus R. Gangemi, Jr., and Joseph J. Torres, "The Corporate Campaign at Caterpillar," *Journal of Labor Research* 17, no. 3 (Summer 1996): 378–92.

25. "Unions Turn to SEC, Seeking Aid in Fighting Corporate 'Villains'," *The Wall Street Journal,* May 18, 1999, A-1.

26. Aaron Bernstein, "Making Nice in Detroit," *Business Week,* June 21, 1999, 46.

27. G. Harrison Darby and Margaret R. Bryant, "When Unions Knock, How Should Employers Answer?" *HRMagazine* 42, no. 7 (July 1997): 124–28.

28. See endnote 5.

29. Jonathan A. Segal, "Unshackle Your Supervisors to Stay Union Free," *HRMagazine* 43, no. 7 (June 1998): 177–84.

30. If over 50 percent of the employees have signed authorization cards, the union can ask the employer for recognition. A union usually will not make a request for recognition unless a substantial majority—often 60 or 70 percent—of employees sign cards. This large percentage is necessary since the employer will likely question the legitimacy of some cards or the eligibility of some workers to be represented or to vote in the election. If the employer does not voluntarily recognize the union, either party can petition for an NLRB certification election to determine whether the union has majority support.

31. Marcus Hart Sandver and Kathryn J. Ready, "Trends in and Determinants of Outcomes in Multi-Union Certification Elections," *Journal of Labor Research* 19, no. 1 (Winter 1998): 165–72.

32. Milton Mayfield and Jacqueline Mayfield, "NLRB Election Delays: Do They Make a Difference?" *Labor Law Journal* 50, no. 3 (March 1999): 53–57.

33. The number of unions associated with the AFL-CIO has steadily declined during the past twenty years. The decline has largely been caused by the mergers of unions through absorptions, amalgamations, or affiliations. Several prominent mergers have been the merger of the International Ladies Garment Workers Union and the Amalgamated Clothing and Textile Workers Union into the Union of Needletrades, Industrial and Textile Employees; the merger of the Packinghouse and Industrial Workers with the United Food & Commercial Workers; and the merger of the Woodworkers with the Machinists. See Gary N. Chaison, "The Form and Frequency of Union Mergers," *Labor Law Journal* 47, no. 8 (August 1996): 493–97.

34. Telephone conversation with Charles Huggins, secretary-treasurer, Arizona State AFL-CIO, Phoenix, July 14, 1999.

35. Renaud Paquet and Isabelle Roy, "Why Do People Get Involved in Local Union Office?" *Journal of Collective Negotiations in the Public Sector* 27, no. 1 (1998): 63–77.

36. Researchers have discussed the erosion of union steward power in contract administration. The loss of power has been attributed to bureaucratization and centralization of labor relations activity within both unions and management hierarchies. While no one doubts the influence—positive or negative—that stewards can have on labor-management relations, the shifting power of the steward is important in deciding labor-management controversies.

37. John T. Delaney, Jack Fiorito, and Paul Jarley, "Evolutionary Politics? Union Differences and Political Activities in the 1990s," *Journal of Labor Research* 20, no. 3 (Summer 1999): 277–95.

38. Marick F. Masters, "AFSCME as a Political Union," *Journal of Labor Research* 19, no. 2 (Spring 1998): 313–49.

39. Data obtained from union web pages, July 14, 1999.

40. Albert A. Blum and I. B. Helburn, "Federal Labor-Management Relations: The Beginning," *Journal of Collective Negotiations in the Public Sector* 24, no. 4 (1997): 255–77.

41. *Code of Federal Regulations* (CFR) 1959–1963 Compilation, 521.

42. George W. Bohlander, "The Federal Service Impasses Panel: A Ten Year Review and Analysis," *Journal of Collective Negotiations in the Public Sector* 24, no. 3 (Fall 1995): 193–200.

43. John Lund and Cheryl L. Maranto, "Public Sector Law: An Update," in *Public Sector Employment* (University of Wisconsin-Madison: Industrial Relations Research Association, 1996), Chapter 1.

44. Richard W. Hurd, "Contesting the Dinosaur Image: The Labor Movement's Search for a Future," *Labor Studies Journal* 22, no. 4 (Winter 1998): 5–30. See also Mark Crouch, "A Change of Image Is Not Enough," *Labor Studies Journal* 22, no. 4 (Winter 1998): 31–42.

45. Del Jones, "Fewer Wear the Union Label," *USA Today,* August 10, 1998, 3-B. See also David Whitford, "Labor's Lost Change," *Fortune,* September 28, 1998, 177–82.

46. Marjorie Valbrun, "To Reverse Declines, Unions Are Targeting Immigrant Workers," *The Wall Street Journal,* May 27, 1999, A-1.

47. Aaron Bernstein, "Andy Stern's Mission Impossible," *Business Week,* June 10, 1996, 73.

48. Jodie Morse, "Unionizing the E.R.," *Time,* July 5, 1999, 62.

49. Tim Blonfield, "80 Area Doctors Organize 1st Union," *Cincinnati Enquirer,* July 22, 1998, 1.

50. De'Ann Weimer, "The Doctor Is in—A Union Meeting," *Business Week,* February 9, 1999, 6.

51. "The Debate over Wage Equity Continues," *HRFocus* 73, no. 3 (March 1996): 8.

52. "AFL-CIO Shows Concern over Pace of Organizing," *Bulletin to Management* 50, no. 10 (March 1999): 74.

53. Constantine Von Hoffman, "Does This Company Need a Union?" *Harvard Business Review* 76, no. 3 (May-June 1998): 24–28. See also Jonathan A. Segal, "Keeping Norma Ray at Bay," *HRMagazine* 41, no. 8 (August 1996): 111–19.

54. Roger D. Staton, "Hiring of Replacement Workers: An Insidious Weapon against Labor or Management's Last Bargaining Chip?" *Labor Law Journal* 45, no. 1 (January 1994): 25–32.

## Answers to HRM 1

1. No. Applicants are considered as employees and, as such, are protected under the law.
2. No. Individual questioning of employees about their union membership or activities is unlawful.
3. No. Except in specific situations (for example, to promote safety), employees have the right to wear union insignia.
4. Yes.
5. Yes. Blacklisting of job applicants or employees is against labor law.
6. No. During an organizing drive, an employer cannot promise improvements in wages or benefits as a means of defeating the union.
7. Yes. Both employers and unions are subject to unfair labor practice charges.
8. No. Employees are allowed union representation during disciplinary hearings.
9. Yes. Employees can be disciplined or discharged for work-related misconduct but not solely because of their union affiliations or union sentiments.
10. Yes. Antiunion remarks are not unlawful, provided they are not coercive.

# chapter 15

# Collective Bargaining and Contract Administration

## AFTER STUDYING THIS CHAPTER, YOU SHOULD BE ABLE TO

**OBJECTIVE 1**
Discuss the bargaining process and the bargaining goals and strategies of a union and an employer.

**OBJECTIVE 2**
Describe the forms of bargaining power that a union and an employer may utilize to enforce their bargaining demands.

**OBJECTIVE 3**
Cite the principal methods by which bargaining deadlocks may be resolved.

**OBJECTIVE 4**
Give examples of current collective bargaining trends.

**OBJECTIVE 5**
Identify the major provisions of a labor agreement and describe the issue of management rights.

**OBJECTIVE 6**
Describe a typical union grievance procedure.

**OBJECTIVE 7**
Explain the basis for arbitration awards.

N egotiating is a major part of our daily lives. We negotiate when buying a car or a home or, sometimes, when setting our salary. Researchers studying the art of negotiating note that the basic techniques of negotiating are applicable to a variety of bargaining arrangements—including labor negotiations. Therefore, while the focus of this chapter is labor-management negotiations, the bargaining principles discussed here are appropriate to diverse situations.

Once a labor organization wins bargaining rights for employees, its two primary functions are to negotiate the labor agreement and resolve member grievances through the grievance-arbitration process. Interestingly, according to labor law, once the union is certified to negotiate for bargaining unit members, it must represent everyone in the unit equally, regardless of whether employees subsequently join the union or elect to remain nonmembers. The labor agreement that ultimately is negotiated establishes the wages, hours, employee benefits, job security, and other conditions under which represented employees agree to work. An employer's negotiators, on the other hand, must come up with an agreement that will allow the employer to remain competitive. The agreement must be one that can be administered with a minimum of conflict and that facilitates HRM.

# The Bargaining Process

**Collective bargaining process**
Process of negotiating a labor agreement, including the use of economic pressures by both parties

Those unfamiliar with contract negotiations often view the process as an emotional conflict between labor and management, complete with marathon sessions, fist pounding, and smoke-filled rooms. In reality, negotiating a labor agreement entails long hours of extensive preparation combined with diplomatic maneuvering and the development of bargaining strategies.[1] Furthermore, negotiation is only one part of the **collective bargaining process**. (See Figure 15.1.) Collective bargaining also may include the use of economic pressures in the form of strikes and boycotts by a union. Lockouts, plant closures, and the replacement of strikers are similar pressures used by an employer. In addition, either or both parties may seek support from the general public or from the courts as a means of pressuring the opposing side.

## Preparing for Negotiations

Preparing for negotiations includes assembling data to support bargaining proposals and forming the bargaining team. This will permit collective bargaining to be conducted on an orderly, factual, and positive basis with a greater likelihood of achieving desired goals. Negotiators often develop a bargaining book that serves as a cross-reference file to determine which contract clauses would be affected by a demand. The bargaining book also contains a general history of contract terms and their relative importance to management.[2] Assuming that the labor agreement is not the first to be negotiated by the parties, preparation for negotiations ideally should start soon after the current agreement has been signed. This practice will allow negotiators to review and diagnose weaknesses and mistakes made during the previous negotiations while the experience is still current in their minds.

**FIGURE 15.1**

The Collective Bargaining Process

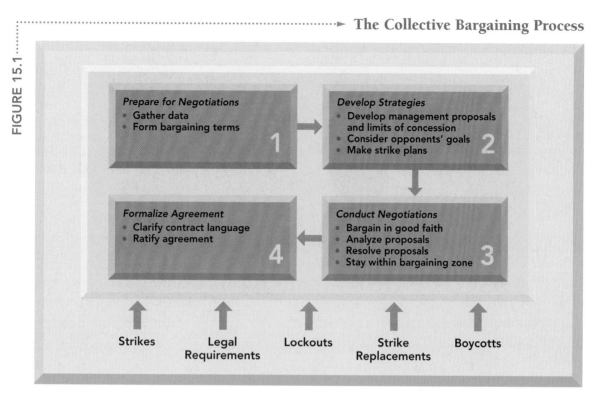

1. **Prepare for Negotiations**
   - Gather data
   - Form bargaining terms

2. **Develop Strategies**
   - Develop management proposals and limits of concession
   - Consider opponents' goals
   - Make strike plans

4. **Formalize Agreement**
   - Clarify contract language
   - Ratify agreement

3. **Conduct Negotiations**
   - Bargain in good faith
   - Analyze proposals
   - Resolve proposals
   - Stay within bargaining zone

Strikes    Legal Requirements    Lockouts    Strike Replacements    Boycotts

### Gathering Bargaining Data

Internal data relating to grievances, disciplinary actions, transfers and promotions, layoffs, overtime, former arbitration awards, and wage payments are useful in formulating and supporting the employer's bargaining position. The supervisors and managers who must live with and administer the labor agreement can be very important sources of ideas and suggestions concerning changes that are needed in the *next* agreement. Their contact with union members and representatives provides them with a firsthand knowledge of the changes that union negotiators are likely to propose.

Data obtained from government publications such as the *Monthly Labor Review* and agencies such as the Department of Labor's Bureau of Labor Statistics can help to support the employer's position during negotiations; information from *The Wall Street Journal* and publications of the Bureau of National Affairs and Commerce Clearing House can also be of use. Each of these data sources can provide information on general economic conditions, cost-of-living trends, and geographical wage rates covering a wide range of occupations.

When negotiating contracts, union bargainers talk about "taking wages out of competition." This term refers to having similar contract provisions—particularly concerning wages and benefits—between different companies in order to prevent one employer from having a favorable labor cost advantage over another. **Pattern bargaining** allows unions to show their members that they are receiving wages and benefits similar to other employees doing like work, and employers are assured that their labor costs are comparable with those of their competitors. Pattern

**Pattern bargaining**
Bargaining in which unions negotiate provisions covering wages and other benefits that are similar to those provided in other agreements existing within the industry or region

"I'm not sure about Coach. He never teaches us anything about contract negotiations."

Reprinted with special permission of King Features Syndicate.

bargaining also prevents union political problems. Employers quite naturally try to minimize increases by citing other employers who are paying lower compensation costs. Other negotiated labor agreements can establish a pattern that one side or the other may seek to follow in support of its own bargaining position. Importantly, while pattern bargaining has lost much of its prominence at the national level, at the local and regional levels, it still plays a significant part in settling the terms of the labor agreement.

### Bargaining Teams

The composition and size of bargaining teams are often a reflection of the desires and practices of the parties. Normally, each side will have four to six representatives at the negotiating table. The chief negotiator for management will be the vice president or manager for labor relations; the chief negotiator for the union will be the local union president or union business agent. Others making up management's team may include representatives from accounting or finance, operations, employment, legal, or training. The local union president is likely to be supported by the chief steward, various local union vice presidents, and a representative from the national union.

Many negotiators, over a period of time, acquire the ability "to read their opponents' minds," to anticipate their actions and reactions. Inexperienced negotiators bargaining for the first time, on the other hand, may misinterpret their opponents' actions and statements and unintentionally cause a deadlock.

The initial meeting of the bargaining teams is a particularly important one because it establishes the climate that will prevail during the negotiations that follow. A cordial attitude, with perhaps the injection of a little humor, can contribute much to a relaxation of tensions and help the negotiations to begin smoothly. This *attitudinal structuring* is done to change the attitudes of the parties toward each other, often with the objective of persuading one side to accept the other side's demands.[3]

## Developing Bargaining Strategies

Negotiators for an employer should develop a written plan covering their bargaining strategy. The plan should consider the proposals that the union is likely to submit, based on the most recent agreements with other employers and the demands that remain unsatisfied from previous negotiations. The plan should also consider the goals the union is striving to achieve and the extent to which it may be willing to make concessions or to resort to strike action in order to achieve these goals.

At a minimum, the employer's bargaining strategy must address these points:

- Likely union proposals and management responses to them
- A listing of management demands, limits of concessions, and anticipated union responses

- Development of a database to support management bargaining proposals and to counteract union demands
- A contingency operating plan should employees strike

Certain elements of strategy are common to both the employer and the union. Generally, the initial demands presented by each side are greater than those it actually may hope to achieve. This is done in order to provide room for concessions. Moreover, each party will usually avoid giving up the maximum it is capable of conceding in order to allow for further concessions that may be needed to break a bargaining deadlock.

## Conducting the Negotiations

The economic conditions under which negotiations take place, the experience and personalities of the negotiators on each side, the goals they are seeking to achieve, and the strength of the relative positions are among the factors that tend to make each bargaining situation unique.[4] Additionally, in today's competitive and complex bargaining environment, resolving differences and promoting cooperation require an analytically grounded process and high levels of problem-solving skill. We are now in the midst of what can be described as a technological shift in the skills and techniques required of labor and management negotiators.

### Bargaining in Good Faith

Once bargaining begins, an employer is obligated to negotiate in good faith with the union's representative over conditions of employment. Good faith requires the employer's negotiators to meet with their union counterparts at a reasonable time and place to discuss these conditions. It requires also that the proposals submitted by each party be realistic. In discussing the other party's proposals, each side must offer reasonable counterproposals for those it is unwilling to accept.

Where an employer argues a financial inability-to-pay position during negotiations, the duty to bargain in good faith requires the employer to furnish relevant financial information to the union if the claim is legitimate and not simply based on unwillingness to meet union wage demands.[5] Finally, both parties must sign the written document containing the agreement reached through negotiations.

The National Labor Relations Board (NLRB) defines the duty to bargain as bargaining on all matters concerning rates of pay, wages, hours of employment, or other conditions of employment.[6] These topics are called *mandatory subjects* of bargaining, and both the employer and the union must bargain in good faith over these issues. The law, however, does not requires either party to agree to a proposal or to make concessions while negotiating these subjects. On other topics, called *permissive issues*—matters that are lawful but not related to wages, hours, or other conditions of employment—the parties are free to bargain, but neither side can force the other side to bargain over these topics. Permissive subjects might include a union demand to ratify supervisory promotions or consultation on setting the price of the organization's product or service. *Illegal subjects* of bargaining would include such issues as the closed shop or compulsory dues checkoff. If a demand were made concerning an illegal item, the NLRB would find a violation of good-faith bargaining under section 8(a)(5) of the Taft-Hartley Act. Where labor and management negotiators cannot agree on whether a bargaining proposal is a mandatory or a permissive issue, the NLRB will decide the dispute.[7] Figure 15.2 illustrates several prevalent examples of bad-faith employer bargaining.

## Analyzing the Proposals

The negotiation of a labor agreement can have some of the characteristics of a poker game, with each side attempting to determine its opponent's position while not revealing its own. Each party will normally try to avoid disclosing the relative importance that it attaches to a proposal so that it will not be forced to pay a higher price than is necessary to have the proposal accepted. As with sellers who will try to get a higher price for their products if they think the prospective buyer strongly desires them, negotiators will try to get greater concessions in return for granting those their opponents want most.

As they develop their collective bargaining proposals, astute negotiators know that some demands are more important to their side than others—either for economic or for political reasons. Therefore the proposals that each side submits generally may be divided into those it feels it must achieve, those it would like to achieve, and those it is submitting primarily for trading purposes. As bargainers discuss the proposals from each side, they are constantly trying to determine the intensity with which each side is committed to its demands. The ability to accurately gauge "commitment" to various proposals can spell the difference between an agreement or a bargaining impasse.

## Resolving the Proposals

Regardless of its degree of importance, every proposal submitted must be resolved if an agreement is to be finalized. A proposal may be withdrawn, accepted by the other side in its entirety, or accepted in some compromise form.

For each bargaining issue to be resolved satisfactorily, the point at which agreement is reached must be within limits that the union and the employer are willing to accept. In a frequently cited bargaining model, Ross Stagner and Hjalmar Rosen call the area within these two limits the **bargaining zone**. In some bargaining situations, such as the one illustrated in Figure 15.3, the solution desired by one party may exceed the limits of the other party. Thus that solution is outside the bargaining zone. If that party refuses to modify its demands sufficiently to bring them within

**Bargaining zone**
Area within which the union and the employer are willing to concede when bargaining

**FIGURE 15.2**

## Examples of Bad-Faith Employer Bargaining

- Refusing to discuss or consider mandatory subjects of bargaining as defined by the NLRB
- Using delaying tactics such as frequent postponements of bargaining sessions
- Withdrawing concessions previously granted
- Insisting that the union stop striking before resuming negotiations
- Unilaterally changing bargaining topics
- Negotiating with individual employees other than bargaining unit representatives
- Engaging in mere surface bargaining rather than honest negotiations
- Refusing to meet with duly appointed or elected union representatives

FIGURE 15.3

## The Bargaining Zone and Negotiation Influences

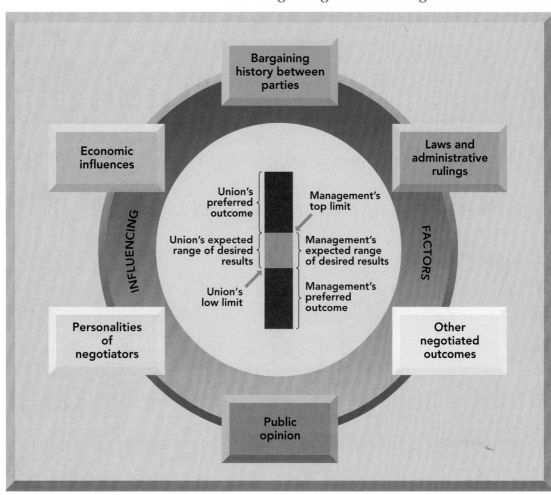

Source: Adapted from Ross Stagner and Hjalmar Rosen, *Psychology of Union-Management Relations* (Belmont, Calif.: Wadsworth Publishing Company, 1965), 96. Adapted with permission from Brooks/Cole Publishing Co.

the bargaining zone or if the opposing party refuses to extend its limit to accommodate the demands of the other party, a bargaining deadlock will result.[8] For example, when bargaining a wage increase for employees, if the union's lowest limit is a 4 percent increase and management's top limit is 6 percent, an acceptable range—the bargaining zone—is available to both parties. If management's top limit is only 3 percent, however, a bargaining zone is not available to either side and a deadlock is likely to occur. Figure 15.3, which is based on the original model by Stagner and Rosen, shows that as bargaining takes place, several important variables influence the negotiators and their ability to reach agreement within the bargaining zone.

## Formalizing the Agreement

When bargaining proposals are finally agreed upon, they must be reduced to clear and unambiguous contract wording. This task, however, is often difficult since the language of labor relations is sometimes open to unintentional confusion. For example, phrases like "just cause discharge," "emergency conditions," or "a day's work" can be given different interpretations dependent upon their application. If an employee works seven hours of an eight-hour shift, and then goes home with the permission of supervision, has the individual technically completed "a day's work" according to the language of the agreement? When ambiguity creeps into a labor contract, arbitration may be required to resolve the dispute.

Before negotiated contracts—called tentative agreements—become binding, they must be ratified (e.g., approved) by the membership of the local union. The bylaws of a local might state that a tentative agreement becomes binding only when 75 percent of the membership votes acceptance. When tentative agreements are not approved, then the parties must return to the bargaining table or face a bargaining impasse.

## Nonadversarial Bargaining

U.S. labor-management negotiations are characterized as adversarial. With adversarial bargaining, negotiators start with defined positions and through deferral, persuasion, trade, or power, the parties work toward the resolution of individual bargaining demands. With traditional bargaining—and its give-and-take philosophy—the results may or may not be to the complete satisfaction of one or both parties. In fact, when one side feels it received "the short end of the stick," bitter feelings may persist throughout the life of the agreement. As noted by one labor negotiator, "adversarial bargaining does little to establish a long-term positive relationship based on open communications and trust. By its nature, it leads to suspicion and compromise."[9] To overcome these negative feelings, labor and management practitioners may use a nonadversarial approach to negotiating. (Figure 15.4 contrasts the differences between adversarial and nonadversarial bargaining.)

**Nonadversarial bargaining**
Problem-solving bargaining based on a win-win philosophy and the development of a positive long-term relationship

**Nonadversarial bargaining**, also called interest-based bargaining (IBB) by the Federal Mediation and Conciliation Service (FMCS), is based on the identification and resolution of mutual interests rather than the resolve of specific bargaining demands.[10] As defined by the FMCS, interest-based bargaining is "a problem-solving process conducted in a principled way that creates effective solutions while improving the bargaining relationship."[11] The focus of nonadversarial bargaining strategy is to discover mutual bargaining interests with the intent of formulating options and solutions for mutual gain.[12] Specifically, during negotiations the parties will

- Present an issue (a topic for discussion) and interests (concerns about an issue)
- Brainstorm options to resolve interests
- Establish a set of standards to evaluate the options
- Evaluate options relative to standards
- Select the most appropriate option and reduce it to writing

Nonadversarial bargaining, or IBB, is novel in both its philosophy and bargaining process. Also distinct are the bargaining tools used to expedite a successful nonadversarial negotiating experience. Rather than using proposals and counterproposals as a means of reaching agreement (as with adversarial negotiations), participants use brainstorming, consensus decision making, active listening, process

FIGURE 15.4

► **Adversarial vs. Nonadversarial Bargaining**

| ADVERSARIAL | NONADVERSARIAL |
|---|---|
| • Discredit opponent's position; attack individuals. | • Address mutual problems and concerns; focus on specific issues—not on individuals or past conflicts. |
| • Present and defend position; provide supporting materials. | • Explore interests of joint concern; clearly define mutual issues. |
| • Continually insist on predetermined bargaining positions. | • Be open-minded to possibilities and/or future opportunities; satisfy others' interests as well as your own. |
| • Negotiate to obtain outcomes for your own best interest. | • Work toward satisfying the interests of all concerned. |
| • Use power, pressure, deferral to obtain desired solutions. | • Define acceptable solutions measured against jointly developed standards; use consensus decision making to reach solutions. |

Source: *Interest-Based Negotiations: Participants' Handbook* (Washington, D.C.: Federal Mediation and Conciliation Service, 1998).

checking, and matrix building to facilitate the settlement of issues. (See Highlights in HRM 1.) An underlying goal of nonadversarial bargaining is to create a relationship for the future based on trust, understanding, and mutual respect.

## The Union's Power in Collective Bargaining

During negotiations, it is necessary for each party to retreat sufficiently from its original position to permit an agreement to be achieved. If this does not occur, the negotiations will become deadlocked, and the union may resort to the use of economic power to achieve its demands. Otherwise, its only alternative will be to have members continue working without a labor agreement once the old one has expired. The economic power of the union may be exercised by striking, picketing, or boycotting the employer's products and encouraging others to do likewise. As managers know well, the ability to engage or even threaten to engage in such activities also can serve as a form of pressure.

### Striking the Employer

A strike is the refusal of a group of employees to perform their jobs. Although strikes account for only a small portion of total workdays lost in industry each year, they are a costly and emotional event for all concerned. Unions usually will seek strike authorization from their members to use as a bargaining ploy to gain concessions that will make a strike unnecessary. A strike vote by the members does not mean they actually want or expect to go out on strike. Rather, it is intended as a vote of confidence to strengthen the position of their leaders at the bargaining table.

Of critical importance to the union is the extent, if any, to which the employer will be able to continue operating through the use of supervisory and nonstriking

# The Tools and Techniques of Interest-Based Bargaining as Described by the FMCS

### Brainstorming
Brainstorming is used to develop creative and innovative ideas. All team members contribute suggestions in a round-robin fashion while a recorder captures ideas without criticism. Brainstorming permits novel ideas to surface, enlarges the pool of ideas including unfamiliar ones, encourages synergy, and discourages evaluation. FMCS brainstorming escapes the boundaries of logical thinking and transcends tradition, precedent, time, staff, and resource constraints.

### Consensus Decision Making
Consensus decision making involves finding a solution acceptable enough that all negotiators can support the decision to some degree. Consensus decision making does not require unanimity nor does it invoke majority vote. Rather, the technique encourages total participation in a give-and-take exchange of thoughts and opinions. Differences are debated and compromises take place. Consensus decison making can be used to establish ground rules, formulate standards, agree upon solutions, or develop a joint statement.

### Active Listening
Active listening is the capacity to hear effectively and understand words, including the emotions and body language of the speaker. It also encourages the asking of questions to verify or expand on the information received. Active listening is particularly useful when selecting an issue, discussing interests, defining standards, or communicating results to constituents.

### Process Checking
Process checking allows for monitoring adherence to the IBB process and the interactions of negotiators. This technique gives team members a structured opportunity to share thoughts and/or observations about negotiations. Importantly, process checking prevents negative behavior from becoming ingrained in the bargaining process. Process checking is employed when a team member perceives that ground rules are violated or when negotiators are not following the IBB process.

### Recording
Recording is the writing of spoken ideas on a flip chart for all to view. It is used to capture ground rules, proposed options, standards, solutions, and/or issues and interests. Recording helps to preserve language and the meaning of oral statements while creating joint ownership of ideas.

### Matrix Building
Matrix building facilitates the evaluation of options against standards. In a matrix formulation, columns represent standards and rows represent options. Negotiators place a "yes" or "no" in each matrix square depending on whether the option satisfies the standards under review.

personnel and employees hired to replace the strikers.[13] In organizations with high levels of technology and automation, and consequently fewer employees, continuing service with supervisors and managers is more likely. Among the highly automated telephone companies, most services can be maintained by supervisors during a strike. According to one authority, "Because of technological change, striking in many industries no longer has the effect of curtailing the employer's operations significantly."[14] Consequently, the greater the ability of the employer to continue operating, the less the union's chances of gaining its demands through a strike.

Since 1985 the number of work stoppages in the United States involving 1,000 or more workers has declined to well under 75 each year. In 1998 the Bureau of Labor Statistics reported 34 such stoppages,[15] a figure that contrasts sharply with the number of strikes reported in the 1960s (282 average each year) and 1970s (288 average each year). HRM practitioners conclude that the decline in the use of the strike by unions can be attributed to the increased willingness of employers to hire replacements when employees strike and the increased automation of employee jobs.

### Picketing the Employer

When a union goes on strike, it will picket the employer by placing persons at business entrances to advertise the dispute and to discourage people from entering the premises. Even when the strikers represent only a small proportion of the employees within the organization, they can cause the shutdown of an entire organization if a sufficient number of the organization's remaining employees (i.e., sympathy strikers) refuse to cross their picket line. Also, because unions often refuse to cross another union's picket line, the pickets may serve to prevent trucks and railcars from entering the business to deliver and pick up goods. For example, a Teamster truck driver may refuse to deliver produce to a food store whose employees are out on strike with the United Food & Commercial Workers Union.

*The national union sanctioned the strike of these local union workers.*

**Boycott**
Union tactic to encourage others to refuse to patronize an employer

### *Boycotting the Employer*

Another economic weapon of unions is the **boycott**, which is a refusal to patronize the employer. A *primary boycott* occurs where a union asks its members or customers not to patronize a business where there is a labor dispute; for example, production employees on strike against a hand tool manufacturer might picket a retail store that sells the tool made by the struck employer. Under most circumstances this type of boycott is legal, provided the union advises consumers to boycott the tools and *not* the neutral store. A union may go a step further, however, and attempt to induce third parties, primarily suppliers of the struck employer, to refrain from business dealings with the employer with whom it has a dispute. A boycott of this type, called a *secondary boycott,* generally is illegal under the Taft-Hartley Act.

## The Employer's Power in Collective Bargaining

The employer's power in collective bargaining largely rests in being able to shut down the organization or certain operations within it. The employer can transfer these operations to other locations or can subcontract them to other employers through **outsourcing**. General Motors outsources to foreign manufacturers many parts used in the assembly of American cars. In exercising their economic freedom, however, employers must be careful that their actions are not interpreted by the NLRB to be an attempt to avoid bargaining with the union.

**Outsourcing**
Act of subcontracting operations to other employers

### *Operating during Strikes*

When negotiations become deadlocked, typically it is the union that initiates action and the employer that reacts. In reacting, employers must balance the cost of taking a strike against the long- and short-term costs of agreeing to union demands. They must also consider how long operations might be suspended and the length of time that they and the unions will be able to endure a strike. An employer who chooses to accept a strike must then decide whether or not to continue operating if it is possible to do so.

Organizations today seem to be more willing to face a strike than they were in former years. Several reasons have been advanced to explain this change, including:

1. Union members seem less willing to support strike activity. Thus the union is less able to maintain strike unity among its members.
2. Because organizations are forced to reduce labor costs to meet domestic and global competition, unions have no choice but to accept lower wages and benefits.
3. Technological advances enhance the employer's ability to operate during a strike.
4. Organizations are able to obtain favorable, often concessionary, contracts.

Should employees strike the organization, employers have the right to hire replacement workers. Striking employees have reemployment rights for one year, beginning when they indicate a desire to return to work, should an opening arise. Employers, however, are not obligated to terminate replacement employees to make openings for striking employees.[16]

**Lockout**
> Strategy by which the employer denies employees the opportunity to work by closing its operations

## *Using the Lockout*

Although not often used, a **lockout** occurs when an employer takes the initiative to close its operations. Besides being used in bargaining impasses, lockouts may be used by employers to combat union slowdowns, damage to their property, or violence within the organization that may occur in connection with a labor dispute.

Under NLRB rulings, employers are granted the right to hire temporary replacements during a legitimate lockout. With this right, employers acquire a bargaining weapon equal in force to the union's right to strike. As one observer noted, "The availability of a lockout-with-replacement strategy improves management's ability to battle a union head-on in the way that unions have battled employers for decades." Employers may still be reluctant to resort to a lockout, however, because of their concern that denying work to regular employees might hurt the organization's image.

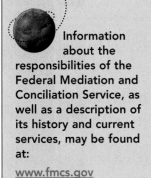

OBJECTIVE 3

## Resolving Bargaining Deadlocks

**USING THE INTERNET**

Information about the responsibilities of the Federal Mediation and Conciliation Service, as well as a description of its history and current services, may be found at:

**www.fmcs.gov**

When a strike or a lockout occurs, both parties are soon affected by it. The employer will suffer a loss of profits and customers, and possibly of public goodwill. The union members suffer a loss of income that is likely to be only partially offset by strike benefits or outside income. The union's leaders risk the possibility of losing members, of being voted out of office, of losing public support, or of having the members vote to decertify the union as their bargaining agent. As the losses to each side mount, the disputing parties usually feel more pressure to achieve a settlement.

### *Mediation and Arbitration*

When the disputing parties are unable to resolve a deadlock, a third party serving in the capacity of either a mediator or an arbitrator may be called upon to provide assistance. A **mediator** serves primarily as a fact finder and to open up a channel of communication between the parties.[17] Typically, the mediator meets with one party and then the other in order to suggest compromise solutions or to recommend concessions from each side that will lead to an agreement without causing either to lose face.[18] Mediators have no power or authority to force either side toward an agreement. They must use their communication skills and the power of persuasion to help the parties resolve their differences.

**Mediator**
> Third party in a labor dispute who meets with one party and then the other in order to suggest compromise solutions or to recommend concessions from each side that will lead to an agreement

The federal government is likely to become involved in labor disputes through the services of the Federal Mediation and Conciliation Service. (See Chapter 14.) The FMCS has been highly successful in resolving bargaining deadlocks.

**Arbitrator**
> Third-party neutral who resolves a labor dispute by issuing a final decision in the disagreement

Unlike a mediator, an **arbitrator** assumes the role of a decision maker and determines what the settlement between the two parties should be. In other words, arbitrators write a final contract that the parties *must* accept. Compared with mediation, arbitration is not often used to settle private-sector bargaining disputes. In the public sector, where strikes are largely prohibited, the use of **interest arbitration** is a common method to resolve bargaining deadlocks.[19] Generally, one or both parties are reluctant to give a third party the power to make the settlement for them. Consequently, a mediator typically is used to break a deadlock and assist the parties in reaching an agreement. An arbitrator generally is called upon to resolve disputes arising in connection with the administration of the agreement, called *rights arbitration* or *grievance arbitration,* which will be discussed shortly.

**Interest arbitration**
> Binding determination of a collective bargaining agreement by an arbitrator

# Trends in Collective Bargaining

Managers see the 21st century as a period of great importance to labor-management relations. Advances in technology, management's antiunion posture, and continued competitive pressures will have their impact. These conditions will affect the attitudes and objectives of both employers and unions in collective bargaining. They will also influence the climate in which bargaining occurs and the bargaining power each side is able to exercise.

## Changes in Collective Bargaining Relationships

While the goal of organized labor has always been to bargain for improved economic and working conditions, large layoffs caused by economic downturns and domestic and global competition have caused both sides to change their bargaining goals and tactics. We are seeing a gradual movement away from direct conflict and toward more labor-management accommodation. Fortunately, labor organizations, such as the Machinists in bargaining with Harley-Davidson; the Paperworkers in bargaining with Champion Paper; the Electrical Workers with General Electric; and the American Federation of State, County, and Municipal Employees with the City of Portland, Maine, have been sufficiently enlightened to recognize the danger of making bargaining demands that will create economic adversity for employers.[20] While cooperative labor relations has long had advocates, today's business environment requires a participative labor-management relationship where both sides work for the advancement of all.[21]

## Facilitating Union-Management Cooperation

Improving union-management cooperation generally requires a restructuring of attitudes by both managers and union officials and members. John Calhoun Wells, director of the Federal Mediation and Conciliation Service, notes, "This cooperative model emphasizes trust, common ground, sharing of information, joint problem solving, risk taking, and innovation."[22] When a cooperative attitude exists, organizations and unions can explore and experiment with new and improved ways of working together, including novel ways of bargaining and resolving areas of disagreement. Also, union-management cooperation programs have a greater chance for success when both parties jointly establish goals and philosophies for mutual gain.

When building a cooperative environment, it is particularly important that union leaders and members believe that management is sincerely interested in their personal well-being, along with improvements in organizational performance.[23] In one study, results showed that union leaders' receptiveness to labor-management cooperation was a function of the extent to which leaders perceived cooperation as a challenge to union survival and a threat to members' well-being.[24] Additionally, a review of meaningful labor-management cooperative endeavors indicates that success depends on an open and honest style of communication grounded in developmental activities. Both supervisors and employees must be trained in participative and problem-solving approaches to problem resolution.[25] In one participative union-management program known to the authors, over 400,000 hours were invested in training managers and employees to interact in a participative manner. The company spent over $5 million in training costs.

## Definition and Forms of Cooperation

Labor-management cooperation can assume any mode of bargaining or joint discussion in which the objective is to improve the well-being of both parties. It is not surprising, therefore, that labor-management programs are of many types. In fact, the purpose and structure of cooperative endeavors largely depends upon the needs and desires of the parties. Areawide labor-management committees are jointly sponsored organizations operating on a geographical or industry basis. They serve to identify common problems—job security or reduced profits, for example—and use joint efforts to resolve them. The Joint Labor-Management Committee (JLMC) in the retail food industry and the Tailored Clothing Technology Corporation (TC2) program in textiles are examples of industry-wide joint committees. Shop committees, department committees, and employee involvement groups are illustrations of union-management efforts at the operating level. For example, at the U.S. Department of Labor, the Employee Involvement/Quality Improvement (EIQI) program has been highly successful in improving organizational effectiveness and the working life of union employees. This program is based entirely on labor-management cooperation and the idea of equal partnership.

Employers implementing cooperative programs must be concerned with the legal implications of these endeavors.[26] The NLRB in the *Electromation, Inc.*, case ruled that where employers establish and support (e.g., dominate) employee groups that discuss topics related to wages, hours, and working conditions, these groups may be deemed labor organizations as identified by Section 2(5) of the National Labor Relations Act. If, however, cooperation groups discuss issues solely

*Replacing traditional labor, robotic welder arms work on the frame of an automobile.*

related to organizational efficiency (e.g., improved productivity or service quality), legal issues may not arise. The proper classification of topics discussed through a cooperative program is the key to avoiding legal difficulties.[27]

## Concessionary Bargaining

Economic adversity and competition motivate a concessionary bargaining stance by management. Research shows that concessions sought by managers have been fairly consistent across industries and are directed toward (1) limiting, freezing, or lowering compensation payments and (2) increasing productivity. To gain wage concessions, employers may offer gainsharing plans (see Chapter 10) that link compensation to productivity or sales. Profit sharing and stock ownership are other plans being offered to motivate employees and reward improvements in performance.

Restrictive work rules are particularly troublesome to employers because, in this age of technology, these rules are detrimental to productivity. Union concessions may include reduction in job classifications or fewer restrictions on work tasks. In return for concessions granted to employers, unions are demanding provisions for greater job security.[28] Unions are also likely to demand provisions restricting the transfer of work, outsourcing (subcontracting), and plant closures by employers. Getting advance notice of shutdowns, as well as severance pay and transfer rights for displaced employees, will be high on the "want lists" of union negotiators. For employees likely to be replaced by technology, unions will bargain for retraining programs as a means to upgrade employee skills.

# The Labor Agreement

The labor agreement is a formal *binding* document listing the terms, conditions, and rules under which labor and management agree to operate. The scope of the agreement (and the length of the written contract) will vary with the size of the employer and the length of the bargaining relationship. Highlights in HRM 2 shows some of the major articles in a labor agreement and also provides examples of some new and progressive contract classes. Two important items in any labor agreement pertain to the issue of management rights and the forms of security afforded the union.

## The Issue of Management Rights

Management rights have to do with conditions of employment over which management is able to exercise exclusive jurisdiction. Since virtually every management right can and has been challenged successfully by unions, the ultimate determination of these rights will depend on the relative bargaining power of the two parties. Furthermore, to achieve union cooperation or concessions, employers have had to relinquish some of these time-honored rights.

### Reserved Rights

In the labor agreement, management rights may be treated as *reserved rights* or as *defined rights*. The **reserved rights** concept holds that "management's authority is supreme in all matters except those it has expressly conceded in the collective

**Reserved rights**
Concept that management's authority is supreme in all matters except those it has expressly conceded to the union in the collective agreement

**HRM 2**

HIGHLIGHTS IN HRM

# Items in a Labor Agreement

*Typical clauses* will cover

- Wages
- Vacations
- Holidays
- Work schedules
- Management rights
- Union security
- Transfers
- Discipline

- Grievance procedures
- No strike/no lockout clause
- Overtime
- Safety procedures
- Severance pay
- Seniority
- Pensions and benefits
- Outsourcing

*Progressive clauses* will cover

- Employee access to records
- Limitations on use of performance evaluation
- Elder care leave
- Flexible medical spending accounts
- Protection against hazards of technology equipment (VDTs)
- Limitations against electronic monitoring
- Procedures governing drug testing
- Bilingual stipends
- Domestic partnership benefits

---

agreement, or in those areas where its authority is restricted by law. Put another way, management does not look to the collective agreement to ascertain its rights; it looks to the agreement to find out which and how much of its rights and powers it has conceded outright or agreed to share with the union."[29]

Reserved rights might include the right of management to determine the product to produce or to select production equipment and procedures. Employers who subscribe to the reserved rights concept prefer not to mention management rights in the labor agreement on the grounds that they possess such rights already. To mention them might create an issue with the union.

### Defined Rights

**Defined rights**

Concept that management's authority should be expressly defined and clarified in the collective agreement

The **defined rights** concept, on the other hand, is intended to reinforce and clarify which rights are exclusively those of management. It serves to reduce confusion and misunderstanding and to remind union officers, union stewards, and employees that management never relinquishes its right to operate the organization. For example, a defined right would include the right of management to take disciplinary action against problem employees. The great majority of labor agreements contain provisions covering management rights. The following is an example of a general statement defining management rights in one labor agreement:

> It is agreed that the company possesses all of the rights, powers, privileges, and authority it had prior to the execution of this agreement; and nothing in this agreement shall be construed to limit the company in any way in the exercise of the regular and customary functions of management and the operation of its business, except as it may be specifically relinquished or modified herein by an express provision of this agreement.[30]

## Forms of Union Security

When a labor organization is certified by the NLRB as the exclusive bargaining representative of all employees in a bargaining unit, by law it must represent all employees in the unit, nonunion and union members alike. In exchange for its obligation to represent all employees equally, union officials will seek to negotiate some form of compulsory membership as a condition of employment. Union officials argue that compulsory membership precludes the possibility that some employees will receive the benefits of unionization without paying their share of the costs. A standard union security provision is dues checkoff, which gives the employer the responsibility of withholding union dues from the paychecks of union members who agree to such a deduction.[31]

Other common forms of union security found in labor agreements include the following:

1. The *closed shop* states that employers will hire only union members. The closed shop is generally illegal in the United States.
2. The *union shop* provides that any employee not a union member upon employment must join the union within thirty days or be terminated.
3. The *agency shop* provides for voluntary membership. However, all bargaining unit members must pay union dues and fees.
4. The *maintenance-of-membership* shop requires that employees who voluntarily join a union must maintain membership during the life of the agreement. Membership withdrawal is possible during a designated escape period.
5. The *open shop* allows employees to join the union or not. Nonmembers do not pay union dues.

Few issues in collective bargaining are more controversial than the negotiation of these agreements. The most popular union security clause, the union shop, is illegal in twenty-one states having right-to-work laws.[32] Right-to-work laws ban any form of compulsory union membership. Section 14(b) of the Taft-Hartley Act permits the individual states to enact legislation prohibiting compulsory union membership as a condition of employment.[33] Generally, right-to-work states are located in the South and West and have been historically agricultural states. (See Figure 15.5.) The right-to-work argument is a heated one with strong supporters on both sides.[34]

Working in conjunction with the union shop clause are the various seniority provisions of the labor agreement. Unions prefer that many personnel decisions (promotions, job transfers, shift assignments, vacations) be based on seniority, a criterion that limits the discretion of managers to make such decisions on the basis of merit.

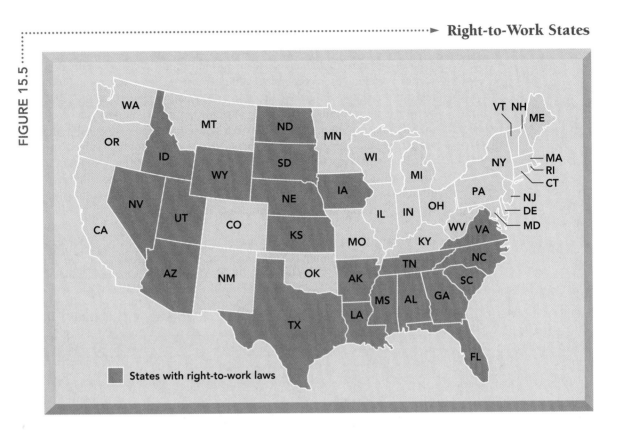

**FIGURE 15.5**

**Right-to-Work States**

States with right-to-work laws

# Administration of the Labor Agreement

Negotiation of the labor agreement, as mentioned earlier, is usually the most publicized and critical aspect of labor relations. Strike deadlines, press conferences, and employee picketing help create this image. Nevertheless, as managers in unionized organizations know, the bulk of labor relations activity comes from the day-to-day administration of the agreement, since no agreement could possibly anticipate all the forms that disputes may take. In addition, once the agreement is signed, each side will naturally interpret ambiguous clauses to its own advantage. These differences are traditionally resolved through the grievance procedure.

## Negotiated Grievance Procedures

**Grievance procedure**
Formal procedure that provides for the union to represent members and nonmembers in processing a grievance

The **grievance procedure** typically provides for the union to represent the interests of its members (and nonmembers as well) in processing a grievance. It is considered by some authorities to be the heart of the bargaining agreement, or the safety valve that gives flexibility to the whole system of collective bargaining.[35] When negotiating a grievance procedure, one important concern for both sides is how effectively the system will serve the needs of labor and management. A well-written grievance procedure will allow grievances to be processed expeditiously and with as little red tape as possible. Furthermore, it should serve to foster cooperation, not conflict, between the employer and the union.

The operation of a grievance procedure is unique to each individual collective bargaining relationship. Grievance procedures are negotiated to address the organization's structure and labor-management philosophy and the specific desires of the parties. Although each procedure is unique, there are common elements among systems. For example, grievance procedures normally specify how the grievance is to be initiated, the number and timing of steps that are to compose the procedure, and the identity of representatives from each side who are to be involved in the hearings at each step. (See Figure 15.6.) When a grievance cannot be resolved at one of the specified steps, most agreements provide for the grievance to be submitted to a third party—usually an arbitrator—whose decision is final. It is not the function of an arbitrator to help the two parties reach a compromise solution. Rather, it is the arbitrator's job to mandate how the grievance is to be resolved.

### Initiating the Formal Grievance

In order for an employee's grievance to be considered formally, it must be expressed orally and/or in writing, ideally to the employee's immediate supervisor.

**FIGURE 15.6**

**Five-Step Grievance Procedure**

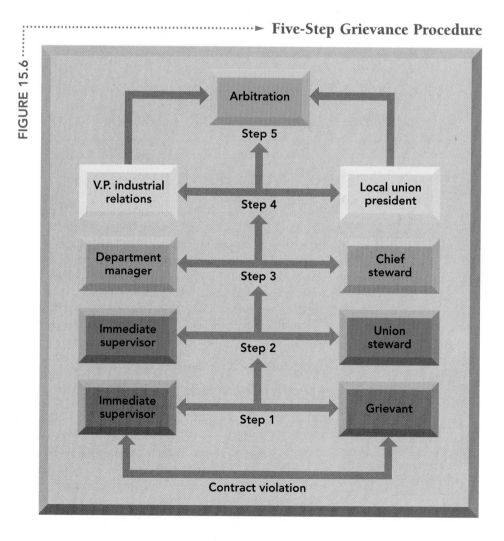

If the employee feels unable to communicate effectively with the supervisor, the grievance may be taken to the union steward, who will discuss it with the supervisor. Since grievances are often the result of an oversight or a misunderstanding, many of them can be resolved at this point. Whether or not it is possible to resolve a grievance at the initial step will depend on the supervisor's ability and willingness to discuss the problem with the employee and the steward. Supervisors should be trained formally in resolving grievances. This training should include familiarization with the terms of the labor agreement and the development of counseling skills to facilitate a problem-solving approach.

In some instances a satisfactory solution may not be possible at the first step because there are legitimate differences of opinion between the employee and the supervisor or because the supervisor does not have the authority to take the action required to satisfy the grievant.[36] Personality conflicts, prejudices, emotionalism, stubbornness, or other factors may also be barriers to a satisfactory solution at this step.

### *Preparing the Grievance Statement*

Most labor agreements require that grievances carried beyond the initial step must be stated in writing, usually on a multicopy form similar to the one shown in Highlights in HRM 3. Requiring a written statement reduces the chance that various versions of the grievance will appear because of lapses in memory. It also forces employees to think more objectively about their grievances. When this is done, grievances that stem from trivial complaints or feelings of hostility are less likely to be pursued beyond the first step.

## Grievance Mediation

If a grievance is to be resolved successfully, representatives of both management and the union must be able to discuss the problem in a rational and objective manner. A grievance should not be viewed as something to be won or lost. Rather, both sides must view the situation as an attempt to solve a human relations problem. When deadlocks arise, however, labor-management practitioners support grievance mediation as a way to resolve employee grievances.

**Grievance mediation** is an effort on the part of a neutral person to assist labor and management in reaching agreement on a grievance that is moving toward or is actually at impasse.[37] With grievance mediation, a neutral mediator is selected from outside the employment relationship to assist the parties in resolving a dispute voluntarily. The role of the mediator is to help the disputing parties resolve the grievance through compromise as if it were a bargaining deadlock.[38] Grievance mediation may be invoked as one step in the formal labor-management grievance procedure or in an ad hoc situation separate from the labor agreement.

Grievance mediators will attempt to use creative problem solving to resolve disagreements. The approach of the mediator may be to bring the parties to a common ground of acceptance or to bring about understanding regarding the facts of the case. If an agreement between the parties is reached, it is recorded and signed by the parties as a legally enforceable document. If the issue is not resolved, the mediator may write an advisory opinion regarding a future settlement. The mediator's opinion may be used as a basis for settlement or for proceeding to arbitration.

**Grievance mediation**
Process where a neutral party assists in the resolution of an employee grievance

**HRM 3**

# Grievance Form: Phoenix Transit System and Teamsters, Local 104

## COMPLAINT RECORD

**Transport, Local Delivery and Sales Drivers, Warehousemen and Helpers, Mining and Motion Picture Production, State of Arizona, Local Union No. 104**

an Affiliate of the International Brotherhood of Teamsters, Chauffeurs, Warehousemen and Helpers of America

Member's name_____ Date_____

Member's address_____ Home phone_____

City_____ State_____ Zip Code_____

Name of company against whom you are filing complaint_____
_____

Explain complaint in detail_____
_____
_____
_____
_____
_____
_____

If complaint is for discharge (give exact reason given by Co.)_____
_____
_____
_____

This will constitute full authority for Transport and Local Delivery Drivers Local 104 or any employee or agent designated by them as my attorney-in-fact, to fully represent me in the processing of this complaint in any manner they deem is in the best interest of myself as the complainant and the Union, and to receive on my behalf any monies due me.

Should this complaint be processed through the grievance procedure,

      (a) I request notification of the time, date and place of hearing    ☐

      (b) I do not request notification of the time, date and place of hearing ☐

I understand and agree that if I attend any hearing on my behalf, I will do so at my own personal expense, and the Union will in no way be obligated for same.

_____

                                             MEMBER'S SIGNATURE

Record of action by Union:_____
_____
_____
_____

Case settled:_____

                                             AGENT

Source: Courtesy of Phoenix Transit System and Teamsters, Local 104, Phoenix, Arizona

## Grievance Arbitration

**Rights arbitration**
Arbitration over interpretation of the meaning of contract terms or employee work grievances

The function of **rights arbitration** is to provide the solution to a grievance that a union and an employer have been unable to resolve by themselves. As mentioned earlier, arbitration is performed by a neutral third party (an arbitrator or impartial umpire). This third party's decision dictates how the grievance is to be settled. Both parties are obligated to comply with the decision.[39]

**USING THE INTERNET**

Check out the American Arbitration Association's web site for more information about the organization and its work:

www.adr.org

### Sources of Arbitrators

An arbitrator must be an individual who is acceptable to both disputing parties. Arbitrators may be retained on a permanent basis; however, most grievances are resolved by arbitrators who are appointed on an ad hoc basis. If both parties are satisfied with an arbitrator's performance, that person may be called upon to resolve subsequent grievances.[40] Typically, arbitrators are professionals such as professors, attorneys, members of the clergy, or retired government labor mediators. Because of their professional backgrounds, they tend to be identified with neither labor nor management and are therefore able to occupy a position of neutrality. The American Arbitration Association, the Federal Mediation and Conciliation Service, and appropriate state agencies maintain lists of available arbitrators.

### The Decision to Arbitrate

In deciding whether to use arbitration, each party must weigh the costs involved against the importance of the case and the prospects of gaining a favorable award. It would seem logical that neither party would allow a weak case to go to arbitration if there were little possibility of gaining a favorable award. Logic, however, does not always prevail. For example, it is not unusual for a union to take a weak case to arbitration in order to demonstrate to the members that the union is willing to exhaust every remedy in looking out for their interests. Union officers also are not likely to refuse to take to arbitration the grievances of members who are popular or politically powerful in the union, even though their cases are weak. Moreover,

**Fair representation doctrine**
Doctrine under which unions have a legal obligation to provide assistance to both members and nonmembers in labor relations matters

under the **fair representation doctrine**, unions have a legal obligation to provide assistance to members who are pursuing grievances. Because members can bring suit against their unions for failing to process their grievances adequately, many union officers are reluctant to refuse taking even weak grievances to arbitration.

Management, on the other hand, may allow a weak case to go to arbitration to demonstrate to the union officers that management "cannot be pushed around." Also, managers at lower levels may be reluctant to risk the displeasure of top management by stating that a certain HR policy is unworkable or unsound. Stubbornness and mutual antagonism also may force many grievances into arbitration because neither party is willing to make concessions to reach an agreement, even when it may recognize that it is in the wrong. Figure 15.7 lists the types of issues most frequently submitted to arbitration in recent years.

### The Arbitration Process

**Submission agreement**
Statement that describes the issues to be resolved through arbitration

The issues to be resolved through arbitration may be described formally in a statement known as a **submission agreement**. Such a statement might read: "Was the three-day suspension of Alex Hayden for just cause? If not, what is the appropriate remedy?" However, grievable issues are also presented orally to the arbitrator by

FIGURE 15.7

► **Issues Most Likely to Be Arbitrated**

| ISSUE | PERCENT OF ALL CASES* |
| --- | --- |
| Discipline and discharge | 30 |
| Arbitrability | 20 |
| Wages | 10 |
| Work assignments and schedules | 9 |
| Promotions and transfers | 7 |
| Management rights | 5 |
| Layoff and recall | 4 |
| Employee benefits | 4 |

*Percentages represent averages for various reporting years and do not add up to 100.

Source: The American Arbitration Association, *Study Times*, selected years.

the two parties at the beginning of the hearing. If minutes and memoranda covering the meetings held at earlier stages of the grievance procedure have been prepared, these are sometimes submitted prior to the formal hearing to acquaint the arbitrator with the issues.

In arbitrating a dispute, it is the responsibility of the arbitrator to ensure that each side receives a fair hearing during which it may present all of the facts it considers pertinent to the case. The procedures for conducting arbitration hearings and the restrictions governing the evidence that may be introduced during these hearings are more flexible than those permitted in a court of law. Hearsay evidence, for example, may be introduced, provided it is considered as such when evaluated with the other evidence presented. The primary purpose of the hearing is to assist the arbitrator in obtaining the facts necessary to resolve a human relations problem rather than a legal one. The arbitrator, therefore, has a right to question witnesses or to request additional facts from either party.[41]

Depending on the importance of the case, the hearings may be conducted in an informal way or in a very formal manner not unlike that of a court trial. If desired by either or both parties, or by the arbitrator, a court reporter may be present during the hearing to prepare a transcript of the proceedings. After conducting the hearing and receiving posthearing briefs (should the parties choose to submit them), the arbitrator customarily has thirty days in which to consider the evidence and to prepare a decision. However, extensions beyond this period are not uncommon. In the majority of labor contracts, the costs of arbitration are shared equally by the parties.

**Arbitration award**
Final and binding award issued by an arbitrator in a labor-management dispute

### The Arbitration Award

The **arbitration award** should include not only the arbitrator's decision but also the rationale for it. The reasoning behind the decision can help provide guidance concerning the interpretation of the labor agreement and the resolution of future disputes arising from its administration. In pointing out the merits of each party's position, the reasoning that underlies the award can help lessen the disappointment and protect the self-esteem of those representing the unsuccessful party. In short, tact and objective reasoning can help to reduce disappointment and hard feelings. However, the foundation for the arbitrator's decision is the labor agreement and the rights it establishes for each party.

In many grievances, such as those involving employee performance or behavior on the job, the arbitrator must determine whether the evidence supports the employer's action against the grievant. The evidence must also indicate whether the employee was accorded the right of due process, which is the employee's right to be informed of unsatisfactory performance and to have an opportunity to respond to these charges. Under most labor agreements an employer is required to have just cause (i.e., a good reason) for the action it has taken, and such action should be confirmed by the evidence presented. When management fails to support its burden of proof (or management's actions were deemed unfair), then it is within the arbitrator's power to reduce the penalty. It is not uncommon, for example, for an arbitrator to reduce a discharge to a suspension without pay for a specified time period.

Importantly, arbitration awards do not establish precedents for future cases. In practice, however, arbitration awards have some influence on the decision of an arbitrator who may seek guidance from decisions of other arbitrators in somewhat similar cases. When preparing arbitration cases, therefore, managers or supervisors may wish to review decisions published by the American Arbitration Association and by such labor services as the Bureau of National Affairs, Commerce Clearing House, and Prentice-Hall.

### How Arbitrators Decide Cases

Because of the importance and magnitude of arbitration in both the union and nonunion setting (see Chapter 13), the process by which arbitrators make decisions and the factors that influence those decisions are of continuing interest to managers. Typically, arbitrators use four factors when deciding cases:

1. The wording of the labor agreement (or employment policy in nonunion organizations)
2. The submission agreement as presented to the arbitrator
3. Testimony and evidence offered during the hearing
4. Arbitration criteria or standards (i.e., similar to standards of common law) against which cases are judged

When deciding the case of an employee discharged for absenteeism, for example, the arbitrator would consider these factors separately and/or jointly. Arbitrators are essentially constrained to decide cases on the basis of the wording of the labor agreement, or employment policy, and the facts, testimony, and evidence presented at the hearing.

Since discipline and discharge issues generally comprise about 30 percent of all rights arbitration, it is informative to understand the reasons given by arbitrators when they overturn managers in these cases. This information will help managers when they prepare cases for arbitration. In one study, five reasons accounted for over 70 percent of all reversal cases:

- The evidence did not support the charge of wrongdoing.
- The evidence supported the charge, but there were mitigating circumstances.
- Management committed procedural errors that prejudiced the grievant's rights.
- The rule was fair, but punishment for its infraction was harsh.
- Management was partly at fault in the incident.[42]

In practice, arbitration decision making is not an exact science. In fact, the decisions of arbitrators can be rather subjective. Arbitrators can, and do, interpret contract language differently (e.g., What does "just cause discharge" actually mean?), they assign varying degrees of importance to testimony and evidence, they judge the truthfulness of witnesses differently, and they give arbitration standards greater or lesser weight as they apply to facts of the case.[43] Each of these influences serves to introduce subjectivity into the decision-making process.[44]

### Expedited Arbitration

**Expedited arbitration**
A faster, less expensive, and less legalistic way to resolve grievances regarding discipline cases, routine work issues, and cases of insignificant monetary cost to the disputing parties

The steel industry, the U.S. Postal Service, and the maritime industry use **expedited arbitration** as a way of overcoming the high costs, time delays, and legalism of grievance arbitration. While each labor agreement may have its own procedures governing the use of expedited arbitration, the following are typical characteristics of this particular arbitration process:

1. The arbitration hearing is held within ten days from the demand for arbitration.
2. The hearing is completed in one day.
3. Awards must be rendered within five days from the close of the hearing, and only short written awards (one or two pages) are required.
4. Hearings are informal; attorneys, legal briefs, and court reporters are not involved.

Expedited arbitration is an effective way to dispose of disciplinary cases, routine work issues, and cases of insignificant monetary cost to the parties.[45] Complex contract-interpretation cases may not be amenable to the expedited procedures.

# SUMMARY

Negotiating a labor agreement is a detailed process. Each side will prepare a list of proposals it wishes to achieve while additionally trying to anticipate those proposals desired by the other side. Bargaining teams must be selected and all proposals must be analyzed to determine their impact on and cost to the organization. Both employer and union negotiators will be sensitive to current bargaining patterns within the industry, general cost-of-living trends, and geographical wage differentials.

Managers will establish goals that seek to retain control over operations and to minimize costs. Union negotiators will focus their demands around improved wages, hours, and working conditions. An agreement will be reached when both sides compromise their original positions and final terms fall within the limits of the parties' bargaining zone.

Traditionally, collective bargaining between labor and management has been adversarial. Presently, there is an increased interest in nonadversarial negotiations—negotiations based on mutual gains and a heightened respect between the parties. What the FMCS calls interest-based bargaining (IBB) is one form of nonadversarial negotiations.

**OBJECTIVE 2** The collective bargaining process includes not only the actual negotiations but also the power tactics used to support negotiating demands. When negotiations become deadlocked, bargaining becomes a power struggle to force from either side the concessions needed to break the deadlock. The union's power in collective bargaining comes from its ability to picket, strike, or boycott the employer. The employer's power during negotiations comes from its ability to lock out employees or to operate during a strike by using managerial or replacement employees.

**OBJECTIVE 3** Mediation is the principal way of resolving negotiating deadlocks. Federal mediators provided by the U.S. Federal Mediation and Conciliation Service seek to assist the negotiators through opening up lines of communication between the parties and offering suggestions to resolve deadlocked proposals. In some situations, interest arbitration is employed to finalize the labor agreement. Interest arbitration is rarely used in the private sector; however, it is used often in the public sector where unions are largely prohibited from striking.

**OBJECTIVE 4** During the late twentieth century several trends in labor relations became evident. These include attempts to develop more cooperative labor-management endeavors and attitudes of less adversarial collective bargaining. Management has used concessionary bargaining to minimize or lower labor costs while improving workplace productivity through the reduction of restrictive work rules. Unions have stressed employee retraining and job security where employer concessions are sought.

**OBJECTIVE 5** The typical labor agreement will contain numerous provisions governing the employment relationship between labor and management. The major areas of interest concern wages (rates of pay, overtime differentials, holiday pay), hours (shift times, days of work), and working conditions (safety issues, performance standards, retraining). To managers the issue of management rights is particularly important. These rights hold that management's authority is supreme for all issues except those shared with the union through the labor agreement.

**OBJECTIVE 6** When differences arise between labor and management they will normally be resolved through the grievance procedure. Grievance procedures are negotiated and thus reflect the needs and desires of the parties. The typical grievance procedure will consist of three, four, or five steps—each step having specific filing and reply times. Higher-level managers and union officials will become involved in disputes at the higher steps of the grievance procedure. The final step of the grievance procedure may be arbitration. Arbitrators will render a final decision to problems not resolved at lower grievance steps.

**OBJECTIVE 7** The submission agreement is a statement of the issue to be solved through arbitration. It is simply the problem the parties wish to have settled. The arbitrator must answer the issue by basing the arbitration award on four factors: the contents of the labor agreement (or employment policy), the submission agreement as written, testimony and evidence obtained at the hearing, and various arbitration standards developed over time to assist in the resolution of different types of labor-management disputes. Arbitration is not an exact science since arbitrators will give varying degrees of importance to the evidence and criteria by which disputes are resolved.

# KEY TERMS

| | | |
|---|---|---|
| arbitration award | fair representation doctrine | outsourcing |
| arbitrator | grievance mediation | pattern bargaining |
| bargaining zone | grievance procedure | reserved rights |
| boycott | interest arbitration | rights arbitration |
| collective bargaining process | lockout | submission agreement |
| defined rights | mediator | |
| expedited arbitration | nonadversarial bargaining | |

## DISCUSSION QUESTIONS

 1. Of what significance is the bargaining zone in the conduct of negotiations? What are some influences affecting negotiated outcomes?

 2. What are some of the possible reasons an employer may be willing to face a strike that could result in a loss of customers and profits?

 3. How does mediation differ from arbitration? In what situations is each of these processes most likely to be used?

 4. What are some of the bargaining concessions generally sought by employers and unions in return for the concessions they may grant?

 5. At an election conducted among the twenty employees of the Exclusive Jewelry Store, all but two voted in favor of the Jewelry Workers Union, which subsequently was certified as their bargaining agent. In negotiating its first agreement, the union demanded that it be granted a union shop. The two employees who had voted against the union, however, informed the management that they would quit rather than join. Unfortunately for the store, the two employees were skilled gem cutters who were the most valuable of its employees and would be difficult to replace. What position should the store take with regard to the demand for a union shop?

 6. What are some of the reasons a union or an employer may allow a weak grievance to go to arbitration?

 7. The discharge of Allen Paige for poor work performance is scheduled for an arbitration hearing. What arguments is each side likely to put forth to support its case?

## Don't I Deserve a Second Chance?

At the arbitration hearing, both parties were adamant in their positions. Nancy McCormick, manager for All-Freight Storage, argued that the grievant, Tom Benedict, was justly terminated for knowingly and willingly falsifying his employment application—a direct violation of company policy and the employee handbook. In his defense, Benedict argued that he had been a good employee during his seven years of employment. Furthermore, at the time of his hiring, he was in desperate need of a job to support himself and his family.

The submission agreement governing the case read, "It is the employer's position that just cause existed for the discharge of Mr. Tom Benedict and the penalty was appropriate for the offense committed." Additionally, the employer introduced into evidence the company handbook that defined just cause termination as

> Just cause shall serve as the basis for disciplinary action and includes, but is not limited to: dishonesty, inefficiency, unprofessional conduct, failure to report absences, falsification of records, violation of company policy, destruction of property, or possession or being under the influence of alcohol or narcotics.

Benedict was hired as inventory control clerk on November 7, 1992, a position he held until his termination on October 25, 1999. According to the testimony of McCormick, the position of inventory control clerk is one requiring a high degree of honesty and integrity by employees. Benedict's performance evaluations showed him to be an average employee, although he had received several disciplinary warnings for poor attendance and one three-day suspension for an "inventory control error."

The termination of Benedict concerned the concealment of his criminal record. When Benedict completed his employment application in 1992, he had checked "no" in a box on the form asking if he had ever been convicted of a felony or misdemeanor—other than minor violations. Additionally, the application provided a statement by which applicants attest to the truthfulness of their answers. The form specifically states, "I understand the truth of my answers is a condition of employment, and that any misrepresentation or omission of facts on this application may cause dismissal." Benedict signed and dated the application October 22, 1992.

During September 1999, All-Freight Storage learned through a recently hired security guard that prior to Benedict's employment in 1992, he had served a total of seven years in state prison for four separate felony convictions for grand theft. He was last released six months prior to his employment by All-Freight Storage. The security guard had previously worked as a guard for the state prison system.

At arbitration, Benedict readily admitted that he had falsified his employment application. His reason was his desperate need for employment and the likelihood that the company would not have hired him had he revealed his criminal record. Since his release from prison he has had no further felony or misdemeanor convictions. Interestingly, in Benedict's state of employment, state law allows criminal records to be sealed after five years from incarceration or completion of probation. Benedict failed to apply for this benefit.

Source: Adapted from an arbitration heard by Dr. Marcus Miller, December 1999. All names are fictitious.

## QUESTIONS

1. Which arguments should be given more weight: those based on company policy, the employee handbook, and the application form or those mitigating arguments offered by the grievant? Explain.
2. How important is it that Benedict's felony conviction bear a relationship to the position of inventory control clerk? Explain.
3. If you were the arbitrator, how would you rule in this case? Explain fully the reasons for your decision.

CASE STUDY 2

## "Just Read the Agreement— That's All You Need"

This case illustrates how seemingly clear contract wording and subsequent verbal discussions can lead to confusion and misunderstanding regarding application of the labor agreement. Introduced at arbitration, held November 22, 1999, was the following submission agreement:

> Did the school district violate the terms and conditions of the 1998–2000 labor agreement between the Western Teachers Association (WTA) and the Western Unified School District (WUSD), specifically Article 9, section 4-A, and Article 9, section 1-A? If so, what is the appropriate remedy?

## Pertinent Labor Agreement Language

*Article 9-4-A*    Student Contact Time. The amount of teacher-student contact time (teaching time) shall be no more than 320 minutes per day in grades 1–6, and no more than 285 minutes per day in kindergarten.

*Article 9-1-A*    Normal Work Day. A normal work day shall be no longer than seven and one-half (7 1/2) hours, including not less than thirty (30) minutes duty-free lunch period.

The grievance alleged that the WUSD violated the bargaining agreement between the parties by increasing the maximum number of minutes per day of student contact (instructional) time as stated in Article 9-4-A of the labor agreement.

The grievance arose from a teacher/administration committee meeting held during February 1999. The meeting was held to discuss early-release days for teacher development. Early-release days are days when students are dismissed early from school in order to provide time for teacher development during the normal school day. At arbitration, it was argued by the WUSD that an oral agreement was reached at the February meeting to increase the number of early-release days from five to eight for the 1999–2000 school year. However, in order to accommodate this change, the school district received oral agreement from Kathy Adams-Hoff, president of WTA, and other WTA members, to alter the maximum daily minutes of teacher contact time. The verbal understanding would extend the maximum number of daily contact minutes on various days to accommodate the loss of instructional minutes on early-release days (Article 9-4-A).

Beginning with the school year in August 1999, the WUSD began implementing the new teacher development policy. On September 17, 1999, the WTA filed a grievance alleging violation of Article 9-4-A. At the hearing, school officials and WTA representatives testified to the wording of the contract and their understanding of the discussions held at the February 1999 committee meeting. Kathy Adams-Hoff did not testify at arbitration for either the WTA or the WUSD. The expressed positions of the parties were

*Western Teachers Association*

1. The WUSD unilaterally increased teacher-student contact time without the approval of the WTA or persons representing the WTA.
2. The language of the labor agreement is clear, unambiguous, and not open to interpretation.
3. The WTA seeks "retroactive impairment" since the WUSD violated the labor agreement. The WUSD should reduce teacher-student contact time to conform with Article 9-4-A. Monetary compensation or compensatory time off should be awarded to affected teachers.

*Western Unified School District*

1. The WUSD did not unilaterally change the labor agreement. Changes were made with the full knowledge and agreement of WTA representatives and the expressed approval of Kathy Adams-Hoff, president of WTA.
2. The change in release days from five to eight was done specifically for the benefit of teachers (e.g., to provide more development time for teachers). The WUSD did not seek to unjustly benefit from this decision.

Source: Adapted from an arbitration heard by George W. Bohlander, November 1999. All names are fictitious.

## QUESTIONS

1. Should the labor agreement wording or the oral discussion of February 1999 be controlling in this case? Explain fully.
2. Is the absence of testimony from Kathy Adams-Hoff harmful or beneficial to either party in this case? Explain fully.
3. If you were chosen to arbitrate this case, how would you rule? Why?
4. If you were to decide in favor of the WTA, what (if any) remedy would you recommend? Explain.

# NOTES AND REFERENCES

1. James G. Baker, "Negotiating a Collective Bargaining Agreement: Law and Strategy—A Short Course for Non-Labor Lawyers," *Labor Law Journal* 47, no. 4 (April 1996): 253–67.
2. Joan A. Fossom, *Labor Relations: Development, Structure, Process,* 7th ed. (Homewood, Ill.: BPI-Irwin, 1999).
3. For the original description of attitudinal structuring, see Richard E. Walton and Robert B. McKersie, *A Behavioral Theory of Labor Negotiations* (New York: McGraw-Hill, 1965). This book is considered a classic in the labor relations field.
4. "Be Nice—And You're Dead Meat," *Business Week,* November 30, 1998, 8.
5. Employers who refuse to pay union demands are not legally required to provide financial data to union representatives. The requirement to provide financial data would normally arise where an employer asserts during negotiations that it cannot survive if it agrees to union wage proposals or that it has no operating profit.
6. The National Labor Relations Board offers an excellent book on the National Labor Relations Act. This book discusses good-faith bargaining as well as other important legal issues—for example, employers covered by the law, unfair labor practices, and election procedures. See *A Guide to Basic Law and Procedures under the National Labor Relations Act* (Washington, D.C.: U.S. Government Printing Office, 1991).
7. John Thomas Delaney and Donna Stockell, "The Mandatory-Permissive Distinction and Collective Bargaining Outcomes," *Industrial and Labor Relations Review* 42, no. 4 (July 1989): 566–81.
8. Ross Stagner and Hjalmar Rosen, *Psychology of Union-Management Relations* (Belmont, Calif.: Wadsworth, 1965): 95–97. This is another classic in the field of labor-management relations.
9. Conversation with Joe Stanley, July 23, 1999, Phoenix, Arizona.
10. George W. Bohlander and Jim Naber, "Nonadversarial Negotiations: The FMCS Interest-Based Bargaining Program," *Journal of Collective Negotiations in the Public Sector* 28, no. 1 (1999): 41–52. The FMCS has a complete and comprehensive program to train labor and management negotiators in the art and techniques of interest-based bargaining (IBB). Information on the IBB program can be obtained from the FMCS national headquarters at 2100 K Street, N.W., Washington, D.C. 20427, or from FMCS district offices.
11. *Interest-Based Negotiations: Participants' Guidebook* (Washington, D.C.: Federal Mediation and Conciliation Service, 1998), 11.
12. Victor G. Devinatz, "What Do We Know about Mutual Gains Bargaining Among Educators?" *Journal of Collective Negotiations in the Public Sector* 27, no. 2 (1998): 79–91.
13. John W. Budd, "Canadian Strike Replacement Legislation and Collective Bargaining Lessons for the United States," *Industrial Relations* 35, no. 2 (April 1996): 245–60.
14. "Strikes Fall to 50-Year Low as Job Insecurities Increase," *The New York Times National,* January 29, 1996, A-1.
15. "Major Work Stoppages Stay near Record Lows in 1998," *Bulletin to Management* 50, no. 9 (March 9, 1999): 69.
16. Employers are cautioned to know their rights and the rights of striking employees and replacement workers during a labor impasse. The National Labor Relations Board has established specific guidelines (rules) that must be followed in order to avoid receiving an unfair labor practice charge. One general rule is that employers must not discipline or threaten striking employees in regard to their legal right to strike.
17. Wendy Trach-Huber and Stephen K. Huber, *Mediation and Negotiation: Reaching Agreement in Law and Business* (Cincinnati, Ohio: Anderson Publishing, 1998).
18. Patrice M. Mareschal, "Providing High Quality Mediation," *Review of Public Personnel Administration* 17, no. 4 (Fall 1998): 55–71.
19. Craig A. Olson and Barbara L. Rau, "Learning from Interest Arbitration: The Next Round," *Industrial and*

*Labor Relations Review* 50, no. 2 (January 1997): 237–51.

20. Patricia Peightal, Dana Souza, Bill Bray, John Rague, Jim Pritchard, and Joseph Thomas, "Labor-Management Cooperation—City of Portland, Maine," *Public Personnel Management* 27, no. 1 (Spring 1998): 85–91. See also Robert E. Allen and Kathleen L. Van Norman, "Employee Involvement Programs: The Noninvolvement of Unions Revisited," *Journal of Labor Research* 17, no. 3 (Summer 1996): 479–95.

21. Sandra Bilooh, "Cooperative Labor-Management Relations as a Strategy for Change: The Critical Role and Opportunity for the Human Resource Professional," *Public Personnel Management* 27, no. 1 (Spring 1998): 1–10.

22. John Calhoun Wells, "Conflictive Partnership: A Strategy for Real World Labor-Management Cooperation," *Labor Law Journal* 47, no. 8 (August 1996): 484–92.

23. Tom Juravich, "Empirical Research on Employee Involvement: A Critical Review for Labor," *Labor Studies Journal* 21, no. 2 (Summer 1996): 52–66; Douglas M. McCabe, "Labor-Management Cooperation: A Business Ethics and Business-Government Relations Perspective," *Labor Law Journal* 47, no. 8 (August 1996): 467–78. See also George W. Bohlander and Marshall H. Campbell, "Forging a Labor-Management Partnership: The Magma Copper Experience," *Labor Studies Journal* 18, no. 4 (Winter 1994): 3–20; George W. Bohlander and Marshall H. Campbell, "Problem-Solving Bargaining and Work Redesign: Magma Copper's Labor-Management Partnership," *National Productivity Review* 12, no. 4 (Autumn 1993): 519–33.

24. Yonatan Reshef and Helen Lam, "Union Responses to Quality Improvement Initiatives: Factors Shaping Support and Resistance," *Journal of Labor Research* 20, no. 1 (Winter 1999): 111–31. See also Robert W. Miller, Richard W. Humphreys, and Frederick A. Zeller, "Structural Characteristics of Successful Cases of Cooperative Union-Management Relations," *Labor Studies Journal* 22, no. 2 (Summer 1997): 44–65.

25. Brenda Paik Sunoo, "Labor-Management Partnerships Boost Training," *Workforce* 78, no. 4 (April 1999): 80–85. See also Marvin J. Levine, "The Union Role in Labor-Management Cooperation," *Journal of Collective Negotiations in the Public Sector* 26, no 3 (1997): 203–22.

26. Michael H. LeRoy, "Are Employers Constrained in the Use of Employee Participation Groups by Section 8(a)(2) of the National labor Relations Act?" *Journal of Labor Research* 20, no. 1 (Winter 1999): 53–71.

27. Mary E. Pivec and Howard Z. Robbins, "Employee Involvement Remains Controversial," *HRMagazine* 41, no. 11 (November 1996): 145–50. See also Mark A. Nordstrom, "Safety Teams May Collide with the NLRA," *National Law Journal,* February 26, 1996, C-6; David A. Dilts, "Labor-Management Cooperation: Real or Nominal Changes in Collective Bargaining?" *Labor Law Journal* 44, no. 2 (February 1993): 124–28.

28. Joann Muller, "Labor Could Back This GM Spin-Off," *Business Week,* August 2, 1999, 62–64.

29. For an expanded discussion of management's reserved rights, see Paul Prasow and Edward Peters, *Arbitration and Collective Bargaining,* 2nd ed. (New York: McGraw-Hill, 1983): 33–34. This book is considered an authority on management rights issues.

30. Labor agreement, Wabash Fibre Box Company and Paperworkers.

31. Susan E. Long, "Unions Can Demand Dues but Not Membership," *HRFocus* 75, no. 12 (December 1998): S11.

32. William J. Moore, "The Determinants and Effects of Right-to-Work Laws: A Review of the Recent Literature," *Journal of Labor Research* 19, no. 3 (Summer 1998): 445–69.

33. Charles W. Baird, "Right to Work Before and After 14(b)," *Journal of Labor Research* 19, no. 3 (Summer 1998): 47–93. See also Morgan O. Reynolds, "The Prospects for Right to Work," *Journal of Labor Research* 19, no. 3 (Summer 1998): 519–28.

34. John T. Delaney, "Redefining the Right-to-Work Debate: Unions and the Dilemma of Free Choice," *Journal of Labor Research* 19, no. 3 (Summer 1998): 425–43.

35. *Grievance Guide,* 9th ed. (Washington, D.C.: BNA Books, 1995). See also Frank Elkouri and Edna Asher Elkouri, *How Arbitration Works,* 4th ed. (Washington, D.C.: Bureau of National Affairs, 1985), 153. This book continues to be a leading reference on the topic of arbitration and the resolution of grievances.

36. David Meyer, "The Political Effects of Grievance Handling by Stewards in a Local Union," *Journal of Labor Research* 15, no. 1 (Winter 1994): 33.

37. Richard R. Block, John Beck, and Robin Olson, "A Look at Grievance Mediation," *Dispute Resolution Journal* 51, no. 4 (October 1996): 54–61.

38. Dennis Sharp, "The Many Faces of Mediation Confidentiality," *Dispute Resolution Journal* 53, no. 4 (November 1998): 56–63.

39. Arbitration awards are not final in all cases. Arbitration awards may be overturned through the judicial process if it can be shown that the arbitrator was prejudiced or failed to render an award based on the essence of the agreement.

40. Some labor agreements call for using arbitration boards to resolve employee grievances. Arbitration

boards, which may be either temporary or permanent, are composed of one or more members chosen by management and an equal number chosen by labor. A neutral member serves as chair.

41. Sharon T. Nelson, "What Kind of Questions Should Arbitrators Ask?" *Journal of Dispute Resolution* 54, no. 1 (February 1999): 53–55.

42. George W. Bohlander, "Police Officer Discipline and Arbitration: The Issue of Conduct Unbecoming," *Journal of Collective Negotiations in the Public Sector* 27, no. 1 (Spring 1998): 1–12. See also George W. Bohlander and Donna Blancero, "A Study of Reversal Determinants in Discipline and Discharge Arbitration Awards: The Impact of Just Cause Standards," *Labor Studies Journal* 21, no. 3 (Fall 1996): 3–18; George W. Bohlander, "Why Arbitrators Overturn Managers in Employee Suspension and Discharge Cases," *Journal of Collective Negotiations in the Public Sector* 23, no. 1 (Spring 1994): 73–89.

43. Dennis Nolan, "Labor and Employment Arbitration: What's Justice Got to Do with It?" *Dispute Resolution Journal* 53, no. 4 (November 1998): 40–48.

44. While arbitration is widely used and championed as an effective method to resolve employee complaints, it is not without its problems. Specifically, arbitration is criticized for taking too much time, being too expensive, causing long delays in resolving relatively simple disputes, being overly legalistic, and being inappropriate for resolving some specific types of cases, namely discrimination cases under EEOC statutes.

45. Nels E. Nelson and A.N.M. Mesquat Uddin, "The Impact of Delay on Arbitrators' Decisions in Discharge Cases," *Labor Studies Journal* 23, no. 2 (Summer 1998): 3–20.

# chapter 16

# International Human Resources Management

AFTER STUDYING THIS CHAPTER, YOU SHOULD BE ABLE TO

 **OBJECTIVE 1**
Identify the types of organizational forms used for competing internationally.

 **OBJECTIVE 2**
Explain how domestic and international HRM differ.

 **OBJECTIVE 3**
Discuss the staffing process for individuals working internationally.

 **OBJECTIVE 4**
Identify the unique training needs for international assignees.

 **OBJECTIVE 5**
Reconcile the difficulties of home-country and host-country performance appraisals.

 **OBJECTIVE 6**
Identify the characteristics of a good international compensation plan.

 **OBJECTIVE 7**
Explain the major differences between U.S. and European labor relations.

In the first chapter of this textbook, we said that one of the chief forces driving HRM today was the globalization of business. According to the U.S. Department of Commerce, in the last twenty-five years U.S. investment overseas has jumped from around $75 billion to almost $750 billion. While estimates vary widely, approximately 70 to 85 percent of the U.S. economy today is affected by international competition. And as we rapidly move toward a more global economy, many organizations are reassessing their approaches to human resources management. To a large degree, the challenge of managing across borders boils down to the philosophies and systems we use to manage people.[1]

The importance of globalization notwithstanding, we have—for the most part—emphasized HRM practices and systems as they exist in the United States. This is not so much an oversight on our part as it is a deliberate pedagogical choice. The topic of international HRM is so important that we wanted to dedicate an entire chapter to its discussion. Our thinking is that now after you have read (and, we hope, discussed) some of the best practices for managing people at work, it may be appropriate to see how some of these HRM systems change as we begin to manage people in an international arena. In this chapter we will observe that much of what has been discussed throughout this text can be applied to international operations, provided one is sensitive to the requirements of a particular international setting.

The first part of this chapter presents a brief introduction to international business firms. In many important respects, the way a company organizes its international operations influences the type of managerial and human resources issues it faces. In addition, we briefly describe some of the environmental factors that also affect the work of managers in a global setting. Just as with domestic operations, the dimensions of the environment form a context in which HRM decisions are made. A major portion of this chapter deals with the various HR activities involved in the recruitment, selection, development, and compensation of employees who work in an international setting. Throughout the discussion the focus will be on U.S. multinational corporations.

# Managing Across Borders

International business operations can take several different forms. A large percentage carry on their international business with only limited facilities and minimal representation in foreign countries. Others, particularly *Fortune* 500 corporations, have extensive facilities and personnel in various countries of the world. Managing these resources effectively, and integrating their activities to achieve global advantage, is a challenge to the leadership of these companies.

Figure 16.1 shows four basic types of organizations and how they differ in the degree to which international activities are separated to respond to the local regions and integrated to achieve global efficiencies. The **international corporation** is essentially a domestic firm that builds on its existing capabilities to penetrate overseas markets. Companies such as Honda, General Electric, and Procter & Gamble used this approach to gain access to Europe—they essentially adapted existing products for overseas markets without changing much else about their normal operations.[2]

A **multinational corporation (MNC)** is a more complex form that usually has fully autonomous units operating in multiple countries. Shell, Philips, and ITT

**International corporation**
Domestic firm that uses its existing capabilities to move into overseas markets

**Multinational corporation (MNC)**
Firm with independent business units operating in multiple countries

Types of Organizations

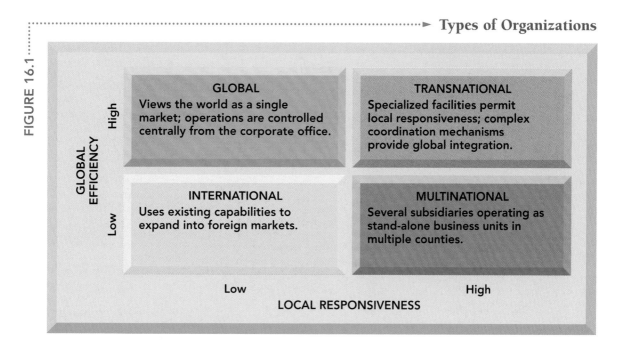

FIGURE 16.1

GLOBAL EFFICIENCY — High / Low

**GLOBAL**
Views the world as a single market; operations are controlled centrally from the corporate office.

**TRANSNATIONAL**
Specialized facilities permit local responsiveness; complex coordination mechanisms provide global integration.

**INTERNATIONAL**
Uses existing capabilities to expand into foreign markets.

**MULTINATIONAL**
Several subsidiaries operating as stand-alone business units in multiple counties.

Low — High
**LOCAL RESPONSIVENESS**

**Global corporation**
Firm that has integrated worldwide operations through a centralized home office

**Transnational corporation**
Firm that attempts to balance local responsiveness and global scale via a network of specialized operating units

are three typical MNCs. These companies have traditionally given their foreign subsidiaries a great deal of latitude to address local issues such as consumer preferences, political pressures, and economic trends in different regions of the world. Frequently these subsidiaries are run as independent companies, without much integration. The **global corporation**, on the other hand, can be viewed as a multinational firm that maintains control of operations back in the home office. Japanese companies such as Matsushita and NEC, for example, tend to treat the world market as a unified whole and try to combine activities in each country to maximize efficiency on a global scale. These companies operate much like a domestic firm, except that they view the whole world as their marketplace.

Finally, a **transnational corporation** attempts to achieve the local responsiveness of an MNC while also achieving the efficiencies of a global firm. To balance this "global/local" dilemma, a transnational uses a network structure that coordinates specialized facilities positioned around the world. By using this flexible structure, a transnational provides autonomy to independent country operations but brings these separate activities together into an integrated whole. For most companies, the transnational form represents an ideal, rather than a reality. However, companies such as Ford, Unilever, and British Petroleum have made good progress in restructuring operations to function more transnationally.[3]

Although various forms of organization exist, in this chapter we will generally refer to any company that conducts business outside its home country as an international business. The United States, of course, has no monopoly on international business. International enterprises are found throughout the world. In fact, some European and Pacific Rim companies have been conducting business on an international basis much longer than their U.S. counterparts. The close proximity of European countries, for example, makes them likely candidates for international trade. As shown in Figure 16.2, approximately two-thirds of the top fifty corporations in the world are headquartered in countries outside the United States.[4]

FIGURE 16.2 ┈┈┈┈┈┈┈┈┈┈┈┈┈┈┈┈┈┈┈┈┈┈┈┈┈┈┈┈┈┈┈┈┈┈┈┈┈┈► The Top 50 Global Firms

| COMPANY | HDQTRS | SALES (1998) | COMPANY | HDQTRS | SALES (1998) |
|---|---|---|---|---|---|
| 1. General Motors | U.S. | 161,315 | 26. Matsushita | Japan | 59,771 |
| 2. DaimlerChrysler | Germany | 154,615 | 27. Philip Morris | U.S. | 57,813 |
| 3. Ford Motor | U.S. | 144,418 | 28. Ing Group | Netherlands | 56,468 |
| 4. Wal-Mart Stores | U.S. | 139,208 | 29. Boeing | U.S. | 56,154 |
| 5. Mitsui | Japan | 109,373 | 30. AT&T | U.S. | 53,588 |
| 6. Itochu | Japan | 108,749 | 31. Sony | Japan | 53,156 |
| 7. Mitsubishi | Japan | 107,184 | 32. Metro | Germany | 52,126 |
| 8. Exxon | U.S. | 100,697 | 33. Nissan Motor | Japan | 51,478 |
| 9. General Electric | U.S. | 100,469 | 34. Fiat | Italy | 50,999 |
| 10. Toyota Motor | Japan | 99,740 | 35. Bank of America | U.S. | 50,777 |
| 11. Royal Dutch/Shell | U.K./Neth. | 93,692 | 36. Nestle | Switzerland | 49,504 |
| 12. Marubeni | Japan | 93,568 | 37. Credit Suisse | Switzerland | 49,143 |
| 13. Sumitomo | Japan | 89,020 | 38. Honda Motor | Japan | 48,747 |
| 14. IBM | U.S. | 81,667 | 39. Assicurazioni Generali | Italy | 48,478 |
| 15. Axa | France | 78,729 | 40. Mobil | U.S. | 47,678 |
| 16. Citigroup | U.S. | 76,431 | 41. Hewlett-Packard | U.S. | 47,061 |
| 17. Volkswagen | Germany | 76,306 | 42. Deutsche Bank | Germany | 45,165 |
| 18. Nippon T&T | Japan | 76,118 | 43. Unilever | U.K./Neth. | 44,908 |
| 19. BP Amoco | U.K. | 68,304 | 44. State Farm Insurance | U.S. | 44,620 |
| 20. Nissho Iwai | Japan | 67,741 | 45. Dai-Ichi Insurance | Japan | 44,485 |
| 21. Nippon Life Insurance | Japan | 66,299 | 46. Veba Group | Germany | 43,407 |
| 22. Siemens | Germany | 66,037 | 47. HSBC Holdings | U.K. | 43,338 |
| 23. Allianz | Germany | 64,874 | 48. Toshiba | Japan | 41,471 |
| 24. Hitachi | Japan | 62,409 | 49. Renault | France | 41,353 |
| 25. U.S. Postal Service | U.S. | 60,072 | 50. Sears Roebuck | U.S. | 41,332 |

These companies are in a strong position to affect the world economy in the following ways:

1. Production and distribution extend beyond national boundaries, making it easier to transfer technology.

2. They have direct investments in many countries, affecting the balance of payments.

3.  They have a political impact that leads to cooperation among countries and to the breaking down of barriers of nationalism.

Despite the successes of foreign competition, the United States remains a formidable foe in international business; in virtually every major global industry, American business continues to be a leader.

## How Does the Global Environment Influence Management?

In Chapter 1, we highlighted some of the global trends affecting human resources management. One of the major economic issues we discussed was the creation of free trade zones within Europe, North America, and the Pacific Rim. Figure 16.3 shows a map of the fifteen member countries of the European Union (EU) whose goal is facilitate the flow of goods, services, capital, and human resources across national borders in Europe in a manner similar to the way they cross state lines in the United States.[5] Despite the political and legal obstacles to unification, most

**FIGURE 16.3**

**The Nations of the European Union**

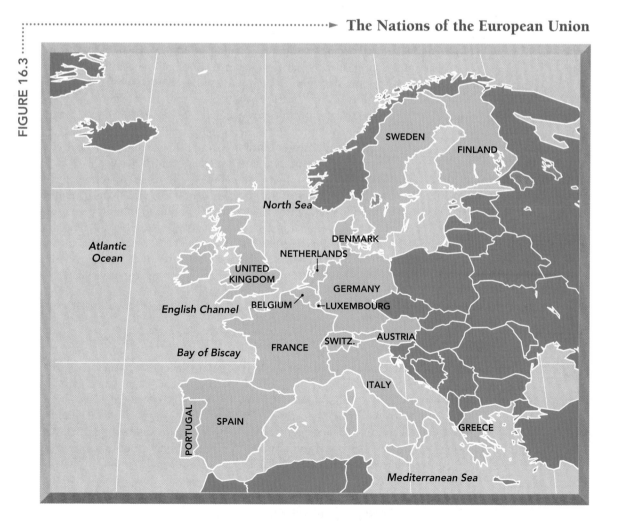

observers agree that ultimately the EU will become a unified buying and selling power that will compete as a major economic player with the United States and Japan. Highlights in HRM 1 describes some of the effects that unification may have on HRM practices within Europe.

A similar transition has been occurring within North America with the passage of NAFTA (discussed in Chapter 1). Some alarmists have feared that NAFTA would lead to a loss of jobs for U.S. companies. Just the opposite has occurred; a recent report by the U.S. Department of Commerce on the merits of NAFTA shows that job growth has surged in all three North American countries: In the United States, there has been a 7 percent increase (12.8 million jobs); in Canada, there has been a 10.1 percent increase (1.3 million jobs); and in Mexico there has been a 22 percent increase (2.2 million jobs).[6]

In addition to Europe and North America, many global companies are also fully engaged in Asia. Although the focus for many years has been on Japan, companies are now operating in a broader range of Asian countries such as Korea, Vietnam, Taiwan, Malaysia, and China (including Hong Kong). Motorola, for example, has invested $1.2 billion in China and its annual sales in that country is more than $3.2 billion (almost 12 percent of its worldwide revenue). Nike is another company that does a good deal of business in Asia, and the stories of its mismanagement in Vietnam and China are now well known.[7]

Beyond the economic issues of world trade, the **cultural environment** (communications, religion, values and ideologies, education, and social structure) has an important influence on decisions in an international setting. Figure 16.4 summarizes the complexity of the cultural environment in which HR must be managed. Culture is an integrated phenomenon, and by recognizing and accommodating taboos, rituals, attitudes toward time, social stratification, kinship systems, and the many other components listed in Figure 16.4, managers will pave the way toward greater harmony and achievement in the **host country**, the country in which an international business operates.

Different cultural environments require different approaches to human resources management. Strategies, structures, and management styles that are appropriate in one cultural setting may lead to failure in another. Managers at Coca-Cola, for example, are quite sensitive to differences among the more than 200 countries within which the company operates. They point out that forging effective relations is a matter of accurate perception, sound diagnosis, and appropriate adaptation.[8] Throughout this chapter we will discuss several HR issues related to adapting to different cultural environments.

**Cultural environment**
Communications, religion, values and ideologies, education, and social structure of a country

**Host country**
Country in which an international corporation operates

**USING THE INTERNET**

EUROPA, the web site of the European Union, is filled with details about the EU's goals and policies:

www. europa.eu.int

## Domestic versus International HRM

The internationalization of U.S. corporations has grown at a faster pace than the internationalization of the HRM profession. Executives in the very best companies around the world still lament that their HR policies have not kept pace with the demands of global competition. And unfortunately, the academic community has not been a particularly good source of answers to international HRM problems. While various journals on international business have published articles on HRM over the years, it was not until 1990 that a journal specifically devoted to this area—the *International Journal of Human Resource Management*—was started.[9]

International HRM differs from domestic HRM in several ways. In the first place, it necessarily places a greater emphasis on functions and activities such as

HRM 1

# HR Issues of a Unified Europe

### Staffing

Unification provides workers the right to move freely throughout Europe and opens labor markets on a pan-European basis. However, unemployment rates vary dramatically across countries throughout Europe. For example, Spain's unemployment rate is improving but still hovers around 18 percent, while countries such as Norway enjoy employment rates around 3 percent. Many of these differences reflect the existence of hard-core unemployed, a problem due to many factors, including political systems, sociocultural differences, and worker training. In some cases, unemployment is the result of racial discrimination. Managers must overcome these problems to take advantage of the labor markets that have been opened to them.

The EU prohibits discrimination against workers and unions. However, while member countries are required to interpret national law in light of EU directives, most companies are still trying to reconcile EU policies with laws in their home countries.

### Training and Development

It has not been easy bringing education up-to-date to prepare Europe's youth and to eliminate the bottlenecks that already exist in many advanced industries. Under a unified Europe, every worker is guaranteed access to vocational training. However, training experts fear that attempts to improve vocational training standards across the European Union will fail unless standards of quality are assured. Germany remains a model of apprenticeship programs and worker development. Firms in other countries are struggling to create transnational employability in the face of inadequate training regulation. Meanwhile, there is a need for "Euroexecutives"—those who speak many languages, are mobile, and are experienced at managing a multicultural workforce.

### Productivity

To be competitive in a global economy, Europeans must increase their level of productivity. Europeans on average work fewer hours, take longer vacations, and enjoy far more social entitlements than do their counterparts in North America and Asia. In contrast to the ten vacation days that U.S. employees receive, in the United Kingdom, France, and the Netherlands workers receive about twenty-five days of paid vacation, and workers in Sweden and Austria receive thirty. In many countries, these periods are established by law and must be reconciled in a unified Europe.

### Compensation and Benefits

Wages also differ substantially across countries throughout Europe. Workers in industrialized countries such as Germany and Switzerland receive an average hourly rate of about $28. Workers in Greece and Portugal, in contrast, have hourly wages between $5 and $9. Market forces are diminishing these differences somewhat, but to be competitive, companies need to bring compensation levels further in line to productivity.

Although pay discrimination is prohibited by law, women workers still tend to be in low-paying jobs. Because of this, the European Commission has proposed "codes of practice on equal pay for work of equal value," similar to comparable worth in the United States.

In addition to wage issues, the EU has also addressed issues related to benefits. Under EU mandate, all workers have the right to social security benefits regardless of occupation or employer. In

(continued)

addition, even persons who have been unable to enter the workforce are given basic social assistance. Several directives on occupational safety and health establish minimal standards throughout Europe.

**Labor Relations**

In the past, powerful trade unions have fiercely defended social benefits. In a unified Europe, unions retain collective bargaining rights laid out under the host country's laws and the right to be consulted regarding company decisions. Stimulating economic growth to create jobs may mean eliminating rigid work rules and softening policies related to social benefits. Union leaders have promised to fight these initiatives.

Sources: James C. Cooper and Kathleen Madigan, "Growth Has Joblessness on the Run," *Business Week*, July 5, 1999, 21; Xan Smiley, "Survey: The Nordic Countries: Well-Oiled Independence," *Economist*, January 23, 1999, N13–N15; "Special Article: Crisis in Brussels: Europe Has to Scratch Its Head," *Economist*, March 20, 1999, 21–27; "Paying Dues: Once a Big Muscle of German Industry, Unions See It All Sag," *The Wall Street Journal*, November 29, 1999, A-1, A-18; Mike Leat, *Human Resource Issues of the European Union* (London: Financial Times Management, 1998); Andrew Martin and George Ross, eds., *The Brave New World of European Labor* (Oxford, England: Berghahn Books, 1999); David Fairlamb, Carol Matlack, John Rossant, Stephen Baker, Gail Edmondson, and Jack Ewing, "Europe's Big Chance," *Business Week*, September 27, 1999, 62; Jennie Walsh, "No Stamp for Passport to EU Training," *People Management* 4, no. 12 (June 11, 1998):15.

## Cultural Environment of International Business

FIGURE 16.4

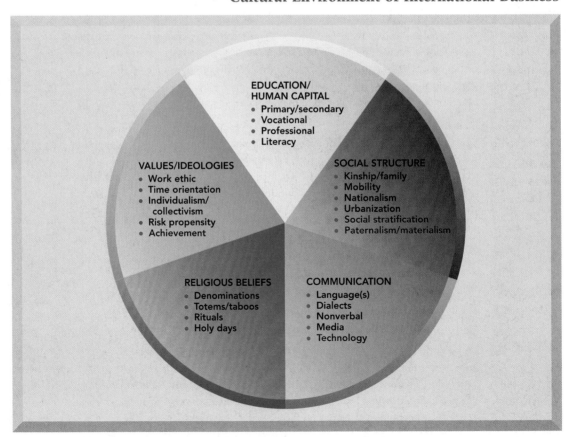

relocation, orientation, and translation services to help employees adapt to a new and different environment outside their own country. Assistance with tax matters, banking, investment management, home rental while on assignment, and coordination of home visits is also usually provided by the HR department. Most larger corporations have a full-time staff of HR managers devoted solely to assisting globalization. McDonald's, for example, has a team of HR directors who travel around the world to help country managers stay updated on international concerns, policies, and programs.

Coca-Cola provides support to its army of HR professionals working around the world. There is a core HR group in the company's Atlanta headquarters that holds a two-week HR orientation twice a year for the international HR staff. This program helps international HR practitioners share information about HR philosophies, programs, and policies established either in Coca-Cola's headquarters or another part of the world that can be successfully adopted by others. The program also provides a foundation for an HR network within the Coca-Cola system that helps participants get a broader view of the company's activities.[10]

The HR department in an overseas unit must be particularly responsive to the cultural, political, and legal environments. For example, companies such as Shell, Xerox, Levi Strauss, Digital, and Honeywell have made a special effort to create codes of conduct for employees throughout the world to make certain that standards of ethical and legal behavior are known and understood. PepsiCo has taken a similar approach to ensuring that company values are reinforced (even while recognizing the need for adapting to local cultures). The company has four core criteria that are viewed as essential in worldwide recruiting efforts: (1) personal integrity, (2) a drive for results, (3) respect for others, and (4) capability.[11]

*PepsiCo has worldwide operations that now include the emerging markets of the Czech Republic, Hungary, India, Poland, Slovakia, and Russia.*

# International Staffing

International management poses many problems in addition to those faced by a domestic operation. Because of geographic distance and a lack of close, day-to-day relationships with headquarters in the home country, problems must often be resolved with little or no counsel or assistance from others. It is essential, therefore, that special attention be given to the staffing practices of overseas units.

There are three sources of employees with whom to staff international operations. First, the company can send people from its home country. These employees are often referred to as **expatriates**, or **home-country nationals**. Second, it can hire **host-country nationals**, natives of the host country, to do the managing. Third, it can hire **third-country nationals,** natives of a country other than the home country or the host country.

Each of these three sources of overseas workers provides certain advantages and certain disadvantages. Some of the more important advantages are presented in Figure 16.5. Most corporations use all three sources for staffing their multinational operations, although some companies exhibit a distinct bias for one or another of the three sources.[12]

As shown in Figure 16.6, at early stages of international expansion, organizations often send home-country expatriates to establish activities (particularly in less-developed countries) and to work with local governments. At later stages of internationalization, there is typically a steady shift toward the use of host-country nationals. There are three reasons for this trend:

1. Hiring local citizens is less costly because the company does not have to worry about the costs of home leaves, transportation, and special schooling allowances.
2. Since local governments usually want good jobs for their citizens, foreign employers may be required to hire them.
3. Using local talent avoids the problem of employees having to adjust to the culture.

## Comparison of Advantages in Sources of Overseas Managers

**FIGURE 16.5**

| HOST-COUNTRY NATIONALS | HOME-COUNTRY NATIONALS (EXPATRIATES) | THIRD-COUNTRY NATIONALS |
|---|---|---|
| Less cost | Talent available within company | Broad experience |
| Preference of host-country governments | Greater control | International outlook |
| Intimate knowledge of environment and culture | Company experience | Multilingualism |
| Language facility | Mobility | |
| | Experience provided to corporate executives | |

FIGURE 16.6

**► Changes in International Staffing over Time**

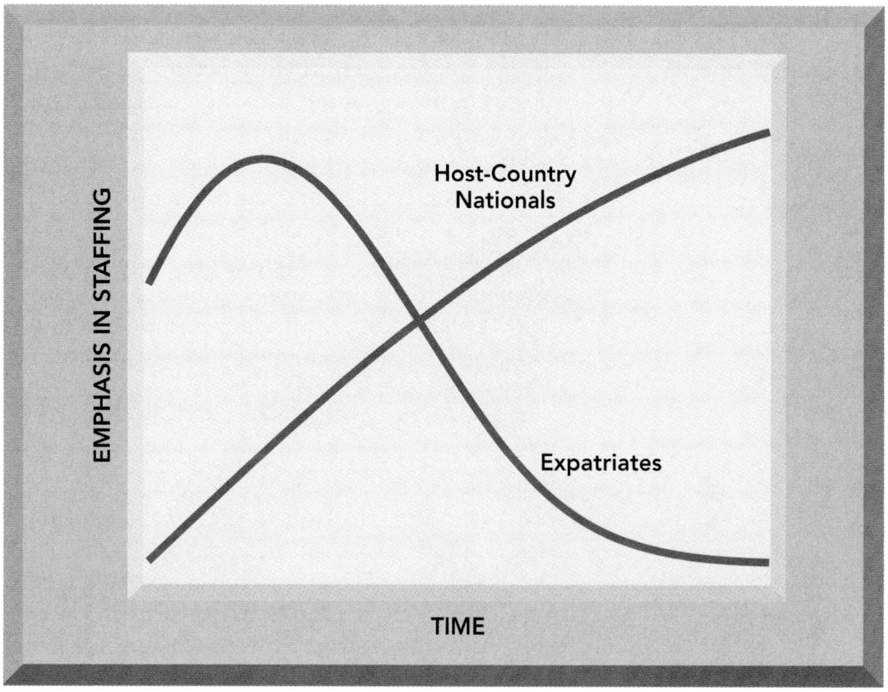

Recently there has also been a trend away from using only expatriates in the top management positions. In many cases, U.S. companies want to be viewed as true international citizens. To avoid the strong influence of the home country, companies frequently change staffing policies to replace U.S. expatriates with local managers. In Honeywell's European Division, for example, twelve of the top executive positions are held by non-Americans.[13]

Companies such as PepsiCo, Asea Brown Boveri (ABB), and IBM have strong regional organizations and tend to hire third-country nationals in addition to host-country nationals. In such cases, companies would tend to use expatriates only when there is need for a specific set of skills or when individuals in the host country require development. Over the years, U.S.–based companies, in particular, have tended to use more third-country nationals.[14]

It should be recognized that while top managers may have preferences for one source of employees over another, the host country may place pressures on them that restrict their choices. Such pressure takes the form of sophisticated government persuasion through administrative or legislative decrees to employ host-country individuals.

## Recruitment

In general, employee recruitment in other countries is subject to more government regulation than it is in the United States. Regulations range from those that cover procedures for recruiting employees to those that govern the employment of foreign labor or require the employment of the physically disabled, war veterans, or

**Work permit, or work certificate**
Government document granting foreign individual the right to seek employment

displaced persons. Many Central American countries, for example, have stringent regulations about the number of foreigners that can be employed as a percentage of the total workforce. Virtually all countries have work-permit or visa restrictions that apply to foreigners. A **work permit**, or **work certificate**, is a document issued by a government granting authority to a foreign individual to seek employment in that government's country.[15]

MNCs tend to use the same kinds of internal and external recruitment sources as are used in their home countries. At the executive level, companies use search firms such as Korn/Ferry or Heidrick & Struggles. At lower levels more informal approaches tend to be useful. While unskilled labor may be readily available in a developing country, recruitment of skilled workers may be more difficult. Many employers have learned that the best way to find workers in these countries is through referrals and radio announcements because many people lack sufficient reading or writing skills.

The laws of many countries require the employment of locals if adequate numbers of skilled people are available. In these cases, recruiting is limited to a restricted population. Specific exceptions are granted (officially or unofficially) for contrary cases, as for Mexican farmworkers in the United States and for Italian, Spanish, Greek, and Turkish workers in Germany and the Benelux (Belgium, the Netherlands, and Luxembourg) countries. Foreign workers invited to come to perform needed labor are usually referred to as **guest workers**. The employment of nonnationals may involve lower direct labor costs, but indirect costs—language training, health services, recruitment, transportation, and so on—may be substantial.[16]

**Guest workers**
Foreign workers invited to perform needed labor

## Selection

As you might imagine, selection practices vary around the world. In the United States managers tend to emphasize merit, with the best-qualified person getting the job. In other countries, however, firms tend to hire on the basis of family ties, social status, language, and common origin. The candidate who satisfies these criteria may get the job even if otherwise unqualified. Much of this is changing—there has been a growing realization among organizations in other nations that greater attention must be given to hiring those most qualified.

### *The Selection Process*

The selection process for international assignments should emphasize different employment factors, depending on the extent of contact that one would have with the local culture and the degree to which the foreign environment differs from the home environment. For example, if the job involves extensive contacts with the community, as with a chief executive officer, this factor should be given appropriate weight. The magnitude of differences between the political, legal, socioeconomic, and cultural systems of the host country and those of the home country should also be assessed.[17]

If a candidate for expatriation is willing to live and work in a foreign environment, an indication of his or her tolerance of cultural differences should be obtained. On the other hand, if local nationals have the technical competence to carry out the job successfully, they should be carefully considered for the job before the firm launches a search (at home) for a candidate to fill the job. As stated previously, most corporations realize the advantages to be gained by staffing international operations with host-country nationals wherever possible.

Selecting home-country and third-country nationals requires that more factors be considered than in selecting host-country nationals. While the latter must of course possess managerial abilities and the necessary technical skills, they have the advantage of familiarity with the physical and cultural environment and the language of the host country. The discussion that follows will focus on the selection of expatriate managers from the home country.

### Selecting Expatriates

One of the toughest jobs facing many organizations is finding employees who can meet the demands of working in a foreign environment. There are several steps involved in selecting individuals for an international assignment. And the sequencing of these activities can make a big difference.

*Step 1: Begin with self-selection.* Employees should begin the process (years) in advance by thinking about their career goals and interest in international work. By beginning with self-selection, companies can more easily avoid the problems of forcing otherwise promising employees into international assignments where they would be unhappy and unsuccessful. In cases where individuals have families, the decisions about relocation are more complicated. Employees should seek out information to help them predict their chances of success living abroad. Companies such as EDS and Deloitte & Touche give the self-selection instruments to their employees to help them think through the pros and cons of international assignments.

*Step 2: Create a candidate pool.* After employees have self-selected, organizations can put together a database of candidates for international assignments. Information on the database might include availability, languages, country preferences, and skills.

*Step 3: Assess core skills.* From the shortlist of potential candidates, managers can assess each candidate on technical and managerial readiness relative to the needs of the assignment. Although there are many factors that determine success abroad, the initial focus should be on the requirements of the job.

*Step 4: Assess augmented skills and attributes.* As shown in Figure 16.7, expatriate selection decisions are typically driven by technical competence as well as professional and international experience. In addition, however, an increasing number of organizations have also begun considering an individual's ability to adapt to different environments. Satisfactory adjustment depends on flexibility, emotional maturity and stability, empathy for the culture, language and communication skills, resourcefulness and initiative, and diplomatic skills.[18]

To be more specific, companies such as Colgate-Palmolive, Whirlpool, and Dow Chemical have identified a set of **core skills** that they view as critical for success abroad and a set of **augmented skills** that help facilitate the efforts of expatriate managers. These skills are shown in Highlights in HRM 2. It is worth noting that many of these skills are not significantly different from those required for managerial success at home.

While these efforts to improve the selection process have helped in many cases, unfortunately the **failure rate** among expatriates has been estimated to range from 25 to 50 percent. What is worse, the average cost of a failed assignment can run as high as from $200,000 to $2.1 million.[19] In contrast to the criteria for selection, the most prevalent reasons for failure among expatriates are not technical or managerial limitations—they sit squarely on family and lifestyle issues. Interestingly, Figure 16.8 shows the major causes of expatriate assignment failure. By far, the biggest factor tends to be a spouse's inability to adjust to his or her new surroundings.[20]

**Core skills**
Skills considered critical to an employee's success abroad

**Augmented skills**
Skills helpful in facilitating the efforts of expatriate managers

**Failure rate**
Percentage of expatriates who do not perform satisfactorily

FIGURE 16.7

▶ **Expatriate Selection Criteria**

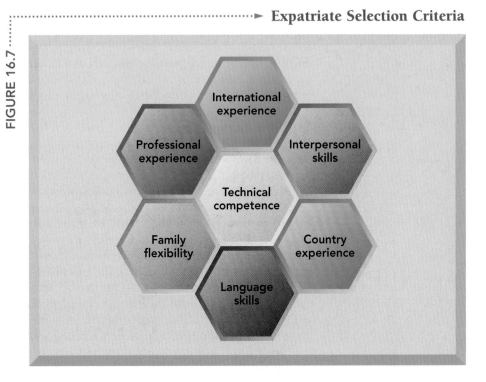

### Women Going Abroad

Traditionally, companies have been hesitant to send women on overseas assignments. Executives may either mistakenly assume that women do not want international assignments, or they may assume that host-country nationals are prejudiced against women. The reality is that women frequently do want international assignments—at least at a rate equal to that of men. And while locals may be prejudiced against women in their own country, they view women first as foreigners (*gaijin* in Japanese) and only secondly as women. Therefore, cultural barriers that typically constrain the roles of women in a male-dominated society may not totally apply in the case of expatriates.

Importantly, in those cases where women have been given international assignments, they generally have performed quite well. The success rate of female expatriates has been estimated to be about 97 percent—a rate far superior to that of men.[21] Ironically, women expatriates attribute at least part of their success to the fact that they are women. Because locals are aware of how unusual it is for a woman to be given a foreign assignment, they frequently assume that the company would not have sent a woman unless she was the very best. In addition, because women expatriates are novel (particularly in managerial positions), they are very visible and distinctive. In many cases, they may even receive special treatment not given to their male colleagues.

### Staffing Transnational Teams

In addition to focusing on individuals, it is also important to note that companies are increasingly using transnational teams to conduct international business.

**HIGHLIGHTS IN HRM**

# Skills of Expatriate Managers

**CORE SKILLS**

Experience
Decision making
Resourcefulness
Adaptability
Cultural sensitivity
Team building
Maturity

**AUGMENTED SKILLS**

Computer skills
Negotiation skills
Strategic thinking
Delegation skills
Change management

**Transnational teams**
Teams composed of members of multiple nationalities working on projects that span multiple countries

**Transnational teams** are composed of members of multiple nationalities working on projects that span multiple countries.[22] These teams are especially useful for performing tasks that the firm as a whole is not yet structured to accomplish. For example, they may be used to transcend the existing organizational structure to customize a strategy for different geographic regions, transfer technology from one part of the world to another, and communicate between headquarters and subsidiaries in different countries.

The fundamental task in forming a transnational team is assembling the right group of people who can work together effectively to accomplish the goals of the team. Many companies try to build variety into their teams in order to maximize

**FIGURE 16.8**

## Causes of Expatriate Assignment Failure

**WHY DO EXPATS FAIL?**

- Family adjustment
- Lifestyle issues
- Work adjustment
- Bad selection

- Poor performance
- Other opportunities arise
- Business reasons
- Repatriation issues

responsiveness to the special needs of different countries. For example, when Heineken formed a transnational team to consolidate production facilities, it made certain that team members were drawn from each major region within Europe. Team members tended to have specialized skills, and members were added only if they offered some unique skill that added value to the team.

### Selection Methods

The methods of selection most commonly used by corporations operating internationally are interviews, assessment centers, and tests. While some companies interview only the candidate, others interview both the candidate and the spouse, lending support to the fact that companies are becoming increasingly aware of the significance of the spouse's adjustment to a foreign environment and the spouse's contribution to managerial performance abroad. However, despite the potential value of considering a spouse's adjustment, the influence of such a factor over the selection/expatriation decision raises some interesting issues about validity, fairness, and discrimination. For example, if someone is denied an assignment because of concerns about his or her spouse, there may be grounds for legal action. This is particularly true now that the Civil Rights Act of 1991 makes it clear that U.S. laws apply to employees working for U.S. companies overseas.

# Training and Development

Although companies try to recruit and select the very best people for international work, it is often necessary to provide some type of training to achieve the desired level of performance. Over time, given the rapidity of change in an international setting, employees may also need to upgrade their skills as they continue on the job. Such training may be provided within the organization or outside it in some type of educational setting.

## Skills of the Global Manager

If businesses are to be managed effectively in an international setting, managers need to be educated and trained in global management skills. In this regard, Levi Strauss has identified the following six skill categories for the **global manager,** or the manager equipped to run an international business:

**Global manager**
Manager equipped to run an international business

- Ability to seize strategic opportunities
- Ability to manage highly decentralized organizations
- Awareness of global issues
- Sensitivity to issues of diversity
- Competence in interpersonal relations
- Skill in building community[23]

Corporations that are serious about succeeding in global business are tackling these problems head-on by providing intensive training. Companies such as AMP, Texas Instruments, Procter & Gamble, Bechtel, and others with large international staffs prepare employees for overseas assignments. (These firms and others, including Coca-Cola, Motorola, Chevron, and Mattel, also orient employees who are still located in the United States but who deal in international markets.) The biggest mistake managers can make is to assume that people are the same everywhere. An organization that makes a concerted effort to ensure that its employees understand and respect cultural differences will realize the impact of its effort on its sales, costs, and productivity.[24]

## Content of Training Programs

There are at least four essential elements of training and development programs that prepare employees for working internationally: (1) language training, (2) cultural training, (3) assessing and tracking career development, and (4) managing personal and family life.[25]

### Language Training

Communication with individuals who have a different language and a different cultural orientation is extremely difficult. Most executives agree that it is among the biggest problems for the foreign business traveler. Even with an interpreter, much is missed.[26]

**USING THE INTERNET**

Thunderbird, at the American Graduate School, is devoted solely to the education of college graduates for international careers. Native speakers of English receive thorough training in *nine* languages. Check it out at:

www.t-bird.edu

When ARCO Products began exploring potential business opportunities in China, the HR department set up a language training class (with the help of Berlitz International) in conversational Mandarin Chinese.[27] While foreign language fluency is important in all aspects of international business, only a small percentage of Americans are skilled in a language other than English. Students who plan careers in international business should start instruction in one or more foreign languages as early as possible. Penn State University recently changed its requirements for all students in business management so that they now include four college semesters of a foreign language. Other programs designed to train participants for international business, such as those offered at the American Graduate School of International Management in Glendale, Arizona, and the Global Management Program at the University of South Carolina, provide intensive training in foreign languages.

Fortunately for most Americans, English is almost universally accepted as the primary language for international business. Particularly in cases where there are many people from different countries working together, English is usually the designated language for meetings and formal discourse. Although English is a required subject in many foreign schools, students may not learn to use it effectively. Many companies provide instruction in English for those who are required to use English in their jobs.

Learning the language is only part of communicating in another culture. One must also learn how the people think and act in their relations with others. The following list illustrates the complexities of the communication process in international business.

1. In England, to "table" a subject means to put it on the table for present discussion. In the United States, it means to postpone discussion of a subject, perhaps indefinitely.
2. In the United States, information flows to a manager. In cultures where authority is centralized (Europe and South America), the manager must take the initiative to seek out the information.

3.  Getting straight to the point is uniquely American. Europeans, Arabs, and many others resent American directness in communication.
4.  In Japan, there are sixteen ways to avoid saying "no."
5.  When something is "inconvenient" to the Chinese, it is most likely downright impossible.
6.  In most foreign countries, expressions of anger are unacceptable; in some places, public display of anger is taboo.
7.  The typical American must learn to treat silences as "communication spaces" and not interrupt them.
8.  In general, Americans must learn to avoid gesturing with the hand.

To understand the communication process, attention must be given to non-verbal communication. Highlights in HRM 3 illustrates that some of our everyday gestures have very different meanings in other cultures. In summary, when one leaves the United States, it is imperative to remember that perfectly appropriate behavior in one country can lead to an embarrassing situation in another.

Since factors other than language are also important, those working internationally need to know as much as possible about (1) the country where they are going, (2) that country's culture, and (3) the history, values, and dynamics of their own organization. Figure 16.9 gives an overview of what one needs to study for an international assignment.

### Cultural Training

Cross-cultural differences represent one of the most elusive aspects of international business. Generally unaware of their own culture-conditioned behavior, most people tend to react negatively to tastes and behaviors that deviate from those of their own culture.

Managerial attitudes and behaviors are influenced, in large part, by the society in which managers have received their education and training. Similarly, reactions of employees are the result of cultural conditioning. Each culture has its expectations

*International assignments provide an employee with a set of experiences that are uniquely beneficial to both the individual and the firm.*

# Nonverbal Communications in Different Cultures

## CALLING A WAITER

In the United States, a common way to call a waiter is to point upward with the forefinger. In Asia, a raised forefinger is used to call a dog or other animal. To get the attention of a Japanese waiter, extend the arm upward, palm down, and flutter the fingers. In Africa, knock on the table. In the Middle East, clap your hands.

## INSULTS

In Arab countries, showing the soles of your shoes is an insult. Also, an Arab may insult a person by holding a hand in front of the person's face.

## A-OKAY GESTURE

In the United States, using the index finger and the thumb to form an "o" while extending the rest of the fingers is a gesture meaning okay or fine. In Japan, however, the same gesture means money. Nodding your head in agreement if a Japanese uses this sign during your discussion could mean you are expected to give him some cash. And in Brazil the same gesture is considered a seductive sign to a woman and an insult to a man.

## EYE CONTACT

In Western and Arab cultures, prolonged eye contact with a person is acceptable. In Japan, on the other hand, holding the gaze of another is considered rude. The Japanese generally focus on a person's neck or tie knot.

## HANDSHAKE AND TOUCHING

In most countries, the handshake is an acceptable form of greeting. In the Middle East and other Islamic countries, however, the left hand is considered the toilet hand and is thought to be unclean. Only the right hand should be used for touching.

## SCRATCHING THE HEAD

In most Western countries, scratching the head is interpreted as lack of understanding or noncomprehension. To the Japanese, it indicates anger.

## INDICATING "NO"

In most parts of the world, shaking the head left and right is the most common way to say no. But among the Arabs, in parts of Greece, Yugoslavia, Bulgaria, and Turkey, a person says no by tossing the head to the side, sometimes clicking the tongue at the same time. In Japan, no can also be said by moving the right hand back and forth.

## AGREEMENT

In addition to saying yes, Africans will hold an open palm perpendicular to the ground and pound it with the other fist to emphasize "agreed." Arabs will clasp their hands together, forefingers pointed outward, to indicate agreement.

Source: S. Hawkins, *International Management* 38, no. 9 (September 1983): 49. Copyright © 1983 by Reed Business Information Ltd. Reprinted with permission.

FIGURE 16.9

### Preparing for an International Assignment

To prepare for an international assignment, one should become acquainted with the following aspects of the host country:

1. Social and business etiquette

2. History and folklore

3. Current affairs, including relations between the host country and the United States

4. Cultural values and priorities

5. Geography, especially its major cities

6. Sources of pride and great achievements of the culture

7. Religion and the role of religion in daily life

8. Political structure and current players

9. Practical matters such as currency, transportation, time zones, hours of business

10. The language

for the roles of managers and employees. For example, what one culture encourages as participative management another might see as managerial incompetence.[28] Being successful as a manager depends on one's ability to understand the way things are normally done and to recognize that changes cannot be made abruptly without considerable resistance, and possibly antagonism, on the part of local nationals. Some of the areas in which there are often significant variations among the different countries will be examined briefly.

A wealth of data from cross-cultural studies reveals that nations tend to cluster according to similarities in certain cultural dimensions such as work goals, values, needs, and job attitudes. Using data from eight comprehensive studies of cultural differences, Simcha Ronen and Oded Shenkar have grouped countries into the clusters shown in Figure 16.10. Countries having a higher GDP per capita in comparison with other countries are placed close to the center.

Ronen and Shenkar point out that while evidence for the grouping of countries into Anglo, Germanic, Nordic, Latin European, and Latin American clusters appears to be quite strong, clusters encompassing the Far Eastern and Arab countries are ill defined and require further research, as do clusters of countries classified as independent. Many areas, such as Africa, have not been studied much at all. It should also be noted that the clusters presented in Figure 16.10 do not include Russia and the former satellites of what was the Soviet Union.[29]

Studying cultural differences can help managers identify and understand work attitudes and motivation in other cultures. In Japan, for example, employees are more likely to feel a strong loyalty to their company, although recent reports show that this may be changing. When compared with the Japanese, Americans may feel little loyalty to their organization. On the other hand, a Latin American tends to work not for a company but for an individual manager. Thus managers in Latin American countries can encourage performance only by using personal influence

FIGURE 16.10

**A Synthesis of Country Clusters**

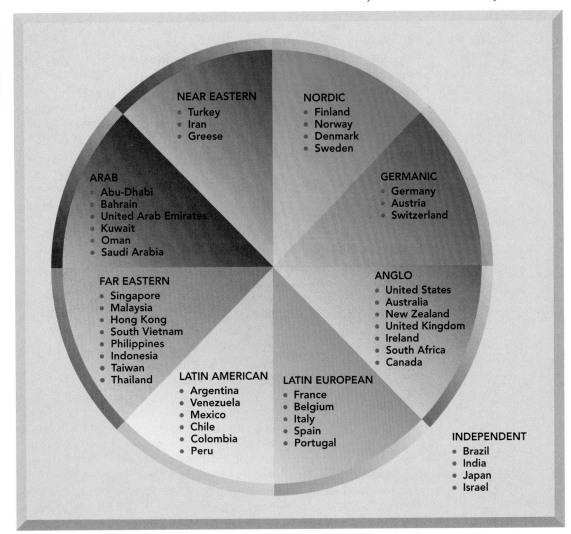

NEAR EASTERN
- Turkey
- Iran
- Greese

NORDIC
- Finland
- Norway
- Denmark
- Sweden

ARAB
- Abu-Dhabi
- Bahrain
- United Arab Emirates
- Kuwait
- Oman
- Saudi Arabia

GERMANIC
- Germany
- Austria
- Switzerland

FAR EASTERN
- Singapore
- Malaysia
- Hong Kong
- South Vietnam
- Philippines
- Indonesia
- Taiwan
- Thailand

ANGLO
- United States
- Australia
- New Zealand
- United Kingdom
- Ireland
- South Africa
- Canada

LATIN AMERICAN
- Argentina
- Venezuela
- Mexico
- Chile
- Colombia
- Peru

LATIN EUROPEAN
- France
- Belgium
- Italy
- Spain
- Portugal

INDEPENDENT
- Brazil
- India
- Japan
- Israel

Source: Simcha Ronen and Oded Shenkar, "Clustering Countries on Attitudinal Dimensions: A Review and Synthesis," *Academy of Management Review* 10, no. 3 (Jult 1985): 435–54. Copyright *Academy of Management Review*. Reprinted with permission of the *Academy of Management Review* and the authors; permission conveyed through the Copyright Clearance Center, Inc.

and working through individual members of a group. In the United States, competition has been the name of the game; in Japan, Taiwan, and other Asian countries, cooperation is more the underlying philosophy.[30]

One of the important dimensions of leadership, whether we are talking about international or domestic situations, is the degree to which managers invite employee participation in decision making. While it is difficult to find hard data on employee participation across different countries, careful observers report that American managers are about in the middle on a continuum of autocratic to democratic decision-making styles. Scandinavian and Australian managers also appear to be in the middle. South American and European managers, especially those from France, Germany, and Italy, are toward the autocratic end of the continuum; Japanese managers are at the most participatory end. Because Far Eastern cultures and religions tend to emphasize harmony, group decision making predominates there.[31]

### Assessing and Tracking Career Development

International assignments provide some definite developmental and career advantages. For example, working abroad tends to increase a person's responsibilities and influence within the corporation. In addition, it provides a person with a set of experiences that are uniquely beneficial to both the individual and the firm. In this way, international assignments enhance a person's understanding of the global marketplace and offer the opportunity to work on a project important to the organization.[32]

To maximize the career benefits of a foreign assignment, two key questions about the employer should be asked before accepting an overseas post: (1) Do the organization's senior executives view the firm's international business as a critical part of their operation? (2) Within top management, how many executives have a foreign-service assignment in their background, and do they feel it important for one to have overseas experience? At Dow Chemical, for example, fourteen of the firm's twenty-two-member management committee, including the CEO, have had overseas assignments. To ensure appropriate career development, Dow appoints what their expatriates refer to as a "godfather," usually a high-level manager who serves as a stateside contact for information about organizational changes, job opportunities, and anything related to salary and compensation. At Exxon, employees are given a general idea of what they can expect after an overseas assignment even before they leave to assume it. With this orientation, they can make a smooth transition and continue to enhance their careers. Colgate-Palmolive and Ciba-Geigy make a special effort to keep in touch with expatriates during the period that they are abroad. Colgate's division executives and other corporate staff members make frequent visits to international transferees.[33]

An increasing number of companies such as Monsanto, 3M, Digital, and GTE are developing programs specifically designed to facilitate **repatriation**—that is, helping employees make the transition back home. The program is designed to prepare employees for adjusting to life at home (which at times can be more difficult than adjusting to a foreign assignment). Employees are given guidance about how much the expatriate experience may have changed them and their families. Monsanto's program is also designed to smooth the employee's return to the home organization and help make certain that the expatriate's knowledge and experience are fully utilized. To do so, returning expatriates get the chance to showcase their new knowledge in debriefing sessions.[34] A repatriation checklist is shown in Highlights in HRM 4.

Unfortunately, not all companies have career development programs designed for repatriating employees. In several recent studies researchers have found that the majority of companies do not do an effective job of repatriation. Here are some general findings:

1. Only about one-third of companies have a repatriation plan in place before the expatriate leaves home.

2. Another third typically don't begin formal repatriation discussions until two to six months before the end of their assignment.

3. The remaining third never have a repatriation discussion at all.

**Repatriation**
Process of employee transition home from an international assignment

**HIGHLIGHTS IN HRM**

# Repatriation Checklist

For employees returning from an overseas assignment, there are guidelines to help make their homecoming easier. Remember, planning for repatriation begins even before a person leaves to go overseas. Then there are things to take care of during their stint abroad, and finally, there are some important things to be considered when they come home.

**Before They Go**
- Make sure you have clearly identified a need for the international assignment. Don't send somebody abroad unnecessarily. Develop a clear set of objectives and expectations.
- Make sure that your selection procedures are valid. Select the employee and also look at the family situation.
- Provide (or fund) language and cultural training for the employee and the employee's family.
- Offer counseling and career assistance for the spouse.
- Establish career planning systems that reward international assignments.

**While They Are Away**
- Jointly establish a developmental plan that focuses on competency development.
- Tie performance objectives to the developmental plan.
- Identify mentors who can be a liaison and support person from home.
- Keep communications open so that the expatriate is aware of job openings and opportunities.
- Arrange for frequent visits back home (for the employee and the family). Make certain they do not lose touch with friends and relatives.

**When They Come Back Home**
- Throw a "welcome home" party.
- Offer counseling to ease the transition.
- Arrange conferences and presentations to make certain that knowledge and skills acquired away from home are identified and disseminated.
- Get feedback from the employee and the family about how well the organization handled the repatriation process.

Source: Adapted from Bennet & Associates, Price Waterhouse, and Charlene Marmer Solomon, "Repatriation Planning Checklist," *Personnel Journal* 14, no. 1 (January 1995): 32.

Not surprisingly, employees often lament that their organizations are vague about repatriation, about their new roles within the company, and about their career progression. It is not at all uncommon for employees to return home after a few years to find that there is *no* position for them in the firm and that they no longer know anyone who can help them. Employees often feel their firms disregard their difficulties in adjusting to life back in the United States. Even in those cases where employees are successfully repatriated, their companies often do not fully utilize the knowledge, understanding, and skills they developed in overseas experiences. And contrary to the reason that many Americans take international assignments in the first place—to gain advancement—evidence suggests that only a fraction are actually promoted. In fact, many employees take jobs at lower levels than their international assignments. This hurts the employee, of course, but it may hurt equally the firm's chances of using that employee's expertise to gain competitive advantage. For these reasons, expatriates sometimes leave their company within a year or two of coming home.[35]

### Managing Personal and Family Life

As noted previously, one of the most frequent causes of an employee's failure to complete an international assignment is personal and family stress. **Culture shock**—a disorientation that causes perpetual stress—is experienced by people who settle overseas for extended periods. The stress is caused by hundreds of jarring and disorienting incidents such as being unable to communicate, having trouble getting the telephone to work, being unable to read the street signs, and a myriad of other everyday matters that are no problem at home. Soon minor frustrations become catastrophic events, and one feels helpless and drained, emotionally and physically.

In Chapter 7, we observed that more and more employers are assisting two-career couples in finding suitable employment in the same location. To accommodate dual-career partnerships, some employers are providing informal help finding jobs for the spouses of international transferees. However, other companies are establishing more formal programs to assist expatriate couples. These include career- and life-planning counseling, continuing education, intercompany networks to identify job openings in other companies, and job-hunting/fact-finding trips. In some cases, a company may even create a job for the spouse—though this is not widely practiced. The U.S. Chamber of Commerce, the U.S. State Department, and various women's organizations have initiated job counseling, networking groups, and assistance programs in several business centers. The available evidence suggests that, while a spouse's career may create some problems initially, in the long run it actually may help ease an expatriate's adjustment process.[36]

## Training Methods

There are a host of training methods available to prepare an individual for an international assignment. Unfortunately, the overwhelming majority of companies provide only superficial preparation for their employees. Lack of training is one of the principal causes of failure among employees working internationally.

In many cases, the employee and his or her family can learn much about the host country through books, lectures, and videotapes about the culture, geography, social and political history, climate, food, and so on. The content is factual and the knowledge gained will at least help the participants to have a better understanding of their assignments. Such minimal exposure, however, does not fully prepare one for a foreign assignment. Training methods such as sensitivity training, which focuses on learning at the affective level, may well be a powerful technique in the reduction of ethnic prejudices. The Peace Corps, for example, uses sensitivity training supplemented by field experiences. Field experiences may sometimes be obtained in a nearby "microculture" where similarities exist.

Companies often send employees on temporary assignments—lasting, say, a few months—to encourage shared learning. These temporary assignments are probably

**Culture shock**
Perpetual stress experienced by people who settle overseas

too brief for completely absorbing the nuances of a culture; however, companies such as AMP and Texas Instruments use them to help employees learn about new ideas and technologies in other regions.[37]

In other instances employees are transferred for a much longer period of time. For example, Fuji-Xerox sent fifteen of its most experienced engineers from Tokyo to a Xerox facility in Webster, New York. Over a five-year period, these engineers worked with a team of American engineers to develop the "world" copier. By working together on an extended basis, the U.S. and Japanese employees learned from each other both the technical and the cultural requirements for a continued joint venture.[38]

## Developing Local Resources

Apart from developing talent for overseas assignments, most companies have found that good training programs also help them attract needed employees from the host countries. In less developed countries especially, individuals are quite eager to receive the training they need to improve their work skills. Oftentimes, however, a company's human capital investment does not pay off. It is very common, for example, for locally owned firms to hire away those workers who have been trained by the foreign-owned organizations.

### Apprenticeship Training

A major source of trained labor in European nations is apprenticeship training programs (described in Chapter 6). On the whole, apprenticeship training in Europe is superior to that in the United States. In Europe, a dual-track system of education directs a large number of youths into vocational training. The German system of apprenticeship training, one of the best in Europe, provides training for office and shop jobs under a three-way responsibility contract between the apprentice, his or her parents, and the organization. At the conclusion of their training, apprentices can work for any employer but generally receive seniority credit with the training firm if they remain in it.

### Management Development

One of the greatest contributions that the United States has made to work organizations is in improving the competence of managers. Americans have a facility for analytical reasoning that is part of their lives. They tend to make decisions on a rational basis and to have a better psychological background for decision making.

Foreign nationals have generally welcomed the type of training they have received through management development programs offered by American organizations. Increasingly, organizations such as the World Bank, Mobil, and Petroleos de Venezuela have entered into partnerships with university executive education programs to customize training experiences to the specific needs of expatriate managers and foreign nationals.

# Performance Appraisal

As we noted earlier, individuals frequently accept international assignments because they know that they can acquire skills and experiences that will make them more valuable to their companies. Unfortunately, one of the biggest problems with managing these individuals is that it is very difficult to evaluate their performance.

Even the notion of performance evaluation is indicative of a U.S. management style that focuses on the individual, which can cause problems in Asian countries such as China, Japan, and Korea and eastern European countries such as Hungary and the Czech Republic. For these reasons, performance appraisal problems may be one of the biggest reasons why failure rates among expatriates are so high and why international assignments can actually derail an individual's career rather than enhance it.[39]

## Who Should Appraise Performance?

In many cases, an individual working internationally has at least two allegiances: one to his or her home country (the office that made the assignment) and the other to the host country in which the employee is currently working. Superiors in each location frequently have different information about the employee's performance and may also have very different expectations about what constitutes good performance. For these reasons, the multirater (360-degree) appraisal discussed in Chapter 8 is gaining favor among global firms such as ABB, Bechtel, and Nordson.[40]

### Home-Country Evaluations

Domestic managers are frequently unable to understand expatriate experiences, value them, or accurately measure their contribution to the organization. Geographical distances pose severe communication problems for expatriates and home-country managers. Instead of touching base regularly, there is a tendency for both expatriates and domestic managers to work on local issues rather than coordinate across time zones and national borders. Information technology has improved this situation, and it is far easier to communicate globally today than it was just a few years ago.[41] But even when expatriates contact their home-country offices, it is frequently not to converse with their superiors. More likely they talk with peers and others throughout the organization.

### Host-Country Evaluations

Although local management may have the most accurate picture of an expatriate's performance—managers are in the best position to observe effective and ineffective behavior—there are problems with using host-country evaluations. First, local cultures may influence one's perception of how well an individual is performing. As noted earlier in the chapter, participative decision making may be viewed either positively or negatively, depending on the culture. Such cultural biases may not have any bearing on an individual's true level of effectiveness. In addition, local management frequently does not have enough perspective on the entire organization to know how well an individual is truly contributing to the firm as a whole.

Given the pros and cons of home-country and host-country evaluations, most observers agree that performance evaluations should try to balance the two sources of appraisal information.[42] Although host-country employees are in a good position to view day-to-day activities, in many cases the individual is still formally tied to the home office. Promotions, pay, and other administrative decisions are connected there, and as a consequence, the written evaluation is usually handled by the home-country manager. Nevertheless, the appraisal should be completed only after vital input has been gained from the host-country manager. As discussed in Chapter 8, multiple sources of appraisal information can be extremely valuable for providing independent points of view—especially if someone is working as part of a team. If there is much concern about cultural bias, it may be possible to have persons of the same nationality as the expatriate conduct the appraisal.

## Adjusting Performance Criteria

As we discussed at the beginning of this chapter, an individual's success or failure is affected by a host of technical and personal factors. Many of these factors should be considered in developing a broader set of performance criteria.

### Augmenting Job Duties

Obviously the goals and responsibilities inherent in the job assignment are among the most important criteria used to evaluate an individual's performance. However, because of the difficulties in observing, documenting, and interpreting performance information in an international setting, superiors often resort to using "easy" criteria such as productivity, profits, and market share. These criteria may be valid—but they are still deficient if they do not capture the full range of an expatriate's responsibility. There are other, more subtle factors that should be considered as well. In many cases, an expatriate is an ambassador for the company, and a significant part of the job is cultivating relationships with citizens of the host country.

### Individual Learning

Any foreign assignment involves learning. As one might guess, it is much easier to adjust to similar cultures than to dissimilar ones. An American can usually travel to the United Kingdom or Australia and work with locals almost immediately. Send that same individual to Hungary or Malaysia, and the learning curve is less steep. The expatriate's adjustment period may be even longer if the company has not yet established a good base of operations in the region. The first individuals transferred to a country have no one to show them the ropes or to explain local customs. Even relatively simple activities such as navigating the rapid transit system can prove to be problematic. The U.S. State Department and defense forces have developed rating systems that attempt to distinguish whether regional assignments are (1) somewhat more difficult than they would be in the United States, (2) more difficult than in the United States, or (3) much more difficult than in the United States. These difficulty factors can be built into the appraisal system.[43]

### Organizational Learning

It is worth noting that bottom-line measures of performance may not fully convey the level of learning gained from a foreign assignment. Yet learning may be among the very most important reasons for sending an individual overseas, particularly at early stages of internationalization and during joint ventures.[44] Even if superiors do acknowledge the level of learning, they frequently use it only as an excuse for less-than-desired performance, rather than treating it as a valuable outcome in itself. What they fail to recognize is that knowledge gained—if shared—can speed the adjustment process for others. However, if the learning is not shared, then each new employee to a region may have to go through the same cycle of adjustment.

## Providing Feedback

Performance feedback in an international setting is clearly a two-way street. Although the home-country and host-country superiors may tell an expatriate how well he or she is doing, it is also important for expatriates to provide feedback regarding the support they are receiving, the obstacles they face, and the suggestions they have about the assignment. More than in most any other job, expatriates are in the very best position to evaluate their own performance.

In addition to ongoing feedback, an expatriate should have a debriefing interview immediately upon returning home from an international assignment. These repatriation interviews serve several purposes:

1. They help expatriates reestablish old ties with the home organization and may prove to be important for setting new career paths.

2. The interview can address technical issues related to the job assignment itself.

3. The interview may address general issues regarding the company's overseas commitments, such as how relationships between the home and host countries should be handled.

4. The interview can be very useful for documenting insights an individual has about the region. These insights can then be incorporated into training programs for future expatriates.

# Compensation

One of the most complex areas of international HRM is compensation. Different countries have different norms for employee compensation. Managers should consider carefully the motivational use of incentives and rewards in foreign countries. For Americans, while nonfinancial incentives such as prestige, independence, and influence may be motivators, money is likely to be the driving force. Other cultures are more likely to emphasize respect, family, job security, a satisfying personal life, social acceptance, advancement, or power. Since there are many alternatives to money, the rule is to match the reward with the values of the culture. For example, Figure 16.11 shows how pay plans can differ on the basis of one cultural dimension: individualism. In individualistic cultures, such as the United States, pay plans often focus on individual performance and achievement. However, in collectively oriented cultures such as Japan and Taiwan, pay plans focus more on internal equity and personal needs.[45]

In general, a guiding philosophy for designing pay systems might be "think globally and act locally." That is, executives should normally try to create a pay plan that supports the overall strategic intent of the organization but provides enough flexibility to customize particular policies and programs to meet the needs of employees in specific locations. After a brief discussion of compensation practices for host-country employees and managers, we will focus on the problems of compensating expatriates.

## Compensation of Host-Country Employees

As shown in Figure 16.12, hourly wages vary dramatically from country to country. Labor costs are one of the biggest motivators for international expansion, but there are many managerial and administrative issues that must be addressed when an organization establishes operations overseas.

FIGURE 16.11

## Individualism and Compensation Strategies

INDIVIDUALISM

| | DOMINANT VALUES | CORPORATE FEATURES | COMPENSATION STRATEGIES | SAMPLE COUNTRIES |
|---|---|---|---|---|
| **HIGH** | • Personal accomplishment<br>• Selfishness<br>• Independence<br>• Individual attributions<br>• Internal locus of control<br>• Belief in creating one's own destiny<br>• Utilitarian relationship with employee | • Organizations not compelled to care for employees' total well-being<br>• Employees look after individual interests<br>• Explicit systems of control necessary to ensure compliance and prevent wide deviation from organizational norms | • Performance-based pay utilized<br>• Individual achievement rewarded<br>• External equity emphasized<br>• Extrinsic rewards as important indicators of personal success<br>• Attempts made to isolate individual contributions (i.e., who did what)<br>• Emphasis on short-term objectives | • United States<br>• Great Britain<br>• Canada<br>• New Zealand |
| **LOW** | • Team accomplishment<br>• Sacrifice for others<br>• Dependence on social unit<br>• Group attributions<br>• External locus of control<br>• Belief in the hand of fate<br>• Moral relationship | • Organizations committed to a high level of involvement in workers' personal lives<br>• Loyalty to the firm critical<br>• Normative, rather than formal, systems of control to ensure compliance | • Group-based performance as important criterion<br>• Seniority-based pay utilized<br>• Intrinsic rewards essential<br>• Internal equity key in guiding pay policies<br>• Personal need (e.g., number of children) as factor in pay received | • Singapore<br>• South Korea<br>• Indonesia<br>• Japan |

Source: L.R. Gomez-Mejia and T. Welbourne, "Compensation Strategies in a Global Context," *Human Resources Planning* 14, no. 1 (1991): 29–41. Reprinted with permission.

FIGURE 16.12

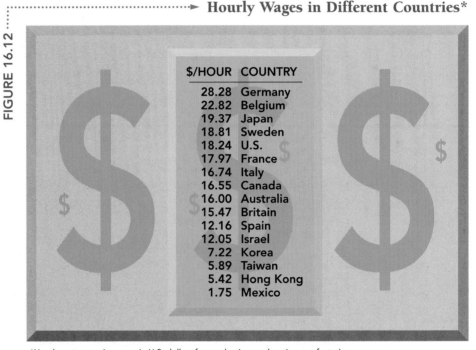

## Hourly Wages in Different Countries*

| $/HOUR | COUNTRY |
|--------|---------|
| 28.28 | Germany |
| 22.82 | Belgium |
| 19.37 | Japan |
| 18.81 | Sweden |
| 18.24 | U.S. |
| 17.97 | France |
| 16.74 | Italy |
| 16.55 | Canada |
| 16.00 | Australia |
| 15.47 | Britain |
| 12.16 | Spain |
| 12.05 | Israel |
| 7.22 | Korea |
| 5.89 | Taiwan |
| 5.42 | Hong Kong |
| 1.75 | Mexico |

*Hourly compensation costs in U.S. dollars for production workers in manufacturing.
Source: Department of Labor.

Host-country employees are generally paid on the basis of productivity, time spent on the job, or a combination of these factors. In industrialized countries, pay is generally by the hour; in developing countries, by the day. The piece-rate method is quite common. In some countries, including Japan, seniority is an important element in determining employees' pay rates. When companies commence operations in a foreign country, they usually set their wage rates at or slightly higher than the prevailing wage for local companies. Eventually, though, they are urged to conform to local practices to avoid "upsetting" local compensation practices.

Employee benefits in other countries are frequently higher than those in the United States. In France, for example, benefits are about 70 percent of wages and in Italy 92 percent, compared with around 40 percent in the United States. Whereas in the United States most benefits are awarded to employees by employers, in other industrialized countries most of them are legislated or ordered by governments. Some of these plans are changing. Defined contribution plans are on the rise, sex equality is becoming important, and stock ownership is being tried.[46]

In Italy, Japan, and some other countries, it is customary to add semiannual or annual lump-sum payments equal to one or two months' pay. These payments are not considered profit sharing but an integral part of the basic pay package. Profit sharing is legally required for certain categories of industry in Mexico, Peru, Pakistan, India, and Egypt among the developing countries and in France among the industrialized countries. Compensation patterns in eastern Europe are also in flux as these countries make the adjustment to more-capitalistic systems.

**USING THE INTERNET**

What salary would a manager need to receive to maintain his/her real current income while working in a foreign city? See the international salary calculator at:

www.homefair.com

## Compensation of Host-Country Managers

In the past, remuneration of host-country managers has been ruled by local salary levels. However, increased competition among different companies with subsidiaries in the same country has led to a gradual upgrading of host-country managers' salaries. Overall, international firms are moving toward a narrowing of the salary gap between the host-country manager and the expatriate. A recent survey of twenty-six countries by Wyatt Company showed that U.S. firms had lost their ranking as the world's compensation leader. In fact, on average, firms in Japan ($387,000), Mexico ($277,000), Argentina ($229,000), Switzerland ($213,000), and Hong Kong ($206,000) all pay managers more than do those in the United States ($195,000).[47]

## Compensation of Expatriate Managers

Compensation plans for expatriate managers must be competitive, cost-effective, motivating, fair and easy to understand, consistent with international financial management, easy to administer, and simple to communicate. To be effective, an international compensation program must

1. Provide an incentive to leave the United States
2. Allow for maintaining an American standard of living
3. Facilitate reentry into the United States
4. Provide for the education of children
5. Allow for maintaining relationships with family, friends, and business associates[48]

**Balance-sheet approach**
Compensation system designed to match the purchasing power in a person's home country

Expatriate compensation programs used by over 90 percent of U.S.-based international organizations rest on the **balance-sheet approach**, a system designed to equalize the purchasing power of employees at comparable positions living overseas and in the home country and to provide incentives to offset qualitative differences between assignment locations.[49] The balance-sheet approach generally comprises the following steps:

*Step 1: Calculate base pay.* Begin with the home-based gross income, including bonuses. Deduct taxes, Social Security, and pension contributions.

*Step 2: Figure cost-of-living allowance (COLA).* Add or subtract a cost-of-living allowance to the base pay. Typically, companies don't subtract when the international assignment has a lower cost of living. Instead, they allow the expatriate to benefit from the negative differential. Often a housing allowance is added in here as well.

*Step 3: Add incentive premiums.* General mobility premiums and hardship premiums compensate expatriates for separation from family, friends, and domestic support systems, usually 15 percent of base salary.

*Step 4: Add assistance programs.* These additions are often used to cover added costs such as moving and storage, automobile, and education expenses.

The differentials element is intended to correct for the higher costs of overseas goods and services so that in relation to their domestic peers expatriates neither gain purchasing power nor lose it. It involves a myriad of calculations to arrive at a total differential figure, but in general, the cost typically runs between three and five times the home-country salary. Fortunately, employers do not have to do extensive research to find comparative data. They typically rely on data published quarterly by the U.S. Department of State for use in establishing allowances to compensate American civilian employees for costs and hardships related to assignments abroad.[50]

# International Organizations and Labor Relations

Labor relations in countries outside the United States differ significantly from those in the United States. Differences exist not only in the collective bargaining process but also in the political and legal conditions. To get a basic idea about labor-management relations in an international setting, we will look at four primary areas: (1) the role of unions in different countries, (2) collective bargaining in other countries, (3) international labor organizations, and (4) the extent of labor participation in management.

## The Role of Unions

The role of unions varies from country to country and depends on many factors, such as the level of per capita labor income, mobility between management and labor, homogeneity of labor (racial, religious, social class), and level of employment. These and other factors determine whether the union will have the strength it needs to represent labor effectively. In countries with relatively high unemployment, low pay levels, and no union funds for welfare, the union is driven into alliance with other organizations: political party, church, or government. This is in marked contrast to the United States, where the union selected by the majority of employees bargains only with the employer, not with other institutions.

Even in the major industrial countries one finds that national differences are great with respect to (1) the level at which bargaining takes place (national, industry, or workplace), (2) the degree of centralization of union-management relations, (3) the scope of bargaining, (4) the degree to which government intervenes, and (5) the degree of unionization.

Labor relations in Europe differ from those in the United States in certain significant characteristics:

1. In Europe, organizations typically negotiate the agreement with the union at the national level through the employer association representing their particular industry, even when there may be local within-company negotiations as well. This agreement establishes certain minimum conditions of employment, which are frequently augmented through negotiations with the union at the company level.

2. Unions in many European countries have more political power than those in the United States, with the result that when employers deal with the union they are, in effect, dealing indirectly with the government. Unions are often allied with a particular political party, although in some countries these alliances are more complex, with unions having predominant but not sole representation with one party.

3. There is a greater tendency in Europe for salaried employees, including those at the management level, to be unionized, quite often in a union of their own.[51]

Like the United States, European countries are facing the reality of a developing global economy. And particularly in Germany and the United Kingdom, unions have been losing some of their power. Ironically, the power of the unions to gain high wages and enforce rigid labor rules has been blamed for hurting the competitiveness of European companies. As the power of unions declines a bit, it has been increasingly evident in Europe that workers are less inclined to make constant demands for higher wages. The trend has been to demand compensation in other ways—through benefits or through greater participation in company decision making.[52] Various approaches to participation will be discussed later.

## Collective Bargaining in Other Countries

We saw in Chapter 15 how the collective bargaining process is typically carried out in companies operating in the United States. When we look at other countries, we find that the whole process can vary widely, especially with regard to the role that government plays. In the United Kingdom and France, for example, government intervenes in all aspects of collective bargaining. Government involvement is only natural where parts of industry are nationalized. Also, in countries where there is heavy nationalization there is more likely to be acceptance of government involvement, even in the nonnationalized companies. At Renault, the French government-owned automobile manufacturer, unions make use of political pressures in their bargaining with managers, who are essentially government employees. The resulting terms of agreement then set the standards for other firms. In developing countries it is common for the government to have representatives present during bargaining sessions to make sure that unions with relatively uneducated leaders are not disadvantaged in bargaining with skilled management representatives.

## International Labor Organizations

The fact that international corporations can choose the countries in which they wish to establish subsidiaries generally results in the selection of those countries that have the most to offer. Certainly inexpensive labor is a benefit that most strategists consider. By coordinating their resources, including human resources, and their production facilities, companies operate from a position of strength. International unions, such as the United Auto Workers, have found it difficult to achieve a level of influence anywhere near that found within a particular industrial nation. Those that have been successful operate in countries that are similar, such as the United States and Canada.

The most active of the international union organizations has been the International Confederation of Free Trade Unions (ICFTU), which has its headquarters in Brussels. Cooperating with the ICFTU are some twenty International Trade Secretariats (ITSs), which are really international federations of national trade unions operating in the same or related industries. The significance of the ITSs from the point of view of management lies in the fact that behind local unions may be the expertise and resources of an ITS. Another active and influential organization is the International Labor Organization (ILO), a specialized agency of the United Nations. It does considerable research on an international basis and endorses standards for various working conditions, referred to as the International Labor Code. At various times and places this code may be quoted to management as international labor standards to which employers are expected to conform.[53]

## Labor Participation in Management

In many European countries, provisions for employee representation are established by law. An employer may be legally required to provide for employee representation on safety and hygiene committees, worker councils, or even on boards of directors. While their responsibilities vary from country to country, worker councils basically provide a communication channel between employers and workers. The legal codes that set forth the functions of worker councils in France are very detailed. Councils are generally concerned with grievances, problems of individual employees, internal regulations, and matters affecting employee welfare.

**Codetermination**

Representation of labor on the board of directors of a company

A higher form of worker participation in management is found in Germany, where representation of labor on the board of directors of a company is required by law. This arrangement is known as **codetermination** and often by its German word, *Mitbestimmung*. While sometimes puzzling to outsiders, the system is fairly simple: Company shareholders and employees are required to be represented in equal numbers on the supervisory boards of all corporations with more than 2,000 employees. Power is generally left with the shareholders, and shareholders are generally assured the chairmanship. Other European countries and Japan either have or are considering minority board participation.[54]

Each of these differences makes managing human resources in an international context more challenging. But the crux of the issue in designing HR systems is not choosing one approach that will meet all the demands of international business. Instead, organizations facing global competition must balance multiple approaches and make their policies flexible enough to accommodate differences across national borders. Throughout this book we have noted that different situations call for different approaches to managing people, and nowhere is this point more clearly evident than in international HRM.

# SUMMARY

**OBJECTIVE 1** There are four basic ways to organize for global competition: (1) The international corporation is essentially a domestic firm that has leveraged its existing capabilities to penetrate overseas markets; (2) the multinational corporation has fully autonomous units operating in multiple countries in order to address local issues; (3) the global corporation has a worldview but controls all international operations from its home office; and (4) the transnational corporation uses a network structure to balance global and local concerns.

**OBJECTIVE 2** International HRM places greater emphasis on a number of responsibilities and functions such as relocation, orientation, and translation services to help employees adapt to a new and different environment outside their own country.

**OBJECTIVE 3** Because of the special demands made on managers in international assignments, many factors must be considered in their selection and development. Though hiring host-country nationals or third-country nationals automatically avoids many potential problems, expatriate managers are preferable in some circumstances. The selection of the latter requires careful evaluation of the personal characteristics of the candidate and his or her spouse.

**OBJECTIVE 4** Once an individual is selected, an intensive training and development program is essential to qualify that person for the assignment. Wherever possible, development should extend beyond information and orientation training to include sensitivity training and field experiences that will enable the manager to understand cultural differences better. Those in charge of the international program should provide the help needed to protect managers from career development risks, reentry problems, and culture shock.

 Although home-country managers frequently have formal responsibility for individuals on foreign assignment, they may not be able to fully understand expatriate experiences because geographical distances pose severe communication problems. Host-country managers may be in the best position to observe day-to-day performance but may be biased by cultural factors and may not have a view of the organization as a whole. To balance the pros and cons of home-country and host-country evaluations, performance evaluations should combine the two sources of appraisal information.

 Compensation systems should support the overall strategic intent of the organization but be customized for local conditions. For

expatriates, in particular, compensation plans must provide an incentive to leave the United States; enable maintenance of an equivalent standard of living; facilitate repatriation; provide for the education of children; and make it possible to maintain relationships with family, friends, and business associates.

 In many European countries—Germany, for one—employee representation is established by law. Organizations typically negotiate the agreement with the union at a national level, frequently with government intervention. Since European unions have been in existence longer than their U.S. counterparts, they have more legitimacy and much more political power. In Europe, it is more likely for salaried employees and managers to be unionized.

## KEY TERMS

augmented skills
balance-sheet approach
codetermination
core skills
cultural environment
culture shock
expatriates, or home-country
  nationals

failure rate
global corporation
global manager
guest workers
host country
host-country nationals
international corporation
multinational corporation (MNC)

repatriation
third-country nationals
transnational corporation
transnational teams
work permit, or work certificate

## DISCUSSION QUESTIONS

 1. What do you think are the major HR issues that must be addressed as an organization moves from an international form to a multinational, to a global, and to a transnational form?

 2. In recent years we have observed an increase in foreign investment in the United States. What effect are joint ventures, such as General Motors–Toyota, likely to have on HRM in the United States?

 3. If you were starting now to plan for a career in international HRM, what steps would you take to prepare yourself?

 4. Describe the effects that different components of the cultural environment can have on HRM in an international firm.

5. Pizza Hut is opening new restaurants in Europe every day, it seems. If you were in charge, would you use expatriate managers or host-country nationals in staffing the new facilities? Explain your thinking.

6. In what ways are American managers likely to experience difficulties in their relationships with employees in foreign operations? How can these difficulties be minimized?

 7. This chapter places considerable emphasis on the role of the spouse in the success of an overseas manager. What steps should management take to increase the likelihood of a successful experience for all parties involved?

 8. Talk with a foreign student on your campus; ask about his or her experience with culture shock on first arriving in the United States. What did you learn from your discussion?

 9. If learning (individual and organizational) is an important outcome of an overseas assignment, how can this be worked into a performance appraisal system? How would a manager assess individual and organizational learning?

 10. If the cost of living is lower in a foreign country than in the United States, should expatriates be paid less than they would be at home? Explain your position.

 11. What are the major differences between labor-management relations in Europe and those in the United States?

 12. Do you believe that codetermination will ever become popular in the United States? Explain your position.

## International HRM at Molex, Inc.

The cover of Molex Inc.'s 1998 annual report boasts: "Everywhere, Anywhere." It's a declaration that speaks volumes about this 60-year-old manufacturer of electronic connectors. Molex is a truly global company—the $1.6 billion firm operates 49 manufacturing facilities in 21 countries and employs 13,000 people worldwide. The company has customers in more than 50 countries and nearly 70 percent of its sales come from outside the United States.

The company has four corporate goals: (1) provide good customer service, (2) fully develop its human resources, (3) build a truly global company, and (4) meet or exceed financial goals. Malou Roth, head of training and development, puts it this way, "The way I've always looked at Molex is, there's only four corporate goals and two of them have to do with people." Every employee has an HR-related element tied to his or her performance goals.

Molex tries to make the goals come alive for its workforce, and its human resources team has a big hand in making that happen. "What I tried to do when I came to Molex 15 years ago was take the basic HR programs and practices that I knew were good ones and make those things standards or consistent practices at every entity in every country," says Roth. For example, as Molex grew rapidly during the '80s, Roth established a standardized employee manual with policies and practices for new employee orientation, salary administration with a consistent grading system, written job descriptions, written promotion and grievance procedures, and performance appraisals. Roth made certain that all the materials were translated into the languages of the countries in which Molex had operations. Local managers were free to add to the programs and be creative with them, but they had to implement minimum HR standards.

According to Kathi Regas, corporate VP of HR for Molex, "Our global HR practices in training and communications helps us build on the strong foundation we have—a common way of managing our employees, strengthening their skills, and improving service to our customers both locally and globally." Yet each local unit has unique needs, so the philosophy has been to hire experienced HR professionals from other companies in the same country in which they have operations. Roth figures you need to hire people who know the language, have credibility, know the law, and know how to recruit. "You can't transfer someone in to do that," says Roth. There are 80 HR staff members in 17 countries where Molex operates.

Part of the Molex philosophy about being global is to have many people moving around the company's operations worldwide to learn from each other. For a medium-size company, having so much worldwide employee movement is unusual—and costly. "But we feel it's really worthwhile because there's nothing like living and working with people outside your home country to make you understand you're really in something bigger than Molex Japan or Molex Germany," explains Roth. Adds Regas: "Our investment in expatriates is critical to building the strong foundation we have of sharing our expertise with each other. It's important for us to respect individual cultures while maintaining Molex's unique global culture."

As one way to maintain the culture, every Molex entity worldwide has to conduct bimonthly communications meetings. They're top-down communications blitzes that bring people up to speed on what's going on in that particular Molex unit. Usually the HR manager kicks off the meeting, and then the general manager or sales manager speaks. Molex also does annual communication meetings, which include the company's chairman, the COO, the executive vice president, the corporate VP of HR, and the VP of HR, in addition to other senior executives of the local entity and the region. They spend a day at each location touring the factory, looking at new equipment and facilities and meeting with employees. "Our annual communications meetings ensure that our employees know they're a part of something much bigger than their local entities," says Regas. "They know our history, our performance, and our plans for the future. This, combined with frequent contact among our employees from entities around the world and common practices, helps maintain our culture and strengthen a global team of employees."

These methods have helped Molex find ways for individuals with varying backgrounds and perspectives to work together. The culture serves as a corporate 'glue' that holds the organization effectively together, while also maximizing the energy of individuals throughout the company's global operations.

**Source:** Condensed from "Molex Makes Global HR Look Easy," by Jennifer Laabs, copyright March 1999. Used with permission of Workforce/ACC Communications, Inc. Web site at http://www.workforce.com. All rights reserved.

## QUESTIONS

1. What are the chief human resources challenges that Molex faces as a global organization?
2. What value is gained from having a standardized HR policy manual for all locations?
3. What value is gained from allowing managers to customize the policies for their local countries?
4. Why is there so much emphasis on company culture and communications in this organization?

## Amgen's Global Workforce

Since its inception, Amgen has grown from a few hundred employees at its headquarters in Thousand Oaks, California, to 3,900 people spanning the globe. Amgen is a biotechnology firm that discovers, develops, manufactures, and markets human therapeutics (drugs) based on advanced cellular and molecular biology.

As soon as the company got ready to launch its first product, Amgen executives decided to establish a facility in Cambridge, England. The company needed to do clinical trials in every country in which they wanted to manufacture or sell a product. Doing the research in England gave the company legitimacy with the British government agencies. Amgen also set up clinical development locations in Australia and Canada and established its European headquarters in Lucerne, Switzerland.

Originally, when the company first began its distribution abroad, Amgen executives would send an American manager to scout the location, collect data, and make an analysis based on a map. These days, the company relies on the expertise and knowledge of locals in the host country. Another factor that determines where Amgen sets up shop is where it can form the best academic and medical collaborations. The company has established a relationship with the University of Toronto because of its parallel research in biotechnology and has also created a joint venture with Japan's Kirin Brewery to distribute Amgen products in China.

According to their vice president of human resources, Ed Garnett, Amgen has developed a global mindset that influences the way they manage people. Garnett puts it this way: "If you're a multinational, you'll have an expatriate program. If you're global, you'll only provide one-way tickets." Indeed, Amgen's HR strategy reflects this premise. To gain competitive advantage, Amgen hires the top international scientists, medical personnel, and global managers, who are either natives of or familiar with Amgen's worldwide locations. Further, approximately 15 percent of Amgen's employees in Thousand Oaks are foreign nationals. With the exception of one worker in Asia, all of Amgen's foreign-based managers are locals or third-country nationals. According to Garnett, "We hire locals for management, but we send expats to help with the integration of processes and special projects." The company has only six expatriates worldwide—and they are deployed only temporarily, to set things up.

What type of employees does Amgen look for? "Global companies need people who've experienced many different business environments," Garnett says. This goes beyond speaking the language and growing up in the country. It requires someone who can execute company directives in any country where Amgen operates. To bolster its global workforce, the company is beefing up its executive development program. While still in the early stages, Amgen's curriculum will include more information about different countries' cultures and business practices, and much of the training will focus on leadership skills like communication, performance management, and decision making.

Another piece of Amgen's continuous training is team building. Transnational teams are commonplace in this company. The company's European HR director, Michael Bentley, noted, "Our teams cut across countries, and in the case of product development, they may cross continents." Because all team members tend to be focused on advancements in cellular and molecular biology—the sciences that will provide products to save and enhance lives—their professional culture unites otherwise very different people. Their commonalities help Amgen reinforce the company's values and still respect the various cultures in which the company operates. The company's values of openness, diversity, risk taking, and scientific collaboration have led to its growing success worldwide.

*Source:* Condensed and adapted from Brenda Paik Sunoo, "Amgen's Latest Discovery," *Personnel Journal* 75, no. 2 (February 1996): 38–45.

### QUESTIONS

1. What inherent problems do you see with Amgen's global staffing approach?
2. What do you think would be the biggest HR problems in managing a transnational team?
3. Would this approach to HR work for other firms? What kinds?

## NOTES AND REFERENCES

1. Peter Dowling, Denice E. Welch, and Randall S. Schuler, *International Human Resource Management: Managing People in a Multinational Context* (Cincinnati, Ohio: South-Western, 1998); Nancy J. Adler, *International Dimensions of Organizational Behavior* (Cincinnati, Ohio: South-Western, 1997); Michael S. Schell and Charlene Marmer Solomon, "Global Culture: Who's the Gatekeeper?" *Workforce* 76, no. 11 (November 1997): 35–39.

2. Christopher A. Bartlett and Sumatra Ghoshal, *Managing across Borders: The Transnational Solution* (Boston: Harvard Business School Press, 1998).

3. Scott A. Snell, Charles C. Snow, Sue Canney Davison, and Donald C. Hambrick, "Designing and Supporting Transnational Teams: The Human Resource Agenda," *Human Resource Management* 37, no. 2: 147–58. See also Charles C. Snow, Scott A. Snell, Sue Canney Davison, and Donald C. Hambrick, "Use Transnational Teams to Globalize Your Company," *Organizational Dynamics,* Spring 1996, 50–67.

4. Jeremy Kahn, "The *Fortune* Global 500: The World's Largest Corporations," *Fortune,* August 2, 1999, 144–46; "Country by Country," *Business Week,* July 13, 1998, 54.

5. Bill Emmott, "The 20th Century: Free to Be European," *Economist* 352, no. 8136 (September 11, 1999): S21–S23.

6. Tom Bagsarian, "NAFTA at 5: A Boon for Customers," *Iron Age New Steel* 15, no. 10 (September 1999): 18–22; "The Real NAFTA Winner," *Business Week,* September 27, 1999, 34.

7. Jeremy Kahn, "China's Tough Markets," *Fortune,* October 11, 1999, 282; Charlene Marmer Solomon, "The Big Question," *Workforce,* Special Supplement, July 1997, 10–16; Philip Knight, "Global Manufacturing: The Nike Story Is Just Good Business," *Vital Speeches of the Day* 64, no. 20 (August 1, 1998): 637–40.

8. Stephen J. Mezias, Ya-Ru Chen, and Patrice Murphy, "Toto, I Don't Think We're in Kansas Anymore: Some Footnotes to Cross-Cultural Research," *Journal of Management Inquiry* 8, no. 3 (September 1999): 323–33; Pan Suk Kim, "Globalization of Human Resource Management: A Cross-Cultural Perspective for the Public Sector," *Public Personnel Management* 28, no. 2 (Summer 1999): 227–243; David Veale, Lynn Oliver, and Kees van Langen, "Three Coca-Cola Perspectives on International Management

Styles," *Academy of Management Executive* 9, no. 3 (August 1995): 74–77.

9. Interested readers can access this journal online. The journal's web site is *www.journals.routledge.com/hr/hrtext.htm*.

10. Maali H. Ashamalla, "International Human Resource Management Practices: The Challenge of Expatriation," *Competitiveness Review* 8, no. 2 (1998): 54–65.

11. Readers interested in codes of conduct and other ethical issues pertaining to international business might read the following: Janice M. Beyer and David Nino, "Ethics and Cultures in International Business," *Journal of Management Inquiry* 8, no. 3 (September 1999): 287–97; Ronald Berenbeim, "The Divergence of a Global Economy: One Company, One Market, One Code, One World," *Vital Speeches of the Day* 65, no. 22 (September 1, 1999): 696–98; Larry R. Smeltzer and Marianne M. Jennings, "Why an International Code of Business Ethics Would Be Good for Business," *Journal of Business Ethics* 17, no. 1 (January 1998): 57–66. See also Charlene Marmer Solomon, "Put Your Ethics to a Global Test," *Personnel Journal* 75, no. 1 (January 1996): 66–74; David J. Cherrington and Laura Zaugg Middleton, "An Introduction to Global Business Issues," *HRMagazine* 40, no. 6 (June 1995): 124–30; Rochelle Kopp, "International Human Resource Policies and Practices in Japanese, European, and United States Multinationals," *Human Resource Management* 33, no. 4 (Winter 1994): 581–99; "Global Companies Reexamine Corporate Culture," *Personnel Journal* 73, no. 8 (August 1994): 12–13.

12. Rosalie L. Tung, "American Expatriates Abroad: From Neophytes to Cosmopolitans," *Journal of World Business* 33, no. 2 (Summer 1998): 125–44; Calvin Reynolds, "Strategic Employment of Third Country Nationals," *Human Resource Planning* 20, no. 1 (1997): 33–93; Donald McNerney, "Global Staffing: Some Common Problems—and Solutions," *HRFocus* 73, no. 6 (June 1996): 1, 4–6.

13. Charlene Marmer Solomon, "Staff Selection Impacts Global Success," *Personnel Journal* 73, no. 1 (January 1994): 88–99; Cecil G. Howard, "Profile of the 21st-Century Expatriate Manager," *HRMagazine* 37, no. 6 (June 1992): 93–100.

14. Calvin Reynolds, "Strategic Employment of Third Country Nationals," *Human Resource Planning* 20, no. 1 (1997): 33–93; Dawn Anfuso, "Coca-Cola's Staffing Philosophy Supports Its Global Strategy," *Personnel Journal* 73, no. 11 (November 1994): 116.

15. Valerie Frazee, "Expert Help for Dual-Career Spouses," *Workforce* 4, no. 2 (March 1999): 18–20; "On the Border," *Government Executive* 31, no. 2 (February 1999): 101–4.

16. Barb Cole-Gomolski, "A Whole New Ball Game for High-Tech Guest Workers," *Computerworld* 32, no. 47 (November 23, 1998): 24; Stuart Rosewarne, "The Globalization and Liberalization of Asian Labor Markets," *World Economy* 21, no. 7 (September 1998): 963–79; Jennifer Hunt, "Japan's 'Guest Workers': Issues and Public Policies," *Industrial and Labor Relations Review* 48, no. 4 (July 1995): 863–64.

17. John P. Harrison and Alfons Westgeest, "Developing a Globally Savvy Staff," *Association Management* 51, no. 2 (February 1999): 58–64; Ingemar Torbiorn, "Staffing for International Operations," *Human Resource Management Journal* 7, no. 3 (1997): 42–52.

18. Allan Halcrow, "Expats: The Squandered Resource," *Workforce* 78, no. 4 (April 1999): 42–48; Valerie Frazee, "Selecting Global Assignees," *Workforce* 3, no. 4 (July 1998): 28–30.

19. Halcrow, "Expats"; "Expat Assignments: Key Is Preparedness," *HRFocus* 75, no. 9 (September 1998): 2; Reyer A. Swaak, "Expatriate Failures: Too Many, Too Much Cost, Too Little Planning," *Compensation and Benefits Review* 27, no. 6 (November–December 1995): 47–55.

20. Carl Quintanilla, "The Number One Reason Overseas Assignments Fail: The Spouse Hates It," *The Wall Street Journal,* January 7, 1997; A-1.

21. Michael Harvey and Danielle Wiese, "The Dual-Career Couple: Female Expatriates and Male Trailing Spouses," *Thunderbird International Business Review* 40, no. 4 (July/August 1998): 359–88; "Women Managers in Asia," *Training and Development* 50, no. 4 (April 1996): 37; Sully Taylor and Nancy Napier, "Working in Japan: Lessons from Women Expatriates," *Sloan Management Review* 37, no. 3 (Spring 1996): 76–84.

22. Snell et al., "Designing and Supporting Transnational Teams."

23. "What Does It Take to Be a Global Manager?" *Quality* 37, no. 3 (March 1998): 34; Sheila Rothwell, "Leadership Development and International HRM," *Manager Update* 4, no. 4 (Summer 1993): 20–32.

24. Cynthia L. Kemper, "Global Training's Critical Success Factors," *Training and Development* 52, no. 2 (February 1998): 35–37; Margaret Kaeter, "Interna-

tional Development," *Training* 32, no. 5 (May 1995): S23–S29.

25. Valerie Frazee, "Send Your Expats Prepared for Success," *Workforce* 4, no. 2 (March 1999): 6–8; Janet D. Lein and Nichole L. Sisco, "Language and Cross-Cultural Training for Expatriate Employees: A Comparison between the U.S. and Germany," *Journal of Language for International Business* 10, no. 2: 47–59.

26. Managers who are interested in setting up a language-training program or who wish to evaluate commercially available language-training programs should consult the "Standard Guide for Use-Oriented Foreign Language Instruction." The seven-page guide is put out by the American Society for Testing and Materials (ASTM), (610) 832-9585, *http://www. astm.org.*

27. Stephen Dolainski, "Language Training Improves Global Business at ARCO," *Workforce* 76, no. 2 (February 1997): 38; Kathryn Tyler, "Targeted Language Training Is Best Bargain," *HRMagazine* 43, no. 1 (January 1998): 61–64; Tom Lester, "Pulling Down the Language Barrier," *International Management* 49, no. 6 (July/August 1994): 42–44; Robert McGarvey and Scott Smith, "Speaking in Tongues," *Training* 31, no. 1 (January 1994): 113–16. See also Stephen H. Wildstrom, "Log On—and Learn a Language," *Business Week,* January 22, 1996, 22.

28. Neil J. Simon, "Competitive Intelligence Personnel: Requirements for the Multicultural Organization," *Competitive Intelligence Magazine* 2, no. 1 (January–March 1999): 43–44; Abbas J. Ali, Ahmed A. Azim, and Krish S. Krishnan, "Expatriates and Host Country Nationals: Managerial Values and Decision Styles," *Leadership and Organization Development Journal* 16, no. 6 (1995): 27–34; Dean B. McFarlan, Paul D. Sweeney, and John L. Cotton, "Attitudes toward Employee Participation in Decision-Making: A Comparison of European and American Managers in a United States Multinational Company," *Human Resource Management* 31, no. 4 (Winter 1992): 363–83.

29. Readers interested in HR-related issues for managing in Russia should see the following: Carl Fey, Pontus Engstrom, and Ingmar Bjorkman, "Doing Business in Russia: Effective Human Resource Management Practices for Foreign Firms in Russia," *Organizational Dynamics* 28, no. 2 (Autumn 1999): 69–74; Ruth May, Carol Bormann Young, and Donna Ledgerwood, "Lessons from Russian Human Resource Management Experience," *European Man-*

*agement Journal* 16, no. 4 (August 1998): 447–459; Martha Cooley, "HR in Russia: Training for Long-Term Success," *HRMagazine* 42, no. 12 (December 1997): 98–106.

30. Mike Bendixen and Bruce Burger, "Cross-Cultural Management Philosophies," *Journal of Business Research* 42, no. 2 (June 1998): 107–14; Clifford C. Hebard, "Managing Effectively in Asia," *Training and Development* 74, no. 12 (December 1995): 113–17.

31. Geert Hofstede, "Cultural Constraints in Management Theories," *Academy of Management Executive* 7, no. 1 (February 1993): 81–94. See also Fons Trompenaars, *Riding the Waves of Culture: Understanding Cultural Diversity in Business* (London: Economist Books, 1993).

32. William E. Franklin, "Careers in International Business: Five Ideas or Principles," *Vital Speeches of the Day* 64, no. 23 (September 15, 1998): 719–21; Ronald Mortensen, "Beyond the Fence Line," *HRMagazine* 42, no. 11 (November 1997): 100–9.

33. Mary A. Scelba, "Developing an Effective Repatriation Process at Chubb and Sons Inc.," *Employee Relations Today* 22, no. 4 (Winter 1995/1996): 55–61; "What You Thought," *Personnel Journal* 75, no. 6 (June 1996): 16; Kenton J. Klaus, "How to Establish an Effective Expatriate Program—Best Practices in International Assignment Administration," *Employment Relations Today* 22, no. 1 (Spring 1995): 59–70.

34. Sherrie Zhan, "Smooth Moves," *World Trade* 12, no. 7 (July 1999): 62–64; Charlene Marmer Solomon, "Repatriation: Up, Down, or Out?" *Personnel Journal* 74, 1 (January 1995): 28–30.

35. Lance J. Richards, "Hiring Multicultural Vagabonds," *Workforce* 3, no. 6 (November 1998): 28–30; Halcrow, "Expats." Also see J. Stewart Black and Mark E. Mendenhall, *Global Assignments: Successfully Expatriating and Repatriating International Managers* (San Francisco: Jossey-Bass, 1992); Solomon, "Repatriation," 28–30.

36. Stephen S. McIntosh, "Breaking through Culture Shock: What You Need to Succeed in International Business," *HRMagazine* 44, no. 6 (June 1999): 184–86; Michael G. Harvey and M. Ronald Buckley, "The Process for Developing an International Program for Dual-Career Couples," *Human Resource Management Review* 8, no. 1 (Spring 1998): 99–123; Nancy Carter, "Solve the Dual-Career Challenge," *Workforce* 2, no. 4 (October 1997): 21–22; Charlene Marmer Solomon, "One Assignment, Two Lives," *Personnel Journal* 75, no. 5 (May 1996): 36–47.

37. Nancy Adler, *International Dimensions of Organizational Behavior* (Cincinnati, Ohio: South-Western, 1997).

38. Snell et al., "Designing and Supporting Transnational Teams."

39. Paul Y. Huo and Mary Ann Von Glinow, "On Transplanting Human Resource Practices to China: A Culture-Driven Approach," *International Journal of Manpower* 16, no. 9 (1995): 3–15; Robert C. Kovach, Jr., "Matching Assumptions to Environment in the Transfer of Management Practices: Performance Appraisal in Hungary," *International Studies of Management and Organization* 24, no. 4 (Winter 1994/1995): 83–99; Gary Oddou and Mark Mendenhall, "Expatriate Performance Appraisal: Problems and Solutions," in Mark Mendenhall and Gary Oddou, eds., *Readings and Cases in International Human Resource Management* (Cincinnati, Ohio: South-Western, 1999), 399–410.

40. Charlene Marmer Solomon, "How Does Your Global Talent Measure Up?" *Personnel Journal* 73, no. 10 (October 1994): 96–108.

41. "10 tips for expatriate management," *HR Focus* 75, no. 3 (March 1998): S8; M. G. Martinsons, "Human Resource Management Applications of Knowledge-Based Systems," *International Journal of Information Management* 17, no. 1 (February 1997): 35–53.

42. Michael Harvey, "Focusing the International Personnel Performance Appraisal Process," *Human Resource Development Quarterly* 8, no. 1 (Spring 1997): 41–62.

43. Mendenhall and Oddou, eds., *Readings and Cases*. See also Kenneth W. Davis, Teun De Rycker, and J. Piet Verckens, "Become a Global Communicator," *Workforce* 2, no. 4 (October 1997): 10–11; Gayle Porter and Judith W. Tansky, "Expatriate Success May Depend on a 'Learning Orientation': Considerations for Selection and Training," *Human Resource Management* 38, no. 1 (Spring 1999): 47–60.

44. Andrew C. Inkpen, "Learning and Knowledge Acquisition through International Strategic Alliances," *Academy of Management Executive* 12, no. 4 (November 1998): 69–80; Oded Shenkar and Jiatao Li, "Knowledge Search in International Cooperative Ventures," *Organization Science* 10, no. 2 (March/April 1999): 134–43; Charlene Marmer Solomon, "Return on Investment," *Workforce* 2, no. 4 (October 1997): 12–18; Dianne J. Cyr and Susan C. Schneider, "Implications for Learning: Human Resource Management in East-West Joint Ventures," *Organizational Studies* 17, no. 2 (1996): 207–26;

Igor Gurkov and Yaroslav Kuz Minov, "Organizational Learning in Russian Privatized Enterprises: The Beginning of Strategic Change," *International Studies of Management and Organization* 25, no. 4 (Winter 1995–1996): 91–117.

45. Timothy D. Dwyer, "Trends in Global Compensation," *Compensation and Benefits Review* 31, no. 4 (July/August 1999): 48–53; George Milkovich and Matt Bloom, "Rethinking International Compensation," *Compensation and Benefits Review* 30, no. 1 (January/February 1998): 15–23; "Japanese Companies Can't Seem to Adjust to U.S. Pay Practices," *HRFocus* 72, no. 2 (February 1995): 14.

46. Mark Sullivan, "European Benefit Issues: Costs to the Multinational Employers," *Compensation and Benefits Management* 12, no. 2 (Spring 1996): 54–60; "Becoming a Global Company: The Implications for the Benefits Department," *Employee Benefit Plan Review* 50, no. 8 (February 1996): 40–44; Jim McKay, "Benefit Trends in Europe," *Employee Benefits* 19, no. 1 (March 1994): 25–29.

47. Jacqueline M. Graves, "U.S. Managers Rank Sixth in Pay," *Fortune,* January 16, 1995, 18; "Want the Big Bucks? Head East—Far East," *Personnel Journal* 74, no. 4 (April 1995): 26.

48. Carolyn Gould, "Expat Pay Plans Suffer Cutbacks," *Workforce* 78, no. 9 (September 1999): 40–46; Carolyn Gould, "What's the Latest in Global Compensation?" *Workforce* Supplement (July 1997): 17–21; Ranae M. Hyer, "Executive Compensation in the International Arena: Back to the Basics," *Compensation and Benefits Review* 25, no. 2 (March-April 1993): 49–54.

49. Valerie Frazee, "Is the Balance Sheet Right for Your Expats?" *Workforce* 77, no. 9 (September 1998): 19–26; Carolyn Gould, "What's the Latest?"

50. *U.S. Department of State Index of Living Costs Abroad, Quarters, Allowances, and Hardship Differentials* (Washington, D.C.: Bureau of Labor Statistics), published quarterly. For recent figures (dated April 1999), see the following web site: *http://www.state.gov/www/perdiems/quarterly_reports/apr99_table1.html.*

51. Andrew Martin and George Ross, eds., *The Brave New World of European Labor: European Trade Unions at the Millennium* (Oxford, England: Berghahn Books, 1999); Haknoh Kim, "Constructing European Collective Bargaining," *Economic and Industrial Democracy* 20, no. 3 (August 1999): 393–426.

52. "Paying Dues: Once the Big Muscle of German Industry, Unions See It All Sag," *The Wall Street*

*Journal,* November 29, 1999, A-1, A-18; Bernard Ebbinyhaus, Jelle Visser, and Bernard Ebbinghaus, *Development of Trade Unions in Western Europe 1945–1995* (New York: Grove's Dictionaries, 1999); "Looking for Work: In Employment Policy, America and Europe Make a Sharp Contrast," *The Wall Street Journal,* March 14, 1994, A-1; "Payroll Policy: Unlike Rest of Europe, Britain Is Creating Jobs, but They Pay Poorly," *The Wall Street Journal,* March 28, 1994, A-1.

53. Interested readers can find more information about international trade unions by checking out the web site for the ICFTU (*http://www.icftu.org/*) as well as the site for the ILO (*http://www.ilo.org/*).

54. Anke Hassel, "The Erosion of the German System of Industrial Relations," *British Journal of Industrial Relations* 37, no. 3 (September 1999): 483–505; Manfred Schumann, "'*Mitbestimmung*'—A German Model for Social Peace," *World Trade* 9, no. 4 (April 1996): 9; Klas Levinson, "Codetermination in Sweden: From Separation to Integration," *Economic and Industrial Democracy* 17, no. 1 (February 1996): 131–42.

# Creating High-Performance Work Systems

## AFTER STUDYING THIS CHAPTER, YOU SHOULD BE ABLE TO

**OBJECTIVE 1**
Discuss the underlying principles of high-performance work systems.

**OBJECTIVE 2**
Identify the components that make up a high-performance work system.

**OBJECTIVE 3**
Describe how the components fit together and support strategy.

**OBJECTIVE 4**
Recommend processes for implementing high-performance work systems.

**OBJECTIVE 5**
Discuss the outcomes for both employees and the organization.

**OBJECTIVE 6**
Explain how the principles of high-performance work systems apply to small and medium-sized, as well as large, organizations.

S o, you've finished reading sixteen (or so) chapters on HRM. Congratulations, textbooks do not always make for the most gripping reading. And if you read this one cover to cover, you were probably cramming for an exam. But before you close this book, think about the following question: What is more difficult, designing effective HR practices or managing them all together as one system?

In the past, HR textbooks simply ended after each individual aspect of HRM was introduced and explained. But in today's competitive environment, many organizations are discovering that it's how the pieces are combined that makes all the difference. After all, managers typically don't focus on staffing, training, and compensation practices in isolation from one another. These HR practices are combined into an overall system to enhance employee involvement and performance. So now that we have talked about the individual pieces, we thought it might be useful to spend some time talking about how they fit together into "high-performance work systems."

**High-performance work system (HPWS)**

A specific combination of HR practices, work structures, and processes that maximizes employee knowledge, skill, commitment, and flexibility

A **high-performance work system (HPWS)** can be defined as a specific combination of HR practices, work structures, and processes that maximizes employee knowledge, skill, commitment, and flexibility. Although there are some noteworthy HR practices and policies that tend to be incorporated within most HPWSs, it would be a mistake for us to focus too much, or too soon, on the pieces themselves. The key concept is the "system." High-performance work systems are composed of many interrelated parts that complement one another to reach the goals of an organization, large or small.

We will start by discussing the underlying principles that guide the development of high-performance work systems and the potential benefits that can occur as a result. Then we will outline the various components of the system, the work-flow design, HR practices, management processes, and supporting technologies. (See Figure 17.1.) We will also describe the ways in which organizations are trying to tie all the pieces of the system together and link them with strategy. We end the chapter with a discussion of the processes organizations use to implement high-performance work systems as well as the outcomes that benefit both the employee and the organization as a whole.

# Fundamental Principles

In Chapter 1, we noted that organizations face a number of important competitive challenges such as adapting to global business, embracing technology, managing change, responding to customers, developing intellectual capital, and containing costs. Side by side with these competitive challenges we noted some very important employee concerns that must be addressed, such as managing a diverse workforce, recognizing employee rights, adjusting to new work attitudes, and balancing work and family demands. We now know that the best organizations go beyond simply balancing these sometimes competing demands; they create work environments that blend these concerns to simultaneously get the most from employees, contribute to their needs, and meet the short-term and long-term goals of the organization.

The notion of high-performance work systems was originally developed by David Nadler to capture an organization's "architecture" that integrates technical

FIGURE 17.1

## Developing High-Performance Work Systems

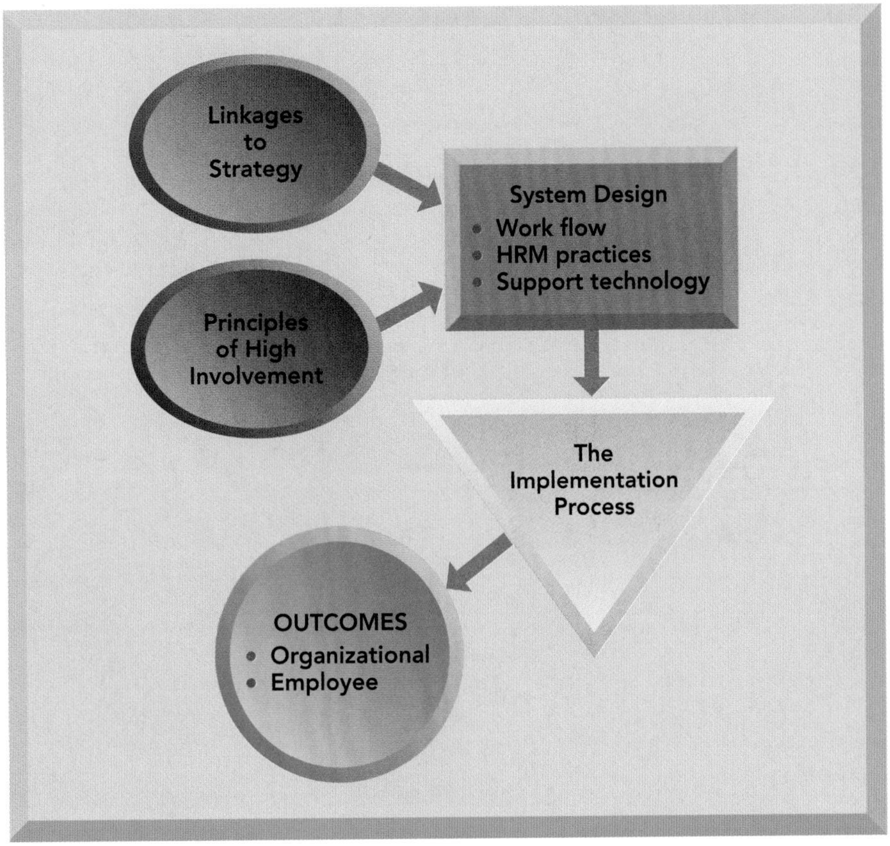

and social aspects of work. Edward Lawler and his associates at the Center for Effective Organization at the University of Southern California have worked with *Fortune* 1000 corporations to identify the primary principles that support high-performance work systems. There are four simple but powerful principles, as shown in Figure 17.2:

- Shared information
- Knowledge development
- Performance-reward linkage
- Egalitarianism[1]

In many ways, these principles have become the building blocks for managers who want to create high-performance work systems. More importantly, they are also quickly becoming the foundation for current theories of human resources management. We will use them as a framework for the rest of the chapter.

## The Principle of Shared Information

The principle of shared information is critical for the success of empowerment and involvement initiatives in organizations. In the past, employees traditionally were

FIGURE 17.2

## Underlying Principles of High-Performance Work Systems

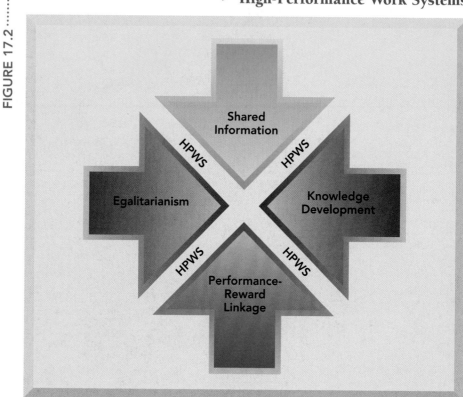

not given—and did not ask for—information about the organization. People were hired to perform narrowly defined jobs with clearly specified duties, and not much else was asked of them. Today much of this is changing as organizations rely on the expertise and initiative of employees to react quickly to incipient problems and opportunities. Without timely and accurate information about the business, employees can do little more than simply carry out orders and perform their roles in a relatively perfunctory way. They are unlikely to understand the overall direction of the business or contribute to organizational success.

On the other hand, when employees are given timely information about business performance, plans, and strategies, they are more likely to make good suggestions for improving the business and to cooperate in major organizational changes. They are also likely to feel more committed to new courses of action if they have input in the decision making. For example, at Magma Copper Company, when the company developed high-performance work teams, a new compensation system based on gainsharing was needed. A special project team composed of employees, managers, and consultants was formed to study the issue and recommend a new payment system. After eleven months of research, a team-based pay structure was implemented that was widely embraced by employees throughout the organization.

The principle of shared information typifies a shift in organizations away from the mentality of command and control toward one more focused on employee commitment. If executives do a good job of communicating with employees, and create a culture of information sharing, employees are perhaps more likely to be willing (and able) to work toward the goals for the organization.[2]

## The Principle of Knowledge Development

Knowledge development is the twin sister of information sharing. As Richard Teerlink, former CEO of Harley-Davidson, noted, "The only thing you get when you empower dummies is bad decisions faster." Throughout this text, we have noted that the number of jobs requiring little knowledge and skill is declining while the number of jobs requiring greater knowledge and skill is growing rapidly. As organizations attempt to compete through people, they must invest in employee development. This includes both selecting the best and the brightest candidates available in the labor market and providing all employees opportunities to continually hone their talents.

High-performance work systems depend on the shift from touch labor to knowledge work. Employees today need a broad range of technical, problem-solving, and interpersonal skills to work either individually or in teams on cutting-edge projects. Because of the speed of change, knowledge and skill requirements must also change rapidly. In the contemporary work environment, employees must learn continuously. Stopgap training programs may not be enough. Employees in high-performance work systems need to learn "real time," on the job, using innovative new approaches to solve novel problems.

## The Principle of Performance-Reward Linkage

A time-tested adage of management is that the interests of employees and organizations naturally diverge. People may intentionally or unintentionally pursue outcomes that are beneficial to them but not necessarily to the organization as a whole. A corollary of this idea, however, is that things tend to go more smoothly when there is some way to align employee and organizational goals. When rewards are connected to performance, employees will naturally pursue outcomes that are mutually beneficial to themselves and the organization. When this happens, some amazing things can result. For example, supervisors don't have to constantly watch to make sure that employees do the right thing. In fact, employees may go out of their way—above and beyond the call of duty, so to speak—to make certain that co-workers are getting the help they need, systems and processes are functioning efficiently, and customers are happy.

Connecting rewards to organizational performance also ensures fairness and tends to focus employees on the organization. Equally important, performance-based rewards ensure that employees share in the gains that result from any performance improvement. For instance, Lincoln Electric has long been recognized for its efforts in linking employee pay and performance.

## The Principle of Egalitarianism

Status and power differences tend to separate people and magnify whatever disparities exist between them. The "us versus them" battles that have traditionally raged between managers, employees, and labor unions have to be replaced by more-cooperative approaches to managing work. More-egalitarian work environments eliminate status and power differences and, in the process, increase collaboration and teamwork. When this happens, productivity can improve if people who once worked in isolation from (or opposition to) one another begin to work together.

Nucor Steel has an enviable reputation not only for establishing an egalitarian work environment but also for the employee loyalty and productivity that stem from that environment. According to John Correnti, Nucor's president and CEO, this happens by making sure that "those who produce the steel know they're the kings of the company." Employees at Nucor don't see executives stepping off a corporate jet or driving a company car. Nucor's headquarters take up the first floor of a small office building next to a mall in Charlotte, North Carolina, not the top floor of a skyscraper. All employees have the same vacation benefits and insurance plans. And all employees are listed alphabetically on the annual report.[3]

Moving power downward in organizations—that is, empowering employees—frequently requires structural changes. Managers often use employee surveys, suggestion systems, quality circles, employee involvement groups, and/or union-management committees that work in parallel with existing organizational structures. In addition, work flow can be redesigned to give employees more control and influence over decision making. Job enlargement, enrichment, and self-managing work teams are typical methods for increasing the power employees have to influence decisions, make suggestions for change, or take action on their own. With decreasing power distances, employees can become more involved in their work; their quality of work life is simultaneously increased and organizational performance is improved.

These four principles—shared information, knowledge development, performance-reward linkage, and egalitarianism—are the basis for designing high-performance work systems. They also cut across many of the topics and HR practices we have talked about elsewhere in this textbook. These principles help us integrate practices and policies to create an overall high-performance work system.

**USING THE INTERNET**

Nucor makes no secret of the importance of its employees. Read about the management philosophy and incentive-based compensation plans at About Nucor at:

# Anatomy of High-Performance Work Systems

**OBJECTIVE 2**

We said at the beginning of this chapter that high-performance work systems combine various work structures, HR practices, and management processes to maximize employee performance and well-being. And although we outlined the principles underlying such systems, their specific characteristics have not as yet been described in detail.

Although it may be premature to claim that there is a foolproof list of "best practices" that can be implemented by every organization for every work situation, there are some clear trends in work design, HR practices, leadership roles, and information technologies that tell us what high-performance work systems look like.[4] Some of these are summarized in Figure 17.3.

## Work-Flow Design and Teamwork

High-performance work systems frequently begin with the way work is designed. Total quality management (TQM) and reengineering have driven many organizations to redesign their work flow. Instead of separating jobs into discrete units,

FIGURE 17.3

## Anatomy of High-Performance Work Systems

| | Shared Information | Knowledge Development | Performance-Reward Linkage | Egalitarianism |
|---|---|---|---|---|
| **Work flow** | | | | |
| • Self-managed teams | | | | |
| • Empowerment | | | | |
| **Staffing** | | | | |
| • Selective recruiting | | | | |
| • Team decision making | | | | |
| **Training** | | | | |
| • Broad skills | | | | |
| • Cross-training | | | | |
| • Problem solving | | | | |
| • Team training | | | | |
| **Compensation** | | | | |
| • Incentives | | | | |
| • Gainsharing | | | | |
| • Profit sharing | | | | |
| • Skill-based pay | | | | |
| **Leadership** | | | | |
| • Few layers | | | | |
| • Coaches/facilitators | | | | |
| **Technologies** | | | | |
| • HRIS | | | | |
| • Communications | | | | |

most experts now advise managers to focus on the key business processes that drive customer value—and then create teams that are responsible for those processes. Federal Express, for example, redesigned its delivery process to give truck drivers responsibility for scheduling their own routes and for making necessary changes quickly. Because the drivers have detailed knowledge of customers and routes, Federal Express managers empowered them to inform existing customers of new products and services. In so doing, drivers now fill a type of sales representative role for the company. In addition, FedEx drivers also work together as a team to identify bottlenecks and solve problems that slow delivery. To facilitate this, advanced communications equipment was installed in the delivery trucks to help teams of drivers balance routes among those with larger or lighter loads.[5]

Similarly, when Colgate-Palmolive opened a plant in Cambridge, Ohio, managers specifically designed teams around key work processes to produce products such as Ajax, Fab, Dynamo, and Palmolive detergent. Instead of separating each stage of production into discrete steps, teams work together in a seamless process to produce liquid detergent, make polyurethane bottles, fill those bottles, label and package the products, and deliver them to the loading dock.

By redesigning the work flow around key business processes, companies such as Federal Express and Colgate-Palmolive have been able to establish a work environment that facilitates teamwork, takes advantage of employee skills and knowledge, empowers employees to make decisions, and provides them with more meaningful work.[6]

## Complementary Human Resources Policies and Practices

Work redesign, in and of itself, does not constitute a high-performance work system. Neither does total quality management or reengineering. Other supporting elements of HRM are necessary to achieve high performance.[7] Several recent studies suggest that both performance and satisfaction are much higher when organizations combine their changes in work-flow design with HR practices that encourage skill development and employee involvement.[8]

### Staffing Practices

Many high-performance work systems begin with highly directive recruitment and selection practices. Recruitment tends to be both broad and intensive in order to get the best pool of candidates from which to choose. Then, by selecting skilled individuals with the ability to learn continuously and work cooperatively, organizations are likely to make up for the time and expense they invested in selection. Talented employees "come up to speed" more quickly and take less time to develop. Too often organizations try to save money by doing a superficial job of hiring. As a consequence, they run the risk of hiring the wrong people and spending more on training and/or outplacement, severance, and recruitment of replacement. Especially in organizations that try to stay lean, perhaps after a painful cycle of downsizing, HPWS can be instrumental for effective performance.[9]

In organizations such as Nissan's Smyrna, Georgia, plant, potential job applicants are drawn from a pool of individuals who have been trained at the state's expense and who seem best suited to working in high-performance teams. In other organizations, like Macy's/Bullocks, General Motors's Saturn division, and Gaines Pet Foods, team members select their teammates. This practice gives employees more control over decisions about who their co-workers will be and forges relationships more quickly than if new members were simply assigned to a team.[10]

### Training and Development

Like recruitment and selection, training is focused on ensuring that employees have the skills needed to assume greater responsibility in a high-performance work environment. For example, Schindler Elevator Corporation provides a sixty-hour prehire training that provides instruction and testing in such subjects as orientation/company history, safety, plant policies and procedures, just-in-time (JIT) techniques, and basic shop math. This prehire training is the foundation upon which the Schindler training program is built. Continuation training is provided in processes, team building, empowerment, and personal educational training needed for individual growth.

Similarly, team members at Saturn receive up to several hundred hours of training in their first few months. Typically, training focuses on technical, problem-solving, and interpersonal skills. Emphasis on teamwork, involvement, and continuous improvement requires that employees develop a broader understanding of work processes performed by others around them rather than rely on just know-

*Schindler-Elevator Corporation provides both prehire and continuation training for its employees.*

**Cross-training**
Training of employees in jobs in areas closely related to their own

ing their own jobs. To accomplish this, organizations increasingly use **cross-training,** that is, the training of employees in jobs in areas closely related to their own. Nurses in the perinatal unit of Cincinnati-based Tri-Health System implemented cross-training in order to facilitate teamwork and cooperation across units; even more, it helps nurses identify trouble spots that cut across several jobs and allows them to suggest areas for improvement.

Beyond individual training, Eastman Chemical has established a training certification process that helps to ensure that intact teams progress through a series of maturity phases. The teams certify their abilities to function effectively by demonstrating knowledge and skills in such areas as customer expectations, business conditions, and safety. Because these skills must be continually updated, Eastman Chemical requires that even certified teams periodically review their competencies.[11]

### Compensation

Another important piece of a high-performance work system is the compensation package. Because high-performance work systems ask many different things from employees, it is difficult to isolate one single approach to pay that works for everyone. As a consequence, many companies are experimenting with alternative compensation plans. In order to link pay and performance, high-performance work systems often include some type of employee incentives. For example, for Saturn employees an average of 10 percent of their pay is linked to goals for quality and training. Other organizational incentives such as gainsharing, profit sharing, and employee stock ownership plans focus employee efforts on outcomes that are beneficial to both themselves and the organization as a whole. The Scanlon Plan, the Rucker Plan, and Improshare, three systems discussed in Chapter 10, are used by companies such as TRW, Weyerhauser, and Xaloy to elicit employee suggestions and reward them for contributions to productivity.

High-performance work systems may also incorporate skill-based pay plans. By paying employees on the basis of the number of different job skills they have, organizations such as Shell Canada, Nortel Networks, and Honeywell hope to create both a broader skill base among employees and a more flexible pool of people to rotate among interrelated jobs. Both of these qualities are beneficial in a high-performance work environment and may justify the added expense in compensation. Honeywell has even experimented with what it calls "intracapital"—a pool of money employees can spend on capital improvements if the company meets profitability goals.[12]

Recall that in addition to linking pay and performance, high-performance work systems are also based on the principle of egalitarianism. To reinforce this principle in two of its plants utilizing high-performance work systems, Monsanto recently abandoned its hourly/management compensation plan and replaced it with an all-salaried workforce.[13] The open pay plan, where everyone knows what everyone else makes, is yet another feature of compensation systems used to create a more egalitarian environment that encourages employee involvement and commitment.

## Management Processes and Leadership

Leadership issues arise at several levels with high-performance work systems. At the executive level there needs to be clear support for a high-performance work environment, for the changes in culture that may accompany this environment, and for the modification of business processes necessary to support the change. These concerns will be addressed in more detail below in our discussion of implementation issues.

Organizations such as Doubletree Hotels, American Express, and Reebok International found that the success of any high-performance work system depends on first changing the roles of managers and team leaders. With fewer layers of management and a focus on team-based organization, the role of managers and supervisors is substantially different in an environment of high-performance work systems. Managers and supervisors are seen more as coaches, facilitators, and integrators of team efforts.[14] Rather than autocratically imposing their demands on employees and closely watching to make certain that the workers comply, managers in high-performance work systems share responsibility for decision making with employees. Typically, the term "manager" is replaced by the term "team leader." And in a growing number of cases, leadership is shared among team members. Kodak, for example, rotates team leaders at various stages in team development. Alternatively, different individuals can assume functional leadership roles when their particular expertise is needed most.

## Supportive Information Technologies

Communication and information technologies are yet one more piece that has to be added to the framework of high-performance work systems. Technologies of

various kinds create an infrastructure for communicating and sharing information vital to business performance. Federal Express, for example, is known for its use of information technology to route packages. Their tracking system helps employees monitor each package, communicate with customers, and identify and solve problems quickly. Sally Industries in Orlando, Florida, uses information technology to assign employees to various project teams. The company specializes in "animatronics," the combination of wires and latex that is used to make humanoid creatures such as are found in Disney's Hall of Presidents. Artisans employed by Sally Industries work on several project teams at once. A computerized system developed by the company helps budget and track the employee time spent on different projects.

But information technologies need not always be so high tech. The richest communication occurs face to face. The important point is that high-performance work systems cannot succeed without timely and accurate communications. (Recall the principle of shared information.) Typically the information needs to be about business plans and goals, unit and corporate operating results, incipient problems and opportunities, and competitor performance.[15]

# Fitting It All Together

Each of these practices highlights the individual pieces of a high-performance work system. And while we have emphasized throughout this text that certain HR practices are better than others, recall that in high-performance work systems the pieces are particularly valuable in terms of how they help the entire system function as a whole. Careful planning helps to make certain that the pieces fit together and are linked with the overall strategic goals of the organization. This philosophy is reflected in the mission statement of Saturn Motors, a model organization for HPWS. Saturn's mission is to "Market vehicles developed and manufactured in the United States that are world leaders . . . through the integration of people, technology, and business systems." Figure 17.4 summarizes the horizontal and vertical linkages needed to fit high-performance work systems together.

## Ensuring Horizontal Fit

**Horizontal fit**
Situation in which all the internal elements of the work system complement and reinforce one another

**Horizontal fit** occurs when all the internal elements of the work system complement and reinforce one another. For example, a first-rate selection system may be of no use if it is not working in conjunction with training and development activities. If a new compensation program elicits and reinforces behaviors that are directly opposed to the goals laid out in performance planning, the two components would be working at cross-purposes.

This is the true nature of systems. Changes in one component impact all the other components. Since the pieces are interdependent, it may be that a new compensation system may have no effect on performance if it is implemented on its own. Horizontal fit means testing to make certain that all of the HR practices, work designs, management processes, and technologies complement one another. The synergy achieved through overlapping work and human resources practices is at the heart of what makes a high-performance system effective.

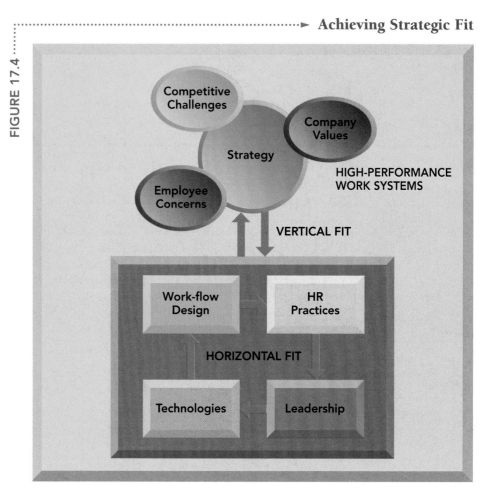

**Achieving Strategic Fit**

FIGURE 17.4

## Establishing Vertical Fit

**Vertical fit**
Situation in which the work system supports the organization's goals and strategies

To achieve **vertical fit**, high-performance work systems must support the organization's goals and strategies. This begins with an analysis and discussion of competitive challenges, organizational values, and the concerns of employees and results in a statement of the strategies being pursued by the organization.[16]

Xerox, for example, uses a planning process known as "Managing for Results," which begins with a statement of corporate values and priorities. These values and priorities are the foundation for establishing three-to-five-year goals for the organization. Each business unit establishes annual objectives based on these goals, and the process cascades down through every level of management. Ultimately, each employee within Xerox has a clear "line of sight" to the values and goals of the organization so she or he can see how individual effort makes a difference.[17]

Efforts such as this to achieve vertical fit help focus the design of high-performance work systems on strategic priorities. Objectives such as cost containment, quality enhancement, customer service, and speed to market directly impact what is expected of employees and the skills they need to be successful. Words such as "involvement," "flexibility," "efficiency," "problem solving," and "teamwork" are not just buzzwords. They are translated directly from the strategic requirements of today's organizations. High-performance work systems are designed to link employee initiatives to those strategies.

# Implementing the System

So far we have talked about the principles, practices, and goals of high-performance work systems. Unfortunately, these design issues compose probably less than half of the challenges that must be met in ensuring system success. Much of what looks good on paper gets messy during implementation. The American Society for Training and Development (ASTD) asked managers and consultants to identify the critical factors that can make or break a high-performance work system. The respondents identified the following as necessary actions for success (see Figure 17.5):

- Make a compelling case for change linked to the company's business strategy.
- Make certain that change is owned by senior and line managers.
- Allocate sufficient resources and support for the change effort.
- Ensure early and broad communication.
- Make certain teams are implemented in a systemic context.
- Establish methods for measuring the results of change.
- Make certain there is continuity of leadership and champions.[18]

Many of these recommendations are applicable to almost any change initiative, but they are especially important for broad-based change efforts that characterize high-performance work systems. Some of the most critical issues are discussed below.

## Building a Business Case for Change

In some organizations, the idea of high-performance work systems is something very new and radically different from the way things customarily work. Any one of the pieces of the system may represent an innovation in HRM: Teamwork, cross-training, skill-based pay, employee involvement, information technology, and the

**FIGURE 17.5** **Implementing High-Performance Work Systems**

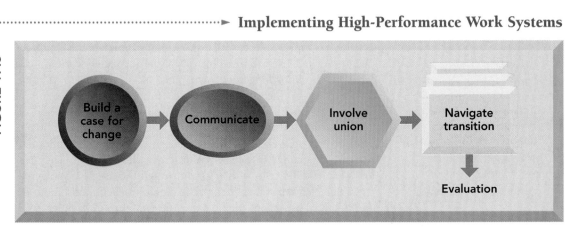

like may be relatively new ideas to some employees and managers. Their combined usage may be downright intimidating. Change can be threatening because it asks people to abandon the old ways of doing things and accept new approaches that, to them at least, are untested.

To get initial commitment to high-performance work systems, managers have to build a case that the changes are needed for the success of the organization. For example, executives at Harley-Davidson tried to institute employee involvement groups without first demonstrating their own personal commitment to the program. Not surprisingly, employees were apathetic and in some cases referred to the proposed changes as just "another fine program" put in place by the personnel department. Harley-Davidson executives learned the hard way that commitment from the top is essential in order to establish mutual trust between employees and managers. In a recent study on the implementation of high-performance work systems, it was found that a member of top management typically played the role of sponsor/champion, and spent a substantial portion of his or her time in that role communicating with employees about the reasons and approaches to change.[19]

One of the best ways to communicate the business needs is to show employees where the business is today—its current performance and capabilities. Then show them where the organization needs to be in the future. The gap between today and the future represents a starting point for discussion. When executives at TRW wanted to make a case for change to high-performance work systems, they used employee attitude surveys and data on turnover costs. The data provided enough ammunition to get conversation going about needed changes and sparked some suggestions about how they could be implemented.

Highlights in HRM 1 shows what happened when BMW bought British Land Rover and began making changes without first talking through the business concerns. Ironically, in this case, BMW unwittingly dismantled an effective high-performance work system.

## Establishing a Communications Plan

The ASTD council on high-performance work systems noted that providing an inadequate communication system is the most frequent mistake companies make during implementation. While we have emphasized the importance of executive commitment, top-down communication is not enough. Two-way communication can result not only in better decisions, it may help to diminish the fears and concerns of employees.

For example, Solectron Corporation, winner of the Baldrige National Quality Award, tried to implement high-performance work systems to capitalize on the knowledge and experience of its employees. A pilot program put in place by the company showed immediate gains in productivity of almost 20 percent after the switch to self-managed teams and team-based compensation. Although Solectron's rapid growth of over 50 percent per year made it unlikely that middle managers would be laid off, many of them resisted the change to a high-performance work system. They resented the loss of status and control that accompanied the use of empowered teams.[20]

If Solectron managers had participated in discussions about operational and financial aspects of the business, they might not have felt so threatened by the change. Open exchange and communication at an early stage pays off

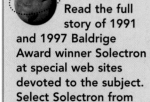

**USING THE INTERNET**

Read the full story of 1991 and 1997 Baldrige Award winner Solectron at special web sites devoted to the subject. Select Solectron from the winners list at:

www.quality.nist.gov/winners/winlist.htm

**HRM 1**

**HIGHLIGHTS IN HRM**

# British Land Rover and BMW Crash Head-on

Some years ago, the British Land Rover Company, a leading manufacturer of four-wheel-drive vehicles, found itself saddled with a notorious reputation for poor quality and productivity. Then it underwent a fundamental transformation. The company instituted extensive training (including giving every employee a personal training fund to be used on any subject), implemented more team-based production methods, reduced the number of separate job classifications, developed more cooperative relations with organized labor, and began a total quality program.

As a result of these changes, productivity soared by 25 percent, quality action teams netted savings worth millions of dollars, and the quality of products climbed. Operating in a very competitive environment, Land Rover produced and sold one-third more vehicles. On the basis of these changes, the company was certified as an "Investors in People—U.K." designee. This national standard recognizes organizations that place the involvement and development of people at the heart of their business strategy.

So far, so good. Then BMW bought the company. In spite of massive evidence documenting the effectiveness of the new management methods and changed culture, BMW began to dictate changes within a manner of months. The changes both undid the cultural transformation and, more to the point, reversed the improvements in quality and efficiency.

later as the system unfolds. Ongoing dialogue at all levels helps to reaffirm commitment, answer questions that come up, and identify areas for improvement throughout implementation. Recall that one of the principles of high-performance work systems is sharing information. This principle is instrumental to success both during implementation and once the system is in place.

## Involving the Union

We mentioned in Chapters 14 and 15 that autocratic styles of management and confrontational approaches to labor negotiations are being challenged by more-enlightened approaches that promote cooperation and collaboration. Given the sometimes radical changes involved in implementing high-performance work systems, it makes good sense to involve union members early and to keep them as close partners in the design and implementation process. Figure 17.6 shows how to "build a bridge" toward a cooperative relationship with unions in implementing high-performance work systems.[21]

FIGURE 17.6

▶ **Builing Cooperation with Unions**

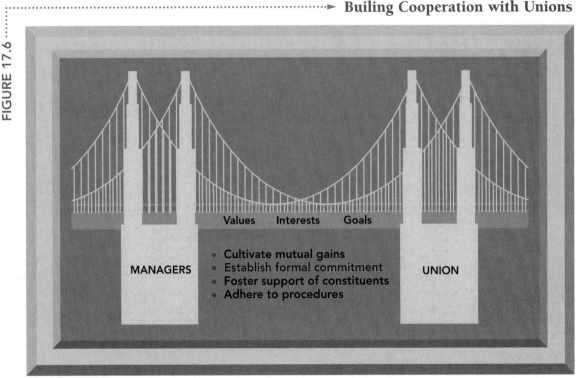

Values    Interests    Goals

MANAGERS

- Cultivate mutual gains
- Establish formal commitment
- Foster support of constituents
- Adhere to procedures

UNION

Source: The Conference Board of Canada.

## Cultivate Mutual Gains

In order to establish an alliance, managers and labor representatives should try to create "win-win" situations, where all parties gain from the implementation of high-performance work systems. In such cases, organizations such as Shell and Weyerhauser have found that "interest-based" (integrative) negotiation rather than positional bargaining leads to better relationships and outcomes with union representatives. Trust is a fragile component of an alliance and is reflected in the degree to which parties are comfortable sharing information and decision making. For some time now, Manitoba Telephone System has involved union members in decisions about work practices, and because of this, company managers have been able to build mutual trust and respect with the union. This relationship has matured to a point where union and company managers now design, select, and implement new technologies together. By working hard to develop trust up front, in either a union or a nonunion setting, it is more likely that each party will understand how high-performance work systems will benefit everyone; the organization will be more competitive, employees will have a higher quality of work life, and unions will have a stronger role in representing employees.[22]

## Establish Formal Commitment

Most labor-management alliances are made legitimate through some tangible symbol of commitment. This might include a policy document that spells out union involvement, letters of understanding, clauses in a collective bargain-

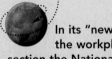

ing agreement, or the establishment of joint forums with explicit mandates. MacMillan Bledel, a wood products company, formed a joint operations committee of senior management and labor representatives to routinely discuss a wide range of operational issues related to high-performance work systems. These types of formal commitments, with investments of tangible resources, serve two purposes: (1) they are an outward sign of management commitment, and (2) they institutionalize the relationship so that it keeps going even if key project champions leave.[23]

### Foster Support of Other Key Constituents

In addition to union leadership, it is critical to have the support of other key constituents. Leaders must ensure that understanding and support are solid at all levels, not just among those in the executive suite. To achieve this commitment, some organizations have decentralized the labor relations function, giving responsibility to local line managers and human resources generalists, to make certain that they are accountable and are committed to nurturing a high-performance work environment. Nortel Networks, for example, formally transferred accountability for labor relations to its plant managers through its collective bargaining agreement with the union. Line managers are now members of the Employee Relations Council, which is responsible for local bargaining as well as for grievance hearings that would formerly have been mediated by HR. Apart from the commitment that these changes create, perhaps the most important reason for giving line managers responsibility for employee relations is that it helps them establish a direct working relationship with the union.

### Adhere to Procedures

Once processes, agreements, and ground rules are established, they are vital to the integrity of the relationship. As Ruth Wright, coordinator of the Council of Industrial Relations Executives, put it, "Procedure is the 'rug' on which alliances stand. Pull it out by making a unilateral management determination or otherwise changing the rules of the game, and the initiative will falter. Procedure keeps the parties focused, and it is an effective means of ensuring that democracy and fairness prevail."[24]

In most cases, a "home-grown" process works better than one that is adopted from elsewhere. Each organization has unique circumstances, and parties are more likely to commit to procedures they create and own.

## Navigating the Transition to High-Performance Work Systems

Building commitment to high-performance work systems is an ongoing activity. Perhaps, in fact, it is never fully completed. And like any change activity, performance frequently falters as implementation gets underway. One of the reasons for this is that pieces of the system are changed incrementally rather than as a total program. Xerox Corporation found that when they implemented teams without also changing the compensation system to support teamwork, they got caught in a bad transition. The teams actually showed poorer performance than did employees working in settings that supported individual contributions. Company executives concluded that they needed to change the entire system at once since piecemeal changes were actually detrimental.[25]

*The transition to high-performance work systems requires a timetable and process for mapping key business processes, redesigning work, and training employees.*

### Build a Transition Structure

Implementation of high-performance work systems proceeds in different ways for different organizations. In organizational start-ups, managers have the advantage of being able to put everything in place at once. However, when organizations have to be retrofitted, the process may occur a bit more clumsily. When Honeywell switched to high-performance work systems in its plant in Chandler, Arizona, employees attended training programs and participated in the redesign of their jobs while the plant was shut down to be reequipped with new technology. When the new plant was reopened, self-managing teams were put in place and a new pay system was implemented for the high-performance workforce.[26]

Not every organization has the luxury of suspending operations while changes are put in place. Nevertheless, establishing an implementation structure keeps everyone on track and prevents the system from bogging down. The structure provides a timetable and process for mapping key business processes, redesigning work, and training employees.

### Incorporate the HR Function as a Valuable Partner

One of the mistakes that organizations can make in implementing high-performance work systems is allocating too few resources to the effort. This means money, of course, but it also means time and expertise. Although line managers typically own the responsibility for implementation, HR managers can be invaluable partners in managing change. For example, Texas Instruments created its High Performance Organization Development unit to facilitate the transition to a high-performance work system. Other organizations such as Merck and Ford Motors have also developed special HR units to manage organizational change. Lever Brothers created a transition team of senior line and HR managers to oversee the implementation of high-performance teams and develop an implementation road map.[27]

## Evaluating the Success of the System

**Process audit**
Determining whether the high-performance work system has been implemented as designed

Once high-performance work systems are in place, they need to be monitored and evaluated over time. There are several aspects of the review process that should be addressed. First, there should be a **process audit** to determine whether the system has been implemented as it was designed and whether the principles of high-performance work systems are being reinforced. Questions such as the following might be included in the audit:

- Are employees actually working together, or is the term "team" just a label?
- Are employees getting the information they need to make empowered decisions?
- Are training programs developing the knowledge and skills employees need?
- Are employees being rewarded for good performance and useful suggestions?
- Are employees treated fairly so that power differences are minimal?

Second, the evaluation process should focus on the goals of high-performance work systems. To determine if the program is succeeding, managers should look at such issues as

- Are desired behaviors being exhibited on the job?
- Are quality, productivity, flexibility, and customer service objectives being met?
- Are quality-of-life goals being achieved for employees?
- Is the organization more competitive than in the past?

Finally, high-performance work systems should be periodically evaluated in terms of new organizational priorities and initiatives. Since high-performance work systems are built on key business processes that deliver value to customers, as these processes and customer relationships change so too should the work system. The advantage of high-performance work systems is that they are flexible and, therefore, more easily adapted. When change occurs, it should be guided by a clear understanding of the business needs and exhibit a close vertical fit to strategy.

# Outcomes of High-Performance Work Systems

There are a wide variety of outcomes that organizations achieve from high-performance work systems and effective human resources management. Recall from Chapter 1 that we have categorized these outcomes in terms of either *employee concerns* such as quality-of-work-life issues and job security or *competitive challenges* such as performance, productivity, and profitability. Throughout the text we have emphasized that the best organizations find ways to achieve a balance between these two sets of outcomes and pursue activities that improve both.

## Employee Outcomes and Quality of Work Life

There are a myriad of potential benefits to employees from high-performance work systems. Because employees are more involved in their work, they are likely to be more satisfied and find that their needs for growth are more fully met. Because they are more informed and empowered, they are likely to feel that they have a fuller role to play in the organization and that their opinions and expertise are valued more. This of course underlies greater commitment. With higher skills and greater potential for contribution, they are likely to have more job security as well as be more marketable to other organizations.

Additionally, as we discussed in Chapter 1, individuals with two- and four-year college degrees are a growing segment of the workforce. If employees with advanced education are to achieve their potential, they must be allowed to utilize their skills and abilities in ways that contribute to organizational success while fulfilling personal job growth and work satisfaction needs. High-performance work systems serve to mesh organizational objectives with employee contributions. Conversely, when employees are underutilized, organizations operate at less than full performance, while employees develop poor work attitudes and habits.[28]

## Organizational Outcomes and Competitive Advantage

There are also several organizational outcomes that result from using high-performance work systems. These include higher productivity, lower costs, better responsiveness to customers, greater flexibility, and higher profitability. Highlights in HRM 2 provides a sample of the success stories that companies have shared about their use of high-performance work systems. [29]

Recall that in Chapter 1 we said that organizations can create a sustainable competitive advantage through people if they focus on four criteria. They must develop competencies in their employees that are

- *Valuable*: High-performance work systems increase value by establishing ways to increase efficiency, decrease costs, improve processes, and provide something unique to customers.

- *Rare:* High-performance work systems help organizations develop and harness skills, knowledge, and abilities that are not equally available to all organizations.

- *Difficult to imitate:* High-performance work systems are designed around team processes and capabilities that cannot be transported, duplicated, or copied by rival firms.

- *Organized:* High-performance work systems combine the talents of employees and rapidly deploy them in new assignments with maximum flexibility.[30]

These criteria clearly show how high-performance work systems in particular, and human resources management in general, are instrumental in achieving competitive advantage through people.

However, for all their potential, implementing high-performance work systems is not an easy task. The systems are complex, and they require a good deal of close partnering among executives, line managers, HR professionals, union representatives, and employees. Ironically, it is this very complexity that leads to competitive advantage. Because high-performance work systems are difficult to implement, organizations that are successful are difficult to copy. The ability to integrate business and employee concerns is indeed rare, and doing it in a way that adds value to customers is especially noteworthy. Organizations such as Wal-Mart, Microsoft, and Southwest Airlines have been able to do it, and as a result they enjoy a competitive advantage.

**HRM 2**

HIGHLIGHTS IN HRM

## The Impact of High-Performance Work Systems

- Ames Rubber Corporation, a New Jersey–based manufacturer of rubber products and office machine components, experienced a 48 percent increase in productivity and five straight years of revenue growth.
- Ashton Photo, a photo-finishing company in Oregon, achieved average productivity increases of 7.5 to 8 percent each year and a 22 percent growth in customers.
- Sales at Connor Formed Metal Products, a San Francisco firm, grew by 21 percent, while new orders rose 34 percent and the company's profit on operations increased 21 percent to a record level.
- Over a seven-year period, Granite Rock, a construction material and mining company in Watsonville, California, experienced an 88 percent increase in market share, its standard for on-time delivery grew from 68 to 95 percent, and revenue per employee was 30 percent above the national average.
- At One Valley Bank of Clarksburg, West Virginia, employee turnover dropped by 48 percent, productivity increased by 24 percent, return on equity grew 72 percent, and profits jumped by 109 percent in three years.
- The Tennessee Eastman Division of the Eastman Chemical Company experienced an increase in productivity of nearly 70 percent, and 75 percent of its customers ranked it as the top chemical company in customer satisfaction.
- A study by John Paul MacDuffie of sixty-two automobile plants showed that those implementing high-performance work systems had 47 percent better quality and 43 percent better productivity.
- A study by Jeff Arthur of thirty steel minimills showed a 34 percent increase in productivity, 63 percent less scrap, and 57 percent less turnover.
- A study by Mark Huselid of 962 firms in multiple industries showed that high-performance work systems resulted in an annual increase in profits of over $3,800 per employee.

Source: Martha A. Gephart and Mark E. Van Buren, "The Power of High Performance Work Systems," *Training and Development* 50, no. 10 (October 1996): 21–36.

## High-Performance Work Systems and the Small and Medium-Sized Employer

We conclude our discussion of high-performance work systems by noting their applicability to small and medium-sized organizations. While many of the examples used to illustrate the popularity of HPWS come from large, well-known companies, the philosophies, principles, and techniques that underlie HPWS are equally appropriate to the management of enterprises of all sizes. It would be wrong to think that the four principles of HPWS identified by Lawler (sharing information with employees, linking pay to performance, training and developing employees, and fostering an egalitarian work culture) are somehow unique to *Fortune* 1000 organizations. Nor would it be correct to surmise that the anatomy of HPWS is applicable only to large corporations. Progressive organizations of all sizes have successfully implemented team-based work systems, implemented staffing practices that select high-quality employees, developed training programs that continually update employee skills, and utilized compensation practices that support specific organizational goals. The key is that they have done these things in a coordinated, integrative manner. These smaller organizations have simply achieved a system approach to organizational design that combines HR practices, work structures, and processes that effectively utilize employee competencies.

Readers of this text will find the principles of HPWS of great assistance as they manage human resources, regardless of organizational size.

# SUMMARY

**OBJECTIVE 1** High-performance work systems are specific combinations of HR practices, work structures, and processes that maximize employee knowledge, skill, commitment, and flexibility. They are based on contemporary principles of high-involvement organizations. These principles include shared information, knowledge development, performance-reward linkages, and egalitarianism.

**OBJECTIVE 2** High-performance work systems are composed of several interrelated components. Typically, the system begins with designing empowered work teams to carry out key business processes. Team members are selected and trained in technical, problem-solving, and interpersonal skills. Reward systems often have group and organizational incentives, though skill-based pay is regularly used to increase flexibility and salaried pay plans are used to enhance an egalitarian environment. Leadership tends to be shared among team members, and information technology is used to make sure that employees have the information they need to make timely and productive decisions.

**OBJECTIVE 3** The pieces of the system are only important in terms of how they help the entire system function. When all the pieces support and complement one another, high-performance work systems achieve internal fit. When the system is aligned with the competitive priorities of the organization as a whole, it achieves vertical fit as well.

**OBJECTIVE 4** Implementing high-performance work systems represents a multidimensional change initiative. High-performance work systems are much more likely to go smoothly if a business case is first made. Top-management support is critical, and so too is the support of union representatives and other important constituents. HR representatives are often helpful in establishing a transition structure to help the implementation progress through its various stages. Once the system is in place, it should be evaluated in terms of its processes, outcomes, and ongoing fit with strategic objectives of the organization.

**OBJECTIVE 5** When implemented effectively, high-performance work systems benefit both the employees and the organization. Employees have more involvement in the organization, experience growth and satisfaction, and become more valuable as contributors. The organization also benefits from high productivity, quality, flexibility, and customer satisfaction. These features together can provide an organization with a sustainable competitive advantage.

**OBJECTIVE 6** The principles of HPWS apply in small and medium-sized organizational work settings as well as in large organizations. Progressive organizations of all sizes have successfully implemented high-performance work systems.

# KEY TERMS

cross-training
high-performance work system
  (HPWS)

horizontal fit
process audit
vertical fit

# DISCUSSION QUESTIONS

 1. Do you think the four principles of high involvement provide an adequate context for designing high-performance work systems? What other concerns or guidelines for developing high-performance work systems would you suggest?

 2. In many cases, organizations use teams as a part of their high-performance work systems. Could such systems be useful in organizations that do not use teams? What special concerns might you have to address?

 3. Although both vertical and horizontal fit are important concerns with high-performance work systems, which do you consider more critical and why?

 4. This chapter places considerable emphasis on the processes involved in implementing high-performance work systems. What are the most critical steps to successful implementation?

 5. How do you think employee-related outcomes and organizational outcomes are related to one another? Is it possible to achieve one set of outcomes without the other? Why or why not?

 6. What concerns must a smaller employer address in trying to implement high-performance work systems? What advantages would a smaller organization have in using such systems?

## HPWS at Tomex Incorporated

Tomex Incorporated, a medium-sized manufacturer of electronic security and surveillance systems, uses high-performance work systems throughout the organization. Because of cutbacks in the defense industry, Tomex has had to focus on private-sector applications for its products. To improve quality, reduce costs, and respond quickly to customer needs, Tomex executives realized that new processes and technologies had to be supported by a much more flexible and empowered workforce. As managers designed a new plant in Buffetton, Pennsylvania, they structured the flow so employees could work more autonomously and with less supervision. Because the production process had 47 percent fewer setups than other plants, Tomex managers reduced the number of job classifications to two so that production workers could rotate jobs as they learned new skills. Jobs were defined broadly and employees were reorganized into self-managed teams empowered to make decisions typically made by managers and supervisors.

The 200 workers in the Buffetton plant are divided into twelve-member teams that schedule their own work, perform statistical analyses, and manage quality. Team members, called "production associates," hold ten-minute meetings at the beginning and end of each shift to discuss problems, focus on goals, and check performance.

The selection process for employees involves several interviews, assessments, and classroom projects to test each applicant's creativity, initiative, problem-solving skills, and interpersonal abilities. Tomex also tries to find people who have a willingness to work in a team-based environment. In fact, in some cases, the company will decline to hire an otherwise promising candidate who expresses no interest in working on teams.

To ensure that employees are highly skilled, Tomex managers make certain that new hires spend more than 30 percent of their time in on-the-job training. In subsequent years, forty hours of mandatory training are required—both on and off the job. Production associates receive training in three principal areas: technical, interpersonal, and group processes.

The company experimented with skill-based pay, but the system was difficult to administer and, according to representatives in the HR department, did not seem to increase flexibility as much as they had hoped. The company currently credits much of its performance improvements to the gainsharing program instituted two years ago. The system, which engages employees in problem-solving activities, has resulted in a greater number of suggestions for performance improvements. In addition to the cost savings, the gainsharing plan has also resulted in employee identification of better ways to work in teams and to share information with one another.

Tomex executives acknowledge that they have always had talented employees but claim that the new work systems allow those employees to exercise more initiative and make greater contributions to the company's performance than ever before. As one executive put it, "Today, the best thing we can do for these folks is give them the support they need and get out of their way. When we do, there's no telling what they're capable of!"

### QUESTIONS

1. What are the key aspects of Tomex's high-performance work system?
2. Does the system achieve both horizontal and vertical fit?
3. What other HR practices might the company consider implementing?

## HPWS at Xerox Corporation

One of the largest companies in the United States to implement high-performance work systems is the Xerox Corporation. The company employs 85,900 people worldwide. Its revenues in 1995 were $16.6 billion. As a result of a total quality management mandate that "improving quality is every employee's job," Xerox introduced their version of empowered teams, what they called "family groups." These family groups are the cornerstone for high-performance work systems throughout the company's service organization around the globe. Xerox's service organizations employ more than 25,000 people, making service the second-largest sector of the company; only manufacturing is larger.

Xerox service managers realized that they could improve productivity if responsibility for decision making moved closer to the point of customer contact. As empowered work groups evolved, the company began to realize that the groups could not function effectively unless other aspects of the company changed as well. Employees complained that they were evaluated and rewarded as individuals despite being organized as teams. Team members were not receiving the kind of information they needed to make decisions. This led Xerox to consider the entire system in which teams operated. And thus high-performance systems were born.

Tom Ruddy, research manager for Xerox's Worldwide Customer Services in Rochester, New York, defines high-performance work systems as "a systems approach to organizational design that optimizes the fit between people, work, information, and technology resulting in maximum organizational performance as measured by customer satisfaction, employee satisfaction, and productivity."

Xerox has a well-defined approach to implementing high-performance work systems throughout the organization. The company recognizes the importance of communication, training, support, and assessment. Perhaps the best example of a transition to HPWS is the Ohio Customer Business Unit (CBU), based in Columbus, one of thirty-seven regional units worldwide.

High-performance work systems were not introduced overnight, but through an incremental process that has taken nearly ten years. The first few steps were timid ones, consisting primarily of training in team dynamics and facilitation skills. Next, Xerox realized the importance of analyzing and reengineering work processes. All of the primary processes such as reliability, parts planning, and team facilitation were analyzed and documented. In each work group, process owners were identified and each team member took on a different role.

As process owners, team members had decision-making responsibility and accountability for such day-to-day decisions as work scheduling and for larger decisions such as hiring and performance reviews. The new responsibilities created some problems. Work-group members were expected to make decisions, but they often lacked relevant information.

In response, Xerox created a management information system to track and summarize key business indicators. Most of the business information is updated monthly. Some information, such as expense reports, is updated weekly. The system also provides teams with indicators of customer satisfaction levels several times a month. At each team meeting, members share information about the company's business plan and its financial performance.

The communication system wasn't the only thing that had to be modified to support high-performance work systems. Teams had to be tied together by common objectives and incentives. They had to be compensated in a way that fostered collaboration between team members and motivated them to work toward team goals. As a result, Xerox moved to a pay-for-performance compensation system called "Workgroup Excellence," which rewards the performance of a team as a whole. Then, within each team, rewards are distributed on the basis of such factors as experience.

Some managers struggled with the new work systems. To increase their understanding, some were sent to Xerox's service operation in Phoenix, Arizona, which had also been experimenting with empowered teams. There they learned that the key to managerial support for work groups was to have managers structured into the work groups themselves. Only after experiencing team dynamics and acquiring the skills to work in teams were the managers able to address the needs of the teams they oversaw.

The Ohio CBU is now the top service organization within Xerox. It maintains customer satisfaction levels around 94 percent on service calls. It also has the lowest maintenance expenses per vehicle of any service unit within Xerox. Evidence of success for other high-performance work systems at Xerox is easy to find. Service organizations report increases in all their target areas. Customer satisfaction has increased by as much as ten points, with each point representing millions of dollars of business. Employee satisfaction has improved 15 percent. Increases of 10 to 15 percent in response time and reliability have occurred as well.

**Source:** Martha A. Gephart and Mark E. Van Buren, "The Power of High Performance Work Systems," *Training and Development* 50, no. 10 (October 1996): 21–36.

### QUESTIONS

1. If you were a manager at Xerox, what concerns would you have with the way the company initially implemented high-performance work systems?
2. What role did information technology play in supporting high-performance work systems?
3. Why do you suppose some Xerox managers resisted the new systems?

## NOTES AND REFERENCES

1. D. A. Nadler and M. S. Gerstein, "Designing High-Performance Work Systems: Organizing People, Work, Technology, and Information," *Organizational Architecture* (San Francisco: Jossey-Bass, 1992): 195–208; E. Lawler III, Susan Albers Mohrman, and Gerald E. Ledford, *Creating High Performance Organizations: Practices and Results of Employee Involvement and Total Quality Management in Fortune 1000 Companies* (San Francisco: Jossey-Bass, 1995).
2. Carlton P. McNamara, "Making Human Capital Productive," *Business and Economic Review* 46, no. 1 (October–December 1999): 10–13; Gerard F. Farias and Arup Varma, "Research Update: High Performance Work Systems: What We Know and What We Need to Know," *Human Resource Planning* 21, 2 (1998): 50–54; Paul E. Tesluk, Robert J. Vance, and John E. Mathieu, "Examining Employee Involvement in the Context of Participative Work Environments," *Group & Organization Management* 24, no. 3 (September 1999): 271–99.
3. Adam Ritt, "Nucor's Investment in Loyalty," *Iron Age New Steel* 14, no. 8 (August 1998): 2.
4. This section is based on several studies related to best practices in human resources management and the development of high-performance work systems. See Arup Varma, Richard W. Beatty, Craig Eric Schneier,

and David O. Ulrich, "High Performance Work Systems: Exciting Discovery or Passing Fad?" *Human Resource Planning* 22, no. 1 (1999): 26–37; Farias and Varma, "Research Update"; J. B. Arthur, "Effects of Human Resource Systems on Manufacturing Performance and Turnover," *Academy of Management Journal* 37 (1994): 670–87; J. B. Arthur, "The Link between Business Strategy and Industrial Relations Systems in American Steel Minimills," *Industrial and Labor Relations Review* 45, no. 3 (1992): 488–506; J. P. MacDuffie, "Human Resource Bundles and Manufacturing Performance: Organizational Logic and Flexible Production Systems in the World Auto Industry," *Industrial and Labor Relations Review* 48, no. 2 (1995): 197–221; M. Huselid, "The Impact of Human Resource Management Practices on Turnover, Productivity, and Corporate Financial Performance," *Academy of Management Journal* 38 (1995): 635–72; P. Osterman, "How Common Is Workplace Transformation and Who Adopts It?" *Industrial and Labor Relations Review* 47, no. 2 (1994): 173–88; Craig Olson and Casey Ichniowski, "What Works at Work: Overview and Assessment," *Industrial Relations* 35, no. 3 (1996): 299–333; Mark A. Youndt, Scott A. Snell, James W. Dean, Jr., and David P. Lepak, "Human Resource Management, Manufacturing Strategy, and Firm Performance," *Academy of Management Journal* 39, no. 4 (August 1996): 836–66.

5.  Jeffrey Kling, "High Performance Work Systems and Firm Performance," *Monthly Labor Review,* May 1995, 29–36. See also Chad Kaydo, "Top of the Charts: FedEx," *Sales and Marketing Management* 150, no. 7 (July 1998): 46, 48; Justin Martin, "So, You Want to Work for the Best . . .," *Fortune,* January 12, 1998, 77–78.

6.  For more information about designing teams around critical work processes, see the following: Ray Dyck and Norman Halpern, "Team-Based Organizations Redesign at Celestica," *Journal for Quality and Participation* 22, no. 5 (September/October 1999): 36–40; Jon-Arild Johannessen, Bjorn Olsen, and Johan Olaisen, "Organizing for Innovation," *Long Range Planning* 30, no. 1 (February 1997): 96–109; Richard Blackburn and Benson Rosen, "Total Quality and Human Resource Management: Lessons Learned from Baldrige Award–Winning Companies," *Academy of Management Executive* 7, no. 3 (1993): 49–66.

7.  Martha A. Gephart and Mark E. Van Buren, "The Power of High Performance Work Systems," *Training and Development* 50, no. 10 (October 1996): 21–36. See also Mark E. Van Buren, "High Performance Work Systems," *Business and Economic Review* 43, no. 1 (October–December 1996): 15–23.

8.  See Varma, Beatty, Schneier, and Ulrich, "High Performance Work Systems"; Peter Berg, "The Effects of High Performance Work Practices on Job Satisfaction in the United States Steel Industry," *Relations Industrielles* 54, no. 1 (Winter 1999): 111–134; Lawler et al., *Creating High Performance Organizations.*

9.  Laurie J. Bassi and Mark E. Van Buren, "Sustaining High Performance in Bad Times," *Training and Development* 51, no. 6 (June 1997): 32–42; Katie Thomas, "Short-Term Downsizing, Long-Term Performance," *Incentive* 171, no. 4 (April 1997): 14.

10.  Michael J. Stevens and Michael A. Campion, "Staffing Work Teams: Development and Validation of a Selection Test for Teamwork Settings," *Journal of Management* 25, no. 2 (1999): 207–28; Eric H. Kessler, and Alok K. Chakrabarti, "Speeding Up the Pace of New Product Development," *Journal of Product Innovation Management* 16, no. 3 (May 1999): 231–47; Judith A. Neal and Cheryl L. Tromley, "From Incremental Change to Retrofit: Creating High-Performance Work Systems," *Academy of Management Executive* 9, no. 1 (1995): 42–54. See also James McCalman, "High Performance Work Systems: The Need for Transition Management," *International Journal of Operations and Production Management* 10, no. 2 (1990): 10–25.

11.  Wayne E. Heaton, "The Secret Strategy," *Production and Inventory Management Journal* 39, no. 1 (1998): 78–81; Leslie Brinley Altimier and John Michael Sanders, "Cross-Training in 3-D," *Nursing Management* 30, no. 11 (November 1999): 59–62; Irving H. Buchen, "Guiding Self-Directed Teams to Realize Their Potential," *National Productivity Review* 17, no. 1 (Winter 1997): 83–90; Mark E. Van Buren and Jon M. Werner, "High Performance Work Systems," *B&E Review,* October–December 1996, 15–23.

12.  Kenneth Mericle and Dong-One Kim, "From Job-Based Pay to Skill-Based Pay in Unionized Establishments: A Three-Plant Comparative Analysis," *Relations Industrielles* 54, no. 3 (Summer 1999): 549–578; Neal and Tromley, "From Incremental Change to Retrofit."

13.  Donald A. Zrebiec and Robert F. Pearse, "Reengineering Managerial and Professional Compensation Systems," *Compensation and Benefits Management,* Summer 1995, 10–19; Steven Rayner, *Recreating the Workplace: The Pathway to High Performance Work Systems* (Essex Junction, Vt.: Oliver Wright, 1993).

14.  Harvey Kolodny, "Building a Foundation for High Performance," *International Journal of Technology Management* 16 (1998): 1–3; Van Buren and Werner, "High Performance Work Systems."

15.  Keith Newton, "The High Performance Workplace: HR-Based Management Innovations in Canada," *International Journal of Technology Management* 16, no. 1–3 (1998): 177–92; Lawler et al., *Creating High Performance Organizations.*

16.  Patrick M. Wright and Scott A. Snell, "Toward a unifying framework for exploring fit and flexibility in strategic human resource management," *Academy of Management Review* 23, no. 4 (October 1998): 756–772; Clair Brown and Michael Reich, "Micro-Macro Linkages in High-Performance Employment Systems," *Organization Studies* 18, no. 5 (1997): 765–81.

17.  Van Buren and Werner, "High Performance Work Systems."

18.  Varma, Beatty, Schneier, and Ulrich, "High Performance Work Systems"; Gephart and Van Buren, "Power of High Performance Work Systems."

19.  Varma, Beatty, Schneier, and Ulrich, "High performance Work Systems"; Gephart and Van Buren, "Power of High Performance Work Systems."

20.  Jeffrey Pfeffer, "When It Comes to 'Best Practices'—Why Do Smart Organizations Occasionally Do Dumb Things?" *Organizational Dynamics,* Summer 1996, 33–44.

21.  Louise Clarke and Larry Haiven, "Workplace Change and Continuous Bargaining," *Relations Industrielles* 54, no. 1 (Winter 1999): 168–91; Ruth Wright,

"Forging Sustainable Alliances in a New Economy," *Canadian Business Review,* Summer 1995, 20–24.

22. Clarke and Haiven, "Workplace Change"; Wright, "Forging Sustainable Alliances."

23. Wright, "Forging Sustainable Alliances."

24. Wright, "Forging Sustainable Alliances."

25. Gephart and Van Buren, "Power of High Performance Work Systems."

26. Neal and Tromley, "From Incremental Change to Retrofit."

27. Nicolay A. M. Worren, Keith Ruddle, and Karl Moore, "From Organizational Development to Change Management: The Emergence of a New Profession," *Journal of Applied Behavioral Science* 35, no. 3 (September 1999): 273–86; Randa A. Wilbur, "Making Changes the Right Way," *Workforce,* Supplement (March 1999): 12–13; Gephart and Van Buren, "Power of High Performance Work Systems."

28. Berg, "The Effects of High Performance Work Practices"; Peter Cappelli and Nikolai Rogovsky, "Employee Involvement and Organizational Citizenship: Implications for Labor Law Reform and Lean Production," *Industrial & Labor Relations Review* 51, no. 4 (July 1998): 633–53.

29. Robert J. Vandenberg, Hettie A. Richardson, and Lorrina J. Eastman, "The Impact of High Involvement Work Processes on Organizational Effectiveness: A Second-Order Latent Variable Approach," *Group & Organization Management* 24, no. 3 (September 1999): 300–39; Jeffrey Pfeffer and John F. Veiga, "Putting People First for Organizational Success," *Academy of Management Executive* 13, no. 2 (May 1999): 37–48; Laurie J. Bassi and Mark E. Van Buren, "The 1999 ASTD State of the Industry Report," *Training and Development,* Supplement (1999): 1–26.

30. John Purcell, "Best Practice and Best Fit: Chimera or Cul-de-Sac?" *Human Resource Management Journal* 9, no. 3 (1999): 26–41; Scott A. Snell, Mark A. Youndt, and Patrick M. Wright, "Establishing a Framework for Strategic Human Resource Management: Merging Resource Theory and Organizational Learning," *Research in Personnel and Human Resource Management* 14 (1996): 61–90.

# Cases

## Case 1

## ConnectPlus: Aligning HRM with Strategic Objectives

Jim Heinrich founded ConnectPlus and has managed the company's operations from its inception. ConnectPlus designs and produces communications software that is sold to customers ranging from the computer industry to independent businesses. Though ConnectPlus has been profitable over the decade of its existence, productivity at the company has recently decreased. Specifically, in the past several years the workers have displayed diminished innovation, higher turnover and absenteeism, and overall sluggish performance.

Because of these trends, Heinrich called a meeting of all the managers to discuss potential courses of action to correct the problems. After a series of discussions, Heinrich and the other managers agreed that they needed to hire a full-time manager to assume sole responsibility for human resources management. In the past, the department managers had assumed basic responsibilities for managing their employees. However, the growth of the company—there are now over 100 employees—coupled with recent increases in absenteeism and turnover, suggested that the human resources responsibilities were large enough to warrant hiring a full-time manager.

After careful consideration, Heinrich decided to hire Judith Thompson to assume the primary responsibilities of developing a systematic HRM function for ConnectPlus. Once Thompson arrived at ConnectPlus, she and Heinrich met to discuss the strategic objectives and long-term goals of the company. Heinrich stated that ConnectPlus must achieve two primary objectives to be successful in the future. First, the company must continue its growth strategy to respond to the expanding demands for its services. Second, it must enhance the innovative nature of its workforce to ensure that it remains up-to-date with competitors and market changes. At the end of their meeting, Heinrich gave Thompson the task of developing an HRM function that could address the absenteeism and turnover problems while helping ConnectPlus attain the two goals he had outlined.

As a first step to achieve this, Thompson began to review the human resources practices used at ConnectPlus. It became clear that the company has relied primarily upon two practices to meet employment needs. First, ConnectPlus recruits at the state university located just ten miles away. If graduating students are not interested or are not appropriate candidates for a certain job, ConnectPlus places advertisements in regional newspapers to seek job candidates with the relevant skills who are willing to relocate. Though this hiring process is not comprehensive, ConnectPlus, because of its potential growth opportunities, has not typically experienced much difficulty in recruiting employees.

Second, ConnectPlus has relied upon an established compensation system that applies to all employees throughout the company. Workers are paid on a salaried basis, with their compensation levels based on the going rate in the market for similar positions. By tying employee compensation to the market average, ConnectPlus has been able to ensure that there is a reasonably high degree of equity between the company's pay levels and the pay levels at other firms. Yearly raises are calculated by considering cost-of-living adjustments and each employee's yearly performance level. The average increases for employee salary levels are between 3 and 7 percent of their base salary.

Thompson now realizes that besides these recruitment and compensation practices, there is really no consistent use of other human resources practices at ConnectPlus. Rather, managers utilize different methods of managing the workers in their respective units. For example, there are no consistent performance appraisal standards used throughout the organization. The criteria used to evaluate employees range from counting days absent to measuring innovation and creativity. Similarly, each manager uses somewhat different tactics in training employees. Some units assign new hires to shadow more experienced employees, who serve as the new hires' mentors. Other managers do not offer any training and assume that the employees come to the job with all the knowledge they need to succeed.

In light of the organization's goals of growth and innovation, Thompson has become quite certain that significant changes need to be made at ConnectPlus. The productivity of employees and the performance of the firm depend on correctly realigning the HR function.

### QUESTIONS

1. Identify the causes that lead to high absenteeism and turnover at ConnectPlus.
2. Suggest specific HRM practices that could facilitate the company's strategic objectives of growth and innovation.
3. ConnectPlus employs twelve sales associates to sell its software products. List and describe various criteria by which sales associates could be evaluated.

## Case 2  Microsoft: Hiring the Supersmart

At Microsoft, the preeminent software developer based in Redmond, Washington, human resources are truly the company's most important asset. Working on the cutting edge of technology in a fast-paced industry, top managers at Microsoft are quick to acknowledge that their success rests primarily on the intellectual talents of their employees. Essentially, Microsoft depends on employees who are learners rather than knowers. Microsoft wants people who understand current technology, who ask questions, and who possess the potential to continue to learn about technological changes. Microsoft wants its people to be able to think flexibly so they can adapt to the changing nature of the industry. As a result, the software company makes significant effort to ensure that they have the right people in their organization. The primary mechanisms they use to accomplish this are innovative recruitment and selection techniques.

Like most organizations, Microsoft relies upon a variety of tools to reach potential applicants. The software company places advertisements in newspapers, accepts applications on their Microsoft World Wide Web page, and recruits at college job fairs. However, to complement these basic practices, Microsoft has developed a reputation for relying upon hiring techniques that mirror the innovative and creative nature that drives the company's success.

All applicants, regardless of recruitment source, go through a rigorous recruiting process. This is a time-consuming task considering that Microsoft receives roughly 12,000 resumes a month. Each resume is logged into a computer database, which recruiters sort through, using keyword searches that indicate skills and abilities valuable to Microsoft.

In addition to this database, there is significant employee involvement in the recruitment process. To help match prospective employees with Microsoft, recruiters are involved in business meetings and solicit feedback from current employees about the needs of jobs throughout the organization. As a result, the recruiters are familiar with the needs of each position. Because Microsoft's goal is to have the smartest employees possible, regardless of their previous experiences, background, and education, the top managers also get involved in recruiting. Even Bill Gates, the highly visible company founder and chairman, has been known to occasionally call potential employees to let them know that Microsoft is interested in bringing them on board.

Microsoft's selection techniques are equally creative. The company does not place a lot of emphasis on traditional selection tests, and recruiters do not usually conduct reference checks or drug tests. Instead, after sorting through resumes and identifying potential employees, recruiters schedule candidates for intensive interview sessions. Rather than using the interview to verify information or seek answers to basic questions, the interviewers at Microsoft are primarily concerned with understanding how potential employees think and learn. For instance, an interviewer may ask an applicant how much water flows through the Mississippi on a daily basis, or why manhole covers are round. The interviewers are not looking for correct answers but are trying to understand an applicant's ability to solve problems by examining how the applicant thinks and what information the applicant requests.

Do these recruiting and selection practices work for Microsoft? It appears so. The individuals who are selected seem to be a good fit for this company. Indeed, the turnover rate for employees is roughly 7 percent a year, a rate far below the industry average. Microsoft is always looking for potential employees who will continually advance the organization. By pushing employees and recruiters to challenge interviewees to assess their true capabilities and potential, Microsoft continually recruits the best talent it can get.

Source: Ron Lieber, "Wired for Hiring: Microsoft's Slick Recruiting Machine," *Fortune*, February 5, 1996, 123–24; George Taninecz, "In Search of Creative Sparks," *Industry Week*, December 4, 1995, 43–47; Stuart J. Johnston, "Microsoft Scrambles to Find 'Brightest,'" *Computerworld*, February 20, 1995, 32; Randall E. Stross, "Microsoft's Big Advantage—Hiring Only the Supersmart," *Fortune*, November 25, 1996, 159–62.

QUESTIONS

1. What are the costs and benefits associated with using such innovative hiring techniques?
2. How successfully would these practices transfer to other firms in the same industry? How successfully would these practices transfer to firms in other industries?
3. What type of training, career development, performance appraisal, and compensation initiatives should be used to complement Microsoft's unique hiring techniques?

## Case 3

# Job Analysis and Hiring Decisions at Ovania Chemical

## Company Background

Ovania Chemical Corporation is a specialty chemicals producer of polyethylene terephthalate (PET) thermoplastic resins primarily used to make containers for soft drinks and bottled water, as well as packaging for food and pharmaceutical products. Though smaller than other chemical producers that produce globally, Ovania has competed successfully in its niche of the U.S. specialty chemical business. Its main plant is located in Steubenville, Ohio, positioned along the Ohio River midway between Pittsburgh, Pennsylvania, and Wheeling, West Virginia. In recent years, advances in technology have altered the nature of chemical production, and like other firms in the industry, Ovania Chemical is taking steps to modernize its facilities. Not surprisingly, these technological changes have been accompanied by redesign in employee jobs. In fact, over the last three years, there have been drastic changes in both the number and the kinds of jobs being performed by employees. The latest change at the Steubenville plant involves the job transformations of the system analyzer position.

## The System Analyzer

Because chemical production involves highly integrated process technologies, someone is needed who can monitor all of the individual components simultaneously. The system analyzer is primarily responsible for this monitoring function. It is one of the most prestigious nonmanagerial jobs in the entire plant, and its importance is likely to grow.

Formerly the position was classified as that of a semiskilled maintenance technician, but as the plant has become more automated, the requirements for the system analyzer job have become much more extensive. Knowledge of pneumatics, hydraulics, information technology, programming, and electrical wiring are all increasingly critical aspects of this job. As these up-skilling trends continue, the three men who currently hold the position admit that they will be incapable of performing adequately in the future. It is estimated that within two years, the tasks, duties, and responsibilities of the system analyzer will have changed by over 70 percent. For these reasons, the decision was made to recruit and select three new people for the rapidly transforming position.

## Job Analysis and New Position Analysis

Ovania's Steubenville plant manager, Jack Sarabe; the HR manager, Emily Claire; and two senior engineers, Dave Packley and Mark Young, formed a selection committee. With the help of two consultants, they first conducted a job analysis for the new position of system analyzer. Although they had to project into the future regarding the specific nature of the job, they collectively felt they had created an accurate depiction of the requirements for someone who would occupy the position. Figure 1 shows a list of the major performance dimensions of the job and a subsample of specific tasks characteristic of each dimension.

From this list of tasks, the selection committee then delineated a set of personal qualities required for anyone who would hold the system analyzer position. These qualities included the twelve abilities shown in Figure 2. The numbers beside each ability indicate the tasks (see Figure 1) to which it is related. The abilities marked with an asterisk (*) were considered by the committee to be "critical." Any applicant not scoring well on each of the critical dimensions would be considered unqualified for the job.

## Anticipated Selection Process

The committee hoped to gain "new blood" for the redesigned system analyzer job and therefore wanted to recruit externally for the best available talent they could find. However, as a matter of policy, management was also deeply committed to the idea of promoting from within. After deliberation, the committee decided to recruit both internally and externally for the new position. It was also decided to especially encourage current system analyzers to "reapply" for the job.

Because there was a two-year lead time before the newly transformed position would be put in place, the committee was very careful not to include in the selection battery any skills or knowledge that could reasonably be trained within that two-year period. Only aptitude or ability factors were incorporated into the selection process, rather than achievement tests.

In a private session, a few of the selection committee members admitted candidly that they had serious doubts whether any woman or minority member currently in the relevant labor market would have requisite credentials to be competitive for the position. The three present system analyzers were white males. However, since Ovania Chemical had a rather unenviable history of employment discrimination charges, the decision was made to do no unnecessary prescreening of applicant qualifications, previous experience, and so on. This strategy was thought to encourage minorities and women to apply for the new position irrespective of their prior employment history.

It should be noted, however, that there was some concern about prejudice if a woman or minority member were to get the job. Word through the grapevine was that many did not consider a woman or minority suitable for such a prestigious position. Moreover, several comments had been heard that a woman would not get down into the treatment tanks to check gauge readings. All of these factors, taken together, made for a very sensitive selection process. Ovania's management, however, was dedicated to making the procedures and decisions fair and objective.

Fifty-six employees applied for the new position of system analyzer. Twenty-one were female; fifteen were black. Only two of the three current system analyz-

FIGURE 1

**Performance Dimensions (Duties and Tasks)**

*Maintaining Spares and Supplies*

1. Anticipates future need for parts and supplies and orders them.
2. Stocks parts and supplies in an orderly fashion.
3. Maintains and calibrates test equipment.

*Troubleshooting*

4. Applies calibration standards to verify operation by subjecting the system to known standards.
5. Decides whether the problem is in the sensor, in the processor, in the process stream, and/or in the sample system.
6. Uses troubleshooting guides in system manuals to determine the problem area.
7. Uses test equipment to diagnose the problem.
8. Makes a general visual inspection of the analyzer system as a first troubleshooting step.
9. Replaces components such as printed circuit boards and sensors to see if the problem can be alleviated.

*Handling Revisions and New Installations*

10. Makes minor piping changes such as size, routing, and additional filers.
11. Makes minor electrical changes such as installing switches and wires and making terminal changes.
12. Uses common pipefitting tools.
13. Uses common electrical tools.
14. Reads installation drawings.

*Record Keeping*

15. Maintains system files showing historical record of work on each system.
16. Maintains loop files that show the application of the system.
17. Updates piping and instrument drawings if any changes are made.
18. Maintains Environmental Protection Agency records and logbooks.
19. Disassembles analyzers to perform repairs on-site or back in the shop.
20. Replaces damaged parts such as filters, electronic components, light source, lenses, sensors, and values.
21. Uses diagnostic equipment such as oscilloscopes, ohmmeters, and decade boxes.
22. Tests and calibrates repaired equipment to ensure that it works properly.
23. Reads and follows written procedures from manuals.

*Routing Maintenance*

24. Observes indicators on systems to ensure that there is proper operation.
25. Adds reagents to systems.
26. Decides whether the lab results or the system is correct regarding results (i.e., resolves discrepancies between lab and analyzer results).
27. Performs calibrations.

**► Abilities and Tasks**

FIGURE 2

Numbers represent tasks cited in Figure 1. Asterisks indicate abilities considered critical by the committee.

| SKILLS | TASK NUMBERS |
| --- | --- |
| *Finger dexterity | 3, 4, 7, 9, 10, 11, 12, 13, 19, 20, 21, 22, 25, 27 |
| *Mechanical comprehension | 3, 5, 6, 8, 9, 10, 12, 13, 7, 14, 19, 20, 22, 23, 24, 27, 11, 17 |
| *Numerical ability | 11, 3, 4, 24, 10, 21, 12, 13, 14, 27 |
| *Spatial ability | 2, 4, 5, 9, 10, 11, 14, 19, 20 |
| *Visual pursuit | 3, 4, 5, 6, 7, 8, 9, 10, 11, 14, 16, 17, 19, 20, 21, 22, 27 |
| *Detection | 2, 3, 5, 6, 8, 9, 10, 14, 19, 20, 23, 7 |
| Oral comprehension | 1, 2, 5, 6, 26, 7, 8, 9, 19, 21, 25 |
| Written comprehension | 1, 15, 16, 17, 18 |
| Deductive reasoning | 1, 5, 3, 6, 7, 8, 9, 10, 11, 19, 21, 20, 22, 2, 26, 27 |
| Inductive reasoning | 1, 3, 5, 6, 7, 8, 9, 10, 11, 19, 21, 20, 22, 2, 26, 27 |
| Reading comprehension | 3, 6, 14, 7, 22, 23, 21, 9, 27 |
| Reading scales and tables | 3, 4, 7, 8, 9, 21, 23, 24, 27, 2, 6, 14 |

ers reapplied for the new position. For now, the company decided that an overall total score of 800 on the twelve tests would be the cutoff score in order for an applicant to be seriously considered for the system analyzer position. This criterion resulted in the primary pool of twenty candidates shown in Figure 3. It should be noted that although each of the aptitude tests has been published, standardized (100 points possible for each test), and validated on other jobs, there are no normative data or validity information for the specific job of the system analyzer. Therefore, the defensibility of the test battery is founded solely upon content validity judgments. Issues regarding the final cutoff scores and method for combining the multiple predictors are problematic for the selection committee.

QUESTIONS

1. How would you go about conducting a job analysis for a job that does not yet exist?
2. Do you think the abilities chosen for selection are content-valid? What other kinds of predictors might be generally useful for employee selection?
3. What reasons did the selection committee have for selecting only those factors that could not be acquired in a two-year training program?
4. Should the concern for women getting down into the dirty treatment tanks have been a selection issue? How might you include this factor in a selection battery?
5. For the abilities termed "critical," what score should someone receive in order to be considered scoring "well" on that test (i.e., cutoff scores)? How

FIGURE 3

Primary Pool of Candidates

| NAME | RACE | SEX | EXTERNAL/ INTERNAL | Finger dexterity | Mechanical comprehension | Numerical ability | Spatial ability | Visual pursuit | Detection | Oral comprehension | Written comprehension | Deductive reasoning | Inductive reasoning | Reading comprehension | Reading scales and tables | | |
|---|---|---|---|---|---|---|---|---|---|---|---|---|---|---|---|---|---|
| Bohlander, G. | W | M | E | 67 | 78 | 74 | 70 | 76 | 62 | 80 | 69 | 71 | 76 | 78 | 82 | = | 883 |
| Baldwin, T. | W | M | I | 83 | 76 | 78 | 76 | 69 | 71 | 90 | 70 | 74 | 72 | 88 | 92 | = | 941 |
| Bittner, D. | W | M | E | 92 | 62 | 88 | 89 | 96 | 85 | 90 | 94 | 93 | 89 | 97 | 87 | = | 1062 |
| Buffett, J. | B | M | E | 87 | 97 | 89 | 61 | 94 | 93 | 75 | 90 | 85 | 96 | 85 | 80 | = | 1032 |
| Denny, A. | B | F | I | 92 | 88 | 72 | 72 | 78 | 79 | 69 | 76 | 81 | 83 | 81 | 78 | = | 949 |
| Egan, M. | W | F | E | 93 | 80 | 76 | 98 | 76 | 88 | 93 | 92 | 93 | 78 | 81 | 92 | = | 884 |
| Granger, D. | W | F | I | 82 | 82 | 79 | 75 | 77 | 73 | 72 | 80 | 81 | 77 | 70 | 80 | = | 856 |
| Haney, H. | W | M | E | 82 | 76 | 76 | 71 | 69 | 80 | 62 | 76 | 75 | 74 | 78 | 67 | = | 810 |
| Kight, G. | W | F | E | 65 | 75 | 72 | 67 | 80 | 74 | 62 | 47 | 66 | 67 | 60 | 80 | = | 815 |
| Kovach, S. | W | M | E | 82 | 87 | 85 | 85 | 83 | 88 | 81 | 80 | 80 | 83 | 84 | 80 | = | 998 |
| Laukitis, T. | B | F | E | 87 | 97 | 63 | 89 | 93 | 90 | 91 | 85 | 86 | 96 | 88 | 89 | = | 1054 |
| Lesko, B.J. | B | F | I | 83 | 84 | 89 | 91 | 80 | 82 | 86 | 88 | 85 | 84 | 90 | 89 | = | 1031 |
| Rom, D. | B | M | I | 80 | 60 | 67 | 66 | 67 | 62 | 74 | 80 | 67 | 72 | 75 | 66 | = | 835 |
| Sara, E. | W | F | I | 89 | 91 | 77 | 93 | 90 | 91 | 88 | 78 | 98 | 80 | 80 | 76 | = | 1021 |
| Sherman, A. | W | F | I | 91 | 82 | 78 | 93 | 92 | 94 | 89 | 77 | 95 | 77 | 81 | 92 | = | 1041 |
| Sauder, C. | W | F | E | 76 | 72 | 78 | 81 | 80 | 72 | 73 | 77 | 75 | 79 | 82 | 82 | = | 927 |
| Snell, J. | W | M | E | 80 | 85 | 84 | 81 | 81 | 80 | 89 | 88 | 84 | 86 | 81 | 82 | = | 1001 |
| Timothy, S. | W | F | E | 82 | 78 | 76 | 71 | 69 | 80 | 62 | 76 | 76 | 70 | 71 | 67 | = | 878 |
| Whitney, J. | W | M | I | 67 | 71 | 70 | 76 | 76 | 62 | 81 | 69 | 71 | 76 | 78 | 82 | = | 815 |
| Wright, P. | W | M | I | 80 | 60 | 57 | 56 | 57 | 62 | 74 | 80 | 69 | 72 | 75 | 65 | = | 887 |

should the test scores be combined (e.g., compensatory, multiple hurdle, combination)?

6. Which three candidates appear most qualified? What are your reservations, if any, about this recommendation?

7. Would this test battery and selection procedure be defensible in court?

## Case 4     Diversity Is in Good Hands at Allstate

In today's competitive environment, companies continue to look for ways to improve their performance and achieve corporate objectives. Whether it is through improvements in production and customer service or investments in workforce development and training, senior executives must implement strategies that distinguish their firms from the competition. The task is not easy, but the team of HR executives at Allstate has found that its diversity strategy has become one of the company's most potent competitive weapons.

It has long been Allstate's position that diversity is neither about political mandates nor legal obligation. Rather the company's vision statement emphasizes competitiveness through diversity: "Diversity is Allstate's strategy for leveraging differences in order to create a competitive advantage." This strategy has two major points: one internally focused, and the other externally focused. According to Joan Crockett, vice president of human resources, the internal diversity focus is about "unlocking the potential for excellence in all workers by providing them the tools, resources and opportunities to succeed." The external focus of diversity is about making certain that the workforce matches the characteristics of the marketplace. As much as possible, the workforce should share the same experiences, backgrounds, and sensitivities as the markets it serves and the communities in which it operates. In this context, Allstate managers view diversity not as a goal, but as a process that is ongoing, measurable, managed, and integrated into the daily life of the company.

In the early days, Allstate's commitment to diversity didn't always link recruitment, development, and retention strategies to business performance. The company focused more on affirmative action and diversity awareness through education and training. And while these initiatives were considered innovative in their day, they had no articulated business outcome. Carlton Yearwood, director of diversity management, notes that programs in the 1960s and 1970s were geared toward assimilating cultural differences into Allstate's culture rather than reformulating the culture to represent diversity. However, these early efforts strengthened the company's commitment to building an organization that reflected the many people and markets it serves. So instead of starting over, the company used those experiences as a foundation for future initiatives. According to Yearwood, the key question became, "How do you take this workforce of differences and bring them together in a more powerful way so that it can impact business results?"

Allstate has taken four specific steps to integrate diversity into its human resources processes. According to Crockett, "Allstate's commitment to affirmative action seeks to ensure that qualified women and minorities are fully integrated into the business, and that every employee has the opportunity to contribute to the company's overall performance."

*Step 1: Succession planning.* Diversity is integrated into Allstate's succession planning through a process that ensures that a diverse slate of candidates is identified and developed for each key position. Allstate's integrated process enables it to track and measure key drivers of career development and career opportunities, ensuring the company's future workforce will be diverse within all levels of the organization. Allstate's succession planning has made a difference that is easy to measure. Employment of women and minorities has grown at a rate far surpassing national averages. Today, 40 percent of Allstate's executives and managers are women, compared with the national average of 32 percent. And 21 percent of its executives and managers are minorities, more than double the national average of 12 percent.

*Step 2: Development.* Allstate's second major diversity initiative is employee development. Development of employees' skills is a critical component for each individual's success. Through the company's employee development process, all employees receive an assessment of their current job skills, as well as a road map for developing the critical skills necessary for advancement within the organization. Options available to employees include education, coaching and mentoring, classroom training, and a variety of other career experiences. Leaders are provided with employee feedback and base future development plans on the input that they receive. In addition, all of Allstate's nonagent employees with service of more than a year have completed diversity training courses, which represent an investment in excess of 640,000 hours in classroom time.

*Step 3: Measurement.* The third key element is measurement. Twice a year the company takes a "snapshot" of all 53,000 employees through a survey called the Diversity Index. As part of a larger on-line employee survey and feedback process called the Quarterly Leadership Measurement System (QLMS), the Diversity Index taps the following questions:

- To what extent does our company deliver quality service to customers regardless of their ethnic background, gender, age, etc.?
- To what extent are you treated with respect and dignity at work? To what extent does your immediate manager/team leader seek out and utilize the different backgrounds and perspectives of all employees in your work group?
- How often do you observe insensitive behavior at work, e.g., inappropriate comments or jokes about ethnic background, gender, age, etc.?
- To what extent do you work in an environment of trust where employees/agents are free to offer different opinions?

Management communicates results of this survey and actively solicits feedback from employees on creating action plans to solve problems and improve work processes.

*Step 4: Accountability and reward.* The compensation system at Allstate is closely linked to the company's diversity goals. For managers at all levels, 25 percent of their merit pay is tied to the diversity index and the QLMS. In addition, incentive compensation for senior leaders, who are eligible for bonuses, also is tied to the measurement system through the QLMS. Karleen Zuzich, assistant vice president of HR, says that embedding diversity into leaders' pay and recognition helps sharpen the focus on the initiative. "What you measure is what people focus on. This really sends a clear signal that management of people and doing that well is really important," she says.

Allstate has received considerable recognition for its diversity efforts. Most recently, the company was among the first companies to be ranked by *Fortune* as one of the "50 Best Companies for Asians, Blacks, and Hispanics." *Minority MBA Magazine* included Allstate on its list of "Top Ten Companies for Minority Managers." *Working Mother, Vista,* and *Hispanic* likewise have cited Allstate. Although accolades such as these are nice, Allstate views them as an opportunity to improve further. According to Crockett, "Through the process of applying for awards and citations like these, we can gain the feedback needed to continually improve our results. We are convinced that the outstanding results Allstate employees deliver every day for shareholders and policyholders are, in part, the fruits of our diversity strategy. And we expect the steps we have taken to embrace diversity as a business strategy to continue paying off in the years to come."

Source: Adapted from Joan Crockett, "Diversity: Winning Competitive Advantage through a Diverse Workforce," *HR Focus* 76, no. 5 (May 1999): 9–10; Joan Crockett, "Diversity as a Business Strategy," *Management Review* 88, no. 5 (May 1999): 62; Louisa Wah, "Diversity at Allstate: A Competitive Weapon," *Management Review* 88, no. 7 (July/August 1999): 24–30.

1. What are the key points to Allstate's diversity strategy and how do they impact competitiveness?
2. How has Allstate integrated diversity with HR practices?
3. In what ways do awards help Allstate improve its diversity efforts?

## Case 5

# The Training and Development Dilemma at Whitney and Company

## Company Background

Whitney and Company is a global management consulting firm that has been growing rapidly, particularly in the United States and western Europe. The firm provides comprehensive business planning and analysis as well as consulting in operational and technical areas such as finance, operations, and information technology. Its client list includes medium-sized firms but its growth tends to focus on *Fortune* 1000 companies. Whitney contracts include manufacturing and service organizations as well as government, health care, and religious organizations. The firm has offices in twenty-four U.S. cities and offices in sixteen other countries. With its world headquarters in Chicago, Whitney employs nearly 27,000 people, the vast majority of whom are young, aggressive professionals.

In light of the tremendous growth of the consulting industry, Whitney has ambitious plans for expanding the firm. It is estimated that in the next five years alone they will need 1,200 new managers and about 200 new partners. Because Whitney maintains a policy of promotion from within, these people will come mainly from the ranks of entry-level employees. There is plenty of incentive for these young professionals to do well; starting salaries for partners average $250,000 (although normally individuals do not reach partner status until they have been with the firm for ten years).

## Training and Development

Given the critical importance of professional talent, Whitney has devoted millions of dollars over the years to create in-house educational and training facilities that are the envy of the industry. The most observable indicator of this dedication is the very plush Corporate Education and Development Center (CEDC) in St. Charles, Illinois, thirty minutes west of Chicago. The 100-acre center provides living and meeting accommodations for approximately 500 persons and includes an impressive facility of classrooms, conference rooms, libraries, and even a television studio. The center also employs a staff of nearly 50 instructors, mostly field managers who rotate on a two-year basis into the CEDC.

Every new Whitney employee spends two weeks at CEDC before receiving a total of three additional months of training at one of nine other regional facilities in Atlanta, Boston, Cleveland, Chicago, Dallas, Denver, Los Angeles, Seattle, and New York. All told, Whitney spends almost $3,500 per employee for training and education each year.

The majority of this investment is on technical and systems training for entry-level consultants. Additionally, employees receive extensive training in the specific industries where they will predominantly work (e.g., oil and gas, telecommunications, banking, health care). The senior staff is particularly aware that Whitney's public image is largely a function of the actions and work quality of their first-level associates. Executives clearly recognize the importance of an expert workforce and spare no expense in this regard.

## Employee Performance

While Whitney affords many opportunities to its employees and spends a great deal of money on professional development, it expects a great deal from its employees in return. Especially in the first two years, it is not at all uncommon for a beginning associate to work seventy-hour weeks. The schedules and traveling are often grueling, and the rewards in the first few years are typically not commensurate. For example, salaries are generally in the mid-$40,000s and the benefit package is only average for a firm of Whitney's size and reputation. The greater payoffs, as indicated before, come when one achieves partner status, but not much earlier.

Nevertheless, Whitney has little trouble attracting very aggressive, energetic students generally right out of college who are eager "to pay their dues" for success in a major firm. Occasionally, however, this aggressiveness has come across as being boorish and callous with clients, especially in the health care industry. There are even situations where clients have discontinued business with Whitney, not because of concerns about expertise, but because of the "fast-in, fast-out style of big-time consulting." While in most cases, Whitney employees gradually learn to interpret the subtleties of client needs, occasionally (and increasingly), employees have been let go because of their lack of personal acumen.

In view of the importance of interpersonal competence at Whitney, some of the training staff has suggested that more attention should be placed on that part of the development of entering employees. But others on staff point out that only two years ago a series of lectures was put into the training program dealing with clients and customer relations. The consensus has been that the program addition has not been well received. They simply do not feel the added expense would be justified. In fact, there is a growing group of senior partners who believe too much is already being spent on education and training, since so many of those trained employees subsequently leave to take jobs with other companies.

The facts in this regard are clear. Only about 50 percent of new hires stay with Whitney beyond their first five years. Approximately 90 percent leave the firm within ten years of employment. Most of these people either start their own firms or go to work for one of Whitney's clients. Comparatively few are fired. Many people think this turnover rate is terribly detrimental to the success of Whitney, especially given the immense expense for training and development. Many others, however, feel the departures are inevitable, given the promotion-from-within policies. Some feel the turnover actually helps business since those who go to work for other companies often convince them to become clients of Whitney—the logic being that former employees are familiar with Whitney's procedures and generally will have respect for the quality of the firm's work.

## The Training and Development Dilemma

Not surprisingly, there is increasing debate regarding the role and importance of education and training at Whitney and Company. It is very difficult to know which parts of the current programs are good and which are not. Likewise, there is the problem of determining if additional training is needed. As Anthony Blaine, one of the training directors, summarized it: "For years we've been throwing tons of training at these people, but we aren't sure if its the right kind, if it's too much, or even if they're catching what we're throwing. We've got to start coming up with some good questions, and then figure out some pretty intelligent answers."

### QUESTIONS

1. What could Whitney do to enhance the value of training?
2. Is the company using the most effective techniques, especially with regard to training for client and customer service? What technique changes would you recommend?
3. How should Whitney decide specifically who needs training? Is it advisable, even cost-efficient, to send everyone through the program?
4. How would Whitney determine whether its education and training programs are of sufficient utility? How would you specifically evaluate the programs?

## Case 6 — Realigning HR Practices at Egan's Clothiers

At the end of fiscal year 2000, revenues at Egan's Clothiers, Inc., had increased 21 percent over 1999 and had increased at a compounded rate of 24 percent over the past five years. That's the good news. The bad news is that costs have risen at an even more rapid rate, thereby shrinking the company's gross margins. As a consequence, Egan's profitability (measured as return on sales and return on net assets) has actually fallen by 14 percent over the past three years.

The retail industry in general has been enjoying growth due to a healthy economy, and this drop in profitability at Egan's is particularly worrisome. In fact, according to Egan's chief financial officer, Richard Coyle, if something isn't done immediately to control material and labor costs, as well as administrative expenses, the company may need to restructure its operations. In the short run, Coyle, company president Karen Egan, and vice president of HR Jim Rooney have put an indefinite freeze on all hiring. Further, they are contemplating layoffs of nearly one-quarter of Egan's sales staff and are weighing the benefits of cutting back on HR-related expenses such as training. Compared to others in the industry, their labor costs are very high.

### Company Background

Gene Egan and Pat Pollock opened their first store in Baldwin, New York, in 1958. The company grew rapidly during the 1980s and now operates a chain of thirty-four medium-sized stores located throughout Connecticut, New York, Pennsylvania, and New Jersey. Since the beginning, Egan's customers have been primarily middle- and upper-middle-class families purchasing sportswear, dresswear, and fashion accessories. The company has established a longstanding tradition of quality and customer service. In addition to its thirty-four stores, the company also maintains two distribution centers and its administrative offices in Stamford, Connecticut. The total employment currently stands at approximately 2,400 people: 15 executives, 40 staff specialists, 40 store managers, 215 sales managers, 250 administrative personnel, 1,600 salespeople, and 240 distribution workers. Except for the employees at the distribution centers, the company is not presently unionized. However, it is no secret that Egan's management has been trying very hard recently to keep current labor organizing activities to a minimum. Especially in these times of growth and change, management views unionism as a threat to the company's success. In this regard, the HR office has been called upon to conduct a program audit of various HR practices utilized at Egan's. The purpose of this audit is to assess the impact of HR policies and practices on employee outcomes (e.g., performance, satisfaction, absenteeism, turnover). The corollary objective of this audit is to identify specific problem areas where policy adjustments may be necessary. The final report to the executive staff will include the HR department's evaluation of current problems and recommendations for implementing changes in HR practices.

## Human Resources Management History

Over the past five years, Egan's has made several changes in order to implement the best HR practices possible. Partially, this has been to circumvent unionization efforts, but primarily it is indicative of Egan's longstanding belief that success in retailing depends on the competencies and efforts of its employees.

The commitment to HR is demonstrated by the fact that in 1998 the company spent $1.3 million on an intranet-based human resources information system (HRIS). The HRIS has successfully automated most employment records (e.g., job titles, salary information, sales levels, attendance, demographics, etc.) and connects each of the retail stores, distribution centers, and executive offices. Also, Egan's has maintained an ongoing training program for the past five years to help salespeople improve their retail selling skills (RSS) and customer service. The annual cost of this program has been roughly $750,000. To further ensure high ability levels in their workforce, the company sets selection standards substantially higher than their competitors. Whereas other retail companies typically hire inexperienced high school students, Egan's generally requires some retailing or sales experience before considering an applicant for employment. While this policy increases overall labor costs, Egan's management has been confident that the added expense is well justified over the long run. However, recently even the strongest proponents of HR have been wondering if it might be a good idea to cut back on training, given the company's current financial picture.

By far the most problematic and volatile HR issues at Egan's have been regarding promotions and salary increases. Because the company promotes from within, and distributes raises on a company-wide basis, comparisons generally have to be made across employees in different jobs and departments. To combat arguments of subjectivity and bias pertaining to these decisions, Egan's links these rewards to objective measures of performance. Specifically, rather than utilizing subjective managerial evaluations of employee performance, ongoing accounts of sales results are maintained for each employee through use of the HRIS. On the basis of this information, each department manager assigns each employee to one of five categories:

Superior—top 10 percent

Very good—next 20 percent

Good—middle 40 percent

Fair—lower 20 percent

Poor—lowest 10 percent

Administrative decisions are then made across departments utilizing these standardized distributions. Additionally, in order to provide constant feedback to each employee concerning his or her relative performance, data are updated and posted daily. It is hoped that this feedback is motivating to employees, and in this way there are no surprises when the time comes for semiannual performance appraisal interviews. It is interesting to note that since these changes have been made in the performance appraisal system, there has not been one formal complaint registered regarding salary or promotion decisions. However, sales managers themselves have mentioned occasionally that they do not feel as comfortable now that they are required to assign employees to the "fair" and "poor" categories.

## HR Outcomes

Despite the concerted efforts of Egan's management to create a first-rate system of human resources management, there are several troubling issues facing the company. The HR practices are not having their desired effects. For example, there have been recent complaints that employees have not been as patient or courteous with customers as they should be. This was best summarized by Paul Kelly, a store manager in White Plains, New York, who noted, "My people are beating up the clientele in order to make a sale—the very opposite of what the RSS program trains them to do." This lapse in customer service is frustrating to management since the RSS training has proven effective in the past. Additionally, there seems to be a great deal of competition *within* departments that is hurting a team effort. Although intergroup rivalries *between* departments has always been viewed as normal and healthy, the lack of intragroup cohesiveness is seen as a problem.

Additionally, Egan's has been plagued with increases in lost and damaged merchandise. Management attributes this to the fact that storage rooms are disorganized and unkempt. This is in sharp contrast to the selling floors, which have remained fairly well orderly and uncluttered. Nevertheless, inventory costs have been increasing at an alarming rate.

Everyone notices that something is wrong. But the behavior patterns are perplexing. Absenteeism has decreased by 23 percent, but employee turnover has actually increased from 13 to over 29 percent, thereby increasing labor costs overall. Unfortunately, many of those leaving the company (43 percent) are rated as very good to superior employees.

As executives in the company look at these trends, they are understandably concerned. The success of the company and its reputation for quality and service depends on solid investments in HR to ensure the best possible workforce. However, the expenses are eroding the company's profits, and worse, it looks now like these investments are not paying off.

### QUESTIONS

1. What overall changes could you recommend to the executive team at Egan's about its HR practices?
2. What are the pros and cons of Egan's performance appraisal system? Do you think it identifies the best employees? Do you think it helps develop employees to perform the best they can?
3. Can increased sales be linked directly and/or indirectly to the appraisal system? How about some of the other performance effects? How would you change the system?
4. How do you account for the fact that absenteeism has decreased at Egan's while turnover has increased?

CASE 7

# The Layoff of Paul Dougherty: A Manager's Tough Decision

Applied Technologies, with fifty-five employees, is a small technological services company that provides technological support to larger firms. When Applied Technologies was created twelve years ago, the company faced virtually no competition and the market seemed to have unlimited potential for growth. However, over the past five years the company has experienced slow growth and diminished profitability. As the industry prospered, more companies entered the market and increased the level of competition. In addition, with the advances in technology, computers, and software capabilities, fewer companies are requesting technological support from contractors. This has become particularly apparent in the computer graphics area. Requests for traditional graphics support services from other companies have declined over 20 percent in the past year alone.

Beverly Meyers, the manager for computer graphics at Applied Technologies, and Mike Peterson, the owner and founder of Applied Technologies, recently began meeting to discuss what they need to do to enhance the company's performance. Both Meyers and Peterson know something must change and, after a series of long discussions, they have determined that Meyers's unit must refocus its emphasis. Specifically, to enhance its customer orientation, that unit must shift from solely providing computer graphics support and move toward providing a greater degree of customer service along with some basic computer support.

Meyers faces a tough decision: She must restructure her unit and lay off one of her four employees. This decision is particularly difficult because all four workers are good employees and they get along very well. As she tries to determine which of the employees will be laid off, Meyers reviews the background and personnel information for each of them:

Paul Dougherty is married and has two children in high school. His wife works evenings as an assistant manager at a local department store to help make ends meet. Dougherty has been with Applied Technologies for just over eight years. He was hired during a period of growth in computer graphics support during the late 1980s and has been a good performer on the job. Dougherty's work is not the best among the four employees, but he is consistent and never complains about his workload.

Shannon Wall is a single mother with a child in elementary school. Wall came to Applied Technologies a year after Dougherty as a highly recruited graphic design specialist. She'd earned both a bachelor's and a master's degree in graphic design from a well-respected university. Meyers had high expectations for Wall, but her performance has slipped the past twenty-four months. The rumor around the office is that she has recently gone through a tough divorce and is in counseling to deal with her problems. Despite her decline in performance, Meyers still thinks Wall has the most potential of her four employees.

Teresa Livingstone is a dedicated worker. In fact, everyone says that she is "married to her job." She has been known to put in twenty hours of work on weekends to make sure that her work is up-to-date. Livingstone has a college degree in marketing with a minor in graphic design. Though her computer graphics skills are not as sizable as those of the other three employees, she has a comprehensive understanding of the marketing side of the business, is capable of bringing in customers, and consistently meets her performance expectations.

Greg Stevens came to Applied Technologies two years ago directly out of college, where he had completed his undergraduate degree in computer graphics. Though Stevens started somewhat slowly, once he had settled into his role at Applied Technologies his performance took off. In fact, he has been the top performer of the four workers for the past year and a half. Although his performance is exceptional, Stevens does not take the marketing side of the business as seriously as he should. As a result, his potential to bring in new business is not as strong as his ability to do the work once a contract is negotiated.

| | Seniority (Years) | Compen-sation | Performance | | | |
|---|---|---|---|---|---|---|
| | | | 1995 | 1996 | 1997 | 1998 |
| Paul Dougherty | 8 | $36,500 | Average | Average | Good | Average |
| Shannon Wall | 7 | $40,500 | High | Good | Average | Low |
| Teresa Livingstone | 3 | $34,000 | | Poor | Average | Average |
| Greg Stevens | 2 | $32,500 | | | Good | High |

After reviewing the personnel information for each of her four employees, Meyers has decided to lay off Paul Dougherty. To help him in his transition, she is committed to aiding him in finding another job. Though it was not an easy decision to make, she feels confident that she has made the right choice.

### QUESTIONS

1. What criteria should be used to determine potential layoff candidates? What emphasis, if any, should be given to nonjob-related factors such as personal problems or a spouse's need to work? Explain.
2. Do you agree with Meyers's decision to lay off Paul Dougherty? Whom would you have laid off in this situation? Provide support for your position.
3. Are there any potential legal implications in Meyers's decision? Explain your answer.

## CASE 8 — Continental Airlines: One Company's Flight to Success

In the past decade, Continental Airlines has had a spotty track record. The airline twice filed for bankruptcy, realized diminished performance culminating in a $613 million loss in 1994, and was ranked dead last in industry indicators such as on-time performance among the major carriers. During these years, employees at Continental had undergone several series of layoffs and withstood both wage cuts and delayed wage increases in an effort to slash Continental's costs. The result of these efforts was a demoralized workforce and a corporate reputation that put Continental near the top of *Fortune*'s list of "least admired" companies.

Despite this history, things have taken a positive turn for the airline in recent years. Since the arrival of Gordon Bethune, Continental's new CEO, the company appears to have made a 180-degree turn and is now a highly productive and profitable carrier. Indeed, all indications are that Continental is back on track. For instance, in 1995, the carrier was number 1 in on-time performance for the first time ever and was highly ranked in baggage handling. Customer complaints are down more than 60 percent, and Continental recently gained the distinction of being the number 1 airline in customer satisfaction among the major U.S. carriers for long-distance flights. Just a few years earlier, Continental was last in this category. Moreover, sick leave and on-the-job injuries have decreased, and applications for employment at Continental are back up again. Perhaps most impressive is that Continental posted an all-time record annual profit in 1995, and in 1996 the price of Continental stock rose over 370 percent.

Compared with their listless efforts in the past, workers at Continental are now operating at a productivity level that is quite impressive. But what is the cause of this turnaround? Granted, the airline industry as a whole has realized greater profitability in recent years, but Continental's feverish change of course has occurred for other reasons as well.

One of the first actions that Bethune took was to refocus the company and streamline operations at Continental. Once in charge of the struggling airline, Bethune eliminated more than 7,000 jobs, dismissed fifty vice presidents and replaced them with twenty new managers, and outsourced much of the carrier's maintenance work. The thrust of this reorientation embodied Bethune's efforts and goals to improve company service while abolishing cut-rate fares and cost-based practices. In addition to these explicit streamlining actions, Bethune also changed several practices that had significant symbolic value in the refocusing effort at Continental. For example, surveillance cameras were removed from executive offices, and the cockpits of planes were scheduled to be cleaned every thirty rather than every ninety days.

Perhaps the most important changes, however, were the actions taken to adjust the human resources management practices to facilitate the achievement of the company's new goals. The first step was to involve the workers in the decision-making processes at Continental. When Bethune arrived and determined that there would have to be layoffs, the employees were given input into the process and decisions. Communication with top management was implemented through a toll-free number established to handle employee complaints. To deal with the sixty calls a day that came in, a committee was created to respond to these problems with a solution within forty-eight hours. Moreover, Bethune invited workers to call his voice mail, and when they called, he called them back.

To demonstrate to the employees that he was serious about their involvement in the company's success, Bethune also changed performance appraisal practices. He ordered departments to focus on specific targets that were important to customer service rather than on traditional cost-based measures. Consequently, the focus of the performance appraisals shifted toward achievement and facilitation of on-time flights. To emphasize the importance of this goal, management devised an incentive system that promised to pay each employee $65 each month the airline finished in the top half of the Department of Transportation's rankings. If they achieved the number 1 ranking, each employee would receive $100. In addition, employees were provided with the information they needed to achieve these goals. Automated systems were put in place to let the staff track problems, and supervisors were able to show workers how their daily actions affected performance indicators. To top it all off, once profits started to come in, Bethune paid employees a postponed wage increase that was not due until 1996.

To build on these achievements, Bethune continues to devise new ways to motivate the workers at Continental. For example, in July of 1996, to acknowledge perfect attendance by employees, seven workers were drawn from a list of thousands to receive new sport utility vehicles at the company's expense.

Since Bethune's arrival in 1994, employees are paying more attention to their work and there has been a sharp improvement in morale. By focusing on the workers and rewarding them for displaying the behaviors and actions necessary to the company's success, Bethune is guiding the company in the right direction. Faced with the challenge to turn Continental Airlines around, Gordon Bethune has gained the confidence of his workers by coming through on his promises. He has the entire company rallying around the future success of Continental.

Source: Wendy Zellner, "Back to 'Coffee, Tea, or Milk?'" *Business Week*, July 3, 1995, 52–56; Scott McCartney, "Back on Course: Piloted by Bethune, Continental Air Lifts Its Workers' Morale," *The Wall Street Journal*, May 15, 1996, A-1, A-8; Wendy Zellner, "The Right Place, the Right Time," *Business Week*, May 27, 1996, 74–76; "America's Most Admired Companies," *Fortune*, March 4, 1996, 90–98.

## QUESTIONS

1. If you were the manager of a distressed organization, what specific steps would you take to turn the organization around?
2. What are the primary causes for the sudden change in employee morale at Continental Airlines?
3. What actions would you take, if any, to ensure that Continental continues its improved performance over the next decade?
4. Explain how different employee contribution techniques (e.g., teams, job enrichment, etc.) could serve to continually improve Continental's performance.

## Case 9          Ill-Fated Love at Centrex Electronics

Nancy Miller-Canton never imagined she would lose her job at Centrex Electronics Corporation (CEC), and certainly not under such unpleasant circumstances. Unfortunately, after eleven years of employment, the last two as a senior product engineer in the firm's military/space division in Atlanta, she made a mistake: She fell in love.

Human resources professionals agree that CEC is highly regarded as a quality employer in the electronics industry. It is a multinational corporation with engineering services and production facilities in Spain, Canada, Hong Kong, Mexico, and Germany. With more than 12,000 employees in the United States, the firm has been named as one of the country's top 100 organizations to work for by several studies. Centrex Electronics is known as a top-paying corporation with proactive employee relations policies. Kathryn Garner, vice president of human resources, is credited with establishing many positive employee rights policies, including those covering drug testing, search and surveillance, access to employee files, and employee smoking. The corporation permits marriage between employees except in cases where "one employee is in a direct reporting relationship with the other."

Miller-Canton joined Centrex Electronics shortly after graduating from Georgia State University in 1982. At that time she was married to Tom Canton, her college sweetheart. In 1988, Canton died suddenly. As a single parent, his widow then became dependent upon her job for the majority of her family's support.

Miller-Canton enjoyed rapid promotions through various engineering positions until reaching her present job as senior product engineer. In 1995, the year before her dismissal, she had been awarded the firm's Engineering Distinction Award for her research and development work in metallography. But in January 1996, one week after receiving a 14.2 percent raise, she was called on the carpet. The question from the military/space division manager was clear and direct: "Are you dating Mike Domzalski?" Domzalski was a former CEC senior engineer who had changed employment in 1994 to work for International Technologies, a direct competitor of CEC. There was no denying the romance. The two had dated while Domzalski was with CEC, and he still played on CEC's softball team. It was widely known among Miller-Canton's friends that she was "extremely fond" of Domzalski.

Now, chastised for her involvement, Miller-Canton was ordered to forget about Domzalski or be demoted. After the meeting she told a friend, "I was so socialized in CEC culture and so devoted to my job that I thought seriously about breaking up with Mike." As she later testified in court, however, she never got the chance because she was dismissed the day after the meeting with her manager.

At the root of Miller-Canton's dismissal was a corporate policy regarding the leakage of confidential product information. The policy seeks to avoid situations where an employee of CEC might be compromised into providing sensitive or confidential information to an employee of a competing organization. Miller-Canton's work in research and development made her subject to the following CEC policy:

> Employees performing jobs where they have access to sensitive or confidential information which could benefit competitors are prohibited from being married to or from having a romantic relationship with individuals employed by competing organizations.

Since Mike Domzalski's work at International Technologies was similar to Miller-Canton's at CEC, the corporation felt their "romantic relationship" made her discharge appropriate. Feeling aggrieved, Miller-Canton engaged the services of an attorney specializing in employee rights claims. In preparing her wrongful-discharge suit, the attorney told her that, given the nature of her case and the continuous erosion of the employment-at-will doctrine, he believed she could win the lawsuit. Furthermore, while gathering background information for the trial, the attorney discovered something that her former division manager didn't know. Shortly before her discharge, no less an authority than former CEC chairman Joseph M. Torell had declared that "CEC employees are responsible for their own off-the-job behavior. We are concerned with an employee's off-the-job conduct only when it reduces the employee's ability to perform normal job assignments."

A jury trial in state court upheld the wrongful-discharge suit and awarded Miller-Canton $425,000 in back pay and punitive damages. Like other trials, however, this one took its toll on the parties involved. "I couldn't function for four or five months after the trial, I was so emotionally upset and drained," Miller-Canton said. She is now employed as an engineer for a computer company; she and Domzalski are no longer dating. "It was a bad experience all around," she says. "There was a real sense of belonging and a feeling of personal job worth at CEC. If I had my way, I'd take my old job back today."

---

Source: This case is adapted from an actual situation known to the authors. All names are fictitious.

QUESTIONS

1. What exceptions to the employment-at-will doctrine would the attorney have used to file the lawsuit?
2. Comment on the confidential information policy adopted by Centrex Electronics. Do you agree with the way it is used?
3. Is dating a "romantic relationship"?

## Case 10     The Last Straw for Aero Engine

The meeting lasted only ten minutes, since all those present quickly agreed that Tom Kinder should be fired. According to management, Kinder had caused the company numerous problems over the last eighteen months, and the incident that Saturday had been "the straw that broke the camel's back." Plant management believed it had to rid itself of a poor employee, one the company had offered numerous opportunities for improvement. It seemed like an airtight case and one the union couldn't win if taken to arbitration.

Tom Kinder had worked for the Aero Engine Company for fourteen years prior to his discharge. He was initially employed as an engine mechanic servicing heavy-duty diesel engines. For his first nine years with Aero Engine, he was considered a model employee by his supervisors and plant management. Kinder was also well liked by his fellow employees. His performance appraisals were always marked "exceptional," and his personnel folder contained many commendation letters from customers and supervisors alike. Supervisor Mark Lee described Kinder as "devoted to his job of building and repairing engines." Through company-sponsored training classes and courses taken at a local trade school, Kinder had acquired the knowledge and experience to build and repair specialty engines used in arctic oil exploration.

The Aero Engine Company, with headquarters in the Midwest, was engaged primarily in the production and maintenance of specialty engines used in drilling, heavy manufacturing, and diesel transportation. The company had experienced very rapid growth in sales volume, number of products produced, and the size of its workforce since 1970. (At the time of Tom Kinder's termination, the company employed about 1,700 employees.) Aero Engine avoided hiring new personnel and then laying them off when they were no longer needed. Company policy stated that layoffs were to be avoided except in extreme circumstances. When heavy workloads arose, the natural solution to the problem was to schedule large amounts of overtime and to hire temporary employees through one of the local temporary help services.

Tom Kinder's work problems had begun approximately five years prior to his discharge when he went through a very emotional and difficult divorce. He was a devoted family man, and the divorce was a shock to his values and his way of life. The loss of his children was particularly devastating to his mental well-being. He became sullen, withdrawn, and argumentative with his supervisors. An absenteeism problem developed and continued until his discharge. Over the eighteen months prior to this termination, Tom was absent twenty-seven complete days and nine partial days and was tardy nineteen times. Twelve months before termination he had been given a written warning that his attendance must improve or he would face further disciplinary action, including possible discharge. Unfortunately, his attendance did not improve; however, he received no further disciplinary action until his discharge on Monday, June 17, 1996.

Management had experienced problems other than absenteeism with Tom Kinder. The quantity and quality of his work had decreased to only an acceptable level of performance. His supervisor had discussed this with him on two occasions, but no disciplinary action was ever instituted. Furthermore, during heavy production periods Kinder would either refuse to work overtime assignments or, once assigned, would often fail to report for work. It was an incident that occurred during a Saturday overtime shift that caused his discharge.

On Saturday, June 15, Kinder was assigned to a high-priority project that required him to build a specialty engine for a large and loyal customer. The big new engine was needed to replace a smaller engine that had exploded on an Alaskan drilling rig. The engine was being put together in a newly constructed plant building located one-half mile from the company's main production facilities. At approximately 9:15 a.m. on that Saturday, Gordon Thompson, Kinder's supervisor, had walked over to the new building to check on the progress of the engine. As Thompson passed by a window, he noticed Kinder sitting at a desk with his feet up, reading a magazine. The supervisor decided to observe him from outside the building. After about twenty-five minutes Kinder had not moved, and Thompson returned to the plant to report the incident to Glenn Navarro, the plant production manager. Neither the supervisor nor the production manager confronted Kinder about the incident.

At 8:15 the next Monday morning, supervisor Thompson and production manager Navarro met with the director of human resources to review the total work performance of Tom Kinder. After this short meeting, all those present decided that Tom Kinder should be fired. Tom's discharge notice read, "Terminated for poor work performance, excessive absenteeism, and loafing." At 10:15 that morning Kinder was called into Navarro's office and told of his discharge. Navarro then handed him his final paycheck, which included eight hours of work for Monday.

Source: This case is based on an actual arbitration heard by George W. Bohlander. All names are fictitious.

QUESTIONS

1. Comment on the handling of this case by the supervisor, production manager, and director of human resources.
2. To what extent were the concepts of good discipline and "just cause" discharge applied?
3. If Tom Kinder's discharge went to arbitration, how would you decide the case? Why? What arguments would labor and management present to support their respective positions?

# Glossary

## A

**Achievement tests**
Measures of what a person knows or can do right now.

**Active listening**
Technique by which a counselor/interviewer allows a person to present views without interruption.

**Adverse impact**
A concept that refers to the rejection of a significantly higher percentage of a protected class for employment, placement, or promotion when compared with the successful, nonprotected class.

**Affirmative action**
Policy that goes beyond equal employment opportunity by requiring organizations to comply with the law and correct past discriminatory practices by increasing the numbers of minorities and women in specific positions.

**Alarm reaction**
Response to stress that basically involves an elevated heart rate, increased respiration, elevated levels of adrenaline in the blood, and increased blood pressure.

**Alternative dispute resolution (ADR)**
Term applied to different types of employee complaint or dispute-resolution procedures.

**Apprenticeship training**
System of training in which a worker entering the skilled trades is given thorough instruction and experience, both on and off the job, in the practical and theoretical aspects of the work.

**Aptitude tests**
Measures of a person's capacity to learn or acquire skills.

**Arbitration award**
Final and binding award issued by an arbitrator in a labor-management dispute.

**Arbitrator**
Third-party neutral who resolves a labor dispute by issuing a final decision in the disagreement.

**Assessment center**
Process by which individuals are evaluated as they participate in a series of situations that resemble what they might be called upon to handle on the job.

**Augmented skills**
Skills helpful in facilitating the efforts of expatriate managers.

**Authorization card**
A statement signed by an employee authorizing a union to act as a representative of the employee for purposes of collective bargaining.

## B

**Balanced scorecard**
Standard for determining executive incentive bonus on the basis of customer satisfaction, ability to innovate, product or service leadership, and the like.

**Balance-sheet approach**
Compensation system designed to match the purchasing power in a person's home country.

**Bargaining unit**
Group of two or more employees who share common employment interests and conditions and may reasonably be grouped together for purposes of collective bargaining.

**Bargaining zone**
Area within which the union and the employer are willing to concede when bargaining.

**Behavior modeling**
Approach that demonstrates desired behavior and gives trainees the chance to practice and role-play those behaviors and receive feedback.

**Behavior modification**
Technique that operates on the principle that behavior that is rewarded, or positively reinforced, will be exhibited more frequently in the future, whereas behavior that is penalized or unrewarded will decrease in frequency.

**Behavior observation scale (BOS)**
A behavioral approach to performance appraisal that measures the frequency of observed behavior.

**Behavioral description interview (BDI)**
An interview in which an applicant is asked questions about what he or she actually did in a given situation.

**Behaviorally anchored rating scale (BARS)**
A behavioral approach to performance appraisal that consists of a series of vertical scales, one for each important dimension of job performance.

**Benchmarking**
Process of measuring one's own services and practices against the recognized leaders in order to identify areas for improvement.

**Bona fide occupational qualification (BFOQ)**
Suitable defense against a discrimination charge only where age, religion, sex, or national origin is an actual qualification for performing the job.

**Bonus**
Incentive payment that is supplemental to the base wage.

**Boycott**
Union tactic to encourage others to refuse to patronize an employer.

**Broadbanding**

Competency-based pay system that collapses many traditional salary grades into a few wide salary bands.

**Burnout**

Most severe stage of distress, manifesting itself in depression, frustration, and loss of productivity.

**Business necessity**

Work-related practice that is necessary to the safe and efficient operation of an organization.

**Business representative**

Normally a paid labor official responsible for negotiating and administering the labor agreement and working to resolve union members' problems.

**Business unionism**

Term applied to the goals of U.S. labor organizations, which collectively bargain for improvements in wages, hours, job security, and working conditions.

**C**

**Career counseling**

Process of discussing with employees their current job activities and performance, their personal and career interests and goals, their personal skills, and suitable career development objectives.

**Career paths**

Lines of advancement in an occupational field within an organization.

**Career plateau**

Situation in which for either organizational or personal reasons the probability of moving up the career ladder is low.

**Charge form**

Discrimination complaint filed with the EEOC by employees or job applicants.

**Codetermination**

Representation of labor on the board of directors of a company.

**Collective bargaining process**

Process of negotiating a labor agreement, including the use of economic pressures by both parties.

**Combined salary and commission plan**

Compensation plan that includes a straight salary and a commission.

**Comparable worth**

The concept that male and female jobs that are dissimilar, but equal in terms of value or worth to the employer, should be paid the same.

**Compensable factors**

Factors—skills, efforts, responsibilities, and working conditions—that can serve to rank one job as more or less important than another.

**Compensatory model**

Selection decision model in which a high score in one area can make up for a low score in another area.

**Competency assessment**

Analysis of the sets of skills and knowledge needed for decision-oriented and knowledge-intensive jobs.

**Competency-based selection**

Hiring based on observation of behaviors shown to distinguish successful employees.

**Compulsory binding arbitration**

Binding method of resolving collective bargaining deadlocks by a neutral third party.

**Computer-assisted instruction (CAI)**

System that delivers instructional material directly through a computer terminal in an interactive format.

**Computer-managed instruction (CMI)**

System normally employed in conjunction with CAI that uses a computer to generate and score tests and to determine the level of training proficiency.

**Concurrent validity**

Extent to which test scores (or other predictor information) match criterion data obtained at about the same time from current employees.

**Consent election**

NLRB election option wherein the petition to hold a representation election is not contested by either the employer or the union.

**Construct validity**

Extent to which a selection tool measures a theoretical construct or trait.

**Constructive discharge**

Situation in which an employee is forced into involuntary resignation because of intolerable working conditions.

**Consumer price index (CPI)**

Measure of the average change in prices over time in a fixed "market basket" of goods and services.

**Content validity**

Extent to which a selection instrument, such as a test, adequately samples the knowledge and skills needed to perform a particular job.

**Contrast error**

Performance-rating error in which an employee's evaluation is biased either upward or downward because of comparison with another employee just previously evaluated.

**Contributory plan**

A pension plan where contributions are made jointly by employees and employers.

**Cooperative training**

Training program that combines practical on-the-job experience with formal educational classes.

**Coordination flexibility**

Organizational flexibility that occurs through rapid reallocation of resources to new or changing needs.

**Core competencies**

Integrated knowledge sets within an organization that distinguish it from its competitors and deliver value to customers.

**Core skills**
Skills considered critical to an employee's success abroad.

**Craft unions**
Unions that represent skilled craft workers.

**Criterion-related validity**
Extent to which a selection tool predicts, or significantly correlates with, important elements of work behavior.

**Critical incident**
Unusual event that denotes superior or inferior employee performance in some part of the job.

**Critical incident method**
Job analysis method by which important job tasks are identified for job success.

**Cross-training**
Training of employees in jobs in areas closely related to their own.

**Cross-validation**
Verifying the results obtained from a validation study by administering a test or test battery to a different sample (drawn from the same population).

**Cultural audits**
Audits of the culture and quality of work life in an organization.

**Cultural environment**
Communications, religion, values and ideologies, education, and social structure of a country.

**Culture shock**
Perceptual stress experienced by people who settle overseas.

**Customer appraisal**
Performance appraisal, which, like team appraisal, is based on TQM concepts and seeks evaluation from both external and internal customers.

### D

**Defined-benefit plan**
A pension plan in which the amount an employee is to receive upon retirement is specifically set forth.

**Defined-contribution plan**
A pension plan that establishes the basis on which an employer will contribute to the pension fund.

**Defined rights**
Concept that management's authority should be expressly defined and clarified in the collective agreement.

**Delphi technique**
Qualitative forecasting method that solicits and summarizes the judgments of a preselected group of individuals.

**Depression**
Negative emotional state marked by feelings of low spirits, gloominess, sadness, and loss of pleasure in ordinary activities.

**Differential piece rate**
Compensation rate under which employees whose production exceeds the standard amount of output receive a higher rate for all of their work than the rate paid to those who do not exceed the standard amount.

**Disabled individual**
Any person who (1) has a physical or mental impairment that substantially limits one or more of such person's major life activities, (2) has a record of such impairment, or (3) is regarded as having such an impairment.

**Discipline**
(1) Treatment that punishes; (2) orderly behavior in an organizational setting; or (3) training that molds and strengthens desirable conduct—or corrects undesirable conduct—and develops self-control.

**Disparate treatment**
Situation in which protected-class members receive unequal treatment or are evaluated by different standards.

**Distress**
Harmful stress characterized by a loss of feelings of security and adequacy.

**Downsizing**
The planned elimination of jobs.

**Dual-career partnerships**
Couples in which both members follow their own careers and actively support each other's career development.

**Due process**
Employee's right to present his or her position during a disciplinary action.

### E

**Earnings-at-risk incentive plans**
Incentive pay plans placing a portion of the employee's base pay at risk, but giving the opportunity to earn income above base pay when goals are met or exceeded.

**E-commerce**
Electronic commerce; use of the Internet to transact business.

**EEO-1 report**
An employer information report that must be filed annually by employers of 100 or more employees (except state and local government employers) and government contractors and subcontractors to determine an employer's workforce composition.

**Elder care**
Care provided to an elderly relative by an employee who remains actively at work.

**Employee assistance programs (EAPs)**
Services provided by employers to help workers cope with a wide variety of problems that interfere with the way they perform their jobs.

**Employee associations**
Labor organizations that represent various groups of professional and white-collar employees in labor-management relations.

**Employee empowerment**

Granting employees power to initiate change, thereby encouraging them to take charge of what they do.

**Employee involvement groups (EIs)**

Groups of employees who meet to resolve problems or offer suggestions for organizational improvement.

**Employee leasing**

Process of dismissing employees who are then hired by a leasing company (which handles all HR-related activities) and contracting with that company to lease back the employees.

**Employee rights**

Guarantees of fair treatment from employers, particularly regarding an employee's right to privacy.

**Employee stock ownership plans (ESOPs)**

Stock plans in which an organization contributes shares of its stock to an established trust for the purpose of stock purchases by its employees.

**Employee teams**

An employee contributions technique whereby work functions are structured for groups rather than for individuals and team members are given discretion in matters traditionally considered management prerogatives, such as process improvements, product or service development, and individual work assignments.

**Employer-intent standard**

Legal basis for a constructive-discharge claim whereby the plaintiff must prove not only that he or she resigned a job because of intolerable working conditions but that the employer intended the conditions to force the resignation.

**Employment-at-will principle**

The right of an employer to fire an employee without giving a reason and the right of an employee to quit when he or she chooses.

**Entrepreneur**

One who starts, organizes, manages, and assumes responsibility for a business or other enterprise.

**Environmental scanning**

Systematic monitoring of the major external forces influencing an organization.

**Equal employment opportunity**

The treatment of individuals in all aspects of employment—hiring, promotion, training, etc.—in a fair and nonbiased manner.

**Equity theory**

Theory of motivation that explains how employees respond to situations in which they feel they have received less (or more) than they deserve based upon their contributions to the job.

**Ergonomics**

An interdisciplinary approach to designing equipment and systems that can be easily and efficiently used by human beings.

**Error of central tendency**

Performance-rating error in which all employees are rated about average.

**Escalator clauses**

Clauses in labor agreements that provide for quarterly cost-of-living adjustments in wages, basing the adjustments upon changes in the consumer price index.

**Essay method**

A trait approach to performance appraisal that requires the rater to compose a statement describing employee behavior.

**Ethics**

Set of standards of conduct and moral judgments that help to determine right and wrong behavior.

**Eustress**

Positive stress that accompanies achievement and exhilaration.

**Exempt employees**

Employees not covered by the overtime provisions of the Fair Labor Standards Act.

**Expatriates, or home-country nationals**

Employees from the home country who are sent on international assignment.

**Expedited arbitration**

A faster, less expensive, and less legalistic way to resolve grievances regarding discipline cases, routine work issues, and cases of insignificant monetary cost to the disputing parties.

**External fit**

Element of strategic planning that focuses on the connection between business objectives and major HR initiatives.

## F

**Factor comparison system**

Job evaluation system that permits the evaluation process to be accomplished on a factor-by-factor basis by developing a factor comparison scale.

**Failure rate**

Percentage of expatriates who do not perform satisfactorily.

**Fair employment practices (FEPs)**

State and local laws governing equal employment opportunity that are often more comprehensive than federal laws.

**Fair representation doctrine**

Doctrine under which unions have a legal obligation to provide assistance to both members and nonmembers in labor relations matters.

**Fast-track program**

Program that encourages young managers with high potential to remain with an organization by enabling them to advance more rapidly than those with less potential.

**Final-offer arbitration**

Method of resolving collective bargaining deadlocks whereby the arbitrator has no power to compromise but must select one or another of the final offers submitted by the two parties.

**Flexible benefits plans (cafeteria plans)**

Benefit plans that enable individual employees to choose the benefits that are best suited to their particular needs.

**Flextime**

Flexible working hours that permit employees the option of choosing daily starting and quitting times, provided that they work a set number of hours per day or week.

**Forced-choice method**

A trait approach to performance appraisal that requires the rater to choose from statements designed to distinguish between successful and unsuccessful performance.

**Four-fifths rule**

Rule of thumb followed by the EEOC in determining adverse impact for use in enforcement proceedings.

**Functional job analysis (FJA)**

Quantitative approach to job analysis that utilizes a compiled inventory of the various functions or work activities that can make up any job and that assumes that each job involves three broad worker functions: (1) data, (2) people, and (3) things.

## G

**Gainsharing plans**

Programs under which both employees and the organization share the financial gains according to a predetermined formula that reflects improved productivity and profitability.

**Global corporation**

Firm that has integrated worldwide operations through a centralized home office.

**Global manager**

Manager equipped to run an international business.

**Globalization**

Trend toward opening up foreign markets to international trade and investment.

**Graphic rating-scale method**

A trait approach to performance appraisal whereby each employee is rated according to a scale of characteristics.

**Grievance mediation**

Process where a neutral party assists in the resolution of an employee grievance.

**Grievance procedure**

Formal procedure that provides for the union to represent members and nonmembers in processing a grievance.

**Guest workers**

Foreign workers invited to perform needed labor.

## H

**Hay profile method**

Job evaluation technique using three factors—knowledge, mental activity, and accountability—to evaluate executive and managerial positions.

**Health maintenance organizations (HMOs)**

Organizations of physicians and health care professionals that provide a wide range of services to subscribers and dependents on a prepaid basis.

**Hearing officer**

Person who holds a full-time position with an organization but assumes a neutral role when deciding cases between the aggrieved employees and management.

**High-performance work system (HPWS)**

A specific combination of HR practices, work structures, and processes that maximizes employee knowledge, skill, commitment, and flexibility.

**Horizontal fit**

Situation in which all the internal elements of the work system complement and reinforce one another.

**Host country**

Country in which an international corporation operates.

**Host-country nationals**

Employees who are natives of the host country.

**Hostile-environment harassment**

Form of harassment that occurs when unwelcome sexual conduct interferes with job performance or creates an intimidating work environment.

**Hot-stove rule**

Rule of discipline that can be compared with a hot stove in that it gives warning, is effective immediately, is enforced consistently, and applies to all employees in an impersonal and unbiased way.

**Hourly work**

Work paid on an hourly basis.

**Human capital**

The knowledge, skills, and capabilities of individuals that have economic value to an organization.

**Human resources information system (HRIS)**

Computerized system that provides current and accurate data for purposes of control and decision making.

**Human resources planning (HRP)**

Process of anticipating and making provision for the movement of people into, within, and out of an organization.

## I

**Improshare**

Gainsharing program under which bonuses are based upon the overall productivity of the work team.

**In-basket training**

Assessment-center process for evaluating trainees by simulating a real-life work situation.

**Indirect compensation**

Compensation comprising an employer's benefits package.

**Industrial engineering**

A field of study concerned with analyzing work methods and establishing time standards.

**Industrial unions**

Unions that represent all workers—skilled, semiskilled, unskilled—employed along industry lines.

**Instructional objectives**

Desired outcomes of a training program.

**Instrumentality**

Perception that elements of a compensation package have value.

**Interest arbitration**

Binding determination of a collective bargaining agreement by an arbitrator.

**Internal fit**

Element of strategic planning that aligns all HR practices with one another to establish a configuration that is mutually reinforcing.

**International corporation**

Domestic firm that uses its existing capabilities to move into overseas markets.

**Internship programs**

Programs jointly sponsored by colleges, universities, and other organizations that offer students the opportunity to gain real-life experience while allowing them to find out how they will perform in work organizations.

## J

**Job**

A group of related activities and duties.

**Job analysis**

Process of obtaining information about jobs by determining what the duties, tasks, or activities of jobs are.

**Job characteristics model**

Job design that purports that three psychological states (experiencing meaningfulness of the work performed, responsibility for work outcomes, and knowledge of the results of the work performed) of a jobholder result in improved work performance, internal motivation, and lower absenteeism and turnover.

**Job classification system**

System of job evaluation by which jobs are classified and grouped according to a series of predetermined wage grades.

**Job description**

Statement of the tasks, duties, and responsibilities of a job to be performed.

**Job design**

Outgrowth of job analysis that improves jobs through technological and human considerations in order to enhance organization efficiency and employee job satisfaction.

**Job enrichment**

Enhancing a job by adding more meaningful tasks and duties to make the work more rewarding or satisfying.

**Job evaluation**

Systematic process of determining the relative worth of jobs in order to establish which jobs should be paid more than others within an organization.

**Job family**

A group of individual jobs with similar characteristics.

**Job posting and bidding**

Posting vacancy notices and maintaining lists of employees looking for upgraded positions.

**Job progressions**

Hierarchy of jobs a new employee might experience, ranging from a starting job to jobs that successively require more knowledge and/or skill.

**Job ranking system**

Simplest and oldest system of job evaluation by which jobs are arrayed on the basis of their relative worth.

**Job specification**

Statement of the needed knowledge, skills, and abilities of the person who is to perform the job.

## K

**Knowledge workers**

Workers whose responsibilities extend beyond the physical execution of work to include planning, decision making, and problem solving.

## L

**Labor market**

Area from which applicants are to be recruited.

**Labor relations process**

Logical sequence of four events: (1) workers desire collective representation, (2) union begins its organizing campaign, (3) collective negotiations lead to a contract, and (4) the contract is administered.

**Leaderless group discussions**

Assessment-center process that places trainees in a conference setting to discuss an assigned topic, either with or without designated group roles.

**Leniency or strictness error**

Performance-rating error in which the appraiser tends to give employees either unusually high or unusually low ratings.

**Lockout**

Strategy by which the employer denies employees the opportunity to work by closing its operations.

**Lump-sum merit program**

Program under which employees receive a year-end merit payment, which is not added to their base pay.

# M

**Management by objectives (MBO)**

Philosophy of management that rates performance on the basis of employee achievement of goals set by mutual agreement of employee and manager.

**Management forecasts**

The opinions (judgments) of supervisors, department managers, experts, or others knowledgeable about the organization's future employment needs.

**Management prerogatives**

Decisions regarding organizational operations over which management claims exclusive rights.

**Manager and/or supervisor appraisal**

Performance appraisal done by an employee's manager and often reviewed by a manager one level higher.

**Managing diversity**

Being aware of characteristics common to employees, while also managing employees as individuals.

**Markov analysis**

Method for tracking the pattern of employee movements through various jobs.

**Material Safety Data Sheets (MSDSs)**

Documents that contain vital information about hazardous substances.

**Maturity curves**

Experience or performance bases for providing salary increases for professional employees.

**Mediator**

Third party in a labor dispute who meets with one party and then the other in order to suggest compromise solutions or to recommend concessions from each side that will lead to an agreement.

**Mentoring functions**

Functions concerned with the career advancement and psychological aspects of the person being mentored.

**Mentors**

Managers who coach, advise, and encourage individuals of lesser rank.

**Merit guidelines**

Guidelines for awarding merit raises that are tied to performance objectives.

**Mixed-standard scale method**

A trait approach to performance appraisal similar to other scale methods but based on comparison with (better than, equal to, or worse than) a standard.

**Multinational corporation (MNC)**

Firm with independent business units operating in multiple countries.

**Multiple cutoff model**

Selection decision model that requires an applicant to achieve some minimum level of proficiency on all selection dimensions.

**Multiple hurdle model**

A sequential strategy in which only the applicants with the highest scores at an initial test stage go on to subsequent stages.

# N

**Negligence**

Failure to provide reasonable care where such failure results in injury to consumers or other employees.

**Nepotism**

A preference for hiring relatives of current employees.

**Noncontributory plan**

A pension plan where contributions are made solely by the employer.

**Nondirective interview**

An interview in which the applicant is allowed the maximum amount of freedom in determining the course of the discussion, while the interviewer carefully refrains from influencing the applicant's remarks.

**Nonexempt employees**

Employees covered by the overtime provisions of the Fair Labor Standards Act.

**Nonfinancial compensation**

Compensation that includes such rewards as employee recognition programs, rewarding jobs, and flexible work hours to accommodate personal needs.

# O

**Ombudsman**

Designated individual from whom employees may seek counsel for the resolution of their complaints.

**On-the-job training (OJT)**

Method by which employees are given hands-on experience with instructions from their supervisor or other trainer.

**Open-door policy**

Policy of settling grievances that identifies various levels of management above the immediate supervisor for employee contact.

**Organization analysis**

Examination of the environment, strategies, and resources of the organization to determine where training emphasis should be placed.

**Organizational capability**

Capacity of the organization to act and change in pursuit of sustainable competitive advantage.

**Orientation**

Formal process of familiarizing new employees with the organization, their jobs, and their work units.

**Outplacement services**

Services provided by organizations to help terminated employees find a new job.

**Outsourcing**

Contracting outside the organization to have work done that formerly was done by internal employees.

## P

**Panel interview**

An interview in which a board of interviewers questions and observes a single candidate.

**Pattern bargaining**

Bargaining in which unions negotiate provisions covering wages and other benefits that are similar to those provided in other agreements existing within the industry or region.

**Pay equity**

An employee's perception that compensation received is equal to the value of the work performed.

**Pay-for-performance standard**

Standard by which managers tie compensation to employee effort and performance.

**Pay grades**

Groups of jobs within a particular class that are paid the same rate or rate range.

**Peer appraisal**

Performance appraisal done by one's fellow employees, generally on forms that are compiled into a single profile for use in the performance interview conducted by the employee's manager.

**Peer-review system**

System for reviewing employee complaints that utilizes a group composed of equal numbers of employee representatives and management appointees, which functions as a jury since its members weigh evidence, consider arguments, and after deliberation vote independently to render a final decision.

**Perquisites**

Special benefits given to executives; often referred to as perks.

**Person analysis**

Determination of the specific individuals who need training.

**Piecework**

Work paid according to the number of units produced.

**Point system**

Quantitative job evaluation procedure that determines the relative value of a job by the total points assigned to it.

**Position**

The different duties and responsibilities performed by only one employee.

**Position analysis questionnaire (PAQ)**

Questionnaire covering 194 different tasks which, by means of a five-point scale, seeks to determine the degree to which different tasks are involved in performing a particular job.

**Positive, or nonpunitive, discipline**

System of discipline that focuses on the early correction of employee misconduct, with the employee taking total responsibility for correcting the problem.

**Predictive validity**

Extent to which applicants' test scores match criterion data obtained from those applicants/employees after they have been on the job for some indefinite period.

**Preferred provider organization (PPO)**

A group of physicians who establish an organization that guarantees lower health care costs to the employer.

**Proactive change**

Change initiated to take advantage of targeted opportunities.

**Process audit**

Determining whether the high-performance work system has been implemented as designed.

**Profit sharing**

Any procedure by which an employer pays, or makes available to all regular employees, in addition to base pay, special current or deferred sums based upon the profits of the enterprise.

**Progressive discipline**

Application of corrective measures by increasing degrees.

**Promotion**

Change of assignment to a job at a higher level in the organization.

**Protected classes**

Individuals of a minority race, women, older persons, and those with disabilities who are covered by federal laws on equal employment opportunity.

## Q

**Quid pro quo harassment**

Form of harassment that occurs when submission to or rejection of sexual conduct is used as a basis for employment decisions.

## R

**Reactive change**

Change that occurs after external forces have already affected performance.

**Real wages**

Wage increases larger than rises in the consumer price index, that is, the real earning power of wages.

**Realistic job preview (RJP)**

Informing applicants about all aspects of the job, including both its desirable and undesirable facets.

**Reasonable accommodation**

Attempt by employers to adjust, without undue hardship, the working conditions or schedules of employees with disabilities or religious preferences.

**Reasonable-person standard**

Legal basis for a constructive-discharge claim whereby the plaintiff must prove that working conditions intolerable to a "reasonable person" forced his or her resignation.

**Recency error**

Performance-rating error in which the appraisal is based largely on the employee's most recent behavior rather than on behavior throughout the appraisal period.

**Recordable case**

Any occupational death, illness, or injury to be recorded in the log (OSHA Form 200).

**Red circle rates**

Payment rates above the maximum of the pay range.

**Reengineering**

Fundamental rethinking and radical redesign of business processes to achieve dramatic improvements in cost, quality, service, and speed.

**Reliability**

Degree to which interviews, tests, and other selection procedures yield comparable data over time and alternative measures.

**Relocation services**

Services provided to an employee who is transferred to a new location, which might include help in moving, in selling a home, in orienting to a new culture, and/or in learning a new language.

**Repatriation**

Process of employee transition home from an international assignment.

**Repetitive motion injuries**

Injuries involving tendons of the fingers, hands, and arms that become inflamed from repeated stresses and strains.

**Replacement charts**

Listings of current jobholders and persons who are potential replacements if an opening occurs.

**Reserved rights**

Concept that management's authority is supreme in all matters except those it has expressly conceded to the union in the collective agreement.

**Resource flexibility**

Organizational flexibility that results when employees can do many different jobs in different ways.

**Reverse discrimination**

Act of giving preference to members of protected classes to the extent that unprotected individuals believe they are suffering discrimination.

**Rights arbitration**

Arbitration over interpretation of the meaning of contract terms or employee work grievances.

**Right-to-know laws**

Laws that require employers to advise employees about the hazardous chemicals they handle.

**Rucker Plan**

Bonus incentive plan based on the historic relationship between the total earnings of hourly employees and the production value created by the employees.

## S

**Scanlon Plan**

Bonus incentive plan using employee and management committees to gain cost-reduction improvements.

**Selection**

Process of choosing individuals who have relevant qualifications to fill existing or projected job openings.

**Selection ratio**

The number of job applicants compared with the number of persons to be hired.

**Self-appraisal**

Performance appraisal done by the employee being evaluated, generally on an appraisal form completed by the employee prior to the performance interview.

**Severance pay**

One-time payment sometimes given to employees being terminated.

**Sexual harassment**

Unwelcome advances, requests for sexual favors, and other verbal or physical conduct of a sexual nature in the working environment.

**Silver handshake**

An early-retirement incentive in the form of increased pension benefits for several years or a cash bonus.

**Similar-to-me error**

Performance-rating error in which an appraiser inflates the evaluation of an employee because of a mutual personal connection.

**Situational interview**

An interview in which an applicant is given a hypothetical incident and asked how he or she would respond to it.

**Skill-based pay**

Pay based on how many skills employees have or how many jobs they can perform.

**Skill inventories**

Files of personnel education, experience, interests, skills, etc., that allow managers to quickly match job openings with employee backgrounds.

**Spot bonus**

Unplanned bonus given for employee effort unrelated to an established performance measure.

**Staffing tables**

Graphic representations of all organizational jobs, along with the numbers of employees currently occupying those jobs and future (monthly or yearly) employment requirements.

**Standard hour plan**
Incentive plan that sets rates based upon the completion of a job in a predetermined standard time.

**Step-review system**
System for reviewing employee complaints and disputes by successively higher levels of management.

**Stipulation election**
NLRB election option wherein the parties seek settlement of representation questions such as the NLRB's jurisdiction or the appropriate employees to be included in the bargaining unit.

**Straight commission plan**
Compensation plan based upon a percentage of sales.

**Straight piecework**
Incentive plan under which employees receive a certain rate for each unit produced.

**Straight salary plan**
Compensation plan that permits salespeople to be paid for performing various duties that are not reflected immediately in their sales volume.

**Stress**
Any adjustive demand caused by physical, mental, or emotional factors that requires coping behavior.

**Structured interview**
An interview in which a set of standardized questions having an established set of answers is used.

**Submission agreement**
Statement that describes the issues to be resolved through arbitration.

**Subordinate appraisal**
Performance appraisal of a superior by an employee, which is more appropriate for developmental than for administrative purposes.

**Succession planning**
Process of identifying, developing, and tracking key individuals for executive positions.

**Supplemental unemployment benefits (SUBs)**
A plan that enables an employee who is laid off to draw, in addition to state unemployment compensation, weekly benefits from the employer that are paid from a fund created for this purpose.

**T**

**Task analysis**
Process of determining what the content of a training program should be on the basis of a study of the tasks and duties involved in the job.

**Team appraisal**
Performance appraisal, based on TQM concepts, that recognizes team accomplishment rather than individual performance.

**Team incentive plan**
Compensation plan where all team members receive an incentive bonus payment when production or service standards are met or exceeded.

**Telecommuting**
Use of microcomputers, networks, and other communications technology such as fax machines to do work in the home that is traditionally done in the workplace.

**Third-country nationals**
Employees who are natives of a country other than the home country or the host country.

**Total quality management (TQM)**
A set of principles and practices whose core ideas include understanding customer needs, doing things right the first time, and striving for continuous improvement.

**Transfer**
Placement of an individual in another job for which the duties, responsibilities, status, and remuneration are approximately equal to those of the previous job.

**Transfer of training**
Effective application of principles learned to what is required on the job.

**Transnational corporation**
Firm that attempts to balance local responsiveness and global scale via a network of specialized operating units.

**Transnational teams**
Teams composed of members of multiple nationalities working on projects that span multiple countries.

**Trend analysis**
A quantitative approach to forecasting labor demand based on an organizational index such as sales.

**U**

**Unfair labor practices (ULPs)**
Specific employer and union illegal practices that operate to deny employees their rights and benefits under federal labor law.

***Uniform Guidelines on Employee Selection Procedures***
Procedural document published in the *Federal Register* to assist employers in complying with federal regulations against discriminatory actions.

**Union shop**
Provision of the labor agreement that requires employees to join the union as a requirement for their employment.

**Union steward**
Employee who as a nonpaid union official represents the interests of members in their relations with management.

## V

**Validity**

Degree to which a test or selection procedure measures a person's attributes.

**Validity generalization**

Extent to which validity coefficients can be generalized across situations.

**Value-added compensation**

Evaluating the individual components of the compensation program to see if they advance the needs of employees and the goals of the organization.

**Variable pay**

Tying pay to some measure of individual, group, or organizational performance.

**Vertical fit**

Situation in which the work system supports the organization's goals and strategies.

**Vesting**

A guarantee of accrued benefits to participants at retirement age, regardless of their employment status at that time.

**Virtual office**

Variant of telecommuting whereby employees are in the field or at some remote location but are working as if they were in the home office.

**Virtual team**

A team with widely dispersed members linked together through computer and telecommunications technology.

**Voluntary protection programs (VPPs)**

Programs that encourage employers to go beyond the minimum requirements of OSHA.

## W

**Wage and salary survey**

Survey of the wages paid to employees of other employers in the surveying organization's relevant labor market.

**Wage curve**

Curve in a scattergram representing the relationship between relative worth of jobs and wage rates.

**Wage-rate compression**

Compression of differentials between job classes, particularly the differential between hourly workers and their managers.

**Work permit, or work certificate**

Government document granting a foreign individual the right to seek employment.

**Workers' compensation insurance**

Federal- or state-mandated insurance provided to workers to defray the loss of income and cost of treatment due to work-related injuries or illness.

**Workforce utilization analysis**

Process of classifying protected-class members by number and by the type of job they hold within the organization.

## Y

**Yield ratio**

Percentage of applicants from a recruitment source that make it to the next stage of the selection process.

# Name Index

# Organization Index

# Subject Index

# Photo Credits

**Chapter 1**
p. 2 ©PhotoDisc, Inc.; p. 9 ©1998 by Nick Downes, from *Harvard Business Review*; p. 21 ©PhotoEdit; p. 26 ©PhotoDisc, Inc.

**Chapter 2**
p. 40 ©PhotoDisc, Inc.; p. 43 ©Corbis/Bettmann; p. 60 Courtesy of the United States Post Office; p. 73 From the *Wall Street Journal*-Permission, Cartoon Features Syndicate

**Chapter 3**
p. 84 ©PhotoDisc, Inc.; p. 100 PEANUTS ©Distributed by United Feature Syndicate. Reprinted by Permission; p. 104 ©Liaison/NASA; p. 113 ©Bonnie Kamin/PhotoEdit

**Chapter 4**
p. 120 ©PhotoDisc, Inc.; p. 126 ©PhotoDisc, Inc.; p. 147 From the *Wall Street Journal*-Permission, Cartoon Features Syndicate; p. 160 ©Michael Newman/PhotoEdit

**Chapter 5**
p. 176 ©PhotoDisc, Inc.; p. 187 From the *Wall Street Journal*-Permission, Cartoon Features Syndicate; p. 195 ©Laura Dwight/Corbis; p. 202 ©Ad Photo/Photri-Microstock

**Chapter 6**
p. 220 ©PhotoDisc, Inc.; p. 227 ©Walter Hodges/Tony Stone Images; p. 237 ©Fernald Ivaldi/Tony Stone Images; p. 246 DILBERT reprinted by permission of United Feature Syndicate, Inc.

**Chapter 7**
p. 272 ©PhotoDisc, Inc.; p. 290 Printed by permission by Mighty Media (www.mightymedia.com); p. 296 ©Dan Bosler/Tony Stone Images; p. 298 Copyright 1983 Pat Brady. Reprinted with Permission.

**Chapter 8**
p. 316 ©PhotoDisc, Inc.; p. 324 ©Stewart Cohen/Tony Stone Images; p. 328 Courtesy Kinko's Ventures, Inc.; p. 346 DILBERT reprinted by permission of United Feature Syndicate, Inc.

**Chapter 9**
p. 360 ©PhotoDisc, Inc.; p. 370 ©1999, Reprinted courtesy of Bunny Hoest and *Parade Magazine*; p. 371 Courtesy Bureau of Labor Statistics; p. 386 ©Bettmann/Corbis

**Chapter 10**
p. 398 ©PhotoDisc, Inc.; p. 406 ©SWCP/Kessler Photography; p. 407 ©Jerry King; p. 412 ©Superstock International

**Chapter 11**
p. 434 ©PhotoDisc, Inc.; p. 452 Reprinted with permission of J.B. Handelsman; p. 463 ©Ken Whitmore/Tony Stone Images; p. 464 ©PhotoDisc, Inc.

**Chapter 12**
p. 474 ©PhotoDisc, Inc.; p. 478 ©PhotoDisc, Inc.; p. 484 ©PhotoDisc, Inc.; p. 505 Reprinted with permission of Wayne Stayskal

**Chapter 13**
p. 518 ©PhotoDisc, Inc.; p. 523 From the *Wall Street Journal*-Permission, Cartoon Features Syndicate; p. 530 ©South-Western College Publishing/Cary Benbow; p. 541 ©Corbis/Bob Rowan, Progressive Image

**Chapter 14**
p. 562 ©PhotoDisc, Inc.; p. 571 ©1996 Bill Burke/Page One; p. 588 ©1996 Bill Burke/Page One

**Chapter 15**
p. 596 Natalie Forbes/©Corbis; p. 600 Reprinted with special permission of King Features Syndicate; p. 607 ©SWCP; p. 611 ©PhotoDisc, Inc.

**Chapter 16**
p. 630 ©PhotoDisc, Inc.; p. 639 ©Corbis; p. 648 ©Corbis

**Chapter 17**
p. 674 ©PhotoDisc, Inc.; p. 683 ©Schindler Mobile® from Schindler Elevator and Escalator; p. 684 STONE SOUP ©1998 Jan Eliot. Reprinted with permission of UNIVERSAL PRESS SYNDICATE. All rights reserved.; p. 692 ©Tony Stone Images